Living with Art

Twelfth Edition

Mark Getlein

McGraw Hill Education

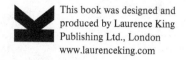

This book was designed and produced by Laurence King Publishing Ltd., London
www.laurenceking.com

Editorial Manager: Kara Hattersley-Smith
Senior Editor: Clare Double
Production Controller: Simon Walsh
Designer: Jo Fernandes
Picture Researcher: Alison Prior
Copy-editor: Angela Koo

LIVING WITH ART, TWELFTH EDITION

8 9 LKV 23

ISBN 978-1-259-91675-5 (bound edition)
MHID 1-259-91675-8 (bound edition)
ISBN 978-1-260-36389-0 (loose-leaf edition)
MHID 1-260-36389-9 (loose-leaf edition)

Portfolio Manager: *Sarah Remington*
Lead Product Developer: *Mary Ellen Curley*
Product Developer: *Betty Chen*
Marketing Manager: *Meredith Leo DiGiano*
Lead Content Project Manager: *Susan Trentacosti*
Project Manager: *Emily Windelborn*
Buyer: *Susan K. Culbertson*
Lead Designer: *David Hash*
Lead Content Licensing Specialist: *Carrie Burger*
Cover Images: *Courtesy of Alexandra Kehayoglou Studio. Photography by Francisco Nocito*
Compositor: *Laurence King Publishing*

Library of Congress Cataloging-in-Publication Data

Names: Getlein, Mark, author.
Title: Living with art / Mark Getlein.
Description: Twelfth edition. | New York, NY : McGraw-Hill Education, [2020]
   | Includes bibliographical references and index.
Identifiers: LCCN 2018042887| ISBN 9781259916755 (hardcover) | ISBN
   9781260363890 (loose-leaf edition)
Subjects: LCSH: Art appreciation.
Classification: LCC N7477 .G55 2019 | DDC 701/.18–dc23
LC record available at https://lccn.loc.gov/2018042887

mheducation.com/highered

BRIEF CONTENTS

CONTENTS

PART ONE: INTRODUCTION 2

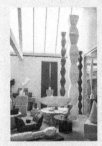

PART TWO: THE VOCABULARY OF ART 80

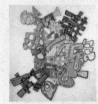

PART THREE: TWO-DIMENSIONAL MEDIA 142

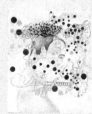

PART FOUR: THREE-DIMENSIONAL MEDIA   244

14 Ancient Mediterranean Worlds 327

15 Christianity and the Formation of Europe 355

16 The Renaissance 372

17 The 17th and 18th Centuries 396

18 Arts of Islam and of Africa 420

19 Arts of Asia: India, China, and Japan 435

Move beyond first impressions. See art in everyday life.

Art is part of our lives,

from the monuments in our communities, to the fashions

we wear and the media images we take in, to the exhibits on display

in museums and galleries. It permeates our daily life.

But why do we study art? How do we talk about art?

Living with Art helps students see art in everyday life by fostering

a greater understanding and appreciation of art. Taking a step further,

Getlein equips students with the tools necessary to analyze,

digest, and uphold a life-long enthusiasm for art.

Understand ART

SmartBook with Learning Resources reinforces concepts, models visual analysis, and draws thematic, cultural, and historical connections as students learn about art and its vocabulary.

Elements and Principles interactive media and **Art Process videos** offer an engaging introduction to core concepts and the vocabulary of art to build comprehension and bring students into the creative process.

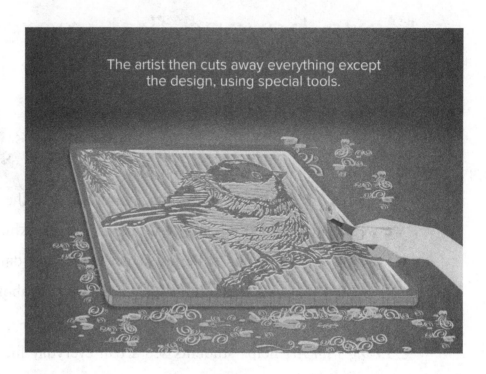

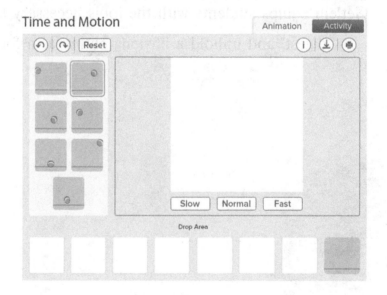

Analyze ART

Connect delivers assessments, analytics, and resources—including SmartBook—that make *Living with Art* a rich learning experience. Featured activities that help students analyze art include:

Interactive Activities, which challenge students to apply their comprehension of concepts to works of art, and to prepare them to describe the art they encounter in their lives.

Guided Viewing Worksheets, which feature links to Google's Arts & Culture site. Questions guide students through learning the process of describing what they see, providing formal analysis of various works of art, discussing their meanings, and ultimately developing informed opinions.

Thematic Worksheets, which encourage students to explore gallery or museum collections in person or online. The worksheets guide them in making connections between works of art by choosing a theme, looking for works that reflect this theme, and supporting their selections with formal and contextual details.

Appreciate ART

Living with Art fosters each student's unique path to appreciation.

Featured essays, such as **Thinking about Art**, focus on **social, historical, and global context**, introducing issues of art over time—how art has been appreciated, interpreted, destroyed, categorized, displayed, fought over, preserved, censored, owned, and studied.

Chapter 3 of *Living with Art* helps students appreciate some of the common **themes of art**. The following themes are further explored in SmartBook and its learning resources in Chapters 14 to 23, and can be incorporated into assignments, lectures, and class discussions:

- The Sacred Realm
- Politics and the Social Order
- Stories and Histories
- Picturing the Here and Now
- Reflecting on the Human Experience
- Invention and Fantasy
- The Natural World
- Art about Art and Its Institutions

The Twelfth Edition

Small, but significant, changes appear in almost every chapter, refreshing the illustration program and clarifying and enlivening the text. Some are detailed in the chapter-by-chapter revision summaries below.

Highlights of this Edition

Part One, which introduces students to art, now includes question prompts throughout the narrative to get them to think critically and understand the purposes of studying art. Related to purpose, each chapter now includes specific learning outcomes or goals. New image selections and the absorption of Crossing Culture essays into the main text narrative emphasize more integrated global coverage. The majority of the Artists essays have been updated to reflect how the artist fits with concepts, topics, and goals set forth for the chapter in which he or she is featured. The presence of Design has been bolstered throughout. The digital edition, or the eBook, includes heavily revised Themes of Art sections for Chapters 14 to 23, exploring themes introduced in Chapter 3 and using the various illustrations that appear in those chapters. The pronunciation guide has been updated to include new artists and terms. Terms, concepts, and visual analysis are modeled in discussions of selected works.

The Revision in Detail

Chapter 1. A new Chinese ceramic vessel is now used as an example to discuss functional and ornamental aspects of the oldest pottery. Doris Salcedo's *Shibboleth* contributes to the coverage of what artists do. An added discussion on artists' sketchbooks, with an example by Giorgio di Giovanni, refreshes the section on the creative process. A section covering Gestalt theory on how we perceive visual information has been revised with a poster for the bicycle company Public.

Chapter 2. A heavily revised introduction to the chapter includes the addition of Yasumasa Morimura's *In praise of Velázquez*, paired with Diego Velázquez's original painting *Las Meninas*. Also included is a discussion of exports, using an ivory work of the Virgin of Immaculate Conception. New illustrations, such as Käthe Kollwitz's *Woman with Dead Child*, refresh the discussion of art and beauty, along with a revised Thinking about Art essay on aesthetics. Two new works by Antonio Pérez de Aguilar and Pablo Picasso introduce the section on art and appearances. Elaine de Kooning's *Bullfight* contributes to the discussion of nonrepresentational art. New paintings—Giorgione's *Adoration of the Shepherds* and El Greco's *Adoration of the Shepherds*—explore the relationship between form and content. Banksy's work adds to the discussion of art and purpose.

Chapter 3. Various themes have been renamed for clarity, and complemented with new examples. William Hogarth's *A Harlot's Progress* illustrates storytelling; Frank Henderson's *Off to War* and Judith Baca's *Great Wall of Los Angeles* are examples of historical recording; an illustration from the *Florentine Codex* shows traditional rituals; and a print from Piranesi's *Il Carceri* ("The Prison") explores the depths of human imagination. Coverage of the Guerrilla Girls can now be found in this chapter's discussion of art and its institutions.

Chapter 4. New visuals support the discussion of various elements. Earth drawings by the Nasca people and Claude Mellan's *Sudarium of St. Veronica* illustrate line. Contour has a new example in Jacques Callot's *Study of a Rearing Horse*. There is added coverage of two broad categories of shape: geometric and organic. Rosalba Carriera's portrait of Gustavus Hamilton and a Puebloan vessel serve as examples of shape. Discussion of light has been expanded with an illustration by Joaquín Sorolla. An Iranian coronation carpet exemplifies color palette; a Navajo rug illustrates color properties; Emmi Whitehorse's work shows monochromatic harmony; Louis Comfort Tiffany's piece displays analogous harmony; and Vermeer offers expressive possibilities of color. A Mexican coconut-shell cup demonstrates how texture can contribute to our understanding and interpretation. Cornelius Norbertus Gijsbrechts's work presents a new example of *trompe l'oeil*. Anish Kapoor's *Cloud Gate* shows three-dimensional space, and the implied-space discussion has been clarified with the example of a Fremont petroglyph. The Artists essay on Albrecht Dürer has been moved to this chapter to support the element of space. An illustration from *Khamsah* exemplifies isometric perspective. Calder's *Carmen* appears in the time and motion section, along with Asif Khan's *MegaFaces Kinetic Facade*.

Chapter 5. Toulouse-Lautrec, Tina Modotti, Childe Hassam, and Enrique Chagoya offer new examples for unity and variety. Degas's *Before the Ballet* supports the discussion of asymmetrical balance. For emphasis and subordination, Georges de La Tour's *The Magdalen with the Smoking Flame* contributes to the coverage. A new work by Robert Jacob Gordon introduces scale, and Calatrava's *Wave* illustrates rhythm, along with Whistler's *Billingsgate* and Ansel Adams's *The Tetons*. The summary section on elements and principles is now more concise.

Chapter 6. New examples illustrate various drawing concepts, materials, and techniques, including Van Lint's drawing for *Farnese Hercules* and Howling Wolf's *Ute Indian*. An Artists essay for Howling Wolf appears in this chapter.

Chapter 7. Girolamo dai Libri's manuscript illumination is an example of tempera. The inclusion of pastel as a painting medium is clarified. Homer's *Key West, Hauling Anchor* freshens the discussion of watercolor. For post-Internet art, there is a new visual by Petra Cortright.

Chapter 8. Woodcut prints are illustrated with Kunisada's *Artisans*, and wood engraving with Posada's *Skeletons as Artisans*. Dürer's intaglio example is replaced with his *Knight, Death, and the Devil*. Cassatt's *The Caress* offers an example of drypoint, and Peale's *Benjamin Franklin* an example of mezzotint. A new Thinking about Art essay on caricatures and cartoons includes discussion of Daumier to support lithography coverage. The Inkjet section is now called Digital to encompass various digital printmaking processes. John Hitchcock's *National Sanctuary* exemplifies three-dimensional printing.

Chapter 9. The chapter is freshened up with new examples across time from Timothy O'Sullivan, Dorothea Lange, Robert Capa, Gertrude Käsebier, Walker Evans, Cindy Sherman, Mungo Thomson, Beryl Korot, and Wafaa Bilal. The Thinking about Art essay on censorship is updated, and a new Artists essay presents Wafaa Bilal.

Chapter 10. A revised introduction to signs and symbols includes an illustration of children playing, Baker's LGBT flag, and Times Square in New York City. Gutenberg's *Biblia Latina* provides an example of typography and layout. Gestalt principles are demonstrated in new posters by J. Howard Miller and Shepard Fairey. Fairey is also highlighted in a new Artists essay. Motion and interactivity are explored in Aaron Koblin's *Data Visualization*. Aleksandr Rodchenko's work explores design and art, and the question of whether design is art is discussed in a new Thinking about Art essay.

Chapter 11. A new example of an eagle-headed deity demonstrates relief. Casting has new visuals with Cellini's *Perseus with the Head of Medusa*. *Voltri VI* replaces the previous Smith selection, and Huma Bhabha offers another example of assembling. A new Artists essay features Martin Puryear. Pedro de Mena's *Ecce Homo* contributes to the coverage of the human figure in sculpture. New works representing time and place include Serpent Mound near Locust Grove, Ohio; Liza Lou's *Trailer*; Steiner and Lenzlinger's *Falling Garden*; and Annette Lawrence's *Coin Toss*. A new Thinking about Art essay dives into public art controversies.

Chapter 12. Clay has a new example: a Chinese bowl with lotus petals and floral scrolls. Metal presents an Italian bracelet in its discussion. This chapter features new Thinking about Art essays, one on grave robbery and preservation and one on engaging tradition. The Thinking about Art essay about the ivory trade is now in this chapter. A new example, a snuff bottle, complements the coverage of lacquerware. A work by Dale Chihuly and a dress by Iris van Herpen enhance the coverage of art, craft, and design.

Chapter 13. Some featured structures have new illustrations. Arata Isozaki and Anish Kapoor's Ark Nova, and Ateliers Jean Nouvel's One Central Park in Sydney, Australia, exemplify new technologies and materials.

Chapter 14. A lyre now shows the refined and luxurious aspect of Sumerian art. The stele of King Naram-Sin is a commemorative piece from Mesopotamia, and a new Thinking about Art essay discusses the destruction of art. The Egypt section now includes a statue of Queen Hatshepsut and the Book of the Dead.

Chapter 15. The introduction to the rise of Christianity has been revised with new images of the Arch of Constantine. A brief introduction connects the section from early Christianity to Byzantium. The European Middle Ages now includes a new illuminated manuscript with the *Book of Kells*, and the High Middle Ages includes a plaque showing *Christ Presenting the Keys to Saint Peter and the Law to Saint Paul*. The transition from the Romanesque to the Gothic era is clarified.

Chapter 16. For the Early Renaissance, Donatello is now represented by the statue of *David* and Botticelli by *Primavera* to link to the discussion of the Medici palace and family. A new Thinking about Art essay touches on the power of patronage and families, complemented by a visual of a cassone with a tournament scene. The inclusion of Giorgione's *Adoration of the Shepherds* and Titian's *Venus of Urbino* offers glimpses of the Venetian Renaissance style. Dürer's engraving *Adam and Eve* provides a marriage of Northern and Italian Renaissance ideas. Sofonisba Anguissola is represented by her *Self-Portrait at the Easel*, which displays Mannerist characteristics.

Chapter 17. More coverage of Rubens is available with a new example, *Presentation of the Portrait of Marie de' Medici*, to show the Baroque style. Claude Lorrain's *Abduction of Europa* offers a look at the more restrained Baroque approach of French artists. Rigaud's *Louis XIV* portrait explores French aristocracy. Classical themes in Baroque paintings can be seen in Velázquez's *The Feast of Bacchus*. There is also added coverage of Dutch still-life paintings, using a work by Van der Ast, and explaining cross-cultural influences. The 18th century starts with a church designed by Balthasar Neumann and a Meissen teapot. Charles Willson Peale's portrait of Washington and Anne-Louis Girodet de Roucy-Trioson's portrait of Jean-Baptiste Belley are new additions to the revolution section.

Chapter 18. Arts of Islamic daily life feature a Persian woman's coat and a bowl with courtly and astrological signs to provide a fuller panorama of artistic production in the Islamic world. The role Islam played in the preservation and dissemination of learning is featured in a new Thinking about Art essay. Islamic and Christian influence can be seen in the arts of Africa, such as the new addition of the Church of St. George in Ethiopia. The inclusion of photography discusses modern African art.

Chapter 19. There is a heavily revised introduction to early Buddhist art in India with a new example, *Green Tara*. Mughal art also has a new visual, *Shah Jahan on Horseback*, and the arts of both India and China feature a new section called Into the Modern Era, paired with illustrations and essays such as the Artists essay on Lala Deen Dayal, and the Thinking about Art essay on the Silk Road. Discussion of Buddhism, Confucianism, and

Daoism falls under one section to focus on the Han and Tang dynasties with a few new visuals. Arts of Japan also includes some new, more diverse examples, such as a samurai's armor, *Welcoming Descent of Amida and Bodhisattvas*, a landscape work by Bokushō Shūshō, and a *shoin* room.

Chapter 20. The chapter starts with a new Dreaming image of an emu and Asmat *bis* poles. Maya work now includes a painted vessel. A sculpture of the Aztec goddess Coatlicue is featured, and a new section called Into the Modern Era expands coverage of the Americas, including a new Artists essay on T. C. Cannon.

Chapter 21. Daumier's *Rue Transnonain*, a new visual, contributes to the discussion of Realism. The Bridging the Atlantic section covers the Americas, not just the United States, featuring a work by José María Velasco. Realism in the Americas is explored in *War News from Mexico*. Expressionism now has a new example with Erich Heckel's *Fränzi Reclining*, and Surrealism with Max Ernst's *Two Children Are Threatened by a Nightingale*. José Clemente Orozco is featured in this chapter, and the coverage of the Bauhaus is updated, including an example of graphic design by Herbert Bayer. The chapter closes with a new Thinking about Art essay about the Nazis' campaign against modern art.

Chapter 22. A new selection for Rauschenberg, *Canyon*, refreshes the discussion of combines, and Saburo Murakami's *Laceration of Paper* contributes to the discussion of happenings. Installation coverage focuses on the work of Dan Flavin, while Bruce Nauman is now featured under body art. Performance art includes a work by Ana Mendieta, and Yoko Ono appears under Conceptual art. Postmodernism covers the work of Damien Hirst and the Young British Artists in a new Thinking about Art essay. For identity, the poster *Silence=Death* is discussed along with Kara Walker's *African't*. Barney's *Cremaster 4* and Baumgartner's *Luftbild* provide new examples of Postmodern media.

Chapter 23. The artist Takashi Murakami and his work is featured alongside other contemporary artists previously discussed. There is a new Thinking about Art essay about the record-setting sales and value of art today.

Supporting Resources for Instructors

Connect Image Bank
Instructors can access a database of images for which McGraw-Hill Education has secured electronic permissions. Instructors can access images by browsing chapters, style/period, medium, and culture, or by searching key terms. Images can be downloaded for use in presentations and assignments you create. The download includes a text file with image captions and information. You can access Connect Image Bank under the library tab in Connect.

Connect Insight
The first and only analytics tool of its kind, Connect Insight™ is a series of visual data displays—each framed by an intuitive question—to provide at-a-glance information regarding how a class is doing: *How are my students doing? How is this student doing? How is this assignment doing? How are my assignments doing? How is my section doing?*

Instructors receive instant student performance results matched with student activity, view real-time analytics so that they can take action early and keep struggling students from falling behind, and are empowered with a more valuable and productive connection between themselves and their students with the transparency Connect Insight™ provides in the learning process.

McGraw-Hill Education's Create
Easily rearrange chapters, combine materials from other content sources, and quickly upload content you have written, such as your course syllabus or teaching notes, using

McGraw-Hill Education's Create. Find the content you need by searching through thousands of leading McGraw-Hill Education's textbooks. Arrange your book to fit your teaching style. Create even allows you to personalize your book's appearance by selecting the cover and adding your name, school, and course information. Order a Create book, and you will receive a complimentary print review copy in 3 to 5 business days or a complimentary electronic review copy via e-mail in about an hour. Experience how McGraw-Hill Education empowers you to teach *your* students *your* way. **create.mheducation.com**

Instructor Resources include an Instructor's Manual, test banks, and lecture PowerPoint slides that can be accessed through Connect.

Acknowledgments

This innovative twelfth edition of *Living with Art* would not have been possible without the contributions of Kelly Donahue-Wallace (University of North Texas). Before lending her expertise to this revision, she created successful online courses, including Art Appreciation for Non-Majors and Art History Survey, for her department. She brings practical expertise in pedagogy to this revision, and she has been instrumental in making sure the twelfth edition is as rigorous and focused as ever. Moreover, she makes it engaging for students so that they leave the class curious about and caring for the art that surrounds them. Professor Donahue-Wallace emphasizes function and theme, focuses on making sure the text builds upon itself with terms and concepts presented in earlier chapters, and incorporates the feedback of her peers.

Numerous reviewers have contributed to the growth and development of *Living with Art* through various editions. We want to express our gratitude to those who have offered valuable feedback on the twelfth edition:

Janine Adkins, Rio Salado College
Rabea Ballin, Lone Star College
Matthew Backer, Lone Star College-CyFair
Kristal Boyers, Palm Beach State College
Susan Braun, Central New Mexico Community College
Rebecca Coleman, East Arkansas Community College
Jennifer Dutcher, Iowa Central Community College
Lisandra Estevez, Winston-Salem State University
Albert Faggard, Lamar State College-Port Arthur
Rachel S. Golden, University of Arkansas at Little Rock
Brenda Hanegan, Delgado Community College
Sarah Hoglund, Boise State University
Kristin Hopkins, Palm Beach State College
Lydia Host, Bishop State Community College
Jeremy Jordan, California State University-Sacramento
Sarah Kaiser, Wright College
Connie LaMarca-Frankel, Pasco-Hernando State College
Joy Lea, Coastal Bend College
Sheila Levi-Aland, Valencia College
John Marshall, Meridian Community College
Roya Mansourkhani, El Centro College
Erin Maurelli, Concordia University
Vicki Mayhan, Richland College
Hallie G. Meredith, Washington State University
John Minkoff, Essex County College
Jacqueline Mitchell, El Paso Community College-Valle Verde
Ralph Parente, Quinsigamond Community College
Barbara Pogue, Essex County College
Richard Ripley, Victor Valley College
Cheyenne Rudolph, Gulf Coast State College
Jennifer Rush, Central New Mexico Community College
Erin Sanders, Delgado Community College
James Scarborough, California State University-Dominguez Hills
Joshua Schutz, Minnesota State University, Mankato
Olivia Schreiner, College of DuPage
Mary Shira, James Madison University
Jennifer Sims, Western Kentucky University
Amy Sluis, Lone Star College-University Park

A Chat with Kelly Donahue-Wallace

What is your approach to pedagogy and teaching art?

A text must teach more and tell less. This edition models the use of art's vocabulary throughout the text, using key terms so that readers understand their applications and *see* what is being discussed in the accompanying images. As I do in the classroom, I draw attention to where the visual element, principle of design, or characteristic of the medium is most visible in the object. The text still tells the story of art, but also teaches readers to see that story in the book's images and in the world around them, because teaching is what is most dear to William "Bill" McCarter, who created *Living with Art*.

How did you capture art globally for this edition of *Living with Art?*

Living with Art always promoted inclusivity, with many women numbering among the artists featured, along with representations of art created around the world. My teaching encompasses the globe; therefore, I found it important to integrate global art and works created by artists from marginalized populations throughout the text. This includes adding works from the Middle East, Latin America, Africa, Australia, and Asia, as well as increasing the representation of Native American and Chicano art.

   The presence of global artists has increased for the Artists essays, and I have tied them more closely to the concepts and issues discussed in the body of their respective chapters.

How did you give more voice to artists in this edition?

I have let the featured artists speak more, adding quotations that reveal their thoughts. Additionally, rather than include a photograph of the artist, I have used a portrait or self-portrait whenever possible. This allows readers to see another artist's response to the featured subject, such as Shepard Fairey's portrait of Robert Rauschenberg, or the artist's own self-representation, such as Howling Wolf's delightful drawing of himself and a friend courting two young ladies.

Why is it important to bridge art and design more, and how did you accomplish this for the twelfth edition?

The text integrates a broad array of media throughout. Printmaking appears beyond the chapter on prints. Crafts appear in the historical chapters. Design is scattered throughout. My goal is to illustrate the fact that visual elements and principles of design are integrated throughout our lives.

Letter from the Author

To the reader,

I'm about to disappear. There I am, below, walking off the page and into the book. When we next meet, in the first chapter, you won't recognize me, for "I" will not appear. An impersonal authority will seem to be speaking, explaining ideas and concepts, imparting information, directing your attention here and there, narrating a history: first this happened, and then that. But you should know that there is someone in particular behind the words, just as there is someone in particular reading them.

I'm walking by a painting of dancers by Matisse. Before that, I've stopped to look at a group of sculptures by Brancusi. Often it's the other way around: I linger for a long time before a painting and walk right by the sculptures without thinking much about them. The works are in the same museum, and I've known them for most of my life. In a way, I think of them as mine—they belong to me because of the hours I have spent looking at them, thinking about them, reading about the artists who made them. Other works in the museum are not mine, at least not yet. Oh, I recognize them on sight, and I know the names of the artists who made them. But I haven't given them the kind of sustained attention it takes to make them a part of my inner world.

Is it perhaps that I don't like them? Like anyone, I am attracted to some works more than others, and I find myself in greater sympathy with some artists than with others. Some works have a deeply personal meaning for me. Others do not, however much I may admire them. But in truth, when looking at a work of art for the first time, I no longer ask whether I like it or not. Instead, I try to understand what it is. These are deep pleasures for me, and I would wish them for you: that through this book you may learn to respond to art in ways that set like and dislike aside, and that you may encounter works you find so compelling that you take the time to make them your own.

Mark Getlein

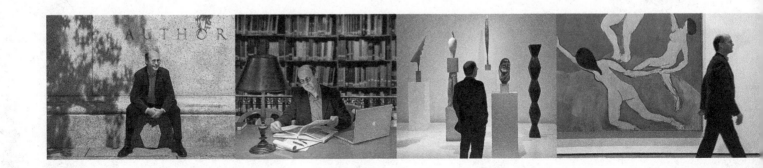

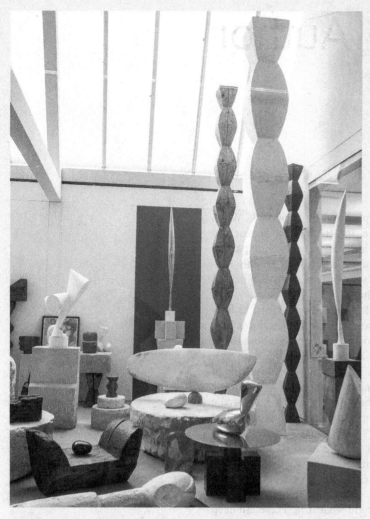

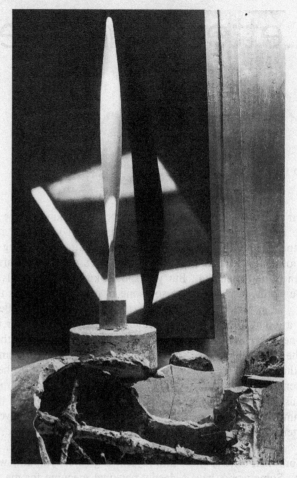

1.2 Constantin Brancusi. *Bird in Space*. ca. 1928–30. Gelatin silver print, 11 ¾ × 9 ⅜".

1.1 Brancusi's studio. Reconstruction at the Musée National d'Art Moderne, Centre Georges Pompidou, by the Renzo Piano Building Workshop. 1992–96.

PART ONE

Introduction

Chapter 1
Living with Art

In this chapter, you will learn to

LO1   recognize why artists make art,

LO2   explain how artists create their works,

LO3   describe the creative process and its objects, and

LO4   discuss how viewers respond to art.

Our simplest words are often the deepest in meaning: birth, kiss, flight, dream. The sculptor Constantin Brancusi spent his life searching for forms as simple and pure as those words—forms that seem to have existed forever, outside of time. Born a peasant in a remote village in Romania, he spent most of his adult life in Paris, where he lived in a single small room adjoining a skylit studio. Upon his death in 1957, Brancusi willed the contents of his studio to the French government, which eventually re-created the studio itself in a museum (**1.1**).

Near the center of the photograph are two versions of an idea Brancusi called *Endless Column*. Pulsing upward with great energy, the columns seem as though they could go on forever. Perhaps they *do* go on forever, and we can see only part of them. Directly in front of the white column, a sleek, horizontal marble form looking something like a slender submarine seems to hover over a disk-shaped base. Brancusi called this simply *Fish*. It does not depict any particular fish but, rather, shows us the idea of something that moves swiftly and freely through the water, the essence of a fish. To the left of the dark column, arching up in front of a patch of wall painted red, is a version of one of Brancusi's most famous works, *Bird in Space*. Here again the artist portrays not a particular bird but, rather, the idea of flight, the feeling of soaring upward. Brancusi said that the work represents "the soul liberated from matter."[1]

A photograph by Brancusi shows another, more mysterious view of *Bird in Space* (**1.2**). Light from a source we cannot see cuts across the work and falls in a sharp diamond shape on the wall behind. The sculpture casts a shadow so strong that it seems to have a dark twin. Before it lies a broken, discarded work. The photograph might make you think of the birth of a bird from its egg, or of a perfected work of art arising from numerous failed attempts, or indeed of a soul newly liberated from its material prison.

Brancusi took many photographs of his work, and through them we can see how his sculptures lived in his imagination even after they were finished. He photographed them in varying light conditions, in multiple locations and combinations, and from close up and far away. With each photograph they seem to reveal a different mood, the way people we know reveal different sides of themselves over time.

Living with art, Brancusi's photographs show us, is making art live by letting it engage our attention, our imagination, our intelligence. Few of us, of course, can live with art the way Brancusi did. Yet we can choose to seek out encounters with art, to make it a matter for thought and enjoyment, and to let it live in our imagination.

You probably already live with more art than you think you do. Very likely the walls of your home are decorated with posters, photographs, or even paintings you chose because you find them beautiful or meaningful. Walking around your community you probably pass by buildings that were designed for visual appeal as well as to serve practical ends. If you ever pause for a moment just to look at one of them—to take pleasure, for example, in its silhouette against the sky—you have made the architect's work live for a moment by appreciating an effect that he or she prepared for you. We call such an experience an *aesthetic* experience. **Aesthetics** is the branch of philosophy concerned with the feelings aroused in us by sensory experiences—experiences we have through sight, hearing, taste, touch, and smell. Aesthetics concerns itself with our responses to the natural world and to the world we make, especially the world of art. What art is, how and why it affects us—these are some of the issues that aesthetics addresses.

This book hopes to deepen your pleasure in the aesthetic experience by broadening your understanding of one of the most basic and universal of human activities—making art. Its subject is visual art, which is art that addresses the sense of sight, as opposed to music or poetry, which are arts that appeal to the ear. It focuses on why and how art has been made around the world. It reaches back to consider works created well before current ideas about art were born and across cultures that have very different traditions of art.

The Impulse for Art

What motivated humans to make the earliest forms of art? No society that we know of, for as far back in human history as we have been able to penetrate, has lived without some form of art. The impulse to make and respond to art appears to be as deeply ingrained in us as the ability to learn language—part of what sets us apart as humans. Where does the urge to make art come from? What purposes does it serve? For answers, we might begin by looking at some of the oldest works yet discovered, images and artifacts dating from the Stone Age, near the beginning of the human experience.

Named for one of the explorers who discovered it in 1994, the Chauvet cave is one of hundreds of caves in Europe whose walls are decorated with images created during the Upper Paleolithic era, the latter part of the Old Stone Age (**1.3**). A number of these caves were already known when the marvels of Chauvet came to light, but the Chauvet cave created a sensation when radiocarbon dating confirmed that at least some of the images on its walls had been painted 32,000 years ago, thousands of years earlier than their accomplished style suggested.

The galleries and chambers of Chauvet teem with over three hundred depictions of animals—lions, mammoths, rhinoceroses, cave bears, horses, reindeer, red deer, aurochs, musk-oxen, bison, and others—as well as palm prints and stenciled silhouettes of human hands. Evidence from this and other Paleolithic sites tells us something of how the paintings were made. Charcoal, naturally tinted red and yellow clays (ochers), and a black mineral called manganese dioxide served as pigments. They were ground to a powder with stone mortars, then mixed with a liquid that bound them into paint—blood, animal fat, and calcium-rich cave water were some of the binders used. Paint was applied to the cave walls with fingers and animal-hair brushes, or sprayed from the mouth or through a hollow reed. Some images were engraved, or scratched, into the rock; others were drawn with a chunk of rock or charcoal held like a pencil. Deep in the interior of the caves, far from any natural light or living areas, the images would have been created and viewed by the flickering light of torches, or of stone lamps that may have burned animal fat using moss wicks.

When Paleolithic cave paintings were first discovered, during the late 19th century, scholars suggested that they had been made purely for pleasure during times of rest from hunting or other occupations. But their presence in deep and difficult-to-reach areas seemed to work against that notion. For Stone Age image-

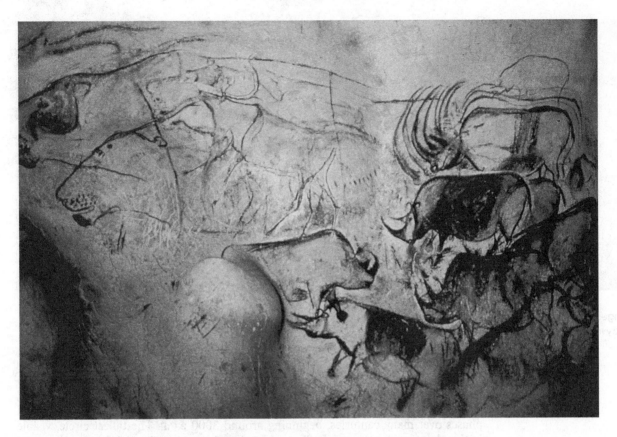

1.3 Left section of the "Lion Panel," Chauvet cave, Ardèche Valley, France. ca. 30,000 B.C.E.
Courtesy the French Ministry of Culture and Communication, Regional Direction for Cultural Affairs—
Rhône-Alpes, Regional Department of Archaeology

makers to have gone to such lengths, their work must have been meaningful. One influential early theory held that the images were a form of magic to ensure success in hunting. Other scholars began to look past individual images to consider each cave as a purposefully structured whole, carefully noting the placement of every image and symbolic marking within it. A related branch of research examines how Paleolithic artists responded to the unique characteristics of each underground space, including the spaces' acoustics. More recently, it has been suggested that the images were used in rituals conducted by shamans—religious specialists who communicate with a parallel spirit world, often through animal spirit go-betweens.

Fascinating as those theories are, they pass over perhaps the most amazing thing of all, which is that there should be images in the first place. The ability to make images is uniquely human. Anthropologists speak of an "explosion" of images during the Upper Paleolithic period, when anatomically modern humans arrived in Europe and began to displace the Neanderthal human population that had been living there for several hundred thousand years. Along with musical instruments, personal ornaments, and portable sculptures, cave paintings were part of a cultural toolkit that must have given our ancestors an advantage over their now-extinct Neanderthal competitors, helping communities to form and thrive in a new environment. If images had not been useful to us, we would have stopped making them. As it is, we have been making them ever since. All images may not be art, but our ability to make them is one place where art begins.

The 20th-century British sculptor Anthony Caro once said that "all art is basically Paleolithic or Neolithic: either the urge to smear soot and grease on cave walls or pile stone on stone."[2] By "soot and grease" Caro meant the cave paintings. With "the urge to pile stone on stone" he had in mind one of the most impressive and haunting works to survive from the Stone Ages—the structure in the south of

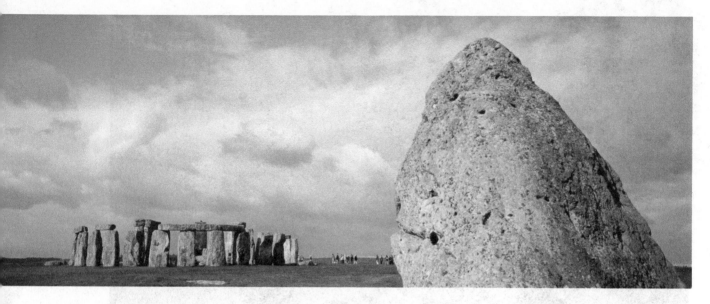

1.4 Stonehenge. Salisbury Plain, England. ca. 3000–1500 B.C.E. Height of stones 13' 6".
Alvis Upitis/Getty Images

England known as Stonehenge (**1.4**). Today much ruined through time and vandalism, Stonehenge at its height consisted of several concentric circles of **megaliths**, very large stones, surrounded in turn by a circular ditch. It was built in several phases over many centuries, beginning around 3000 B.C.E. The tallest circle, visible in the photograph here, originally consisted of thirty gigantic upright stones capped with a continuous ring of horizontal stones. Weighing some 50 tons each, the stones were quarried many miles away, hauled to the site, and laboriously shaped by blows from stone hammers until they fitted together.

Many theories have been advanced about why Stonehenge was built and what purpose it served. Recent archaeological research has confirmed that the monument marks a graveyard, perhaps that of a ruling dynasty. The cremated remains of up to 240 people appear to have been buried there over a span of some five hundred years, from the earliest development of the site until the time when the great stones were erected. Other findings show that the monument did not stand alone but was part of a larger complex, perhaps a religious complex used for funerary rituals. What is certain is that Stonehenge held meaning for the Neolithic community that built it. For us, it stands as a compelling example of how old and how basic is our urge to create meaningful order and form, to structure our world so that it reflects our ideas. This is another place where art begins.

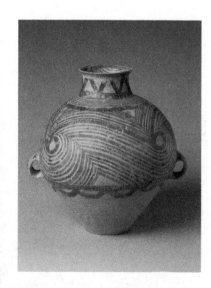

1.5 Jar (*Hu*). Neolithic, Majiayao culture, China. ca. 2650–2350 B.C.E. Earthenware with painted decoration, height 13 ⅜".
Metropolitan Museum of Art, New York. Charlotte C. and John C. Weber Collection, Gift of Charlotte C. and John C. Weber, 1992

Stonehenge was erected in the Neolithic era, or New Stone Age. The Neolithic era is named for the new kinds of stone tools that were invented, but it also brought such important advances as the domestication of animals and crops, and the development of the technology of pottery, as people discovered that fire could harden certain kinds of clay. With pottery, storage jars, food bowls, and all sorts of other practical objects came into being. Yet much of the world's oldest pottery seems to go far beyond purely practical needs (**1.5**). This elegant painted ceramic vessel was made around 2650 B.C.E. in what is now China. The pot is functional, but its ornamentation is not. Great care and skill have gone into making this utilitarian item pleasing to the eye. It is covered in concentric lines that change direction several times across the shoulder of the pot. Here is a third place we might turn to for the origins of art—the urge to explore the aesthetic possibilities of new technology. What are the limits of clay? the early potters must have wondered. What can be done with it? How can we make it more pleasing for the viewer?

To construct meaningful images and forms, to create order and structure, to explore aesthetic possibilities—these characteristics seem to be part of our nature as human beings. From them, art has grown, nurtured by each culture in its own way.

What Do Artists Do?

In our society, we tend to think of art as something created by specialists, people we call artists, just as medicine is practiced by doctors and bridges are designed by engineers. In other societies, virtually everyone contributes to art in some way. Yet no matter how a society organizes itself, it calls on its art-makers to fulfill similar roles.

First, artists *create places for some human purpose*. Stonehenge, for example, was probably created as a place where a community could gather for rituals. Closer to our own time, Maya Lin created the Vietnam Veterans Memorial as a place for contemplation and remembrance (**1.6**). During the Vietnam War—one of our most painful national memories—thousands of young men and women lost their lives in a distant conflict that was increasingly questioned and protested at home. By the war's end, the nation was so bitterly divided that returning veterans received virtually no recognition for their services. In this atmosphere of continuing controversy, Lin's task was to create a memorial that honored the human sacrifice of the war while neither glorifying nor condemning the conflict itself.

At the heart of the memorial is a long, tapering, V-shaped wall of black granite, inscribed with the names of the missing, the captured, and the dead—some 58,000 names in all. Set into the earth exposed by slicing a great wedge from a gently sloping hill, it suggests perhaps a modern entrance to an ancient burial mound, although in fact there is no entrance. Instead, the highly polished surface acts as a mirror, reflecting the surrounding trees, the nearby Washington Monument, and the visitors themselves as they pass by.

Entering along a walkway from either end, visitors are barely aware at first of the low wall at their feet. The monument begins just as the war itself did—almost unnoticed, a few support troops sent to a small and distant country, a few deaths in the nightly news. As visitors continue their descent along the downward-sloping path, the wall grows taller and taller until it towers overhead, names upon names upon names. Often, people reach out to touch the letters, and as they do, they touch their own reflections reaching back. At the walkway's lowest point, where the wall is at its highest, a corner is turned. The path begins to climb upward, and the wall begins to fall away. Drawn by a view of either the Washington Monument or the Lincoln Memorial, visitors leave the war behind.

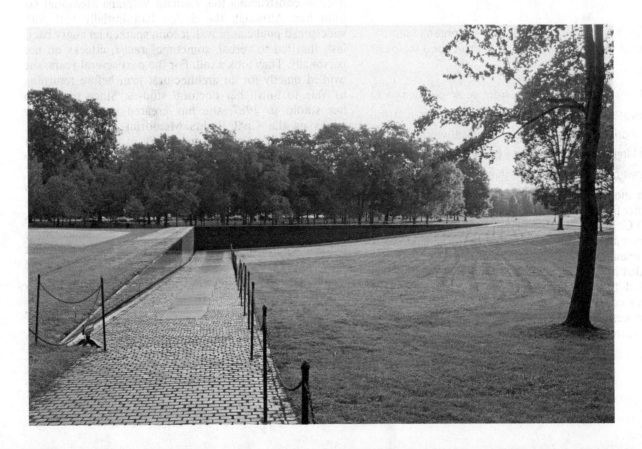

1.6 Maya Lin. Vietnam Veterans Memorial, Washington, D.C. 1982. Black granite, length 492'.
mike black photography/Getty Images

Maya Lin (born 1959)

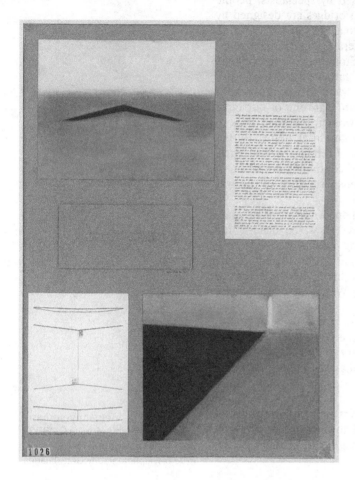

How do Lin's works provide a space for contemplation? What kind of artist is Lin—is she an architect or a sculptor?

"Each of my works originates from a simple desire to make people aware of their surroundings, not just the physical world but also the psychological world we live in," Maya Lin has written. "I create places in which to think, without trying to dictate what to think."[3]

The most famous of Maya Lin's places for thought was also her first, the Vietnam Veterans Memorial in Washington, D.C. Lin created the design seen here in response to an open call for proposals for the memorial, and it was selected unanimously from the more than 14,000 entries that flooded in. We can imagine the judges' surprise when they dialed the winner's telephone number and found themselves connected to a dormitory at Yale University, where Lin was a twenty-two-year-old undergraduate student in architecture.

As with much of Lin's work, the memorial's powerful form was the product of a long period of reading and thinking, followed by a moment of intuition. On a trip to Washington to look at the site, she writes, "I had a simple impulse to cut into the earth. I imagined taking a knife and cutting into the earth, opening it up, an initial violence and pain that in time would heal. The grass would grow back, but the initial cut would remain a pure flat surface in the earth with a polished, mirrored surface, much like the surface on a geode when you cut it and polish the edge."[4] Engraved with the names of the dead, the surface "would be an interface, between our world and the quieter, darker, more peaceful world beyond. . . . I never looked at the memorial as a wall, an object, but as an edge to the earth, an opened side."[5] Back at school, Lin gave her idea form in the university dining hall with two decisive cuts in a mound of mashed potatoes.

Maya Lin was born and grew up in Athens, Ohio. Her father, a ceramist, was chair of the fine arts department at Ohio University, while her mother, a poet, taught in the department of English there. Both parents had immigrated to the United States from China before Maya was born. Lin readily credits the academic atmosphere and her family's everyday involvement with art for the direction her life has taken. Of her father, she writes simply that "his aesthetic sensibility ran throughout our lives."[6] She and her brother spent countless hours after school watching him work with clay in his studio.

Lin admits that it took a long time to put the experience of constructing the Vietnam Veterans Memorial behind her. Although the design had initially met with widespread public approval, it soon sparked an angry backlash that led to verbal, sometimes racist, attacks on her personally. They took a toll. For the next several years, she worked quietly for an architectural firm before returning to Yale to finish her doctoral studies. Since setting up her studio in 1987, she has created such compelling works as the Civil Rights Memorial in Montgomery, Alabama; *Wave Field*, an earthwork at the University of Michigan in Ann Arbor; and the Langston Hughes Library in Clinton, Tennessee.

Critics are often unsure about whether to classify Lin as an architect or a sculptor. Lin herself insists that one flows into the other. "The best advice I was given was from Frank Gehry (the only architect who has successfully merged sculpture and architecture), who said I shouldn't worry about the distinctions and just make the work,"[7] she recalls. That is just what she continues to do.

Maya Lin. Vietnam Veterans Memorial. Competition drawing. 1982. Library of Congress/Maya Lin

In a quiet, unobtrusive way, the place that Maya Lin created encourages a kind of ritual, a journey down into a valley of death, then up toward hope, healing, and reconciliation. Like Stonehenge, it has served to bring a community together.

A second task artists perform is to *create extraordinary versions of ordinary objects*. Just as the Neolithic vessel we looked at earlier is more than an ordinary drinking cup, so the textile here is more than an ordinary garment (**1.7**). Woven in West Africa by artists of the Asante people, it is a spectacular example of a type of textile known as *kente*. *Kente* is woven in hundreds of patterns, each with its own name, history, and symbolism. Traditionally, a newly invented pattern was shown first to the king, who had the right to claim it for his own exclusive use. Royal *kente* was reserved for ceremonial occasions. Rich, costly, and elaborate, the cloth distinguished its wearer as special too, an extraordinary version of an ordinary human being.

A third important task for artists has been to *record and commemorate*. Artists create images that help us remember the present after it slips into the past, that keep us in mind of our history, and that will speak of our times to the future. Illustrated here is a painting created in the early 17th century by an artist named Manohar, one of several painters employed in the royal workshops of the emperor Jahangir, a ruler of the Mughal dynasty in India (**1.8**). At the center of the painting we see Jahangir himself, seated beneath a sumptuous canopy. His son Khusrau, dressed in a yellow robe, offers him the precious gift of a golden cup. The painting commemorates a moment of reconciliation between father and son, who had had a violent falling out. The moment did not last, however. Khusrau would soon stage an armed rebellion that cost him his place in line to the throne.

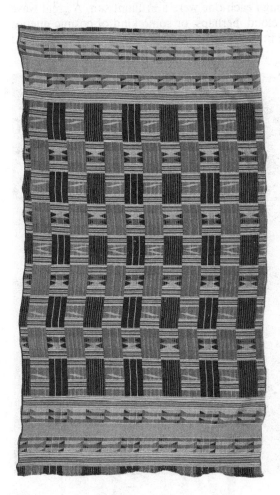

1.7 *Kente* cloth, from Ghana. Asante, mid-20th century. Cotton, 6' 5 ¼" × 3' 9".
The Newark Museum/Art Resource, NY

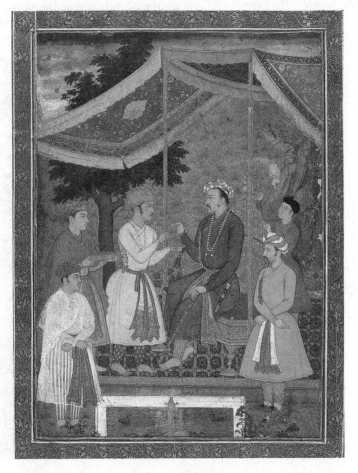

1.8 Manohar. *Jahangir Receives a Cup from Khusrau*. 1605–06. Opaque watercolor on paper, 8 ³⁄₁₆ × 6".
The British Museum, London. © The Trustees of the British Museum/Art Resource, NY

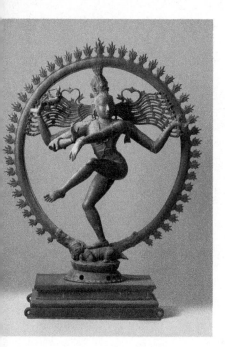

1.9 *Shiva Nataraja.* India. 10th century C.E. Bronze, height 5' ¼". Rijksmuseum, Amsterdam. On loan from the Asian Art Society in The Netherlands

Although the intricate details of Mughal history may be lost on us today, this enchanting painting gives us a vivid glimpse into their vanished world as they wanted it to be remembered.

A fourth task for artists is to *give tangible form to the unknown*. They portray what cannot be seen with the eyes, or events that can only be imagined. An anonymous Indian sculptor of the 10th century gave tangible form to the Hindu god Shiva in his guise as Nataraja, Lord of the Dance (**1.9**). Encircled by flames, his long hair flying outward, Shiva dances the destruction and rebirth of the world, the end of one cycle of time and the beginning of another. The figure's four arms communicate the complexity of this cosmic moment. In one hand, Shiva holds the small drum whose beat summons up creation; in another hand, he holds the flame of destruction. A third hand points at his raised foot, beneath which worshipers may seek refuge, while a fourth hand is raised with its palm toward the viewer, a gesture that means "fear not."

A fifth function artists perform is to *give tangible form to feelings and ideas*. The statue of Shiva we just looked at, for example, gives tangible form to ideas about the cyclical nature of time that are part of the religious culture of Hinduism. In *The Starry Night* (**1.10**), Vincent van Gogh labored to express his personal feelings as he stood on the outskirts of a small village in France and looked up at the night sky. Van Gogh had become intrigued by the belief that people journeyed to a star after their death, and that there they continued their lives. "Just as we take the train to get to Tarascon or Rouen," he wrote in a letter, "we take death to reach a star."[8] Seen through the prism of that idea, the night landscape inspired in him a vision of great intensity. Surrounded by halos of radiating light, the stars have an exaggerated, urgent presence, as though each one were a brilliant sun. A great wave or whirlpool rolls across the sky—a cloud, perhaps, or some kind of cosmic energy. The landscape, too, seems to roll on in waves like an ocean. A tree in the foreground

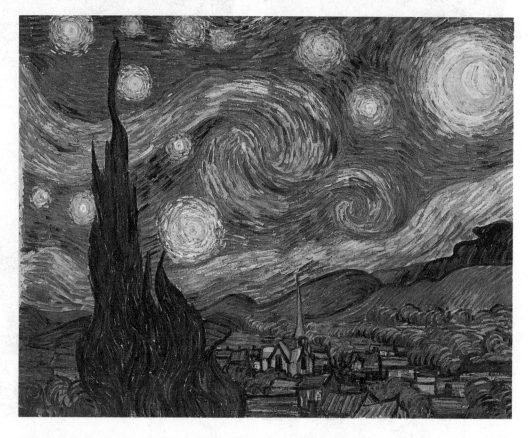

1.10 Vincent van Gogh. *The Starry Night.* 1889. Oil on canvas, 29 × 36 ¼".
The Museum of Modern Art, New York. Acquired through the Lillie P. Bliss Bequest, 472.1941. Digital Image © The Museum of Modern Art/Licensed by SCALA/Art Resource, NY

Vincent van Gogh (1853–1890)

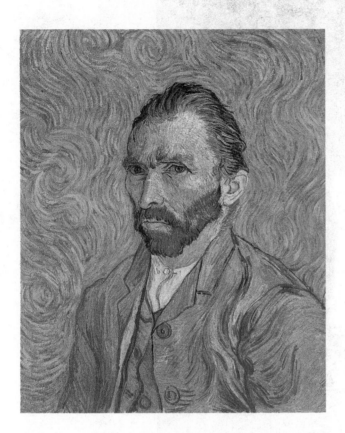

How did Van Gogh explain the appearance of his work? How does his style reflect his suffering and his response to it?

The appeal of Van Gogh for today's art lovers is easy to understand. A painfully disturbed, tormented man who, in spite of his great anguish, managed to create extraordinary art. An intensely private, introspective man who wrote eloquently about art and about life. An erratic, impulsive man who had the self-discipline to construct an enormous body of work in a career that lasted only a decade.

Vincent van Gogh was born in the Netherlands, the son of a Dutch Protestant minister. He did not begin to take a serious interest in art until the age of twenty-seven, when he had but ten years left to live. In 1886, he went to stay in Paris with his brother Theo, an art dealer, who was always his closest emotional connection.

Vincent's letters to Theo represent a unique document in the history of art. They reveal a sensitive, intelligent artist pouring out his thoughts to someone uniquely capable of understanding them. In 1883, while still in the Netherlands, he wrote to Theo: "In my opinion, I am often

rich as Croesus, not in money, but (though it doesn't happen every day) rich, because I have found in my work something to which I can devote myself heart and soul, and which gives inspiration and significance to life. Of course my moods vary, but there is an average of serenity. I have a sure *faith* in art, a sure confidence that it is a powerful stream, which bears a man to harbor, though he himself must do his bit too; and at all events I think it such a great blessing, when a man has found his work, that I cannot count myself among the unfortunate. I mean, I may be in certain relatively great difficulties, and there may be gloomy days in my life, but I shouldn't want to be counted among the unfortunate nor would it be correct."[9]

Life as an artist in France was not easy for Van Gogh, and he suffered emotional problems. He realized that his instability had got out of hand, and he committed himself to an asylum, where–true to form–he continued to work prolifically at his painting. In one letter to Theo, Van Gogh wrote, "My dear brother–I'm still writing to you between bouts of work–I'm ploughing on like a man possessed, more than ever I have a pent-up fury for work, and I think that this will contribute to curing me."[10]

Van Gogh's style exaggerates and distorts objects and colors for expressive effect. He explained his approach in a letter to his brother: "The effects colours produce through their harmonies or discords should be boldly exaggerated. It's the same as in drawing–the precise drawing, the right colour–is not perhaps the essential element we should look for."[11] Van Gogh exceeded the optical truth of his subjects in order to convey deeper emotion. Describing a painting of a man that he planned to make, the artist wrote: "I'll paint him, then, just as he is, as faithfully as I can–to begin with. But the painting isn't finished like that. To finish it, I'm now going to be an arbitrary colourist. I exaggerate the blond of the hair, I come to orange tones, chromes, pale lemon. Behind the head–instead of painting the dull wall of the mean room, I paint the infinite. I make a simple background of the richest, most intense blue that I can prepare, and with this simple combination, the brightly lit blond head, against this rich blue background achieves a mysterious effect, like a star in the deep azure."[12]

Most of the work we admire so much was done in the last two and a half years of his life. Vincent (as he always signed himself) received much sympathetic encouragement during those years, both from his brother and from an unusually perceptive doctor and art connoisseur, Dr. Gachet, whom he painted several times. Nevertheless, his despair deepened, and in July of 1890 he died from a self-inflicted gunshot.

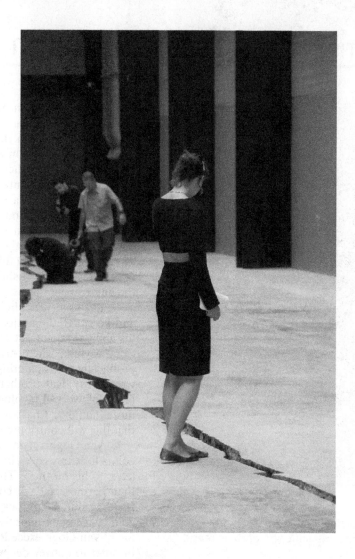

writhes up toward the stars as though answering their call. In the distance, a church spire points upward as well. Everything is in turbulent motion. Nature seems alive, communicating in its own language while the village sleeps.

Finally, artists *refresh our vision and help us see the world in new ways.* Habit dulls our senses. What we see every day we no longer marvel at, because it has become familiar. Through art we can see the world through someone else's eyes and recover the intensity of looking for the first time. Doris Salcedo's *Shibboleth* (**1.11**) is a simple cement floor with huge cracks running through it. The work, referring to the immigrant experience in Europe, was commissioned by the Tate Modern in London. The title comes from a biblical story in which a community used the word *shibboleth* to determine who belonged and who did not. The huge cracks forced visitors to pay attention to the most mundane part of the environment: the floor. Together with the title, the cracked floor's seeming instability helped viewers see and feel what life is like under unstable and uncertain conditions.

Creating and Creativity

While thinking about how to represent a painful moment in American history, Maya Lin could have noticed how the monument's site was on a rolling hill between the Lincoln and Washington monuments, but then moved on. Standing in a field more than a century ago, Van Gogh could have had his vision of the night sky, then returned to his lodgings—and we would never have known about it. We all experience the moments of insight that put us where art begins. For most of us, such moments are an end in themselves. For artists, they are a beginning, a kind of raw material that sets a creative process in motion.

Creativity is a word that comes up often when talking about art, but what is creativity exactly? Are we born with it? Can it be learned? Can it be lost? Are artists more creative than other people? If so, how did they get that way? Creativity has been broadly defined as the ability to produce something that is both innovative and useful within a given social context. Although the exact nature of creativity remains elusive—there is no definitive test for it—psychologists agree that creative people tend to possess certain traits: Creative people have the ability to generate numerous ideas, many of them quite original, then to analyze their ideas, selecting the most promising ones to develop. They redefine problems and seek connections between seemingly unrelated ideas. They tend to have a playful side, but they are also capable of long periods of intense, concentrated work. They take risks, remain open to experience, and do not feel restricted by existing knowledge or conventional solutions.

Recently, advances in brain monitoring and imaging technology have allowed neuroscientists to investigate creativity from their own point of view, with fascinating, though inconclusive, results. Using magnetic resonance imaging (MRI) to monitor white matter—the tissue that transmits signals from one area of the brain to another—one group of researchers discovered that nerve traffic (i.e., signal transmission) in a creative brain is slower and more meandering in key areas, perhaps allowing more novel and varied ideas to be linked up. Another study compared the brain activity of trained musicians and nonmusicians as they improvised on a keyboard. Researchers found that, when improvising, the trained musicians shut down the part of the brain that reads and sorts through incoming stimuli. By doing this, they blocked out potential distractions, allowing themselves to focus exclusively on the music they were making. Years of training had made an extra level of concentration available to them.[13]

Looking at a work of art, we know we are seeing the result of a creative process, but we rarely have access to the process itself. Artists' sketchbooks offer a glimpse of the early steps in creating works of art. A sketchbook is like a journal where artists record observations of the world and ideas for new works in the form of drawings. The drawings may be accompanied by notes, as Leonardo da Vinci famously did (see 5.22). The images range from incomplete sketches rapidly done to record a fleeting impression, to fully worked-out and complete drawings that may even be painted. The page of a sketchbook belonging to the Italian artist Giorgio di Giovanni (1.12) has both types. At the top of the page, Giovanni has quickly

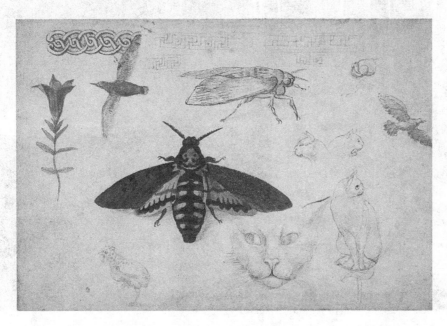

1.12 Giorgio di Giovanni. *Studies of a Gentian Moth, Birds, Cats, Interlacing Motif, and Greek Frets.* 1530–40. Pen, ink, watercolor, and chalk on paper, 7 3/16 × 10 7/16".
The Metropolitan Museum of Art, New York. Gift from the family of Howard J. Barnet, in his memory, 2001

drawn a decorative pattern of interlocking lines that he had likely seen in an ancient Roman building. In the middle, however, the artist has carefully rendered a moth, even painting it in lifelike colors. The cats, chicken, flower, and birds fall somewhere in between. Like other artists, Giovanni kept this batch of drawings to call upon when he needed one of these subjects in a painting.

Sometimes artists leave behind sketches or photographs that document the entire creative process for a single work of art. In the case of Mike Kelley's *Kandors Full Set* (**1.13**), we are lucky enough to have a text by the artist that relates how the work came to have the form we see, and through it we can witness something of the creative process in action.

A fictional city on the fictional planet of Krypton, Kandor is the place where Superman, the comic-book hero, was born. In the Superman story, we learn that Krypton was destroyed. Kandor, however, was miniaturized and stolen before the disaster. It eventually ended up in Superman's possession; he keeps it under a glass bell jar in his Fortress of Solitude.

The subject of Kandor first occurred to Kelley when he was asked to participate in a museum exhibit on the theme of the new century in 1999–2000. Kelley was drawn to Kandor because the Superman artists of the past had imagined it as a "city of the future," much like cities in old science-fiction films. His initial idea was to use the Internet, a new medium just then coming into popular use, to reach out to Superman fans, asking them to contribute information and ideas about Kandor to a Web site. From their input, models of the city would be created for exhibit in the museum. Web site participants would be flown to the opening of the exhibition, showing that the project had created a community, and that fears that the Internet would isolate people and disconnect them from reality were unfounded.

Kelley's initial idea had to be modified almost immediately: The museum's budget could not cover setting up a Web site, much less travel expenses for the participants. Another idea then took shape. During his research for the project, Kelley had received from a collector photocopies of every image of Kandor that had appeared in the Superman series. He was intrigued to find that the city had

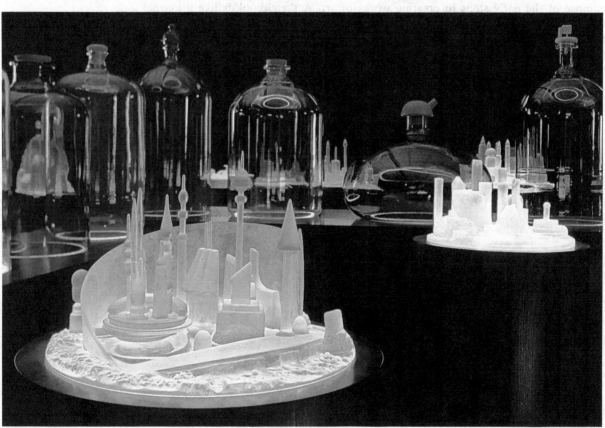

1.13 Mike Kelley. *Kandors Full Set*, detail. 2005–09. Cast resin, blown glass, illuminated pedestals; dimensions variable.
Punta della Dogana, François Pinault Foundation, Venice. Photo Fredrik Nilsen, Courtesy Gagosian Gallery. Art © Mike Kelley Foundation for the Arts. All Rights Reserved/Licensed by VAGA, New York, NY

never been drawn the same way twice. There had never been a standardized image for the artists to follow. In the unstable image of Superman's childhood home, Kelley found a link to one of his own artistic preoccupations: the partial and unrecoverable nature of childhood memories, including memories of the spaces in which childhood unfolds.

Kelley asked a digital animator to create a video of Kandor's constantly shifting shape, and he commissioned architects to begin a scale model of Kandor that drew freely on the photocopied images. The architects worked continuously as part of the exhibition, which included signage that advertised Kandor as though it were a housing development in progress. Kandor would be completed in the year 419500, one billboard announced—Kelley's estimate of how long it would take to build a model of every building in every version of the city. The project had shifted in meaning from Kelley's original concept, becoming a work about failure—failure to recapture the past, and the failure of so many optimistic visions of the future to come true.

The theme of Kandor was so rich that Kelley continued with it, this time focusing on the bell jar that kept the miniature city alive. He decided to commission twenty jars of blown colored glass, reproducing designs that appeared in the Superman images. Using the figures from the cartoon panels as a guide to scale, the largest jars were to be over 40 inches in height. One famous glass center after another told him that it was physically impossible to blow a vessel that large, but Kelley persevered, finally locating a glass blower who agreed to take on the challenge.

Kelley wanted to create a sense of motion and atmosphere inside the jars. He experimented with a number of methods to achieve this, including having particles of various substances blown around inside each jar by a compressor. This solution proved too noisy, but videos made of the swirling particles were captivating. Kelley worked with a composer to develop a soundtrack for the whirling, atmospheric patterns of each video. He had hoped to project the videos onto the bottles, but he found the results disappointing. Still, the videos were so compelling that he decided to include them in the exhibition, projected onto the walls. The jars, he decided, would now house models of twenty versions of Kandor cast in colored, translucent resin. Set on bases that Kelley designed after the Superman images, and lit from below, the models seem to glow from within. Only ten of the models were completed in time for the projected exhibit in 2007, but Kelley eventually finished all twenty, showing the complete set for the first time in 2010. Visitors wandered around a darkened room amid a display of luminous, jewel-like cities, empty bell jars, and haunting videos. Kelley had created an enchanted space, a prolonged meditation on memory, loss, and desire.[14]

We can see many of the traits of creativity at work in Kelley's narrative of his Kandor projects: the leap of imagination that led him to link Kandor to the museum's proposal, the flexibility with which he responded to setbacks by generating new ideas, the way continued reflection on the theme deepened its meaning for him and suggested new forms, his willingness to experiment and take risks, and, not least, the persistence and concentration that allowed him to see the project through to completion.

The profession of artist is not the only one that requires creativity. Scientists, mathematicians, teachers, business executives, doctors, librarians, computer programmers—people in every line of work, if they are any good, look for ways to be creative. Artists occupy a special place in that they have devoted their lives to opening the channels of *visual* creativity.

Can a person learn to be more creative? Absolutely, say researchers. The key to creativity is the ability to alternate quickly between two modes of thinking—generating ideas and analyzing them—and this ability can be consciously cultivated. Furthermore, by regularly practicing a creative activity, people can learn to tap into the brain's creative network more rapidly and effectively. Creativity may not bring happiness, but it promotes a richer, more engaged life, and it is as essential to looking at art as it is to making it. We close this chapter by considering what creative looking might entail.

Looking and Responding

Science tells us that seeing is a mode of perception, which is the recognition and interpretation of sensory data—in other words, how information comes into our eyes (ears, nose, taste buds, fingertips) and what we make of it. In visual perception, our eyes take in information in the form of light patterns; the brain processes these patterns to give them meaning. The role of the eyes in vision is purely mechanical. Barring some physical disorder, vision functions the same way for everyone. The brain then has to make sense of it.

The field of psychology has found that there are some commonalities in the ways we perceive visual information. In particular, graphic designers apply a series of principles from Gestalt theory when they work. Gestalt theory is based on the assumption that the whole is more than the sum of its parts. Our minds interpret visual information in predictable ways in order to make sense of what our eyes see. For example, we perceive that things located close together in an image, or that are the same color or size, are related. The letters in the poster for the bicycle company Public (**1.14**) are located near each other and two large ovals. They also share color and thickness with the ovals, so we assume that they belong together and act as a group. This group suggests the shape of a bicycle even though the form is not fully described and lots of typical bike parts are missing: spokes, seat, frame. Our mind nevertheless completes the bike to help us understand the overall image.

The mind's role in making sense of the visual information we perceive, however, is highly subjective. Simply put, given the same situation, we do not all notice

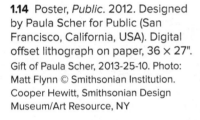

1.14 Poster, *Public*. 2012. Designed by Paula Scher for Public (San Francisco, California, USA). Digital offset lithograph on paper, 36 × 27". Gift of Paula Scher, 2013-25-10. Photo: Matt Flynn © Smithsonian Institution. Cooper Hewitt, Smithsonian Design Museum/Art Resource, NY

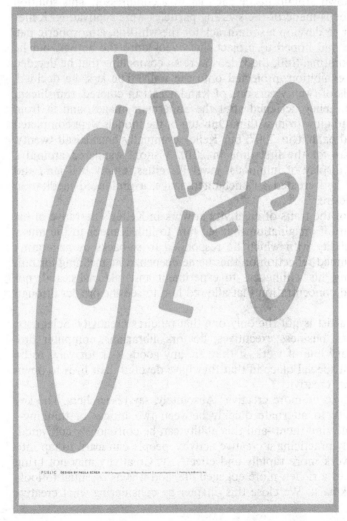

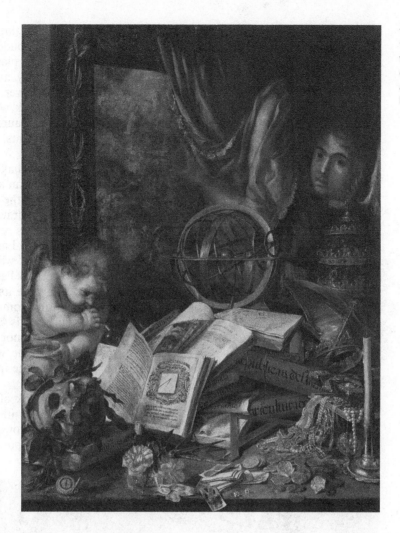

1.15 Juan de Valdés Leal. *Vanitas*. 1660. Oil on canvas, 51 ¾ × 39 ¹⁄₁₆". Wadsworth Atheneum, Hartford, Connecticut. The Ella Gallup Sumner and Mary Catlin Sumner Collection Fund, 1939.270

the same things, nor do we interpret what we see in the same way. One reason for differences in perception is the immense amount of detail available for our attention at any given moment. To navigate efficiently through daily life, we practice what is called selective perception, focusing on the visual information we need for the task at hand and relegating everything else to the background. But other factors are in play as well. Our mood influences what we notice and how we interpret it, as does the whole of our prior experience—the culture we grew up in, relationships we have had, places we have seen, knowledge we have accumulated.

The subjective nature of perception and interpretation explains why a work of art may mean different things to different people, and how it is that we may return to a favorite work again and again, noticing new aspects of it each time. It explains why the more we know, the richer each new encounter with art will be, for we will have more experience to bring to it. It explains why we should make every effort to experience as much art in person as possible, for physical dimensions also influence perception. The works reproduced in this book are miniaturized. Many other details escape reproduction as well.

Above all, the nature of perception suggests that the key to looking at art is to become aware of the process of looking itself—to notice details and visual relationships, to explore the associations and feelings they inspire, to search for knowledge we can bring to bear, and to try to put what we see into words. A quick glance at Juan de Valdés Leal's *Vanitas* (**1.15**) reveals a careless jumble of objects with a cherub looking over them. In the background, a man looks out at us from the shadows. But what are the objects? And what are the cherub and the man doing? Only if we begin to ask and answer such questions does the message of the painting emerge.

In the foreground to the left is a timepiece. Next to it are three flowers, each one marking a stage in the brief life of a bloom across time: budding, then blossoming, then dying as its petals fall away. Then come dice and playing cards, suggesting games of chance. Further on, a cascade of medals, money, and jewelry leads up to an elaborate crown, suggesting honors, wealth, and power. At the center, books and scientific instruments evoke knowledge. Finally, back where we began, a skull crowned with a laurel wreath lies on its side. Laurel traditionally crowns those who have become famous through their achievements, especially artistic achievements.

Over this display the cherub blows a bubble, as though making a comment on the riches before him. A bubble's existence is even shorter than a flower's—a few seconds of iridescent beauty, and then nothing. When we meet the man's gaze, we catch a glimpse of a wing: He is an angel, a messenger. He has drawn back a heavy curtain with one hand and is pointing at a painting he has thus revealed with the other. "Look at this," he all but speaks. The painting depicts the Last Judgment. In Christian belief, the Last Judgment is the moment when Christ will appear again. He will judge both the living and the dead, accepting some into Paradise and condemning others to Hell. The universe will end, and with it, time itself.

We might paraphrase the basic message of the painting something like this: "Life is fleeting, and everything we prize and strive for during it is ultimately meaningless. Neither wealth nor beauty nor good fortune nor power nor knowledge nor fame will save us when we stand before God at the end of the world." Without taking the time to perceive and reflect on the many details of the image, we would miss its message completely.

Vanitas is Latin for "vanity." It alludes to the biblical Book of Ecclesiastes, a meditation on the fleeting nature of earthly life and happiness in which we read that in the end, "all is vanity." The title wasn't invented or bestowed by the artist, however. Rather, it is a generic name for a subject that was popular during his

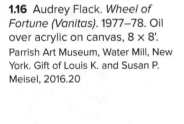

1.16 Audrey Flack. *Wheel of Fortune (Vanitas).* 1977–78. Oil over acrylic on canvas, 8 × 8'. Parrish Art Museum, Water Mill, New York. Gift of Louis K. and Susan P. Meisel, 2016.20

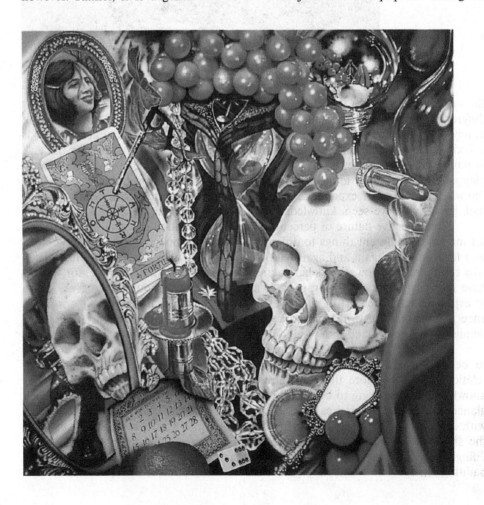

lifetime. Numerous *vanitas* paintings have come down to us from the 17th century, and together they show the many ways that artists treated its themes.

Closer to our own time, the painter Audrey Flack became fascinated by the *vanitas* tradition, and she created a series of her own, including *Wheel of Fortune (Vanitas)* (**1.16**). Knowing something of the tradition Flack is building on, we can more easily appreciate her updated interpretation. As ever, a skull puts us in mind of death. An hourglass, a calendar page, and a guttering candle speak of time and its passing. The necklace, mirrors, powder puff, and lipstick are contemporary symbols of personal vanity, while a die and a tarot card evoke the roles of chance and fate in our lives. As in the painting by Valdés Leal, a visual echo encourages us to think about a connection, in this case between the framed oval photograph of a young woman and the framed oval reflection of the skull just below.

Flack may be painting with one eye on the past, but the other is firmly on our society as it is now. For example, she includes modern inventions such as a photograph and a lipstick tube, and she shuns symbols that no longer speak to us directly, such as laurels and a crown. The specifically Christian context is gone as well, resulting in a more general message that applies to us all, regardless of faith: time passes quickly, beauty fades, chance plays a bigger role in our lives than we like to think, death awaits.

Despite their differences, both Flack and Valdés Leal provide us with many clues to direct our thoughts. They depict objects that have common associations and then trust us to add up the evidence. The stark geometry of Maya Lin's Vietnam Veterans Memorial (see 1.6) does not provide such obvious clues. Like much abstract art, this wall cut into a grassy hillside leaves interpretation to the viewer. Is it a wound or gash? Is it the earth opening to accept the bodies of the fallen? In the end, what we see in the memorial depends on what we bring to it, and if we approach the task sincerely, there are no wrong answers.

The Vietnam Veterans Memorial will never mean exactly the same for the artist and every viewer, nor should it. An artist's work grows from a lifetime of experiences, thoughts, and emotions; no one else can duplicate them exactly. Works of art hold many meanings. The greatest of them seem to speak anew to each generation and to each attentive observer. The most important thing is that some works of art come to mean something for *you*, that your own experiences, thoughts, and emotions find a place in them, for then you will have made them live.

Notes to the Text

1. Quoted in Friedrich Teja Bach, "Brancusi: The Reality of Sculpture," *Constantin Brancusi 1876-1957* (Philadelphia Museum of Art, 1995), p. 24.

2. Quoted in Liz Dawtrey et al., *Investigating Modern Art* (London: Yale University Press in association with the Open University, 1996), p. 139.

3. Maya Lin, *Boundaries*, copyright © 2000 by Maya Lin Studio, Inc. Reprinted with the permission of SSA, a division of Simon & Schuster, Inc. All rights reserved.

4. Ibid.

5. Ibid.

6. Ibid.

7. Ibid.

8. Vincent van Gogh. Letter to Theo van Gogh, July 9, 1888, Letter 506. Translated and edited by Robert Harrison, copyright © 2018 WebExhibits. http://webexhibits.org/vangogh/letter/18/506.htm.

9. Vincent van Gogh. Letter to Theo van Gogh, March 11, 1883, Letter 274. Translated by Mrs. Johanna van Gogh-Bonger, edited by Robert Harrison, copyright © 2018 WebExhibits. http://webexhibits.org/vangogh/letter/12/274.htm.

10. Vincent van Gogh. Letter to Theo van Gogh, September 5-6, 1889, Letter 800, *Vincent van Gogh: The Complete Letters*, copyright © 2009 Van Gogh Museum, Enterprises B.V.

11. Ibid., June 5, 1888, Letter 602.

12. Ibid., August 18, 1888, Letter 663.

13. For details about these experiments and for information about creativity in general, see

R. Jung et al., "White Matter Integrity, Creativity, and Psychopathology: Disentangling Constructs with Diffusion Tensor Imaging," *PLoS ONE*, vol. 5, no. 3 (March 2010), journals.plos.org/plosone/article?id=10.1371/journal.pone.0009818; Po Bronson and Ashley Merryman, "The Creativity Crisis," *Newsweek*, July 10, 2010, newsweek.com/creativity-crisis-74665; Patricia Cohen, "Charting Creativity: Signposts of a Hazy Territory," *The New York Times*, May 8, 2010, nytimes.com/2010/05/08/books/08creative.html; Robert J. Sternberg, "What Is the Common Thread of Creativity? Its Dialectical Relation to Intelligence and Wisdom," *American Psychologist*, vol. 56, no. 4 (April 2001), pp. 360–62; Mihaly Csikszentmihalyi, "The Creative Personality," *Psychology Today*, July 1, psychologytoday.com/articles/199607/the-creative-personality 1996. All articles accessed April 27, 2018.

14. Kelley's account, necessarily truncated here, is well worth reading in its entirety. It can be found in Mike Kelley, *Kandors* (Cologne: Jablonka Galerie; Munich: Hirmer Verlag, 2010), pp. 53–60.

Chapter 2
What Is Art?

In this chapter, you will learn to

LO1   explain relationships between artists and their audience,

LO2   discuss the relationship between art and beauty,

LO3   categorize art by its appearance,

LO4   examine art for its meaning, and

LO5   summarize some purposes for art.

Art is something that has great value in many societies. Around the world, art museums are as much a point of civic pride as new sports stadiums, pleasant shopping districts, public libraries, and well-maintained parks. From daring structures designed by famous architects to abandoned industrial buildings reclaimed as exhibition spaces, new museums are encouraged by city governments eager to revitalize neighborhoods and attract tourists. Inside museums, art is made available in many ways, not only in the galleries themselves, but also in shops that offer illustrated books, exhibition catalogs, and photographs of famous artworks reproduced on posters, calendars, coffee mugs, and other merchandise. The prestige of art is such that many of us visit museums because we feel it is something we ought to do, even if we're not exactly sure why.

But what is art? This is not an easy question to answer. By far the most famous work of Western art is the *Mona Lisa* (**2.1**). Leonardo da Vinci painted this portrait during the early years of the 16th century. The sitter or person pictured was a woman named Lisa del Giocondo (née Gherardini). Leonardo portrayed her seated on a balcony that overlooks a landscape of rock and water. Her left forearm rests on the arm of her chair; her right hand settles gently over her left wrist. She turns her head to look at us with a hint of a smile.

The portrait dazzled Leonardo's contemporaries, to whom it appeared almost miraculously lifelike. The *Mona Lisa*'s current fame, however, is a product of our own modern era. The painting first went on view to the public in 1797, when it was placed in the newly created Louvre Museum in Paris. Writers and poets of the 19th century became mesmerized by what they took to be the mystery and mockery of the sitter's smile. They described her as a dangerous beauty, a fatal attraction, a mysterious sphinx, a vampire, and other fanciful things. The public flocked to gaze. When the painting was stolen from the museum in 1911, people stood in line to see the empty space where it had been. When the painting was recovered two years later, its fame grew.

Today, still in the Louvre, the *Mona Lisa* attracts millions of visitors every year. Crowds gather. People standing toward the back raise their cameras over their heads to get a photograph of the famous masterpiece in the distance. Those patient enough to make their way to the front find their view obscured by glare from the bulletproof glass box in which the priceless painting is encased. The layer of protective varnish covering the paint surface has crackled and yellowed with age. Cleaning techniques exist, but who would take the risk with this irreplaceable work of art?

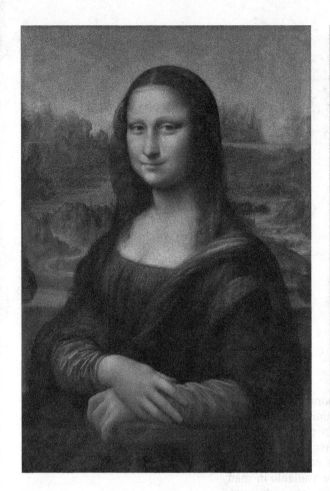

2.1 Leonardo da Vinci. *Mona Lisa*. ca. 1503–05. Oil on panel, 30 ¼ × 21".

Musée du Louvre, Paris. Photo © RMN-Grand Palais/Art Resource, NY

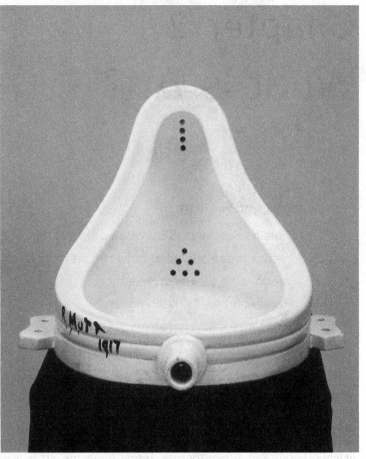

2.2 Marcel Duchamp. *Fountain*. 1917/1964. Edition Schwartz, Milan. Ceramic compound, height 14".

Indiana University Art Museum, Bloomington. Partial gift of Mrs. William Conroy. © Association Marcel Duchamp/ADAGP, Paris/Artists Rights Society (ARS), New York 2019

What about Marcel Duchamp's *Fountain* (**2.2**)? It is a type of art known as a *ready-made*. This means that Duchamp did not *make* this urinal but only *designated* it as a work of art. He made this designation by entering *Fountain* into a New York art exhibition under a pseudonym, R. Mutt, which he slopped on in black paint as a signature. Here, we see a replica because Duchamp never intended for his ready-mades to be permanent. His project was to find an object—he insisted that it be an object with no aesthetic interest whatsoever—and exhibit it as art. After the exhibition, the object was to be returned to life.

Fountain was pure provocation. The exhibition organizers had stated that all works of art submitted for the exhibition would be accepted, and Duchamp wanted to see whether they really meant it. Yet as Duchamp well knew, *Fountain* also raised interesting philosophical questions: Does art have to be made by an artist? Is art a form of attention? If we have spent our lives perfecting this form of attention on various acknowledged masterpieces, can we then bestow it on absolutely anything? If so, how is an art object different from any other kind of object? Does art depend on context, on being shown in an "art place" such as a museum or a gallery? Can something be art in one place and not another? Is *Fountain* still art today, or was it art only for the time that Duchamp said it was?

These examples show that the ideas we have about art have changed and been tested. Even our use of the word *art* has a history. During the Middle Ages, the formative period of European culture, *art* was used in roughly the same sense as *craft*. Both words had to do with skill in making something. Forging a sword, weaving cloth, carving a cabinet—all these were spoken of as arts, for they involved specialized skills.

Beginning around 1500, during the period known as the Renaissance, painting, sculpture, and architecture came to be thought of as more elevated forms of art, but it was not until the 18th century that the division became formalized. It was then, during the period we know as the Enlightenment, that philosophers grouped painting, sculpture, and architecture together with music and poetry as the *fine arts* on the principle that they were similar kinds of activities—activities that required not just skill but also genius and imagination, and whose results gave pleasure as opposed to being useful. As the 19th century began, the word *fine* tended to drop away, leaving only *art*, often capitalized to distinguish it from earlier uses and underscore its new prestige. Also during the Enlightenment, the philosophical field of aesthetics came into being and began to ask questions: What is the nature of art? Is there a correct way to appreciate art? Are there objective criteria for judging art? Can we apply our concept of art to other cultures? Can we apply it backward to earlier eras in our own culture?

Duchamp's *Fountain* also raises questions about the role of artists in the production of a work of art. In his capacity as Spanish court painter, Diego Velázquez created his masterpiece, *Las Meninas* (*The Maids of Honor*) (**2.3**). At left, we see the painter demonstrating the role of an artist: to create a work of art with his own hands. Velázquez represents himself working on a very large canvas. Scholars debate what he might be painting. Perhaps it is the young princess, the *infanta*, who stands regally at center surrounded by her attendants (*meninas*), one of whom is a dwarf.

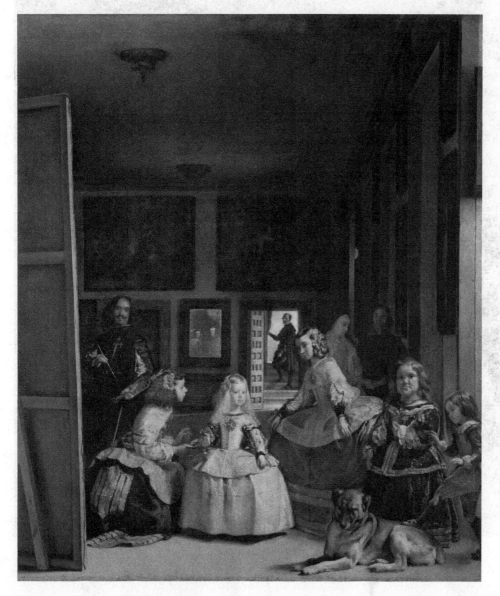

2.3 Diego Velázquez. *Las Meninas* (*The Maids of Honor*). 1656. Oil on canvas, 10' 5 ¼" × 9' ¾".
Museo del Prado, Madrid, Spain. Photograph Erich Lessing/Art Resource, NY

Or perhaps Velázquez is actually painting the king and queen, whom we see reflected in a mirror on the far wall.

Whatever the case, Velázquez used this painting to make a clear statement about the identity of the artist as creative genius. He came up with the idea for the image. He decided on the size, the colors, and the lighting. He figured out how to arrange or compose the princess and other figures on the canvas. He studied their faces, clothes, and poses and determined how to render them. He used his unique style of drawing and painting to execute the work. When the painting was finished, Velázquez's choices, decisions, and style were admired by the king, and the work was hung in the royal palace.

Contemporary Japanese artist Yasumasa Morimura, on the other hand, challenges the nature of this creative role. Morimura creates photographs that re-create well-known works from European and American art history, transforming them by inserting himself into the image. His 2013 *In praise of Velázquez* (**2.4**) copies many of Velázquez's artistic choices: composition, colors, lighting, figures, and dress. Morimura also includes his self-portrait, as Velázquez did. However, every figure in Morimura's photograph is a self-portrait; the artist dressed as each char-

2.4 Yasumasa Morimura. *In praise of Velázquez: Distinguished ones in confinement.* 2013. Chromogenic print, 30 ¹¹⁄₁₆ × 25 ⁹⁄₁₆".
© Yasumasa Morimura; Courtesy of the artist and Luhring Augustine, New York

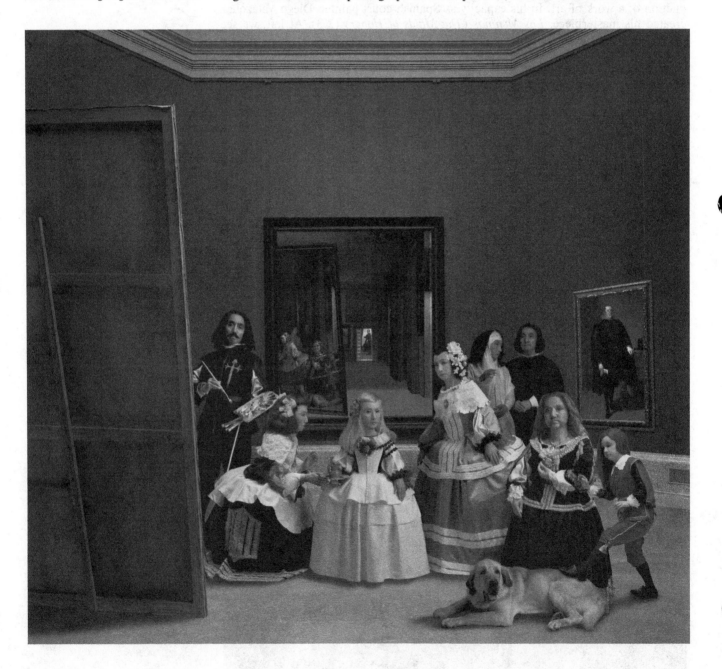

acter, photographed himself, and later assembled the photographs into a single image. Morimura re-created the *Las Meninas* painting inside the gallery at Madrid's Prado Museum where the original painting hangs (Velázquez's work is visible in the background of the newer work). Morimura appropriated the Spanish painter's painting and transformed it into his own creation; he took from Velázquez and made something new. But his work, like Duchamp's ready-made, raises questions about the artist's role in the creative process. Who owns the idea for a work of art? What is originality?

Many answers have been proposed to questions about what art is and what artists do, but the fact that philosophers still debate them should tell us that the questions are not easy. This chapter will not give any definitive answers. Rather, we will explore topics that touch on some common assumptions that many of us have about art and artists. We will look at where our ideas come from and compare them with ideas that were current earlier and elsewhere. Our goal is to arrive at an understanding of art as we find it today, in the early 21st century.

Artist and Audience

Yasumasa Morimura works within today's art world. He attended art school, where he honed his skills and ideas. He works in a studio, where he comes up with the concepts for his images and executes them. He exhibits this work in galleries and museums, special locations principally dedicated to the display of art for a viewing public. Art critics review his shows, evaluating his work for its beauty, ideas or concepts, and execution. Good reviews—or simply their own taste—lead art collectors to purchase Morimura's photographs for display in their homes and offices. Other works are purchased by museums and still others are resold through auction sales. While all this happens to work he has already created, Morimura continues making art and exhibiting it in galleries.

This world of independent artists, art schools, galleries, critics, collectors, and museums is familiar to us today. We may think of it as the way things have always been, but to the 15th-century Italian artist Andrea del Verrocchio, it would have seemed strange indeed. One of the foremost artists of the early Renaissance, Verrocchio did not create what he wanted to but what his clients, known as patrons, asked him to. He did not work alone but ran a workshop staffed with assistants and apprentices—a small business, essentially—that produced paintings, altarpieces, sculptures, banners, objects in precious metals, and architecture. He did not hope to have his art enshrined in museums, for there were no museums. Instead, displayed in public spaces, private residences, civic buildings, churches, and monasteries, the products of his workshop became part of the fabric of daily life in Florence, the town where he lived and worked.

One of Verrocchio's best-known works is a statue of the biblical hero David (**2.5**). The work was commissioned by Piero de' Medici, the head of a wealthy and powerful Florentine family, for display in the Medici family palace. Piero's sons later sold it to the City of Florence, which had adopted the story of David and his victory over Goliath as an emblem of its own determination to stand up to larger powers. Thereafter, the statue was displayed in the city hall.

Verrocchio had learned his skills as all artists of the time did, by serving as an apprentice in the workshop of a master. Boys (the opportunity was available only to males) began their apprenticeship between the ages of seven and fifteen. In exchange for their labor they received room and board and sometimes a small salary. Menial tasks came first, together with drawing lessons. Gradually apprentices learned such essential skills as preparing surfaces for painting and casting statues in bronze. Eventually, they were allowed to collaborate with the master on important commissions. When business was slow, they might make copies of the master's works for sale over the counter. Verrocchio trained many apprentices in his turn, including a gifted teenager named Leonardo da Vinci. The *David* may actually be a portrait of him.

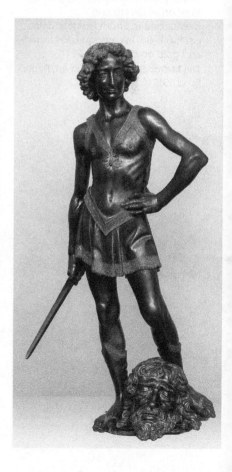

2.5 Andrea del Verrocchio. *David.* ca. 1465. Bronze with gold details, height 3' 11 ¼".
Museo Nazionale del Bargello, Florence.
Erich Lessing/Art Resource, NY

Our next three artists also learned through apprenticeship and served as court artists, working for a powerful patron. Dasavanta, Madhava Khurd, and Shravana were employed in the royal workshops of Akbar, a 16th-century emperor of the Mughal dynasty in India. Their job, for which they were paid a monthly salary, was to produce lavishly illustrated books for the delight of the emperor and his court. Akbar ascended to the throne at the age of thirteen, and one of his first requests was for an illustrated copy of the *Hamzanama*, or *Tales of Hamza*. Hamza was an uncle of the Prophet Muhammad, the founder of Islam. The stories of his colorful adventures were (and still are) beloved throughout the Islamic world. Much as the Spanish king turned to his court artist, Diego Velázquez, to represent his daughter, Akbar relied on Dasavanta, Madhava Khurd, and Shravana to give form to his vision.

Illustrating the 360 tales of the *Hamzanama* occupied dozens of artists for almost fifteen years. The painting here, attributed to Dasavanta, Shravana, and Tara, portrays an episode with Hamza's allies, Princes Qasim and Badi'uzzaman (**2.6**). A single artist would sometimes be responsible for an entire illustration, but more often the paintings were the result of collaboration, with each artist contributing what he did best.

Verrocchio and the artists working at the Mughal court knew their patrons. They produced work in response to specific commissions ordering a sculpture of a biblical hero or a manuscript of a venerable historical person. Much other art, however, has been produced on speculation, with artists creating works to respond

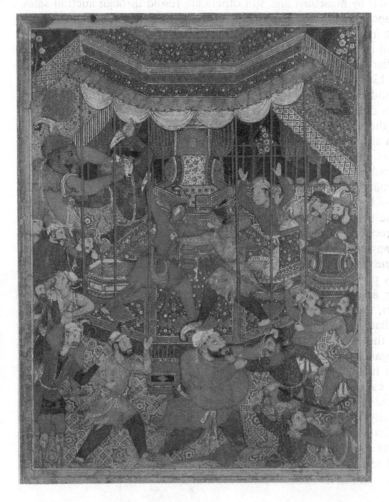

2.6 Dasavanta, Shravana, and Tara (attr.). "Hamza's Heroes Fight in Support of Qasim and Badi'uzzaman," from *Hamzanama*. ca. 1564–69. Ink, opaque watercolor, and gold on cloth, 27 × 21¼".
The Metropolitan Museum of Art, Rogers Fund, 1918

to a general demand for a type of image. The *Virgin of the Immaculate Conception* (2.7) was carved by an unknown artist in the Philippine islands. The sculpture represents the Virgin Mary and illustrates the Catholic doctrine of Mary's conception without the stain of original sin. Mary is pictured as a young woman standing with her hands clasped. The sculpture leans slightly to the left because it was carved from a curved ivory elephant tusk. This natural curvature helps Mary look humble and submissive. Glass eyes, inserted through the back of the head, make the image more lifelike, and gold paint and a silver halo add a heavenly luxury.

The artist responsible for this sculpture never met the person who ultimately purchased it. Beginning in the late 16th century, large workshops in Manila employed artists from what is today the Philippines and China to make luxury goods and religious images. These artists worked under the direction of European missionaries. They created sculptures such as this one as export items to be sent across the Pacific Ocean to Latin America and Europe. Buyers in Mexico City, Madrid, or Rome purchased the objects both for their religious theme and because of their "exotic" source on the other side of the world. European colonization and global trade spurred similar workshops in what are now China, India, and Sri Lanka. At each, local artists worked on speculation, responding to the demand for export goods.

Our final artist takes us out of the realm of professional training, career paths, and intended audiences altogether. James Hampton had no particular training in art, and the only audience he ever sought during his lifetime was himself. Hampton worked for most of his adult life as a janitor for the federal government in Washington, D.C., but for many years he labored secretly on an extraordinary work called *Throne of the Third Heaven of the Nations' Millennium General Assembly* (2.8). Discovered after his death in a garage that he had rented, the work represents Hampton's vision of the preparation for the Second Coming as described in the biblical Book of Revelation. Humble objects and cast-off furniture are here transformed by silver and gold foil to create a dazzling setting ready to receive those who will sit in judgment at the end of the world.

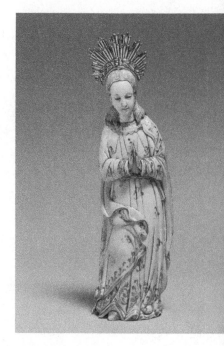

2.7 *Virgin of the Immaculate Conception.* 18th century. Ivory, height 10".
The Metropolitan Museum of Art, New York. Gift of Loretta Hines Howard, 1964

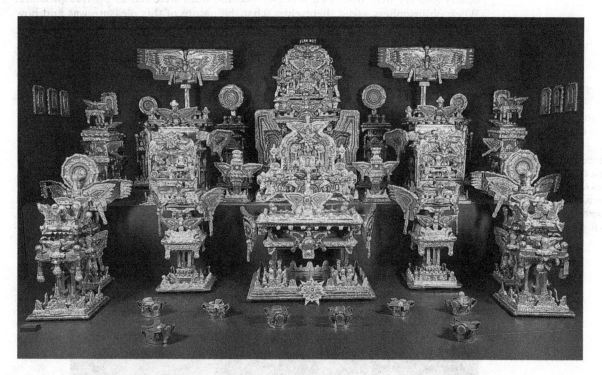

2.8 James Hampton. *Throne of the Third Heaven of the Nations' Millennium General Assembly.* ca. 1950–64. Gold and silver aluminum foil, colored kraft paper and plastic sheets over wood, paperboard, and glass; 180 pieces, 105 × 27 × 14 ½'.
National Museum of American Art, Smithsonian Institution, Washington, D.C. Photo Smithsonian American Art Museum, Washington, D.C./Art Resource, NY

We do not know whether Hampton considered himself an artist or whether he intended his work to be seen as art. He may have thought only about realizing a spiritual vision. The people who opened his garage after his death might easily have discarded *Throne of the Third Heaven of the Nations' Millennium General Assembly* as a curiosity. Instead, they recognized it as an example of outsider art, meaning art created by a self-taught artist. Outsider art has recently attracted the interest of collectors and arts institutions. Today, Hampton's work is in a museum collection and on view to the public.

Our contemporary ideas about art carry with them ideas about the person who makes it, the artist, and the people it is for, the audience. We take it for granted that the artist's task is to pursue his or her own vision of art; to express his or her own ideas, insights, and feelings; and to create as inner necessity dictates. We believe these things so strongly that we recognize people such as James Hampton as artists and accept a broad range of creations as art. We assume that art is for anyone who takes an interest in it, and through museums, galleries, books, magazines, and academic courses we make it available to a wide public. Other times and places did not necessarily share these ideas, and most visual creators across history have worked under very different assumptions about the nature of their task, the purpose it served, and the audience it was for.

Art and Beauty

Beauty is deeply linked to our thinking about art. Aesthetics, the branch of philosophy that studies art, also studies the nature of beauty. Many of us assume that a work of art should be beautiful, and even that art's entire purpose is to be beautiful. Why should we think that way, and is what we think true?

During the 18th century, when our modern concept of art came into being, beauty and art were discussed together because both were felt to provide pleasure. When philosophers asked themselves what the nature of this pleasure was and how it was perceived, their answer was that it was an intellectual pleasure and that we perceived it through a special kind of attention called disinterested contemplation. By "disinterested" they meant that we set aside any personal, practical stake we might have in what we are looking at. For example, if we are examining a peach to

2.9 Edward Weston. *Cabbage Leaf.* 1931. Gelatin silver print, 7 ⁹⁄₁₆ × 9 ⁷⁄₁₆".

The Museum of Modern Art, New York. Gift of T. J. Maloney. Digital image © The Museum of Modern Art/Licensed by SCALA/Art Resource, NY. © 2019 Center for Creative Photography, Arizona Board of Regents/Artists Rights Society (ARS), New York

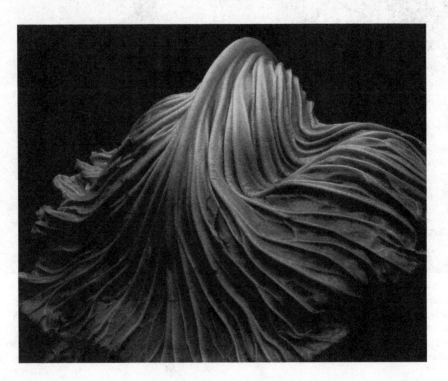

see whether it is ripe enough to eat, we are contemplating it with a direct personal interest. If we step back to admire its color, its texture, its roundness, with no thought of eating it, then we are contemplating it disinterestedly. If we take pleasure in what we see, we say the peach is beautiful.

Edward Weston's photograph *Cabbage Leaf* embodies this form of cool, distanced attention (**2.9**). Gazing at the way the light caresses the gracefully arching leaf, we can almost feel our vision detaching itself from practical concerns (good for coleslaw, or is it too wilted?). As we look, we become conscious of the curved object as a pure form, and not a thing called "cabbage leaf" at all. It looks perhaps like a wave crashing on the shore, or a ball gown trailing across a lawn. Letting our imagination play in this way is part of the pleasure that philosophers described.

But is pleasure what we always feel in looking at art? For a print such as Käthe Kollwitz's *Woman with Dead Child*, "sadness" might be a more appropriate word (**2.10**). Kollwitz has borrowed the theme of a mother with a dead child from the *pietà,* a standard subject in Christian art picturing Mary, the mother of Jesus, holding her son after he was taken down from the Cross. The artist used herself and her son as models to represent the mother's profound grief over her child's death. The woman wraps her body around her son and envelops him one last time. Although the subject matter is both sad and moving, as opposed to pleasurable, many people may still find the print beautiful.

Some theories link beauty to formal qualities such as symmetry, repeated lines, simple geometrical shapes, and the play of colors. Here, for example, Kollwitz has posed the mother in a roughly triangular shape, from the top of her head to the knee and foot of her left leg. The softly undulating lines that define her body parts repeat throughout the image. The mother's round head is mirrored by the slightly smaller head of her child. Although different versions of this print have different colors, the gray figures contrast with the color in the background. If we find Kollwitz's *Woman with Dead Child* beautiful, perhaps those are the qualities we are reacting to.

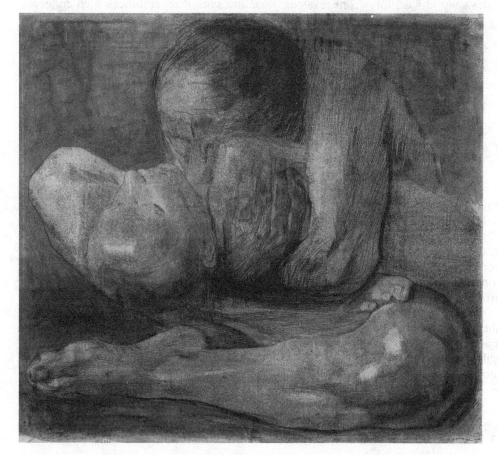

2.10 Käthe Kollwitz. *Woman with Dead Child*, 3rd state. 1903. Soft-ground etching with engraving, printed in black and overworked with gold and pencil on thick cream wove paper, 16 5/16 × 18 9/16".
Yale University Art Gallery. © 2019 Artist Rights Society, NY

Aesthetics

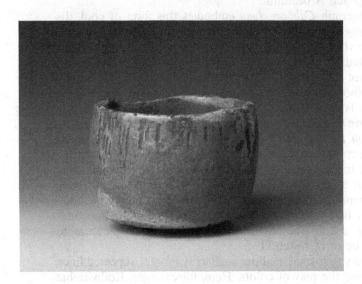

What is the definition of *aesthetics*? What do the aesthetics of various cultures encountered so far tell us about their creative expression and values? How have aesthetic preferences shaped what we see in museums?

The word *aesthetics* was coined in the early 18th century by a German philosopher named Alexander Baumgarten. He derived his word from the Greek word for "perception"—*aisthanomai*—and he used it to name what he considered to be a field of knowledge, the knowledge gained by sensory experience combined with feelings. Aesthetics is a branch of philosophy concerned with notions of the beautiful in works of art. We also speak of an aesthetic as a set of principles or characteristics of what is considered beautiful in a particular time and place.

In Baumgarten's time, Western audiences viewed the Classical art of ancient Greece and Rome and the Italian Renaissance as the most aesthetically pleasing. They measured all art against these standards, and considered art without roots to the ancient Mediterranean to be ugly or "primitive." Collectors in Paris, London, and New York would display these works in anthropological collections rather than in art museums.

This kind of cultural prejudice changed over the course of the 20th century, and today we understand that exploring the aesthetics of other cultures can help us to appreciate what expressive forms they value and why. For example, the tea bowl shown here was formed by hand in the Japanese province of Shigaraki during the late 16th or early 17th century. By the aesthetic standards of 18th- and 19th-century Western culture, this small vessel is not beautiful. Yet for the Japanese culture that produced it, the bowl reflects two key concepts that form part of Japanese tastes: *wabi* and *sabi. Wabi* embraces such concepts as naturalness, simplicity, understatement, and impermanence. *Sabi* adds overtones of loneliness, old age, and tranquility. The two terms are central to the aesthetics that developed around the austere variety of Buddhism known as Zen. They are especially connected with the Zen-inspired practice we know as the tea ceremony. Through its connection with the tea ceremony and with Zen Buddhist spiritual ideals, this simple bowl partakes in a rich network of meanings and associations that are valued in its context.

Whether or not the Japanese tea bowl looks as "beautiful" as a Greek vase to us is irrelevant, just as whether or not Manohar's portrait of Jahangir (see 1.8) looks as "beautiful" as the *Mona Lisa* (see 2.1). Our opinions are shaped by the aesthetic preferences we were raised with. Each of the works in this book reflects a different, and equally valuable, aesthetic. One is not better than the next. All are beautiful and worthy of study within their own contexts and within this book as we seek to appreciate art.

Hon'ami Kōetsu (attr.) Teabowl. Edo period, 17th century. Kyoto ware, height 3 ¾". H. O. Havemeyer Collection, Bequest of Mrs. H. O. Havemeyer, 1929. The Metropolitan Museum of Art.

To contemplate the formal beauty of Kollwitz's print, we detach ourselves from the pitiable subject matter in somewhat the same way that Edward Weston detached himself from any feelings he might have had about cabbages to create his photograph. But not all art makes this sort of detachment so easy. An image such as Francisco de Goya's *Saturn Devouring One of His Children* seems to shut down any possibility for aesthetic distance (**2.11**). It grabs us by the throat and shows us a vision of pure horror.

A Spanish painter working during the decades around the turn of the 19th century, Goya lived through tumultuous times and witnessed terrible acts of cruelty, stupidity, warfare, and slaughter. As an official painter to the Spanish court, he painted lighthearted scenes, tranquil landscapes, and dignified portraits, as asked. In works he created for his own reasons, he expressed his increasingly pessimistic view of human nature. *Saturn Devouring One of His Children* is one of a series of nightmarish images that Goya painted on the walls of his own house. By their compelling visual power and urgent message, we recognize them as extraordinary art. But we must admit that they leave notions of pleasure and beauty far behind.

Art can indeed produce pleasure, as the first philosophers of aesthetics noted. But it can also inspire sadness, horror, pity, awe, and a full range of other emotions. The common thread is that in each case we find the experience of looking to be valuable for its own sake. Art makes looking worthwhile. Similarly, art can be

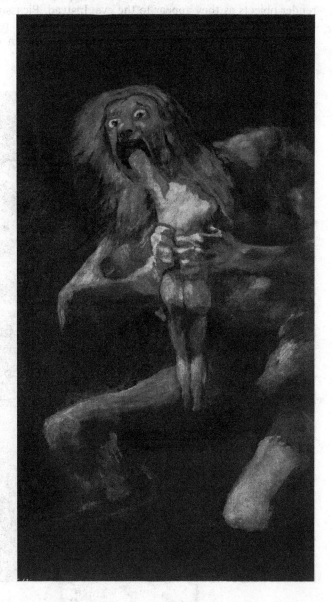

2.11 Francisco de Goya. *Saturn Devouring One of His Children.* ca. 1820–22. Wall painting in oil on plaster (since detached and transferred to canvas), 57 ⅞ × 32 ⅝".

Museo del Prado, Madrid. Image copyright Museo Nacional del Prado/ Art Resource, NY beautiful, but not all art tries to be beautiful, and beauty is not a requirement for art. Beauty remains a mysterious concept, something that everyone senses, many disagree about, and no one has yet defined. Artists are as fascinated by beauty as any of us and return to it again and again, though not always in the form we expect. Often, they seek out beauty in new places—in a cabbage leaf, for example.

Art and Appearances

The two artworks seen here both picture things from everyday life, yet they appear very different. The bread, baskets, vessels, and other items in Antonio Pérez de Aguilar's painting (**2.12**) look the way they do in nature. This truth to natural appearance had been a goal of Western art since the Renaissance, and European colonization brought the lifelike style of painting to the Americas in the 16th century. Painting in Mexico in the 18th century, Pérez de Aguilar took pains to render on the canvas the textures, shapes, colors, lighting, and spaces of his subject as they appeared to his eye.

Although Pablo Picasso mastered this traditional technique while still a teenager, he soon abandoned it for a style of art known as Cubism. His drawing and collage *Bottle of Vieux Marc, Glass, Guitar and Newspaper* (**2.13**) does not try to render objects as they appear to the eye. Instead, Picasso distorted and broke apart the objects he pictured. He also altered the viewer's relationship to them. Some items we see from above and some from the side. In doing so, Picasso rejected traditional Western techniques.

2.12 Antonio Pérez de Aguilar. *Painter's Cupboard.* 1769. Oil on canvas, 49 ¼ × 38 ⅝".
Museo Nacional de Arte, Mexico. The Artchives/Alamy Stock Photo

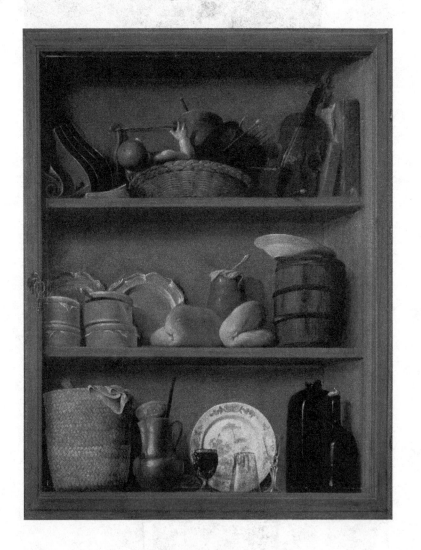

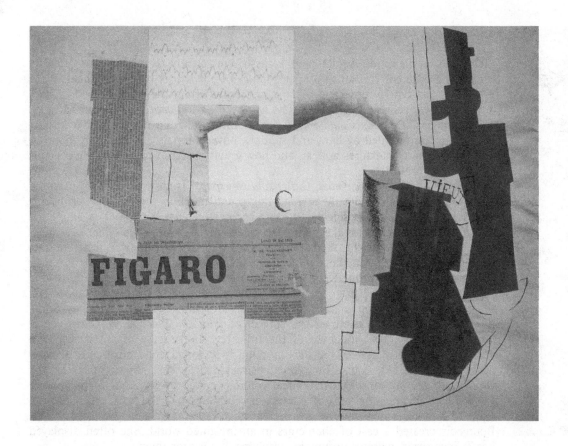

2.13 Pablo Picasso. *Bottle of Vieux Marc, Glass, Guitar and Newspaper*. 1913. Printed papers, 18 ⅜ × 24 ⅝".

© Tate, London/Art Resource, NY. © 2019 Estate of Pablo Picasso/Artists Rights Society (ARS), New York

Picasso was part of a generation of artists who opened up new territory for Western art to explore. These artists had been trained in traditional skills, and yet they set off on paths where those skills were not required. Many people wish they hadn't. Many people feel that art should aim at representing appearances as faithfully as possible, that artists who do not do this are not good artists, and that works such as *Bottle of Vieux Marc, Glass, Guitar and Newspaper* are not good art, or perhaps not even art at all.

Where do we get these ideas? The simple answer is that we get them from our own artistic heritage. For hundreds of years, Western art was distinguished among the artistic traditions of the world by precisely the concerns that Picasso and others turned their backs on. The elevation of painting and sculpture to a higher status during the Renaissance had gone hand in hand with the discovery of new methods for making optically convincing representations. From that time until almost the end of the 19th century, a period of about five hundred years, techniques for representing the observable world of light and shadow and color and space—the techniques evident in *Painter's Cupboard*—formed the foundation upon which Western art was built.

Why did art change all of a sudden? There are many reasons, but Picasso, when asked, pointed to one in particular: photography. "Why should the artist persist in treating subjects that can be established so clearly with the lens of a camera?" he asked.[1] Photography had been developed not long before the artists of Picasso's generation were born. They were the first generation to grow up taking it for granted. Photography is now so pervasive that we need to take a moment to realize how revolutionary that change was. From the time of Paleolithic cave paintings until about 160 years ago, images had to be made by hand. Suddenly, there was a mechanical way based on chemical reactions to light. For some artists, photography meant the end of painting, for manual skills were no longer needed to create a visual record. For Picasso, it meant liberation from a lifetime spent copying nature. "Now we know at least everything that painting isn't," he said.[2]

If the essence of art was not visual fidelity, however, what was it? Thus began the adventure of the 20th century.

Representational and Abstract Art

The works by Pérez de Aguilar and Picasso refer clearly to the visible world, yet each has a different relationship to it. *Painter's Cupboard* is **representational**. Pérez de Aguilar set out to represent—that is, to present again—the visible world in such a way that we recognize a likeness. The word *representational* covers a broad range of approaches. *Painter's Cupboard* is very faithful to visual experience, recording how forms are revealed by light and shadow, how materials and colors respond to light, how different textures appear, and how gravity makes weight felt. We call this approach **naturalistic**.

Bottle of Vieux Marc, Glass, Guitar and Newspaper is **abstract**. Picasso used the appearances of the world only as a starting point, much as a jazz musician begins with a standard tune. He selected certain aspects of what he saw, then simplified and fragmented them to make his image. A fragment of the edge of an oval table appears on the lower right. A shape that recalls part of the body of a guitar rests in the middle. A form on the right bearing the word "VIEUX" suggests the shape of a bottle. Pieces of printed paper are glued to the surface. Are they supposed to be resting on the table? If so, do we see the table from the top or from the side?

Like representation, abstraction embraces a broad range of approaches. Some of us might be able to decipher the subject of *Bottle of Vieux Marc, Glass, Guitar and Newspaper* without the help of the title, but the process of abstraction can continue much further, until the starting point is no longer recognizable. In *Woman with Packages* (**2.14**), Louise Bourgeois abstracted the visual impact of a standing woman all the way to a slender vertical column topped by an egg-shaped element. *Woman with Packages* belongs to a series of sculptures that the artist called *Personages*. A personage is a fictional character, as in a novel or a play. Like a writer, Bourgeois created a cast of characters in an imagined world. She often displayed her *Personages* in pairs or groupings, implying a story for them.

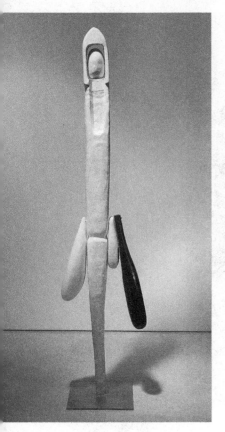

2.14 Louise Bourgeois. *Woman with Packages*. 1949. Bronze, polychromed, 65 × 18 × 12".
Collection the Easton Foundation; Photo Christopher Burke. Art © The Easton Foundation/Licensed by VAGA, New York, NY

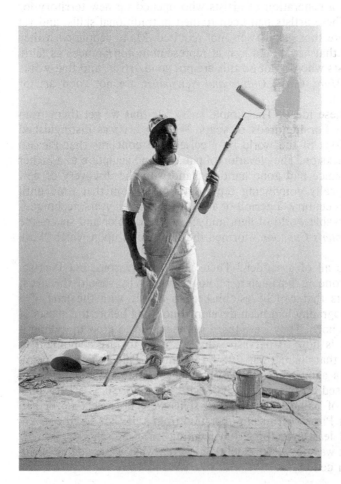

2.15 Duane Hanson. *Housepainter III*. 1984/1988. Autobody filler, polychromed, mixed media, with accessories; life-size.
Hanson Collection, Davie, Florida. Courtesy Mrs. Duane Hanson. Art © Estate of Duane Hanson/Licensed by VAGA, New York, NY

At the opposite end of the spectrum from Bourgeois's radically simplified forms are representational works so convincingly lifelike that we can be fooled for a moment into thinking that they are real. The word for this extreme optical fidelity is ***trompe l'oeil*** (pronounced tromp-loy), French for "fool the eye," and one of its modern masters was Duane Hanson. Hanson's sculptures portray ordinary people carrying out ordinary activities—cleaning ladies and tourists, museum guards and housepainters (**2.15**). Like a film director searching for an actor with just the right look for a role, Hanson looked around for the perfect person to "play" the type he had in mind. Once he had found his model (and, we may imagine, talked him or her into cooperating), he set the pose and made a mold directly from the model's body. Painted in lifelike skin tones and outfitted with hair, clothing, and props, the resulting sculptures can make us wonder how much distance we actually desire between art and life.

By opening Western art up to a full range of relationships to the visible world, artists of the 20th century created a bridge of understanding to other artistic traditions. For example, sculptors working many centuries ago in the Yoruba kingdom of Ife, in present-day Nigeria, also employed both naturalistic and abstract styles. Naturalistic portrait sculptures in brass were created to commemorate the kingdom's rulers (**2.16**). Displayed on altars dedicated to royal ancestors, each head was accompanied by a smaller, abstract version (**2.17**). The two heads relate to concepts that are still current in Yoruba thought today. The naturalistic head represents the outer, physical reality that can be perceived by the senses, and the abstract head represents the inner, spiritual reality that can be perceived only by the imagination. Similarly, Louise Bourgeois's *Woman with Packages* (see 2.14) could be said to portray the inner essence of the subject, whereas Duane Hanson's *Housepainter III* (see 2.15) is about how abstract concepts such as "housepainter" are rooted in the particular details of an individual.

Somewhere between naturalism and abstraction lies stylization. **Stylized** describes representational art that conforms to a preset style or set of conventions for depicting the world. The Chinese porcelain bowl illustrated in **2.18**, for example, is decorated with a depiction of a dragon flying through clouds in pursuit of a motif known as the flaming pearl. A band of clouds rings the rim of the bowl as well. The clouds are stylized, defined by lines that spiral inward like a snail shell or a

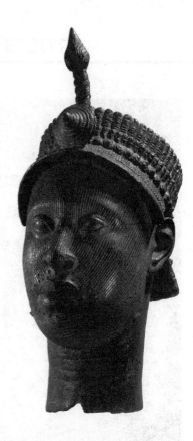

2.16 Head of a king, from Ife. Yoruba, ca. 13th century. Brass, life-size.

The British Museum, London. Werner Forman Archive/Universal Images Group/Getty

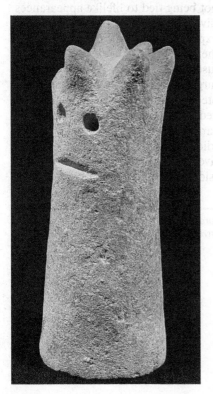

2.17 Cylindrical head, from Ife. Yoruba, ca. 13th–14th century. Terra cotta, height 6 ⅜".
National Museum, Ife, Nigeria. André Held/akg-images

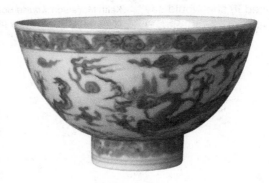

2.18 Bowl. China. 1506–21. Porcelain painted in underglaze blue and overglaze enamels, diameter 6 ⅜".
The Metropolitan Museum of Art, New York. Gift of Stanley Herzman, in memory of Adele Herzman, 1991, 1991.253.54. Image copyright © The Metropolitan Museum of Art. Image source: Art Resource, NY

Louise Bourgeois (1911–2010)

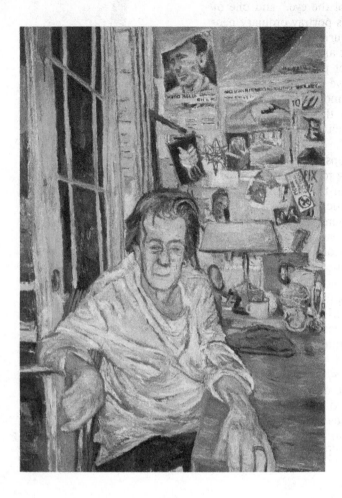

How do Bourgeois's works express emotion? How did she use abstraction to communicate her feelings?

Well into her ninth decade, Louise Bourgeois made art whose unsparing emotional honesty and restless formal inventiveness left far younger artists in awe. Her influence on art was profound. Explaining his portrait of Bourgeois seen here, painter Keith Mayerson said that artists would visit to gain her approval of their work: "[Y]ou would come up and present to her, and if she liked it, she would say 'Very good,' and would send you to the moon for weeks."[3]

Louise Bourgeois was born in Paris in 1911. Her parents were restorers of antique tapestries, and as a teenager Louise helped out by drawing missing parts so that they could be rewoven. Her home life was difficult and she lived through challenging times for Europe. After earning an undergraduate degree in philosophy, she studied art history at the Ecole du Louvre (a school attached to the famous museum) and studio art at the Ecole des Beaux Arts (the School of Fine Arts, France's most prestigious art school). Bourgeois was a restless student, however, and her dissatisfaction with official art education and its traditional techniques led her to explore alternative paths, most valuably a period of study with the painter Fernand Léger. In 1938 she married Robert Goldwater, a young American art historian who was in Paris doing research. The couple moved to New York that same year.

It was in America that Bourgeois discovered herself as an artist. "When I arrived in the United States from France I found an atmosphere that allowed me to do as I wanted," she told an interviewer.[4] Bourgeois exhibited frequently, gaining her first solo show of paintings in 1945. She exhibited her first sculptures four years later. The work, including *Woman with Packages* of 1949, was abstract and reduced forms to simple, organic shapes.

Bourgeois's abstract art expressed deep emotion, particularly through images of the body. She explained once, "It is not an image I am seeking. It's not an idea. It is an emotion you want to recreate, an emotion of wanting, of giving, and of destroying."[5] Abstraction offered a way to explore emotions by not being tied to lifelike appearances. As she explained, "I live in a world of emotions and my only obligation is to express them. I will try any material, shape or form to get there."[6]

In 1982, the Museum of Modern Art held a retrospective exhibit of Bourgeois's work, only the second such show it had ever devoted to a female artist. The attention the exhibition generated fueled an astonishing late flowering of creativity in the artist, and masterpieces poured forth from Bourgeois's studio, to worldwide acclaim. Among many honors she received was the National Medal of Arts, awarded to her by President Bill Clinton in 1997.

Keith Mayerson. *Louise Bourgeois at Her Salon.* 2008. Oil on linen, 42 × 30". Courtesy private collection. Image Marlborough Contemporary Gallery

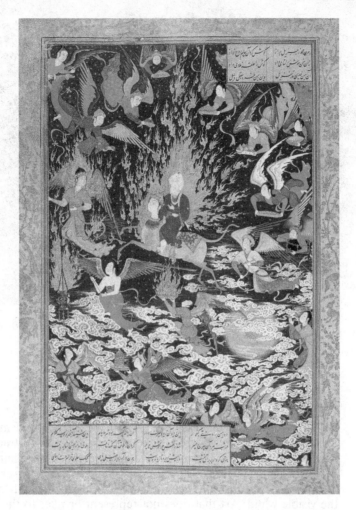

scroll. The individual clouds near the dragon are each formed from a bouquet of four scrolls and three trailing elements that wave like silk scarves in the breeze. The band of clouds around the rim is made of symmetrical, mushrooming scroll forms linked by waves of trailing scrolls.

Scrolling clouds were a convention in Chinese art for many centuries, appearing on embroidered robes, porcelain decoration, and paintings. They are especially associated with apparitions of divine beings, including dragons. If you look ahead to the Chinese Buddhist painting illustrated in 19.19, you will see at the upper left a depiction of paradise set on a bank of scrolling clouds. They were painted more than six hundred years before the clouds on the porcelain bowl, but they are stylized in the same way.

Chinese culture was highly influential, and scrolling clouds were adopted by artists in Korea, Vietnam, and Japan. To the West, they were taken up by Persian artists, as in this illustration of *The Ascent of the Prophet Muhammad* (**2.19**). Persian artists also adopted the Chinese convention of depicting radiating light as stylized flames. The single stylized flame that issues from the flaming pearl on the porcelain bowl—a writhing, branching form—is multiplied many times to indicate the light radiating from Muhammad, his miraculous mount, and the archangel Gabriel, who according to tradition guided Muhammad on his nighttime journey through the heavens.

Nonrepresentational Art

Even as Picasso and others experimented with abstraction, seeing how far art could go without severing its ties to the visible world, other artists at the beginning of the 20th century came to believe that only by abandoning these ties could art progress and realize its true nature. Instead of imitating or interpreting appearances, they

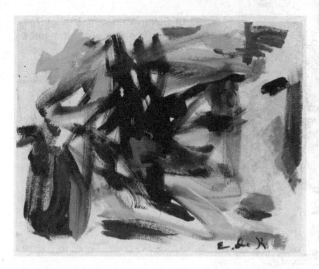

2.20 Elaine de Kooning. *Bullfight.* 1960. Acrylic on paper, 19 ¼ × 24 ⅝". Museum of Modern Art, New York. Larry Aldrich Foundation Fund/Digital Image © The Museum of Modern Art/Licensed by SCALA/Art Resource, NY

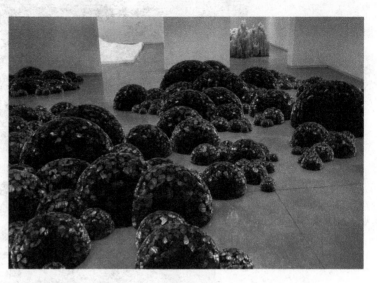

2.21 Tara Donovan. *Untitled (Mylar).* 2008. Mylar and hot glue, site-specific, dimensions variable.
Boston Globe / Contributor/Getty Images

found meaning and expressive power in the elements of art itself—in line, shape, form, and color. They referred to their art variously as abstract, nonrepresentational, and nonobjective. In this book, we reserve the term abstract for works such as Picasso's *Bottle of Vieux Marc, Glass, Guitar and Newspaper* (see 2.13) and Louise Bourgeois's *Woman with Packages* (see 2.14), which retain clues to their origins in the visible world. Art that does not represent or refer to the world outside itself we call **nonrepresentational** or **nonobjective**.

American painter Elaine de Kooning's *Bullfight* is an example of nonrepresentational art (**2.20**). It does not rely on any representations or pictures of things. There are thick strokes of brightly colored paint made in large, sweeping motions. There is nothing in the painting that is recognizable. There is no bull, sand, or matador. Although *Bullfight* contains no visual references to the real world, its title helps viewers to interpret what they see, as the brushstrokes express the movement, fear, fury, and pain we might associate with bullfights.

Nonrepresentational art never supplanted representational approaches, as some of its early practitioners predicted. Instead, it has taken its place as one of the possibilities available to contemporary artists, who continue to find ways to enliven it. Tara Donovan, for example, makes large-scale installations from accumulations of ordinary objects. She has stacked transparent plastic buttons until they resemble groups of stalagmites, covered a ceiling with an undulating blanket of Styrofoam cups, and stacked wooden toothpicks into a 3-foot-tall cube. Here, her chosen material is Mylar, scrolled and gathered into spheres, the spheres joined in a way that suggests that the sculpture grew by itself, and might grow still more as we watch (**2.21**).

Style

Terms such as *naturalistic* and *abstract* categorize art by the way it relates to the appearances of the visible world. A work of art, of course, has a place in the visible world itself. It has its own appearance, which is the result of the artist's efforts. A term that helps us to categorize art by its own appearance is *style*. **Style** refers to a distinctive, recognizable ensemble of recurring characteristics. If a person we know always wears jeans and cowboy boots, we identify that person with a certain style of dress. If a family has furnished their living room entirely in antiques except for one very modern chair, we would recognize a mix of styles. But if they do this in every room of their house, and in every house they live in, then we would say that mixing styles is their style, and we would call it eclectic, meaning drawing on many sources.

In the visual arts, as in other areas of life, style is the result of a series of choices, in this case choices an artist makes in creating a work of art. As we grow more familiar with a particular artist's work, we begin to see a recurring pattern to these choices—characteristic subject matter or materials, distinctive ways of drawing or of applying paint, preferences for certain colors or color combinations. For example, now that you have seen two paintings by Van Gogh (see 1.10 and the self-portrait on page 11), you can see certain traits they have in common, such as heightened color, thickly applied paint, distinct brushstrokes, distorted and exaggerated forms, and flamelike or writhing passages. Each subsequent work by Van Gogh that you come across will fine-tune what you already know about his style, just as what you already know will provide a framework for considering each new work.

One theory of art maintains that style is what distinguishes artists from other skillful makers. Not all people who set out to make art eventually develop an individual style, but all artists do. An enjoyable way to get a sense of the great range of individual styles is to compare works that treat similar subjects, as in the following three depictions of a woman having her hair combed. The first is a **woodcut** by the 18th-century Japanese artist Kitagawa Utamaro (**2.22**), the second a drawing in pastel by the 19th-century French artist Edgar Degas (**2.23**), and the third an oil painting by the 20th-century American artist Susan Rothenberg (**2.24**).

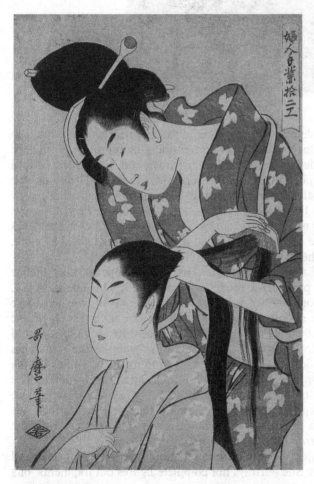

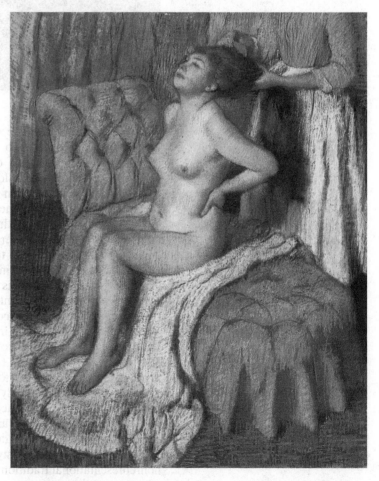

2.22 Kitagawa Utamaro. *Hairdressing*, from *Twelve Types of Women's Handicraft*. ca. 1798–99. Polychrome woodblock print, 15 3/16 × 10".
Library of Congress, Washington, D.C. Library of Congress Prints and Photographs Division Washington, D.C. FP 2 - JPD, no. 2191

2.23 Edgar Degas. *Woman Having Her Hair Combed*. ca. 1886–88. Pastel on paper, 29 1/8 × 23 7/8".
The Metropolitan Museum of Art, New York, H. O. Havemeyer Collection. Bequest of Mrs. H. O. Havemeyer, 1929, 29.100.35. Image copyright © The Metropolitan Museum of Art. Image source: Art Resource, NY

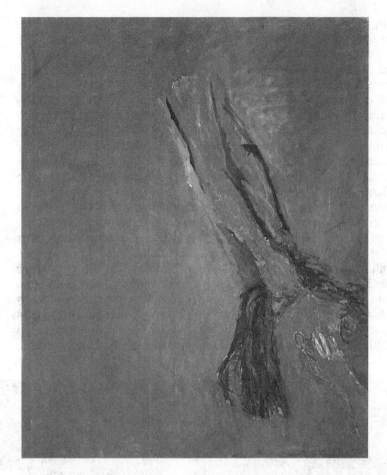

Utamaro's women are slightly stylized. They do not appear as they would in life, but instead conform to his community's conventions for representing figures: elegant, flat, and with little descriptive detail. Their robes, too, are stylized into a series of sinuous curves. Slender black lines describe the faces and features, the robes and their folds, even the individual strands of hair. We could take away the color altogether, and the lines would still tell us everything we need to know. Color is applied evenly, with no lighter or darker variations. This makes the robes seem flat, as though they were cut out of patterned paper. The background is blank, and gives no hint of where the scene is set.

Edgar Degas worked in a naturalistic style. His woman appears more lifelike and individualized, and was probably a model who posed for him in his studio. Faint lines describe the contours of her body and the chair she sits on, but these lines are not the sole source of information about the figure, as in the Japanese work. Colors are applied in individual strokes that remain distinct even as they build up in layers. Variations in color depict light and shadow, showing us the roundness and weight of the woman's body and sculpting the deep folds of the ruffles on the upholstered chair. Not all forms are depicted with equal attention to detail. The woman's body is very finely observed, whereas the outer areas of the image are treated more freely. The background is suggested rather than really described, yet the scene is clearly set in an interior. The composition is quite daring, with the servant's body cropped suddenly at the upper torso.

Susan Rothenberg's style is a unique combination of representational and nonrepresentational traditions. She portrays not complete figures but fragments, bits of representation that seem to surface like memories in a nonrepresentational painting. Here, two arms detach themselves from the red. Their hands grasp a dark mass—we understand it as hair only when we notice the small ear to the right that indicates a human head. A hand at the lower right offers a hair tie to secure the ponytail.

Each of these artists formed his or her style within a particular culture during a particular historical moment. Artists working in the same culture during the same period often have stylistic features in common, and in this way individual styles contribute to our perception of larger, general styles. General styles fall into several categories. There are *cultural styles* (Aztec style in Mesoamerica), *period* or *historical styles* (Gothic style in Europe), and *school styles*, which are styles shared by a particular group of like-minded artists (Cubist style). General styles provide a useful framework for organizing the history of art, and familiarity with them can help us to situate art and artists that are new to us in a historical or cultural context, which often helps understanding. But it is important to remember that general styles are constructed after the fact, as scholars discern broad trends by comparing the work of numerous individual artists. Cultures, historical periods, and schools do not create art. Individuals create art, working with (and sometimes pushing against) the possibilities that their time and place hold out to them.

Art and Meaning

"What is the artist trying to say?" is a question many people ask when looking at a work of art, as though the artist were trying to tell us in images what he or she could have said more clearly in a few words. As we saw in Chapter 1, meaning in art is rarely so simple and straightforward. Rather than a definitive meaning that can be found once and for all, art inspires interpretations that are many and changeable.

According to some theories of art, meaning is what distinguishes art from other kinds of skilled making. Art is always *about* something. One brief definition of art, in fact, is "embodied meaning." Viewers who wonder what the artist is trying to say are thus right to expect their experience of art to be meaningful, but they may misunderstand where meaning can be found or underestimate their own role in making it. Understanding art is a cultural skill and, like any cultural skill, must be learned.

Key terms related to meaning are form and content; materials and techniques; iconography; and context. We will look at them in turn.

Form and Content

In thinking about art, philosophers have found it useful to distinguish two aspects, form and content. **Form** is the physical appearance of the work, everything the eye registers about it, such as colors, shapes, and internal organization. **Content** is what the work of art is about, its meaning. For representational and abstract works, content begins with the objects or events the work depicts, its **subject matter**.

Two paintings allow us to explore the intimate relationship of form and content (2.25 and 2.26). Both feature the same subject matter—the shepherds visiting the infant Jesus. The two paintings, created within a century of each other, are inspired by a passage from the biblical Gospel of Luke. Both include the newborn, his mother, Joseph, the shepherds, animals, and angels. Yet their form clearly differs, and thus their meaning diverges as well.

Adoration of the Shepherds (**2.25**) by Giorgione is naturalistic. It is an evening scene and the figures occupy a dimly lit interior space. Mary and Joseph appear on the right in rich garments and bear themselves regally. They proudly show off the newborn. The shepherds gaze upon the infant Jesus and bow toward the child, almost like visitors to a royal court. Other small figures occupy the landscape, seemingly unaware of the event. The scene is calm and peaceful. The only features that distinguish this visit to a newborn from others are the child's central location and the small angels that look down on the scene and invite the viewer to adore the child. The form of this painting gives it a meaning that communicates the serene yet majestic birth of the faith's savior.

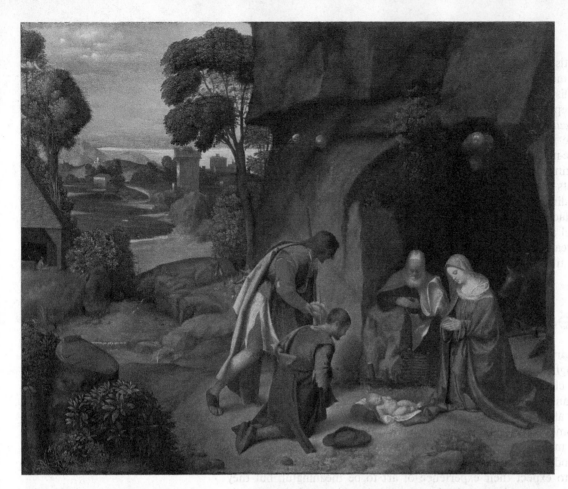

2.25 Giorgione. *Adoration of the Shepherds*. 1505–10. Oil on panel, 35 ¾ × 43 ½".
Courtesy National Gallery of Art, Washington, D.C.

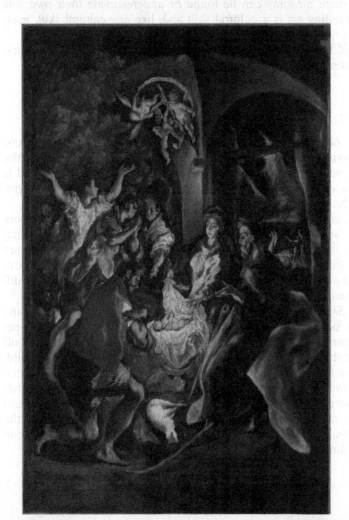

2.26 El Greco. *Adoration of the Shepherds*. 1605. Oil on canvas, 56 ⅞ × 39 ⅞".
Rogers Fund, 1905/Metropolitan Museum of Art

Adoration of the Shepherds (**2.26**) by El Greco offers a very different atmosphere. It is moody and unnatural. The figures are stylized, with elongated limbs, small heads, and dramatic poses. Their expressions range from astonishment to reverence. The setting is unclear, with clouds hovering before a doorway in the background. The only light in the painting shines brilliantly from the infant's body and illuminates the figures with an otherworldly glow. The shadows almost seem to dance, as if the infant's glow came from a flame. Otherwise the painting is dark. The form of El Greco's painting results in content that emphasizes the mystery of Jesus's birth, distancing the event from normal events in our world.

We could summarize the difference in content by saying that Giorgione's *Adoration of the Shepherds* celebrates Jesus as king while El Greco's plumbs the mystical aspects of the Christian religion. By approaching the same theme with a different form, each painter expressed a different message. We as viewers then interpret the form to arrive at the content.

Materials and Techniques

The two paintings of the *Adoration of the Shepherds* are made using oil paint applied with brushes to wood or canvas stretched over a wooden frame. Oil paint, brushes, and canvas were relatively new when Giorgione painted, but were standard materials by El Greco's day—they don't represent significant choices on his part. Similarly, Auguste Rodin probably took white marble and the technique of carving for granted when he created *The Kiss*, one of his most famous works (**2.27**). White marble had long been a standard material for sculpture in Europe, and carving was the standard way to shape it.

With Janine Antoni's *Gnaw*, in contrast, what it is made of and how it was made are the first things that grab our attention (**2.28**). The artist has reached far beyond traditional art materials and techniques, and her choices are fundamental

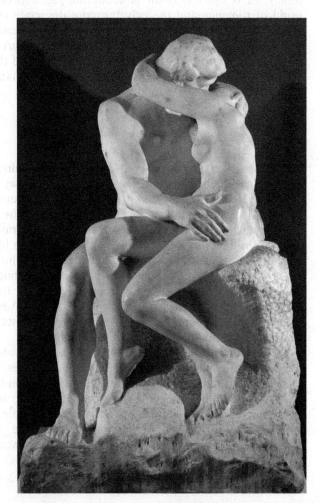

2.27 Auguste Rodin. *The Kiss*. 1886–98. Marble, height 5' 11 ¼". Musée Rodin, Paris. Erich Lessing/Art Resource, NY

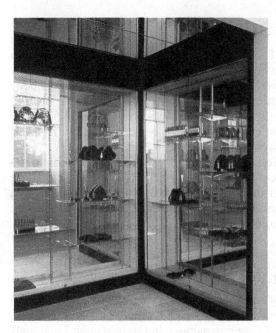
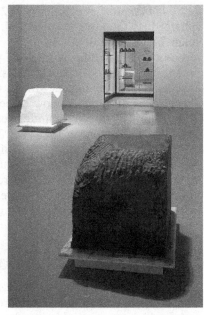

2.28 Janine Antoni. *Gnaw*. 1992. Two installation views and three details. 600 lbs chocolate cube and 600 lbs lard cube gnawed by the artist, 45 heart-shaped packages of chocolate made from chewed chocolate removed from chocolate cube, and 150 lipsticks made with pigment, beeswax, and chewed lard removed from lard cube. Each cube 24 × 24 × 24".

The Museum of Contemporary Art, Los Angeles. © Janine Antoni. Courtesy of the artist and Luhring Augustine, New York

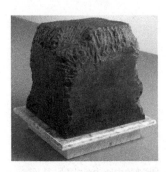

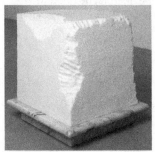

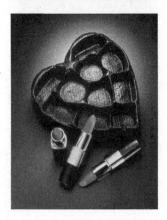

to the work's content. *Gnaw* consists of a 600-pound cube of chocolate and a similar one of lard, each gnawed at by the artist herself. The chewed portions of lard were made into lipsticks, and the chocolate was made into heart-shaped, partitioned boxes for fancy gift chocolates. These are displayed in a nearby showcase, as though in an upscale boutique. Chocolate has strong associations with love, as both a token of affection and a substitute for it. Lard summons up obsessions with fat and self-image, which in turn are linked to culturally imposed ideals of female beauty, as is lipstick. *Gnaw* is about the gap between the prettified, commercial world of romance and the private, more desperate cravings it both feeds on and causes. The gnawed blocks of chocolate and lard resemble the base of Rodin's statue after the couple have gone, and perhaps that is part of the message as well. *The Kiss* wants to convince us that love is beautiful, and that we are beautiful when we are in love. Not always, *Gnaw* replies, and the romantic illusions that works such as *The Kiss* inspire are part of the problem.

Iconography

In talking about form and content in the two paintings of the *Adoration of the Shepherds*, we relied on something so basic you may not even have noticed it. In fact, it was our very first step: we recognized the subject matter. The title was our point of departure, and we looked for elements in the paintings that represented it. We know what shepherds look like, and what adoration looks like. Other objects depicted in the paintings required some research to identify. The glowing infant in the center is Jesus, the winged figures are angels, the young woman closest to the infant is Mary, and the older man is Joseph, although he is easier to identify in Giorgione's painting than in El Greco's. Today that information is standard knowledge, and almost any description of images of the Adoration of the Shepherds will include it. But at some point it was new, and artists adopted these characters as standard elements in images of this subject.

This kind of background information about subject matter is the domain of iconography. **Iconography**, literally "describing images," involves identifying, describing, and interpreting subject matter in art. Iconography is an important activity of scholars who study art, and their work helps us to understand meanings that we might not be able to see for ourselves. For example, unless you are schooled in Japanese Buddhism, you would not recognize the subject matter of the *Amida Buddha* (**2.29**). To understand the content of this work, we must read the parts of the image that help us to identify it. These signs or symbols within the work help us to arrive at the object's meaning.

Our investigation begins with the title, which leads us to the most basic question of all: Who is Amida Buddha? In the Buddhist faith, a buddha is a fully enlightened being. The historical Buddha was a spiritual leader who lived in India perhaps as early as the 6th century B.C.E. His insights into the human condition form the basis of the Buddhist religion. As Buddhism developed, it occurred to believers that if there had been one fully enlightened being, there must have been others. In Japan, where Buddhism quickly spread, the most popular buddha has been Amida, the Buddha of the Western Paradise.

We could have identified this figure as Buddha even without knowing the title. The iconography of the historical Buddha image was established early on and became a convention through the centuries, being reused for other buddha figures. Buddha wears a monk's robe, a single length of cloth that drapes over the left shoulder. He sits in the cross-legged position of meditation. His ears are elongated, for in his earthly life, before his spiritual awakening, he wore the customary heavy earrings of an Indian prince. The form resembling a bun on the top of his head is a protuberance called the *ushnisha*. It symbolizes his enlightenment. Sculptors also developed a repertoire of hand gestures for the Buddha image, each gesture having its own meaning. Here, Amida Buddha's hands form the gesture of teaching, which symbolizes Buddha's role in helping others on the path toward enlightenment.

The iconography of this statue is readily available to us because it forms part of a tradition that has continued unbroken since it first developed almost two thousand years ago. Often, however, traditions change and meanings are forgotten. We cannot always tell with certainty what images from the past portray, or what they meant to their original viewers. Such is the case with one of the most famous images in Western art, the *Arnolfini Double Portrait* by Jan van Eyck (**2.30**). Painted with entrancing naturalism and *trompe l'oeil* detail, the work portrays a man and a woman, their hands joined. He has taken off his shoes, which lie on the floor next to him; hers can be seen on the floor in the background. Seemingly pregnant, she stands next to a bed draped in rich red fabric. Overhead is a chandelier with but one candle. On the floor between the couple stands an alert little dog. A mirror on the far wall (**2.31**) reflects not only the couple but also two men standing in the doorway to the room and looking in—standing, that is, where we are standing as we look at the painting. Over the mirror the painter's signature reads "Jan van Eyck was here."

By the time the painting ended up in the National Gallery in London in 1842, it had changed hands so many times that even the identity of the couple had been forgotten. Researchers working from old documents soon identified them as Giovanni di Arrigo Arnolfini, a rich merchant, and his wife, Giovanna Cenami, also from a socially prominent family. But what was the purpose of the painting? What, exactly, does it depict? Who was its patron? One influential theory claims that the painting records a private marriage ceremony and served as a sort of marriage certificate. The men reflected in the mirror are none other than Jan van Eyck and a friend, who had served as witnesses. Moreover, almost every iconographic detail of the painting has a symbolic meaning related to the sacrament of marriage. The bride's seemingly pregnant state alludes to fertility, as does the red bed of the nuptial chamber. The single candle signifies the presence of God at the ceremony, and the dog is a symbol of marital fidelity and love. The couple have cast off their shoes as a sign that they stand on sacred ground.

Another, more recent, theory claims that the painting does not depict a marriage but a ceremony of betrothal, an engagement. It commemorates the alliance of two prominent and well-off families. In this view, the iconographic details do not carry specific symbolism, although many of them serve to underscore the couple's affluence. Canopied beds, for example, were status symbols and as such were commonly displayed in the principal room of the house. Candles were enormously expensive, and burning one at a time was common thrift. The shoes were of a style worn by the upper class and were probably taken off routinely upon going indoors. The dog is simply a pet: everyone had dogs.

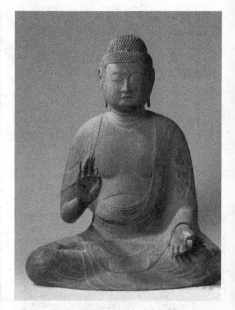

2.29 *Amida Buddha*, from Japan. 1125–75. Wood with traces of lacquer, height 34 ¼". Rijksmuseum, Amsterdam

2.30 Jan van Eyck. *Arnolfini Double Portrait*. 1434. Oil on wood, 33 × 22 ½".

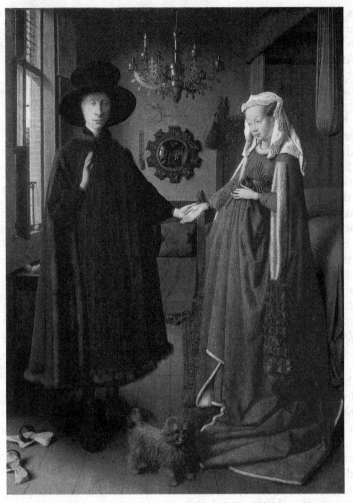

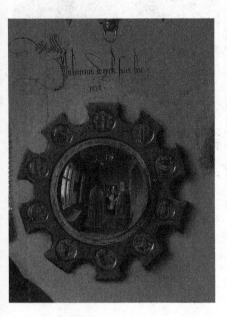

2.31 *Arnolfini Double Portrait*, detail of mirror and rosary.

Still more recent research questions the identity of the sitters and leads to further possible interpretations. The man may not be Giovanni di Arrigo Arnolfini but, rather, his cousin Giovanni di Nicolao Arnolfini. The woman would presumably be Giovanni di Nicolao's second wife, his first wife having died before the painting was made. The painting portrays neither a marriage nor a betrothal, but is a straightforward portrait of a prosperous couple. A fourth theory points out that we have no direct evidence that Giovanni di Nicolao remarried, and maintains that the woman is indeed his first wife, Costanza Trenta. She may have died in childbirth, perhaps even as the painting was in progress. We are looking at a commemorative image: the man is alive, the woman is not. Iconographic details related to the couple's hands have also been used to support this interpretation. The man turns his raised right hand toward the woman to bid her farewell; her right hand slips from his left, signifying that she is no longer of this world.[7]

All these theories are supported by impressive research and reasoning. Each carefully analyzes the symbols in the painting and considers them in light of the era's iconographic conventions. Some scholars believe one theory, some another. Viewers will continue to find their own meanings in this magical painting, but we may never know just what it signified for its original audience.

Context

Art does not happen in a vacuum. Strong ties bind a work of art to the life of its creator, to the tradition it grows from and responds to, to the audience it was made for, and to the society in which it circulated. These circumstances form the **context** of art, the personal, social, cultural, and historical setting in which it was created, received, and interpreted.

This chapter has already made use of the kind of insight that context can provide. Near the beginning, we considered the fame of Leonardo's *Mona Lisa* (see 2.1). In the discussion of the Philippine *Virgin of the Immaculate Conception* (see 2.7), we examined how colonization and trade led to the production of export items.

The type of context that especially concerns us here is the social context of art, including the physical setting in which art is experienced. The piece shown in figure **2.32** portrays a work of art as we might see it today in a museum. Isolated against a dark background and dramatically lit, the gilded carving gleams like a rare and precious object. We can admire the harmony of the sculpture's gently rounded forms in much the same way that we contemplated the light flowing over Edward Weston's cabbage leaf earlier in the chapter (see 2.9). Yet the sculpture was not made primarily to be looked at in this way. In fact, it was not made to be seen in a museum at all.

Photo **2.33** shows similar sculptures in their original context, as they were made to be seen and used by the Akan peoples of West Africa. The men in the photograph are officials known as linguists. Linguists serve Akan rulers as translators, spokespersons, advisers, historians, and orators. Every local chief employs at least one linguist, and more powerful chiefs and kings may be attended by many. As a symbol of office, a linguist carries a staff topped with a wooden sculpture covered in gold leaf. Each sculptural motif is associated with one or more proverbs, often about the nature of leadership or the just use of power. In the photograph here, for example, the staff at the far left portraying two men seated at a table calls forth the proverb "Food is for its owner, not for the one who is hungry," meaning that the chieftaincy belongs to the man who has the right to it, not just to anyone who wants it.

In an Akan community, the aesthetic attention we directed at the sculpture (see 2.32) would have been the unique privilege of the artist who carved the work and the linguist who owned it. Other members of the community would have glimpsed the figure only during public occasions of state. More meaningful to them would have been the authority that the staffs symbolized and the pageantry they contributed to—a lavish visual display that reaffirmed the social order of the Akan world.

Museums are the principal setting our society offers for encounters with art. Yet the vast majority of humankind's artistic heritage was not created with museums in mind. It was not made to be set aside from life in a special place but, rather, to

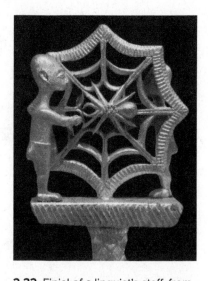

2.32 Finial of a linguist's staff, from Ghana. Asante, 20th century. Wood and gold, height 11 ¼".
Musée Barbier-Mueller, Geneva.
World History Archive / Alamy Stock Photo

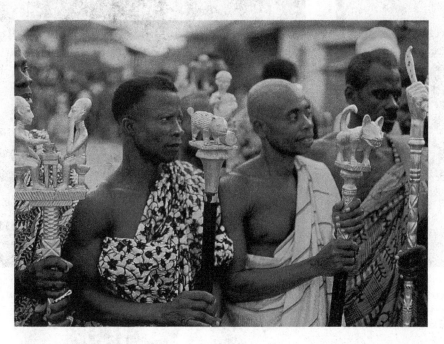

2.33 Akan (Fante) linguists at Enyan Abaasa, Ghana, 1974.
Photo Professor Herbert M. Cole

be part of life—both the lives of individuals and the lives of communities. Its meaning, like that of the Akan linguist staff, was united with its use. This is as true for Western art as it is for the art of other cultures. Image **2.34** shows Titian's *Assumption* in isolation, as we might expect to find it in a museum or an art book. "Assumption" names another standard subject of Christian art—that of Mary, the mother of Jesus, being accepted bodily into heaven at her death. Titian has imagined Mary being borne upward amid a crowd of angels, her garments swirling about her, into a golden glory. Above, God appears to welcome her; below, witnesses marvel at the miracle.

Titian's masterpiece does not reside in a museum, however, or on the white pages of an art book. It towers up behind the main altar of the Church of the Frari in Venice, in the exact location for which the artist painted it. Image **2.35** is a photograph that captures something of the experience of seeing Titian's work in context. Now we understand that the painting is part of a richly worked, massive stone altarpiece, with fluted columns, marble inlay, and gilded carving. A statue of Christ crowns the ensemble, flanked by two monks. We can see how the tall, arched shape of the painting repeats the pointed arches of the church itself, and we can appreciate how the painting's bold composition projects clearly into the cavernous interior.

But all these ways of looking are still ways of looking at art. At its unveiling in 1518, the painting was seen through the eyes of faith. We need to imagine the effect it produced when Christianity was the central cultural force of Venetian life. Citizens filling the Church of the Frari would have felt the truth of their beliefs through the splendor of the architecture echoing with music, the pageantry of the

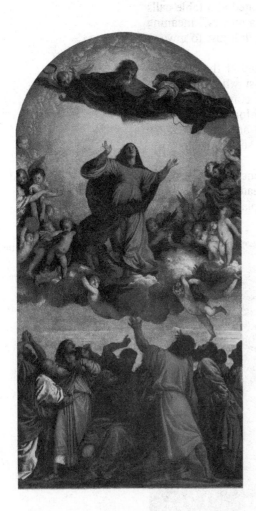

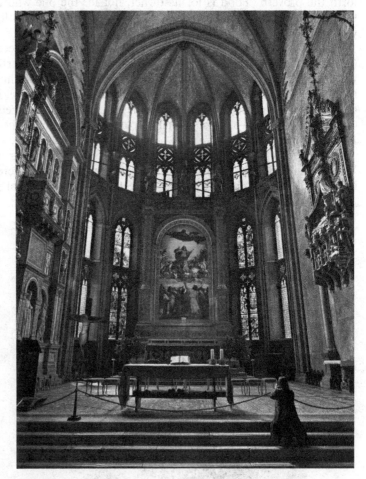

2.34 Titian. *Assumption.* 1518. Oil on wood, 22' 7 ¾" × 11' 11 ⁵⁄₁₂".
Church of the Frari, Venice. akg-images/Cameraphoto

2.35 *Chiesa dei Frari, Venice.*
Hercules Milas / Alamy Stock Photo

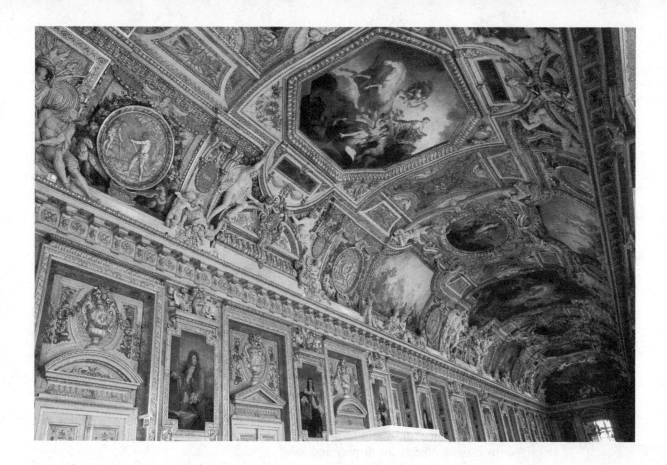

2.36 Interior of the Louvre Museum, Paris.
© Epictura/Alamy Stock Photo

rituals, and the glorious vision of a miracle made present through Titian's skill and imagination. In Struth's photograph, light falls on a small group of tourists who have paused to look at the famous painting. They have come to look at art, as though the church were a museum. And yet for a moment they seem transfigured.

The museum as we know it today—a building housing a collection of art and open to the public—developed in Europe during the decades leading into the 19th century, the same decades that witnessed the social upheavals that inaugurated our modern era, including the American and French revolutions. The Louvre Museum in Paris (**2.36**), where the *Mona Lisa* hangs today, was originally a royal palace. Its walls and ceilings were decorated with paintings and sculptures that celebrated the monarchy, and its enormous rooms were filled with art from antiquity to the present. After the French Revolution, the palace became a public museum, allowing visitors to see the vast royal art collection. The same occurred in other nations, where Western museums displayed art that had previously belonged to the aristocracy or the Church, or to vanished civilizations such as ancient Rome and Egypt. All these objects were removed from the contexts that originally gave them meaning. Placed in a museum, their new function was to be works of art.

Whereas the first museums were concerned only with the art of the past, many museums now exhibit the work of living artists. Along with galleries that display (and usually sell) art, and a circuit of international exhibitions that survey current artistic trends, they are the principal context for the art of our time. Our artists work with these institutions and spaces in mind, and as viewers we expect to see their work in these settings.

Art and Purpose

During the 20th century, many Western artists began to feel that something important had been lost when art was separated from life and placed in a separate, privileged realm. Seen in the larger context of consumer culture, where shopping and window-shopping were favorite leisure activities, were museums and galleries really

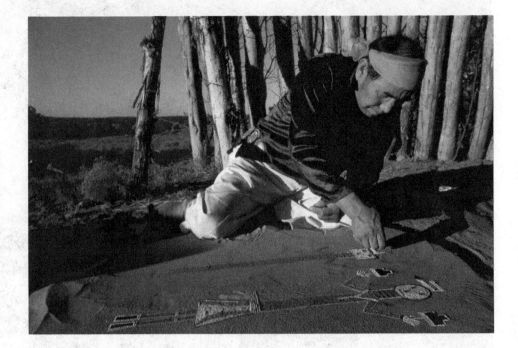

2.37 Navajo man creating a sand painting.
© Ted Spiegel, Getty Images

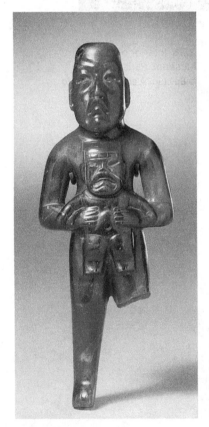

2.38 Standing figure holding supernatural effigy. Olmec, 800–500 B.C.E. Jade, height 8 ⅝".
The Collection of Robin B. Martin, The Guennol Collection, Brooklyn Museum of Art, New York. Photo © Justin Kerr K4838

so different from department stores and boutiques? Despite the talk of meaning and spiritual value, did the role of the artist in modern society come down in the end to making objects for display and sale?

Sometimes a slight shift in perspective is all it takes to open up new ways of thinking. A painting, for example, is indeed an object. But it is also the result of a process, the activity of painting. In questioning the purpose of art and the role of the artist in contemporary culture, many artists began to shift their focus away from the products of art to its processes, considering how they might be meaningful in themselves.

Many cultures, however, retained the connection of art and its context even in the face of modern consumer culture. The Navajo practice of sand painting, for example, is one of the most famous instances of an art where product and process cannot be separated, for the painting, its making, and its unmaking are all equally important. Sand painting is part of a ceremony in which a religious specialist known as a singer, or *hataali*, calls upon spirit powers to heal and bless someone who is ill. The ceremony begins as the singer chants a Navajo legend. At a certain point, he begins making the painting by sifting colored sand through his fingers onto the earthen floor. The photograph shown here depicts a Navajo man demonstrating the technique of sand painting (**2.37**). Actual sand painting is viewed as a sacred activity, and photography is not usually permitted. The painting acts as an altar, a zone of contact between earthly and spirit realms, and together with the chanting it attracts the spirits, the Holy People. When the painting is completed, the patient is instructed to sit at its center. The singer begins to touch first a portion of the painting and then the patient, gradually transferring the powers of healing. When the ceremony is over, the painting is unmade—swept with a feather staff into a blanket, then carried outside and deposited safely so that it does not harm anyone with the sickness it has taken on.

The Navajo *hataali* is a shaman, a type of religious specialist common to many cultures. A shaman is a person who acts as a medium between the human and spirit worlds. A jade carving from the ancient Mesoamerican Olmec culture gives visual form to ideas about the power of shamans (**2.38**). Standing in a pose of meditation, the shaman holds up a small, stylized creature whose fierce, animated expression contrasts vividly with his own trancelike gaze. The iconographic details of the creature's headband, catlike eyes, snub nose, and large, downturned mouth identify him as the infant man-jaguar, a supernatural being mingling animal and human traits. The navels of the creature and the shaman are aligned, as on an axis linking the cosmic and earthly realms. In Olmec belief, the creature probably served as the shaman's contact in the supernatural world.

The person who most directly adopted the idea of the artist as a kind of shaman and art as a tool of spiritual healing was Joseph Beuys. In his 1965 work *How to Explain Pictures to a Dead Hare*, he covered his head in honey and gold leaf and appeared in a gallery cradling a dead hare in his arms (**2.39**). Walking about the room, he spoke quietly and tenderly to the animal as he brought it close to the pictures on display. On the floor in the middle of the gallery was a withered fir tree that Beuys stepped over from time to time, still cradling the hare. Beuys's performances—he called them Actions—did not result in an object at all. They were ritual-like events that, for those who chose to reflect on them, touched on issues of art, society, and nature. Beuys believed that an artist's role in a materialistic society was to remind people of human and spiritual values. He also thought that artists should be concerned with how these values point to the need for social and political change.

Rituals combining artistic processes and performance have a very long history around the world. The masquerades of Africa, for example, constitute one of the most varied and compelling world traditions of art in performance (**2.40**). Masquerades serve to make otherworld spirits physically present in the human community. The photograph here shows a procession of nature spirits entering a community of the Bwa people of West Africa. Raffia costumes and carved and painted masks completely disguise the performers' human identities, which are believed to be subsumed into the spirit identities of the masks. Masks are called upon during times when the cooperation of spirits and the natural forces they control is especially needed. For example, masks may appear at festivals surrounding the planting and harvesting of crops, or during the initiation of young people into adulthood, or at funerals, when their help is needed to ensure that the spirit of the deceased leaves

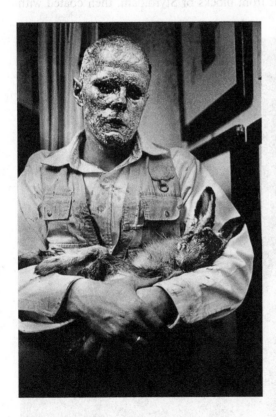

2.39 Joseph Beuys performing *How to Explain Pictures to a Dead Hare*. 1965. Photo Walter Vögel. Courtesy Ronald Feldman Fine Arts, New York. © 2019 Artists Rights Society (ARS), New York/VG Bild-Kunst, Bonn

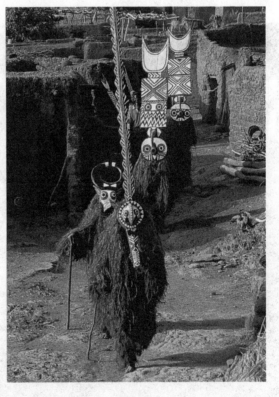

2.40 Bwa masqueraders, Burkina Faso. Carol Beckwith/Angela Fisher, Robert Estall Photo Library

the human community and takes its place in the spirit world of ancestors. When Western scholars first became interested in African masks, they tended to discuss them formally as sculptures, for this was the standard Western category of art that masks most resembled. Today our broader understanding of art encourages us to see masks as an element in a larger art form, the masquerade, which is based in performance.

Viewers, too, have a process related to art, the process of experiencing and reflecting on a work. Being in a gallery or museum is itself an experience, and artists have taken this into account in various ways. One result was a new art form called **installation**, in which a space is presented as a work of art that can be entered, explored, experienced, and reflected on.

Kara Walker's installation *A Subtlety* was created for a space that was already intensely evocative on its own, the cavernous warehouse of the Domino Sugar Refinery in Brooklyn, New York (**2.41**). At its height, the Domino Factory had been the largest sugar refinery in the world. It was shuttered in 2004 after 148 years of continuous operation, all but one of its buildings slated for demolition. Sponsored by an arts organization, Walker's installation allowed the general public to enter the warehouse for the first and last time before it disappeared. The audience walked around and through the space to experience her installation.

As viewers walked between the sculptures, they experienced how the past was still present in the warehouse. The sweet and acrid odor of burnt sugar still hung in the air. Molasses still oozed from the blackened walls and puddled on the floor. *A Subtlety* brought another aspect of sugar's past into the mix, its historical reliance on slavery: the vast sugar plantations founded by European colonists in Brazil and the Caribbean were worked by African slaves. The most imposing element of Walker's installation was a monumental sphinx with distinctly African features and a kerchief tied around her head. Blindingly white, she seemed to be made of solid sugar. (In fact, the sculpture was built from blocks of Styrofoam, then coated with

2.41 Kara Walker. *At the behest of Creative Time Kara E. Walker has confected: A Subtlety, or the Marvelous Sugar Baby, an Homage to the unpaid and overworked Artisans who have refined our Sweet tastes from the cane fields to the Kitchens of the New World on the Occasion of the demolition of the Domino Sugar Refining Plant*. Installation view: A project of Creative Time, Domino Sugar Refinery, Brooklyn, New York. May 10–July 6, 2014. Styrofoam, resin, sugar, and molasses; height of sphinx figure 35'.
Photo: Jason Wyche. Artwork © 2015 Kara Walker

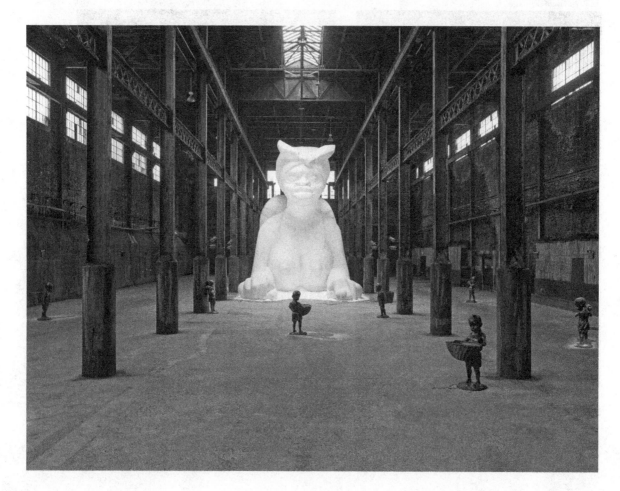

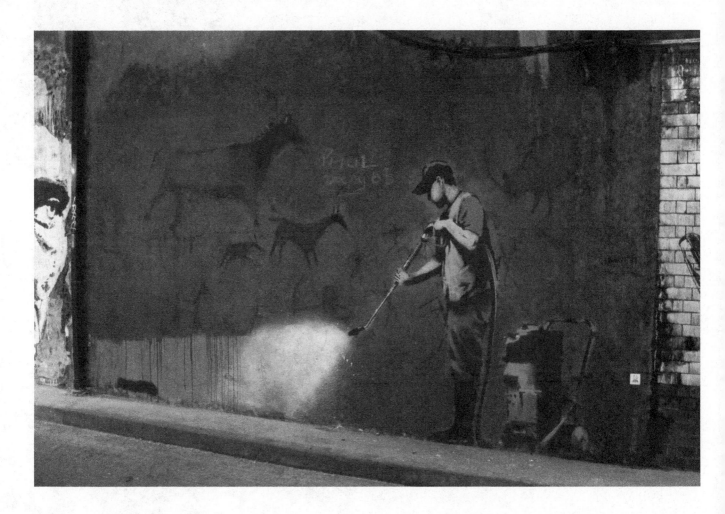

2.42 Banksy. Mural (now painted over) on Leake Street, London. 2008.

David Reed/Alamy Stock Photo

30 tons of sugar.) Scattered around the warehouse were her attendants, fifteen life-size sculptures of African children carrying large baskets or lugging bunches of bananas. Some were made of caramel-colored sugar and gradually disintegrated over the course of the exhibition. Others, cast in resin and coated with molasses, remained, mute witnesses to their companions' end.

Walker brought art into a specialized space, evoking a connection between what took place there and larger social and historical issues. Other artists have worked in the opposite direction, placing works of art into the everyday visual world. The street artist known only as Banksy paints images (**2.42**) on the walls of buildings owned by private individuals, companies, and governments. The paintings, many made using a stencil technique with spray paint for rapid execution, are commonly satirical social commentaries that sometimes combine text and image. Their purpose is to raise questions and to entertain.

The Banksy mural painting seen here comments on our attitudes toward street art. It depicts a city worker mindlessly power-washing a prehistoric rock painting off the wall, much as workers routinely scrub unauthorized graffiti from walls today. The painting draws a parallel between modern street art and the cave paintings of prehistory that we now consider to be priceless treasures of human patrimony. Yet, like graffiti artists, the cave painters did not have permits or government authorization to paint their images. They simply made their work for the public to see.

The questions that artists of the 20th century posed about the nature of their task, and the great formal variety of their responses to those questions, served to map the territory of the word *art*. We now understand that art can manifest itself in many more ways than the 18th-century philosophers who invented the category ever dreamed of. A painting, a sculpture, a video, an installation, a Web site, a computer program, a concept, a performance, an action—all these and more may be presented and understood as art.

Notes to the Text

1. Gyula Halasz Brassai, *Picasso and Company* (New York: Doubleday, 1966), pp. 46–47.

2. Quoted in Mario De Micheli, *Scritti di Picasso* (Milan: Feltrinelli, 1964), p. 42.

3. "Keith Mayerson Talks with Erin Leland," *Bad at Sports*, blog. Available at badatsports. com/2014/keith-mayerson-talks-with-erin-leland, accessed September 15, 2017.

4. Louise Bourgeois, *Destruction of the Father, Reconstruction of the Father: Writings and Interviews, 1923-1997* (London: Violette, 1998), p. 266.

5. Louise Bourgeois, "Self-Expression Is Sacred and Fatal: Statements," in Christiane Meyer-Thoss, *Louise Bourgeois: Designing for Free Fall* (Zürich: Ammann Verlag, 1992), p. 194.

6. Suzanne Isabelle Trimble (aka Bella Land), "Louise Bourgeois in Conversation," *Third Text*, 23:6, 2009, p. 787.

7. For the first theory, see Erwin Panofsky, *Early Netherlandish Painting, Its Origins and Character* (Cambridge, MA: Harvard University Press, 1953); for the second, see Edwin Hall, *The Arnolfini Betrothal* (Berkeley: University of California Press, 1994); for the identity of the sitters, see Lorne Campbell, "Portrait of Giovanni(?) Arnolfini and His Wife," *National Gallery Catalogues: The Fifteenth Century Netherlandish Paintings* (London: National Gallery Company Ltd., 1998), pp. 174-211; for the fourth theory, see Margaret L. Koster, "The Arnolfini Double Portrait: A Simple Solution," *Apollo*, September 2003, pp. 3-14.

Chapter 3
Themes of Art

In this chapter, you will learn to

LO1   compare representations of the sacred realm,

LO2   identify how works of art reflect politics and the social order,

LO3   explain the story or history represented in works of art,

LO4   describe how artists represent everyday life,

LO5   discuss how art is used to reflect on the human experience,

LO6   recognize invention and fantasy in art,

LO7   characterize the representation of the natural world in art, and

LO8   restate how artists respond to art and its institutions.

In extending our modern concept of art across cultures and backward in time, we observe that peoples throughout history have created visually meaningful forms. Whether those forms be paintings or textiles, buildings or ceramics, they have in common that they are *about* something. This "aboutness" is what allows us to experience them as art. But what sorts of things are they about?

One way to begin exploring the elusive concept of "aboutness" is to consider some broad areas of meaning that have been reflected in the arts of many cultures throughout human history. We can call these areas of meaning *themes*. No doubt, every person setting out to name the most important themes in art would produce a different list. This chapter proposes eight themes, from the sacred realm to art about art and its institutions. Each one allows us to range widely over the world's artistic heritage, setting works drawn from different times and places in dialogue by showing how their meanings begin in a shared theme.

Just as a work of art can hold many meanings and inspire multiple interpretations, so it may reflect more than one theme. As you read this chapter, you may find yourself considering works discussed earlier in the light of the new theme at hand, or thinking about how a newly encountered work also reflects themes discussed earlier. This is as it should be. Themes are not intended to reduce art to a set of neat categories. Rather, they provide a framework for exploring how complex a form of expression it can be.

The Sacred Realm

Who made the universe? How did life begin, and what is its purpose? What happens to us after we die? For answers to those and other fundamental questions, people throughout history have turned to a world we cannot see except through faith, the sacred realm of the spirit. Gods and goddesses, spirits of ancestors, spirits of nature, one God and one alone—each society has formed its own view of the sacred realm and how it interacts with our own. Some forms of faith have disappeared into history; others have remained small and local; while still others, such as Christianity and Islam, have become major religions that draw believers from all over the world. From earliest times, art has played an important role in our relationship with the sacred, helping us to envision it, to honor it, and to communicate with it.

Many works of architecture have been created to provide settings for rituals of worship and prayer, rituals that formalize contact between the earthly and the divine realms. One such work is the small marvel known as the Sainte-Chapelle, or holy chapel (3.1), in Paris. The chapel was commissioned in 1239 by the French king Louis IX to house an important collection of relics that he had just acquired, relics he believed to include pieces of the True Cross, the Crown of Thorns, and other instruments of Christ's Passion. The king's architects created a soaring vertical space whose walls seem to be made of stained glass. Light passing through the glass creates a dazzling effect, transforming the interior into a radiant, otherworldly space in which the glory of heaven seems close at hand.

The Sainte-Chapelle is a relatively intimate space, for it was intended as a private chapel for the king and his court. In contrast, the Great Mosque at Córdoba, Spain, was built to serve the needs of an entire community (3.2). A mosque is an Islamic house of worship. Begun during the 8th century, the Great Mosque at Córdoba grew to be the largest place of prayer in western Islam. The interior of the prayer hall is a vast horizontal space measured out by a forest of columns. Daylight enters through doorways placed around the perimeter of the hall. Filtered through the myriad columns and arches, it creates a complex play of shadows that makes the extent and shape of the interior hard to grasp. Alternating red and white sections break up the visual continuity of the arch forms. Oil lamps hanging in front of the focal point of worship would have created still more shadows.

In both the Sainte-Chapelle and the Great Mosque at Córdoba, architects strove to create a place where worshipers might approach the sacred realm. The builders of the Sainte-Chapelle envisioned a radiant vertical space transformed by colored light, whereas the architects of the Great Mosque at Córdoba envisioned a disorienting horizontal space fractured by columns and shadows. In both buildings, the everyday world is shut out, and light and space are used to create a heightened sense of mystery and wonder.

3.1 Interior, upper chapel, Sainte-Chapelle, Paris. 1243–48.
Art Resource, NY

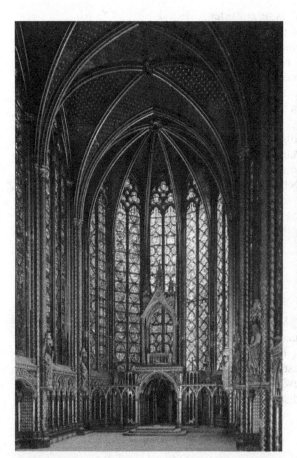

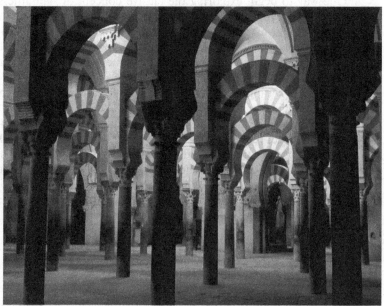

3.2 Interior, Great Mosque, Córdoba, Spain. Begun 786 C.E.
Photo Scala, Florence

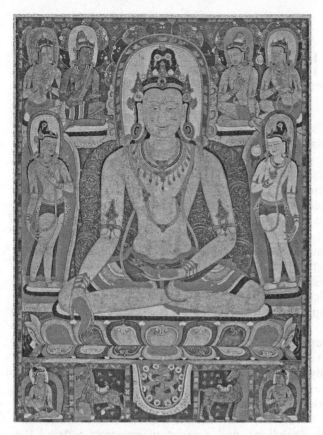

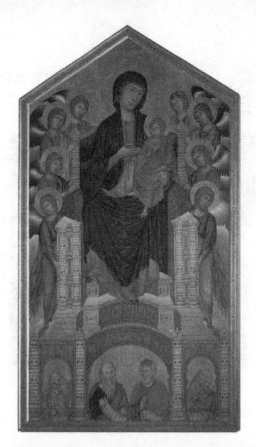

3.3 *Rathnasambhava, the Transcendent Buddha of the South.* Tibet. 13th century C.E. Opaque watercolor on cloth, height 36 ½". Los Angeles County Museum of Art. From the Nasli and Alice Heeramaneck Collection, Museum Associates Purchase (M.78.9.2)

3.4 Cimabue. *Madonna Enthroned.* ca. 1280–90. Tempera on wood, 12' 7 ½" × 7' 4". Galleria degli Uffizi, Florence. © Quattrone, Florence

The sacred realm cannot be seen with human eyes, yet artists throughout the ages have been asked to create images of gods, goddesses, angels, demons, and all manner of spirit beings. Religious images may serve to focus the thoughts of the faithful by giving concrete form to abstract ideas. Often, however, their role has been more complex and mysterious. For example, in some cultures, images have been understood as a sort of conduit through which sacred power flows; in others, they serve as a dwelling place for a deity, who is called upon through ritual to take up residence within.

Our next two images, one Buddhist and one Christian, were made at approximately the same time but some four thousand miles apart, the Buddhist image in Tibet, the Christian one in Italy. The Buddhist painting portrays Rathnasambhava, one of the Five Transcendent Buddhas, seated in a pose of meditation on a stylized lotus throne (**3.3**). Many of his iconographic details are similar to the *Amida Buddha* (see 2.29) from the last chapter. He has an *ushnisha* and sits in a meditative pose. His right hand makes the gesture of bestowing vows; his left, the gesture of meditation. Unlike other buddhas, however, the Five Transcendent Buddhas are typically portrayed in the bejeweled garb of Indian princes, rather than just featuring elongated earlobes. Arranged around Rathnasambhava are *bodhisattvas*, also in princely attire. Bodhisattvas are enlightened beings who have deferred their ultimate goal of *nirvana*—freedom from the cycle of birth, death, and rebirth—in order to help others attain that goal. All wear halos signifying their holiness. The buddha, being the most important of the personages depicted, dominates the painting as the largest figure. He faces straight in front, in a pose of tranquility, while the others around him stand or sit in relaxed postures.

The second example, painted by the 13th-century Italian master Cimabue, depicts Mary, mother of Christ, with her son (**3.4**). While in the last chapter we saw the Christ child adored by shepherds, in this painting the infant and his mother sit tranquilly on a throne. The gold background places them in a heavenly realm.

Iconoclasm

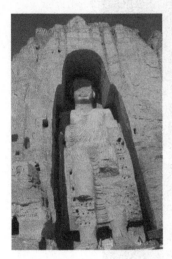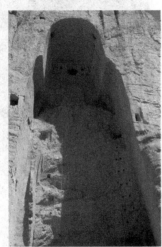

In arguments for iconoclasm, why is worshiping artworks themselves not the same as worshiping what they represent? On the other hand, how can art communicate religious beliefs, practices, and values?

On February 26, 2001, the Islamic fundamentalist rulers of Afghanistan, the Taliban, issued an edict that stunned the world: all statues in the country must be destroyed, for they were being worshiped and venerated by unbelievers. The order targeted statues large and small, those housed in museums and those on view in public places. But the statues that caught the public's attention were a pair of monumental buddhas. Carved into the living rock of a cliff face sometime between the 3rd and 7th centuries, they were originally cared for by Buddhist monks and visited by pilgrims during religious festivals. The monks and pilgrims left centuries ago, but the statues had survived. It seemed scarcely credible that they were about to be blown up, but that is exactly what happened. In early March, despite international diplomatic efforts, the statues were destroyed.

Why would statues be destroyed in the name of religion? Like many other religions, Islam has at its core a set of texts that invite interpretation. One of these, the Tradi-tions of the Prophet, contains two objections to representational images. The first objection is that making images usurps the creative power of God; the second is that images can lead to idolatry, the worship of the images themselves. Historically, these warnings have led Muslims generally to avoid representational images in religious contexts such as mosques or manuscripts of the Qur'an, their holy book. Interpreted more radically, they have sometimes been used to forbid all representational images, no matter what their context. Our word for the destruction of images does not come from Islam, however, but from Christianity, which also has a history of destroying images in the name of spiritual purity. The word is *iconoclasm*.

Iconoclasm is derived from the Greek for "image breaking." It was coined to describe one side of a debate that raged for more than a century in the Christian empire of Byzantium (see page 359). Byzantine churches, monasteries, books, and homes were decorated with depictions of Christ, of the saints, and of biblical stories and personages. Yet during the 8th century, a movement arose against such depictions, and a series of emperors ordered the destruction of images throughout the realm. Again, the objection was idolatry. Christianity too has at its core a set of texts. The most important of these is the Bible, which contains a very clear warning against making images. The warning comes directly from God as the second of the Ten Commandments.

Centuries after the Byzantine episode, iconoclasm arose in western Europe when newly forming Protestant movements of the 16th century accused Catholics of idolatry. Protestant mobs ransacked churches, smashing stained glass, destroying paintings, breaking statues, whitewashing over frescoes, and melting down metal shrines and vessels. To this day, Protestant churches are comparatively bare.

Images have played an important role in almost every religion in the world. Many religions embrace them wholeheartedly. In Buddhism, for example, making religious images is viewed as a form of prayer. In Hinduism they may provide a dwelling place for a deity. The modern Western invention of "art" has meant that many of these images have been moved to museums, and in the end this may have been part of the Taliban's point. We may not worship images for the deities they represent, but do we worship art?

(left) Large Buddha, Bamiyan, Afghanistan. 3rd–7th century C.E. Stone, height 175'. © Jenny Matthews/Alamy Stock Photo
(right) The empty niche after the statue was destroyed. March 2001. Marion Kaplan/Alamy Stock Photo

Mary's right hand indicates the Christ child, who raises his own right hand in a gesture of benediction. On both sides of her are figures of angels, heavenly spirit-messengers. Again, all wear shimmering gold halos signifying their holiness. As in the Buddhist painting, the most important personage dominates the composition, is the largest figure, and holds a serenely frontal pose.

We should not conclude from the remarkable formal similarity of these works that any communication or influence took place between Italy and Central Asia. A safer assumption is that two artists of different faiths independently found a format that satisfied their pictorial needs. Both the Buddha and the Virgin are important, serene holy figures. Bodhisattvas and angels, who are always more active, attend them. Therefore, the artists, from their separate points of view, devised similar compositions.

Politics and the Social Order

Of the many things we create as human beings, the most basic and important may be societies. How can a stable, just, and productive society best be organized? Who will rule, and how? What freedoms will rulers have? What freedoms will citizens have? How is wealth to be distributed? How is authority to be maintained? Many answers to those questions have been posed throughout history, and throughout history the resulting order has been reflected in art.

In many early societies, earthly order and cosmic order were viewed as interrelated and mutually dependent. Such was the case in ancient Egypt, where the pharaoh (king) was viewed as a link between the divine and the earthly realms. The pharaoh was considered a "junior god," a personification of the god Horus and the son of the sun god, Ra. As a ruler, his role was to maintain the divinely established order of the universe, which included the social order of Egypt. He communed with the gods in temples only he could enter, and he wielded theoretically unlimited power over a country that literally belonged to him.

When a pharaoh died, it was believed that he rejoined the gods and became fully divine. Preparations for this journey began even during his lifetime, as vast tombs were constructed and outfitted with everything he would need to maintain his royal lifestyle in eternity. The most famous of these monuments are the three pyramids at Giza (**3.5**), which served as the tombs of the pharaohs Menkaure, Khafre, and Khufu. Thousands of years later, the scale of these structures is still

3.5 The Great Pyramids, Giza, Egypt. Pyramid of Menkaure (foreground), ca. 2500 B.C.E.; Pyramid of Khafre (center), ca. 2530 B.C.E.; Pyramid of Khufu (in background), ca. 2570 B.C.E. Radius Images/Alamy Stock Photo

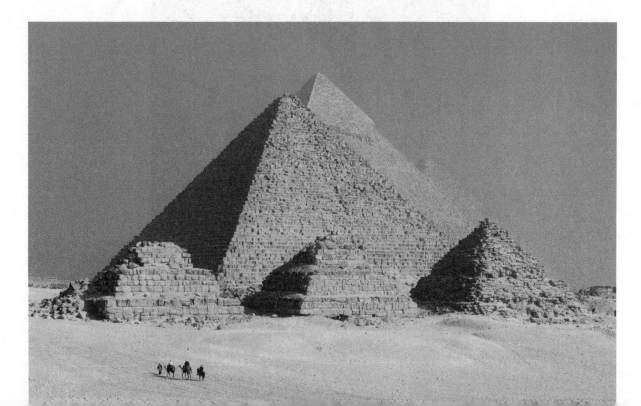

awe-inspiring. The largest pyramid, that of Khufu, originally reached a height of about 480 feet, roughly the height of a fifty-story skyscraper. Its base covers more than 13 acres. More than two million blocks of stone, each weighing over 2 tons, went into building it. Each block had to be quarried with hand tools, transported to the site, and set in place without mortar. Tens of thousands of workers labored for years to build such a tomb and fill its chambers with treasures.

The pyramids reflect the immense power of the pharaohs who could command such forces, but they also reflect the beliefs underlying the social order that granted its rulers such power in the first place. In the Egyptian view, the well-being of Egypt depended on the goodwill of the gods, whose representative on earth was the pharaoh. His safe passage to the afterlife and his worship thereafter as a god himself were essential for the prosperity of the country and the continuity of the universe. No amount of labor or spending seemed too great to achieve those ends.

Visitors to the pyramids at Giza originally arrived by water, disembarking first at one of the temples that sat on the riverbank (each pyramid had its own). From there, they would have walked along a long, raised causeway to a second temple at the base of the pyramid, which itself could not be entered. The temples contained numerous shrines to the dead pharaoh, each with its own life-size statue of him. Statues lined the causeways as well, and still more were inside the pyramid itself. Before our modern mass media, it was art that served to project the presence and authority of rulers to the people throughout their lands. During the days of the Roman Empire, in the first centuries of our era, an official likeness of a new emperor was circulated throughout the realm so that local sculptors could get busy making statues for public places and civic buildings.

One of the finest of these ancient Roman works to come down to us is a bronze statue of the emperor Marcus Aurelius (**3.6**). Seated on his mount, he extends his arm in an oratorical gesture, as if delivering a speech. His calm in vic-

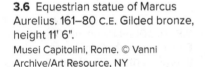

3.6 Equestrian statue of Marcus Aurelius. 161–80 C.E. Gilded bronze, height 11' 6".
Musei Capitolini, Rome. © Vanni Archive/Art Resource, NY

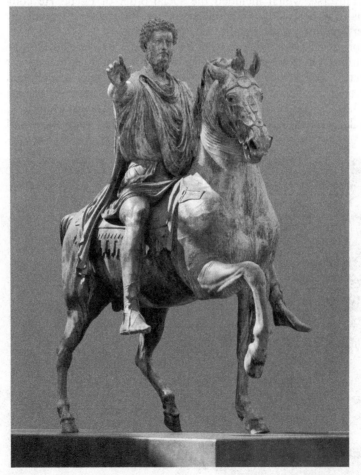

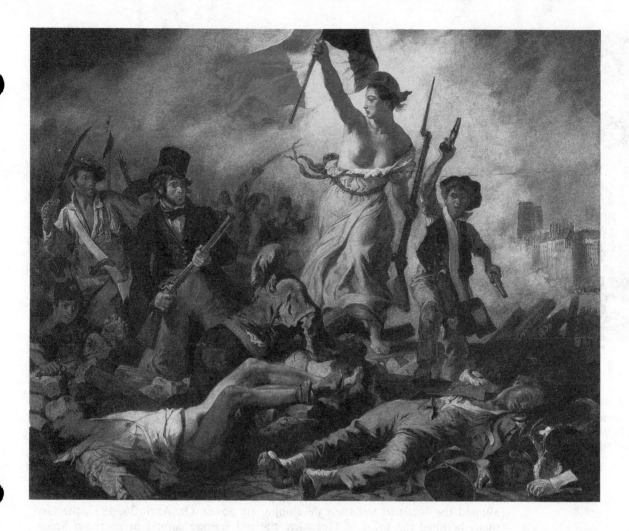

3.7 Eugène Delacroix. *Liberty Leading the People, 1830*. 1830. Oil on canvas, 8' 6" × 10' 10". Musée du Louvre, Paris. Erich Lessing/ Art Resource, NY

tory contrasts with the spirited motions of his horse, which was originally shown raising its hoof over a fallen enemy, now lost. The Roman fashion for beards came and went, like all fashions. But the emperor's beard in the statue is a significant iconographic detail, and part of the way he wanted to be portrayed. Beards were associated with Greek philosophers, and Marcus Aurelius's beard signals his desire to be seen as a philosopher-king, an ideal he genuinely tried to live up to.

During the often violent transition into our modern era, art remained deeply involved with politics and the social order. The perspective of the artist changed profoundly, however. Instead of exclusively serving those in power, the artist was now a citizen among other citizens and free to make art that took sides in the debates of the day. Eugène Delacroix's *Liberty Leading the People* leaves no doubt about the artist's support for the Revolution of 1830, a popular uprising in Paris that toppled one government and installed another (**3.7**). Delacroix completed the painting in the very same year, and it retains the passion of his idealized view of the insurrection and the hopes he had for the future it would bring. At the center is Liberty herself, personified as a Greek statue come to life. Holding the French flag high, she rallies the citizens of Paris, who surge toward us brandishing pistols and sabers as though about to burst out of the painting. Before them lie the bodies of slain government troops.

Delacroix painted the work on his own, without a patron. When the painting was displayed to the public in 1831, it was bought by none other than Louis-Philippe, the "citizen-king" that the revolution had put in power. But perhaps the image was a little *too* revolutionary, for the new king returned the painting to Delacroix after a few months. In fact, *Liberty Leading the People* did not go on permanent public display until 1863, after a vast urban-renewal program had minimized the possibility of angry citizens again taking control of the streets.

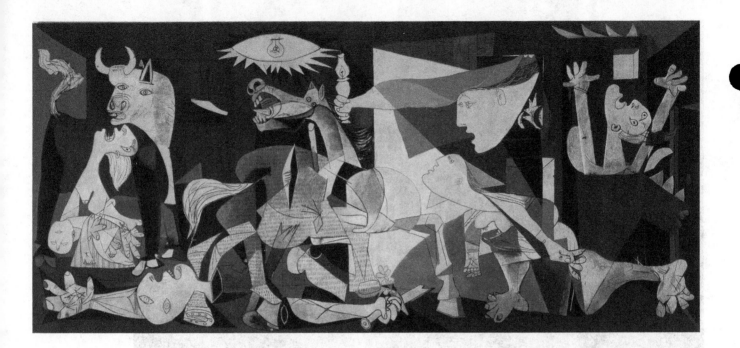

3.8 Pablo Picasso. *Guernica*. 1937.
Oil on canvas, 11' 5 ½" × 25' 5 ¾".
Museo Nacional Centro de Arte Reina
Sofia, Madrid. © 2019 Estate of Pablo
Picasso/Artists Rights Society (ARS),
New York

Where Delacroix glorifies violence in the service of democracy in *Liberty Leading the People*, Pablo Picasso condemns the violence that fascism unleashed against ordinary citizens in *Guernica*, one of the most famous paintings of the 20th century (**3.8**). *Guernica* depicts an event that took place during the Spanish Civil War, when a coalition of conservative, traditional, and fascist forces led by General Francisco Franco were trying to topple the liberal government of the fledgling Spanish Republic. In Germany and Italy, the fascist governments of Hitler and Mussolini were already in power. Franco willingly accepted their aid, and in exchange he allowed the Nazis to test their developing air power. On April 26, 1937, the Germans bombed the town of Guernica, the old Basque capital in northern Spain. There was no real military reason for the raid; it was simply an experiment to see whether aerial bombing could wipe out a whole city. Being totally defenseless, Guernica was devastated and its civilian population massacred.

At the time, Picasso, himself a Spaniard, was working in Paris and had been commissioned by his government to paint a **mural** for the Spanish Pavilion of the Paris World's Fair of 1937. For some time, he had procrastinated about fulfilling the commission; then, just days after news of the bombing reached Paris, he started *Guernica* and completed it in little over a month. The finished mural shocked those who saw it, and it remains today a chillingly dramatic protest against the brutality of war.

At first encounter with *Guernica*, the viewer is overwhelmed by its presence. The painting is huge—more than 25 feet long and nearly 12 feet high—and its stark, powerful imagery seems to reach out and engulf the observer. Picasso used no colors; the whole painting is done in white and black and shades of gray, possibly to echo the visual impact of news photography. (Newspapers at the time were illustrated with black-and-white photographs; newsreels shown in cinemas were also in black and white. Television did not yet exist.) Although the artist's symbolism is very personal (and he declined to explain it in detail), we cannot misunderstand the scenes of extreme pain and anguish throughout the canvas. At far left, a shrieking mother holds her dead child, and at far right, another woman, in a burning house, screams in agony. The gaping mouths and clenched hands speak of disbelief at such mindless cruelty.

Like *Liberty Leading the People*, *Guernica* has had an interesting political afterlife. Franco's forces were triumphant. Picasso refused to allow *Guernica* to reside in Spain while Franco was in power, and so for years it was displayed at the Museum of Modern Art in New York. When Franco died, in 1975, the painting was returned to Spain, but there another debate ensued: Where in Spain should it stay? The town of Guernica wanted it. So did the town where Picasso was born. Madrid, the Spanish capital, won out in the end. The Basque Nationalist Movement, which would like to see the Basque territories secede from Spain, considers that Madrid kidnapped their rightful cultural property. *Guernica* is now displayed behind bulletproof glass.

Stories and Histories

Deeds of heroes, tragic legends, folktales passed down through generations, episodes of television shows that everyone knows by heart—shared stories are one of the ways we create a sense of community. Artists have often turned to stories for subject matter, especially stories whose roots reach deep into their culture's collective memory. When images tell a story, we say that they are **narrative**.

Storytelling to effect social change is at the heart of William Hogarth's art. The print seen here (**3.9**) is the first image in a series of six prints titled *A Harlot's Progress*. The image introduces us to an innocent country girl, Mary Hackabout, who has arrived in London. The parson who was to serve as Mary's guardian in the city appears befuddled in the background, leaving Mary to be met by an older woman. Unfortunately, the older woman runs a brothel and recruits Mary into prostitution. A series of tragedies ensues and the story ends with Mary's death after serving time in prison.

Hogarth used symbols within the narrative to hint at Mary's sad fate in this image. A pile of pans on the left side of the print is about to topple over, just as Mary's life is soon to descend into misery. To the right, the head of a dead goose flops over the side of Mary's basket to signify metaphorically that her goose is cooked. Hogarth used conventional iconographic details like these to help his viewers understand the image's meaning. His strategy was successful, and his moralizing serial prints became so popular that he sold subscriptions in advance to thwart forgeries.

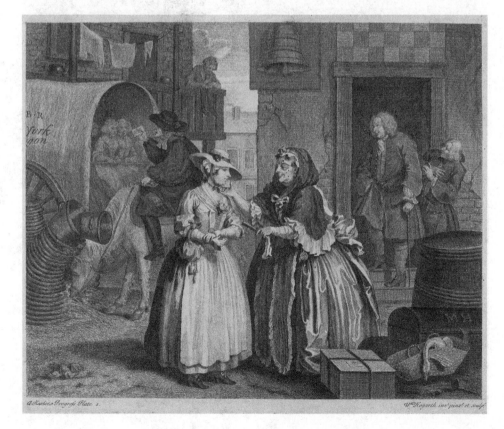

3.9 William Hogarth. *A Harlot's Progress*, plate 1. 1732. Engraving. Image courtesy National Gallery of Art, Washington, D.C.

The Arapaho artist Frank Henderson told the story of his people in *Off to War* (**3.10**). The Arapaho lived in the mountains and plains of the western United States until Anglo-American incursion forced them onto a reservation in the Oklahoma Territory in 1867. Henderson recorded the history of the Arapaho people as their horse-based culture was converted to an agrarian society confined within the reservation's boundaries.

Henderson depicted two warriors leaving for battle in this drawing. They wear traditional regalia and their horses charge excitedly across the page. Plains Indian artists had previously made images like this on their tipis, depicting significant events and celestial symbols in stylized line drawings. Once restricted to the reservation, artists turned to a different material. Henderson made his drawing on a ledger, a bound book made for recording financial transactions. Ledger art by Henderson and other artists recorded history for their communities, and these images remain an important source for understanding the histories of Native American peoples.

Judith Baca and her team of artists share Henderson's interest in recording history, using the concrete walls of a drainage canal. Baca's *Great Wall of Los Angeles* (**3.11**) is a half-mile-long history of the area from prehistory to the 20th century. The goal of this ongoing project is to represent the histories of the diverse populations of Los Angeles who are underrepresented in history books and school curricula. Baca collaborates with historians and other artists to picture events that have received little attention, but deeply affect people's lives. The scene shown here represents the roles of Asians and Latinos on the frontier in the 19th century. It also pictures how the 1848 Treaty of Guadalupe-Hidalgo brought California and other western and southwestern territories into the United States, splitting the

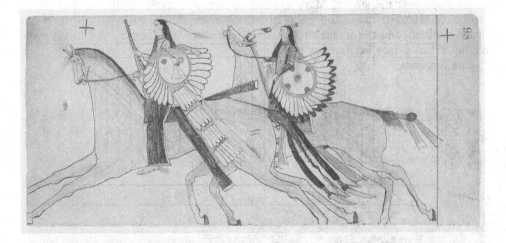

3.10 Frank Henderson. *Off to War*. 1882. Pencil, colored pencil, and ink on paper, 5 ⅜ × 11 ⅞".
Metropolitan Museum of Art, New York/ Gift of Charles and Valerie Diker, 1999

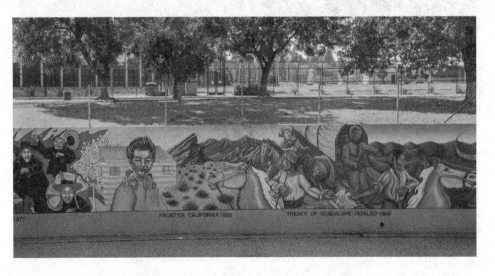

3.11 Judith Baca. *Great Wall of Los Angeles: Frontier California 1880 and Treaty of Guadalupe Hidalgo 1848*. Begun 1974. Mural painting.
The Citizens of the Planet/UIG via Getty Images

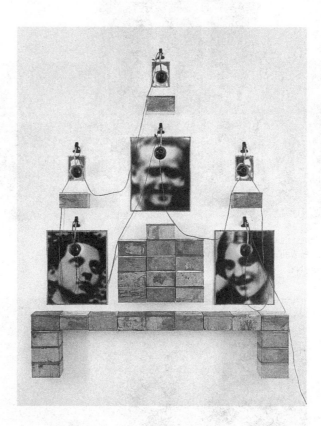

3.12 Christian Boltanski. *Altar to the Chases High School*. 1987. Photographs, tin biscuit boxes, and six metal lamps; 6' 9 ½" × 7' 2 ½". The Museum of Contemporary Art, Los Angeles. Gift of Peter and Eileen Norton, Santa Monica, California. 89.28. Photo Paula Goldman. © 2019 Artists Rights Society (ARS), New York/ADAGP, Paris

region's Latino population. Unlike Hogarth's prints and Henderson's ledger art, Baca's narrative storytelling is public. It recalls Mexican murals of the 20th century that made similarly strong political and social statements. The *Great Wall of Los Angeles* is the longest mural painting in the world, and is still growing.

History has furnished artists with many stories, for history itself is nothing more than a story we tell ourselves about the past, a story we write and rewrite. In *Altar to the Chases High School* (**3.12**), Christian Boltanski draws on our memory of the historical episode known as the Holocaust, the mass murder of European Jews and other populations by the Nazis during World War II. Chases was a private Jewish high school in Vienna. Boltanski began with a photograph that he found of the graduating class of 1931. Eighteen years old in the photograph, the students would have been twenty-five when Austria was annexed by Germany at the start of the war. Most of them probably perished in the death camps. Boltanski rephotographed each face, then enlarged the results into a series of blurry portraits. The effect is as though someone long gone were calling out to us; we try to recognize them, but cannot quite. Our task is made even more difficult by the lights blocking their faces, lights that serve as halos on the one hand, but also remind us of interrogation lamps. We wonder, too, what the stacked tin boxes might hold. Ashes? Possessions? Documents? They have no labels, just as the blurred faces have almost no identities.

Picturing the Here and Now

The social order, the world of the sacred, history and the great stories of the past—all these are very grand and important themes. But art does not always have to reach so high. Sometimes it is enough just to look around us and notice what our life is like here, now, in this place, at this time.

Among the earliest images of daily life to have come down to us are those that survived in the tombs of ancient Egypt. Egyptians imagined the afterlife as resembling earthly life in every detail, except that it continued through eternity.

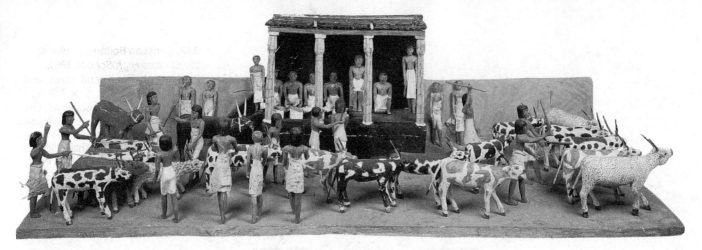

3.13 Model depicting the counting of livestock, from the tomb of Meketre,
Deir el-Bahri. Dynasty 11, 2134–1991 B.C.E. Painted wood, length 5' 8".
Egyptian Museum, Cairo. Scala/Art Resource, NY

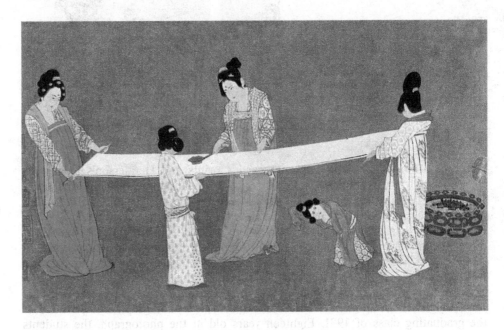

3.14 *Court Ladies Preparing Newly
Woven Silk*, detail. Attributed to
the emperor Huizong (1082–1135),
but probably by a court painter.
Handscroll, ink, colors, and gold
on silk; height 14 ½".
Museum of Fine Arts, Boston. Pictures
from History/Bridgeman Images

To ensure the prosperity of the deceased in the afterlife, scenes of the pleasures
and bounty of life in Egypt were painted or carved on the tomb walls. Sometimes
models were substituted for paintings (**3.13**).

This model is one of many found in the tomb of an Egyptian official named
Meketre, who died around 1990 B.C.E. Meketre himself is depicted at the center,
seated on a chair in the shade of a pavilion. Seated on the floor to his left is his
son; to his right are several scribes (professional writers) with their writing materials ready. Overseers of Meketre's estate stand by as herders drive his cattle before
the reviewing stand so that the scribes can count them. The herders' gestures are
animated as they coax the cattle along with their sticks, and the cattle themselves
are beautifully observed in their diverse markings.

Another model from Meketre's tomb depicts women at work, spinning and
weaving cloth. They would probably have been producing linen, which Egyptians
excelled at. In China, the favored material since ancient times has been silk. *Court
Ladies Preparing Newly Woven Silk* (**3.14**) is a scene from a long handscroll depicting women weaving, ironing, and folding lengths of silk. The painting is a copy
made during the 12th century of a famous 8th-century work by Zhang Xuan, now
lost. In this scene, four ladies in their elegant robes stretch a length of silk. The woman
facing us irons it with a flat-bottomed pan full of hot coals taken from the brazier
visible at the right. A little girl too small to share in the task clowns around for our

benefit. If this is a scene from everyday life, it is a very rarefied life indeed. These are ladies of the imperial court, and the painting is an exercise just as much in portraying beautiful women as it is in showing their virtuous sense of domestic duty.

Daily work is also the subject of a painting made in Mexico in 1575. *Feather Workers* (**3.15**) is part of the manuscript known as the *Florentine Codex*. This bound book was written by Friar Bernadino de Sahagún with the assistance of native Mexican artists and informants. The text is in Spanish and the Aztec language, Nahuatl. As a missionary, Sahagún created the book as a general history of the Indians of central Mexico as he worked to convert them to Christianity. He recorded their traditional religious rituals, gods, agricultural practices, and arts. In the scene shown here, artists make clothing and regalia out of brightly colored feathers. They use whole feathers and individual barbs from birds kept in the Aztec ruler's private aviary. Examples of their work appear in the two panels below. A feather mosaic shield like the one in the middle panel is discussed later (see 20.12).

Living in New York in the 1960s, Robert Rauschenberg found that the visual impact of daily life had outgrown the ability of any single image to convey it. Instead, to communicate the energy and vitality of his time and place, Rauschenberg treated his canvas like a gigantic page in a scrapbook. The result is a kind of controlled chaos in which photographic images drawn from many sources are linked by a poetic process of free association. *Windward*, for example, includes images of the Statue of Liberty, a bald eagle against a rainbow, the Sistine Chapel with Michelangelo's famous frescoes (upper left), Sunkist oranges, Manhattan rooftops and their distinctive water towers (in red), building facades (in blue), and construction workers in plaid shirts and hard hats (in blue, lower right) (**3.16**). Part of our pleasure as viewers lies in teasing out their visual and conceptual connections.

The Statue of Liberty and the eagle are symbols of the United States, while the statue is more specifically a tourist attraction of New York. Sunkist oranges are

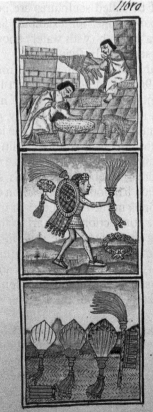

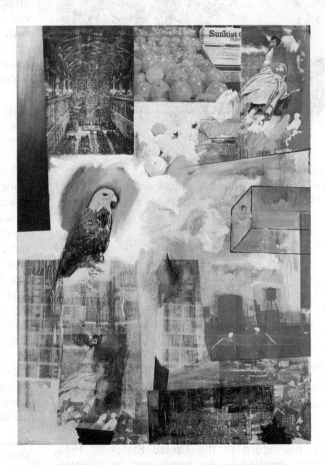

3.15 Bernardino de Sahagún. *Florentine Codex: Feather Workers*. 1575–77. Ink and pigment on paper.
Mexico City, Biblioteca Manuel Gamio del Museo del Templo Mayor. DeAgostini/Getty Images

3.16 Robert Rauschenberg. *Windward*. 1963. Oil and silkscreened ink on canvas, 8' × 5' 10".
Fondation Beyeler, Riehen/Basel. akg-images. Art © Robert Rauschenberg Foundation/Licensed by VAGA, New York, NY

Robert Rauschenberg (1925–2008)

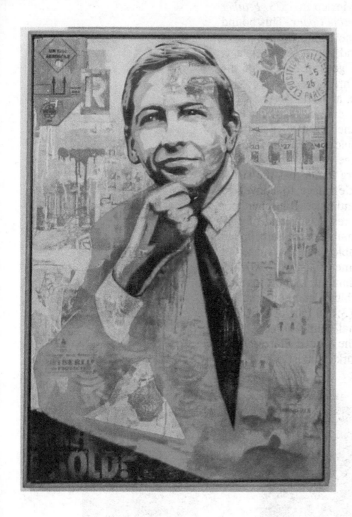

How should we categorize the works of Rauschenberg? How does his style capture the culture and the events of his time? What are some of his dominant themes?

Born in Port Arthur, Texas, Milton Rauschenberg—who later became known as Bob and then Robert—had no exposure to art as such until he was seventeen. His original intention to become a pharmacist faded when he was expelled from the University of Texas within six months, for failure (he claims) to dissect a frog. After three years in the Navy during World War II, Rauschenberg spent a year at the Kansas City Art Institute; then he traveled to Paris for further study. At the Académie Julian in Paris he met the artist Susan Weil, whom he later married.

Upon his return to the United States in 1948, Rauschenberg enrolled in the now-famous art program headed by the painter Josef Albers at Black Mountain College in North Carolina. Many of his long-term attachments and interests developed during this period, including his close working relationship with the avant-garde choreographer Merce Cunningham. In 1950 Rauschenberg moved to New York, where he supported himself partly by doing window displays for the fashionable Fifth Avenue stores Bonwit Teller and Tiffany's.

Rauschenberg's work began to attract critical attention soon after his first one-man exhibition at the Betty Parsons Gallery in New York. The artist reported that between the time Parsons selected the works to be exhibited and the opening of the show, he had completely reworked everything, and that "Betty was surprised." More surprises were soon to come from this steadily unpredictable artist.

The range of Rauschenberg's work makes him difficult to categorize. In addition to paintings, prints, and combination pieces, he produced extensive set and costume designs for dances by Cunningham and others, as well as graphic design for magazines and books. "Happenings" and performance art also played a role in his work from the very beginning. Rauschenberg used objects that he found around him in his paintings. One has an actual stuffed bird attached to the front of the canvas. Another consists of a bed, with a quilt on it, hung upright on the wall and splashed with paint. Works that might be called sculptures are primarily **assemblages** of ordinary items; for example, *Sor Aqua* (1973) is composed of a bathtub (with water) above which a large chunk of metal seems to be flying.

Rauschenberg explained his interest in images from daily life in an interview in 1965. He described the art he made in New York City as "unbiased documentation of my observations, and by observations I mean that literally, of my excitement about the way in the city you have on one lot a forty story building and right next to it you have a little wooden shack. One is a parking lot and one is this maze of offices and closets and windows where everything is so crowded. . . . It was this constant, irrational juxtaposition of things that I think one only finds in the city." Later in the same interview, discussing the connection of his art to the here and now, Rauschenberg explained, "The one thing that has been consistent about my work is that there has been an attempt to use the very last minutes in my life and the particular location as the source of energy and inspiration, rather than retiring to some kind of other time, or dream, or idealism."[1]

We get from Rauschenberg a sense of boundaries being dissolved—boundaries between media, between art and nonart, between art and life. As he said: "The strongest thing about my work . . . is the fact that I chose to ennoble the ordinary."[2]

an American product, but Rauschenberg likes their name as well: sun-kissed, kissed by the sun. In a repeat of the image directly below, he paints white all the oranges but one. The single orange becomes a sun, and the rest are clouds. "Sun-kissed" also applies to the rainbow, which is moist air kissed by the sun. It applies more generally to a clear day in New York, and in the company of the eagle and the statue it evokes the sentiments expressed in one of our most popular patriotic songs, which begins "O beautiful for spacious skies." Again and again we find the optimistic gesture of raising up: Liberty raises her torch high, the rooftops hold aloft their water towers, the Sistine Chapel holds up its great vaulted ceiling, the construction workers build a skyscraper.

Reflecting on the Human Experience

An Egyptian official, a lady of the imperial Chinese court, and artists in 16th-century Mexico would all have had very different lives. They would have known different stories, worshiped different deities, seen different sights, and had different understandings of the world and their place in it. Yet they also would have shared certain experiences, just by virtue of being human. We are all of us born, we pass through childhood, we mature into sexual beings, we search for love, we grow old, we die. We experience doubt and wonder, happiness and sorrow, loneliness and despair.

Surely one of the most common of human wishes is to talk, if only we could, for even a brief moment, with someone who is no longer here. Many religions embrace the idea that the dead form a vast spirit community capable of helping us. Many rituals have been devised to honor ancestors and appease their spirits. But all the rituals in the world do not compensate for the ache we sometimes feel when we wish we could speak to those who came before—to tell them what we have become, to ask for guidance, to compare experiences, to explain, to listen.

Meta Warrick Fuller's poignant sculpture *Talking Skull* depicts that wish being granted (**3.17**). Kneeling before the skull, naked and vulnerable, the boy seems to hear an answer to his plea. On one level, *Talking Skull* embodies a universal message about the desire for communion beyond the boundaries of our brief lifetime. But it is also a specifically African-American work that addresses the traumatic

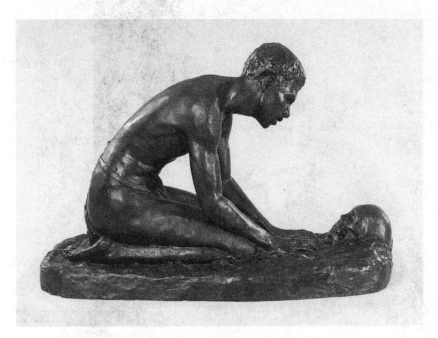

3.17 Meta Warrick Fuller. *Talking Skull*. 1937. Bronze, 28 × 40 × 15". Museum of African American History, Boston and Nantucket

rupture with ancestral culture that slavery had caused. Fuller was a pioneering African-American artist. Born in 1877, she pursued her artistic training in both the United States and Europe, mastering the conservative, academic style that brought mainstream recognition to artists in her day. Like many of her generation, she sought out themes that would help American blacks reconnect with and take pride in their African heritage.

Looking at Fuller's sculpture, we enter into the boy's thoughts through empathy. Fuller counts on this ability, and her artistry facilitates it by giving us numerous clues: the pose, the nakedness, the intense gaze, the open mouth. In *Self-Portrait with Monkeys* (**3.18**), the Mexican artist Frida Kahlo does not provide us with an easy way into her thoughts. She seems, rather, to hold us at arm's length with her gaze, to insist that we cannot truly know her.

Kahlo began to paint while recovering from a streetcar accident that left her body shattered and unable to bear children. She would know periods of crippling pain for the rest of her life, and would undergo dozens of operations. Her first work was a self-portrait, as though to affirm that she still existed. She continued to paint self-portraits over the course of her career. In them she expressed her experience as a woman, as an artist, as a Mexican. Often, as here, she painted herself as the still center of a busy visual field. Wearing an embroidered Mexican dress, she regards us coolly, skeptically. Or perhaps it is herself in the mirror whom she sees.

Her two pet monkeys seem both protective and possessive in their gestures. Their gazes tell us no more than hers, but she and they clearly share an understanding that excludes us. Behind them two more monkeys peer out from the foliage. Next to her head, as though she were thinking it, a bird-of-paradise flower displays its extravagant, flamelike petals—exotic, proud, desirable, and slightly menacing. European visitors admired Kahlo's paintings for their dream imagery, but she herself rejected such praise. "I never painted dreams," she said. "I painted my own reality."[3]

3.18 Frida Kahlo. *Self-Portrait with Monkeys*. 1943. Oil on canvas, 32 1/16 × 24 3/16".
Jacques and Natasha Gelman Collection. akg-images. © 2019 Banco de México Diego Rivera Frida Kahlo Museums Trust, Mexico, D.F./Artists Rights Society (ARS), New York

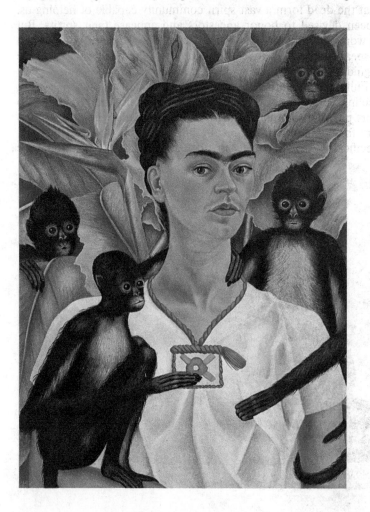

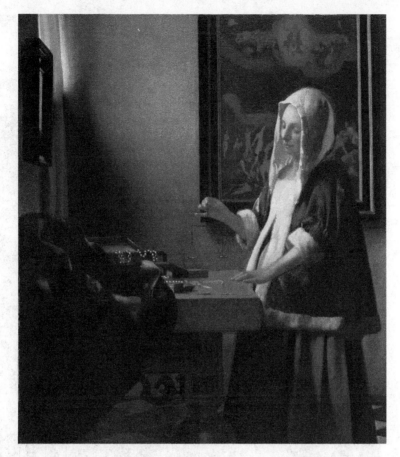

One of the most reticent yet complete evocations of our existence and its fundamental questions is the Dutch painter Johannes Vermeer's quiet masterpiece *Woman Holding a Balance* (**3.19**). Stillness pervades the picture. A gentle half-light filtered through the curtained window reveals a woman contemplating an empty jeweler's balance. She holds the balance and its two glinting trays delicately with her right hand, which falls in the exact center of the composition. The frame of the painting on the wall behind catches the light, drawing our attention.

The painting is a depiction of the Last Judgment, when according to Christian belief Christ shall come again to judge, to weigh souls. On the table, the light picks out strands of pearls. Jewels and jewelry often serve as symbols of vanity and the temptations of earthly treasure. Light is reflected, too, in the surface of the mirror, next to the window. The mirror suggests self-knowledge, and indeed if the woman were to look up, she would be facing directly into it. Scholars have debated whether the woman is pregnant or whether the fashion of the day simply makes her appear so. Either way, we can say that her form evokes pregnancy, the miracle of birth, and the renewal of life.

Birth, death, the decisions we must weigh on our journey through life, the temptations of vanity, the problem of self-knowledge, the question of life after death—all these issues are gently touched on in this most understated of paintings.

Invention and Fantasy

Renaissance theorists likened painting to poetry. With words, a poet could conjure an imaginary world and fill it with people and events. Painting was even better, for it could bring an imaginary world to life before your eyes. Poetry had long been considered an art, and the idea that painting was comparable to it is one of the factors that led to painting being considered an art as well.

One of the most bizarrely inventive artists ever to wield a brush was the Netherlandish painter Hieronymus Bosch. When we first encounter his *Garden of*

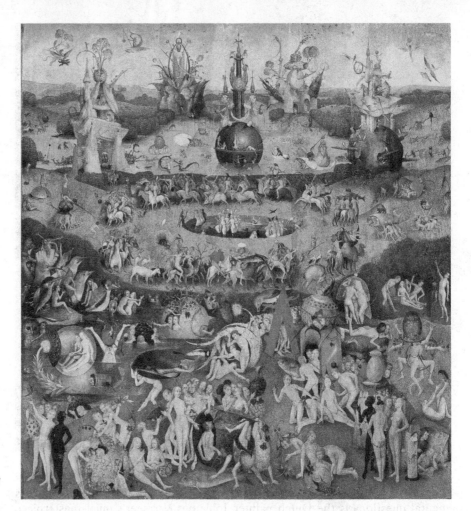

3.20 Hieronymus Bosch. *The Garden of Earthly Delights*, center section. ca. 1505–10. Oil on panel, 7' 2 ⅝" × 6' 4 ¾".
Museo del Prado, Madrid. Erich Lessing/ Art Resource, NY

Earthly Delights (**3.20**), we might think we have wandered into a fun house of a particularly macabre kind. *The Garden of Earthly Delights* is the central and largest panel of a **triptych**, a painting in three sections. The outer two sections, painted both front and back, can close like a pair of shutters over this central image. Closed, they depict the creation of the world; open, they illustrate the earthly paradise of Eden (left) and Hell (right). Between Eden and Hell, Bosch set *The Garden of Earthly Delights*, which depicts the false paradise of love—false because, although deeply pleasurable, it can lead humanity away from the bonds of marriage toward the deadly sin of Lust, and thus damnation. Hundreds of nude humans cavort in a fantasy landscape inhabited by giant plants and outsized birds and animals. The people are busy and inventive in the things they do to and with one another (and to and with the animals and plants). They seem to be having a fine time, but their goings-on are so strange that we are both intrigued and repelled by them. Can these truly be delights?

While Bosch imagined an earthly paradise, Giovanni Battista Piranesi created a subterranean dungeon using a printmaking technique known as **etching**. He called the sixteen prints in this series *Il Carceri* ("The Prison") (**3.21**), and explained that they were "capricious inventions" from his own imagination. The etchings picture an underground prison of ambiguous spaces, stairways to nowhere, and soaring, dark vaults. We see this architecture from a low vantage point to emphasize its size. Piranesi filled his frightening spaces with machines and tiny figures. After printing an initial run or state of the prints, Piranesi returned to his images and made them even darker and more ominous, like the one seen here. He added chains, ladders, and spiked objects that look like torture devices. He even added spikes to the top of the sawhorse on the right that gives this print its title. Piranesi drew these additional elements with slashing, aggressive strokes, with the result that the form adds to the scary content. Texts in some of the images refer to the ancient Roman justice system under some of its more brutal emperors. Piranesi likely also created the

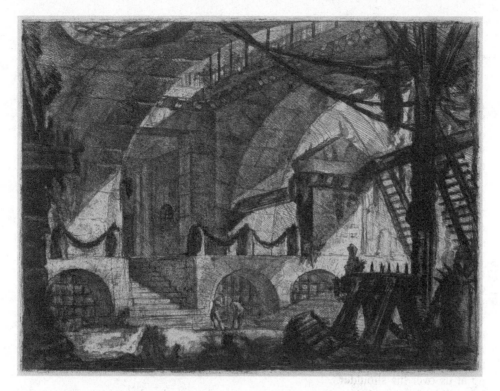

etchings in response to the Enlightenment's celebration of reason. His work anticipates the movement known as Romanticism that would soon react to the rationality of Enlightenment with stories of monsters and high-keyed emotion.

A far more benign imagination was that of Henri Rousseau. Rousseau worked in France during the late 19th and early 20th centuries. He was acquainted with all the up-and-coming artists of the Parisian scene, and sometimes he exhibited with them. The naiveté of his expression came not so much from ignorance of formal art tradition as from indifference to that tradition. Rousseau loved to paint jungle scenes, but they were wholly products of fantasy, for in fact he never left France. Instead, he assembled his exotic visions from illustrated books, from travel magazines, and from sketching trips to the zoo, the natural history museum, and especially the great tropical greenhouses of the Paris botanical garden. Entering them, he said, was like walking into a dream. In his last painting, he gave this dream to a young woman (**3.22**). Reclining nude on a velvet sofa, she seems unsurprised to find herself in a dense forest of stylized foliage, serenaded by a dark-skinned musician wearing a loincloth. Perhaps it is his music that has cast this spell in which giant lotuses grow on land, lions are as tame as house cats, and a full moon shines during the day.

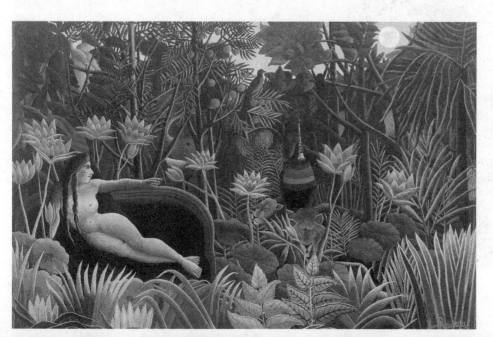

The Natural World

As humans, we make our own environment. From the first tools of the earliest hominids to today's towering skyscrapers, we have shaped the world around us to our needs. This manufactured environment, though, has its setting in quite a different environment—that of the natural world. Nature and our relationship to it are themes that have often been addressed through art.

During the 19th century, many American painters set themselves the American landscape as a subject. One of the first of these was Thomas Cole, who as a young man had immigrated to America from England. Cole's most famous painting is *The Oxbow*, which depicts the great looping bend (oxbow) of the Connecticut River as seen from the heights of nearby Mount Holyoke, in Massachusetts (**3.23**). To the left, a violent thunderstorm darkens the sky as it passes over the mountain wilderness. To the right, emerging into the sunlight after the storm, a broad settled valley extends as far as the eye can see. Fields have been cleared for grazing and crops. Minute plumes of smoke mark scattered farmhouses, and a few boats dot the river. Cole even gives us a role to play: we have accompanied him on his painting expedition and climbed up a little higher for an even better view. On a promontory to the right, we see the artist's umbrella and knapsack. A little to the left and down from the umbrella, Thomas Cole himself, seated in front of a painting in progress, looks up at us over his shoulder.

Cole developed the painting in his studio from a sketch he had made at the site, though he also introduced a number of inventions to make a more effective composition. The shattered and gnarled trees in the left foreground, for example, are a device he often used, and even the storm itself is probably a fiction, although

3.23 Thomas Cole. *The Oxbow (View from Mount Holyoke, Northampton, Massachusetts, After a Thunderstorm).* 1836. Oil on canvas, 4' 3 ½" × 6' 4".
The Metropolitan Museum of Art, New York. Gift of Mrs. Russell Sage, 1908, 08.228. Image copyright © The Metropolitan Museum of Art. Image source: Art Resource, NY

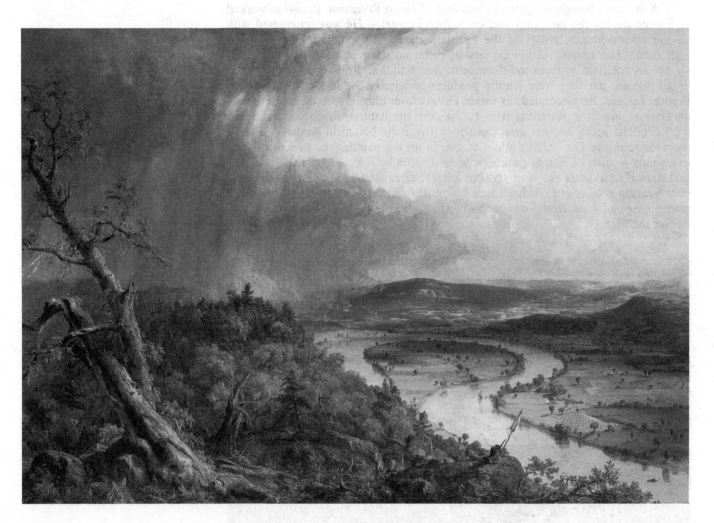

he certainly could have seen such storms. But the view of the river bend from the mountain, a famous sight in Cole's day, is largely faithful to his observation.

In contrast, the painter of *Shade of Pines in a Cloudy Valley* (3.24) may never have seen the view they depict nor would their audience have expected them to. Landscape is the most important and honored subject in the Chinese painting tradition, but its purpose was never to record the details of a particular site or view. Rather, painters learned to paint mountains, rocks, trees, and water so that they could construct imaginary landscapes for viewers to wander through in the mind's eye. Whereas Cole's painting places us on the mountain and depicts what can be seen from a fixed position, the artist here suspends us in midair and depicts a view that we could see only if we were mobile, like a bird.

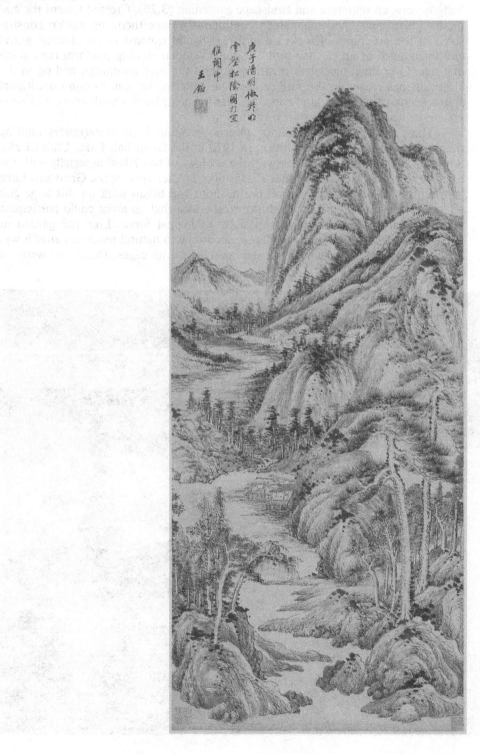

3.24 *Shade of Pines in a Cloudy Valley,* 1660. Ink and color on paper. Heritage Arts/Heritage Images/Getty Images

In his inscription, Wang Jian writes that his painting was inspired by a work by the early 14th-century master Zhao Mengfu, who in turn admired Dong Yuan, a 10th-century painter known for a view of this same region. In just a couple of sentences, Wang Jian situates himself in a centuries-old tradition of painterly and poetic meditations on the Xiao and Xiang rivers and the Jiuyi Mountains they flow through, a landscape rich in historical, literary, and artistic associations. All of that was more important to the painter and his audience than topographical accuracy.

Nature has been more than a subject for art; it has also served as a material for art. The desire to portray landscapes has been matched by the desire to create them for the pleasure of our eyes. A work such as the famed stone-and-gravel garden of the Buddhist temple of Ryoan-ji in Kyoto, Japan, seems to occupy a position halfway between sculpture and landscape gardening (**3.25**). Created toward the end of the 15th century and maintained continuously since then, the garden consists solely of five groupings of rocks set in a rectangular expanse of raked white gravel and surrounded by an earthen wall. A simple wooden viewing platform runs along one side. Over time, moss has grown up around the rock groupings, and oil in the clay walls has seeped to the surface, forming patterns that call to mind traditional Japanese ink paintings of landscape. The garden is a place of meditation, and viewers are invited to find their own meanings in it.

The simplicity of Ryoan-ji finds an echo in *Spiral Jetty*, an **earthwork** built by the American artist Robert Smithson in 1970 in the Great Salt Lake, Utah (**3.26**). Smithson had become fascinated with the ecology of salt lakes, especially with the microbacteria that tinge their water shades of red. After viewing the Great Salt Lake in Utah, he leased a parcel of land on its shore and began work on this large coil of rock and earth. Smithson was drawn to the idea that an artist could participate in the shaping of landscape almost as a geological force. Like the garden at Ryoan-ji, *Spiral Jetty* continued to change according to natural processes after it was finished. Salt crystals accumulated and sparkled on its edges. Depths of water in

3.25 Stone and gravel garden, Ryoan-ji Temple, Kyoto. ca. 1488–1500, with subsequent modifications.
© Vanni Archive/Art Resource, NY

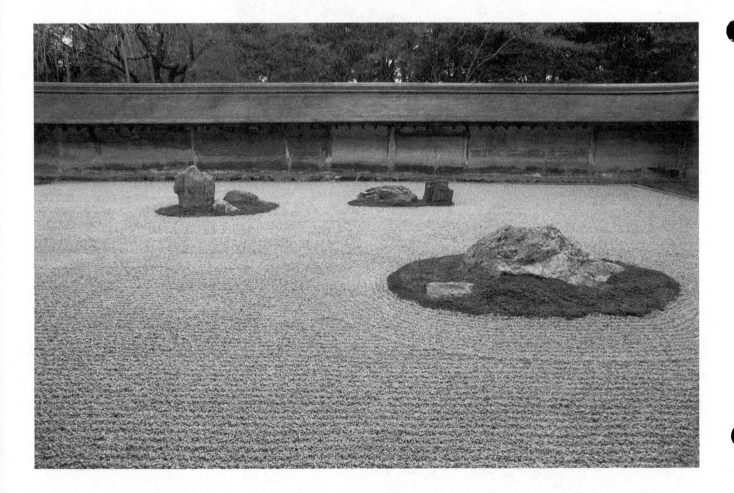

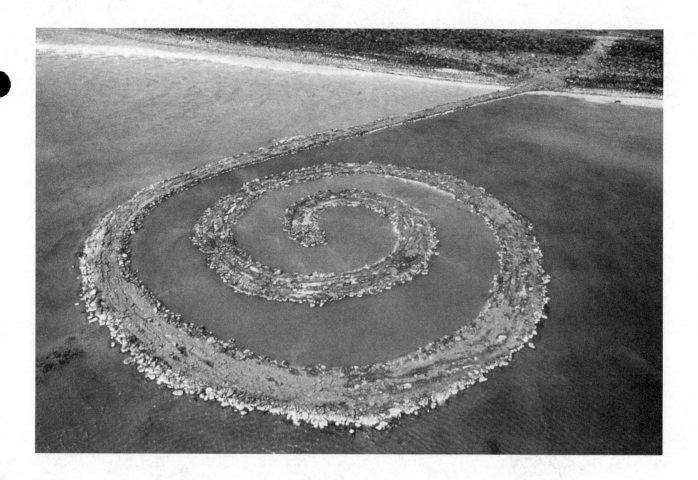

3.26 Robert Smithson. *Spiral Jetty*. Great Salt Lake, Utah. April 1970. Black rock, salt crystals, earth, red water (algae); 3 ½ × 15 × 1500'. DIA Center for the Arts, New York. Courtesy of James Cohan Gallery, New York and Shanghai © Holt-Smithson Foundation/VAGA, New York. Photo: Gianfranco Gorgoni

and around it showed themselves in different tints of transparent violet, pink, and red. *Spiral Jetty* was submerged by the rising waters of the lake soon after it was created. Following droughts in the early 2000s, it resurfaced, transformed by a coating of salt crystals.

Art about Art and Its Institutions

Artists learn to make art by looking at art. They look at the art of the past to learn about their predecessors, and they look at the art of the present to situate themselves amid its currents and get their bearings. In Chapter 2, we saw Yasumasa Morimura appropriate an image by the Spanish 17th-century artist Diego Velázquez in order to raise questions about self and the nature of creativity. When he did this, he made art about art itself—about learning, making, and viewing it; about its nature and social setting; about specific movements, styles, or works.

Jeff Wall is an artist who often sets up a dialogue with earlier art in his work. *A Sudden Gust of Wind (after Hokusai)* (**3.28**) shows him thinking about Hokusai's *Ejiri in Suruga Province* (**3.27**). Wall takes seriously the idea, touched on in Chapter 2, that photography has taken over from painting the project of depicting modern life. But he does not practice photography in a straightforward way, going into the world to take pictures of objects he sees or events he witnesses. Instead, he uses the technology of photography to construct an image, much as a painter organizes a painting or a film director goes about making the artificial reality of a film. He builds a set or scouts a location, he sets up the lighting or waits for the right weather, and he costumes and poses his models. Often, as here, he uses digital technology to combine many separately photographed elements into a single image. Wall displays the finished works as large-format transparencies lit from behind. *A Sudden Gust of Wind* is almost the size of a billboard, a glowing billboard.

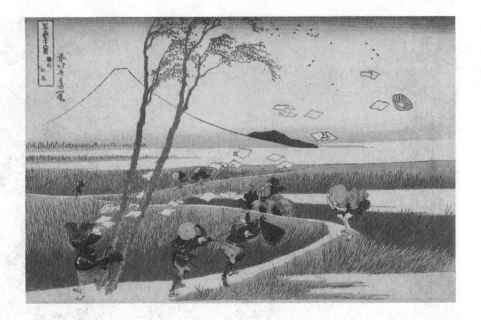

3.27 Hokusai. *Ejiri in Suruga Province*, from *Thirty-Six Views of Mt. Fuji*. ca. 1831. Polychrome woodblock print, 9 ⅝ × 14 ⅞".
Honolulu Museum of Art, Gift of James A. Michener, 1991, 21941

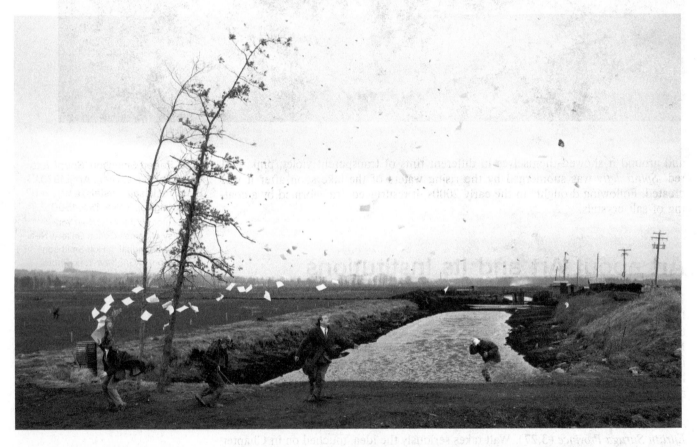

3.28 Jeff Wall. *A Sudden Gust of Wind (after Hokusai)*. 1993. Transparency in lightbox, 7' 6 ⅞" × 12' 4 ⁵⁄₁₆".
Photo courtesy Marian Goodman Gallery, New York. © Jeff Wall

Typically, what Wall wants us to see comes into focus only once we have the "art behind the art" in mind. Hokusai's *Ejiri in Suruga Province* is from *Thirty-Six Views of Mt. Fuji*, a series of views of daily life in Japan linked by the presence of the serene mountain in the distance. Like Hokusai, Wall sets his scene in a nondescript place, a flat land that is nowhere in particular. He re-creates the two trees, the travelers, and the wind-scattered papers. But there is no sublime mountain in the background, nothing to give the scene a larger meaning or sense of purpose. Without knowing Hokusai's print, we would not realize that the most powerful presence in Wall's photograph is an absence, the mountain that is not there.

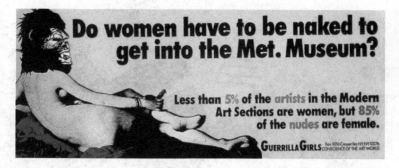

3.29 Guerrilla Girls. "Do women have to be naked to get into the Met. Museum?" 1989. Screenprint on paper, 11 × 28".
Copyright © by Guerrilla Girls.
www.guerrillagirls.com

Some artists comment on the figures and institutions of the art world: artists, schools, critics, auction houses, collectors, galleries, and museums. The activist group known as the Guerrilla Girls came into being in 1985, shortly after the opening of a huge exhibition at New York's Museum of Modern Art. The show, titled *International Survey of Contemporary Painting and Sculpture*, included works by 169 artists, fewer than 10 percent of whom were women. The Guerrilla Girls, an anonymous group of women artists, protested the absence of women from this and similar exhibitions. They produced a poster that asked in bold type, "WHAT DO THESE ARTISTS HAVE IN COMMON?" Underneath were the names of forty-two prominent artists—all male. The poster text continued, "They all allow their work to be shown in galleries that show no more than 10 percent women or none at all."

More posters followed. One asked, "Do women have to be naked to get into the Met. Museum?" (**3.29**), and noted the underrepresentation of women artists in the Metropolitan Museum of Art's collection. The poster uses a photograph of a painting by the 19th-century French artist Jean-Auguste-Dominique Ingres to represent the abundance of women's bodies displayed in museums. A gorilla mask is superimposed over her head, as the Guerrilla Girls wear this kind of mask when they appear in public. These posters drew attention to art institutions that promoted white male artists, all but ignoring women and minority artists. The works achieved almost instant chic, partly because of their excellent graphic design and partly because of the Guerrilla Girls' aura of mystery. The group remains active today.

Notes to the Text

1. "Oral history interview with Robert Rauschenberg, 1965 Dec. 21." Archives of American Art, Smithsonian Institution. Available at www.aaa.si.edu/collections/interviews/oral-history-interview-robert-rauschenberg-12870, accessed September 17, 2017.
2. Barbara Rose, *An Interview with Robert Rauschenberg* (New York: Elizabeth Avedon Editions, 1987), p. 59. Information in this biography is adapted from *Robert Rauschenberg* (Washington, D.C.: National Collection of Fine Arts, 1976).
3. Quoted in "Mexican Autobiography," *Time*, April 27, 1953.

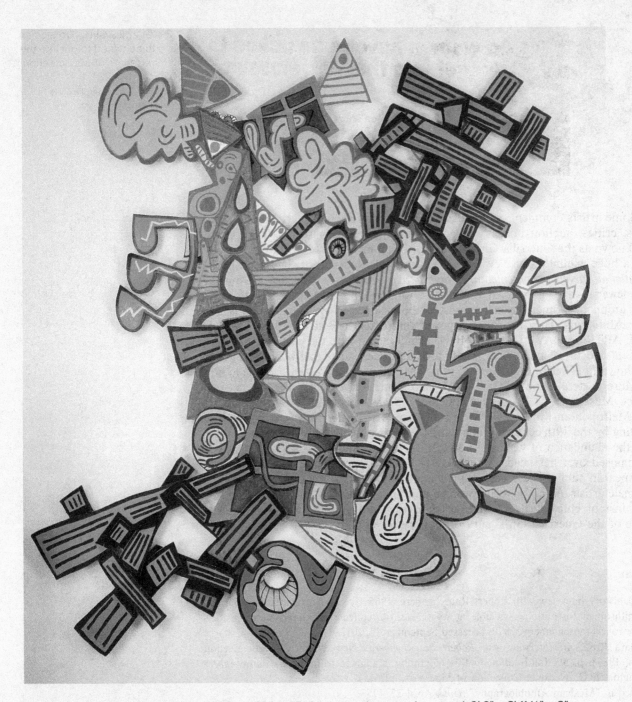

4.1 Elizabeth Murray. *The Sun and the Moon.* 2004–05. Oil on panel mounted on wood, 9' 9" × 8' 11 ½" × 2".
The Phillips Collection, Washington, D.C.

PART TWO

The Vocabulary of Art

Chapter 4
The Visual Elements

In this chapter, you will learn to

LO1   identify types of line,

LO2   explain how artists create shape and mass,

LO3   describe how real and implied light function in art,

LO4   characterize the use of color and the theories relating to it,

LO5   distinguish actual and visual texture as used in art,

LO6   discuss the strategies for creating space in two-dimensional art, and

LO7   relate how time and motion appear in art.

At first glance, Elizabeth Murray's *The Sun and the Moon* looks like nothing so much as a controlled explosion of colorful jigsaw-puzzle pieces (**4.1**). As we look longer, some of the pieces come into focus. There's a pink-and-red figure, a person, stepping over. . .is it an orange cat? We can make out the cat's two ears, its open mouth (with a representation of sound coming out, as in a cartoon), and its long, curling tail, which laces through. . .is it a window frame? Other elements are less clear, although by now we suspect that they, too, must represent abstractions of sights and sounds.

Murray's painting strikes a clever balance between what we see in abstract terms (an orange shape) and what we eventually realize is represented (a cat). But shapes are not the only thing that our eyes take in as we try to make sense of the painting. We distinguish the colors and notice their range, from pale yellow to dark violet. We notice that the shapes are outlined, and that some lines inside the shapes seem to suggest texture, as in the blue-green lattice formation in the upper right, which may represent pieces of wood. We see that certain shapes repeat, although not regularly enough to form a pattern. We notice the spaces between the pieces of the painting, and we observe that light from above has caused the pieces of the painting to cast shadows, suggesting that they have some mass, like a shallow sculpture.

The eight terms that helped us to analyze our visual experience of Murray's painting—line, shape, mass, light, color, texture, pattern, and space—are the ingredients that an artist has available in making any work of art. Called the visual or formal elements, they are the elements that we perceive and respond to when we look at a work's form. We will examine each one in this chapter. During the 20th century, time and motion were added to the traditional list of elements by artists seeking to expand and modernize artistic practice, and this chapter considers them as well.

Line

Strictly defined, a line is a path traced by a moving point. You poise your pencil on a sheet of paper and move its point along the surface to make a line. Yet lines are not confined to scribbling on a page. Some can reach immense proportions.

The gigantic earth drawings known as the Nasca Lines (**4.2**) are just that—lines. They are the work of the Nasca people of southern Peru. Created sometime in the first millennium C.E., the lines were made by removing the top layer of weathered stones from the desert floor. The exposed sand is lighter in color. Some of the drawings are long, straight lines up to 30 miles long. Others are geometric patterns, animals, plants, and humanlike forms. The lines seen here seem to define the shape of a hummingbird. The feathers and beak are formed by perfectly parallel lines that come together at the end. The shape the lines create can be seen completely only from the sky, leading experts to wonder how the drawings were used. Such immense drawings would have taken many people and a long time to create. Whatever their meaning, these lines in the Peruvian desert clearly meant a great deal to the Nasca people who created them.

The French artist Claude Mellan's line engraving (**4.3**) pictures the image of Christ's face miraculously transferred to Saint Veronica's handkerchief. What is more remarkable about the print than its subject is the fact that the entire image consists of a single line. The line begins at the tip of Christ's nose and continues in concentric circles until it runs out of paper. Even then, the lines pick up as if they continued. The artist accomplished this by cutting the line into the copper plate, which he slowly turned as he worked. Where Mellan wanted darker tones, he made the line wider. This single line defines the whole image: facial features and their physical shape, hair, and even cloth. Viewers of this print delighted in Mellan's playful use of line and were impressed by his precision and control.

While the lines of the Nasca drawings and Mellan's print seem very still, other lines create the sense of motion. Sarah Sze's installation *Hidden Relief* prominently features lines that "draw" curves, circles, rules, and lattice formations in the air (**4.4**). Sze assembles her works from commonplace industrial products such as measuring sticks, string, lamps, ladders, toothpicks, plastic tubes, and kitchen implements. In her hands, we become aware of them as visual elements, bits of ready-

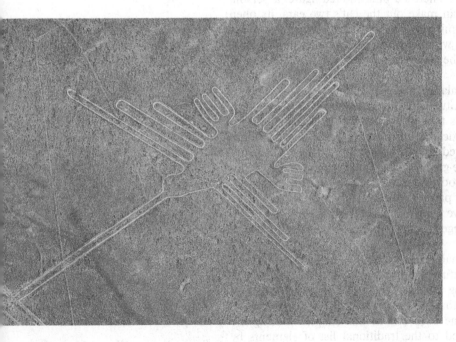

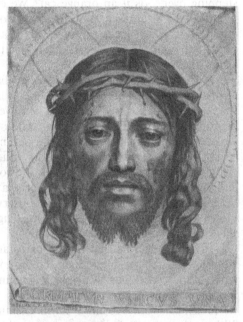

4.2 High angle view of Nasca lines, Nasca, Peru.
Glow Images

4.3 Claude Mellan. *Sudarium of St. Veronica.* 1649. Engraving, 17 × 12 ½".
National Gallery of Art, Washington/Rosenwald Collection

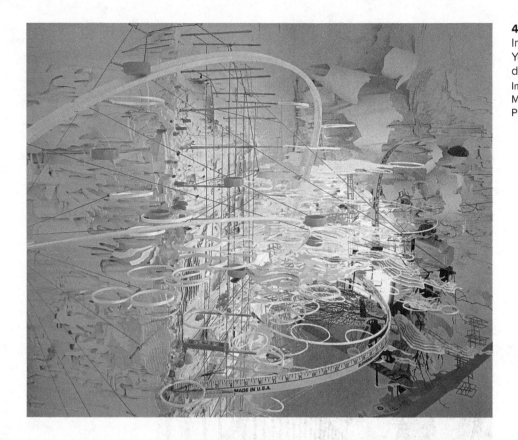

4.4 Sarah Sze. *Hidden Relief*. 2001.
Installation at the Asia Society, New
York. 2001–04. Mixed media,
dimensions variable.
Image courtesy the artist and Victoria
Miro, London/Venice. © Sarah Sze.
Photo © Sarah Sze and Frank Oudeman

made line, mass, color, and shape. (The squat blue cylindrical forms here are
plastic bottle caps; the white circles are slices of Styrofoam cups.) Installed in a
corner of a room, *Hidden Relief* is not particularly large, but Sze's close-up photograph makes it seem like a universe. Our eyes follow the roller-coaster ride of the
yellow arcs, spin like figure skaters through the flock of white circles, and speed
down the taut string lines that converge on the yellow lamp as we explore this
strange new world.

The ways that the Nasca artists, Mellan, and Sze use line—to record the borders of form, to describe surfaces and shapes, and to convey direction and motion—
are the primary functions of line in art. We look more closely at them below.

4.5 Jacques Callot. *Study of a
Rearing Horse*. ca. 1616. Pen and
ink, 12 ¾ × 7 ¼".
Digital image courtesy of the Getty's
Open Content Program

Contour and Outline

Strictly speaking, an outline defines a two-dimensional shape. For example, drawing
with chalk on a blackboard, you might outline the shape of your home state. On
a dress pattern, dotted lines outline the shapes of the various pieces. But if you
were to make the dress and then draw someone wearing it, you would be drawing
the dress's contours. Contours are the boundaries we perceive of three-dimensional
forms, and **contour lines** are the lines we draw to record those boundaries. Jacques
Callot used pen and ink to make a contour drawing of a horse (**4.5**). We see the
edges of the horse's legs, hindquarters, shoulders, neck, and head. Callot even used
contour lines to define the boundaries of the tail and mane.

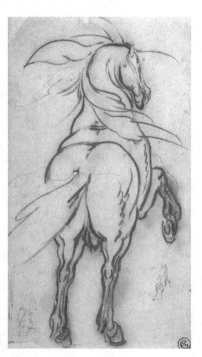

Direction and Movement

In following the looping lines of Sarah Sze's *Hidden Relief*, we were doing what
comes naturally. Our eyes tend to follow lines to see where they are going, like a
train following a track. Artists can use this tendency to direct our eyes around an
image, and to suggest movement.

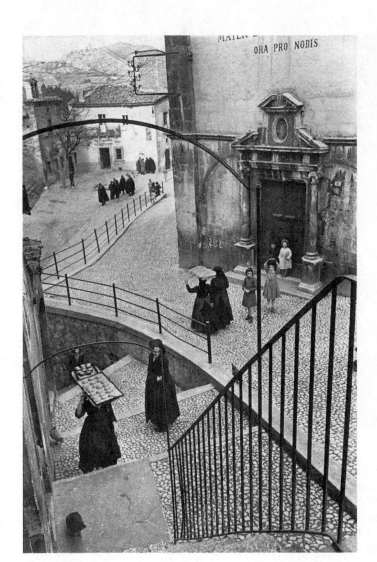

4.6 Henri Cartier-Bresson. *Aquila, Abruzzi, Italy*. 1951. Gelatin silver print, 14 ⅛ × 9 ½".
© Henri Cartier-Bresson/Magnum Photos

Directional lines play an important role in Henri Cartier-Bresson's photograph of a small Italian town (**4.6**). For Cartier-Bresson, the success of a photograph hinged on what he called the "decisive moment." Here, for example, what probably drew his attention was the woman climbing the stairs and balancing a tray of bread on her head. The small loaves resemble the paving stones so closely that it looks as though a piece of the street were suddenly in motion. Visual coincidences like this delighted Cartier-Bresson, but the decisive moment for the photograph occurred just as the woman was framed by the lines of the iron archway, creating a picture within a picture. Our eyes slide down the line of the steeply pitched railing right to her. Other railing lines carry our eyes into the background, where a cluster of town-dwellers stand in the open square. Without the lines of the iron railings, our eyes would not move so efficiently through the picture, and we might miss what Cartier-Bresson wants us to notice.

You may have noticed that the lines your eyes followed most readily were diagonal lines. Most of us have instinctive reactions to the direction of line, related to our experience of gravity. Flat, horizontal lines seem placid, such as the horizon line or a body in repose. Vertical lines, such as those of an upright body or a skyscraper jutting up from the ground, may have an assertive quality; they defy gravity in their upward thrust. But the most dynamic lines are the diagonals, which almost always imply action. Think of a runner hurtling down the track or a skier down the slope. The body leans forward, so that only the forward motion keeps it from toppling over. Diagonal lines in art have the same effect. We sense motion because the lines seem unstable; we half expect them to topple over.

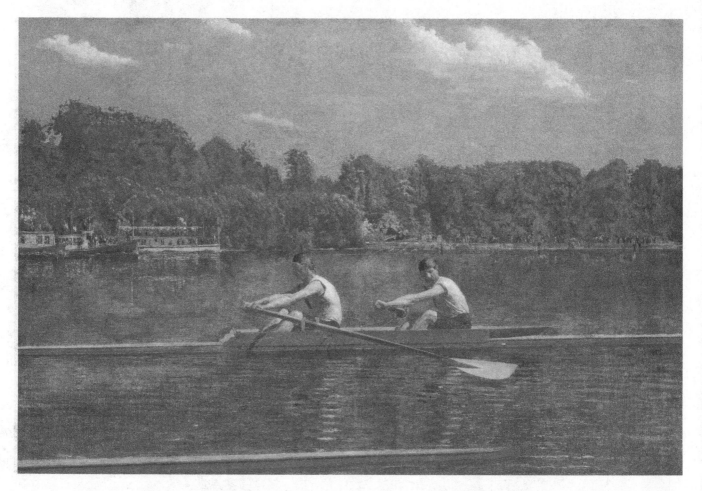

4.7 Thomas Eakins. *The Biglin Brothers Racing*. 1872. Oil on canvas, 24 ⅛ × 36 ¹⁄₁₆".
Image courtesy of the Board of Trustees, National Gallery of Art, Washington, D.C., Chester Dale Collection, Gift of Mr. and Mrs. Cornelius Vanderbilt Whitney 1953.7.1

Thomas Eakins's *The Biglin Brothers Racing* (**4.7**) is stabilized by the long, calm horizontal of the distant shore. The two boats in the foreground are set on the gentlest of diagonals—only a hint, but it is enough to convey their motion. More pronounced diagonals are found in the men's arms and oars. In rowing, arms and oars literally provide the power that sets the boat in motion. In Eakins's painting, their diagonals provide the visual power. If you place a ruler over the near oar and then slide it slowly upward, you will see that the treetops to the left and the clouds in the sky repeat this exact diagonal (**4.8**). It is as if the swing of the oar set the entire painting in motion. The subdued diagonals of Eakins's painting perfectly capture the streamlined quality of sculling, in which slender boats knife smoothly and rapidly through the calm water of a river or lake.

Eakins's painting demonstrates that we experience more than literal drawn lines as lines. In fact, we react to any linear form as a line. For example, we can talk about the line of the men's arms or the line of an oar. Oars and arms are not lines, but they are linear. They act as lines in the work of art. We also react to lines

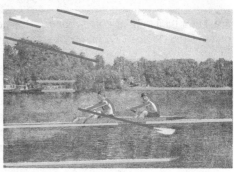

4.8 Linear analysis of *The Biglin Brothers Racing*.

Image courtesy of the Board of Trustees, National Gallery of Art, Washington, D.C., Chester Dale Collection, Gift of Mr. and Mrs. Cornelius Vanderbilt Whitney 1953.7.1

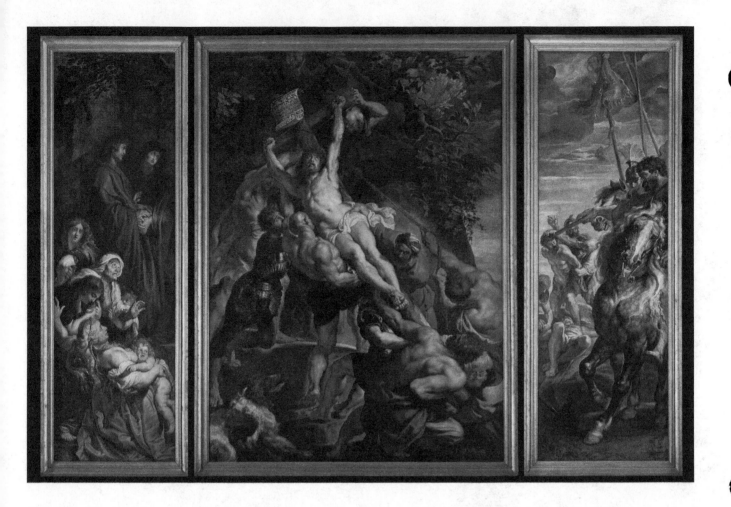

4.9 Peter Paul Rubens. *The Raising of the Cross*. 1609–11. Oil on panel, 15' 1 ⅞" × 11' 1 ½".
Onze Lieve Vrouwekerk, Antwerp Cathedral, Belgium/Peter Willi/Bridgeman Images

formed by edges. For example, the white contours of the men's backs contrast strongly with the dark behind them, and we perceive the edges of the backs as lines.

There is a great contrast in linear movement, and thus in emotional effect, between Eakins's work and the next illustration, Peter Paul Rubens's *Raising of the Cross* (**4.9**). Rubens's theme is the moment when the cross-bound Christ is hoisted into the vertical position. He imagines this work done by large, muscular men. As they pull the cross, their bodies, Christ's body, and the cross itself form a large diagonal line that runs from the bottom right corner of the painting to the top left. The main diagonal is repeated by another consisting of the rope and the pulling man farthest right. These lines intersect smaller diagonals made of legs and backs on the left side. These secondary lines seem to push the main diagonal toward the viewer. Picked out by the light, Christ's body directs our eye toward his face as he looks heavenward.

Implied Lines

In addition to actual lines, linear forms, and lines formed by edges, our eyes also pick up on lines that are only implied. A common example from everyday life is the dotted line, where a series of dots are spaced closely enough that our mind connects them. The 18th-century French painter Jean-Antoine Watteau created a sort of dotted line of amorous couples in *The Embarkation for Cythera* (**4.10**). Starting with the seated couple at the right, our eyes trace a line that curves in a gentle S and leaves us evaporating into the gauzy air with the infant cupids (**4.11**). Cythera is the mythological island of love. Watteau specialized in elegant scenes in which aristocratic men and women gather in a leafy setting to play at love. Often, as here, the scenes are tinged with a gentle melancholy.

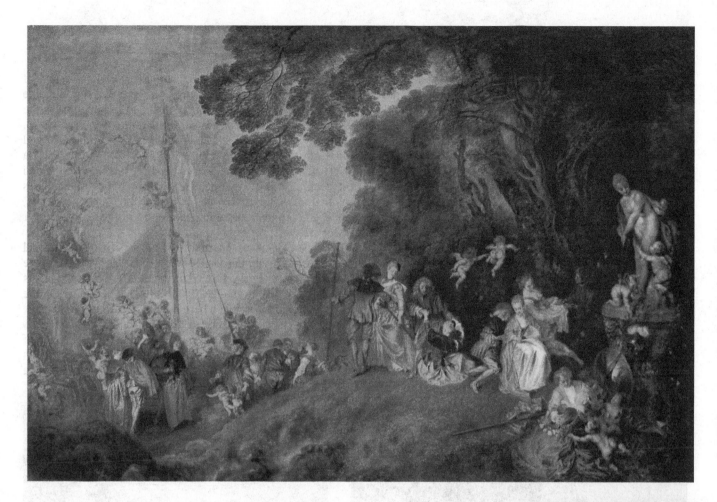

4.10 Jean-Antoine Watteau. *The Embarkation for Cythera*. 1718–19(?). Oil on canvas, 4' 21 ³⁄₁₆" × 6' 4 ³⁄₈".
Schloss Charlottenburg, Staatliche Schlösser und Gärten Berlin. The Picture Art Collection / Alamy Stock Photo

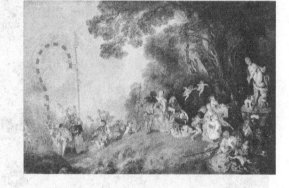

4.11 Linear analysis of *The Embarkation for Cythera*.
Schloss Charlottenburg, Staatliche Schlösser und Gärten Berlin. The Picture Art Collection / Alamy Stock Photo

In representational art, the same directional cues we follow in life can create implied lines. When a person stops on a street corner and gazes upward, other passersby will also stop and look up, following the "line" of sight. When someone points a finger, we automatically follow the direction of the point. Watteau uses these implied lines here as well. Looking at the painting, we are drawn eventually to the statue of Venus at the far right. We could be "stuck" there if it were not for her extended arm, which directs our attention down to the first couple below, where the winding procession begins. In addition, most of the couples look at each other, but the most prominent gazes are directed to the right, especially that of the woman who turns at the crest of the hill to look at the couple behind her. The graceful procession toward the shore is undercut by the constant tug of backward glances, and in following them we too are gently pulled back. It is this that gives the painting its slight air of melancholy, prompting many scholars to wonder whether the couples are heading toward the island of love, or leaving it.

Shape and Mass

A **shape** is a two-dimensional form, and any two-dimensional image is a system of interlocking shapes. Each shape within the image occupies an area with identifiable boundaries. Boundaries may be created by line (a square outlined in pencil on white paper), a shift in texture (a square of unmowed lawn in the middle of mowed lawn), or a shift in color (blue polka dots on a red shirt). A **mass** is a three-dimensional form that occupies a volume of space. We speak of a mass of clay, the mass of a mountain, the masses of a work of architecture. Shapes and masses can be divided into two broad categories: geometric and organic. Geometric shapes and masses approximate the regular, named shapes and volumes of geometry, such as a square, triangle, circle, cube, pyramid, and sphere. Organic shapes and masses are irregular and evoke the living forms of nature.

Rosalba Carriera's portrait of Gustavus Hamilton (**4.12**) is a two-dimensional work. It was painted while the young Irishman visited Venice. He is dressed for the Venice Carnival, with a mask pushed off to the side of his head. The painting defines different shapes within the figure by using changes in color. The boundary of the triangular shape of Hamilton's right side is visible where the blue coat meets the black headscarf and fur collar. Carriera also used texture to distinguish shapes. The triangular area of the white linen shirt is bordered by the fur of the collar and the lace of the headscarf. The whole figure creates a roughly triangular shape. This is known as a **positive shape**. But there is another shape in this image. It is the gray arching area

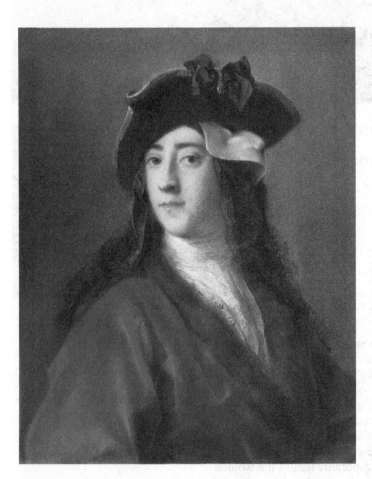

4.12 Rosalba Carriera. *Gustavus Hamilton*. 1730. Pastel on paper, 22 ¼ × 16 ⅞".
Metropolitan Museum of Art, New York/Purchase, George Delacorte Fund Gift, in memory of George T. Delacorte Jr., and Gwynne Andrews, Victor Wilbour Memorial, and Marquand Funds, 2002

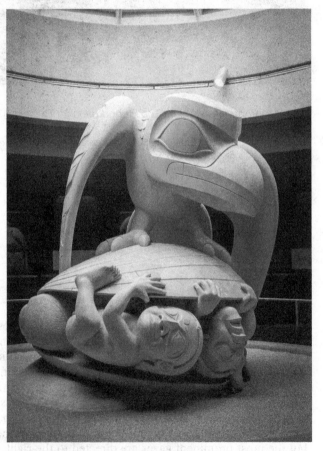

4.13 Bill Reid. *The Raven and the First Men*. 1980.
Laminated yellow cedar, height 6' 2 ¼".
Felix Choo / Alamy Stock Photo

of the background. In fact, any shape created on a limited, two-dimensional surface creates a second, complementary shape known as a **negative shape**.

There are lots of shapes in Bill Reid's monumental sculpture *The Raven and the First Men* (**4.13**), but the mass of space displaced in this work is considerable. Carved from blocks of laminated cedar, the work depicts the birth of humankind as told in the creation stories of the Haida in the Pacific Northwest Coast. The giant bird is a spirit hero called Raven. It was he who discovered the first humans hiding in a clam shell and coaxed them out into the world. The photograph of Reid's sculpture shows how light and shadow reveal the three-dimensional form of a mass to us, letting us sense where it bulges outward or recedes, where it is concave and where convex. The mass of the clam shell is substantial and is topped by the mass of the bird. We see these as positive masses, yet we also see negative shapes between the bird's wings and its body. But we cannot fully understand mass from a single two-dimensional photograph such as this one. We would have to walk around the sculpture in person, or have it slowly circled with a video camera, to get a complete idea of its form.

We perceive shapes by mentally detaching them from their surroundings and recognizing them as distinct and coherent. We refer to this relationship as figure and ground. A **figure** is the shape we detach and focus on; the **ground** is the surrounding visual information the figure stands out from, the background. In *Gustavus Hamilton*, the figure is Hamilton's body and clothing while the ground is the gray background behind him. In the photograph of *The Raven and the First Men*, we easily recognize the sculpture as the principal figure and the rest of the image as the ground. The figures in both of these works determine what the shapes of the ground are. In the photograph of Reid's sculpture, for example, negative shapes appear between the bird's wings and its body. Artists learn to pay equal attention to positive and negative shapes in their work, and we will be better viewers for cultivating this habit as well.

On the pitcher by an artist of the ancient Puebloan people of the American Southwest (**4.14**), on the other hand, the distinction between figure and ground or positive and negative shapes is not so clear. Covering the vessel are lines that end in triangular shapes. Over much of the pitcher, the lines are clearly black drawn on a white ground. But things are not so clear when we reach the center. While we may initially see black lines ending in black triangles, it is just as easy to reverse this perception and see white lines ending in white triangles. This play of figure and field, or positive and negative, brings the surface to life and makes the pitcher more engaging.

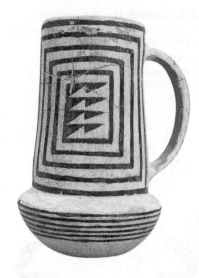

4.14 Jar (*olla*). Black on white pitcher. Pueblo period, ca. 1000 C.E. Height 8".
Maxwell Museum of Anthropology, Albuquerque. Werner Forman Archive/ Bridgeman Images

Implied Shapes

Diagram **4.15** shows three black circles, each with a wedge taken out, but the very first thing that most of us see is a floating white triangle. Our mind instantly perceives the visual information as a whole—even though that whole doesn't exist! This is called *reification*, when we do not need to see the whole of a thing for our minds to fill in the gaps. Reification is one of the principles of Gestalt theory. The lines of each wedge and their position in relation to one another cause us to see the triangle formed of negative space at the center.

Through optical puzzles such as this triangle, psychology provided a scientific explanation for something that artists had been doing intuitively for centuries, using implied shapes to unify their compositions. In *The Madonna of the Meadows* (**4.16**), Raphael has grouped the figures of Mary, the young John the Baptist (left), and the young Jesus (right) so that we perceive them as a single, triangular whole. Mary's head defines the apex, and John the Baptist the lower left corner. Defining the lower right corner is Mary's exposed foot, which draws our eye because of the way the pale flesh contrasts with the darker tones around it. Just as artists use implied lines to help direct our eyes around a composition, Raphael used this implied shape to create a sense of order, so that we perceive the work of art as a unified and harmonious whole.

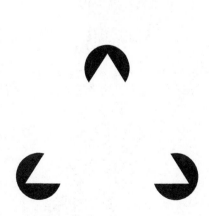

4.15 The triangle that isn't there.

4.16 Raphael. *The Madonna of the Meadows*. 1505. Oil on panel, 44 ½ × 34 ¼".
Kunsthistorisches Museum, Vienna. Photograph Erich Lessing/Art Resource, NY

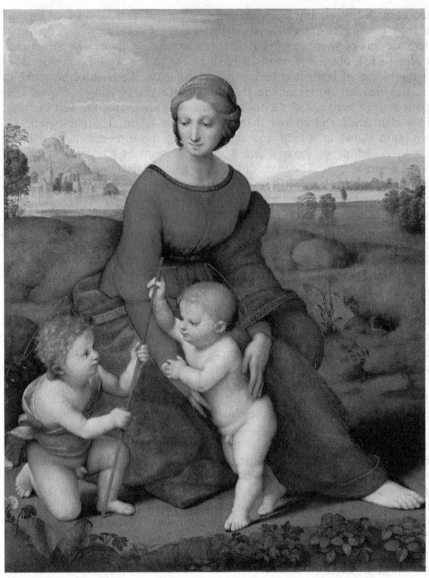

Light

To our distant ancestors, light seemed so miraculous that the sun was often considered to be a god and the moon a goddess. Today we know that light is a type of radiant energy, and we have learned how to generate it ourselves through electricity, yet our day-to-day experience of the varying qualities and effects of light is no less marvelous.

Light is a key visual element in works of art. When we talk about light in art, we refer to real light and the representation of light. Real light refers to how an object interacts with light in its environment. At Sainte-Chapelle (see 3.1), natural light passes through the colored glass of the stained-glass windows to create a dramatic, jewel-like effect. The gold background and halos in Cimabue's *Madonna Enthroned* (see 3.4) were designed to reflect the light of candles and windows in the church where it originally hung. As light falls on Bill Reid's *The Raven and the First Men* (see 4.13), some areas are highlighted while the areas under the raven and inside the clam shell are in shadow. Each artist made these works keeping in mind how the architecture, painting, and sculpture would interact with the light around it. Other artists represent light to suggest that objects have mass in their two-dimensional works of art.

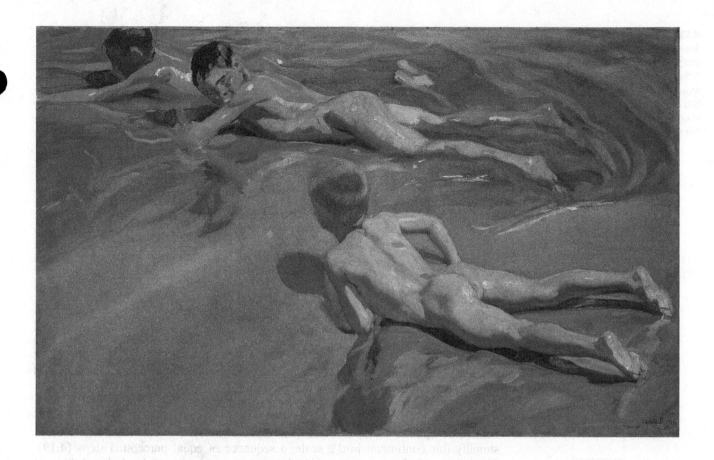

Light is represented in works of two-dimensional art to define and describe figures and spaces. The Spanish painter Joaquín Sorolla has been called the "Painter of Light." His luminous *Boys on the Beach* (**4.17**) shows his mastery of representing light using paint. The painting pictures three boys lying on wet sand while seawater swirls around them. Sorolla depicts light in several ways. Note how each boy's reflection appears beside him. This is light reflected on the wet sand. Light also creates reflections on the boys' bodies. Sorolla uses small patches of white paint to simulate the glare of light reflecting off wet skin. These white patches all appear on the boys' left sides because Sorolla wants us to see that they all share the light of the same hot sun, which is above and to the right of the painting. The light from the sun creates shadows under the boys' heads; these shadows fall opposite the sun.

4.17 Joaquín Sorolla y Bastida. *Boys on the Beach*. 1909. Oil on canvas, 46 ⅜ × 72 ⅘".
Prado Museum. Heritage Image Partnership Ltd./Alamy Stock Photo

Implied Light: Modeling Mass in Two Dimensions

The most fundamental purpose that light serves for us is to reveal the material world to our eyes in a way that helps us to understand forms and spatial relationships. The representation of light in art plays the same role. Artists use light and shadow to **model** objects in two-dimensional works, meaning to give them a three-dimensional appearance. We cannot see the source of light in Manuel Álvarez Bravo's photograph *The Visit* (**4.18**), but we understand from the way the shadows fall that it is off to the right, and that the statues are facing almost directly into it. Reading the light and shadows, we understand the masses of the robed sculptures. This is because our experience in the world tells us that three-dimensional objects are highlighted where they are closest to the light and then increasingly shaded the farther away they are. Therefore, these figures must also have mass and bulk.

Black-and-white film has transposed the colors of the original scene into their relative **values**, shades of light and dark. Value exists in a seamless continuum from

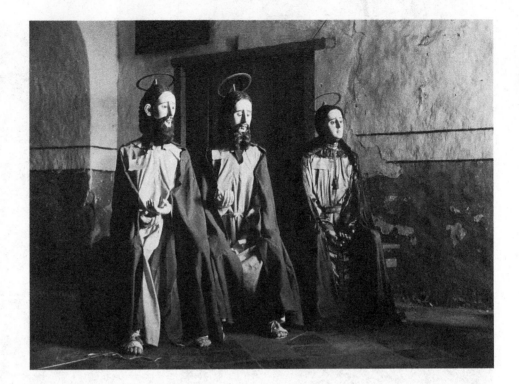

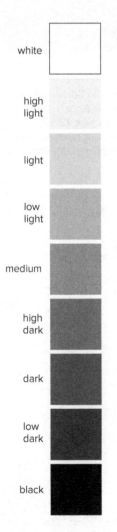

white

high light

light

low light

medium

high dark

dark

low dark

black

4.19 Value scale in gray.

white (the lightest value) to black (the darkest value). For convenience, we often simplify this continuum into a scale, a sequence of equal perceptual steps (**4.19**). The value scale here goes from black to white in nine steps (including both end points). Our eyes are more sensitive than film and can distinguish a greater and more subtle range of values. Nevertheless, thanks to black-and-white photography, we can readily understand the idea that the world we see in full color can also be expressed in shades of light and dark, and that every color can also be spoken of in terms of its value.

Photography easily demonstrates how value models mass for our eyes. But photography was invented only in the mid-19th century. Long before then, European painters had become interested in modeling mass in two dimensions through value. Discovered and perfected by Italian painters during the Renaissance, the technique is called **chiaroscuro**, Italian for "light/dark." With chiaroscuro, artists employ values—lights and darks—to record contrasts of light and shadow in the natural world, contrasts that model mass for our eyes. One of the great masters of chiaroscuro was Leonardo da Vinci. His unfinished drawing of *The Virgin and St. Anne with the Christ Child and John the Baptist* (**4.20**) shows the miraculous effects he could achieve. Working on a middle-value brown paper, Leonardo applied charcoal for a range of darks and white chalk for lighter values. The figures seem to be breathed onto the paper, bathed in a soft, allover light that comes from everywhere and nowhere. The roundness that Leonardo's mastery conveys is immediately evident if we look between the heads of the two children at the raised hand of Saint Anne. Drawn with a contour line but not modeled, it looks jarringly flat, as though it does not yet belong to the rest of the image.

Leonardo used continuous tones in his drawing, values that grade evenly into one another. But value can also be indicated with surprising richness by line alone. In the etching shown here, Rembrandt made use of lines (**4.21**). Taking the pale gray of the paper as the highest value, Rembrandt indicated the next step down in value with **hatching,** areas of closely spaced parallel lines, as on the neck, shoulder, and left forearm. Darker values were achieved through additional sets of parallel lines laid across the first, a technique called **cross-hatching**. Seen from up close, the effect seems coarse, but at a certain distance the dark hatch marks seem to average out with the lighter paper into nuanced areas of gray, an effect of perception that is called optical mixing.

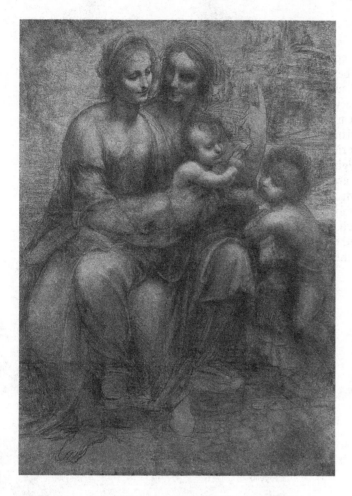

4.20 Leonardo da Vinci. *The Virgin and St. Anne with the Christ Child and John the Baptist.* ca. 1499–1500. Charcoal, black and white chalk on brown paper, 54 ⅞ × 39 ⅞".
© National Gallery, London/Art Resource, NY

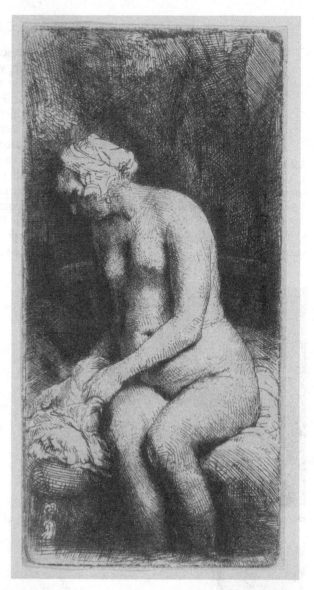

4.21 Harris Brisbane Dick Fund, 1917/ The Metropolitan Museum of Art

Another technique for suggesting value is **stippling**, in which areas of dots average out through optical mixing into values (**4.22**). As with hatching, the depth of the value depends on density: The more dots in a given area, the darker it appears.

Color

It is probably safe to say that none of the visual elements gives us as much pleasure as color. Many people have a favorite color that they are drawn to. They will buy a shirt in that color just for the pleasure of clothing themselves in it, or paint the walls of their room that color for the pleasure of being surrounded by it. Various studies have suggested that color affects a wide range of psychological and even physiological responses. One particular shade of pink, known as Baker-Miller pink, has been shown to calm agitated or aggressive behavior, producing a tranquilizing effect that lasts for about half an hour. In Tokyo, blue lighting installed at the ends of train platforms has been effective in reducing the number of people who attempt suicide by diving in front of oncoming trains. A recent German study suggests that seeing the color green can boost creativity. The mechanism involved in these color responses is still unclear, but such studies indicate that color affects the human brain and body in powerful ways.

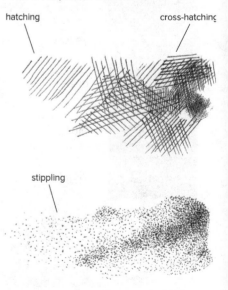

4.22 Techniques for modeling mass with lines: hatching, cross-hatching, and stippling.

Color Theory

Much of our present-day color theory can be traced back to experiments made by Sir Isaac Newton, who is better known for his work with the laws of gravity. In 1666, Newton passed a ray of sunlight through a prism, a transparent glass form with nonparallel sides. He observed that the ray of sunlight broke up or **refracted** into different colors, which were arranged in the order of the colors of the rainbow (**4.23**). By setting up a second prism, Newton found he could recombine the rainbow colors into white light, like the original sunlight. These experiments proved that colors are actually components of light.

In fact, all colors are dependent on light, and no object possesses color intrinsically. You may own a red shirt and a blue pen and a purple chair, but those items have no color in and of themselves. What we perceive as color is reflected light rays. When light strikes the red shirt, for example, the shirt absorbs all the color rays except the red ones, which are reflected, so your eye perceives red. The purple chair reflects the purple rays and absorbs all the others, and so on. Both

4.23
a. White light separated into spectral colors by a prism.
© Science Photo Library/Alamy Stock Photo

b. The colors of the visible spectrum.

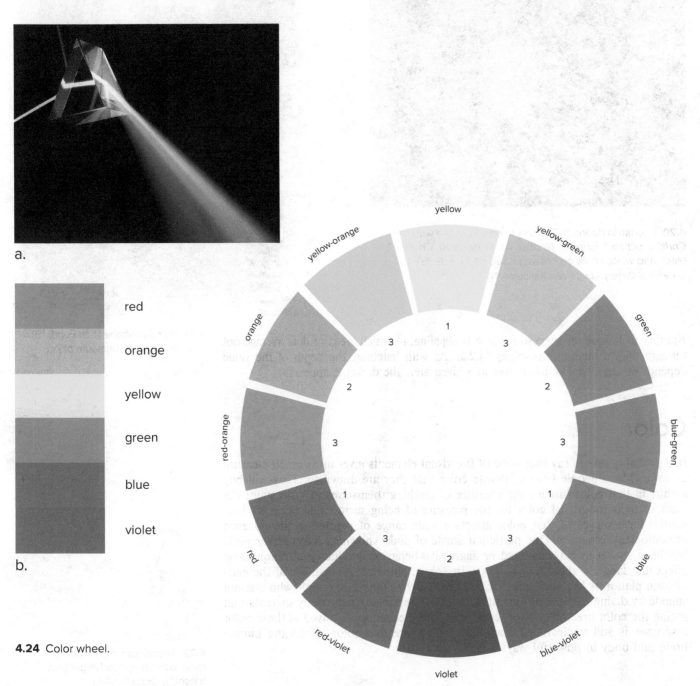

a.

red

orange

yellow

green

blue

violet

b.

4.24 Color wheel.

the physiological activity of the human eye and the science of electromagnetic wavelengths take part in this process.

If we take the colors separated out by Newton's prism—red, orange, yellow, green, blue, and violet—add the transitional color red-violet (which does not exist in the rainbow), and arrange these colors in a circle, we have a **color wheel (4.24)**. Different theorists have constructed different color wheels, but the one shown here is fairly standard.

Primary Colors—red, yellow, and blue—are labeled with the numeral 1 on the color wheel. They are called primary because (theoretically at least) they cannot be made by any mixture of other colors.

Secondary Colors—orange, green, and violet—are labeled with the numeral 2. Each is made by combining two primary colors.

Intermediate Colors, also known as **tertiary colors**, labeled number 3, are the product of a primary color and an adjacent secondary color. For instance, mixing yellow with green yields yellow-green. This kind of mixing takes place in painting on a palette. **Palette** refers to the wooden board on which artists traditionally set out and combine their pigments, but it also refers to the range of pigments they select.

We speak of the colors on the red-orange side of the wheel as **warm colors**, perhaps because of their association with sunlight and firelight. The colors on the blue-green side are **cool colors**, again probably because of their association with sky, water, shade, and so on. A work of art may have a predominantly warm or cool palette.

The Iranian coronation carpet shown in figure **4.25** has a cool palette: blue, light blue, and green. This palette makes the warmer reds stand out. Secondary colors such as the green and tertiary colors such as the yellow-oranges and beige play supporting roles in this work. They frame the warm reds and cool blues and greens in the vines that spiral through the carpet.

4.25 Iranian coronation carpet. ca. 1520–30. Textile. Los Angeles County Museum of Art

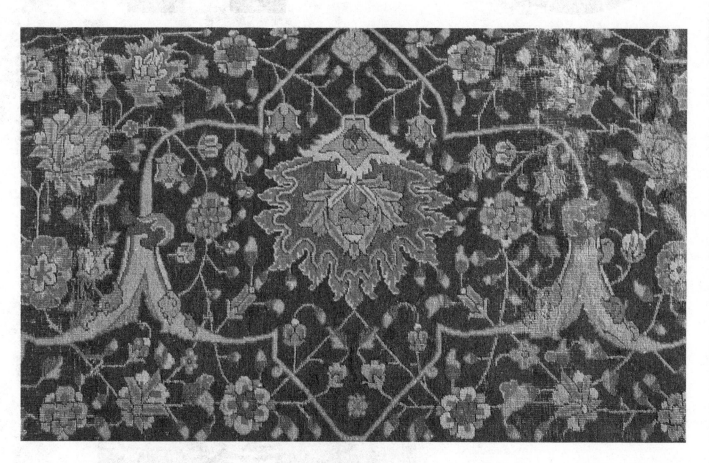

Color Properties

Any color has three properties: hue, value, and intensity.

Hue is the name of the color according to the categories of the color wheel—green or red or blue-violet.

Value refers to relative lightness or darkness. Most colors are recognizable in a full range of values; for instance, we identify as "red" everything from palest pink to darkest maroon. In addition, all hues have what is known as a normal value—the value at which we expect to find that hue. We think of yellow as a "light" color and violet as a "dark" color, for example, even though each has a full range of values. Figure **4.26** shows the hues of the color wheel in relation to a gray value scale (**a**), and the hue blue taken through a range of values (**b**).

4.26 Color value and intensity.
a. The spectral colors and their corresponding gray-scale values.
b. Blue in a range of values.
c. Yellow-orange progressively dulled with gray.
d. Yellow-orange progressively dulled with blue-violet.

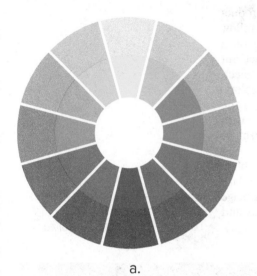

a.

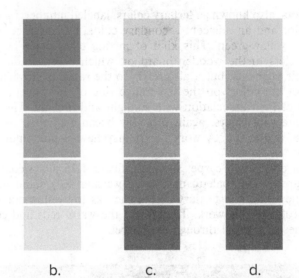

b.　　　c.　　　d.

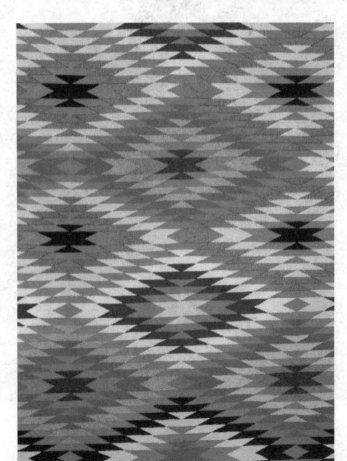

4.27 Diamond-pattern blanket rug. 1885. Textile.
Ericbvd/Getty Images

A color lighter than the hue's normal value is known as a **tint**; for example, pink is a tint of red. A color darker than the hue's normal value is called a **shade**; maroon is a shade of red.

Intensity—also called **chroma** or **saturation**—refers to the relative purity of a color. Colors may be pure and saturated, as they appear on the color wheel, or they may be dulled and softened to some degree. The purest colors are said to have high intensity; duller colors, lower intensity. To lower the intensity of a color when mixing paints or dyes, the artist may add a combination of black and white (gray) or may add a little of the color's complement, the hue directly opposite it on the color wheel. Figure 4.26 shows a saturated yellow-orange lowered first with gray (**c**) and then with blue-violet (**d**).

The Navajo weaver of this diamond-pattern blanket rug (**4.27**) used the primary hues red and yellow as the dominant colors. Three different values of red appear, from a lighter orange-red tint to a darker ruby-red shade. The colors in the rug are highly saturated, although the yellows have a lower intensity with the addition of gray or another dark color on the opposite side of the color wheel. The saturated, warm reds appear to pop out.

Light and Pigment

Colors behave differently depending on whether an artist is working with light or with pigment. In light, as Newton's experiments showed, white is the sum of all colors. People who work directly with light—such as lighting designers who illuminate settings for film, theater, or video productions—learn to mix color by an additive process, in which colors of light mix to produce still lighter colors. For example, red and green light mix to produce yellow light. Add blue light to the mix and the result is white. Thus red, green, and blue form the lighting designer's primary triad (**4.28a**).

Pigments, like any other object in the world, have to our eyes the color that they reflect. A red pigment, for example, absorbs all the colors in the spectrum except red. When pigments of different hues are mixed, the resulting color is darker and duller, because together they absorb still more colors from the spectrum. Mixing pigments is thus known as a subtractive process (**4.28b**). The closer two pigments are to being complementary colors on the color wheel, the duller their mixture will appear, for the more they will subtract each other from the mix. For example, whereas red and green light mix to produce yellow light, red and green pigment mix to produce a grayish brown or brownish gray pigment.

Color Harmonies

A color harmony, sometimes called a color scheme, is the selective use of two or more colors in a single composition. We tend to think of this especially in relation to interior design; you may say, for instance, "The color scheme in my kitchen is blue and green with touches of brown." But color harmonies also apply to the pictorial arts, although they may be more difficult to spot because of differences in value and intensity.

Monochromatic harmonies are composed of variations on the same hue, often with differences of value and intensity. A painting all in reds, pinks, and maroons would be considered to have a monochromatic harmony. In *Chanter* (**4.29**), Emmi Whitehorse mainly used tints and shades of blue in her interpretation of the symbols found in Navajo rock art. Notice how this mostly monochromatic palette of cool blues makes the red element at the bottom stand out.

Complementary harmonies involve colors directly opposite each other on the color wheel, such as red and green. Complementaries "react" with each other more vividly than with other colors, and thus areas of complementary color placed next to or even near each other make both hues appear more intense. We see this in the

4.28
a. Light primaries and their additive mixtures.
b. Pigment primaries and their subtractive mixtures.

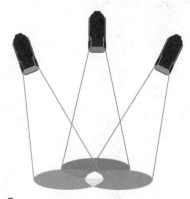

a.

b.

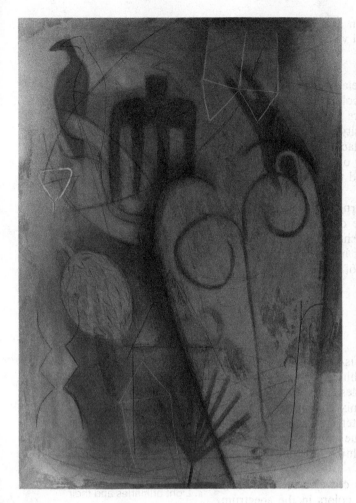

4.29 Emmi Whitehorse. *Chanter*. 1991. Oil on paper, mounted on canvas, 39 ⅛ × 28".
Saint Louis Art Museum. Museum Shop Fund. 37:1991.
© Emmi Whitehorse

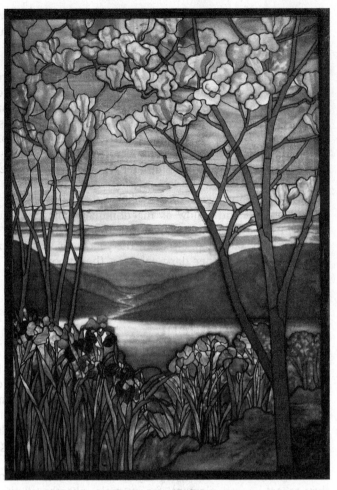

4.30 Louis Comfort Tiffany. *Magnolias and Irises*. 1908. Stained glass, 60 ¼ × 42".
The Metropolitan Museum of Art, New York. Anonymous Gift, in memory of Mr. and Mrs. A. B. Frank, 1981

red form at the bottom of Whitehorse's *Chanter*, which appears more intense surrounded by so much blue. Similarly, the glow of the yellow stars in Van Gogh's *Starry Night* (see 1.10) owes much to the blue background. The orange catlike form in Elizabeth Murray's *The Sun and the Moon* (see 4.1) would not draw as much attention without the green elements nearby. Raphael's contrast of red gown and blue robe makes the Madonna's figure stand out in *The Madonna of the Meadows* (see 4.16).

Analogous harmonies combine colors adjacent to one another on the color wheel, as in Louis Comfort Tiffany's *Magnolias and Irises* (**4.30**), which moves from light blues and greens to deep purples. The analogous colors of the window—which was designed for a mausoleum—create a calm, introspective feeling for mourners.

Triadic harmonies are composed of any three colors equidistant from each other on the color wheel. The *Ascent of the Prophet Muhammad* attributed to Sultan Muhammad (see 2.19) and Elaine de Kooning's *Bullfight* (see 2.20) both contrast blues, reds, and yellows for bold effects. In his mature works, Piet Mondrian famously limited his colors to the primary triad of red, yellow, and blue (see *Trafalgar Square*, 21.28). The same triadic harmony in another guise dominates Jean-Auguste-Dominique Ingres's *Jupiter and Thetis* (see 21.1). Paul Gauguin's *Te Aa No Areois* (see 21.10) owes a great deal to the triadic harmony of blue-green, red-violet, and yellow-orange, as well as to the complementary opposition of blue-green and red-orange.

Numerous other color harmonies have been identified and named. Artists themselves, however, are more likely to speak generally of working with a **restricted palette** or an **open palette**. Working with a restricted palette, artists limit themselves to a few pigments and their mixtures, tints, and shades. For an example of a painting created with a restricted palette, look again at Antonio Pérez de Aguilar's *Painter's Cupboard*, in Chapter 2 (see 2.12). For an example of a painting created with an open palette, look again at Manohar's *Jahangir Receives a Cup from Khusrau*, in Chapter 1 (see 1.8).

Optical Effects of Color

Certain uses and combinations of colors can "play tricks" on our eyes or, more accurately, on the way we perceive colors registered by our eyes. One effect we have already touched on is **simultaneous contrast**, where complementary colors appear more intense when placed side by side. Simultaneous contrast is related to another fascinating optical effect, **afterimage**. Prolonged staring at any saturated color fatigues the receptors in our eyes, which compensate when allowed to rest by producing the color's complementary as a ghostly afterimage in the mind. You can experience this effect by following the instructions in the caption to figure **4.31**.

Another effect of color is that some hues seem to "advance," others to "recede." We noticed how the red in the Navajo diamond-pattern blanket rug (see 4.27) seemed to project toward us. Interior designers know that if you place a bright red chair in a room, it will seem larger and farther forward than the same chair upholstered in beige or pale blue. Thus, color can dramatically influence our perception of space and size. In general, colors that create the illusion of large size and advancing are those with the warmer hues (red, orange, yellow), high intensity, and dark value; small size and receding are suggested by colors with cooler hues (blue, green), low intensity, and light value.

Colors can be mixed in light or pigment, but they can also be mixed by the eyes. When small patches of different colors are close together, the eye may blend them to produce a new color. This is called **optical color mixture**, and it is an important feature in the painting of Georges Seurat.

Seurat was familiar with the color theories of simultaneous contrast and afterimage, which seemed to hold out the possibility of placing painting on a scientific footing. Most artists blend their colors, either on a palette or on the canvas itself, to produce gradations of hue, but Seurat did not. Instead, he laid down his paints by placing many thousands of tiny dots—or points—of pure color next to each other, a process that came to be called **pointillism**. From a distance of a few inches, a painting such as *Evening, Honfleur* appears to be nothing but a jumble of colored dots (**4.32**). As the viewer steps back, however, the dots gradually coalesce into shapes, and an image emerges of the shore at Honfleur, a seaside town in France. Seurat's dots never quite fuse entirely. They remain just distinct enough to give the surface of the painting a lively texture, and they create a sort of shimmer as their colors interact. In a letter he sent from Honfleur to his friend the painter Paul Signac, Seurat spoke of the sea as being "an almost indefinable gray."[1] His technique of optical mixing is well suited to producing just such indefinable colors. Seurat

4.31 Demonstration of complementary color afterimage. Stare for a time at the black dot in the middle of the colored square. Then, with your eyes unfocused, stare at the white square beside it. The colors will appear in ghostly reverse, with a blue-green inner square and a red outer square.

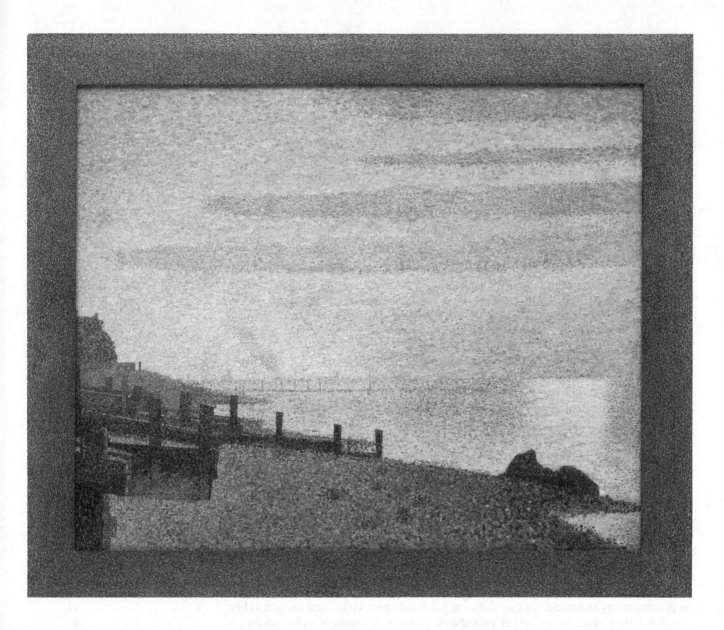

4.32 Georges Seurat. *Evening, Honfleur*. 1886. Oil on canvas, 25 ¾ × 32".
The Museum of Modern Art, New York. Gift of Mrs. David M. Levy. 266.1957. Digital Image © The Museum of Modern Art/Licensed by SCALA/Art Resource, NY

sometimes painted frames for his paintings using the same pointillist technique; *Evening, Honfleur* has one of the few frames to have survived. We can see how Seurat used contrasting values and complementary colors on the frame to make the sky, sea, and sand seem more luminous. Fundamentally blue, it tilts subtly toward violet, green, orange, and red as it makes its way around the painting.

Optical mixing is perhaps most familiar to us today through computers, whose screen images are made up of discrete units called pixels, short for "picture elements." Most computer users have noticed that enlarging an image eventually causes it to disintegrate into its component pixels, which appear as squares of color set in a grid pattern. Reversing the process, we can watch as the pixels grow smaller and the image comes back into focus.

In works such as *Hendrix*, Devorah Sperber explores our brain's capacity for assembling images from discrete units of visual information by using spools of colored thread as the equivalent of pixels (**4.33**, **4.34**). Just as pixels are digital samplings of an original image, so Sperber's thread colors match crude samplings of a photograph of the musician Jimi Hendrix, turned upside down. Seen from a few feet away in person, the 1,292 spools form a large, gridded, seemingly nonrepresentational composition. If we were to step back far enough, an image would gradually come into focus, but Sperber spares us the trouble by placing a clear acrylic sphere in front of the work. The sphere acts as a lens, gathering in visual

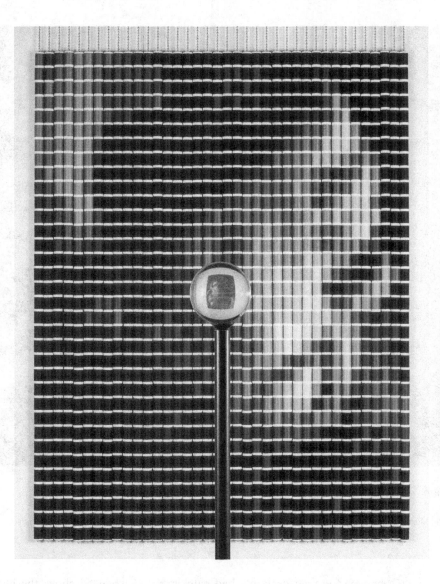

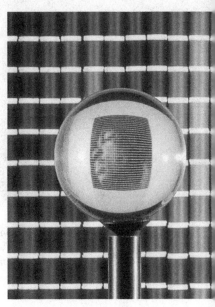

4.33 Devorah Sperber. *Hendrix.* 2009. 1,292 spools of thread, stainless-steel ball chain and hanging apparatus, clear acrylic sphere, and metal stand; panel of spools 60 × 48", viewing sphere set at a distance of 5'.
Courtesy of the artist

4.34 Devorah Sperber. *Hendrix.* 2009. Detail.
Courtesy of the artist

information, miniaturizing it, and rotating it 180 degrees. (Our eyes work the same way.) The illustration in figure 4.34 shows how Hendrix's face comes into focus in the viewing sphere, and also how the spools themselves appear from up close. By providing a way for us to see the image and its components at the same time, Sperber makes us aware of the brain's role in constructing our visual reality.

Expressive Possibilities of Color

Color affects us on such a basic level that few would deny that we have a direct emotional response to it. The problem comes when we try to find universal principles, for we quickly discover that emotional responses to color are both culturally conditioned and intensely personal. For most people brought up in America, red and green have strong cultural associations with Christmas. Vincent van Gogh, however, once made a painting of a café interior that juxtaposed red and green to suggest what he called "the terrible passions of humanity."[2] For the German painter Franz Marc, blue was the color of male spirituality. In India, it is associated with the Hindu deity Krishna, who is traditionally depicted with blue skin, for sacred texts describe him as being the color of water-filled clouds. As the color of the sky and the ocean, blue is often associated with freedom. It is a "cool" color and has been shown to have a calming effect. Artists have therefore often used it to express feelings of tranquility.

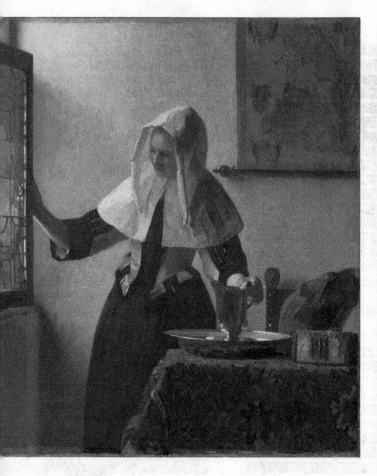

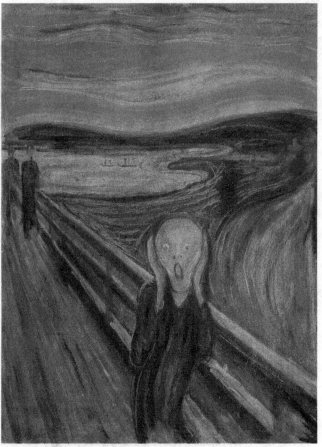

4.35 Johannes Vermeer. *Young Woman with a Water Pitcher*. 1662. Oil on canvas, 18 × 16".
The Metropolitan Museum of Art, New York, Marquand Collection, Gift of Henry G. Marquand, 1889

4.36 Edvard Munch. *The Scream*. 1893. Tempera and casein on cardboard, 36 × 29".
Nasjonalgalleriet, Oslo/Bridgeman Images. © 2019 Artists Rights Society (ARS), New York

Johannes Vermeer certainly had calm in mind when he chose the blues that dominate his *Young Woman with a Water Pitcher* (**4.35**). The different hues and values of blue are cool and create a quiet mood. Blue contributes significantly to the subdued feeling of the painting, although it does not create it all alone. The filtered, bluish light that comes in through the window and the woman's slow movement evoke the viewer's memories of tranquil mornings at home, and these elements also play a role in the emotional "temperature" of the work.

Edvard Munch's harrowing painting *The Scream* uses color for a very different expressive effect (**4.36**). "It was a time when life had ripped my soul open," the artist wrote in his diary. "The sun was going down. . . . It was like a flaming sword of blood. . . . The sky was like blood sliced with strips of fire. . .I felt a great scream—and I heard, yes, a great scream—the colors in nature broke the lines of nature, the lines and colors vibrated with motion. . . . I painted the picture Scream then."[3] Munch uses red to express horror, blood, and anguish. But how, outside of his diary, are we to know that Munch did not intend simply to depict a splendid sunset? As with Vermeer's domestic scene, color does not carry the entire expressive burden by itself. Whereas Vermeer's painting is characterized by soft light and a slow pace, here unstable diagonals and swirling lines dominate. The line of the horizon is almost obliterated. The figure in the foreground clasps his hands over his ears to block out the piercing sound. His head has become a death's head; his body wavers unsteadily. In contrast, the two pedestrians in the background remain unaffected. Evidently, they hear nothing out of the ordinary. The scream is a silent one, the interior cry of a soul projected onto nature.

Texture and Pattern

Texture refers to surface quality—a perception of smooth or rough, flat or bumpy, fine or coarse. Our world would be bland and uninteresting without contrasts of texture. Most of us, when we encounter a dog or a cat, are moved to pet the animal, partly because the animal likes it, but also because we enjoy the feel of the fur's texture against our hands. In planning our clothes, we instinctively take texture into account. We might put on a thick, nubby sweater over a smooth cotton shirt and enjoy the contrast. We look for this textural interest in all facets of our environment. Few people can resist running their hands over a smooth chunk of marble or a glossy length of silk or a drape of velvet. This is the outstanding feature of texture: It makes us want to touch it.

Actual Texture

Actual texture is literally tactile, a quality we can experience through touch. It would be a pleasure to run our hands along the smooth industrial surfaces around the perimeter of Mona Hatoum's steel *Dormiente* (**4.37**). But anyone who has ever scraped their knuckles on a kitchen grater would be very careful about exploring the rough texture of the two central fields. *Dormiente* is Italian for "sleeping person." The title asks us to imagine this large-scale grater as a bed, thus encouraging us to contemplate the exact experience we would rather not consider: the intimate contact of our vulnerable flesh with its jagged metal protrusions. "In my work I often take familiar, everyday things and make them unfamiliar, reveal the uncanny in them," Hatoum says. "I like it when something is simultaneously attractive and forbidding—both seductive and dangerous."[4]

Like any other visual element, texture can contribute to our understanding and interpretation of a work. The Mexican coconut-shell cup shown here (**4.38**) brings together two distinct materials: coconut shell and silver. The artist carved

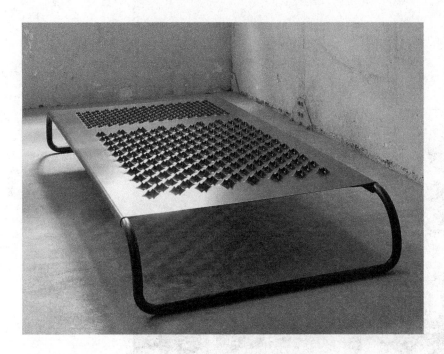

4.37 Mona Hatoum. *Dormiente*. 2008. Mild steel, 10 ⅝ × 90 ⁹⁄₁₆ × 39 ⅜".
Photo Aurelien Mole. Courtesy GALLERIA CONTINUA San Gimignano/Beijing/Les Moulins and White Cube

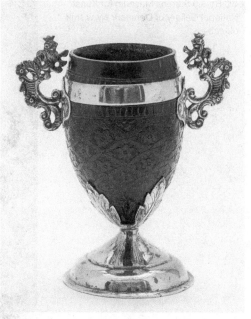

4.38 Coconut-shell cup (*coco chocolatero*). 17th–18th century. Height 4 ½".
Gift of Ronald A. Belkin, Long Beach, California, in memory of Charles B. Tate (M.2015.69.3), Los Angeles County Museum of Art

small flowers into the polished shell but left roughened areas behind them for a contrast of textures. The silver handles and base provide a smooth and hard texture. Bringing these disparate materials and their textures together created meaning. It reminded the cup's viewers of the meeting of Europeans and far-distant civilizations through colonization. The coconut shell represented Asia or the Americas, while the silver symbolized European culture.

Visual Texture

That we can appreciate the textures of Hatoum's *Dormiente* or the coconut-shell cup in a photograph shows that texture has a visual component as well as a tactile one. In fact, even before touching a surface, we have formed an idea of its texture by observing the way it reflects light and associating what we see with a sense memory of touch. Its texture is visible and so can be depicted visually.

Naturalistic painting can suggest the texture of objects in the world in the same way that photography does, by faithfully recording the way light plays over their surfaces. Centuries before photography was invented, Dutch **still-life** painters delighted in capturing visual texture in paint. Cornelius Norbertus Gijsbrechts was part of a group of these painters who were so skilled in simulating what the eye sees that their works came to be known as *trompe l'oeil* paintings. *Trompe l'oeil* is French for "fool the eye" and Gijsbrechts's *Trompe l'Oeil with Studio Wall and Vanitas Still Life* (**4.39**) does just that. Notice how the artist meticulously describes the rough texture of the wood wall, the sticky viscosity of the paint running down the painter's palette, the smoothness of the glass bottles, and the soft flexibility of the canvas pulling away from the wood stretcher. Each visual texture fools our eyes into thinking that it is real.

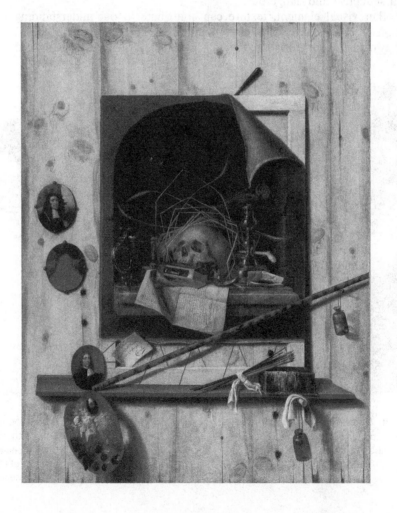

4.39 Cornelius Norbertus Gijsbrechts. *Trompe l'Oeil with Studio Wall and Vanitas Still Life*. 1668. Oil on canvas, 59 ⅞ × 46 ½". CC BY 3.0 Statens Museum for Kunst/ National Gallery of Denmark www.smk. dk/ccby

Our word *texture* is derived from the Latin *textus*, the past participle of *textere*, "to weave." It is easy to imagine how the experience of appreciating woven cloth by touching it was transferred to the experience of touching surfaces in general. In addition to its literal meaning, we have also come to use the word figuratively in a variety of ways, often for things we can imagine as woven. For example, we could describe a poem as woven of words, a symphony as woven of notes played by many instruments, and a painting as woven of brushstrokes. In each case, we can speak of the work's texture—aural texture for the poem and the symphony, and visual texture for the painting. Earlier in this chapter we spoke of the lively texture produced by Seurat's pointillist technique (see 4.32), for the dots seem to weave a tapestry of color. Paintings by Van Gogh also have a characteristic visual texture, created by his typically short, unblended brushstrokes (see 1.10).

Pattern

Pattern is any decorative, repetitive motif or design. Pattern can create visual texture, although visual texture may not always be seen as a pattern. An interesting aspect of pattern is that it tends to flatten our perception of mass and space. The self-portrait here by the African photographer Samuel Fosso illustrates the visual "buzz" and spatial ambiguity that patterns can produce (**4.40**). Everything clamors for our attention at once. Elements that should stay calmly in the background or firmly underfoot seem to come forward to meet us. For example, look at the area surrounding the legs of the chair. It seems flat, but our minds know that the chair takes up space, so it must have depth. In the middle of it all sits the artist, dressed as an outrageous parody of a traditional ruler. (For an example of the sort of royal display that Fosso is mocking, see 18.14.)

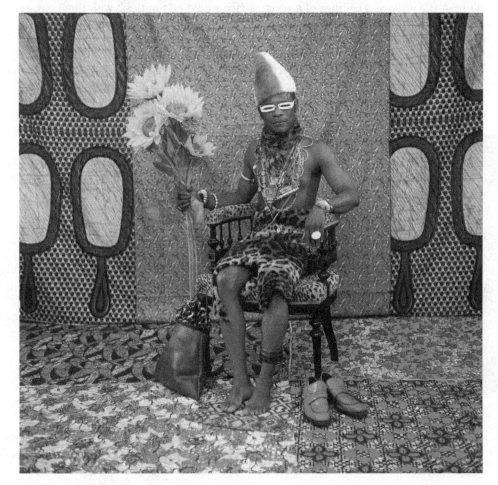

4.40 Samuel Fosso. *The Chief: He Who Sold Africa to the Colonists*, from *Self-Portraits I–V*. 1997. Chromogenic print, 20 × 20".
© CNAC/MNAM/Dist. RMN-Grand Palais/ Art Resource, NY

Space

The word *space*, especially in our technological world, sometimes conveys the idea of nothingness. We think of outer space as a huge void, hostile to human life. A person who is "spaced out" is blank, unfocused, not really "there." But the space in and around a work of art is not a void, and it is very much there. It is a dynamic visual element that interacts with the lines and shapes and colors and textures of a work of art to give them definition. Consider space in this way: How could there be a line if there were not the spaces on either side of it to mark its edges? How could there be a shape without the space around it to set it off?

Three-Dimensional Space

Sculpture, architecture, and all other forms with mass exist in three-dimensional space—that is, the actual space in which our bodies also stand. These works of art take their character from the ways in which they carve out volumes of space within and around them.

Anish Kapoor's sculpture *Cloud Gate* (**4.41**) occupies a lot of space. Located in a park in Chicago, the polished steel sculpture is more than 65 feet wide and rises more than 30 feet in the air. This mass, inspired by liquid mercury, exists in three-dimensional space just as its viewers do. Walking around and under the sculpture reminds us of the space the sculpture takes up and the space we share with it. We are also reminded of the real space where the sculpture is by looking at the reflections on the polished surface. The sculpture interacts with this space as we see ourselves, the park, and the Chicago skyline reflected back to us.

Architecture in particular can be thought of as a means of shaping space. Without the walls and ceilings of a room, space would be limitless; with them, space suddenly has boundaries, and therefore volume. Whereas from the outside we appreciate a work of architecture for its sculptural masses, from the inside we experience it as a shaped space or a sequence of shaped spaces. Frank Gehry's Guggenheim Museum in Bilbao, Spain (**4.42**), helps us to see how architecture shapes space. There are no vertical walls and flat ceilings to create a box of interior space here. Instead, Gehry molds and complicates the space. The main space in the middle of

4.41 Anish Kapoor. *Cloud Gate.* 2006. Steel, 33 × 66 × 42'.
© McGraw-Hill Education/Jill Braaten

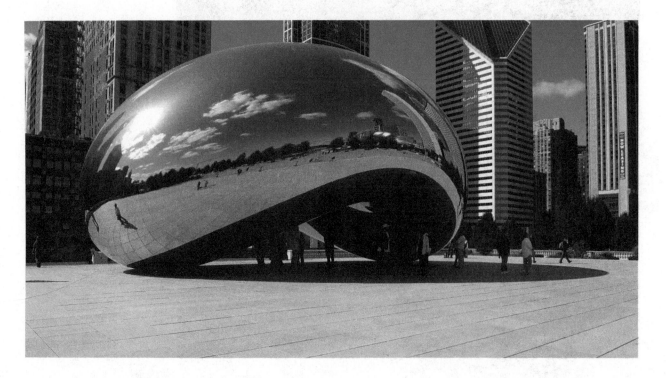

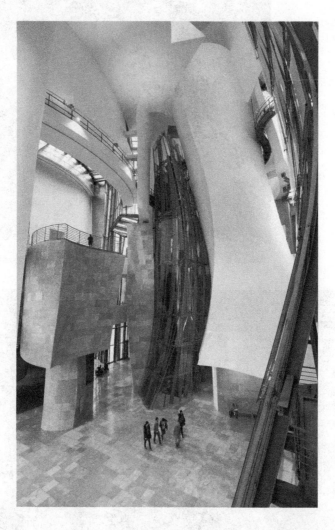

4.42 Frank Gehry. Interior, Guggenheim Museum Bilbao.
David Herraez/Alamy Stock Photo

the photograph swells and bends to follow the lines of the building. Some spaces are concave and some are convex. Each of the openings—a balcony, a passageway, a staircase—fragments the space and invites visitors to explore each area.

Implied Space: Suggesting Depth in Two Dimensions

Architecture, sculpture, and other art forms that exist in three dimensions work with actual space. When we view the work, we inhabit the same space it does, and we need to walk around it or through it to experience it completely. With painting, drawing, and other two-dimensional art forms, the actual space is the flat surface of the work itself, which we tend to see all at once. This literal surface is called the **picture plane**, and some works of art make no attempt to suggest more space than its flat surface. This petroglyph of a lizard (**4.43**) from the Utah desert was pecked on the surface of the rock. The image is completely flat. The artist, who belonged to the Fremont culture, allowed the image to rest entirely on the picture plane and made no attempt to suggest three dimensions.

Quantities and dimensions of space can be implied in two-dimensional art. For example, if you take an ordinary notebook page and draw a tiny dog in the center, the page has suddenly become a large space, a field for the dog to roam about in. If you draw a dog that takes up the entire page, the page has become a much smaller space, just big enough for the dog. Perhaps the petroglyph's artist thought of the surface of the rock as a space for the lizard to inhabit.

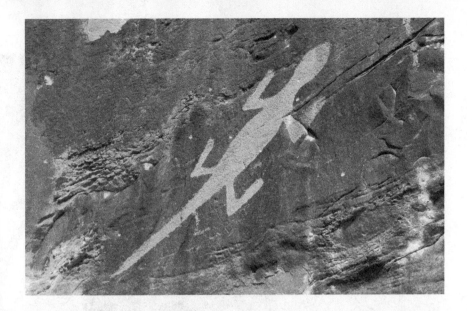

4.43 Fremont lizard petroglyph. 600–1200 C.E. Rock art.
Ingram Publishing/SuperStock

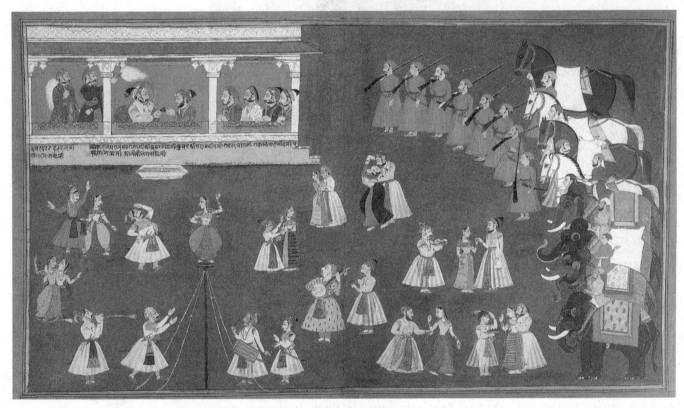

4.44 *Maharana Amar Singh II, Prince Sangram Singh, and Courtiers Watch the Performance of an Acrobat and Musicians*. Rajasthan, Mewar. ca. 1705–08. Ink, opaque watercolor, and gold on paper; 20 ½ × 35 ¾".
The Metropolitan Museum of Art, New York. Gift of Mr. and Mrs. Carl Bimel, Jr. 1996 (1996.357)

Suppose now that you draw two dogs and perhaps a tree, and you want to show where they are in relation to one another. One dog is behind the tree, say, and the other is running toward it from a distance. These relationships take place in the third dimension, depth. There are many visual cues that we use to perceive spatial relationships in depth. One of the simplest is overlap: we understand that when two forms overlap, the one we perceive as complete is in front of the one we perceive as partial. A second visual cue is position: seated at a desk, for example, we look down to see the objects closest to us and raise our head to see objects that are farther away.

Many artistic cultures have relied entirely on those two basic cues to imply depth in two dimensions (**4.44**). In this lively scene of an Indian prince's entertainment, spatial distance is communicated by location on the page and by overlapping. We understand that the performers toward the bottom of the page are nearer to us than those higher up, and that the overlapping elephants and horses are standing next to each other in a row that recedes from us. The most important person in the scene is the prince, and the painting makes this clear. Framed by the architectural setting, he sits amid his courtiers and attendants, all of whom are looking at him. The prince, too, is depicted in profile and does not seem to be watching the performance. Yet this seeming inattention is not to be taken literally. The prince would certainly have watched such a wonderful event. Indian artists favored profile views, for they give the least information about depth, and so lend themselves well to the overall flatness of Indian painting.

LINEAR PERSPECTIVE The sense of space in the Indian painting is conceptually convincing, but not optically convincing. For example, we understand perfectly well that the prince's pavilion is on the far side of the acrobats, but there is actually no evidence to tell our eyes that it is not hovering in the air directly over them. Similarly, we understand that the elephants and horses represent rounded forms even though they appear to our eyes as flat shapes fanned out like a deck of cards on the picture plane. Together, the flatness of traditional Indian painting, the preference for profiles, the use of saturated colors, and the conceptual construction of space make up a coherent system for depicting the world. They work together to give Indian artists tremendous flexibility in assembling complex, vivid, and visually delightful scenes such as this one while preserving narrative clarity.

The chiaroscuro technique of modeling developed by Italian artists of the 15th century also forms part of a larger system for depicting the world. Just as Renaissance artists took note of the optical evidence of light and shadow to model rounded forms, they also developed a technique for constructing an optically convincing space to set those forms in. This technique, called **linear perspective**, is based on the systematic application of two observations:

- Forms seem to diminish in size as they recede from us.

- Parallel lines receding into the distance seem to converge, until they meet at a point on the horizon line where they disappear. This point is known as the **vanishing point**.

You can visualize this second idea if you imagine gazing down a straight highway. As the highway recedes farther from you, the two edges seem to draw closer together, until they disappear at the horizon line (**4.45**).

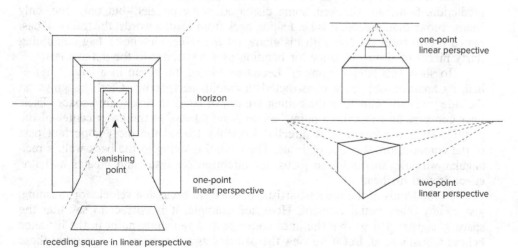

horizon

vanishing point

one-point linear perspective

receding square in linear perspective

one-point linear perspective

two-point linear perspective

4.45 Basic principles of linear perspective.

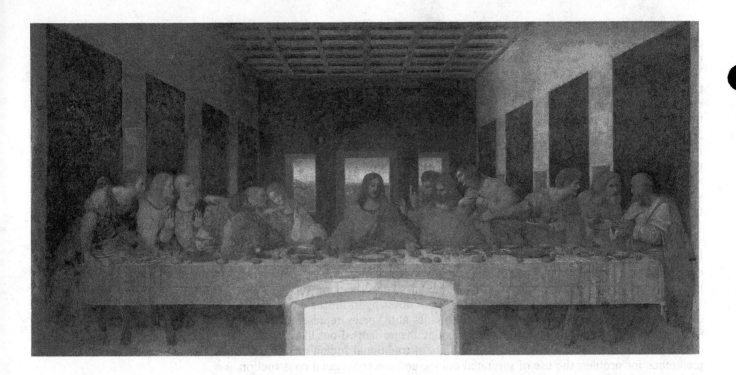

4.46 Leonardo da Vinci. *The Last Supper* (after restoration). ca. 1495–97. Fresco, 15' 1 ⅛" × 28' 10 ½". Refectory, Santa Maria delle Grazie, Milan. © Quattrone, Florence

The development of linear perspective profoundly changed how artists viewed the picture plane. For medieval European artists, as for Indian artists, a painting was primarily a flat surface covered with shapes and colors. For Renaissance artists, it became a window onto a scene. The picture plane was reconceived as a sort of windowpane, and the painted view was imagined as receding from it into the distance in the way our eye sees real space.

Leonardo da Vinci used linear perspective to construct space for his portrayal of *The Last Supper* (**4.46**). It was, above all, the measurable quality of the space created through linear perspective that intrigued Renaissance artists. Here, regular divisions of the ceiling measure out the recession, giving the figures a logical space to occupy.

Painted on a monastery wall in Milan, *The Last Supper* depicts the final gathering of Jesus Christ with his disciples, the Passover meal they shared before Jesus was brought to trial and crucified. Leonardo captures a particular moment in the story, as related in the Gospel of Matthew in the Bible. Jesus, shown at the center of the composition, has just said to his followers: "One of you shall betray me." The disciples, Matthew tells us, "were exceeding sorrowful, and began every one of them to say unto him, Lord, is it I?"

In Leonardo's portrayal, each of the disciples reacts differently to the terrible prediction. Some are shocked, some dismayed, some puzzled—but only one, only Judas, knows that, indeed, it is he. Falling back from Jesus's words, the traitor Judas, seated fourth from the left with his elbow on the table, clutches a bag containing thirty pieces of silver, his price for handing over his leader to the authorities.

To show this fateful moment, Leonardo places the group in a large banquet hall, its architectural space constructed in careful perspective. Cloth hangings on the side walls and panels in the ceiling are drawn so as to recede into space. Their lines converge at a vanishing point behind Jesus's head, at the exact center of the picture. Thus, our attention is directed forcefully toward the most important part of the composition, the face of Jesus. The central opening in the back wall, a rectangular window, also helps to focus our attention on Jesus and creates a "halo" effect around his head.

In the hands of the greatest artists, perspective became a vehicle for meaning, just as any other visual element. Here, for example, it is correct to say that the space is constructed so that the lines converge at a vanishing point in the distance behind Christ's head. But if we view the painting as a flat surface, we see that these lines can also be interpreted as radiating from Christ's head, as all of creation radiates from the mind of God. Leonardo has purposefully minimized Christ's shoulders so that his arms, too, take part in the system of radiating lines. Spreading his hands, then, God opens space to this moment, which He had foreseen since the beginning of time.

FORESHORTENING   For pictorial space to be consistent, the logic of linear perspective must apply to every form that recedes into the distance, including objects and human and animal forms. This effect is called **foreshortening**. You can understand the challenge presented by foreshortening by closing one eye and pointing upward with your index finger in front of your open eye. Gradually shift your hand until your index finger is pointing away from you and you are staring directly down its length and into the distance. You know that your finger has not changed in length, and yet it appears much shorter than it did when it was upright. It appears foreshortened.

Hans Baldung Grien portrays two foreshortened figures in *The Groom and the Witch* (**4.47**). The groom, lying perpendicular to the picture plane, is foreshortened. If we were to shift him so that he lay parallel to the picture plane with his head to the left and his feet to the right, we would have to stretch him back out. The horse, standing at a 45-degree angle to the picture plane, is also foreshortened, with the distance between his rump and his forequarters compressed by the odd angle at which we see him.

Foreshortening presented great difficulties to artists, for the complex, organic masses of a horse or a man do not offer the simple receding lines of architecture. Baldung Grien's teacher, Albrecht Dürer, left us this wonderful image of an artist wrestling logically with a problem of extreme foreshortening (**4.48**). From our point of view, the woman lies parallel to the picture plane. From the point of view of the artist, however, she is directly perpendicular to it. Her knees are closest to him, her head farthest away. He has actually constructed a picture plane in the form of a gridded window through which he looks at his model. On the table before him lies a sheet of paper, gridded to match. Standing on the table within the embrace of his arms is an obelisk whose tip just reaches his eye. The obelisk serves to focus his glance, making sure that every time he returns his gaze to the model, it is at exactly the same height.

Our artist will work slowly back and forth. Looking across the tip of the obelisk with one eye open, he will observe his model through the grid. Looking down, he will open both eyes and quickly draw from memory what he saw, using the grid lines as reference points. Looking up again, he will refocus one eye on his model over the obelisk and memorize another small bit. Glance by glance, he will complete the drawing.

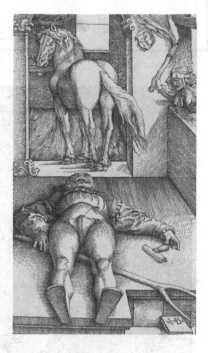

4.47 Hans Baldung Grien. *The Groom and the Witch*. ca. 1540. Woodcut, 13 15/16 × 7 7/8".
Image courtesy of the Board of Trustees, National Gallery of Art, Washington, D.C., Gift of W. G. Russell Allen 1941.1.100

4.48 Albrecht Dürer. *Draftsman Drawing a Reclining Nude*, from *The Art of Measurement*. ca. 1527. Woodcut, 3 × 8 ½".
The Metropolitan Museum of Art, New York, Gift of Henry Walters, 1917

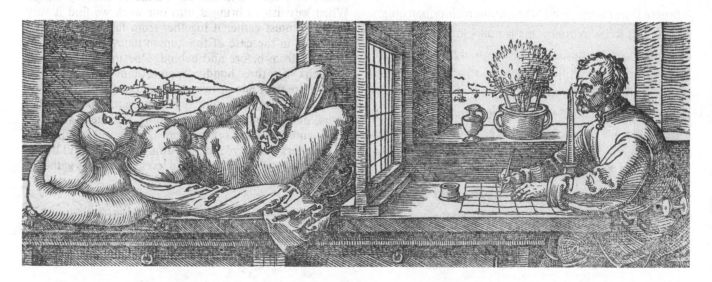

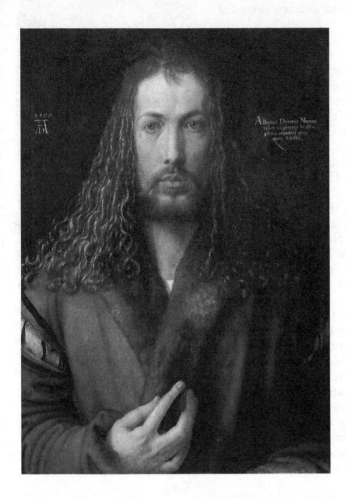

What motivated Dürer to write about perspective and proportion? How did his theories appear in his art? What is his definition of aesthetics?

Albrecht Dürer is the first of the northern European artists who seems to us "modern" in his outlook. Unlike most of his colleagues, he had a strong sense of being an *artist*, not a craftsman, and he sought—and received—acceptance in the higher ranks of society. Moreover, Dürer appears to have understood his role in the history of art, sensing that his work would exert great influence on his contemporaries and on artists of the future. That awareness led him to date his works and sign them with the distinctive "AD" (visible in the left background of his self-portrait)—a fairly unusual practice at the time.

Born in the southern German city of Nuremberg, Dürer was the son of a goldsmith, to whom he was apprenticed as a boy. At the age of fifteen, young Albrecht was sent to study in the workshop of Michael Wolgemut, then considered a leading painter in Nuremberg. He stayed with Wolgemut for four years, after which he began a four-year period of wandering through northern Europe before returning home to open his own studio.

Dürer made a great many paintings and drawings, but it is his output in prints (engravings, woodcuts, and etchings) that is truly extraordinary. Many people would argue that he was the greatest printmaker who ever lived. His genius derived partly from an ability to unite the best tendencies in northern and southern European art of that period, for Dürer was a well-traveled man. In 1494 he visited Italy, and he returned in 1505, staying two years in Venice, where he operated a studio. He brought back to Germany the Italian ideas about representing the body in space. Upon his return to Nuremberg, Dürer took his place among the leading writers and intellectuals of the town, authoring texts on geometry and proportion inspired by his Italian sojourns.

When he prepared his treatise on measurements and perspective, Dürer explained that German art had to that point no method for representing bodies in their spaces. Artists needed to learn the art of measurement, as he called it, which was the "true foundation for all painting." He attempted to teach artists how to draw with measurement, explaining, "I have proposed to myself to propound the elements for the use of all eager students of Art and to instruct them how they may employ a system of measurement with rule and compass, and thereby learn to recognize the real truth, seeing it before their eyes."[5] In other words, Dürer's system allowed artists to understand the underlying geometry of what they saw.

As a Renaissance artist, Dürer was also fascinated by perfection and by an ideal of beauty. He wrote: "What beauty is, I know not, though it adheres to many things. When we wish to bring it into our work we find it very hard. We must gather it together from far and wide, and especially in the case of the human figure throughout all its limbs from before and behind. One may often search through two or three hundred men without finding amongst them more than one or two points of beauty which can be made use of. You, therefore, if you desire to compose a fine figure, must take the head from some, the chest, arm, leg, hand, and foot from others; and likewise, search through all members of every kind. For from many beautiful things something good may be gathered, even as honey is gathered from many flowers."[6]

Albrecht Dürer. *Self-Portrait at Age 28*. 1500. Oil on wood, 26 5/16 × 19 5/16". Alte Pinakothek, Munich. classicpaintings/Alamy Stock Photo

Dürer's image illustrates well the strengths and drawbacks of linear perspective. It is a scientifically accurate system for rendering space and relationships within space as we perceive them standing in one fixed place, with one eye open, staring at fixed points along one eye level. But in life we have two eyes, not one, and they are always in motion. Nevertheless, the principles of linear perspective dominated Western views of space for almost five hundred years, and they continue to influence us through images generated by the camera, which also shows the view seen by one eye (the lens) staring at a point on a fixed level (the center focus).

ATMOSPHERIC PERSPECTIVE   Staring off into a series of hills, you may notice that each succeeding range appears paler, bluer, and less distinct. This is an optical effect caused by the atmosphere that interposes itself between us and the objects we perceive. Particles of moisture and dust suspended in the atmosphere scatter light. Of all the colors of the spectrum, blue scatters the most; hence the sky itself appears to be blue, and things take on a bluish tinge as their distance from us increases. The first European artist to apply this observation systematically was Leonardo da Vinci, who called the effect "aerial perspective." A more common term today is **atmospheric perspective**.

Atmospheric perspective is the third and final element of the optically based system for representing the world that was developed during the Renaissance. For as long as naturalism remained a goal of Western art, these three techniques—modeling form through value, constructing space with linear perspective, and suggesting receding landscape through atmospheric perspective—remained central to painting.

John Frederick Kensett's view of *Lake George* is an exquisite example of beautifully modulated atmospheric perspective (**4.49**). With its rocky outcropping, fallen tree trunk, green leaves, and water grasses, the shore in the foreground is clear and detailed. Small islands nearby are less distinct, but the trees are still green. Marking

4.49 John Frederick Kensett. *Lake George*. 1869. Oil on canvas, 3' 8 ⅛" × 5' 6 ⅜".
The Metropolitan Museum of Art, New York. Bequest of Maria DeWitt Jesup, from the collection of her husband, Morris K. Jesup, 1914. 15.30.61. Image © The Metropolitan Museum of Art

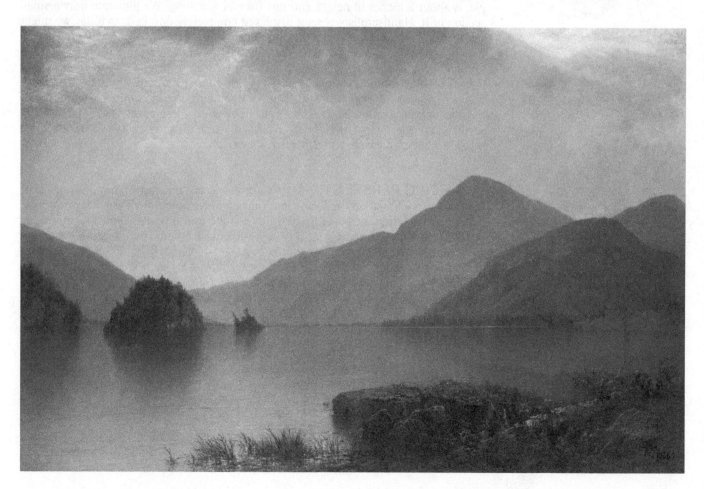

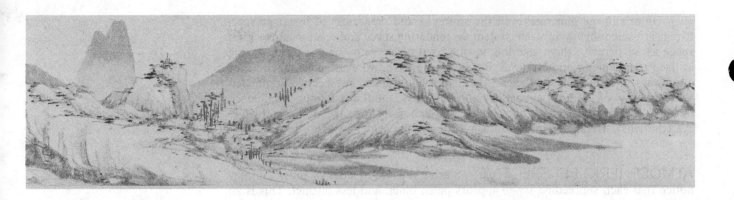

4.50 Shen Zhou. *Autumn Colors among Streams and Mountains.* ca. 1490–1500. Handscroll, ink on paper, image 8 ⅛" × 21' ¼".
The Metropolitan Museum of Art, New York. Gift of Douglas Dillon, 1979. 1979.75.1. © 2014. © The Metropolitan Museum of Art. Image source: Art Resource, NY

our progression into the distance, the three hills along the farther shores grow progressively more hazy and tinged with blue, which takes over completely as the farthest hill follows the curve of the lake away from us and disappears from view.

Chinese and Japanese painters also developed a technique of atmospheric perspective to suggest broad vistas of receding landscape. In Shen Zhou's *Autumn Colors among Streams and Mountains* (**4.50**), the gentle hills along the shore are built up from layers of contour strokes, anchored by local gray washes, and detailed with barren tree trunks and black dots indicating foliage. The mountains that rise in the distance, in contrast, are simply rendered in washes of pale gray ink. The colors of the title are left to the viewer's imagination.

Autumn Colors among Streams and Mountains is an example of a handscroll, an intimate format of painting developed in China. Small enough to be held in the hands, as the name indicates, a handscroll was commonly only a foot or so in height, but many feet long. *Autumn Colors among Streams and Mountains*, for example, is about 8 inches in height and just over 21 feet long. We illustrate only a small section of it. Handscrolls were not displayed completely unrolled, as today we might see them in museums. Rather, they were kept rolled up and taken out for viewing only occasionally. Viewers would savor the painting slowly, setting it on a table and unrolling a foot or two at a time. Working their way from one end of the scroll to the other, they journeyed through a landscape that commonly alternated stretches of open water and lowlands with hills and mountains. In *Autumn Colors among Streams and Mountains*, Shen Zhou paid homage to the quartet of painters known as the Four Masters of the Yuan Dynasty by imitating their styles one after the other—an added pleasure for cultivated viewers.

ISOMETRIC PERSPECTIVE   As we have seen, the converging lines of linear perspective are based on the fixed viewpoint of an earthbound viewer. The viewpoint in Chinese painting, however, is typically mobile and airborne, and so converging lines have no place in their system of representation. Islamic painting often employs an aerial viewpoint as well, so that scenes are depicted in their totality, as God might see and understand them. To suggest regular forms such as a building receding from the picture plane, Chinese and Muslim painters use diagonal lines, but without allowing parallels to converge. This system is known as **isometric perspective** (**4.51**).

4.51 Basic principles of isometric perspective.

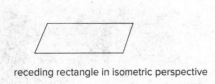

receding rectangle in isometric perspective

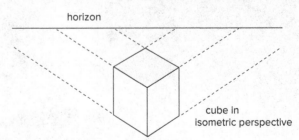

horizon

cube in isometric perspective

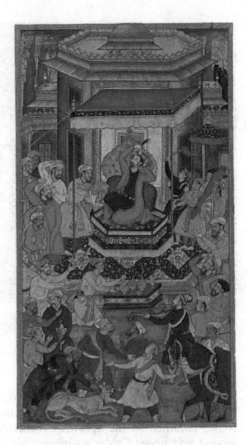

4.52 Bim Gujarati. *Alexander the Great Enthroned at Persepolis*, from *Khamsah* by Nizami Ganjavi. 1595. Ink and pigments on light brown paper, 13 ⅜ × 8 ⁷⁄₁₆".
Acquired by Henry Walters and bequeathed to the Walters Art Museum, Baltimore, Maryland

In the page illustrated here from a manuscript of the *Khamsah* by the Azerbaijani poet Nizami Ganjavi, the canopy over the head of the seated figure is portrayed using isometric perspective (**4.52**). The sides recede to the right in parallel diagonal lines; the rear edge is as wide as the wall nearest us. The painting pictures the ancient Greek king Alexander the Great enthroned at the palace at Persepolis in Iran. Alexander conquered much of the territory between Greece and India during his thirteen-year reign. He spent several months at Persepolis, celebrating his defeat of the Persians who had once sacked the Greek city of Athens. From his throne, Alexander appears here receiving Persian courtiers and being cared for by their servants.

Time and Motion

Time and motion have always been linked to art, if only because time is the element in which we live and motion is the very sign of life. It was only during the 20th century, however, that time and motion truly took their places as elements of Western art, and this was for the simple reason that through advances in science and technology, daily life itself became far more dynamic, and the nature of time and its relationship to space and the universe more a matter for thought.

During the 1930s, the American artist Alexander Calder set sculpture in motion with works that Marcel Duchamp called mobiles. Constructed from abstract forms suspended on slender lengths of wire, they respond with their own weight to the lightest currents of air. Calder also created works that Jean Arp dubbed stabiles—sculptures that did not move but sat still on the ground like everyone else's. Often, he combined the two ideas, as in *Carmen* (**4.53**), where a black stabile holds aloft a red-and-yellow mobile. The mobile is almost always in motion, reminding the viewer that time is constantly passing.

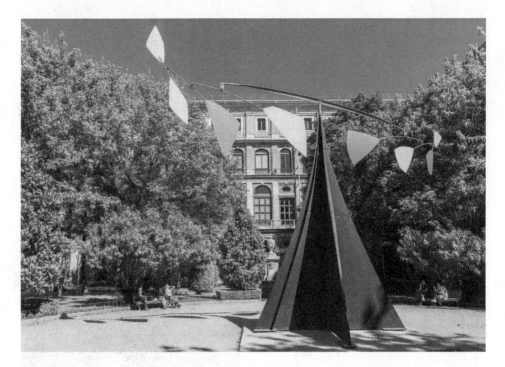

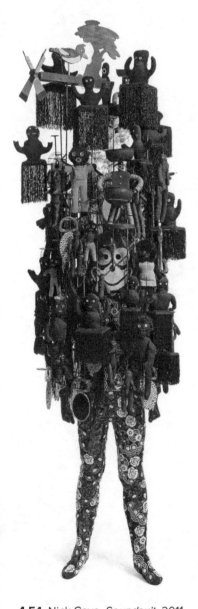

Art that moves is called **kinetic** art, from the Greek word *kinetos*, "moving." Calder is considered to be one of its founders. But motion in the experience of art is not confined to the artworks themselves. As viewers, we also move, walking around and under Calder's *Carmen*, for example, to experience what it looks like from different distances and angles. We walk through architecture to explore its spaces; we draw near to and away from paintings to notice details or allow them to blur back into the whole. As we saw in Chapter 2, artists of the 20th century became increasingly conscious of the viewer's motion over time, especially in the context of gallery and museum spaces.

Nick Cave makes art that depends for its full effect on the motion of the performer. Cave makes sculptures he calls *Soundsuits* (**4.54**). Although we can appreciate them in a gallery setting, where they stand motionless before us, most of them are made to be worn and danced. Like masquerades, the great African art form (see 2.40), Cave's *Soundsuits* are art that is meant to be seen in motion.

Soundsuits take their name from the first one Cave made, during the racially tense times of the early 1990s. An amateur video documenting the brutal beating of an African-American man by members of the Los Angeles police force had been widely shown on the news media. Riots broke out in several cities after a jury acquitted three of the four officers involved. "I started thinking about myself more and more as a black man,"[7] Cave recalls, "as someone who was discarded, devalued, viewed as less than." Sitting one day on a park bench, he began to consider the twigs that lay on the ground around him as similarly rejected, valueless things. He gathered up armfuls of them and brought them back to his studio, where he cut them into 3-inch lengths and wired them to a bodysuit he had made, completely covering it from head to toe. Cave had intended the work as a sculpture, but he immediately realized that he could wear it. "I put it on and jumped around and was just amazed. It made this fabulous rustling sound. And because it was so heavy, I had to stand very erect, and that alone brought the idea of dance back into my head."[8] Just as important, Cave realized, he could disappear into the suit, and no one could tell from the outside whether he was black, white, orange, or purple. Since that initial impulse to give form to feelings in the face of events, Cave has created hundreds of *Soundsuits* using scavenged materials and items purchased from thrift shops, flea markets, and garage sales. They dance before us, a race of joyous, mysterious, silly, mournful, disturbing, majestic, extravagant beings that make their own music. We could put one on and join in.

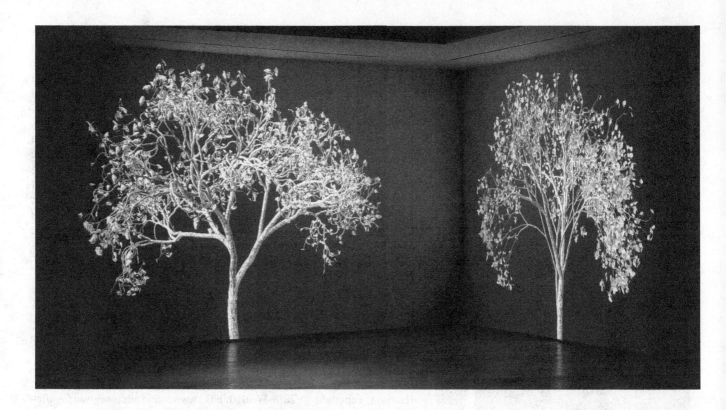

The Greek word *kinetos* also gave us the word *cinema*, certainly the most significant new art form of the 20th century. Film and, later, video provided artists with new ways to work with time and motion. As these technologies become increasingly affordable and available, artists experimented with them more and more, to the point where video became an important medium for contemporary art.

More recently, digital animation technology has allowed artists to create videos that do not necessarily rely on camera images. A beautiful example is Jennifer Steinkamp's installation *Dervish* (**4.55**). The installation was named for the order of Sufi mystics known in English as whirling dervishes, who enter into a state of spiritual ecstasy by means of a spinning dance. *Dervish* consisted of four digitally animated images of trees, each called *Dervish*, projected onto the walls of a darkened room. (The photograph here shows two of the trees.) Each individual branch, leaf, and blossom seemed alive as the trees twirled slowly, first one way and then the other, their virtual roots holding firm in the virtual ground, their trunks twisting like wrung laundry. Even more magically, each tree cycled through the seasons as it swayed, with spring blossoms giving way to summer foliage, then autumn colors, then bare branches.

To create her trees, Steinkamp began with an image of a maple. She modified each element digitally until she had created a tree that resembled no known tree at all, a completely artificial and virtual tree. Her only rule in her art, she says, is that everything must be simulated. Each *Dervish* can be programmed to display whatever season the viewer is in the mood for, or to change seasons on cue (the sound of a slamming door, for example, could cause spring to turn into summer). With strategies such as these, many digital artists surrender ultimate control over their creations.

Asif Khan's *MegaFaces Kinetic Facade* (**4.56**) also uses digital images to make kinetic art. Created for the 2014 winter Olympic games in Sochi, Russia, Khan's installation recalls monumental sculpture that commemorates heroes and world leaders. Yet the artist wanted to include not just Olympic athletes in his installation, but also people of every age, gender, nationality, and sexual preference. He began with three-dimensional scans of the faces of people at thirty sites across Russia. In Sochi, LED lights on projecting arms re-created the scanned portraits in three dimensions. Three portraits at a time, each more than 25 feet tall and up to

4.55 Jennifer Steinkamp. *Dervish*, detail. 2004. Video installation at Lehmann Maupin Gallery, New York, January 10–February 14, 2004. Each tree 12 × 16' (size variable). Courtesy of the artist and Lehmann Maupin, New York and Hong Kong

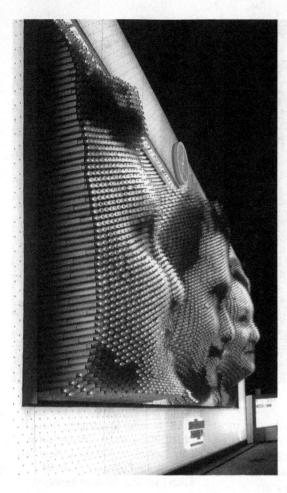

4.56 Asif Khan. *MegaFaces Kinetic Facade*. 2014. Installation with LED lights, 59' × 24' 3".
© Asif Khan. Photo Scott Easton

7½ feet deep, emerged from a wall for a short time, then disappeared. For Sochi visitors, the installation was a constantly moving and changing array of faces. For the people whose faces were scanned, a text message alerted them to watch the webcam when their portraits were displayed and allowed the kinetic sculpture to reach and involve people well beyond its immediate environment.

Line, shape, mass, light, value, color, texture, pattern, space, time, and motion—these are the raw materials, the elements, of a work of art. To introduce them, we have had to look at each one individually, examining its role in various works of art. However, we do not perceive the elements one at a time but together, and almost any given work of art is an example not of one element but of many. In the next chapter, we examine how artists organize these elements into art, how this organization structures our experience of looking, and how an understanding of the visual elements and their organization can help us to see more fully.

Notes to the Text

1. Cited in Henri Dorra and John Rewald, *Seurat: L'Oeuvre peint, biographie et catalogue critique* (Paris: Les Beaux-Arts, 1959), pp. 1–li.
2. Vincent van Gogh. Letter to Theo van Gogh, September 8, 1888, Letter 533. Translated by Mrs. Johanna van Gogh-Bonger, edited by Robert Harrison, copyright © 2018 WebExhibits. www.webexhibits.org/vangogh/letter/18/533.htm, accessed April 27, 2018.
3. J. Gill Holland, ed. and transl., *The Private Journals of Edvard Munch: We Are Flames Which Pour Out of the Earth* (Madison: University of Wisconsin Press, 2005), pp. 64–65.
4. Quoted in Urs Steiner and Samuel Herzog, "'Es kommt auf die Idee an': Ein Gespräch mit der palästinensisch-britischen Künstlerin Mona Hatoum," *Neue Zürcher Zeitung*, November 20, 2004. Available at nzz.ch/articleA07HX-1.336931, accessed April 27, 2018.
5. William Martin Conway and Lina Eckenstein, *Literary Remains of Albrecht Dürer* (London: Cambridge University Press, 1889), p. 212.
6. Robert Goldwater and Marco Treves, eds., *Artists on Art: From the 14th to the 20th Century* (New York: Pantheon, 1972), p. 82.
7. Quoted in Jori Finkel, "I Dream the Clothing Electric," *New York Times*, March 31, 2009. Available at nytimes.com/2009/04/05/arts/design/05fink.html, accessed April 27, 2018.
8. Ibid.

Chapter 5
Principles of Design

In this chapter, you will learn to

LO1   describe how artists create unity and variety,

LO2   identify types of balance found in art,

LO3   explain how artists emphasize and subordinate parts of a work,

LO4   relate how scale and proportion function in art,

LO5   characterize the use of rhythm in art, and

LO6   analyze formal elements and principles of design.

When an artist sets about making any work, he or she is faced with infinite options. How big or small? What kinds of lines and where should the lines go? What kinds of shapes? How much space between the shapes? How many colors and how much of each one? What amounts of light and dark values? Somehow, the elements discussed in Chapter 4—line, shape, mass, light, color, texture, pattern, space, and possibly time and motion—must be organized in such a way as to satisfy the artist's expressive intent. In two-dimensional art, this organization is often called **composition**, but the more inclusive term, applicable to all kinds of art, is **design**. The task of making the decisions involved in designing a work of art would be paralyzing were it not for certain guidelines that, once understood, become almost instinctive. These guidelines are usually known as the *principles of design*.

All of us have some built-in sense of what looks right or wrong, what "works" or doesn't. Some—including most artists—have a stronger sense of what "works" than others. If two families each decorate a living room, and one room is attractive, welcoming, and pulled together while the other seems drab and uninviting, we might say that the first family has better "taste." Taste is a common term that, in this context, describes how some people make visual selections. What we really mean by "good taste," often, is that some people have a better grasp of the principles of design and how to apply them in everyday situations.

The principles of design are a natural part of perception. Most of us are not conscious of them in everyday life, but artists usually are very aware of them, because they have trained themselves to be aware. These principles codify, or explain systematically, our sense of "rightness" and help to show why certain designs work better than others. For the artist they offer guidelines for making the most effective choices; for the observer an understanding of the principles of design gives greater insight into works of art.

The principles of design most often identified are unity and variety, balance, emphasis and subordination, scale and proportion, and rhythm. This chapter illustrates works of art that show these principles very clearly. But *any* work of art, regardless of its form or the culture in which it was made, could be discussed in terms of the principles of design, for they are integral to all art.

Unity and Variety

Unity is a sense of oneness, of things belonging together and making up a coherent whole. Variety is difference, which provides interest. We discuss them together because the two generally coexist in a work of art. A solid wall painted white certainly has unity, but it is not likely to hold your interest for long. Take that same blank wall and ask fifty people each to make a mark on it and you will get plenty of variety, but there probably will be no unity whatever. In fact, there will be so *much* variety that no one can form a meaningful visual impression. Unity and variety exist on a spectrum, with total blandness at one end, total disorder at the other. For most works of art, the artist strives to find just the right point on that spectrum—the point at which there is sufficient visual unity enlivened by sufficient variety.

The first thing that strikes us when we look at Henri de Toulouse-Lautrec's *Divan Japonais* (**5.1**) is the repetition of similar curving shapes in gray and black: musical instruments, arms, elbows, letters. This repetition unifies the composition, tying the parts together. At the same time, we also see that not everything in the image is black or gray; there are different colors. The purse, stage, chair, cane, and gentleman's hair are yellow; the middle woman's hair is orange and her lips are red.

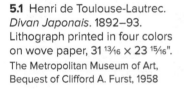

5.1 Henri de Toulouse-Lautrec. *Divan Japonais*. 1892–93. Lithograph printed in four colors on wove paper, 31 ¹³⁄₁₆ × 23 ¹⁵⁄₁₆". The Metropolitan Museum of Art, Bequest of Clifford A. Furst, 1958

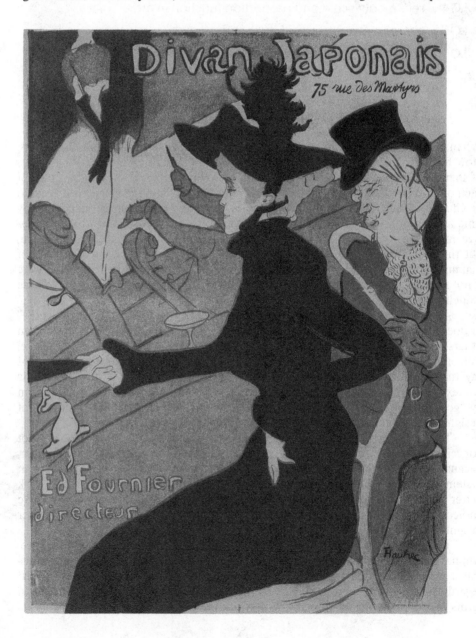

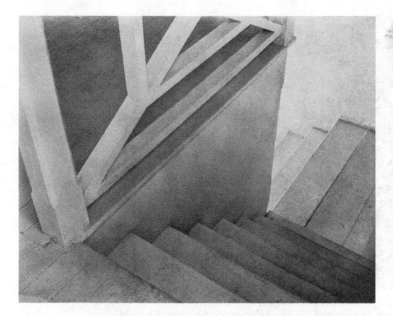

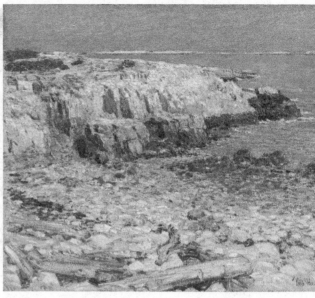

5.2 Tina Modotti. *Stairs*. 1924–26. Gelatin silver print, 7 ¼ × 9 ⁷⁄₁₆".
The Metropolitan Museum of Art, Ford Motor Company Collection, Gift of Ford
Motor Company and John C. Waddell, 1987. 1987.1100.43

5.3 Childe Hassam. *A North East Headland*. 1901. Oil on
canvas, 25 ⅛ × 30 ¹⁄₁₆".
Image courtesy National Gallery of Art, Washington, D.C.

These colors add variety and make this poster more interesting. Yet, by using so
many yellow objects, the artist unified the work as well. Toulouse-Lautrec got the
idea for this composition by observing people at the theater, but when he translated
what he saw into a work of art, he exercised his artistic license by repeating shapes
and contrasting colors. He understood that this unity and variety in the composition
made the image "work" better and made it more engaging for his viewers.

The unity of Tina Modotti's photograph *Stairs* (**5.2**) is easy to see. Rectangles
and triangles abound. Each step, railing, and plank of wood is a rectangle. Each
corner and intersection of two stairs or planks forms a triangular shape. The repetition of these shapes unifies the composition. The monochromatic array of gray
hues ties the work together as well. Still, the photograph has lots of variety. The
direction of the rectangles changes from the second story, where the photograph is
taken, to the top section of stairs, the landing, and the lower section of stairs. There
is also a strong diagonal created by the brightly lit cross-bar within the second-story
railing. Looking closely reveals that the texture differs in each section, from the
scuffed wood stairs to the smooth wall. Each of these elements adds variety and
makes the image more interesting.

Childe Hassam's painting *A North East Headland* (**5.3**) also exhibits a great
deal of unity. Much of the landscape consists of the circular rocks that line the
shore. Some are larger, others are smaller, but all share the same shape and a gray
or brown hue. The unity of these rocks is contrasted by the texture of the water
offshore. The irregular shoreline also provides variety, as do the two logs in the
foreground that contrast with the round stones. The dominance of analogous blues
and grays unifies the work, while the spots of yellow, green, and brown offer variety.
Hassam made this painting while visiting an island off the coast of Maine. His goal
was to capture the fleeting effects of light on the natural environment. Yet, he
demonstrated his artistic skill by composing the work with unity and variety.

The three works we have just considered demonstrate *visual* unity—unity based
on the elements of shape, line, color, and so on. Art can also be unified *conceptually*—that is, through a unity of ideas. Annette Messager relies largely on conceptual
unity in her assemblage *Mes Voeux* (French for "my wishes") (**5.4**). If we think
about what the photographs have in common, we realize that they all portray isolated body parts—knee, throat, mouth, ear, hand. The framed texts ask not only to
be looked at but also to be read. Two repeat the word *tenderness* over and over

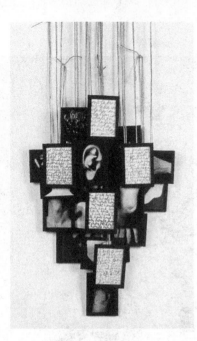

5.4 Annette Messager. *Mes Voeux.* 1989. Framed photographs and handwritten texts, suspended with twine, 59 × 15 ¾".
Courtesy the artist and Marian Goodman Gallery, Paris. © 2019 Artists Rights Society (ARS), New York/ADAGP, Paris

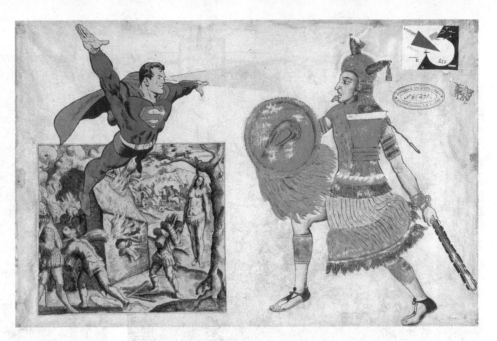

5.5 Enrique Chagoya. *Uprising of the Spirit* (*Elevación del espíritu*). 1994. Acrylic and oil on paper, 48 × 72".
© Enrique Chagoya. Gift of Ann and Aaron Nisenson in memory of Michael Nisenson (AC1995.183.9). Digital image © 2019 Museum Associates/LACMA. Licensed by Art Resource, NY

again; another, the word *shame*. Understanding the grouping as a kind of body itself places *consolation* at the head, *tenderness* at the arms, *shame* at the genitals, and *luck* at the legs. Repeating shapes and restricted color give visual unity to the work, but it is conceptual unity that asks for our interpretation.

Conceptual unity characterizes Enrique Chagoya's *Uprising of the Spirit* (**5.5**). This large painting features Superman seeming to battle an Aztec emperor carrying a feather shield and wearing feather garments like those pictured in the *Florentine Codex* discussed in Chapter 3 (see 3.15). Below them is a scene of atrocities committed against indigenous Americans in the 16th century. Chagoya appropriated all these images: the emperor's image came from a 16th-century Mexican manuscript, Superman from popular comic books, and the scene of atrocities from a 16th-century European print. These disparate elements are unified conceptually by the artist's critique of colonialism and his own heritage as a Mexican-American raised with Mexican and American cultural influences. By having a modern American superhero square off against an ancient Aztec emperor, Chagoya brings us into the contemporary era and references 20th-century political and social issues.

Balance

Forms within a work of art have **visual weight**. A rocky outcropping looks heavy while a feather looks light. The apparent "heaviness" or "lightness" of these forms within the composition is gauged by how insistently they draw our eyes. When visual weight is equally distributed to either side of a felt or implied center of gravity, we feel that the composition is balanced.

Symmetrical Balance

With **symmetrical** balance, the forms of a composition mirror each other across a central axis, an imaginary horizontal or vertical line that divides the composition in half. The two halves of the composition thus correspond exactly, with the axis as the center of gravity. For example, the colorful shapes in Haruka Kojin's *reflectwo* mirror each other across a horizontal axis (**5.6**). The upper and lower halves of the work correspond exactly. *Reflectwo* evokes a wooded shoreline reflected in a still water surface. It was inspired by an experience the artist had as a university student while walking late one night along a river near her school: So perfectly did a tall tree join with its reflection that it seemed as though a gigantic tower were floating in the air before her, perfect and eternal. She felt disoriented, lost in space, as in a dream. Kojin gave form to her vision by using fabric petals from artificial flowers, flattened, grouped, and suspended by threads from the ceiling. *Reflectwo* seems to float before us, beautiful and eerie. The petal groupings are hung in depth, some farther forward, some farther back, so that their relationships shift slightly as viewers move, the perfect symmetry of the whole revealing itself for a moment and then vanishing, like Kojin's vision.

The Tabernacle Polyptych with the Madonna and Child and Scenes from the Life of Christ (**5.7**) also exhibits symmetrical balance. This tiny sculpture is a shrine, created for private devotion at home by its wealthy patron. It is a polyptych, which means that it has several panels, two to either side of the central section. These fold so that the shrine could travel with its owner. The central section and its figures of Mary and Christ form a central axis, and the panels are symmetrically paired on each side. The work's symmetry is not absolute. The Christ child rests

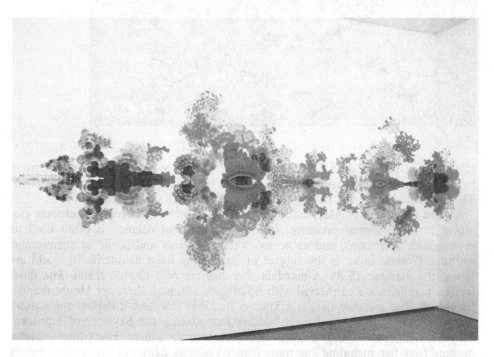

5.6 Haruka Kojin. *reflectwo*. 2007. Installation at the Museu de Arte Moderna de São Paulo, April 10–June 22, 2008. Artificial flower petals, acrylic, string, dimensions variable.
Courtesy the artist and SCAI the Bathhouse, Tokyo

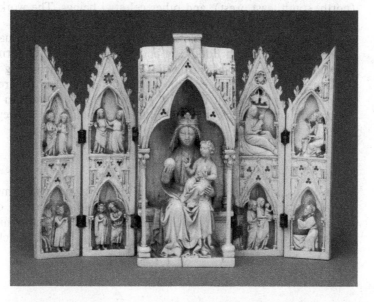

5.7 Tabernacle Polyptych with the Madonna and Child and Scenes from the Life of Christ. ca. 1275–1300. Ivory with traces of original gilding and polychromy; silver hinges, 3 ¾ × 5 ¼" (with open wings).
The Metropolitan Museum of Art, New York, Robert Lehman Collection, 1975

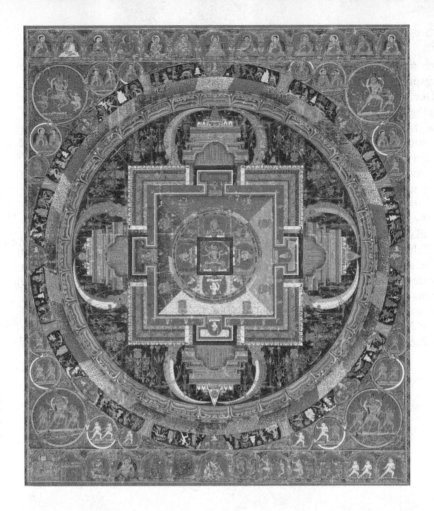

5.8 Mandala of Jnanadakini. Late 14th century. Distemper on cloth, without mount 29 ½ × 33".
The Metropolitan Museum of Art, New York. Purchase, Lita Annenberg Hazen Charitable Trust Gift, 1987, 1987.16

off-center on his mother's knee, for example. Yet the work possesses symmetrical balance because the visual weight of the orb that Mary holds balances the child. The panels to either side of the axis also exhibit equal visual weight.

The placement of Mary and Christ at the center of the ivory tabernacle creates a forceful, formal presence. Indeed, symmetrical balance is often used to express order, harmony, and authority, whether earthly and social or cosmic and spiritual. Cosmic order is the subject of one of the most distinctive of world art forms, the mandala (**5.8**). A **mandala** is a diagram of a cosmic realm. The most famous mandalas are connected with Buddhism, although there are Hindu mandalas as well. The mandala here is a Tibetan Buddhist one, and it depicts the cosmic realm emanating from the female buddha Jnanadakini, the Sky-goer of Transcendental Insight, who is shown seated in its centermost square. Everything radiates outward from her, including four more female buddhas, deities of the cardinal points (north, south, east, west), and other celestial beings. The work therefore has both symmetrical balance and **radial balance**.

The word *mandala* means "circle" in Sanskrit, the ritual language of early South Asia, where both Buddhism and Hinduism first took form. For practitioners, a mandala serves to focus meditation in the goal of achieving enlightenment. The basic message of its clear geometry and symmetry is this: We are living in a universe that makes sense, even if its logic and order are hidden from us during our brief lifetimes. Much religious art uses symmetrical balance to convey the same message.

Asymmetrical Balance

When you stand with your feet flat on the floor and your arms at your sides, you are in symmetrical balance. But if you thrust an arm out in one direction and a leg out in the other, your balance is **asymmetrical** (not symmetrical). Similarly, an asymmetrical composition has two sides that do not match. If it seems to be balanced, that is because the visual weights in the two halves are very similar. What looks "heavy" and what looks "light"? The only possible answer is, that depends. We do not perceive absolutes but relationships. The heaviness or lightness of any form varies depending on its size in relation to other sizes around it, its color in relation to other colors around it, and its placement in the composition in relation to the placement of other forms there. The drawing **5.9** illustrates some very general precepts about asymmetrical or informal balance:

1. A large form is visually heavier than a smaller form.
2. A dark-value form is visually heavier than a light-value form of the same size.
3. A textured form is visually heavier than a smooth form of the same size.
4. A complex form is visually heavier than a simple form of the same size.
5. Two or more small forms can balance a larger one.
6. A smaller dark form can balance a larger light one.

Those are only a few of the possibilities. Keeping them in mind, you may still wonder, but how does an artist actually go about balancing a composition? The answer is unsatisfactory but true: The composition is balanced when it looks balanced. An understanding of visual weights can help the artist to achieve balance or see what is wrong when balance is off, but it is no exact science.

In Gustav Klimt's *Death and Life* (**5.10**), asymmetrical balance dramatizes the opposition between life, envisioned to the right as a billowing form of light-hued patterns and slumbering human figures, and death, a dark skeletal presence at the far left, robed in a chilling pattern of grave markers. The two halves of the painting are linked by the gaze that passes between death and the woman he has come to claim. Klimt has placed her face exactly on the vertical axis of the painting, which here serves as a sort of symbolic border between life and death. The only waking

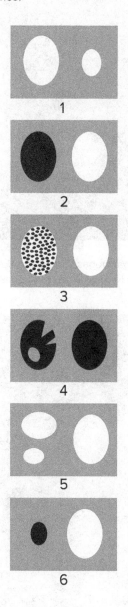

5.9 Some principles of visual balance.

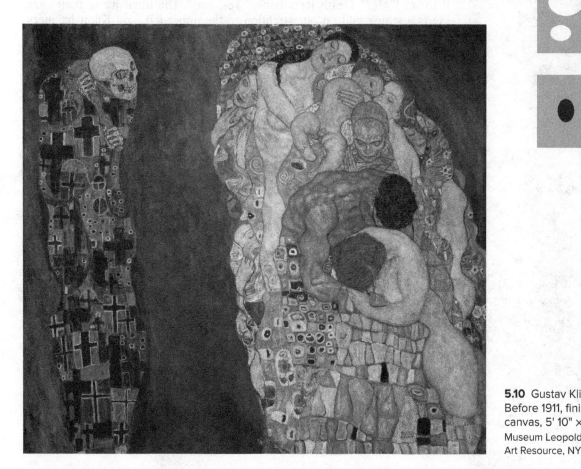

5.10 Gustav Klimt. *Death and Life.* Before 1911, finished 1915. Oil on canvas, 5' 10" × 6' 6".
Museum Leopold, Vienna. Erich Lessing/ Art Resource, NY

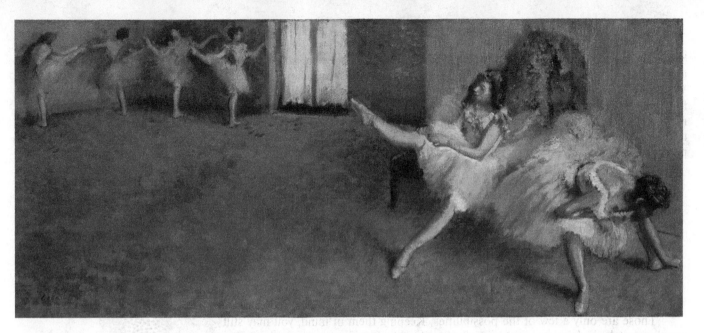

5.11 Edgar Degas. *Before the Ballet*. 1890–92. Oil on canvas, 15 ¾ × 35".
Courtesy National Gallery of Art, Washington, D.C.

5.12 Tawaraya (Nonomura) Sōtatsu. *The Zen Priest Choka*. Edo period,
late 16th–early 17th century. Hanging scroll, ink on paper, 37 ¹¹⁄₁₆ × 15 ³⁄₁₆".
Cleveland Museum of Art, Ohio/Norman O. Stone and Ella A. Stone Memorial Fund/
Bridgeman Images

person in the dreaming cloud of life, she smiles awkwardly and gestures as
if to say, "Me?" Death leers back, "Yes, you." The intensity of their gaze
exerts a strong pull on our attention to the upper left, and Klimt balances
this with an equal pull of visual weight to the right and down.

Space exaggerates the asymmetrical balance of Edgar Degas's *Before
the Ballet* (**5.11**). Two dancers occupy the right foreground of the painting.
They are large and well lit. This attracts the viewer's attention. One dancer
pulls at her stockings, creating an implied diagonal line that stretches from
her leg back to the four dancers warming up in the background. They are
smaller and occupy a shadowier space. The four figures visually balance the
weight of the two foreground figures; their darkened area of the dance studio has as much visual weight as the light figures of the two foreground
dancers. The painting is thus asymmetrically balanced. Degas learned this
approach by studying Japanese prints that employed asymmetrical balance.
It helped him to break the "rule" of earlier Western art that placed the most
significant forms in the middle and arrayed lesser forms symmetrically
around them.

The Japanese approach Degas admired is found in Tawaraya Sōtatsu's
ink painting of *The Zen Priest Choka* (**5.12**). In fact, it would be difficult to
imagine a more daringly asymmetrical composition. The forms are placed
so far to the left as to be barely on the page. Sōtatsu relies on an implied
line of vision both to balance the composition and to reveal its meaning.
We naturally raise our eyes to look at the form of the priest sitting in the
tree–that's all there is to look at. We then follow the direction of his gaze
down to. . .nothing. Meditation on emptiness is one of the exercises pre-
scribed by Zen Buddhism, and this ingenious painting makes that clear. Our
eyes repeatedly seek out the priest, who repeatedly sends us back to focus
on nothingness.

Depth, or the lack of it, is fascinating in Édouard Manet's *A Bar at
the Folies-Bergère* (**5.13**). The barmaid seems to stand before a large interior
that recedes far into the distance. Actually, she is wedged into a narrow

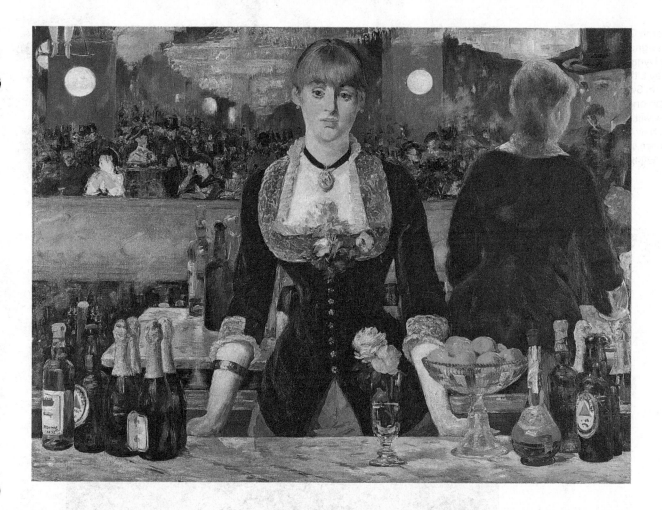

5.13 Édouard Manet. *A Bar at the Folies-Bergère*. 1881–82. Oil on canvas, 3' 1 ¾" × 4' 3 ¼".
© Samuel Courtauld Trust, The Courtauld Gallery, London/ Bridgeman Images

space between the marble bar and a large mirror, which reflects all that she can see but cannot participate in. Her own reflection is displaced to the right, where we see that she is waiting on a man who must be standing where we are standing as we view the painting. Around the central, symmetrical form of the barmaid Manet scatters a dazzling display of visual weights and counterweights. The large, dark form of the barmaid's reflection, the bowl of oranges next to the green bottle on the bar, the bottles to either side and their reflections in the mirror, the massive chandeliers and the moonlike white globes in the background, the woman in white who props her elbows on the balcony, even the green-clad feet of the trapeze artist visible at the upper left corner—all have a role to play.

Balance, then, encourages our active participation in looking. By using balance to lead our eyes around a work, artists structure our experience of it. As an important aspect of form, balance also helps to communicate a mood or meaning. The promise of an unchanging, eternal paradise is embodied in the stable, symmetrical balance of the Jnanadakini Mandala (see 5.8), just as the dramatic confrontation of life and death is embodied in the dynamic asymmetrical balance of Klimt's *Death and Life* (see 5.10).

Emphasis and Subordination

Emphasis and subordination are complementary concepts. Emphasis means that our attention is drawn more to certain parts of a composition than to others. If the emphasis is on a relatively small, clearly defined area, we call this a **focal point**. Subordination means that certain areas of the composition are deliberately made less visually interesting, so that the areas of emphasis stand out.

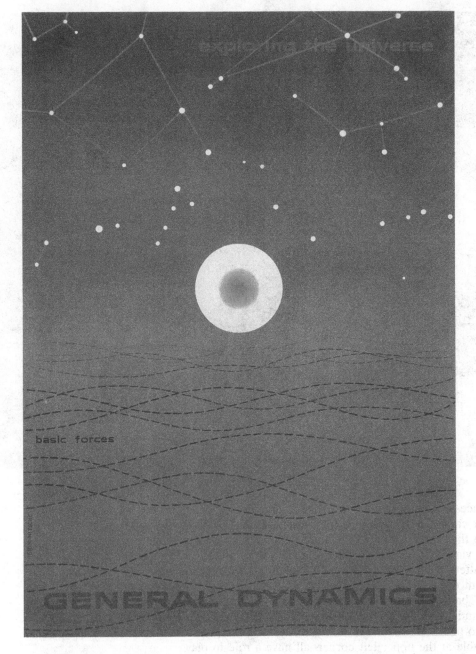

5.14 Poster, General Dynamics, 1956. Designed by Erik Nitsche for General Dynamics Corporation. Printed by Lithos R. Marsens (Lausanne, Switzerland). Offset lithograph on paper, 52 × 37 ⁹⁄₁₆". Cooper Hewitt, Smithsonian Design Museum, New York, NY, U.S.A. Gift of Arthur Cohen and Daryl Otte in memory of Bill Moggridge, 2013-42-12. Photo: Matt Flynn

A poster designed in 1956 by Erik Nitsche (**5.14**) represents a glowing atom, celestial constellations, and waving lines that suggest the ocean's rhythmic movement or oscillating sound waves. The poster was created as part of the General Dynamics Corporation's campaign to help American audiences embrace scientific research that used atomic energy. The designer employed several strategies to emphasize the atom, which appears like a nurturing sun rather than the potentially destructive force that threatened human existence during the Cold War. Its contrasting, high-value colors and placement in the center of the image draw attention to its concentric circles and warm glow. Conversely, the tertiary, low-value colors and analogous color scheme of the constellations and oscillating waves subordinate their role in the composition. Together, the atom and its surroundings create a harmonious whole, with the atom playing a starring role in the universe.

In *The Banjo Lesson* (**5.15**), Henry Ossawa Tanner also used size and placement to emphasize the figures of the old man and the young boy. Tanner set the pair in the foreground, and he posed them so that their visual weights combine to form a single mass, the largest form in the painting. Strongly contrasting values of

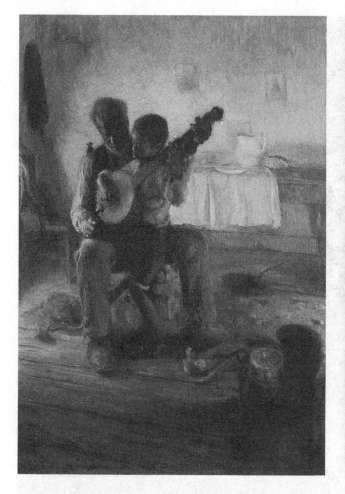

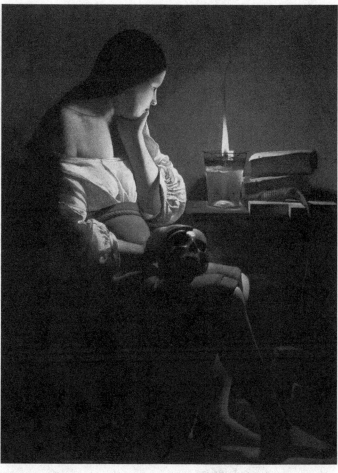

5.15 Henry Ossawa Tanner. *The Banjo Lesson*. 1893. Oil on canvas, 49 × 35 ½".
Collection of Hampton University Museum, Hampton, Virginia US 919-H

5.16 Georges de La Tour. *The Magdalen with the Smoking Flame*. ca. 1638–40. Oil on canvas, 46 ¹/₁₆ × 36 ⅛".
LACMA – Los Angeles County Museum of Art

dark skin against a pale background add further emphasis. Within this emphasized area, Tanner uses directional lines of sight to create a focal point on the circular body of the banjo and the boy's hand on it. Again contrast plays a role, for the light form of the banjo is set amid darker values, and the boy's hand contrasts dark against light. Tanner has subordinated the background so that it does not interfere, blurring the detail and working in a narrow range of light values. Imagine, for example, if one of the pictures depicted hanging on the far wall were painted in bright colors and minute detail. It would "jump out" of the painting and steal the focus away from what Tanner wants us to notice.

In his painting *The Magdalen with the Smoking Flame* (**5.16**), the French painter Georges de La Tour used size and placement for emphasis but also relied on light. Mary Magdalen sits beside a table with a burning candle. The flame casts light on her face and upper body, and creates the focal point of the painting. The rest of the image is darker, with some areas completely hidden in the shadows. The light draws our attention to Mary's pensive expression, body, and billowy blouse. When our eye follows the line of her arm, we come to her hand resting on a skull. Even though the symbol of mortality is an important part of this painting, it is a subordinate visual element. La Tour draws our attention with line and rewards our careful observation with this significant iconographic detail. Other important symbols also lurk in the subordinate portions of the painting, including books, a wooden cross, and the whip Mary uses to punish her sinful body. Our eye, however, is always drawn back to her brilliantly illuminated face, as the artist intended.

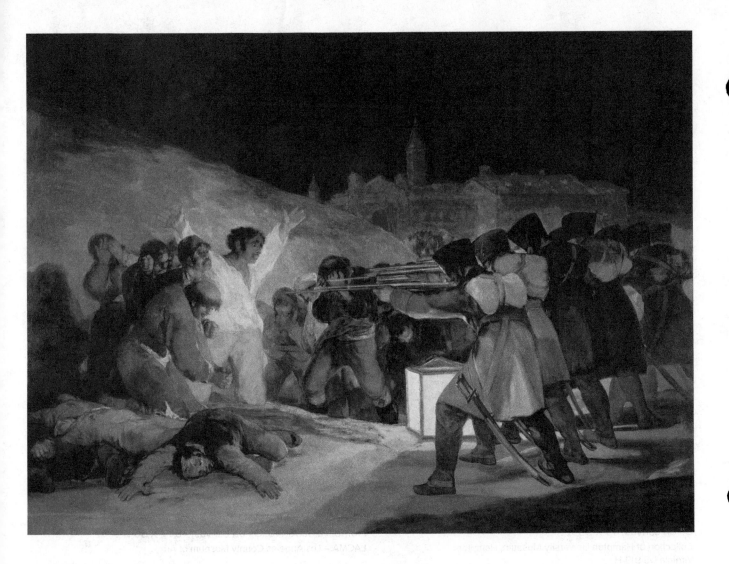

5.17 Francisco de Goya. *Executions of the Third of May, 1808*. 1814–15. Oil on canvas, 8' 9" × 13' 4". Museo del Prado, Madrid. Photo Erich Lessing/Art Resource, NY

Francisco de Goya used almost the same strategy in *Executions of the Third of May, 1808* (**5.17**). Brightly illuminated colors—white, yellow, and red—demand our attention by creating a dramatic focal area against a background of earth tones and black. A man is about to die; there is the blood of those who have preceded him, and a lantern that casts a light as harsh as the sound of a scream. The scene is set as minimally as possible so that nothing distracts our attention from the terrible slaughter. A barren hillside. Madrid. Darkness. The event Goya depicted occurred during the invasion of Spain by Napoleon, when a popular uprising in Madrid was brutally suppressed by occupying French soldiers.

In addition to dramatic contrasts in value, Goya uses psychological forces to direct not only our attention but also our sympathy. As in La Tour's painting, faces serve as focal points. The victims of the firing squad have faces, and we can read their expressions; the soldiers are faceless, as though they are not even human. They lunge forward as we look at them, creating directional forces that send us back again to the incipient martyr, his hands flung outward in a gesture of crucifixion.

Scale and Proportion

Proportion and scale both have to do with size. **Scale** means size in relation to a standard or "normal" size. Normal size is the size we expect something to be. For example, a model airplane is smaller in scale than a real airplane; a 10-pound prize-winning tomato at the county fair is a tomato on a large scale. We measure normal size based on our experience and what we know. Robert Jacob Gordon helped viewers to understand the normal size of a giraffe (**5.18**) by providing a measuring stick along the left side of his drawing. More importantly, he included a human figure to show that the normal size of the animal is very large. Viewers use this information to understand how big giraffes are compared to humans.

Artists sometimes play with scale and our experience of "normal" sizes. The artist Claes Oldenburg delights in the effects that a radical shift in scale can produce. In *Plantoir*, created with Coosje van Bruggen, he presents a humble gardening tool on a heroic scale (**5.19**). Perhaps it is a monument, but to what? Part of the delight in coming across a sculpture by Oldenburg and Van Bruggen is the shock of having our own scale overthrown as the measure of all things. Many fairy tales and adventure stories tell of humans who find themselves in a land of giants. In the sculptures of Oldenburg and Van Bruggen, the giants seem to have left an item or two behind.

Proportion refers to size relationships between parts of a whole, or between two or more items perceived as a unit. For example, the proportions of each part of the giraffe's body in the drawing by Gordon are naturalistic. The head is in the correct proportion to the size of the neck, the body, the legs, and the feet. The proportions of the giraffe generally agree with our knowledge of giraffes from media and visits to the zoo. Gordon's goal was to depict accurately the likeness of a giraffe, so he drew the proportions he saw.

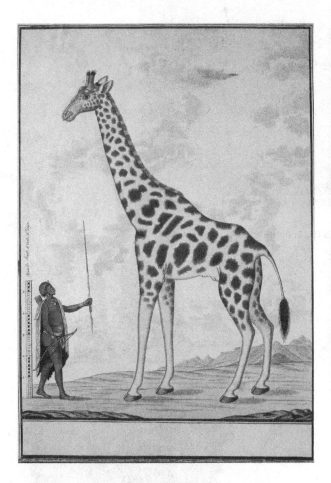

5.18 Robert Jacob Gordon. *Giraffa camelopardalis (Giraffe)*. 1779. Paper, paint, ink, watercolor, and pencil on paper, 26 × 18 ⅞".
Robert Jacob Gordon/Rijksmuseum. RP-T-1914-17-148

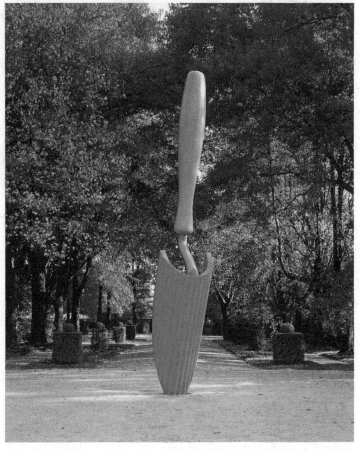

5.19 Claes Oldenburg and Coosje van Bruggen. *Plantoir*. 2001. Stainless steel, aluminum, fiber-reinforced plastic, painted with polyurethane enamel, height 23' 11".
Edition of 3, 1 Fundação de Serralves, Porto, Portugal. Purchase financed by funds donated by João Rendeiro, European Funds and Fundação de Serralves. Photo courtesy the Oldenburg van Bruggen Studio. Copyright 2001 Claes Oldenburg and Coosje van Bruggen

Many artistic cultures have developed a fixed set of proportions for depicting a "correct" or "perfect" human form. Ancient Egyptian artists, for example, relied on a squared grid to govern the proportions of their figures (5.20). Unfinished fragments such as this give us a rare insight into their working methods, for in finished works the grid is no longer evident. Egyptian artists took the palm of the hand as the basic unit of measurement. Looking at the illustration, you can see that each palm (or back) of a hand occupies one square of the grid. A standing figure measures 18 units from the soles of the feet to the hairline, with the knee falling

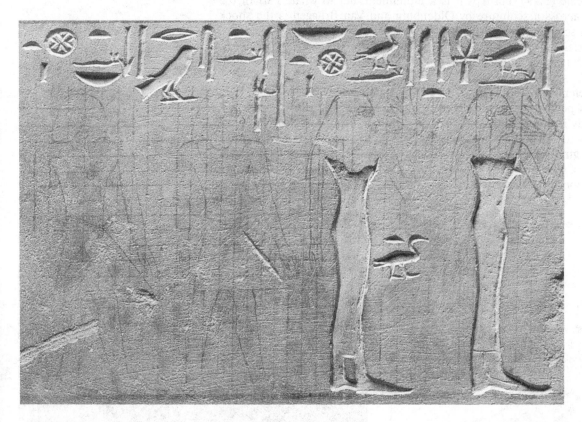

5.20 Stela of the sculptor Userwer, detail. Egypt. Dynasty 12, 1991–1783 B.C.E. Limestone.
© The Trustees of the British Museum, London/Art Resource, NY

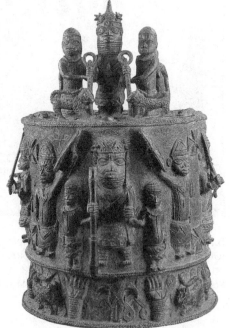

5.21 A royal altar to the hand (*ikegobo*). Benin. 18th century. Brass, height 17 ¾".
© The Trustees of the British Museum, London/Art Resource, NY

at horizontal 6, the elbow at horizontal 12, the nipple at 14, and so on. The shoulders of a standing male were 6 units wide; the waist about 2½ units.

Artists have often varied human proportions for symbolic or aesthetic purposes, as in this royal altar from the African kingdom of Benin (**5.21**). Cast in brass, the altar is dedicated to the king's hand, a symbol of physical prowess. Hands are depicted around its base, where they alternate with rams' heads. The king is shown seated atop the altar, flanked by attendants in a symmetrical composition. The composition expresses a social hierarchy. As the most important person, the king is the focal point at the center. He is also portrayed on a larger scale than his attendants. The use of scale to indicate relative importance is called **hierarchical scale**. Proportionally, the king's head takes up a full third of his total height. "Great Head" is one of the terms used in praise of the king, who is felt to rule his subjects just as the head, the seat of wisdom and judgment, rules the body. Representations of the king make these ideas manifest through proportion.

Among the many ideas from ancient Greece and Rome that were revived during the Renaissance was the notion that numerical relationships held the key to beauty, and that perfect human proportions reflected a divine order. Leonardo da Vinci was only one of many artists to become fascinated with the ideas of Vitruvius, a Roman architect of the first century B.C.E. whose treatise on architecture, widely read during the Renaissance, related the perfected male form to the perfect geometry of the square and the circle (**5.22**). Leonardo's figure stands inside a square defined by his height and the span of his arms, and a circle centered at his navel.

A proportion that has fascinated many artists and architects since its discovery by the ancient Greeks is the ratio known as the golden section. A golden section

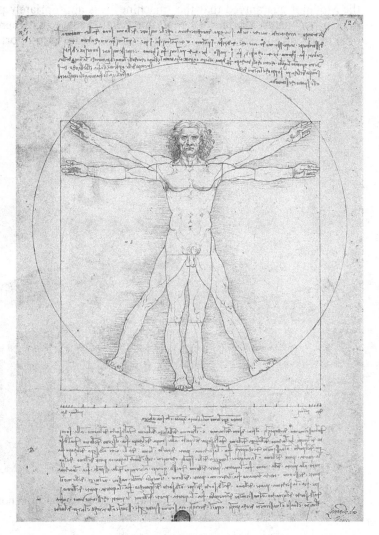

5.22 Leonardo da Vinci. *Study of Human Proportions According to Vitruvius.* ca. 1485–90. Pen and ink, 13 ½ × 9 ¾".
Gallerie dell'Accademia, Venice. Cameraphoto Arte, Venice/Art Resource, NY

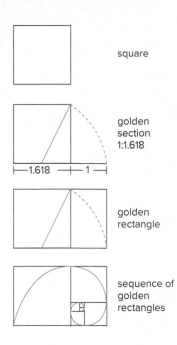

square

golden section 1:1.618

|— 1.618 —|— 1 —|

golden rectangle

sequence of golden rectangles

5.23 Proportions of the golden section and golden rectangle.

divides a length into two unequal segments in such a way that the smaller segment has the same ratio to the larger segment as the larger segment has to the whole. The ratio of the two segments works out as approximately 1 to 1.618. The golden section is more easily constructed than it is explained: Figure **5.23** takes you through the steps.

A rectangle constructed using the proportions of the golden section is called a golden rectangle. One of the most interesting characteristics of the golden rectangle, as figure 5.23 shows, is that when a square is cut off from one end, the remaining shape is also a golden rectangle—a sequence that can be repeated endlessly and relates to such natural phenomena as the spiraling outward growth of a shell.

Artists and architects have often turned to the golden section when seeking a rational yet subtle organizing principle for their work. During the 20th century, the French architect Le Corbusier related the golden section to human proportions in a tool he called the Modulor (**5.24**). The Modulor is based on two overlapping golden sections. The first extends from the feet to the top of the head, with the section division falling at the navel; the second extends from the navel to the tip of an upraised hand, with the section division falling at the top of the head. Using the height of an average adult, Le Corbusier derived several series of measurements based on the golden section.

Le Corbusier offered the Modulor to architects as a tool that could help them arrive at proportions that were both poetic and practical. He used the Modulor himself in many of his own buildings, including the Villa Savoye (**5.25**). The layout of the spaces and the size and location of windows are based on the golden section. Le Corbusier called this house a "machine for living in." Basing its proportions on the Modulor guaranteed that the "machine" was appropriately proportioned for its human occupants. Corbusier's Modulor acknowledges that there are no absolutes, only relationships, and that we experience the world in proportion to ourselves.

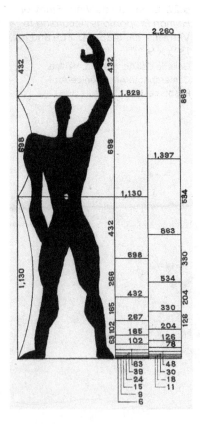

5.24 Le Corbusier. *The Modulor.* 1945.

Courtesy Fondation Le Corbusier. © Fondation Le Corbusier/© F.L.C./ADAGP, Paris/Artists Rights Society (ARS), New York 2019

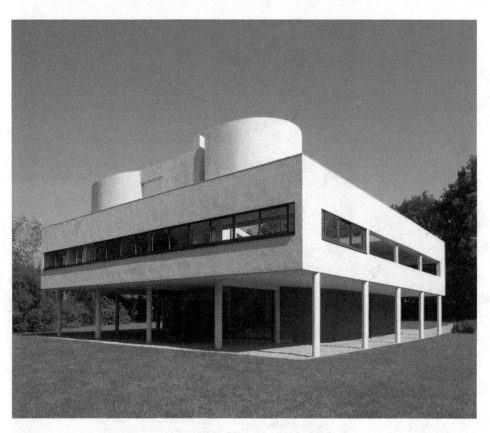

5.25 Le Corbusier. Villa Savoye (Villa les Heures Claires), view from northwest. 1928–31.
Bildarchiv Monheim GmbH/Alamy Stock Photo

Rhythm

Rhythm is based on repetition, and it is a basic part of the world we find our-selves in. We speak of the rhythm of the seasons, which recur in the same pattern every year, the rhythm of the cycles of the moon, the rhythm of waves upon the shore. These natural rhythms measure out the passing of time, organizing our experi-ence of it. To the extent that our arts take place in time, they, too, structure expe-rience through rhythm. Music and dance are the most obvious examples. Poetry, which is recited or read over time, also uses rhythm for structure and expression. Looking at art takes time as well, and rhythm is one of the means that artists use to structure our experience.

Santiago Calatrava's monumental sculpture *Wave* (**5.26**) exhibits rhythm through its construction and its motion. The work is made of 129 bronze bars lined up side by side. This arrangement creates a short, choppy rhythm when seen from the side. When the bars are set in motion, they rise and fall in sequence, and remind us of the rhythm of ocean waves that are constantly rising and falling. The rhythmic motion is reflected in the water below the sculpture, and can even be heard when the sculpture groans as it moves.

Even without motion, any of the visual elements can take on a rhythm within a work through repetition. The sailboat masts in James Abbott McNeill Whistler's

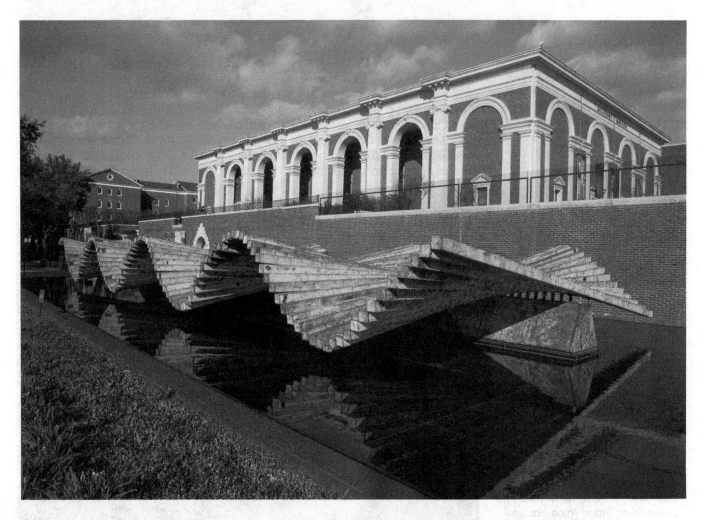

5.26 Santiago Calatrava. *Wave*. 2002. Steel, bronze, nylon, and granite reflecting pool, 79 ¼ × 816 × 312".
Meadows Museum, SMU, Dallas. Gift of the Rosine Foundation Fund of the Communities Foundation of Texas
through the generous vision of Mary Anne and Richard Cree, MM.02.01/© 2019 Artists Rights Society (ARS),
New York/VEGAP, Madrid

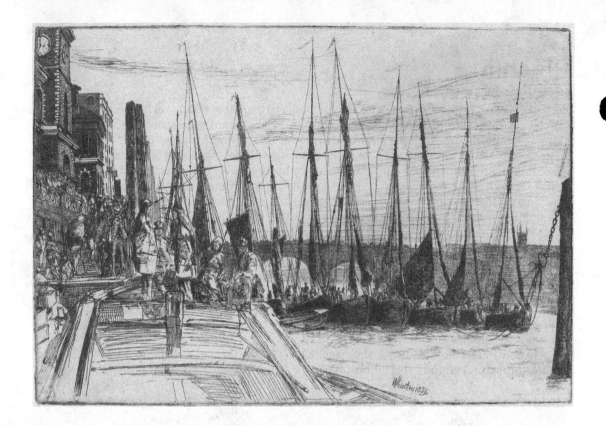

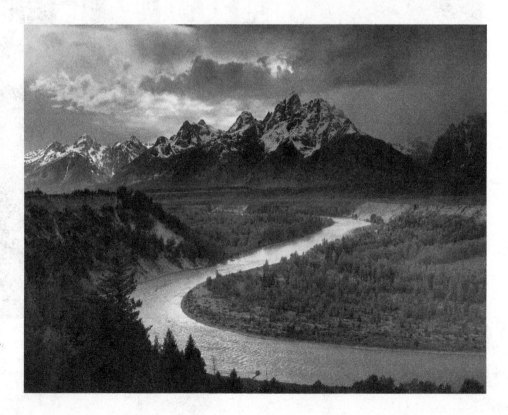

5.27 James Abbott McNeill Whistler. *Billingsgate*. 1859. Etching, 6 × 8 ¾".
Courtesy National Gallery of Art, Washington, D.C./Rosenwald Collection

etching *Billingsgate* (**5.27**) create a rhythm as our eyes move across the image. The line of masts crosses the composition. It is continued by the vertical lines created on the right by a dock post and on the left by the smokestacks and buildings on the shore. This continuous rhythm unifies the image, but the slight variations in the masts' angles—only the center one is perfectly vertical—gives variety to the rhythm.

Ansel Adams's photograph *The Tetons–Snake River, Grand Teton National Park, Wyoming* (**5.28**) also has rhythm, but the artist did not create it. Instead, he selected a place to photograph that already had visual rhythm. The river in the

5.28 Ansel Adams, *The Tetons—Snake River, Grand Teton National Park, Wyoming*. 1942. Gelatin silver print, 15 ½ × 19".
National Archives and Records Administration

Ansel Adams (1902–1984)

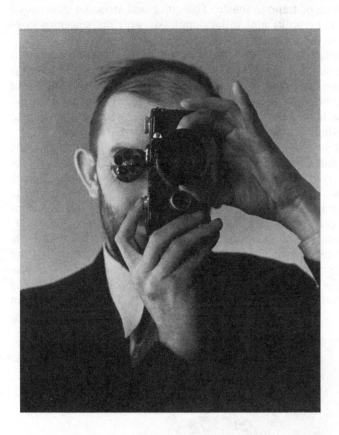

How did Ansel Adams describe the photographer's role? How would you describe his approach to landscape photography? In what ways does nature have an impact on your experience?

This picture was taken by the famous American photographer Edward Weston, who took the picture of a cabbage leaf in Chapter 2 (see 2.9). This photograph is a portrait of the photographer Ansel Adams, who was Weston's friend and colleague. Adams acts as a photographer in this portrait. He looks out from behind his camera and captures what he sees with the click of the shutter. In order to make a good photograph, Adams explained, "[Y]ou begin to *see* the picture—visualize it—and you make it."[1]

Ansel Adams was raised in the San Francisco Bay Area in California, where he developed a deep love for nature. Although he spent much of his life taking landscape photographs, he once explained that he took all kinds of jobs, "from morgue photography and surgical photography . . .to commercial advertisements and architecture."[2] He is best known, however, for his photographs of Yosemite and other sites in the western United States. His goal, as he described it, was helping others to see the beauty of nature through his photographs. He hoped that his pictures would move people to preserve nature for posterity.

Adams's photographs are different from Weston's. He once said of Weston, "[H]is work never moved me, never stirred me to do anything different. . . . I was bothered by [Weston's] emphasis on shape and form."[3] While Weston looked closely at his subjects' forms, Adams's pictures capture the grandeur and drama of the sites he photographed. Weston wanted us to see the form regardless of the subject, while Adams wanted us to see the subject in all its glory.

Composition, shape, and rhythm are essential elements in Adams's work. He looked for the right location from which to take his pictures and positioned himself to capture the site's scale and richness. As he explained, "[T]he external world is nothing but a chaotic infinity of shapes, and the photographer's problem is to isolate the shapes, both for meaning and for their inherent potential to produce forms within the format of the image."[4] He described how learning to see the shapes and rhythms in nature challenges all art students: "[S]eaweed has a shape, the faucet has a shape, the pipe has a shape—think of a square and how the rhythm is—oh boy, they really do begin to see that there *are* relationships of shapes."[5]

The world continues to admire the way Adams captured the relationships of shapes, and he is widely recognized as one of the greatest photographers of the 20th century. His obituary in the *New York Times* in 1984 described it well: "In a career that spanned more than 50 years, Mr. Adams combined a passion for natural landscape, meticulous craftsmanship . . . and a missionary's zeal for his medium to become the most widely exhibited and recognized photographer of his generation."[6]

Edward Weston. *Ansel Adams (After He Got a Contax Camera)*. 1936. Photograph, 4 ⅝ × 3 ¹¹⁄₁₆". Collection Center for Creative Photography, Gift of Ansel and Virginia Adams/Art Resource, New York. © 2019 Center for Creative Photography, Arizona Board of Regents/Artists Rights Society (ARS), New York

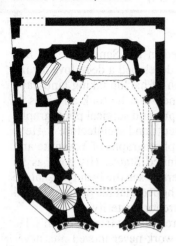

5.29 Plan of San Carlo alle Quattro Fontane, Rome.

foreground repeats a slow, looping movement. It swoops to the left then swings to the right before moving to the left again. The viewer's eye meanders along this easy, soft rhythm. The mountains in the background, on the other hand, have a jagged staccato rhythm like a piece of frenetic music. The quick and irregular alternation of the basic repeating unit of peaks and valleys contrasts with the smoothness of the river, adding variety to the image.

Earlier, we discussed how architects use proportion to create harmonious masses and spatial volumes—the positive and negative elements of a building. Through rhythm, they can articulate those proportions. When we articulate our speech, we take care to pronounce consonants and vowels clearly so that each syllable is distinct. Our goal is to be understood. Similarly, architects use rhythm to divide a building into distinct visual units so that we can grasp its logic.

The Baroque architect Francesco Borromini used rhythm to articulate the interior of the church of San Carlo alle Quattro Fontane in Rome (**5.29**). The floor plan reveals the alternation of projecting and receding elements punctuated by columns attached to the wall. The rhythm defines each part of the church, from the entryway to the side altars and the main altar. The entire church architecture seems to move continuously in and out around the viewer who stands inside.

The exterior face or facade of Borromini's church (**5.30**) continues this rhythmic distinction of visual units. Notice how the edges and the central section of the facade come forward. The areas in between recede away from the street. This projection and recession create a repeating rhythm. They also cause constantly shifting patterns of light and shadow as the sun moves through the sky. The facade's rhythm

5.30 Francesco Borromini. San Carlo alle Quattro Fontane, Rome. 1665–67. Facade.
Scala/Art Resource, NY

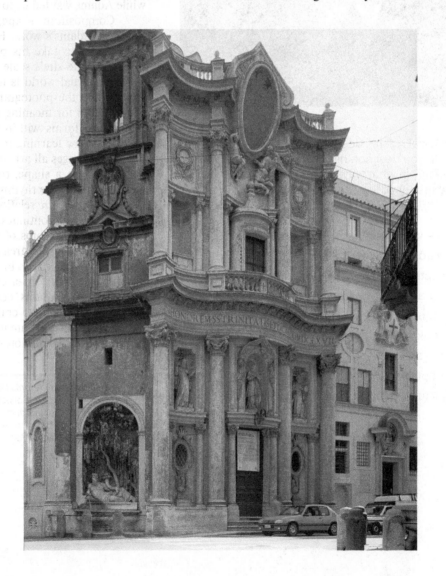

is also established by the repetition of columns separated by niches. The whole surface seems to be in constant, undulating motion, like a ship at sea. This dramatic effect was admired in the 17th century as rhythm and movement became hallmarks of Western architecture.

Elements and Principles: A Summary

In the second chapter of this book, we examined two paintings of the *Adoration of the Shepherds* to explore how form could suggest meaning (see 2.25 and 2.26). This chapter and the preceding one have introduced the vocabulary of formal analysis, the terms that help us see and describe what we see. In the process, we have examined many artworks, each from a particular formal point of view—as an example of line, value, balance, rhythm, and so on. Before leaving this section, we should analyze one work more fully to show how these points of view combine into a more complete way of seeing, and to suggest again how form invites interpretation. The work we will look at is Pablo Picasso's *Girl Before a Mirror* (**5.31**).

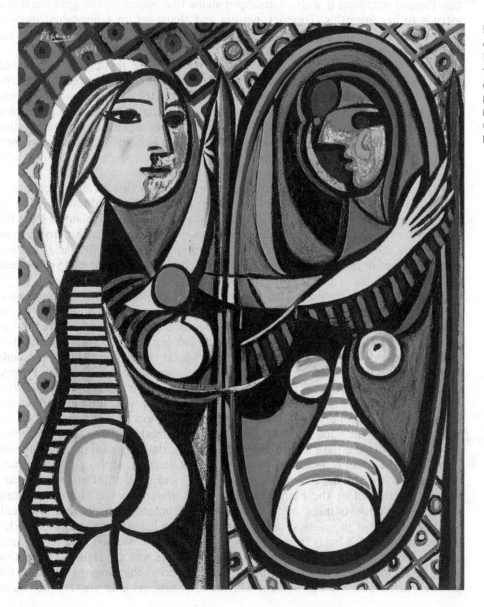

5.31 Pablo Picasso. *Girl Before a Mirror*. 1932. Oil on canvas, 5' 4" × 4' 3 ¼".

The Museum of Modern Art, New York. Gift of Mrs. Simon Guggenheim. Digital image © The Museum of Modern Art/Licensed by SCALA/Art Resource, NY. © 2019 Estate of Pablo Picasso/Artists Rights Society (ARS), New York

Oriented vertically, *Girl Before a Mirror* is over 5 feet in height. The woman and her reflection occupy almost the entire canvas. Thus, she is not miniaturized, as in the illustration in this book, but portrayed larger than life-size. The scale of the painting and of the woman represented in it makes a powerful impression when seen in person. We confront the work on an equal footing as a presence that rises up before us.

The design is based on symmetrical balance, with the woman on the left and her mirror image on the right. The left post of the mirror falls near the vertical axis, dividing the composition in two. The fundamental symmetry draws our attention to the ways in which the two sides are *not* alike, for it sets them in opposition. The unity of the symmetrical balance is contrasted by the variety in what appears on each side of the axis. Indeed, the reflection of the girl's face in the mirror does not double her exactly. Warm colors are reflected as cool colors, and firm shapes become fluid. This alteration of the reflection puts the image in a mysterious, shadowy realm of uncertainty—perhaps the girl's thoughts, perhaps her unconscious, perhaps her soul, perhaps her mortality.

A composition divided so cleanly in two could easily break apart, and Picasso uses several means to unify the two halves. The most important is the girl's gesture as she reaches out to the far edge of the mirror, almost in an embrace. The gesture links the girl and her reflection, and it is so important to the composition that Picasso reinforces it with a red-striped shape that begins on the girl's chest and extends to her fingertips. Together, gesture and shape set up a pendulum motion, and as we look at the painting, our eyes swing rhythmically back and forth from one side to the other.

Overall, the unity of the composition rests on the rhythmical curves and repeating circles of the girl and her reflection, culminating in the great oval of the mirror itself. A second unifying device is the lushly painted wallpaper, which extends across the entire canvas. Its diagonal geometric grid acts as a foil for the sweeping organic curves of the girl, and it is almost as important a presence in the painting as she is. Color unifies the composition as well, for although the colors are brilliantly varied, they fall generally in the same range of intensities and values, with the important exception of the girl herself.

And what of the girl? Picasso directs our attention first of all to her face, a natural focal point. He emphasizes it by painting one half bright yellow and by surrounding her head with an oval of white and green that both isolates it from the busy pattern of the background and provides enough visual weight to balance the form of the mirror. He also modifies its proportions so that her facial features occupy the entire space of her head. With her yellow hair, circular half-yellow face, and white aura, she is like the sun of the painting, its source of light.

The pale violet portion of her face is depicted in profile, gazing at the mirror. With the addition of the yellow portion, she turns her head to look at us—or at Picasso. Cool, pale colors set off by black shapes and lines draw our attention to her body, which is also divided vertically. The left portion is clothed in a striped garment, perhaps a bathing suit; the right portion is nude. The swell of the belly evokes childbearing and the renewal of life. In a remarkable X-ray view, Picasso even paints through her skin to the womb inside, envisioned as another circle. Her biological destiny is emphasized in the mirror image as well, for this part of her body is reflected confidently. Picasso draws our attention to it through an abrupt shift in value—in the dark world of the mirror, the breasts and the belly are white.

Picasso did not have a checklist as he worked, dutifully adding the visual elements in the correct proportions of unity, variety, balance, scale, proportion, and rhythm. His student days were far behind him, and such thinking was by now second nature. But as the numerous reworkings evident in the finished painting show, he changed his mind often and made constant adjustments as he worked. Why? Any number of reasons, probably—because the balance was off, because his eye was not traveling freely over the canvas, because there was too much focus here and not enough there, because the mood of the colors was not right. The painting is the result of all his decisions, a project he stopped at the moment when, as the picture's first viewer, he was content with what he saw. As later viewers, we articulate the elements and principles to make ourselves aware of the dynamic of seeing. With experience, this becomes second nature to us as well.

Notes to the Text

1. "Conversations with Ansel Adams: Oral history transcript, 1972–1975," University of California Bancroft Library, 1978, p. 17.
2. Ibid., p. 104.
3. Ibid., p. 56.
4. Ibid., p. 152.
5. Ibid., p. 367.
6. John Russell, "Ansel Adams, Photographer, Is Dead," *New York Times*, April 24, 1984, available at nytimes.com/1984/04/24/obituaries/ansel-adams-photographer-is-dead.html. Accessed September 27, 2017.

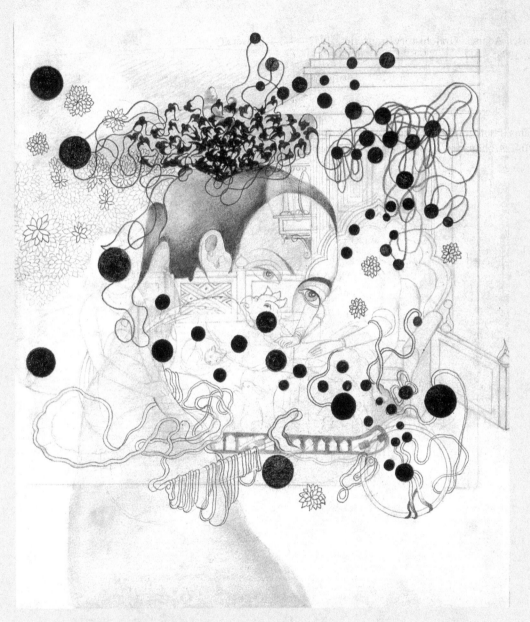

6.1 Shahzia Sikander. *1*, from *51 Ways of Looking* (Group B). 2004. Graphite on paper, 12 × 9".
© Shahzia Sikander. Image courtesy Sikkema Jenkins & Co., New York

PART THREE

Two-Dimensional Media

Chapter 6

Drawing

In this chapter, you will learn to

LO1   identify the various materials used for drawing, and

LO2   discuss the ways in which artists employ paper as a medium.

Everybody draws. We routinely give children drawing materials so that they can entertain and express themselves, and they take to it so naturally that there can scarcely be a person above the age of two who has never made a drawing. A pebble scraped across a flat stone will draw a line. A stick dragged through the snow. The shaft of a feather in smooth, wet sand. Our finger on a fogged-up windowpane.

Even if we have left the habit of drawing behind with our childhood, we retain a familiar connection to it. Perhaps it is this connection that makes drawings by even the most accomplished artists feel somehow not so far removed from our own experience. This is where we overlap.

Shahzia Sikander's drawing was executed in pencil on paper—ordinary materials that most of us have close at hand (**6.1**). Working in a beautifully controlled range of values, the artist created an image of layered images. In the faintest image, the deepest layer, we can make out an architectural setting, a fragment of a South Asian palace. Before it, a figure—male, it seems, although the head and the torso fade away—is seated on an ornate chair. A woman sits on the floor nearby, and between them we can distinguish a curled-up cat, an inquisitive rabbit, and a mythical beast, a griffin. Perhaps these are part of a story she is telling him, like Scheherazade. In the next layer, a woman's head and pale bust command our attention. Her hairstyle suggests that she may be a *gopi*, one of the female cowherds who appear in Hindu mythology as companions and lovers of the god Krishna. In traditional depictions, the *gopis* gather adoringly around the god. The *gopi* here, however, seems to have floated free of the role that the tales assign to her. She rises before us as an individual, a contemplative woman. Like the other figures, though, she is a fragment. She cannot speak. Where her lower face would be, the topmost layer of imagery takes precedence: a system of tangled lines, starburst blossoms, dark circles hung like planets, and a flock of small *gopi* hairdos.

Many older drawings we see today were never intended for exhibition. Preliminary sketches for paintings or sculptures, ideas quickly jotted down for later development, studies that linger on a detail of the visible world (see 1.12), they retain a kind of intimacy that can offer fascinating glimpses into the creative process. Pablo Picasso, mindful of his own legacy, began early on to date and save all his sketches. Thanks to that habit, we have almost a complete visual record of his creative process. Illustrated here is his first sketch for his great antifascist painting *Guernica* (**6.2**; for the completed work see 3.8). Much changed between this first rapidly sketched idea and the final painting, but one essential gesture is already in place: The horror will be revealed to us by the light of a lamp held by a figure leaning out of an upper-story window.

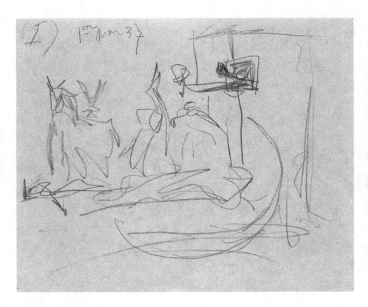

6.2 Pablo Picasso. First composition study for *Guernica*. May 1, 1937. Pencil on blue paper, 8 ¼ × 10 ⅝".
Museo Nacional Centro de Arte Reina Sofia, Madrid. © 2019 Estate of Pablo Picasso/Artists Rights Society (ARS), New York

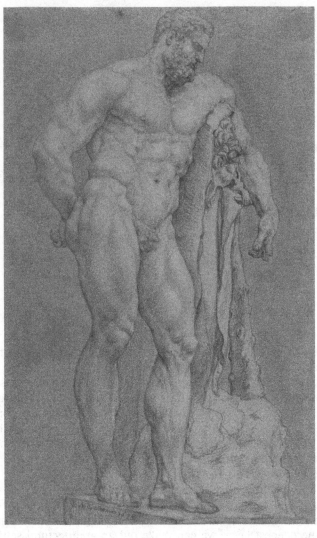

6.3 Peter van Lint. *Farnese Hercules*. 1639. Black chalk heightened with white chalk, on blue paper. Sheet 16 ¾ × 10 ⁷⁄₁₆".
The Metropolitan Museum of Art, New York. The Elisha Whittelsey Collection, The Elisha Whittelsey Fund, 2006/Public Domain

Many artists have traditionally learned by making drawings of other artists' work. They did so to learn how earlier artists made their images, but also to develop their "eye," meaning their taste or preference for the great art of the past. Studying and drawing works from ancient Greece and Rome was standard practice for Western artists from the 15th century until well into the 19th. Like many artists, the Flemish artist Peter van Lint traveled to Italy, where he created a drawing of the famous sculpture known as the *Farnese Hercules* (**6.3**). The sculpture is a Roman copy of a Greek original discovered during excavations of a Roman bath. It depicts the hero Hercules leaning on his club and the skin of the lion he defeated. Van Lint studied the sculpture to learn the style of ancient art. He also used the drawing to develop his own skill in chiaroscuro, and he carefully modeled each muscle to suggest three dimensions in a two-dimensional drawing.

Drawings are not always preliminary steps toward a final work of art in another medium. As Sikander's work shows, drawings can be the final product. This has been true throughout history, even before paper was readily available. Among the oldest representational images we know of are the Paleolithic cave drawings in southern France (see 1.3, 14.1) and in Spain, some engraved on the cave walls with a hard stone, others drawn with a chunk of charcoal. With the development of pottery during the Neolithic era, fired clay became a surface for drawing in many cultures. Later, the Greeks drew on vases, picturing heroes, gods, and common people in red and black designs (see 14.23). The Greeks also drew and wrote on papyrus, a paperlike material developed in ancient Egypt that was made from pressed plant stems. Rivaling papyrus was a later invention, parchment. Made from treated animal skins, it was widely used throughout the Roman Empire and continued as the surface of choice in medieval Europe. The ancient Chinese drew on silk, their special material, and many Chinese artists still do. It is the Chinese, too, who are credited with the invention of paper, which spread rapidly through the Muslim world and into Europe by the 12th century. By 1500 the Western world experienced a boom in drawing that continues to this day.

Before buffaloes were nearly driven to extinction, the native peoples of the American plains used animal hides to make drawings. The subjects were determined by the artist's gender: Women made conceptual drawings of supernatural subjects while men made representational images of heroic deeds. When U.S. policy confined native peoples to reservations during the latter part of the 19th century, some artists turned to common ledger books (**6.4**, and see 3.10) to make their drawings. Working alone or in collaboration, they filled the books' pages with drawings made in pencil, crayon, and paint. These narrative drawings picture battles, hunts, and community rituals in a drawing style characterized by prominent contour lines, flat colors, and limited details of setting or context.

Howling Wolf of the Southern Cheyenne people depicts himself battling a Ute in the drawing seen here. The artist is identified by the pictograph of a howling wolf drawn above his head. He wears his battle regalia and attacks the Ute scout with both a spear and a pistol. The Ute returns fire as he flees on horseback, and bullets whiz past the artist. Howling Wolf drew the image with an ink pen, then colored it with watercolor paint. As with most ledger drawings, figures are presented with a frontal view of the torso and a profile view of the head. Both faces are identical because ledger artists used clothing and accessories to identify a person, adding name pictographs for highly significant subjects. The horse's head is similarly less important than the line and flow of its body in motion.

Today, artists have a wide array of drawing surfaces and materials to choose from. Some materials have their origins in the distant past; others were developed more recently. In this chapter, we examine some of the traditional materials that have been used for drawing, and the effects they can produce. Then we look briefly at how the most common drawing surface, paper, became a medium in its own right.

6.4 Howling Wolf. *Ute Indian.* 1874–75. Pen, ink, and watercolor on ledger paper, 7 ⅞ × 12 ⅜". Allen Memorial Art Museum, Oberlin College, Ohio/Gift of Mrs. Jacob D. Cox/ Bridgeman Images

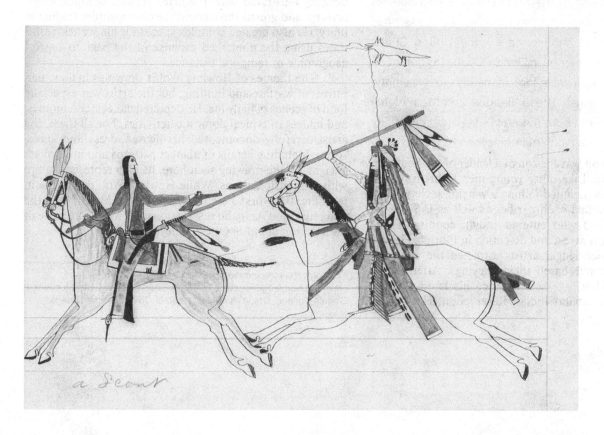

Howling Wolf (1849–1927)

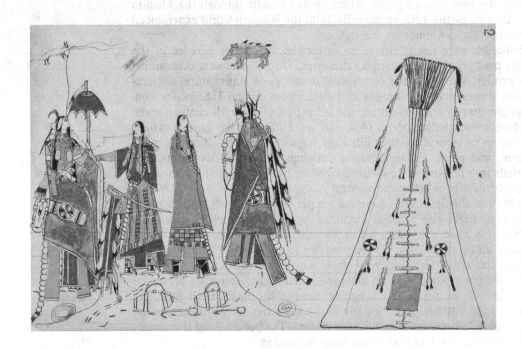

How would you describe Howling Wolf's drawing style? What themes did he represent in his art? How were his ledger drawings received?

The ledger drawing of the artist Howling Wolf and his friend Feathered Bear courting two girls was made while Howling Wolf was imprisoned by the United States government at Fort Marion in Florida. During his detention from 1875 to 1878, Howling Wolf made most of his eighty-six ledger drawings. These images create a highly personal statement about the artist's life and community during a tumultuous moment in American history.

Howling Wolf was the son of a leader of the Southern Cheyenne people. Like other young men in his tribe, his path to manhood included joining a warrior society. With this group, he battled enemy tribes as well as U.S. troops and Anglo settlers who entered Indian country. These activities led to his arrest and detention in Florida. He and the other detainee ledger artists attracted the attention of tourists, who purchased their drawings. After his release in 1878, Howling Wolf rejoined his family on the Cheyenne and Arapaho Indian Reservation. He died in

1927 in a car accident in Houston, Texas, while working for a wild west show.

While Howling Wolf's drawings share many characteristics with other ledger art, he is known for his complex patterning using saturated complementary colors. In the drawing illustrated here, the artist repeats oranges, grays, browns, and greens throughout the composition, leading to unity. He also created complex spaces for his scenes, sometimes using the unmarked expanse of the page to suggest geographic or temporal distance.

The themes of Howling Wolf's drawings include narratives of warfare and hunting, but the artist was especially fond of scenes of daily life. He depicted dances, ceremonies, and images of typical domestic activities. For all these, the artist carefully documented his figures' dress and accessories, including details of blanket patterns and breastplate designs. In the drawing seen here, he also represents a tipi with geometric designs. While Howling Wolf drew little in later life, the works he completed at Fort Marion and the Cheyenne and Arapaho reservation offer a treasure trove of information about Southern Cheyenne life.

Howling Wolf. *Howling Wolf and Feathered Bear*. Pen, ink, and watercolor on ledger paper. 7 ⅞ × 12 ⅜". Allen Memorial Art Museum, Oberlin College, Ohio/Gift of Mrs. Jacob D. Cox/Bridgeman Images

Materials for Drawing

Drawing media can be divided into two broad groups: dry media and liquid media. Dry media are generally applied directly in stick form. As the stick is dragged over a suitably abrasive surface, it leaves particles of itself behind. Liquid media are generally applied with a tool such as a pen or a brush. Although some media are naturally occurring, most of today's media are manufactured, usually by combining powdered **pigment** (coloring material) with a **binder**, a substance that allows it to be shaped into sticks (for dry media) or to be suspended in fluid (for liquid media), and to adhere to the drawing surface.

Dry Media

GRAPHITE   A soft, crystalline form of carbon first discovered in the 16th century, graphite is a naturally occurring drawing medium. Pure, solid graphite need only be mined, then shaped into a convenient form. Dragged across an abrasive surface, it leaves a trail of dark gray particles that have a slight sheen.

Graphite was adopted as a drawing medium soon after its discovery. But pure, solid graphite is rare and precious. (In fact, there is only one known deposit.) More commonly, graphite must be extracted from various ores and purified, resulting in a powder. Toward the end of the 18th century, a technique was discovered for binding powdered graphite with fine clay to make a cylindrical drawing stick. Encased in wood, it became what we know as a pencil, today the most common drawing medium of all.

Varying the percentage of clay in the graphite compound allows manufacturers to produce pencils that range from very hard (lots of clay) to very soft (a minimal amount of clay). The softer the pencil, the darker and richer the line it produces. The harder the pencil, the more pale and silvery the line. In his drawing *Prince Amongst Thieves with Flowers* (**6.5**), Chris Ofili used a comparatively soft pencil for

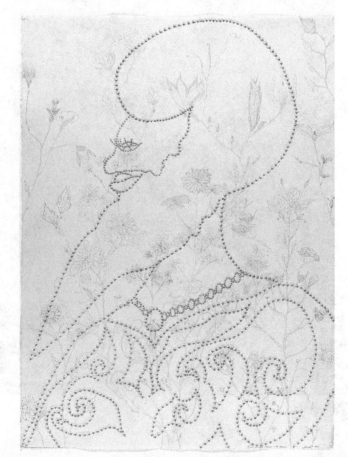

6.5 Chris Ofili. *Prince Amongst Thieves with Flowers*. 1999. Pencil on paper, 29 ¾ × 22 ¼".
The Museum of Modern Art, New York. Gift of David Teiger and the Friends of Contemporary Drawing, 393.1999. Digital image © The Museum of Modern Art/Licensed by SCALA/Art Resource, NY. Courtesy the Artist, Victoria Miro, London/Venice © Chris Ofili

the image of the bearded man and a harder pencil for the pale but still precise flowers in the background. From a standard viewing distance, the lines that define the figure seem to be made of dots. But as the viewer draws closer, the dots reveal themselves to be tiny heads, each sporting an afro, a black hairstyle popular during the 1970s. A British artist of African ancestry, Ofili often uses imagery associated with the sense of black identity that emerged during the 1960s and 1970s, treating it with a complicated mixture of nostalgia, irony, affection, and respect.

METALPOINT **Metalpoint**, the ancestor of the graphite pencil, is an old technique that was especially popular during the Renaissance. Few artists use it now, because it is not very forgiving of mistakes or indecision. Once put down, the lines cannot easily be changed or erased. The drawing medium is a thin wire made of a relatively soft metal such as silver, set in a holder for convenience. The drawing surface must be prepared by covering it with a **ground**, a preliminary coating of paint. Traditional metalpoint ground recipes call for a mixture of bone ash, glue, and white pigment in water. As the point of the wire is drawn across the dried ground, it leaves behind a thin trail of metal particles that soon tarnish to a pale gray.

Metalpoint drawings are characterized by a fine, delicate line of uniform width. Making thrifty use of a single sheet of paper, Filippino Lippi drew two figure studies in metalpoint on a pale pink ground, building up the areas of shadow with fine hatching and cross-hatching, then delicately painting in highlights in white (**6.6**). Hatching is most visible on the right arm of the nude figure, while a grid of

6.6 Filippino Lippi. *Figure Studies: Standing Nude and Seated Man Reading*. ca. 1480. Metalpoint, highlighted with white gouache, on pale pink prepared paper, 9 ⅝ × 8 ½".

The Metropolitan Museum of Art, New York. Harris Brisbane Dick Fund, 1936, 36.101.1. Image © The Metropolitan Museum of Art

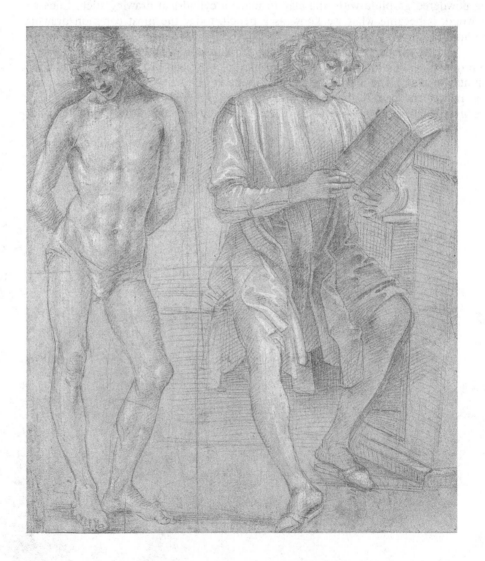

cross-hatched lines can be seen clearly on the torso of the clothed man. The models were probably workshop apprentices. Renaissance apprentices often posed for one another and for the master, and thus found their way into innumerable paintings. The figure on the left, for example, may well have been incorporated into a painting as Saint Sebastian, who was typically depicted with his arms bound and wearing only a loincloth.

CHARCOAL   Charcoal is charred wood. Techniques for manufacturing it have been known since ancient times. The best-quality artist's charcoal is made from special vine or willow twigs, slowly heated in an airtight chamber until only sticks of carbon remain—black, brittle, and featherlight. Natural charcoal creates a soft, scattered line that smudges easily and can be erased with a few flicks of a cloth. For denser, more durable, or more detailed work, sticks of compressed charcoal are available, as are charcoal pencils made along the same lines as graphite pencils. Yvonne Jacquette's *Three Mile Island, Night I* illustrates well the tonal range of charcoal, deepening from sketchy, pale gray between the buildings to thick, velvety black for the structures and water (**6.7**). The artist's angled cross-hatches help to model the round reactors. Jacquette has made a specialty out of depicting landscape as seen from an airplane. With the popularization of air travel during the second half of the 20th century, this view became common. Although we might consider it fundamental to our modern experience of the world, it has rarely been treated in art.

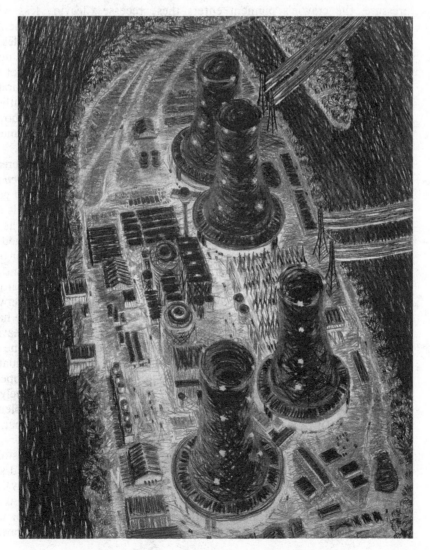

6.7 Yvonne Jacquette. *Three Mile Island, Night I*. 1982. Charcoal on laminated tracing paper, 4' 13⁄16" × 3' 2".
Hirshhorn Museum and Sculpture Garden, Washington, D.C. HMSG 83.153. Courtesy DC Moore Gallery, New York, NY

CRAYON, PASTEL, AND CHALK The dry media we have discussed so far—graphite, metalpoint, and charcoal—allow artists to work with a range of values on the gray scale. With crayon, pastel, and chalk, a full range of colors becomes available.

Crayons and pastels are made of powdered pigments, the same as those used to make paints, mixed with a binder. For crayons, the binder is a greasy or waxy substance. The coloring crayons we give to children, for example, use a wax binder. Finer, denser, more brilliant versions of these crayons have been developed for artists. Another children's product, a crayon using a binder of wax and oil, has also inspired an artist-quality equivalent. Known somewhat confusingly as oil pastels, they are as brilliant as artist-quality wax crayons but with a creamier consistency that facilitates blending. Crayons made with waxy or greasy binders, in contrast, tend to favor discrete strokes that can be layered but not blended.

Perhaps the most well-known artist's crayon is the conté crayon. Developed in France at the turn of the 19th century, it consists of compressed pigment compounded with clay and a small amount of greasy binder. Initially conceived as a substitute for natural black and red chalks (discussed later), conté crayons have since become available in a full range of colors.

One artist who comes readily to mind in discussing conté crayon drawings is Georges Seurat. In Chapter 4, we looked at Seurat's painting technique, pointillism, in which tiny dots of color are massed together to build form. Seurat also did many drawings. By working in conté crayon on rough-textured paper, he could approximate the effect of color dots in paint. The crayon clings to the raised portion of the paper surface, leaving white paper visible in the recessed areas. With more pressure, the crayon's pigment enters these recesses, leaving less white page. *Café-concert* is one of several drawings Seurat made of an entertainment that was all the rage in his day (**6.8**). People of all classes flocked to the cafés and their vibrant nightlife. Artists went as well, attracted by the effects of the lighting, the colorful personalities of the performers, and the fascinating social mix of the crowd. By simplifying his forms and downplaying any sense of motion, Seurat tends to bring out the eerie side of almost any situation. Here, the distant, brightly lit female performer is watched rather spookily by an impassive audience of bowler-hatted men. Her figure was made by lightly drawing on the paper, while the men's silhouettes needed a heavier application of the crayon.

Another artist attracted to the café-concerts was Edgar Degas. Whereas Seurat's drawing was made from the back of the hall, Degas's *The Singer in Green* (**6.9**) puts us right on stage next to the performer, who touches her shoulder in a gesture that Degas borrowed from one of his favorite café singers. Degas created his drawing in **pastel**. Pastel consists of pigment bound with a nongreasy binder such as a solution of gum arabic or gum tragacanth (natural gums made from hardened sap) and water. The principle is simple enough that artists can manufacture their own if they choose, mixing pigment and binder into a doughy paste, then rolling the paste into sticks and letting it dry. Available in a full range of colors and several degrees of hardness, pastel is often considered a borderline medium, somewhere between painting and drawing. Artists favor soft pastels for most work, reserving the harder ones for special effects or details. Because they are bound so lightly, pastels leave a velvety line of almost pure pigment. They can be easily blended by blurring one color into another, obliterating individual strokes and creating smoothly graduated tones. Here, Degas has blended the tones that model the girl's face and upper torso as she is lit from below by the footlights. Her dress is treated more freely, with the individual strokes still apparent. The background is suggested through blended earth tones and roughly applied blue-greens that show the texture of the paper, flattening the space of the image.

For geologists, "chalk" is the name for a kind of soft, white limestone. In art, the word has been used less precisely to name three soft, finely textured stones that can be used for drawing: black chalk (a composite of carbon and clay), red chalk (iron oxide and clay), and white chalk (calcite or calcium carbonate). Like graphite, these stones need only be mined and then cut into convenient sizes for use. Seurat used discrete touches of white chalk to heighten his conté crayon drawing of the

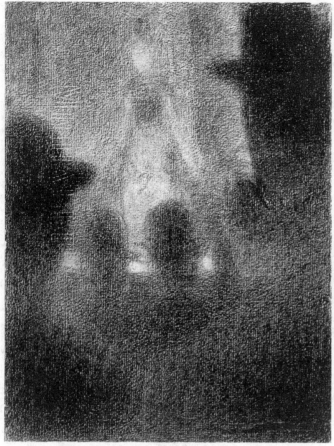

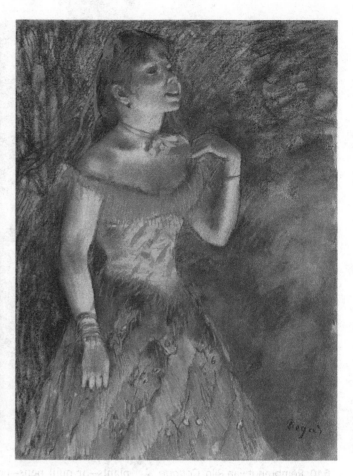

6.8 Georges Seurat. *Café-concert*. ca. 1887. Conté crayon heightened with white chalk, 12 ⁵⁄₁₆ × 9 ¼".
© Cleveland Museum of Art, Ohio/Leonard C. Hanna, Jr. Fund/ Bridgeman Images

6.9 Edgar Degas. *The Singer in Green*. ca. 1884. Pastel on light blue laid paper, 23 ¾ × 18 ¼".
The Metropolitan Museum of Art, New York. Bequest of Stephen C. Clark, 1960, 61.101.7

Café-concert (see 6.8). Natural chalks have largely been replaced today by conté crayons and pastels, although they are still available to artists who seek them out.

Liquid Media

PEN AND INK   Drawing inks generally consist of ultrafine particles of pigment suspended in water. A binder such as gum arabic is added to hold the particles in suspension and help them adhere to the drawing surface. Inks today are available in a range of colors. Historically, however, black and brown inks have predominated, manufactured from a great variety of ingenious recipes since at least the 4th century B.C.E.

There are endless ways to get ink onto paper. You could soak a bit of sponge with it and swipe a drawing onto the page. You could use your fingertips, or a twig. But if you want a controlled, sustained, flexible line, you'll reach for a brush or a pen. Traditional artist's pens are made to be dipped in ink, then set to paper. Depending on the qualities of the nib—the part of a pen that conveys ink to the drawing surface—the line a pen makes may be thick or thin, even in width or variable, stubby and coarse or smooth and flowing.

Today most pen nibs are made of metal, but this is a comparatively recent innovation, dating only from the second half of the 19th century. Before then, artists generally used either reed pens—pens cut from the hollow stems of certain

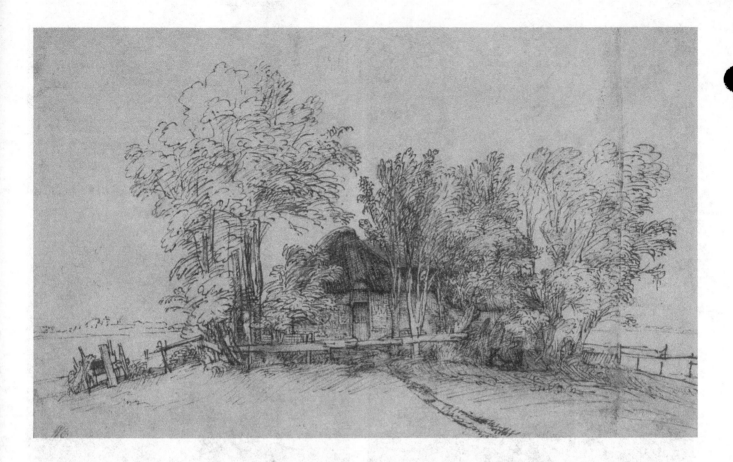

6.10 Rembrandt van Rijn. *Cottage among Trees*. 1648–50. Pen and brown ink, brush and brown wash, on paper washed with brown, 6 ¾ × 10 ⅞".
The Metropolitan Museum of Art, New York. H. O. Havemeyer Collection, Bequest of Mrs. H. O. Havemeyer, 1929, 29.100.939

plants—or quill pens—pens cut from the hollow shafts of the wing feathers of large birds. Both reed and quill pens respond sensitively to shifts in pressure, lending themselves naturally to the sort of varied, gestural lines we see in Rembrandt van Rijn's *Cottage among Trees* (**6.10**). Rembrandt applied more pressure to draw the thick lines of the fence and less for the thin, wispy lines describing the far distance. One of the greatest draftsmen who ever lived, Rembrandt made thousands of drawings over the course of his lifetime. Many record ideas for paintings or prints, but many more are simply drawings done for the pleasure of drawing.

The wind-tossed foliage of the asymmetrically balanced trees shows Rembrandt's virtuosity at its most rapid, loose, and effortless. The solid volumes of the cottage were more slowly and methodically built up with hatches and cross-hatches. Here and there, Rembrandt used a **wash**—ink diluted with water and applied with a brush—to give greater solidity to the cottage and to soften the shadows beneath the trees. Before beginning his drawing, he prepared the paper by applying an allover wash of pale brown. By tinting the paper, Rembrandt lowered the contrast between the dark ink and the ground, creating a more atmospheric, harmonious, and unified image.

A more recently developed type of ink pen is the rapidograph, a metal-tipped instrument that channels a reservoir of ink into a fine, even, unvarying line. Compared with the line traced by a reed or quill pen, a line drawn with a rapidograph can seem mechanical and impersonal. In fact, the rapidograph was invented as a tool for technical drawing, such as the drawings that illustrate architectural systems in Chapter 13. Before the advent of the computer, architects often used the rapidograph to draw precise images of buildings they were planning.

Julie Mehretu deliberately evokes the association of the rapidograph with architecture in drawings such as the untitled example here (**6.11**). Composed in an inverted triangle or cone, fragments of urban plans along with details of buildings and infrastructure seem caught up in an explosive whirlwind. The architectural elements' impersonal and mechanical lines are typical of rapidograph drawings. Mehretu's works thrive on the contrast between their seemingly apocalyptic subject

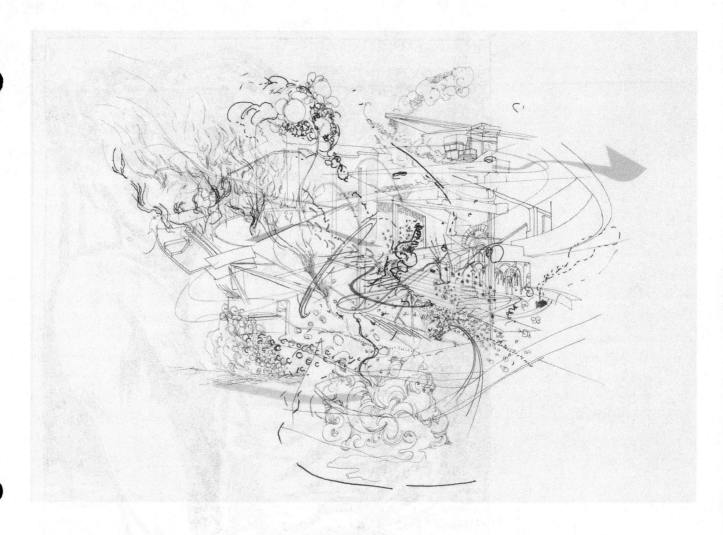

matter and their cool, detached style, a style in which the even line of the rapido-graph plays an important role. Mehretu makes her drawings on translucent Mylar, a polyester film used in architectural drafting. Often, as in the drawing here, she works on multiple, superimposed sheets of Mylar, so that elements placed on an underlayer appear as though seen through a fog.

6.11 Julie Mehretu. *Untitled*. 2001. Ink, colored pencil, and cut paper on Mylar, 21 ½ × 27 ⅜". Seattle Art Museum, Gift of the Contemporary Art Project, Seattle, 2002.30. Courtesy Marian Goodman Gallery, New York. © Julie Mehretu

BRUSH AND INK The soft and supple brushes used for watercolor can also be used with ink. In *No Title (Not a single . . .)*, Raymond Pettibon used a fine brush to draw the slender, even lines of the text at the upper left (**6.12**). He used a larger brush and a looser, more varied stroke to create contour lines and the hatches that model the figures. These lines show quite clearly that they were made by a brush, tapering at both ends and swelling in the middle. The text of Pettibon's drawing is taken from an 18th-century novel by Laurence Sterne that relates an anecdote that ultimately reaches back to a 2nd-century writer called Lucian of Samosata. In an essay, Lucian recounts the strange tale of the ancient Greek town of Abdera, whose citizens fell under the spell of a play in which the hero pleads with Cupid, the god of love. The next day, the hero's speech was on every man's lips; for weeks afterward, men spoke only of love. "Not a single armorer had a heart to forge one instrument of death," Sterne writes in his retelling. "Friendship and Virtue met together and kiss'd each other in the street—the golden age returned." Pettibon juxtaposes a phrase from this ancient tale with an ambiguous image from our own day and age. The nature of the encounter between the two men is far from clear. If it is amorous, it is also furtive and fearful.

The concept of using a brush for drawing shows how difficult it can be to define where drawing leaves off and painting begins. We tend to classify Pettibon's

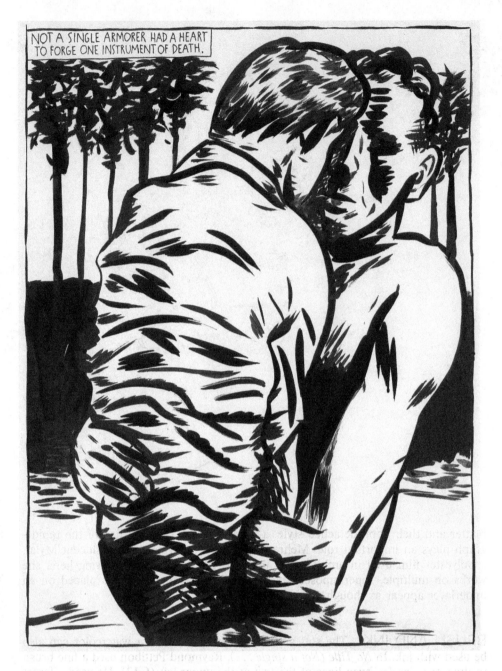

NOT A SINGLE ARMORER HAD A HEART TO FORGE ONE INSTRUMENT OF DEATH.

6.12 Raymond Pettibon. *No Title (Not a single. . .).* 1990. Brush, pen and ink on paper, 23 ½ × 18".
The Museum of Modern Art, New York. Gift of the Friends of Contemporary Drawing. 249.2000. Digital Image © The Museum of Modern Art/Licensed by SCALA/Art Resource, NY Courtesy the artist, David Zwirner, New York/London and Regen Projects, Los Angeles

work as a drawing because it was created on paper, is in black and white, and is largely linear in character—that is, Pettibon used the brush largely to make lines. Taken together, these characteristics are more closely associated with the Western tradition of drawing than with painting. But if we shift our focus to China or Japan, we find a long tradition of works made with brush and black ink on paper, often linear in character, which by custom we call paintings. Turn back, for example, to Shen Zhou's *Autumn Colors among Streams and Mountains* (see 4.50) or ahead to Ni Zan's *Rongxi Studio* (see 19.23). Both were created with brush and ink on paper, and both are primarily linear. Yet within the cultural traditions of East Asia, both are clearly associated with the practice of painting.

Drawing and Beyond: Paper as a Medium

Our word "paper" is derived from the Latin word *papyrus*, which the ancient Romans used to designate both a plant that grew along the banks of the Nile River and the writing material that the ancient Egyptians made from it. Paper as we know it today—wool or plant fibers, beaten to a pulp, mixed with water, then spread in a thin layer over a fine mesh surface and left to dry—may have reminded later Europeans of Egyptian papyrus, but in fact it was invented in China. By the second century B.C.E. Buddhist monks spread news of the paper-making technique across Asia as they traveled, eventually reaching the Muslim world in the 8th century. Europeans learned paper-making from Muslim neighbors, and by the 13th century paper was being manufactured in the West.

For centuries an artisanal product, made by hand one sheet at a time, paper began to be produced by machine during the 19th century. Instead of individual sheets, machines manufactured paper in continuous rolls more than 12 feet wide at a rate of hundreds of feet per minute. Printing, too, became industrialized, with steam-driven rotary printers capable of turning out millions of pages per day. By the early 20th century, paper had become the ubiquitous material we know today. In the form of newspapers, magazines, advertising posters, and other products, it flooded daily life with printed words and images.

In 1912, this new visual reality found its way into art in a revolutionary way: not through representation, but literally. The first step was taken by Picasso, who pasted a bit of patterned oilcloth onto a painting of a still life. But it was Picasso's friend Georges Braque who later that year began to experiment in earnest with bringing pieces of industrially printed paper directly into his drawings (**6.13**). Here, rectangular shapes sliced from a newspaper and from a roll of imitation-wood-grain

6.13 Georges Braque. *Still Life on Table: "Gillette."* 1914. Charcoal, pasted paper, and gouache, 18 ⅞ × 24 ⅜".
Musée National d'Art Moderne, Centre Georges Pompidou, Paris. © CNAC/MNAM/Dist. RMN-Grand Palais/Art Resource, NY © 2019 Artists Rights Society (ARS), New York/ADAGP, Paris

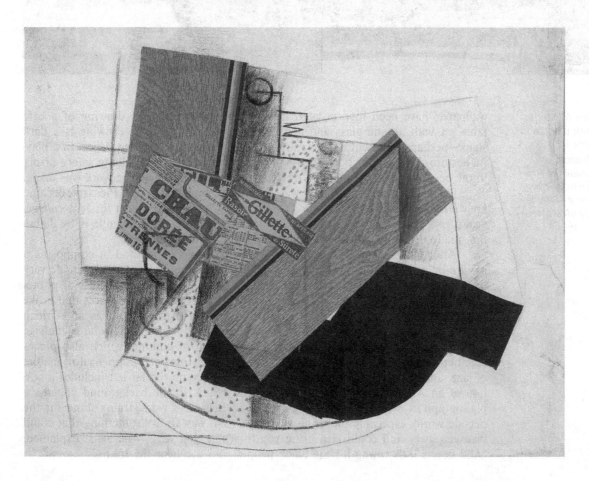

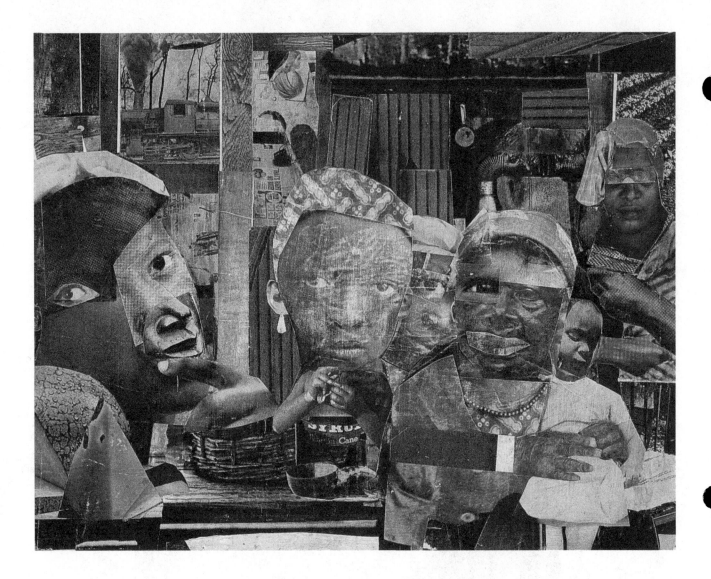

6.14 Romare Bearden. *Mysteries.* 1964. Collage, polymer paint, and pencil on board, 11 ¼ × 14 ¼".
Museum of Fine Arts, Boston. Photograph © 2015 Museum of Fine Arts, Boston, Ellen Kelleran Gardner Fund 1971. 63. Art © Romare Bearden Foundation/Licensed by VAGA, New York, NY

wallpaper have been incorporated into an abstracted charcoal drawing of a café table set with a wine glass and a bottle. Also pasted onto the drawing is a dark shape—perhaps representing a shadow—cut from a piece of painted paper. In a playful gesture, Braque included a razor-shaped advertisement for Gillette safety razors in the center of the composition, drawing our attention to how the work was made.

Braque's invention, which was taken up immediately by Picasso, became known as *papier collé*, French for "pasted paper." A broader term for it is *collage*, again from the French for "pasting" or "gluing." Whereas papier collé is by definition made of paper, **collage** does not imply any specific materials.

After Picasso and Braque, many artists adopted this method of composing a picture by gathering bits and pieces from various sources. An artist who made very personal use of collage was Romare Bearden. Pieced together from bits of photographic magazine illustrations, *Mysteries* (**6.14**) is one of a series of works that evoke the texture of everyday life as Bearden had known it growing up as an African American in rural North Carolina. In Bearden's hands, the technique of collage alludes both to the African-American folk tradition of quilting, which also pieces together a whole from many fragments, and to the rhythms and improvisatory nature of jazz, another art form with African roots. The face on the far left includes a portion of an African sculpture (the mouth and nose). In the background appears a photograph of a train. A recurring symbol in Bearden's work, trains stand for the outside world, especially the white world. "A train was always something that could take you away and could also bring you to where you were," the artist explained. "And in the little towns it's the black people who live near the trains."[1]

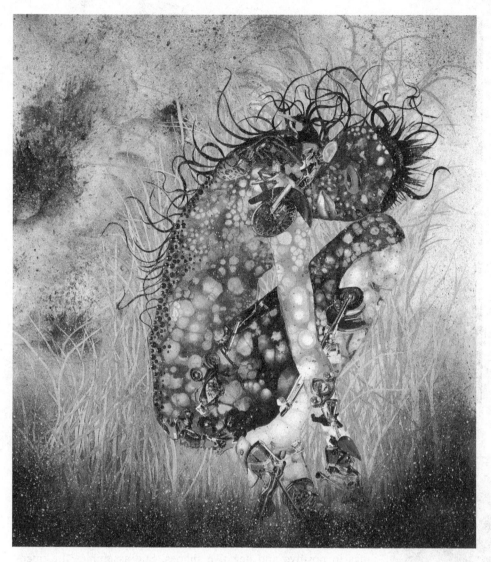

6.15 Wangechi Mutu. *Hide and Seek, Kill or Speak*. 2004. Paint, ink, collage, and mixed media on Mylar, 48 × 42".
Photo Gene Ogami. Courtesy of the artist and Susanne Vielmetter Los Angeles Projects

The Kenyan-born artist Wangechi Mutu uses collage to link her work to the larger world of photographic images that circulate in media such as fashion magazines and *National Geographic*. *Hide and Seek, Kill or Speak* depicts a woman crouching in the African grasslands (**6.15**). Her hair writhes down the length of her spine like a mane, suggesting that in some way she is an animal. Her body is spotted and marbled, evoking expensive designer fabrics but also camouflage or disease. Collaged elements cut from photographs of a motorcycle transform her feet into high-heeled machines and her forearms and hands into mechanical extensions. Her lips, eyes, and ear are cut from photographs as well. The title of the work evokes the deadly conflicts that have so often erupted in African societies. (The splattered gray in the background might indicate an explosion.) Yet the image of the woman is disturbingly ambiguous, made of clashing signs of glamour and violence, danger and desire. The different spatial systems from the collaged photographs—some are flat while others suggest three dimensions—also lend an air of uneasiness to the image.

In *Untitled (cut-out 4)* Mona Hatoum also relies on clashing signs, this time of innocence and experience (**6.16**). Here, too, space is flattened and filled with negative shapes. Silhouettes of two men with guns confront their mirror image again and again. Naively stylized starbursts stand in for exploding grenades or bombs. Two medallions that look like blossoms turn out to have skulls for petals. Delicate, miniaturized, decorative, and lethal, the scenes were made from a single sheet of tissue paper, folded, cut, and opened up—the technique we teach to children so they can delight in making paper snowflakes or chains of people holding hands.

6.16 Mona Hatoum. *Untitled (cut-out 4)*. 2009. Tissue paper, 10 ⅝ × 13 ⅛".
Courtesy Galerie Chantal Crousel. Photo Florian Kleinefenn. Art © Mona Hatoum

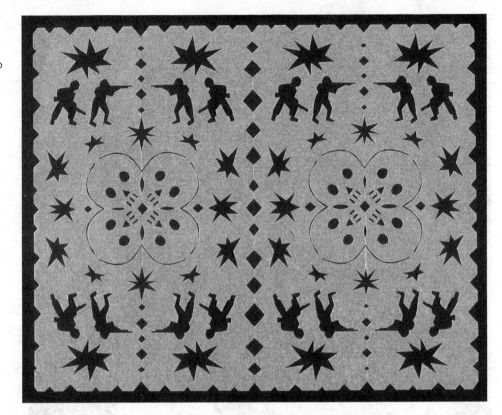

6.17 Mia Pearlman. *Inrush*. Installation at the Museum of Arts and Design, New York, October 7, 2009–April 4, 2010. Paper, India ink, paper clips, tacks, 16 × 5 × 4'.
© Mia Pearlman

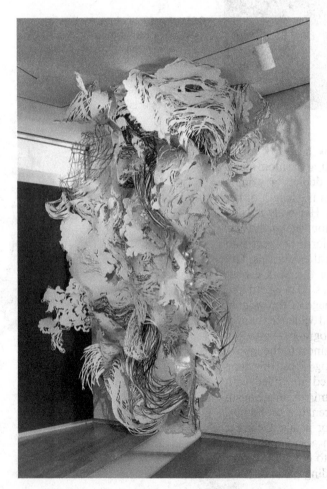

Paper's flatness is challenged by Mia Pearlman, who takes paper into the realm of sculpture. She uses paper to make site-specific installations such as *Inrush* (**6.17**). We can think of Pearlman's installations as exploded drawings. She begins by making line drawings in brush and ink on large rolls of paper. Then she cuts out selected areas to make versions of the drawings in positive and negative shapes. She assembles the open-work drawings on site to create delicate yet turbulent sculptural forms, often setting them in front of a window so they seem lit from within. For the artist, "these drawings and their shadows capture a weightless world in flux, frozen in time, tottering on the brink of being and not being."[2] Easily available, inexpensive, lightweight, and ubiquitous, paper has grown from a self-effacing support for drawings to take on a starring role.

Notes to the Text

1. Quoted in Sharon F. Patton, *African-American Art* (Oxford: Oxford University Press, 1998), p. 188.
2. Taken from the artist's statement in *Slash: Paper Under the Knife* (New York: Museum of Arts and Design, 2009), p. 172.

Chapter 7
Painting

In this chapter, you will learn to

LO1   describe the ancient technique of painting in encaustic,

LO2   identify the advantages and disadvantages of the wall-painting technique of fresco,

LO3   compare works created with tempera dating from the Renaissance and the 20th century,

LO4   discuss the unique characteristics of oil paints,

LO5   distinguish between pastel, watercolor, gouache, and other similar media,

LO6   explain the benefits introduced with the invention of modern acrylic paints,

LO7   note how artists have exploited paint and painting beyond traditional practices,

LO8   summarize the new territory of post-Internet art, and

LO9   outline the technical and creative possibilities of working with mosaic and tapestry.

To the Muslim ruler Akbar, writing in the 16th century, it seemed that painters had a unique appreciation of the divine, for "in sketching anything that has life . . . [a painter] must come to feel that he cannot bestow individuality upon his work, and is thus forced to think of God, the Giver of Life, and will thus increase his knowledge." In the opinion of Zhang Yanyuan, a Chinese painter and scholar who lived some seven centuries earlier, painting existed "to enlighten ethics, improve human relationships, divine the changes of nature, and explore hidden truths." Leonardo da Vinci proudly claimed that "painting embraces and contains within itself all things produced by nature," and for the 17th-century Spanish playwright Pedro Calderón de la Barca, painting was "the sum of all arts . . . the principal art, which encompasses all the others."[1]

Clearly, painting has inspired extravagant admiration in cultures where it is practiced. Even today, if you ask ten people to envision a work of art, nine of them are likely to imagine a painting. But what is a painting, exactly? What is it made of, and how? This chapter examines some of the standard media and techniques that painters have used across the centuries. We begin with some basic concepts and vocabulary.

Paint is made of **pigment**, powdered color, compounded with a **medium** or **vehicle**, a liquid that holds the particles of pigment together without dissolving them. The vehicle generally acts as or includes a **binder**, an ingredient that ensures that the paint, even when diluted and spread thinly, will adhere to the surface. Without a binder, pigments would simply powder off as the paint dried.

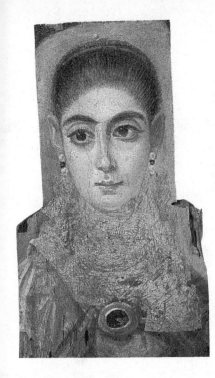

7.1 *Young Woman with a Gold Pectoral*, from Fayum. 100–50 C.E. Encaustic on wood, height 12 ⅝". Musée du Louvre, Paris. Erich Lessing/Art Resource, NY

Artist's paints are generally made to a pastelike consistency and must be diluted to be brushed freely. Aqueous media can be diluted with water. **Watercolors** are an example of an aqueous medium. Nonaqueous media require some other diluent. Oil paints are an example of a nonaqueous medium; these can be diluted with turpentine or mineral spirits. Paints are applied to a **support**, which is the canvas, paper, wood panel, wall, or other surface on which the artist works. The support may be prepared to receive paint with a **ground** or **primer**, a preliminary coating.

Some pigments and binders have been known since ancient times. Others have been developed only recently. Two techniques perfected in the ancient world that are still in use today are encaustic and fresco, and we begin our discussion with them.

Encaustic

Encaustic paints consist of pigment mixed with wax and resin. When the colors are heated, the wax melts and the paint can be brushed easily. When the wax cools, the paint hardens. After the painting is completed, there may be a final "burning in" as a heat source is passed close to the surface of the painting to fuse the colors.

Literary sources tell us that encaustic was an important technique in ancient Greece. (The word *encaustic* comes from the Greek for "burning in.") The earliest encaustic paintings to have survived, however, are funeral portraits created during the first centuries of our era in Egypt, which was then under Roman rule (**7.1**). Portraits such as this were set into the casings of mummified bodies to identify and memorialize the dead (see 14.34). The saturated colors of this painting, almost as fresh as the day they were set down, testify to the permanence of encaustic. The modeling that defines the shape of the face—the shadows to either side of the nose and the brilliantly lit tip that make this feature seem three dimensional—makes the portrait lifelike even if its subject was not alive.

The technique of encaustic was forgotten within a few centuries after the fall of the Roman Empire, but it was redeveloped during the 19th century, partly in response to the discovery of the Roman-Egyptian portraits. One of the foremost contemporary artists to have experimented with encaustic is Jasper Johns (**7.2**). *Numbers in Color* is painted in encaustic over a collage of paper on canvas. Encaustic allowed Johns to build up a richly textured paint surface. (Think of candle drippings.) Moreover, wax will not harm the paper over time as oil paint would.

Fresco

With **fresco**, pigments are mixed with water and applied to a plaster support, usually a wall or ceiling coated in plaster. The plaster may be dry, in which case the technique is known as *fresco secco*, Italian for "dry fresco." But most often when speaking about fresco, we mean *buon fresco*, "true fresco," in which paint made simply of pigment and water is applied to wet lime plaster. As the plaster dries, the lime undergoes a chemical transformation and acts as a binder, fusing the pigment with the plaster surface.

Fresco is above all a wall-painting technique, and it has been used for large-scale murals since ancient times. Probably no other painting medium requires such careful planning and such hard physical labor. The plaster can be painted only when it has the proper degree of dampness; therefore, the artist must plan each day's work and spread plaster only in the area that can be painted in one session. (Michelangelo could cover about one square yard of wall or ceiling in a day.) Work may be guided by a full-size drawing of the entire project, called a **cartoon**. Once the cartoon is finalized, its contour lines are perforated with pinprick-size holes. The drawing is transferred to the prepared surface by placing a portion of the

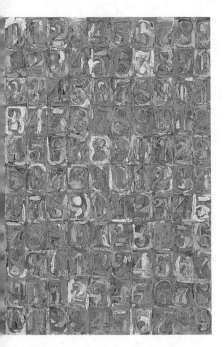

7.2 Jasper Johns. *Numbers in Color*. 1958–59. Encaustic and collage on canvas, 5' 6 ½" × 4' 1 ½". Albright-Knox Art Gallery, Buffalo, New York. Gift of Seymour H. Knox, Jr., 1959. Albright Knox Art Gallery/Art Resource, NY. Art © Jasper Johns/Licensed by VAGA, New York, NY

cartoon over the damp plaster and rubbing pigment through the holes. The cartoon is then removed, leaving dotted lines on the plaster surface. With a brush dipped in paint, the artist "connects the dots" to re-create the drawing, then the work of painting begins.

There is nothing tentative about fresco. Whereas in some media the artist can experiment, try out forms, and then paint over them to make corrections, in fresco every touch of the brush is a commitment. The only way an artist can correct mistakes or change the forms is to let the plaster dry, chip it away, and start all over again.

Frescoes have survived to the present day from the civilizations of the ancient Mediterranean (see 14.31), from China and India, and from the early civilizations of Mexico. Among the most spectacular in Western art are the magnificent frescoes of the Italian Renaissance.

While Michelangelo was at work on the frescoes of the Sistine Chapel ceiling (see 16.9), Pope Julius II asked Raphael to decorate the walls of several rooms in the Vatican Palace. Raphael's fresco for the end wall of the Stanza della Segnatura, a room that may have been the Pope's library, is considered by many to embody the ideas of Renaissance art. It is called *The School of Athens* (**7.3**) and depicts the Greek philosophers Plato and Aristotle at the center of a symmetrical composition. They and their followers and students are framed by the arch. The "school" in question means the two schools of philosophy represented by these two Classical thinkers—Plato's the more abstract and metaphysical, Aristotle's the more earthly and physical.

Everything about Raphael's composition celebrates the Renaissance ideals of perfection, beauty, naturalistic representation, balance, order, and noble principles. The towering architectural setting is drawn in linear perspective with the vanishing

7.3 Raphael. *The School of Athens.* 1510–11. Fresco, 26 × 18'.
Stanza della Segnatura, Vatican, Rome.
Scala/Art Resource, NY

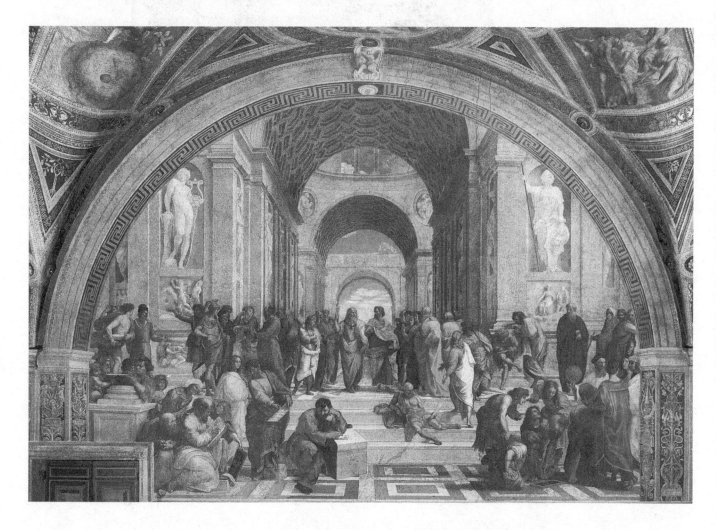

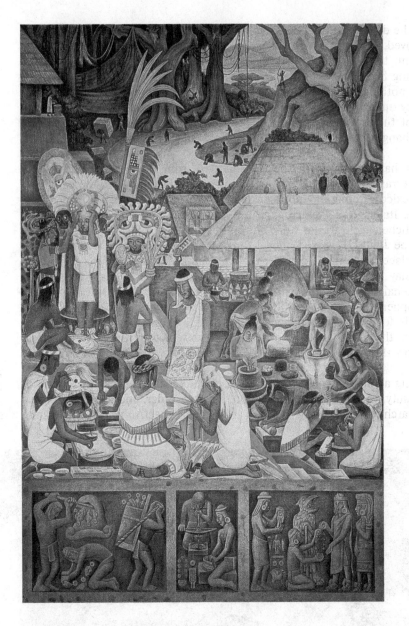

7.4 Diego Rivera. *Mixtec Culture.* 1942. Fresco, 16' 1 ⅝" × 10' 5 ⅝". Palacio Nacional, Mexico City. Art Resource/Bob Schalkwijk © 2019 Banco de México Diego Rivera Frida Kahlo Museums Trust, Mexico, D.F./Artists Rights Society (ARS), New York

point falling between the two central figures. The figures, perhaps influenced by Michelangelo's figures on the Sistine ceiling, are idealized—more perfect than life, full-bodied, and dynamic. The groups of bodies are balanced to either side of the central axis, and the architecture orders the space. *The School of Athens* reflects Raphael's vision of one Golden Age—the Renaissance—and connects it with the Golden Age of Greece two thousand years earlier.

The most celebrated frescoes of the 20th century were created in Mexico, where the revolutionary government that came into power in 1921 after a decade of civil war commissioned artists to create murals about Mexico itself—the glories of its ancient civilizations, its political struggles, its people, and its hopes for the future. *Mixtec Culture* (**7.4**) is one of a series of frescoes painted by Diego Rivera in the National Palace in Mexico City. Mixtec people still live in Mexico, as do descendants of all the early civilizations of the region. The Mixtec kingdoms were known for their arts, and Rivera has portrayed a peaceful community of artists at work. To the left, two men, probably nobles, are being fitted with the elaborate ritual headdresses, masks, and capes that were a prominent part of many ancient Mexican cultures. To the right, smiths are melting and casting gold. In the foreground are potters, sculptors, feather workers, mask makers, and scribes. In the background, people pan for gold in the stream.

Tempera

Tempera is an aqueous medium like watercolor that dries to a tough, insoluble film. Its colors retain their brilliance and clarity for centuries. Technically, tempera is paint in which the vehicle is an emulsion, which is a stable mixture of an aqueous liquid with an oil, fat, wax, or resin. A familiar example of an emulsion is milk, which consists of minute droplets of fat suspended in liquid. A derivative of milk called casein is one of the many vehicles that can be used to make tempera colors. The most famous tempera vehicle, however, is another naturally occurring emulsion, egg yolk. Tempera dries very quickly, and so colors cannot be blended easily once they are set down. Although tempera can be diluted with water and applied in a broad wash, painters who use it most commonly build up forms gradually with fine hatching and cross-hatching strokes, much like a drawing. Traditionally, tempera was used on a wood panel support prepared with a ground of **gesso**, a mixture of white pigment and glue that sealed the wood and could be sanded and rubbed to a smooth, ivorylike finish.

An exquisite example of tempera painting as it was practiced during the Renaissance is a scene of holy women at a tomb by Girolamo dai Libri (**7.5**). It

7.5 Girolamo dai Libri. *Manuscript Illumination with the Holy Women at the Tomb.* ca. 1490–1500. Tempera and gold on parchment, 5 15/16 × 5 9/16".

The Metropolitan Museum of Art, New York, Bequest of Millie Bruhl Frederick, 1962

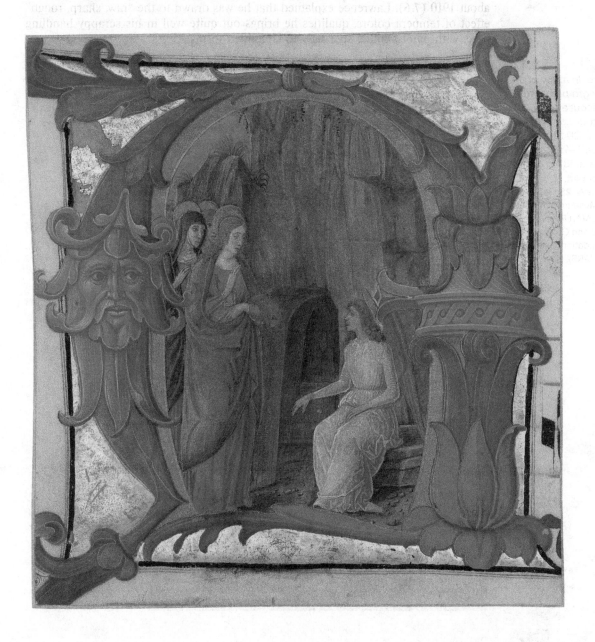

pictures the three women who visit the tomb of Christ after his crucifixion, only to discover that it is empty. An angel sits next to the tomb's entryway. This painting is a manuscript illumination, meaning that it is painted in a handmade book. The narrative appears within a letter A painted maroon, blue, and green at the head of a song in the manuscript. A blue face on the left side of the letter is a decorative element. The saturated colors are typical of tempera paintings. Libri has built up the forms of his work slowly and patiently through layers of small, precise brush-strokes. The shimmering gold provides textural variation and an air of holiness.

Workshop apprentices would have made Libri's colors fresh daily, grinding the pigments with water to form a paste, then mixing the paste with diluted egg yolk. They would have made just enough for one day's work, since tempera colors do not keep. Not long after Libri's time, tempera fell out of favor in Europe. The technique was forgotten until the 19th century, when it was revived, based on descriptions in an early Renaissance artist's handbook. Today, tempera is available commercially in tubes, although many painters still prefer to make their own.

One modern painter who experimented with both commercial and handmade tempera was Jacob Lawrence. Like Libri, Lawrence used tempera to make images that tell a story, in this case the story of the Great Migration—the migration of thousands of African Americans from the South to the North of the U.S. beginning about 1910 (**7.6**). Lawrence explained that he was drawn to the "raw, sharp, rough" effect of tempera colors, qualities he brings out quite well in his scrappy handling here, with paint applied sparingly to simplified forms.

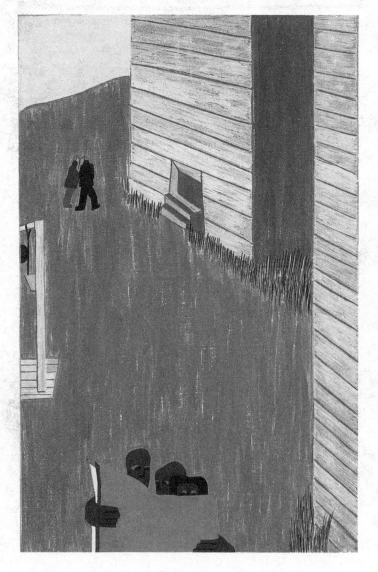

7.6 Jacob Lawrence. *In many of the communities the Negro press was read continually because of its attitude and its encouragement of the movement.* Panel 20 from *The Migration Series.* 1940–41. Tempera on composition board, 18 × 12".

The Museum of Modern Art, New York, Gift of Mrs. David M. Levy, 28.1942.10. Digital image © The Museum of Modern Art/Licensed by SCALA/Art Resource, NY © 2019 The Jacob and Gwendolyn Knight Lawrence Foundation, Seattle/Artists Rights Society (ARS), New York

Jacob Lawrence (1917–2000)

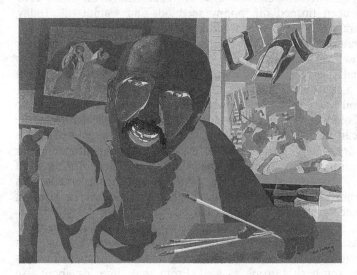

Why did Lawrence use tempera? What themes from his personal life did he share through his art? Why did he make images in series?

In the 1920s, the New York City neighborhood known as Harlem experienced a tremendous cultural upsurge that has come to be called the Harlem Renaissance. Many of the greatest names in black culture—musicians, writers, artists, poets, scientists—lived or worked in Harlem at the time, or simply took their inspiration from its intellectual energy. To Harlem, in about 1930, came a young teenager named Jacob Lawrence, relocating from Philadelphia with his mother, brother, and sister. The flowering of the Harlem Renaissance had passed, but there remained enough momentum to help turn this child into one of the most distinguished American artists of his generation.

Lawrence studied at the Harlem Art Workshop from 1932 to 1934 and received much encouragement from two noted black artists, Charles Alston and Augusta Savage.

By the age of twenty, Lawrence had begun to exhibit his work. A year later he, like so many others, was being supported by the WPA Art Project, a government-sponsored program to help artists get through the economic void of the Great Depression.

Tempera was one of Lawrence's preferred painting media. After being told that his tempera paintings revealed his "addiction" to design, pattern, and color, Lawrence responded, "I liked design. I used to do things like rugs by seeing the pattern—this was when I was about twelve or thirteen. . . . I used to make these very symmetrical designs in very bright primary and secondary colors. . . . And then I did masks. . . . And again they were very symmetrical."[2] The tempera paintings the artist completed as an adult share these qualities.

The themes of Lawrence's work came from his own experience, from black experience: the hardships of poor people in the ghettos, the violence that greeted blacks moving from the South to the urban North, the upheaval of the civil rights movement during the 1960s. He was inspired by the Mexican muralists to focus on social issues. Although Lawrence did paint individual pictures, the bulk of his production was in narrative, storytelling series, such as *The Migration Series* and *Theater*, some of them containing as many as sixty images.

Many people would call Lawrence's paintings instruments of social protest, but his images, however stark, have more the character of reporting than of protest. It is as though he is telling us, "This is what happened, this is the way it is." What happened, of course, happened to black Americans, and Lawrence the world-famous painter did not seem to lose sight of Lawrence the youth in Harlem. He said, "My belief is that it is most important for an artist to develop an approach and philosophy about life—if he has developed this philosophy he does not put paint on canvas, he puts himself on canvas."[3]

Oil

Oil paints consist of pigment compounded with oil. Historically, the most commonly used oils have been linseed oil, poppy seed oil, and walnut oil. Today, commercial manufacturers of artist's colors often grind darker pigments with linseed oil and light pigments such as white and yellow with poppy seed oil or safflower oil, which do not yellow over time, as linseed oil tends to do. What all these oils have in common is that they will dry at room temperature, leaving the pigment particles suspended in a transparent film.

Unlike tempera, oil paint dries very slowly, allowing artists far more time to manipulate the paint. Colors can be laid down next to each other and blended softly and seamlessly. They can be painted wet-on-wet, with a new color painted into a color that is not yet dry. They can be scraped away partially or altogether for revisions or effects. Again unlike tempera, oil paint can be applied in a range of consistencies, from very thick to very thin. Oil paintings can also be made with **glazes**—thin veils of translucent color like stained glass applied over a layer of opaque paint. This creates a luminous, glowing effect.

Oil was known as a medium in western Europe as early as the 12th century, but it did not begin its rise to popularity until two centuries later. By the 15th century, oil paint had eclipsed tempera as the medium of choice in northern Europe. It would soon conquer southern Europe as well. From that time for about five hundred years, the word "painting" in Western culture was virtually synonymous with "oil painting." Only since the 1950s, with the introduction of acrylics (discussed later in this chapter), has the supremacy of oil been challenged.

A beautiful example of oil painting from its first decades of popularity is *A Goldsmith in His Shop* by Petrus Christus (**7.7**). The scene is set in the prosperous Netherlandish city of Bruges, where Christus spent his career. A richly dressed

7.7 Petrus Christus. *A Goldsmith in His Shop*. 1449. Oil on wood, 38 ⅝ × 33 ½".
The Metropolitan Museum of Art, New York. Robert Lehman Collection, 1975, 1975.1.110. © 2014. Image © The Metropolitan Museum of Art

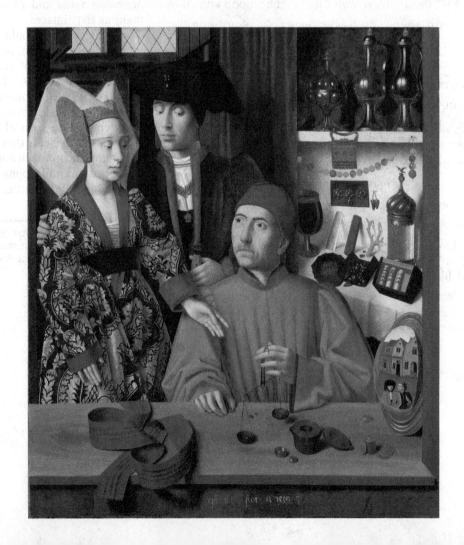

young couple is paying a visit to the local goldsmith. Soon to be married (her betrothal girdle is displayed on the counter), they have come to purchase a ring. The seated goldsmith holds a jeweler's balance with a ring in one tray and a weight in the other. Gold coins and additional weights are stacked on the counter. A convex mirror reflects the streetscape outside and two passersby, one of whom carries a falcon perched on his gloved hand. To the right, a green curtain has been drawn back to reveal a fascinating display of the goldsmith's raw materials—coral, crystal, porphyry, seed pearls, and beads. Finished products are displayed as well—rings, brooches, a gold-lidded crystal container, and polished pewter vessels with gold fittings.

When oil paints were first introduced, most artists, including Christus, continued working on wood panels. Gradually, however, artists adopted canvas, which offered two great advantages. For one thing, the changing styles favored larger and larger paintings. Whereas wood panels were heavy and liable to crack, the lighter linen canvas could be stretched to almost unlimited size. Second, as artists came to serve distant patrons, their canvases could be rolled up for easy and safe shipment. Canvas was prepared by stretching it over a wooden frame, sizing it with glue to seal the fibers and protect them from the corrosive action of oil paint, and then coating it with a white, oil-based ground. Some painters then applied a thin layer of color over the ground, most often a warm brown or a cool, pale gray.

Painting as practiced by artists such as Christus is a slow and time-consuming affair. The composition is generally worked out in advance down to the least detail, drawn on the ground, then built up methodically, with layer after layer of opaque paints and glazes. Artists who favor a less fussy, more spontaneous approach may work directly in opaque colors on the white ground, a technique sometimes called **alla prima** (ahl-lah pree-mah), Italian for "at first." Also known as "direct painting" or "wet-on-wet," *alla prima* implies that the painting was completed all at once, in a single session, although in fact it may only look that way.

Amy Sillman's *Nut* takes advantage of oil paint's unique characteristics in a contemporary way (**7.8**). The surface has been worked and reworked, with colors brushed on, brushed over, scraped away, and reapplied, now in a thinned,

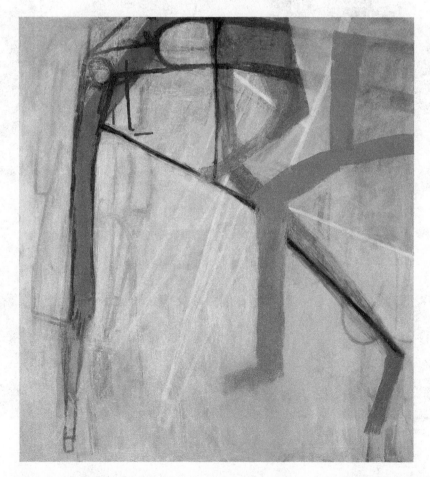

7.8 Amy Sillman. *Nut*. 2011. Oil on canvas, 7' 7" × 7'.
Image courtesy Gladstone Gallery, New York and Brussels. Artwork © 2015 Amy Sillman

translucent layer (the long green form), now in thick, opaque strokes (the lavender Y-form). Underlayers are allowed, even encouraged, to show through as traces of the painting's development. It's impossible to say what memories or experiences triggered *Nut*, but the painting evolved in a way that allows us to distinguish (perhaps) two legs, a dangling arm, and a hand poised over the hem of a woman's coat drawn in an underlayer. Diagrammatic lines in white, green, and violet form a sort of scaffolding.

Pastel, Watercolor, Gouache, and Similar Media

In the last chapter we learned that classifying materials is not always black and white. Like ink, which can be drawn with a pen or painted with a brush, pastel is a medium that exists somewhere between drawing and painting. It is a dry medium, not wet like paint, and it is drawn, not brushed, onto the surface. We saw an example of Degas's pastel drawing *The Singer in Green*, made by drawing on the paper with pastel sticks consisting of pigment and binder (see 6.9). But once pastel is drawn on, the artist can treat the material like paint, moving it around with a stiff paintbrush either with or without the help of water. Degas used this technique to blend the colors of the dancer's skin. Adding water can also turn a thin layer of pastel into a watery wash for a light tint of color.

The American painter Georgia O'Keeffe used pastel for her *White Shell with Red* (**7.9**). The work reveals the intense, saturated color typical of pastel. The rich red hill in the background allows the pearly white shell tinged with yellow and pink to stand out as the focal point. O'Keeffe drew the image with pastel. She then

7.9 Georgia O'Keeffe. *White Shell with Red*. 1938. Pastel, 21 ⅝ × 27 ⅝". The Art Institute of Chicago/Art Resource, NY

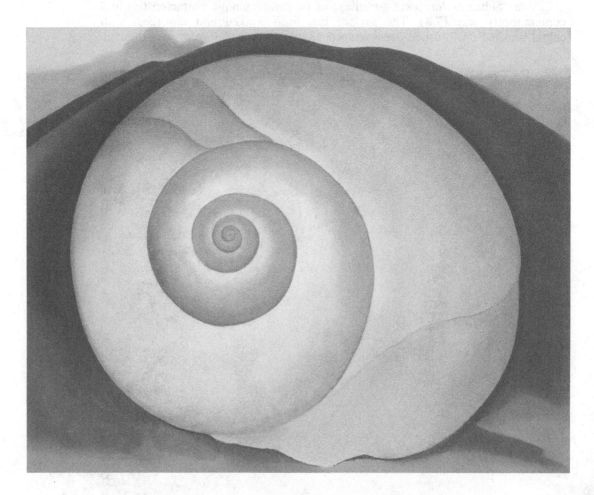

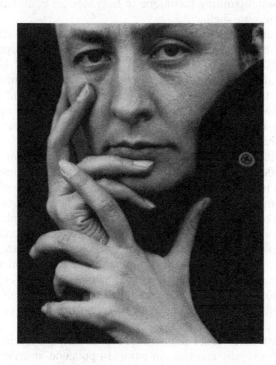

What types of image did Georgia O'Keeffe paint? How would you describe the style of her paintings? How do her paintings reflect her love of the Southwest desert? How did she use the pastel medium?

"At last! A woman on paper!" According to legend, that was the reaction of the famed photographer and art dealer Alfred Stieglitz in 1916, when he first saw the work of Georgia O'Keeffe. Whether accurate or not, the quotation sums up Stieglitz's view of O'Keeffe as the first great artist to bring to her work the true essence and experience of womanhood. Ultimately, much of the critical art world came to share Stieglitz's opinion.

Georgia O'Keeffe studied at the School of the Art Institute of Chicago and the Art Students League in New York. By 1912, she was teaching in Amarillo, Texas—the beginning of a lifelong infatuation with the terrain of the Southwest. In 1914, O'Keeffe moved back to New York, where she and other American artists saw the increasingly abstract art of the European Modernists. Exhibitions of her art were well received. Visitors and critics appreciated her spare, almost abstract, forms and pure colors, as seen in the pastel *White Shell with Red* (see 7.9). After splitting her time between New York and the Southwest for several years, O'Keeffe moved permanently to New Mexico in 1949.

While she is most widely known for her close-up paintings of flowers, O'Keeffe also created landscapes and studies of natural objects found around her New Mexico home, which she called Ghost Ranch. "I have wanted to paint the desert and I haven't known how," she wrote. "So I brought home my bleached bones as symbols of the desert. . . . The bones seem to cut sharply to the center of something that is keenly alive in the desert even tho' it is vast and empty and untouchable."[4] These striking works combine the white bone, parched landscape, and brilliant blue sky to capture the essence of the desert.

O'Keeffe's images feature bright colors, simplified forms, and uncluttered compositions. Her goal was not to record faithfully what she saw. Instead, as she explained, "I had to create an equivalent of what I felt about what I was looking at."[5] As a result, she produced expressive paintings that highlight the beauty of natural shapes. O'Keeffe believed that the colors and shapes in her paintings communicated in ways that words could not.

O'Keeffe's style of painting was unique; she did not adhere to any particular "school" or artistic movement. This singular approach reflected the same fierce independence that led her to abandon New York for a solitary life in the desert. The move was made, she explained, when she became aware of the many restrictions that had been placed upon her. Her art, she decided, would not become one of those things, and she embraced a style unlike that of her peers: "I decided I was a very stupid fool for not at least painting as I wanted to."[6]

While O'Keeffe is known today as one of the greatest American artists of the 20th century, she viewed herself differently. "I don't think I have a great gift," she once said. "It isn't just talent. You have to have something else. You have to have a kind of nerve . . . and a lot of very, very hard work."[7]

Alfred Stieglitz. *Georgia O'Keeffe*. 1918. Gelatin silver print, 4 ½ × 3 ⅗" (image/paper/first mount); 12 ½ × 10" (second mount). The Art Institute of Chicago/Art Resource, NY

smoothed the drawing strokes with a brush and her fingers so that the colors blended seamlessly. The paler pink in the lower section of the painting may indicate that she used water to thin the pastel for a less intense effect. A master of playing with scale, the artist used her pastel painting technique to help viewers contemplate the form and beauty of this common shell.

Watercolor consists of pigment in a vehicle of water and gum arabic, a sticky plant substance that acts as the binder. As with drawing, the most common support for watercolor is paper. Also like drawing, watercolor is commonly thought of as an intimate art, small in scale and free in execution. Eclipsed for several centuries by the prestige of oil paints, watercolors were in fact often used for small and intimate works. Easy to carry and requiring only a glass of water for use, they could readily be taken on sketching expeditions outdoors (see Giorgio di Giovanni's sketch, 1.12), and were a favorite medium for amateur artists.

The leading characteristic of watercolors is their transparency. They are applied not thickly, like oil paints, but thinly in translucent washes. Although opaque white watercolor is available, it is reserved for special uses. More usually, the white of the paper serves for white, and dark areas are built up through several layers of transparent washes, which take on depth without ever becoming completely opaque. Winslow Homer's *Key West, Hauling Anchor* (**7.10**) is a perfect example of what we might think of as employing a "classic" watercolor technique. Controlled and yet spontaneous in feeling, it gives the impression that the paint is still wet, with color bleeding beyond the drawn pencil lines. Homer achieved this effect by laying washes without waiting for the previous application to dry. The white of the paper serves as the boat's white hull, and loose, open brushstrokes add a casual and laid-back quality.

Gouache is watercolor with inert white pigment added. Inert pigment is pigment that becomes colorless or virtually colorless in paint. In gouache, it serves to make the colors opaque, which means that when used at full strength, they can completely hide any ground or other color they are painted over. The poster paints given to children are basically gouache, although not of artist's quality. Like water-

7.10 Winslow Homer. *Key West, Hauling Anchor*. 1903. Watercolor, 14 × 21 ¹³⁄₁₆".
Courtesy National Gallery of Art, Washington, D.C. Gift of Ruth K. Henschel in memory of her husband, Charles R. Henschel

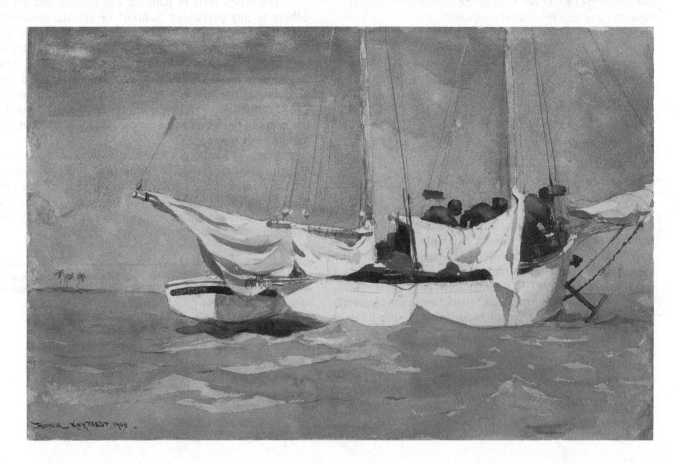

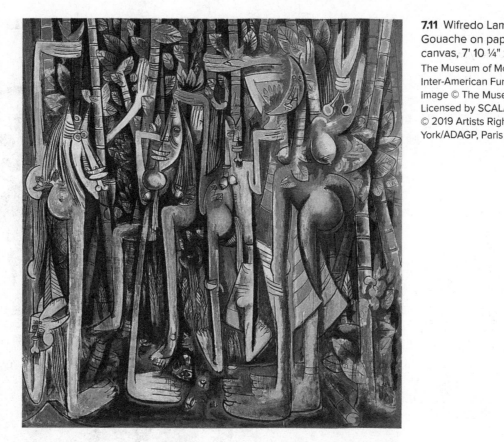

7.11 Wifredo Lam. *The Jungle*. 1943. Gouache on paper mounted on canvas, 7' 10 ¼" × 7' 6 ½".

The Museum of Modern Art, New York. Inter-American Fund 140.1945. Digital image © The Museum of Modern Art/ Licensed by SCALA/Art Resource, NY. © 2019 Artists Rights Society (ARS), New York/ADAGP, Paris

color, gouache can be applied in a translucent wash, although that is not its primary use. It dries quickly and uniformly and is especially well suited to large areas of flat, saturated color. The Cuban painter Wifredo Lam exploited both the transparent and the opaque possibilities of gouache in *The Jungle* (**7.11**). Human and animal forms mingle in this fascinating work, which contains references to Santería, a Caribbean religion that combines West African and Roman Catholic beliefs.

Acrylic

The enormous developments in chemistry during the early 20th century had an impact in artists' studios. By the 1930s, chemists had learned to make strong, weatherproof, industrial paints using a vehicle of synthetic plastic resins. Artists began to experiment with these paints almost immediately. By the 1950s, chemists had made many advances in the new technology and had also adapted it to artists' requirements for permanence. For the first time since it was developed, oil paint had a challenger as the principal medium for Western painting.

These new synthetic artists' colors are broadly known as **acrylics**, although a more exact name for them is polymer paints. The vehicle consists of acrylic resin, polymerized (its simple molecules linked into long chains) through emulsion in water. As acrylic paint dries, the resin particles coalesce to form a tough, flexible, and waterproof film.

Depending on how they are used, acrylics can mimic the effects of oil paint, watercolor, gouache, and even tempera. They can be used on prepared or raw canvas, and also on paper and fabric. They can be layered into a heavy **impasto** like oils, or diluted with water and spread in translucent washes like watercolor. Like tempera, they dry quickly and permanently. (Artists using acrylics usually rest their brushes in water while working, for if the paint dries on the brush, it is extremely difficult to remove.)

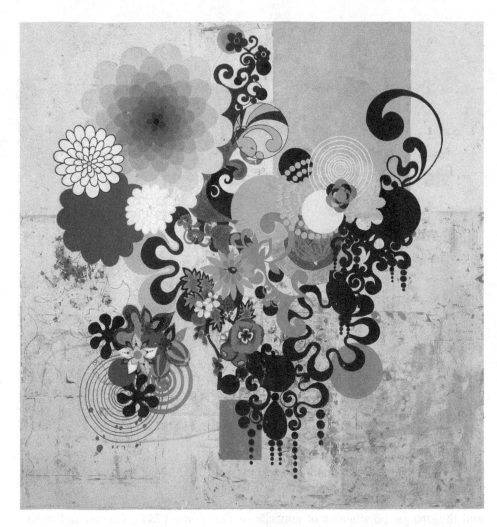

7.12 Beatriz Milhazes. *Mariposa*. 2004. Acrylic on canvas, 8' 2" × 8' 2". © Beatriz Milhazes. Courtesy James Cohan, New York

The Brazilian painter Beatriz Milhazes has developed an unusual technique for working with acrylics. To create a painting such as *Mariposa* (**7.12**), Milhazes first paints each motif separately on a sheet of clear plastic. When the paint has dried, she glues the motif face-down onto the canvas and peels away the plastic backing, revealing the motif's smooth underside. Motif by motif, element by element, Milhazes builds up her painting as though she were making a collage. The technique demands that the artist plan ahead, for each motif must be painted in reverse, both in the way its colors are layered (since it is the underside that will show) and in its orientation (since attaching it face-down will reverse right and left).

Painting and Beyond: Off the Wall!

Most of the paintings we have looked at in this chapter are **easel paintings**—a term for paintings executed on an easel or similar support. An easel is a portable stand that props up a painting in progress vertically so that the artist can work facing it, in the position that a viewer will eventually take. The painting that Diego Velázquez depicts himself working on in *Las Meninas* is propped up against an easel, for example (see 2.3). Unlike frescoes or murals, easel paintings are portable objects, generally rectangular in format, that can be hung on any wall big enough to accommodate them.

Easel painting came into prominence during the Renaissance, and it has dominated the Western painting tradition ever since. Chances are that if you were asked to imagine a painting, it is an easel painting that would come to mind. Modern artists seeking new means of expression (and having new things to express) have pushed the boundaries of easel painting, imagining other ways for paintings to be made and experienced. In the 1940s, for example, Jackson Pollock did away with the easel and spread his canvas on the floor so that he could spatter and drip paint onto it from above (see 22.1). A few years later, Pollock's younger colleague Helen Frankenthaler followed his lead, placing raw, unprimed canvas on the floor and flooding it with thinned paint that soaked into the fabric like dye (see 22.5). During the 1960s, Lynda Benglis took their ideas a step further, pouring her colors directly onto the floor . . . and leaving them there (**7.13**).

Working with large cans of latex into which she had stirred pigments, Benglis poured overlapping flows of vivid color onto the floor, creating works she called "fallen paintings." Many of her fallen paintings, like the one she is shown working on in the illustration here, were site-specific and temporary, created in an exhibition space and then discarded when the exhibition was over. Others were created in her studio and then removed from the floor, making them portable and permanent. With Benglis, painting not only left the wall but also broke free of traditional geometric formats, for the shape of the fallen paintings was determined by the flow of the latex. Benglis's fallen paintings have a sculptural presence, like a very low relief, and they share the viewer's space in the way that sculpture does.

A number of artists have since worked in the space that Benglis and others opened up between painting, sculpture, and installation. One is the Berlin-based

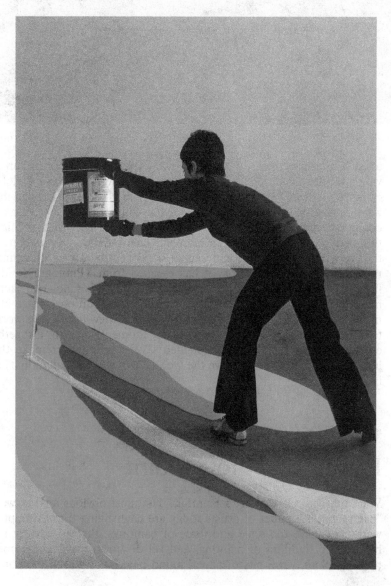

7.13 Lynda Benglis painting on the floor with pigmented latex, University of Rhode Island, 1969.
Henry Groskinsky/The LIFE Picture Collection/Getty Images. Courtesy Cheim & Read, New York. Art © Lynda Benglis/Licensed by VAGA, New York

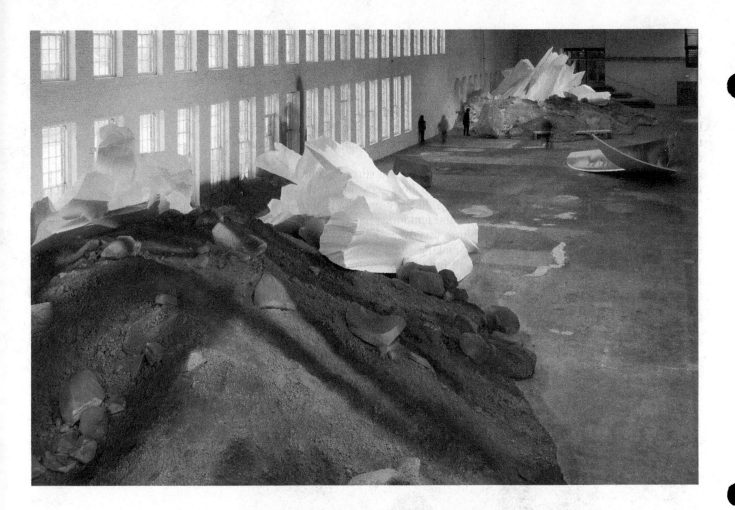

7.14 Katharina Grosse. *One Floor Up More Highly*, detail. 2010. Installation at Mass MoCA, December 22, 2010–October 31, 2011. Soil, wood, acrylic, Styrofoam, acrylic on glass-fiber-reinforced plastic, and acrylic on canvas.
Photo Arthur Evans. © 2015 Artists Rights Society (ARS), New York/VG Bild-Kunst, Bonn

artist Katharina Grosse, whose exuberant spray-painted colors run riot over walls, windows, fiberglass sculptures, fabricated boulders, articles of clothing, and piles of earth in *One Floor Up More Highly* (**7.14**). Huge, elongated blocks of white Styrofoam establish a visual link with the white walls of the space. The artist has compared the Styrofoam blocks to crystallized light, like sunlight so blinding that it obscures our view for a moment. Unavoidably, the illustration here gathers the work into the traditional rectangular view of an easel painting, as though reclaiming it for the territory it has escaped from. (Photography does this to our lived experience all the time, whether we notice it or not.) In fact, the artist did not intend the work to be a composition in the traditional sense at all. It was not meant to appear unified from a certain point of view *outside* the work. It was meant to be experienced from *inside*, moment by moment. "We put it together as we move, every second anew," Grosse explained. "We continually remake this surrounding just as we do when we perceive the world. To see the installation as a coherent unit is an illusion."[8]

The Idea of a Painting: Painting without Paint

What makes a work of art a painting? The most obvious answer would seem to be "paint," but a number of artists today are challenging that assumption. They make works that have the scale and force of paintings, that are clearly informed by the history and tradition of painting, and yet do not use paint as a medium. Instead, they use cloth, yarn, bits of paper, found objects, and even the computer.

The Californian artist Petra Cortright makes digital paintings. She is part of a movement called post-Internet art—a group of artists who use digital images found online as the basis for their artworks. Cortright collects digital pictures much as traditional Western artists have gathered drawings in sketchbooks. She then transforms these found pictures with the help of image-making software. These altered files serve as the basic elements of her art and she layers them, sometimes a dozen or more in one image. The finished artwork lives on the Internet. To display her digital paintings beyond a computer, the artist prints them on aluminum.

Cortright's *007 goldeneye_all characters cheat* (**7.15**) was created digitally and then printed on a large sheet of aluminum. The metal support offers its own reflective quality, making Cortright's brightly colored digital painting even more brilliant. The image recalls the work of the Impressionist painter Claude Monet (see 21.6), with green and white water lilies in a pond at the bottom. Flowers are a common theme in Cortright's art. The painting is otherwise abstract. Large streaks of highly saturated red and yellow fill much of the surface, contrasted with smaller lines in blue and white. All seems to be in motion.

Cortright's streaks and lines of color look as if they were made with a paintbrush rather than a printer. Notice the streaking effect where the yellow and red blend into each other, and the squiggly white lines on the right edge that look as though they were made by hand. These marks are the artist's homage to the essence of her medium—the painting made with brushes—but in a contemporary, high-tech form. She even calls them brushstrokes. Unlike the strokes of paint brushed onto canvas or paper, however, Cortright's digital marks can be reused and recombined to make new digital paintings. They can also live entirely inside a computer, be copied infinite times by the artist in whatever sizes she pleases, and travel electronically in an instant. Cortright's digital paintings may celebrate the essence of painting, but they push the medium into new territory.

7.15 Petra Cortright. *007 goldeneye_all characters cheat.* 2013. Digital painting on aluminum, 48 × 64".

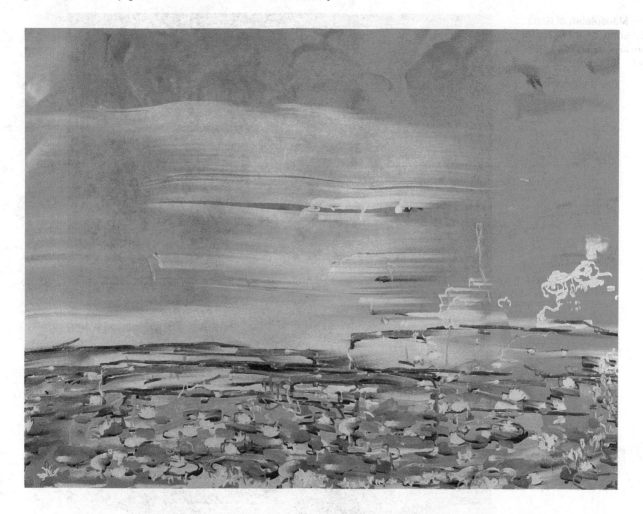

Sumptuous Images: Mosaic and Tapestry

When painting rose to prominence during the Renaissance, it found itself in the company of two other highly esteemed techniques for creating monumental, two-dimensional images: mosaic and tapestry. Painters were often called upon to create designs for these media, which were then carried out by specialized workshops.

Mosaic is made of small, closely spaced particles called **tesserae** (singular **tessera**) embedded in a binder such as mortar or cement. Tesserae function similarly to the dots in a pointillist painting: each one contributes a small patch of pure color to the construction of an image, which comes into focus at a certain distance (see 4.32). Like fresco, mosaic is well suited to decorating architectural surfaces such as walls and ceilings. Unlike fresco, however, mosaic is sturdy enough to stand up to the elements, and so it can be used for floors and outdoor surfaces as well.

The ancient Greeks made floor mosaics using small pebbles as tesserae. Later, the practice arose of fabricating tesserae from natural materials such as colored marble or manufactured materials such as glass. The ancient Romans adopted the technique of mosaic along with many other aspects of Greek artistic culture, using it not only for floors but also for walls and ceilings. After Christianity came to power within the Roman Empire, mosaic was used to decorate churches and other Christian religious buildings.

The Mausoleum of Galla Placidia contains some of the most beautiful of these early Christian mosaics to have come down to us (**7.16**). Galla Placidia was a Roman empress and patron of the arts who lived during the first half of the 5th

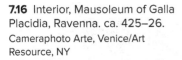

7.16 Interior, Mausoleum of Galla Placidia, Ravenna. ca. 425–26. Cameraphoto Arte, Venice/Art Resource, NY

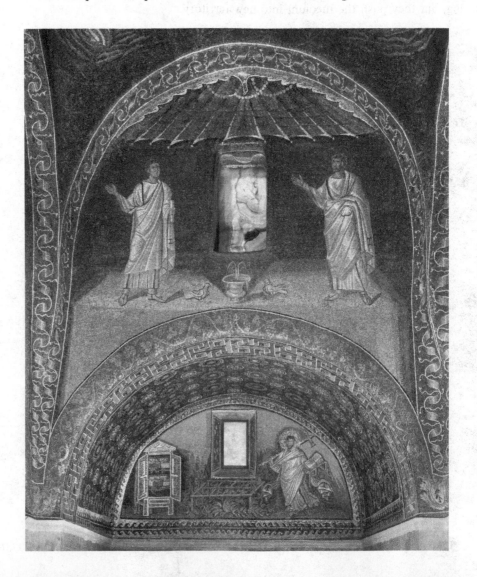

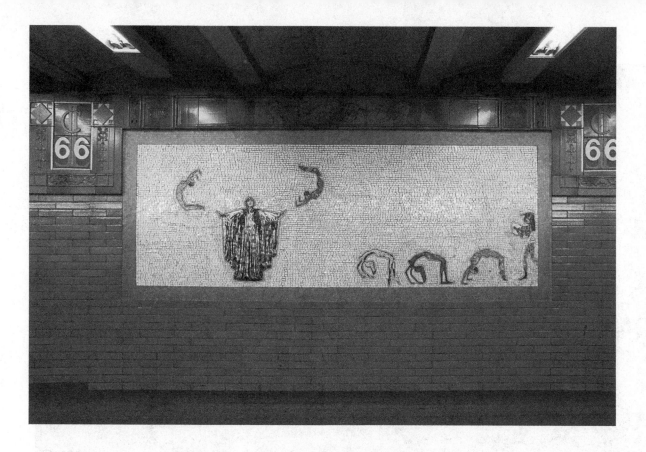

century. Her name has long been associated with this small mausoleum, and although scholars no longer believe that she was buried in it, she may well have sponsored its construction. The entire upper portion of the interior is covered with mosaics made of glass tesserae. In the detail illustrated here, two apostles standing to either side of an alabaster window panel raise their hands in greeting. In the smaller scene below we see an open cabinet containing the four books of the Gospels, a gridiron set over a roaring fire, and a man carrying a cross over his right shoulder and holding an open book in his left hand. The speckles we see in the blue background and the gold floor are individual tesserae. Yet notice how the robes seem to have smooth transitions between shaded and illuminated areas. Up close, these are rows of tesserae in lighter and darker tones. From a distance, the colors seem to blend.

The 15th-century Renaissance painter Domenico Ghirlandaio spoke of mosaics as "painting for eternity." Although their brilliant colors and glittering surfaces may not actually last forever, mosaics are far more durable than paintings, and that is part of their appeal. Ghirlandaio himself designed several mosaics, as did a number of other Renaissance artists, including Raphael. Nevertheless, mosaic was largely abandoned in favor of fresco, which was faster, far less costly, and better suited to the new Renaissance interest in naturalism.

Interest in mosaic revived in the 19th century, and a number of important workshops were established. Rich with historical associations, mosaic has since reclaimed a place in artistic practice. A recent example is Nancy Spero's *Artemis, Acrobats, Divas, and Dancers* (**7.17**). The whole work consists of forty-eight panels of glass mosaic set into the tile walls of a New York City subway station. The station serves Lincoln Center, home to many performing-arts organizations. A small repertoire of figures—ancient Egyptian musicians, arching acrobats, dancers ancient and modern, the ancient Greek goddess Artemis, and a glamorously robed diva (female opera singer)—appear again and again in various combinations across the panels, as though taking part in a theatrical performance or a ritual. The diva, illustrated here, was a new image for Spero, but many of the other figures had appeared often in her paintings over the years, reflecting her ongoing themes and concerns. The white tesserae in the background are large and easy to see, but the figures are composed of smaller individual pieces of tile whose colors seem to blend together.

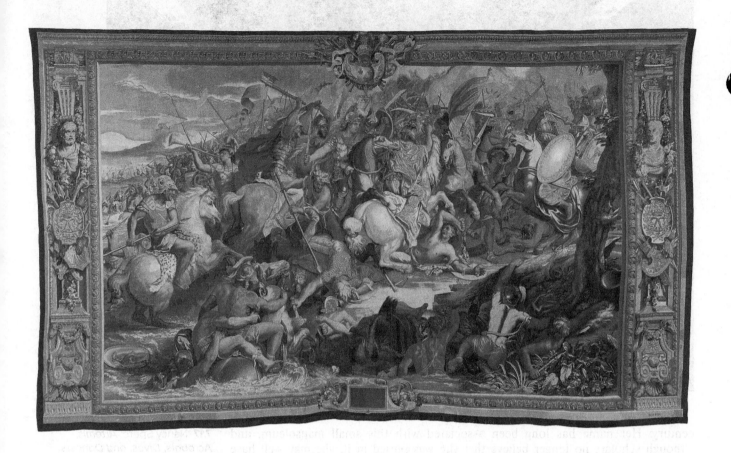

7.18 Charles Le Brun. *The Battle of the Granicus*, from a five-piece set of the *Story of Alexander*. 1680–87. Wool, silk, and gilt-metal-wrapped silk thread; 15' 11" × 27' 8 ⅝". Kunsthistorisches Museum, Vienna. © RMN-Grand Palais/Art Resource, NY

Tapestry refers to a particular weaving technique, and also to the wall hangings made using it. Weaving involves interlacing two sets of threads at right angles to each other. One set of threads, called the warp, is held taut, usually by a loom. The second set, called the weft, is passed through the warp threads, winding over and under them in a set pattern. In ordinary cloth weaving, the weft thread passes back and forth from one edge of the warp to the other, evenly building up a textile. In tapestry weaving, weft threads do not cross the entire warp but, rather, are woven in locally to build up zones of color. You can imagine the warp of a tapestry as a blank canvas stretched out on the loom. (The warp threads are not dyed.) The weft threads are the weaver's palette of colors.

Tapestry weave has been used in many cultures to create textiles such as rugs or garments. In Europe, it was also used to create monumental pictorial wall hangings. Tapestry production began in Europe during the Middle Ages; the earliest surviving examples date from the 11th century. The cloth hangings helped to keep drafty castles a little warmer, and were easy to transport as nobles moved between houses. The hangings were commonly woven in sets that illustrated a theme or depicted episodes from a famous story. Starting during the Renaissance, prominent painters were commissioned to design tapestries. As with frescoes, designs for tapestry were produced as cartoons—full-scale painted drawings on paper. The cartoons were then sent to weaving workshops to be translated into tapestry.

The Battle of the Granicus, designed by the painter Charles Le Brun for the French king Louis XIV, shows how closely tapestry and painting became intertwined (**7.18**). *The Battle of the Granicus* began as a painting, one of five monumental canvases narrating the life of the ancient Macedonian conqueror Alexander the Great. The king had commissioned the paintings from Le Brun, and he was so taken with them that he ordered that they be reproduced as tapestries. Le Brun prepared two sets of cartoons for two different tapestry workshops, and he fleshed out the five monumental scenes with six smaller ones. Eight sets of the tapestries were woven in all. One set was installed in a room in the royal residence; the others were saved for ceremonial display or given by the king as diplomatic gifts.

More than 27 feet long and almost 16 feet in height, *The Battle of the Granicus* reproduces a slightly cropped and lightly reworked version of Le Brun's original painting. Massed in a dramatic diagonal, Alexander's men surge up from the River Granicus and into battle against the forces of Persia. Alexander himself is depicted at the center wearing a magnificent plumed helmet, a sword in his outstretched right hand, his face a mask of fury. The turbulent scene is set in a woven frame flanked by borders depicting architectural ornaments—sculpted busts, garlands, shields, weapons, and the royal emblem and motto. In other words, the tapestry does not merely depict the scene itself, but also suggests a framed painting of the scene hung in a rich architectural setting.

The passing of the aristocratic world that prized and commissioned tapestries coincided with the modern formulation of "art," in which painting and sculpture took pride of place. Tapestry was now spoken of as a decorative art or a craft. (We discuss these categories further in Chapter 12.) Tapestry workshops were still a focus of national pride, however, and artists continued to work with them. In fact, the principles of simultaneous contrast and optical blending, discussed in Chapter 4, were first articulated by the director of a tapestry workshop interested in the effects of juxtaposing differently colored threads. During the 20th century, tapestry gave rise to the new medium of fiber art, as more and more artists grew interested in weaving. (For more about fiber art, see Chapters 12 and 22.) Today, when our definition of art has expanded to embrace a broad variety of media and techniques, a number of artists have again turned to realizing their ideas as tapestries.

One such artist is Pae White, who has exhibited tapestries depicting such unlikely subjects as crumpled aluminum and lazily curling smoke (**7.19**). Instead of a cartoon, White begins with a digital photograph. Working closely with a tapestry workshop in Belgium, she settles on the color palette and weaving patterns that will best give the image material form. A digital file of weaving instructions is prepared, and the tapestry is woven from them on a computer-controlled loom.

Forty feet long, *Still, Untitled* reprises the scale of the monumental tapestries of the past, inviting us to draw comparisons between then and now. Gone are the complex historical, mythological, and allegorical subjects that intrigued and flattered aristocratic patrons such as Louis XIV. Those aren't for us, in our time and place. We content ourselves with humbler fare, the everyday beauty of a plume of smoke, frozen by photography so that we can take in every detail. An intriguing aspect of tapestry is that the image is not *on* the material, the way paint is on canvas, but, rather, embedded *in* the material, part of its essence. White has described her smoke tapestries as "cotton's dream of becoming something else"[9]—a dense, textured, weighty textile dreaming about being as insubstantial and fleeting as a wisp of smoke.

7.19 Pae White. *Still, Untitled*. 2010. Cotton and polyester tapestry, 12 × 40'.

Collection of Sandretto Re Rebaudengo, Turin. © Pae White. Courtesy the artist, Greengrassi and Neugerriemschneider, Berlin

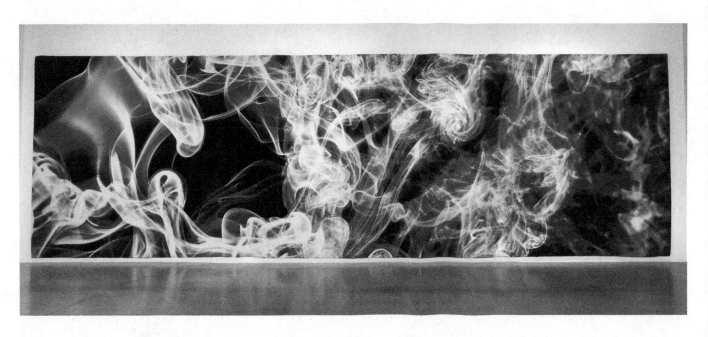

Notes to the Text

1. Akbar cited in Vidya Dehejia, *Indian Art* (London: Phaidon, 2000), p. 309; Zhang cited in Richard Barnhardt et al., *Three Thousand Years of Chinese Painting* (New Haven: Yale University Press, 1997), p. 10; Leonardo cited in Martin Kemp, *Leonardo on Painting* (New Haven and London: Yale University Press, 1989), p. 201; Calderón de la Barca cited in Anita Albus, *The Art of Arts* (Berkeley: University of California Press, 2000), p. vii.

2. "Oral history interview with Jacob Lawrence, October 26 1968." Available at aaa.si.edu/collections/interviews/oral-history-interview-jacob-lawrence-11490, accessed September 28, 2017.

3. Black Mountain College Records, 1946; quoted in Ellen Harkins Wheat, *Jacob Lawrence: American Painter* (Seattle: Seattle Art Museum, 1986), p. 73.

4. Nancy J. Scott, *Georgia O'Keeffe* (London: Reaktion Books, 2015), p. 161.

5. Ibid., p. 14.

6. Ibid., p. 96.

7. Ibid., p. 195.

8. Quoted in Ati Maier, "Katharina Grosse," *BOMB*, no. 115 (Spring 2011). Available at bombmagazine.org/articles/katharina-grosse, accessed April 27, 2018.

9. Quoted in Diana Kamin, "Pae White," *2010: Whitney Biennial* (New York: Whitney Museum of American Art, 2010), p. 122.

Chapter 8
Prints

In this chapter, you will learn to

LO1   describe relief printmaking processes and their characteristics,

LO2   distinguish intaglio printmaking processes and their advantages,

LO3   characterize the use of lithography,

LO4   identify characteristics of screenprinting,

LO5   explain the unique qualities of monotype,

LO6   relate digital prints to other printmaking processes, and

LO7   discuss recent approaches to printmaking.

If you have ever accidentally tracked mud into the house in your sneakers, then you understand the basic principle of making a **print**. When you stepped in the mud, some of it stuck to the raised surfaces of the sole of your sneakers. When you stepped on the floor afterward, the pressure of your weight transferred the mud from the raised surfaces of your sneaker to the floor, leaving a footprint. If you took a second step, the print you made was probably fainter, because there wasn't as much mud left on the sneaker. You would have to step in the mud again to produce a second print as good as the first one. With a little practice, you could probably make a row of sneaker prints that were almost exactly identical.

In the vocabulary of printmaking, the sole of your sneaker served as a **matrix**, a surface on which a design is prepared before being transferred through pressure to a receiving surface such as paper. The printed image it left is called an *impression*. You probably didn't make your own sneaker, but an artist makes a matrix to create prints from it. A single matrix can be used to create many impressions, all of them almost identical, and each of them considered to be an original work of art. For that reason, printmaking is called an art of multiples.

With the development of industrial printmaking technology during the modern era, we have come to recognize a difference in value between original artists' prints and mass-produced reproductions. Artists' prints include Hogarth's *A Harlot's Progress* (see 3.9), Hiroshige's *Riverside Bamboo Market* (see 19.36), and Piranesi's "The Sawhorse" (see 3.21), and reflect each artist's vision. Mass-produced reproductions have more commercial purposes and include such works as the images in this book, an advertisement like the General Dynamics printed ad (see 5.14), or a poster bought in a museum shop. Today, two broadly agreed-upon principles distinguish original artists' prints from commercial reproductions.

The first is that the artist performs or oversees the printing process and examines each impression for quality. The artist signs each impression he or she approves; rejected impressions must be destroyed. The second is that there may be a declared limit to the number of impressions that will be made. This number, called an **edition**, is also written by the artist on each approved impression, along with the number of the impression within that edition. For example, a print numbered 10/100 is the tenth impression of a limited edition of one hundred. Once the entire edition has been

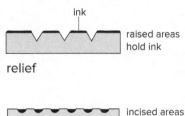
relief

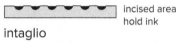
raised areas hold ink

intaglio

incised areas hold ink

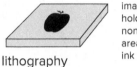
lithography

image area holds ink; non-image areas repel ink

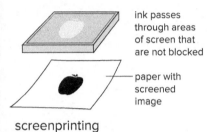
screenprinting

ink passes through areas of screen that are not blocked

paper with screened image

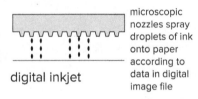
digital inkjet

microscopic nozzles spray droplets of ink onto paper according to data in digital image file

8.1 Five basic print methods.

printed, approved, signed, and numbered, the printing surface is canceled (by scratching cross marks on it) or destroyed so that no further prints can be made from it.

Prints, however, were made for hundreds of years before these standards were in place. From the beginning, they have served to disseminate visual information and to bring the pleasure of owning art within reach of a broad public.

Three historical methods for making art prints—relief, intaglio, and lithography—were joined in the 20th century by screenprinting and in the 21st by digital printing. This chapter takes up each method in turn, then closes with a look at some innovative ways in which contemporary artists are using printed images.

Relief

The term **relief** describes any printing method in which the image to be printed is *raised* from a background. Think of a rubber stamp. When you look at the stamp itself, you may see the words "First Class" or "Special Delivery" standing out from the background in reverse. You press the stamp to an ink pad, then to paper, and the words print right side out—a mirror image of the stamp. All relief processes work according to this general principle, as seen in this illustration of the basic processes used to make prints (**8.1**). The top diagram illustrates relief printing. Notice how the ink rests on the raised part of the matrix. The ink is not in the recessed areas.

Any surface from which the background areas can be carved away is suitable for relief printing. You may have made a relief print from a potato or an apple when you were a child. For artists, the material most commonly associated with relief printing is wood.

Woodcut

To make a **woodcut**, the artist first draws the desired image on a block of wood. Then all the areas that are not meant to print are cut and gouged out of the wood so that the image stands out in relief. When the block is inked, only the raised areas take the ink. Finally, the block is pressed on paper, or paper is placed on the block and rubbed to transfer the ink and make the print.

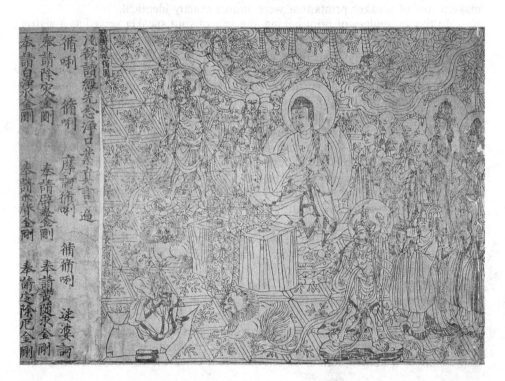

The earliest surviving woodcut image was made in China (**8.2**). Dated 868 C.E., this portrayal of the Buddha preaching appears at the beginning of the world's earliest known printed book, a copy of the Diamond Sutra, an important Buddhist text. The image probably reproduces an original drawing in brush and ink, executed in the slender, even-width lines that Chinese writers likened to iron wire. Although only one copy survives, the edition of the sutra must have been quite large, for a postscript at the end of the 18-foot-long scroll tells us that the project was undertaken at the expense of one Wang Jie, "for universal free distribution." Two great Chinese inventions, paper and printing, are here united.

In Europe, woodblocks had been used to print patterns on textiles since as early as the 6th century C.E., but it was not until the introduction of paper that printing anything else became practical. Soon after, in the mid-15th century, the invention of the printing press and movable type launched Europe's first great "information revolution." For the first time in the West, information could be widely disseminated. Woodcuts quickly found a place as book illustrations, for the block could be placed on the same framework as the type letters, and the entire page inked and printed at the same time. As in China, the first printed books in Europe were illustrated with woodcuts.

With the introduction of **engraving** and other printmaking techniques discussed later in this chapter, woodcut gradually fell out of favor with European artists. Compared with these later techniques, it seemed coarse and unrefined. Those very qualities drew artists to woodcut again in the early 20th century, when many rejected the refinement of the past in favor of bolder, starker, more urgent images, such as *The Widow II*, by Käthe Kollwitz (**8.3**). A woman lies dead on the ground with her child's body across her chest. The image is stark, and Kollwitz used the black ink and white page to create dramatic chiaroscuro. She also revealed the process of making a woodcut. The traces of the cut-away portions of the block are visible below the figure. They represent the energy and even the violence of the cutting and gouging that cleared this area away. *The Widow II* is from a portfolio of seven prints called *War*. Created in the aftermath of World War I, the prints evoke the trauma of the war from the perspective of those left behind, mainly women.

8.3 Käthe Kollwitz. *The Widow II,* from *Krieg (War)*. 1923. Woodcut, 11 ¹³⁄₁₆ × 20 ⅞".

The Museum of Modern Art, New York. Gift of the Arnhold Family in memory of Sigrid Edwards. © 2019 Artists Rights Society (ARS), New York/VG Bild-Kunst, Bonn

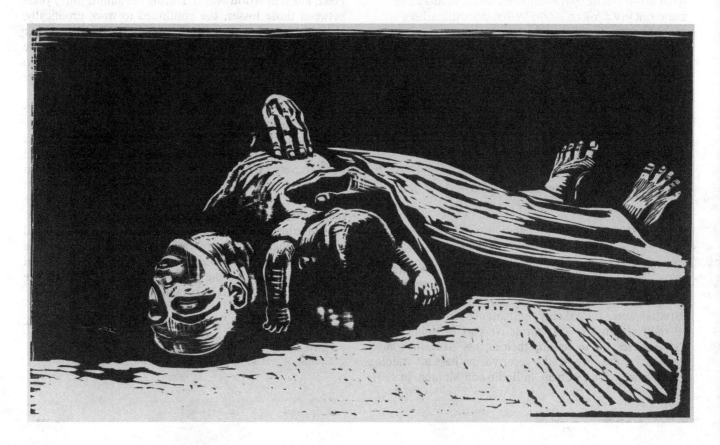

Käthe Kollwitz (1867–1945)

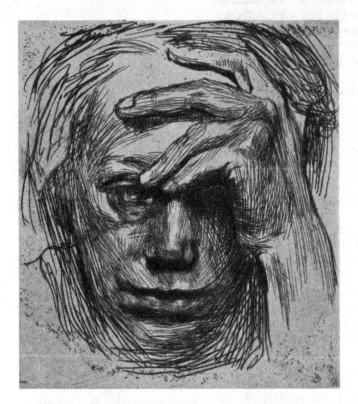

What are some defining elements and principles that stand out in Kollwitz's works? What does the artist's concentration on black and white reveal about her style and themes? How do her works show her political and emotional struggles?

Käthe Kollwitz's art is bold and powerful. Her prints, drawings, and sculptures communicate profound grief and deep introspection. Her art champions the strength of women and explores the overwhelming but sometimes painful power of love. Her self-portraits, like the one seen here, are raw and unflinching studies of her aging face, with the experiences of her life etched into her skin. They are portraits of her soul and the life she led.

Käthe Schmidt was born in Königsberg (then in Prussia, now called Kaliningrad and part of Russia), the second child in an intellectually active middle-class family. Her parents were remarkably enlightened in encouraging all their children to take an active part in political and social causes and to develop their talents—in Käthe's case, a talent for drawing. Käthe received the best art training then available for a woman, in Berlin and Munich. In 1891,

after a seven-year engagement, she married Karl Kollwitz, a physician who seems to have been equally supportive of his wife's career. The couple established themselves in Berlin, where they kept a joint doctor's office and artist's studio for fifty years.

During her student days, Kollwitz had gradually focused on line and had come to realize that draftsmanship was her genius. Her conventional artistic training must have intensified the shock when she "suddenly saw that I was not a painter at all."[1] She concentrated then on drawings and prints—etchings and woodcuts early on; lithographs when her eyesight grew weaker. She also produced images sculpted in stone.

Five major themes dominate Kollwitz's art: the artist herself, in a great many self-portraits and images for which she served as model; the ties between mothers and their children; the hardships of the working classes, usually interpreted through women's plight; the unspeakable cruelties of war; and death as a force unto itself. As a socialist, Kollwitz identified passionately with the sufferings of working people; as a mother, she identified with the struggle of women to keep their children safe.

Kollwitz bore two sons—Hans in 1892 and Peter in 1896. The first of many tragedies that marked her later life came in 1914, with the death of Peter in World War I. She lived long enough to see her beloved grandson, also named Peter, killed in World War II. During the almost thirty years between those losses, she continued to work prolifically, but her obsession with death never left her. One of her most powerful works is a stone memorial she carved for the cemetery where her son Peter was buried. It represents two parents: the father suffering in stoic silence and the mother bent over with grief.

Few artists have so touchingly described their attempts to achieve a certain goal, and their continual frustration at falling short. In Kollwitz's case, the artistic goals were generally realized, but the emotional and political goals—never: "While I drew, and wept along with the terrified children I was drawing, I really felt the burden I am bearing. I felt that I have no right to withdraw from the responsibility of being an advocate. It is my duty to voice the sufferings of men, the never-ending sufferings heaped mountain-high. This is my task, but it is not an easy one to fulfill. Work is supposed to relieve you. . . . Did I feel relieved when I made the prints on war and knew that the war would go on raging? Certainly not."[2]

Käthe Kollwitz. *Self-Portrait with Hand on Her Forehead.* 1910. Etching, 6 × 5 ⅜". Metropolitan Museum of Art, Gift of Leo Wallerstein, 1942 © 2019 Artists Rights Society (ARS), New York/VG Bild-Kunst, Bonn

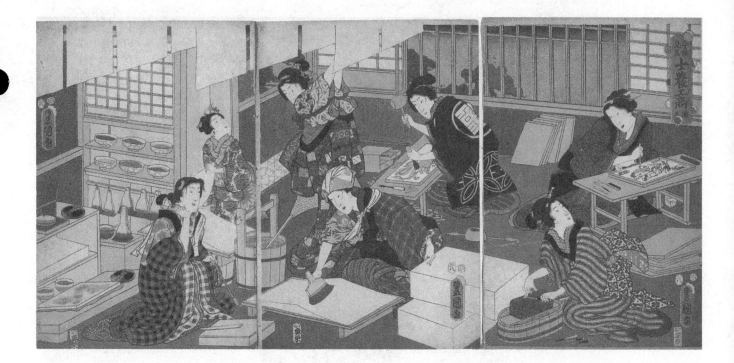

By the 14th century, China had advanced to the next step in woodcut by using multiple blocks to print images in full color. A few centuries later, this technique was transmitted to Japan, where during the 18th century it was brought to a level of perfection that would make Japanese prints famous the world over (see 2.22, 3.27, and 19.35).

Produced by the thousands and cheaply sold, woodblock prints in Japan were a popular art even if they never enjoyed the prestige of painting. Utagawa Kunisada's *Artisans* (**8.4**) is a fanciful depiction of how Japanese woodcut prints were made. In the background, a woman in a black robe carves one of the blocks using a mallet and chisel. A smaller chisel rests nearby for finer cutting. To the right, another woman pierces a piece of paper to transfer a drawing to the block before cutting. The colors available for printing images are seen on the left. The woman in the center foreground prepares the paper to receive the ink transferred from the matrix. Printed papers hang from the rafters to dry. While this woodcut pictures a print-making shop's operations, it is fanciful for having women do the work and for the large size of the printed images it depicts. *Artisans*, for example, is just barely larger than a sheet of notebook paper.

Artisans was printed using at least a dozen cut blocks, one for each color. One of the blocks, known as the line block or key block, printed all the contour lines you see. Other blocks printed the green floor, the blue sky outside the window, the pink walls, and so on. Each block was printed individually. This meant that the artist had to carefully align his block for each printing so that the color or line would show up in the right place and within its contour lines. This process is known as **registration**, and printmakers took great pains to avoid unwanted gaps or overlapping in the colors. If you look very carefully, you will find registration errors in this print, including the spot of white paper visible in the bucket and next to the thumb of the woman sharpening the tool in the foreground.

8.4 Utagawa Kunisada. *Artisans*. 1857. Color woodblock print, 10 × 14 ½".
The Metropolitan Museum of Art, New York. Gift of Cole J. Younger, 1975

Wood Engraving

Like a woodcut, a **wood engraving** uses a block of wood as a matrix. But whereas a woodcut matrix is created on a surface cut *along* the grain, a wood engraving matrix is created on a surface cut *across* the grain, an end-grain block. If you imagine a piece of lumber—say a 1-foot length of 2-by-4—then a woodcut would use one of the 4-by-12-inch sides, whereas a wood engraving would use one of the 2-by-4-inch cut

8.5 José Guadalupe Posada. *Skeletons as Artisans*. 1890–1910. Wood engraving, 4 ¾ × 7 ½". The Metropolitan Museum of Art, New York. Gift of Jean Charlot, 1930

ends. Sanded to mirror smoothness and worked with finely pointed tools, an end-grain block can be cut with equal ease in any direction and lends itself well to detail.

The tools used for wood engraving cut fine, narrow channels that can show as white lines when the block is inked and printed. In José Guadalupe Posada's wood engraving *Skeletons as Artisans* (**8.5**), the white lines are visible in the hat, the shoes, the vest, and in the dark areas of the skeletons' skulls. But wood engraving can also have black lines, just as with woodcuts. The black lines are created by cutting away everything but the line, leaving it in relief to be printed. All the contour lines in Posada's print were made in this way.

The play of positive and negative—of white lines on a black surface, and black lines on a white surface—adds to the humorous and chaotic qualities of Posada's farcical image. Posada regularly used skeletons or *calaveras* to comment on Mexican society. He adopted these figures from the imagery of the Mexican Day of the Dead, which honors the deceased. In this wood engraving, Posada casts *calaveras* as artisans hard at work making clothing, painting signs, and doing carpentry. The artist satirizes the drudgery of our everyday lives, reminding us that life is short. Posada would also use skeletons to poke fun at political figures, the elite, and other members of Mexican society. The unrefined appearance of *Skeletons as Artisans* reflects his attempt to communicate to a broad, popular audience.

Linocut

A linoleum cut, or **linocut**, is very similar to a woodcut. Linoleum, however, is much softer than wood. The relative softness makes linoleum easier to cut, but it also limits the number of crisp impressions that can be produced, since the block wears down more quickly during printing. Linoleum has no grain, so it is possible to make cuts in any direction with equal ease.

John Muafangejo's *Men Are Working in Town* shows the almost liquid ease with which linoleum can be cut (**8.6**). One of southern Africa's most beloved artists, Muafangejo devoted most of his artistic career to linocuts. Among his recurring themes was the daily life of the region's tribal peoples, who at the time were restricted to "homelands" established under a system of racial segregation known as apartheid. Muafangejo himself was a member of the Ovambo people. Dividing his image into three registers, Muafangejo depicts men working in town and in the

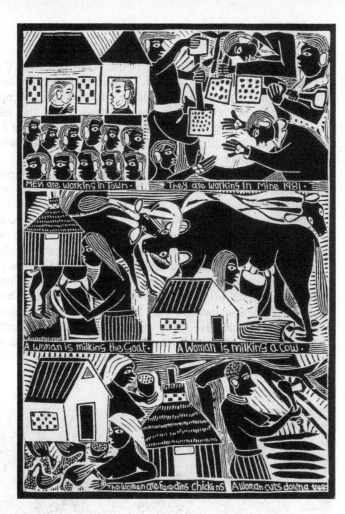

mines, while women milk livestock, feed chickens, and cut down trees. Text labels each activity. Muafangejo wanted his art to be clear, and he said that his style was a "teaching style." Among the things he taught was a generous vision of a society based on racial harmony. In the words of one of his most famous prints, he urged "hope and optimism in spite of the present difficulties."

Intaglio

The second major category of printmaking techniques is **intaglio** (from an Italian word meaning "to cut"), which includes several related methods. Intaglio is exactly the reverse of relief, in that the areas meant to print are *below* the surface of the printing plate. The artist uses a sharp tool or acid to make depressions—lines, grooves, or pits—in a metal plate. When the plate is inked, the ink sinks into the depressions. Then the surface of the plate is wiped clean. When dampened paper is brought into contact with the plate under pressure, the paper is pushed into the depressions to pick up the image.

There are six basic types of intaglio printing: engraving, drypoint, mezzotint, etching, aquatint, and photogravure.

Engraving

The oldest of the intaglio techniques, engraving developed from the medieval practice of incising (cutting) linear designs in armor and other metal surfaces. The armorer's art had achieved a high level of expertise, and it was just a short step to realizing that the engraved lines could be filled with ink and the design transferred to paper.

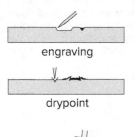
engraving

drypoint

mezzotint

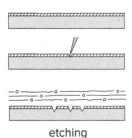
etching

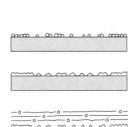
aquatint

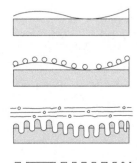
photogravure

The basic tool of engraving is the burin, a sharp, V-shaped instrument used to cut lines into the metal plate (**8.7**). Shallow cuts produce a light, thin line; deeper gouges in the metal result in a thicker and darker line. Engraving is closely related to drawing in pen and ink in both technique and the visual effect of the work. Looking at a reproduction, it is hard to tell an engraving from a fine pen drawing. In both media, modeling and shading effects are usually achieved by hatching, cross-hatching, or stippling.

Until the invention of lithography and photography in the 19th century, engravings were the principal way in which works of art were reproduced and disseminated. Professional engravers were extraordinary draftsmen, capable of making extremely accurate copies of drawings, paintings, statues, and architecture. During the Renaissance, the awakening interest in ancient Roman art was fed by engravings, for no sooner was a newly discovered statue unearthed than it was recorded in a drawing, which was then engraved and distributed across Europe.

One of the greatest Renaissance printmakers was Albrecht Dürer. Although he considered himself primarily a painter, it was prints that brought Dürer his greatest renown. (They also brought him a steady income. Toward the end of his life, he noted that he would have made more money if he had stuck to engravings.) In 1513 and 1514, Dürer created three prints so technically and artistically sophisticated that they have become known as the Master Engravings. One of these is *Knight, Death, and the Devil* (**8.8**).

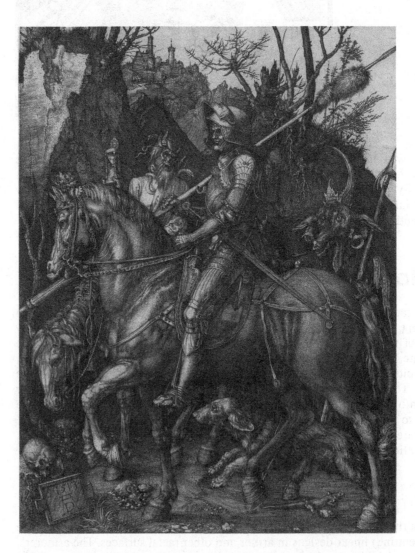

8.8 Albrecht Dürer. *Knight, Death, and the Devil.* 1513. Engraving, 9 ¹¹⁄₁₆ × 7 ³⁄₈".
Rijksmuseum, Amsterdam

A knight on horseback rides through an inhospitable landscape. His loyal dog trots alongside, past a lizard and a skull. Personifications of death and the devil stand next to the path. Death appears as a skeletal figure wearing a crown filled with snakes. He carries an hourglass to remind the knight of the inevitability of his demise. The devil is a horned beast with goat legs and a reptilian tail. This engraving's rich chiaroscuro modeling is accomplished entirely with fine hatching, cross-hatching, and stippling. This creates the illusion of the horse's three-dimensional body and the crevices and projections of the rocky hillside. Dürer's array of lines also help us to understand the various textures pictured in the engraving, from the downy fur of the tail tied to the knight's lance, to the scaly hardness of the devil's horns.

Drypoint

Drypoint is similar to engraving, except that the cutting instrument used is a drypoint needle. The artist draws on the plate, usually a copper plate, almost as freely as one can draw on paper with a pencil. As the needle scratches across the plate, it raises a burr, or thin ridge of metal (see 8.7). If left in place, the burr will hold ink along with the incised line, producing a soft, slightly blurred line when printed. The burr can also be scraped away, in which case the incised line only will hold ink, producing a fine, delicate line. Because intaglio prints are made using a roller press that exerts great pressure, drypoint burrs are quickly worn down. This means that only a few good copies can be made.

We can see the difference between the scraped and unscraped drypoint lines in Mary Cassatt's *The Caress* (**8.9**). Notice how some lines seem to have indistinct edges and a velvety appearance, such as along the child's arm or in the mother's hair. These lines have not had their burr removed. The scraped lines are crisper,

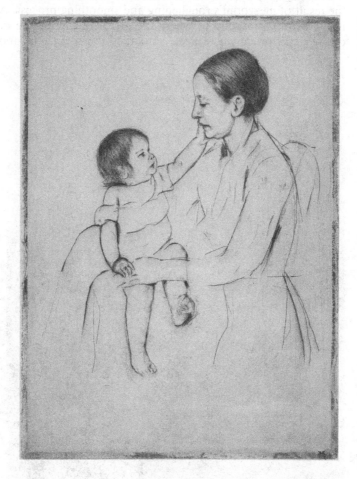

8.9 Mary Cassatt. *The Caress*. 1891. Drypoint, 7 ¾ × 5 ¾".
The Metropolitan Museum of Art, New York. Gift of Arthur Sachs, 1916

with edges that are easier to distinguish. Drypoint's scratchy quality and the subtle value variations possible with this intaglio process are visible in the figures' hair and in the soft modeling of their faces.

Mezzotint

Almost all the major printmaking techniques developed anonymously. We do not know who the first person was to make a woodcut, or who first realized that the lines incised into metal for decoration could also hold ink and be pressured into printing. With **mezzotint**, however, we know precisely who invented it, and when: it was devised by a 17th-century amateur artist named Ludwig von Siegen, who lived in Utrecht, in the Netherlands. In 1642, Von Siegen sent a print created with his new technique to the king of the Netherlands, with a letter boasting that "there is not a single engraver, a single artist of any kind, who can account for, or guess how this work is done."[3] Mezzotint was indeed something new in printing, a method for producing finely graded tonal areas—areas of gray shading into one another—without using line.

Mezzotint relies on pits in the plate rather than lines. It is also a reverse process, in which the artist works from dark to light. To prepare a mezzotint plate, the artist first roughens the entire plate with a sharp tool called a rocker. If the plate were inked and printed after this stage, it would print a sheet of paper entirely black, because each tiny pit would catch and hold the ink. Lighter tones can be created only by smoothing or rubbing out these rough spots so as not to trap the ink. To do this, the artist goes over portions of the plate with a burnisher (a smoothing tool) and/or a scraper to wear down the roughened pits and their burrs (see 8.7). Where the burrs are partially removed, the plate will print intermediate values. The lightest values print in areas where the burrs are smoothed away entirely.

The grainy appearance of Charles Willson Peale's *Benjamin Franklin* (**8.10**) is the result of mezzotint's roughening and smoothing process. All the tiny dots visible in the print correspond to where the artist roughened the plate. The lighter areas of the jacket reveal where Peale smoothed down the burr and pits in the dark coat

8.10 Charles Willson Peale. *Benjamin Franklin*. 1787. Mezzotint, 6 ⅜ × 5 ⅛".
Metropolitan Museum of Art, New York. Bequest of Charles Allen Munn, 1924

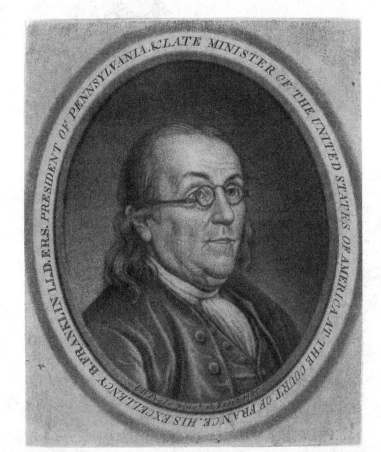

to create the illusion of mass. The dark areas at the top of the right shoulder, under the hair, and on the back of the head are where the artist left the roughened plate alone to create shadows. While Peale created the image of this hero of American history in mezzotint, he used an engraver's burin to cut the letters in the frame.

Mezzotint found immediate favor as a method for reproducing famous paintings in black and white, thus making them available to a broad audience. Artists liked how mezzotint used tone rather than line to simulate the colors in paintings. Although less often used today for original prints than other techniques, it is still the first choice for artists who want a seamless range of values at their disposal, especially if they work on a small scale.

Etching

Etching is done with acids that "eat" lines and depressions into a metal plate much as sharp tools cut those depressions in the other methods. To make an etching, the artist first coats the entire printing plate with an acid-resistant substance called a **ground**, made from beeswax, asphalt, and other materials. Next, the artist draws on the coated plate with an etching needle. The needle removes the ground, exposing the bare metal in areas meant to print. Then the entire plate is dipped in acid (see 8.7). Only the portions of the plate exposed by the needle are eaten into by the acid, leaving the rest of the plate intact. Finally, the ground is removed, and the plate is inked and printed. Etched lines are not as sharp and precise as those made by the engraver's burin, because the biting action of the acid is slightly irregular. But drawing with the etching needle is not as physically demanding as cutting with a burin, allowing for freer and more fluid lines.

Rembrandt van Rijn, who was a prolific printmaker, made hundreds of etchings. Unfortunately, many of his plates were not canceled or destroyed. Long after his death, and long after the plates had worn down badly, people greedy to produce yet more "Rembrandts" struck impressions from the plates. These later impressions lack detail and give us little idea of what the artist intended. To get a true sense of Rembrandt's genius as an etcher, we must look at prints that are known to be early impressions, such as *Christ Preaching* (**8.11**). Using only line, Rembrandt gives us a world made of light and shade. He has set his scene in a humble quarter of town,

8.11 Rembrandt van Rijn. *Christ Preaching*. ca. 1652. Etching, 6 ⅛ × 8".
Rijksmuseum, Amsterdam
RP-P-1961-1022

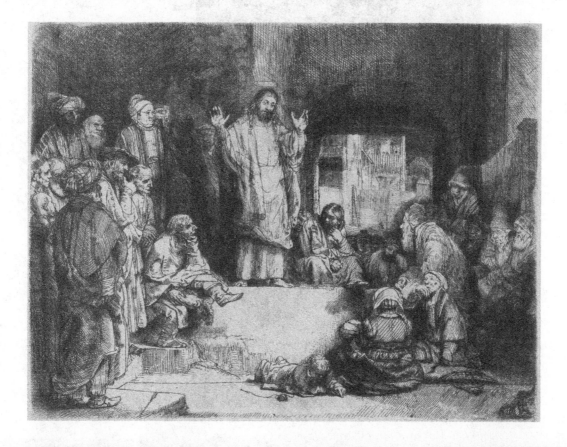

possibly modeled on the Jewish section of the Amsterdam he knew well. Barefoot and bathed in sunlight, Christ preaches to the small but curious crowd that has gathered. His attention falls for a moment on the little boy in the foreground, who, too young to understand the importance of what he is hearing, has turned away to doodle with his finger in the dust. Rembrandt's greatness lay in part in his ability to imagine and portray such profoundly human moments.

Aquatint

A variation on the etching process, **aquatint** is a way of achieving flat areas of tone—gray values or intermediate values of color. Aquatint was invented around 1650 by a Dutch printmaker named Jan van de Velde, but it was not until the technique was included in two French printmaking manuals more than a century later that it finally became widely known among artists.

To prepare a plate for aquatint, the artist first dusts it with finely powdered resin. The plate is then heated so that the resin sticks to it. Resin resists acid, so when the plate is immersed in acid, the acid will bite all around the resin particles, producing a pitted surface that holds ink evenly. The longer the acid bath, the deeper the bite; the deeper the bite, the more ink it will hold, and the darker it will print. To achieve a variety of tones with the same plate, the artist works in stages. First, areas that are not to be bitten at all, where the white of the paper will show untouched, are **stopped out**—painted with an acid-resistant varnish. The plate is then immersed in acid until the bite is deep enough to print the lightest desired tone. The areas that are to print in the lightest tone are then stopped out, and the plate is returned to the acid until the bite is deep enough to produce the second lightest tone. These areas are then stopped out, and the plate is returned to the acid yet again. The process continues until the full range of desired tones has been achieved. The resin and stop-out varnish are then scrubbed away using a solvent, and the plate is ready to be inked and printed.

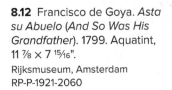

8.12 Francisco de Goya. *Asta su Abuelo* (*And So Was His Grandfather*). 1799. Aquatint, 11 ⅞ × 7 ¹⁵⁄₁₆".
Rijksmuseum, Amsterdam
RP-P-1921-2060

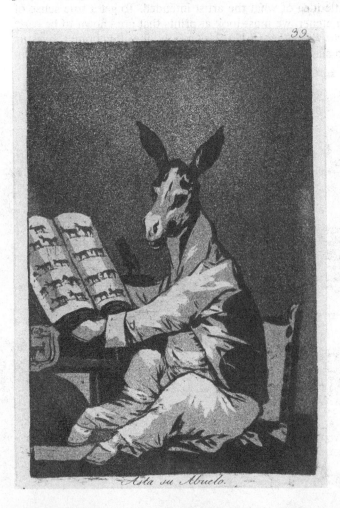

The Spanish artist Francisco de Goya used aquatint for his satirical print *Asta su Abuelo* (*And So Was His Grandfather*, **8.12**). Goya depicts an ass proudly displaying his family genealogy. It's clear that he comes from a long line of asses. Goya's immediate target was the Spanish aristocracy of his day, which inherited power and privilege thanks to noble pedigrees that went back for centuries. The areas that appear lightest on the sleeve, pants, and page have been protected from the acid. The areas that are darkest, such as the figure's back and ears, have spent the longest time in the acid. The graininess of the distinct tonal areas is typical of aquatint and shows the location of the resin grains.

Because aquatint prints not lines but only areas of tone, it is usually combined with one of the other intaglio techniques—drypoint, etching, or engraving (see 21.14). By combining techniques, the intaglio artist can get almost any result he or she wishes. Because the artist can achieve effects ranging from the most precisely drawn lines to the most subtle areas of tone, the possibilities for imagery are much greater than with the relief methods.

Photogravure

Developed during the 19th century, **photogravure** is an etching technique for printing photographic images. Like mezzotint, photogravure can print continuous tones, tones that shade evenly from light to dark. Like aquatint, it uses powdered resin to create a plate that can hold tone. We describe the process here for a black-and-white photograph, though color photographs can also be printed.

To create a photogravure, a full-size positive transparency of the photographic image is placed over a sheet of light-sensitized gelatin tissue (gelatin backed with paper) and exposed to ultraviolet light. The gelatin hardens in proportion to the amount of light it is exposed to, beginning on the surface and extending gradually downward. Thus, light passing through a blank area on the transparency will eventually harden the entire thickness of the gelatin; during the same amount of exposure time, light passing through gray areas will harden the gelatin only partway down, leaving a soft lower layer.

After exposure, the gelatin tissue is attached face down to a copper plate, reversing the image. (The paper backing is now on top.) The plate is placed in a bath of warm water, which causes the paper to float free and the soft gelatin to dissolve away, leaving only the hardened gelatin attached to the plate. What remains is a low relief of the image in hardened gelatin in which lighter areas are raised (the gelatin layer is thicker) and darker areas are sunken (the gelatin layer is thinner). This gelatin surface is now dusted with resin, as for aquatint, and the plate is heated to bind the resin to the surface. When the plate is immersed in acid, the acid eats through the gelatin and into the plate below, etching it. Because the gelatin varies in thickness, the bite will vary in depth: By the time the acid has eaten through the thickest layers of gelatin to reach the plate, the lowest layers will be deeply etched. The deeply etched areas will print velvety darks; the barely etched areas will print pale tones.

Photogravure was initially used to print photographs and photographic reproductions of paintings as book illustrations. Alfred Stieglitz used photogravure for *The Steerage* (**8.13**). In 1907, Stieglitz was aboard ship on his way to Europe, traveling first class. One day as he was walking the deck, he happened to look down into the lowest-class section, called steerage. Before him he saw a perfectly composed image—the smokestack leaning to the left at one end, the iron stairway leaning to the right at the other, the chained drawbridge cutting across, even such details as the round straw hat on the man looking down and the grouping of women and children below. Stieglitz knew he had only one unexposed photographic plate left (the equivalent of one exposure at the end of a roll of film). He raced to his cabin to get his camera. When he returned, the scene was exactly the same; no one had moved. That one plate became *The Steerage*.

Photogravure's characteristically broad tonal range is visible throughout *The Steerage*. The values shift from the white of the walkway to the darkest, velvety black

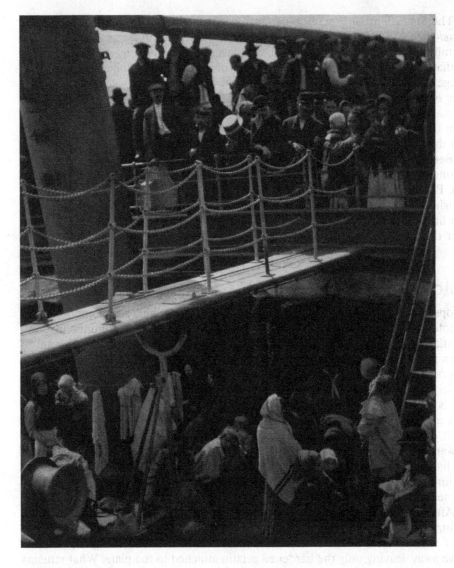

under the deck. If we had the opportunity to inspect the image with a magnifying glass, we would see the graininess of the powdered resin that etched the plate. Even from a distance we see the soft edges characteristic of photogravure.

Lithography

Like mezzotint, **lithography** owes its existence to a single inventor, in this case a young German actor and playwright named Alois Senefelder. While living in Munich during the 1790s, Senefelder began to experiment with etching processes in an effort to find an inexpensive way to print music, which had traditionally been engraved. Too poor to invest much money in copper plates, he tried working on the smooth Bavarian limestones that lined the streets of Munich, which he excavated from the street and brought to his studio. One day, when he was experimenting with ingredients for drawing on the stone, his laundress appeared unexpectedly, and Senefelder hastily wrote out his laundry list on the stone, using his new combination of materials—wax, soap, and lampblack. Later, he decided to try immersing the stone in acid. To his delight he found that his laundry list appeared in slight relief on the stone. That event paved the way for his development of the lithographic process. Although the relief aspect eventually ceased to play a role, the groundwork for lithography had been laid.

Lithography is a **planographic** process, which means that the printing surface is flat—not raised as in relief or depressed as in intaglio. It depends, instead, on the principle that oil and water do not mix. To make a lithographic print, the artist first draws the image on the stone with a greasy material—usually a grease-based lithographic crayon or a greasy ink known by its German name, *tusche*. The stone is then subjected to a series of procedures, including treatment with an acid solution, that fix the drawing (bind it to the stone so that it will not smudge) and prepare it to be printed. To print the image, the printer dampens the stone with water, which soaks into the areas *not* coated with grease. When the stone is inked, the greasy ink sticks to the greasy drawing and is repelled by the water-soaked background areas. Although limestone is still the preferred surface for art prints, lithographs can also be made using zinc or aluminum plates.

For artists, lithography is the most direct and effortless of the print media, for they can work as freely with lithographic crayons and tusche on stone as they do with regular crayons and ink on paper. Preparing the stone for printing and the printing itself are highly specialized skills, however, and artists usually work on their lithographs at a printer's workshop, often directly under the printer's guidance.

Honoré Daumier's *Nadar Elevating Photography to the Heights of Art* (**8.14**) is a lithograph made for a French newspaper. It pokes fun at the photographer Gaspar-Félix Tournachon, who went by the nickname Nadar. Photography was invented in the late 1830s and quickly gained popularity, especially among the middle class that had portraits taken at the photography studios that Daumier shows covering the city of Paris. Nadar owned one of these studios, but also experimented with aerial photography. Some artists, however, were skeptical about the merits of the new

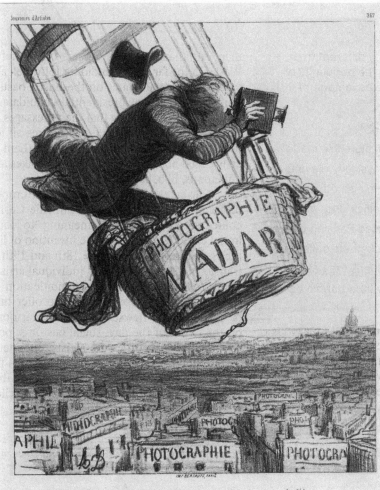

8.14 Honoré Daumier. *Nadar Elevating Photography to the Heights of Art*. 1862. Lithograph, 10 ½ × 8 ¹¹⁄₁₆".
Courtesy National Gallery of Art, Washington, D.C.

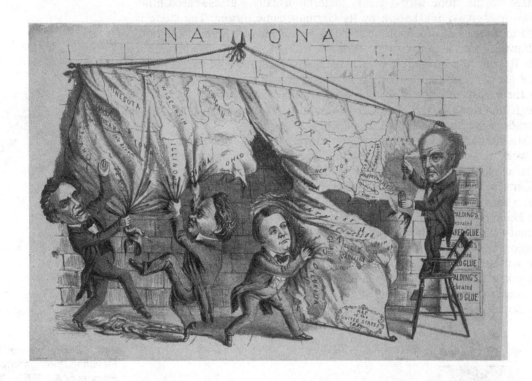

What are caricatures and how are they different from cartoons? How did lithography affect the popularity of caricature? How did caricaturists take advantage of newspapers?

Honoré Daumier was a master of caricature. He made fun of Nadar by showing him trying to physically elevate the status of his photography (see 8.14). He also ridiculed politicians by drawing them with big bellies and voracious appetites for collecting taxes. He teased Parisian women for following fashion trends. He mocked art gallery visitors for not understanding the exhibitions they attended. Each time Daumier published a new lithographic caricature, the people of France clamored to see it.

A caricature is an image of a person that exaggerates features for expressive effect. Daumier's caricatures made noses or bellies larger, or bodies thinner, than they were in life. A cartoon is a humorous drawing that may or may not include caricatures. Usually the desired effect of both a caricature and a cartoon is humorous, although sometimes the humor is mean-spirited and hurtful to the person or group depicted.

In the cartoon seen here, candidates in the 1860 U.S. presidential election greedily claim portions of the national map. Abraham Lincoln appears on the left, claiming the West. On the far right, candidate John Bell attempts to glue together the small states on the East Coast. The cartoon's humor pokes fun at presidential candidates fighting for a share of voters, knowing that their messages appeal more to one region than another. It caricatures all four candidates by exaggerating their heads and giving them small, dramatically posed bodies, and humorously makes all four look like impetuous, ill-behaved children.

Caricature became popular in Europe after the Renaissance. The Italian artist Annibale Carracci may have coined the term *caricatura*, meaning "to load" or "change," in the early 16th century. The invention of lithography and the rise of newspapers in the 18th and 19th centuries then transformed the art from an individual artist's playful doodling to a major form of communication. Lithography's rapid production allowed artists to offer timely images to be inserted into newspapers. Their cartoons commented on the issues of the day: social customs, politics, and current events. Sometimes the artists' commentary exceeded legal boundaries. Daumier's publisher was fined and jailed for the artist's lithographic caricatures of the French king. Still today, caricatures have the power to rile viewers, even sparking violent reactions.

Dividing the National Map. 1860. Lithograph, sheet 14 1/16 × 20 5/8".
Library of Congress Prints and Photographs Division [LC-USZ62-10493]

mechanical image-making process, believing that the camera did all of the work. Daumier plays with the distinction between high- and low-brow art in this lithograph, comparing Nadar's physical elevation to the social elevation he sought for his art.

Daumier's satirical image shows the ease of drawing in lithography. The crayon lines that describe the basket, hair, and flowing cloth are loose and sketchy. We can imagine the artist's hand quickly drawing these lines. The top hat, jacket, and pants are more carefully treated to model the round cylinder of the hat or the bulky mass of the figure. Notice the use of hatching to create value on the arm. In other areas, Daumier used tusche to create flat areas of tone without lines, as seen in the even washes of gray over the city and across the side of the figure's face. Up close, these flat areas and the lines of Daumier's lithograph reveal the graininess of the limestone on which the artist drew.

Color lithographs can be made by using one stone for each color. To ensure correct registration, an outline of the image is first transferred to each stone using a nongreasy substance that will not print. The stones are then worked and prepared in the normal way. Elizabeth Catlett employed flat colors, patterned grounds, and precise contours for her color lithograph *Singing Their Songs* (**8.15**). This is one of a series of prints that Catlett made based on lines from Margaret Walker's remarkable poem "For My People." A touchstone of African-American literature, "For My People" builds its considerable power through repetition, with each stanza lifting its voice again in dedication. Catlett echoes this device, dividing her composition into four spaces, the way a poem is divided into stanzas, and using each space to celebrate a new group—the people singing their songs, the people saying their prayers, the wise elders looking on, the young with their eyes on the future.

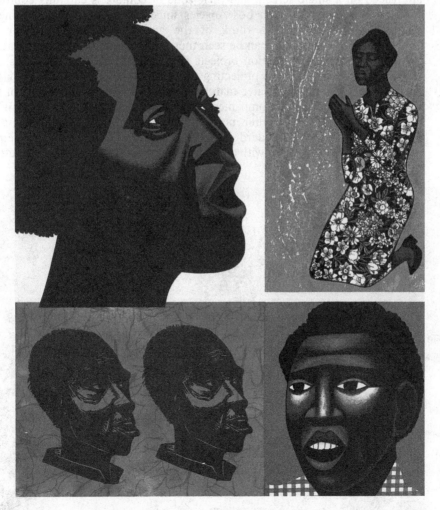

8.15 Elizabeth Catlett. *Singing Their Songs*. 1992. Color lithograph, 23 × 19".

Moore Energy Resources Elizabeth Catlett Collection. Art © Catlett Mora Family Trust/Licensed by VAGA, New York, NY

Screenprinting

To understand the basic principle of **screenprinting**, you need only picture the lettering stencils used by schoolchildren. The stencil is a piece of cardboard from which the forms of the alphabet letters have been cut out. To trace the letters onto paper, you simply place the stencil over paper and fill in the holes with pencil or ink.

Today's art screenprinting works much the same way. The screen is a fine mesh of silk or synthetic fiber mounted in a frame, rather like a window screen. (Silk is the traditional material, so the process has often been called **silkscreen** or **serigraphy**—"silk writing.") Working from drawings, the printmaker stops out (blocks) screen areas that are *not* meant to print by plugging the holes, usually with some kind of glue, so that no ink can pass through. Then the screen is placed over paper, and the ink is forced through the mesh with a tool called a squeegee. Only the areas not stopped out allow the ink to pass through and print on paper (see 8.1).

To make a color screenprint, the artist prepares one screen for each color. On the "blue" screen, for example, all areas not meant to print in blue are stopped out, and so on for each of the other colors. The preparation of multiple color screens is relatively easy and inexpensive. For that reason, it is not unusual to see serigraphs printed in ten, twenty, or more colors. Color screenprinting requires careful registration so that the image prints correctly.

Ed Ruscha's screenprint *Standard Station* (**8.16**) takes advantage of the medium's ability to produce broad areas of flat, uniform color. Popularly used for such humble purposes as printing T-shirts and posters, screenprinting is well suited to the banal, everyday subject matter of a roadside gasoline station. The two-toned background was created using a technique called split fountain, in which two colors are placed on a single screen, and their zone of contact is carefully controlled.

Ed Ruscha has lived in Los Angeles since his student days, and one way to understand his work is to think of the giant white letters of the famous "HOLLYWOOD" sign that can be seen there against the hills. The dramatic diagonal of Ruscha's gasoline station projects the word "STANDARD" across the page as boldly as a beam of light projecting a film title onto a screen. Indeed, the sign itself resembles a movie theater marquee. Standard Oil was the name of the first and most famous of all oil companies. But Ruscha leaves out the word "oil" so that "standard" can take on its other meanings as well: a norm, a benchmark, a banner, a flag. His image of a standard station slyly links two fundamental elements of American life, our love affair with the movies, and our love affair with the automobile.

8.16 Ed Ruscha. *Standard Station*. 1966. Screenprint, 19 ⅝ × 36 ¹⁵⁄₁₆". The Museum of Modern Art, New York. John B. Turner Fund, 1386.1968. Digital image © The Museum of Modern Art/Licensed by SCALA/Art Resource, NY. Photography by Robert McKeever. © Ed Ruscha. Courtesy Gagosian Gallery

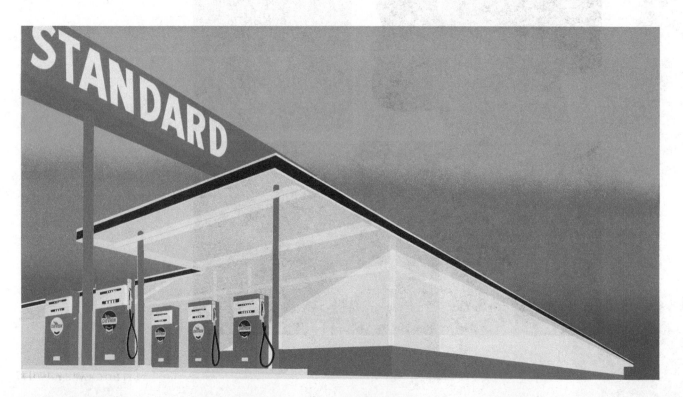

Monotype

There is one major exception to the rule, stated at the beginning of this chapter, that prints are an art of multiples. That exception is the **monotype**. Monotypes are made by an indirect process, like any other print, but, as the prefix "mono" implies, only one print results. To make a monotype, the artist draws on a metal plate or some other smooth surface, often with diluted oil paints. Then the plate is run through a press to transfer the image to paper. Or the artist may simply place a sheet of paper on the plate and hand-rub it to transfer the image. Either way, the original is destroyed or so altered that there can be no duplicate impressions. If a series of prints is planned, the artist must do more work on the plate.

Monotype offers several technical advantages. The range of colors is unlimited, as is the potential for lines or tones. No problems arise with cutting against a grain or into resistant metal. The artist can work as freely as in a direct process such as painting or drawing. Yet the medium is not as simple and straightforward as it seems, for the artist cannot be quite sure how the print will look when it comes through the press. Transferred by pressure from a nonabsorbent surface such as metal to the absorbent surface of paper, colors may blend and spread and contours may soften. The textures of brushstrokes on the plate disappear into flatness on the paper. Differences between plate and print may be minute or dramatic, and the artist may try to control them as much as possible, or play with the element of chance that they bring to the creative process.

Nicole Eisenman's whimsical untitled monoprint depicts a romantic encounter between an unshaven man and a pet bird that seems to take them both by surprise (**8.17**). Brushstrokes from where the paint was laid down on the plate are clearly visible in the sky and on the man's hand and torso. Eisenman enjoys visual puns, and the image may have been inspired by our idiom for a quick, light kiss: a peck on the lips.

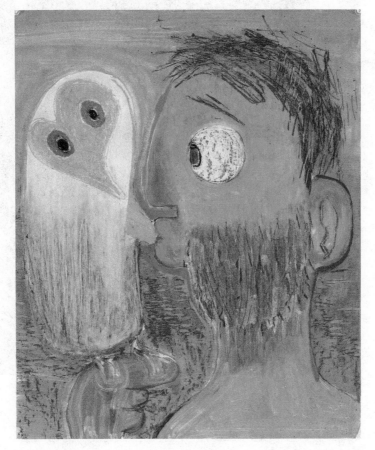

8.17 Nicole Eisenman. *Untitled.* 2012. Monoprint on paper, 23 ½ × 19 ½", unique.
Private Collection, New York. Courtesy the artist and Koenig & Clinton, New York

Digital

According to the traditional definition, a print is made from a matrix. For a woodcut or a wood engraving, for example, the matrix is a piece of wood; for a lithograph, the matrix is a slab of stone. Within the past few years, however, this definition has been blurred by the acceptance of digital prints as a fine-art medium. The inkjet printers used for digital fine-art prints are more sophisticated versions of the printers that many people have connected to their home computer. Like a home printer, a high-quality printer creates an image from a digital file by spraying mists of ink at a receptive surface such as a sheet of paper; there is no matrix. A high-quality printer is capable of printing with more colors than a home-grade printer, however, and it uses finer, pigment-based inks formulated to resist fading or altering in color over time.

Digital prints are easy to identify under magnification. The color is applied as dots of cyan, magenta, yellow, and black that overlap to produce a full range of hues. Looking closely at a digital print reveals a massive field of irregularly spaced colorful spots.

If digital prints sound like the digital paintings we discussed in the previous chapter, then it is true that the two mediums have a lot in common. Like Petra Cortright (see 7.15), the British artist Fiona Rae generates the initial compositions for her paintings on the computer. "I use Photoshop as if it were a sophisticated

8.18 Fiona Rae. *Cute Motion!!* 2006. Inkjet with hand collage, 29 × 23". Edition of 40.

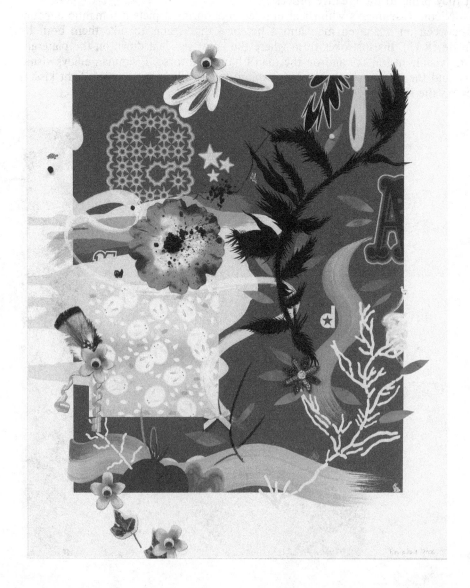

photocopier," she says. "I can feed an image into it and flip the colors around to come up with a set of colors that might have taken me years to figure out by hand."[4] Once the composition has reached a certain point, Rae freely paints a version of it onto a large canvas and continues from there. To create her inkjet print *Cute Motion!!*, she revisited a digital composition linked to one of her paintings and developed it further on its own (**8.18**). Brushstrokes, paint drips, graphic symbols, flowers, letter forms, plant forms, tiny animals, and more all clamor for space and attention in a sort of joyful cacophony. Each print is finished by hand with three-dimensional elements pasted on—googly eyes, small beaded flowers, tiny fuzzy spheres, and a small satin bow. *Cute Motion!!* is definitely not taking itself too seriously. This is art that just wants to have fun.

Recent Directions: Printing on the World

Thanks to industrial versions of engraving, lithography, screenprinting, and digital printmaking, images are routinely printed on almost every imaginable surface around us—balloons, clothing, ceramics, packaging, textiles, wallpaper, decals, electronics, and more. Perhaps it should not surprise us, then, that artists are increasingly taking printed images into the third dimension as well. Like drawing and painting, prints today have left the wall to find a place in sculptures and installations.

John Hitchcock has a long history of experimenting with prints in three dimensions. One project covered the floor and walls of a gallery in prints of tanks and helicopters. Another screenprinted on synthetic fabric naugahyde and stretched prints over wood frames to recall indigenous dwellings. In *National Sanctuary* (**8.20**), Hitchcock screenprinted on naugahyde cut in the shape of a buffalo hide and paper folded into the shape of skulls. He installed these in the shape of a tornado seemingly under siege by attacking helicopters. The screenprint process provided boldly graphic imagery with flat, uniform areas of color. The screens bearing images of birds, lines, and the letter X were used repeatedly on the hides and skulls.

With his three-dimensional prints, Hitchcock participates in the long tradition of printmakers who challenge the social and political status quo. With its easy and rapid dissemination and relative cheapness, printmaking has been the ideal medium for propaganda, subversion, and criticism. Käthe Kollwitz used prints to criticize warfare (see 8.3), William Hogarth turned to engraving to comment on social ills (see 3.9), and Daumier employed lithography to poke fun at the new medium of photography (see 8.14). In *National Sanctuary*, Hitchcock comments on the destruction of war and on damage to the environment. The combination of helicopters, birds, and buffalo from the artist's childhood home near Fort Sill, Oklahoma, reference control and identity.

With Caledonia Curry, better known as Swoon, prints move to walls outside. Swoon makes large linocuts and woodcuts on lightweight paper, cuts the images free of their ground, then pastes them up on urban walls and barriers (**8.21**). "For me pasting is about many things," she says, "and one of them is about declaring the walls of the city a public sounding board for our dreams, desires, and collective identity. I see these walls as a ground level, reachable and seeable-by-the-masses bulletin board for a million voices needing outlets. And I am one of them."[6]

Swoon's subjects are ordinary people, looked at closely, she says. She created the portrait illustrated here while traveling in Brazil in 2011. A young Kamayurá

8.20 John Hitchcock. *National Sanctuary*. 2016. Screenprint, installation, dimensions variable. © John Hitchcock. Photo courtesy of the Museum of Wisconsin Art

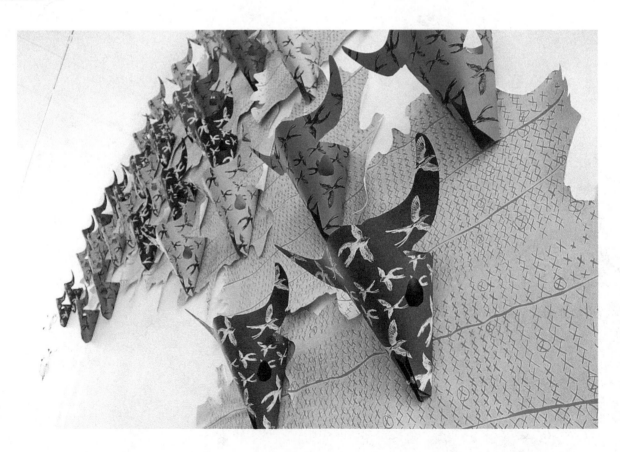

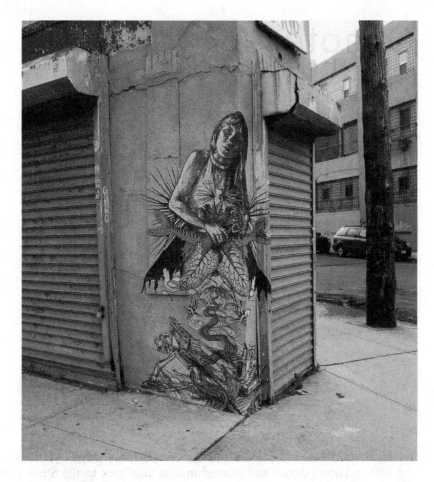

8.21 Swoon (Caledonia Curry).
Untitled (Kamayurá Woman). 2011.
Street installation in Brooklyn, New
York, 2014. Hand-colored linocut,
height approx. 8'.
Photo © Jaime Rojo

woman rises like a spirit over a construction site, holding before her an emblematic arrangement of vegetation and wildlife. The Kamayurá are one of several indigenous peoples who were then fighting the Brazilian government's project to build a huge hydroelectric dam on the Xingu River, the principal river of their region and a major tributary of the Amazon. (They and the environmental groups protesting alongside them did not prevail. As of this writing, the dam is almost finished, and thousands of people living along the river have been displaced.)

Swoon began her career as a street artist, but her work quickly drew the attention of an adventurous gallery owner, who invited her to create an installation. A number of museums have since followed his lead, bringing some of Swoon's prints back inside while others remain pasted to walls around the world.

Notes to the Text

1. Martha Kearns, *Käthe Kollwitz: Woman and Artist* (Old Westbury, NY: Feminist Press, 1967), p. 48.
2. Ibid., p. 164.
3. Quoted in Carol Wax, *The Mezzotint: History and Technique* (New York: Abrams, 1990), p. 15.
4. Fiona Rae, "Artist Fiona Rae on How She Paints," *The Observer*, September 19, 2009. Available online as "Artist Fiona Rae Loves to Show Off in Paint," theguardian.com/artand-design/2009/sep/20/artist-fiona-rae-on-painting, accessed April 27, 2018.
5. Quoted in Peter Crimmins, "Nothing Virtual About Philagrafika Arts Festival," *WHYY News and Information*, January 28, 2010. Available at whyy.org/articles/nothing-virtual-philagrafika-arts-festival, accessed April 27, 2018.
6. Quoted in "CUT & PASTE, an Interview with Swoon," March 27, 2013. Available at destroy-thee.wordpress.com/2013/03/27/cut-paste-an-interview-with-swoon, accessed April 27, 2018.

Chapter 9

Camera and Computer Arts

In this chapter, you will learn to

LO1   describe photographic processes and styles,

LO2   explain the history and art of film,

LO3   discuss how artists have used video, and

LO4   recognize how the Internet is used in art.

In the world of art, the camera and the computer were born yesterday. Although the earliest known drawn and painted images date back to the Stone Age, and the earliest surviving print was made well over one thousand years ago, images recorded by a camera or created on a computer belong entirely to our own modern era.

The camera relies on a natural phenomenon known since antiquity: that light reflected from an object can, under controlled circumstances, project an image of that object onto a surface. It was not until the 19th century, however, that a way was found to capture and preserve such a projected image. With that discovery, photography was born, and after photography, film and video, which recorded the projected image in motion over time.

The computer, too, is rooted in discoveries of earlier times. The first true computer, an electronic machine that could be programmed to process information in the form of data, was built around 1938. Early computers were so large that a single machine occupied an entire room. Over the following decades, technological advances chipped away at the size even as they made computers faster, more powerful, more affordable, and easier to use. Beginning in about 1980, the pace of change accelerated so dramatically that we have come to speak of a digital revolution. The personal computer, the compact disc, the scanner, the World Wide Web, the digital video disk, and the digital camera appeared in rapid succession, together making it possible to capture, store, manipulate, and circulate text, images, and sound as digital data. With the digital revolution, the camera and the computer became intertwined.

Camera and computer technology is essential to business, advertising, education, government, mass media, and entertainment. It has commercial applications and personal applications, and it is widely available to both professional organizations and individual consumers. Among these individuals are artists, who have carved out a space for human expression within the vast flow of information and images that the camera and the computer have enabled. This chapter explores the camera arts—photography, film, and video—from their beginnings through the digital revolution. Then it looks at how artists have worked with the possibilities opened up by the global reach of the Internet.

Photography

The earliest written record that has come down to us of the principle behind photography is from a Chinese philosopher named Mo Ti, who lived during the 5th century B.C.E. Mo Ti noticed that light passing through a pinhole opening into a darkened chamber would form an exact view of the world outside, but upside down. A century or so later, the Greek philosopher Aristotle observed similar phenomena and wondered what caused them. Early in the 11th century C.E., the Arab mathematician and physicist Abu Ali Hasan Ibn al-Haitham, known in the West as Alhazen, set up an experiment in a dark room in which light from several candles passed through a pinhole in a partition, projecting images of the candle flames onto a surface on the other side. From his observations, Alhazen deduced (correctly) that light travels in straight lines, and he theorized (also correctly) that the human eye works along this same principle: Light reflected from objects passes through the narrow opening of the iris, projecting an image of the outside world onto a surface in the dark interior. Alhazen's works circulated in translation in Europe, where early scientists continued his investigations into the behavior of light, but it was not until the Renaissance that a practical device was developed to harness those principles. It was known as the *camera obscura*, Latin for "dark room."

You can make a camera obscura yourself. Find a light-tight room, even a closet or a very large cardboard box. Pierce a small hole, no bigger than the diameter of a pencil, in one wall of the room to admit light. Inside, hold a sheet of white paper a few inches from the hole. You will see an image of the scene outside the room projected on the paper—upside down and rather blurry, but recognizable.

With the development of lenses during the 16th century, the camera obscura could be made to focus the image it projected. Artists of the time, concerned with making optically convincing representations through perspective and chiaroscuro, welcomed this improved camera obscura as a drawing tool. The illustration here (**9.1**) appeared in a book called *The Great Art of Light and Shadow*, published in 1646. It depicts an elaborate version of a portable camera obscura (note the poles on the ground for carrying it). The roof and the fourth wall have been left out of the illustration to allow us to peer inside. Each of the four outer walls had a lens at its center. (Two lenses are shown here, at left and right.) Entering through a trapdoor in the floor (marked F), the artist stood in an inner chamber made of four

9.1 *Camera Obscura*, in cutaway view. 1646. Engraving.
Image courtesy of the Board of Trustees, National Gallery of Art, Washington, D.C. Gift of The Circle of the National Gallery of Art

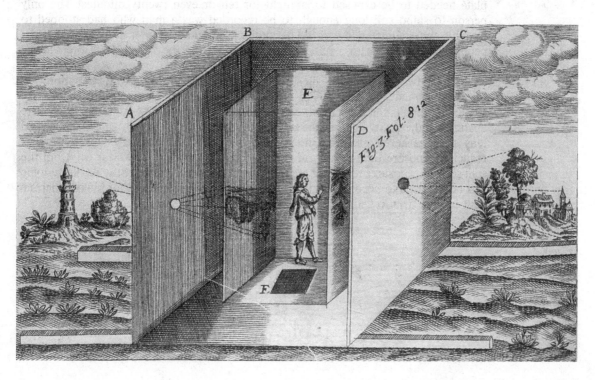

translucent paper screens. (The man here is drawn in miniature—the chamber was not really quite so large!) Each lens projected its view onto the paper chamber, and the artist traced the projections from the other side (thus not getting in the way of the light). It was none other than Leonardo da Vinci who first suggested this arrangement.

The Still Camera and Its Beginnings

Despite the sophistication of modern photographic equipment, the basic mechanism of the camera is simple, and it is no different in theory from that of the camera obscura. A camera is a light-tight box (**9.2**) with an opening at one end to admit light, a lens to focus and refract the light, and a light-sensitive surface to receive the light-image and hold it. The last of these—the holding of the image—was the major drawback of the camera obscura. It could project an image, but there was no way to preserve the image, much less walk away with it in your hand. It was to this end that a number of people in the 19th century directed their attention.

One of those investigators was Joseph Nicéphore Niépce, a French inventor. Working with a specially coated pewter plate in the camera obscura, Niépce managed, in 1826, to record a fuzzy version of the view from his window after an exposure of eight hours. Although we may now consider Niépce's "heliograph" (or sun-writing), as he called it, to be the first permanent photograph, the method was not really practical.

Niépce was corresponding with another Frenchman, Louis-Jacques-Mandé Daguerre, who was also experimenting with methods to fix the photographic image. The two men worked separately and communicated in code to keep their progress from prying eyes. When Niépce died in 1833, his son Isidore continued the experiments. It was Daguerre, however, who in 1837 made the breakthrough, recording in his studio an image that was clear and sharp, by methods that others could duplicate easily. Daguerre's light-sensitive surface was a copper plate coated with silver iodide, and he named his invention the **daguerreotype**.

Daguerre made the image illustrated here in 1839, the year the French government announced his discovery to the world (**9.3**). In the entrancing detail characteristic of daguerreotypes, it records a seemingly deserted boulevard in Paris. In fact, the boulevard was a bustling thoroughfare. To record an image, Daguerre's plate needed to be exposed to sunlight for ten or even twenty minutes! The only person to stand still long enough to be recorded was a man who had stopped to have his shoes shined. He and the partially obscured shoeshiner are among the first people ever to appear in a photograph, and certainly the first to have their image taken without knowing it.

In the two years after Daguerre's discovery was made public, dramatic improvements were made. From England came a better method for fixing the final image so that it didn't continue to change in the light, and also a more light-sensitive coating for the plate, that reduced exposure time. From Vienna came an improved lens that gathered sixteen times as much light as previous lenses, further reducing exposure time to around thirty seconds. Although still a far cry from the split-second exposures that later technology would make possible, the daguerreotype was now poised to become the first commercially viable method for making permanent images from reflected light.

9.2 The basic parts of a camera.

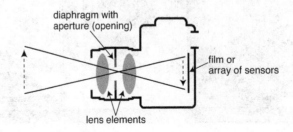

diaphragm with
aperture (opening)

film or
array of sensors

lens elements

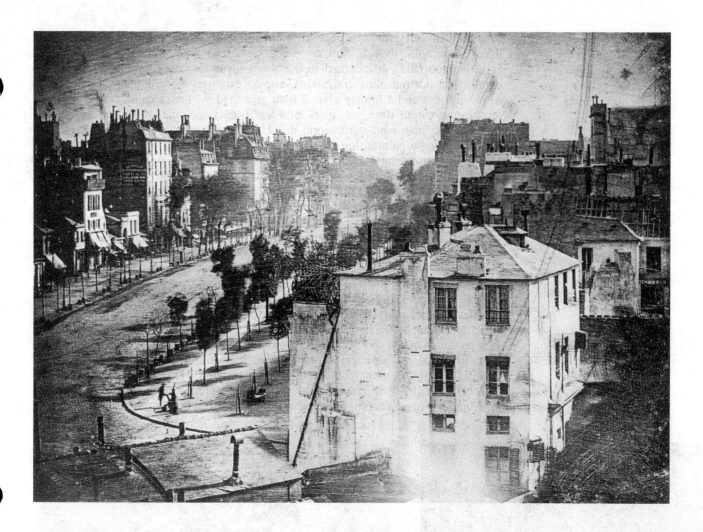

9.3 Louis-Jacques-Mandé Daguerre. *Le Boulevard du Temple*. 1839. Daguerreotype.
Bayerisches Nationalmuseum, Munich.
GraphicaArtis/Getty Images

Daguerre's invention caused great excitement throughout Europe and North America. Entrepreneurs and the general public alike were quick to see the potential of photography, especially for portraits. It is hard to realize now, but until photography came along only the rich could afford to have their likenesses made, by sitting for a portrait painter. Within three years of Daguerre making his first plate, a "daguerreotype gallery for portraits" had opened in New York, and such galleries soon proliferated.

Yet for all its early success, the daguerreotype was ultimately a blind alley for photography. The process produces a *positive* image, an image in which light and dark values appear correctly. This image is unique and cannot be reproduced. The plate is the photograph. The future of photography instead lay in technology that produced a *negative* image, one in which light and dark values were reversed. This negative could be used again and again to create several positive images on light-sensitive paper. Instead of a single precious and delicate object, photography found its essence as an art of potentially unlimited, low-cost multiples. An early version of the negative/positive print process was the calotype, which used a paper negative. Toward the middle of the 19th century, the vastly superior collodion process was developed, which produced a negative on glass.

Portraits remained an important use of the new medium, providing a steady source of income for commercial photographers. The printmaker Daumier poked fun at the proliferation of portrait studios in his lithograph of the photographer Nadar (see 8.14). One of the finest portraitists of the time, however, was an amateur, an English woman named Julia Margaret Cameron. Cameron's social circle included some of the most famous writers, artists, and intellectuals of her time, and she drew on her friendships to create memorable portraits of such luminaries as the naturalist Charles Darwin, the American poet Henry Wadsworth Longfellow, the Shakespearean actress Ellen Terry, and the poet Alfred, Lord Tennyson. Some of Cameron's loveliest photographs, though, portray someone who was not famous at all, her niece Julia Jackson (**9.4**). In contrast to the sharp focus and even lighting preferred by commercial portrait photographers, Cameron explored more poetic effects, with a softened focus and a moody play of light and shadow. Julia's calm, forthright gaze reaches out to our time from hers. She was twenty-one years old and about to be married to a man who would soon die. Her second marriage would produce two daughters, one a painter, the other the novelist Virginia Woolf.

Early photography required long exposure times and bulky equipment. This meant that photographers could not yet capture action. The renowned Civil War photographer Timothy O'Sullivan created images that have become part of the American cultural identity, yet none pictures a battle underway. Instead, photographs such as *A Harvest of Death* (**9.5**) capture the quieter, but still powerful, moments before or after the fighting. *A Harvest of Death* was taken in the aftermath of the Battle of Gettysburg in July of 1863, when more than 7,000 men died. The bodies spread across the landscape in O'Sullivan's photograph stand for the thousands more found nearby. The men seen standing and on horseback in the background represent those charged with the grim task of burying the dead in land that would soon become Gettysburg National Cemetery. O'Sullivan's photograph was published in an 1866 album of pictures of the Civil War that Americans purchased as a reminder of the sad events.

To make his photograph, O'Sullivan had to transport his large camera, chemicals, and darkroom to the battlefield in a wagon. He prepared the glass plate and, before it dried, inserted it into the camera perched on a large tripod. After allowing light to pass through the focused lens for several seconds, O'Sullivan closed

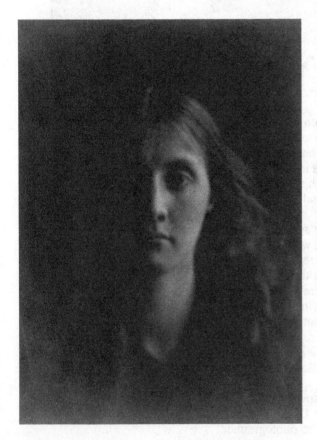

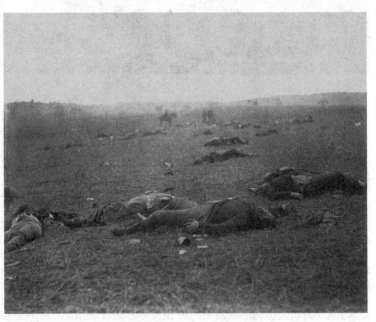

9.5 Timothy O'Sullivan. *A Harvest of Death*. 1863. Albumen print from glass negative, 5 ¹³⁄₁₆ × 8 ¹³⁄₁₆".
The J. Paul Getty Museum, Los Angeles. Digital image courtesy of the Getty's Open Content Program

9.4 Julia Margaret Cameron. *Julia Jackson*. 1867. Albumen print from glass negative, 10 ¹³⁄₁₆ × 8 ⅛".
The Metropolitan Museum of Art, New York. Purchase, Joseph Pulitzer Bequest, 1996, 1996.99.2. Image © The Metropolitan Museum of Art

the aperture and stored the plate without exposing it to ambient light. Once back in the studio, he printed the negative. Only then could he truly see the image he had captured.

This cumbersome process had changed by the 1880s, when technical advances reduced exposure time to a fraction of a second, allowing cameras to capture life as it happened, without asking it to pose. Then, in 1888, an American named George Eastman developed a camera called the Kodak, which changed photography forever. Unlike earlier cameras, the Kodak was lightweight and handheld, which meant it could be taken anywhere. Sold with the slogan "You press the button, we do the rest," the camera came loaded with a new invention, a roll of film, enough for one hundred photographs. Users simply took the pictures (which quickly became known as "snapshots") and sent the camera back to the company. Their developed and printed photographs were returned to them along with their camera, reloaded with film.

The Kodak and cameras like it opened photography up to amateurs, and it quickly became a popular hobby. Although serious photographers continued (and still continue) to oversee the development and printing of their own work, they, too, benefited from the portable, lightweight technology. Almost anywhere a person could go, a camera could now go; almost anything a person could see, a camera could record. Daily life, the life any one of us lives, became photography's newest and perhaps most profound subject. It remains so even in today's age of digital photographs.

Bearing Witness and Documenting

One way in which photography changed the world was in the sheer quantity of images that could be created and put into circulation. Whereas a painter might take weeks or even months to compose and execute a scene of daily life, a photographer could produce dozens of such scenes in a single day. But what purpose could this facility be put to? What was the advantage of quantity and speed? One early answer was that photography could record what was seen as history unfolded, or preserve a visual record of what existed for a time. We could call these purposes "bearing witness" and "documenting," and they continue to play important roles today.

Photographs bearing witness to events appear in newspapers and magazines the world over, but it wasn't always this way. Newspapers during the 19th century were illustrated with wood engravings or lithographs. Artists were sent as reporters to major news events or drew images after the fact based on eyewitness accounts. The Civil War images that appeared with newspaper articles still had to be drawn, and even suitable photographs had to be recopied as engravings or lithographs, for the technology did not yet exist to print photographs commercially on ordinary paper. Then, around 1900, the first process for photomechanical reproduction—high-speed printing of photographs along with type—came into being, and with it a new concept, photojournalism.

Photojournalism quickly became concerned about more than just getting a photograph to illustrate an article. Although a single photograph may be all the general public sees at the time, photojournalists often create a significant body of work around an event, a place, or a culture. A historical episode that brought out the best in many of the finest photographers of the day was the Great Depression in the United States. The Great Depression, which began in 1929 and lasted until the onset of World War II, caused hardship for photographers as well as for the population as a whole. To ease the first problem and document the second, the Farm Security Administration (FSA) of the U.S. Department of Agriculture subsidized photographers and sent them out to record conditions across the nation. One of those photographers was Dorothea Lange.

Dorothea Lange's travels for the FSA took her to nearly every part of the country. In one summer alone she logged 17,000 miles in her car. Lange devoted her attention to the migrants who had been uprooted from their farms by the combined effects of Depression and drought. Lange's best-known image from this time

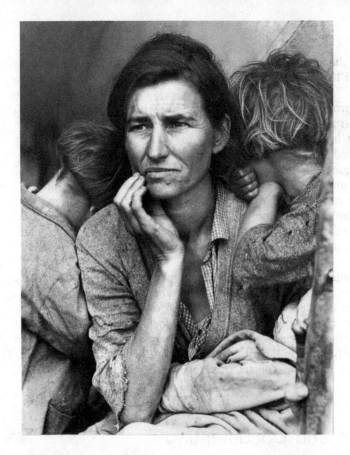

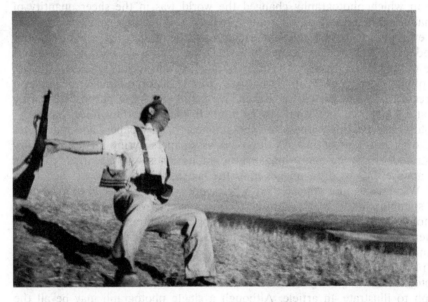

is the haunting *Migrant Mother* (**9.6**). From this worried mother and her tattered clothing, from the two children who huddle against her, hiding their faces from the stranger with the camera, Lange created a photograph that touched the hearts of the world. "I do not remember how I explained my presence or my camera to her but I do remember she asked me no questions," the photographer recalled years later. "I made five exposures, working closer and closer from the same direction. I did not ask her name or her history . . ."[1] FSA photos like this one were offered free to newspapers and magazines.

A photograph can capture a fleeting moment's terrible consequences. Robert Capa was a Hungarian photojournalist working in Spain during the Spanish Civil War. His photograph *The Falling Soldier* (**9.7**) was taken at the precise moment a bullet struck the fighter. The shot's force pushes the soldier backward and he loses

Censorship

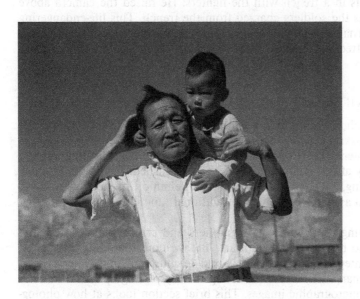

What is censorship? Why is art sometimes censored? How was Dorothea Lange's photography censored? What boundaries, if any, should be imposed on artists? How much of the public's reaction should artists take into consideration?

Censorship occurs when groups or individuals suppress words or pictures they find offensive, indecent, or dangerous. Censorship's goal is to keep these texts and images out of public view. Art has a long history of being censored. Governments have censored seditious images or those that give away military secrets. Organized religions have censored pictures that violate their teachings or morals. Individual artists have self-censored by opting not to represent a theme or issue that might upset viewers or cause controversy.

Dorothea Lange's photographs of the American Great Depression have secured her a place in American history, but even she was not immune to censorship. In 1942, Lange photographed the internment camps where Japanese Americans were held against their will during World War II. She had been hired by the U.S. government to take the pictures, yet the photographs were not distributed. Instead, the U.S. Army put her photographs, such as the image of a grandfather with his grandson seen here, in a folder labeled "Impounded," and her work was shut away in the National Archives. The government censored the photographs as a record of its shameful treatment of American citizens. The collection was not published until 2006, more than 60 years after the war ended.

Prints, paintings, and even sculptures have been censored. In 1857, an Italian nobleman sent an extravagant gift to Queen Victoria of England: a life-size plaster cast of Michelangelo's famous statue of *David* (see 16.8). The Queen sent it off to a museum still in its crate. When she came to have a look at the statue, its nudity so shocked her that officials commissioned a sculptor to create a large white fig leaf to cover the statue's genitals. The leaf was removable. Notified of an upcoming visit by sensitive ladies, museum officials would rush to put the fig leaf in place. After the visitors had departed, they would take it off again.

Photography seems to invite special scrutiny, thanks to its ability to capture reality. U.S. military authorities kept documentary photographers away from the front lines in World War I and controlled which photographs were published during World War II. Newspaper and magazine editors have cropped, blurred, or obscured upsetting or supposedly indecent images ranging from photographs of deceased soldiers to paparazzi pictures of topless sunbathers. Even in 2016, the social media site Facebook censored the famous 1972 photograph of a nude Vietnamese child burned by napalm, initially arguing that its nudity was indecent.

Fine-art photography has been censored as well. In 1990, a museum director was indicted on obscenity charges (although later acquitted) for exhibiting photographs by Robert Mapplethorpe. Members of the U.S. Congress found these and other images so offensive that they permanently eliminated direct government grants to individual artists. One of the images that offended politicians at about the same time was Andres Serrano's *Piss Christ*, a photograph of a Crucifixion submerged in urine. This picture was also censored in Australia in 1997, when a visitor to a museum exhibition attacked the photograph, causing the museum to end the show. In 2011, the Smithsonian Institution removed a video by the artist David Wojnarowicz that showed ants crawling on a Crucifixion. Each of these works was censored for offending viewers' religious beliefs or sense of decency.

Dorothea Lange. *Manzanar Relocation Center, Manzanar, California, July 2, 1942. Grandfather and grandson of Japanese ancestry at the War Relocation Authority center.* 1942. National Archives Records of the War Relocation Authority

his grip of the gun he holds. This image embodies photography's potential to communicate the frenzied brutality of warfare. It may have been the first photograph to capture the moment of death on the battlefield. Capa explained that when he took the picture he was in a trench with the fighters. He raised the camera above his head and clicked as the soldiers charged from the trench. This life-endangering approach to photojournalism has come to define wartime photography, and photographers have been frequent casualties in global conflicts.

Photography and Art

The development of photography has been seen as freeing painting and sculpture from practical tasks such as recording appearances and events, and it is certainly true that Western artists began to explore the potential of abstraction and nonrepresentation only after photography was well established. Ironically, to many people's way of thinking, the older forms took the definition of "art" with them, leaving photography to assume many of the traditional functions of art with none of the rewards.

From the beginning there were photographers and critics who insisted that photography could also be practiced as an art. Today, more than 180 years later, photography is fully integrated into the art world of museums and galleries, and many artists who are not primarily photographers work with photographic images. This brief section looks at how photography found its way both as an art and into art.

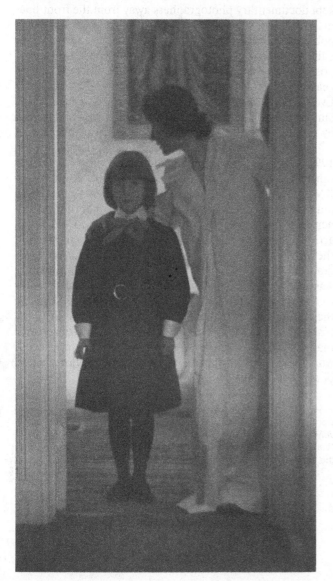

9.8 Gertrude Käsebier. *Blessed Art Thou Among Women.* 1899. Platinum print, 9 1/16 × 5 3/16". The Metropolitan Museum of Art, New York. Alfred Stieglitz Collection, 1933

One characteristic of photographs that disqualified them as art in many people's eyes was their sharply detailed objectivity, which seemed to preclude personal expression. Another stumbling block was the medium's increasing popularity and ease. In the 20th century, the Kodak camera brought photography within reach of almost everyone, reinforcing the notion that it was simply a matter of framing the view and pushing a button. As Eastman's slogan promised, "we do the rest."

It was precisely "the rest" that obsessed the photographers of the international Pictorialist movement in the late 19th and early 20th centuries—the most influential of the movements that sought to have photography accepted as an art. Pictorialists embraced labor-intensive printing techniques that allowed them to blur unwanted detail, enhance tonal range, soften focus, and add highlights and delicate veils of color, resulting in images that drew close to painting in their effects. A classic example of Pictorialism in America is Gertrude Käsebier's *Blessed Art Thou Among Women* (**9.8**). The photograph pictures a mother standing with her daughter in a well-appointed home. Along with the title, the mother's gown and protective pose suggest that motherhood is a religious calling. The photograph exhibits Pictorialism's typical soft focus and subtle tones, distinguishing it from the crisp edges and strong tones of documentary photography.

Pictorialism flourished from 1889 until the outbreak of World War I, during which time it successfully demonstrated that photographs could be as beautiful and expressive as paintings. But with developments such as abstraction, Cubism, and nonrepresentation, painting was changing, and photography would change as well. In retrospect, the image that most clearly foretold the new direction was *The Steerage*, by Alfred Stieglitz (see 8.13). The type of photography that Stieglitz championed came to be known as "pure" or "straight" photography. Practitioners of straight photography consider it a point of honor not to crop or manipulate their photographs

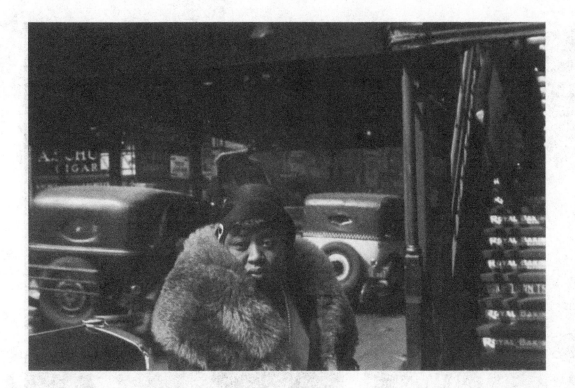

9.9 Walker Evans. *6th Avenue/ Forty-Second Street.* 1929. Gelatin silver print, 4 ¾ × 7 ⁵⁄₁₆".
The J. Paul Getty Museum. Digital image courtesy of the Getty's Open Content Program

in any way. The composition is entirely visualized in advance, framed with the viewfinder, then photographed and printed. With its emphasis on formal values and faithfulness to the essence of the medium, the aesthetic of straight photography was enormously influential for much of the 20th century.

Walker Evans's *6th Avenue/Forty-Second Street* (**9.9**) represents the straight approach to photography. Captured on the streets of New York in 1929, the photograph pictures the city's hustle and bustle. A well-dressed woman walks along the sidewalk, a man descends from an elevated train platform, and cars roll by. The composition is filled with horizontal, vertical, and diagonal lines, from the train trestle and stairway column to the steps and line of car roofs. The hard surfaces throughout the photograph are contrasted by the soft textures of the woman's hat and fur coat. Her presence brings a warm humanity to the impersonal technology of the modern city. Yet for all its artistic qualities, Evans's photograph is the composition the photographer saw through his viewfinder, not the result of darkroom manipulation.

Evans, Käsebier, and Stieglitz practiced photography as an art. Other artists have made photography itself part of the subject of their art, examining its role in society, the particular vision of the world it promotes, and the assumptions we make about it. One of the first artists to look critically at photography was Hannah Höch. Born in 1889, Höch came of age during the decades when photomechanical reproduction first allowed photographic images to appear in newspapers, periodicals, posters, and advertising. Everyday life was suddenly flooded with images, and a constant flow of secondhand reality began to compete with direct experience.

Höch's response was to use these "found" images as a new kind of raw material. In works such as *Cut with the Kitchen Knife . . .* (**9.10**), she combined images and letters she had clipped from printed sources to portray the overwhelming experience of a modern city with its masses of people and machines. The word *dada* that appears in several places refers to the art movement that Höch belonged to. **Dada** was formed in 1916 as a reaction to the unprecedented slaughter of World War I, which was then being fought. The word *dada* itself has no meaning, for, faced with the horror of mechanized killing and the corruption of the societies that allowed it, Dada refused to make sense in traditional ways. A Dada manifesto written in 1918, the year the war ended, called for an art "which has been visibly shattered by the explosions of the last week, which is forever trying to collect its

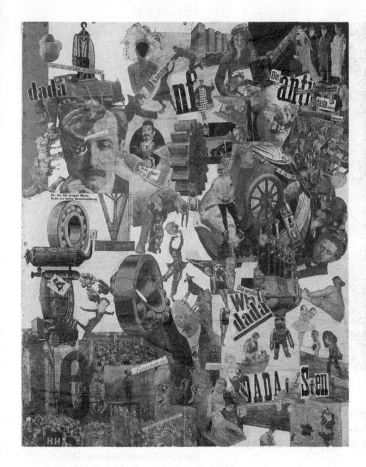

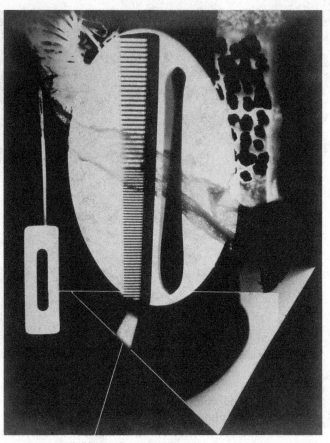

9.10 Hannah Höch. *Cut with the Kitchen Knife Dada through Germany's Last Weimar Beer Belly Cultural Epoch.* 1919. Collage, 44 ⅞ × 35 ⅜".

bpk Bildagentur/Nationalgalerie, Staatliche Museen, Berlin, Germany/ Photo: Jörg P. Anders/Art Resource, NY © 2019 Artists Rights Society (ARS), New York/VG Bild-Kunst, Bonn

9.11 Man Ray. *Champs délicieux, second rayogram.* 1922. Rayogram, silver salt print, 8 ¾ × 7 ½".

Image copyright © The Metropolitan Museum of Art, New York. Image source: Art Resource, NY © Man Ray Trust/Artists Rights Society (ARS), NY/ADAGP, Paris 2019

limbs after yesterday's crash. The best and most extraordinary artists will be those who every hour snatch the tatters of their bodies out of the frenzied cataract of life."[2] Höch, for her part, spent her life snatching bits and pieces from the frenzied cataract of images.

Another artist formed by the ideas of Dada was Emmanuel Radnitzky, better known as Man Ray. Trained as a painter, Man Ray initially learned photography to document his paintings. When a year or two later he turned his attention to the art of photography itself, he reacted with characteristic Dada abandon: He threw away the camera. Instead of placing himself before the world armed with a camera and film, Man Ray retired to the darkroom and began to experiment with the light-sensitive paper that photographs are printed on. He discovered that an object placed on the paper would leave its own shadow in white when the paper darkened upon exposure to light. Working with that simple idea, he invented a technique he called the rayograph (also known as the rayogram, **9.11**). Through such simple strategies as shifting the objects over time, suspending them at various heights over the paper, removing some and adding others, or shifting the light source, Man Ray created mysterious images that looked like ordinary photographs but did not correspond to preconceived ideas of what a photograph was. Rayographs are far removed from the ideal of straight photography championed by Stieglitz and his followers. If we think of photography as a tool for making images instead of as a tool for recording the world, then there are no right or wrong ways to use it—only choices, discoveries, and experiments.

Cindy Sherman also embraces photography itself as part of the subject of some of her photographs. Sherman draws on familiar images from magazines and film to create photographs of herself as someone else. The characters that Sherman invents seem to represent types rather than individuals—the abandoned girlfriend, the vengeful hussy, the pert secretary, the society drunk, the party girl, the androgynous youth, and many others. As we look, we realize that these are categories that we ourselves bring to the images, for the photographs are all called simply *Untitled*. Here, for example, is *Untitled #48* (**9.12**). It pictures Sherman as a young woman standing alone on a dark road, a suitcase resting beside her. As you invent a story for the woman Sherman portrays, you will find that you have made assumptions about what kind of person she is, assumptions based in part on the stereotypes you have absorbed through the photographic images—films, television shows, and advertising—that surround us.

One complaint that had been lodged against photography from the very beginning was that it recorded the world in black and white instead of in full color. Early techniques for color were in place by about 1910, but it was not until the 1930s that color began to be widely used, and then only in advertising. Serious photographers continued for decades to prefer black and white, feeling that color lacked dignity and was suitable only for vulgar commercial photography. Such prejudices began to crumble during the 1960s and 1970s. Today many artists have adopted color photography as a primary means of making images.

The computer has also been welcomed as a natural extension of the medium by many artists who work with photography. Developed during the 1990s, digital cameras use no film at all but, instead, store photographs as data. For photojournalists, digital cameras allow images to be transmitted back to a newspaper over the Internet. For artists, the technology allows them to gather photographic images, feed them into a computer, work with them, and print the end product as a photograph.

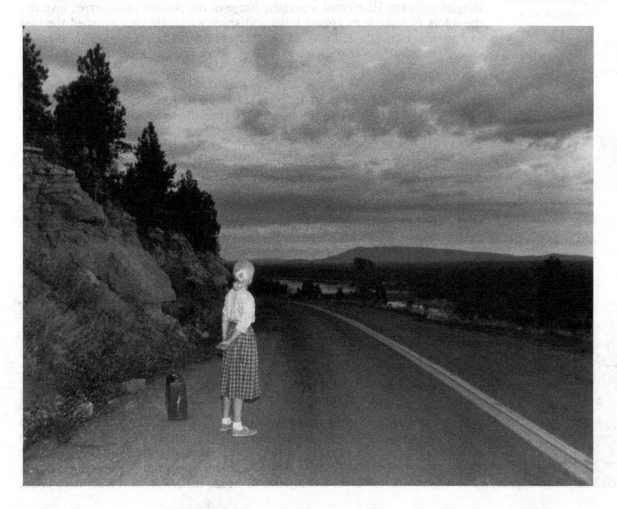

9.12 Cindy Sherman. *Untitled #48*. 1978. Gelatin silver print, 7 7/16 × 9 7/16".
© 2019 Cindy Sherman. Image courtesy Metro Pictures, New York

9.13 Mungo Thomson. *Negative Space (STScl-PRC2012-10a)*. 2012. Inkjet on vinyl, length 93'.

Collection Walker Art Center, Minneapolis. Gift of Collectors' Council Acquisitions Fund (Maurice and Sally Blanks, Bruno Freeman, Katharine L. Kelly, Ron Lotz and Randy Hartten, Carla McGrath and Cole Rogers, Leni and David Moore, Jr./ The Moore Family Fund for the Arts of The Minneapolis Foundation, Brian J. Pietsch and John T. Walsh, Rebecca C. and Robert Pohlad, Alan Polsky, Gregory Stenmoe), and the Babe and Julie Davis Acquisition Fund, 2012

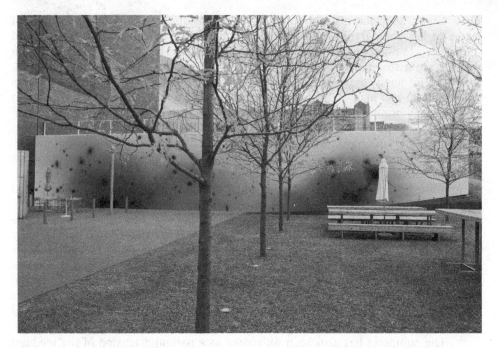

9.14 Thomas Ruff. *Substratum 12 III*. 2003. C-print and Diasec, 8' 4" × 5' 5 ½".

Courtesy the artist and VG Bild-Kunst © 2019 Artists Rights Society (ARS), New York/VG Bild-Kunst, Bonn

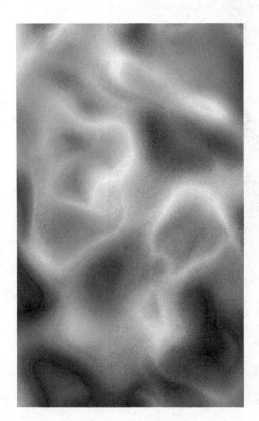

Mungo Thomson's *Negative Space (STScl-PRC2012-10a)* (**9.13**) began with digital photographs taken by the Hubble Space Telescope and transmitted back to Earth. NASA makes these photographs available to the public through the Internet. Thomson took the NASA photograph and manipulated it on the computer using imaging software. He created a negative image of the positive photograph, inverting the colors to make stars appear black and space white. He then cropped the view to a narrow rectangle and printed the 93-foot-long mural on vinyl. The inversion process resulted in a bright and engaging abstract image made by the click of a single button in the imaging software.

Thomas Ruff also looks to the Internet in series of works he calls *Substrata*, meaning "underlayers" (**9.14**). His process is more involved than Thomson's, as he uses images taken from Japanese manga (comic books) and anime (animated films). Ruff layers the images one on top of the other, making them difficult to decipher individually. He manipulates the resulting image, blurring the contours until all traces of recognizable representation have disappeared, then prints the result. Like Thomson, Ruff works on a very large scale. *Substratum 12 III*, illustrated here, is over 8 feet in height.

In the tradition of Man Ray, Ruff has produced photographs without the aid of a camera at all. The raw material he uses, anime and manga images, depicts stories about fantasy worlds. When Ruff finds the images, they are doubly disconnected from reality: once by their imaginary subject matter, and a second time through their virtual existence on the Internet. Layering and blurring them, he further dissolves their stories until they have no memory of their former life, existing only as a glowing, pulsating, jewel-toned field of light on a monitor. Then he gives them material form as a photograph.

Film

Throughout history, artists have tried to create the illusion of motion in a still image. Painters have drawn galloping horses, running people, action of all kinds—never being sure that their depictions of the movement were "correct" and lifelike. To draw a running horse with absolute realism, for instance, the artist would have to freeze the horse in one moment of the

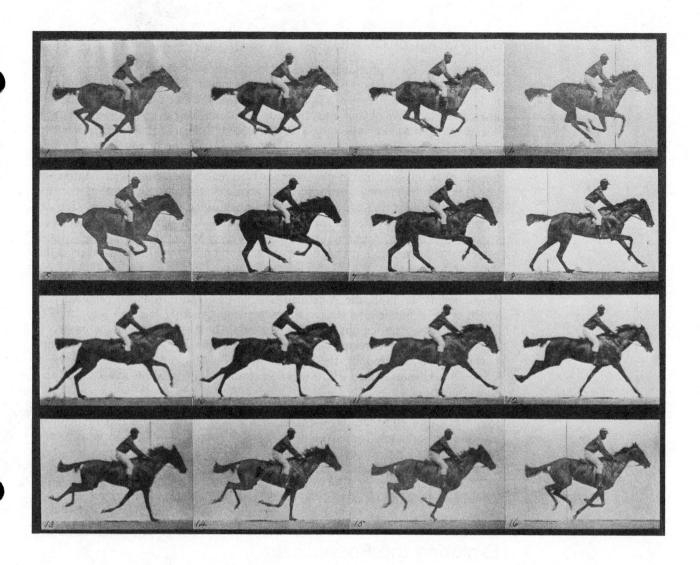

9.15 Eadweard Muybridge. *Horse Galloping*. 1878. Collotype, 9 ³⁄₁₆ × 12".

Library of Congress Prints and Photographs Division, Washington, D.C. LC-USZ62-52703

run, but because the motion is too quick for the eye to follow, the artist had no assurance that a running horse ever does take a particular pose. In 1878, a man named Eadweard Muybridge addressed this problem, and the story behind his solution is a classic in the history of photography.

Leland Stanford, a former governor of California, had bet a friend 25,000 dollars that a horse at full gallop sometimes has all four feet off the ground. Since observation by the naked eye could not settle the bet one way or the other, Stanford hired Muybridge, who was known as a photographer of landscapes, to photograph one of the governor's racehorses. Muybridge devised an ingenious method to take the pictures. He set up twenty-four cameras, each connected to a black thread stretched across the racecourse. As Stanford's mare ran down the track, she snapped the threads that triggered the cameras' shutters—and proved conclusively that a running horse does gather all four feet off the ground at certain times (**9.15**). Stanford won the bet, and Muybridge went on to more ambitious studies of motion. In 1887, he published *Animal Locomotion*, his most important work. With 781 plates of people and animals in sequential motion, *Animal Locomotion* allowed the world to see for the first time what positions living creatures really assume when they move.

Muybridge's experiments in the 1880s had two direct descendants. One was stop-motion photography, which became possible as both films and cameras became faster and faster. The other was *continuous*-motion photography. Undoubtedly, Muybridge had whetted the public's appetite to see *real* motion captured on film. The little room with a view had glimpsed a different world, a world that does not stand still but spins and moves and dances.

The Origins of Motion Pictures

Film depends on a phenomenon called persistence of vision. The human brain retains a visual image for a fraction of a second longer than the eye actually records it. If this were not true, your visual perception of the world would be continually interrupted by blinks of your eyes. Instead, your brain "carries over" the visual image during the split second while the eyes are closed. Similarly, the brain carries over when still images are flashed before the eyes with only the briefest space between them. Motion-picture film is not real motion but a series of still images projected at a speed of twenty-four frames per second, which makes the action seem continuous.

Interest in moving pictures really pre-dates the development of the still camera. As early as 1832, a toy was patented in Europe in which a series of drawn images, each slightly different from the next, was made to spin in a revolving wheel so that the image appeared to move. Eadweard Muybridge later applied this principle to his multiple photographic images, spinning them in a wheel he called the zoopraxiscope.

Commercial applications of the motion picture, however, awaited three major developments. In 1888, the American George Eastman introduced celluloid film, which made it possible to string images together. Another big step was taken by Thomas Edison, the famous American inventor. It was in Edison's laboratory, in 1894, that technicians created what was apparently the first genuine motion picture. Lasting only a few seconds, the film was made on celluloid. Its "star" was one of Edison's mechanics, a man who could sneeze amusingly on command. Its title: *Fred Ott's Sneeze*.

One major problem remained: There was no satisfactory method for projecting the films to an audience. Here the challenge was taken up by two Frenchmen, brothers appropriately named Lumière (*lumière* means "light"), who in 1895 succeeded in building a workable film projector. In December of that year, they held the first commercial film screening in history, showing a program of ten short films to a paying audience in a large Paris café. From that point the motion-picture industry was off and running.

Exploring the Possibilities

From the beginning of motion pictures, there was no doubt about what the new technology would do best: at last visual art could tell stories. Paintings had always been able to allude to stories, or imply stories, or depict episodes from stories. Photography could do those things as well. But with film, stories could unfold over time and in motion, as they did in life or on stage in the theater.

One early film that the Lumière brothers showed told a brief, real-life story about a train pulling into a station. It was a documentary of something that had happened. Of course, not all stories we tell are set in the present time or the real world, at least not in the parts of it where a camera can travel. They may be set in an imaginary future, or in the historical past, or at the bottom of the sea, or at the center of the Earth. Early filmmakers, already familiar with the tricks that photography could play, quickly set out to explore the new medium's ability to tell imaginary tales. A wonderful early example is *A Trip to the Moon* by the French filmmaker Georges Méliès (**9.16**). Méliès made his film in 1902, when space travel was far in the future. One of the first science-fiction films ever made, *A Trip to the Moon* tells the story of a group of scientists who travel to the moon. How do they get there? They invent a "space-gun," which looks a lot like a cannon, and shoot themselves into space in a capsule that looks like a giant bullet. After landing smack in the moon's eye (ouch!), the adventurers do battle with a race of underground moon beings. The moon people win, and take the invaders prisoner. But the scientists manage to escape and return to Earth, where they are greeted by a cheering crowd.

Méliès created his fourteen-minute film in a studio using painted scenery, just like that for a theatrical production. By the simple means of stop-motion photography, he also created sophisticated special effects. For example, on the moon, an

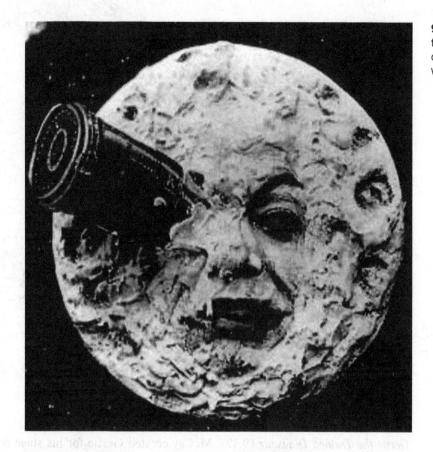

9.16 The space capsule lands, frame from *A Trip to the Moon*, directed by Georges Méliès. 1902. World History Archive/Alamy Stock Photo

opened umbrella belonging to one of the scientists suddenly turns into a giant mushroom. Méliès filmed the umbrella, then stopped the camera, replaced the umbrella with the mushroom, and began filming again. When the film was shown, the transformation seemed to happen by magic.

Méliès made his films using human actors. Other early filmmakers quickly discovered that stories could be "acted" by objects or drawings that seemed to come to life by themselves, a magical effect called animation, meaning "bringing to life." Animation takes advantage of the fact that although a film camera can shoot continuously as motion unfolds, it can also shoot a single frame of film at a time. If you place, say, a spoon on a table, then shoot a single frame of it, then shift the spoon slightly and shoot another frame, then shift it again and shoot a third frame, when the film is projected, the spoon will appear to move by itself. Animating objects in this way is called pixilation, and early filmmakers were quite inventive with it. A French film made in 1907 included a sequence in which a knife buttered a piece of breakfast toast all by itself.

Hand-drawn animation works on the same frame-by-frame principle, except that in this case it is a drawing or a cartoon that is photographed, not an object. To imagine the work involved, look back at Muybridge's sequential photographs of a horse galloping (see 9.15). If you drew each of those images and photographed your drawings in sequence, you would produce a very short animated film. Animation is a time-consuming and laborious way of making a movie, for between twelve and twenty-four drawings are required per *second* of running time to create the illusion of smooth motion. An animated cartoon only three minutes long may thus require up to 4,320 individual drawings!

One of the pioneers of animation in the United States was Winsor McCay. Before turning to animation, McCay was already famous for his innovative comic strip *Little Nemo*, which he began drawing for the *New York Daily Herald* in 1905. He was also a successful stage performer, where he appeared as a chalk-talk artist—someone who told stories and illustrated them at the same time on a chalkboard. McCay made several short animated features, but his most famous creation was

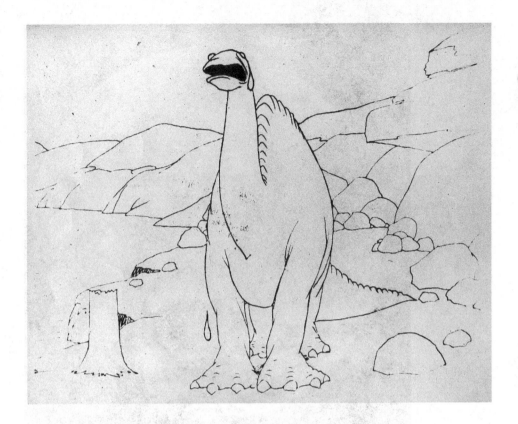

Gertie the Trained Dinosaur (**9.17**). McCay created Gertie for his stage act. He had her projected onto a large sketchpad set on an easel. The effect was as though one of his own drawings had suddenly come to life. McCay interacted with the cartoon as it played, scolding Gertie, for example, who reacted by acting contrite. Gertie was not the first animal character invented for animated features, but she was the first to have a distinct personality, and as such she is the ancestor of Mickey Mouse, Donald Duck, Bugs Bunny, and other famous animated animal characters.

When it came to filming a story, early filmmakers looked naturally to theater as a model. At their most basic, they set up a camera in front of a staged performance and let it record the view, as though the camera were an audience member who stared straight ahead and never blinked. In fact, however, as audience members we don't quite sit and stare at the entire stage. We focus here and there, we follow the action. We concentrate sometimes on the setting, sometimes on a face, sometimes on a gesture. Filmmakers soon realized that the camera could do those things as well, entering the story and making it more vivid for spectators. A camera could film from close up or from a distance; it could film from above or from below or to one side; it could film while moving toward or pulling back from or gliding alongside a view; it could film while turning from left to right or right to left or scanning from high to low or low to high. In all those ways, a camera could film a shot, a continuous sequence of frames. Planning what kinds of shot to film quickly became an important aspect of gathering the "raw material" for a movie. The shots were then edited—pieced together to create storytelling sequences, which were in turn joined to create a complete film.

Editing quickly emerged as fundamental to effective filmmaking. One of the most influential early masters of editing was the Soviet Russian filmmaker Sergei Eisenstein. Many filmmakers had concerned themselves with editing for clarity and continuity, making sure that shots followed each other smoothly and logically so that the audience could follow the story. Eisenstein, however, became just as interested in the expressive possibilities of editing, including changing the rhythm of how quickly one shot succeeded another, breaking a single action down into several shots, and alternating shots of different subjects so that viewers would understand a symbolic connection between them.

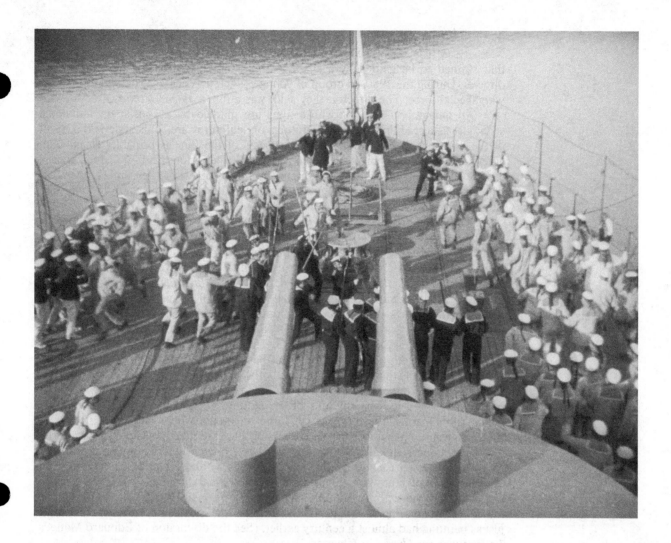

9.18 Scene from *Battleship Potemkin*, directed by Sergei Eisenstein. 1925.
World History Archive/Alamy Stock Photo

Many of Eisenstein's editing techniques can be seen in *Battleship Potemkin* (**9.18**), a 1925 film that became an international hit. The movie tells the story of an uprising by sailors angered at how unjustly they have been treated by their ship's officers. In one scene, a sailor's anger boils over while he and some shipmates are washing dishes. He raises a dish over his head and smashes it to bits on the counter. Eisenstein used ten shots for the action, editing them together in such a rapid and violent rhythm that the brief moment stands apart from everything that happened before, its full importance clear.

With special effects, animation, and editing, the fundamental possibilities of film as a visual medium were identified and explored by the very first generation of filmmakers. A steady stream of technological advances since then has provided today's filmmakers with a far more sophisticated set of tools to work with, but the essential elements of filmmaking have not changed.

Film and Art

Film was hailed initially as a wonderful medium for creating popular entertainments and disseminating information. Yet from the beginning, there were people who claimed that, like photography, it could be practiced as an art. During the 1920s, the expression "art cinema" came into use, usually to indicate an independent movie that did not conform to popular storytelling techniques or aim to please a mass audience. Often, these films were shown by small, specialized theaters, by cinema societies, or even by art museums—a network of venues that existed apart from the major commercial theaters. In such a collaborative medium as film, who was the artist? The actors? The writers? The editor who put it together? All of them were artists in a way. The most satisfying films, most viewers agreed, were those that seemed to be guided by a single vision. Many felt that this person was the director. During the 1950s, a group of young French film critics articulated this view with special force: The director, they said, was a film's *auteur*, French for "author."

An **auteur** is a director whose films are marked by a consistent, individual style, just as a traditional artist's paintings or sculptures are. This style is the result of the director's control over as many aspects of the film as possible. Usually, an auteur will be closely involved in conceiving the idea for the film's story and in writing the script. He or she will direct the film, work with the camera operators to plan and frame each shot, then work closely with the editor when the final film is assembled.

The young critics behind the auteur concept were hoping to become filmmakers themselves, and their writings described the kinds of film they admired and wanted to make. And make them they did, in the process launching a vibrant movement known as the New Wave. One of the first New Wave films to appear was Jean-Luc Godard's *Breathless* (**9.19**). The story of *Breathless* is fairly simple. A handsome petty criminal (Michel, played by Jean-Paul Belmondo) steals a car and heads north to Paris. On the way, he shoots a policeman who has pulled him over for speeding. In Paris, he meets up with a pretty American student journalist he knows (Patricia, played by Jean Seberg). They talk, make love, go to the movies, steal cars, and plan to escape to Italy. But Patricia does not want to be in love, and to prove to herself that she isn't, she calls the police and turns Michel in.

The revolutionary nature of *Breathless* does not lie in the story, however, but in the way it is told. The rhythms of the editing are fast and nervous, giving the film a spontaneous, youthful energy. Jump cuts—cuts where either the figures or the background change abruptly, interrupting the smooth visual flow—abound. The camera is sometimes unsteady, as though it were being held by someone walking. The dialogue is part gangster film, part philosophy, and includes quotations from famous works of literature. Finally, the film contains allusions to famous films of the past, and the actors play characters who have been formed as much by the movies as by anything else. With the New Wave, the movies became self-conscious, just as painting had almost a century earlier. (See the discussion of Édouard Manet's *Le Déjeuner sur l'herbe* in Chapter 21.)

We might say that film called a new kind of artist into being, someone as finely attuned to words as to images, gifted in structuring an experience that unfolds over time, able to communicate and collaborate with actors and production specialists, and as aware of the heritage of great films as painters are of the heritage of great paintings. As for traditionally trained visual artists, the expense of making a film, together with the specialized equipment and technical knowledge involved, generally kept them from experimenting with the new medium. It would not be until the invention of video, discussed later in this chapter, that visual artists began to work with recorded time and motion in significant numbers. Nevertheless, alongside the rich, international history of the film industry runs a slender history of films by artists.

One artist who had an unusually prolific engagement with film was Andy Warhol. Warhol was one of the leading artists of the Pop art movement during the 1960s. "Pop" is short for popular, and nothing was more popular by that time than the movies. Affordable film cameras had become widely available to the general public, leading to a thriving scene in underground or experimental filmmaking. Warhol had rented a large loft space in downtown New York. He called it the Factory, for it was a place where his art was to be manufactured—by himself, his assistants, his friends, hangers-on, visiting celebrities, and all manner of people. In that setting, Warhol began making films. His early films were all silent and filmed in black and white. They resemble his paintings of the time in that they challenge our idea that something will "happen." For example, his film *Kiss* (1963) consisted of close-ups of couple after couple, kissing for three minutes, much like his paintings of soup cans consisted of can after can of soup, sometimes all the same flavor, sometimes different flavors. An even more radical film, *Empire*, followed the next

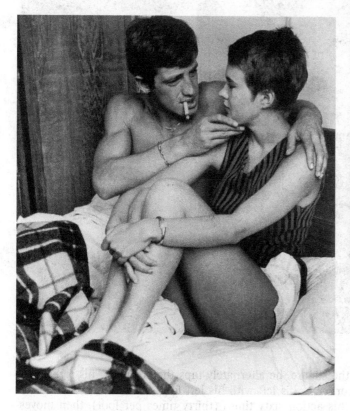

9.19 Jean-Paul Belmondo and Jean Seberg in a scene from *Breathless*, directed by Jean-Luc Godard. 1960.
© Impéria/Courtesy Photofest

9.20 Andy Warhol. *Empire*. 1964. 16mm film, black and white, silent; 8 hours 5 minutes at 16 frames per second.
© 2015 The Andy Warhol Museum, Pittsburgh, PA, a museum of Carnegie Institute. All rights reserved

year (**9.20**). Warhol and some friends set up a rented camera on the 44th floor of a building with a view of the Empire State Building. They filmed the famous skyscraper for more than six hours, from dusk until around 3 a.m. During all that time, the camera did not move. The composition shown in the illustration here did not change. The reels of film were then spliced end to end and projected at a slower speed, producing an eight-hour film. What was the film about? *Empire*, Warhol said, was a way of watching time pass.

Artists also began to use film to document actions or activities that they were proposing as art. One of the most influential artists to do this was Bruce Nauman. As a young artist just at the start of his career, Nauman had begun teaching at the San Francisco Art Institute, where as a new faculty member he found himself isolated. "I had no support structure for my art then . . . . there was no chance to talk about my work," he later recalled. "And a lot of things I was doing didn't make sense so I quit doing them. That left me alone in the studio: this in turn raised the fundamental question of what an artist does when left alone in the studio. My conclusion was that [if] I was an artist and I was in the studio, then whatever I was doing in the studio must be art. . . . At this point art became more of an activity and less of a product."[3]

Nauman began structuring activities by naming them, thereby setting limits. Then he filmed himself performing the activities in his studio. Typical activities had bland, descriptive titles such as *Bouncing Two Balls Between the Floor and Ceiling with Changing Rhythms* or *Dance or Exercise on the Perimeter of a Square (Square Dance)* (**9.21**). The plain titles were matched by plain, unedited camera work. Like Warhol in *Empire*, Nauman set the camera on a stand, turned it on, and let it record whatever happened in front of it.

For *Dance or Exercise on the Perimeter of a Square (Square Dance)*, Nauman outlined a square on his studio floor with masking tape and marked the midpoint of each side. The dance (or exercise) he devised is repetitive: standing at the

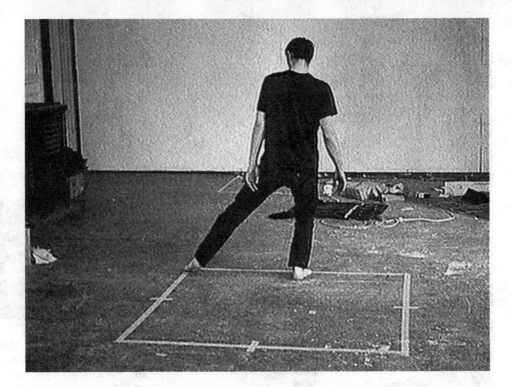

9.21 Bruce Nauman. *Dance or Exercise on the Perimeter of a Square (Square Dance)*. 1967–8. 16mm black-and-white film with sound, transferred to video, length 8:24 min.

Courtesy Electronic Arts Intermix, New York. © 2019 Bruce Nauman/Artists Rights Society (ARS), New York

midpoint of a length of the square, he alternately taps the corner to his right with his right foot, then the corner to his left with his left foot, in time to the beat of a metronome. He repeats this action sixty times (thirty times per foot), then moves to the next midpoint. He works his way around the square clockwise facing outward, then counterclockwise facing inward. Then the video ends. Without being a dancer, Nauman conceived of the activities as dance problems, and he practiced each piece extensively before performing it for the camera, becoming aware of his body in space and gaining control over the movements.

Video

Warhol made virtually all his films during the five years between 1963 and 1968. During those same years, another technology that could record and play back images in motion was made available to the general public, and it quickly became more popular with artists than film had ever been. That technology was video.

Just as radio had been invented to allow sound captured by a microphone to be transmitted over the air, so video was invented to do the same for moving images captured by a camera. A video camera converts a moving image into electronic signals. The signals are transmitted to a monitor, which decodes them and reconstitutes the image for display. The most famous monitor, of course, is the television. First demonstrated in the United States in 1939 in connection with the opening of the New York World's Fair, television sets became standard fixtures in American homes by about 1950.

Artists took quickly to video. They appreciated how it could be recorded and then played back immediately on a monitor, eliminating the wait for film to be developed. The monitors that displayed the video, moreover, lent themselves well to exhibition in gallery spaces where new art was shown.

Beryl Korot's *Text and Commentary* (**9.22**) is a five-channel video installation that displays video on five monitors. Typical of early video art, *Text and Commentary* has a grainy, black-and-white appearance. The work represents the artist weaving on a loom, with the recordings made from above at different distances. The five weavings Korot created while she filmed hang nearby in the installation. Each video features sequences of views of the yarn. Experiencing the installation takes time, as Korot carefully choreographed the moving images that appear on each screen. The

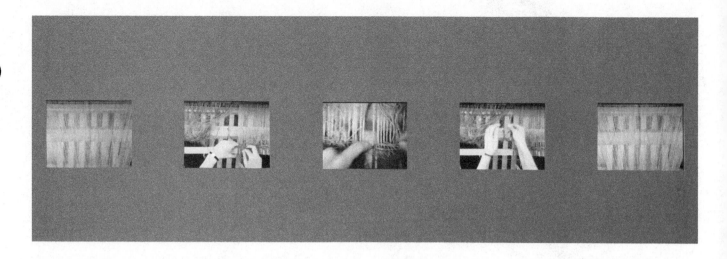

artist's close views of the yarn turn the textiles she creates into abstractions of line and pattern on the screens. These abstract forms are then reconstituted as real objects by the weavings hanging beside them. The combination of abstract views and real objects reinforces Korot's goal to create a dialog between old and new technologies. Weaving is one of the earliest arts, while video is one of the newest. Viewers looking back and forth between the two see a small piece of the history of human ingenuity.

During the 1990s, digital video became available, along with technology that allowed video stored digitally on disk to be projected onto a wall or some other surface instead of being fed to a monitor. Because it can be fed into a computer for further manipulation, digital video gives artists access to the same programs that today's filmmakers use for editing, adding a soundtrack, and creating special effects. A project by the Iranian-born artist Shirin Neshat shows how the worlds of the video artist and the filmmaker have drawn closer together.

Neshat created a series of five large-scale video installations inspired by *Women Without Men*, a novel by the contemporary Iranian writer Shahrnush Parsipur (**9.23**). *Women Without Men* tells the story of a small group of women who live briefly together in a house with a large garden not far from the Iranian capital of Teheran. They come together by chance, each one having suffered and then escaped the world of male authority in her own way. Each of Neshat's brief videos takes up the story of one of the women in the book, but it does not retell the story literally.

9.22 Beryl Korot. *Text and Commentary.* 1976–77. Video installation, 30 min.
© Beryl Korot. Courtesy Bitforms Gallery

9.23 Shirin Neshat. Production still from *Women Without Men.* 2008. Video, length approx. 20 min.
© Shirin Neshat. Courtesy Gladstone Gallery, New York and Brussels

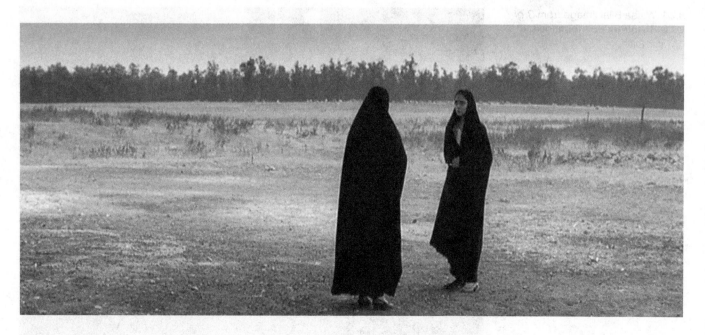

Rather, it meditates freely on the story's events, themes, and imagery. Repeating imagery links the videos in subtle ways, as does the choice of actors, some of whom play more than one role across the series. Shown in gallery or museum spaces, the videos are projected onto the walls, each in its own room. Viewers can wander from one to the other in any order, as they choose.

Neshat also made a full-length feature film inspired by the book, just as an independent filmmaker might. In contrast to the videos, the film offers a clearer story, with characters whose development over time is more evident. The two projects illustrate how at least one artist draws a distinction between videos for a gallery setting and an art audience, and film for a theater setting and a cinema audience.

The Internet

Thus far in this book, we have discussed the computer as a tool that expands the possibilities of older art forms such as printmaking, photography, film, and video. In addition to being a tool, the computer is a place. Images can be created, stored, and looked at on a computer without being given a traditional material form at all. With the development of the Internet, the World Wide Web, and browser applications capable of finding and displaying Web pages, a computer became a gateway to a new kind of public space, one that was global in scope and potentially accessible to everyone. Not only could anyone find information on the Internet, but also anyone could claim a presence on the Internet by creating a site on the World Wide Web, a Web site.

Art that uses the Internet as a medium is known as Internet art or, more casually, net art. Since its beginnings in the 1990s, net art has typically taken the form of e-mails, Web pages, or software—a set of step-by-step instructions that can be executed by a computer. Net art is often interactive, allowing visitors to explore a space that has been created on the Internet or to influence an image as it evolves on the computer monitor.

Wafaa Bilal uses the camera and the Internet to tell stories about himself and his interaction with the world. In 2010, Bilal had a camera temporarily implanted on the back of his head. As he went about his daily activities, the camera captured one image every minute and transmitted it to the Internet as *3rdi* (**9.24**). The photographs depict his immediate past—those things he had left behind within the last

9.24 Wafaa Bilal. Image from *3rdi*. 2010–11. Internet performance.
© Wafaa Bilal

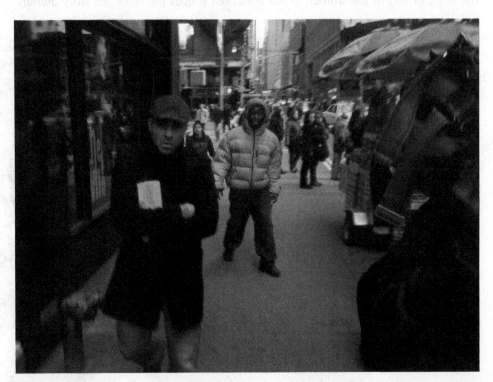

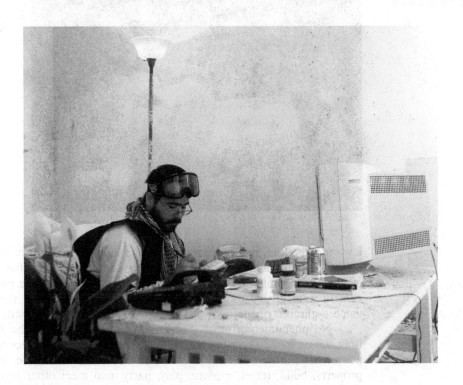

What is Wafaa Bilal's goal for his art? What message does he send with his interactive Internet performances? How does the public respond?

Wafaa Bilal was born in Iraq in 1966. As a young artist, he was arrested for making art critical of the dictator Saddam Hussein and his political party. In 1991, he fled Iraq rather than participate in the invasion of Kuwait. After living in a refugee camp, Bilal eventually settled in the United States. He completed art school and started a career as an art professor in New York City.

Bilal uses his body as an integral part of his art. In *3rdi* (see 9.24), he embedded a camera in the back of his head. The camera was later removed, but the pictures showed the places his body moved through and the people he encountered. This Internet performance had two aspects, as Bilal explained. It provided a personal trace of his life, "But by having the camera on my head, it also makes people aware of how much we are under surveillance."[4]

The artist also used his body in *Domestic Tension*, the Internet performance work pictured here. When Bilal left Iraq, his family stayed behind. His brother was killed in 2004 by bombs dropped by the American armed forces. *Domestic Tension* (also known as *Shoot an Iraqi*) was Bilal's response to this event and the U.S. war against Iraq. Inspired by a news story about American drone pilots stationed in the United States while their drones flew in Iraq, the artist linked a paintball gun to the Internet. He placed the gun in a Chicago art gallery and then occupied that space for the next month. People visiting the corresponding website controlled the gun. They tracked and shot at him over 65,000 times. Unlike the make-believe action that takes place in most online games, moving a mouse or clicking a button in *Domestic Tension* had very real consequences. The project crossed the line between the virtual and real worlds, raising questions about identity, violence, and warfare.

The artist's body was also part of the art in a 2010 piece entitled . . . *and Counting*. To visualize American and Iraqi deaths from the war in Iraq, Bilal turned his back into a map of Iraq. He tattooed a red dot for each U.S. casualty near the location where the soldier fell. Dots for Iraqi soldiers or civilians like his brother were visible only under ultraviolet light. This difference drew attention to the invisibility of the Iraqi casualties compared to the media coverage of American deaths. The entire tattooing event was broadcast live on the Internet. Bilal explained in a recent interview that this project, like much of his work, was intended to "establish a virtual platform to engage people in a political dialogue in which they may otherwise have been unable or unwilling to engage."[5]

Wafaa Bilal. Detail from *Domestic Tension*. 2007. Internet performance. © Wafaa Bilal

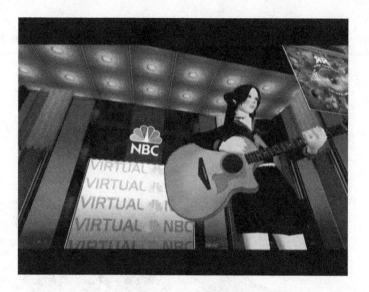

9.25 Cao Fei (China Tracy). *i.Mirror*. 2007. Single-channel video with sound, running time 28 min.
Courtesy the artist and Lombard Freid Projects, New York

few seconds. Bilal had no control over the images. He did not choose the scene or crop the photograph for a more pleasing or artistic composition. He did not review all the photographs in order to choose the best ones. All the pictures taken by his camera were posted to the Web site. Visitors could retrace the artist's steps and catch a glimpse of the lives of the people who crossed his path.

No phenomenon more clearly illustrates the idea of the Internet as a place than the online, 3-D virtual-reality environment known as Second Life. Millions of people from around the world are "residents" of Second Life, where they can buy property, build, travel, explore, play, party, and meet other residents. Before they can do any of those things, however, they must select and name their avatar, the animated persona who will represent them in the virtual world.

The Chinese artist Cao Fei is present on Second Life as an avatar named China Tracy. For six months, Cao recorded China Tracy's experiences in Second Life on video. From those many hours of material she created a three-part, thirty-minute film called *i.Mirror* (**9.25**). The opening credits announce it as "a Second Life documentary film by China Tracy."

The first part of *i.Mirror* is dominated by images of emptiness and solitude. The second part chronicles a delicate romance between China Tracy and a man she meets, Hug Yue. Young and handsome in Second Life, he turns out to be an older American in real life, and toward the end of their bittersweet encounters, he meets her more honestly as an older avatar. The third part of *i.Mirror* documents some unknown residents of Second Life, at first singly, then in loving couples, and finally as they are drawn by music to dance together.

A melancholy and yet ultimately hopeful film, *i.Mirror* is an example of a new artistic practice called machinima, from "machine cinema," in which real-time computer-generated 3-D video from such sources as online games or Second Life is recorded and used as raw material for a film, just as traditional filmmakers use shots of live actors in the real world.

Recently, many observers have discerned the beginnings of a post-Internet era. "Post-Internet" does not mean that the Internet is over, but that it is no longer new. We are accustomed to its presence. A generation has grown up that has always known it. Post-Internet art may reside online or it may take the form of an object, often one that embodies critical thinking about the Internet itself—its visual culture, its networks of information and communication, and its role in our experience of the world.

A clever and thought-provoking example of post-Internet art is Aram Bartholl's ongoing project *Map* (**9.26**). The central element of *Map* is a large wooden sculpture that materializes the marker Google drops on its online maps to indicate a location. When the map is switched to satellite view, the pin remains, now seemingly part of the real world. Bartholl scaled his sculpture to the size the pin appears to

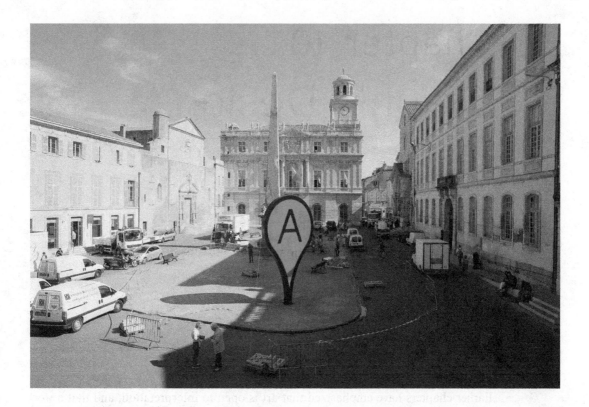

9.26 Aram Bartholl. *Map.* 2006–10. Public installation at Arles, France, July 2011. Wood, color, wire, screws, glue, and nails; height 19' 8 ¼". Photo Anne Fourès. © Aram Bartholl

be in the satellite view's highest magnification, when we have zoomed in as close as the program will allow. (The pin itself does not change size when the view is magnified; only its scale in relation to the objects in the view changes.) Bartholl brings his sculptural marker to a city and sets it up temporarily in the place that Google Maps designates as the city's center. "Transferred to physical space, the map marker questions the relation of the digital information space to everyday life public city space," he writes. "The perception of the city is increasingly influenced by geolocation services."[6]

Communications technology of the modern age, the camera, and the computer have transformed our world. They were not developed with art in mind, yet because artists choose to work with them, they have yielded new art forms for our era.

Notes to the Text

1. From Dorothea Lange, 'The Assignment I'll Never Forget' *Popular Photography*, Feb 1960, pp. 263–266.

2. Richard Huelsenbeck's "Dadaist Manifesto," quoted in Matthew Gale, *Dada & Surrealism* (London: Phaidon, 1997), p. 121.

3. Ian Wallace and Russell Keziere, "Bruce Nauman Interviewed," *Vanguard*, 8/1 (February 1979), pp. 15–18. Vancouver Art Gallery Association. Reproduced by permission of Ian Wallace.

4. Cited in Ashley Rawlings, "Remote Repercussions: Wafaa Bilal," *ArtAsiaPacific*, March/April 2011. Available at artasiapacific.com/Magazine/72/RemoteRepercussionsWafaaBilal, accessed April 27, 2018.

5. Anjali Kamat and Wafaa Bilal, "Interview with Iraqi Artist Wafaa Bilal," *The Arab Studies Journal* 18:1 (2010), p. 316.

6. Aram Bartholl, https://arambartholl.com/map.html. Reproduced with permission.

Chapter 10
Graphic Design

In this chapter, you will learn to

LO1   describe the use of signs and symbols in design,

LO2   explain the roles of typography and layout,

LO3   discuss how graphic design uses words and images,

LO4   identify motion and interactivity in graphic design, and

LO5   relate graphic design and art.

Earlier chapters have emphasized that art is open to interpretation, and that a work of art can hold many meanings. This chapter explores meaning from another point of view, for a graphic designer's task is to try to limit interpretation and to control meaning as much as possible. Graphic design has as its goal the communication of some *specific* message to a group of people, and the success of a design is measured by how well that message is conveyed. The message might be "This is a good product to buy," or "This way to the elevators (or restrooms or library)," or any of countless others. If it can be demonstrated that the public received the intended message—because the product sold well or the traveler found the right services—then the design has worked.

Graphic designers attend to the visual presentation of information as it is embodied in words and/or images. Books, newspapers, magazines, advertisements, packaging, Web sites, television and film credits, road signs, and corporate logos are among the many items that must be designed before they can be printed or produced.

Graphic design is as old as civilization itself. The development of written languages, for example, entailed a lengthy process of graphic design, as scribes gradually agreed that certain **symbols** would represent specific words or sounds. Over the centuries, those symbols were refined, clarified, simplified, and standardized—a process involving generation after generation of anonymous design work. The field as we know it today, however, has its roots in two more recent developments: the invention of the printing press in the 15th century and the Industrial Revolution of the 18th and 19th centuries.

Anyone can write a notice to be posted on a door. The printing press made it possible to devise a notice that could be reproduced hundreds of times and distributed widely. Someone, however, had to decide exactly how the notice would look; they had to design it. How would the words be placed on the page? Which words should be in large type, which in small? Should there be a border around them? An image to accompany them?

The Industrial Revolution, for its part, dramatically increased the commercial applications of graphic design. Before the Industrial Revolution, most products were grown or produced locally to serve a local population. A person who wanted a new pair of shoes, say, could walk down the road to the village cobbler, or perhaps wait for the monthly fair at which several cobblers from neighboring towns might appear. With the advent of machines, huge quantities of goods were produced in centralized factories for wide distribution. For manufacturers to succeed in this newly competitive and anonymous environment, they had to market both themselves and their wares through advertising, distinctive packaging, and other graphic means. At the same time, the invention of faster presses, automated typesetting, lithography, and photography expanded designers' capabilities, and the growth of newspapers and magazines expanded their reach.

Today international commerce, communications, and travel continue to feed the need for graphic design; and technological developments, most notably the computer, continue to broaden its possibilities.

Signs and Symbols

On the most basic level, we communicate through symbols. The sound of the syllable *dog*, for example, has no direct relation to the animal it stands for. In Spanish, after all, the syllables *perro* indicate the same animal. Each word is part of a larger symbolic system, a language. Visual communication is also symbolic. Letters are symbols that represent sounds; the lines that we use to draw representational images are symbols for perception.

Symbols convey information or embody ideas. Some are so common that we find it difficult to believe they didn't always exist. Who, for example, first used arrows to indicate directions? We follow them instinctively now, but at some point they were new and had to be explained. We all recognize the symbol for children playing (**10.1**). It is one of the universal symbols that communicates essential information across language barriers. The silhouette of two children on a teeter-totter appears against a yellow background. We interpret the round heads and simplified bodies to represent children. Our driver's education in the United States teaches us that traffic signs with a yellow background tell us to proceed with caution, and diamond-shaped signs signify possibly hazardous conditions. Yet even these common and relatively simple symbols were the work of graphic designers who brainstormed, researched, drew, and created prototypes to test their designs.

10.1 Children at Play traffic sign.
Shutterstock/James Laurie

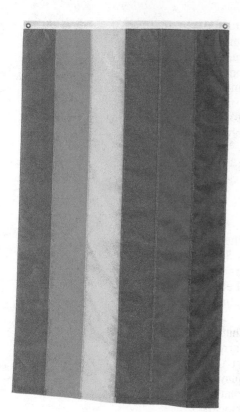

While some signs refer to simple concepts, other symbols embody more complex ideas and associations. The familiar LGBT flag (**10.2**) was created in 1978 to represent the gay, lesbian, bisexual, and transgender community. It was made by the designer Gilbert Baker, whom the activist Harvey Milk hired to make a flag for San Francisco's Gay Freedom Day parade. As a designer, Baker thought about what flags are, how they are seen, and what they are supposed to accomplish. Most importantly, he considered how to represent the gay community in a positive and uplifting way. At the time, the only symbol of gay identity was a pink triangle used by the Nazis to identify homosexuals. Baker turned to nature and the sky. He used the rainbow as his symbol and the design was universally understood to represent inclusion and acceptance, even without any text or images.

Among the most pervasive symbols in our visual environment today are logos and trademarks, which are symbols of an organization or a product. An impressive number of these are the work of Paul Rand, one of the most influential of all American graphic designers (**10.3**). Simple, clear, distinctive, and memorable, each of these corporate logos has become familiar to millions of people around the world, instantly calling to mind the company and its products or services. As with any symbol, a logo means nothing in itself. It is up to an organization to make its logo familiar and to persuade people through sound business practices to associate it with such virtues as service, quality, and dependability.

Because symbols serve as focal points for associations of ideas and emotions, one of the most effective ways for a company to change its image is to redo its logo. United Parcel Service has updated its logo since the original design was made (**10.4**). The new logo emphasizes continuity with the past by retaining essential elements of Rand's original 1960s design, even as it adds a fresh, dynamic look by suggesting reflective, three-dimensional forms instead of flat shapes. The new design does away with Rand's string-tied package, which no longer conveys the range of services that UPS provides. The upper edge of the shield form now curves into space. An asymmetrical brown interior field curves up to meet it, creating a strong sense of movement.

A logo like this often serves as the fundamental element of a brand identity program, a larger design undertaking that unifies a brand's overall visual presence. Guidelines for **typography**, color palette, layout, and imagery are developed for application to letterheads, business cards, packaging, marketing materials, Web sites, office design, and more to project a consistent image that reflects how the brand wants to be perceived. This branding has been so effective in the case of UPS that we all recognize its brown trucks and uniforms. UPS now even uses its branded color in its advertising tagline, asking customers to "see what brown can do for you."

A photograph of New York City's Times Square at night (**10.5**) shows the importance of graphic design in creating a brand identity. How many companies do you recognize in this picture? The car manufacturer Toyota appears at the top. We recognize its name and the red color, but also its typography. The designed name is Toyota's **wordmark**, or **logotype**—a standardized text logo using a font that Toyota chose. Like other savvy companies, Toyota mandates that its dealers and service providers use this logotype. The capital letters are easily readable and look sturdy and modern. The sign also uses a symbol mark, the large oval with two smaller interlocking ovals resembling the letter T inside. The ovals suggest motion and fast cars on test tracks. This mark has come to be identified with the company through its brand identity program as much as the ABC logo seen here on the left

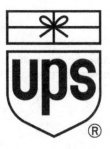

10.3 Paul Rand. Logo for UPS. 1961.
Paul Rand Archives, Yale University

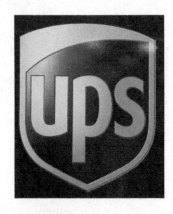

10.4 UPS logo (2003)
© AngiePhotos/iStock

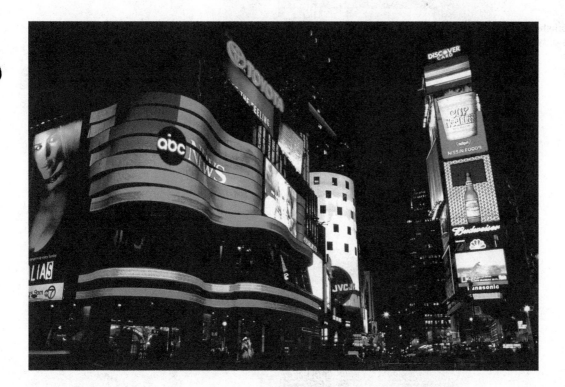

and NBC's multicolored peacock mark on the right. As parts of larger branding packages created by graphic designers, these logotypes, symbol marks, and logos help customers come to know a company and choose it over its competitors.

10.5 Times Square at night.
© TongRo Image Stock/Alamy

Typography and Layout

Cultures throughout history have appreciated the visual aspects of their written language. In China and Japan, and in Islamic cultures, calligraphy is considered an art. Although personal writing in the West has never been granted that status, letters for public architectural inscriptions have been carefully designed since the time of the ancient Romans, whose alphabet we have inherited. With the invention of movable type around 1450, the alphabet again drew the attention of designers. Someone had to decide on the exact form of each letter, creating a visually unified alphabet that could be mass-produced as a **typeface**, a style of type. No less an artist than Albrecht Dürer turned his attention to the design of well-balanced letter forms (**10.6**). Constructing each letter within a square, Dürer paid special attention to the balance of thick and thin lines and to the visual weight of the serifs—the short cross-lines that finish the principal strokes (at the base of the As, for example).

The letters Dürer designed would have been cast in metal, with the reversed letter in relief above the body of each piece of type (labeled as "Fig. 4" in **10.7**). Type without letters served as spacers. The metal type would have been set (placed in position) by hand before printing in small trays called sticks and locked together ("Fig. 5"). Finally, sticks with each line of text were assembled as a group ("Fig. 6") and the page was ready for printing. Today type is created and set by digital and photographic methods. The design of typefaces continues to be an important and often highly specialized field, and graphic designers have literally thousands of styles to choose from.

10.6 Albrecht Dürer. Letters, from *Treatise on Measurement*. 1525. J. Paul Getty Museum, GRI Digital Collections 1385-140

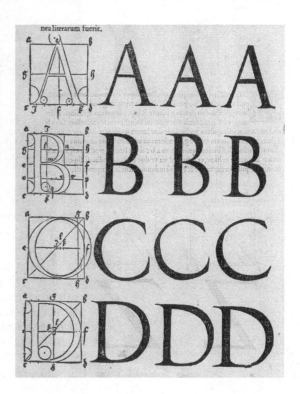

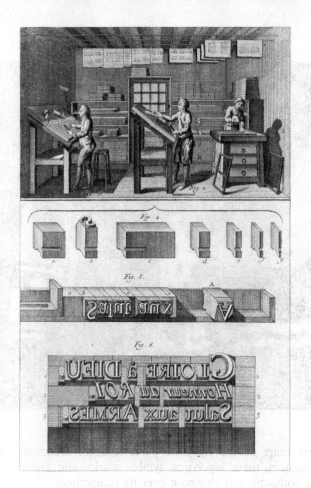

10.7 Three printers in a workshop setting type, and examples of type and spacers set for printing. Library of Congress Prints and Photographs Division [LC-USZ62-110399]

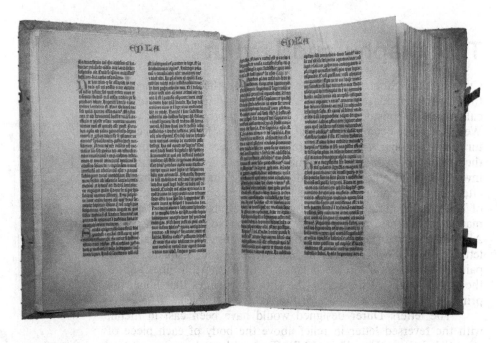

10.8 Johannes Gutenberg. *Biblia Latina*. 1454. Ink on paper, each page 12 1/16 × 17 1/2". Rare Books and Special Collections Division, Library of Congress 52002339

Having selected the typeface, a designer's next concern is **layout**, or how text and images (if any) appear on the page. Layout is significant in design because one of the most important tasks of a graphic designer is to devise visual presentations that make potentially confusing information easier to grasp. It includes such specifications as the dimensions of the page, the width of the margins, the sizes and styles of type for text and headings, the style and placement of running heads or feet (lines at the top or bottom of the page that commonly give the chapter or part title and page number), and many other elements.

Johannes Gutenberg is credited with the invention of movable type and the printing process. He adapted the wine press to serve as a printing press, and invented the small metal letters that could be combined to make words. His *Biblia Latina*, also known as the *Gutenberg Bible* (**10.8**), was the first major book to be printed using the new process—a technological breakthrough that soon replaced the slow process of making books by hand. The bible's layout is based on earlier manuscript books, but it is challenging for the modern reader. Text appears in 40 to 42 lines organized into two columns on each page. The borders are wide, but the style of type that Gutenberg had to work with—known as Gothic—is difficult to read. Breaks between paragraphs are marked by colored letters that were hand-drawn, but otherwise the text runs together in a dense block.

Since Gutenberg's day, designers have learned a great deal about creating layouts that assist readers. This book, for example, places a single column of text asymmetrically on the page, leaving a slender outer column (for captions) and a one-inch inner margin. Each spread (two facing pages) is thus fundamentally symmetrical, with left and right pages in mirror image. Illustrations are placed to relieve and even disguise this symmetry, and the page-makeup artists took pains to arrange each spread in a pleasing asymmetrical composition.

Word and Image

Among the services offered by printers in the 15th century was the design and printing of single sheets called broadsides. Handed out to town-dwellers and posted in public spaces, broadsides argued political or religious causes, told of recent events, advertised upcoming festivals and fairs, or circulated woodcut portraits of civic and religious leaders. They were the direct ancestors not only of advertising and posters but also of leaflets, brochures, newspapers, and magazines.

With the development of color lithography in the 19th century, posters came into their own as the most eye-catching form of advertising, for color printing was not yet practical in magazines or newspapers, and television was still a hundred years away. Among the most famous of all 19th-century posters are those created by Henri de Toulouse-Lautrec for the cabarets and dance halls of Paris (**10.9**). In this poster for a famous dance hall called the Moulin Rouge, the star performer, La Goulue, is shown dancing the cancan, while in the foreground rises the wispy silhouette of another star attraction, Valentin, known as "the boneless one." The flattened, simplified forms and the dramatically cropped composition show the influence of the Japanese prints that were so popular in Europe at the time.

Toulouse-Lautrec integrates text and image through color, line, and the Gestalt principles that guide designers. The red letters echo the red stockings and red polka-dot blouse worn by La Goulue. The black letters mirror the silhouetted background figures. The artist outlines the words "Moulin Rouge" in the same manner that he outlines the dancers and the yellow clouds of smoke. The letters also share Valentin's tallness or the curves of the dancers' bodies. The poster uses the Gestalt principles of similarity and uniform connectedness; objects are united by both color and line. Proximity, another Gestalt principle, also lets us know that La Goulue and Valentin are related to each other and to the Moulin Rouge. The whole experience of this poster is more than the sum of its individual elements. Toulouse-

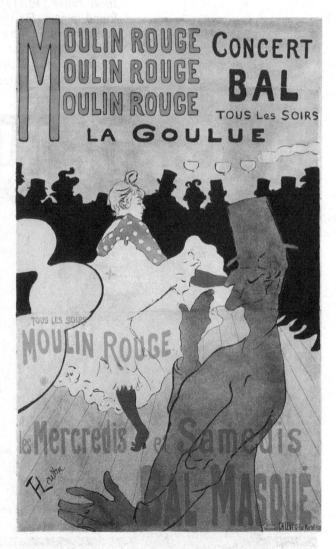

10.9 Henri de Toulouse-Lautrec. *La Goulue at the Moulin Rouge*. 1891. Poster, lithograph printed in four colors, 6' 2 ⅘" × 3' 9 ¹³⁄₁₆".
The Metropolitan Museum of Art, New York. Harris Brisbane Dick Fund, 1932, 32.88.12. Image © The Metropolitan Museum of Art

Lautrec's posters were so effective that they were immediately recognized as collectors' items, and instructions circulated secretly for detaching them from the kiosks on which they were pasted.

Gestalt principles are also at work in the famous 1942 poster of *We Can Do It!* (**10.10**) by J. Howard Miller. The poster, commonly known as *Rosie the Riveter*, pictures one of the many women who joined the workforce during World War II. The woman in the poster is a factory employee wearing work clothes and a bandana over her hair. Her flexed arm embodies the muscle women and men put to work to support the war effort. The poster's inspirational slogan and the woman's arm are the focal points. Her head and arm form a line that continuously draws the viewer's eye back to the text and its uplifting message, given in a sans serif typeface. The figure and the text stand out from the background, thanks to the use of saturated complementary colors. Repeated curving shapes and lines tie the work together to create an effective and powerful message.

Toulouse-Lautrec drew his image on a lithographic stone and Miller worked on paper. Today most graphic design is done on a computer, generating digital files that will be sent to an industrial printer. The graphic designer and street artist Shepard Fairey uses several different materials and tools to make works such as *Ideal Power* (**10.11**). He both draws elements freehand and uses photocopies of found images. He then scans these into the computer and manipulates their color and composition—for example, by adding typography, like the simulated newspaper text that appears in the background here. This produces what Fairey refers to as a "digital sketch," which he then turns into stencils for screenprinting in layers, creating the bold and graphic quality that his work is known for.

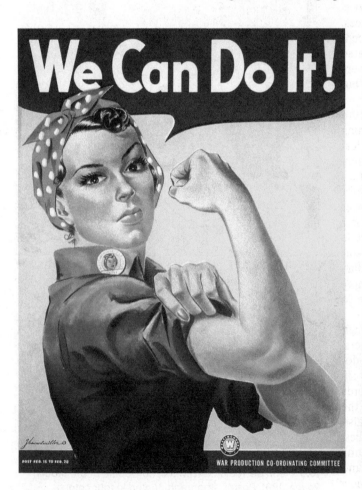

10.10 J. Howard Miller. *We Can Do It!* 1942. Offset lithography, 17 × 22".

Pictorial Press Ltd/Alamy Stock Photo

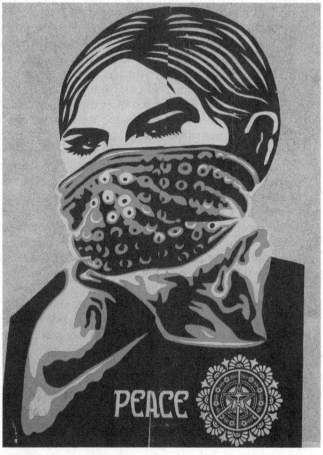

10.11 ArtAngel / Alamy Stock Photo. Screenprint, 18 × 24".

© Shepard Fairey

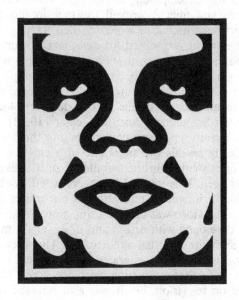

How did Shepard Fairey begin to use Andre the Giant's sticker? What was his purpose for the sticker campaign? How does Fairey reconcile the differences between art and design?

Shepard Fairey blurs the lines between graphic design, street art, and traditional fine art. His work defies labels, but it began to capture the world's imagination with the stencil of Andre the Giant seen here. While in art school, Fairey began posting stickers featuring the wrestler's face with the word "OBEY" around town. People were curious about the mysterious stickers, starting Fairey on a decades-long campaign that used Andre the Giant's face as its main symbol. As he explains, "The sticker has no meaning but exists only to cause people to react, to contemplate and search for meaning in the sticker."[1]

Fairey's body of work has included stickers, clothing, album covers, movie posters, fine-art prints, and murals. In 2008, he created a poster of presidential candidate Barack Obama's likeness with the word "HOPE." Made as street art to promote the candidate Fairey supported, the poster proved immensely popular and became the unofficial symbol of Obama's campaign. Viewers found it uplifting and powerful. The Smithsonian Institution acquired a copy of it for its collection, and the new president even wrote Fairey a letter of thanks.

Whether creating a fine-art print or a sticker, Fairey works in a boldly graphic style. His images are dominated by large, flat areas of red, black, light blue, and tan. He does not use hatching to model his forms. Instead, flat colors placed side by side suggest shading. His compositions are symmetrical, and all design rests on the surface of the page. Typography always enjoys a prominent role in his images, too, frequently shaping the meaning of the work—as with the command to "OBEY."

Fairey cherishes the intersection of art and design. As he explained in a recent interview, "For so long [art and design] have been two separate worlds." At his design agency, Fairey sees this intersection as a competitive advantage. "It's helped us as an agency because we can do our own illustrations and people want a style that no one else can provide, but yet we can do all of the technical side of design too."[2]

While Fairey's career is still in full bloom, he has already enjoyed immense success. He has shown his work at exhibitions around the world, and major museums have purchased his images. Fairey's many awards recognize his political activism and his artistry, including the honorary doctorate he received from the Pratt Institute in 2015.

Shepard Fairey's *OBEY* posted near Old Street, London.
David Crausby / Alamy Stock Photo

Motion and Interactivity

With the development of film and television, graphic design was set in motion. Words and images worked together in film titles, television program titles, and advertisements, all of which needed to be designed. With the digital revolution, a new element was added for designers to work with, interactivity—the possibility of give-and-take between users and technology by means of an interface.

In the forefront of today's motion graphics are designers who generate videos on a computer by writing code. A dramatic example is this video about the Audi TT sedan, created by the British designers Matt Pyke at Universal Everything and Karsten Schmidt at PostSpectacular (**10.12**). As the video begins, vividly colored lines stream rapidly away from us into the depths of a black space. Their swarming gradually reveals the silhouette of a car that pivots and then drives away, leaving the lines swirling in the turbulence of its wake. The effect is magical, for the car is never seen. It is implied by the void left by the streaming lines. This relies on the Gestalt principle of reification as our minds fill in the missing car.

The video was created using a programming language called Processing, which was developed with artists and designers in mind. Pyke and Schmidt used Processing to create a virtual wind tunnel. The streaming lines in the video indicate wind flow. The program generated video in real time at full, high-definition resolution, with no further production work necessary. The video ran as a traditional advertisement on television, but it was also released on the Internet as a viral video to be forwarded from person to person and posted on sharing sites around the world.

As we have seen, graphic design can reveal information by organizing facts or data in a visually coherent way. We can see this at work in an interactive setting on a Web site called *Graffiti Archaeology* (**10.13**). Graffiti or street art is somewhat ephemeral. It gets painted over by city officials and by other graffiti artists. Walls get torn down and train cars move. *Graffiti Archaeology* compiles photographs and reassembles them as photo-collages. The site takes isolated facts—in this case,

10.12 Matt Pyke (Universal Everything) and Karsten Schmidt (PostSpectacular). *High Performance Art*. 2007. Viral/HD television video for Audi TT Movement.
© Universal Everything

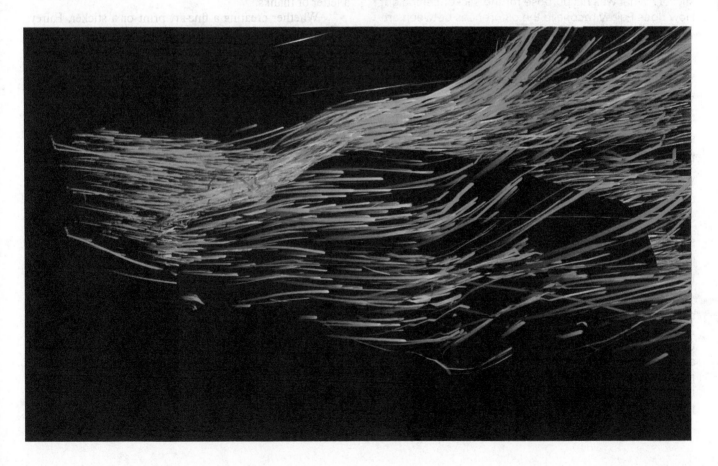

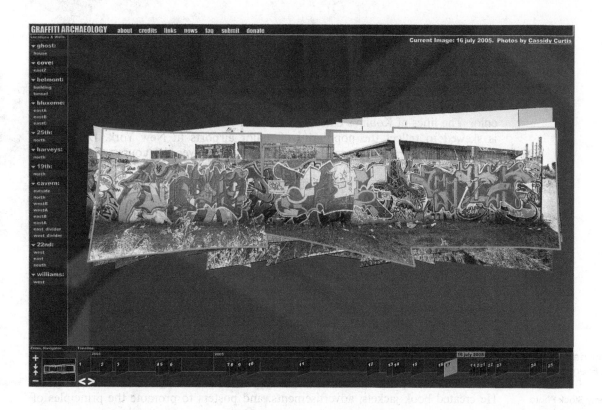

individual photographs of graffiti—and sets them in a structure that reveals the information they contain. Its design presents the information so that we can easily retrieve it.

Designed by Cassidy Curtis, *Graffiti Archaeology* makes visible the evolution of graffiti sites over time as graffiti writers paint on top of one another's work. To the left is a list of sites, grouped by general area. When a site is selected, all the available images for it are loaded onto the screen, with the most recent layer displayed on top. A graphic display at the bottom of the screen shows how many layers of photographs are available and situates them on a timeline. Moving backward in time, we can peel back layer after layer of imagery to see what is hidden underneath. At the lower left, zoom controls and a navigator allow us to examine images in greater detail.

10.13 Cassidy Curtis. *Graffiti Archaeology*. 2004–present. Interactive Web site. Web page illustrated is layer 17 of the graffiti site eastZ, featuring works by ZEROS, AWAKE, and anonymous artists.
Courtesy Cassidy Curtis. Photo © Cassidy Curtis

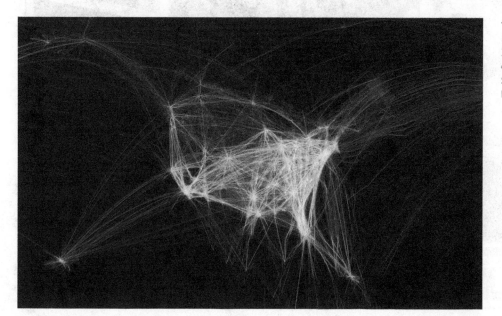

10.14 Aaron Koblin. *Data Visualization: Flight Patterns*. 2005–08. Video.
Cooper Hewitt, Gift of Aaron Koblin/ Smithsonian Design Museum/Art Resource, NY

Aaron Koblin's *Data Visualization: Flight Patterns* (**10.14**) puts data in motion. This video, also created using Processing, traces the flight patterns of airplanes traveling over a 24-hour period in the United States. The source of Koblin's information was the Federal Aviation Administration's flight records. Koblin plotted each of the 140,000 flights over the span of a day. As the planes move to and from American airports, they appear as colorful lines. Each type of plane is a different color. The lines of Koblin's data trace the shape of the United States, but the shape is skewed to reflect the popularity of major airports in New York, Dallas, Los Angeles, and Chicago. Since the data is visualized over the course of a day, the time differences across the nation are captured, with the East Coast lighting up early and the West Coast remaining active later.

Graphic Design and Art

Graphic design is all around us, part of the look of daily life. Many art museums maintain collections of graphic design, which overlaps with art in interesting ways. Indeed, as we saw with Shepard Fairey, many artists have worked as graphic designers, and many graphic designers also make art.

The work of Aleksandr Rodchenko spans the gap between art and design. *Books (Please)! On Every Subject* (**10.15**) is a poster designed to promote a state publisher. Rodchenko began his career as a painter, but his Communist politics led him to abandon painting, which he viewed as elitist, for design's functional purpose. He created book jackets, advertisements, and posters to promote the principles of

10.15 Aleksandr Rodchenko. *Books (Please)! On Every Subject.* 1924. Poster.
Pictorial Press Ltd/Alamy Stock Photo

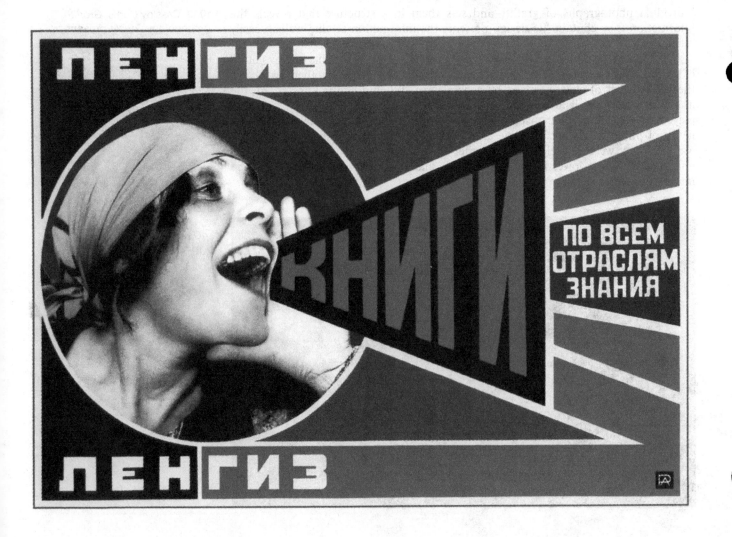

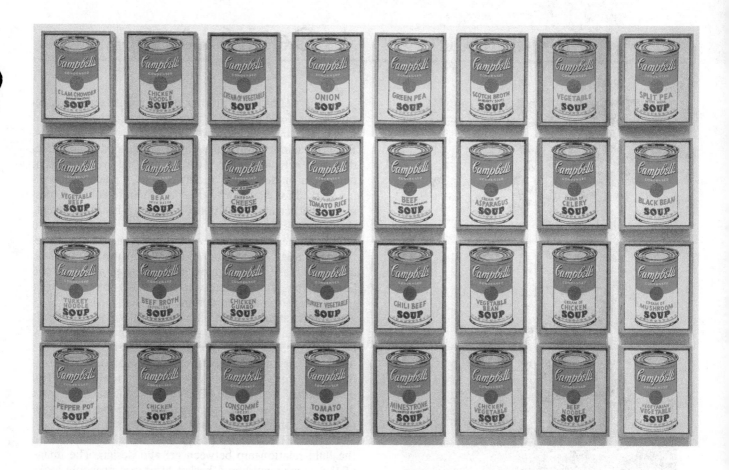

the Russian Revolution. He worked in a style known as **Constructivism**, which used abstraction and geometric shapes that emphasized the formal elements of line, color, and texture. As seen here, Rodchenko also liked to integrate photography into his work, combining its realism with shapes in rich, saturated colors.

One of the earliest artists to acknowledge the power of graphic design to become part of our personal world was Andy Warhol (**10.16**). His famous images of Campbell's soup cans are often talked about in the context of the history of art, for they signaled the arrival of a new kind of subject matter. Some viewers have seen them as a criticism of mass production and consumer culture; others have seen them as a celebration of those same things. But one thing they certainly are is a collection of affectionate portraits of a very successful graphic design, the Campbell's soup label.

Campbell's first unveiled its red-and-white label in 1898. The gold medal was added in 1900, after the product won a gold medal at an international exhibition. For almost a century afterward, the label remained unchanged, a visual fact of daily life that accompanied several generations of Americans from childhood through old age. When asked why he painted the soup cans, Warhol answered, "I just paint things I always thought were beautiful—things you use every day and never think about."[3] Campbell's finally changed its soup labels in 1999, twelve years after Warhol's death. From that point on, viewers coming into contact with Warhol's paintings for the first time had to be told that soup cans really looked like that once.

Whereas Warhol painted portraits of graphic design, Barbara Kruger appropriated its methods. Kruger worked for years as a graphic designer and art director for glossy magazines, where she became expert in the ways that words and images are used together to influence readers. She made use of her experience in works such as *Untitled (Your Gaze Hits the Side of My Face)* (**10.17**), which combines words and images in the manner of a poster or an advertisement. The image is a found photograph of a sculpture of a woman's head (note the block base). It can neither see nor speak. Passive and motionless, it exists only to be looked at. The words, in

10.16 Andy Warhol. *Campbell's Soup Cans*. 1962. Synthetic polymer paint on 32 canvases, each 20 × 16". Overall installation 97 × 163".

Is Design Art?

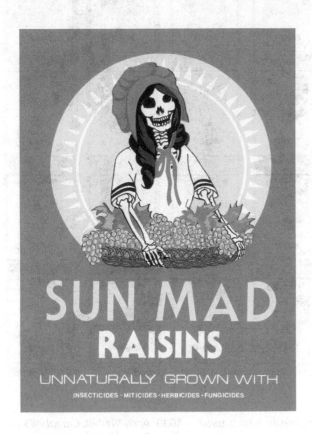

Is design art? How are the two different? Why do artists and designers debate this issue? Do you think art and design are the same?

Is the UPS logo (see 10.3) art? What about the neon signs on Times Square (see 10.5)? Few would say yes. But what about work in which the artist's hand is more visible, such as Toulouse-Lautrec's *La Goulue* (see 10.9) or Ester Hernandez's *Sun Mad*, created to protest the working conditions of American farmworkers? Are these examples of art, design, or both?

At the beginning of this chapter, we read that a graphic designer creates work to convey a specific message, avoiding ambiguity and divergent interpretations. The designer is under contract to a client who seeks to communicate specific information about a product or service. The graphic designer has a creative role, but must respond to the client's needs.

This definition of graphic design would seem to separate design from art, which represents the artist's idea and may inspire many interpretations and hold many meanings. But art was not always this way. The ideas of artistic freedom and artistic license are very new. As we have seen, before our modern ideas about art were in place, artists often worked for clients who expected them to convey a message, whether about religious doctrine, a historical event, the power of a great ruler, or an episode from a favorite tale. Even the style of the work was not at the artist's discretion until relatively recently in the Western world. Instead, artists such as the anonymous sculptor responsible for the Stela of the sculptor Userwer (see 5.20) followed strict rules to conform to their community's standards.

Some argue that graphic design is not art because it is commercial. It is used to sell things and to make money for the client. Yet, works of art sometimes also promote the industry or typical products of a region. Doesn't Cornelius Norbertus Gijsbrechts's *Trompe l'Oeil with Studio Wall and Vanitas Still Life* (see 4.39) advertise the painter's work and talent? Doesn't the *Virgin of the Immaculate Conception* (see 2.7) promote Asian ivory and overseas trade?

Ester Hernandez's poster seen here helps us to see the fluid relationship between art and design. The image of the woman holding a basket of grapes probably looks familiar. You know it from the packaging used for a popular brand of raisins. The image appears on every box of raisins as part of the company's branding effort. The company uses the image repeatedly so that consumers link it to the company and its products. Hernandez borrowed and adapted the brand image so that viewers would understand her protest. She maintained the commercial look but transformed the woman into a skeleton poisoned by the pesticides and chemicals of modern farming. Hernandez also mass-produced her poster using the screenprint process to spread her message, just as the work of graphic designers is reproduced in branding and marketing campaigns.

Hernandez, Warhol, Toulouse-Lautrec, and others help us to appreciate that the line between art and design is not always clear. Designers today, like artists throughout history, communicate and bend new technology to the principles of clarity and visual elegance that have been at the core of graphic design since scribes first developed writing.

Ester Hernandez. *Sun Mad*. 1982. Screenprint on paper, 20 × 15".
© 1982 Ester Hernandez, Gift of Tomás Ybarra-Frausto, 1995.50.32.
Smithsonian American Art Museum, Washington, D.C./Art Resource, NY

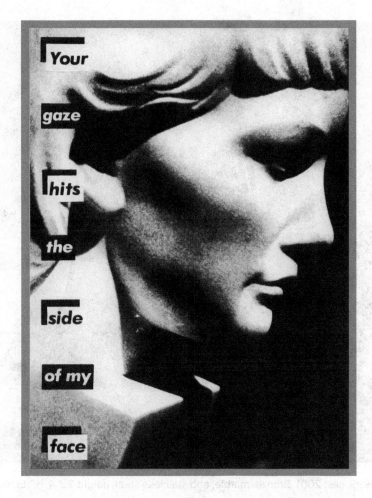

10.17 Barbara Kruger. *Untitled (Your Gaze Hits the Side of My Face).* 1981. Photograph, 55 × 41".
© Barbara Kruger. Courtesy Mary Boone Gallery, New York

contrast, are visually more dynamic. Every other word punches out toward us, asserting itself and disrupting our reading. The woman's face is a natural focal point, and each time we are drawn back to it we enact the statement: Again and again, our gaze hits the side of her face until we become aware of our looking as a kind of aggression.

Notes to the Text

1. Shepard Fairey, "Manifesto," 1990. Available at obeygiant.com/propaganda/manifesto, accessed October 27, 2017.
2. "Interview with Shepard Fairey," *Art Prostitute* (n.d.). Available at obeygiant.com/articles/art-prostitute-magazine-interview, accessed October 27, 2017.
3. Quoted in "Art. The Slice of Cake School," *Time,* May 11, 1962, p. 52.

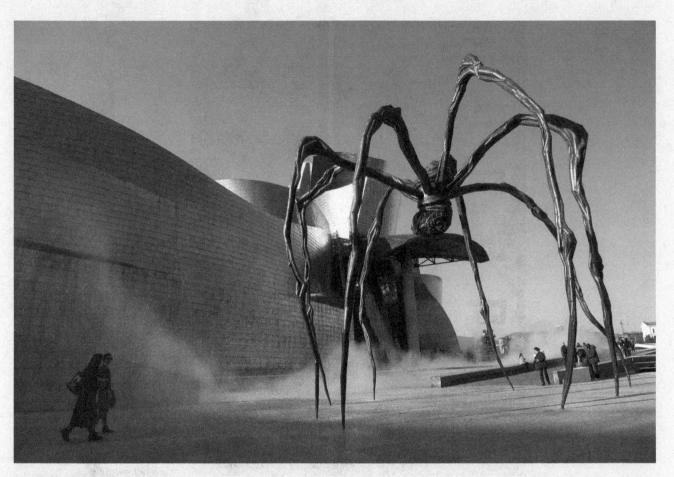

11.1 Louise Bourgeois. *Maman*. 1999, cast 2001. Bronze, marble, and stainless steel, height 29' 4 ⅜". Edition 2/6 + A.P.
ANDER GILLENEA/AFP/Getty Images

PART FOUR

Three-Dimensional Media

Chapter 11

Sculpture and Installation

In this chapter, you will learn to

LO1 identify methods and materials used to make sculpture,

LO2 describe how the human figure has been represented in sculpture, and

LO3 discuss how time and place are incorporated into sculpture and installation art.

Visitors arriving at the Guggenheim Museum Bilbao find it guarded by a very strange and unsettling presence: a nearly 30-foot-tall bronze sculpture of a spider (**11.1**). Even less expected is the spider's name: *Maman*, French for "mom." For the artist Louise Bourgeois, *Maman* is a metaphor for her own mother as seen through a child's eyes—awesomely tall, protective, patient, and skilled. Perhaps the association of mother and spider was born from the strange logic of dreams. Bourgeois's mother wove and repaired tapestries for a living; a female spider spins a web to provide for herself and a cocoon to protect her young. Viewers make their own associations and explore their own feelings as they circle the bronze figure, or wander into the open cage of *Maman*'s cascading legs, or gaze upward at the compact body with its clutch of eggs suspended high overhead.

    Maman is a sculpture **in the round**—a freestanding work that can be viewed from any angle, for it is finished on all sides. Not all sculpture is finished in the round. The work shown in **11.2** from the ancient Middle East is an example of a **relief** sculpture, in which forms project from but remain attached to a background surface. A relief is meant to be viewed frontally, the way we view a painting. Artists in many cultures have animated the surfaces of important objects and architecture with relief sculpture. The carving illustrated here is a deity with the body of a man, wings, and the head of an eagle. It once hung on the walls of a palace in present-day Iraq that was covered in relief carvings picturing the ruler and different gods. The deity pictured here is using a pine cone to sprinkle water from the bucket he holds. His body is robust, with individual muscles and even tendons visible. His clothing, sandals, hair, and wings have meticulously described texture and detail. The plants to either side are stylized in a repeating pattern of identical leaves. The markings that run across the middle of the sculpture are cuneiform text, a writing system developed in the ancient Middle East.

    This work of an eagle-headed deity is carved in **low relief**—sometimes called by its French name, **bas-relief**—a technique in

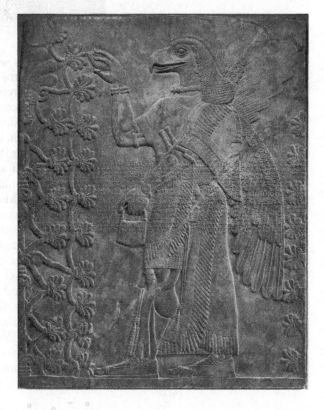

11.2 Eagle-headed deity. From Nimrud, present-day Iraq, 9th century B.C.E. Alabaster, 88 × 83 × 3".
Los Angeles County Museum of Art

11.3 *Durga Slaying the Buffalo Demon.* 13th century C.E. Schist, 34 × 21 ¼ × 10 ½".
Los Angeles County Museum of Art

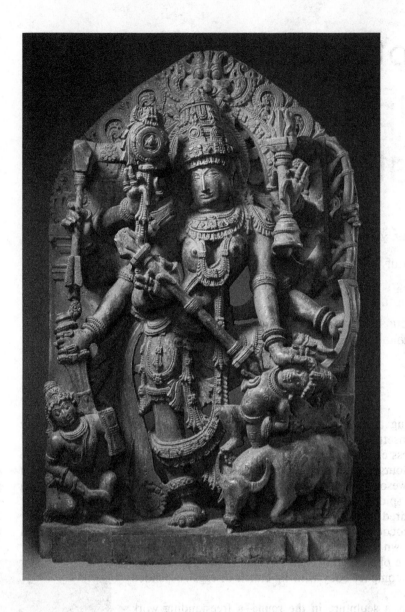

which figures project only slightly from the background. Coins, for example, are modeled in low relief, as you can see by examining the portrait of Abraham Lincoln on the one-cent coin. A sculpture in which forms project more boldly from their background is called **high relief**. Forms modeled in high relief generally project to at least half their understood depth. Foreground elements may be modeled in the round, detaching themselves from the background altogether, as in the 13th-century relief from India shown in **11.3**. The panel depicts a battle between the goddess Durga and the buffalo demon Mahisha. In the center, the eight-armed Durga stands victorious over Mahisha and his supporters, who appear below. Each of Durga's hands holds a weapon the gods gave her to battle the demon. The figures in this dynamic composition are all carved well away from the background, some considerably more than half-round, including Durga's arms, the buffalo, and the fallen fighter on the right. The mask and ornamentation in the background, on the other hand, are in much lower relief.

In the round, low relief, and high relief are traditional categories for classifying sculpture. As we shall see, sculpture today is anything but traditional. In addition to works in bronze, wood, and stone, we will encounter works in fiberglass, fabric, and fluorescent light. We will look at works meant to last for eternity and works meant to last for a morning. And we will explore how an increasing awareness of sculpture's relationship to its surrounding space inspired artists to create spaces themselves as art, inaugurating a new artistic practice called installation.

Methods and Materials of Sculpture

There are four basic methods for making a sculpture: modeling, casting, carving, and assembling. **Modeling** and **assembling** are considered additive processes. The sculptor begins with a simple framework or core or nothing at all and *adds* material until the sculpture is finished. **Carving** is a subtractive process in which one starts with a mass of material larger than the planned sculpture and *subtracts*, or takes away, material until only the desired form remains. **Casting** involves a **mold** of some kind, into which liquid or semiliquid material is poured and allowed to harden.

Let us consider each of these methods in more detail and look as well at some of the materials they are used with.

Modeling

Modeling is familiar to most of us from childhood. As children, we experimented with play dough or clay to construct lopsided figures of people and animals. For sculpture, the most common modeling material is clay, an earth substance found in most parts of the world. Wet clay is wonderfully pliable; few can resist the temptation to squeeze and shape it. As long as clay remains wet, the sculptor can do almost anything with it—add more and more clay to build up the form, gouge away sections, pinch it outward, scratch into it with a sharp tool, smooth it with the hands. But when a clay form has dried and been fired (heated to a very high temperature), it becomes hard. Fired clay, sometimes called by the Italian name **terra cotta**, is surprisingly durable. Much of the ancient art that has survived was formed from this material.

The portrait vessel seen here (**11.4**) was made by the Moche people of South America using modeling and a pre-prepared mold. The clay was pressed into the mold to establish the basic shape. Then the face was modeled by hand, sensitively worked with tools of stone and wood. Finally, the sculpted head was painted. Moche portrait vessels have individualized features, such as the broad nose and piercing eyes of this figure. The headdress and ear ornaments identify this as a ruler. Works like this were used in rituals, placed in tombs, and given as diplomatic gifts to neighboring communities.

In some ways modeling is the most direct of sculpture methods. The workable material responds to every touch, light or heavy, of the sculptor's fingers. Sculptors often use clay modeling in the same way that painters traditionally have used drawing, to test ideas before committing themselves to the finished work. As long as the clay is kept damp, it can be worked and reworked almost indefinitely.

Casting

In contrast to modeling, casting seems like a very *indirect* method of creating a sculpture. Sometimes the sculptor never touches the final piece at all. Metal, and specifically bronze, is the material we think of most readily in relation to casting. Bronze can be superheated until it flows, will pour freely into the tiniest crevices and forms, and then hardens to extreme durability. Even for a thin little projection, like a finger, there is no fear of its breaking off. Also through casting, the sculptor can achieve smooth, rounded shapes and a glowing, reflective surface, such as we see in this Indian sculpture of the bodhisattva Avalokiteshvara (**11.5**). Cast in bronze and then gilded (covered with a thin layer of gold), the smooth, gleaming surfaces of the body contrast with the minutely detailed jewelry, hairstyle, and flowers, demonstrating the ability of metal to capture a full range of effects. In Buddhism,

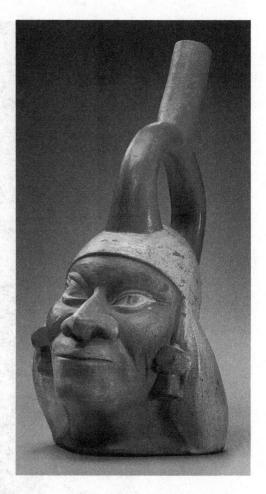

11.4 Stirrup-spout portrait vessel. Moche, central Andes, 300–450 C.E. Clay and pigment, 10 ½ × 4 15⁄16". Yale University Art Gallery

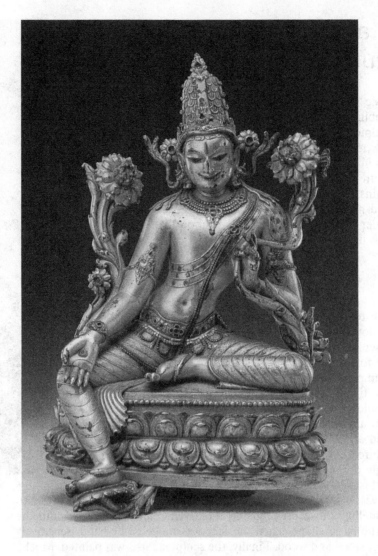

11.5 *The Bodhisattva Avalokiteshvara*, from Kurkihar, Bihar, Central India. Pala dynasty, 12th century. Gilt bronze, height 10". Patna Museum, India. © Dirk Bakker/ Bridgeman Images

bodhisattvas are those spiritually advanced beings who have chosen to delay their own buddhahood in order to help others. Avalokiteshvara is the most popular and beloved of these saintly presences. He is depicted here in princely garb, his hair piled high, seated in a relaxed and sinuous pose on a stylized lotus throne. Lotus blossoms, symbols of purity, twine upward beside him.

The most common method for casting metal is called the **lost-wax** process. Dating back to the third millennium B.C.E., the basic concept is simple and ingenious. We describe it here as it was practiced by the African sculptors of ancient Ife to create heads such as the one illustrated in Chapter 2 (see 2.16).

First, a core is built up of specially prepared clay (**11.6**; **a**). Over this core, the sculptor models the finished head in a layer of wax (**b**). When the sculpture is complete, wax rods and a wax cup are attached to it to form a sort of "arterial system," and metal pins are driven through the wax sculpture to the core inside (**c**). The whole is encased in specially prepared clay (**d**). When the clay has dried, it is heated so that the wax melts and runs out (hence "lost wax") and the clay hardens (**e**). The lost wax leaves a head-shaped void inside the block. Where the wax rods and block were, channels and a depression called a pouring cup remain. The pins hold the core in place, preserving the space where the wax was. Next, the mold is righted, and molten metal is poured into the pouring cup. The metal enters the mold through the channels, driving the air before it (**f**). When the metal bubbles up through the air channels, it is a sign that the mold is probably filled. Metal, therefore, has replaced the wax, which is why casting is known as a replacement method. When the metal has cooled, the mold is broken apart, freeing the head (**g**).

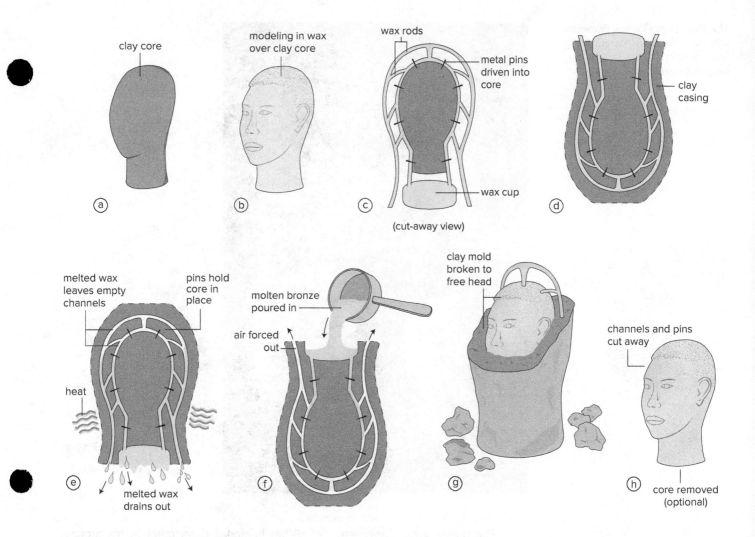

The channels, now cast in metal as well, are cut away, the clay core is removed (if desired), holes or other flaws are patched or repaired, and the head is ready for smoothing and polishing (**h**).

A sculpture cast in this way is unique, for the wax original is destroyed in the process. Standard practice today is a variation called indirect or investment casting, which allows multiples to be made. In this method, the artist finishes the sculpture completely in clay, plaster, or other material. A mold is formed around the solid sculpture (today's foundries use synthetic rubber for this mold). The mold is removed from the sculpture in sections, then reassembled. Melted wax is painted or "slushed" inside the mold to build up an inner layer about three-sixteenths of an inch thick. After it has hardened, this wax casting is removed from the mold and checked against the original sculpture for accuracy: it should be an exact duplicate, but hollow. The wax casting is fitted with wax rods, pierced with pins, then encased in solid plaster, which both fills and surrounds it, just as in figure 11.6d. This plaster is called the *investment*. From this point on, the process is the same: the investment is heated so that the wax melts and runs out, metal is poured into the resulting void, and the investment is broken away to free the casting. The key difference is that the mold that makes the wax casting is reusable; thus, multiple wax versions of an original can be prepared and multiple bronzes of a sculpture cast. All but the simplest sculptures are cast in sections, which are then welded together. (Imagine two halves of an eggshell being cast separately in metal, then welded together to form a hollow metal egg.) As with prints (see Chapter 8), each casting is considered an original work of art, and a limited edition may be declared and controlled.

11.6 The lost-wax casting process.

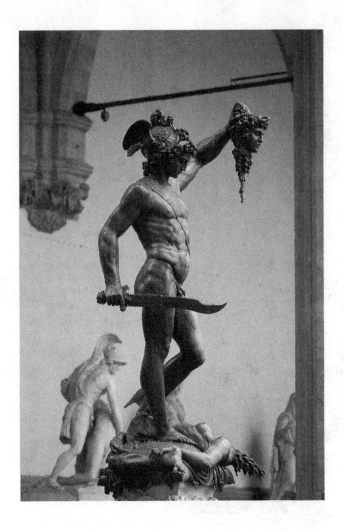

11.7 Benvenuto Cellini. *Perseus with the Head of Medusa*. 1554. Bronze, height 126".
Adam Eastland/Alamy Stock Photo

The Italian artist Benvenuto Cellini left behind a description of his process of lost-wax casting for the sculpture of *Perseus with the Head of Medusa* (**11.7**). The work pictures the idealized figure of the Greek mythological hero Perseus, the son of Zeus. He was sent to fight the gorgon Medusa, a snake-haired monster who turned to stone anyone who looked at her beautiful face. Using a mirrored shield that allowed him to see only her reflection, Perseus slew Medusa, severing her head. Along with the blood flowing from her neck came the winged horse Pegasus, whom the goddess Athena tamed and gave to Perseus.

Cellini's sculpture was created for Duke Cosimo I de' Medici of Florence. The work was cast in two parts: the decapitated body he stands on and the figure of Perseus with the head. But the sculptor's design for the hero made casting difficult. The molten bronze needed to flow up Perseus's arm into the head as well as into the hero's own elaborate helmet. Cellini described the casting in a highly dramatic passage in his autobiography. Rising from his bed while suffering from a high fever, he saw that his molten bronze was not flowing properly. In a feverish frenzy, he ordered his studio assistants to hurl 200 pieces of his pewter housewares into the furnace. Bronze began to stream through the mold, reaching even the most distant points of the work. The shop workers cheered, and Cellini fell to his knees, thanking God.

Any material that hardens from a liquefied state can be cast to make sculpture. Artists use metals, ceramics, plastics, and even blood in their cast works. Janine Antoni used chocolate and soap for *Lick and Lather* (**11.8**). The work features fourteen busts, seven made of chocolate and seven made of soap. Antoni's work addresses what she calls the rituals we perform as we go about our daily lives: We eat, we bathe, we move. She considers identity in her art, and her goal for *Lick and Lather* is to explore ideas of beauty and desire. Antoni chose the number seven for

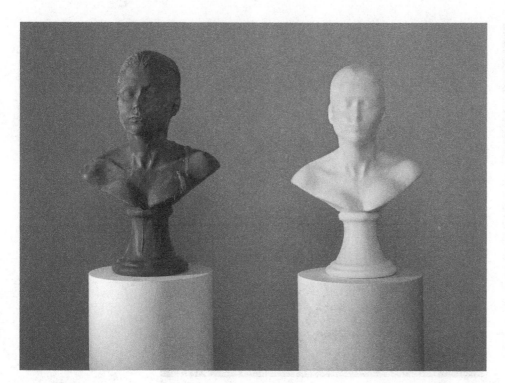

11.8 Janine Antoni. *Lick and Lather*. 1993. Cast chocolate and soap, 24 × 16 × 13" each.
© Janine Antoni; Courtesy of the artist and Luhring Augustine, New York

the busts to refer to Classical proportion systems that make the height of a female body seven times the height of her head.

As she does for much of her work, Antoni used her own body to make the art. She created a mold of her head in the manner of Classical portrait busts. She then filled the mold with the two materials in their liquid state. When they cooled and hardened, the realistic busts exactly reproduced her image. Then the artist manipulated each bust. She licked and nibbled the chocolate sculptures and washed herself with those made of soap. Each bust is therefore slightly different and reminds viewers of the artist's presence.

Carving

Carving is more aggressive than modeling, and more direct than casting. In this process, the sculptor begins with a block of material and cuts, chips, and gouges away until the form of the sculpture emerges. Wood and stone are the principal materials for carving, and both have been used by artists in many cultures throughout history.

Tilman Riemenschneider, one of the foremost German sculptors of the late Middle Ages, carved his *Virgin and Child on the Crescent Moon* in limewood (**11.9**). A soft wood with a close, uniform grain, limewood carves easily and lends itself well to Riemenschneider's detailed, virtuosic style. Mary stands in a gentle, stylized S-curve, as though she might move at any moment. The infant Jesus is even more animated, and his body twists in a spiral motion. Like many artists of his time, Riemenschneider depicted Jesus unclothed and in motion to emphasize the completeness of his incarnation as a man.

Limewood was native to southern Germany, where Riemenschneider lived and worked. Northern German sculptors generally worked with oak, which was in plentiful supply in their own region. Ancient Olmec artists, in contrast, may have had more complex reasons for using basalt for their monumental stone carvings (**11.10**). Certainly, they went to great lengths to quarry and transport it. Boulders weighing up to 44 tons seem to have been dragged for miles to the riverbank, then floated by barge to a landing point near their final destinations. Olmec sculptors shaped the hard stone using still harder stone tools, probably quartz blades. Carved in a broad style of plain surfaces and subtle modeling, the monumental sculptures are

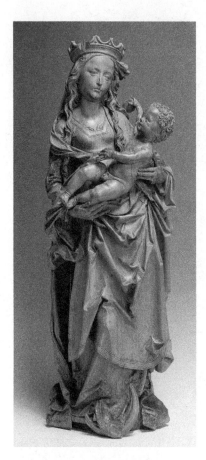

11.9 Tilman Riemenschneider. *Virgin and Child on the Crescent Moon.* ca. 1495. Limewood, height 34 ⅛".

Museum für Angewandte Kunst, Cologne. Sammlung Wilhelm Clemens. A 1156 CL. Photo © Rheinisches Bildarchiv Köln, rba_c017585

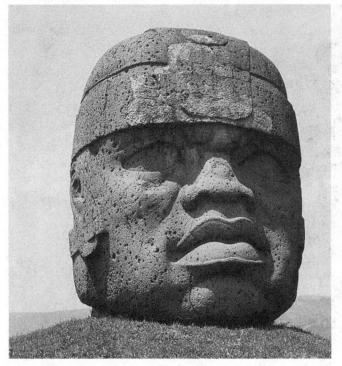

11.10 Colossal head. Olmec, 1500–300 B.C.E. Basalt, height approx. 8'.

Museo de Antropología, Veracruz. Werner Forman/Art Resource, NY/ Anthropology Museum, Veracruz University, Jalapa

thought to represent Olmec rulers. Scholars believe that basalt was selected for its symbolic value. A volcanic stone that emerges in molten form from the Earth's interior, basalt was associated with the awesome power of nature. It was thus a fitting material for rulers, who were believed to have the awesome power of journeying to the spirit world and back.

Assembling

Assembling is a process by which individual pieces or segments or objects are brought together to form a sculpture. Some writers make a distinction between assembling, in which parts of the sculpture are simply placed on or near each other, and constructing, in which the parts are actually joined together through welding, nailing, or a similar procedure. This book uses the term *assemblage* for both types of work.

The 20th-century American sculptor David Smith came to assemblage in an unusual way. While trying to establish himself as an artist, Smith worked as a welder. Later, when he began to concentrate on sculpture, he adapted his welding skills to a different purpose. His mature works broke new ground in both materials and forms (**11.11**). Smith's *Voltri VI* is an abstract assemblage made of steel, a material closely identified with our modern era. Steel had been produced in small quantities since ancient times for such purposes as swords and armor, but only during the second half of the 19th century was the technology developed for mass-producing the metal, making steel widely and cheaply available for the first time. The architecture of the 20th century would not have been possible without it. For *Voltri VI*, Smith assembled steel pieces he found in an Italian factory, combining wheels, tools, and pieces of scrap metal. *Voltri VI* resembles a chariot or a train car carrying vertical, curved pieces the sculptor referred to as clouds.

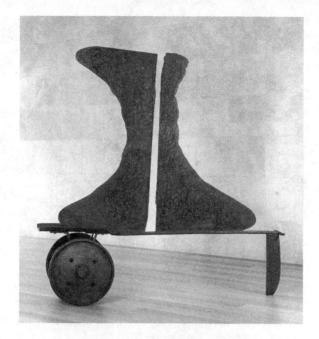

11.11 David Smith. *Voltri VI*. 1962. Steel, 98 ⅞ × 102 ¼ × 24".
Nasher Sculpture Center. Raymond and Patsy Nasher Collection © 2019 Estate of David Smith/Licensed by VAGA, New York, NY

The artist Roxy Paine uses stainless steel for his outdoor sculptures, constructing organic forms—life-size, naturalistic trees he calls Dendroids (**11.12**). The pair of trees here lean toward each other, their branches joined at the tips. The longer we look, the less like any known trees they seem. Of course, they cannot grow, but are they dead? The branches seem a little too animated, like crooked whips or jagged bolts of lightning. The trunks and branches are not textured to imitate bark but, instead, are blatantly artificial—smooth, gleaming, cylindrical lengths of stainless steel welded together, the joints clearly evident. And where are the leaves? There is something magical about Paine's trees, as though we had stumbled onto a punishment in a fairy tale.

11.12 Roxy Paine. *Conjoined*. 2007. Stainless steel and concrete, 40 × 45'.
Modern Art Museum of Fort Worth, Texas. Courtesy of the artist and Paul Kasmin Gallery, New York © Roxy Paine

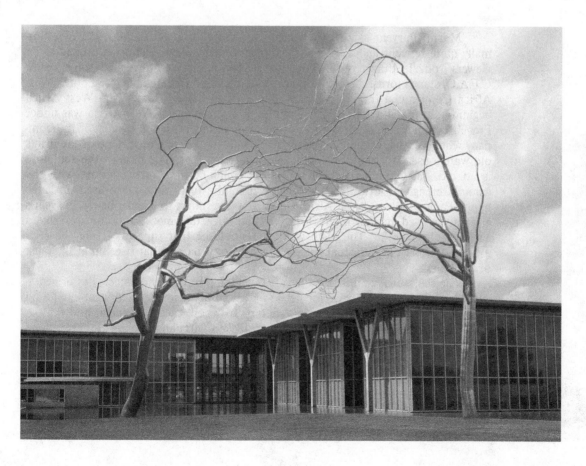

11.13 Martin Puryear. *C.F.A.O.* 2006–07. Painted and unpainted pine and found wheelbarrow, 8' 4 ½" × 6' 5 ½" × 5' 1".
Courtesy the artist and Donald Young Gallery, Chicago

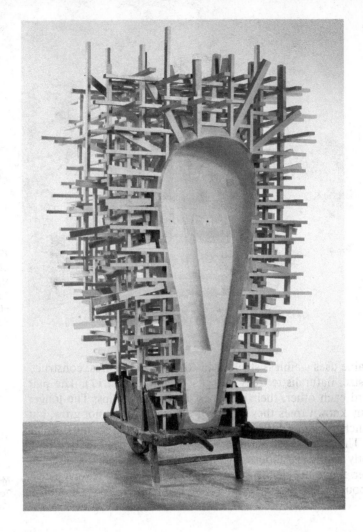

11.14 Huma Bhabha. *Athos.* 2006. Wood, clay, wire, Styrofoam, metal stud, and acrylic paint, 77 × 28 × 29 ½".
Courtesy Salon 94

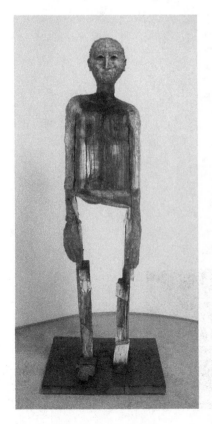

Martin Puryear assembled wooden elements to create *C.F.A.O.* (**11.13**). Normally quite reticent about what his sculptures might mean, the artist prefers to let viewers "puzzle things out."[1] For this sculpture, he has furnished some clues. C.F.A.O. stands for Compagnie Française de l'Afrique Occidentale, the French West Africa Company, a trading company that sailed between France and West Africa beginning in the late 19th century, at a time when much of West Africa was under French colonial rule. Puryear first came into contact with the history of the company when he was teaching in West Africa with the Peace Corps. One of the firm's old warehouses still stood in the village where he lived. The base of the sculpture is an old, rustic French wheelbarrow. Its rough-hewn planks contrast with the smooth, elongated form it bears, an interpretation of a white mask used in dance by the Fang people. Like all African masks, it gives form to a spirit being. Puryear's elegantly carved version is much larger than an actual mask, and concave, like a shallow tub or coffin. The plain wooden scaffolding that supports it may be seen as a kind of bristling spiritual energy, like a halo of flames that rises up at the back of the mask.

The sculptor Huma Bhabha began assembling from found objects out of necessity. Materials were expensive for her as an art student, so she used what she found and combined it into organic forms. Scraps of wood, pieces of metal and plastic, Styrofoam containers and packing pieces, chicken wire, and sticks—all these served as building blocks for sculptures such as *Athos* (**11.14**). We see the diverse materials lashed together, along with clay molded around the head, hands, and back to suggest skin. Each of these materials is meaningless on its own, but is activated and energized when assembled into the work. The figurative work is haunting, with a passive face and helpless pose. The pathetic figure seems little like his namesake from *The Three Musketeers* by Alexandre Dumas, or the giant Athos who battled the gods in Greek mythology.

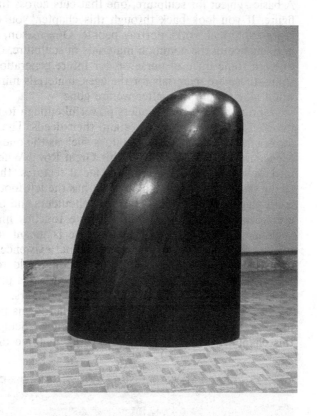

How would you describe Martin Puryear's work? What is his goal for his art? What sculptural processes does he use?

The African-American sculptor Martin Puryear was born in Washington, D.C., but is a world traveler. He went to Africa after college to "live among the people who lived in the part of the world that stamped me."[2] After working in the Peace Corps in Sierra Leone, Puryear studied art in Sweden and Japan before returning to the United States. As he traveled, the artist studied the crafts of each nation and came to appreciate the historical role of the anonymous craftsman.

Puryear delights in working with the materials he chooses, from found wood scraps to granite. *Self*, seen here, for example, appears to be a solid mass but is instead made from thin sheets of wood, layered one atop the next, that transform a simple shape into a complex construction. He began his lifelong love affair with materials as a young man, making wood furniture and canoes. His abstract sculpture celebrates materials, and the viewer always appreciates the labor and effort that went into its making. *Self* reveals the artist's hand that smoothed and polished the wood to its glossy sheen.

Puryear's work usually has no story to tell, but is instead a celebration of form. As he has explained, "Whether it's through beauty or through ugliness or whatever quality you put into the work, that is what the work can be about." Granting viewers this freedom of interpretation means that his art "feels like it's got a lot more potential for evolution and change and open-endedness" than other abstract sculpture.[3] To bring the work closer to the viewer, Puryear does not put his sculpture on a pedestal. Instead, the works rest directly on the ground, sharing the viewer's space.

Puryear has enjoyed immense success in his career. His work is owned by major museums around the world, and the National Gallery of Art and the Museum of Modern Art have held retrospective exhibitions of his work. He has been recognized with both a Guggenheim Fellowship and a MacArthur Foundation Fellowship, also known as the "Genius Grant." In 2011, Puryear received the National Medal of Arts from President Barack Obama.

Martin Puryear. *Self*. 1978. Polychromed red cedar and mahogany, 69 × 48 × 25". © Martin Puryear, Joslyn Art Museum, Omaha, Nebraska, Museum purchase in memory of Elinor Ashton, 1980.63

The Human Figure in Sculpture

A basic subject for sculpture, one that cuts across time and cultures, is the human figure. If you look back through this chapter, you will notice that almost all the representational works portray people. One reason, certainly, must be the relative permanence of the common materials of sculpture. Our life is short, and the desire to leave some trace of ourselves for future generations is great. Metal, terra cotta, stone—these are materials for the ages, materials mined from the Earth itself. Even wood may endure long after we are gone.

From earliest times, rulers powerful enough to maintain a workshop of artists have left images of themselves and their deeds. The royal tombs of ancient Egypt, for example, included carved statues such as the one illustrated here of the pharaoh Menkaure and Khamerernebty, his Great Royal Wife (**11.15**). Portrayed with idealized, youthful bodies and similar facial features, the couple stand proudly erect, facing straight ahead. Although each has the left foot planted slightly forward, there is no suggestion of walking, for their shoulders and hips are level. Menkaure's arms are frozen at his sides, while his wife touches him in a formalized gesture of "belonging together." This formal pose is meant to convey not only the power of the rulers but also their serene, eternal existence. The pharaoh, after all, ruled as a "junior god" on Earth and, at death, would rejoin the gods in immortality. Egyptian rulers must have been pleased with this pose, for their artists repeated it again and again over the next two thousand years.

A second reason for the many human forms portrayed in sculpture is a little more mysterious. We might call it "presence." Sculpture, as pointed out earlier in this chapter, exists wholly in our world, in three dimensions. To portray a being

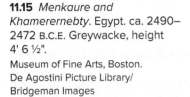

11.15 *Menkaure and Khamerernebty.* Egypt. ca. 2490–2472 B.C.E. Greywacke, height 4' 6 ½".
Museum of Fine Arts, Boston.
De Agostini Picture Library/ Bridgeman Images

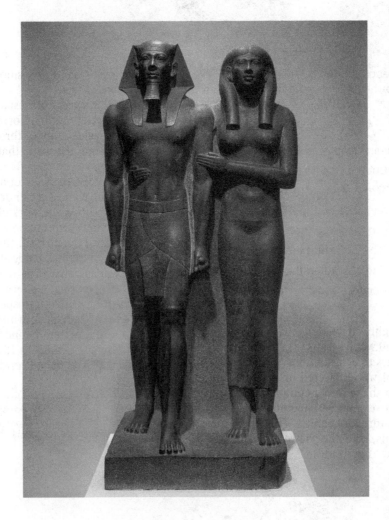

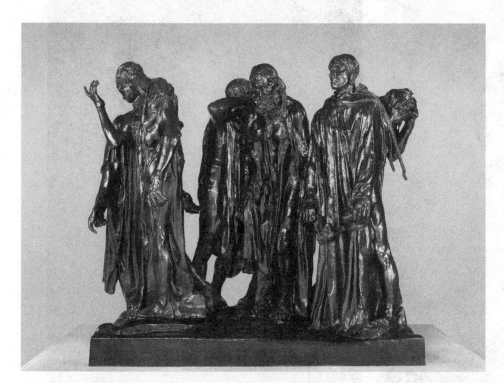

11.16 Auguste Rodin. *The Burghers of Calais*. Modeled 1884–1917, cast 1919–21. Bronze, 6' 10 ½" × 7' 10" × 6' 3".
Metropolitan Museum of Art, New York, Gift of Iris and B. Gerald Cantor, 1989

in sculpture is to bring it into the world, to give it a presence that is close to life itself. In the ancient world, statues were often believed to have an ambiguous, porous relationship to life. In Egypt, for example, the Opening of the Mouth ceremony that was believed to help a dead person reawaken in the afterlife was performed not only on his or her mummified body but also on his or her statue. In China, the tomb of the first emperor was "protected" by a vast army of terra-cotta soldiers, buried standing in formation (see 19.16). A famous Greek myth tells of the sculptor Pygmalion, who fell so in love with a statue that it came to life.

Sculptors are often called on to memorialize the heroes and heroines of a community, people whose accomplishments or sacrifices are felt to be worthy of remembrance by future generations. Auguste Rodin's group of cast bronze figures known as *The Burghers of Calais* (**11.16**) was commissioned in 1884 by the French city of Calais to honor six prominent townsmen of the 14th century, when France and England were engaged in the protracted conflict known as the Hundred Years War. The men had offered their lives to ransom Calais from the English, who had laid siege to it for more than a year, starving its citizens. A famous chronicle of the time preserves the men's names, and Rodin, moved by it, imagined them as individuals, each facing death and defeat in his own way, whether in pride, anger, sorrow, resignation, or despair. Barefoot, with ropes around their necks and dressed only in their robelike shirts, as the English king had demanded, the men pace in an irregular circle, carrying the heavy key to the city gates. Sympathetic viewers must pace alongside them, for there is no angle from which all their faces are visible.

Among the human images that artists are most often asked to make present in the world through sculpture are those connected with religion and the spirit realm. The Japanese sculptor Kaikei carved and painted this wood image of the Shinto deity Hachiman in 1201 for a newly refurbished shrine (**11.17**). Patron and protector of warriors, Hachiman is often portrayed in the guise of a Buddhist monk. Kaikei has imagined him sitting cross-legged on a lotus pedestal, his long sleeves flowing gracefully over his knees. In his right hand he delicately holds a priest's walking staff made of bronze. The freely jangling rings at the top served to warn small creatures that someone was coming so they had time to get out of the way and avoid being stepped on. Cradled in his lap, his left hand originally held a rock-crystal rosary. The coloring heightens the realism of Kaikei's style, bringing the statue even closer to seeming capable of speech.

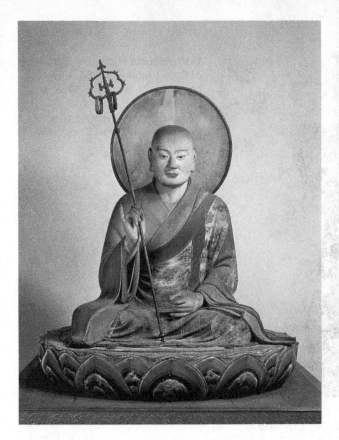

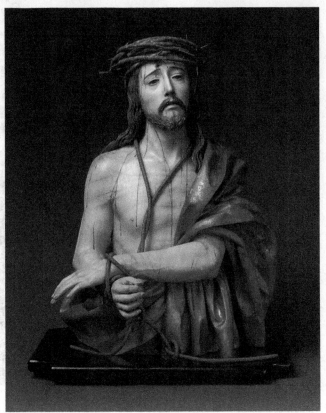

11.17 Kaikei. *Hachiman in the Guise of a Monk*. 1201.
Polychrome wood, height 34 ½".
Todai-ji temple, Nara. © DeA Picture Library/Art Resource, NY

11.18 Pedro de Mena. *Ecce Homo*. 1674–85. Polychromed
wood, 26 ¼ × 21 × 16 ⅛".
Metropolitan Museum of Art, New York, Purchase, Lila Acheson
Wallace Gift, Mary Trumbell Adams Fund, and Gift of Dr. Mortimer
D. Sackler, Theresa Sackler and Family, 2014

Speech also seems imminent in the Spanish sculptor Pedro de Mena's *Ecce Homo* (**11.18**). The work represents Christ after his arrest and torture. Pontius Pilate places a crown of thorns on his head and mockingly displays him to the crowd, stating, "*Ecce homo*," meaning "Behold the man." Mena's goal for the sculpture was to picture this painful and sad moment in Christ's life with the utmost drama. He used painted wood to make the image as realistic as possible. He also simulated real flesh by layering naturalistic pigments and varnish in a process Spanish sculptors called incarnation. After each layer dried it was sanded until the painted skin took on a lifelike glow, and bruised flesh was distinguished from unblemished areas. Drips of red paint simulate blood. Mena and his fellow Spanish sculptors also sometimes enhanced the realism of their sculpture with glass eyes inserted into the head, ivory teeth and fingernails, and real hair and clothing. In this case, the red cloak wrapped around the body is painted over gold leaf to look like silk or brocade. The effect is moving, and the sculpture evokes an emotional response from its viewers, who feel Christ's pain and sorrow.

The human figure is also the most common subject of traditional African sculpture, but in fact the sculptures rarely represent humans. Instead, they generally represent spirits of various kinds. The masterful carving shown in **11.19** by a Baule sculptor of a seated woman carrying a child on her back depicts a spirit spouse. A formal pose and an impassive face are used to express the dignity of an otherworldly being. Baule belief holds that each person has, in addition to an earthly spouse, a spirit spouse in the Other World. If this spirit spouse is happy, all is well. But an unhappy or jealous spirit spouse may cause trouble in one's life. A remedy is to give the spirit spouse a presence in this world by commissioning a statue (called a "person of wood"). The statue is made as beautiful as possible to encourage the spirit to take up residence within it, and it is placed in a household shrine and tended to with gifts and small offerings.

Portrayals of rulers, heroes and heroines, and religious or spirit figures unite the many sculptural traditions of the world. Western culture, however, is marked as well by a tradition of sculpting the human figure for its own sake and of finding the body to be a worthy subject for art. This we owe ultimately to the ancient Greeks. Cultivating the body through gymnastics and sport was an important part of Greek culture, and they admired their athletes greatly. (The Olympics, after all, were a Greek invention.) Not surprisingly, perhaps, they came to believe that the body itself was beautiful. From the many athletic bodies on view, sculptors derived an ideally beautiful body type, governed by harmonious proportions. They gave these idealized, perfected bodies to images of gods and mythological heroes, who were usually depicted nude, and also to images of male athletes, who actually did train and compete unclothed. Finally, Greek artists developed a distinctive stance for their standing figures. Called **contrapposto**, it can be seen in this statue of an athlete scraping himself off after a workout (**11.20**).

Contrapposto, meaning "counterpoise" or "counterbalance," sets the body in a gentle S-shaped curve through a play of opposites (**11.21**). Here, the athlete's weight rests on his left foot, so that his left hip is raised and his right leg is bent and relaxed. To counterbalance this, his right shoulder is raised. By portraying the dynamic interplay of a standing body at rest, contrapposto implies the potential for motion inherent in a living being. We can easily imagine that a moment earlier the athlete's weight was arranged differently, and that it will shift again a moment from now.

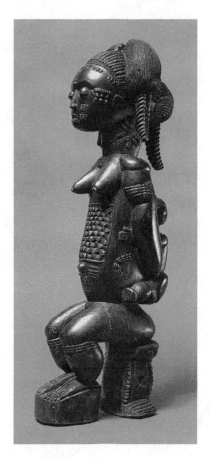

11.19 *Spirit Spouse*, from Ivory Coast. Baule, early 20th century. Wood, height 17 ⅛".
University of Pennsylvania Museum, Philadelphia. Purchased from J. Laporte, 29-12-68

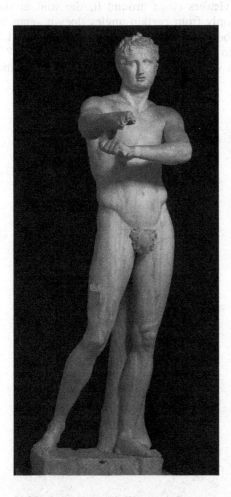

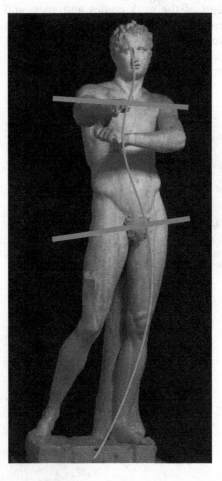

11.20 *Apoxyomenos (Scraper)*. Roman copy of a bronze original by Lysippos, ca. 320 B.C.E. Marble, height 6' 8 ¾".
Musei Vaticani, Museo Pio Clementino, Rome. Scala/Art Resource, NY

11.21 The dynamics of contrapposto.
Musei Vaticani, Museo Pio Clementino, Rome. Scala/Art Resource, NY

Since antiquity, the body has continued to serve as a subject through which sculptors express feelings and ideas about the human experience, particularly in the West. For Kiki Smith, who came of age artistically during the decade around 1990, the body is a subject that connects the universal and the personal in a unique way. "I think I chose the body as a subject, not consciously, but because it is the one form that we all share," she has said. "It's something that everybody has their own authentic experience with."[4] *Honeywax* depicts a woman, her knees and right hand drawn up to her chest, her left arm relaxed at her side, her eyes closed (**11.22**). It is hard to say whether she is retreating from the world or about to be born into it. Although Smith set the work on the floor, the figure's pose is that of a person suspended—in air, in fluid, in a dream. Translucent and easily injured, the wax surface suggests human skin, vulnerability, and impermanence. Within the history of sculpture, wax is the material of lost-wax casting, the material that will be discarded to make way for something else, something durable. "I feel I'm making physical manifestations of psychic and spiritual dilemmas," Smith has said. "Spiritual dilemmas are being played out physically."[5] Her words might just as easily have been spoken by Pedro de Mena about his *Ecce Homo* expressing the human experience.

The body at the center of Antony Gormley's *Quantum Void III* is an absence, a void within a field of energy (**11.23**). The photograph illustrated here makes the body-shaped void clear for purposes of documentation, but the experience of seeing the work in person is very different. Made from lengths of slender stainless-steel bars welded each to the next in branching formation, the sculpture dissolves in the sunlight into a formless dazzle. As viewers circle around it, the void at the heart of the work comes and goes, and only from certain angles does it seem to resolve itself into the form of a human body. "The body is central to my work," Gormley has written. "How does it feel to be alive? What is it to be conscious?"[6] *Quantum Void III* can be understood as a visual response to those most basic and profound questions.

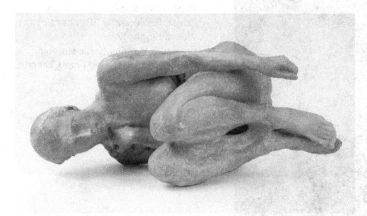

11.22 Kiki Smith. *Honeywax*. 1995.
Beeswax, 15 ½ × 36 × 20", unique.
Milwaukee Art Museum, Gift of
Contemporary Art Society. M1996.5
© Kiki Smith, courtesy Pace Gallery

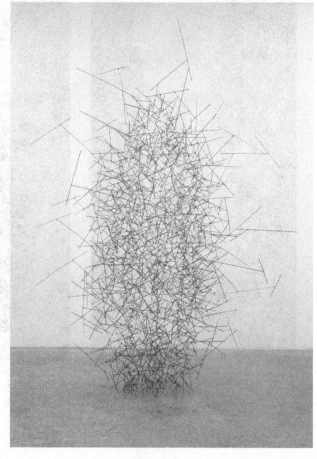

11.23 Antony Gormley. *Quantum Void III*.
2008. 2mm square-section stainless-steel
wire, 8' 4" × 7' 7 ¾" × 5' 10 ⅞".
© Antony Gormley. Photo © Stephen White,
courtesy White Cube

Working with Time and Place

We live in an environment sculpted by the forces of nature. Millions of years ago, drifting continents collided, the shock sending up towering mountain ranges. Glaciers advanced and retreated, gouging out lakes and valleys, creating hills and waterfalls, grinding down rock faces, and distributing boulders. Rivers carved channels and canyons. Still today mountains are slowly being pushed upward, the ocean constantly rearranges the shoreline, and wind shifts the desert sands. Some shapings happen quickly, others take millions of years. Some last for centuries, others for only a moment.

People, too, have worked to sculpt the landscape. Often, the shaping is purely practical, such as digging a canal to enable boats to penetrate inland, or terracing a hillside so that crops can grow. But just as often, we have shaped places for religious purposes or for aesthetic contemplation and enjoyment. When the Western category of art was first formulated, landscape gardening was often mentioned along with painting and sculpture. In Chapter 3, we looked at one of the most famous gardens in the world, the stone and gravel garden at Ryoan-ji Temple (see 3.25). We also looked at Robert Smithson's *Spiral Jetty*, a coil of rock and earth extending into the Great Salt Lake in Utah (see 3.26).

Spiral Jetty is an earthwork, a work of art made for a specific place using natural materials found there, especially the earth itself. Earthworks were one of the ways in which artists of Smithson's generation tried to move away from inherited ideas about art as an object that could be bought and sold. As with many developments of those years, earthworks built bridges of understanding to other world traditions. One of the most famous earthworks in the United States is the Serpent Mound, near Locust Grove, Ohio (**11.24**). For almost five thousand years, numerous Eastern American peoples built large-scale earthworks as burial sites and ceremonial centers. Serpent Mound was long thought to have been formed by the Hopewell people during the early centuries of our common era. Recently, however, scientific methods have suggested a date of around 1070 C.E., long after the decline of Hopewell culture. Serpent Mound contains no burials, and one archaeologist has suggested that the mound may have been created in response to a celestial event, the sighting of Halley's comet, which flamed through the skies in 1066.[7]

11.24 Serpent Mound, near Locust Grove, Ohio.
Mark Burnett/Alamy Stock Photo

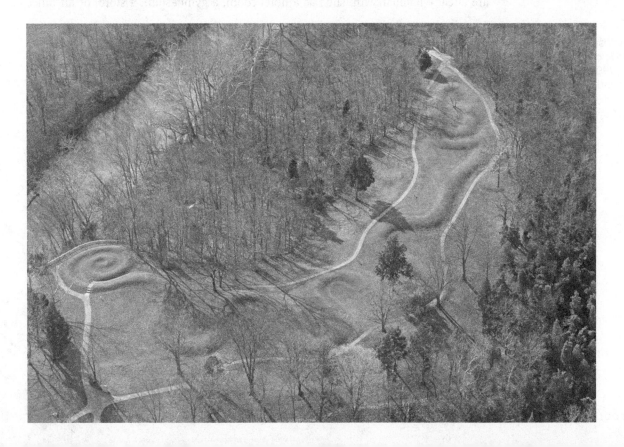

Earthworks such as Serpent Mound and *Spiral Jetty* enter into the natural world and participate in its changes—the rain and snow that fall, the vegetation that grows and blossoms, even eventual decay. For artists such as Smithson, participating in natural processes was part of the art. Smithson assumed that his work would change slowly over time, and he embraced those changes as part of the ongoing life of his sculpture. In the earthworks of Andy Goldsworthy, the element of time moves to center stage (**11.25**). Goldsworthy makes earthworks that are ephemeral, often from such fleeting materials as ice, leaves, or branches. Many of his works last no more than a few hours before the wind scatters them, or the tide sweeps them away, or, in the case of *Reconstructed Icicles, Dumfriesshire, 1995*, the sun melts them. Goldsworthy tries to go into nature every day and make something from whatever he finds. He documents his work in photographs, including photographs that record the work's disappearance over time, as nature "erases" it. "Time and change are connected to place," he has written. "Real change is best understood by staying in one place."[8]

Photographs bring us views of Serpent Mound, *Spiral Jetty*, and *Reconstructed Icicles, Dumfriesshire*, by framing them in a two-dimensional composition and making them a focal point. In fact, such works are incidents in the landscape, like other incidents—a tree, a rock, a stream, a hill. We would experience them quite differently in person, with the land extending endlessly and our eyes free to look in any direction. Artists have more control over our experience in a shaped, delimited space such as a room. The art form known as installation, introduced in Chapter 2 (see 2.41), grew from this observation. Originally, "installation" referred to the placement of artworks in an exhibition space—where the pictures were hung or the sculpture was positioned. Gallery and museum workers speak of "installing a show," by which they mean setting the art in place. Often, an "installation shot" is made—a photograph documenting the exhibition.

Just as an installation shot gathers a space and everything in it into a single image, so artists began to conceive of a space and everything in it as a single work of art. This new approach came to be known as installation, or installation art. With installation art, an artist modifies a space in some way and then asks us to enter, explore, and experience it. Some installations may remind us of places our mind invents in dreams. Others have been compared to sets for a play or a film—a place where something happened or is about to happen. Still others resemble places we are already familiar with, such as a hotel room, a gymnasium, a store, or an office.

11.25 Andy Goldsworthy. *Reconstructed Icicles, Dumfriesshire, 1995*. Icicles, reconstructed and refrozen. © Andy Goldsworthy. Courtesy Galerie LeLong, New York

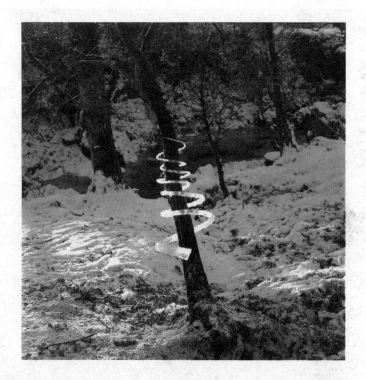

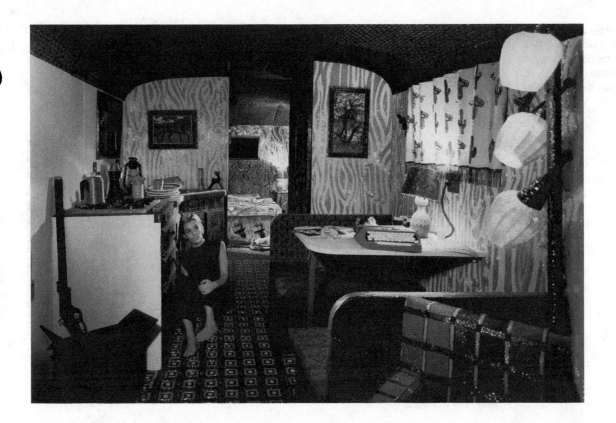

11.26 Liza Lou. *Trailer*. 1998–2000. Interior: Glass beads, velvet, wood, wire, plaster, found objects, electrical parts. Television sound from *Force of Evil* (1948) on continuous loop. Installation, 10 × 8 × 40'.
© Liza Lou. Photo Mick Haggerty

The idea of a room remains at the heart of many installations. A room is a space set apart from the rest of the world. It may be a place of refuge, of discovery, of secrets, or even of imprisonment. The room in Liza Lou's *Trailer* (**11.26**) was the interior of a 1949 Spartan Mobile Mansion. She found the trailer abandoned in the woods and remade the interior completely. As with much of her work, the artist applied small glass beads to every surface: walls, dishes, seats, typewriter, lamp. The beads drew attention to each item that would otherwise go unnoticed for its mundane functionality. Lou used the beads to make everyday objects beautiful and unpleasant things approachable.

Lou began working with beads after a visit to a craft store while she was in art school. She found the beads more engaging than paint and began using tweezers to apply them to objects she found or made. Her professors did not appreciate her change of medium, but Lou used the beads to draw attention to labor, to materials and their qualities, and to the women artisans who have historically toiled without recognition. The bead work attracted worldwide attention when Lou exhibited a kitchen she had crafted from found objects and papier-maché, and covered in millions of brightly colored beads. In 2002, the creative value of her work was recognized with a $500,000 MacArthur Foundation "Genius Grant."

Trailer's sparkly finish belies its mysterious and grim story. Lou provided a narrative for this installation, basing the story on a history she invented for the trailer. Imagining that it had been abandoned for a bad reason, Lou re-created an interior decor for a lonely, despairing hunter. The beads covering all the surfaces have a dark palette, with lots of silver, black, and white. The books on the shelves are about killing and the art on the wall pictures guns. A magazine on the table is titled *Men Today: Flesh Farm of Horror*. A television inside the trailer plays a 1948 film, *Force of Evil*, and the movie's dialog fills the space. Lou's dark story continues in the back part of the trailer, where discarded bottles and a gun rest next to legs outstretched on the floor. The viewer is left to complete the story, as the rest of the figure is unseen.

In *Trailer*, Lou created a work of art that could be entered so that viewers were immersed in the experience. The installation Gerda Steiner and Jörg Lenzlinger created for the 2003 Venice Biennale—an exhibition of contemporary art held every

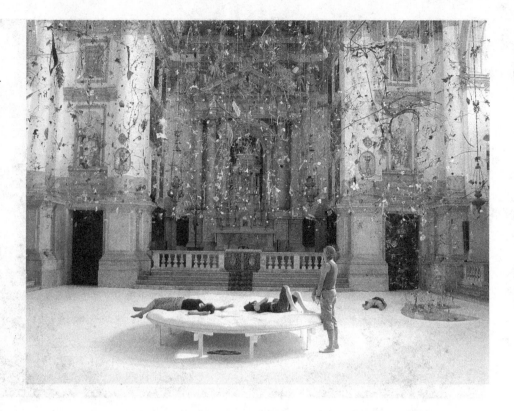

two years in Venice, Italy—operates similarly. To make *Falling Garden* (**11.27**), the artists strung common items on long threads hanging from the ceiling of a 17th-century church. The found objects include plastic berries, real cow dung, discarded paper, leaves, silk flowers, bones, and even a rubber snake. Visitors lay on a circular couch set above a grave in the church's floor. As they gazed upward, the viewers saw a "garden," inspired by the story of Saint Eustace and his vision of a crucifix on a deer's forehead. The artists imagined this falling garden to be the forest where the deer lived. The installation used the vast space of the vaults strung with colorful items to transform the visitor's experience of the church.

Previous chapters have explored how light can be used to create a sense of place, as with the colored light that suffuses the Sainte-Chapelle in Paris (see 3.1). Another artist who devoted his career to exploring the effects of light on our perception of space was Dan Flavin. Flavin's means were simple, and they never varied: He made constructions from standard, commercially available fluorescent light tubes and fixtures. At first Flavin focused his attention on the lights themselves as sculptural objects, but he quickly came to realize, as he put it, that "the actual space of the room could be disrupted and played with" through light.[9] *Untitled (to Karin and Walther)* (**11.28**) consists of four blue fluorescent lights arranged in a square and standing on the floor in a corner. Two lights face inward, two outward. From these simple means a whole range of blues arises as light reflects off the white walls and radiates into the room.

Flavin was associated with **Minimalism**, an art movement of the 1960s. Like other movements of those years, Minimalism was part of an ongoing argument about the appropriate purpose, materials, and look of art in the modern era. Minimalist artists believed that art should offer a pure and honest aesthetic experience instead of trying to influence people through images or transmit the ego of the artist through self-expression. They favored materials associated more with industry or construction than with art, and they let those materials speak for themselves.

Annette Lawrence's installation *Coin Toss* (**11.29**) was inspired in part by Minimalist art. The work consists of steel cables strung diagonally across a concourse at AT&T Stadium in Arlington, Texas. The stadium, where the Dallas Cowboys football team plays, is massive, with large open areas surrounding entryways. Like all installations, *Coin Toss* forces the viewer to see one of those spaces, to think

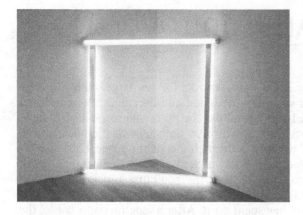

11.28 Dan Flavin. *Untitled*. 1960s. Fluorescent light fixtures.
© Stephen Flavin/Artists Rights Society (ARS), New York.
Photo: GINIES/SIPA/Newscom

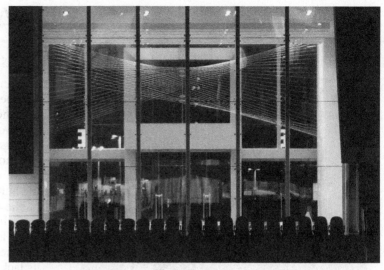

11.29 Annette Lawrence. *Coin Toss*. 2009. Stranded cable, 14 × 45'.
© Annette Lawrence

about its shape and purpose, and to be conscious of our movement through it. The hourglass shape created by the cables is meant to recall the repeated turning of a coin during the opening coin toss at a football game. The work seems to change and move as you walk beneath it, and the installation changes the visitor's experience of the stadium.

Although Lawrence's work is a permanent installation that forms part of a unique art collection at the stadium, several of the works we have examined in this section no longer exist. This is not because they were lost or destroyed, but because they were not meant to last in the first place. The idea of impermanent sculpture may surprise us at first, but in fact most of us not only are familiar with it but also have made it. An outdoor figure modeled in snow on a cold winter afternoon is destined to melt before spring, but we take pleasure in sculpting it anyway. Castles and mermaids modeled in wet sand by the shore will be washed away when the tide comes in, but we still put great energy and inventiveness into creating them. For festivals and carnivals the world over, weeks and even months are spent creating elaborate figures and floats, all for the sake of a single day's event.

Since the 1960s, many artists have been intrigued by these kinds of event and activity—by the way they bring people together, focus their energy, and intensify life for a moment before disappearing. In their different ways, festivals and sandcastles suggested answers to such questions as how to bring art closer to daily life, and how to make art without making an object that could be sold and owned.

Among the most famous artists to work with these ideas were the husband-and-wife team of Christo and Jeanne-Claude. For more than five decades, they planned and carried out vast art projects involving the cooperation of hundreds of people. The last work they completed together was *The Gates* (**11.30**), a project for New York City's Central Park. Hundreds of paid workers arrived from all over the country to help Christo and Jeanne-Claude set up 7,503 saffron-colored, rectangular gateways along the 23 miles of the park's footpaths. Rolled up and secured against the high horizontal beam of each gate was a saffron-colored banner of nylon fabric. On the opening day of the project, the workers went from gate to gate freeing the banners, which unfurled and began to billow in the wind as the pale winter sunlight played over and through them. *The Gates* remained in place for sixteen days, attracting four million visitors from all over the world. The American composer Aaron

Public Art Controversies

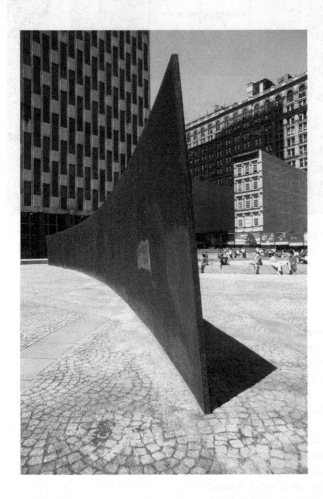

What happens when people do not like the art that is installed in public places? What makes public art controversial? What is the value of public art?

Christo and Jeanne-Claude's *The Gates* was well received by New Yorkers and visitors to the city who walked beneath it. Yet, not everyone liked this public art. Some people complained that it was a safety hazard. Others argued that it interfered with the beauty of the park. Other projects by the pair have similarly riled local populations concerned with environmental impact, cost, and danger. While the temporary nature of projects by Christo and Jeanne-Claude makes criticism short-lived, what happens when permanently installed public art causes controversy?

In 1979, Richard Serra was hired to create a public sculpture for an open plaza at a New York City federal building. The artist, known for his large-scale Minimalist steel sculpture, designed and executed a long arc that stretched 120 feet across the plaza and stood 12 feet high. The work drew attention to the shape of the plaza and to visitors' movement through this public space. Criticism began, however, as soon as Serra installed *Tilted Arc* in 1981. Some complained that the sculpture blocked access to the building. Others found the work ugly and not worth the public money spent on it. After a lengthy court battle, the sculpture was removed and has never been displayed again.

The design of Maya Lin's Vietnam Veterans Memorial (see 1.6) also stirred controversy. Some people found its lack of familiar images and symbols of heroism and sacrifice to be a political statement against the war. Some felt that the abstract design looked like a gash in the earth, or compared it to Serra's failed *Tilted Arc*. Two magazines even likened the names of the fallen soldiers carved into the monument to reports of traffic accident fatalities. While the criticism did not result in design changes or the memorial's removal, it did lead authorities to commission a figurative sculpture of three soldiers to be placed nearby. Despite early criticism, most visitors today find Lin's memorial to be an appropriate and moving way to honor the deceased soldiers.

The National Mall, where Lin's memorial rests, has seen other public art controversies as well. The 2011 monument to the civil rights leader Dr. Martin Luther King, Jr., was criticized for its foreign artist as well as for the quotations chosen to accompany the sculpted figure. The record for the longest public art controversy on the mall belongs to the Franklin Delano Roosevelt monument. Designs selected in 1959 and 1966 were scrapped following public criticism. A monument designed in 1974 was finally built in 1997, but even this design had its critics. Some wanted the monument to picture Roosevelt in a wheelchair, even though the president never let himself be photographed with his chair visible. A compromise was struck and the final design included a small wheel visible beneath the seated president's cloak. A second figure of the president added to the monument in 2001 shows the wheelchair completely.

Public art engages with a broad population. It can be expensive and may be funded by taxpayer money. The works are commissioned by governments or other entities that may not have consulted with communities or other constituencies. Each of these characteristics can make works of public art controversial. Yet public art can also educate us, make us think, lift our spirits, bring us solace, and beautify our spaces.

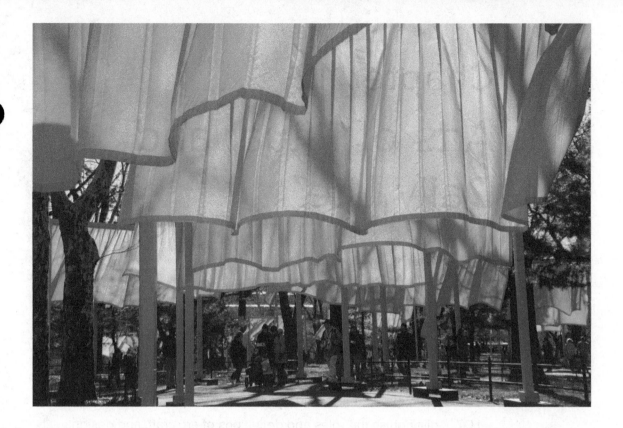

Copland once wrote an orchestral piece called *Fanfare for the Common Man*. In a similar spirit, *The Gates* was like a majestic ceremonial walkway for everyone. After sixteen days, the project was removed. The materials it was made of—steel, vinyl, and nylon fabric—were all recycled, and the park was left as pristine as it had been before.

Christo and Jeanne-Claude accepted no funding from outside sources for such projects, preferring instead to raise the money themselves by selling drawings and collages generated during the planning stages, as well as early artworks. They were careful to emphasize that their art was not just the result, but the entire process, from planning through removal, including the way it energized people and created relationships.

11.30 Christo and Jeanne-Claude. *The Gates*. 1979–2005. Installation in Central Park, New York City, February 12–27, 2005.
Volz/LAIF/Camera Press. © Christo and Jeanne-Claude 2005

Notes to the Text

1. Quoted in Peter Boswell, "Martin Puryear," in Martin Friedman et al., *Sculpture Inside Outside* (New York: Rizzoli, 1988), p. 197.

2. Quoted in Farah Nayeri, "Martin Puryear's Works Mine African-American History," *New York Times*, October 15, 2017. Available at nytimes.com/2017/10/15/arts/martin-puryear-artist-parasol.html, accessed November 4, 2017.

3. "Martin Puryear, Abstraction and 'Ladder for Booker T. Washington,'" *Art21*, 2003. Available at art21.org/read/martin-puryear-abstraction-and-ladder-for-booker-t-washington, accessed November 4, 2017.

4. Quoted in Helaine Posner, *Kiki Smith/Helaine Posner*; interview by David Frankel (Boston: Bulfinch, 1998), p. 12.

5. Ibid., p. 32.

6. Quoted in "The Body Is the Most Potent and Intelligent Object," *The Guardian*, April 22, 2004. Reproduced by permission of the Antony Gormley Studio.

7. The suggestion was made by Bradley Lepper. See David Hurst Thomas, *Exploring Ancient Native America: An Archaeological Guide* (New York: Macmillan, 1994), p. 133.

8. Andy Goldsworthy, "Time, Change, Place," *Time* (New York: Abrams, 2000), p. 7.

9. Quoted in David Batchelor, *Minimalism* (Cambridge: Cambridge University Press, © 1997 Tate Gallery), p. 55.

Chapter 12

Arts of Ritual and Daily Life

In this chapter, you will learn to

LO1   explain how clay is transformed into functional objects,

LO2   describe how art is made with glass,

LO3   discuss techniques for making objects in metal,

LO4   relate wood to its artistic functions,

LO5   summarize techniques and use of fiber arts,

LO6   describe art made of ivory, jade, and lacquer, and

LO7   distinguish the roles and definitions of art, craft, and design.

As we saw in Chapter 2, our modern concept of art took shape in the West during the 18th century. It was then that European philosophers separated painting, sculpture, and architecture from other kinds of skilled making and placed them together with poetry and music in a new category called the fine arts. More than two centuries separate us from that moment, and over that time the new grouping has come to seem natural to us, just part of the way the world is. Yet, in fact, the grouping is not natural but cultural.

In this chapter, we look at the context that "art" was lifted from, objects made with great skill and inventiveness, rewarding to contemplate and imbued with meaning. They were made to be touched, to be handled, to be used or worn in daily life or in ritual settings such as religious ceremonies. Because of that, they possess a special human intimacy. Even if we see them now in a museum, we know that they once were used by their owners, who took them into their lives.

We begin by introducing a range of widely used media—clay, glass, metal, wood, fiber, ivory, jade, and lacquer—illustrated with objects fashioned before our system of fine art arose, and with objects from cultures where that separation never occurred. We then look briefly at how Western thinking about these arts has changed and been challenged in the centuries since fine art was born.

Clay

Ceramics, from the ancient Greek word *keramakos*, meaning "of pottery," is the art of making objects from clay, a naturally occurring earth substance. When dry, clay has a powdery consistency; mixed with water, it becomes **plastic**—that is, moldable and cohesive. In this form it can be modeled, pinched, rolled, or shaped between the hands. Once a clay form has been built and permitted to dry, it will hold its shape, but it is very fragile. To ensure permanence, the form must be fired in a kiln, at temperatures ranging between about 1,200 and 2,700 degrees Fahrenheit, or higher. Firing changes the chemical composition of the clay so that it can never again be made plastic.

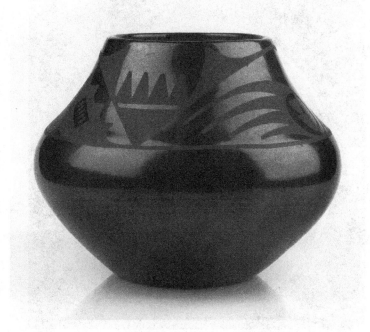

12.1 María and Julián Martínez. Jar. ca. 1939. Blackware, height 11 ⅛". Smithsonian American Art Museum, Washington, DC / Art Resource, NY

Nearly every culture we know of has practiced ceramics. The earliest known ceramics are from China and have been dated to as early as 20,000 years ago. Pottery almost as old has been discovered at sites in Japan. A major requirement for most ceramic objects is that they be hollow, that they have thin walls around a hollow core. There are two reasons for this. First, many ceramic wares are meant to contain things—food or liquids, for instance. Second, a solid clay piece is difficult to fire and may very well explode in the kiln. To meet this need for hollowness, ceramists over the ages have developed specialized forming techniques.

One such technique is called slab construction. The ceramist rolls out the clay into a sheet, very much as a baker would roll out a pie crust, and then allows the sheet to dry slightly. The sheet, or slab, can then be handled in many ways. It can be curled into a cylinder, draped over a mold to make a bowl, shaped into free-form sculptural configurations, or cut into shapes that can be pieced together.

Another technique for making a thin, hollow form is coiling. The ceramist rolls out ropelike strands of clay, then coils them upon one another and joins them together. A vessel made from coils attached one atop the other will have a ridged surface, but the coils can be smoothed completely to produce a uniform, flat wall. The native peoples of the southwestern United States made extraordinarily large, finely shaped pots by coiling. During the 20th century, the tradition was revived by a few supremely talented individuals, including the famous Pueblo potter María Martínez (**12.1**).

Martínez worked with the local red clay of New Mexico. The distinctive black tonalities of her finished pots were produced by the firing process. After building, smoothing, and air-drying her pots, Martínez laboriously burnished them to a sheen with a smooth stone. Next, a design was painted on with **slip** (liquid clay). The pot was then fired. Partway through the firing, the flames were smothered, and the pot blackened in the resulting smoke. Areas painted with slip remained matte (dull), while burnished areas took on a high gloss. The glossy and matte areas create interlocking positive and negative shapes.

By far the fastest method of creating a hollow, rounded form is by means of the potter's wheel. Potters in the ancient Near East were using a rotating disk, today called a slow wheel, to speed the making of coil pots by around 4000 B.C.E., but the true potter's wheel, known as the fast wheel, seems to have been invented first in China a little over a thousand years later. Despite some modern improvements and the addition of electricity, the basic principle of wheel construction remains

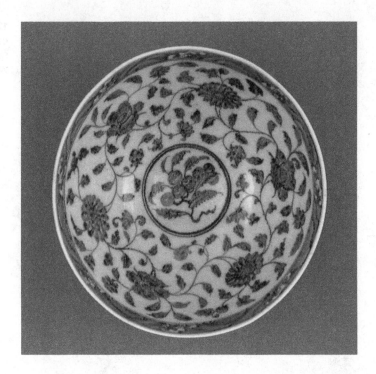

the same as it was in ancient times. The wheel is a flat disk mounted on a vertical shaft, which can be made to turn rapidly either by electricity or by foot power. The ceramist centers a mound of clay on the wheel and, as the wheel turns, uses their hands to "open," lift, and shape the clay form—a procedure known as throwing. Throwing on the wheel always produces a rounded or cylindrical form, although the thrown pieces can later be reshaped, cut apart, or otherwise altered.

The Chinese bowl illustrated here (**12.2**) would have been thrown on a wheel by a specialist at one of the great ceramic centers of imperial China, where thousands of workers produced ceramics on an industrial scale using assembly-line methods. The bowl is made of **porcelain**, a ceramic made by mixing kaolin, a fine white clay, with finely ground petunse, also known as porcelain stone. When fired at a high temperature, elements in the mixture fuse into a glassy substance, resulting in a hard, white, translucent ceramic. The secret of porcelain was discovered and perfected in China, and for hundreds of years potters elsewhere tried without success to duplicate it.

After being shaped, the bowl was painted with blue pigment then dipped in a glaze. Ceramic glazes consist of powdered minerals in water. When fired, they fuse into a nonporous, glasslike coating that bonds with the clay body. Glazes may be formulated so that they yield a color when fired, but the classic glaze for white porcelain was transparent. It was probably made chiefly from very finely ground petunse, an ingredient in the porcelain itself.

The motifs painted on the bowl carried a symbolic meaning for Chinese viewers. The lotus flowers are a symbol of purity or of the Buddha, who is frequently depicted sitting on a lotus-blossom throne. The other flowers may be peonies, which represent wealth and honor.

Glass

If clay is one of the most versatile of materials, glass is perhaps the most fascinating. Few people, when presented with a beautiful glass form, can resist holding it up to the light, watching how light changes its appearance from different angles.

Although there are numerous formulas for glass, its principal ingredient is usually silica, or sand. The addition of other materials can affect color, melting point, strength, and so on. When heated, glass becomes molten, and in that state it can be shaped by several different methods. Unlike clay, glass never changes chemically as it moves from a soft, workable state to a hard, rigid one. As glass cools, it hardens, but it can then be reheated and rendered molten again for further working.

According to a legend recorded by the ancient Roman author Pliny, the secret of making glass was discovered accidentally by seafaring Phoenician traders. Debarking from their ships on the eastern Mediterranean shore, the traders made a fire on the beach and set their cooking cauldrons over it on lumps of "nitrum" from their cargo. (Nitrum was a valued substance that seems to have been either potash or soda.) The heat melted the nitrum, which fused with the sand to create a transparent liquid that cooled as glass. Delightful as the story is, archaeological evidence suggests that glass was first manufactured further inland, in the region today divided between eastern Syria and northern Iraq. From there, the technology spread throughout the ancient Near East, including Egypt, where this bottle in the shape of a pomegranate was made (**12.3**).

The most familiar way of shaping a hollow glass vessel such as a bottle is by blowing: The glass artist dips up a mass of molten glass at the end of a long metal tube and, by blowing into the other end of the tube, produces a glass bubble that can be shaped or cut while it is hot and malleable. The bottle here, however, was shaped by a more ancient method known as sand-core casting. In that method, a core of compacted clay and sand was made in the shape of the cavity of the intended vessel. Wrapped in cloth and set on the end of a long rod, the core was plunged into a vat of molten glass, then removed for further work such as smoothing and decoration. After the glass had cooled, the core was scraped out.

Glass was a luxury product in the ancient world. This bottle probably held pomegranate juice, which was appreciated as a beverage and also used for medicinal purposes. A red fruit filled with hundreds of edible, garnet-colored seeds, the pomegranate has been associated by many peoples with fertility and renewal. The ancient Egyptians were no exception, and they included pomegranates and images of pomegranates in their burials to help promote rebirth in the afterlife. This little bottle, then, would have taken part in a rich network of associations that gave it meaning beyond its humble function.

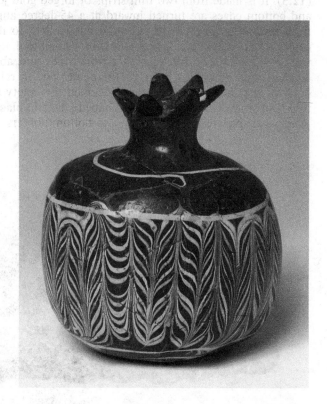

12.3 Bottle in the shape of a pomegranate. Egypt. ca. 1550–1307 B.C.E. Sand-core glass, height 4".
The Newark Museum, Gift of Mrs. Eugene Schaefer, 1950, 50.1249. Photo Newark Museum/Art Resource, NY

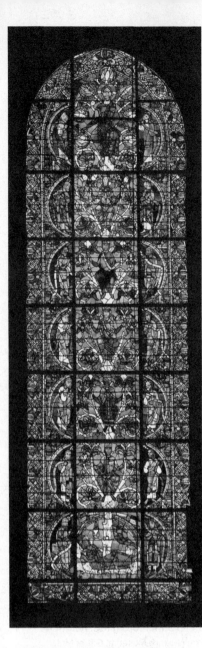

12.4 *Tree of Jesse*, west facade, Chartres Cathedral, France. ca. 1150–70. Stained glass.
Sites & Photos/Capture Ltd/Alamy Stock Photo

A special branch of glasswork, **stained glass** is a technique used for windows, lampshades, and similar structures that permit light to pass through. Stained glass is made by cutting sheets of glass in various colors into small pieces, then fitting the pieces together to form a pattern. Often, the segments are joined by strips of lead, hence the term *leaded* stained glass. The 12th and 13th centuries in Europe were a golden age for stained glass. In the religious philosophy that guided the building of the great cathedrals of that time, light was viewed as a spiritually transforming substance. The soaring interiors of the new cathedrals were illuminated by hundreds of jewel-like windows such as the one illustrated here from the Cathedral of Notre-Dame at Chartres, France (**12.4**). The central motif is a branching tree that portrays the royal lineage of Mary, mother of Jesus. The tree springs from the loins of the biblical patriarch Jesse, depicted asleep at the base of the window. Growing upward, it enthrones in turn four kings of Judaea, then Mary, then Jesus himself.

Metal

Ever since humans learned to work metals, they have made splendid art, as well as functional tools, from this versatile family of materials. One distinctive aspect of metal is that it is equally at home in the mundane and the sublime—the bridge that spans a river or the precious ring on a finger; the plow that turns up the earth or the crown on a princess's head. Whatever the application, the basic composition of the material is the same, and the methods of working it are similar.

As discussed in Chapter 11, metal can be shaped by heating it to a liquid state and pouring it into a mold, a process known as casting (see 11.6). Another ancient metalworking technique is **forging**, in which metal is shaped by hammer blows. Some metals are heated to a high temperature before being worked with hammers, a technique known as hot forging. Iron, for example, is almost always hot-forged. Other metals can be worked at room temperature, a technique known as cold forging. Gold is an example of a metal that can be forged cold.

This bracelet from Italy testifies to the skills of ancient Roman goldsmiths (**12.5**). It is made from two thin strips of forged gold joined with a hinge. The top and bottom edges are turned inward at a 45-degree angle. This keeps the bracelet from resting flat against the skin and allows light to illuminate the design in the center. Created by piercing the gold with a small tool, opening tiny holes, the open-work decoration consists of meandering vines and abstracted flowers. The large emeralds and blue glass beads in the center rest in raised settings that also allow light to pass through. Pearls once occupied the empty settings, two of which have thin gold straps to hold irregularly shaped pearls in place. Emeralds, sapphires, and pearls also appeared along the top and bottom borders. Roman women wore brace-

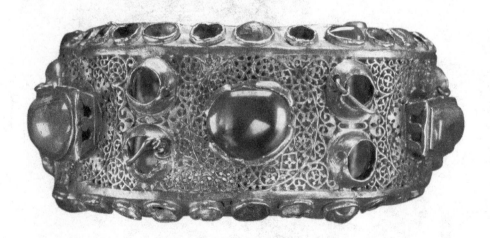

12.5 Bracelet. Roman Empire, 375–95 C.E. Gold, emeralds, sapphires, and glass, 1 ⅛ × 2 ¼".
Digital image courtesy of the Getty's Open Content Program

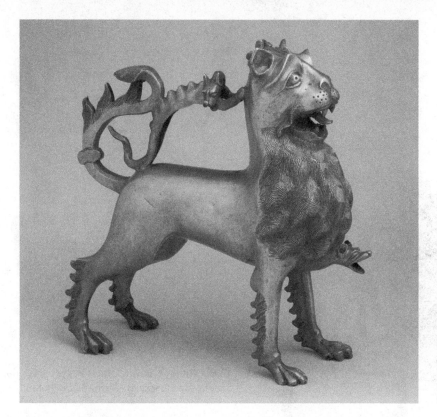

12.6 Lion aquamanile. Nuremberg. ca. 1400. Latten alloy, height 13 ⅛". The Metropolitan Museum of Art, New York. The Cloisters Collection, 1994, 1994.244. Image © The Metropolitan Museum of Art

lets like this to display their wealth, along with brooches, earrings, necklaces, and rings. Men wore only rings, though sometimes on every finger.

A wealthy client was also responsible for this medieval European aquamanile (**12.6**). Derived from the Latin for water (*aqua*) and hand (*manus*), an aquamanile held water used for ritual hand-washing. Aquamaniles were used by priests, who wash their hands at the altar before celebrating Mass (the central Roman Catholic rite of worship). They were also used in secular settings by aristocrats and wealthy merchants, whose dinner rituals included washing their hands in water perfumed with orange peel and herbs. Often fashioned in the form of animals, the fanciful metal vessels seem to have been an Iranian invention. Certainly they were used for centuries in the Islamic world before passing into the Christian culture of medieval Europe.

Modeled in wax and then cast in latten—an alloy of copper, like bronze and brass—the lion aquamanile here stands just over a foot tall. Water would have flowed into a waiting basin from the spigot issuing from the mouth of the dragon's head that juts from the lion's chest. Another dragon rises up on the lion's back to serve as a handle for lifting the vessel. The lion was a popular motif for European aquamaniles, perhaps because its symbolism could be adapted to both religious and secular settings. In a religious context, the lion could symbolize Jesus Christ. It was also the symbol of Saint Mark, one of the four gospel writers. In a secular context, the lion was a royal symbol suitable for the table of a noble family.

Wood

Widely available, renewable, and relatively easy to work, wood has been used by almost all peoples across history to fashion objects for ritual or daily use. As an organic material, however, wood is vulnerable—heat and cold can warp it, water can cause it to rot, fire will turn it to ash, and insects can eat away at it. We must assume that only a small fraction of the wooden objects made over the centuries have survived.

The most common product of the woodworker's art is furniture. The basic forms of furniture are surprisingly ancient. The chair, for example, seems to have

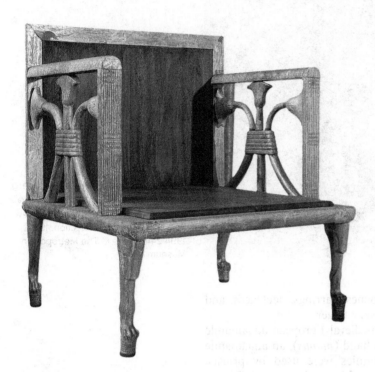

12.7 Chair of Hetepheres. Egypt, Dynasty 4, reign of Sneferu, 2575–2551 B.C.E. Wood and gold leaf, height 31 5/16".
Egyptian Museum, Cairo. Scala/Art Resource, NY

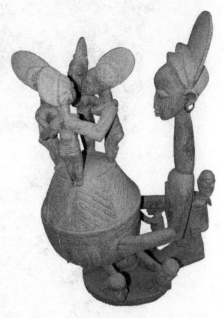

12.8 Olumeye Bowl, Yoruba People, Nigeria.
Sabena Jane Blackbird / Alamy Stock Photo

been developed in Egypt around 2600 B.C.E. Massive thrones for rulers and humble stools for ordinary people had existed earlier, but the idea of a portable seat with a back and armrests was an innovation (**12.7**). Miraculously preserved by the dry desert climate of Egypt, this chair, one of the oldest known, shows that artistic attention was lavished on furniture from the very beginning. The chair's legs are carved as the legs and paws of a lion, an emblem of royal power. Within the open frames of the armrests are carved bouquets of papyrus flowers, a symbol of Lower (northern) Egypt.

The repetition of the papyrus motif in numerous contexts across the centuries allowed scholars of Egyptian art to decipher its symbolic meaning. With the *Olumeye* bowl (**12.8**) by the great Yoruba sculptor Olowe of Ise, in contrast, much of the meaning is lost, for some of the iconographic elements are unique, and the original context in which the bowl was used is no longer known.

Olumeye is a Yoruba word meaning "one who knows honor." It refers to the kneeling woman Olowe depicted holding the lidded bowl. She is a messenger of the spirits, and she kneels in respect and devotion. *Olumeye* bowls were common in Yoruba culture. Often, they were used to store kola nuts, which were offered to guests as a sign of hospitality and to deities during worship. Of the many *olumeye* bowls to have come down to us, however, only this one includes a kneeling nude male among the small figures supporting the bowl, and only this one features four women dancing in a circle on the lid. Both subjects are unprecedented in Yoruba art.

If we knew who had commissioned the bowl from Olowe, or what context the bowl was used in, or what visual materials Olowe had been inspired by, we might be able to recover the meaning of these unusual elements or better explain their presence. As it is, we can only marvel at the mastery displayed in the carving itself. The lid is carved from a single piece of wood. Even more astonishing, the base—

including the bowl, the *olumeye*, and the supporting figures—is also carved from a single piece. Olowe permitted himself a further bravura touch by carving a freely rolling head *inside* the cage formed by the supporting figures beneath the bowl. This, too, was an innovation, and its meaning is likewise unclear.

Fiber

A fiber is a pliable, threadlike strand. Almost all naturally occurring fibers are either animal or vegetable in origin. Animal fibers include silk, wool, and the hair of such animals as alpacas and goats. Vegetable fibers include cotton, flax, raffia, sisal, rushes, and various grasses. Fibers lend themselves to a variety of techniques and uses. Some can be spun into yarn and woven into textiles. Others can be pressed into felt or twisted into rope or string. Still others can be plaited to create baskets and basketlike structures such as hats.

The art of basketry is highly valued by many Native American peoples, including the Pomo, whose ancestral lands are in present-day California (**12.9**). Legend tells that when a Pomo ancestor stole the sun from the gods to light the dark Earth, he hung it aloft in a basket that he moved across the sky. The daily journey of the sun reenacts that original event. Pomo baskets are thus linked to larger ideas about the universe and about the transfer of knowledge from gods to humans at the beginning of the world.

Traditionally a woman's art, basket weaving began with the harvesting of materials. This activity, too, was endowed with ritual significance, for it involved following ancestral paths into the landscape to find the traditional roots, barks, woods, rushes, and grasses. In the basket here, willow and bracken fern root were used to produce a pattern of alternating lights and darks. Feathers, clamshell beads, and glass beads procured through trade were woven into the surface. Somewhere in the basket, the weaver included a small, barely noticeable imperfection. Called a *dau*, it serves as a spirit door, letting benevolent spirits into the basket and allowing evil ones to leave. Feather baskets were produced as gifts for important or honored people, and they were usually destroyed in mourning when the person died.

Textile is the fiber art we are most intimately familiar with, for we clothe ourselves in it. The very first textiles were probably produced by felting, a technique in which fibers are matted and pressed together. Another ancient technique still in use today is weaving.

Weaving involves placing two sets of parallel fibers at right angles to each other and interlacing one set through the other in an up-and-down movement, generally on a loom or frame. One set of fibers is held taut; this is called the warp. The other set, known as the weft or woof, is interwoven through the warp to make

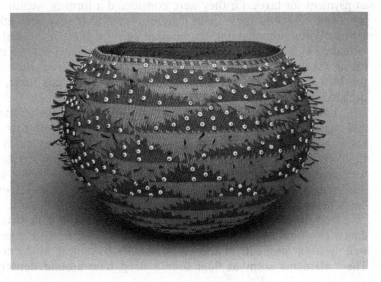

12.9 Wedding basket. ca. 1895. Plant fibers, feathers, and glass and clamshell beads. 24 x 25".
The Art Institute of Chicago, Mrs. Leonard S. Florsheim, Jr., Endowment; African and Amerindian Art Purchase Fund

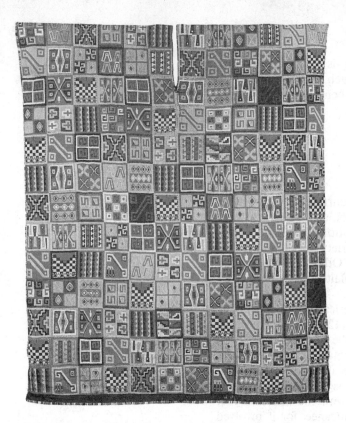

12.10 Tunic, from Peru. Inca, ca. 1500. Wool and cotton, 35 ⅞ × 30".
Dumbarton Oaks Research Library and Collections, Washington, D.C. Photo © Justin Kerr K4311.1

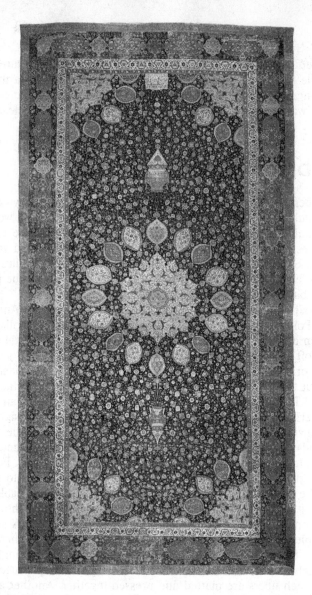

12.11 Ardabil carpet. Persia (Tabriz?). 1539–40. Wool pile on undyed silk warps, length 34' 5 ¾".
Victoria and Albert Museum, London. HIP/Art Resource, NY

a textile. Nearly all textiles, including those used for our clothing, are made by some variation of this process.

The ancient Incas, whose civilization flourished in the mountains of Peru during the 15th century, held textiles in such high regard that they draped gold and silver statues of their deities with fine cloth offerings. Textiles were also accepted as payment for taxes, for they were considered a form of wealth. Standardized patterns and colors on Inca tunics instantly signaled the wearer's ethnicity and social status. Woven around 1500, the fascinating royal tunic illustrated here (**12.10**) is a virtual catalog of such patterns, although scholars have not yet succeeded in identifying them all. The black-and-white checkerboard pattern, for example, represents the Inca military uniform in miniature. By wearing this tunic, the king visually declared his role in Inca society.

Islamic cultures have focused a great deal of aesthetic attention on carpets and rugs. Among the most famous Islamic textiles is the pair of immense rugs known as the Ardabil carpets, of which we illustrate the one in the collection of London's Victoria and Albert Museum (**12.11**). Like most Islamic carpets, they were created by knotting individual tufts of wool onto a woven ground. The labor was minute and time-consuming: the London Ardabil carpet has over three hundred knots per square inch, or over twelve million knots in all!

The design features a central sunburst medallion with sixteen radiating pendants. Two mosque lamps, one larger than the other, extend from the medallion as well. Quarter segments of the medallion design appear in the corners of the rug. These elements seem to float over a deep blue ground densely patterned with

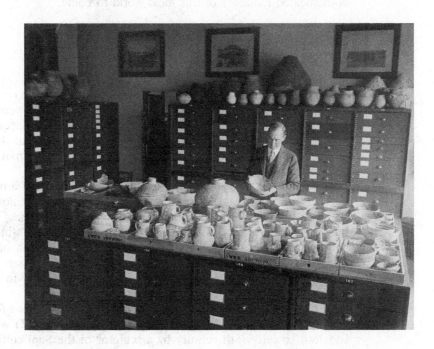

What is the Native American Graves Protection and Repatriation Act? What led to this law? How do you feel about the excavation of burial goods?

A visit to a museum offers the opportunity to see art from around the world and across time. We rarely think about where the art came from and how the museum came to possess and display it. Some museums began as royal or noble collections acquired over centuries through commissions, purchases, and war booty. The discipline of archaeology also helped to expand museum collections. University-trained archaeologists went out into the field, conducted excavations, and brought their discoveries back to the museums that sponsored their digs. But, as a dramatic scene in the film *Indiana Jones* illustrates, archaeology has not always been sensitive to cultural difference. When Jones removes a gold sculpture from a subterranean chamber, he is met by indigenous fighters angered at his theft of their holy object.

What Hollywood dramatizes happened repeatedly in the 19th and 20th centuries. In the United States, museums and universities sponsored excavations of Native American sites throughout the nation. Archaeologists conducted their research into indigenous cultures by digging up graves and ruins and taking their finds back home for study. They removed textiles, jewelry, pottery, and other objects found in burial locations. They also took skeletons, filling museum and university storage vaults with human remains. The scientists' goal was research and preservation, but they ignored the fact that they were disturbing sacred sites and disinterring human beings. They relied on the marginalized status of Native Americans to extract objects without the permission of their living descendants.

As Native Americans pursued civil rights in the second half of the 20th century, they drew attention to the issue. In 1990, the United States government passed the Native American Graves Protection and Repatriation Act (NAGPRA). The new law prohibited excavation of native graves or sacred sites. It also required all federal institutions and those receiving federal funds to return the objects and remains that had been removed in the past.

Many in the Native American community view NAGPRA as a victory over exploitation and marginalization. Some scientists, on the other hand, argue that museums and other institutions are better equipped to preserve the remains and sacred objects. They also object to abandoning the research potential these materials represent. While NAGPRA continues to be revised, the law made great strides toward insuring that all Americans are treated with decency and respect. For museums, the law has led to many returned items, but also to a greater understanding of the culturally sensitive items they collect and display.

Man examining pottery. 1923. Photograph. Harris & Ewing Collection (Library of Congress)

flowers, making the carpet a sort of stylized garden. (In a similar figure of speech, we talk of a field in springtime as being "carpeted in flowers.") Paradise in Islam is imagined as a garden, and such flower-strewn carpets represent a luxurious, domesticated reminder of this ideal world to come.

Ivory, Jade, and Lacquer

A porcelain vase, a glass beaker, and a wool tunic might have been made as luxury items or intended for a social elite, but the materials they were made of—sand, clay, animal hair—were common enough. With ivory, jade, and lacquer, we arrive at rarer materials. Ivory and jade have been considered precious in themselves. Lacquer is unique to East Asia, where it has been the basis of an important artistic tradition for some three thousand years.

Technically, ivory may refer to the teeth and tusks of a number of large mammals. In practice, it is elephant tusks that have been the most widely sought-after and treasured form. Today considered an endangered species, Asian elephants once ranged from the coast of Iran through the Indian subcontinent, southern China, and Southeast Asia. African elephants once roamed much of the continent south of the Sahara desert. Trade in elephant tusks arose in ancient times and continued unchecked well into the 20th century, bringing raw ivory to cultures that did not have local access to it.

Ivory from African elephants was particularly admired for its ease of carving and its durability. The ivory vessel illustrated here (**12.12**) was carved during the late 15th or early 16th century by a sculptor of the Sapi culture, which flourished then along the West African coast in the region of present-day Sierra Leone. The

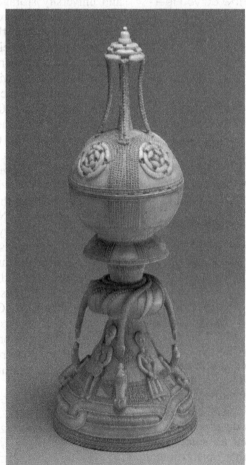

12.12 Lidded saltcellar. Sapi artist, Sierra Leone, 15th–16th century. Ivory, height 11 ¾".
The Metropolitan Museum of Art, New York. Gift of Paul and Ruth W. Tishman, 1991.435a,b. Image © The Metropolitan Museum of Art

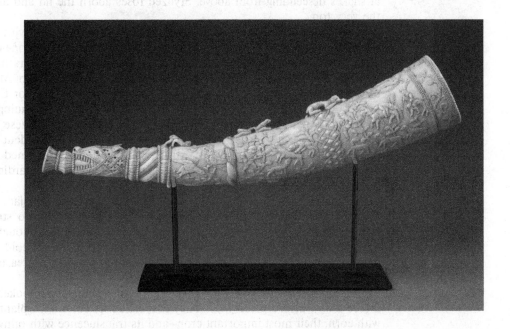

Why did artists and patrons turn to ivory as a material? How did ivory and ivory objects reach far-distant locations? What impact did the ivory trade have on the world's elephant populations?

Elephant ivory is a beautiful material that polishes to a yellowish sheen. It is durable and easy to work, allowing artists such as the Sapi carver who made this trumpet to make intricate, detailed objects. This trumpet is less than 2 feet long, but the surface is covered in small decorative and figurative designs.

Ivory once moved around the world within a global network. The ivory for the tabernacle polyptych (see 5.7) was acquired in Africa and carved in Europe. The ivory for the *Virgin of the Immaculate Conception* (see 2.7) was acquired on the Asian mainland and sculpted in the Philippines. The hunting trumpet seen here was created by a Sapi artist working in what is now Sierra Leone. Like the sculpture of the Virgin Mary, the horn was made for export to Europe. It traveled from its point of origin along a trade route created by Portuguese explorers who scoured Africa for slaves, spices, and raw materials.

Like the *Virgin of the Immaculate Conception*, the elephant tusk's shape affects the horn's appearance. It curves and widens along its length. The mouth of the horn at the tusk's tip is an animal head. The remaining decorations alternate between purely ornamental designs and narrative images. These storytelling scenes picture hunters and were chosen to meet the demands of European collectors.

Many cultures around the world have relied on ivory for small, portable luxury items like these. Acquiring the raw material means killing the elephant, which has dramatically reduced the world's elephant populations. Between 3 and 5 million elephants roamed Africa in the mid-19th century. Today, the World Wildlife Fund estimates that only 415,000 remain in the wild. To preserve existing populations, the Convention on International Trade in Endangered Species of Wild Fauna and Flora recommended banning the sale of ivory in 1989. Countries around the world have slowly complied. Today the ivory trade in India is prohibited to protect remaining Indian elephants; the trade in Africa is restricted, monitored, and periodically suspended. These laws have slowed the killing of elephants, but the United Nations estimates that even now 100 elephants are still killed daily for their tusks.

Unknown (Sapi). Trumpet. 1490–1530. Ivory, 3 ½ × 20 ¾". Yale University Art Gallery

vessel was created for a Portuguese patron. A lidded bowl atop an elaborate pedestal, it resembles a European chalice, although it was made to store salt. Male and female attendants ring the base, alternating with vigilant dogs that bare their teeth at snakes descending from above. Stylized roses adorn the lid and an acorn rests at the very top.

Many African peoples associated elephants symbolically with rulers, for they were seen to be mighty, powerful, wise, and long-lived. For Europeans, ivory represented luxury and global exploration. Early Portuguese explorers had been deeply impressed by the skill of the ivory carvers they encountered in Africa, and for a century or so they commissioned works such as this saltcellar for European collectors. A stunning example of African artistry, the vessel is intriguing for the way it mingles African and European forms and imagery. The Portuguese client probably supplied the African artist with visual materials, such as woodcut illustrations of roses, a flower not found in West Africa. The Sapi artist combined the foreign elements with the local belief in snakes as spirits and in dogs as guardians with special powers to see ghosts.

Jade is a common name for two minerals, nephrite and jadeite. Ranging in color from white through shades of brown and green, the two stones are found principally in East and Central Asia and Central America. Although their underlying structures differ, they share the extreme hardness, the ice-cold touch, and the mesmerizing, translucent beauty that have caused jade to be treasured in cultures lucky enough to have access to it.

The ancient Olmecs, whose jade figure of a shaman we looked at in Chapter 2 (see 2.38), prized green jade. They associated its color with plant life—especially with corn, their most important crop—and its translucence with rainwater, on which agricultural bounty depended. In China, jade of all colors has been prized and carved for some six thousand years. In early Chinese belief, the stone was credited with magical properties.

The Chinese jade basin (**12.13**) seen here was carved in high relief. The exterior features stylized dragons with long snouts and sharp talons. The dragons twist and turn through a cloudy sky, chasing flaming pearls. A landscape of tall mountains appears at the bottom of the vessel. In China, pearls are symbols of power, spiritual

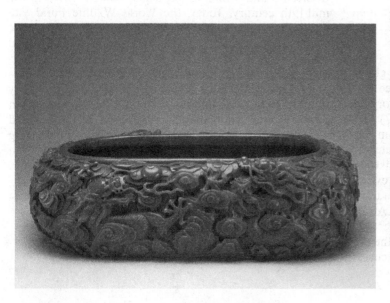

12.13 Jade basin. 1774. Jade, 7 ⅝ × 29 ¹⁵⁄₁₆ × 16 ¹⁵⁄₁₆".
The Metropolitan Museum of Art, New York. Gift of Heber R. Bishop, 1902

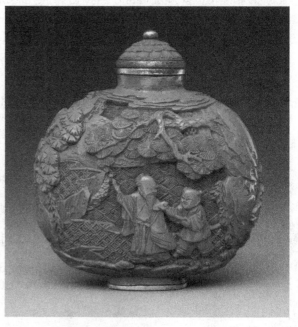

12.14 Snuff bottle with figures in a landscape. China. 18th century. Carved red lacquer, 3 ¼ × 2 ⅜".
The Metropolitan Museum of Art, New York. Bequest of Edmund C. Converse, 1921

energy, and the moon. Dragons, who represent good fortune and cosmic energy and covet pearls in Chinese lore, are also closely associated with the emperor. A poem carved inside this basin was written by Emperor Qianlong.

Lacquer is made from the sap of a tree that originally grew only in China. Harvested, purified, colored with dyes, and brushed in thin coats over wood, the sap hardens into a smooth, glasslike coating. The technique demands great patience, for up to thirty coats of lacquer are needed to build up a substantial layer, and each must dry thoroughly before the next can be applied. Ancient Chinese artisans used lacquer to create trays, bowls, storage jars, and other wares that were lightweight and delicate-looking yet water-resistant and airtight. Exported along with other luxury goods over the long overland trade route known as the Silk Road, Chinese lacquerware was admired as far away as the Roman Empire.

Knowledge of lacquer spread early from China to Korea and Japan, as did cultivation of the sap-producing tree. Asian artists developed a variety of techniques for decorating lacquerware. In China, a favorite method was to apply layer after layer of red lacquer, building up a surface thick enough to be carved in relief (**12.14**). The scene on the snuff bottle illustrated here depicts two men walking in a landscape. The carving is in high relief. The rocks and trees to each side represent the last of the applied layers, and the diamond-shaped pattern between the two figures is cut into the earliest. Tobacco was introduced to China by European merchants who brought it from the Americas. While Europeans carried their powdered tobacco in boxes, the Chinese found medicinal bottles more suitable and began producing small snuff bottles in the 18th century. Early examples were made for the imperial court, but a taste for these practical yet beautiful objects soon spread outside the palace. The elaborate carving of this snuff bottle suggests that it was made for a very wealthy client.

In Japan, artists perfected the art of decorating lacquerware with inlays of mother-of-pearl and sprinklings of gold and silver powder. The writing box illustrated here (**12.15**) features a motif of maple leaves. The leaves are scattered around a *bugaku* hat, a hat worn in traditional court dances performed by members of the aristocracy. For a cultivated Japanese audience, the combination would bring to mind a famous episode from the *Tale of Genji*, a classic work of Japanese literature,

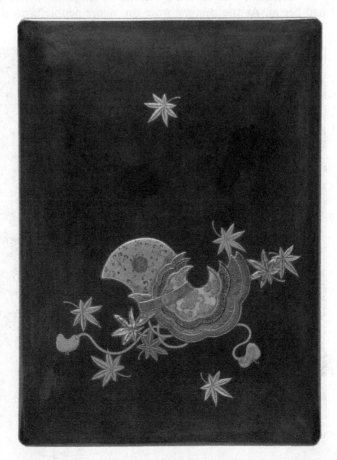

12.15 Writing box. Style of Ogawa Haritsu, Japan. 18th century. Gold and glazed pottery on colored lacquer inlaid with mother-of-pearl, 1 ½ × 7 × 9 ½".
The Metropolitan Museum of Art, New York. The Howard Mansfield Collection, Purchase, Rogers Fund, 1936, 36.100.141a-e. © 2014. Image © The Metropolitan Museum of Art

in which the young, radiantly handsome Prince Genji dances before the emperor and his court as autumn leaves fall around him. The box's hat and leaves are made of mother-of-pearl, gold, and red lacquer. As its name suggests, a writing box housed a set of writing implements. The inside, often decorated as well, was typically configured to hold an inkstone and ink stick, brushes, a water dropper, a small knife, and an ink-stick holder.

Art, Craft, Design

When painting and sculpture were placed in the new category of fine art in the West, the skilled activities they were formerly associated with—textiles, ceramics, metalwork, furniture making, and so on—were grouped together under various names, each of which suggested a contrast with fine art. They were referred to as decorative arts, suggesting that they were primarily ornamental; applied arts, suggesting that they were fundamentally utilitarian; and even minor arts, suggesting that they were inherently less important. The English language offered up another word, craft, which, like the word "art," originally meant skill.

During that same historical period, the Industrial Revolution was transforming Western societies. The handmade world, which had existed since the beginning of human culture, was giving way to a world in which many objects used in daily life were mass-produced by machines. Small workshops were being replaced by large factories, and the nature of work itself was being transformed. Many social thinkers of the 19th century criticized those developments, and their criticism of industrialization went hand in hand with their criticism of the new distinction between fine art and craft. They pointed to the loss of dignity and pride in one's work that resulted from factory labor. They objected to the glorification of the fine arts over crafts and to the lower esteem in which people who worked with their hands were now held. They mourned the loss of the satisfaction to be had in making things by hand and the pleasure experienced in using them, and they worried about the effect it would have on the human spirit.

Criticism was especially strong in England, where the Industrial Revolution had begun. As the century wore on, many people grew determined to carve out a

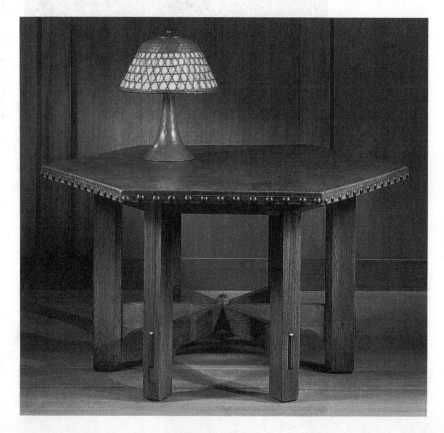

12.16 Gustav Stickley's Craftsman Workshop. Library table. 1910–12. Oak, leather, and brass, 29 ⅞ × 55 ½ × 49".

Los Angeles County Museum of Art. Gift of Max Palevsky and Jodie Evans in honor of the museum's twenty-fifth anniversary M.89.151.14

place for handmade objects in the new industrial order. They set up workshops and studios. They taught themselves and one another such skills as pottery, bookbinding, furniture making, and weaving. They held exhibits and formed societies, most famously, in 1887, the Arts and Crafts Exhibition Society. The Arts and Crafts movement, as it came to be known, spread quickly throughout Europe and to the United States, where its most vocal proponent was Gustav Stickley. In 1901, Stickley began to publish an influential magazine called *The Craftsman*, which introduced the ideals of the Arts and Crafts movement to a broad public. Several years later, he founded the Craftsman Workshop, where the hexagonal library table illustrated here was built (**12.16**). Made of American oak, its simple lines, forthright construction, and unadorned surfaces epitomized the style that Stickley favored for what he called "a democratic art."

The Arts and Crafts movement began to wane after a few decades, but its influence can be felt to this day. One of its legacies is the vibrant presence of studio crafts in our cultural life, independent artists who practice such skills as woodworking, glassblowing, and weaving. An example is the glass artist Dale Chihuly, a detail view of whose *Macchia Forest* we illustrate here (**12.17**). Seeing stained-glass windows like the *Tree of Jesse* (see 12.4) inspired Chihuly to work with brightly colored glass. The artist uses a full palette of 300 colors to create the organic, bell-like forms he calls *macchia*, Italian for "spots." He uses one color for the inside of the form, another for the outside, and a complementary color for the lip. Chihuly adds a layer of colored glass chips between the interior and exterior layers to create the spotted effect. Like other forms by the artist, the *macchia* are created by heating colored glass rods until they melt, then blowing through a long stainless-steel pipe to create the final shape. Chihuly displays his *macchia* either alone or in groups, allowing light to pass through the glass walls for a luminescent effect.

While Chihuly uses traditional glassblowing techniques, Jeroen Verhoeven enlisted the help of computer-aided design and manufacturing technology (CAD/CAM) to create *Cinderella*, a curvaceous table made of plywood (**12.18**). *Cinderella* was inspired by the forms of 17th- and 18th-century Dutch furniture. Verhoeven researched and drew example after example, simplifying their contours. He scanned his drawings into a computer and fused them using 3-D morphing software to create a hybrid form, an elegant table turning into a bulbous cabinet, like an enchantment in a fairy tale. The virtual design was digitally "sliced" like a loaf of bread into fifty-seven slices, which were cut and shaped individually by computer-controlled woodworking machines, then glued together and finished by hand. Verhoeven issued *Cinderella* in a limited edition, as artists do for prints or cast sculptures.

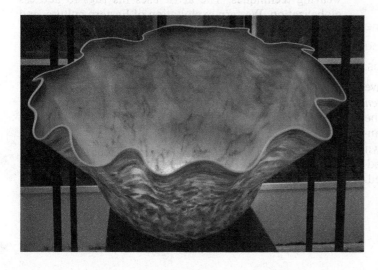

12.17 Dale Chihuly. *Macchia Forest*, detail. 2005. Glass.
Randy Duchaine/Alamy Stock Photo

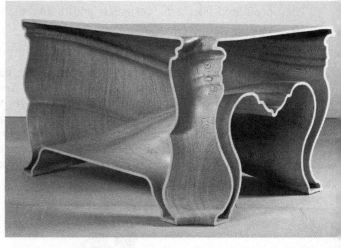

12.18 Jeroen Verhoeven. *Cinderella* table. 2005. Plywood, 31 ½ × 52 × 40".
Courtesy the artist and Blain/Southern. Photo Matthew Hollow, 2013

Engaging Tradition

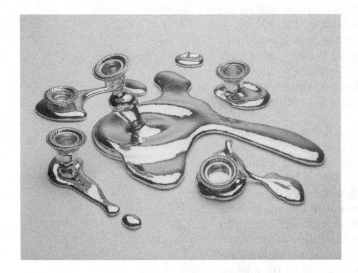

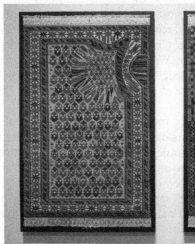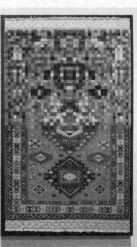

What is the role of traditional crafts in contemporary art? How have artists engaged cultural traditions in their art? How do artists update traditional craft media?

When painting and sculpture were elevated to the status of fine art at the beginning of the modern age, they came to be associated with male artists, even though women painted and sculpted as well. Textiles, ceramics, and other crafts became so-called women's work. If a woman wanted to be taken seriously as an artist in the mid-20th century, she needed to paint. In the 1960s, however, some feminist artists embraced the traditional craft media as a way to represent a woman's perspective and experience. They promoted fiber arts, ceramics, and metals as fine arts, making potent statements about civil rights and female empowerment in quilts, clay vessels, and weavings.

Contemporary artists working in craft media have also raised other questions. In *Candelabrum: Seven Fragments*, the artist Myra Mimlitsch-Gray challenges the craft artist's relationship with the past. Sterling-silver candlesticks are traditional heirloom objects, passed down from generation to generation. They are precious commodities, but are sometimes melted down to be repurposed.

Mimlitsch-Gray's candelabrum reminds us of the grandiose silver services of the past, but is melted to the point that it can no longer serve its intended purpose. Or can it? The artist challenges us to see the candelabrum as a dynamic form rather than a static, unchanging object. She plays with the notion of its usefulness as we wait for the silver forms to become something else.

The artist Faig Ahmed calls upon the long rug-weaving tradition of his native Azerbaijan for his textile arts. Rugs produced in the Middle East, Central Asia, South Asia, and Russia were created originally for religious use and to warm and adorn homes. Western merchants coveted the works, and such rugs have been staples in well-appointed homes since the Renaissance. Ahmed's rugs are designed on the computer but then handcrafted by women using traditional weaving techniques. The artist uses his rugs to address globalization, Western exploitation of Eastern culture, and regional identity. His work engages tradition but brings to it very modern political questions.

(left) Myra Mimlitsch-Gray. *Candelabrum: Seven Fragments*. 2003. Silver, height 9". © The Artist. Cranbrook Centennial Acquisition, Museum Purchase with funds from George Gough Booth and Ellen Scripps Booth by exchange CAM 2003.6. Photograph by R. H. Hensleigh and Tim Thayer
(right) Faig Ahmed. *Hollow* (2011) and *Pixelate Tradition* (2011). Rugs, 59 × 39 ⅜" each. Malcolm Park editorial/Alamy Stock Photo

"For me, it's a manifesto," Verhoeven said of his creation. "It's about showing what our high-tech tools would be capable of if they were fully used. We have at our disposal the most fantastic slaves, whose possibilities we are completely wasting. We use them to mass-produce boring objects, whereas in fact these tools of the 21st century could produce art. Just like Cinderella, who was much more than a cleaning woman but whose talents remained hidden because they weren't used."[1]

Another legacy of the Arts and Crafts movement has been a recurrent questioning of the distinction between fine art and craft. In the 1960s, many artists working with crafts media began to claim a place in the fine-art world, and many artists working in the fine-art system reached out to use materials and forms associated with crafts—a crossover that continues today. These practitioners have insisted that we think harder about just what, if anything, distinguishes one category from the other, and they have built bridges of understanding to other cultures where such a division never arose.

Perhaps it should not surprise us that potters were among the first to practice their craft as an art. Clay, after all, had long led a double life, used at once for sculpture and for ceramics. The Danish ceramist Merete Rasmussen uses the traditional coiling technique to build nonrepresentational sculptural forms in stoneware. *Red Twisted Form* illustrates her special fascination with continuous surfaces (**12.19**). A single flowing ribbon with no beginning and no end, *Red Twisted Form* curls around itself, opening up negative spaces, delighting in the play between convex and concave surfaces, inviting us to take a visual ride on its roller coaster. "I work with the idea of a composition in three dimensions, seeking balance and harmony," Rasmussen writes. "The finished form should have energy, enthusiasm, and a sense of purpose."[2]

Ceramics had a comparatively easy time finding a place in the system of fine art, for clay had a long history as a sculptural medium. Fiber, on the other hand, faced greater resistance. The path was clearer in Europe, where the tradition of collaboration between artists and tapestry workshops had been kept alive. (For more about tapestry, see Chapter 7.) During the 1960s, exhibitions of contemporary tapestry included increasing numbers of ambitious, large-scale works in fiber by independent artists. Much of the new work abandoned tapestry's centuries-old link with painting. Made from rough, natural fibers and using such techniques as knotting, braiding, and crochet, it demanded to be understood as sculpture.

Among the many artists working with fiber today is the young Brazilian Maria Nepomuceno, who uses colorful rope and beaded necklaces to construct quirky biomorphic forms (**12.20**). Arranged on the floor as though they had propagated

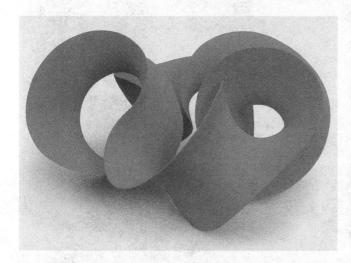

12.19 Merete Rasmussen. *Red Twisted Form*. 2012. Stoneware clay with colored slip, 21 ⅝ × 35 ⁷⁄₁₆ × 35 ⁷⁄₁₆".
Victoria and Albert Museum, London. Courtesy the artist. Photo © Merete Rasmussen

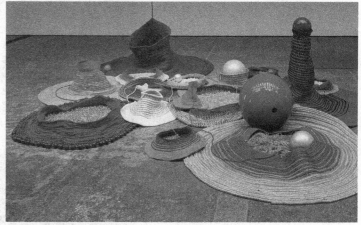

12.20 Maria Nepomuceno. *Untitled*. 2010. Ropes, beads, and fabric, 14' 5 ⅓" × 11' 9 ⅞". Installation, May 7–June 12, 2010, Victoria Miro, London N1.
© Maria Nepomuceno. Image courtesy the artist and Victoria Miro, London/Venice

themselves there, they suggest a colony of brilliant anemones in a tropical coral reef. Cheerfully sensuous and uninhibited, their craters filled with beads like eggs or spawn, they overlap and touch and send out exploratory tendrils toward one another.

Nepomuceno's art was profoundly influenced by the experience of giving birth. She has compared the rope she works with to an umbilical cord through which life nourishes new life, the present connects to the future. She builds her forms by coiling the rope in spirals, a movement she associates with whirlpools, galaxies, and the DNA spiral of life itself. She speaks of the beads as fertile points capable of multiplying themselves into infinity. Themes of fertility and generation are clearly present in *Untitled*. Even if we can't put a name to these creatures, we know what they are up to.

In works such as *Between Earth and Heaven*, the contemporary Ghanaian artist El Anatsui takes his formal inspiration from textiles, although the material he works with is not fiber but metal (**12.21**). In its visual splendor, *Between Earth and Heaven* draws on the tradition of African royal textiles such as *kente* (see 1.7). *Kente*, too, was an art of recycling, for it was originally made of silk fabric imported from China. African weavers patiently separated the silk fabric into threads, which they then rewove in patterns that expressed their own culture.

As we have seen, the Arts and Crafts movement heightened public awareness of the value of handmade objects and traditional skills in the face of industrialization. Most of the movement's leading voices fully recognized the value of mass production in making goods available to a greater number of people at affordable prices, and they appreciated the ability of machines to facilitate dull, repetitive tasks. However, the ideals of the movement encouraged cooperation between artists and manufacturers. In this new relationship, an artist's task was no longer to make an object but to design an object that could be made by industrial methods. Writing in *The Craftsman*, Gustav Stickley referred to such objects as industrial art. Within a few years, the field had become known as design.

One task of designers is to translate technological and scientific advances into functional, approachable, visually rewarding objects for our lives. The designer Iris van Herpen makes wearable garments that combine fashion, nature, and technology. Her otherworldly designs are inspired by such diverse phenomena as the movement

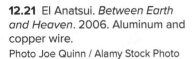

12.21 El Anatsui. *Between Earth and Heaven*. 2006. Aluminum and copper wire.
Photo Joe Quinn / Alamy Stock Photo

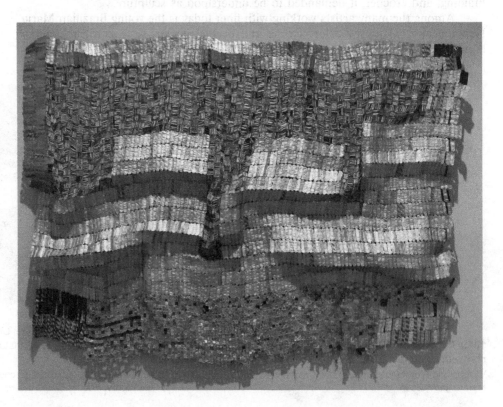

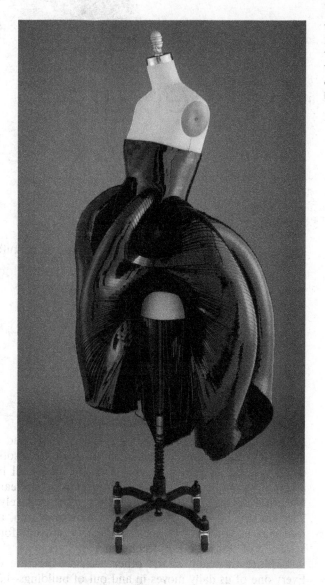

12.22 Iris van Herpen. *Dress*. 2012–13. PVC, silk, metal. The Metropolitan Museum of Art, New York, Gift of Iris van Herpen, in honor of Harold Koda, 2016 (2016.185)/Art Resource, NY

of water or the charge of electricity. She explores materials beyond traditional fabric, sometimes printing entire garments on a 3-D printer. *Dress* (**12.22**) combines plastic PVC, silk, and metal. To create the design, Van Herpen imagined that one day garments would be able to transform themselves into other shapes to respond to the environment. The result is a dress that looks alive yet also mechanical. Van Herpen designs using computers, but her work relies as much on the skill and attention of a human maker as it does on machines. As she explains, "I could not express myself without the help of technology or without the help of the handwork. If one of the two would not be there, it would not make sense."[3]

Notes to the Text

1. Quoted in Valérie Bougault, "La Table Cendrillon de Jeroen Verhoeven," *Connaissance des Arts*, September 2009, p. 102. Translation by the author.

2. From the artist's statement on her Web site, www.mtereterasmussen.com. Reproduced with permission.

3. Allison McNearney, "In Dallas With One of Fashion's Most Innovative Designers: Iris van Herpen, Who Weaves Cutting-edge Technology with Couture Craftsmanship, Brought T to Texas," *New York Times*, May 23, 2017. Available at nytimes.com/2017/05/23/t-magazine/fashion/iris-van-herpen-dallas-museum-art.html, accessed November 11, 2017.

Chapter 13

Architecture

In this chapter, you will learn to

LO1   explain structural systems used in architecture, and

LO2   discuss how new architectural technology and materials respond to current concerns.

Architecture satisfies a basic, universal human need for a roof over one's head. More than walls, more than a chair to sit on or a soft bed to lie on, a roof is the classic symbol of protection and security. We've all heard the expression "I have a roof over my head," but it would be unusual to hear someone say, "I'm all right because I have walls around me." Of course, in purely practical terms a roof does keep out the worst of the elements, snow and rain, and in warm climates just a roof may be sufficient to keep people dry and comfortable. The roof seems to be symbolic of the nature of architecture.

More than any of the other arts, architecture demands structural stability. Every one of us daily moves in and out of buildings—houses, schools, stores, banks, and movie theaters—and we take for granted, usually without thinking about it, that they will not collapse on top of us. That they do not is a tribute to their engineering; if a building is physically stable, it adheres faithfully to the principles of the particular *structural system* on which its architecture is based.

Structural Systems in Architecture

Since the time of the earliest human settlements, architects have tackled the challenge of erecting a roof over empty space, setting walls upright, and having the whole stand secure. Their solutions have depended upon the materials they had available, for, as we shall see, certain materials are better suited than others to a particular structural system. There are two basic families of structural systems: the shell system and the skeleton-and-skin system.

In the shell system one building material provides both structural support and sheathing (outside covering). Buildings made of brick or stone or adobe fall into this category, and so do older (pre-19th-century) wood buildings constructed of heavy timbers, the most obvious example being the log cabin. The structural material comprises the walls, marks the boundary between inside and outside, and is generally visible as the exterior surface. It may also serve as the ceiling of the building, and even, although more rarely, the roof.

The skeleton-and-skin system might be compared to the human body, which has a rigid bony skeleton to support its basic frame and a more fragile skin for sheathing. We find it in the tipi of the American Plains Indians, which consists of a conical skeleton of wooden poles covered with a skin made of animal hides. We find it again in modern skyscrapers, with their steel frames (skeletons) supporting the structure and a sheathing (skin) of glass or some other light material.

The task of any structural system is to channel the forces that act upon a building safely to the ground. Architects speak of these forces as *loads*. The first and most important of these loads is the building's own weight, which is caused by gravity. Gravity is constantly pulling the building toward Earth, as though daring it to fail. The building's weight is a permanent and unchanging load, but there are other loads that come and go, such as people moving through the building, furnishings placed in the building, snow that accumulates on the roof, wind that blows against the sides, earth that settles beneath its foundations, and even earth that trembles beneath it, as in an earthquake.

No matter what materials it is made of or how complicated its structure, a building handles these loads in just two ways: pushing and pulling. When an element is pushed, we say it is in *compression*. When an element is pulled, we say it is in *tension*. An element in compression becomes shorter. An element in tension lengthens. These changes are rarely visible to the naked eye, but they nevertheless occur.

You can get a sense of the forces of tension and compression by imagining yourself as a structural material. Two friends raise you up high overhead, their arms locked. One holds you by your ankles, the other braces your shoulders. You are horizontal, facing the floor, as rigid as you can be. The three of you have now formed an opening—a doorway, say, that people could pass through. The two people holding you up are in compression. Your weight is pushing down on them, and eventually their knees may buckle or their elbows give way if they are not strong enough. And you? Your situation is a little more complicated. Your front side is under tension, but your back side is under compression. You will feel this when you start to sag: your stomach muscles will make it clear that they are stretching, and your back will tell you that it is being scrunched.

To withstand the stresses induced by loads, then, structural materials must possess **tensile strength** (be able to withstand tension) and/or compressive strength (be able to withstand compression). Wood, stone, concrete, and steel, our most commonly used materials, all possess both tensile strength and compressive strength, although not always in equal measure. Stone and concrete have excellent compressive strength but little tensile strength. Wood is virtually equal in compressive and tensile strength, but it is not nearly as strong as steel, our strongest construction material.

With these basic concepts in mind, we can turn to some of the structural systems that architects have developed, and look at some famous buildings that use them. We take up the systems roughly in the chronological order in which they were invented.

Load-Bearing Construction

Another term for load-bearing construction is "stacking and piling." This is the simplest method of making a building, and it is suitable for brick, stone, adobe, ice blocks, and certain modern materials. Essentially, the builder constructs the walls by piling layer upon layer, starting thick at the bottom, getting thinner as the structure rises, and usually tapering inward near the highest point. The whole may then be topped by a lightweight roof, perhaps of thatch or wood. This construction is stable, because its greatest weight is concentrated at the bottom and the weight diminishes gradually as the walls grow higher.

Load-bearing structures tend to have few and small openings (if any) in the walls, because the method does not readily allow for support of material above a void, such as a window opening. Yet it would be a mistake to think that such basic methods must produce basic results. The Great Friday Mosque at Djenné, in Mali,

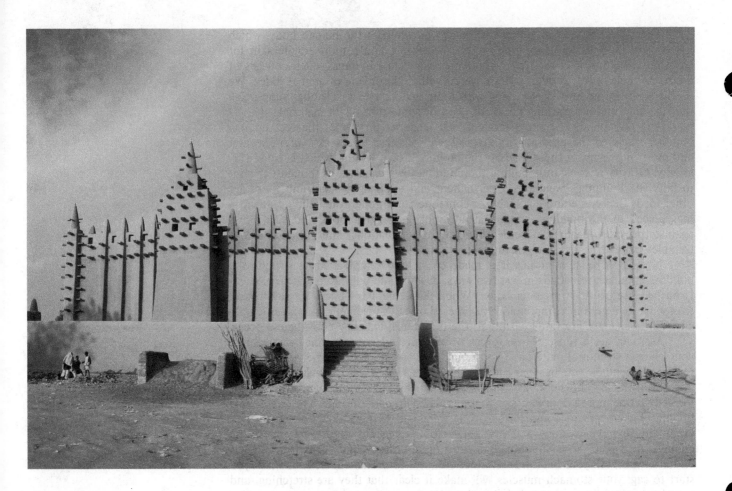

is a spectacular example of monumental architecture created from simple techniques and materials (**13.1**). Constructed of **adobe** (sun-dried brick) and coated with mud plaster, the imposing walls of this mosque have a plastic, sculptural quality. The photograph shows well the gentle tapering of the walls imposed by the construction technique, as well as the small size of the windows that illuminate the covered prayer hall inside. The protruding wooden poles serve to anchor the scaffolding that is erected every few years so that workers can restore the mosque's smooth coating of mud plaster.

Post-and-Lintel

After stacking and piling, **post-and-lintel** construction is the most elementary structural method, based on two uprights (the posts) supporting a horizontal crosspiece (the **lintel**, or beam; see diagram). This configuration can be continued indefinitely, so that there may be one very long horizontal supported at critical points along the way by vertical posts to carry its weight to the ground. The posts are in compression; the lintel is in compression on its upper side and tension on its lower side—your situation when you were being lifted by your friends. The most common materials for post-and-lintel construction are stone and wood.

Post-and-lintel construction has been, for at least four thousand years, a favorite method of architects for raising a roof and providing open space underneath. On a smaller scale, it is used to open up windows and doorways in load-bearing construction, the lintel bearing the weight of the material above and protecting the void below. The ruins of a portion of the ancient Egyptian temple of Luxor illustrate the majesty and also the limits of post-and-lintel construction in stone (**13.2**). Carved as bundles of stems capped by stylized papyrus-flower buds, the stone columns support rows of heavy stone lintels, with each lintel spanning two columns.

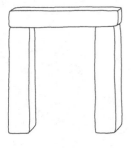

post-and-lintel

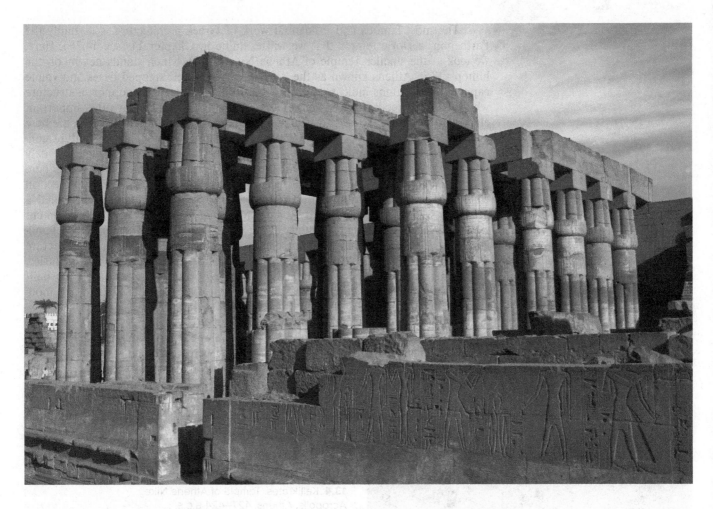

13.2 View of the hypostyle from the temple of Luxor, Egypt. Begun ca. 1390 B.C.E. Height of columns 30'.
© Prisma Archivo/Alamy Stock Photo

The lintels would in turn have supported slabs of stone that served as both ceiling and roof. Because stone does not have great tensile strength, the supporting columns must be closely spaced. A large hall erected in post-and-lintel construction was thus a virtual forest of columns inside. We call such spaces **hypostyle** halls, from the Greek for "beneath columns." Ancient Egyptians associated hypostyle halls with the primal swamp of creation, where, according to Egyptian belief, the first mound of dry land arose at the dawn of the world. To make that connection clear, they designed their columns as stylized versions of plants that grew in the marshes of the Nile. Surrounded by load-bearing walls pierced high up by small windows, the hypostyle halls of Egyptian temples were dark and mysterious places.

In ancient Greece, the design of post-and-lintel buildings, especially temples, became standardized in certain features. Greek architects developed and codified three major architectural styles, roughly in sequence. We know them as the Greek **orders**. The most distinctive feature of each was the design of the column (**13.3**). By the 7th century B.C.E., the **Doric** style had been introduced. A Doric column has no base, nothing separating it from the floor below; its **capital**, the topmost part between the shaft of the column and the roof or lintel, is a plain stone slab above a rounded stone. The **Ionic** style was developed in the 6th century B.C.E. and gradually replaced the Doric. An Ionic column has a stepped base and a carved capital in the form of two graceful spirals known as **volutes**. The **Corinthian** style, which appeared in the 4th century B.C.E., is yet more elaborate, having a more detailed base and a capital carved as a stylized bouquet of acanthus leaves.

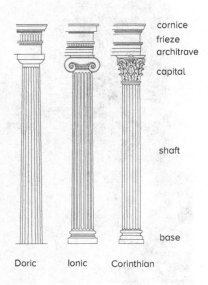

cornice
frieze
architrave
capital

shaft

base

Doric   Ionic   Corinthian

13.3 Column styles of the Greek orders.

The most famous and influential work of Greek architecture is certainly the Parthenon, a Doric temple that we will examine in Chapter 14 (see 14.26). Here, we look at the smaller Temple of Athena Nike (13.4), which stands nearby on the hilltop site in Athens known as the Acropolis. With their stepped bases and volute capitals, the columns indicate that this is an Ionic temple. They support a structure whose remains, reconstructed here in a line drawing (13.5), display other important elements of Greek architecture. The plain, horizontal stone lintels of Egypt are here elaborated into a compound structure called an **entablature**. The entablature consists of three basic elements. The simple, unadorned band of lintels immediately over the columns is the **architrave**. The area above the architrave is the **frieze**, here ornamented with sculpture in relief. The frieze is capped by a shelflike projection called a **cornice**. The entablature in turn supports a triangular element called a **pediment**, which is itself crowned by its own cornice. Like the frieze, the pediment would have been ornamented with sculpture in relief. If these elements look familiar to you, it is because they have passed into the vocabulary of Western architecture and form part of the basis of the style we refer to broadly as classical. For centuries, banks, museums, universities, government buildings, and churches have been built using the elements first codified and named by the Greeks, then adapted and modified by the Romans.

Many of the great architectural traditions of the world are based on post-and-lintel construction. The architectural style developed in China provides a good contrast to that of Greece, for while its principles were developed at about the same time, the standard material is not stone but wood. We know from terra-cotta models found in tombs that the basic elements of Chinese architecture were in place by the 2nd century B.C.E. During the 6th century C.E., this architectural

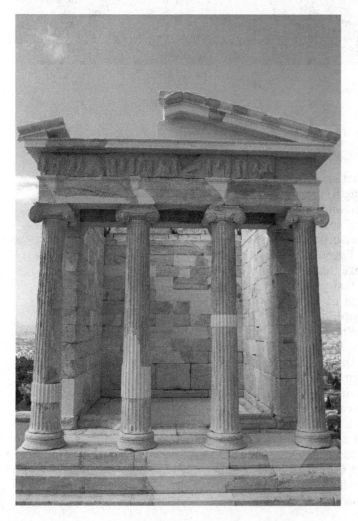

13.4 Kallikrates. Temple of Athena Nike, Acropolis, Athens. 427–424 B.C.E.
Greek photonews/Alamy Stock Photo

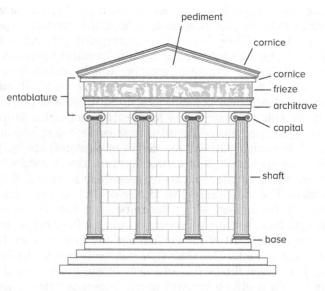

13.5 Elevation, Temple of Athena Nike.

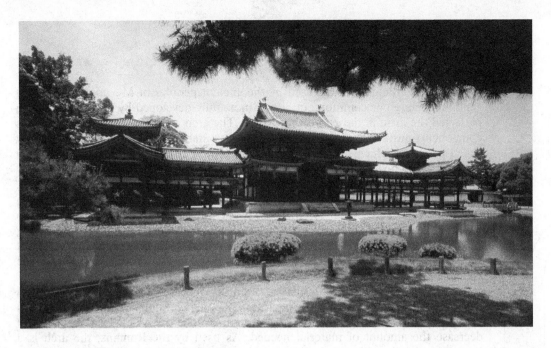

13.6 Byodo-in Temple, Uji, Japan. Heian period, ca. 1053.
Glow Images

vocabulary was adopted by Japan, along with other elements of Chinese culture. We illustrate it here with a Japanese building, the incomparable Byodo-in (**13.6**).

Built as a palace, Byodo-in was converted to a Buddhist shrine after the death of the original owner in 1052 C.E. Our first impression is of a weighty and elaborate superstructure of gracefully curved roofs resting—lightly, somehow—on slender wooden columns. The effect is miraculous, for the building seems to float; but how can all of that weight rest on such slender supports? The answer lies in the cluster of interlocking wooden brackets and arms that crowns each column (**13.7**). Called bracket sets, they distribute the weight of the roof and its large, overhanging eaves evenly onto the wooden columns, allowing each column to bear up to five times the weight it could support directly. Chinese and Japanese architects developed many variations on the bracket set over the centuries, making them larger or smaller, more elaborate or simpler, more prominent or more subtle.

The distinctive curving profile of East Asian roofs is made possible by a stepped truss system (**13.8**). (Western roofs, in contrast, are usually supported by a rigid triangular truss, as in the Greek pediment.) By varying the height of each level of the truss, builders could control the pitch and curve of the roof. Taste in roof styles varied over time and from region to region. Some roofs are steeply pitched and fall in a fancifully exaggerated curve, almost like a ski jump; others are gentler, with a subtle, barely noticeable curve.

The post-and-lintel system, then, offers potential for both structural soundness and grandeur. When applied to wood or stone, however, it leaves one problem unsolved, and that is the spanning of relatively large open spaces. The first attempt at solving this problem was the invention of the round arch.

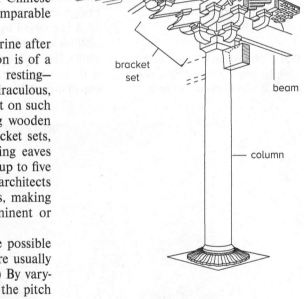

13.7 Bracket system.

From A Pictorial History of Chinese Architecture by Liang Ssu-ch'eng, foreword by Wilma Fairbank, originally published by Massachusetts Institute of Technology, 1984

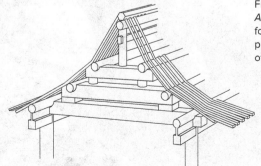

13.8 Stepped truss roof structure.

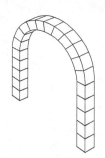

round arch

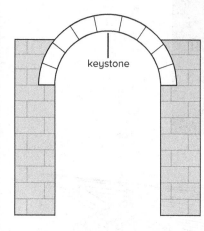

keystone

round arch with outward
thrust contained

13.9 Pont du Gard, Nîmes, France.
Early 1st century C.E. Length 902'.
Apply Pictures/Alamy Stock Photo

Round Arch and Vault

Although the round **arch** was used by the ancient peoples of Mesopotamia several centuries before our common era, it was most fully developed by the Romans, who perfected the form in the 2nd century B.C.E. The arch is a compressive structure. Its components push against one another to achieve stability. This makes it particularly suited to stone, which has high compressive strength. An arch is not stable until it is complete, however. During construction, it must be supported from below by a temporary wooden framework called a centering. Once the centering is in place, wedge-shaped blocks of stone are set along its arch-shaped top, beginning at both ends simultaneously. When the topmost block, called the **keystone**, is wedged into place, the two sides of the arch meet and lean against each other. The centering can be removed, for the arch is now self-supporting. An arch exerts an outward thrust at its base. Unless the arch sits directly on the ground, this thrust must be countered or contained (see diagram).

The arch has many virtues. In addition to being an attractive form, it enables the architect to open fairly large spaces in a wall without risking the building's structural soundness. These spaces admit light, reduce the weight of the walls, and decrease the amount of material needed. As used by the Romans, the arch is a perfect semicircle, although it may seem elongated if it rests on columns.

Among the most elegant and enduring of Roman structures based on the arch is the Pont du Gard at Nîmes, France (**13.9**), built in about 15 C.E., when the empire was nearing its farthest expansion. The Pont du Gard consists of three tiers of **arcades**—rows of arches set on columns or, as here, massive piers. It functioned as an aqueduct, a structure for transporting water, and its lower level served as a footbridge across the river. That it stands today virtually intact after two thousand years (and is crossed by cyclists on the route of the famous Tour de France bicycle race) testifies to the Romans' brilliant engineering skill. Visually, the Pont du Gard exemplifies the best qualities of arch construction. Solid and heavy, obviously durable, it is shot through with open spaces that make it seem light and its weight-bearing capabilities effortless.

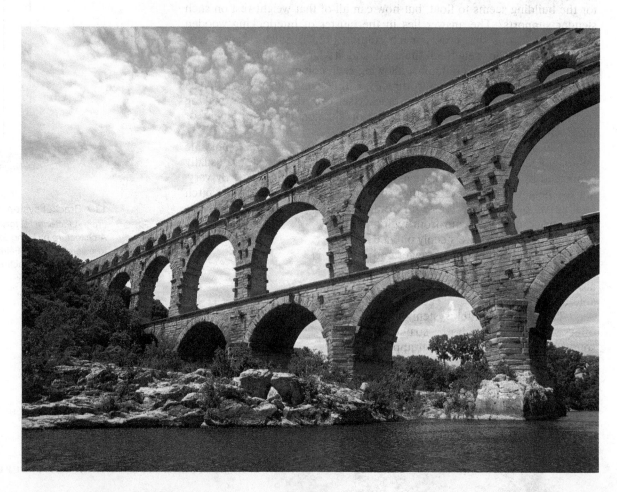

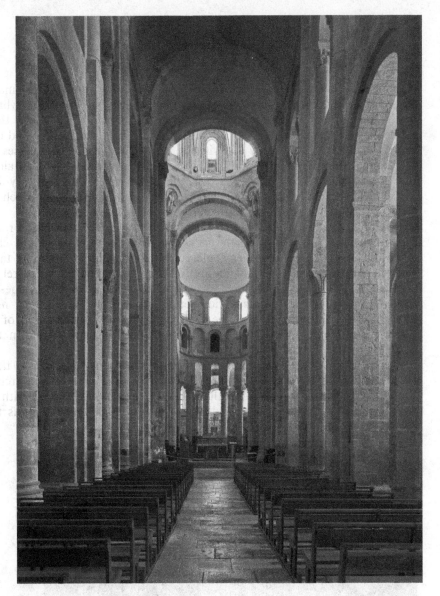

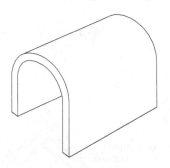

barrel vault

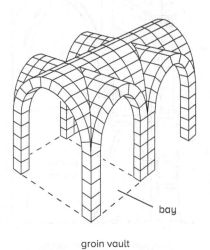

bay

groin vault

13.10 Interior, abbey church of Sainte-Foy, Conques, France. ca. 1050–1120.
© Achim Bednorz, Cologne

When the arch is extended in depth—when it is, in reality, many arches placed flush one behind the other—the result is called a **barrel vault**. This vault construction makes it possible to create large interior spaces. The Romans made great use of the barrel vault, but for its finest expression we look many hundreds of years later, to the churches of the Middle Ages.

The abbey church of Sainte-Foy (**13.10**), in the French city of Conques, is an example of the style that was prevalent throughout western Europe from about 900 to 1200—a style known as **Romanesque**. (For an aerial photograph and plan of the church, see 15.14 and 15.15.) Earlier churches had used the Roman round arch to span the spaces between interior columns that ultimately held up the roof. There were no ceilings, however. Rather, worshipers looked up into a system of wooden trusses and the underside of a pitched roof. Imagine looking directly up into the attic of a house and you will get the idea. With the Romanesque style, builders set a stone barrel vault as a ceiling over the **nave** (the long central area), hiding the roof structure from view. The barrel vault unified the interior visually, providing a soaring, majestic climax to the rhythms announced by the arches below.

On the side aisles of Sainte-Foy (not visible in the photograph), the builders employed a series of **groin vaults**. A groin vault results when two barrel vaults are crossed at right angles to each other, thus directing the weights and stresses down into the four corners. By dividing a space into rectangular segments known as **bays**, each of which contains one groin vault, the architects could cover a long span safely and economically. The repetition of bays also creates a satisfying rhythmic pattern.

Pointed Arch and Vault

Although the round arch and the vault of the Romanesque era solved many problems and made many things possible, they nevertheless had certain drawbacks. For one thing, a round arch, to be stable, must be a semicircle; therefore, the height of the arch is limited by its width. Two other difficulties were weight and darkness. Barrel vaults are both literally and visually heavy, calling for huge masses of stone to maintain their structural stability. They exert an outward thrust all along their base, which builders countered by setting them in massive walls that they dared not weaken with light-admitting openings. The **Gothic** period in Europe, which followed the Romanesque, solved those problems with the pointed arch.

The pointed arch, although seemingly not very different from the round one, offers two advantages. Because the sides arc up to a point, weight is channeled down to the ground at a steeper angle, and therefore the arch can be taller. The vault constructed from such an arch also can be much taller than a barrel vault. In addition, a pointed arch exerts far less outward thrust at its base than does a round arch. Architects of the Gothic period found they did not need heavy masses of material throughout the curve of the vault, as long as the major points of intersection were reinforced. These reinforcements, called **ribs**, are visible in the nave ceiling of Reims Cathedral (**13.11**).

The light captured streaming into the nave of Reims Cathedral in the photograph vividly illustrates another important feature of Gothic church architecture: windows. Whereas Romanesque cathedrals tended to be dark inside, with few and small window openings, Gothic builders strove to open up their walls for large

13.11 Nave, Cathedral of Notre-Dame de Reims, France. 1211–ca. 1290.
Scala/Art Resource, NY

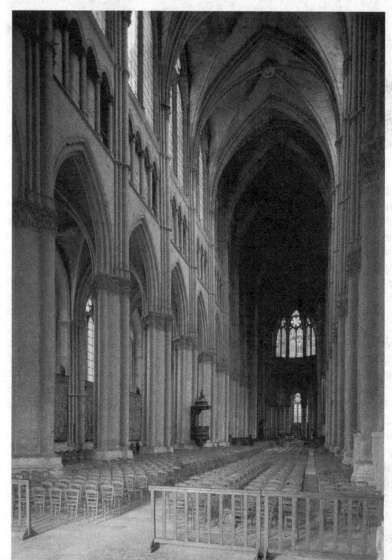

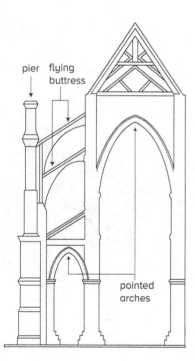

Elements of Gothic architecture

pier flying buttress

pointed arches

13.12 East end, Cathedral of Notre-Dame de Reims.
Sergii Zinko/Alamy Stock Photo

stained-glass windows. (Most of the stained-glass windows in Reims Cathedral have suffered damage and been replaced with clear glass, which is why the light is so evident in the photograph.) Fearing that the numerous window openings could disastrously weaken walls that were already under pressure from the outward thrust of arches, Gothic builders reinforced their walls from the outside with **buttresses**, **piers**, and a new invention, **flying buttresses**. The principles are easy to understand if you imagine yourself using your own weight to prop up a wall. If you stand next to a wall and press the entire length of your body against it, you are a buttress. If you stand away from the wall and press against it with outstretched arms, your body is a pier, and your arms are flying buttresses. The illustration here of the exterior of Reims Cathedral shows the Gothic system of buttresses, piers, and flying buttresses, as well as the numerous windows that made them necessary (**13.12**).

Dome

A **dome** is a curved vault built to cover an interior space. The most common type of dome takes the form of a "shell of rotation"—that is, a form generated by rotating an arch about a vertical central axis. If the arch is a round Roman arch, a half-circle, then the shell of rotation will be a hemisphere, a half-globe, which is the form taken by many domes.

Sliced vertically, a dome is an arch form. Sliced horizontally, a dome is a complete circle. These two aspects are united in a single, continuous surface. Because of this, domes differ from arches in two significant ways. First, a dome can be much thinner in relation to its span than an arch can. Second, a dome exerts far less outward thrust at its base, because the circles, called parallels, act like restraining hoops, preventing the dome from opening up. The upper portion of a dome is in compression. In the lower portion, however, the parallels are in tension, which increases as they near the base. Because domes are generally built of stone, brick, or concrete, all of which have low tensile strength, the base of a dome must be reinforced in some way to prevent cracks from developing. The base of the great dome of St. Peter's Basilica in Rome, for example, is encircled by embedded iron chains (see 16.10).

Like so many other architectural structures, the dome was perfected under the incomparable engineering genius of the Romans, and one of the finest domed buildings ever erected dates from the early 2nd century. It is called the Pantheon, which means a temple dedicated to "all the gods"—or, at least, all the gods who were venerated in ancient Rome (**13.13**, **13.14**, **13.15**). As seen from the inside, the Pantheon has a perfect hemispherical dome soaring 142 feet above the floor, resting upon a cylinder almost exactly the same in diameter—140 feet. The dome is made of concrete, which would have been applied over wooden centering erected in the interior, although exactly how this centering was constructed remains a mystery. The ceiling is **coffered**—ornamented with recessed rectangles, or coffers, which lessen its weight. Only about 2 feet thick at its highest point, the dome increases dramatically in thickness toward its base as a series of step rings appear on the outer surface. The rings add weight to the base of the dome and increase its stability. At the very top of the dome is an opening 29 feet in diameter called an **oculus**, or eye, thought to be symbolic of the "eye of Heaven." This opening provides the sole (and plentiful) illumination for the building. In its conception, then, the Pantheon is amazingly simple, equal in height and width, symmetrical in its structure,

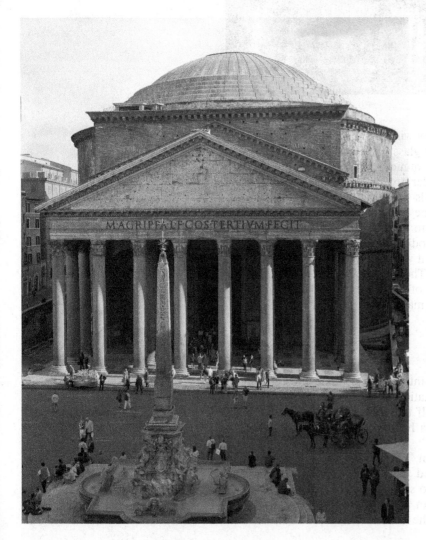

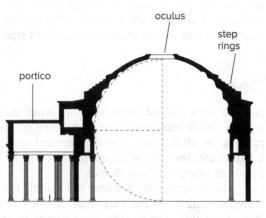

13.13 Pantheon, Rome. 118–26 C.E.
akg-images/Pirozzi

13.14 Section drawing of the Pantheon.

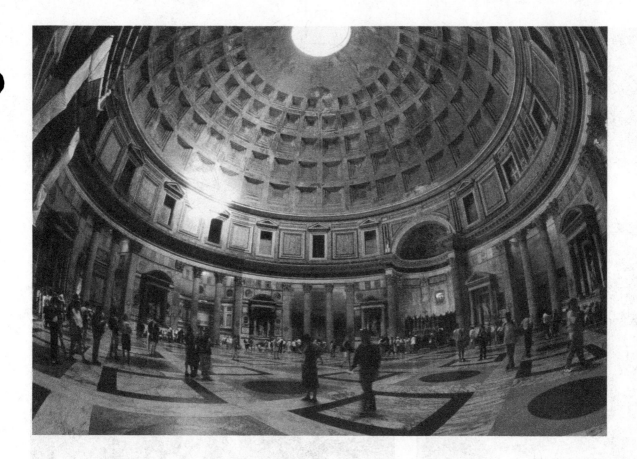

round form set upon round form. Yet because of its scale and its satisfying proportions, the effect is overwhelming.

13.15 Interior of the Pantheon.
Grant Faint/Getty Images

The combined structural possibilities of the dome and the vault enabled the Romans to open up huge spaces such as the Pantheon without interior supports. Another important factor that allowed them to build on such a scale was their use of concrete. Whereas Greek and Egyptian buildings had been made of solid stone, monumental Roman buildings were made of thick concrete, tamped down into parallel brick walls as though into a mold, then faced with stone veneer to look as though they were made of solid stone. An important technological breakthrough, the use of concrete cut costs and enabled building on a grand scale.

Visitors enter the Pantheon through the rectangular **portico**, or porch, that is joined somewhat incongruously to it. Here we recognize the characteristic form of the Greek temple as inherited by the Romans: post-and-lintel construction, Corinthian order, entablature, and pediment. In Roman times, an approach to the building was constructed to lead to the portico while obscuring the rest of the temple. Thinking that they were entering a standard post-and-lintel temple, visitors must have been stunned to see the enormous round space open up before their eyes. Tourists today experience the same theatrical surprise.

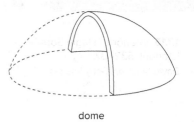

dome

The Pantheon is a **rotunda**, a round building, and its dome sits naturally on the circular **drum** of the base. Often, however, architects wish to set a dome over a square building. In that case, a transitional element is required between the circle (at the dome's base) and the square (of the building's top). An elegant solution can be found in Hagia Sophia (the Church of the Holy Wisdom) in Istanbul (**13.16**, **13.17**). Designed by two mathematicians, Anthemius of Tralles and Isidorus of Miletus, Hagia Sophia was built as a church during the 6th century, when Istanbul, then called Constantinople, was the capital of the Byzantine Empire. When the Turks conquered the city in the 15th century, Hagia Sophia was converted for use as a mosque. It was at that time that the four slender towers, **minarets**, were added. The building is now preserved as a museum. In sheer size and perfection of form, it was the architectural triumph of its time and has seldom been matched since then.

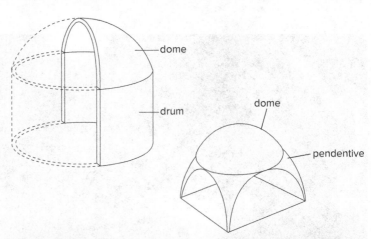

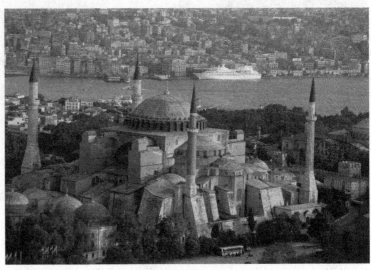

13.17 Hagia Sophia, Istanbul. 532–37.
Harvey Lloyd/Image Bank/Getty Images

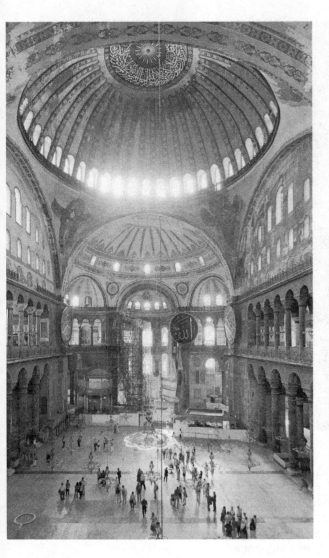

13.16 Interior of Hagia Sophia,
Istanbul. 532–37.
David Madison/Getty Images

The dome of Hagia Sophia rises 183 feet above the floor, with its weight carried to the ground by heavy stone piers—in this case, squared columns—at the four corners of the immense nave. Around the base of the dome is a row of closely spaced arched windows, which make the heavy dome seem to "float" upward. (The exterior view makes it clear that these windows are situated between buttresses that ring the base of the dome, containing its outward thrust and compensating for any structural weakening caused by the window openings.) Each of the four sides of the building consists of a monumental round arch, and between the arches and the dome are curved triangular sections known as **pendentives**. It is the function of the pendentives to make a smooth transition between rectangle and dome.

The domes of the Pantheon and Hagia Sophia serve primarily to open up vast interior spaces. Seen from the outside, their hemispherical form is obscured by the buttressing needed to contain their powerful outward thrust. Yet the dome is such an inherently pleasing form that architects often used it for purely decorative purposes, as an exterior ornament to crown a building. In that case, it is often set high on a drum, a circular base, so that it can be seen from the ground. A famous example of a building crowned by an ornamental dome is the Taj Mahal, in Agra, India (**13.18**).

The Taj Mahal was built in the mid-17th century by the Muslim emperor of India, Shah Jahan, as a tomb for his beloved wife, Arjumand Banu. Although the Taj is nearly as large as Hagia Sophia and possessed of a dome rising some 30 feet higher, it seems comparatively fragile and weightless. Nearly all its exterior lines

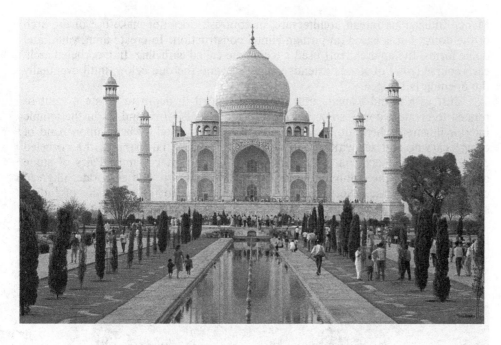

13.18 Taj Mahal, Agra, India.
1632–53.
Monique Pietri/akg-images

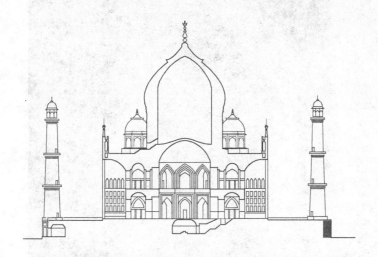

13.19 Section, Taj Mahal.

reach upward, from the graceful pointed arches, to the pointed dome, to the four slender minarets poised at the outside corners. The Taj Mahal, constructed entirely of pure white marble, appears almost as a shimmering mirage that has come to rest for a moment beside the peaceful reflecting pool.

The section drawing (**13.19**) clarifies how the dome is constructed. Over the underground burial chambers of Shah Jahan and his wife, the large central room of the tomb rises to a domed ceiling. Over this, on the roof of the building, sits a tall drum crowned by a pointed dome. A small entryway gives access to the inside for maintenance purposes, but it is not meant to be visited. The exterior is shaped in a graceful, bulging S-curve silhouette that obscures the actual drum-and-dome structure evident in the cutaway view.

Corbeling

Islamic architects knew the use of the arch and the dome because Islam came of age in a part of the world that had belonged first to the Roman and then to the Byzantine Empire. When Islamic rulers settled in India, their architects brought these construction techniques with them, resulting in such buildings as the Taj

Mahal. Indigenous Indian architecture, in contrast, does not make use of the arch or the dome, but is based on post-and-lintel construction. To create arch, vault, and dome forms, Indian architects used a technique called **corbeling**. In a corbeled arch, each course (row) of stones extends slightly beyond the one below, until eventually the opening is bridged.

Just as a round Roman arch can be extended in depth to create a vault or rotated to create a dome, so corbeling can create vault forms and, as in the temple interior illustrated here, dome forms (**13.20**). Ornamented by band upon band of ornate carving and set with figures of the sixteen celestial nymphs, the corbeled dome rests on an octagon of lintels supported by eight columns. Pairs of stone brackets between the columns provide additional support. The elaborate, filigreed carving that decorates every available surface testifies to the virtuosity of Indian stoneworkers, in whose skillful hands stone was made to seem as light as lace.

Although to the naked eye a corbeled arch may be indistinguishable from the round arch described previously, it does not function structurally as a round arch does, channeling weight outward and downward, and so does not enable the construction of large, unobstructed interior spaces.

13.20 Interior of the Jain temple of Dilwara, Vimala Temple, Mount Abu, South Rajasthan, India. Completed 1032.
John Henry Claude Wilson/ Robert Harding

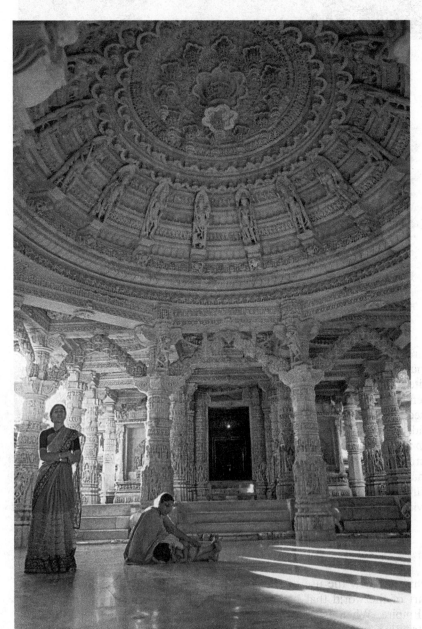

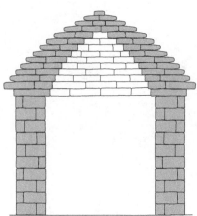

corbeled dome

Cast-Iron Construction

With the perfection of the post-and-lintel, the arch, and the dome, construction in wood, stone, and brick had gone just about as far as it could go. Not until the introduction of a new building material did the next major breakthrough in structural systems take place. Iron had been known for thousands of years and had been used for tools and objects of all kinds, but only after the Industrial Revolution was it produced in sufficient quantities to be used as a building material. The structural value of iron was demonstrated brilliantly in a project that few contemporary observers took seriously.

In 1851 the city of London was planning a great exhibition, under the sponsorship of Prince Albert, husband of Queen Victoria. The challenge was to house under one roof the "Works of Industry of All Nations," and the commission for erecting a suitable structure fell to Joseph Paxton, a designer of greenhouses. Paxton raised in Hyde Park a wondrous building framed in cast iron and sheathed in glass—probably the first modern skeleton-and-skin structure ever designed (**13.21**). The Crystal Palace, as Paxton's creation came to be known, covered more than 17 acres and reached a height of 108 feet. Thanks to an ingenious system of prefabrication, the entire project was completed in less than nine months.

Visitors to the exhibition considered the Crystal Palace a curiosity—a marvelous one, to be sure, but still an oddity outside the realm of architecture. They could not have foreseen that Paxton's design, solid iron framework clothed in a glass skin, would pave the way for 20th-century architecture. In fact, Paxton had taken a giant step in demonstrating that as long as a building's skeleton held firm, its skin could be light and non-load-bearing. Several intermediary steps would be required before this principle could be translated into today's architecture.

13.21 Joseph Paxton. Crystal Palace, Hyde Park, London. 1851. View of the exterior of the north transept. Engraving, 1851.
IAM/akg-images

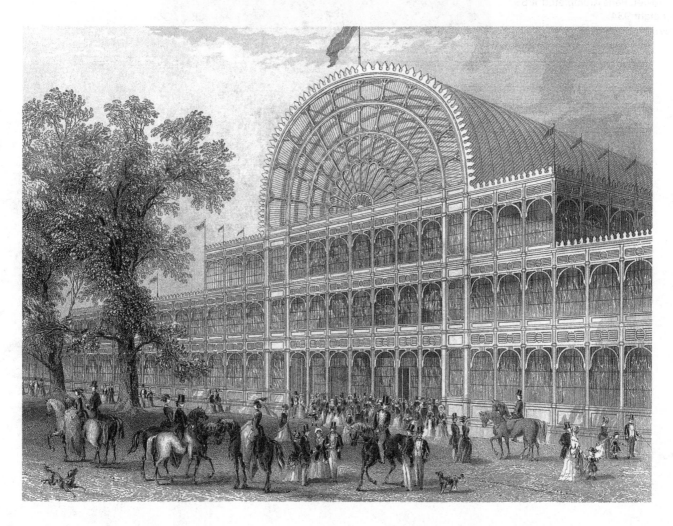

Another bold experiment in iron construction came a few decades later just across the English Channel, in France, and involved a plan that many considered to be foolhardy, if not downright insane. Gustave Eiffel, a French engineer, proposed to build in the center of Paris a skeleton iron tower, nearly 1,000 feet tall, to act as a centerpiece for the Paris World's Fair of 1889. Nothing of the sort had ever been suggested, much less built. In spite of loud protests, the Eiffel Tower (**13.22**) was constructed, at a cost of about a million dollars—an unheard-of sum for those times. It rises on four arched columns, which curve inward until they meet in a single tower thrusting up boldly above the cityscape of Paris.

The importance of this singular, remarkable structure for the future of architecture rested on the fact that it *was* a skeleton that proudly showed itself without the benefit of any cosmetic embellishment. No marble, no glass, no tiles, no skin of any kind—just clean lines drawn in an industrial-age product. Two concepts emerged from this daring construction. First, metal in and of itself can make beautiful architecture. Second, metal can provide a solid framework for a very large structure, self-sustaining and permanent. Today the Eiffel Tower is the ultimate symbol of Paris, and no tourist would pass up a visit. From folly to landmark in a century—such is the course of innovative architecture.

Iron for structural members was not the only breakthrough of the mid-19th century. The Industrial Revolution also introduced a new construction element that was much humbler but equally significant in its implications for architecture: the nail. For want of that simple little nail, most of the houses we live in today could not have been built.

13.22 Alexandre Gustave Eiffel. Eiffel Tower, Paris. Completed 1889. Iron, height 934'.
Photov.com/AGE Fotostock

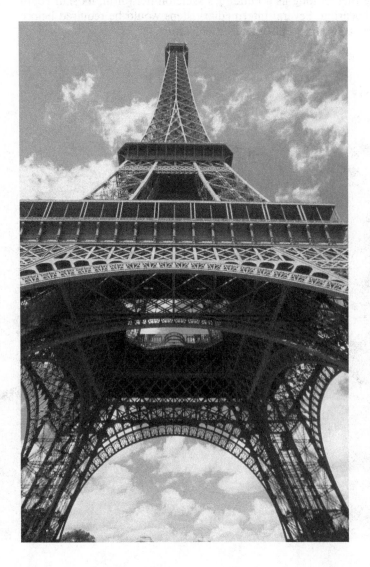

Balloon-Frame Construction

So far in this chapter, the illustrations have concentrated on grand and public buildings—churches, temples, monuments. These are the glories of architecture, the buildings we admire and travel great distances to see. We should not forget, however, that the overwhelming majority of structures in the world have been houses for people to live in, or domestic architecture.

Until the mid-19th century, houses were of shell construction. They were made of brick or stone (and, in warmer climates, of such materials as reeds and bamboo) with load-bearing construction, or else they were post-and-lintel structures in which heavy timbers were assembled by complicated notching and joinery, sometimes with wooden pegs. Nails, if any, had to be fabricated by hand and were very expensive.

In about 1833, in Chicago, the technique of balloon-frame construction was introduced. Balloon-frame construction is a true skeleton-and-skin method. It developed from two innovations: improved methods for milling lumber and mass-produced nails. In this system, the builder first erects a framework or skeleton by nailing together sturdy but lightweight boards (the familiar 2-by-4 "stud"), then adds a roof and sheathes the walls in clapboard, shingles, stucco, or whatever the home-owner wishes (**13.23**). Glass for windows can be used lavishly, as long as it does not interrupt the underlying wood structure, since the sheathing plays little part in holding the building together.

When houses of this type were introduced, the term "balloon framing" was meant to be sarcastic. Skeptics thought the buildings would soon fall down, or burst just like balloons. But some of the earliest balloon-frame houses stand firm today, and this method is still the most popular for new house construction in Western countries.

The balloon frame, of course, has its limitations. Wood beams 2 by 4 inches thick cannot support a skyscraper ten or fifty stories high, and that was the very sort of building architects had begun to dream of late in the 19th century. For such soaring ambitions, a new material was needed, and it was found. The material was steel.

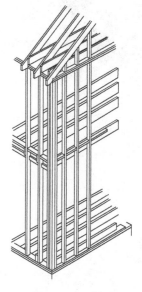

balloon-frame construction

13.23 Balloon-frame house under construction.
gmnicholas/E+/Getty Images

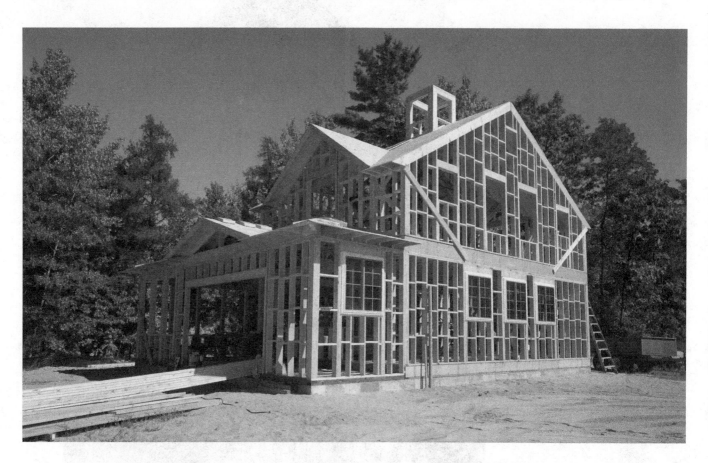

Steel-Frame Construction

Although multistory buildings have been with us since the Roman Empire, the development of the skyscraper, as we know it, required two late-19th-century innovations: the elevator and steel-frame construction. Steel-frame construction, like balloon framing, is a true skeleton-and-skin arrangement. Rather than piling floor upon floor, with each of the lower stories supporting those above it, the builders first erect a steel "cage" that is capable of sustaining the entire weight of the building; then they apply a skin of some other material. But people could hardly be expected to walk all the way to the top of a ten-story building, to say nothing of a skyscraper. Hence, another invention made its appearance, the elevator.

What many consider to be the first genuinely modern building was designed by Louis Sullivan and built between 1890 and 1891 in St. Louis. Known as the Wainwright Building (**13.24**), it employed a steel framework sheathed in masonry. Other architects had experimented with steel supports but had carefully covered their structures in heavy stone so as to reflect traditional architectural forms and make the construction seem reliably sturdy. Centuries of precedent had prepared the public to expect bigness to go hand in hand with heaviness. Sullivan broke new ground by making his sheathing light, letting the skin of his building echo, even celebrate, the steel framing underneath. Regular bays of windows on the seven office floors are separated by strong vertical lines, and the four corners of the building are emphasized by vertical piers. The Wainwright Building's message is subtle, but we cannot mistake it: The nation had stopped growing outward and started growing *up*.

13.24 Louis Sullivan. Wainwright Building, St. Louis. 1890–91.
Raymond Boyd/Getty Images

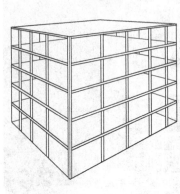

steel-frame construction

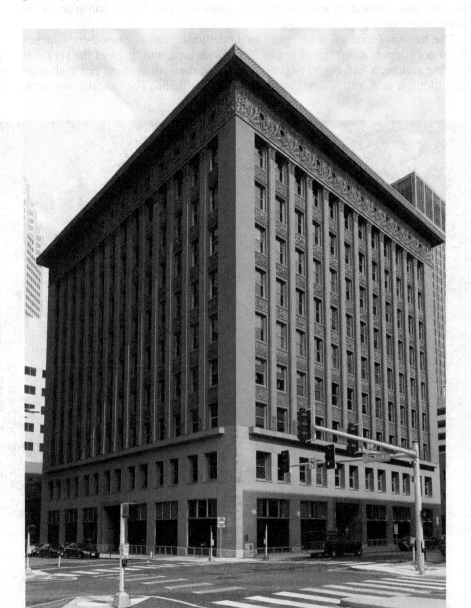

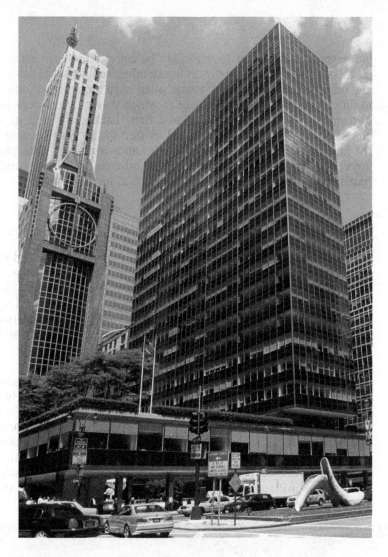

13.25 Gordon Bunshaft of Skidmore, Owings, and Merrill. Lever House, New York. 1952. Sandra Baker/Alamy Stock Photo

Sullivan's design looks forward to the 20th century, but it nevertheless clings to certain architectural details rooted in Classical history, most notably the heavy cornice (the projecting roof ornament) that terminates upward movement at the top of the building. In a very few decades, even those backward glances into the architectural past would become rare.

Toward the middle of the 20th century, skyscrapers began to take over the downtown areas of major cities, and city planners had to grapple with unprecedented problems. How high is too high? How much airspace should a building consume? What provision, if any, should be made to prevent tall buildings from completely blocking out the sunlight from the streets below? In New York and certain other cities, ordinances were passed that resulted in a number of look-alike and architecturally undistinguished buildings. The laws required that if a building filled the ground space of a city block right up to the sidewalk, it could rise for only a certain number of feet or stories before being "stepped back," or narrowed; then it could rise for only a specified number of additional feet before being stepped back again. The resultant structures came to be known as "wedding-cake" buildings. A few architects, however, found more creative ways of meeting the airspace requirement. Those working in the **International style** designed some of the most admired American skyscrapers during the 1950s and 1960s. International style architecture emphasized clean lines, geometric (usually rectilinear) form, and an avoidance of superficial decoration. The "bones" of a building were supposed to show and to be the only ornament necessary. A classic example of this pure style is Lever House.

Lever House in New York (**13.25**), designed by the architectural firm of Skidmore, Owings, and Merrill and built in 1952, was heralded as a breath of fresh air in the smog of look-alike structures. Its sleek, understated form was widely copied but never equaled. Lever House might be compared to two shimmering glass dominoes, one resting horizontally on freestanding supports, the other balanced upright and off-center on the first. At a time when most architects of office buildings strove to fill every square inch of airspace to which they were entitled—both vertically and horizontally—the elegant Lever House drew back and raised its slender rectangle aloof from its neighbors, surrounded by free space. Even its base does not rest on the ground but rides on thin supports to allow room for open plazas and passageways beneath the building. Practically no other system of construction except steel-frame could have made possible this graceful form.

Suspension and Cable-Stayed Structures

In the structural systems we have examined thus far, an elevated expanse such as a flat ceiling or a road over a river would be supported from below. Thus, arches support the footbridge on the lower level of the Pont du Gard (13.9), and columns support the lintels and stone slab ceiling of the temple of Luxor (13.2). With **suspension** and **cable-stayed** structures, such expanses are supported primarily from above, hung from a higher point by means of cables. We illustrate both systems here with bridges, their most common application, but they can also be used to support roofs and even floors.

The Golden Gate Bridge in San Francisco embodies the grace and power of suspension (**13.26**). Two thick, steel-wire cables are draped over twin towers set into the bed of the Golden Gate (the strait of water that links the Pacific Ocean to the San Francisco Bay) and anchored securely on either shore. These main cables in turn support vertical suspender cables attached to the deck below. The deck thus hangs from the main cables. Suspension bridges came into their own with the development of steel-wire rope in the 19th century, but the principle of suspension is far older. In Peru, for example, the ancient Inca constructed suspension bridges

13.26 Golden Gate Bridge, San Francisco. 1937. Joseph B. Strauss, chief engineer; O. H. Ammann, Charles Derleth, Jr., and Leon S. Moisseiff, consulting engineers; Irving F. Morrow, consulting architect.
© ventdusud/Getty Images

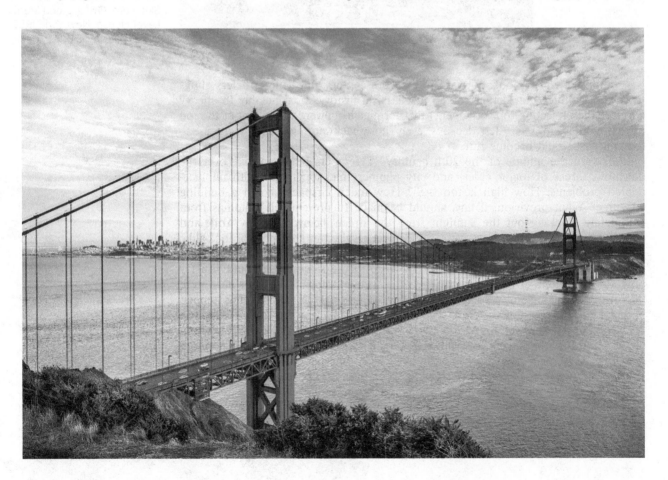

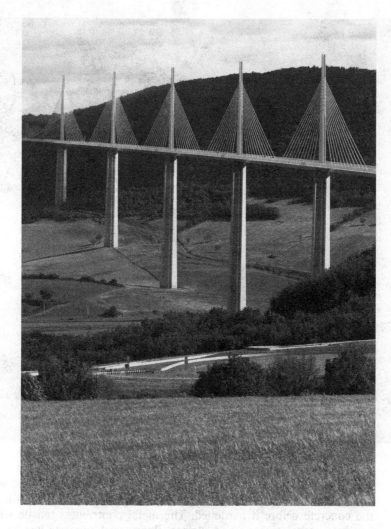

13.27 Foster and Partners. Millau Viaduct, Millau, France. 1993–2004. © Martial Colomb/Photographer's Choice RF/Getty Images

out of fiber rope to carry their mountain roads across gorges and canyons. Attached to stone anchors on either side of the void, the rope suspension system supported a wooden footpath.

Cable-stayed structures bear a superficial resemblance to suspension structures, but they operate on a different principle. With a suspension bridge, the suspender cables rise vertically to the main cables, which sag in a parabolic curve between the towers. These main cables are the primary load-bearing structure. With a cable-stayed bridge, the suspender cables rise on an incline and attach to the towers themselves. The towers are thus the primary load-bearing structure. The Millau Viaduct, designed by the English architect Norman Foster in collaboration with a team of French engineers, is a stunning example of a cable-stayed bridge (**13.27**). One of the tallest bridges in the world, the Millau Viaduct carries a four-lane highway for over 1½ miles across the valley of the River Tarn, near Millau, in the south of France. Seven concrete piers rise from the valley floor to the deck. A steel mast rises from each pier, bearing eleven pairs of suspender cables, here called "stays," that reach down to the deck.

Reinforced Concrete

Concrete is an old material that was known and used by the Romans. A mixture of cement, gravel, and water, concrete can be poured, will assume the shape of any mold, and then will set to hardness. Its major problem is that it tends to be brittle and has low tensile strength. This problem is often observed in the thin concrete slabs used for sidewalks and patios, which may crack and split apart as a result of

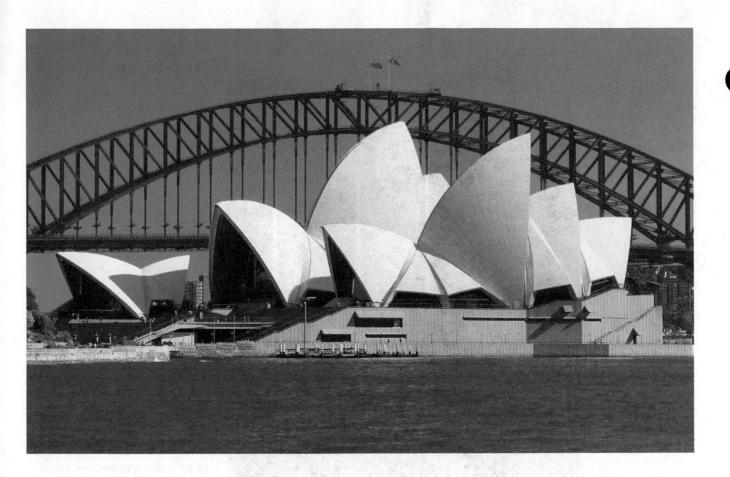

13.28 Jørn Utzon. Sydney Opera House, Australia. 1959–72. Reinforced concrete, height of highest shell 200'.
Album/Raga/Prisma/akg-images

weight and weather. Late in the 19th century, however, a method was developed for reinforcing concrete forms by embedding mesh or rods made of iron or steel inside the concrete before it hardened. The metal contributes tensile strength, while the concrete provides shape and surface. Reinforced concrete has been used in a wide variety of structures, often in those with free-form, organic shapes. Although it may seem at first to be a skeleton-and-skin construction, reinforced concrete actually works more like a shell, because the metal and concrete are bonded permanently and can form structures that are self-sustaining, even when very thin.

Precast sections of reinforced concrete were used to create the soaring shell-like forms of the Sydney Opera House in Australia (**13.28**). The Opera House, which is really an all-round entertainment complex, is almost as famous for its construction difficulties as it is for its extraordinary design. So daring was its concept that the necessary technology virtually had to be invented as the project went along. Planned as a symbol of the great port city in whose harbor it stands, the Opera House gives the impression of a wonderful clipper ship at full sail. Three sets of pointed shells, oriented in different directions, turn the building into a giant sculpture in which walls and roof are one.

One type of structure facilitated by reinforced concrete is the **cantilever**, a projecting form supported at only one end. The American architect Frank Lloyd Wright made poetic use of the cantilever in one of his greatest works, the Edgar J. Kaufmann House, popularly known as Fallingwater (**13.29**). Wright designed Fallingwater for a wooded site beside a stream with a little waterfall. His clients, the Kaufmann family, assumed he would design a house with a view of the waterfall. Instead, Wright set the house over the falls, so that the sound of the water would become part of their lives. The vertical core of the house is made from stone quarried nearby, giving Fallingwater a conceptual as well as a visual unity with the landscape around it. Cantilevered terraces made of reinforced concrete project boldly from the core. Two of them seem to hover directly over the waterfall, rhythmically echoing the natural cantilever of its massive stone ledge.

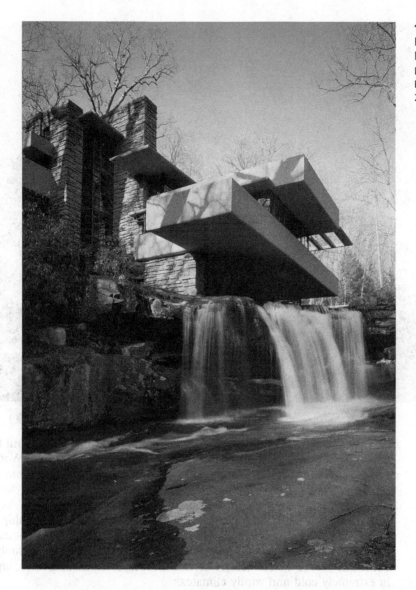

13.29 Frank Lloyd Wright. Fallingwater, Mill Run, Pennsylvania. 1936.
Library of Congress Prints and Photographs Division [HABS PA, 26-OHPY.V,1–87 (CT)]

Geodesic Domes

Of all the structural systems, probably the only one that can be attributed to a single individual is the **geodesic dome**, which was developed by the American architectural engineer R. Buckminster Fuller. Fuller's dome is essentially a bubble, formed by a network of metal rods arranged in triangles and further organized into tetrahedrons. (A tetrahedron is a three-dimensional geometric figure having four faces.) This metal framework can be sheathed in any of several lightweight materials, including wood, glass, and plastic.

The geodesic dome offers a combination of advantages never before available in architecture. Although very light in weight in relation to size, it is amazingly strong, because its structure rests on a mathematically sophisticated use of the triangle. Because it requires no interior support, all the space encompassed by the dome can be used with total freedom. A geodesic dome can be built in any size. In theory, at least, a structurally sound geodesic dome 2 miles across could be built, although nothing of that scope has ever been attempted. Perhaps most important for modern building techniques, Fuller's dome is based on a modular system of construction. Individual segments—modules—can be prefabricated to allow extremely quick assembly of even a large dome. And finally, because of the flexibility in choice of sheathing materials, there are virtually endless options for climate and light control.

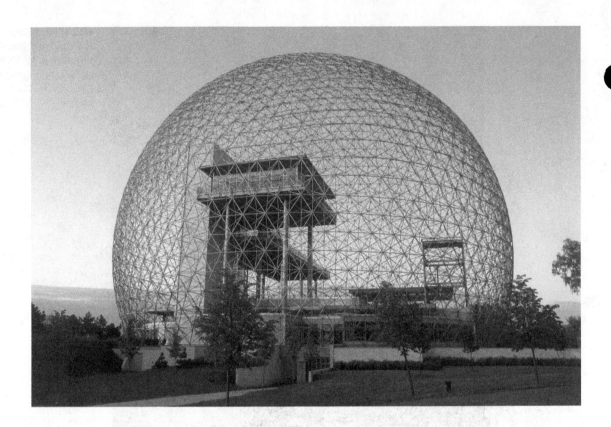

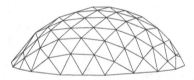

geodesic dome

Fuller patented the geodesic dome in 1954, but it was not until thirteen years later, when his design served as the U.S. Pavilion at the Montreal World's Fair, that the public's attention was awakened to its possibilities. The dome at Expo 67 (**13.30**) astonished the architectural world and fairgoers alike. It was 250 feet in diameter (about the size of a football field rounded off) and, being sheathed in translucent material, lit up the sky at night like a giant spaceship set down on Earth. After Expo 67, some people predicted that before long all houses and public buildings would be geodesic domes. That dream has faded considerably, but Fuller's dome has proved well suited for scientific research stations, homes, and even hotels in extremely cold and windy climates.

New Technology, New Materials, Current Concerns

Like all areas of human creativity, architecture has been affected by the evolution of digital technology. This section looks first at some of the possibilities opened up by using computers to link design and fabrication. It then examines how modern fabrics are being used to create lightweight, portable structures; how architects are responding to the needs of communities; and the ongoing challenge of developing environmentally responsible buildings.

Digital Design and Fabrication

Also known as computer-aided design and manufacturing (CAD/CAM), digital design and fabrication is very much what it sounds like: digital technology is used to help design an object; then digital design data is fed to computer-driven (computer numerical controlled, or CNC) machinery, which automatically fabricates the object.

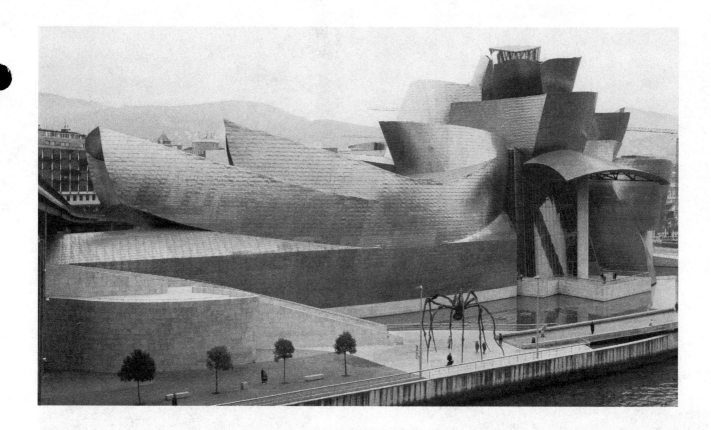

13.31 Frank Gehry. Guggenheim Museum Bilbao, Spain. 1997.

akg-images/Album/Angel Manzano

Linking design and manufacturing by means of computers was pioneered in the 1960s by the electronics, aeronautic, and automotive industries, which could afford to invest in the large, mainframe computers of the day. With the development of personal computers during the years around 1980, digital technology was adopted in numerous work environments, including architecture studios. Many architects began to use two-dimensional drawing programs to help generate the thousands of drawings that guide construction. Today, most architects work with more powerful three-dimensional modeling programs as part of the design process. Linked with the potential of digital fabrication, these programs have expanded the possibilities for the forms architecture can take.

One of the first architects to take advantage of digital design and fabrication was Frank Gehry. Gehry had become interested in complex curving forms, but he didn't know how to communicate them to a contractor so that they could be built. A search for solutions turned up a three-dimensional modeling program called CATIA, which had been developed for the French aerospace industry. The world got its first look at what CATIA could do for architecture when Gehry unveiled his next major project, the Guggenheim Museum Bilbao (**13.31**; for the interior, see 4.42).

Gehry's design for the building began with gestural sketches on paper and proceeded to the construction of a wood-and-paper model. The model was scanned into CATIA, which mapped it in three dimensions. CATIA enabled Gehry's team to work within the construction budget by allowing them to follow every design decision through to its practical consequences in regard to construction methods and exact quantities of materials. In essence, the program built and rebuilt a virtual museum many times before the actual museum was begun. Information from CATIA then guided the digital fabrication of building components: CNC machines milled limestone blocks and cut glass for curved walls, cut the titanium panels that cover the exterior, and cut, folded, and bolted the underlying steel framework of the building.

The Guggenheim Museum Bilbao is a satellite museum of the Solomon R. Guggenheim Museum in New York. Another famous museum of modern and contemporary art, the Pompidou Center in Paris, recently opened its own satellite

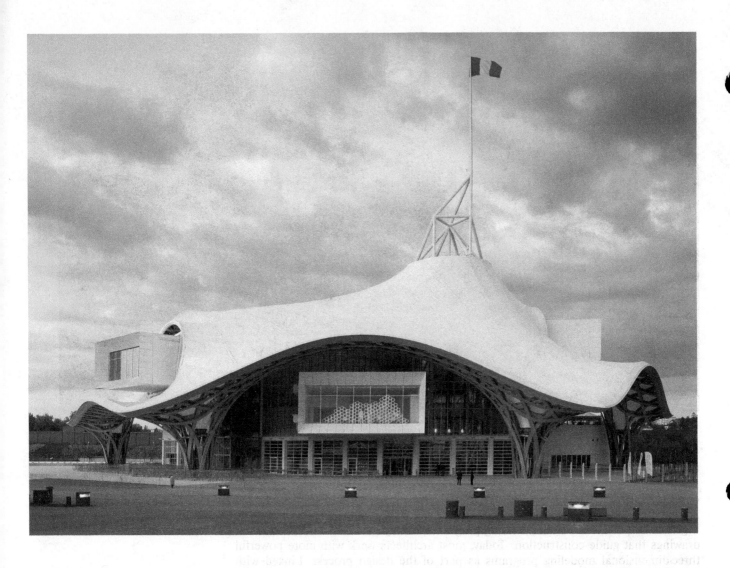

13.32 Shigeru Ban. Centre Pompidou-Metz, Metz, France. 2010.
flashover/Alamy Stock Photo

museum in Metz, France. Designed by Shigeru Ban, the Centre Pompidou-Metz is another example of the new architectural forms enabled by digital design and fabrication (**13.32**). The most spectacular element of the Pompidou-Metz is the undulating white canopy that shelters the center's galleries and atrium spaces. The canopy is supported by a structure made of laminated wooden ribs woven in an open, hexagonal pattern. To create the wooden structure, the curving geometry of the roof was digitally mapped. Sections (slices) were automatically derived to profile the rise and fall of each individual rib, then translated into instructions for CNC wood-milling machinery. All in all, some 1,800 double-curved segments of wood, totaling over 59,000 feet, were individually fabricated to create the structure. Ban took his inspiration for the unusual roof from a Chinese woven bamboo hat that he had found. Weavers have produced such hats for thousands of years, but only with the development of CAD/CAM technology has an architect been able to imitate them.

Fabric Architecture

Shigeru Ban's ingenious wooden lattice is covered with Teflon-coated fiberglass fabric. The stain-resistant, self-cleaning membrane is translucent, allowing daylight to filter into the interior. In the evening, when the building is lit inside, the silhouette of the wooden structure shows through the membrane to the outside. The fabric Ban used is a modern invention, but the idea of fabric architecture is an ancient one. Stone Age peoples first made tents of tree branches covered with animal skins

Architecture as Social Space

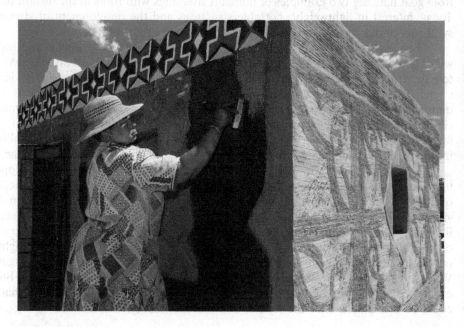 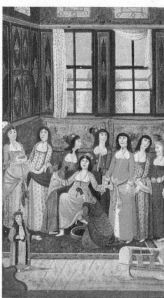

How is architecture a social space? What role does gender play in the construction and use of buildings?

Architecture is more than walls and ceilings. Buildings serve us and the societies in which we live. Social notions of gender are regularly reflected in architecture. Gender has also been a factor in the construction, decoration, and use of some works of architecture.

During the African dry season, women in Lesotho paint colorful murals on the walls of their homes. The practice is called *litema*, which derives from the Basotho word for "cultivation," and the purpose of such murals is to encourage ancestors to send rain. Because agriculture is a traditional women's task in the Basotho community, these paintings are made exclusively by women. The designs are abstract geometric patterns that represent planted fields. Each color has a symbolic meaning: red symbolizes blood and fertility, white is purity, and black represents the ancestors who send the annual rains. When the rainy season washes the designs away, the women repaint the walls to renew the cycle.

Women were not just responsible for the exteriors of traditional Pueblo Indian dwellings. They constructed the homes as well because they, not their male partners, owned the homes. When couples married, the husband moved into his wife's house. Pueblo multi-family structures such as Taos Pueblo were built by women using bricks made of a mixture of dirt, water, and straw, known as adobe. The structures employed load-bearing construction as rows of sun-dried adobe bricks were stacked one upon the other. Even today, women maintain these homes by reapplying adobe plaster every year or two.

A different social use of architecture appears in the Turkish painting of a harem, a private area of retreat and solace away from the business of the court. Its name is derived from the Arabic for a forbidden or inviolable place. Although the sultan occupied the rooms with his family, the harem came to be seen as a space for women. This painting pictures a woman giving birth surrounded by the women of the court. Romantic descriptions by European travelers of the harems they encountered in Ottoman palaces spread a distorted view of these private spaces.

(left) Basotho woman painting a house. imageBROKER/Alamy Stock Photo
(right) Unknown Turkish artist. *Birth in a Harem*. 1775–1800. Opaque watercolor and gold on paper, 8 ⅝ × 5 ⅛". Los Angeles County Museum of Art

as early as 40,000 years ago. Later, as the first cities were raised, nomadic peoples continued to live in tents. The yurts of Central Asia, made of felt over a wooden framework, and the tents of Middle Eastern Bedouin peoples, made of fabric woven from goat hair, are two examples of nomadic dwellings with roots in the distant past. Today, interest in lightweight, portable structures and the development of stronger synthetic fabrics have inspired a new wave of fabric architecture.

The key to fabric architecture is tension: For fabric to bear weight and resist wind, it must be pulled taut. For that reason, fabric structures are also known as tensile structures or tensile membrane structures. One way to tense fabric is to stretch it over a framework. The most familiar example of this principle is the umbrella: When you open an umbrella, the fabric is drawn taut by slender metal ribs, creating a portable roof that protects you from the rain. The tension of the fabric in turn prevents the ribs from buckling and constrains their movement, allowing them to be much thinner and lighter than they would otherwise need to be.

Zaha Hadid's innovative Burnham Pavilion is made of panels of fabric zipped tight over a framework of bent aluminum and steel tubing (**13.33**). Fabric is stretched over the inside of the pavilion as well, where it serves as a projection screen for videos. Light-emitting diodes (LEDs) set between the inner and outer fabric skins illuminate the pavilion at night so that it glows in a sequence of colors—green, orange, blue, violet. A product of computer-aided design, the curved form sits lightly on the ground, as though it has just touched down and might soon be off again. We could think of Burnham Pavilion as contemporary nomadic architecture. Built on-site for a centennial celebration in Chicago in 2009, it was designed so that it could be dismantled after the festival and erected elsewhere as desired.

13.33 Zaha Hadid Architects. Burnham Pavilion. Installation in Millennium Park, Chicago. 2009. Zaha Hadid Architects. Photo Michelle Litvin

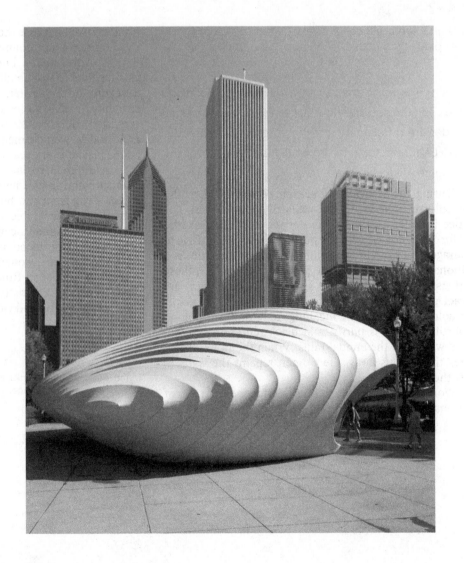

Zaha Hadid

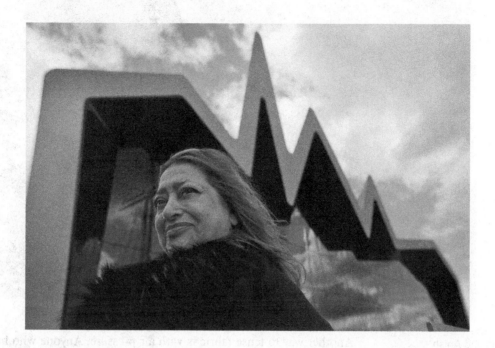

How did Hadid capture a "raw, vital, earthy quality"? Why did the architect have so much difficulty getting her projects realized early in her career? Why do you think her designs became so popular?

Zaha Hadid did not shy away from strong statements. "I don't design nice buildings," she told an interviewer. "I don't like them. I like architecture to have some raw, vital, earthy quality."[1] Indeed, "nice" is a word that critics have never applied to Hadid's work, reaching instead for adjectives such as spectacular, visionary, futuristic, sensuous, and transformative. "Hadid is not merely designing buildings," wrote one critic; "she is reimagining domestic, corporate, and public space."[2]

Zaha Hadid was born in Baghdad in 1950 into an intellectual family. She was educated in Iraq, Switzerland, Lebanon, and England. She became fascinated by the Russian avant-garde painters of the early 20th century, and her conviction grew that Modernism was an unfinished project. She took up painting as a design tool and adapted the formal vocabulary of the Russians she admired. Her paintings so little resembled traditional architectural renderings that many people had a hard time understanding them as buildings at all. Hadid insisted that they could be built and that her unusual technique allowed her to envision an architecture that would express more complex flows of space and capture the dynamism of fragmented and layered geometric forms.

Hadid's early years as an architect were difficult. Her firm entered competition after competition, winning several, yet almost nothing was built. She reached the 21st century with only one significant building to her name and a reputation as a "paper architect"—brilliant in theory, but impractical and untested. Hadid looked back on this period philosophically: "During the days and years we were locked up in Bowling Green Lane with nobody paying attention to us, we all did an enormous amount of research, and this gave us a great ability to reinvent and work on things."[3]

Then, finally, Hadid's luck turned. A series of commissions received during the late 1990s were completed, and the public got its first sustained look at the architecture of Zaha Hadid: the Bergisel Ski Jump in Austria (2002), the Center for Contemporary Art in Cincinnati (2003), the Phaeno Science Center in Wolfsburg, Germany (2005), and the BMW Central Building in Leipzig, Germany (2005). Hadid's buildings could indeed be built, and they were ravishing. In 2004, she was awarded the coveted Pritzker Architecture Prize, the first woman to be so honored.

Hadid completed major projects in Europe, the United States, the Middle East, and Asia. Commissions poured in until her death. She was as philosophical about her late popularity as she was about her years of neglect: "I think it's fantastic, and I'm very grateful for it, but I don't take it so seriously that it affects my life. I believe that when there are good moments, you have to recognize them and enjoy them, and that's it."[4]

Zaha Hadid pictured outside the Riverside Museum, Glasgow, Scotland. Drew Farrell/Alamy Stock Photo

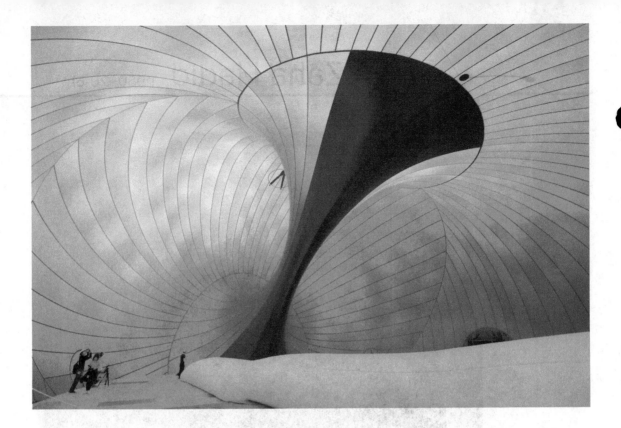

13.34 Arata Isozaki and Anish Kapoor. Ark Nova. 2011.

The Asahi Shimbun via Getty Images

Another way to tense fabric is with air pressure. Anyone who has ever inflated an air mattress will understand immediately how rigid and firm an air-filled structure can be. Air was first used as a structural support in the 19th century, with the invention of the inflatable rubber tire. The development of synthetic fabrics in the mid-20th century led visionary architects to experiment with inflatable structures during the 1960s. After a lull, inflatable architecture is today undergoing something of a revival.

Designed by the architect Arata Isozaki and the sculptor Anish Kapoor, Ark Nova (**13.34**) is an inflatable concert hall. It is made of rectangular panels of plastic fabric and is roughly 95 feet wide by 118 feet long. While it soars to a height of 65 feet when fully inflated, the structure is not a single, uninterrupted volume. Its organic, orblike shape is pierced by a fabric tube that juts diagonally through the interior. Guests enter through a narrow doorway into the vast space that glows reddish-purple. The seams of Ark Nova's fabric membrane look like the ribs of an animal. With room for 500 guests, the structure is fully mobile and accommodates several stages. It is transported by truck, erected temporarily, and then removed, leaving no trace behind.

Isozaki and Kapoor named their inflatable structure after the biblical ark that rescued humans and animals from a great flood. Japan suffered a magnitude-9 earthquake in 2011. The resulting tsunami destroyed much of the country's northeastern coastline, and more than 15,000 people died. The designers wanted to find a way to help the nation heal. They explained, "We named the Project Ark Nova, or 'new ark,' with the hope that it will become a symbol of recovery immediately after the great earthquake disaster."[5] While the structure cannot save people from natural catastrophes, Ark Nova inspires and restores its visitors with music and theatrical performances.

Architecture and Community

Architecture plays an important role in nurturing and sustaining communities. Our sense of having a common life as citizens depends in part on our having public spaces that belong to everyone, places we can enjoy as equals. We need buildings to house the institutions of civic life—schools, courthouses, libraries, and hospitals.

And of course we need dwellings, not only for our individual good, but also for the common good of the community as a whole. In this section we look at a public space, a dwelling, and a civic building, with one twist: Each project not only helps to strengthen and sustain a community, but also involved a community to make it happen.

The Spanish city of Seville is known for its magnificent Gothic cathedral, its beautiful royal palace, and its archive of priceless documents chronicling the Spanish Empire in the Americas and the Philippines. Designated World Heritage Sites, all three are clustered around the intimate Plaza del Triunfo, where they draw more than two million visitors to the city each year. The fate of a large square nearby, in contrast, had been far less glamorous. Uninspiring and unvisited, the Plaza de la Encarnación had at one time been the site of a large and bustling covered market. In 1973, however, the market was razed to make way for a parking lot. Later plans to move the parking lot underground had to be shelved when an archaeological dig turned up the remains of an ancient Roman colony beneath the square.

Looking to revitalize the plaza, the Seville urban-planning department held an international competition to solicit ideas. The winner was the Berlin architect Jürgen Mayer, whose firm submitted plans for a sinuous wooden canopy called Metropol Parasol (**13.35**). Taking his inspiration from the vast vaulted spaces of the city's cathedral, Mayer envisioned Metropol Parasol as a cathedral without walls. Rising majestically from six large trunks, its billowing "mushrooms" meet overhead to form a continuous lattice that flows for almost 500 feet, providing shifting patterns of shade to the square below. At street level, the structure houses an indoor farmers' market and the entrance to an underground museum dedicated to the Roman excavation. Broad staircases that encourage lounging in the sun and serve as meeting places lead to an elevated terrace with cafés and restaurants. A walkway winds along the top of the parasols, culminating in a panoramic viewing deck that overlooks the

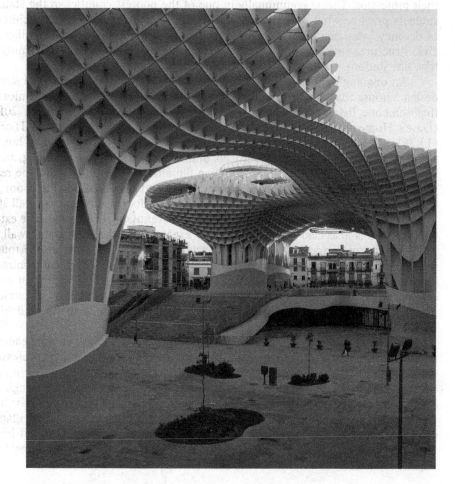

13.35 J. Mayer H. and Partner. Metropol Parasol, Plaza de la Encarnación, Seville. 2004–11.
© Fernando Alda, Seville

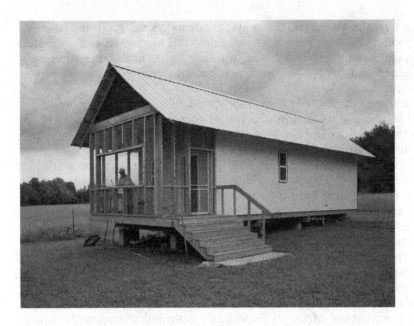

rooftops of Seville. Designed to serve as a contemporary landmark, Metropol Parasol responds to the needs of the local community and attracts tourists to a part of town they might otherwise have ignored.

Our next work involved the efforts of a different kind of community, a community of architecture students. Rural Studio is a satellite school for architecture students at Auburn University, in Alabama. It was founded in 1993 to provide hands-on experience and to expose students to the social and ethical dimensions of their profession. Living communally in one of the poorest counties in the state, the students practice what one of the founders of the program called "an architecture of decency," designing and building houses for poor individuals and families, and civic structures such as community centers, chapels, sports facilities, learning centers, fire stations, and animal shelters for local communities in dire need.

An ongoing project at Rural Studio is the 20K Home. Each year, the students design a house that can be built for $20,000—their estimate of the biggest mortgage that someone living on median social security could reasonably afford. 20Kv08 (Dave's Home) was designed and built in 2009 for local resident David Thornton (**13.36**). Set on an elevated foundation, 20Kv08 is a plain, 600-foot-square box. The screened-in front porch opens onto an uninterrupted kitchen and living area. A wood-burning stove provides heat; a ceiling fan aids ventilation. Toward the rear of the house, an interior core encloses a bathroom and divides the living room from the bedroom at the rear. From the bedroom, a back door opens onto a small stoop. The roof is made of galvanized metal, which can eventually be recycled. The exterior of the house is also clad in metal, with the exception of the front porch wall. The wall Mr. Thornton and his visitors are likely to sit by, to look at, and to touch is made of wood. As an ultimate test, the house was erected by local contractors instead of by the students themselves. The cost: approximately $12,500 for materials and $7,500 for labor. Eventually, Rural Studio hopes to develop a catalog of inexpensive designs that can be adapted to different needs and made available for rural housing.

Our third project was built by the community itself, under the leadership of an architecture student who saw a need. Before beginning her professional studies, the German architect Anna Heringer had spent a year volunteering for a nongovernmental development organization in Rudrapur, a village in Bangladesh. She returned to Rudrapur regularly as a student, and when it came time for her to develop a master's thesis, she decided to design a building for the village. A comprehensive study suggested that Rudrapur's long-term interests would be best served by a new school, and so Heringer set about designing one, hoping that it might be realized.

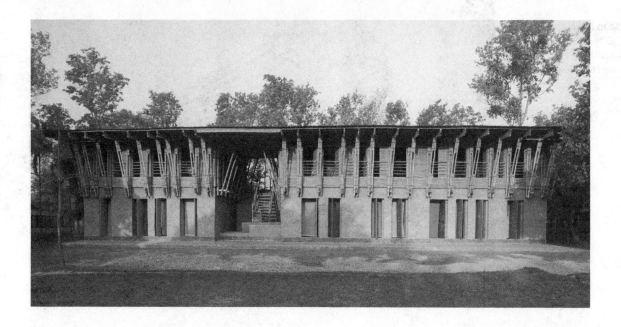

13.37 Anna Heringer and Eike Roswag. METI Handmade School, Rudrapur, Bangladesh. 2004–06. Photo by Kurt Hörbst. Courtesy Anna Heringer

The villagers wanted a school of brick or concrete, materials they associated with progress and viewed as far more stable than their own traditional earthen structures. But Heringer's studies in earth architecture suggested that local traditions needed only to be updated with more sophisticated construction techniques, such as a brick foundation, a layer of plastic to protect the mud walls from ground moisture, the addition of straw to the earth mixture for stability, and thicker walls. She designed a building made of bamboo and cob, a mixture of clay, earth, sand, straw, and water. Her proposal was accepted, and the result is the METI Handmade School (**13.37**).

Working under the direction of Heringer and three colleagues, the villagers built the school by hand. The water buffalo used to mix the cob were the only additional "equipment." The thick cob walls of the first story support a lightweight second story made of joined and lashed bamboo. Deep eaves provide shade and protect the walls from potentially damaging rains. Lengths of vibrantly colored, locally made fabric hang in the doorways and line the bamboo ceiling. Villagers can maintain the school themselves using the skills they learned while constructing it. Those skills have already been put to use on another project: Heringer returned to Rudrapur a year later to oversee a workshop that paired local architecture students with the newly skilled villagers to design and build several two-story cob houses. Heringer hopes that these young architects will carry what they learned to other regions of Bangladesh, and that this modern version of the region's traditional architecture will contribute to the country's ecological balance and economic development. "Architecture," she says, "is a tool to improve lives."[6]

Sustainability: Green Architecture

For more than 250 years, we have been living in the industrial age, which began when inventors discovered how to manufacture energy by harnessing the power of steam, which they created with heat generated by burning fossil fuels—coal and, later, oil. The steam engine was born, followed a century later by the internal combustion engine and the turbine.

During the 19th century, industry produced iron and steel in such large quantities that they became available as building materials. The Crystal Palace (see 13.21) and the Eiffel Tower (see 13.22) were conceived as showpieces for the kind of structure this made possible. Processing coal also produced coal gas, which was piped through cities and into buildings as fuel for street lamps and houselights, lighting the night on a large scale for the first time. But night was truly conquered

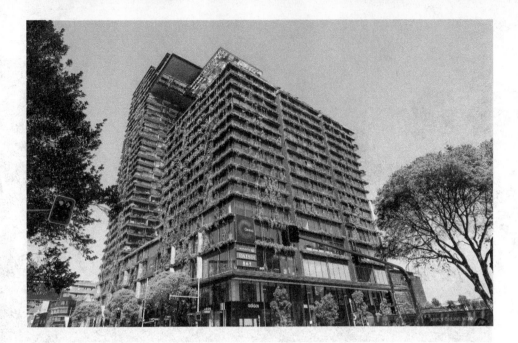

13.38 Ateliers Jean Nouvel and PTW Architects. One Central Park, Sydney, Australia. 2014.
Paul Lovelace/Alamy Stock Photo

when inventors discovered how to convert the energy into electricity, and then how to convert electricity into light with the incandescent lamp.

During the first decades of the 20th century, industrial methods for making sheet glass were developed, the advent of low-wattage fluorescent lamps made it practical to illuminate vast interior spaces artificially, and the triumph of air-conditioning allowed buildings to be sealed off from the natural environment around them. Lever House (see 13.25) epitomizes the aesthetic that developed around these new materials and technologies. Grids of concrete and steel sheathed in glass, their walls and ceilings hide pipes that invisibly deliver and remove hot and cold water, ducts that circulate air and regulate its temperature and humidity, and cables that make electricity available for lighting, appliances, and machines. Such buildings have since been erected all over the world.

Like other benefits of industrialization, these buildings come at a significant cost to the environment, and one that we cannot continue to pay indefinitely. The question of whether we can create a healthier and less wasteful human habitat is at the heart of green architecture. Green architecture addresses the materials that buildings are made of, the construction methods used to make them, and the technology used to heat and cool them, to light their interior spaces, and to supply them with electricity and water. We have already seen these concerns at work in Anna Heringer's METI Handmade School (see 13.37), which favored local materials over brick and concrete, both of which are energy-intensive—that is, much energy is needed to make them.

Since the mid-19th century, city planners have recognized the value of public green spaces. For example, Central Park in New York City was created as a recreational site and respite from the city's concrete and asphalt. Yet parks also help the environment, cutting temperatures by eliminating some of the heat caused by urban development. One Central Park in Sydney, Australia (**13.38**), conserves water and energy, and pays homage to its namesake with green space not just on its grounds, but also on its surface. Built by Ateliers Jean Nouvel and PTW Architects, the twin buildings feature 250 native Australian plant species, which grow on the side of the building. To install the plants on a vertical surface, a botanist placed their roots in felt and crafted a drip irrigation system served by an on-site water-recycling plant. Other plants rest on horizontal balconies, decks, and rooftop gardens. As they grow and die off with the seasons, the plants give the building an ever-changing appearance.

Plants and recycled water are not the only green features at the site. One Central Park has an on-site thermal, low-carbon energy plant to meet the building's heating, cooling, and electricity demands. The architects also added a large, canti-levered heliostat or deck covered in reflective panels that juts out from the building.

These mirrors turn slightly with the sun to reflect its light onto the spaces below. When the sun goes down, LED lights embedded among the reflective panels entertain visitors with a colorful display.

Increasing public awareness of environmental concerns has created a growing interest in healthy, green, efficient homes. To encourage innovation in green architecture, the United States Department of Energy hosts the Solar Decathlon, a competition in which teams of college students vie to design, build, and operate the most appealing, energy-efficient, and affordable solar-powered house. Held every other year, the popular event has inspired European and Chinese versions, creating a family of international Solar Decathlons. In 2013, the competition was held in Irvine, California, where top honors went to LISI House by Team Austria (**13.39**).

Designed as a dwelling for two people, LISI (for "Living Inspired by Sustainable Innovation") was quickly assembled on-site from prefabricated components scaled to fit neatly into standard international shipping containers. At the heart of the house is an open living area flanked on two sides by floor-to-ceiling sliding glass doors and on the other two sides by service cores that function as weight-bearing walls. One service core houses an open kitchen and numerous storage cupboards. The other, visible in the photograph, houses a bedroom, a bathroom, and a utility room for the automated systems that run the house. The glass doors open onto two patios north and south, effectively doubling the amount of living space when the weather permits. The entire plan—patios, living area, core units, and entrance ramp— is crowned by a cornice that supports a white textile facade. Filtering sunlight like a veil of foliage, the facade is essentially a wrap-around curtain that can be adjusted to enclose the house completely, shade selected areas as desired, or open the house to the world.

LISI House generates more energy than it needs from photovoltaic panels hidden on the roof. Two efficient air–water heat pumps provide hot water for domestic use, and hot and cold water for space heating and cooling. The heating and cooling water is piped into a multifunctional system beneath the floor that regulates the indoor climate, adjusting the temperature and providing fresh air. An energy-recovery ventilation unit acts as a heat exchanger between exhaust air and fresh intake air to keep the living spaces comfortable and healthy. Automated screens and awnings provide shade to help maintain cool temperatures. An innovative shower tray recovers thermal energy from drain water through a heat exchanger, significantly lowering the net amount of energy used for daily hygiene. Everything happens invisibly, leaving the occupants to enjoy the handsome wood interior and generous outdoor spaces.

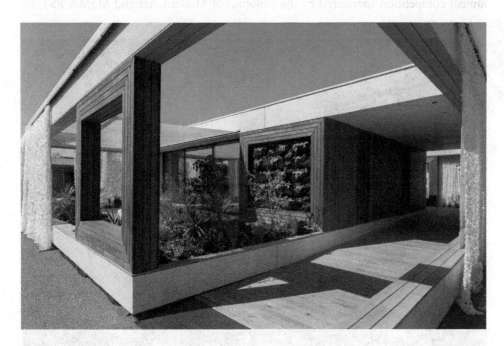

13.39 Team Austria. LISI House, Irvine, California. October 10–13, 2013.
Jason Flakes/U.S. Department of Energy Solar Decathlon

Over 90 percent of LISI House is made of wood, and not only the portions you might expect: In an effort to use every part of the tree, Team Austria chose an insulation material made from wood fiber and cellulose, and manufactured the chairs from bark. Wood is a renewable resource and our only carbon-neutral construction material—that is, the energy needed to transform trees into lengths of lumber is offset by the carbon dioxide that trees absorb as they grow. Often used for houses, it has always been considered too weak to support a large, multistory building. Lately, however, environmental concerns have inspired architects to take another look at its potential for larger structures.

One prominent advocate of wood construction is Michael Green, an architect in Vancouver, British Columbia. His recently completed Wood Innovation and Design Centre was conceived as a showcase for the structural potential of timber (13.40). Rising to a height of 97 feet, it is as of this writing the tallest all-timber building in North America. The key to endowing wood with enough strength to replace steel and concrete is lamination, the gluing together of many thin layers to form one thick one. Plywood is a familiar type of laminated wood product. Less familiar are cross-laminated timber, laminated strand lumber, laminated veneer lumber, and glue-laminated timber. Collectively, these and other engineered wood products are known as massive timber, or mass timber. In the Wood Innovation and Design Centre, mass timber serves for beams, flooring, and walls. With the exception of the ground-floor slab and mechanical elements in the penthouse, there is no concrete in the building at all. Green deliberately kept the design simple so that it could be easily replicated by other architects and engineers.

The Wood Innovation and Design Centre is eight stories tall, but far taller buildings are possible. In 2012, Green published a system for constructing mass-timber towers in seismically active areas such as Vancouver. His feasibility study projected towers up to thirty stories in height. "But we stopped at 30 stories only because at the time that was considered so beyond the comprehension of the public," he says.[7]

Since the dawn of architecture, wood has been virtually the only organic material widely used for construction. Some architects believe that one path to a sustainable future lies in using biological or bio-engineering systems to manufacture new organic building materials. An architect involved in this line of research is David Benjamin, head of the Living Architecture Lab at Columbia University in New York and cofounder of The Living, a research and design studio.

In 2014, Benjamin got an opportunity to put some new ideas into practice, when The Living was selected as the winner of the Young Architects Program, an annual competition sponsored by the Museum of Modern Art and MoMA PS1, its

13.40 Michael Green Architecture. Wood Innovation and Design Centre, Prince George, British Columbia. 2014.
Photo Ema Peter, courtesy Michael Green Architecture

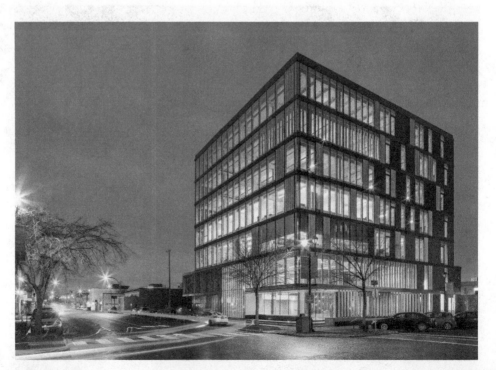

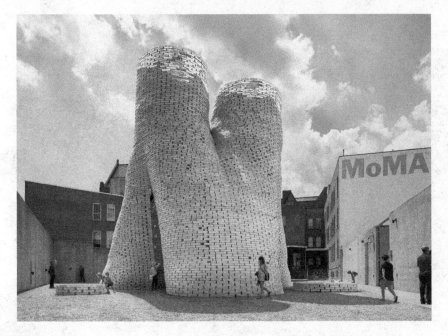

13.41 The Living. *Hy-Fi*. 2014. Installation at MoMA PS1, Queens, New York, June 26–September 7, 2014.
© David Benjamin. Photo Amy Barkow

affiliate institution. The Young Architects Program was founded to encourage and showcase innovation in architecture. Working within guidelines that address environmental issues such as sustainability and recycling, each year's winner must construct a temporary outdoor installation in the courtyard of MoMA PS1 that will provide shade, water, and seating for visitors. The Living responded with a circular tower called *Hy-Fi* (**13.41**).

Hy-Fi was built with organic bricks made from chopped corn husks and mycelium, a living mushroom-root material. Packed into a mold, the mixture self-assembles in a few days into a lightweight object. When it is completely dry, it is ready to use. The molds used to form the bricks for *Hy-Fi* can be seen at the top of the tower. Made of a new daylighting mirror film developed by the 3M Company, they reflected sunlight down into the interior. While it was in use, *Hy-Fi* created an agreeable microclimate by drawing in cool air at the bottom and pushing out hot air at the top. Irregularly spaced openings between the bricks cast shifting sunspots on the walls and floor. When the installation was taken down, the molds were returned to 3M for use in further research, and the bricks were sent to be composted. *Hy-Fi* was the first sizable structure whose construction involved almost no carbon emissions. It arose from the earth and returned to the earth. It was a temporary building and now belongs to the past, but the ideas behind it will carry into the future.

Notes to the Text

1. Quoted in Jonathan Glancey, "'I Don't Do Nice,'" *The Guardian*, October 9, 2006. Available at theguardian.com/artanddesign/2006/oct/09/architecture.communities, accessed April 27, 2018.

2. Quoted in Richard Morrison, "Forever Thinking Outside the Boxy," *The Times*, June 27, 2007. Available at thetimes.co.uk/article/for-ever-thinking-outside-the-boxy-wq0vb8ktb06, accessed April 27, 2018.

3. Hans Ulrich Obrist, ed., *Zaha Hadid/Hans Ulrich Obrist: The Conversation Series* (Köln: Verlag der Buchhandlung Walther König, 2007), p. 89.

4. Ibid., p. 91.

5. Amy Frearson, "Ark Nova by Arata Isozaki and Anish Kapoor," September 26, 2013. Available at dezeen.com/2013/09/26/ark-nova-by-arata-isozaki-and-anish-kapoor-completes, accessed November 24, 2017.

6. Anna Heringer, www.anna-heringer.com. Reproduced with permission.

7. Quoted in Henry Fountain, "Towers of Steel? Look Again," *New York Times*, September 23, 2013. Available at nytimes.com/2013/09/24/science/appeal-of-timber-high-rises-widens.html.

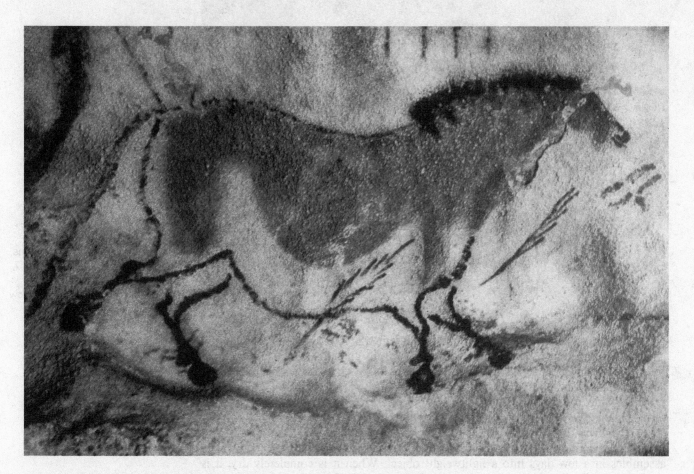

14.1 *Horse and Geometric Symbol.* Cave painting, Lascaux, France. ca. 13,000 B.C.E.

PART FIVE

Arts in Time

Chapter 14
Ancient Mediterranean Worlds

In this chapter, you will learn to

LO1   recognize the forms and themes of prehistoric art,

LO2   describe the art and architecture of Mesopotamia,

LO3   identify the appearance, subjects, and purpose of Egyptian art,

LO4   explain Aegean painting, sculpture, and architecture, and

LO5   discuss the art of the Classical world.

An important factor in understanding and appreciating any work of art is some knowledge of its place in time. When and where was it made? What traditions was the artist building on or rebelling against? What did society at that time expect of its artists? What sort of tasks did it give them?

For that reason, the last part of this book is devoted to a brief survey of art as it has unfolded in time. We focus mainly on the Western tradition, but we also examine the development of art in the cultures of Islam and Africa; of India, China, and Japan; and of Oceania, Australia, and the early Americas. Each of these developed unique forms of artistic expression that responded to local interests and conditions. Yet, as we have seen already, cultures from around the globe interact and exchange ideas. Cultural encounter and exchange introduce new ways of thinking about art, about the roles that art can play in society, and about the formal directions that art can take. Today, more than at any other time in history, the entire range of humankind's artistic past nourishes its present around the globe.

The Oldest Art

The title of this chapter narrows our focus from the entire globe to the region around the Mediterranean Sea. It is here—in Africa, the Near East, and Europe—that the story of Western art begins. In these lands, beginning around 3000 B.C.E., numerous ancient civilizations arose, overlapped, and interacted; learned from one another and conquered each other; and finally transformed into the world we know today.

These civilizations—the "worlds" of our title—were preceded by far older human societies about which we know very little. Scattered evidence of their existence reaches us over a vast distance of tens of thousands of years, fascinating, mysterious, and mute. In Chapter 1, we looked at a detail from the wall paintings in the Chauvet cave in present-day France (see 1.3). Dating from later in the Upper Paleolithic Period are the paintings of the caves at Lascaux, also in France (see **14.1**). Until the discovery of the Chauvet cave in 1994, the images at Lascaux were the oldest known paintings in Europe. The horse illustrated has fascinated scholars because of its seemingly pregnant condition, the feathery forms near its forelegs, and the mysterious geometric symbol depicted above it. The paintings at Chauvet are even more finely executed, based on observation of living animals, and they must surely

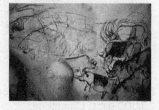

1.3 "Lion Panel," Chauvet cave

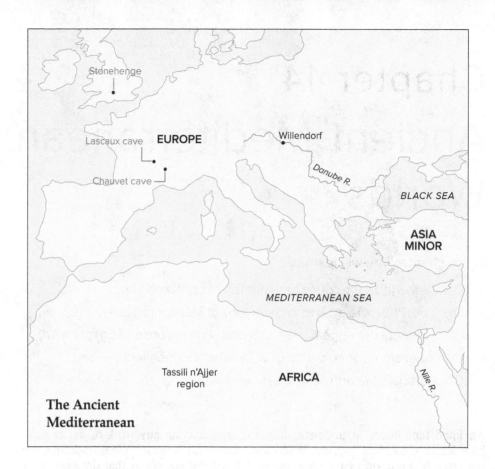

The Ancient
Mediterranean

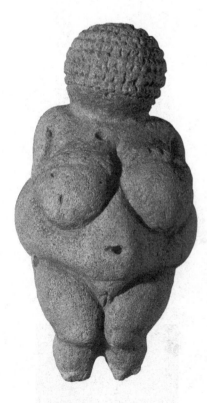

14.2 Female figure from Willendorf.
ca. 23,000 B.C.E. Limestone,
height 4 ⅜".
Erich Lessing/Art Resource, NY

be the result of a long tradition whose origins go back even further in time. As at Chauvet, the paintings at Lascaux are almost all of animals. Experts agree that these naturalistic images are meaningful, although what their exact meaning is remains obscure.

The question of why a work of art was made arises also with ancient sculptures. Nearly as old as the Chauvet cave paintings is a little female statuette that often serves as an emblem of art history's beginnings. It is made of stone, was formed about 25,000 years ago, and was found near Willendorf, a town in present-day Austria (**14.2**). Less than 5 inches tall, the rounded figure is small enough to fit comfortably in the palm of a hand. Its face is obscured by a minutely detailed hairstyle that covers the entire head. The body's proportions are exaggerated. Skinny arms bend at the elbows to rest on a pair of heavy breasts. The ballooning midsection tapers down to legs that end just below the knees.

Numerous Paleolithic female statuettes have been found across a broad region. Carved of wood, ivory, and stone, or modeled in clay, they were produced over a period of thousands of years and in a variety of styles. Scholars long assumed that they were fertility figures, used in some symbolic way to encourage pregnancy and childbirth. Today's more cautious experts suggest that it is unlikely that a single explanation can account for all of them. The most we can say is that they testify to a widely shared belief system that evolved over time.

The Paleolithic Period, or Old Stone Age, gradually gave way to the Neolithic, or New Stone Age, beginning around 9000 B.C.E. and continuing for the next four thousand years. The Neolithic is named for new types of stone tools that were developed, but these tools were only one aspect of what in fact was a completely new way of life. Instead of gathering wild crops as they could find them, Neolithic people learned to cultivate fruits and grains. Farming was born. Instead of following migrating herds to hunt, Neolithic people learned to domesticate animals. Dogs, cattle, goats, and other animals served variously for help, labor, meat, milk, leather, and so on. Dugout boats, the bow and arrow, and the technology of pottery—clay hardened by heat—vastly improved the standard of living. Settled communities grew up and, with them, architecture of stone and wood. The most famous work of

Neolithic architecture in Europe is the monument of megaliths known as Stonehenge, in England, which we discussed in Chapter 1 (see 1.4).

Tantalizing glimpses of daily life in the Neolithic Period survive in the rock paintings of the Tassili n'Ajjer region of Algeria, in northern Africa (**14.3**). Today Tassili n'Ajjer is part of the Sahara, the world's largest desert. At the time these images were painted, roughly between 5000 and 2000 B.C.E., the desert had not yet emerged. Instead, the region was a vast grassland, home to animals, plants, and the people we see depicted here—five women, gathered near their cattle. Other images painted on the rock walls at Tassili n'Ajjer depict women harvesting grain or occupied with children, men herding cattle, and enclosures that may represent dwellings. The figures depict the essence of human and animal bodies in actively posed, stylized silhouettes. They were painted on the rock wall in differing scales and without a single, defined picture plane.

The art that has come down to us from the Stone Age is fragmentary and isolated: ancient cave paintings; a small statue of a woman; a circular stone monument; paintings on rock walls in the desert. Our examples are separated from one another by thousands of years and thousands of miles. Each one must have been part of a long local artistic tradition that stretched back into the past and continued for many millennia afterward. Yet for each one, we are faced with questions: "What came before, what came after, and where is it?"

In studying art of the past, it is important to keep in mind that the cultures we examine most fully are not necessarily those in which the most art was made or the best art was made. They are, rather, the cultures whose art has been found or preserved. Art has been produced at all times and in all places and by all peoples. But for it to be available to future generations for study, it must survive—possibly even after the culture that produced it has disappeared. Certain conditions foster the preservation of art, and the ancient cultures that we are able to study in depth across time fulfill most of them.

First, the artists worked in durable materials such as stone, metal, and fired clay. Second, the local environment was not destructive to artworks; for instance, the hot, dry climate of Egypt provides an excellent milieu for preservation. Third, the culture was highly organized, with stable population centers. Great cities normally house the richest troves of artwork in any culture, for they are where

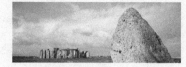
14.3 *Women and Cattle.* Rock painting at Tassili n'Ajjer, Algeria. Pastoralist style, after 5000 B.C.E.
Brother Luck / Alamy Stock Photo

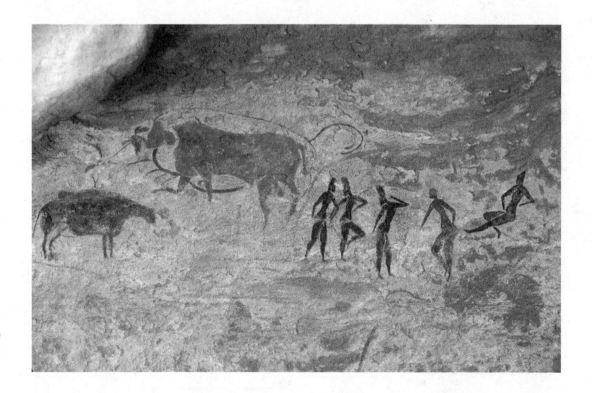

rulers dwell, wealth is accumulated, and artists congregate. Fourth, the culture had a tradition of caching its artworks in places of limited or no accessibility. A huge portion of the ancient art that has survived comes from tombs or underground caves.

The first cultures of the ancient Mediterranean world to meet most of these conditions arose in Mesopotamia—a region in the Near East (today more widely known as the Middle East)—and in Egypt, in northeastern Africa. Here, for the first time, we find a coherent, reasonably intact artistic production about which we have come to know a good deal. It is no accident that the civilizations of both Mesopotamia and Egypt developed along the banks of mighty rivers—the Tigris and Euphrates in Mesopotamia, and the Nile in Egypt. Rivers provided both a means of transportation and a source of water. Water enabled irrigation, which in turn allowed vaster and more reliable farming, which in turn supported larger and denser populations. Cities developed, and with them social stratification (the division of society into classes such as rulers, priests, nobles, commoners, and slaves), the standardization of religions and rituals, the creation of monumental architecture, and the specialization that allowed some people to farm, some to be merchants, and others to make art.

Our study of ancient Mediterranean worlds properly begins here, in the lands along the great rivers.

Mesopotamia

The region known to the ancient world as Mesopotamia occupied a large area roughly equivalent to the present-day nation of Iraq. Fertile soil watered by the Tigris and Euphrates rivers made Mesopotamia highly desirable, but a lack of natural boundaries made it easy to invade and difficult to defend. Successive waves of

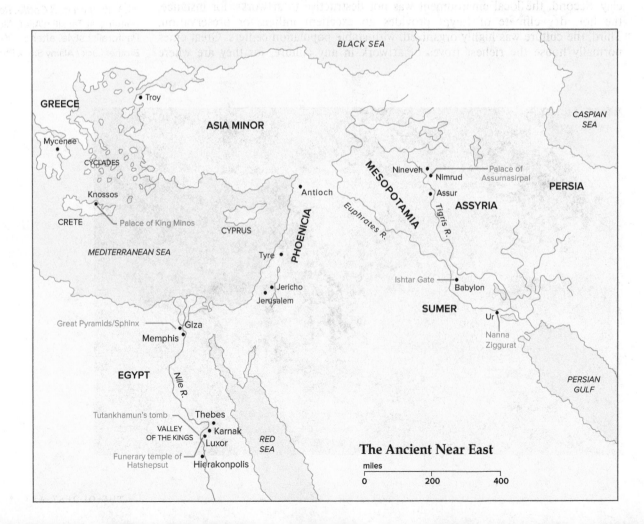

The Ancient Near East

miles
0   200   400

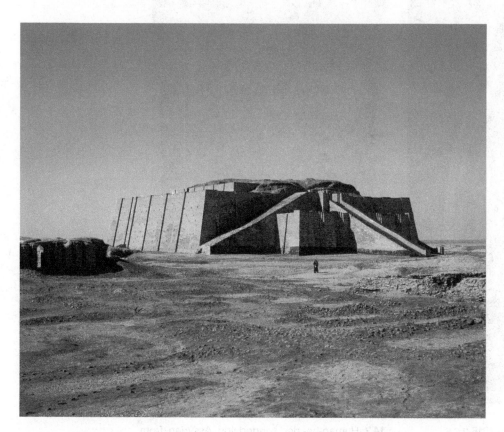

14.4 Nanna Ziggurat, Ur (present-day Muqayyar, Iraq). ca. 2100–2050 B.C.E.
Janzig/MiddleEast/Alamy Stock Photo

people conquered the region in ancient times, and each new ruling group built on the cultural achievements of its predecessors. Thus, we can speak with some justice of a continuing Mesopotamian culture.

The first cities of Mesopotamia arose in the southernmost area, a region called Sumer. By about 3400 B.C.E., some dozen Sumerian city-states—cities that ruled over their surrounding territories—had emerged. The Sumerians were the first people to leave behind them not just artifacts but also words: The wedge-shaped marks that they pressed into damp clay to keep track of inventories and accounts developed over time into a writing system capable of recording language. Called *cuneiform* (Latin for "wedge-shaped"), it served as the writing system of Mesopotamia for the next three thousand years.

Lacking stone, the Sumerians built their cities of sun-dried brick using the load-bearing construction technique. The largest structure of a Sumerian city was the **ziggurat**, a temple or shrine raised on a monumental stepped base (**14.4**). The example illustrated here, partially restored but still missing its temple, was dedicated to the moon god Nanna, the protective deity of the Sumerian city of Ur. In the flat land of Sumer, ziggurats were visible for miles around. They elevated the temple to a symbolic mountaintop, a meeting place for Heaven and Earth. Here priests and priestesses communicated with the gods and the faithful placed small figures offering their prayers.

The refined and luxurious aspect of Sumerian art is evident in this lyre (**14.5**) found in a queen's burial in what is now Iraq. The stringed instrument features a gold bull's head and a panel of lapis lazuli, shell, and limestone. The scenes on the panel depict a lion-headed eagle, bulls, and a man-bull holding aloft two leopards by the tail. Other lyres feature similar narratives, which may reference heroic epics, although their exact meaning is unknown.

By 2300 B.C.E., the Sumerian city-states had been conquered by their neighbors to the north, the Akkadians. Under their ruler Sargon I, the Akkadians established the region's first empire. Although it crumbled quickly, the empire seems to have extended all the way from the shores of the Mediterranean to the Persian Gulf. Sargon I's grandson Naram-Sin commemorated his victory over the Lullubi people

14.5 Queen's lyre. Iraq. 2600 B.C.E. Mixed media.
© The Trustees of the British Museum/ Art Resource, NY

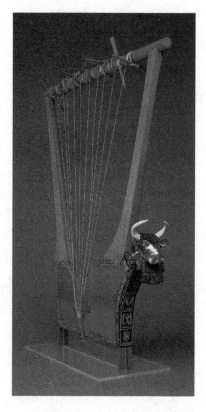

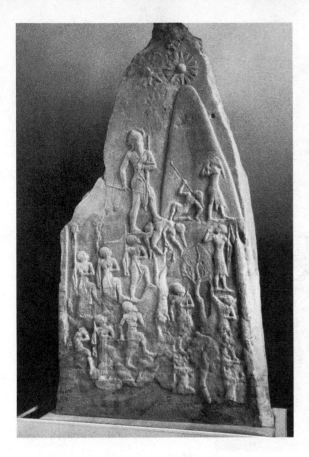

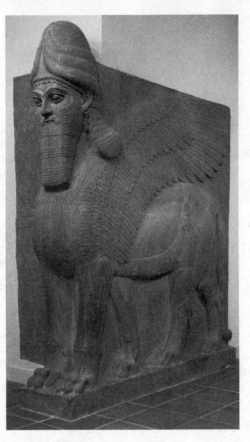

14.6 Stele of King Naram-Sin. 2254–2218 B.C.E.
Limestone, height 6' 6 ¾".
INTERFOTO/Alamy Stock Photo

14.7 Human-headed winged lion. Assyrian, from
Nimrud. 883–859 B.C.E. Limestone, height 10' 2 ½".
The Metropolitan Museum of Art, New York. Gift of John D.
Rockefeller, Jr., 1932, 32.143.2. Image © The Metropolitan
Museum of Art

of eastern Mesopotamia with the monumental Stele of King Naram-Sin (**14.6**). It pictures the Akkadian king dressed in godlike regalia and striding confidently over the defeated soldiers. Hierarchy of scale makes him larger than both his soldiers and the enemy in order to show his importance. His idealized anatomy indicates his strength and political might, while cuneiform text cut into the mountain recounts his victory. Viewers of this public monument would have had little trouble appreciating the king's might.

A more stable and long-lived Mesopotamian empire was established by the Amorites, who consolidated their rule over the region by about 1830 B.C.E. and established a capital at Babylon. The most important legacy of the Babylonian Empire is not artistic but legal: a set of edicts and laws compiled under the ruler Hammurabi (ruled ca. 1792–1750 B.C.E.). Known as Hammurabi's Code, it is the only complete legal code to survive from the ancient world, and it has provided historians with valuable insight into the structure and concerns of Mesopotamian society.

Mesopotamia's history was marked by almost continuous warfare and conquest, and a major goal of architecture was the erection of mighty citadels to ensure the safety of temples and palaces. Such a citadel was that of the Assyrian ruler Assurnasirpal II, built at Nimrud in the 9th century B.C.E. Based in northern Mesopotamia, the Assyrians had been gathering power and territory since before 1100 B.C.E. Their military strength increased significantly under Assurnasirpal II, and within a few centuries, they would amass the largest empire the region had seen by that time. Assurnasirpal's palace had gates fronted by monumental stone slabs carved into enormous human-headed winged beasts, a bull and a lion. The lion (**14.7**) wears a horned cap indicating divine status. Its body has five legs, so that from the front it appears motionless but from the side it is understood to be walking. Visitors to the citadel were meant to be impressed—and no doubt intimidated—by these majestic creatures.

Destroying Works of Art

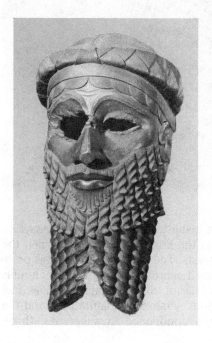

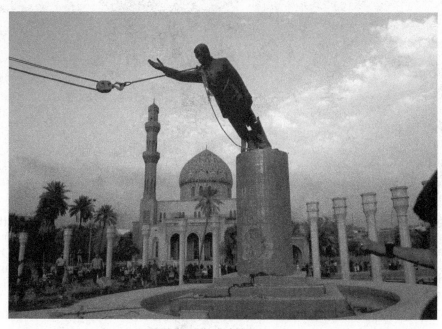

Why are works of art destroyed? What prompts the destruction?

In April 2003, American troops entered the Iraqi capital of Baghdad after defeating the troops of President Saddam Hussein. Almost immediately, Iraqi citizens began to destroy images of the dictator. Chains and ropes thrown around a sculpted portrait in the city's al-Fardous Square helped to topple the monumental likeness seen here. Participants and onlookers then jumped on the statue and beat it, just as they did with other fallen portraits of the leader.

The destruction of portraits like Saddam Hussein's is nothing new. The portrait of an Akkadian ruler (Sargon I?) was intentionally damaged almost 2,500 years ago by a vandal who gouged at its eye. Whether this act was for political or personal reasons is unknown. It is clear, however, that the work of art stood in for the person it represented, allowing the person to attack the ruler, even if just in effigy.

Removing portraits and other works of art following changes of regime or political ideology is common throughout history. In the mid-20th century, Germany rushed to remove portraits of Adolf Hitler, along with other Nazi symbols. Tearing down a sculpted portrait, painting over a mural, or chipping away a relief carving of a swastika symbolized the end of the Third Reich. In contemporary times, American states and cities grapple with the removal of monuments to Confederate soldiers. More than likenesses, the monuments represent the institution of slavery the Confederacy fought to preserve.

Politics is not the only reason art has been intentionally destroyed. Destruction for religious purposes accounts for much of it, as we saw in Chapter 3's Thinking About Art discussion on iconoclasm. Personal feelings also play a role. In 1956, someone threw acid at Leonardo da Vinci's *Mona Lisa* (see 2.1). In 1975, a man angry at the Rijksmuseum slashed Rembrandt's *Sortie of Captain Banning Cocq's Company of the Civic Guard* (*The Night Watch*) (see 17.12). While mental illness played a role in both of these outbursts, the attacks targeted works of art in part because we hold these objects in such high regard. We treat art as precious and special. Attempting to destroy it attracts attention.

(left) Head of an Akkadian Ruler (Sargon I?), from Nineveh, Iraq. ca. 2250 B.C.E. Bronze, height 12". Museum of Antiquities, Baghdad. www.BibleLandPictures.com/Alamy Stock Photo
(right) Iraqi President Saddam Hussein's statue in Baghdad's al-Fardous Square is pulled down on April 9, 2003, with the help of U.S. Marines. Trinity Mirror/Mirrorpix/Alamy Stock Photo

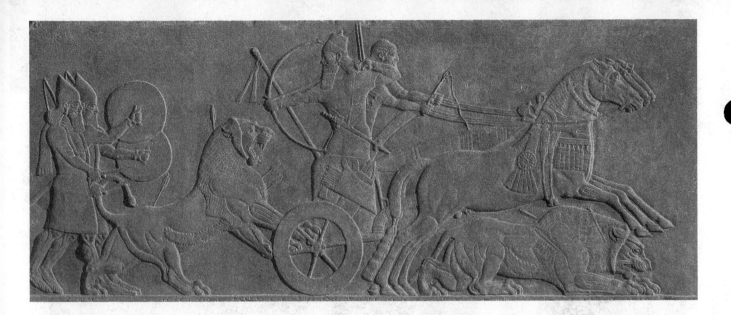

14.8 *Lion Hunt*, from the palace complex of Assurnasirpal II, Kalhu (present-day Nimrud, Iraq). ca. 850 B.C.E. Alabaster, height 39".
© The Trustees of the British Museum, London/Art Resource, NY

The walls of the palace were lined with alabaster reliefs depicting Assyrian triumphs and royal power. A popular subject is the lion hunt (**14.8**), in which the king is depicted slaying the most powerful of beasts. The ceremonial hunt was probably carried out as it is pictured here, with armed guards releasing captive animals into an enclosure for the king to kill from his chariot. Slaying lions was viewed as a fitting demonstration of kingly power. The lions' anatomy is naturalistic, and the many overlapping figures show the sculptor's confidence in suggesting three-dimensional space.

When the Babylonians again came to power in Mesopotamia, late in the 7th century B.C.E., they formed a kingdom now called the Neo-Babylonian. These "new" Babylonians surely must be ranked among the great architects of the ancient world. They developed a true arch before the Romans did, and were masters of decorative design for architecture. Moreover, like their forebears, they had a formidable leader in the person of Nebuchadnezzar, an enthusiastic patron of the arts who built a dazzling capital city at Babylon.

A genuine planned city, Babylon was constructed as a square, bisected by the Euphrates River, with streets and broad avenues crossing at right angles. Because stone is scarce in this region of Mesopotamia, the architects made liberal use of glazed ceramic bricks. Babylon must have been a city of brilliant color. Its main thoroughfare was the Processional Way, at one end of which stood the Ishtar Gate (**14.9**), built about 575 B.C.E. and now restored in a German museum. The gate

14.9 Ishtar Gate (restored), from Babylon. ca. 575 B.C.E. Glazed brick, height 48' 9".
bpk Bildagentur/Vorderasiatisches Museum, Staatliche Museen, Berlin, Germany/Olaf M.Teßmer/Art Resource, NY

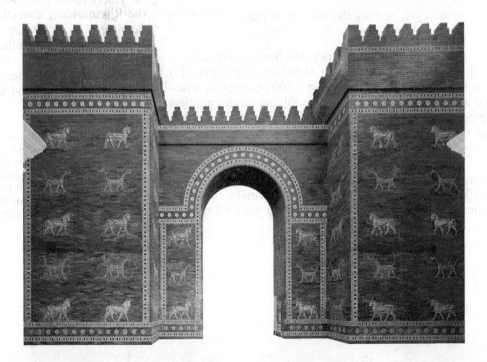

consists of thousands of glazed mud bricks, with two massive towers flanking a central arch. On ceremonial occasions, Nebuchadnezzar would sit under the arch in majesty to receive his subjects. The walls of the gate are embellished with registers of glazed ceramic animals, probably meant as spirit-guardians.

The history of Mesopotamia parallels in time that of its neighbor to the southwest, the kingdom of Egypt, with which it had regular contact. In Egypt, however, we will find considerably less political turmoil. Protected to the south by a series of cataracts (rocky, unnavigable stretches of the Nile) and to the east and west by vast deserts, Egypt during much of its long history was spared the waves of immigration and invasion that continually transformed Mesopotamia.

Egypt

The principal message of Egyptian art is continuity—a seamless span of time reaching back into history and forward into the future. The Greek philosopher Plato wrote that Egyptian art did not change for ten thousand years; although that is an exaggeration, there were many features that remained stable over long periods. The Sphinx (**14.10**), the symbol of this most important characteristic of Egyptian art, is the essence of stability, order, and endurance. Built about 2530 B.C.E. and towering to a height of 66 feet, it faces the rising sun, seeming to cast its immobile gaze down the centuries for all eternity. The Sphinx has the body of a reclining lion and the head of a man, thought to be the pharaoh Khafre, whose pyramid tomb is in the center (see 3.5). Egyptian kings ruled absolutely and enjoyed semidivine status, taking their authority from the sun god, Ra, from whom they were assumed to be descended. Both power and continuity are embodied in this splendid monument.

An even earlier relic from Egyptian culture, the so-called *Palette of Narmer* (**14.11**), illustrates many characteristics of Egyptian art. The palette (so named because it takes the form of a slab for mixing cosmetics) portrays a victory by the forces of Upper (southern) Egypt, led by Narmer, over those of Lower (northern)

RELATED WORKS

3.5 Pyramids at Giza

14.10 The Great Sphinx, Giza. ca. 2530 B.C.E. Limestone, height 66'. Nort/Shutterstock

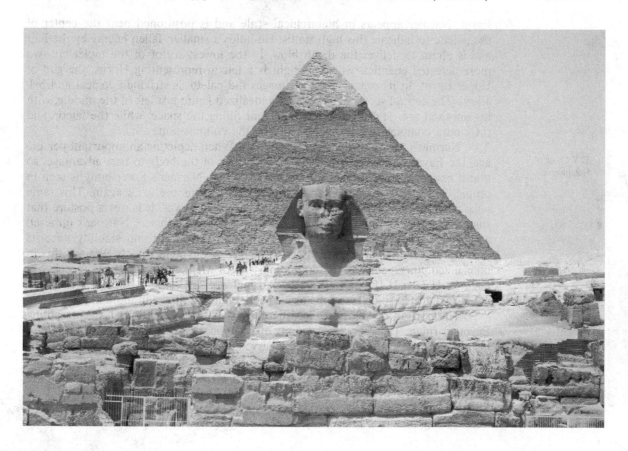

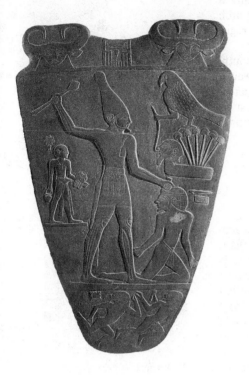

14.11 *Palette of Narmer*, from Hierakonpolis. ca. 3100 B.C.E. Slate, height 25". Egyptian Museum, Cairo. Werner Forman/Art Resource, NY

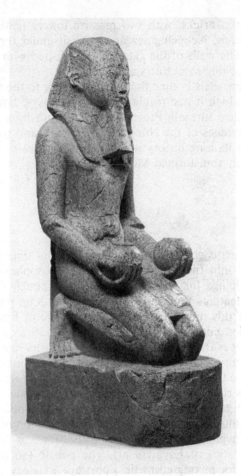

14.12 Large kneeling statue of Queen Hatshepsut. ca. 1479–1458 B.C.E. Granite, height 102 ¹⁵/₁₆". Metropolitan Museum of Art, New York, Rogers Fund, 1929

RELATED WORKS

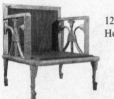

12.7 Chair of Hetepheres

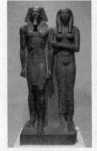

11.15 *Menkaure and Khamerernebty*

Egypt. Narmer appears in hierarchical scale and is positioned near the center of the palette to indicate this high status. He holds a smaller, fallen enemy by the hair and is about to deliver the death blow. In the lowest sector of the tablet are two more defeated enemies. At upper right is a falcon representing Horus, the god of Upper Egypt. In its organization of images the palette is strikingly logical and balanced. The central section has Narmer's idealized figure just left of the middle, with his upraised arm and the form of a servant filling the space, while the falcon and the victim complete the right-hand side of the composition.

Narmer's pose is typical of Egyptian art. When depicting an important personage, the Egyptian artist strove to show each part of the body to best advantage, so that it could be "read" clearly by the viewer. Thus, Narmer's lower body is seen in profile, his torso full front, his head in profile, but his eye front again. This same pose recurs throughout most two-dimensional art in Egypt. It is not a posture that suggests much motion, apart from a stylized gesture like that of Narmer's upraised arm. But action was not important to Egyptian art. Order and stability were its primary characteristics, as they were the goals of Egyptian society. We see this in official sculptures, such as the double portrait of Menkaure and Khamerernebty in Chapter 11 (see 11.15), and also in less formal works. Common people, such as the palette's defeated soldiers, on the other hand, could be shown in more natural poses.

The portrait of Menkaure also demonstrates the conventions for representing Egyptian rulers. He wears the symbols of his office: a headdress, a kilt, and a false beard. The same symbols appear in the carved portrait of Queen Hatshepsut (**14.12**), one of the few female rulers in Egypt's history. Egyptian artists developed the conventions for representing rulers by picturing male kings. Even when representing a female ruler, the desire for continuity dictated that the queen be represented as a man. Not only does she wear the headdress, kilt, and false beard, but also she has a young, idealized male body.

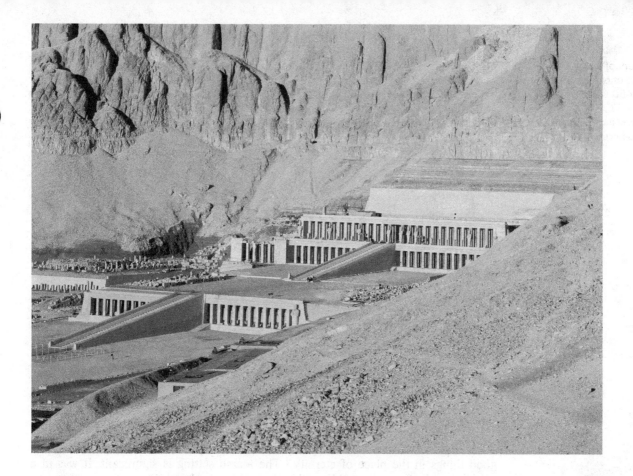

The sculpture of Hatshepsut, which pictures her making an offering to the god Amun-Re, was made for her royal funerary temple (**14.13**). While once Egyptians built massive pyramids with adjacent funerary complexes for their deceased rulers (see 3.5), by Hatshepsut's day, royal burials were more discreet. Funerary temples, on the other hand, became majestic sites for the worship of the deceased ruler, who had rejoined the gods in immortality. Rising in a series of three broad terraces, the post-and-lintel temple dedicated to Hatshepsut continues *into* the steep cliffs behind it, from which an inner sanctuary was hollowed out. More than two hundred statues of the queen once populated the vast complex, which contained shrines to several Egyptian deities as well as to Hatshepsut and her father, the ruler Thutmose I.

Egyptian painting reveals the same clear visual design and illustrative skill as the works in stone. A fragment of a wall painting taken from a tomb chapel in Thebes depicts a man named Nebamun, posed very much like the figure of Narmer (**14.14**). Again we see the lower body with its striding legs in profile, the torso and shoulders full front but with a nipple in profile, the face in profile, and the eye from the front again. Once more, hierarchy of scale means that, as the most important person in the scene, he is larger than the other figures.

As a mid-level official, Nebamun would have been buried in a sealed chamber dug somewhere beneath his painted chapel. He and his tawny cat are shown hunting birds in a marsh. Nebamun's idealized body is young, handsome, and athletic, the form he hopes to have in eternity. He holds a throw stick in one hand and grasps three flapping egrets with the other. The small, elegant woman standing behind him on the papyrus skiff is his wife, Hatshepsut. The still smaller girl between his legs is their daughter. All are depicted in the formal, dignified poses suited to elite members of society. Birds and butterflies fill the air. The birds are shown in profile, the view that gives the most information. The same goes for the fish in the water below. All are depicted in such closely observed detail that we can identify many of the species.

The scene represents an elite ideal of earthly leisure, now transposed to the afterlife. An inscription near Hatshepsut reads in part, "Taking enjoyment, seeing

14.13 Funerary temple of Hatshepsut, Deir el-Bahri. ca. 1460 B.C.E.
© Radius Images/Corbis

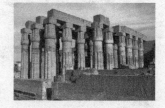

13.2 Temple of Luxor

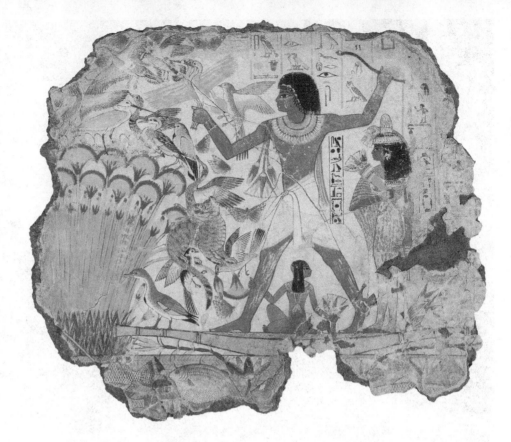

14.14 Fragment of a wall painting from the tomb of Nebamun, Thebes. ca. 1450 B.C.E. Paint on plaster, height 32".
© The Trustees of the British Museum, London/Art Resource, NY

good things in the place of eternity." The marsh setting is significant. It was in a marsh that the Egyptian goddess Isis prepared her husband, Osiris, for resurrection, and where life itself began at the time of creation. A marsh is thus a site where life renews itself, just as the man will renew himself by rising from death. Nebamun's victorious pose proclaims his ability to triumph in the journey to the afterlife, which was thought to be fraught with peril.

Egyptians' journey into the afterlife was guided by texts known as books of the dead (**14.15**). Written on papyrus scrolls, the books were placed in burials to help the deceased. They contained spells and hymns and pictured the dead person interacting with the gods. In the scene shown here, the scribe Hunefer's heart is

14.15 Book of the Dead of Hunefer. ca. 1292–1189 B.C.E. Papyrus.
© The Trustees of the British Museum, London/Art Resource, NY

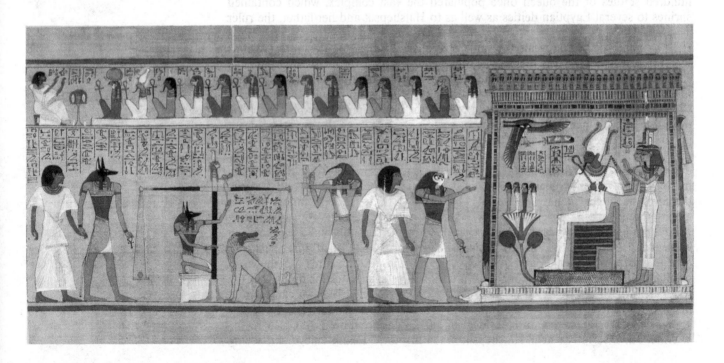

weighed by the jackal-headed god Anubis. Hunefer then walks with the god Horus to see the throned Osiris. Hieroglyphs above the figures offer a spell. The work preserves the conventions of Egyptian art, with the typical Egyptian view of the body mixing frontal and profile views, formal and rigid poses, and a logical and balanced composition.

One brief period in the history of Egyptian culture stands apart from the rest and therefore has fascinated scholars and art lovers alike. This was the reign of pharaoh Amenhotep IV, who came to power about 1353 B.C.E. For a civilization that prized continuity above all else, Amenhotep was a true revolutionary. He changed his name to Akhenaten and attempted to establish monotheism (belief in one god) among a people who had traditionally worshiped many gods. He built a new capital at what is now called Tell el-Amarna, so historians refer to his reign as the Amarna period. Akhenaten was apparently quite active in creating a new style of art for his reign, and under his direction the age-old, rigid postures of Egyptian art gave way to more relaxed, naturalistic, and even intimate portrayals.

In the charming domestic scene depicted in this limestone relief (**14.16**), Akhenaten and his queen, Nefertiti, sit facing each other on cushioned thrones. Akhenaten tenderly holds one of their three daughters, who gestures toward her mother and sisters. Seated on Nefertiti's lap, the older daughter looks up at her mother as she points across to her father; the youngest daughter tries to get her mother's attention by caressing her cheek. Above, Akhenaten's god, Aten, the sun-disk, shines his life-giving rays upon them. The sculpture is an example of **sunken relief**. In this technique, the figures do not project upward from the surface. Instead, outlines are carved deep into the surface, and the figures are modeled within them, from the surface down.

Akhenaten's reforms did not last. After his death, temples to the old gods were restored and temples that had been built to Aten were dismantled. The city of el-Amarna was abandoned, and the traditional Egyptian styles of representation were reimposed. Thus it is that the immobile mask of eternity greets us again in the stunning gold burial mask of Akhenaten's son and successor, the young Tutankhamun (**14.17**). He wears the regalia of office and has an idealized and timelessly youthful face.

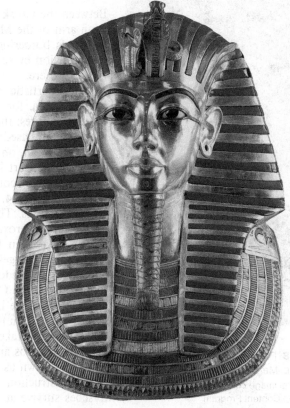

14.17 Burial mask of Tutankhamun. ca. 1323 B.C.E. Gold, inlaid with blue glass and semiprecious stones, height 21¼".
Egyptian Museum, Cairo. Scala/Art Resource, NY

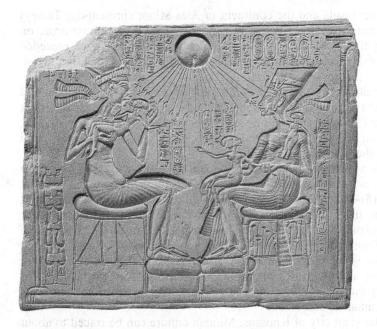

14.16 *Akhenaten and His Family*, from Akhetaten (present-day Tell el-Amarna). ca. 1345 B.C.E. Painted limestone relief, 12¼ × 15¼".
bpk Bildagentur/Aegyptisches Museum, Staatliche Museen, Berlin, Germany/Art Resource, NY

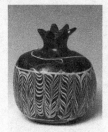

12.3 Bottle in the shape of a pomegranate

From earliest times, Egyptians buried their most lavish art in royal tombs. Rulers were sent into eternity outfitted with everything they would need to continue life in the sumptuous style they had known on Earth—furniture, jewelry, chariots, clothing, and artifacts of all kinds. From earliest times as well, grave robbers have coveted that buried treasure—and not for its artistic merits. Most of the royal tombs that have been discovered in modern times have been empty, their fabulous contents looted long ago. It was not until 1922 that modern eyes could assess the full splendor of ancient Egypt. In that year, the English archaeologist Howard Carter discovered the tomb of Tutankhamun, its treasures virtually intact after three thousand years.

Tutankhamun—quickly dubbed "King Tut" by the newspapers of the time—was a relatively minor ruler. The tombs of the great would have been far more lavish. Yet even Tutankhamun's tomb was a virtual warehouse of priceless objects, superbly crafted of alabaster, precious stones, and, above all, gold—gold in unimaginable quantities. Gold in Egyptian thought signified more than mere wealth. It was associated with the life-giving rays of the sun and with eternity itself. The flesh of the gods was believed to be gold, which would never decay. Tutankhamun's solid gold coffin, and the solid gold face mask that rested on the head and shoulders of his mummified body inside, were meant to confer immortality. Projecting over the young king's forehead are the alert heads of a cobra and a vulture, symbols of the ancient protective goddesses of Lower and Upper Egypt.

When Tutankhamun died, around 1323 B.C.E., Egyptian civilization was already ancient—a continuous culture that looked back confidently on some 1,700 years of achievement and power. Egypt would continue for 1,300 years into the future, but its years of supremacy were waning. Other, younger cultures were gathering force elsewhere around the Mediterranean. Two of these upstarts, Greece and Rome, would eventually conquer Egypt. We turn our attention to Greece next, after a brief look at some of the cultures that preceded it on the islands of the Aegean Sea.

The Aegean

Between the Greek peninsula and the continent of Asia Minor (present-day Turkey) is an arm of the Mediterranean Sea known as the Aegean. Greek culture arose on the lands bordering this small "sea within a sea," but the Greeks were preceded in the region by several fascinating cultures that thrived on the islands that are so plentiful there.

The artistic cultures of the Aegean parallel in time those of Egypt and Mesopotamia, for the earliest begins about 3000 B.C.E. There were three major Aegean cultures: the Cycladic, centered on a group of small islands in the Aegean; the Minoan, based on the island of Crete at the southern end of the Aegean; and the Mycenaean, on the mainland of Greece.

Cycladic art is a puzzle, because we know almost nothing about the people who made it. It consists almost exclusively of nude female figures such as the one illustrated here (14.18)—simplified, abstract, composed of geometric lines and shapes and projections. The figures vary in size from the roughly 1½-foot height of our example to approximately life-size, but they are much alike in style. Most of the figures have been found in burial settings. This, together with the standardized iconography, suggests some sort of ritual use. It seems likely that the figures were associated with ideas about fertility; they may well represent a female deity. To modern eyes, the Cycladic figurines seem astonishingly sophisticated in their sleek abstraction of the human figure.

Centered on the great city of Knossos, Minoan culture can be traced to about 3000 B.C.E. We take the name from a legendary king called Minos, who supposedly ruled at Knossos and whose queen gave birth to the dreaded creature, half-human, half-bull, known as the Minotaur. The palace at Knossos (14.19) features post-and-lintel construction with painted columns topped by pillow-like capitals. Numerous frescoes survive at Knossos—some fragmentary, some restored—and from these we

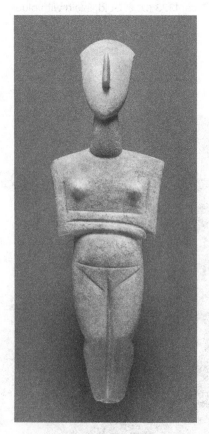

14.18 Female figure. Cycladic, 2400 B.C.E. Marble, height 16".
Digital image courtesy of the Getty's Open Content Program

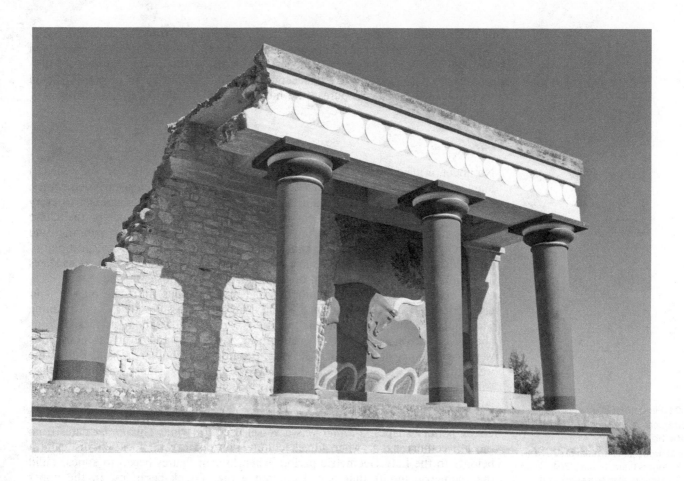

have formed an impression of a lighthearted, cheerful people devoted to games and sport. The fresco seen here pictures a charging bull in a landscape. Many graceful curves—the bull's back and horns, the rolling hills—reinforce our experience of motion, captured to the split second. Other murals feature acrobats leaping over bulls, servants carrying wine vessels, sea life, dancers, and landscapes.

Mycenaean culture, so called because it formed around the city of Mycenae, flourished on the south coast of the Greek mainland from about 1600 to 1100 B.C.E. Like the Minoans, the Mycenaeans built palaces and temples, but they are also noted for their elaborate burial customs and tombs—a taste apparently acquired from the Egyptians, with whom they had contact. It seems probable that Egypt or Nubia was also the source of the Mycenaeans' great supplies of gold, for they alone among the Aegean cultures were master goldsmiths. Burial places in and around Mycenae have yielded large quantities of exquisite gold objects, such as a *rhyton*, or drinking cup, in the shape of a lion's head (**14.20**). The craftsmanship of this vessel is wonderful, contrasting smooth planar sections on the sides of the face with the more detailed snout and mane.

The Classical World: Greece and Rome

When we use the word "Classical" in connection with Western civilization, we are referring to the two cultures discussed next in this chapter—ancient Greece and ancient Rome. The term itself indicates an aesthetic bias, for anything "classic" is supposed to embody the highest possible standard of quality, to be the very best of its kind. If true, this would mean that Western art reached a pinnacle in the few hundred years surrounding the start of our common era and has not been equaled

14.19 Northern entrance to Knossos palace with bull fresco, Crete. ca. 1500 B.C.E. Fresco, height approx. 32".
Branislav Petkovic/Alamy Stock Photo

14.20 *Rhyton* in the shape of a lion's head, from Mycenae. ca. 1550 B.C.E. Gold, height 8".
National Museum, Athens. akg-images

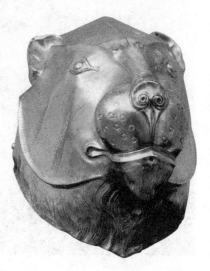

in the millennium and a half since then. This is a controversial idea that many would dispute vehemently. Few can deny, however, that the ancient Greeks and Romans *intended* to achieve the highest standards. Art and architecture were matters of public policy, and it was accepted that there could be an objective, shared standard for the best, the purest, the most beautiful.

Greece

No doubt, a major reason we so respect the ancient Greeks is that they excelled in many fields. Their political ideals serve as a model for contemporary democracy. Their poetry and drama and philosophy survive as living classics, familiar to every serious scholar. Greek philosophers, in fact, were the first to speculate on the nature and purpose of art, although they did not call it that. Sculpture, painting, and architecture were discussed as *techne*, roughly "things requiring a special body of knowledge and skill to make," a large category that included such products as shoes and swords. The idea survives in our words *technology* and *technique*.

Greek architecture and sculpture had an enormous influence on the later civilizations of Rome and, through Rome, Europe. We assume that Greek painting was equally brilliant, for ancient historians wrote vividly about it. Descriptions abound of such marvels as fruit painted so convincingly that even ravenous birds were fooled, and of rival artists striving to outdo one another in skill. But of the works themselves almost nothing has survived. Instead, we must content ourselves with images painted on terra-cotta vessels, which archaeologists have uncovered in large quantities.

An early example is the *krater* illustrated here (**14.21**). One of many standard Greek pottery shapes, a *krater* was a vessel used for wine. This *krater* dates from the 8th century B.C.E., when Greek culture first comes into focus. Stylistically it belongs to the Late Geometric period, when human figures began to appear amid the geometric motifs that had decorated earlier Greek ceramics. In the upper

14.21 Hirschfeld Workshop (attr.). *Krater.* ca. 750–735 B.C.E. Terra cotta, height 42 ⅝".
The Metropolitan Museum of Art, New York. Rogers Fund, 1914, 14.130.14. Image © The Metropolitan Museum of Art

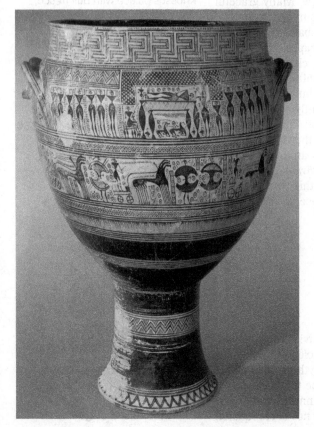

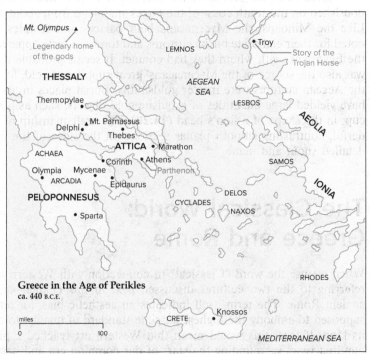

Greece in the Age of Perikles
ca. 440 B.C.E.

register, a narrative scene of a funeral ceremony is depicted. We see the deceased laid out on a four-legged couch. The checkerboard pattern above probably represents the textile that covered him. Wasp-waisted mourners stand to either side, slapping their heads and tearing their hair in grief. In the lower register, a procession of foot soldiers and horse-drawn chariots passes by. The highly abstracted figures are only beginning to break free from their flat, geometric world. Notice, for example, the triangular torsos of the mourners and the squares framed by their arms and shoulders.

The *krater* not only depicts a funeral but also served as a grave marker itself. It was found in the Dipylon Cemetery, a burial ground near the entrance to ancient Athens. Other funerary vessels have been found with a hole punched through the base, suggesting that libations—offerings of wine and water—were poured into them to pass directly into the earth of the grave beneath. Compared with the lavish burials of Egyptian pharaohs, the burial customs of the Greeks were bleak. Tombs of the Egyptian elite were fitted out for a luxurious life in eternity, since that is what they expected. The Greeks were not so optimistic. Death was death. The next world was imagined as a gray and shadowy place of little interest.

The sculptural tradition of Greece begins with small bronze figures of horses and men in styles much like the figures on the *krater* we just examined. At some point, however, Greek sculptors seem to have begun looking closely at the work of their neighbors the Egyptians, with whom they were in contact. Egyptian influence is clear in this life-size statue of a young man (**14.22**). Not only does the work reproduce the characteristic Egyptian pose—one leg forward, arms at the sides, hands clenched (see 11.15)—but it even follows the Egyptian grid system of proportions (see 5.20). Like Egyptian works, too, the block of original stone can still be sensed in the squared-off appearance of the finished sculpture.

In other respects, however, this figure is radically different from Egyptian works. Whereas Egyptian sculptors left their figures partially embedded in the granite block they were carved from, the Greek figure is released completely from the stone, with space between the legs and between the arms and the body. Whereas Egyptian men were depicted wearing loincloths, the Greek figure is nude. His neck ornament and elaborately braided hairstyle suggest that despite this nudity he is carefully groomed and appropriately dressed. His nudity, in other words, is a positive statement, not a temporary absence of clothing. Finally, whereas Egyptian statues depict specific individuals—rulers and other members of the elite—the Greek statue depicts an anonymous boy. Thousands of such figures were carved—perhaps as many as 20,000—all of them in the same pose, and all nude, young, and idealized, with broad-shouldered, slim-waisted, and fit bodies. They were placed as offerings in sanctuaries to the gods and set as grave markers in cemeteries. Scholars refer to them generically by the Greek word for youths or boys, *kouroi* (singular **kouros**). Statues of maidens, *korai* (singular **kore**), were also carved, although these are fewer in number and always fully clothed.

Kouroi and *korai* were created largely during the 6th century B.C.E., in the **Archaic** period of Greek art, so called because what would later be leading characteristics can be seen in their early form. In the *kouros* depicted here, the earliest known example, the treatment of the body and the face is still fairly abstract. As the tradition evolved, sculptors aimed increasingly at giving their statues a lifelike, convincing presence. They observed human bodies more attentively and copied them more faithfully, leading eventually to a style we know as naturalism. One reason for this was that many statues depicted gods. The Greeks imagined their gods in thoroughly human form, many of them highly idealized, dazzlingly beautiful, and eternally young. Every sanctuary contained a statue of the god or goddess it was dedicated to, and the more believable the statue was, the more present to believers the deity seemed.

Created only sixty years after the *kouros* we have been looking at, the amphora (storage vessel) illustrated next shows how rapidly Greek art evolved toward naturalistic representation (**14.23**). It also shows us something of the culture that made men's bodies available for direct observation. Created by the potter Andokides and a painter whom we recognize only as the "Andokides Painter," the vessel is one of

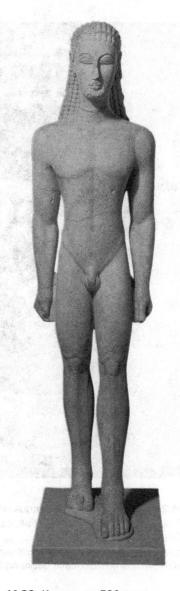

14.22 *Kouros*. ca. 580 B.C.E. Marble, height 6' 4".
The Metropolitan Museum of Art, New York. Fletcher Fund, 193.2 32.11.1. Image © The Metropolitan Museum of Art

RELATED WORKS

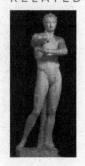

11.20 *Apoxyomenos*, after Lysippos

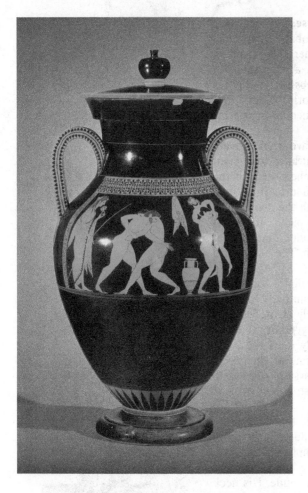

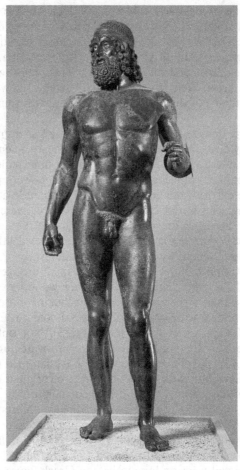

14.23 Andokides and the "Andokides Painter."
Amphora with gymnasium scene. ca. 520 B.C.E.
Terra cotta, height 22 13/16".
bpk Bildagentur/Antikensammlung, Staatliche Museen,
Berlin, Germany/Photo Ingrid Geske/Art Resource, NY

14.24 "Warrior A," discovered in the sea near Riace,
Italy. ca. 450 B.C.E. Bronze, with bone and glass eyes,
silver teeth, and copper lips and nipples, height 6' 8".
Museo Archaeologico Nazionale, Reggio Calabria, Italy.
Scala/Art Resource, NY

the earliest examples of the red-figure style, which evolved toward the end of the Archaic period. In the red-figure style, the ground is painted black, while figures are left mostly unpainted, with only thin black lines to describe the forms. The red that results is the natural color of fired earth. Earlier Archaic pottery had employed the reverse color scheme, with black figures painted on a red ground.

The amphora is decorated with a scene set in a gymnasium. From childhood on, exercise at the gymnasium was as much a part of Greek education as learning mathematics, music, and philosophy. Male citizens were in constant training, for they also formed their city's army. Greek athletes trained and competed in public in the nude. The scene on the amphora depicts two pairs of men wrestling. A trainer stands watching them, holding a flower up to his face. The flower, a symbol of beauty, indicates that the toned bodies of the athletes are to be as openly admired as their wrestling ability. Well-developed male bodies were on constant display, and their beauty was celebrated and depicted in art. There was an erotic component to this, but also a moral one, for beauty was felt to go hand in hand with nobility and goodness. Men in ancient Greece had public lives, and their bodies were public bodies. Women were largely confined to the domestic realm, and their bodies were not for public display, either in life or in art.

The Greek concern with lifelike representation flowered fully in statues such as this bronze warrior (**14.24**). Here is an idealized, virile male body, its anatomy distilled from observing hundreds of athletic physiques. The warrior stands in a relaxed yet vigilant **contrapposto**—the pose the Greeks invented to express the potential for motion inherent in a standing human. Bronze was the favored material for freestanding sculpture in ancient Greece, yet very few examples survive. The metal was too valuable for other purposes—especially weapons—and most ancient sculptures were melted down centuries ago. If it were not for marble copies of bronze works commissioned by later Roman admirers, we would know far less than we do about Greek art. The statue here is one of two life-size warrior figures discovered off the coast of Riace, Italy, in 1972. They had escaped destruction only by being lost at sea.

The Riace warriors were created during the **Classical** period of Greek art, which dates from 480 to 323 B.C.E. Although all ancient Greek and Roman art is broadly known as Classical, the art produced during these decades was considered by later European scholars to be the finest of the finest. During this period, Greece consisted of several independent city-states, often at war among themselves. Chief among the city-states—from an artistic and cultural point of view, if not always a military one—was Athens.

Like many Greek cities, Athens had been built around a high hill, or acropolis. Ancient temples on the Acropolis had crumbled or been destroyed in the wars. In about 449 B.C.E., Athens' great general Perikles came to power as head of state, and set about rebuilding. He soon embarked on a massive construction program, meant not only to restore the past glory of Athens but also to raise it to a previously undreamed-of splendor.

Perikles' friend the sculptor Phidias was given the job of overseeing all architectural and sculptural projects on the Acropolis. The work would continue for several decades, but it took an amazingly short time given the ambitious nature of the scheme. By the end of the century, the Acropolis probably looked much like the reconstruction shown here (**14.25**). The large, columned building at lower right in the photo is the Propylaea, the ceremonial gateway to the Acropolis through which processions winding up the hill would pass. At left in the photo, the building with columned porches is the Erechtheum, placed where Erechtheus, legendary founder of the city, supposedly lived.

14.25 Reconstruction of the Acropolis, Athens.
Roger Payne/Private Collection. © Look and Learn/Bridgeman Images

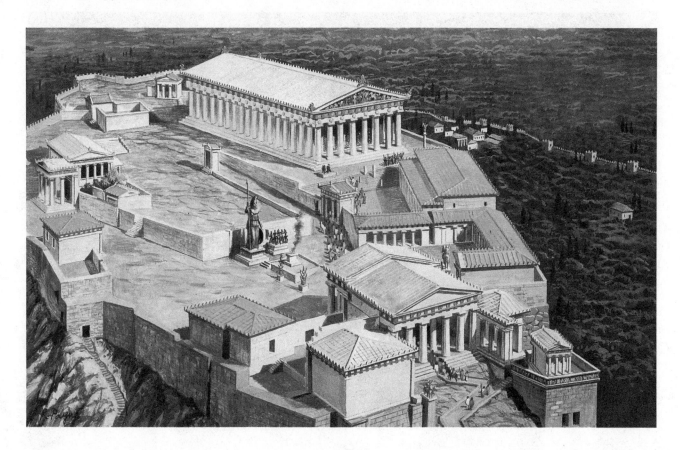

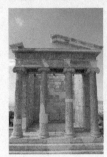

13.4 Kallikrates,
Temple of
Athena Nike

But the crowning glory of the Acropolis was and is the Parthenon (**14.26**). Dedicated to the goddess Athena *parthenos*, or Athena the warrior maiden, the Parthenon is a Doric-style temple with columns all around the exterior and an inner row of columns on each of the short walls. The roof originally rose to a peak, leaving a pediment (visible in the reconstruction) at each end. The pediments were decorated with sculptures, as was the frieze. In the manner of Greek temples, the Parthenon was painted in vivid colors, principally red and blue. The architects Iktinos and Kallikrates, directed by Phidias, completed the structure in just fifteen years.

The Parthenon has been studied in greater detail than perhaps any other building in the Western tradition, for it served generations of European architects as a model of perfection. Research has discovered numerous painstaking refinements that contribute to the temple's pleasing effect. First, a repeating ratio harmonizes its dimensions. The temple is a little more than twice as long as it is wide. The exact ratio is 9:4. This same ratio appears again when we compare the distance between the columns (measured from central axis to central axis) and the diameter of the columns. It appears for a third time in the dimensions of the facade: take away the steps and the pediment, and the width-to-height ratio of the facade is again 9:4. Legend claims there are no straight lines in the Parthenon, but that is probably a romantic exaggeration. Many of the lines we expect to be straight, however, are not. Instead, the builders adjusted the physical lines of the temple so they would appear to be straight. For example, tall columns that are absolutely straight may *appear* to bend inward at the center, like an hourglass, so the columns on the Parthenon have been given a slight bulge, known as **entasis**, to compensate for the visual effect. Also, a long horizontal, such as the Parthenon's porch steps, may appear to sag in the middle; to correct for this optical illusion, the level has been adjusted, rising about 2½ inches to form an arc that is higher at the center. A large building rising perpendicular to the ground may loom over the visitor and seem to be leaning forward; to avoid this impression, the architects of the Parthenon tilted the whole facade back slightly. Corner columns, seen against the sky, would have

14.26 Iktinos and Kallikrates. Parthenon, Athens. 447–432 B.C.E. DAJ/Getty Images

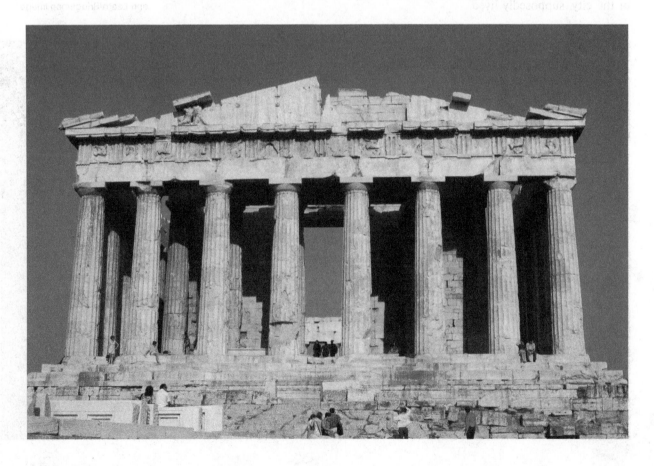

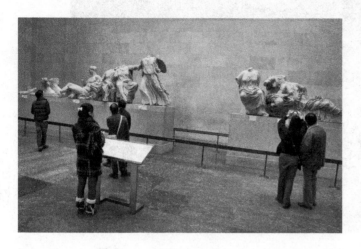

If the intentions of removing artifacts from their places of origin are for conservation and education, should such artifacts be returned when situations improve in the places of origin? How do politics, history, and technology factor into ownership of works of art?

Like most monumental buildings in antiquity, the Parthenon was originally ornamented with a rich program of sculpture. Only about half of its sculptures survive today, and of those, half are in the British Museum in London. How they got there and whether they should be returned is the subject of this essay.

To set the stage, we must sketch in a quick history of Greece. The Parthenon was built in the city-state of Athens during the 5th century B.C.E. Three centuries later, Greece was subsumed into the growing empire of Rome. The western portion of the Roman Empire disintegrated during the 5th century C.E.; the eastern portion continued for a thousand more years as Byzantium, a Greek-speaking Christian empire ruled from Constantinople (present-day Istanbul). In 1453, Constantinople was conquered by Muslim forces, and Greece was absorbed into the Ottoman Empire, where it remained until modern times.

In 1799, Thomas Bruce, 7th Earl of Elgin, was appointed ambassador of England to the Ottoman court. By that time, the Parthenon was in ruins. Early Christians had converted it into a church, in the process destroying many of its sculptures. During the 17th century, invading Venetian forces had fired on the Parthenon, which the Ottomans had been using to store gunpowder. The resulting explosion caused severe damage. Lord Elgin arrived with a plan to make plaster copies of the remaining Parthenon sculptures and send them back to England, but he quickly became convinced that the sculptures themselves needed to be removed to preserve them for posterity. As a diplomatic favor, the Ottoman court granted him a royal mandate to proceed. Detaching the sculptures from the building and shipping them to England took five years; Elgin paid for it out of his own personal fortune. He had intended to donate the marbles to the nation, but severe financial problems prompted him to ask for compensation. In the end, the British Museum, funded by Parliament, purchased the marbles for a fraction of what Elgin had spent to obtain them. The sculptures were first shown to the public in 1817, and they have been on permanent display ever since, the object of scholarly research and conservation efforts.

Not long after Elgin shipped the Parthenon marbles to England, Greece launched a war of independence against the Ottomans, which ended with a Greek victory in 1832. Almost immediately, Greek calls for the return of the marbles were heard. These calls have recurred regularly and with increasing frequency over the years. The British Museum has refused. The argument on both sides has taken many forms, but the trump card in the British response has always been this: How would you care for them? Indeed, sculptures left behind by Lord Elgin remained on the Parthenon until 1977, slowly decaying in the increasingly polluted air of modern Athens. Even after they were taken down, most were stored out of the public view, for Greek plans to build a state-of-the-art museum repeatedly came to naught—until recently.

In 2002, work began on a new museum designed by the Swiss-born architect Bernard Tschumi. Situated at the foot of the Acropolis, it opened to the public in June 2009 and includes a large gallery designed especially to display the Parthenon marbles. As of this writing, the British Museum has said that it would consider loaning the marbles to Greece for a limited time on the condition that British ownership is officially recognized. The Greek government has refused to borrow the marbles on these terms, and has suggested instead that negotiations be mediated by a third party, the United Nations Educational, Scientific and Cultural Organization (UNESCO). The British Museum declined to participate. Should the marbles be returned?

The Parthenon's east pediment sculpture at the British Museum. 438–432 B.C.E., Greece. David Lyons/Alamy Stock Photo

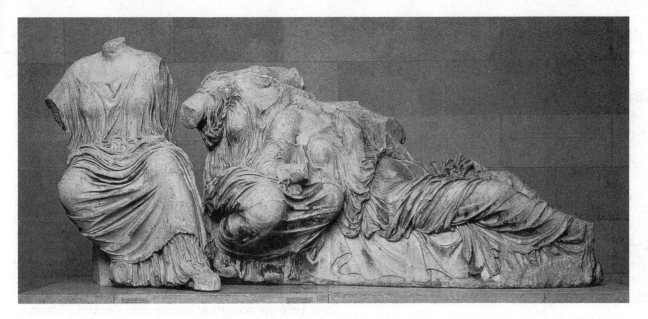

14.27 *Three Goddesses*, from the east pediment of the Parthenon.
ca. 438–432 B.C.E. Marble, over life-size.
The British Museum, London. Scala/Art Resource, NY

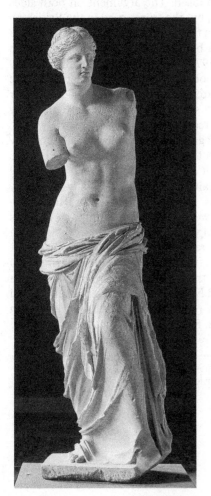

14.28 *Aphrodite of Melos* (also
called *Venus de Milo*). ca. 150 B.C.E.
Marble, height 6' 10".
Musée du Louvre, Paris. Erich Lessing/
Art Resource, NY

seemed thinner than inside columns, which have the building as a backdrop; therefore, the outside columns were made slightly heavier than all the others.

The inner chamber of the Parthenon once housed a monumental statue of Athena, made by Phidias himself of gold and ivory and standing 30 feet tall atop its pedestal. Contemporary sources tell us that Phidias was an artist of unsurpassed genius, but we must take their word for it, since neither the Athena nor any of his other sculptures are known to survive. Other sculptures from the Parthenon have been preserved, however, and these were probably made by Phidias' students, under his supervision.

The Parthenon sculptures represent a high point in the long period of Greek experimentation with carving in marble. One existing sculpture group, now in the British Museum, depicts *Three Goddesses* (**14.27**). In Perikles' time, this group stood near the far right side of the east pediment; if you imagine the figures with their heads intact, you can see how the composition fit into the angle of the triangle. Carved from marble and now headless, these goddesses still seem to breathe and be capable of movement, so convincing is their roundness. The draperies flow and ripple naturally over the bodies, apparently responding to living flesh underneath.

The last phase of Greek art is known as **Hellenistic**–a term that refers to the spread of Greek culture eastward through Asia Minor, Egypt, and Mesopotamia–lands that had been conquered by the Macedonian Greek ruler Alexander the Great. The beginning of the Hellenistic era is usually dated to Alexander's death in 323 B.C.E.

Hellenistic sculpture developed in several stylistic directions. One was a continuing Classical style that emphasized balance and restraint, as seen in one of the most famous extant Hellenistic works, the *Aphrodite of Melos*, also known as the *Venus de Milo* (**14.28**). Venus was the Roman equivalent of Aphrodite, the Greek goddess of love, beauty, and fertility. Sculptors of the late Classical period had begun admitting female nudes into the public realm–although only as goddesses or mythological characters. This statue exemplifies the ideal of female beauty that resulted. Her twisting pose may be explained by the theory that her missing arms once held a shield propped up on her raised knee. She would have been admiring her own reflection in a mirror, her draperies slipping provocatively as she contemplated her beauty.

A second Hellenistic style overthrew Classical values in favor of dynamic poses and extreme emotions. One of the best-known examples of this style is the *Laocoön Group* (**14.29**), which we know from what is probably a Roman copy of a Greek bronze of the 2nd century B.C.E.

Laocoön was a priest of the sun god Apollo, and his story involves one of the most famous events in Greek mythology. In the last year of the war between the Greeks and the Trojans, the Greeks devised a fabulous ruse to overrun the city of Troy. They built a giant wooden horse, concealed inside it a large number of Greek soldiers, and wheeled it up to the gates of Troy, claiming it was an offering for the goddess Athena. While the people of Troy were trying to decide whether to admit the horse, their priest, Laocoön, suspected a trick and urged the Trojans to keep the gates locked. This angered the sea god, Poseidon, who held bitter feelings toward Troy, and he sent two dreadful serpents to strangle Laocoön and his sons. The sculpture depicts the priest and his children in their death throes, entwined by the deadly snakes.

Compared with statues from the Classical period, such as the Riace warrior (14.24), the *Laocoön Group* seems theatrical. Its subject matter, filled with drama and tension, would have been unthinkable three centuries earlier. The Classical sculptor wanted to convey an outward serenity, and thus showed the hero in perfection but not in action, outside time, not throwing the spear but merely holding it. Hellenistic sculptors were far more interested than their predecessors in how their subjects reacted to events. Laocoön's reaction is a violent, anguished one, and the outlines of the sculpture reflect this. The three figures writhe in agony, thrusting their bodies outward in different directions, pushing into space. Unlike earlier figures, with their dignified reserve, this sculpture projects a complicated and intense movement.

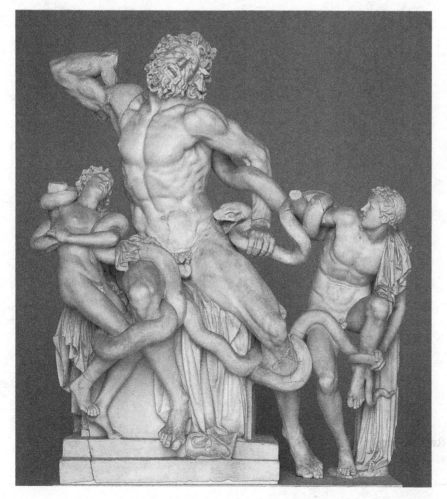

14.29 *Laocoön Group*. Roman copy, late 1st century B.C.E.–early 1st century C.E., of a Greek bronze(?) original, possibly by Agesander, Athenodorus, and Polydorus of Rhodes. Marble, height 8'.
Musei Vaticani, Rome. Nimatallah/ akg-images

Rome

The year 510 B.C.E. is usually cited as the beginning of the Roman era, for it was then, according to ancient historians, that the Roman Republic was founded. There followed a long period of expansion and consolidation of territories brought under Roman rule. Roman legions swept eastward through Greece into Mesopotamia, west and north as far as Britain, across the sea to Egypt, and throughout the rim of northern Africa. In 27 B.C.E., when Augustus took the title of "caesar," Rome officially became an empire.

Rome came of age during the Hellenistic period, when the prestige of Greek culture was at its height in the ancient Mediterranean world. The Romans were great admirers of Greek achievements in the arts. Many works were taken from Greece and brought to Rome. Statues and paintings were commissioned from Greek artists, and copies were made in marble of Greek bronze originals, such as the *Laocoön Group* (see 14.29) illustrated earlier.

One aspect of Hellenistic art was a tendency toward realistic portrayals of individuals, as opposed to idealized portrayals of *types* of people. No longer forever young and perfect, an athlete such as a boxer might be portrayed as the survivor of years of physically punishing bouts, his face lined, his body thickening with the onset of middle age. Roman sculptors excelled at this realism in their portrait busts of ordinary citizens, who wanted to be remembered as individuals.

One such example is the *Funerary Portrait of Gratidia M. L. Chrite and M. Gratidius Libanus* (**14.30**). This double portrait was once attached to a tomb. Mausoleums lined the main roads leading out of Rome, and portraits such as this were set into their facades so that the dead seemed to be looking out of a window onto the living. The man is old. We see the folds of his sunken face and the lines

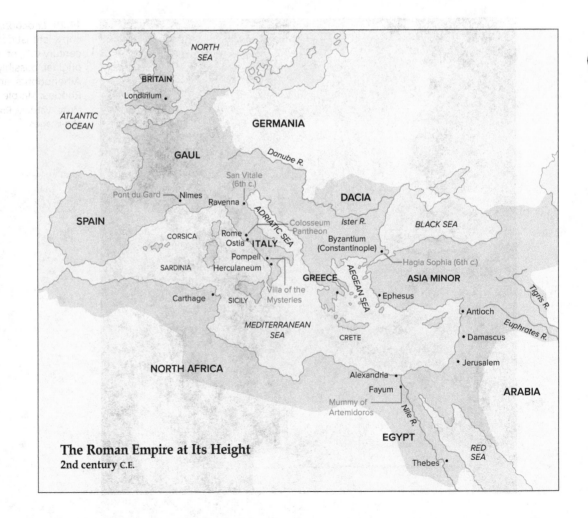

The Roman Empire at Its Height
2nd century C.E.

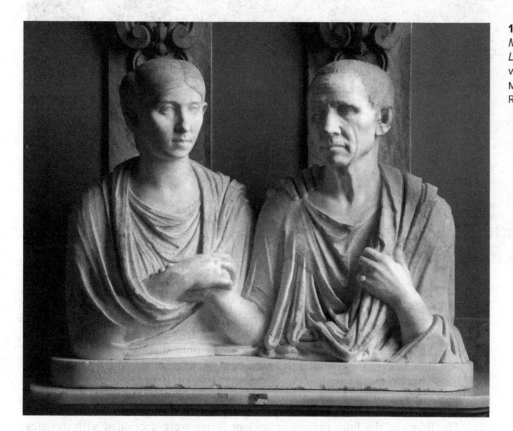

14.30 *Funerary Portrait of Gratidia M. L. Chrite and M. Gratidius Libanus*. 10 B.C.E.–10 C.E. Marble with traces of color, height 23 ¾". Museo Pio Clementino, Musei Vaticani, Rome. © Vanni Archive/Art Resource, NY

on his brow, but also the laugh lines at the edges of his eyes. His wife's image seems more idealized. Perhaps she was younger, or perhaps this was a request. Their right hands are joined in a gesture from the Roman marriage ceremony. Her left hand rests affectionately on his shoulder; his left hand draws our attention to the heavy folds of his toga, a symbol of Roman citizenship. An inscription that was once nearby states that he was Greek in origin and suggests that he was the son of a freedman, an ex-slave. No wonder the right to wear the toga of a full citizen meant so much to him.

The greatest honor that could be bestowed on a Roman ruler was a portrayal in bronze on horseback. Equestrian statues of emperors crowded the Roman forum, their gilt surfaces gleaming. A description of Rome dating from around 320 C.E. speaks of twenty-three such statues. The Greeks, too, had honored their leaders with equestrian statues. Yet of all these only a single example has survived, the statue of Marcus Aurelius that we looked at in Chapter 3 (see 3.6). The equestrian statues of rulers and soldiers that ornament cities around the world are the direct descendants of this fine work.

The Romans were equally masterful at painting, but were it not for a tragedy that occurred in 79 C.E., we would know little more about Roman painting than we do about the Greek. In that year Mt. Vesuvius, an active volcano, erupted and buried the town of Pompeii, about 100 miles south of Rome, along with the neighboring town of Herculaneum. The resulting lava and ash spread a blanket over the region, and this blanket acted as a kind of time capsule. Pompeii lay undisturbed, immune to further ravages of nature, for more than sixteen centuries. Then, in 1748, excavations were undertaken, and their findings were made public by the famous German archaeologist Joachim Winckelmann. Within the precincts of Pompeii the diggers found marvelous frescoes that were exceptionally well preserved. Pompeii was not an important city, so we cannot assume that the most talented artists of the period worked there. In fact, there is some evidence to suggest that the fresco painters were not Roman at all, but immigrant Greeks. Nevertheless, these wall paintings do give some indication of the styles of art practiced within the empire at the time.

RELATED WORKS

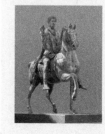

3.6 Equestrian statue of Marcus Aurelius

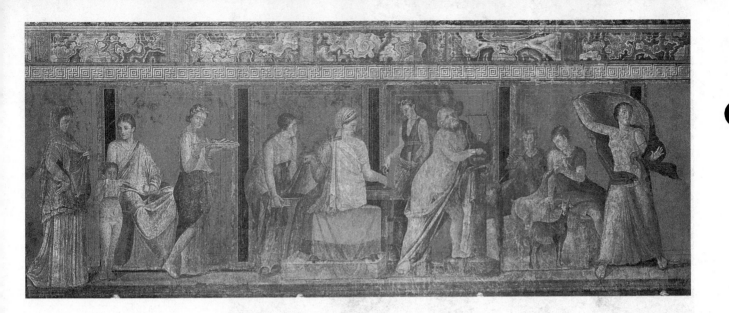

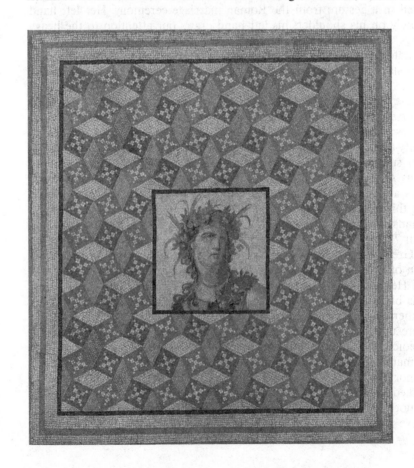

14.31 Wall painting, from Villa of the Mysteries, Pompeii. ca. 50 B.C.E. Fresco.
Scala/Art Resource, NY

One fresco, from a house known as the Villa of the Mysteries (**14.31**), shows a scene believed to represent secret cult rituals associated with the Greek wine god, Dionysus—known to the Romans as Bacchus. The figures stand as though on a ledge, in shallow but convincing space, interacting only slightly with one another. Although the artist has segmented the mural into panels separated by black bands, the figures overlap these panels so freely that there is no strong sense of individual episodes or compartments. Rather, the artist has established two rhythms—one of the figures and another of the dividing bands—giving a strong design unity.

The floors of the finer houses in ancient Rome were decorated with mosaics (**14.32**). The panel illustrated here once adorned a home at a seaside resort. At the center is the bust of a female personification of Spring. She wears a crown and necklace of flowers and fruits. To make the figure lifelike, the artist modeled the

14.32 Mosaic floor panel. 2nd century C.E. Stone, tile, and glass, 89 × 99".
The Metropolitan Museum of Art, New York. Purchase, Joseph Pulitzer Bequest, 1938

face and neck. He used darker tesserae to simulate shadows falling on her three-dimensional figure. The surrounding areas are filled with geometric forms that play with space. The white diamonds appear to be the tops of boxes, while the gray squares look like the vertical sides of the box. Or are the yellow diamonds the sides and the reddish squares the top? It is an optical illusion.

For all their production in sculpture and painting, the Romans are best known for their architecture and engineering. We saw two of their masterpieces, the Pont du Gard and the Pantheon, in Chapter 13 (see 13.9, 13.13, 13.15). But the most familiar monument—indeed, for many travelers the very symbol of Rome—is the Colosseum (**14.33**).

The Colosseum was planned under the emperor Vespasian and dedicated in 80 C.E. as an amphitheater for gladiatorial games and public entertainments. A large oval covering 6 acres, the Colosseum could accommodate some 50,000 spectators—about the same number as most major-league baseball stadiums today. Few of the games played inside, however, were as tame as baseball. Gladiators vied with one another and with wild animals in bloody and gruesome contests.

Even in its ruined state, this structure displays the genius of the Romans as builders. The Colosseum rises in four stories, each of which corresponds to a seating level inside. Archways on the first three stories open onto the barrel-vaulted corridors that ring the interior. The upper two tiers of arches once held statues; the street-level arches served as numbered entrances. (Some of the original numbers can still be seen.) The arches are framed by ornamental engaged or half-columns, with each tier distinguished by a different order: Tuscan on the first level, Ionic on the second, and Corinthian on the third. (The plain Tuscan order was a Roman addition to the Greek orders.) The columns appear to support a horizontal entablature that separates each level, but this is also decorative. On the fourth level, the columns give way to flat pilasters and the arches give way to small windows, which originally alternated with large bronze shields. Tall masts once ringed the top of the wall. They served to suspend a gigantic awning over the interior, shading at least some seats from the hot Roman sun. The arena consisted of a wooden stage covered with sand and fitted with trapdoors. Beneath it was a warren of stone corridors (still visible today), cells for animals, hoisting equipment, and a subterranean passageway that led to a nearby gladiator training camp. The building was fitted with an intricate drainage system for rainwater, and its massive foundations are set almost 40 feet into the ground. The Romans built things to last.

RELATED WORKS

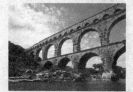

13.9 Pont du Gard

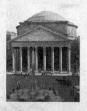

13.13 Pantheon

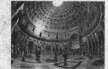

13.15 Interior of the Pantheon

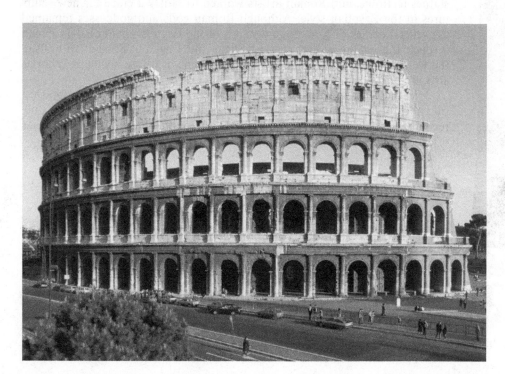

14.33 Colosseum, Rome. 72–80 C.E.
Adam Woolfitt/Robert Harding

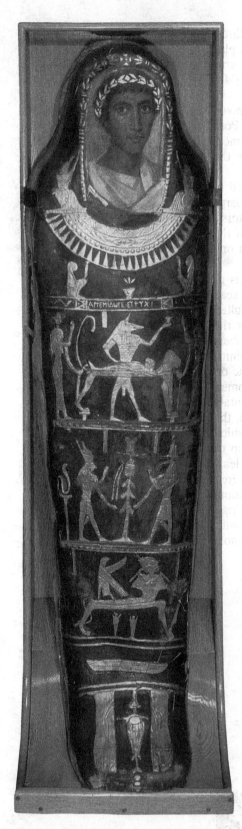

By the year 100 of our common era, the Roman Empire ringed the entire Mediterranean Sea. It extended eastward through Asia Minor and into Mesopotamia, westward through Spain, northward into England, and south across North Africa and Egypt. Yet the many cultures that came under Roman rule did not cease to be themselves and suddenly become Roman. Instead, the empire extended its umbrella over a vast array of cultures, languages, and religions, all of which now mingled freely, thanks to Roman rule and Roman roads.

Our last illustration gives us a glimpse of the multicultural world of late Rome (**14.34**). The illustration shows the mummy of a young man named Artemidoros, from Fayum, Egypt. It dates from sometime in the 2nd century C.E. Egypt was then part of the Roman Empire, and Artemidoros was a Roman subject. Artemidoros, however, is a Greek name, and it is written in Greek letters on his mummy. Why a Greek in Egypt? Alexander the Great had conquered Egypt in 323 B.C.E. For the next three hundred years, Egypt was ruled by a Greek dynasty, the Ptolemies. Greeks constituted an elite part of the population, but although they preserved their own language, they adopted the Egyptian religion, with its comforting belief in an eternal afterlife. Thus, the body of Artemidoros, an Egyptian of Greek ancestry and identity, was mummified for burial, and on his mummy are depicted ancient Egyptian gods, including Anubis, the jackal-headed god of the dead, visible at the center just under Artemidoros' name.

Rome conquered Egypt from the last of the Ptolemies, the celebrated queen Cleopatra, in 30 B.C.E. Greek remained the principal administrative language of Egypt, even under Roman rule. Roman customs and fashions, however, were widely imitated by Egyptians who wanted to appear "up to date." One such custom was the funeral portrait, a commemorative painting of a recently deceased person. Thus, Artemidoros' mummy includes a funeral portrait, painted in encaustic on wood in a Greek–Roman style. What are we to call Artemidoros? Roman-Greek-Egyptian? After thousands of years of history, cultural identities could have many layers in the ancient Mediterranean world.

Influence flowed from Rome's conquests back to Rome, as well. Like the Greeks before them, the Romans were fascinated by Egyptian culture, which was so much older than their own. They imported many Egyptian statues to Rome, and Roman artists worked to satisfy a craze for new sculptures in the Egyptian style. Although Roman gods and goddesses remained the official deities of Rome, the worship of the Egyptian goddess Isis spread through the empire as far away as Spain and England. So did Mithraism, the worship of the sun god of the Persians, some of whose ancient territories also fell under Roman rule.

In these heady if sometimes perplexing times, who could have foreseen that the future would belong to a completely new religion that had only recently arisen in the eastern part of the vast empire? Based on the teachings of an obscure Jewish preacher named Jesus, it was called Christianity.

14.34 Mummy case of Artemidoros, from Fayum. 100–200 C.E. Stucco casing with portrait in encaustic on limewood with added gold leaf, height 5' 7 ¼".
© The Trustees of the British Museum, London/Art Resource, NY

Chapter 15
Christianity and the Formation of Europe

In this chapter, you will learn to

LO1   describe the art made to support the rise of Christianity,

LO2   explain the art and architecture of Byzantium,

LO3   discuss the objects and buildings made in Europe during the Middle Ages, and

LO4   identify the characteristics of art that anticipated the Renaissance.

According to tradition, Jesus, known as the Christ or "anointed one," was born in Bethlehem during the reign of Emperor Augustus. In time his followers would become so influential in world affairs that our common calendar takes as its starting point the presumed date of Jesus's birth, calling it "year 1." As a matter of fact, the 6th-century calendar-makers who devised this plan were wrong in their calculations. Jesus probably was born between four and six years earlier than they had supposed, but the calendar has nevertheless become standard.

The faith preached by the followers of Jesus spread with remarkable speed through the Roman Empire; yet, that empire itself was about to undergo a profound transformation. Overextended, internally weakened, and increasingly invaded, it would soon disintegrate. The western portion would eventually reemerge as western Europe—a collection of independent, often warring kingdoms united by a common religious culture of Christianity. The eastern portion would survive for a time as the Byzantine Empire, a Christianized continuation of a much-diminished Roman Empire. The Near East, Egypt, North Africa, and most of Spain, meanwhile, would become the heartlands of yet another new religious culture, Islam. (We will discuss the arts of Islam in Chapter 18.)

This chapter continues the story of the Western tradition with the rise of Christianity, the arts of Byzantium, and the formation of western Europe.

The Rise of Christianity

Christianity was but one of numerous religions in the late Roman Empire, but it quickly became one of the most popular and well organized. Rome's attitude toward this new cultural force within its borders varied. Often, the faith was tolerated, especially since it came to attract an increasing number of wealthy and influential people. At other times, Christians were persecuted, sometimes officially and sometimes by mobs. One reason for the persecutions was that Christians refused to worship the gods and goddesses of the state religion, including the emperor himself, in addition to their own god. Clearly, such people were a threat to the political stability and well-being of the empire.

Christianity's situation changed abruptly in the year 313, when the Roman emperor Constantine issued an edict of tolerance for all religions. Not only were all faiths now free to practice openly, but also Constantine himself patronized Christianity. While battling his political enemies in 312, Constantine had had a vision of a cross with the inscription *In hoc signo vinces*, or "In this sign, conquer." He interpreted this to mean that following Christian teachings and worshiping the Christian god would lead him to victory. He won the battle and converted to the Christian faith. His Triumphal Arch (**15.1**), a monument erected to commemorate his victories, pictures the battle that secured his imperial title as well as scenes of past emperors' triumphs and personifications of victory. The relief sculpture is

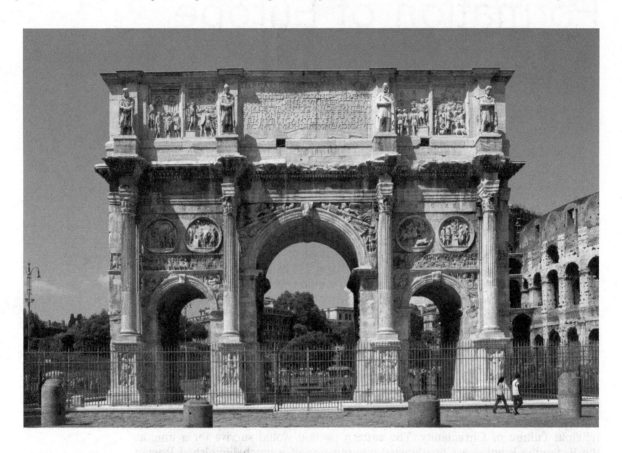

15.1 Arch of Constantine, Rome. 312–15 C.E. Marble.
Peter Noyce/Alamy Stock Photo

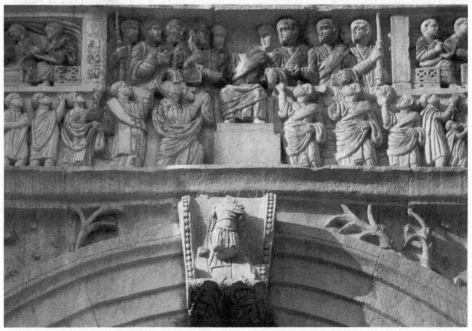

15.2 Constantine and his court, from the Arch of Constantine.
funkyfood London - Paul Williams/Alamy Stock Photo

arrayed across the marble structure, which features a central barrel-vaulted passageway flanked by two smaller openings. A tall attic story includes an inscription celebrating Constantine's strength and divine inspiration. Erected in the center of Rome next to the Colosseum, the arch symbolized the emperor's power and his imperial lineage.

To decorate his arch, Constantine borrowed relief sculptures made for his predecessors Trajan, Hadrian, and Marcus Aurelius. These images employ the naturalistic style of Classical art. Reliefs commissioned by Constantine, on the other hand, reveal a very different approach. The panel picturing Constantine and his court (**15.2**) features small, stereotyped figures, drapery described with thick lines, and limited spatial depth. The style of art in the Roman Empire had changed. The beauty of the human body was no longer important to artists. Now art emphasized symbolism and narrative clarity, with signs borrowed from pagan art but repurposed with Christian meaning. The idealized bodies and individualized faces of the Classical era had been replaced with stylized figures and generic facial features. Art reflected the Christian shift of attention from the well-being of the body to the cultivation of the soul.

Most early worship took place in private homes, although only one such early house-church has been discovered. Some of the earliest Christian art has been preserved in underground burial chambers that were later forgotten. The sarcophagus containing the remains of the Roman patrician Junius Bassus (**15.3**) employs the same simplified style as Constantine's reliefs, as well as a fascinating assortment of Roman imagery borrowed for Christian purposes. The sarcophagus represents stories from Jesus's life and scenes from the Bible within a high-relief, architectural setting. In the upper, central section, Jesus appears between two figures. The artist based his divine likeness on Roman images of the youthful, beardless sun god Apollo. The enthroned Jesus shows his dominion over heaven and earth by resting his feet on another borrowed sign: a Roman personification of the heavens. These and other Roman symbols became a convenient and familiar vocabulary from which Christian artists and patrons drew the images of the new faith.

15.3 Sarcophagus of Junius Bassus. 359 C.E. Marble, height 48". Lanmas/Alamy Stock Photo

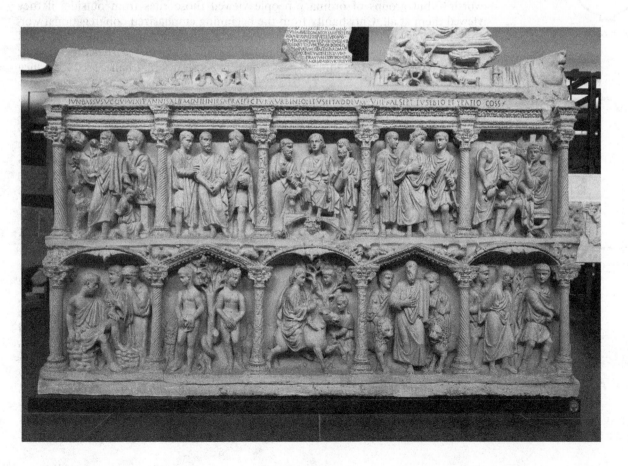

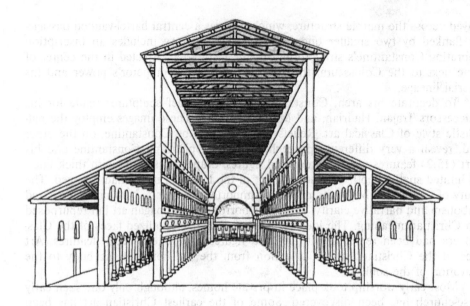

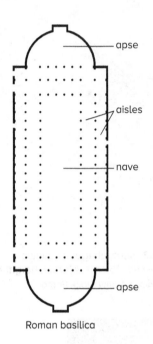

apse

aisles

nave

apse

Roman basilica

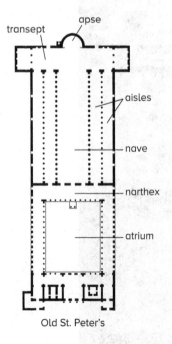

transept

apse

aisles

nave

narthex

atrium

Old St. Peter's

15.5 Plan of a Roman basilica (top) and plan of Old St. Peter's (bottom).

Christian buildings also borrowed from Roman models. Under Constantine's imperial sponsorship, architects raised a series of large and opulent churches at key locations in the empire. One of these was Old St. Peter's, built on the spot in Rome where it was believed that Peter, Jesus's first apostle, had been buried. This structure was demolished in 1506 to make way for the "new" St. Peter's, which is still standing (see 16.10), but contemporary descriptions and drawings have enabled scholars to make informed guesses about its design (**15.4**).

What should a church look like? Most Roman, Greek, and even Egyptian and Mesopotamian temples had essentially been conceived as dwelling places for the gods they were dedicated to. Priests might enter to perform rites of sacrifice and worship, but groups of ordinary people viewed those rites from outside, if they viewed them at all. Christianity from the beginning emphasized congregational worship, and so a fundamentally different kind of building was needed, one that could contain a lot of people. Roman architects already had such a structure in their repertoire of standard building types, a multipurpose meeting hall called a **basilica** (**15.5**, top).

As the plan shows, a basilica was basically a long, rectangular hall. Entrances might be on the long or the short sides (here, they are on the long sides). At one or both ends (both, in this example) might be a curved section called an **apse**. To admit light, the open central space, called the **nave**, extended up higher than the surrounding **aisles**. This upward extension was called the **clerestory**, and it was pierced with windows called clerestory windows. If you look back at the drawing of Old St. Peter's (see 15.4), you can now clearly see the central nave with its clerestory windows and the lower side aisles that buttress it. In the distance, at the far end of the nave, is an apse.

A plan of Old St. Peter's (**15.5**, bottom) makes this clear and also shows an additional element. The basilica form is designed with the entry on one of the short sides. Inside we find the wide central nave flanked by narrower aisles. At the far end is the apse. A natural focal point for anyone entering the church, the apse provides a setting for the altar, the focal point of Christian worship. In addition, this far wall is extended slightly to each side of the building. The extensions create a lengthwise section perpendicular to the nave called a **transept**. Together, nave and transept form a cross, a fundamental Christian symbol. Preceding the church was an atrium. An open courtyard surrounded by a covered walkway, the atrium was a standard element of Roman domestic architecture. The arm of the walkway directly in front of the church served as an entry porch called a **narthex**. The elements here—nave, aisles, clerestory, apse, transept, and narthex—formed the basic vocabulary of church architecture in the West for many centuries. We will use these words often in this chapter.

Byzantium

In 324, Constantine made another decision with far-reaching consequences: Judging that the empire could be more securely ruled from the East, he ordered his architects and engineers to transform the ancient Greek colony of Byzantio, known in Latin as Byzantium, into a new capital city called Constantinople (present-day Istanbul, in Turkey). Six years later, he moved his administration there.

The actual territory ruled from Constantinople varied greatly over the centuries. At first, it was the entire Roman Empire. By the time the city was conquered by Islamic forces in 1453, it was a much-reduced area. But no matter the actual extent of their dominion, the title Byzantine rulers inherited was "emperor of all the Romans." They viewed themselves as the legitimate continuation of the ancient Roman Empire, with one important difference: Byzantium was Christian. Whereas Constantine had extended his protection and patronage to Christianity, his successors went one step further—they made Christianity the official state religion. Church and state were intertwined in Byzantium, and its art marries the luxurious splendor of a powerful earthly kingdom—its gold and silver and jewels—with images that focus on an eternal, heavenly one.

The great masterpiece of early Byzantine architecture is the Hagia Sophia, which we examined in Chapter 13 (see 13.16, 13.17). A smaller gem of the early Byzantine style is San Vitale, built during the 6th century in Ravenna, Italy, which was then under Byzantine control (15.6, 15.7). San Vitale does not follow the cross plan that became standard for Western churches but, instead, uses a central plan favored in the East. Central-plan churches are most often square with a central dome, as is the Hagia Sophia. San Vitale, however, takes the unusual form of an octagon. Although an apse protrudes from one wall and a narthex is attached to two others, the fundamental focus of the building is at its center, over which rises a large dome. The major axis of a central-plan church is thus vertical, from floor to dome, or symbolically from Earth to the vault of heaven.

The interior of San Vitale is decorated in glittering mosaics. Gold and plant motifs in glass and ceramic tesserae create a feeling of otherworldly paradise and splendor. The scene over the apse represents a youthful Jesus flanked by angels and saints. He is dressed in imperial purple robes and sits on a globe to symbolize his power. The vault before the apse depicts Jesus as a sacrificial lamb held aloft in a wreath by four angels. Mosaics to either side depict the stories of Abraham

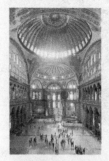

13.16 Interior of the Hagia Sophia

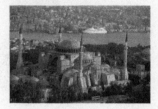

13.17 Hagia Sophia

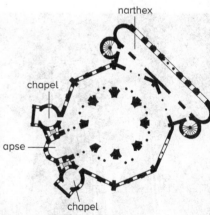

15.6 Plan of San Vitale.

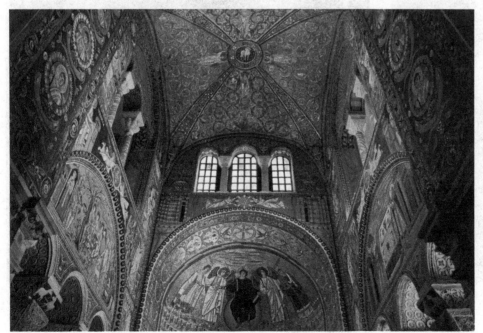

15.7 Interior, San Vitale, Ravenna. ca. 547.
AGF Srl/Alamy Stock Photo

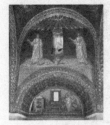

7.16 Mausoleum
of Galla Placidia

and Isaac, and Cain and Abel. The figures and spaces are flat and static. Bodies appear to have no substance beneath the drapery. Less attention is paid to the figures than to the symbols they wear and carry. The purpose of San Vitale's mosaic imagery was informational, with the goal of helping the faithful to understand the stories and teachings of Christianity.

The mosaics at San Vitale also had a political purpose. They include portrayals of the emperor Justinian and the empress Theodora (**15.8**), under whose patronage the church was built. These images conveyed the rulers' symbolic presence in this distant portion of their empire. In the view seen here, the empress makes an offering accompanied by members of the court. Her purple wrap, halo, and crown identify her royal stature, a fact reinforced by the shell niche that hovers above her head and makes her the focal point of the image. Her face is identical to those of her female attendants, so we must read the symbolism of her garments and the artist's composition in order to identify her.

Mosaic continued as a favored Byzantine technique, resulting in such masterpieces as the interior of the 12th-century Cathedral of Monreale, in Sicily (**15.9**). Set in the half-dome crowning the apse illustrated here is a large figure of Christ as *Pantokrator*, Greek for "Ruler of All." A standard element of later Byzantine iconography, the *Pantokrator* image emphasizes the divine, awe-inspiring, even terrifying majesty of Christ, as opposed to his gentle, approachable, human incarnation as Jesus. Directly below Christ is Mary, the mother of Jesus, enthroned with the Christ child on her lap. She is flanked by angels and saints. Hierarchy of scale dictates that Christ as *Pantokrator* is larger than his mother, while she is larger than the male saints surrounding her.

As at San Vitale in Ravenna, we can see here how Byzantine artists had moved away from the naturalism and realism of Greece and Rome toward a flattened, abstracted style. Like the artists of ancient Egypt, Byzantine artists strove to portray often complex religious doctrines and beliefs, not scenes from daily life. Their subject was not the impermanent earthly world of the flesh but the eternal and sacred

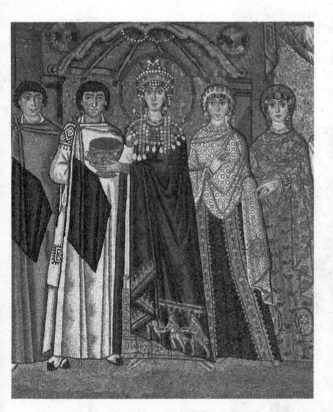

15.8 *Empress Theodora and Retinue*, detail.
San Vitale, Ravenna. ca. 547. Mosaic.
akg-images/Cameraphoto

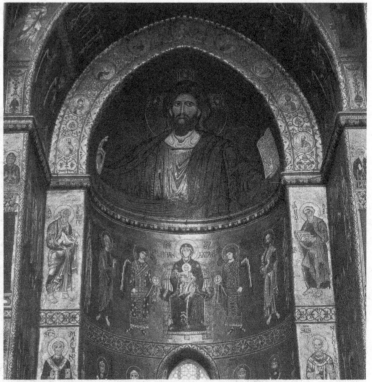

15.9 *Christ as Pantokrator*. Cathedral of Monreale,
Sicily. Before 1183. Mosaic.
Bridgeman Images

world of the spirit. By de-emphasizing the roundness, the weight, the "hereness" of human bodies in this world, they emphasize that what we are looking at is not in fact *here*, but *there*. The glittering gold background of the mosaics is typical, and it sets the figures in a Byzantine vision of heavenly splendor.

A distinctive form of Byzantine art is the **icon**, named after the Greek word for "image," *eikon*. In the context of Byzantine art, an icon is a specific kind of image, either a portrait of a sacred person or a portrayal of a sacred event. Icons were most commonly painted in tempera on gilded wood panels. But other media were also used, including miniature mosaics, precious metals, and ivory (**15.10**). Ivory was a luxury material in Byzantium, and thus it is likely that this exquisitely carved image was made in Constantinople itself, perhaps for a member of the imperial court. The icon portrays Mary, called the Mother of God, enthroned in majesty, a subject that can also be seen in the mosaic we just examined. As in the mosaic, she displays her son Jesus, who blesses onlookers with his right hand. In his left hand he holds a scroll. Angels appearing from the sky in the upper corners marvel at the sight, spreading their hands in awe. Icons had a mysterious status in the Byzantine world. They were not images as we understand them, but points of contact with the sacred realm. Divine power flowed through them into the world, and through them believers could address their prayers to the sacred presence they saw portrayed. Some icons were believed to have been miraculously created; others were believed to have worked miracles.

By the time this icon was carved, vast changes had occurred in the territories that Constantinople was built to rule. Constantine's vision of a unified Roman Empire did not prevail: The territory was simply too vast. His successors partitioned the empire into eastern and western halves, each with its own emperor. Within 150 years, the western empire had fallen, overwhelmed by a massive influx of Germanic peoples arriving from the north and east. Constantinople again claimed authority over the entire empire, but could not enforce it. The Western Church, based in Rome, preserved its imperial organization and religious authority, but true political and military power had passed to the local leaders of the newcomers, who settled throughout the lands of western Europe. It is to these peoples and their art that we now turn our attention.

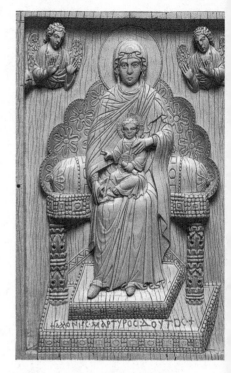

15.10 Plaque with *Enthroned Virgin and Child*. Byzantine (Constantinople?), ca. 1050–1200. Ivory, with traces of red from original gilding; 10 × 6 ⅞".
The Cleveland Museum of Art, Ohio. Gift of J. H. Wade/Bridgeman Images

The Middle Ages in Europe

The Middle Ages is the name that historians long ago gave to the period in Europe between the defeat of the last western Roman emperor in 476 and the beginnings of the Renaissance in the 15th century. To those early historians, the period was a dark one of ignorance and decline, an embarrassing "middle" time between one impressive civilization and another. Today we view the Middle Ages as a complex and fascinating period worthy of study in its own right. During these centuries, Europe was formed, and a distinctive Christian culture flowered within it. Far from ignorant, it was a time of immense achievement.

The Early Middle Ages

The kingdoms of the early Middle Ages in Europe were inhabited by descendants of migratory tribes that had traveled southward and westward on the continent during the 4th and 5th centuries. Ethnically Germanic, these peoples emerged, for the most part, from the north-central part of Europe, or what today we would call northern Germany and Scandinavia. The Romans referred to them as "barbarians" (meaning "foreigners"). They regarded them as crude, but they also admired their bravery and employed them increasingly as mercenaries. Nevertheless, the massive influx of barbarian tribes into Roman lands—sometimes as settlers, sometimes as invaders and conquerors—brought about the empire's ultimate collapse, near the end of the 5th century.

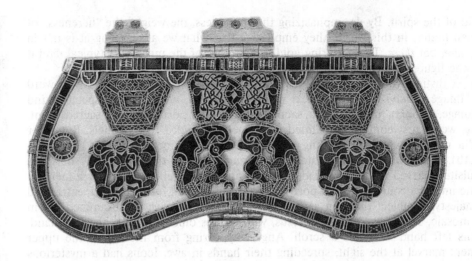

By the year 600, the migrations were essentially over, and kingdoms whose area roughly approximated the nations of modern Europe had taken form. Their inhabitants had steadily been converted to Christianity. For purposes of this discussion, we will focus initially on the people who settled in two areas—the Angles and Saxons in Britain, and the Franks in Gaul (modern France).

On the island of Britain northeast of London (then Londinium) was Sutton Hoo, where the grave of an unknown 7th-century East Anglian king was found. Objects discovered at the burial site include a superb gold-and-enamel purse cover (**15.11**), with delicately made designs. The motifs are typical of the **animal style** prevalent in the art of northwestern Europe at that time—a legacy, very likely, from the migratory herdsmen who were these people's ancestors. Animal-style images were often accompanied by **interlace**, patterns formed by intricately interwoven ribbons and bands. We can see interlace clearly in the upper-center medallion of the Sutton Hoo purse cover, where it is combined with abstracted animals.

Among the most important artistic products of the early Middle Ages were copies of Christian scriptures. In the days before the printing press, each book had to be copied by hand. During the early Middle Ages, this copying was carried out in monasteries; monks, educated by the Church, were the only literate segment of the population. Monks not only copied texts but also **illuminated** them—furnished them with illustrations and decorations. The illumination here (**15.12**) was probably made by Irish monks working in Scotland. It is the first page of the Gospel of Matthew—one of the four accounts in the Bible of the life and works of Jesus—and it shows how the monks adapted animal style and interlace to a Christian setting. The text spells out "Liber" or "Book" in highly stylized letters. Each letter consists of multiple interlace patterns in different widths and colors, some terminating in stylized animal heads. Matthew appears twice holding his Gospel text, first to the left of the letters and again at the top of the page. In both cases, his figure is flat and abstracted, with no suggestion of its mass or three-dimensionality. He is entirely spirit, not substance.

In France, a different style of art was taking root, called **Carolingian** after the emperor Charlemagne. Charlemagne, or Charles the Great, was a powerful Frankish king whose military conquests eventually gave him control over most of western Europe. Like his father before him, Charlemagne was asked by the pope for military help against the Lombards, a Germanic tribe that had conquered Ravenna and besieged Rome. In 800, he intervened yet again on the pope's behalf, this time to restore order in Rome. On Christmas Day that year, a grateful pope crowned Charlemagne *Romanorum Imperator*, Emperor of the Romans. It was the first time the title had been used in the West in more than 300 years.

Even before being crowned emperor, Charlemagne was well aware of his preeminence among the rulers of Europe. Frankish kings had traditionally moved from palace to palace throughout their realm. Charlemagne, while continuing this custom, also decided to build a permanent and more magnificent capital in Aachen,

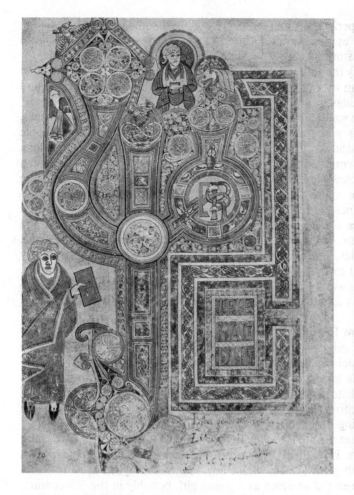

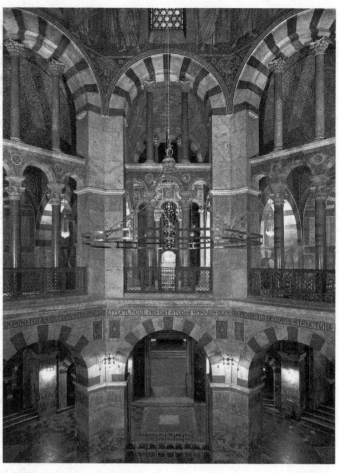

15.12 Gospel of Matthew, from the *Book of Kells*. ca. 800 C.E. Tempera and gold on vellum.
The Print Collector/Alamy Stock Photo

15.13 Interior, palace chapel of Charlemagne, Aachen. 792–805.
© Achim Bednorz, Cologne

in present-day Germany. With papal permission, he transported marble, mosaics, and other materials from buildings in Rome and Ravenna for his project. It is likely that he brought artisans as well, who worked side by side with their Frankish colleagues. The chapel from Charlemagne's monumental palace complex has survived, for it was later incorporated into Aachen Cathedral (**15.13**).

The basic plan of the chapel was probably inspired by San Vitale in Ravenna, which Charlemagne had visited several times (see 15.6, 15.7). It was an appropriate choice for a ruler determined to revive the idea of the Roman Empire. Like San Vitale, the chapel consists of a domed octagonal core with a surrounding aisle and upper gallery. But Charlemagne's architects created a weightier and more rectilinear interior, featuring Roman arches set on massive piers, and they covered the aisles with stone vaulting. The central plan of Charlemagne's chapel links it to the many central-plan churches of the Byzantine Empire to the east. The Roman arches, massive piers, and stone vaulting, in contrast, foretell the next style to emerge in Europe, the Romanesque.

The High Middle Ages

Historians generally divide the art and architecture of the high Middle Ages into two periods: the Romanesque, from about 1050 to 1200, and the Gothic, from about 1200 into the 15th century, which was created in northern France and spread from there.

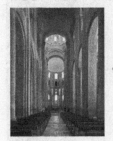
The Romanesque period was marked by a building boom. Contemporary commentators were thrilled at the beautiful churches that seemed to be springing up everywhere. Later art historians called the style of these buildings Romanesque, for despite their great variety they shared certain features reminiscent of ancient Roman architecture, including an overall massiveness, thick stone walls, round arches, and barrel-vaulted stone ceilings.

One reason for the sudden burst of building was the popularity of pilgrimages. In the newly prosperous and stable times of the 11th and 12th centuries, people could once again travel safely. Although some made the trip all the way to Jerusalem, in the Holy Land, most confined their pilgrimages to sites associated with Christian saints in Europe. Churches—and also lodgings and other services—arose along the most popular pilgrimage routes as way stations for these large groups of travelers.

The earliest Romanesque pilgrimage church still standing is the abbey church of Sainte-Foy, in France (**15.14**, **15.15**). This aerial photograph makes clear the church's cross-form plan. Even from the exterior we can distinguish the nave, the slightly shorter aisles, and the transept. Two square towers flank the entry portal, and an octagonal tower marks the intersection of the transept and the nave. The round arches of the windows are continued in the interior, which has a barrel-vaulted nave and groin-vaulted aisles. The interior of Sainte-Foy is illustrated in Chapter 13 (see 13.10).

The plan shows how Romanesque architects modified church design to accommodate large crowds of pilgrims. Aisles now line the transept as well as the nave and continue in a semicircle around the back of the apse, allowing visitors to circulate freely. The aisle around the apse is called an **ambulatory**, Latin for "walkway." Small chapels radiate from the ambulatory. The apse itself is now preceded by an area called the choir. Together, apse and choir served as a small "church within a church," allowing monks to perform their rites even as pilgrims visited.

Pilgrims stopping at Sainte-Foy would have come to see the relics of Saint Foy herself, which were kept there in a statue made of gold hammered over a wooden core and set with gems (**15.16**). Saint Foy, known in English as Saint Faith, was supposed to have been put to death as a young girl, possibly in the 3rd century, for refusing to worship pagan gods.

15.14 Aerial view of Sainte-Foy, Conques, France. ca. 1050–1120.
Erich Lessing/Art Resource, NY

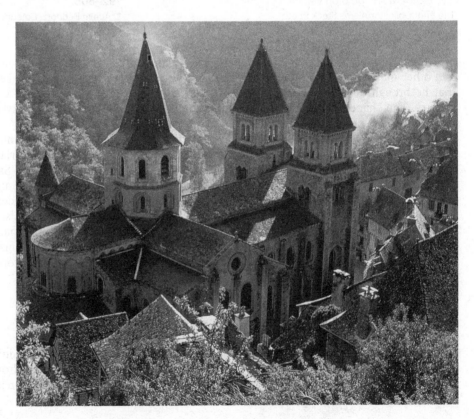

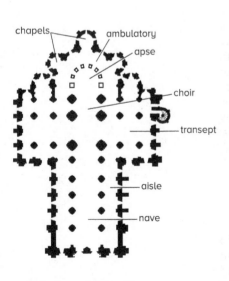

15.15 Plan of Sainte-Foy.

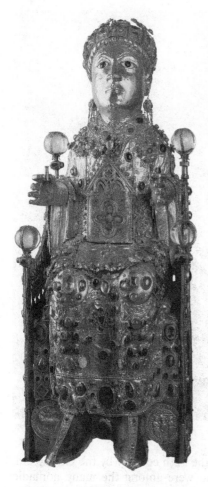

15.16 Reliquary statue of Saint Foy. Late 10th–early 11th century. Gold and gemstones over a wooden core, height 33 ½". Cathedral Treasury, Conques, France. akg-images/Paul M. R. Maeyaert

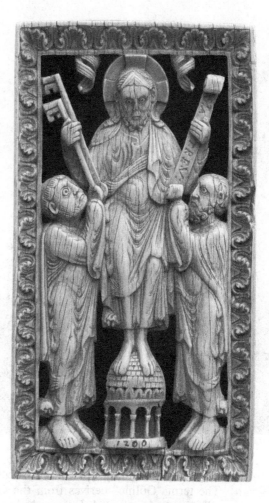

15.17 Plaque with *Christ Presenting the Keys to Saint Peter and the Law to Saint Paul*. ca. 1150–1200 C.E. Ivory, 5 ¹⁵⁄₁₆ × 3 ⅜ × ⅜". The Metropolitan Museum of Art, New York, The Cloisters Collection, 1979

The reliquary statue of Saint Foy is a fine example of the treasures that were offered to and displayed in medieval churches. The plaque with *Christ Presenting the Keys to Saint Peter and the Law to Saint Paul* (**15.17**) was also made for a church. This ivory relief features Jesus standing on a domed structure that represents heavenly Jerusalem. He offers keys and a scroll to Peter and Paul, who receive these gifts reverentially with hands covered. The keys refer to Jesus's statement to Peter: "[T]hou art Peter, and upon this rock I will build my church; and the gates of hell shall not prevail against it. And I will give unto thee the keys of the kingdom of heaven" (Matthew 16:18–19). This statement was interpreted to designate Peter as the first leader or pope of the Catholic faith. Keys remain the symbol of the pope even today. The scroll Jesus gives Paul is the law, which Paul received and interpreted for those he converted to Christianity. By the Middle Ages, Paul's writings guided much of Christian practice.

This small carved plaque commemorating the foundation of Western Christianity also reveals typical Romanesque visual characteristics. The figures are stylized and elongated, with a hierarchy of scale that makes Jesus larger than his followers. The clothing they wear falls in patterned folds that do little to describe the three-dimensional bodies beneath. The figures' faces are stereotyped rather than individualized. The symmetrical composition emphasizes symbols over nature, like Early Christian or Byzantine art. The frame, however, reveals Roman inspiration, with the same acanthus leaves we might find on a Roman column capital or mosaic design.

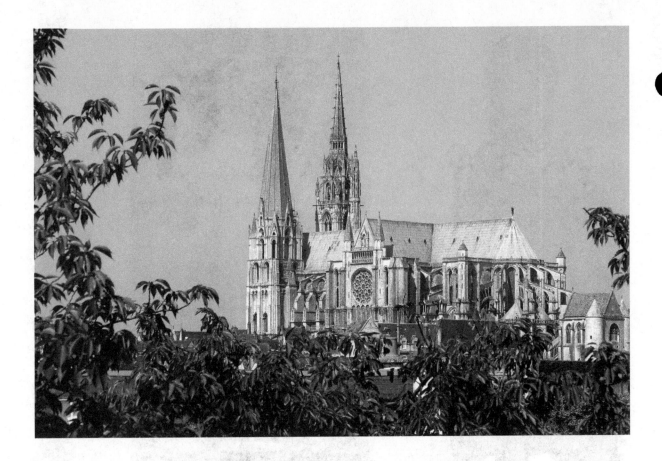

15.18 Chartres Cathedral, France. Begun 1134, completed ca. 1260.
Iconotec/Alamy Stock Photo

The Romanesque period was succeeded in the 12th century by the Gothic era. The term "Gothic" derives from the Goths, who were among the many nomadic tribes sweeping through Europe during the 4th and 5th centuries. It was applied to this style by later critics in the Renaissance, who considered the art and architecture of their immediate predecessors to be vulgar and "barbarian." Yet people in the 12th century found the new style to be beautiful and an appropriately lavish way of honoring the faith.

The Gothic style was started by a powerful French abbot named Suger, who wanted to enlarge and remodel his church, the abbey church of Saint-Denis, near Paris. Inspired by early Christian writings, he came to believe that an ideal church should have certain characteristics: It should appear to reach up to heaven, it should have harmonious proportions, and it should be filled with light. To fulfill those goals, his architects responded with pointed arches, ribbed vaulting, flying buttresses, and stained-glass windows so large they seemed like translucent walls. Finished in two stages in 1140 and 1144, the graceful, light-filled interior of Saint-Denis immediately attracted attention and imitation. Gothic style was born, the creation of a brilliant architect whose name the good abbot did not record.

The cathedral at Chartres, in France, shows the soaring quality of Gothic architecture (**15.18**). Here, the unadorned, earthbound masses of the Romanesque have given way to ornate, linear, vertical elements that direct the eye upward. Clearly visible are the flying buttresses that line the nave and apse to contain the outward thrust of the walls. Because portions of Chartres were built at different times, the cathedral also allows us to see something of the evolution of Gothic style. For example, the first thing most people notice about the west facade of the cathedral (**15.19**) is the mismatched corner towers and spires. The north (left) tower was built first (not including its spire), between 1134 and 1150. Its plain, unadorned surfaces and solid masses are still fundamentally Romanesque. The south (right) tower and its spire were completed next, between 1142 and 1160. Designed in the very earliest Gothic style, they are conceived so that each level grows out of the one before, and all the elements work together to lead the eye upward.

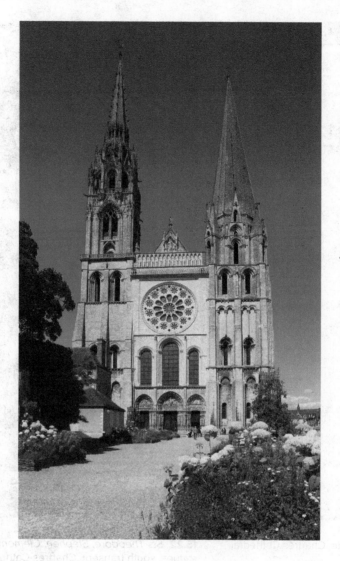

15.19 West facade, Chartres Cathedral.
Louise Heusinkveld/Getty Images

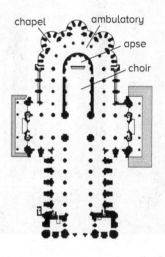

15.20 Plan of Chartres Cathedral.

chapel   ambulatory
apse
choir

The towers, south spire, and facade had originally been built as additions to an older Romanesque church that stood on the site. When a fire in 1194 burned this older part of the church to the ground, it was rebuilt over the course of the next sixty years in the Gothic style we see today. The plan (**15.20**) shows the familiar cross form, but the choir and ambulatory have taken on much larger proportions compared with those at Sainte-Foy. The soaring, open spaces of the interior were created with ribbed vaulting and pointed arches much like those we saw in Chapter 13 in the cathedral at Reims, built around the same time (see 13.11). The final addition to Chartres was the spire atop the north (left) tower. Built in the early 16th century, it illustrates the last phase of Gothic style—a slender, elongated, and highly ornamental style called Flamboyant, French for "flamelike."

Sculpture in the Middle Ages was often created to embellish architecture. Over two thousand carved figures decorate the exterior of Chartres Cathedral. Concentrated especially around principal entryways, they serve as a transition between the everyday world of the town and the sacred space within, forming a sort of "welcoming committee" for the faithful as they enter. Like the architecture itself, the sculptures were created at different times, and in them, too, we can appreciate the evolution of Gothic style.

Early Gothic style can be seen in the elongated and flattened bodies of these 12th-century carvings from the principal entry of the cathedral (**15.21**). In fact, it is difficult to believe that there are actual bodies under the draperies at all. The linear folds of the draperies are not so much sculpted as incised—drawn into the stone with a chisel. We can think of them as a sculptural equivalent of the garments in the Byzantine mosaic we looked at earlier (see 15.9), created around the same time.

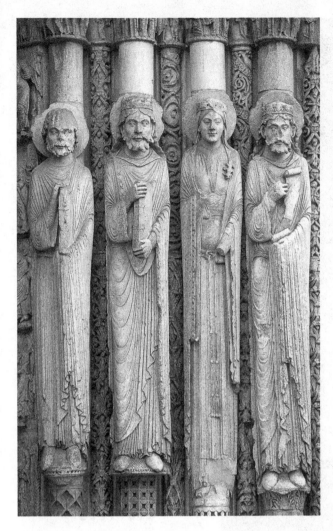

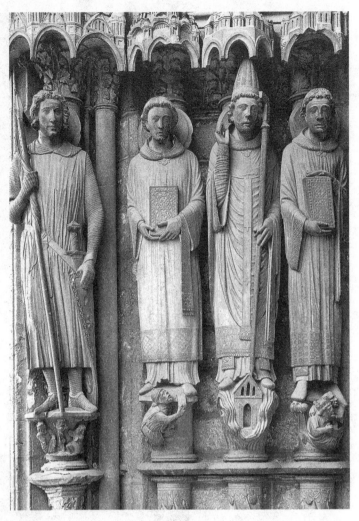

15.21 Door jamb statues, west facade, Chartres Cathedral. ca. 1145–70.
Schütze/Rodemann/akg-images

15.22 *Sts Theodore, Stephen, Clement, and Lawrence*, door jamb statues, south transept, Chartres Cathedral. 13th century.
Peter Willi/Bridgeman Images

Carved a mere hundred years later, this second group of figures (**15.22**) displays the mature Gothic style. Whereas the bodies of the earlier statues took the form of the columns they adorned, the bodies here are more fully rounded and have begun to detach themselves from their architectural supports. The three saints on the right still seem to float somewhat, as though suspended in midair, but the figure of Saint Theodore at the far left truly stands, his weight on his feet. A sense of underlying musculature is evident in armor covering his arms, and his garment, although not yet fully naturalistic, is carved with an awareness of a body underneath. It would remain for another era to conceive of the body *first*, and then figure out how clothing would drape over it.

The glory of Gothic cathedrals is their magnificent stained glass. Chartres contains over 150 stained-glass windows. Their motifs include stories from the Bible, lives of the saints, signs of the zodiac, and donors from every level of society, from knights and nobles to tradespeople such as butchers and bakers. Among the most resplendent medieval windows are the great radiating, circular groupings called rose windows (**15.23**). This rose window, one of three at Chartres, is dedicated to Mary, the mother of Jesus. She is depicted at its center enthroned as the Queen of Heaven. Radiating from her are windows portraying doves and angels, biblical kings, symbols of French royalty, and prophets. Like the gold of Byzantine mosaics, the gemlike colors of stained glass represent a medieval vision of heavenly splendor.

Although all art of the Middle Ages was imbued with Christian culture, not all of it was made for religious settings. Royal and noble households and, as the period drew to its close, wealthy merchant families would have owned not only paintings and carvings of religious subjects for private devotion but also fine carved furniture, illuminated books, and objects to grace daily life, such as the aquamanile illustrated in Chapter 12 (see 12.6). But the most treasured medieval possessions, more valuable by far than paintings, were tapestries—large woven hangings (15.24). Often created in cycles that told a story or followed a theme, sumptuous tapestries were hung in great halls and private chambers. The tapestry illustrated here is from a cycle of six hangings known as *The Lady and the Unicorn*, woven for a member of a wealthy French family named Le Viste toward the end of the 15th century. The unicorn is a mythical beast that, according to legend, can be tamed only by a beautiful young girl. Here, it also stands in for Le Viste himself in amorous pursuit. The lion, too, signals Le Viste's presence by holding up a standard bearing the family coat of arms. Five of the tapestries are devoted to the five senses. The subject of the tapestry here is smell: A servant offers a basket of flowers, while on the bench behind the lady, a monkey sniffs at a blossom he has stolen.

The genteel elegance of the tapestry is typical of the Gothic style. The figures are long and graceful, with a slight curve at the hip. Light modeling suggests their

RELATED WORKS

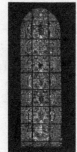

12.4 *Tree of Jesse*, Chartres Cathedral

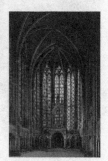

3.1 Sainte-Chapelle

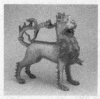

12.6 Lion aquamanile

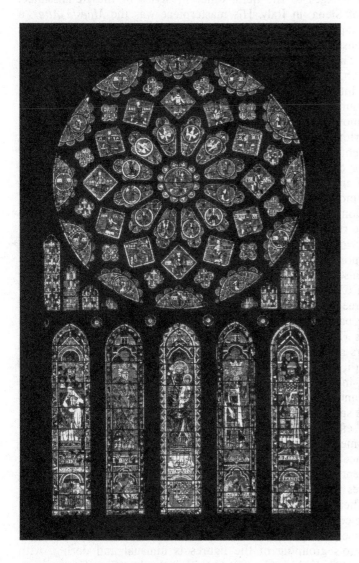

15.23 Rose window and lancets, north transept, Chartres Cathedral. 13th century. Diameter of rose window 42'.
Angelo Hornak/Alamy Stock Photo

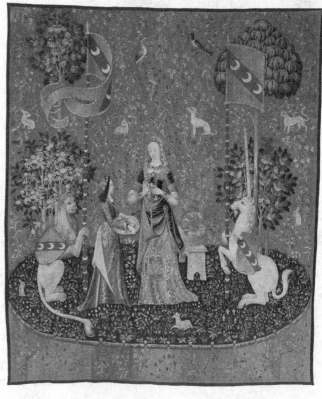

15.24 *Smell*, from *The Lady and the Unicorn*. Late 15th century. Wool and silk, 12' ½" × 10' 6 ¾".
Musée National du Moyen Age–Thermes de Cluny, Paris. Erich Lessing/Art Resource, NY

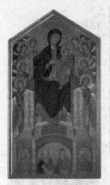

3.4 Cimabue,
*Madonna
Enthroned*

15.25 Duccio. *Christ Entering
Jerusalem*, detail of the *Maestà
Altar*. 1308–11. Tempera on panel,
40 × 21".

Museo dell'Opera Metropolitana, Siena.
Scala/Art Resource, NY

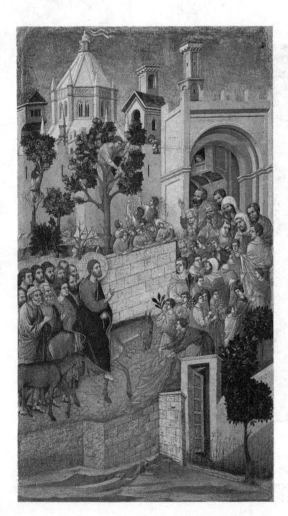

three-dimensional bodies. The plants are carefully described for their shapes and textures, as is the animal fur. Yet the flat space created by the patterned red background and the lion's odd anatomy contradict the tapestry's overall naturalism. Artists had yet to embrace picturing the world as their eyes saw it.

Toward the Renaissance

The Gothic style lasted in northern Europe into the early 16th century. By that time, however, it was overlapping with far different ideas about art that had their origins in the south, in Italy. Living in the heart of what was the ancient Roman Empire, Italians were surrounded with the ruins of the Classical world. More treasures lay buried in the earth, awaiting excavation. All that was needed was an intellectual climate that encouraged an interest in such things. That climate eventually arose, and we call it the Renaissance. But the Renaissance did not happen all at once. Many developments prepared the way—some in scholarship, some in political thought, others in art.

The last two artists in this chapter were influential in making the shift from art styles of the Middle Ages to the quite different styles of the Renaissance. Duccio was an artist of Siena, in Italy. His masterpiece was the *Maestà Altar*, a multisection tempera-on-panel painting meant to be displayed on the altar of a church, of which we illustrate the part showing *Christ Entering Jerusalem* (**15.25**). What is most interesting about this painting is Duccio's attempt to create believable space in a large outdoor scene—a concern that would absorb painters of the next century. Christ's entry into the city, celebrated now on Palm Sunday, was thought of as a triumphal procession, and Duccio has labored to convey the sense of movement and parade. A strong diagonal thrust beginning at the left with Christ and his disciples cuts across the picture to the middle right, then shifts abruptly to carry our attention to the upper left corner of the painting—a church tower that is Christ's presumed goal. The architecture plays an important role in defining space and directing movement. This was Duccio's novel, almost unprecedented, contribution to the art of the period, the use of architecture to demarcate space rather than to act as a simple backdrop.

Duccio's contemporary, a Florentine artist named Giotto, made an even more remarkable break with the art traditions of the Middle Ages. In his most famous work, a cycle of frescoes on the walls of the Scrovegni Chapel in Padua, Giotto used a grid of decorative bands to create three registers of rectangular picture spaces. In each picture space, he painted an episode from the life of the Virgin Mary. One episode is *The Lamentation* (**15.26**), which depicts Mary, Saint John, and others mourning the dead Christ. The scene has been composed as though it were on a stage and we the viewers are an audience participating in the drama. In other words, space going back from the picture plane seems to be continuous with space in front of the picture plane, the space in which we stand. Accustomed as we are now to this "window" effect in painting, it is difficult to imagine how revolutionary it was to medieval eyes, which were used to predominantly flat, decorative space in painting. Moreover, Giotto seems to have developed this concept of space largely on his own, with little artistic precedent. The figures in *The Lamentation* are modeled to look round and full-bodied. Their drapery reveals the bulk of the body beneath. Clustered low in the composition, these figures enhance the effect of a real event taking place just out of our reach.

Giotto's grouping of the figures is unusual and daring, with Christ's body half-hidden by a figure with its back turned. This arrangement seems casual and almost random, until we notice the slope of the hill directing our attention to the heads of Christ and the Virgin,

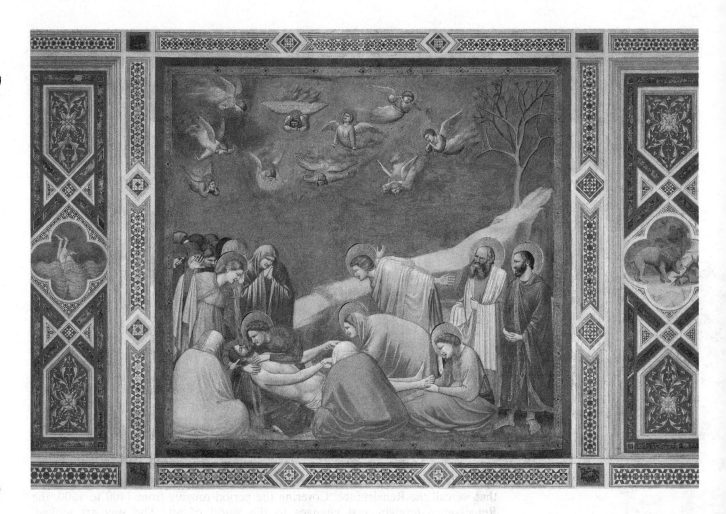

15.26 Giotto. *The Lamentation*, detail from the Scrovegni Chapel, Padua. ca. 1303–05. Fresco.
De Agostini Picture Library/A. Dagli Orti/ Bridgeman Images

which are the focal point of the composition. Yet another innovation—perhaps Giotto's most important one—was his interest in depicting the psychological and emotional reactions of his subjects. The characters in *The Lamentation* interact in a natural, human way that gives this and the artist's other religious scenes a special warmth. The angels observing the scene are particularly moving, each revealing grief through pose and facial expression.

Neither Duccio nor Giotto had an especially long career. Each did his most significant work in the first decade of the 14th century. Yet in that short time the course of Western art history changed dramatically. Both artists had sought a new direction for painting—a more naturalistic, more human, more engaging representation of the physical world—and both had taken giant steps in that direction. Their experiments paved the way for a flowering of all the arts that would come in the next century.

Chapter 16
The Renaissance

Throughout the Middle Ages, painters were considered skilled crafts workers on a level with goldsmiths, carpenters, and other tradespeople. By the mid-16th century, in contrast, Michelangelo could claim that "in Italy great princes as such are not held in honor or renown; it is a painter that they call divine."[1] From anonymous crafts workers to divinely talented individuals more honored and renowned than princes—what had happened?

The simplest answer is that Michelangelo lived and worked during the time that we call the Renaissance. Covering the period roughly from 1400 to 1600, the Renaissance brought vast changes to the world of art. The way art looked, the subjects it treated, the way it was thought about, the position of the artist in society, the identities and influence of patrons, the cultures that served as points of reference—all these things changed. We might even say that the Renaissance was the time when the concept of "art" began to take shape, for it was during these centuries that painting, sculpture, and architecture began to earn their privileged positions in Western thought.

The word *renaissance* means "rebirth," and it refers to the revival of interest in ancient Greek and Roman culture that is one of the key characteristics of the period. Scholars of the day worked to recover and study as many Greek and Latin texts as possible. Referring to themselves as humanists, they believed that a sound education should include not only the teachings of the Church and the study of early Christian writers but also the study of the liberal arts—grammar, rhetoric, poetry, history, politics, and moral philosophy—about which the pre-Christian world had much to teach.

Renaissance humanists believed in the pursuit of knowledge for its own sake. Above all, they held that humankind was not worthless in the eyes of God, as the Church had taught during the Middle Ages. Rather, humankind was God's finest and most perfect creation. Reason and creativity were God's gifts, proof of humankind's inherent dignity. People's obligation to God was thus not to tremble and submit but, rather, to soar, striving to realize their full intellectual and creative potential.

The implications of these ideas for art were tremendous. Artists became newly interested in observing the natural world, and they worked to reproduce it as accurately as possible. Studying the effects of light, they developed the technique of chiaroscuro; noting that distant objects appeared smaller than near ones, they developed the system of linear perspective; seeing how detail and color blurred with distance, they developed the principles of atmospheric perspective.

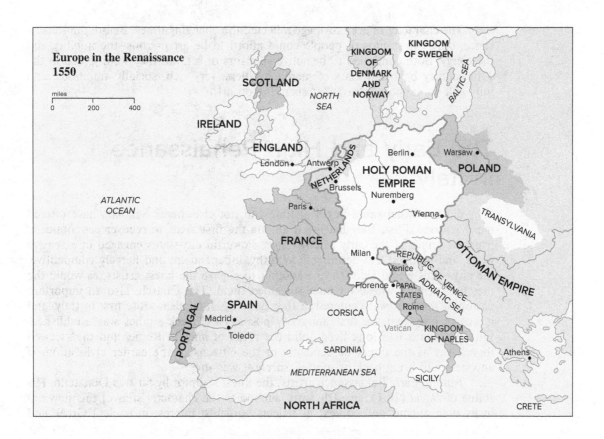

Europe in the Renaissance 1550

The nude reappeared in art, for the body was held to be the noblest of God's creations. "Who is so barbarous as not to understand that the foot of a man is nobler than his shoe," said Michelangelo, "and his skin nobler than that of the sheep with which he is clothed?"[2] To portray the body with understanding, artists studied anatomy, even going so far as to dissect cadavers.

Under the influence of the ancient Greek philosopher Plato, whose works were newly available, beauty became equated with moral goodness. Renaissance artists sought an idealized beauty, one they created by taking the most beautiful features of numerous examples and combining them. "Be on the watch to take the best parts of many individual faces," wrote Leonardo da Vinci.[3] The German Renaissance painter Albrecht Dürer advised the same: "You, therefore, if you desire to compose a fine figure, must take the head from some, the chest, arm, leg, hand, and foot from others. . . . For from many beautiful things something good may be gathered, even as honey is gathered from many flowers."[4]

The ten-volume treatise on architecture by the Roman writer Vitruvius was read avidly in an attempt to understand Classical thought and practice, including ideas about beauty and harmonious proportions. Roman ruins still standing were studied in detail—described, measured, analyzed, and drawn. Excavations revealed still more examples, along with astonishing statues such as the *Laocoön Group* (see 14.29), which served as an inspiration and ideal for Renaissance artists.

Perspective and chiaroscuro, close observation of nature, the study of anatomy, theories of beauty and proportion—these established painting, sculpture, and architecture as intellectual activities allied with science, rhetoric, music, and mathematics. Artists were no longer mere crafts workers, but learned persons whose creative powers were viewed as almost miraculous. The greatest artists were considered a breed apart, constituting a class of their own that transcended the social class determined by birth—not nobility, not bourgeoisie, not clergy, but a separate and elite category of people respected not because of who they were but because of what they could do. They lived in the courts of the nobles and the popes, they moved freely in good society, their company was sought after, their services in demand.

The character of art patronage reflected the changing times. Before the Renaissance, only two groups of people could afford to be art patrons—the nobility and the clergy. Both continued to be active sponsors of art, but they were joined in the 15th century by a new class of merchant-rulers, very rich, socially ambitious, and fully able to support extravagant spending on art.

The Early and High Renaissance in Italy

Why did the **Renaissance** begin in Italy and not elsewhere? Scholars have offered many reasons. First, Italy had been among the first areas to recover economically from the chaos of the early Middle Ages. Powerful city-states engaged in extensive trade, and banking had developed. Wealthy, independent, and fiercely competitive, the city-states would vie with one another to engage the finest artists, as would the merchant-princes whose fortunes sustained them. The Church, also an important patron of the arts, was centered in Italy as well. Humanism arose first in Italy, and it was in Italy that the first university position in Greek studies was established. Finally, Italians had long lived amid the ruins of ancient Rome, and they viewed themselves as the direct descendants of the citizens of the earlier civilization. If anyone could bring back its glories, surely it was they.

Among Early Renaissance artists, the finest sculptor by far was Donatello. His statue of *David* (**16.1**), an early work, embodies the characteristics of this new era in its style, theme, and context. It reflects humanist interest in ancient Greek and

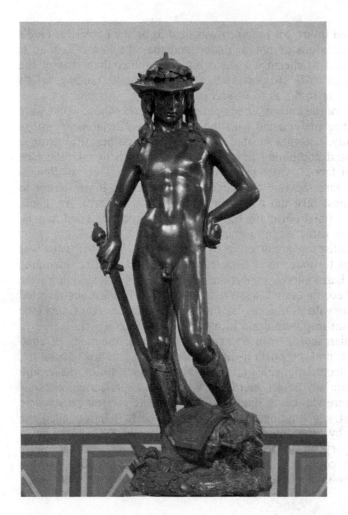

16.1 Donatello. *David*. ca. 1440. Bronze, height 62 ¼".
Bargello, Florence. Peter Barritt/Alamy Stock Photo

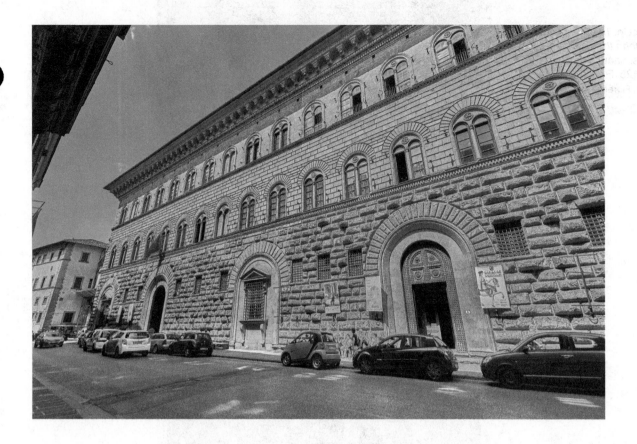

16.2 Michelozzo di Bartolomeo. Palazzo Medici Riccardi, Florence. 1444–84.

Rik Hamilton/Alamy Stock Photo

Roman art by celebrating the nude human (especially male) body as God's most perfect creation. This sculpture was the first full-round nude sculpture to be made since antiquity. The young David stands in contrapposto, and his body is naturally proportioned. His pensive face and confident pose are expressive as he stands over the severed head of Goliath. Donatello created the sculpture for the Medici family, wealthy bankers who placed it in their palace in Florence. The story of the underdog David defeating the more powerful Goliath was a metaphor for the stance taken by Florence against larger states such as Milan—a theme that was soon to be taken up again by Michelangelo. The Medici family sought to link themselves to Florence by commissioning this image for their home. When the family was driven from the city at the end of the 15th century, Florentine citizens took this highly symbolic sculpture and installed it in a public square.

The Medici palace (**16.2**), where Donatello's *David* originally stood, is in the heart of Florence. As with the sculpture, the palace's patron, Cosimo de' Medici, took great pains to use his home to embody both the new ideas about art and his family's important role in the Florentine republic. Although much of the building was inspired by ancient Greek and Roman architecture, the architect, Michelozzo di Bartolomeo, used heavy, roughly hewn stone on the lower level. This visually linked the new building to the city's medieval palaces, including the town hall, known today as the Palazzo Vecchio. Double windows topped by arches on the second and third stories provided another visual link. The clear separation of floors, the round arches, and the elaborate cornice that tops the new Medici palace, on the other hand, were inspired by Classical architecture. So, too, was the courtyard surrounded by columns inside the palace, which was based on the floor plan of ancient Roman villas. This courtyard is where Donatello's sculpture of *David* stood for the admiration of the Medicis' customers and peers.

Classical architecture also inspired the artist Masaccio. He painted *Trinity with the Virgin, St. John the Evangelist, and Donors* (**16.3**) to appear as if within an architectural setting. He painted the holy figures occupying the space under an arch leading to a coffered barrel vault. The painting's donors appear to kneel next to Corinthian pilasters framing the arch and supporting an entablature. Masaccio

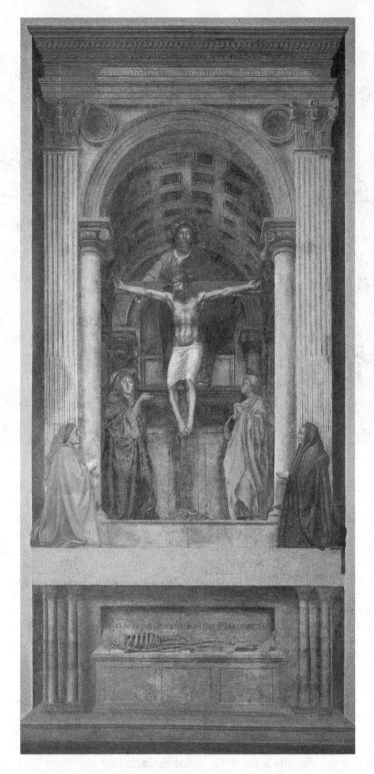

16.3 Masaccio. *Trinity with the Virgin, St. John the Evangelist, and Donors*. Santa Maria Novella, Florence. 1425. Fresco, 21′ 9″ × 9′ 4″.
© Quattrone, Florence

painted the architecture of this fresco in the church of Santa Maria Novella in Florence, using the new technique of linear perspective to construct a deep, convincing space as a setting for his figures.

Masaccio has arranged the figures in a stable triangle that extends from the head of God the Father, who stands over the dead Christ, through the two donors to either side of the holy grouping and outside their sacred space. Triangular (or pyramidal) organization would remain a favorite device of Italian Renaissance artists. Earlier, we noticed it in Raphael's *The Madonna of the Meadows* (see 4.16). Masaccio's composition is organized by a vanishing point located directly under the Cross, at the midpoint of the ledge on which the donors kneel. Five feet above the floor, it is at the eye level of an average viewer. For visitors to the church, the

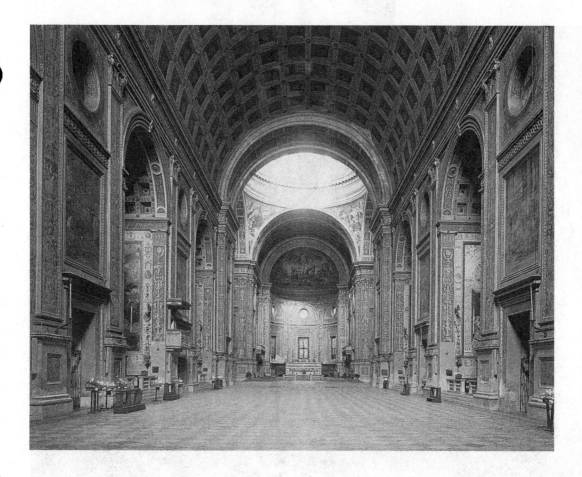

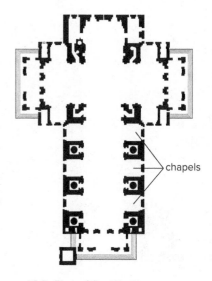

16.4 Leon Battista Alberti. Interior, Sant'Andrea, Mantua. 1470–93. Scala/Art Resource, NY

painting is thus designed to present as convincing an illusion as possible that the sacred scene is really present before them.

Even the architectural setting that Masaccio has painted is in the new Renaissance style. We can see the sort of interior that inspired him in the church of Sant'Andrea in Mantua (**16.4**, **16.5**), by the architect Leon Battista Alberti. The photograph at 16.4 is taken looking up the nave toward the apse; the light in the middle distance is entering through the dome that rises over the intersection of the transept and the nave.

The interior is structured around the geometric shapes of the circle and the square. The aisles of the standard basilica plan have given way to a procession of square, barrel-vaulted chapels along a majestic barrel-vaulted nave. The space of the crossing where the transept and nave meet makes a square. Above is the circular base of the dome. The vast interior space composed of geometric volumes harks back to Roman examples such as the Pantheon (see 13.13). Renaissance humanists believed that the circle and square were perfect shapes that reflected God's singular perfection. This belief was shared by Leonardo da Vinci, who tried to make his perfectly proportioned man fit within both a square and a circle (see 5.22).

In addition to Christian themes, Renaissance artists turned to stories of Greek and Roman gods and goddesses for subject matter, as did many Renaissance poets. An example is *Primavera* (**16.6**), by Sandro Botticelli. Born in 1445, Botticelli belonged to the third generation of Renaissance artists. Early in his career, he had the great fortune to enjoy the patronage of the Medici, who commissioned this painting. The Medici sponsored an academy—a sort of discussion group—where humanist scholars and artists met to discuss Classical culture and its relationship to Christianity. The reconciliation of these two systems of thought gave rise to a philosophy known as Neo-Platonism, after the Greek philosopher Plato.

The painting is an allegory of spring. It features Venus, the Roman goddess of love and beauty, in the center. Her son Cupid flies above her and shoots his arrow toward the three women known as Graces. They embody female charm and

chapels

16.5 Plan of Sant'Andrea.

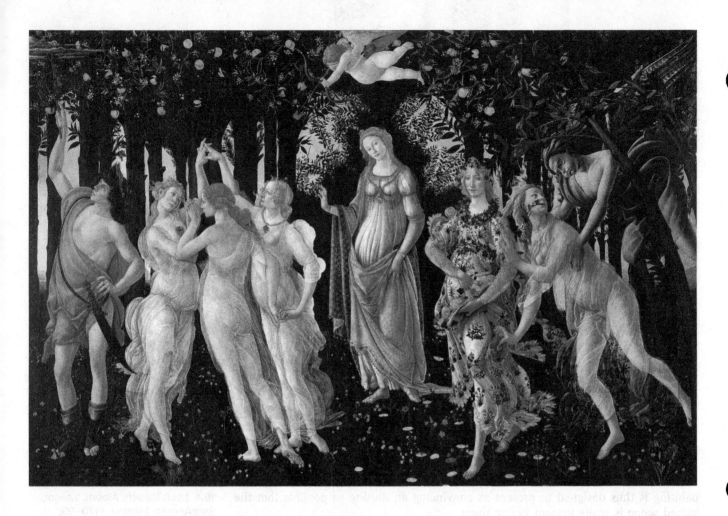

16.6 Sandro Botticelli. *Primavera.*
1481–84. Tempera on panel,
80 × 123 ½".
Alamy Stock Photo

beauty. To the left is Mercury, the messenger god. He uses his caduceus to drive away the clouds. On the opposite side, Zephyrus, the wind, captures the fleeing spring nymph Chloris. According to ancient myth, Chloris becomes Flora, who stands beside her in Botticelli's painting.

Art historians debate the precise meaning of this painting. It may be that it is also an allegory of love and birth. Symbols from the Medici family arms, such as the caduceus and golden orbs—appearing here as fruit in the trees—raise the possibility that this painting celebrated the Medici lineage and the hope that Medici brides would produce an abundance of healthy babies, just as Flora and Chloris offer flowers. Medici intimates would have understood this symbolism. Botticelli's work displays the rarefied and learned side of Renaissance art. It was painted not for a large public but for a cultivated audience of initiates.

Although Botticelli's unusual linear style and shallow modeling were an exception to Renaissance norms, they were highly appreciated by the Medici circle. Venus, for example, looks as though she might be modeled in high relief, but not fully rounded. The Three Graces are also inspired by ancient sculpture, but appear somewhat flattened. The implied space is shallow, with the grove of trees serving almost as a backdrop, as in a theatrical production.

Works like the *Primavera* hung in the great homes of wealthy Italian nobles, merchants, and bankers. They represented a family's power and social status within this elite community. A cassone featuring a tournament scene (**16.7**) was created to commemorate a marriage between two of these families. Their coats of arms are carved into the gilded wood. Cassoni were bedchamber chests for storing housewares. Families commissioned them as gifts for the bride to take to her new home. This example by an anonymous Florentine artist pictures a tournament like the ones that were held to celebrate weddings. The painting shows men from both families engaging in acts of bravery before onlookers and a backdrop of the city. The chest

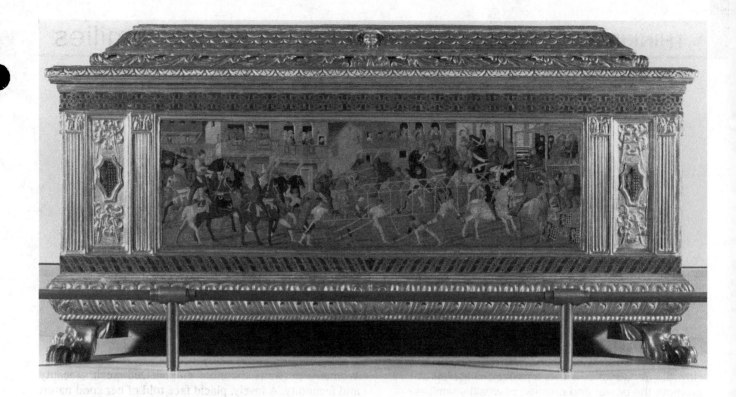

16.7 Cassone with tournament scene. 1455–65. Painted and gilded wood, 15 × 51¼".
© National Gallery, London/Art Resource, NY

bearing the painted panel employs the Classical architectural elements we saw in Sant'Andrea to demonstrate the patron's modern tastes and learning.

The period known as the High Renaissance was a brief but glorious time in the history of art. In barely twenty-five years, from shortly before 1500 to about 1520, some of the most celebrated works of Western art were produced. Many artists participated in this brilliant creative endeavor, but the outstanding figures among them were unquestionably Leonardo da Vinci, Michelangelo, and Raphael.

The term "Renaissance man" is applied to someone who is very well informed about, or very good at doing, many different, often quite unrelated, things. It originated in the fact that several of the leading figures of the Renaissance were artistic jacks-of-all-trades. Michelangelo was a painter, sculptor, poet, architect—incomparably gifted at all. Leonardo was a painter, inventor, sculptor, architect, engineer, scientist, musician, and all-round intellectual. In our age of specialization, those accomplishments seem staggering, but during the heady years of the Renaissance nothing was impossible.

Leonardo is the artist who most embodies the term "Renaissance man"; many people consider him to have been the greatest genius who ever lived. He was possessed of a brilliant and inquiring mind that accepted no limits. Throughout his long life, he remained absorbed by the problem of how things work, and how they might work. A typical example of his investigations is the well-known *Study of Human Proportions* (see 5.22), in which the artist sought to establish ideal proportions for the human body by relating it to the square and the circle. Above and below the figure is Leonardo's eccentric mirror writing, which he used in notes and journals.

Leonardo's interest in mathematics is also evident from his careful rendering of perspective. In Chapter 4, we examined his masterpiece *The Last Supper* (see 4.46), which uses one-point linear perspective to organize the many figures in the composition and set them into deep space. Yet another interest, experimental painting techniques, served the artist less well in *The Last Supper*. Rather than employing the established fresco method, Leonardo worked in a medium he devised for the *Last Supper* project, thus dooming his work to centuries of restoration.

Leonardo's rival in greatness was Michelangelo, who began his career in Florence but also worked in Rome. Michelangelo had established his reputation as

RELATED WORKS

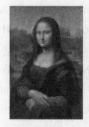

2.1 Leonardo, *Mona Lisa*

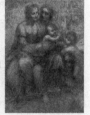

4.20 Leonardo, *The Virgin and St. Anne*

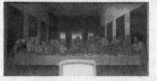

4.46 Leonardo, *The Last Supper*

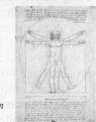

5.22 Leonardo, *Study of Human Proportions*

Art and the Power of Families

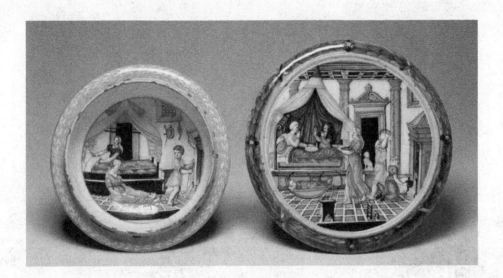

How did Renaissance artists and patrons use art to promote the power and prestige of wealthy families? What categories of object did they use to accomplish this goal? How are women represented in this art?

Botticelli's *Primavera* and the Florentine cassone with a tournament scene reveal the importance of family in the Italian Renaissance. Status in medieval and Renaissance society depended on the family of your birth. Nobility and its social and political benefits were tied to lineage. Titles passed down from parents to their children. Failing to produce an heir meant the title and its perks passed to another family. Non-noble bankers and merchants wanted to keep wealth within the family and to add to it through the generations. Cultivating the family line was thus central to Renaissance culture.

Strategic marriages were key to family success. A well-chosen match merged the status, wealth, and influence of the two families. The children born from the pairing perpetuated the lineage. In an era when many children died before the age of five, this meant that big families were needed to guarantee succession. Girls were raised solely to bring honor to the family, remaining pure until marriage and then producing large families to carry on the line.

Renaissance art helped families to promote themselves and the safety of their lineage. Portraits such as Leonardo's *Mona Lisa* (see 2.1) represent a common approach. Such works were frequently produced in pairs, with the portrait of the wife mirroring the image of her husband. Portraits not only recorded the likeness of a loved one, but also exhibited the qualities that aided the family line.

Women's portraits therefore emphasized wealth, beauty, and fecundity. A lovely, placid face told of her good nature and piety. Rich clothes and jewelry spoke to the fortune of her family or husband. Crossed arms or flowers held near her abdomen hinted at the many healthy babies she would produce. A landscape in the background suggested the vast landholdings she controlled. Men's portraits portrayed their subjects' military prowess, intelligence, wealth, culture, and political acumen.

The cassone and paintings such as Botticelli's *Primavera* celebrated marriages. Other works celebrated births. The bowl and tray from a childbirth set were part of a series of objects created to aid and commemorate the birth of heirs. Families commissioned works like these in anticipation of the happy event, and emblazoned them with their coats of arms. They gave the objects as gifts to the expectant mother to be used during and after the birth.

The bowl and tray seen here picture the postpartum moments. The scene on the left takes place in the birthing chamber. A nurse swaddles the baby lying on her lap. A servant makes the birthing bed and another dries cloth by the fire. On the right, the new mother is installed in her opulent bedchamber. Notice the Classical columns and the coffered ceiling. She has fulfilled her duty to produce a healthy heir, and takes nourishment to restore her energy. The newborn sleeps in a cradle beside the bed. The mother's attendants serve her food on trays made specially for this purpose. Such wood or ceramic birthing trays similarly bore images that alluded to family lineage and the desire for many healthy heirs.

Bowl and tray from a childbirth set (interior view). 1530–50. Earthenware with tin glaze, 4 ⅛ × 7 ¹⁵⁄₁₆". The Walters Art Museum, Baltimore, Maryland, acquired by Henry Walters, 1910

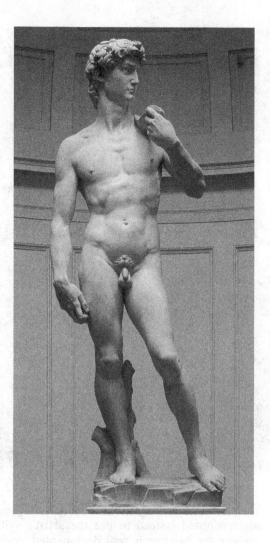

16.8 Michelangelo. *David*. 1501–04. Marble, height 18'. Galleria dell'Accademia, Florence. © Quattrone, Florence

a sculptor by the age of twenty-five. A year later he received the commission for a colossal image of the biblical hero David (**16.8**), the subject taken up a half-century earlier by Donatello (see 16.1). The *David* statue reveals Michelangelo's debt to Classical sculptures. *David* is not, however, a simple restatement of Greek art. The Greeks knew how bodies looked on the outside. Michelangelo knew how they looked on the inside, how they worked, because he had studied human anatomy and had dissected corpses. He translated this knowledge into a figure that seems to be made of muscle and flesh and bone, though all in marble.

There are other characteristics that make *David* a Renaissance sculpture, not a copy of a Greek one. For one thing, it has a tension and an energy that are missing from Greek art. Hellenistic works such as the *Laocoön Group* (see 14.29) expressed these qualities through physical contortions, but to have this energy coiled within a figure standing quietly was new. David is not so much standing in repose as standing in readiness. Another Renaissance quality is the expression on David's face. Classical Greek statues tended to have calm, even vacant expressions. But David is young and vibrant—and angry, angry at the forces of evil represented by the giant Goliath. Contemporary Florentines found this David a fitting emblem for their small but proud city, which had recently battled giants by expelling the ruling Medici family and then founding a republic. They placed the statue in the city square in front of the seat of the new government, near the Donatello *David* they had seized from the Medici. (Both sculptures have since been moved indoors.)

Not long after completing the *David*, Michelangelo embarked on the masterpiece that has become his best-known work, the ceiling frescoes of the Sistine Chapel in the Vatican, in Rome (**16.9**). He had been called to Rome by Pope Julius II, who wanted the artist to design his tomb, a large monument with numerous

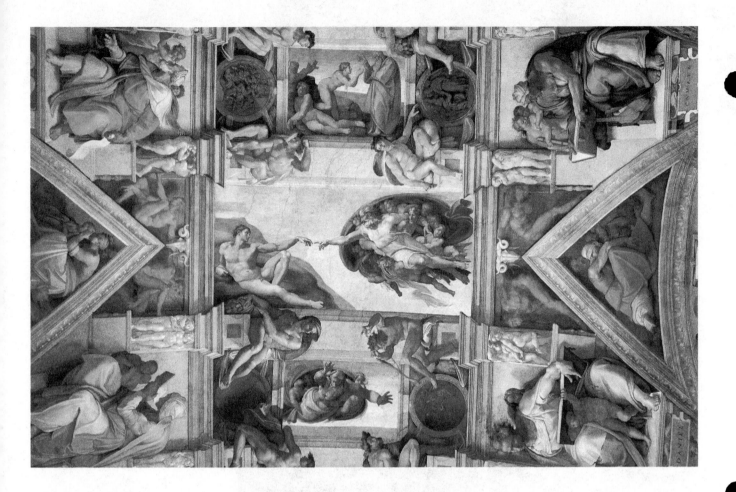

16.9 Michelangelo. Sistine Chapel ceiling, detail showing, from bottom to top: God Dividing the Waters from the Dry Land, with the Persian Sibyl (left) and Daniel (right); The Creation of Adam; The Creation of Eve, with Ezekiel (left) and the Cumaean Sibyl (right). 1508–12. Fresco.

Javier Larrea/Robert Harding

sculptures. Michelangelo set to work, but a year later Julius abandoned that project and proposed instead to use the artist's skill as a painter. Michelangelo, whose distaste for painting is well documented, resisted the plan, but in the end he was forced to capitulate.

The Sistine Chapel, named after an earlier pope called Sixtus, has a high, vaulted ceiling 128 feet long and 44 feet wide. Under Sixtus it had been decorated with a fresco of gilt stars on a deep blue ground. Along the sides were painted niches set with standing figures representing Christ, Saints Peter and Paul, and thirty popes who had been canonized as saints. Julius wanted all this taken down and replaced with a new fresco. Michelangelo signed the contract in 1508 and began work immediately—making detailed drawings, ordering pigments, overseeing the design and construction of the scaffolding, and assembling a team of a dozen or so assistants. The assistants would procure supplies, grind colors, prepare the plaster surface, prepare and transfer the cartoons, and paint repetitive or decorative elements, leaving Michelangelo free to paint everything else. Day after day for the next four years, Michelangelo and his assistants stood side by side on the scaffolding, painting the ceiling just overhead.

To tame the vast expanse of the ceiling vault, Michelangelo invented an illusionistic architecture. Painted to look like stone, its lintels, cornices, pedestals, and supporting sculptural figures create a large grid that divides the surface into discrete zones. In the niches thus created along the sides, Michelangelo portrayed Old Testament prophets and ancient Greek sibyls—women gifted with prophecy. All were believed to have predicted the coming of Christ. Along the central spine of the ceiling, the painted architecture frames a series of nine pictorial spaces. Here, Michelangelo depicted scenes from Genesis, from the creation of the world through the story of Noah and the Flood. The detail of the ceiling illustrated here shows, from bottom to top: God, his hands outstretched, his cloak billowing, looking down at the Earth as he separates the waters from the dry land; the creation of Adam,

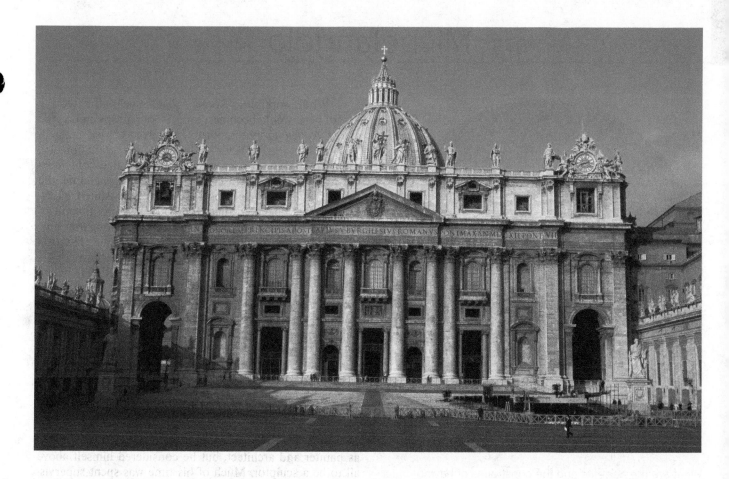

with the dynamic figure of God about to pass the spark of life to the languid first man; and God creating Eve as Adam slumbers. The Genesis scenes alternate rhythmically in size across the ceiling–large, small, large, small–creating the effect of a pulse or a heartbeat. The small scenes are framed by four nude youths holding garlands and ribbons that support bronze shields, painted as though decorated with reliefs illustrating still more biblical scenes. The youths are known by the Italian name for them, *ignudi*, and their meaning is much debated. They may be some kind of perfected beings, perhaps even angels.

The ceiling frescoes were an immediate success, and Michelangelo continued as a papal favorite, although his commissions were not always in his preferred line. Just as Pope Julius had urged the sculptor to work as a painter, one of Julius's successors, Pope Paul III, encouraged the sculptor to work as an architect. In 1546, Paul named Michelangelo the official architect of the new St. Peter's, one of the four most important churches in Rome. This structure would be erected on the site of *old* St. Peter's (see 15.4), dating from the early Christian era in the 4th century. By the time he began work on the project, Michelangelo was an old man, well into his seventies and physically tired, but his creative vigor was undiminished.

Construction on the new church had already begun, based on a plan by an architect named Bramante, who had died in 1514. Michelangelo revised Bramante's plan, gathering its elaborate fussiness into a bold and harmonious design (**16.10** and **16.11**). Central and cross plans here merge in a new idea that relates the powerfully symbolic cross to the geometric forms that Renaissance artists loved, the square and the circle. Michelangelo did not live to see his church finished. The magnificent central dome was completed after his death by another architect, who modified its silhouette. During the 17th century, the nave was lengthened and the facade remodeled. The plan seen here suggests the building that Michelangelo conceived. An organic whole with pulsating contours and a powerful upward thrust, it is the architectural equivalent of his muscular nudes.

16.10 Michelangelo. St. Peter's Basilica, Vatican. ca. 1546–64 (dome completed 1590 by Giacomo della Porta).
akg-images/Stefan Drechsel

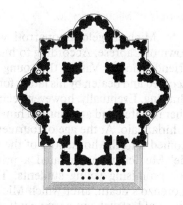

16.11 Plan of St. Peter's.

Michelangelo (1475–1564)

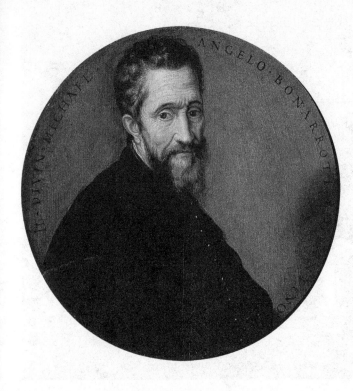

What are the benefits and the constraints of having patrons? How did Michelangelo depict the human figure through sculpture? What did Michelangelo think of his art and his role as artist?

He is beyond legend. His name means "archangel Michael," and to his contemporaries and those who came after, his stature is scarcely less than that of a heavenly being. He began serious work as an artist at the age of thirteen and did not stop until death claimed him seventy-six years later. His equal may never be seen again, for only a particular time and place could have bred the genius of Michelangelo.

Michelangelo Buonarroti was born in the Tuscan town of Caprese. According to his devoted biographer and friend, Giorgio Vasari, the young Michelangelo often was scolded and beaten by his father for spending too much time drawing. Eventually, however, seeing his son's talent, the father relented and apprenticed him to the painter Domenico Ghirlandaio. At the age of fourteen, Michelangelo was welcomed into the household of the wealthy banker Lorenzo de' Medici, who operated a private sculpture academy for promising young students. There he remained until Lorenzo's death, after which Michelangelo, just seventeen years old, struck out permanently on his own.

While working in Rome, Michelangelo attracted the first of what would become a long list of patrons among the clergy. A *Pietà* (Virgin mourning the dead Christ) made in 1500 and now in St. Peter's established his reputation as a sculptor. Within a dozen years of that, he had completed the two works most closely associated with his name: the *David* statue and the ceiling frescoes in the Sistine Chapel. Michelangelo believed that God had given him the gift of art, and that using this gift was a pious act. No matter how beautiful this work, Michelangelo claimed that, "The true work of art is but a shadow of the divine perfection."

From his teenage years until his death, Michelangelo never lacked highly placed patrons. He served—and survived—six popes, and in between accepted commissions from two emperors, a king, and numerous members of the nobility. All his life he struggled to keep a balance between the work he wanted to do and the work demanded of him by his benefactors. His relationships with these powerful figures were often stormy. Pope Julius II famously nagged him about how long the Sistine Chapel fresco was taking, while the artist grumbled about how long the pope took to pay him.

Michelangelo served these masters, at various times, as painter and architect, but he considered himself above all to be a sculptor. Much of his time was spent supervising the quarrying of superior stones for sculptural projects. His greatest genius lay in depictions of the human figure, whether in marble or in paint. Vasari writes that "this extraordinary man chose always to refuse to paint anything save the human body in its most beautifully proportioned and perfect forms." Michelangelo believed that the bodies he sculpted already resided in the stone, writing, "Every block of stone has a statue inside it and it is the task of the sculptor to discover it."

Michelangelo formed a number of passionate attachments during his life. These inspired the artist, always a sensitive and gifted poet, to write numerous sonnets. One of his most poignant verses, however, was written as a commentary on his labors up on the scaffold under the Sistine Chapel ceiling. We might find it amusing if it were not so heartfelt:

> I've grown a goiter by dwelling in this den—
> As cats from stagnant streams in Lombardy,
> Or in what other land they hap to be—
> Which drives the belly close beneath the chin;
> My beard turns up to heaven; my nape falls in,
> Fixed on my spine; my breast-bone visibly
> Grows like a harp: a rich embroidery
> Bedews my face from brush-drops thick and thin. . .[5]

Workshop of Frans Floris. *Portrait of Michelangelo Buonarroti*. 16th century. Oil on wood, diameter 11 ¾". Kunsthistorisches Museum, Vienna. Erich Lessing/Art Resource, NY

The concentration of artistic energy in Rome during the Renaissance was such that while Michelangelo was working on the Sistine ceiling, his slightly younger rival Raphael was only a few steps away, painting his fresco *The School of Athens* (see 7.3) in the private library of the same pope, Julius II. Raphael also painted a portrait of the aged pope (**16.12**). Raphael pictures Julius in his red velvet papal cape and hat. He wears several rings, including the traditional pope's ring. The green cloth in the background has the symbol of the papacy, the crossed keys, woven into the textile. Pope Julius sits on a throne with two acorns at the top—symbols of his della Rovere family lineage (*rovere* means "oak tree" in Italian). The jewelry, family symbols, and sumptuously painted, rich fabrics tell of the worldly splendor of the Church in Rome. The keenly observed face conveys without flattery the power and ambition that drove Julius II and other popes. This likeness was so true, according to Giorgio Vasari, that viewers quaked, feeling that the pope was truly present.

After Rome and Florence, the third great artistic center of Italy was Venice. Located on the water at the north end of the Adriatic Sea, the Republic of Venice was a cultural crossroads and a major trade center. Spices and luxury goods from Asia and the Near East flowed through the port on their way to western Europe. Venice was also famous for the glass that had been produced there since antiquity. It was coveted throughout the western world, and helped to solidify Venice's reputation as a city of luxury and beauty. So, too, did the work produced by its painters.

Giorgione's *Adoration of the Shepherds* (see 2.25) gave us a glimpse of the style of Venetian Renaissance art. The colors are saturated and almost glowing, as Giorgione and other Venetian artists took advantage of oil paint's glazes to build luminous layers of color. The fabrics worn by the shepherds seem luxurious, perhaps referring to the textiles that passed through the city. Giorgione's image reveals a special sensitivity to the way light functions. The lights and shadows falling on Joseph's head and body are based on careful study of nature. It has been said that their watery home made Venetian artists particularly sensitive to light.

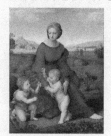

4.16 Raphael, *The Madonna of the Meadows*

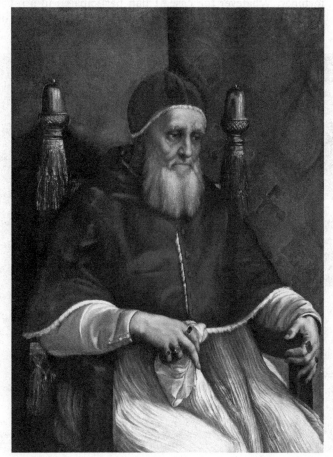

16.12 Raphael. *Pope Julius II.* 1511–12. Oil on panel, 42 ¾ × 31 ⅞".
Peter Horree/Alamy Stock Photo

Giorgione's fellow painter in Venice was Titian, and, while Giorgione died in his early thirties, Titian lived a long and productive life. We have seen the clarity of his style in the *Assumption* (see 2.34). A Venetian saturated red appears throughout the composition and helps to unify it. The deep shadows and glowing, heavenly light convey a drama that is echoed in the frenzied poses of Mary and the apostles below her. The painting conveys all of the order, balance, and unity of Renaissance art in Florence and Rome, but adds a uniquely Venetian sensuality that brings the scene to life.

Another painting by Titian, known as the *Venus of Urbino* (**16.13**), offers even greater emphasis on the senses. It is a feast for the eyes. The viewer can almost feel the texture of the bed sheet, the fabric wall covering, the dog's fur, and the woman's hair and skin. The colors are rich and saturated, with passages of red repeated across the canvas: bed, flowers, dress. Titian's command of linear perspective is demonstrated by the convincing illusionistic space the figures occupy, although the green backdrop keeps the viewer's eye in the foreground. There, the woman's gaze meets ours as she coyly lowers her head and displays her body for our viewing. Such sensuality caused paintings like this to spend most of the time covered, only to be revealed for a select audience.

As with some Venetian Renaissance art, the subject of Titian's *Venus of Urbino* is not entirely clear. She is not Venus—that is a title the painting acquired later—but is instead a mortal woman in her bedchamber. The servants in the background are occupied with two cassoni like the example discussed earlier (see 16.7). They do not seem to notice their mistress's nudity, and she seems to have eyes only for the viewer. It has been suggested that this was a painting created for a marriage bedchamber, which would explain the presence of the cassoni. The new bride offers herself to her husband. The flowers in her hand represent those used in wedding ceremonies, and the dog at her feet symbolizes her loyalty. Another interpretation sees this as a painting of a courtesan who displays herself for her wealthy client. Venice was a rich city and known for attracting beautiful women seeking their fortunes. Whatever the case, Titian participated in a renewed interest in representing the nude figure, referencing the nymphs and graces of ancient art.

16.13 Titian. *Venus of Urbino*. 1538. Oil on canvas, 46 ⅞ × 65".
Artepics/Alamy Stock Photo

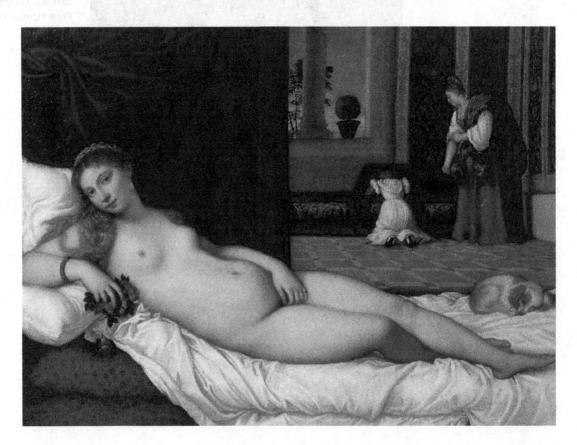

The Renaissance in the North

In the northern countries of western Europe—Switzerland, Germany, northern France, and the Netherlands—the Renaissance did not happen with the sudden drama that it did in Italy, nor were its concerns quite the same. Northern artists did not live among the ruins of Rome, nor did they share the Italians' sense of a personal link to the creators of the Classical past. Instead of the exciting series of discoveries that make the Italian Renaissance such a good story, the Northern Renaissance style evolved gradually out of the late Middle Ages, as artists became increasingly entranced with the myriad details of the visible world, and better at capturing them.

We can see this fondness for detail in one of the most famous works of the late Middle Ages, the illuminated prayer book known as *Les Très Riches Heures* ("the very rich hours"). The book was created at the beginning of the 15th century by three artist brothers, the Limbourgs, for the Duke of Berry, brother to the king of France.

Meant for daily religious devotion, the *Très Riches Heures* contains a calendar, with each month's painting featuring a typical seasonal activity of either the peasantry or the nobility. Our illustration shows the *February* page (**16.14**). At top in the lunette (half-moon shape), the chariot of the Sun is shown making its progress through the months and signs of the zodiac. Below, the Limbourgs depict their notion of lower-class life in the year's coldest month.

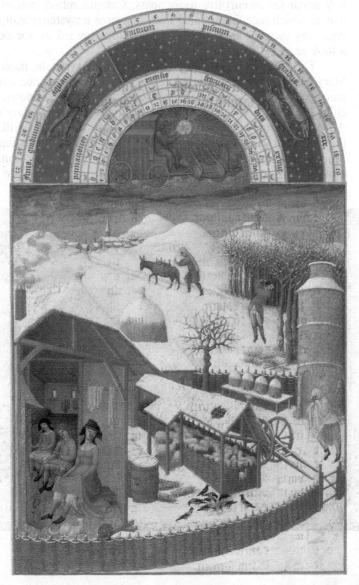

16.14 Limbourg brothers. *February*, from *Les Très Riches Heures du Duc de Berry*. 1416. Illumination, 8 ⅞ × 5 ⅜".
Musée Condé, Chantilly. © RMN-Grand Palais/Art Resource, NY

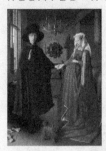

2.30 Van Eyck, *Arnolfini Double Portrait*

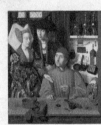

7.7 Christus, *A Goldsmith in His Shop*

16.15 Robert Campin. *Mérode Altarpiece*. ca. 1426. Oil on panel, 25 ³⁄₁₆ × 24 ⁷⁄₈" (center), 25 ³⁄₈ × 10 ¾" (each wing).
The Metropolitan Museum of Art, New York. The Cloisters Collection, 1956, 56.70. Image © The Metropolitan Museum of Art

This view of everyday life focuses on a small peasant hut with its occupants clustered around the fire, their garments pulled back to get maximum benefit from the warmth. With a touch of artistic license, the Limbourgs have removed the front wall of the hut so we can look in. Outside the cozy hut we see what may be the earliest snow-covered landscape in Western art. Sheep cluster in their enclosure, a peasant comes rushing across the barnyard pulling his cloak about his face to keep in the warm breath. From there the movement progresses diagonally up the slope to a man chopping firewood, another urging a donkey uphill, and finally the church at the top.

To appreciate the wealth of detail, we should bear in mind that this is a miniature, barely 9 inches high. So acute is the Limbourgs' observation, on so tiny a scale, that we understand the condition of each character—the exertion of the woodcutter, the chill of the running figure, the nonchalant poses of the couple in the hut, and the demure modesty of the lady in blue.

The Limbourgs' manuscript marks a high point in a medieval tradition dating back hundreds of years (see 15.12). Within a few decades, however, the printing press would be invented, and the practice of copying and illustrating books by hand would gradually die out. In the meantime, an increasing number of Northern artists were turning to painting on panel with the newly developed medium of oil paint. An early master of the medium was Robert Campin, a prominent artist in the Flemish city of Tournai, in present-day Belgium. The subject of his *Mérode Altarpiece* (**16.15**) is the Annunciation, in which Mary hears that she will bear the son of God. Campin painted this work in about 1426, right around the time that the principles of linear perspective were discovered in Italy. The Italian system did not make its way north for seventy-five more years. Campin relied instead on intuitive perspective, in which receding parallel lines converge unsystematically. He uses it here with charming inconsistency, tilting the tabletops toward us, for example, so we can get a look at everything that sits on them.

The Annunciation setting is replete with symbols, most of them referring to Mary's purity: the lilies on the table, the just-extinguished candle, the white linen, among others. At upper left, between two round windows, the tiny figure of a child carrying a cross flies down a light ray toward Mary's ear, signifying that the infant Jesus will enter Mary's womb through God's will, not through human impregnation. The right wing of the altarpiece shows Joseph, who will become Mary's husband, at work in his carpenter shop. By tradition, Joseph is making a mousetrap, symbolic of the Devil being "trapped" by the soon-to-come Jesus,

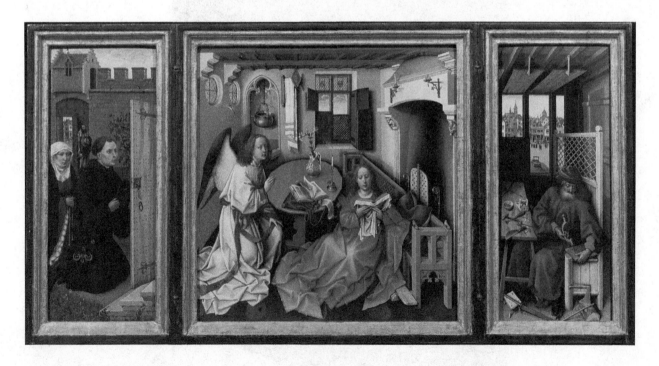

bringing good to banish evil. In the left wing, the donors, who commissioned the painting, kneel to witness the holy scene.

No recitation of this picture's details should overshadow its sheer beauty. Mary's face, modest above her crimson gown, is among the loveliest in all Renaissance art. The angel, with his luminous face and brilliant gold wings, displays an unearthly radiance. Both central figures wear robes that flow into rivers of sculptural folds. The *Mérode Altarpiece* is only about 2 feet in height. Its exquisitely rendered details, its clear colors, and the artist's skillful placement of light and shadow combine to give it a jewel-like quality.

Northern artists' preoccupation with decoration and surface and *things* derives naturally from their heritage. The North had a long tradition of painted miniatures, manuscript illuminations, stained glass, and tapestries—all decorative arts with a great deal of surface detail. Whereas the Italian masters were obsessed with structure—accurate perspective and the underlying musculature of the body—Northern artists perfected their skill at rendering the precise outer appearance of their subjects. They were unsurpassed at capturing in paint the textures of satin or velvet, the sheen of silver and gold, the quality of skin to its last pore and wrinkle.

It was Albrecht Dürer (see 8.8) who more than any other artist attempted to fuse Italian ideas and discoveries with the Northern love of meticulous observation. Dürer had visited Italy as a young artist in 1494 and returned for a longer stay in 1505. He came to share the Italian preoccupation with problems of perspective, ideal beauty, and harmony. In his view, Northern art had relied too heavily on instinct and lacked a firm grounding in theory and science. Toward the end of his life, he summarized his philosophy of art by writing and illustrating two important works, *Treatise on Measurement* and *Four Books on Human Proportions*.

Dürer's engraving of *Adam and Eve* (**16.16**) marries Northern and Italian Renaissance ideas. Like his Northern peers and predecessors, Dürer describes the surface texture of each of the elements in the print in excruciating detail. The image is also filled from edge to edge and foreground to far distance. Nothing is left out,

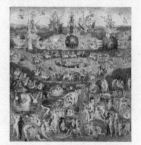

3.20 Bosch, *The Garden of Earthly Delights*

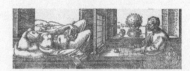

4.48 Dürer, *Draftsman Drawing a Reclining Nude*

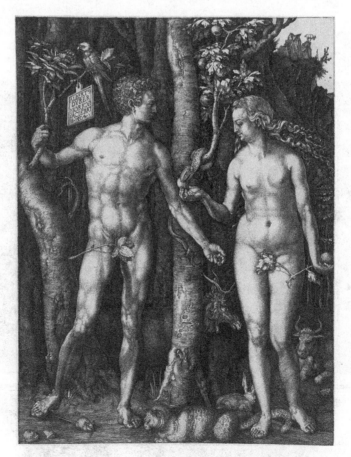

16.16 Albrecht Dürer. *Adam and Eve*. 1504. Engraving, 9 ⅞ × 7 ⁹/₁₆".
Rijksmuseum, Amsterdam

and many of the animals and plants carry important symbolic meanings. The Italian influence appears in the monumental nudes that fill the center of the picture plane. Both figures are based on Classical sculptures the artist saw while traveling in Italy. Dürer also embraced the Italian notion of the artist as intellectual, signing his print in Latin.

Although Dürer's Adam and Eve are calm and restrained, religious art of the Northern Renaissance could also be harsh in its emotionalism—far harsher than that of Italy. Northern art abounds in truly grim Crucifixions, gory martyrdoms of saints, and inventive punishments for sinners. Italian artists did sometimes undertake those subjects, but they never dwelt so fondly on the particulars.

Matthias Grünewald, a German artist active in the early 16th century, painted the Crucifixion of Christ as the center of his great masterpiece, the *Isenheim Altarpiece* (**16.17**). Originally, the altarpiece resided in the chapel of a hospital devoted to the treatment of illnesses afflicting the skin, including syphilis. This setting helps to explain the horrible appearance of Christ's body on the Cross—pockmarked, bleeding from numberless wounds, tortured beyond endurance. Without question, the patients in the hospital could identify with Christ's sufferings and thus increase their faith.

In Grünewald's version of the Crucifixion, the twists and lacerations of the body speak of unendurable pain, but the real anguish is conveyed by the feet and hands. Christ's fingers splay out, clutching at the air but helpless to relieve the pain. His feet bend inward in a futile attempt to alleviate the pressure of his hanging body. To the left of the Cross, the Virgin Mary falls in a faint, supported by Saint John, and Mary Magdalene weeps in an agony that mirrors Christ's own. Opposite her, the Lamb of God, symbol of Christ, cradles a cross as blood flows from his breast into a chalice. To the right, John the Baptist directs our attention to the pitiful figure and says, "He must become greater, I must become less." Grünewald's interpretation of the Crucifixion is in keeping with a stark Northern tradition in which depictions of extreme physical agony were commonplace. Yet, like Dürer, Grünewald also displayed his familiarity with Italian ideas. On the left side of the

16.17 Matthias Grünewald. *Isenheim Altarpiece* (exterior). 1515. Panel, 8' 10" × 10' 1". Musée d'Unterlinden, Colmar/ Bridgeman Images

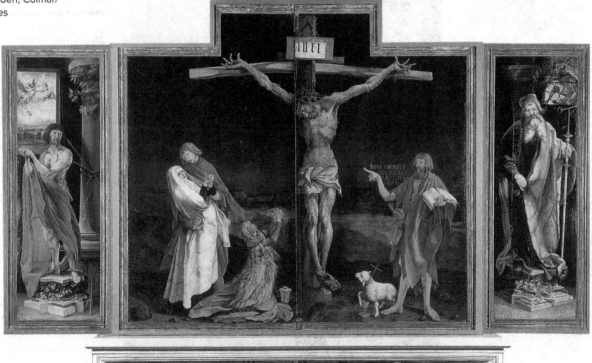

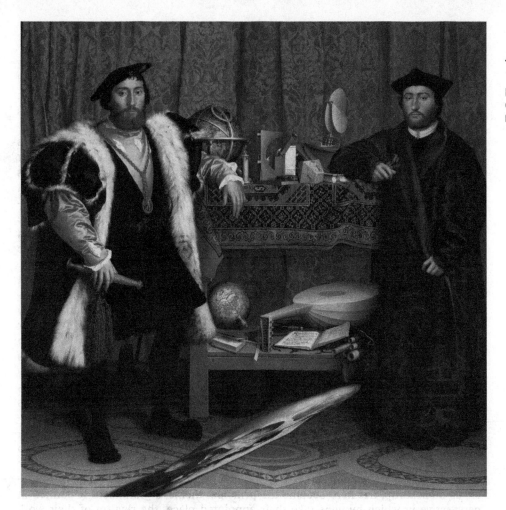

16.18 Hans Holbein the Younger. *The Ambassadors.* 1533. Oil on panel, 6' 9 ½" × 6' 10 ½". © National Gallery, London/Art Resource, NY

painting, a Classically proportioned Saint Sebastian stands beside a Classical column and before a landscape displaying atmospheric perspective.

An artist who matured in the climate of thought that Dürer had created was the German painter Hans Holbein. Although not as intellectual as Dürer, Holbein recognized the need to grapple with the issues that Dürer had introduced. He mastered perspective and studied Italian paintings. Under their influence his modeling softened and his compositions grew more monumental. He did not lose the great Northern gift for detail, however, as his masterpiece known as *The Ambassadors* makes clear (**16.18**).

Holbein painted *The Ambassadors* in England, where his skill as a portraitist earned him the position of court painter to King Henry VIII. The painting was commissioned by the man on the left, Jean de Dinteville, the French ambassador to England. To the right is his friend Georges de Selve, a French bishop who also served as an ambassador. They look out at us from either side of a table richly laden with objects symbolizing the four humanist sciences: music, arithmetic, geometry, and astronomy. The imported Islamic rug speaks of contacts with the wider world, and the globe placed on the lower shelf reminds us that the Renaissance was also the age of European exploration and discovery. Close inspection reveals that the lute resting on the lower shelf has a broken string and that the book before it is open to a hymn by Martin Luther. The broken string symbolizes discord: Europe was no longer in harmony because of the difficult issues raised by Martin Luther's recent accusations against the Church in Rome. The movement Luther started, known as the Reformation, would very soon divide Europe permanently into Protestant countries and Catholic countries. The religious unity that had characterized the Middle Ages would be gone forever.

The strangest element in the painting is the amorphous diagonal shape that seems to float in the foreground. Dinteville's personal motto was *memento mori*, Latin for "remember you must die." Holbein acknowledged this with a human skull,

RELATED WORKS

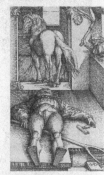

4.47 Grien, *The Groom and the Witch*

stretched as though made of rubber. The skull is painted to come into focus when the painting is viewed up close and at an angle. Death thus cuts across life and shows itself by surprise. Holbein's painting celebrates worldly splendor and human achievement even as it reminds us that death will eventually triumph. It stands as a portrait of two men, a portrait of a friendship, and a portrait of an era.

Protestant reforms of the 16th century included an attitude toward religious images that ranged from wariness to outright hostility. Images of saints and other figures, reformers felt, had all too often been thought to possess sacred powers themselves. In their view, the Church in Rome had encouraged those beliefs, which amounted to idol worship. The walls of Protestant churches were bare: "The kingdom of God is a kingdom of hearing, not of seeing," said Martin Luther.[6] One result was that Northern artists turned increasingly to the everyday world around them for subject matter, and one of the most fruitful subjects they began to explore was landscape.

We opened this brief survey of Northern Renaissance art with a manuscript page by the Limbourg brothers depicting a peasant household with a winter landscape in the background (see 16.14). *The Harvesters* (**16.19**), by the 16th-century Netherlandish painter Pieter Bruegel the Elder, advances the season to late summer and shows us how far painting has come in 150 years. Like the February page from the *Très Riches Heures*, *The Harvesters* formed part of a cycle depicting the months of the year. In the foreground, a group of peasants have paused for their midday meal in the shade of a slender tree. No doubt they have been working in the fields since dawn. The little group sits, chatting and eating. One man has loosened his breeches and stretched out for a nap. In the middle ground, the still unmowed portion of the field stretches out like a golden carpet. Some people are still at work, the men mowing with their scythes, the women stooping to gather the wheat into sheaves. Beyond there opens a vast panorama, a peaceful, domesticated landscape stretching as far as the eye can see. Landscape, which served the Limbourg brothers as a backdrop, has here become the principal theme, a grand setting painted in perspective in which humans take their appointed place, the rhythm of their work and lives falling in with the rhythm of the seasons and of creation.

16.19 Pieter Bruegel the Elder. *The Harvesters*. 1565. Oil on panel, 3' 10 ½" × 5' 3 ¼".
The Metropolitan Museum of Art, New York. Rogers Fund, 1919, 19.164. Image © The Metropolitan Museum of Art

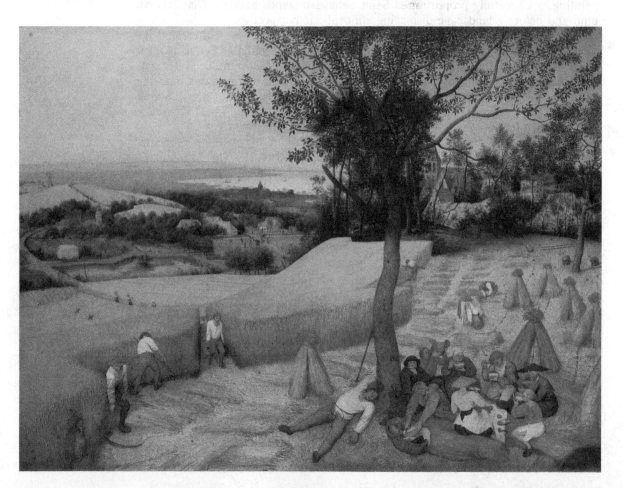

The Late Renaissance in Italy

Scholars generally date the end of the High Renaissance in Italy to the death of Raphael in 1520. The next generation of artists came of age in the shadow of this great period and with two of its most venerated artists, Titian and Michelangelo, still going strong. Of the various artistic trends that emerged, the one that has interested art historians most is known as **Mannerism**.

The word Mannerism comes from the Italian *maniera*, meaning "style" or "stylishness," and it was originally used to suggest that these painters practiced an art of grace and sophistication. Later critics characterized Mannerism as a decadent reaction against the order and balance of the High Renaissance. Today, however, most scholars agree that Mannerism actually grew out of possibilities suggested by the work of High Renaissance artists, especially Michelangelo, whose influence on the next generation was enormous. His own late work also changed to reflect new ideas.

Agnolo Bronzino's bizarre *Allegory* (**16.20**) illustrates some of the fascinating and unsettling characteristics of Mannerism. In an allegory, all the figures and objects also stand for ideas or concepts, and we should be able to "decode" their interaction, perhaps to draw a moral lesson. But the allegory here is so obscure that scholars have yet to reconstruct it. This fondness for elaborate or obscure subject matter is typical of Mannerist artists and the highly cultivated audience they painted for. Also typical is the "forbidden" erotic undercurrent. We recognize Venus and Cupid in the foreground. They are mother and son, but their interaction hints at a different sort of relationship, and both are clearly arranged for our erotic appraisal as well. The elongated figures and twisting S-shaped poses are part of the Mannerist repertoire, as is the illogical picture space—a shallow, compressed zone filled with an impossible number of people.

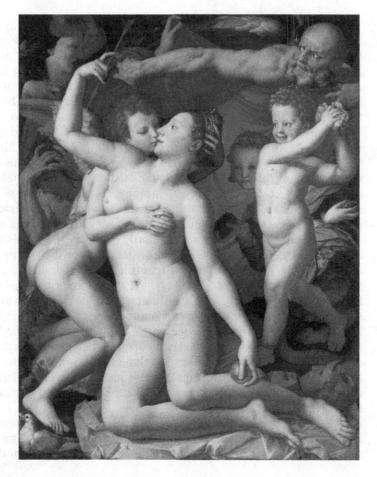

16.20 Agnolo Bronzino. *Allegory (Venus, Cupid, Folly, and Time)*. ca. 1545. Oil on wood, 5' 1" × 4' 8 ¾".
© National Gallery, London/Art Resource, NY

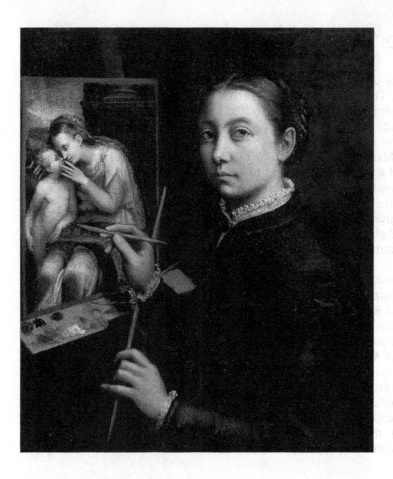

16.21 Sofonisba Anguissola.
Self-Portrait at the Easel. 1556.
Oil on canvas, 26 × 22".
Heritage Image Partnership Ltd/Alamy
Stock Photo

Bronzino's painting is an extreme example of the highly artificial and self-conscious aspects of Mannerist art. But Mannerist elements can also be seen in less exotic works, such as Sofonisba Anguissola's *Self-Portrait at the Easel* (**16.21**). The first woman artist known to have achieved celebrity among her contemporaries, Anguissola was born about 1535 in Cremona, Italy, the eldest of six sisters and one brother. She was well educated and was trained in painting; by about age twenty-two, she had attracted the admiring attention of Michelangelo.

In *Self-Portrait at the Easel*, which may have been created for one of her fans, Anguissola pictures herself as an artist in the act of painting. She has a paintbrush in her right hand, which she keeps steady by resting on a maul stick. The painting she works on displays Mannerist characteristics. The figures have elongated bodies and there is a certain obscurity of meaning. Is this Mary kissing a young Christ? Anguissola looks out of the picture at the viewer who witnesses her making this painting. Her gaze is direct and uncompromising. The painting makes an emphatic assertion of her identity as an artist participating in the trends of her era.

The Protestant Reformation in northern Europe drew large numbers of people away from the Roman Catholic Church. Deeply wounded, the Church of Rome regrouped and struck back. The Catholic Counter-Reformation, begun in the second half of the 16th century and continuing into the 17th, aimed to preserve what strength the Church still had in the southern countries and perhaps recover some lost ground in the north. The concerns of the reformers extended to art, which they recognized as one of their strongest weapons. They insisted that all representations of sacred subjects conform strictly to the teachings of the Church and that artists arrange their compositions to make those teachings evident. They also understood and encouraged art's ability to appeal to the emotions, to engage the hearts of the faithful as well as their intellects.

The Last Supper (**16.22**) by the Venetian painter Tintoretto is an excellent example of the art encouraged by the Counter-Reformation. The greatest painter of the generation after Titian, Tintoretto developed his style from the virtuosic brush-

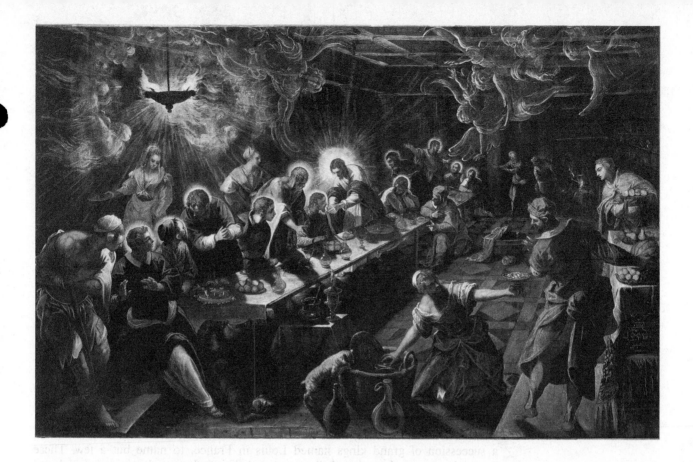

16.22 Tintoretto. *The Last Supper.* 1592–94. Oil on canvas, 12' × 18' 8". San Giorgio Maggiore, Venice. akg-images/Cameraphoto

work and dramatic lighting effects of Titian's late works. Here, Tintoretto chose to portray the central theological moment of the Last Supper, when Christ breaks bread and gives it to his disciples to eat—the basis for the Christian sacrament of communion. The dramatic diagonal of the table sweeps our eyes into the picture and toward the figure of Christ, who stands near the very center of the canvas. His potentially obscure position in the distance is compensated for by the light that radiates from his head. Lesser glows of saintliness shine from the heads of his apostles, who sense the importance of the moment. Only Judas, who will soon betray Christ, fails to emit the light of understanding. He is seated close to Jesus, but alone on the opposite side of the table, a symbolic placement that is both obvious and effective. Witnesses from heaven crowd into the scene from above, swirling in excitement. Although unseen by the servants, who go about their business, they are visible to us, who are left in no doubt that a miracle is taking place.

Comparing Tintoretto's version of the Last Supper with Leonardo's High Renaissance fresco (see 4.46), we can see that what was internalized, subtle, and intellectual has here become externalized, exaggerated, and emotional. Tintoretto's work prepares us well for the next era in art, for key elements of his *Last Supper*—the dramatic use of light, the theatricality, the heightened emotionalism, and even the diagonal composition—would play prominent roles in a style soon to be taken up across all of Europe during the Baroque.

Notes to the Text

1. Quoted in R. Goldwater and M. Treves, eds., *Artists on Art: From the Fourteenth to the Twentieth Century* (New York: Pantheon, 1972), p. 69.

2. Ibid., p. 70.

3. Ibid., p. 52.

4. Ibid., p. 82.

5. Ibid., pp. 60–61.

6. Quoted in Hans Belting, *Likeness and Presence: A History of the Image before the Era of Art* (London and Chicago: University of Chicago Press, 1994), p. 465.

Chapter 17

The 17th and 18th Centuries

In this chapter, you will learn to

LO1   recognize the characteristics of the Baroque era,

LO2   explain the art and architecture of the 18th century, and

LO3   describe art that was inspired by revolutions in the 18th century.

The period encompassing the 17th and 18th centuries in Europe has often been called "The Age of Kings." Some of the most powerful rulers in history occupied the thrones of various countries during this time: Frederick the Great of Prussia, Maria Theresa of Austria, Peter the Great and Catherine the Great of Russia, and a succession of grand kings named Louis in France, to name but a few. These monarchs governed as virtual dictators, and their influence dominated social and cultural affairs of the time as well as political matters.

This same period could equally be called "The Age of Colonial Settlement." By the early 17th century, the Spanish, the Portuguese, the Dutch, the English, and the French had established permanent settlements in North and South America. The first successful English colony was at Jamestown, in Virginia, where a party led by John Smith arrived in 1607. Thirteen years later, the plucky little ship *Mayflower* made landing in what is now Massachusetts. The settlers endured many hardships as they struggled through their first winters in the New World. At Jamestown the colonists went through a period still known as the "starving time." Ironically, the "starving time" in North America coincided exactly with a European style so opulent that its name is now synonymous with extravagance: the Baroque.

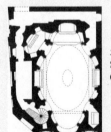

5.29 Plan of San Carlo alle Quattro Fontane

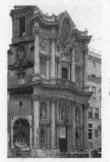

5.30 Facade of San Carlo alle Quattro Fontane

The Baroque Era

Baroque art differs from that of the Renaissance in several important respects. Whereas Renaissance art stressed the calm of reason, **Baroque** art is full of emotion, energy, and movement. Colors are more vivid in Baroque art than in Renaissance art, with greater contrast between colors and between light and dark. In architecture and sculpture, where the Renaissance sought a classic simplicity, the Baroque favored ornamentation, as rich and complex as possible. Baroque art has been called dynamic, sometimes even theatrical. This theatricality was on display in the work of Francesco Borromini, whose church of San Carlo alle Quattro Fontane was studied earlier in this book (see 5.29, 5.30). It is also clearly evident in the work of another of the Baroque's leading interpreters, the artist Gianlorenzo Bernini.

Bernini would have been a fascinating character in any age, but if ever an artist and a style were perfectly suited for each other, this was true of Bernini and the Baroque. Largely for his own pleasure, he was a painter, dramatist, and composer. In architecture and sculpture, however, his gifts rose to the level of genius. Bernini's talents are on full display in the Cornaro Chapel in the church of Santa Maria della Vittoria in Rome (**17.1**). In this small alcove, the funeral chapel of

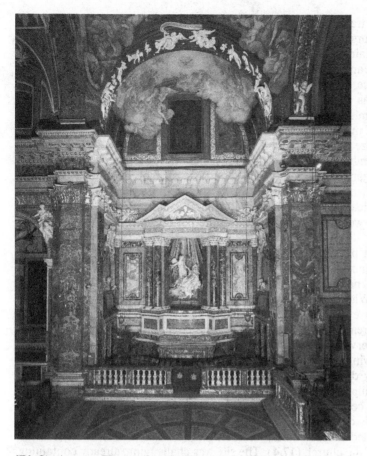

17.1 Gianlorenzo Bernini. Cornaro Chapel, Santa Maria della Vittoria, Rome. 1642–52.
akg-images/Pirozzi

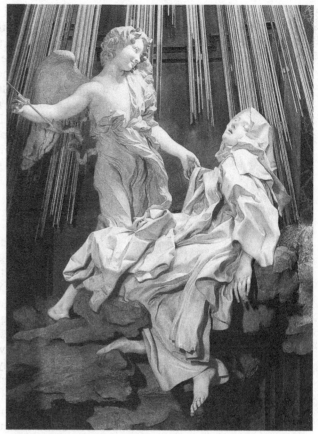

17.2 Gianlorenzo Bernini. *St. Teresa in Ecstasy*, from the Cornaro Chapel. 1642–52. Marble and gilt bronze, life-size.
Scala/Art Resource, NY

Cardinal Federigo Cornaro, Bernini integrated architecture, painting, sculpture, and lighting into a brilliant ensemble. On the ceiling is painted a vision of Heaven, with angels and billowing clouds. At either side of the chapel sit sculptured figures of the Cornaro family, donors of the chapel, in animated conversation, watching the drama before them as though from opera boxes. The whole arrangement is lit dramatically by sunlight streaming through a yellow-glass window.

The centerpiece of the chapel is Bernini's sculptured group known as *St. Teresa in Ecstasy* (**17.2**). Teresa was a Spanish mystic, founder of a strict order of nuns, and an important figure in the Counter-Reformation. She claimed to be subject for many years to religious trances, in which she saw visions of Heaven and Hell and was visited by angels. It is in the throes of such a vision that Bernini has portrayed her. Teresa wrote:

> Beside me, on the left hand, appeared an angel in bodily form, such as I am not in the habit of seeing except very rarely. . . . He was not tall but short, and very beautiful; and his face was so aflame that he appeared to be one of the highest rank of angels, who seem to be all on fire. . . . In his hands I saw a great golden spear, and at the iron tip there appeared to be a point of fire. This he plunged into my heart several times so that it penetrated to my entrails. When he pulled it out, I felt that he took them with it, and left me utterly consumed by the great love of God. The pain was so severe that it made me utter several moans. The sweetness caused by this intense pain is so extreme that one cannot possibly wish it to cease. . . . This is not a physical, but a spiritual pain, though the body has some share in it—even a considerable share.

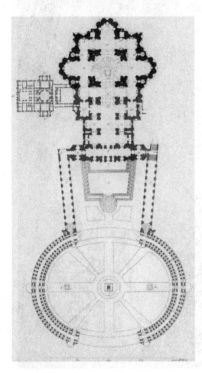

17.3 Carlo Maderno and Gianlorenzo Bernini. Plan of St. Peter's, Rome.
Chronicle/Alamy Stock Photo

Just as Bernini transformed the chapel itself into a sort of theater complete with sculpted spectators, he set the drama of Saint Teresa as if on a stage. We can imagine that the curtains have just parted, revealing Teresa in a swoon, ready for another thrust of the angel's spear. She falls backward, yet is lifted up on a cloud, the extreme turbulence of her garments revealing her emotional frenzy. The angel, wielding his spear, has an expression on his face of tenderness and love; in other contexts he might be mistaken for a Cupid. Master of illusions, Bernini has anchored the massive blocks of marble into the wall with iron bars so that the scene appears to float. The gilt bronze rods depicting heavenly rays of light are themselves lit from above by a hidden window: This little stage set has its own lighting. The deeply cut folds of the swirling garments create abrupt contrasts of light and shadow, dissolving solid forms into flamelike flickerings. As we stand before the chapel, our experience is also theatrical, for we can both watch the ecstasy and watch people watching the ecstasy; we are both caught up in the performance and aware of it *as* a performance.

One of the great projects of Baroque Rome was the completion of St. Peter's, which had been designed by Michelangelo (see 16.10, 16.11). During the early 17th century, an architect named Carlo Maderno transformed Michelangelo's central plan into a basilica. With the addition of three bays to the east side of the church, Maderno created a nave (**17.3**). The new axis allowed for more dramatic processions and accommodated greater numbers of visitors, who could visit side chapels without disturbing religious services. The nave also added drama to the interior, focusing attention on and drawing visitors toward the main altar at the far end of the church. Maderno additionally designed a monumental facade for St. Peter's that is more restrained than the sculptural play of Borromini's San Carlo alle Quattro Fontane but nevertheless contains columns and niches that project and recede across its surface.

Upon Maderno's death, Bernini continued the redecoration of the interior of St. Peter's and designed a spectacular colonnade (row of columns) to enclose the vast square in front of the church (**17.4**). The site was challenging, already containing an obelisk and fountains that Bernini was required to accommodate. His solution solved this problem and another: the distance of the obelisk and fountains from the church's facade. Bernini created a dynamic oval to contain the existing objects and a trapezoid to condense the space between the oval and the facade. This creates the illusion that the church is closer to the oval than it really is, as seen in this later etching. From a bird's-eye perspective, the colonnade seems to form two huge arms that embrace visitors to one of Christendom's most holy sites.

17.4 Giovanni Battista Piranesi. *View of St. Peter's*. 1750. Etching.
bpk Bildagentur/Kunstbibliothek, Staatliche Museen, Berlin, Germany/Art Resource, NY. Photo: Knud Petersen

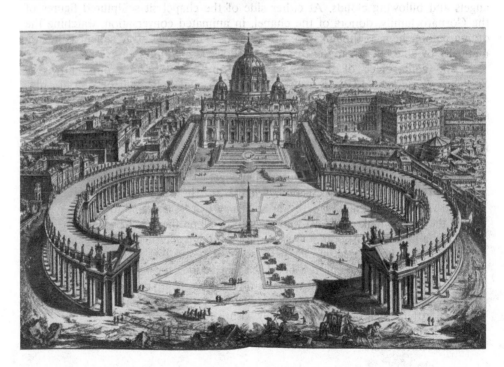

Unlike architecture or sculpture, a painting cannot literally project its figures into the viewer's space. Baroque artists, however, learned to create a similar effect by lighting their figures dramatically and plunging the backgrounds into shadow. The most influential proponent of this type of painting was Caravaggio. His magnificent *Entombment of Christ* (**17.5**) is an example of the theatrical treatment of light and shadow. The *Entombment* depicts the crucified Christ being lowered into an open grave. The body is held by two of Christ's followers—his disciple Saint John and the Jewish ruler Nicodemus, to whom Christ had counseled that a man must be "born again" to enter Heaven. The group also includes the three Marys—Christ's mother, the Virgin Mary, at left; Mary Magdalene, center; and Mary Cleophas, at right—who look on in despair. Caravaggio's structure is a strong diagonal leading from the upraised hand at top right down through the cluster of figures to Christ's face. The light source seems to be somewhere outside the top left edge of the picture. Light falls on the participants in different ways, but always enhances the sense of drama. Mary Magdalene's face, for example, is almost totally in shadow, but a bright light illuminates her shoulder to create a contrast with the bowed head. Light also catches the pathetic outstretched hand of the Virgin. Christ's body is the only figure lit in its entirety; the others stand in partial darkness.

The perspective of the painting places the viewer's eye level at the slab on which the grouping stands. Set on a diagonal, the slab seems to project forward from the picture plane and into our space, involving us in the action. We may imagine ourselves standing in the grave that is about to receive Christ: Perhaps that is why Nicodemus looks at us. Caravaggio painted this work to hang over an altar,

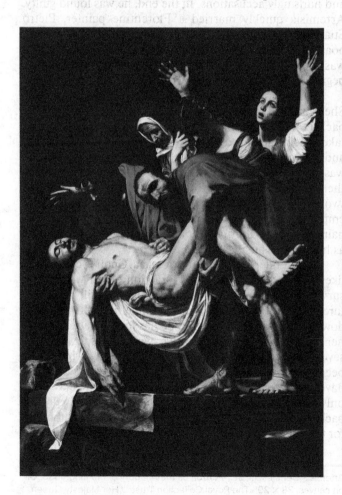

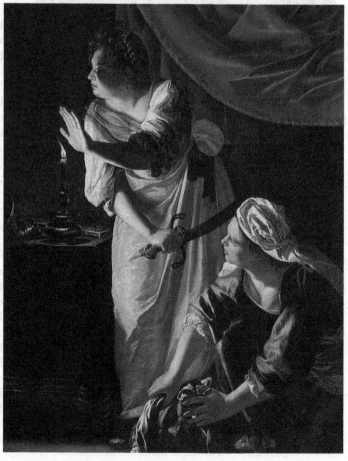

17.5 Caravaggio. *Entombment of Christ*. 1604. Oil on canvas, 9' 9 ⅛" × 6' 7 ¾".
Vatican Museums and Galleries, Vatican City/De Agostini Picture Library/Bridgeman Images

17.6 Artemisia Gentileschi. *Judith and Maidservant with the Head of Holofernes*. ca. 1625. Oil on canvas, 6' ½" × 4' 7 ¾".
Detroit Institute of Arts/Gift of Mr Leslie H. Green/Bridgeman Images

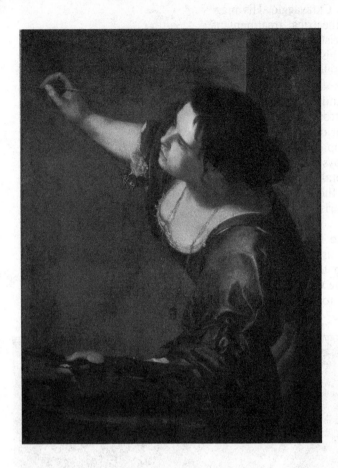

How was Gentileschi able to achieve success in an era that limited women's access to art careers? Compared with Michelangelo, how does she depict the human figure in her works? In the small amount of her work we have access to, what subject matter does she tend to portray?

"I will show Your Most Illustrious Lordship what a woman can do," Artemisia Gentileschi wrote to a patron.[1] She knew full well the prejudices that were arrayed against her. She also knew her own worth: "I have seen myself honored by all the kings and rulers of Europe to whom I have sent my works, not only with great gifts, but also with the most favored letters. . ."[2] It was the simple truth. By dint of talent and ceaseless work, she had become successful, admired, and sought after, and this at a time when women artists were so unusual as to be curiosities.

Artemisia Gentileschi was born in Rome in 1593. Her father, Orazio, was a well-known painter. He was also in all likelihood her teacher. Orazio probably began teaching his daughter to paint subjects considered suitable for women, such as portraits and still life. But at some point he must have recognized the extent of her talent, for the earliest painting we have from her hand depicts a biblical story, *Susanna and the Elders*, and features a large female nude. Mastery of the human form and an elevated literary subject signaled that Artemisia would stake her claim as a history painter, a true rarity for a woman. She was only seventeen years old.

The following year, Artemisia was raped by a friend of her father's, the painter Agostino Tassi. Afterward, Tassi promised to marry her, and because of this she consented to regular relations with him. When after a time he refused to fulfill his promise, Orazio dragged him to court. A transcript of the trial testimony survives, and it makes disturbing reading. Artemisia recounts her version of events in detail and without flinching. Tassi denies all and hurls ugly accusations. In the end, he was found guilty. Artemisia quickly married a Florentine painter, Pietro Stiattesi. Her father found her a patron in Florence, proudly boasting in a letter that his daughter was so skilled that she was without peer. And so it was in Florence that Artemisia began her career.

Our knowledge of Artemisia's trajectory is spotty. She remained in Florence for six years. We find her next back in Rome, having separated from her husband and taken their daughter with her. Then she appears in Genoa and Venice, followed by a stretch of time in Naples. She was briefly summoned to London by the English court, then returned to Naples for the rest of her days. She had two daughters, both of whom she trained as painters. She employed her younger brothers as couriers to deliver her paintings across Europe. Her brother Francesco also served as her business manager.

Our understanding of Artemisia Gentileschi's art is likewise incomplete, for only a fraction of her works have survived. Contemporary writers praised her skill at portraiture and still life, yet only one example of each has come down to us. The story of her rape has focused attention on her images of strong, assertive women, especially the several paintings of Judith slaying Holofernes, which have been seen as her psychological revenge on Tassi. Yet we have no entry into her thoughts, and such images form only a small part of her known output. We must finally fall back on her own words to a patron: "The works will speak for themselves."[3]

Artemisia Gentileschi. *Self-Portrait as the Allegory of Painting*. 1630. Oil on canvas, 38 × 29". The Royal Collection Trust © Her Majesty Queen Elizabeth II, 2015/Bridgeman Images

and the head of a priest standing at the altar would have been at the ideal viewing level, the level of the slab. During the most solemn moment of the Mass, the priest holds the communion bread aloft and repeats the words Christ spoke at the Last Supper, "This is my body." The raised bread would have been visibly juxtaposed with the body in the painting, restoring to the words an intense emotional impact.

Artemisia Gentileschi followed Caravaggio's approach effectively in *Judith and Maidservant with the Head of Holofernes* (**17.6**). The artist took her subject from the biblical story of Judith.[4] According to the scripture, Judith, a pious and beautiful Israelite widow, volunteered to rescue her people from the invading armies of the Assyrian general Holofernes. Judith charmed the general, accepted his invitation to a banquet, waited until he drank himself into a stupor, then calmly beheaded him, wrapped his head in a sack, and escaped. Other of Gentileschi's paintings show the decapitation in progress. Here, she focuses on the moments after the gory deed is done. She poses Judith tensely, caught in the wavering light from a single candle, one hand still clutching the bloody sword, the other poised in a gesture of silence. These Baroque devices heighten the sense of danger, the urgency of deeds committed in the dark of night.

Although Baroque artistic principles were taken up across Europe, each country developed them in its own way. The Flemish artist Peter Paul Rubens created a particularly exuberant and dynamic Baroque style. Although he spent most of his life in Antwerp (in present-day Belgium), Rubens had traveled to Italy and studied the works of Italian masters, including Caravaggio. He also visited and worked for several royal courts, including Paris, where he created a series of twenty-four monumental paintings of the life of the queen mother Marie de' Medici. The purpose of the paintings was to celebrate the French monarchy and Marie's right to rule following the death of her husband, Henri IV. In the canvas seen here (**17.7**), Henri receives a portrait of his betrothed, Marie, held aloft by Cupid and the god of

RELATED WORKS

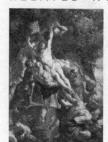

4.9 Rubens, *The Raising of the Cross*

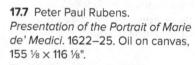

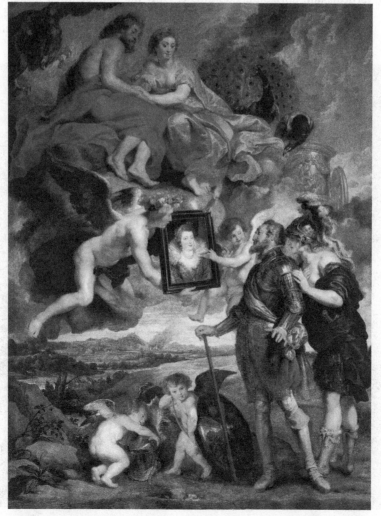

17.7 Peter Paul Rubens. *Presentation of the Portrait of Marie de' Medici.* 1622–25. Oil on canvas, 155 ⅛ × 116 ⅛".
The Artchives/Alamy Stock Photo

marriage, Hymen. The goddess Minerva speaks into the king's ear, telling him about Marie's virtues, while the king and queen of the gods, Jupiter and Juno, look on approvingly from the heavens.

Rubens's Baroque style is seen in the grand diagonal composition that links the king to the gods above. The colors are vivid and saturated, with reds, blues, and golds repeated to unify the image. The play of light and shadow is dramatic, with bright highlights giving way to deeper shadows than the sunny day would seem to produce. Textures glisten, from the silk garments worn by Minerva and Juno to Henri's hard metal armor. Within their garments, each figure possesses a heroic physique. Jupiter and Juno are particularly robust, and their theatrically staged drapery cascades out into the roiling clouds nearby. The entire painting seems to quiver with potential energy and movement, despite its quiet theme.

Although the French monarchy appreciated Rubens's exuberant approach, French artists favored a more restrained, "classical" version of Baroque style. The order and balance of the Renaissance were retained, though infused with a new theatricality and grandeur, even in landscape paintings. Foremost among French landscapists was Claude Lorrain, who actually spent most of his career in Rome. Steeped in the philosophy and history of the Classical past, he created paintings that merged Italian vistas with ancient themes. An example is his painting *Coast View with the Abduction of Europa* (**17.8**). This was based on a story that comes from Greek and Roman mythology. Europa was an ancient Phoenician noblewoman; because of her beauty, the god Zeus wanted her as his own. He transformed himself into a bull so that she would not know his identity. When Europa hopped on the bull's back, Zeus abducted her by swimming away across the sea. He took her to the Greek island of Crete, where Europa bore him three children, including the future king Minos, whose palace we saw in Chapter 14 (see 14.19).

Claude's visual response to this story is far removed from the emotionalism of Caravaggio or the energy of Rubens. In place of their active diagonals, calm verticals and horizontals dominate. Only the manipulation of light marks the painting as Baroque. Zones of light and shadow alternate across the canvas, and the artist captures the hazy glow typical of a coastal sunrise or sunset. In the fore-

17.8 Claude Lorrain (Claude Gellée). *Coast View with the Abduction of Europa.* 1645? Oil on canvas, 37 ⅞ × 66". Digital image courtesy of the Getty's Open Content Program

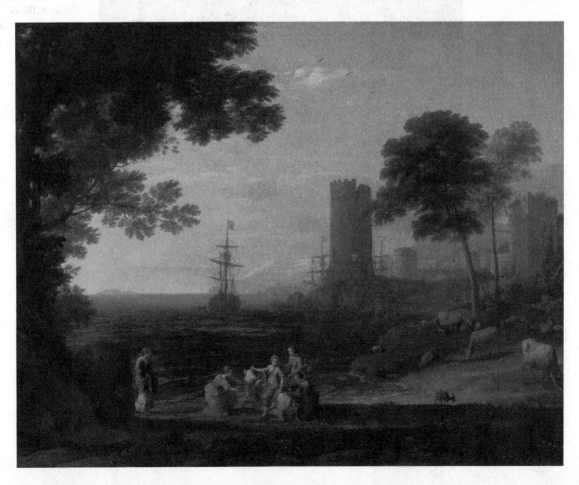

ground, Europa climbs on the bull beside a tree that frames one side of the composition. Another tree to the right and slightly farther away draws our eyes into the painting. The nearby tower does the same, and by following these milestones we eventually reach the mountain and clouds in the distance. The town we see in the distance is not ancient and instead looks more like the ports of medieval or Renaissance Italy. The ship anchored in the bay is also contemporary. Claude's theme may have been taken from ancient mythology, but he modernized the setting to place the event in the here and now.

To grasp fully the flavor of the Baroque in France, we should look at a king who for all time exemplifies the term "absolute monarch"—Louis XIV. Louis ascended the throne of France in 1643, at the age of four. He assumed total control of the government in 1661 and reigned, in all, for seventy-two years. During that time, he made France the artistic and literary center of Europe, as well as a political force to be reckoned with. Showing the unerring instincts of a master actor, he created an aura around his own person that bolstered the impression of divinity. Each day, for example, two ceremonies took place. In the morning, half the court would file into Louis's chambers, in full pageantry, to participate in the king's *lever*—his "getting up." At night, the same cast of characters arrived to play ritual roles in the king's *coucher*—his "going to bed."

The king's godlike power is on display in Hyacinthe Rigaud's *Louis XIV* (**17.9**). The huge portrait pictures the king standing in his throne room, dominating the composition. A curtain is pulled back to reveal the regal person and the symbols of his right to rule. The ermine robe that cascades around him bears the fleur-de-lis symbol of France. The scepter in the king's hand and the crown resting beside it signify royal authority, while the sword on the king's hip shows his might. The king is himself the perfect example of rulership as he gazes confidently out of the painting. He is dressed in the fashionable clothing that he promoted at court, including shoes with heels. Rigaud's treatment of texture creates an almost tangible impression

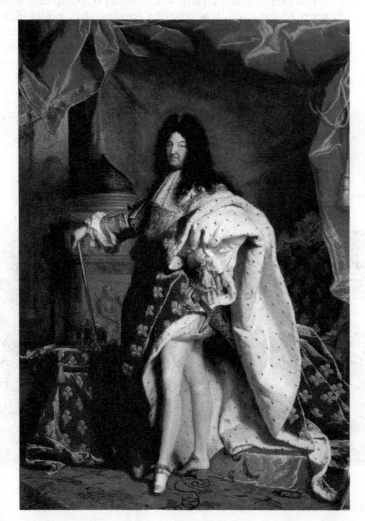

17.9 Hyacinthe Rigaud. *Louis XIV*. 1701. Oil on canvas, 9' 2" × 6' 3". World History Archive/Alamy Stock Photo

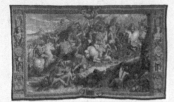

7.18 Le Brun, *Battle of the Granicus*

of the soft ermine and the stiff gold brocade threads of his garments. Colors are rich and dramatically contrasted, with complementary reds, blues, and golds framing the monarch's person. The theatrical lighting highlights the king, while everything else recedes into the shadows.

A life in which the simple act of climbing into and out of bed required elaborate ceremony surely also needed an appropriate setting, and Louis did not neglect this matter. He summoned Bernini from Rome to Paris to work on completion of the Louvre Palace (although the final design of the building was the work of others). But Louis's real love was the Palace of Versailles, in a suburb of the capital, which he rebuilt substantially, and to which he moved his court in 1682. It was from this remarkable structure that the power of kingship flowed forth.

In all, Versailles occupies an area of about 200 acres, including extensive formal gardens and several grand châteaux. The palace itself, redesigned and enlarged during Louis's reign, is an immense structure, more than a quarter of a mile wide (**17.10**). The view here shows the central portion of the palace, overlooking fountains and gardens that stretch for more than 4 miles. Sculpture such as the resting river god in this photograph represents Classical themes meant to symbolize the king's power. The exterior of the palace also reflects the continuing Classical tendencies of France, with a vocabulary of arches, columns, and entablatures. The interior revels in full Baroque splendor. As in Bernini's Cornaro Chapel (see 17.1), although on a much grander scale, architecture, sculpture, and painting are united, creating a series of lavish settings for the pageantry of Louis XIV and his court. Of the countless rooms inside, the most famous is the Hall of Mirrors, which rests just above the sculpture's scepter in this photograph. This grand hall is 240 feet long and lined with large reflective glasses. In Louis's time, the Hall of Mirrors was used for the most elaborate state occasions, and even in the 20th century it served as the backdrop for momentous events, such as the signing of the treaty ending World War I.

The French court clearly was a model of pomp and pageantry, and the Spanish court to the south was eager to emulate that model. King Philip IV of Spain reigned for a shorter time than his French counterpart, and could not begin to match Louis in either power or ability. Philip had one asset, however, that Louis never quite managed to acquire—a court painter of the first rank. That painter was one of the geniuses of Spanish art: Diego Velázquez.

17.10 Jules Hardouin-Mansart. Palace of Versailles. 1678–1715. Shutterstock/onairda

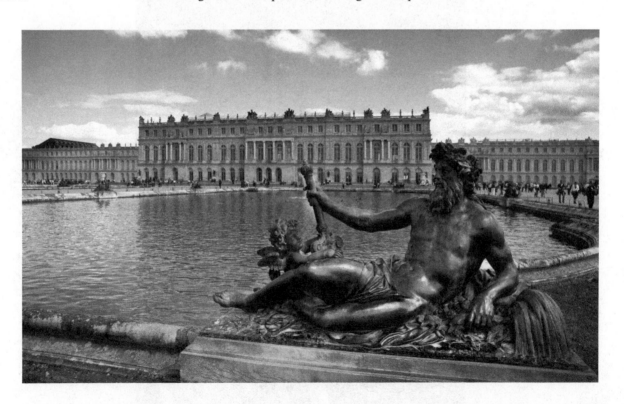

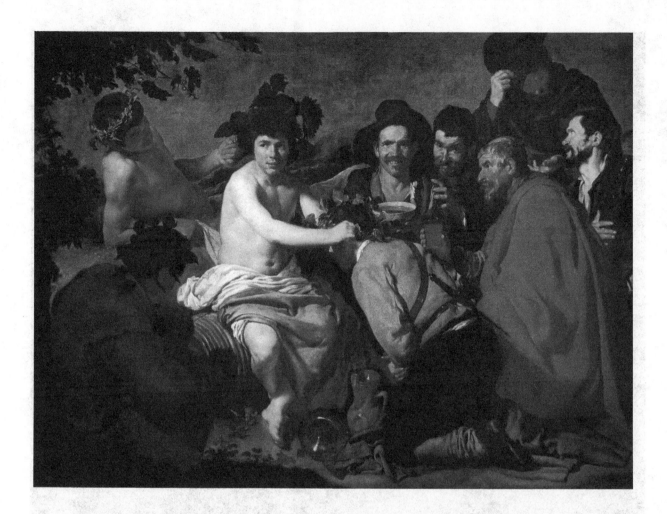

17.11 Diego Velázquez. *The Feast of Bacchus*. 1629. Oil on canvas, 88 9/16 × 64 15/16".
Peter Barritt/Alamy Stock Photo

In his capacity as court painter, Velázquez created his masterpiece, *Las Meninas* (*The Maids of Honor*) (see 2.3). The work pictures the artist at work on a painting for Philip IV. Although it shows a formal occasion, the painting of an official portrait, Velázquez has given the scene a warm, "everyday" quality. Like Caravaggio, Velázquez used light to create drama and emphasis, but light also serves here to organize and unify a complex space. What could have been a very disorderly scene has been pulled together by the device of spotlighting, much as a designer of stage lighting would control what an audience sees in a theater. The theatricality of the Baroque is more subtle in Velázquez than in Bernini, but it is no less skillful.

The Baroque interest in Classical themes is also represented in Velázquez's painting of *The Feast of Bacchus* (also known as *The Merry Topers*) (**17.11**). Yet, the Spanish painter's treatment of the god of wine is far from the heroic idealization of Rubens's Jupiter. Velázquez instead chose to represent the god as a common man, much like Caravaggio's treatment of religious characters. Bacchus is a ruddy young man with a soft physique. His companions are not the nymphs and satyrs of Greek and Roman lore. They instead look familiar to us, as if Velázquez found his models in the local saloon. Their humble clothes, rosy cheeks, and drooping eyes convince us of their inebriation. This realism humanizes the subject, much as Pedro de Mena's *Ecce Homo* (see 11.18) evoked pity for Jesus's suffering with its realistic treatment.

To end this discussion of 17th-century art, we move north, to the Netherlands. The Dutch Baroque, sometimes called the "bourgeois Baroque," is quite different from Baroque movements in France, Spain, and Italy. In the north, Protestantism was the dominant religion, and the outward symbols of faith—imagery, ornate churches, and clerical pageantry—were far less important. Dutch society, and particularly the wealthy merchant class, centered not on the Church but, instead, on the home and family, business and social organizations, the community. These interests were best represented by the most famous Dutch painter, Rembrandt van Rijn.

RELATED WORKS

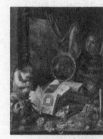

1.15 Valdés Leal, *Vanitas*

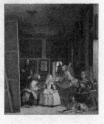

2.3 Velázquez, *Las Meninas*

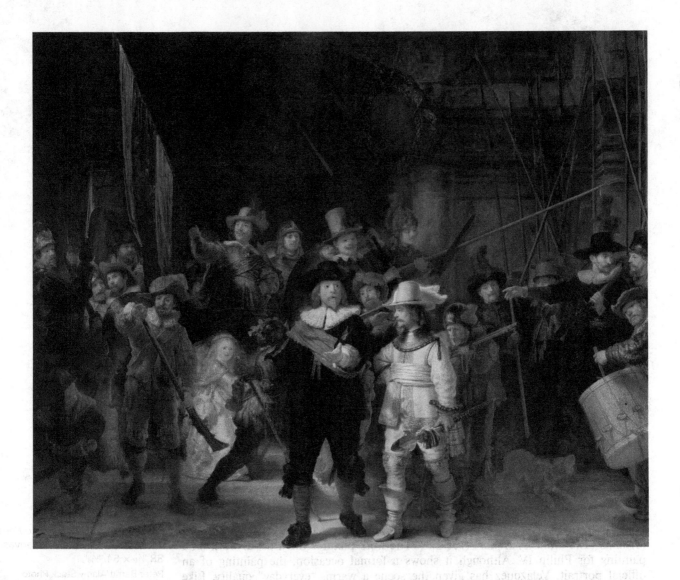

RELATED WORKS

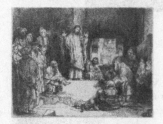

8.11 Rembrandt, *Christ Preaching*

Rembrandt's principal teacher, a painter named Pieter Lastman, had traveled in his youth to Italy, where he had come under the influence of Caravaggio. Returning to the Netherlands to establish his career, he brought with him the new kind of dramatic lighting that Caravaggio had invented. We can see how Rembrandt incorporated this lighting into his own personal style in the famous group portrait *Sortie of Captain Banning Cocq's Company of the Civic Guard* (**17.12**).

The painting portrays a kind of private elite militia. Such groups had played a prominent role in defending the city during the recent wars against Spanish domination; although by Rembrandt's time their function was largely ceremonial, they were still widely respected, and all the most important men of the town belonged to one. Dutch civic organizations often commissioned group portraits, and painters usually responded by portraying the members seated around a table or lined up for the 17th-century equivalent of a class photograph. Rembrandt's innovation was to paint individual portraits within the context of a larger activity, a call to arms. This makes the painting both a portrait and a **genre painting**—a painting that focused on a scene of everyday life.

Rembrandt composes the figures naturally, in deep space, with Captain Cocq, resplendent in a red sash, at the center. The composition builds on a series of broad V shapes, pointing upward and outward. The nested V shapes make the picture seem to burst out from its core—and may have made its subjects feel they were charging off heroically in all directions, into battle. Lest this geometric structure seem rigid, Rembrandt has "sculpted" it into greater naturalness through his dramatic lighting of the scene. Light picks out certain individuals: Captain Cocq

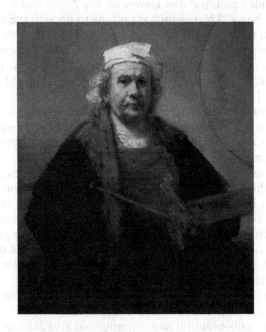

What do Rembrandt's numerous self-portraits tell us about the artist? What functions do light and darkness have in his art? What makes Rembrandt's work so accessible to us?

Of the few artists classified as "greatest of the great," Rembrandt seems the most accessible to us. His life encompassed happiness, success, heartbreak, and failure—all on a scale larger than most of us are likely to know. Through his many self-portraits and his portraits of those he loved, we can witness it all.

Born in the Dutch city of Leiden, Rembrandt Harmenszoon van Rijn was the son of a miller. At fourteen, he began art lessons in Leiden, and he later studied with a master in Amsterdam. By the age of twenty-two, he had pupils of his own. About 1631 he settled permanently in Amsterdam, having by then attracted considerable fame as a portrait painter. Thus began for Rembrandt a decade of professional success and personal happiness—a high point that would never come again in his life.

In 1634, Rembrandt married Saskia van Uijlenburgh, an heiress of good family, thus improving his own social status. The artist's portraits were in demand, his style was fashionable, and he had money enough to indulge himself in material possessions, especially to collect art. One blight on this happy period was the arrival of three children, none of whom survived. But in 1641, Rembrandt's beloved son Titus was born.

Rembrandt's range as an artist was enormous. He was a master not only of painting but also of drawing and of the demanding printmaking technique of etching. (It is said that he went out sketching with an etcher's needle as other artists might carry a pencil.) In all media, Rembrandt created strong contrasts of light and dark that set the mood of the work. In many of his images, shadows partially obscure the main figure's face. Yet only by looking into the shadows do we see the person's character. In the self-portrait seen here, for example, the sorrowful eyes reveal age, wisdom, and perhaps resignation or regret. Rembrandt's art rewards slow looking; only then can we appreciate the full scope of its meaning.

Besides the many portraits he made, Rembrandt displayed unparalleled genius with other themes, including landscapes, religious scenes, and images of his family engaged in daily activities. He infused all of his work with a sense of familiarity and intimacy. His images are accessible to us because they are filled with ordinary people like us. Every character contributes to the work, adding a unique, individual human presence. Regardless of the subject of the painting, drawing, or print, the people in Rembrandt's art engage in everyday activities, experiencing emotions we all feel.

In 1642, Rembrandt's fortunes again changed, this time for the worse. Saskia died not long after giving birth to Titus. The artist's financial affairs were also in great disarray, no doubt partly because of his over-indulgence in buying art and other precious objects. Although he continued to work and to earn money, Rembrandt showed little talent for money management. Ultimately he was forced into bankruptcy and had to sell not only his art collection but even Saskia's burial plot. In about 1649, Hendrickje Stoffels came to live with Rembrandt, and she is thought of as his second wife, although they did not marry legally. She joined forces with Titus to form an art dealership in an attempt to protect the artist from his creditors. Capping the long series of tragedies that marked Rembrandt's later life, Hendrickje died in 1663 and Titus in 1668, a year before his father.

Rembrandt's legacy is almost totally a visual one. He does not seem to have written much. Ironically, one of the few recorded comments comes in a letter to a patron, begging for payment—payment for paintings that are now considered priceless and hang in one of the world's great museums. "I pray you my kind lord that my warrant might now be prepared at once so that I may now at last receive my well-earned 1244 guilders and I shall always seek to recompense your lordship for this with reverential service and proof of friendship."[5]

Rembrandt van Rijn. *Portrait of the Artist*. ca. 1663–65. Oil on canvas, 45 × 37". The Iveagh Bequest, Kenwood House, London/© English Heritage Photo Library/Bridgeman Images

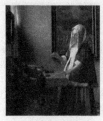

3.19 Vermeer,
*Woman Holding
a Balance*

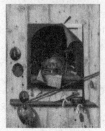

4.39 Gijsbrechts,
*Trompe l'Oeil
with Studio Wall
and Vanitas Still
Life*

himself; the drummer at far right; the lieutenant at Cocq's side, awaiting orders; and especially the little girl in a golden dress, whose identity and role in the picture remain a mystery.

For many years Rembrandt's painting was known as *The Night Watch*, and it is still informally called by that name. The reason has nothing to do with the artist's intent. A heavy layer of varnish on top of the oil paint, combined with smoke from a nearby fireplace, had gradually darkened the picture's surface until it seemed to portray a nighttime scene. No one alive could remember it any differently. It was only when the work was cleaned in the mid-20th century that the light-filled painting we know today reemerged. Even now, though, some members of the group can be seen more clearly than others, and viewers have often wondered how that could have been acceptable to the militia. Documents have revealed that each member contributed to the commission according to how prominently he would appear in the finished painting, and history records no complaints about the results.

In addition to group portraits and genre scenes, Dutch artists made many **still life** paintings. These works, which picture only assembled fruits, foods, or other objects, were very popular with Dutch patrons. Paintings such as Balthasar van der Ast's *Still Life with Fruit and Flowers* (**17.13**) amaze us with their detailed and realistic renderings of common items arrayed across a table. Water drips from grapes, leaves begin to curl with age, and spots form on ripe fruit. Van der Ast was one of a group of artists who specialized in still-life painting. He gained particular fame for including shells, insects, and lizards among his flowers.

The declining role for overtly religious art in Protestant society led prosperous Dutch merchants to commission still-life paintings like Van der Ast's for their homes. These paintings were not only beautiful and engaging, but also demonstrated the patron's wealth. While some still-life paintings are filled with humble objects, many picture tables covered in valuable items from around the world. Van der Ast's painting includes two examples of Chinese porcelain: the plate and vase. These objects were acquired through trade with Asia, and signaled Dutch overseas activity. The tulips in the painting also symbolize wealth. The Dutch experienced what has been called tulipmania in the 17th century. Tulips had been introduced to Europe from Asia a hundred years earlier, and the Dutch had become smitten. Collectors paid outrageous sums of money for a single bulb of a particularly coveted variety.

17.13 Balthasar van der Ast. *Still Life with Fruit and Flowers*. 1620–21. Oil on canvas, 15 ⅜ × 27 ⅝". Rijksmuseum, Amsterdam, purchased with the support of the Vereniging Rembrandt

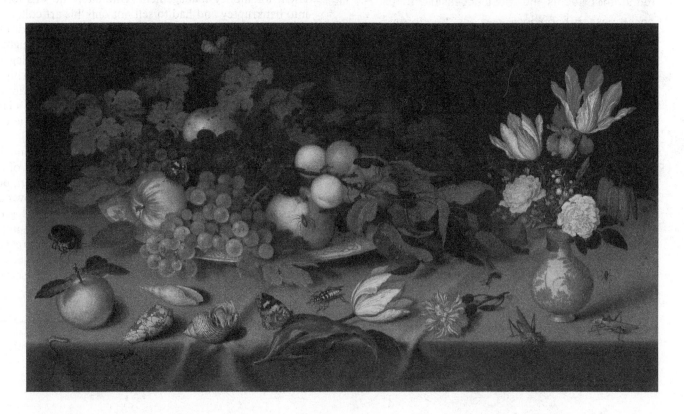

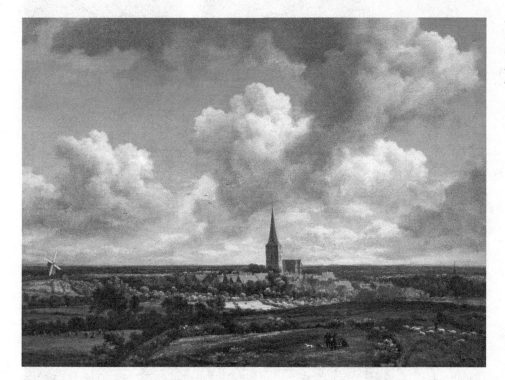

17.14 Jacob van Ruisdael. *View of Ootmarsum*. ca. 1660–65. Oil on canvas, 23 ¼ × 28 ⅞". Alte Pinakothek, Munich. Peter Horree / Alamy Stock Photo

Fortunes were made and lost trading these precious flowers. The tulips lying on the table and resting in the vase in Van der Ast's painting may therefore have cost their owner as much as or more than the Chinese porcelain.

The 17th century was also a great period for landscape painting in the Netherlands. The Dutch were proud of having taken their new nation back from Spanish control, as well as of the feats of engineering that kept the land from being swamped by the ocean. Typical of Dutch landscape painting was the work of Jacob van Ruisdael, which pictures the land and the quiet spirituality of Dutch society. Van Ruisdael's *View of Ootmarsum* (**17.14**) shows not only the famed flatness of the Dutch landscape but also the artist's reaction to that flatness as an expression of the immense, limitless grandeur of nature. The artist makes a contrast between the land—where human order has been established in the form of buildings and cultivation—and the sky, with its billowing clouds, yielding to the wind, which mere people can never tame. The horizon line is set quite low, and, significantly, only the church steeple rises up in silhouette against the sky, perhaps symbolizing that humankind's one connection with the majesty of nature is through the Church.

Despite this emphasis on the church building, Van Ruisdael's art is essentially secular, as is that of Rembrandt. Although religious subjects continued to appear in art—and do so even now—never again would religious art dominate as it did in the Renaissance and Italian Baroque periods. No doubt, this is largely because of changes in sponsorship; popes and cardinals would become less important as patrons, while kings, wealthy merchants, and the bourgeoisie would become more so. We can follow this increasing secularization of art as we move out of the 17th century and into the 18th.

The 18th Century

The first half to three-quarters of the 18th century is often thought of as the age of **Rococo**—a development and extension of the Baroque style. The term *rococo* was a play on the word *baroque*, but it also refers to the French words for "rocks" and "shells," forms that appeared as decorative motifs in architecture, in furniture,

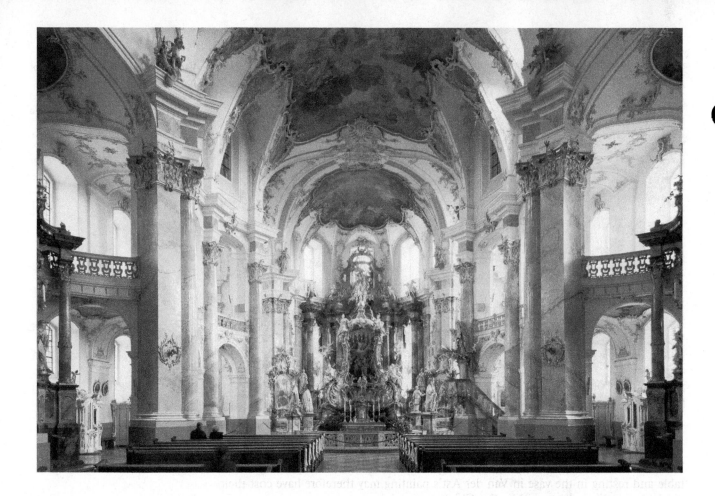

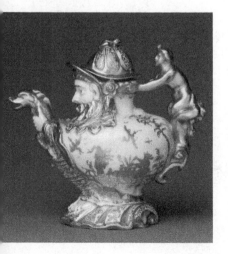

and occasionally in painting. Like the Baroque, Rococo is an extravagant, ornate style, but there are several points of contrast. Baroque, especially in the south, was an art of cathedrals and palaces; Rococo was more intimate, suitable for the aristocratic home and the drawing room. Baroque colors are intense; Rococo leans more toward the gentle pastels. Baroque is large in scale, massive, dramatic; Rococo has a smaller scale and a lighthearted, playful quality.

The Rococo style of architecture originated in France but was soon exported. We find some of the most developed examples in Germany, especially in Bavaria. The church of Vierzehnheiligen (**17.15**) demonstrates amply why the word *rococo* has come to mean "elaborate and profuse." Designed by Balthasar Neumann, the church is a perfect riot of sinuous, twisting architectural and decorative forms. Every line moves, curls, and twists back on itself. Scrolls and plant forms adorn and enliven the surfaces. The light, analogous hues used throughout the building are soft and pleasant, even in the paintings on the ceiling. The serious drama of the Baroque has given way to a theatrical, lighthearted playfulness. Rococo was, above all, a sophisticated style, and Vierzehnheiligen shows us the height of that sophistication.

The same Rococo spirit was applied to every form of art. Elegant homes in European cities were ornamented and outfitted with highly decorated and sophisticated materials. The Meissen firm in Germany produced porcelain tableware to suit refined tastes. Inspired by the Chinese wares flooding into Europe via overseas trade, Meissen developed the first porcelain production in Europe. Its white vessels were formed into fanciful shapes (**17.16**) and decorated in gold or colorful enamel paint. Many of the images painted onto Meissen objects were inspired by Chinese motifs. This teapot's scene, with figures and animals in a landscape, reflects European tastes for Chinese-looking images. The shape of the pot likely derives from European mythology. A nude female forms the handle, and the spout is a beast held by a godlike male character. His helmet, topped by a frog, serves as the pot's lid. We can imagine how ornate and delightful a host's table appeared when outfitted with the full set of cups and saucers that once accompanied this teapot.

Sophistication was paramount in painting, as well. In Chapter 4, we looked at *The Embarkation for Cythera* by Jean-Antoine Watteau (see 4.10). Painted around 1718–19, it stands at the very beginning of the Rococo style. The dreamlike world Watteau invented must have appealed to French aristocrats weary of the formal grandeur of Versailles and the ceremonial character of daily life there. Even the new king, Louis XV, seems to have found his role exhausting, for he created within the palace a modest apartment that he could escape to and where he could live, if only for a few hours, like a simple (if rather well-off) gentleman.

Just over half a century later, the aging king's mistress, the Countess du Barry, commissioned one of the last masterpieces of Rococo art, a set of four large paintings by Jean-Honoré Fragonard called *The Progress of Love*, of which we illustrate *The Pursuit* (**17.17**). Through a lushly overgrown garden in the grounds of some imaginary estate, an ardent youth chases after the girl who has captured his heart. He holds out to her a single flower, plucked from the abundance that surrounds them. She, surprised while sitting with her friends, flees, but so prettily that we know it is all a game. She will surely not run *too* fast. Above, a statue of two cupids seems to participate, watching over this latest demonstration of their powers to see how it will all turn out. The painting's complex composition, decorative appearance, small details, and analogous pastel color scheme of zones of blue/green and yellow/beige typify the Rococo style.

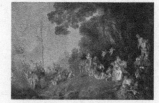

4.10 Watteau, *The Embarkation for Cythera*

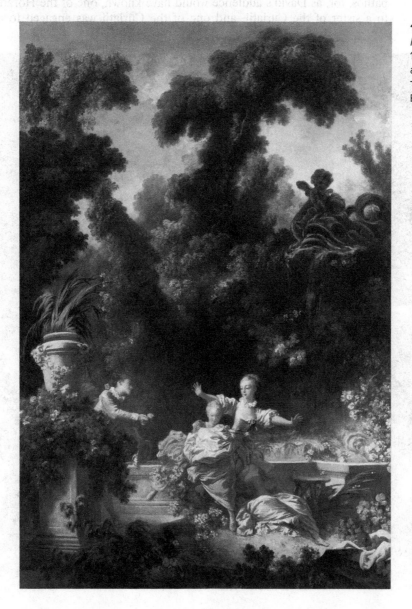

17.17 Jean-Honoré Fragonard. *The Pursuit*, from *The Progress of Love*. 1771–73. Oil on canvas, height approx. 10' 5".
The Frick Collection, New York/Bridgeman Images

Madame du Barry had commissioned these paintings to decorate a new pavilion she had just had built on her estate. Although Fragonard never painted a lovelier set of works, his patron rejected them. She considered them too old-fashioned and sentimental. Rococo taste had run its course. Seriousness was now in vogue, together with an artistic style called **Neoclassicism** ("new classicism"). Since 1748, excavations at the Roman sites of Pompeii and Herculaneum in Italy had been uncovering wonders such as the wall paintings we looked at in Chapter 14 (see 14.31). Patrons and artists across Europe were newly fascinated by the Classical past, and their interest was encouraged by rulers and social thinkers hoping to foster civic virtues such as patriotism, stoicism, self-sacrifice, and frugality—virtues they associated with the Roman Republic.

Among the many young artists who flocked to Italy to absorb the influence at first hand was a young painter named Jacques-Louis David. Upon his return to France, David quickly established himself as an artist of great potential, and it was none other than the new king, Louis XVI, who commissioned his first resounding critical success, *The Oath of the Horatii* (**17.18**).

The painting depicts the stirring moment when three Roman brothers, the Horatii of the painting's title, swear before their father to fight to the death three brothers from the enemy camp, the Curiatii, thus sacrificing themselves to spare their fellow citizens an all-out war. The subject combines great patriotism with great pathos, for, as David's audience would have known, one of the Horatii was married to a sister of the Curiatii, and one of the Curiatii was engaged to a sister of the

17.18 Jacques-Louis David. *The Oath of the Horatii*. 1784–85. Oil on canvas, approx. 11 × 14'. Musée du Louvre, Paris. © RMN-Grand Palais/Art Resource, NY

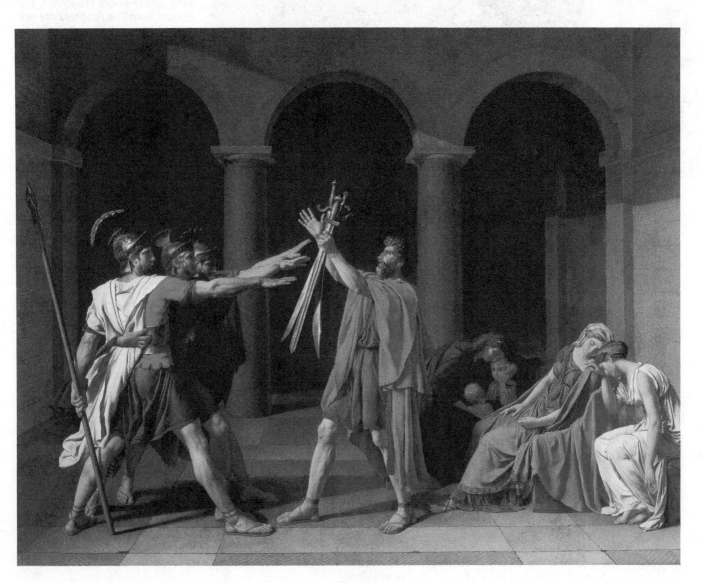

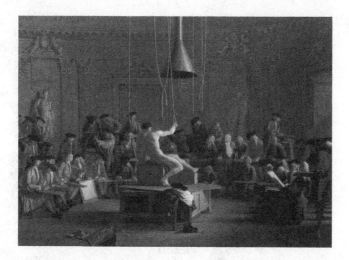

Why did artists want to be accepted by academies? What were some of the accomplishments that academies encouraged? Did academies impose limitations and labels that hindered artistic expression?

The painting seen here pictures work in an 18th-century art academy. A model is posed, with a rope to keep his arm aloft. Artists—both students and working professionals who were members of the academy—study the model and draw what they see. They discuss their art, and representatives of the academy critique and correct it. As revealed by the drawing resting on the floor in the foreground, and the sculptures standing along the back wall, the goal of the drawing session and critique was to develop the skill of drawing in the Classical style.

Academies were one of the many ways in which Renaissance humanists had attempted to revive Classical culture. Their model was the celebrated Academy of the ancient Greek philosopher Plato, which earned its name from the park in Athens where the brilliant thinker met with his students, the Akademeia. Early Renaissance academies were private, informal gatherings that brought small groups of scholars and artists together to discuss ideas. In 1563, however, the artist Giorgio Vasari persuaded Cosimo de' Medici, a wealthy art patron, to sponsor a formal academy devoted to art, the Academy of Design, in Florence. By founding the first public academy, Vasari sought to underscore the prestige of art as an intellectual endeavor and to solidify the social status that artists had achieved during the Renaissance. Over the course of the next two centuries, art academies were founded across Europe. By the close of the 18th century, they were at the center of artistic life, closely aligned with the goals of the monarchy.

Academies were inherently conservative. Their aim was to maintain official standards of skill and taste by perpetuating models of greatness from the past, especially the Classical past. Although women artists could often be accepted as members, only men could enroll as students, for academic training revolved around mastering the human figure, and it was deemed improper for young girls to gaze upon naked models. Students began by copying drawings, then advanced to drawing fragments of Classical statues—isolated heads, feet, torsos. They learned to draw gestures, poses, and facial expressions that expressed a great variety of dramatic situations and emotions. They studied anatomy. Eventually they progressed to drawing from live models, as seen here. They came to know the human form so thoroughly that they could draw it from memory, creating complex compositions without recourse to models at all.

This emphasis on mastering the human form was linked to the belief that the greatest subject for art was history, including biblical and mythological scenes, historical events, and episodes from famous literary works. After history, portraiture had the most prestige. Then, in descending order, came genre painting, still life, and landscape. This hierarchy was upheld in several ways. Competitions held at the academy required mastery of the most important themes. Upon completing their education, academy-trained artists applied to become members of the academy, with the right to show their work in the institution's exhibitions. These exhibitions celebrated and promoted historical, mythological, religious, and literary works. Finally, many academy members sought royal appointments and pensions, which were granted principally to artists specializing in historical subjects.

Michel-Ange Houasse. *Drawing Academy*. Royal Palace of Spain. akg-images/Album/Oronoz

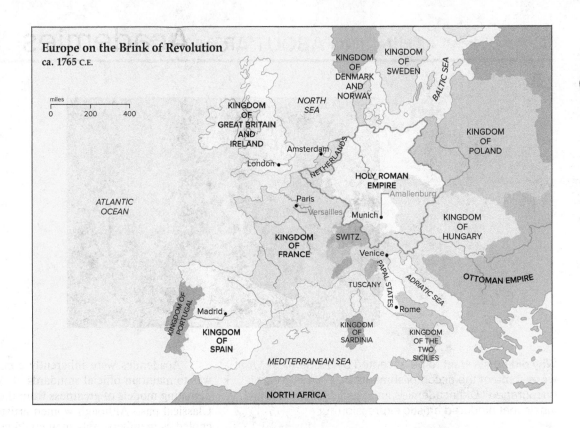

Europe on the Brink of Revolution
ca. 1765 C.E.

Horatii. David paints these two women at the right. They are overcome with emotion, knowing that tragedy is the only possible outcome. In fact, of the six brothers, only one, one of the Horatii, will survive the bloody combat. Arriving home, he finds his sister in mourning for her slain fiancé. Outraged at her sorrow, he kills her.

Gone are the lush gardens and pastel colors of the Rococo. In their place, David has conceived an austere architectural setting beyond which there is merely darkness. Spread across the shallow foreground space, the dramatically lit figures are portrayed in profile as though carved in relief. The composition is orderly and stable, with the father serving as the central axis. The creamy brushstrokes and hazy atmosphere of Fragonard have given way to a smooth finish and a cool, clear light. Colors are muted, except for the father's tunic, which flows like a river of blood next to the three gleaming swords.

Along with the stern "Roman family values" promoted by Neoclassicism, the late 18th century was under the spell of a new taste for simplicity and naturalness. One of the people most taken by the new informality was Louis XVI's queen, Marie-Antoinette. Another advocate of all that was unaffected was the queen's favorite portrait painter, Élisabeth Vigée-Lebrun. Inspired in part by the spareness of Classical costume (note the women in David's painting) and in part by an ideal of the "innocent country girl," Vigée-Lebrun coaxed her highborn models into posing in airy white muslin dresses, their hair falling loosely about their shoulders, a straw bonnet tied with a satin ribbon on their head, and a flower or two in their hands.

In an attempt to repair the queen's reputation with the public as both frivolous and flirtatious, however, Vigée-Lebrun was asked to paint a different sort of portrait of the queen—*Marie-Antoinette and Her Children* (**17.19**). Here, Marie-Antoinette is portrayed as a devoted and beloved mother. She is a woman who knows that her place is in the home, not meddling in politics or advertising her charms. In a gesture meant to tug at viewers' heartstrings, her elder son, the heir to the throne, draws our attention to an empty cradle; his youngest sibling had recently died in infancy. The queen's formal velvet gown and the glimpse of the fabled Hall of Mirrors in the background are meant to convey that she is aware of the seriousness of her position and fully capable of the quiet dignity needed to fulfill it.

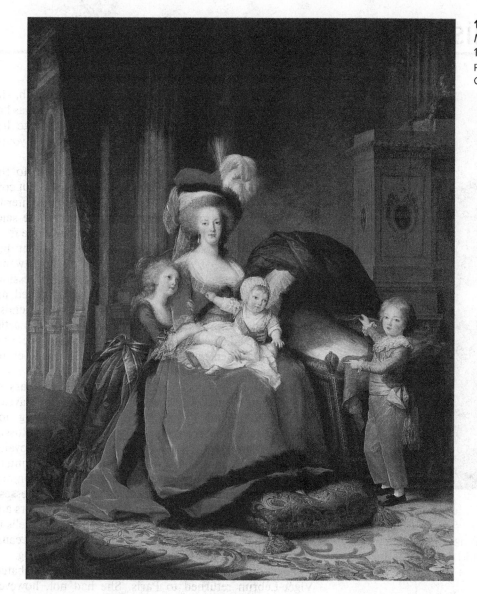

17.19 Élisabeth Vigée-Lebrun. *Marie-Antoinette and Her Children.* 1787. Oil on canvas, 8' 8" × 6' 10". Palace of Versailles, France. © RMN-Grand Palais/Art Resource, NY

The portrait came too late; far too much damage had already been done for a single painting to repair. The nation was teetering on the brink of financial disaster. Popular opinion blamed the deficit on the queen's extravagant ways and also suspected her of shocking personal vices. Vigée-Lebrun herself recorded that when the frame for the large canvas was carried into the Salon, where the painting was to be shown to the public for the first time, voices were heard saying, "There is the deficit."

Although Vigée-Lebrun later made several copies of her own portraits of the queen, she never again painted Marie-Antoinette from life. Within two years, revolution had swept the country, ultimately destroying the monarchy and the aristocracy. The artist fled and took refuge outside France. The queen died by the guillotine.

Revolution

The leaders of the French Revolution continued to evoke the example of Rome and to admire Roman civic virtues. Neoclassicism became the official style of the Revolution and Jacques-Louis David its official artist. David served the Revolution as propaganda minister and director of festivals. As a deputy to the National

Élisabeth Vigée-Lebrun (1755–1842)

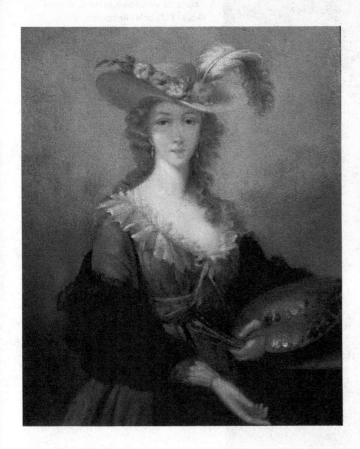

How did Vigée-Lebrun display her steadfast and calm personality in this self-portrait? In her other works? What was it about her style that attracted the attention of aristocratic clients?

From her self-portrait she gazes directly at us, her viewers—calm, self-possessed, sure of her talent, sure of her place in the world. She holds a palette and brushes in her hand; we have momentarily interrupted her work on a painting. She will not be interrupted for long. Throughout her remarkable life, Élisabeth Vigée-Lebrun knew where she was going and remained steadfastly on that path.

Born in Paris, the daughter of a portrait painter, Élisabeth Vigée was convent-educated and encouraged from an early age to draw and paint. At eleven she began serious art studies. After her father's untimely death, she resolved to work as a painter, and by age fifteen she was her family's chief financial provider. Patrons flocked to her studio, eager to have their portraits done by the young artist, and her fees soared.

In 1778, Vigée-Lebrun earned membership to the French Royal Academy. Her selection was not without controversy. As she explained, "Mr. Pierre, the first Painter to the King, made strong opposition, not wishing, he said, that women be admitted."[6] In 1779, a summons came from the Palace of Versailles. Marie-Antoinette sought her services, and Vigée-Lebrun made the first of some twenty portraits of the queen. At their initial portrait session, "The imposing air of the Queen at first frightened me greatly," but the two women went on to become friends.[7] Their relationship was a splendid advantage for the artist initially, but a dangerous liability as resentment of the monarchy grew. When revolution came in 1789, Vigée-Lebrun fled the country.

Then commenced Vigée-Lebrun's twelve years of "exile" from France. And what an exile it was! She traveled first to Rome and Vienna, then to St. Petersburg and Moscow, spending six years altogether in czarist Russia. Wherever she went she was treated like visiting royalty, entertained lavishly, and invited to join the local painters' academy. She was also overwhelmed with portrait commissions. Kings and queens, princesses, counts, duchesses—she painted them all, in between the elaborate dinners and balls to which they invited her. In her memoirs she tells us that she failed to paint Catherine the Great, only because the empress died just before the first scheduled sitting.

In 1801, the furies of the revolution having abated, Vigée-Lebrun returned to Paris. She had not, however, quite satisfied her urge to travel. Only after a three-year stay in London and two visits to Switzerland did she finally settle down to write her memoirs and paint the survivors of the French nobility. She died in her eighty-seventh year, having painted more than 600 portraits. Her memoirs conclude with these words: "I hope to end peacefully a wandering and even a laborious but honest life."[8] And she did.

Élisabeth Vigée-Lebrun. *Self-Portrait*. 1782. Oil on canvas, 31 × 26 ¾".
The Pushkin State Museum of Fine Arts, Moscow. HIP/Art Resource, NY

Convention of 1792, he was among those who voted to send his former patron Louis XVI to the guillotine. One of the events orchestrated by David was the funeral of the revolutionary leader Jean-Paul Marat. David staged the exhibition of Marat's embalmed cadaver to the public, and he memorialized the leader's death in what has become his most famous painting, *The Death of Marat* (**17.20**).

A major figure in the Revolution, Jean-Paul Marat was the fiery voice of the radical political faction called the Jacobins. Because of a painful skin ailment, he spent his days in the bathtub, which was fitted out with a writing desk so that he could work, and there he received callers. A woman named Charlotte Corday, who sympathized with a rival political faction called the Girondins, gained entry to his apartment and stabbed him to death.

In lesser hands Marat's demise could have been laughable—a naked man murdered in his tub. But David has invested the event with all the pathos and dignity of Christ being lowered into his tomb (see Caravaggio's *Entombment of Christ*, 17.5). Marat is shown, in effect, as a kind of secular Christ martyred for the Revolution. All the forms are concentrated in the lower half of the shallow composition, and light bathes the fallen leader in an unearthly glow, both of these devices contributing to the sense of tragedy. Marat's face and body could be those of a fallen Greek warrior, sculpted in marble by an ancient master. David's purpose in this work was to transform a man whom many considered Satan himself into a sainted hero. He projected the image the leaders of the Revolution wished to have of themselves, just as Vigée-Lebrun's art had projected the self-image desired by the French monarchs.

Three other revolutions occurred at more or less the same time as that in France. One was the American Revolution, ending just six years before the French.

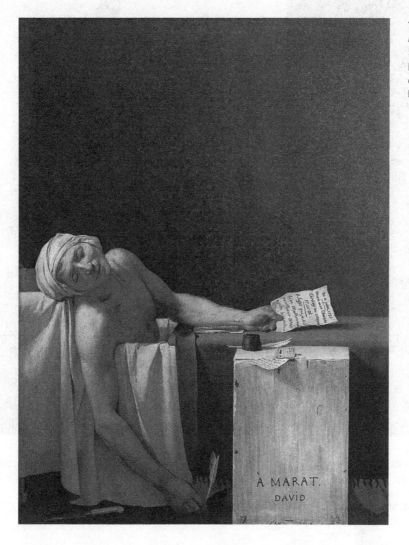

17.20 Jacques-Louis David. *The Death of Marat.* 1793. Oil on canvas, 5' 5" × 4' 2 ½".
Musée d'Art Ancien, Musées Royaux des Beaux-Arts, Brussels. © RMN-Grand Palais/Art Resource, NY

During the relatively brief period covered by this chapter, the American colonists had progressed from the "starving time" of Jamestown to a nation of people capable of independence and self-government. The American colonies' war against British rule was led by George Washington, who became the new nation's first president.

The American artist Charles Willson Peale painted Washington's portrait (**17.21**) while the war still raged. The painting captures an image of an American leader. The flags of the military units Washington defeated at the Battle of Princeton lie at his feet as the vanquished soldiers are led from the battlefield by his troops. On the right side of the painting is an assembly of symbols of the general's military might. The new American flag flies above an obedient page leading a well-trained horse. Both direct their attention toward their leader, who leans against the cannon that secured his victories. Washington dominates the composition, a pillar of strength silhouetted against a stormy sky that clears in his wake. We may compare his confident, casual pose and direct gaze to Louis XIV's formality and haughty superiority (see 17.9). Unlike the godlike absolute monarch, however, Washington appears to us in Peale's painting as both a hero and a compassionate and thoughtful human being.

The second revolution took place in what is today Haiti. Slaves on the island of Saint-Domingue rose up against French colonial authorities in 1791. Jean-Baptiste

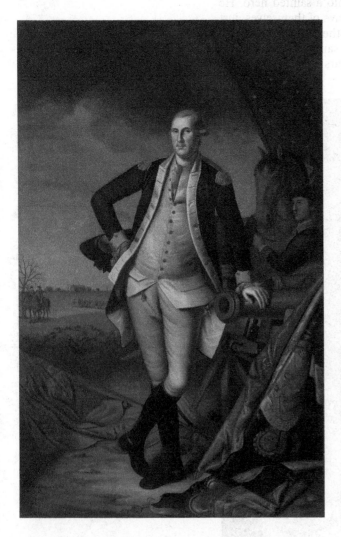

17.21 Charles Willson Peale. *George Washington at the Battle of Princeton*. 1781. Oil on canvas, 95 × 61".
Given by the Associates in Fine Arts and Mrs. Henry B. Loomis in memory of Henry Bradford Loomis, B.A. 1875 © Yale University Art Gallery

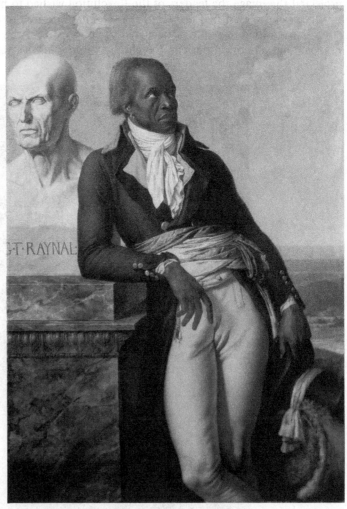

17.22 Anne-Louis Girodet de Roucy-Trioson. *Portrait of Jean-Baptiste Belley*. 1797. Oil on canvas, 62 ¹³⁄₁₆ × 44 ⁷⁄₁₆".
INTERFOTO/Alamy Stock Photo

Belley (**17.22**) fought in the Haitian Revolution that sought an end to slavery and the creation of an independent nation. While the war dragged on, Belley was elected to represent Saint-Domingue at the French National Convention. His speech imploring fellow French citizens to end slavery helped to bring about its abolition in France and its territories in 1794. Apart from a brief return to Saint-Domingue, Belley remained in France, representing the interests of his people, and he died there in 1805.

Belley's portrait was painted by Anne-Louis Girodet de Roucy-Trioson, a student of Jacques-Louis David. The painting embodies many of the qualities of the Neoclassical style, with its seriousness, clarity, and lack of ornamentation. Girodet represents the Haitian politician leaning against the bust of the French abolitionist philosopher Guillaume-Thomas Raynal, who wrote a history that was critical of France's colonial system. Belley wears the uniform of the French National Convention and gazes heavenward. His casual pose, much like Washington's, helps to humanize him. The landscape behind leads to the sea, hinting at Belley's distant home.

The third revolution of this time was not a political uprising but an economic and social upheaval. Many would argue that the Industrial Revolution, which began slowly in the last half of the 18th century, is still going on.

It is difficult to overestimate the impact—social, economic, and ultimately political—of the change from labor done by hand to labor done by machine. Within a few decades, the machine drastically altered a way of life that had prevailed for millennia. People who had formerly worked in their homes or on farms suddenly were herded together in factories, creating a new social class—the industrial worker. Fortunes were made virtually overnight by members of another new class—the manufacturers. Naturally, all this upheaval was reflected in art. At the beginning of the 19th century, then, Western civilization faced a totally new world.

Notes to the Text

1. Artemisia Gentileschi, letter to Don Antonio Ruffo, January 30, 1649, in Mary D. Garrard, *Artemisia Gentileschi: The Image of the Female Hero in Italian Baroque Art* (Princeton: Princeton University Press, 1989), pp. 390-91.

2. Artemisia Gentileschi, letter to Galileo Galilei, October 9, 1625, in ibid., pp. 383-84.

3. Artemisia Gentileschi, letter to Don Antonio Ruffo, March 13, 1649, in ibid, pp. 391-92.

4. The Book of Judith is one of the so-called deuterocanonical books, books that do not appear in the Hebrew Bible, the Tanakh. Often cited by the early Church Fathers, the Book of Judith has officially been considered canonical by the Catholic Church since the Council of Carthage in 397, and thus was included by Saint Jerome in the Vulgate, the Latin translation of the Bible that came to be considered definitive. In shaping the Protestant Bible, Martin Luther moved the deuterocanonical books to the Apocrypha, a collection of adjunct, noncanonical texts. Later Protestant Bibles either follow his example or omit the book altogether. Reacting to the Protestant challenge, the Council of Trent reaffirmed the canonical status of the Book of Judith in 1546. For Gentileschi, as for other Catholic artists—including Michelangelo, who depicted Judith with the head of Holofernes on the Sistine ceiling, and Caravaggio, who painted a particularly gory version of the beheading—the Book of Judith was biblical.

5. Joan Kinneir, *The Artist by Himself* (New York: St. Martin's, 1980), p. 101.

6. Louise-Élisabeth Vigée-Lebrun, *Memoirs of Madame Vigée LeBrun*, trans. Lionel Strachey (New York: Doubleday, Page & Company, 1903), p. 34.

7. Ibid., p. 26.

8. Ibid., pp. 20, 21, 214.

Chapter 18

Arts of Islam
and of Africa

In this chapter, you will learn to

LO1   explain the appearance and purpose of Islamic arts, and

LO2   describe the function and meaning of African arts.

The ancient civilizations discussed in Chapter 14 culminated with the growth of the Roman Empire, which by 100 C.E. encompassed the entire Mediterranean region. In Chapter 15 we saw the empire divided into eastern and western halves after the death of the emperor Constantine. The eastern portion continued for a time as Byzantium. The western portion, after an unstable period, emerged as Europe, which we left in the last chapter on the brink of our own modern age. But what of the lands along the southern shores of the Mediterranean, the lands of North Africa, Egypt, the Near East, and Mesopotamia? The answer is the religious culture of Islam, and thus it is with Islam that our brief exploration of artistic traditions beyond the West begins. (The story of Western art resumes with Chapter 21.)

Arts of Islam

Islam arose during the early 7th century C.E. on the Arabian Peninsula. There, according to Islamic belief, God—who had spoken through such prophets as Abraham, Moses, and Jesus—spoke directly to humanity for the last time. Through the angel Gabriel, He revealed His word to the Prophet Muhammad. Stunned by the revelations, Muhammad began to preach. At the heart of his message was *islam*, Arabic for "submission," meaning submission to God. Those who accepted Muhammad's teachings were called Muslims, "those who submit." Collected and set in order after his death, the revelations Muhammad recited make up the Qur'an ("recitation"), the holy book of Islam.

In 622, Muhammad emigrated from the city of Mecca northward to the city of Medina. Known as the *hijra*, this move marks the year 1 in the Islamic calendar, the beginning of a new era. In Medina Muhammad became a political leader as well as a spiritual one, and much of the Arabian Peninsula was brought into the Islamic community. After Muhammad's death in 632, his successors led Arab armies to victory after victory, and by the middle of the 8th century, Islamic rule extended from Spain and Morocco in the west to the borders of India in the east.

Islam transformed the Arab peoples from a collection of warring tribes with a largely oral culture to a people united by faith, anchored by the written word, and sovereign over vast territories. These new conditions nurtured the growth of a new artistic culture. The need for places to worship and palaces for rulers inspired works of monumental architecture; the establishment of princely courts supported the production of luxury arts such as fine textiles and ceramics; and the centrality of the Qur'an led to a flowering of book arts, including calligraphy and illustration. Wherever Islam extended its influence, local artistic traditions were transformed by

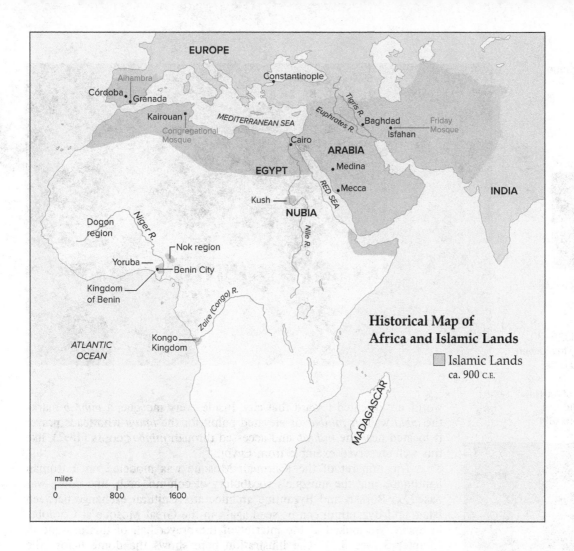

Historical Map of Africa and Islamic Lands

☐ Islamic Lands
ca. 900 C.E.

Islamic patronage. At the same time, converts from many lands transformed Islam itself into a true world religion. From its beginnings as an Arab faith, Islam became a spiritual and intellectual environment in which many cultures have thrived.

Architecture: Mosques and Palaces

One of the first requirements of Islamic rulers in new lands was a suitable place for congregational prayer, a mosque (from the Arabic *masjid*, "place for bowing down"). Early Islamic architects drew their inspiration from descriptions of the Prophet's house in Medina. Like most houses in Arabia, Muhammad's residence was built of sun-dried brick around a central courtyard. An open porch made of palm trunks supporting a roof of palm fronds ran along one wall, providing shade and shelter. There the Prophet had preached to the gathered faithful.

The Congregational Mosque at Kairouan, in Tunisia, shows how those elements were translated into monumental form (**18.1**). The shaded porch of Muhammad's house became a large prayer hall (the covered structure to the right). Just as the roof of Muhammad's porch was supported by rows of palm trunks, the roof of the hall is supported inside by rows of columns. The courtyard before the prayer hall is lined with covered arcades (rows of arches). Over the entry to the courtyard rises a large, square tower called a minaret. From its height a crier calls the faithful to prayer five times a day.

Two domes visible on the roof to the right side of the photograph mark the prayer hall's center aisle. A worshiper entering from the courtyard and walking up this aisle would be walking toward the *mihrab*, an empty niche set into the far wall. This is the *qibla* wall, which indicates the direction of Mecca. Muhammad told his followers to face Mecca during prayer, and all mosques, no matter where in the

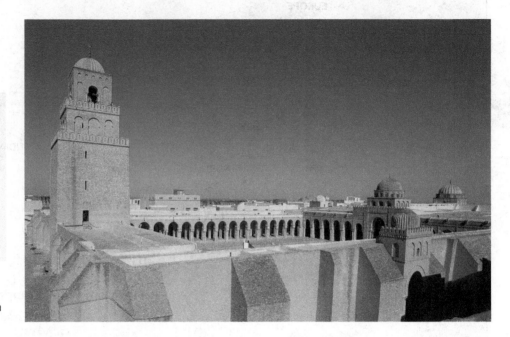

18.1 Congregational Mosque, Kairouan. 836 and later.
Bojan Pavlukovic/Alamy Stock Photo

RELATED WORKS

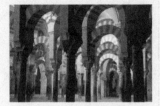

3.2 Interior, Great Mosque, Córdoba

18.2 *Minbar* doors. ca. 1325–30. Rosewood and mulberry inlaid with carved ivory, ebony, and other woods, 77 ¼ × 35".
The Metropolitan Museum of Art, New York. Edward C. Moore Collection, Bequest of Edward C. Moore, 1891

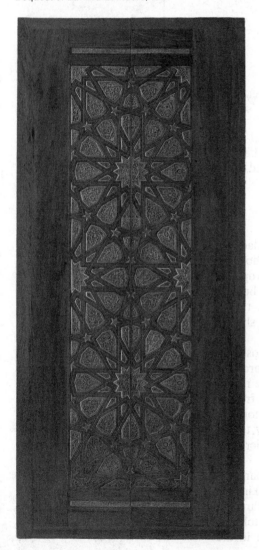

world, are oriented toward that city. Inside every mosque, a *mihrab* marks the *qibla* wall. A *minbar* or elevated pulpit for the *imam* who leads prayer is located near the *mihrab* and accessed through *minbar* doors (**18.2**), like this well-preserved example from Egypt.

The minaret of the Kairouan Mosque was modeled on a Roman lighthouse, and the mosque's vocabulary of column, arch, and dome was based on Roman and Byzantine architecture. Cultural exchange between Islam and Byzantium can be seen again in the Great Mosque at Córdoba, in Spain. We looked at the interior of the prayer hall of this mosque in Chapter 3 (see 3.2). The illustration here shows the dome before the *mihrab* (**18.3**). Eight intersecting arches rising from an octagonal base lift a fluted, melon-shaped dome over the hall below. Light entering through windows opened up by the arches plays over the glittering gold mosaics that cover the interior. Gold mosaics may remind you of Byzantine churches (see 15.9). In fact, the 10th-century ruler who commissioned the mosaics sent an ambassador to the Byzantine emperor requesting a master artisan to oversee the work. The emperor reportedly sent him not only the artisan but also a gift of 35,000 pounds of mosaic tesserae.

Whereas the mosaics in a Byzantine church might depict Jesus, Mary, and saints, the mosaics here do not portray any people, or God himself. The Qur'an contains a stern warning against the worship of idols, and in time this led to a doctrine forbidding images of animate beings in religious contexts. As a result, artists working for Islamic patrons poured their genius into decorative geometric patterns and stylized plant forms—the curving tendrils, stems, foliage, and flowers seen both in the Córdoba mosaics and in the Egyptian *minbar* doors. Arabic script, too, became an important element of decoration. A passage from the Qur'an appears in an octagonal band over the arches at the Great Mosque in Córdoba.

To the east, Islamic civilization was colored by the culture of Persia (present-day Iran), which had been Byzantium's great rival before its empire fell to Arab armies. During the 12th century, Persian architecture inspired a new form of mosque, illustrated here by one of the earliest and most influential examples, the Friday Mosque at Isfahan, in Iran (**18.4**). The photograph shows the view from the entrance to the courtyard. Directly ahead is a large, vaulted chamber whose pointed-arch opening is set in a rectangular frame. This is an *iwan*, a form that served to mark the entry to a royal reception hall in Persian palaces.

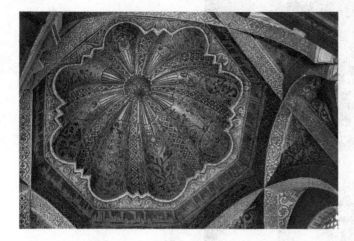

18.3 Dome in front of the *mihrab*, Great Mosque, Córdoba. ca. 965. Mosaic.
Images & Stories/Alamy Stock Photo

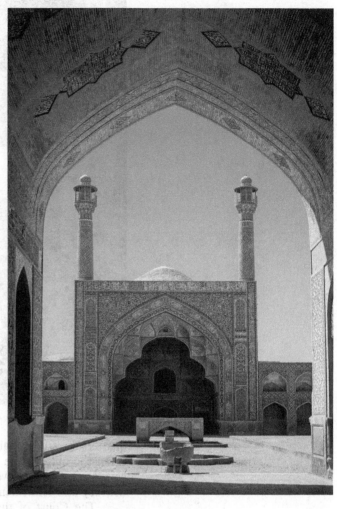

18.4 *Qibla iwan*, Friday Mosque, Isfahan. Rebuilt after 1121–22 (with later work).
© Daniel Boiteau/Alamy

Each side of the mosque's courtyard is set with an *iwan*. This symmetrical four-*iwan* plan became standard in Persia, and its influence extended west to Egypt and east into Central Asia and India. The Taj Mahal in India, for example, is based on Persian architectural forms, and each of its four facades is set with an *iwan* (see 13.18). The photograph of the Friday Mosque at Isfahan was taken from the shade of the entry *iwan*, whose great pointed arch frames the view. Across the courtyard is the *qibla iwan*, oriented toward Mecca. Its interior seems to be formed of triangular scoops as though it had been hollowed out by a giant spoon. Added during the 14th century, these niche-like scoops, *muqarnas*, are one of the most characteristic of Islamic architectural ornaments. Two slender minarets rise above the *qibla iwan*, which served as a prayer hall for the ruler and his court.

The blue glazed tile mosaic that blankets every surface of the entryway at Isfahan was a specialty of Persian artists. Glazed tile had been used to decorate buildings in the region since the ancient civilizations of Mesopotamia (see 14.9). Inscriptions flow across the exterior, brilliant white on a deep-blue ground. The rest is patterned in stylized flowering plants that seem to multiply into infinity, as though a garden with blossoms as numerous as the stars had spread itself like a carpet over the building.

After roughly a century of unity under Arab leadership, Islamic lands were ruled by regional dynasties, and Arab dynasties took their place alongside dynasties founded by African, Persian, Turkish, and Central Asian groups. Little survives of the sumptuous palaces built for those rulers, for palaces were commonly destroyed or abandoned when a dynasty fell from power. A rare exception is the Alhambra, in Granada, Spain. Constructed largely during the 14th century under the Nasrid dynasty, the Alhambra was a royal city of gardens, palaces, mosques, baths, and

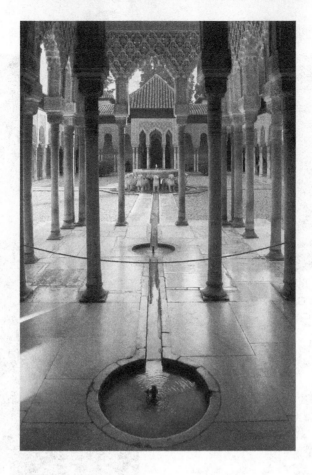

18.5 Court of the Lions, Alhambra Palace, Granada. Mid-14th century. © PIXTAL

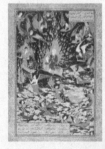
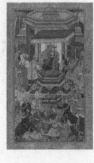
quarters for artisans, all built within the protective walls of an older hilltop fortress. From the outside, the Alhambra looks every inch the forbidding fortress it began as. Once inside, however, visitors find themselves in a sheltered world of surpassing delicacy and refinement (**18.5**).

The Court of the Lions, shown here, takes its name from the stone lions supporting the fountain at its center. Water brought from a distant hill flows through the Alhambra in hidden channels, surfacing in fountains and pools. Indoor and outdoor spaces also flow into each other through open entryways, porches, and pavilions. Here, stucco screens carved in lacy openwork patterns and "fringed" with *muqarnas* are poised on slender columns, allowing light and air to filter through. The Nasrids were to be the last Islamic dynasty in Spain. Christian kings had already reclaimed most of the peninsula, and in 1492 Granada fell to Christian armies as well, ending almost eight hundred years of Islamic presence in western Europe.

Book Arts

Writing out the Qur'an—which Islamic scholars commonly memorize—is viewed as an act of prayer. **Calligraphy** thus became the most highly regarded art in Islamic lands, and great calligraphers achieved the renown Europeans accorded to painters and sculptors. As a religious text, the Qur'an was never illustrated with images of animate beings. Instead, artists ornamented manuscripts with geometric patterns and stylized plant forms, just as they did mosques. An example is this page from a Qur'an copied in 1307 by a famous calligrapher named Ahmad al-Suhrawardi (**18.6**). The top and bottom bands of the painted frame are ornamented in gold with interlacing plant forms and a line of text in an archaic style of Arabic script called Kufic. Ahmad's own bold and graceful calligraphy fills the framed area. One of the most gifted students of an even more famous calligrapher named Yaqut al-Musta'simi, Ahmad lived and worked in Baghdad, which was a major center for book production and scholarship.

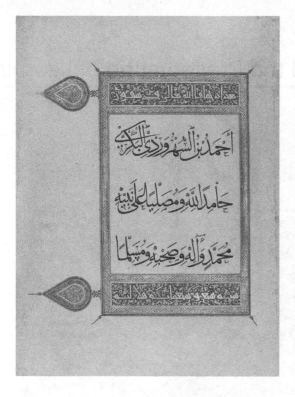

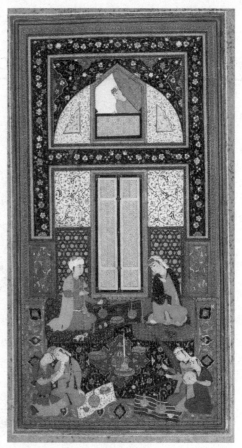

18.6 Ahmad al-Suhrawardi, calligrapher. Page from a copy of the Qur'an. Baghdad, 1307. Ink, colors, and gold on paper, 20 ³⁄₁₆ × 14 ½".
The Metropolitan Museum of Art, New York. Rogers Fund 1955, 55.44. Image © The Metropolitan Museum of Art

Although the Qur'an could not be illustrated with images, other books could. Books were the major artistic outlet for painters in Islamic culture. Working with the finest pigments and brushes that tapered to a single hair, artists created scenes of entrancing detail, such as *Bahram Gur and the Princess in the Black Pavilion* (**18.7**). Bahram Gur was a pre-Islamic Persian king whose legendary exploits were often recounted in poetry. *Haft Manzar* ("seven portraits"), by the 16th-century Persian poet Hatifi, tells of Bahram Gur's infatuation with the portraits of seven princesses. He eventually wins them all and builds for each a pavilion decorated in a different color. The Russian princess is housed in a red pavilion, the Greek princess in a white one. Here, Bahram Gur visits the Indian princess in her black pavilion.

The complex, flattened architectural setting and strong colors mark the style of the artist Shaykhzada, whose signature appears on the work. Floor coverings piled pattern on pattern are tilted toward the picture plane, whereas the brass vessels set on them are seen in perspective. The king and his princess sit demurely on their individual carpets before a wall ornamented with glazed tiles. The setting above resembles the square frame and arched opening of an *iwan*, the pervasive Persian architectural form that might well have graced a pavilion built for an Indian princess.

Arts of Daily Life

Western thinking about art has tended to relegate decorative art such as rugs and ceramics to "minor" status. Islamic cultures, although holding book arts in especially high esteem, have generally considered all objects produced with skill and taste to be equally deserving of praise and attention. Carpets and other textiles, for example, are an important facet of Islamic art. We saw one of the most famous of all Persian textiles in Chapter 12, the Ardabil carpet (see 12.11). We also considered a contemporary response to that tradition in the work of Faig Ahmed (see Thinking about Art: Engaging Tradition in Chapter 12).

18.7 Shaykhzada. *Bahram Gur and the Princess in the Black Pavilion*, from a manuscript of Hatifi's *Haft Manzar*. Bukhara, 1538.
The Picture Art Collection / Alamy Stock Photo

RELATED WORKS

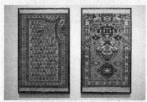

Chapter 12, Thinking About Art
Ahmed, *Hollow* and *Pixelate Tradition*

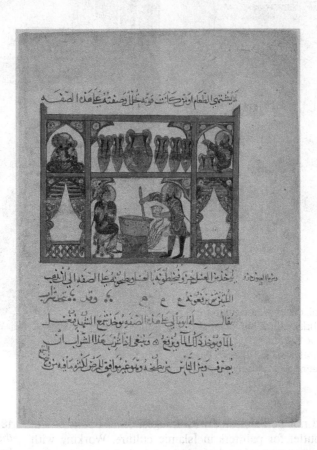

How was knowledge transmitted before printing? What role did Muslim scholars play in the preservation of ancient learning?

After the defeat of the last Roman emperor, Europeans became less interested in the here and now and more concerned with the Christian afterlife, leading early historians to call this period the "dark ages." During the same era, Islam spread throughout the Mediterranean basin and into the east. Muslim scholars and thinkers studied ancient texts and explored questions beyond religion, preserving knowledge that might otherwise have disappeared. The Muslim rulers of Iraq even created the House of Wisdom in Baghdad, dedicated to translating and preserving texts from throughout the known world, and open to scholars of all faiths. Medical knowledge was one area that benefited from Muslim interest.

The Greek physician Dioscorides wrote a five-volume treatise on medicine while serving as a medic for the Roman army. *De Materia Medica* ("On Medical Material") described medicinal plants and their curative properties. It became the most authoritative pharmacological book in the ancient world. Dioscorides's manuscript was copied over and over by scribes and artists working in Europe. Scholars in India and the Islamic world studied the manuscript as well, and translators and scribes added local knowledge.

The version of *De Materia Medica* seen here was written by Abdullah ibn al-Fadl, who worked in Baghdad. The page shown pictures a physician making medicine from honey, which was thought to restore the appetite. The central panel shows the doctor preparing a bowl of the medicine for a patient who sits to the other side of the cauldron. This narrative scene was an addition to the Dioscorides illustrations, which typically featured only drawings of plants. This new illustration therefore pictures the scene as if it took place in Baghdad, with local dress, architecture, and vessels.

"Preparing Medicine from Honey," from a dispersed manuscript of an Arabic translation of *De Materia Medica* of Dioscorides, Baghdad. 1224. Ink, opaque watercolor, and gold on paper, 12 ⅜ × 9". The Metropolitan Museum of Art, New York. Bequest of Cora Timken Burnett, 1956, © Metropolitan Museum of Art

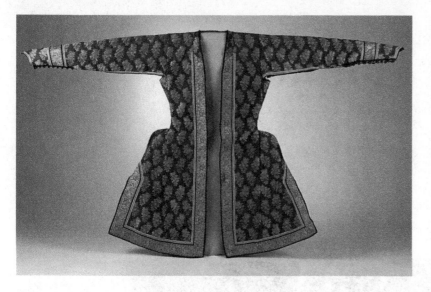

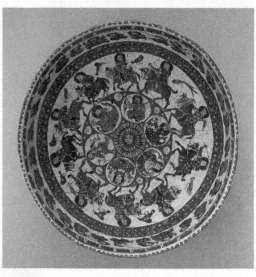

18.8 Woman's coat. 18th century. Metallic thread brocaded on silk, 37 × 63".
The Los Angeles County Museum of Art

18.9 *Bowl with Courtly and Astrological Signs.*
Late 12th or early 13th century. Ceramic, 3 ¾ × 7 ⅜".
The Metropolitan Museum of Art, New York. Purchase, Rogers Fund, and Gift of The Schiff Foundation, 1957

This Persian woman's coat (**18.8**) was made in Iran during the Safavid dynasty. Like the manuscript by Bahram Gur, it offers a glimpse of Safavid sartorial splendor, when male and female courtiers dressed in fine garments decorated with figural and ornamental designs. Persian courtiers wore bright colors in complementary combinations, with robes or tailored jackets over loose pants. Silk production and distribution was controlled by the Safavid ruler, who gave embroidered silk and velvet as diplomatic gifts to Persia's allies.

The jacket with narrow sleeves, cinched waist, round hips, and flared skirt was a common garment for Safavid women in the 18th century. This was a new silhouette in Persia, and it reveals a taste for the tailored shapes of contemporary European fashions. Persian women wore coats like this over a loose tunic and pants, and under a long veil known as a *chador*. The coat's ornamental designs are embroidered in gold- and silver-wrapped thread on blue silk fabric. The fine detail and intricate patterns allow us to see the skill of the Persian maker, and to appreciate the wealth of the Safavid court and the stylishness of the coat's owner.

Ceramic arts were also celebrated in the Muslim world. The *Bowl with Courtly and Astrological Signs* (**18.9**) was created in Persia around the year 1200. The bowl's interior pictures the sun in the center. Five planets and the moon occupy the next ring, each depicted in human form. Although the sun appears in the middle, Islamic astrologers believed that the earth was the center of the universe and other planets revolved around it. Princes on horseback appear in the next ring, while the upper edge of the interior has seated courtiers. By combining astrological personifications and members of the royal family, the bowl gives earthly rulers a divine right to govern. We are meant to understand that earthly princes are part of the natural forces that govern life on Earth. European rulers made similar claims, tracing their lineages back to biblical figures and the gods of ancient Greek and Roman mythology. The prayer book created for the Duke of Berry similarly depicted his domains under signs of the zodiac (see 16.14).

Arts of Africa

When Arab armies invaded Africa in the 7th century C.E., their first conquest was the Byzantine province of Egypt, the site of Africa's best-known early civilization. Chapter 14 introduced ancient Egypt in the context of the Mediterranean world, for its interaction with Mesopotamia, Greece, and Rome is an important part of

RELATED WORKS

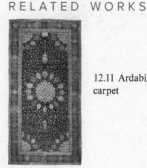

12.11 Ardabil carpet

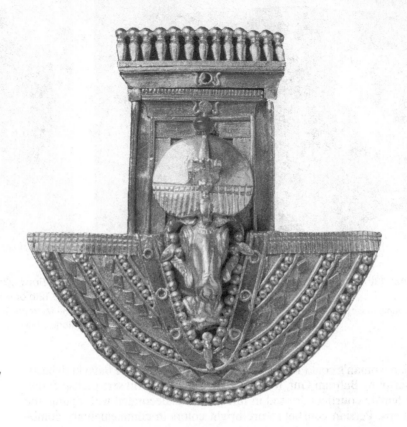

18.10 Ornament from the tomb of Queen Amanishakheto. Kush, Meroitic period, 50–1 B.C.E. Gold with glass inlay, height 2 ½".
bpk Bildagentur/Staatliches Museum Aegyptischer Kunst, Munich, Germany/ Photo: Margarete Buesing/Art Resource, NY

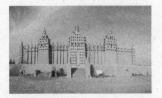
Western art history. But it is useful to remember that Egyptian culture arose in Africa and was the creation of African peoples.

The Nile that nourished Egypt also supported kingdoms farther to the south, in a region called Nubia. Nubia was linked by trade networks to African lands south of the Sahara, and it was through Nubia that the rich resources of Africa—ebony, ivory, gold, incense, and leopard skins—flowed into Egypt. The most famous Nubian kingdom was Kush, which rose to prominence during the 10th century B.C.E. and lasted for over 1,400 years. The gold ornament illustrated here comes from a Kushan royal tomb, the pyramid of Queen Amanishakheto (**18.10**). A sensitively modeled ram's head protrudes from the center of the ornament, a symbol in Kush, as in Egypt, of the solar deity Amun. Over the ram's head, the disk of the sun rises before a faithful representation of an entryway to a Kushan temple.

Carrying their conquests farther west across the Mediterranean coast of Africa, Arab armies quickly routed Byzantine forces from the Roman coastal cities. Far more difficult to subdue were the African people known as Berbers. Berber kingdoms were well known to the ancient Mediterranean world. In the days of the Roman Empire, Berbers mingled with the Roman population in Africa and occasionally rose to high rank in the Roman army. One Berber general became a Roman emperor. After the Islamic conquests, Berbers gradually converted to Islam, and Islamic Berber dynasties held sway in Morocco, Algeria, and Spain. Berber groups were also involved in the long-distance trade across the Sahara that linked the Mediterranean coast with the rest of the continent to the south. Along those ancient trade routes, Islam spread peacefully through much of West Africa, eventually resulting in such African Islamic art as the mosque at Djenné, in Mali (see 13.1).

Islam was not the only foreign religion to make inroads in Africa. Christianity arrived very early, and Jesus's disciple Mark established himself in Alexandria, Egypt. Ethiopia was especially friendly to Christian teachings, and Christianity became its official religion in the 4th century. Eleven rock-cut churches in Ethiopia remain as evidence of the spread of the faith. The Church of St. George at Lalibela (**18.11**) has a central plan in the shape of a cross. Cut directly into volcanic rock, it was made in the 12th century for King Lalibela as part of his plan to turn Ethiopia into a new Jerusalem. He may have been inspired to do so by news that

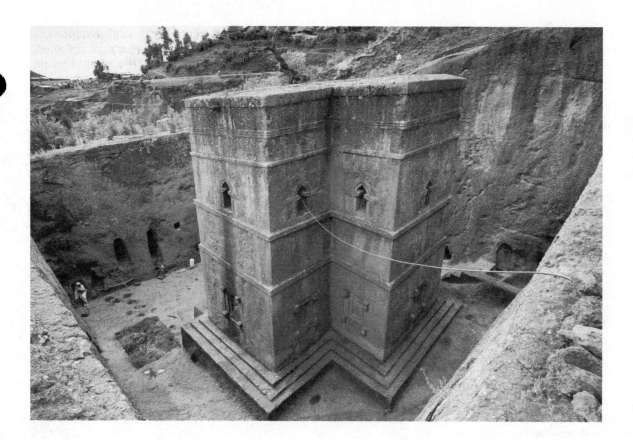

18.11 Church of St. George, Lalibela, Ethiopia. 12th century.
imageBROKER/Alamy Stock Photo

the Holy Lands had been seized by Muslims. The church's interior, hollowed from the stone, has aisles separated by columns and topped by high arches. Relief carvings and paintings adorn the walls, and windows allow light into the surprisingly spacious interior. Other rock-hewn churches are similarly impressive, and Lalibela continues to attract pilgrims even today.

The Africa that Islamic and Christian travelers found south of the Sahara was and is home to literally hundreds of cultures, each with its own distinctive art forms. More than any other artistic tradition, the arts of Africa challenge us to expand our ideas about what art is, what forms it can take, what impulses it springs from, and what purposes it serves. Much of the history of these arts is lost to us, in part for the simple reason that most art in Africa has been made of perishable materials such as wood. Nevertheless, excavations during the 20th century have revealed many fascinating works in stone, metal, and terra cotta, including sculptures such as this terra-cotta head (**18.12**).

18.12 Head, fragment of a larger figure. Nok, 500 B.C.E.–200 C.E. Terra cotta, height 14 ³⁄₁₆".
The National Commission for Museums and Monuments, Lagos © Dirk Bakker/Bridgeman Images

The smooth surfaces and D-shaped eyes are characteristic of works from the culture known as Nok, named after the town in Nigeria where the first examples of its art were found. Scientific testing suggests that most Nok works were made between 500 B.C.E. and 200 C.E., or around the time of ancient Greece and Rome. Broken off at the neck, the life-size head here probably formed part of a complete figure. Judging by the few complete figures that have been recovered, its elaborate, sculptural hairstyle would have been complemented by lavish quantities of jewelry and other ornaments.

It seems likely that Nok culture influenced later cultures in the region, although we cannot say for sure. What is certain is that two of the most sustained art-producing cultures of Africa arose some centuries later, not far from the Nok region. One is the kingdom of Benin, which began to take shape during the 13th century. Located in a region of Nigeria south of the Nok sites, Benin continues to the present day under a dynasty of rulers that dates back to the first century of its existence.

Like the rulers of ancient Egypt, the kings of Benin are viewed as sacred beings. Sacred kingship is common to many African societies, and art is often used to dramatize and support it. In Chapter 5, we looked at a brass altar to the Benin

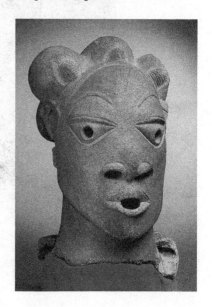

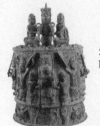

5.21 Royal altar, Benin

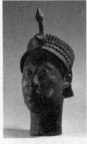

2.16 Yoruba brass head

king's hand (see 5.21). The altar conveyed the king's centrality through symmetrical composition, his importance through hierarchical scale (he is larger than his attendants), and the symbolic role of his head through proportion (the head takes up one-third of his total height).

These elements can be seen again in this altar to the hand (**18.13**), which is created to honor an individual's achievements. Because this object is made from brass, the individual being celebrate is a royal member. Hierarchical scale, along with wardrobe and appearance, highlight the positions and roles of the figures.

In 1897, British forces attacked the Benin palace and took much of the art it contained—works in brass, ivory, terra cotta, and wood produced over a period of about four hundred years. As a result, objects like the ones shown in the photograph here can be found in museums around the world. Examining a brass head or a carved tusk from Benin is a rewarding experience, but these objects were not meant to be seen in isolation, much less in a museum. Rather, they were intended to take their place as elements in a larger, composite work of art—the assemblage of a sacred altar.

According to oral tradition, the current dynasty of Benin rulers was founded by a prince from the Yoruba city of Ife, to the northwest. Yoruba rulers, too, were considered sacred, and artists sculpted portrait heads in their honor. We saw two of these sculptures in Chapter 2: a naturalistic work from the 13th century representing the ruler's outer, physical head and an abstract work representing his inner, spiritual head (see 2.16, 2.17). Although Yoruba artists no longer make such works, Yoruba kings are still regarded as sacred, and art still serves to dramatize their exceptional nature.

18.13 The Michael C. Rockefeller Memorial Collection, Bequest of Nelson A. Rockefeller, 1979/The Metropolitan Museum of Art

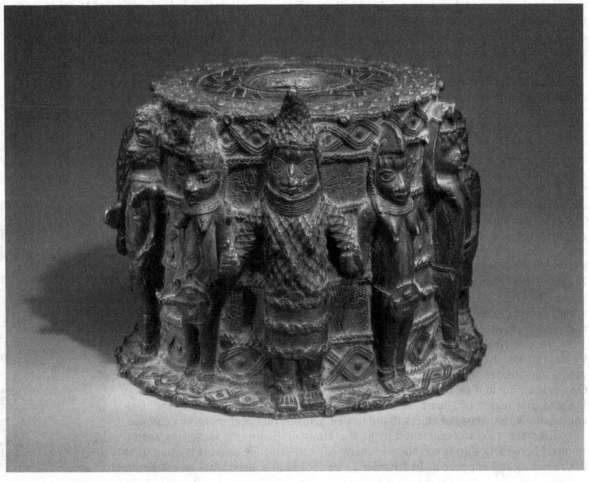

Taken in 1977, the photograph here shows the Yoruba ruler Ariwajoye I seated in his regal robes (**18.14**). His right hand grasps a beaded staff, and on his head is a cone-shaped beaded crown. Abstracted faces of the king's ancestors stare out from the crown; their dark, white-rimmed eyes are easily discernible. At the pinnacle of the crown is a beaded bird, and numerous bird heads protrude from the cone. The birds refer to the female ancestors whose powers the king must draw on. Known as Our Mothers, they are believed to be able to transform themselves into night birds. A beaded veil obscures the ruler's face, for his subjects are not allowed to gaze directly on a sacred being. The crown gives form to the idea that the living king is one with his godly ancestors, for in wearing it his head merges with theirs, and their many eyes look out.

Similar ideas are conveyed by a spectacular beaded display piece commissioned by a Yoruba king in the early 20th century (**18.15**). The base of the piece resembles the conical royal crown. As on the crown, faces of ancestors stare out from the front and back. Over this base rises the figure of a royal wife with a magnificent crested hairstyle and a child on her back. It is as though the bird at the pinnacle of Ariwajoye's crown had turned back into one of the female ancestors who guarantees his power. The woman carries an offering bowl with a small bird on its lid. Female attendants flock around her body, while four protective male figures with guns ring the crown at the base. Male power is here seen as based in

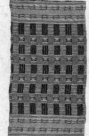
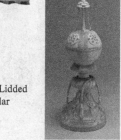
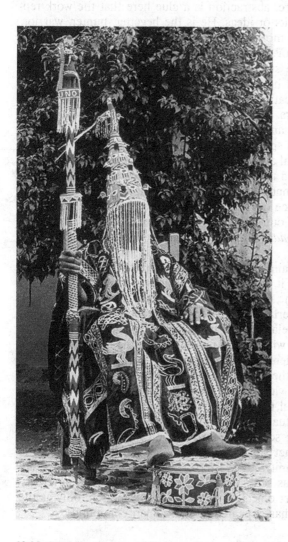

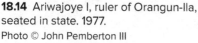

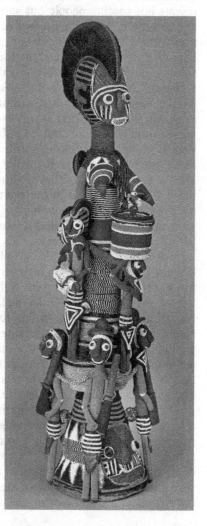

18.14 Ariwajoye I, ruler of Orangun-Ila, seated in state. 1977.
Photo © John Pemberton III

18.15 Display piece. Yoruba, early 20th century. Cloth, basketry, beads, fiber, height 41 ¾".
© The Trustees of the British Museum, London/Art Resource, NY

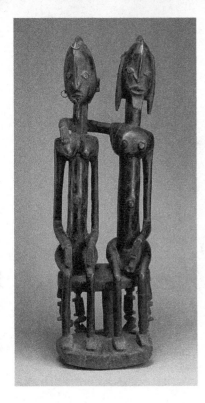

18.16 *Seated Couple*. Dogon, 18th–early 19th century. Wood and metal, height 29".
The Metropolitan Museum of Art, New York. Gift of Lester Wunderman, 1977, 1977.394.15. Image © The Metropolitan Museum of Art

strength, whereas female power, greater and more mysterious, generates ritual (the offering) and new life (the child).

Complementary gender roles are also the subject of this elegant sculpture by an artist of the Dogon people, who live in present-day Mali (**18.16**). The sculpture portrays a couple seated side by side, rendered in a highly conventionalized, abstract manner. The stool they share links them physically and symbolically, as does the man's arm placed around the woman's shoulder. With their tilted heads, tubular torsos, angular limbs, horseshoe-shaped hips, and evenly spaced legs, the two bodies are almost mirror images of each other. Yet within this fundamental unity, differences appear. The man, slightly larger, speaks for the couple through his gestures, while the woman is quiet. His right hand touches her breast, suggesting her role as a nurturer. His left hand rests above his own genitals, signaling the idea of procreation. On her back, not visible here, she carries a child; on his back he carries a quiver. As often in African sculpture, abstraction is a clue here that the work represents not specific people but spirits or ideas. He is the begetter, hunter, warrior, and protector; she is the life-bearer, mother, and nurturer. Together with their child they form a family, the basic unit of a Dogon community. The four small figures beneath the stool may refer to the support they receive from ancestors or other spirits. The carving probably would have been kept in a shrine, where it served as a kind of altar—a site for communication between this world and the world of spirits, including the spirits of ancestors.

Art in Africa often serves as an agent to bring about some desired state of affairs, usually through contact with spirit powers. Among the best-known and most visually compelling works of spiritual agency are the power figures, *minkisi* (singular *nkisi*, "medicine"), of the Kongo and neighboring peoples of central Africa (**18.17**). *Minkisi* are containers. They hold materials that allow a ritual specialist to harness the powers of the dead in the service of the living. Almost any container can be a *nkisi*, but the most famous *minkisi* outside Africa are statues of ferocious hunters such as the one here. Called *minkondi* (singular *nkondi*), they hunt down and punish witches and wrongdoers.

A *nkondi* begins its life as a plain carved figure, commissioned from a sculptor like any other. In order to empower it, the ritual specialist adds packets of materials to its surface, materials linked to the dead and to the dire punishments the *nkondi* will be asked to inflict. Other materials may be added as well. This example has bits of cloth, plant fibers, and porcelain added to it. Mirrors in his eyes and abdomen enable him to see approaching witches and move between the human and spirit worlds. Working on behalf of a client who has sought his help, or even a whole community, the specialist invokes the *nkondi* and provokes it into action, particularly by driving iron nails or blades violently into it. Over the years, nails and other materials accumulate, offering visual testimony to the *nkondi*'s fearsome prowess.

The great African art of spiritual agency, and perhaps the greatest of African arts, is the masquerade. Involving sculpture, costume, music, and movement, a masquerade does not merely contact spirit powers to effect change; it brings the spirits themselves into the community. In Western museums, African masks are commonly exhibited and admired as sculpture. But in Africa a mask is never displayed in public as an isolated, inert object. It appears only in motion, only as the head or face of a spirit being that has appeared in the human community.

RELATED WORKS

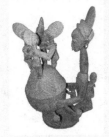

12.8 Olumeye Bowl, Yoruba People, Nigeria

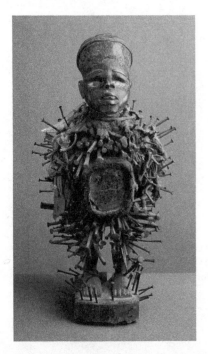

18.17 Male figure (*nkisi-nkondi*). Kongo. 18th–19th century. Wood, iron, cloth, mirror, leopard tooth, fiber, and porcelain, 18 × 8 × 3 ½".
Yale University Art Gallery

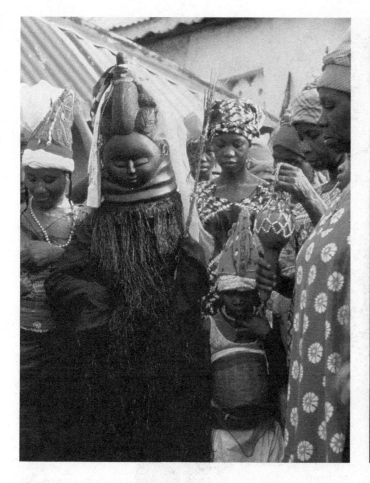

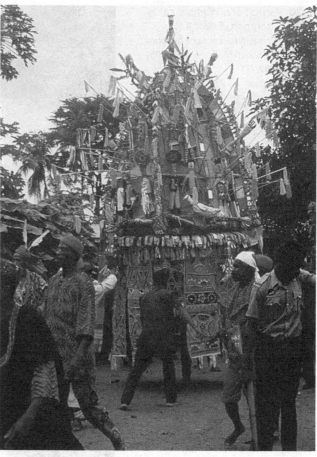

18.18 Temne Nowo masquerade
with attendants, Sierra Leone. 1976.
Photo Frederick John Lamp

18.19 *Ijele* masquerade at an Igbo second
burial ceremony, Achalla, Nigeria. 1983.
Photo courtesy Elizabeth Evanoff Etchepare. Image
number UCSB 88-8751

The mask photographed here represents the water goddess Nowo (**18.18**), the guiding spirit of a Temne women's organization called Bondo, which regulates female affairs. Bondo prepares young girls for initiation into adult status, and afterward presents them to the community as fully mature women. As in many African societies, young people deemed ready for initiation are taken from their families. Isolated together away from the community, they learn the secrets of adulthood and undergo physical ordeals. During this time, they are considered to be in a vulnerable "in between" condition, neither children nor adults. They need the protection, guidance, and sponsorship of spirits to make the transition successfully from one stage of life to the next.

The Nowo mask appears here accompanied by several attendants as part of a Bondo ceremony. The lustrous black mask represents a Temne ideal of feminine beauty and modesty. The rings around the base are compared to the chrysalis of a moth: Just as the caterpillar emerges from its chrysalis transformed, so girls emerge from Bondo as women. The rings are also seen as ripples of water, for Nowo is said to have risen out of the depths of a pool or river, where female spirits dwell. The white scarf tied to Nowo's elaborate hairstyle indicates her empathy for the initiates under her care, whose bodies are painted white during their isolation as a sign of their "in between" state.

Even our preconceived ideas of what a mask *is* must be discarded when faced with the extraordinary spectacle of *ijele* (**18.19**). The most honored mask of the Igbo people of Nigeria, *ijele* appears at the funeral of an especially important man, welcoming his spirit to the other world and easing his transition from one stage of

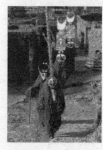

2.40 Bwa
masqueraders

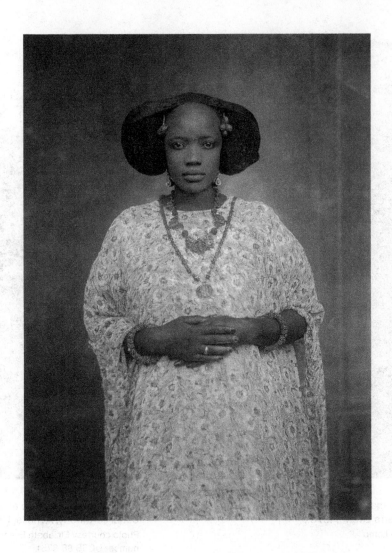

18.20 *Portrait of a Woman*. ca. 1910. Photograph, 6 ½ × 4 ½". The Metropolitan Museum of Art, New York. Gift of Susan Mullin Vogel, 2015. Art Resource, NY

being to the next. The meanings of *ijele* are fluid and layered. In its towering aspect, *ijele* resembles an anthill—structures that in Africa may reach a height of 8 feet and which the Igbo regard as porches to the spirit world. *Ijele* is also a venerable tree, the symbol of life beneath whose branches wise elders meet to discuss weighty matters. Amid the tassels, mirrors, and flowers on *ijele*'s "branches" are numerous sculpted figures of people, animals, and other masks—a virtual catalog of the Igbo and their world. Multiple large eyes suggest the watchfulness of the ever-present (though usually invisible) community of spirits. Majestic in appearance, *ijele* nevertheless moves with great energy, dipping, whirling, shaking, and turning. It is the great tree of meaning—of life itself—appearing briefly in the human community.

African artists have not only practiced what we might call traditional arts. They have also participated in the mediums and trends of contemporary global art. Photography arrived in Africa less than a year after its invention in 1839. European explorers brought cameras to document their trips, and soon African artists began taking photographs. Some African photographers opened portrait studios in larger cities, while others traveled from town to town, setting up temporary studios in order to photograph local residents. This photograph by an unknown Senegalese artist (**18.20**) pictures a woman finely dressed and decked out in gold and silver jewelry. She follows local custom that required women to cover all but their hands and feet, and she wears her hair in a popular local style that wove wool into the hair. Her direct gaze and her peaceful pose with hands resting across her body make this a compelling and beautiful example of African photography. Unlike the European photographers who turned their African subjects into exotic specimens for curious European viewers, this artist represented the Senegalese woman with dignity and respect for her culture.

Chapter 19

Arts of Asia: India, China, and Japan

In this chapter, you will learn to

LO1   explain the styles, themes, and history of Indian arts,

LO2   describe the appearance and subjects of Chinese arts, and

LO3   discuss the history of the arts in Japan.

The previous chapter took us from the Mediterranean world into Asia with the spread of Islam to the east. This chapter continues our eastward journey with a brief look at three of the most influential civilizations of Asia: India, China, and Japan.

In truth, these civilizations have already appeared "behind the scenes" many times in this story of art. Chapter 14, for example, pointed out that the regions of Mesopotamia and Egypt were in contact with each other from early on. But Mesopotamia was also in contact with India to the east, where an impressive civilization had arisen in the Indus River Valley. Akkadian writings from around 2300 B.C.E.

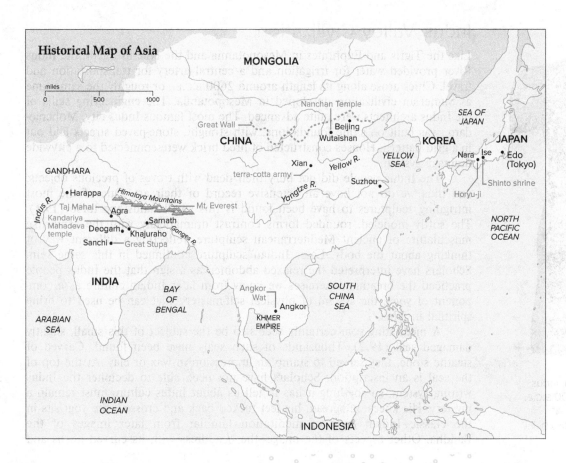

Historical Map of Asia

mention the presence of Indus merchants and ships in Mesopotamia, along with their valuable goods of copper, gold, ivory, and pearls. Later, during the days of the Roman Empire, a long network of trade routes called the Silk Road allowed the citizens of Rome to enjoy the lacquerware and silk textiles of China. Rome had only the vaguest idea about where these exquisite products came from. China, more curious, avidly collected information about Rome and other Western lands. Still later, during the Renaissance, European explorers stumbled on the island nation of Japan. Japanese artists of the time delighted in recording the appearance of these exotic visitors from the West, whose customs were so strange.

Closer and more influential, however, were the contacts between these three Asian cultures themselves. China's greatest exports were writing, urban planning, administration, and philosophy, all of which it transmitted to Japan, together with styles of painting and architecture. India's greatest export was the religion of Buddhism, which travelers and missionaries brought over the Silk Road to China, and which then passed from China to Japan. With these paths of contact in mind, we begin our look at the arts of Asia.

Arts of India

The area of India's historical territories is so large and distinct that it is often referred to as a subcontinent. Another name for it is South Asia. Jutting out in a great triangle from the Asian landmass, South Asia is bordered along most of its northern frontier by the Himalaya Mountains, the tallest mountain range in the world. To the northwest, the mountain range known as the Hindu Kush gradually descends to the fertile valley of the Indus River, in present-day Pakistan.

Indus Valley Civilization

Like the Tigris and Euphrates in Mesopotamia and the Nile in Egypt, the Indus River provided water for irrigation and a central artery for transportation and travel. Cities arose along its length around 2600 B.C.E., or roughly the same time as Sumerian civilization developed in Mesopotamia. The engineering skills of the Indus architects were quite advanced. The most famous Indus city, Mohenjo-daro, was built on stone foundations, with straight, stone-paved streets laid out in a grid pattern. Houses constructed of fired brick were connected to a citywide drainage system.

The Indus people did not bury their dead with troves of precious objects, and thus we do not have an extensive record of their art. One of the most intriguing sculptures to have been found is this small sandstone torso (19.1). The softly modeled, rounded forms contrast dramatically with the armorlike musculature of ancient Mediterranean sculpture, reflecting a different way of thinking about the body. Later Indian sculpture continued in this same vein. Scholars have interpreted the relaxed abdomen as a sign that the Indus people practiced the breathing exercises we know from later Indian culture as a component of yoga, the system of physical self-mastery that can be used to bring spiritual insights.

A meditating yogi certainly seems to be the subject of this small, slightly damaged seal (19.2). Thousands of such seals have been found. Carved of steatite stone, they served to stamp an impression in wax or clay. At the top of the seal is an inscription. Scholars have not been able to decipher the Indus writing system, so anything it has to tell us about Indus culture must remain a mystery. His knees outspread, his feet tucked back and crossed, the yogi sits in the classic Indian pose of meditation familiar from later images of the Buddha. Other aspects of the image—the headdress with its curved horns and

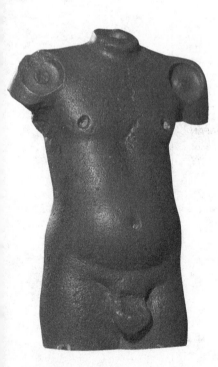

19.1 Torso, from Harappa. Indus Valley civilization, ca. 2000 B.C.E. Red sandstone, height 3 ¾".
National Museum of India, New Delhi/ Bridgeman Images

the small animals in the background—suggest the later Hindu god Shiva. We saw Shiva in his guise as Nataraja in Chapter 1 (see 1.9), but in another guise he is known as Lord of Beasts.

Indus culture began to disintegrate around 1900 B.C.E. Until recently, scholars believed that the cities were conquered by invaders entering the subcontinent from the northwest, a nomadic people who called themselves Aryas, "noble ones." However, new findings have overturned the idea of conquest, suggesting instead that Mohenjo-daro was abandoned after the Indus River changed its course and that other cities were ruined when a parallel river ran dry. During those same centuries, the Aryas began to arrive.

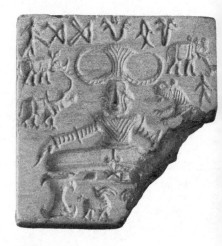

19.2 "Yogi" seal, from Mohenjo-daro. Indus Valley civilization, 2300–1750 B.C.E. Steatite, 1 ⅜ × 1 ⅜".
National Museum of India, New Delhi/Bridgeman Images

Buddhism and Its Art

Beginning around 800 B.C.E., urban centers again arose in northern India, and by the 6th century B.C.E., numerous principalities had taken shape. During this time, Aryan religious practice became increasingly complex. The priestly class of Aryan society, brahmins, grew powerful, for only they understood the complicated sacrificial rituals that were now required. Brahmins also began to impose rigid ideas about social order derived from the Vedas, their sacred texts. Disturbed by these developments, many sages and philosophers of the day sought a different path, preaching social equality and a more direct and personal access to the spiritual realm. Of these numerous leaders, the one who would have the most lasting impact on the world was Siddhartha Gautama, later known as the Buddha.

Gautama was born a prince of the Shaka clan in northern India, near present-day Nepal. His dates are traditionally given as 563–483 B.C.E., although recent research suggests that he lived slightly later, dying around 400 B.C.E. According to tradition, his life was transformed when a series of chance encounters brought him face to face with suffering, sickness, and mortality. These, he realized, were our common fate. What was to be done? Renouncing his princely comforts, he studied with the spiritual masters of the day and tried every accepted path to understanding, but to no avail. He withdrew into meditation until one day, finally, everything became clear. He was *buddha*, "awakened."

Buddha accepted the belief, current in the India of his day, that time is cyclical and that all beings, even gods and demons, are condemned to suffer an endless series of lives unless they can gain release from the cycle. His insight was that we are kept chained to the world by desire. His solution was to extinguish desire by cultivating nonattachment, and to that end he proposed an eightfold path of moral and ethical behavior. By following this path, we too may awaken, see through the veil of illusion to the true nature of the world, and free ourselves from the cycle of life, death, and rebirth.

Buddha attracted followers from all walks of life, from beggars to kings, both men and women. After his death, his cremated remains were distributed among eight memorial mounds called **stupas**. During the 3rd century B.C.E., a Buddhist king named Ashoka called for these remains to be redistributed among a much larger number of stupas, including this one at Sanchi (**19.3**). A stupa is a solid earthen mound faced with stone. Over it rises a stylized parasol that symbolically shelters and honors the relics buried inside. Pilgrims come to be near the energy that is believed to emanate from the Buddha's remains. They visit the stupa by ritually walking around it. The two stone fences evident in the photograph, one at ground level and one higher up, enclose paths for circling the stupa.

Four gateways erected late in the 1st century B.C.E. punctuate the outer enclosure at Sanchi. Their cross-bars are carved in relief with stories from the Buddha's life, although they do not show the Buddha himself. Early Buddhist art avoided depicting the Buddha directly. Instead, sculptors indicated his presence through symbols. A pair of footprints, for example, indicated the ground where he walked; a parasol indicated space he occupied and an empty chair represented his seated presence. That artists should have avoided depicting the Buddha directly is not so surprising. After all, the entire point of his teaching was that he was in his last

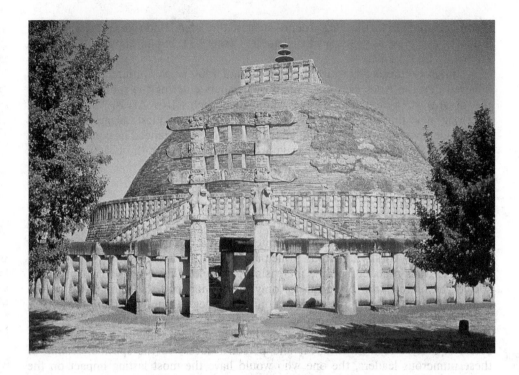

earthly life. Henceforth, he would have no bodily form. Besides, the Buddha had lived 550 lives before his final one. Clearly, he had passed through many bodily forms. Nevertheless, the Buddhist community must eventually have felt the need for an image to focus their thoughts.

Toward the end of the 1st century C.E., images of the Buddha began to appear in northern India, influenced by interaction with Greek culture. Regions bordering on India were part of the extensive Hellenistic world. Hellenistic culture was particularly vital in a region called Bactria, which bordered the mountains of the Hindu Kush. During the 1st century B.C.E., Bactria was conquered by a people of Chinese origin called the Kushans, who eventually established an empire that reached across northern India, where they encountered and embraced Buddhism. Having no monumental art of their own, the Kushans also embraced the Hellenistic culture of Bactria and used it to celebrate their Buddhist faith.

The Greeks had long envisioned their gods in sculpture as perfected humans. Under Kushan rulers, this Hellenistic heritage and the desire for an image of the Buddha merged in fascinating figures such as the one shown here (**19.4**). Modeled on statues of the Greek god Apollo, who was typically portrayed as a handsome youth, the Buddha stands in gentle contrapposto, the great contribution of the Greeks to art. His robe, reminiscent of a Roman toga, hangs in heavy folds over a naturalistically muscled body. This fascinating Hellenistic–Indian hybrid style disappeared with the end of the Kushan Empire in the 3rd century C.E., but its effects were lasting. Contrapposto spread throughout India, where it is a prominent feature of later Hindu art. And the Buddha image was started on its long history.

A different and more enduring image of the Buddha emerged in the 5th century C.E. in the workshops at Sarnath, in northern India (**19.5**). Typical of Sarnath style, the robe the seated Buddha wears molds itself discreetly to the smooth, perfected surfaces of his body. The neckline and the hanging sleeves are almost the only signs that he is wearing a robe at all. Seated in the pose of meditation, the Buddha forms the *mudra* (hand gesture) that indicates preaching. He is understood to be preaching his first sermon, known as the Sermon at Deer Park. (Note the two deer carved in relief to either side of him.) Other attributes of the Buddha include the bump on his head, which signifies his enlightenment. While in the earlier work this resembled hair gathered in a topknot, the Sarnath figure depicts it as a cranial swelling covered by hair. Both works, however, give the Buddha long, pierced earlobes to represent the princely wealth he rejected.

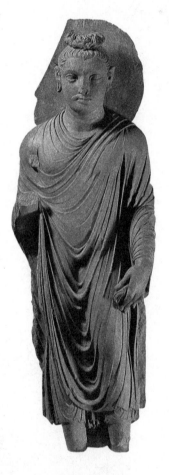

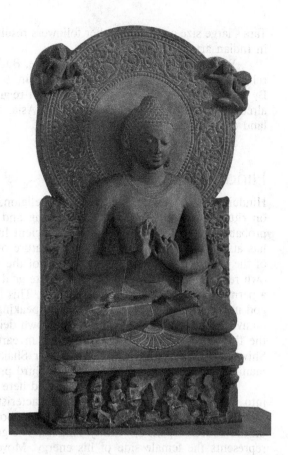

19.5 *Buddha Preaching the First Sermon*, from Sarnath. ca. 465–85 C.E. Sandstone, height 5' 3".
Archaeological Museum, Sarnath.
akg-images/Album/Oronoz

The Buddha is commonly accompanied by bodhisattvas, saintly beings who have delayed their own release in order to help others attain enlightenment. To show that bodhisattvas are still earthly beings, both males and females are typically shown outfitted in jewels. The bodhisattva Tara (**19.6**) is here shown with earrings, bracelets, and strings of beads in a manuscript painting made on the Indian subcontinent. The *mudra* of her right hand tells us that she is giving offerings to the followers who gather around her. She stands in the exaggerated contrapposto adapted from Hellenistic art. Like the torso from Mohenjo-daro, her body is soft and round and she is remarkably voluptuous. Indian artists typically depicted women in this way to symbolize fertility and abundance, as the female form was considered auspicious.

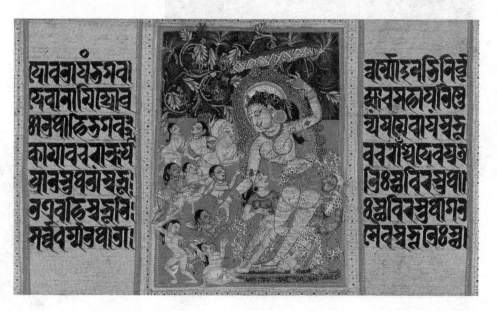

19.6 *Green Tara Dispensing Boons to Ecstatic Devotees*, folio from a manuscript of the Ashtasahasrika Prajnaparamita (Perfection of Wisdom). Early 12th century. Watercolor on palm leaf, 2 ¾ × 16 ⁷⁄₁₆".
The Metropolitan Museum of Art, New York. Purchase, Lila Acheson Wallace Gift, 2001

Tara's large size compared to her followers results from the hierarchy of scale found in Indian art.

When the painting of Tara was made, Buddhism was no longer the dominant religion in India. In fact, Tara figured in both Buddhist and Hindu legends. By the end of the 14th century, Hinduism reigned in India and Buddhism, having already spread to China and Southeast Asia, would virtually disappear from the land of its birth.

Hinduism and Its Art

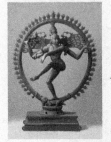

1.9 *Shiva Nataraja*

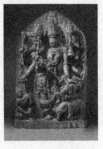

11.3 *Durga Slaying the Buffalo Demon*

Hinduism developed as the older Vedic religion, with its brahmins and its emphasis on ritual sacrifice, evolved in its thinking and mingled with local Indian beliefs, probably including those hinted at in ancient Indus art. Like Buddhism, Hinduism has at its core a belief in the cyclical nature of time, including the cosmic cycles of the creation, destruction, and rebirth of the world, and the briefer cycles of our own repeating lives within it. The ultimate goal is liberation from these cycles into a permanent state of pure consciousness. This liberation will be granted to us by a god in return for our devotion. Strictly speaking, Hinduism is not one religion but many related faiths, each one taking its own deity as supreme. We have met two of the three principal deities of Hinduism in earlier chapters of this book—the god Shiva (see 1.9) and the goddess Devi or Shakti ("power"), whom we saw in her manifestation as Durga (see 11.3). The third principal deity is Vishnu.

Carved in stone, the relief illustrated here depicts Vishnu dreaming the world into existence (**19.7**). Wearing his characteristic cylindrical crown and depicted much larger than those surrounding him to show his importance, Vishnu slumbers on the coiled serpent of infinity, Ananta. The goddess Lakshmi holds his foot. She represents the female side of his energy. Moved by her, Vishnu dreams the god Brahma into existence. Brahma appears at the center of the uppermost row of figures, sitting in a meditative pose on a lotus blossom that is understood to grow from Vishnu's navel. Brahma in turn will create the world of space and time by thinking, "May I become Many."

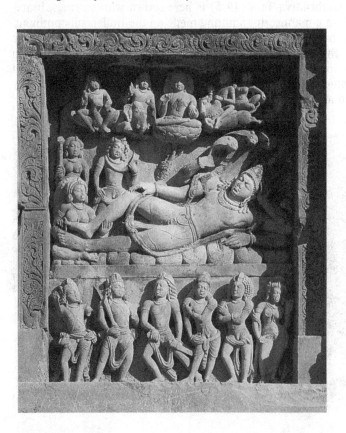

19.7 *Vishnu Dreaming the Universe*, relief panel, temple of Vishnu, Deogarh, Uttar Pradesh. Early 6th century C.E.
Giraudon/Bridgeman Images

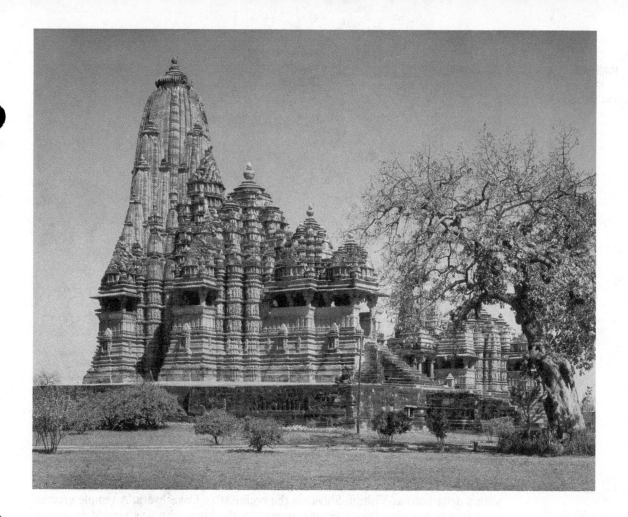

19.8 Kandariya Mahadeva Temple, Khajuraho, Madhya Pradesh, India. ca. 1000 C.E.
© Borromeo/Art Resource, NY

This relief appears on the exterior of one of the earliest surviving Hindu stone temples, a small structure dating from around 500 C.E. Temple architecture evolved rapidly over the ensuing centuries, and by 1000 C.E. monumental forms had been perfected. A masterpiece of the monumental temple as it developed in northern India is the Kandariya Mahadeva (**19.8**, **19.9**). Dedicated to Shiva, the temple rests on a stone platform that serves to mark out a sacred area and separate it from the everyday world. Visitors climb the stairs, visible to the right, and proceed through a series of three halls, each of which is distinguished on the exterior by a pyramidal roof. These roofs grow progressively taller, culminating in a majestic curving tower called a *shikhara*. Conceived as a cosmic mountain ringed around with lesser peaks, the *shikhara* rises over the heart of the temple, a small, dark, cavelike chamber called a *garbhagriha* ("womb-house"). The *garbhagriha* houses a statue of the deity, a statue in which the god is believed to be truly present.

Indian architects worked with post-and-lintel construction techniques, and thus the interior spaces of Hindu temples are not large. They do not need to be, for Hindu religious practice is not based on congregational worship. Instead, devotees approach the deity individually with such gifts as flowers, food, and incense. These are offered as sacrifices by a brahmin, who receives them at the entrance to the *garbhagriha*.

Like the form of the temple itself, the sculptures on its exterior represent the energies of the god radiating outward into the world. The myriad Hindu gods and goddesses in their many guises are favorite subjects. On northern temples such as the Kandariya Mahadeva, voluptuous women and sensuous loving couples are depicted as well (**19.10**). The presence of women is mandated in the texts that guided northern architects, and it demonstrates how belief in such auspicious presences as *yakshi*, nature spirits embodying ideas of fertility and abundance, found a place in Hinduism.

From as early as the 2nd century B.C.E., India exerted an influence on developing cultures in Southeast Asia. Kingdoms of Southeast Asia adopted both Buddhism

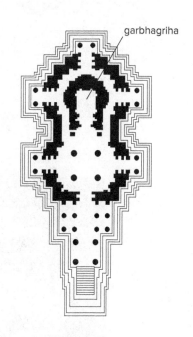

garbhagriha

19.9 Plan of the Kandariya Mahadeva Temple.

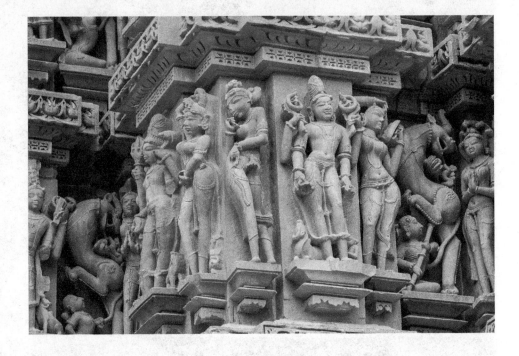

19.10 Sculpture, Kandariya Mahadeva Temple, Khajuraho.
JTB MEDIA CREATION, Inc./Alamy Stock Photo

and Hinduism, and they created their own styles of the art forms that came with them. Among the greatest architectural treasures of Southeast Asia is Angkor, the capital of the Khmer kingdom. The Khmer kingdom dominated the region of present-day Cambodia and much of the surrounding area between the 9th and 15th centuries. Taking the title *devaraja*, "god-king," Khmer rulers identified themselves with a deity such as Vishnu, Shiva, or the bodhisattva Lokeshvara. A temple erected to the deity was also thus a temple erected to the king, who was viewed as one of the deity's earthly manifestations. The finest and largest example is the beautiful temple complex known as Angkor Wat (**19.11**).

19.11 Angkor Wat, Cambodia.
ca. 1113–50 C.E.
Hugo/Flickr RF/Getty Images

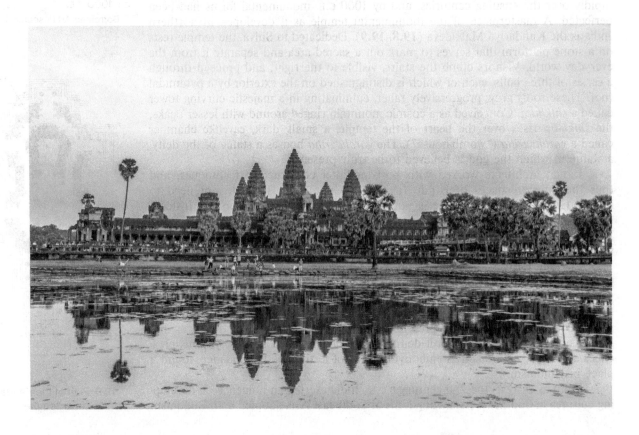

Built in the early 12th century under the patronage of the god-king Suryavarman II and dedicated to Vishnu, Angkor Wat consists of five shrines on a raised, pyramidal stone "mountain." Each shrine houses a *garbhagriha*, the womb-like dwelling place of the deity. Colonnaded galleries connect and enclose the five shrines, their walls carved with reliefs depicting dancing figures, celestial beings, and the many guises and adventures of Vishnu (see 19.7). Visitors approach the complex by a long walkway that originally crossed over a surrounding moat. Like Hindu temples in India, the plan of Angkor Wat is based on a mandala, a diagram of a cosmic realm, and thus the entire site reflects the meaning and order of the spiritual universe.

Jain Art

The Jain religion traces its beginnings to a sage named Mahavira, who lived during the 6th century B.C.E. Like the Buddha, Mahavira left the comforts of home in his youth to pursue spiritual wisdom. Upon achieving enlightenment, he became known as the Jina, or "victor." In the religion developed by his followers, Mahavira is considered to have been the last in a line of twenty-four Jinas. Unlike Buddhism, the Jain religion did not become a world faith, yet within India it has remained an important presence.

In Chapter 13, we looked at the interior of a Jain temple (see 13.20). The hundreds of Jain temples constructed between the 11th and 16th centuries testify to the wealth of the merchants and traders who were the primary adherents of the Jain faith. Jains also commissioned thousands of illuminated manuscripts for donation to temple libraries (**19.12**). The scene reproduced here is from a manuscript of the Kalpasutra, a work that narrates the lives of the Jain saints. The symmetrical composition depicts the bathing of Mahavira at his birth. The newborn Jina sits on the lap of the god Shakra, who seems to hover over a highly stylized depiction of Mount Meru, the sacred celestial mountain. Two attendant gods hold up vessels of water in preparation for the bath. Above, two water buffalo genuflect, recognizing the divine nature of the infant before them. The decorative flatness of the style, with its wiry, linear drawing and intense, bulging eyes, is typical of Jain manuscript painting.

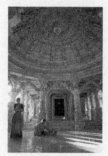

13.20 Interior, Jain temple

19.12 Illustration depicting the *Lustration of the Infant Jina Mahavira*, detail of a folio from a manuscript of the Kalpasutra. Gujarat, late 14th century. Opaque watercolor on paper, folio size 3 ½ × 10 ¹⁵⁄₁₆".
The Metropolitan Museum of Art, New York. Cynthia Hazen Polsky and Leon B. Polsky Fund, 2005, 2005.35. Image © The Metropolitan Museum of Art

Mughal Art and Influence

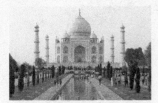

13.18 Taj Mahal

A new culture developed in India with the arrival of the Mughals, an Islamic people from Central Asia who established an empire on the subcontinent beginning in the 16th century. Like most Islamic groups from Central Asia, the Mughals were influenced by Persian culture. In India, Persian forms mingled with Indian elements to create a uniquely Indian form of Islamic art. The most beloved work of Mughal architecture is the Taj Mahal (see 13.18). In Chapters 13 and 18, we pointed out the Persian aspects of the monument: its *iwan* entryways, its central domed interior, and its crowning ornamental onion-shaped dome. (To review the form of an *iwan*, see 18.4.) Looking at the building again, you can see that it rests on a stone platform in the manner of Hindu temples. The open, domed pavilions that sit on the roof and cap the four minarets are *chattri*, a traditional embellishment of Indian palaces.

Illustrated books were a second great Persian artistic tradition. The Mughal painting atelier was directed by Persian painters, who introduced new techniques, styles, subjects, and materials to the subcontinent. The influence of such Mughal masterpieces as the *Hamzanama* (see 2.6) was felt in Indian courts, where painters absorbed the Mughal love of detail and jewel-toned palette, while retaining the decorative flatness and saturated color of earlier Indian manuscript painting (see 19.12). An example of the new style that resulted is *Maharana Amar Singh II, Prince Sangram Singh, and Courtiers Watch the Performance of an Acrobat and Musicians* (see 4.44).

One of the most striking examples of Mughal painting in India is *Shah Jahan on Horseback* (**19.13**). It was painted by the court artist Payag, who worked for three Mughal emperors—Shah Jahan's grandfather Akbar, his father, Jahangir, and Shah Jahan himself—during his long career at the Indian court. The artist's signature appears in tiny script on the bow resting on the horse's saddle. Shah Jahan, who

19.13 Payag. *Shah Jahan on Horseback*. 1630. Ink, opaque watercolor, and gold on paper, 15 ⁵⁄₁₆ × 10 ⅛".
The Metropolitan Museum of Art, New York. Purchase, Rogers Fund and The Kevorkian Foundation Gift, 1955

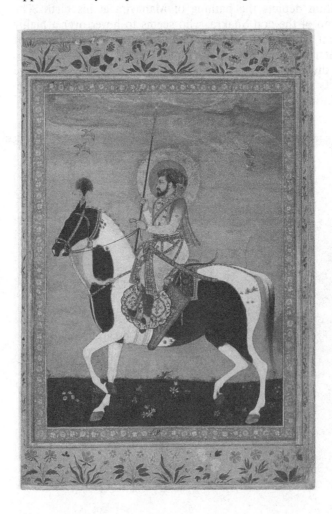

built the Taj Mahal to honor his dead wife, sits atop a majestic steed. A gold halo surrounds his head to show his power. Both horse and rider are decked out in jewels and finery. Payag's painting style is characterized by observed naturalism, seen in the details of the horse's anatomy and the individual hairs of the emperor's beard. It also has very little modeling, and the highly lifelike figures are flat and still. The flowers in the painting and its border are typical of Mughal art. Shah Jahan had covered the Taj Mahal with flowers of multicolored inlaid stone to create a paradise-like setting for his lost love. Payag depicts them in this painting with sufficient detail to identify individual plants.

Into the Modern Era

Although it was in decline by the 18th century, the Mughal Empire survived in India until the mid-19th century. In 1858, the British imposed colonial rule that would not end until 1947. Yet even under foreign control, Indian culture persisted and art continued to be made using traditional themes, media, and techniques. New technology also appeared. Photography was introduced by the British colonial authorities, and cities such as Delhi soon had photography studios run by both foreigners and Indians. As occurred in Africa, some photographs became postcards sent by British colonizers to European friends and family to illustrate the "exotic" lands and people they were encountering. Yet photography also supported the interests of the local people, and Indian amateur and professional photographers formed clubs and exhibited their work in the second half of the 19th century.

Like people around the world, Indians were eager to have photographic portraits made. Lala Deen Dayal photographed this family (**19.14**) in the late 19th century. They are members of the elite group known as Marathas, as identified by the father's jacket and hat. The family wears expensive jewelry and luxurious clothes. The boy in the middle has on a British-style uniform, as the Marathas were recruited as fighters by the British authorities. As in all studio portraits, the family is posed

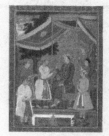

1.8 Manohar, *Jahangir Receives a Cup from Khusrau*

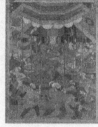

2.6 *Hamzanama* illustration

19.14 Lala Deen Dayal. *Portrait of a Group of (Maratha) Brahmans.* Late 19th century. Photograph. Paul Fearn/Alamy Stock Photo

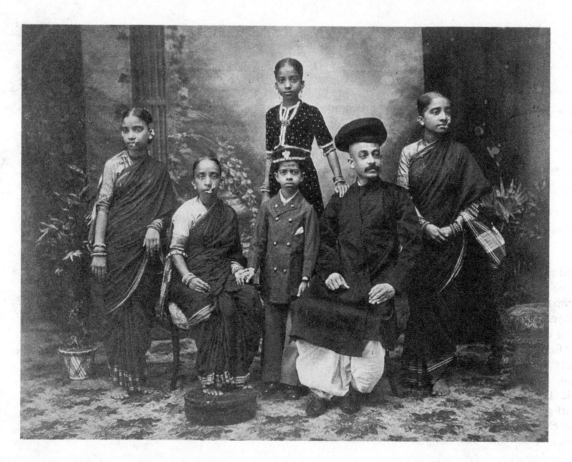

Lala Deen Dayal (1844–1905)

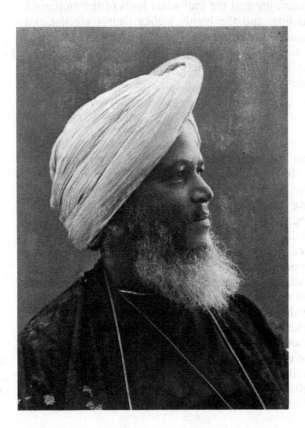

How do Lala Deen Dayal's photographs reflect his context? How did Dayal demonstrate his understanding of global trends in photography?

Lala Deen Dayal is widely considered the most important photographer working in 19th-century India. He photographed everyone, from the wealthiest and most powerful princes, maharajas (Indian rulers), and British colonial governors to the humblest residents of the South Asian subcontinent. He captured the grandeur and majesty of India's historical monuments and the devastation caused by natural disasters.

Dayal was trained as an engineer, but his photography skills soon drew the attention of the local maharaja. With his encouragement and the patronage of British colonial representatives, Dayal established himself as a photographer. By the late 19th century, Dayal and his sons had photographic studios in Bombay, Indore, and Secunderabad.

Dayal's customers were both British and Indian, including the Nizam (Prince) of Hyderabad, who gave Dayal the noble title of Raja. The Nizam also named him as his court photographer. Queen Victoria of England, in her role as Empress of India, also recognized Dayal, making him "Photographer to Her Majesty and Queen" in 1887.

Dayal's photographs offer a glimpse of life in 19th-century India. British colonial rule is well represented in his body of work, with photographs of British governors, military figures, and their families. He even photographed the future King George V on a visit to the region. At the same time, Dayal captured the spectacular wealth of the Indian princely class, taking photographs of their palaces, courts, and courtiers. While subject to England in matters of foreign policy, the Indian princes maintained rule over their ancestral territories. They also controlled local peoples, whom Dayal photographed at his studio and in the field.

While much of his work bears witness to history as it documents people and places, Dayal also used the camera to make artistic images. Pictorialist photography flourished during his lifetime. His bucolic landscapes and majestic waterfalls demonstrate his artistic use of composition, lighting, and focus. They remind us of 19th-century landscape paintings and demonstrate that photography could be beautiful, not just informative.

Raja Lala Deen Dayal. Late 19th century. Photograph. Paul Fearn/Alamy Stock Photo

446

before a backdrop, with plants added to either side. Dayal placed the group in a roughly symmetrical composition around a central axis. The combination of traditional and European-style setting is typical of colonial photography in this era.

Arts of China

Unlike India, China is not protected to the north by intimidating mountains. The vast and vulnerable northern frontier is one of the themes of Chinese history, for it resulted in a constant stream of influence and interaction. Peaceful contacts produced fruitful exchanges between China, India, Central Asia, and Persia. But repeated invasion and conquest from the north also shaped Chinese thinking and Chinese art.

Fundamental features of the Chinese landscape are the three great rivers that water its heartland, the Yellow in the north and the Yangtze and the Xi in the south. The Yellow River is traditionally spoken of as the "cradle of Chinese civilization." Advanced Neolithic cultures built settlements along it from around 5000 B.C.E., but recent archaeological research has found Neolithic sites together with artifacts in jade and ceramic over a much broader area, giving us a more complicated and still incomplete picture of the early stages of Chinese culture. All we can say now is that over time these many distinct Neolithic cultures seem to have merged.

The Formative Period: Shang to Qin

The history of China begins firmly with the Shang dynasty (ca. 1500–ca. 1050 B.C.E.), whose kings ruled from a series of capitals in the Yellow River Valley. Archaeologists have discovered foundations of their palaces and walled cities, and excavations of royal tombs have yielded thousands of works in jade, lacquer, ivory, precious metals, and bronze. The illustration here shows a bronze *jia*, a vessel for wine (**19.15**). Valued and valuable possessions of elite families, bronze vessels were used at banquets for ritual offerings of food to ancestors.

Visible on each side of the *jia* is the most famous and mysterious of Shang decorative motifs, the stylized animal or monster face known as the *taotie*. Its two horns curling away from the raised center axis are clearly distinguishable, as are the staring eyes just beneath them. The *taotie* may relate to shamanism, the practice of communicating with the spirit world through animal go-betweens. Birds appear in a band above the *taotie*, the legs of the vessel are decorated with stylized dragons, and an animal of some kind sits on the lid. Whether directly associated with shamanism or not, animals both fantastic and real are a haunting presence in Shang art.

Around 1050 B.C.E., the Shang were conquered by their neighbors to the northwest, the Zhou, who ruled for the next eight hundred years. The first three hundred years of this longest dynasty were peaceful. During later centuries, however, the states over which the Zhou presided grew increasingly independent and treacherous, finally descending into open warfare. The deteriorating situation inspired much thought about how a stable society could be organized. One of the philosophers of the day was Confucius, who lived around the turn of the 5th century B.C.E. His ideas about human conduct and just rule would later be placed at the very center of Chinese culture.

In 221 B.C.E., the state of Qin (pronounced "chin") claimed victory over the other states, uniting all of China into an empire for the first time. The first emperor, Shihuangdi, was

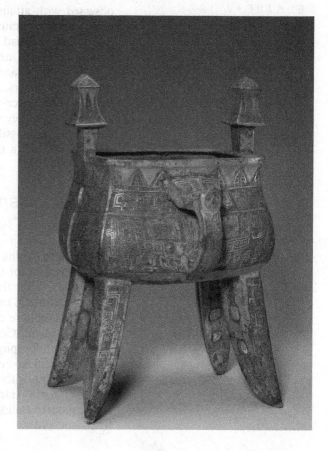

19.15 Chinese artist, active 13th-12th century BCE; Fangjia wine vessel; 13th-12th century BCE; Culture: China, Shang dynasty; Bronze; 13 ¾ × 9 ⅛ × 8 ⁷⁄₁₆ in., 13 lb. (34.93 × 23.18 × 21.43 cm, 5.9 kg)
The Minneapolis Institute of Art, Bequest of Alfred F. Pillsbury

19.16 Excavated figures from the terra-cotta army guarding the tomb of Shihuangdi, First Emperor of Qin (d. 210 B.C.E.). Xian, China.
Julia Hiebaum/Robert Harding

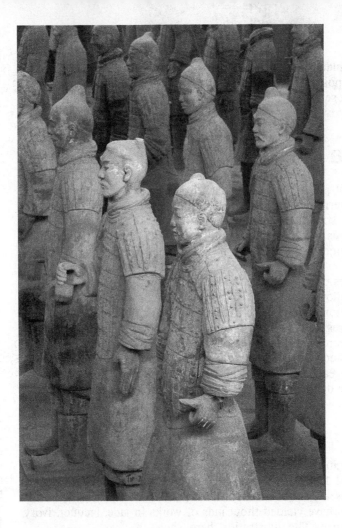

RELATED WORKS

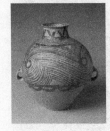

1.5 Jar (*Hu*)

obsessed with attaining immortality. Work on his underground burial site began even before he united China and continued until his death. The mound covering the burial itself had always been visible, but the accidental discovery in 1974 of a buried terra-cotta army guarding it was one of the most electrifying moments in 20th-century archaeology (**19.16**). Row upon row, the life-size figures stand in their thousands—soldiers, archers, cavalrymen, and charioteers—facing east, the direction from which danger was expected to come. Time has bleached them to a ghostly gray, but when they were new, they were painted in lifelike colors, for only by being as realistic as possible could they effectively protect the emperor's tomb behind them, about half a mile to the west.

Confucianism, Daoism, and Buddhism: Han and Tang Dynasties

Our name for China comes from the first dynasty, Qin. Chinese historians, however, reviled the Qin for their brutal rule. Ethnic Chinese instead refer to themselves as Han people, after the dynasty that overthrew the Qin. Han rule endured, with one brief interruption, from 206 B.C.E. to 220 C.E. During those centuries, many features of Chinese culture came into focus, including the central roles played by two systems of thought, Confucianism and Daoism.

The philosophy of Confucius is pragmatic; its principal concern is the creation of a peaceful society. Correct and respectful relations among people are the key, beginning within the family, then extending outward and upward all the way to the emperor. Han rulers adopted Confucianism as the official state philosophy, in the process elaborating it into a sort of religion in which social order was linked to cosmic order.

Confucius urged people to honor ancestors and Heaven, as the Zhou deity was called. Apart from that, he had little to say about spiritual matters. For answers to questions about what lies beyond the physical world, the Chinese turned to Daoism. Daoism is concerned with bringing human life into harmony with nature. A *dao* is a "way" or "path." The Dao is the Way of the Universe, a current that flows through all creation. The goal of Daoism is to understand the Way and be carried along by it, and not to fight it by striving. The first Daoist text, the famous *Dao De Jing* ("the Way and its power") dates to around 500 B.C.E.; the material it draws together is much older.

Among scholars, Daoism continued as a philosophy, but on a popular level it also became a religion; and in doing so it absorbed many folk beliefs, deities, and mystical concerns, including the search for immortality. The glazed ceramic incense burner shown here (**19.17**) was created for a burial and depicts a dreamy afterlife. It has relief carvings of tigers and **chimeras** between stylized waves along the side. Followers of Daoism hoped to occupy a world with these animals upon attaining immortality. The lid is carved in the shape of the mountains where the holy immortals lived. Smoke from burning incense would have wreathed this natural world in clouds of fog, adding to its otherworldly appearance.

Not long after the end of the Han dynasty, invaders from inner Asia conquered the northern part of China. The imperial court fled to the south. For the next 250 years, China was divided. Numerous kingdoms—many under non-Chinese rulers—rose and fell in the north, while six weak dynasties succeeded one another in the south. The tumultuous period ended with the foundation of the Tang dynasty, which restored the great capital of Chang'an. This period, from the 7th to the 10th century, is widely considered one of the greatest periods of Chinese history, marked by the invention of woodcut printing and increased trade with the Near East via the Silk Road.

The educated elite continued to follow Daoist philosophy during the Tang dynasty. To converse brilliantly, to wander the landscape, to drink, and write poetry were still suitable occupations. At the same time, Confucianism, with its stern emphasis on duty to society, remained the official ideal, and Confucian themes continued to appear in art. The Funerary Sculpture of a Pair of Officials (**19.18**) illustrates the rigidity of the Confucian social hierarchy. The large ceramic sculptures depict two court officials dressed in the formal attire and headgear of their

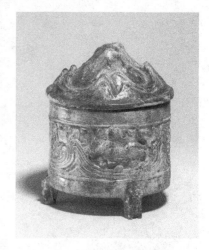

19.17 Incense burner. 220–206 B.C.E. Glazed earthenware, 9 ¾". © The Trustees of the British Museum, London/Art Resource, NY

RELATED WORKS

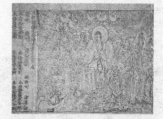

8.2 Preface to the Diamond Sutra

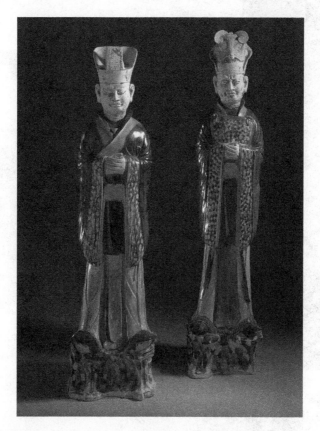

19.18 Funerary Sculpture of a Pair of Officials. 700–800 C.E. Molded earthenware with incised decoration, polychrome (sancai) glaze, and traces of paint, 47 ½ × 11 × 12" and 45 ¼ × 11 × 12". Los Angeles County Museum of Art. Gift of Leon Lidow (M.75.77.1-.2)

office. They stand with hands clasped and eyes fixed, as if they await instructions from their superior. The pair was buried with a nobleman, along with other ceramic figures depicting people and objects to accompany him into the afterlife. These glazed, molded figures demonstrate that the nobleman's venerability and social status were thought to remain with him even after death.

Buddhism had begun to filter into China during the Han dynasty, when missionaries from India arrived via the Silk Road. During the Six Dynasties period, it spread increasingly through the divided north and south. In the first century of the Tang dynasty (the 7th century C.E.), virtually the entire country adopted the Buddhist religion, and vast quantities of art were created for the thousands of monasteries, temples, and shrines that were founded.

The most popular form of Buddhism in China was the sect called Pure Land, named for the Western Paradise where the buddha Amitabha dwells. The fragment of a hanging scroll illustrated here (**19.19**) portrays a bodhisattva leading the soul of a fashionably plump, well-dressed Tang lady to her eternal reward in the Western Paradise, imagined in the upper left corner as a Chinese palace. The magnificently attired bodhisattva is a Chinese fantasy of an Indian prince. In his right hand he holds an incense burner; his left hand holds a lotus flower and a white temple banner. Flowers fall about the couple, symbols of holiness and grace. The painting's thin, black contour lines, flat colors, and limited spatial depth are typical of Tang dynasty painting.

Much Buddhist art of the Tang dynasty was destroyed during the 9th century, when Buddhism was briefly persecuted as a "foreign" religion. One building that somehow escaped destruction is the Nanchan Temple (**19.20**). Little Chinese architecture has survived from before 1400, and thus the Nanchan Temple, although small, takes on added importance. Like all important buildings in China, it is raised

19.19 *Bodhisattva Guide of Souls.* Tang dynasty, late 9th century C.E. Ink and colors on silk, height 31 ⅝". © The Trustees of the British Museum, London/Art Resource, NY

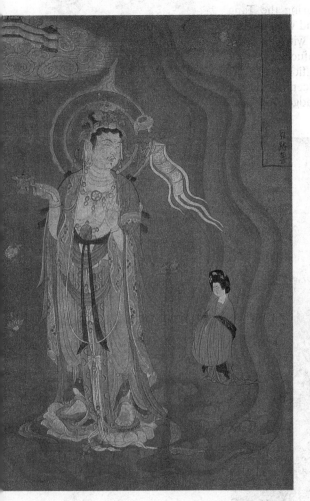

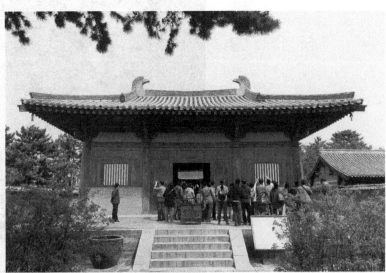

19.20 Nanchan Temple, Shanxi Province, China. 782 C.E.
Xinhua/Alamy Stock Photo

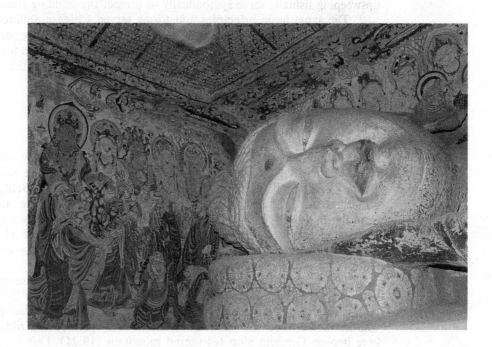

What was the Silk Road? What role did it play in the transmission of goods and ideas?

How are you connected to the rest of the world? Your phone? The Internet? Travel? Before the modern era, most people never traveled more than a few miles from their homes. Only intrepid voyagers visited faraway lands, where they saw people from different cultures living lives quite distinct from their own. The Silk Road was one path for this kind of exploration.

The Silk Road was not a single road. It was a network of trade routes reaching from China to Europe. It had ancient roots, as goods such as silk, horses, spices, and jade made their way from Asia all the way to western Europe, where they have been found in tombs and archaeological excavations. The Italian explorer Marco Polo famously traveled this route in 1269, reaching China before returning to Venice nearly a quarter-century later. Yet, not everything transported along the Silk Road was highly prized. Experts believe that the bubonic plague made the same journey from central Asia to Europe. The Black Death, as it was called, killed millions in the mid-14th century.

Ideas also traveled along the Silk Road. Like other religions, Buddhism spread with the help of traders and merchants who traveled the network. The sculpture seen here is from a Buddhist shrine in the Mogao Caves in Dunhuang, China. The city of Dunhuang was a stopping point along the road, where several routes came together. Just as importantly, it had an oasis where travelers restored their water supplies and watered their pack animals. Nearly 500 caves cut into the nearby hillside transformed the area into an immense complex of Buddhist shrines tended by Buddhist monks.

The reclining Buddha in this photograph is inside one of the caves. We see the cranial swelling atop his head familiar from other Buddha images. The dot between his eyes symbolizes his spiritual insight. The reclining figure represents the Buddha just before he died and was released from the mortal cycle of life, death, and rebirth. The cave's ceiling is covered in tiny, repeating Buddhas. This kind of visual repetition is comparable to the ritual chanting of a mantra during meditation. The cave walls are painted with bodhisattvas dressed in fine clothing and jewels. The sculpture is made of wood, straw, and plaster, while the walls are painted using the dry fresco technique.

While Dunhuang is one of the more spectacular examples, it is just one Silk Road site that allowed travelers to see and experience new and unfamiliar cultures.

Sleeping Statue of Buddha in Mogao Caves, Dunhuang. © DeA Picture Library/Art Resource, NY

above ground level by a stone platform. Wooden columns capped by bracket sets bear the weight of the tiled roof with its broad, overhanging eaves. The gentle curve of the roof draws our eyes upward to the ridge, where two ornaments based on upsweeping fishtails serve symbolically to protect the building from fire.

The same basic principles and forms served Chinese architects for temples, palaces, and residences. Multiplied a hundredfold, this pleasing, sturdy temple lets us imagine the grandeur of the multistoried palaces of the Tang, just as the painted bodhisattva, multiplied into a cast of hundreds, lets us imagine the vanished murals that were the glory of Tang Buddhist art.

The Rise of Landscape Painting: Song

China splintered again after the fall of the Tang, but was quickly reunited under the rulers of the Song dynasty (960–1279 C.E.). Artists during the Song continued to create works for Buddhist and Daoist temples and shrines. Sculpture played an important role in these contexts. The altar of a Buddhist shrine consists of figures from the Buddhist pantheon set on a platform and protected by a railing. A visitor to a large temple might find inside the entire assembly of Heaven—buddhas, bodhisattvas, lesser deities, guardians, and other celestial beings—carved as life-size figures and arranged to reflect the hierarchy of paradise.

The bodhisattva Guanyin, known in India as Avalokiteshvara (see 11.5), became the object of special affection in China. As Guanyin of the Southern Seas, he was believed to reside high on a mountain and offer his special protection to all who traveled the sea. Carved from wood and richly painted and gilded, the sculpture here depicts Guanyin atop his sacred mountain (**19.21**). Left leg dangling down, right leg drawn up, he sits in a position known as the pose of royal ease, as befits his princely nature. He would have been surrounded on his altar by attendants, making his high status even clearer. Cascading swags of drapery animate this serene figure, whose benevolent gaze is like a beacon of calm in the storm, saving us from shipwreck, both at sea and in life. The sculptor has given Guanyin a lithe, slightly feminized body. Chinese Buddhism gradually began to imagine Guanyin as a female deity, and many later depictions show her wearing flowing white robes.

We do not know who carved Guanyin with such virtuosity. Chinese thinking about art did not concern itself with sculpture and architecture, but valued above all the "arts of the brush," calligraphy and painting. Often, paintings were preserved for future generations through the practice of copying. Many famous works of the Tang are known to us only through Song copies, such as Zhang Xuan's *Court Ladies Preparing Newly Woven Silk* (see 3.14). The Tang dynasty was viewed by later writers as the great age of figure painting, and Song copies help us to see why. Song painters, in turn, cast their own long shadow over the future with landscape.

The Song style of monumental landscape was largely the creation of Li Cheng, whose *Solitary Temple amid Clearing Peaks* is illustrated here (**19.22**). Li built on the work of his predecessors of the early 10th century, when landscape first became an independent subject for painting. In his hands, the elements they had explored—shifting perspectives, monochrome ink, vertical format, flowing water, shrouding mists, and a buildup of forms culminating in towering mountains—were gathered into a newly harmonious and spacious whole. Typically, paths are offered for us to walk in and people for us to identify with. Entering the painting with the traveler on the donkey at the lower left, we can cross the rustic bridge to a small village where people are talking and working. A glimpse of a stepped path farther up gives us access to the temple in the middle distance. But, also typically, there is a limit to how high we can climb. Mists separate the middle distance from the towering presences that rise up suddenly in the background. At this point, we must leave the painting and draw back, and when we do, we see a totality that is hidden from us in daily life: the whole of nature and our small place in it. Yet in this view of nature we seem to distinguish an ordering principle, and our place, although small, is in harmony with it: The temple raises its tower upward, and the mountains continue the gesture.

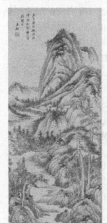
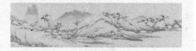

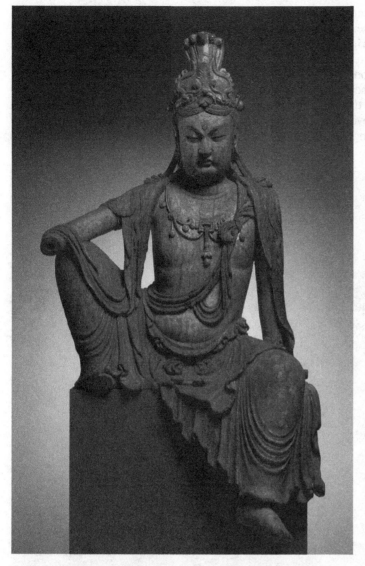

19.21 Unknown (Chinese sculptor, active 1175–1234); Seated Guanyin; late 1100s–1200s; Culture; China, late Northern Song dynasty (960–1127) - Jin dynasty (1115–1234); Wood with polychromy and gilding; overall: 138 cm (54 ⁵⁄₁₆ in.); The Cleveland Museum of Art, Purchase from the J. H. Wade Fund 1984.70

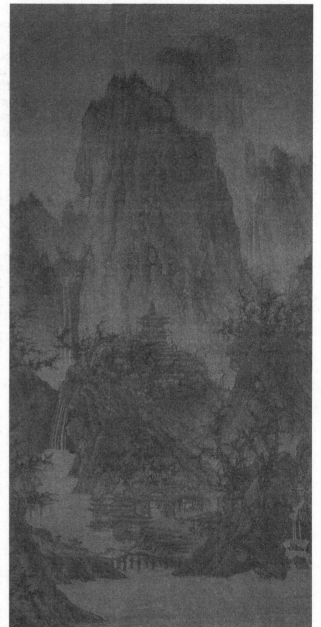

Li Cheng's vision of nature ordered by some higher force and human life in harmony with it clearly echoes the ideas of Daoism. In fact, some art historians believe that such paintings may originally have been understood to portray the Daoist Isle of the Immortals. Yet we can also view the painting from a Confucian perspective as a mirror of the order of China itself, with the emperor towering above, surrounded by his officials, as well as through a Buddhist lens as the great example of the Buddha flanked by bodhisattvas.

19.22 Li Cheng (attrib.). *A Solitary Temple amid Clearing Peaks*. Northern Song dynasty, ca. 960. Hanging scroll, ink and slight color on silk, height 3' 8".
Art Collection 2 / Alamy Stock Photo

Scholars and Others: Yuan and Ming

During the Song dynasty, a new social class began to make itself felt in Chinese cultural life: scholars. Scholars were the product of an examination system designed to recruit the finest minds for government service. Candidates spent many years studying for the grueling test, which became the gateway to political power, social prestige, and wealth. Scholars did not study anything so practical as administration, however. Their education was in the classic texts of philosophy, literature, and history, and its purpose was to produce the Confucian ideal of a cultivated person, right-thinking and right-acting in all situations. Among their accomplishments, scholars were expected to write poetry and practice calligraphy. During the Song dynasty, they also took an interest in painting.

The ideals of scholar painting were formed within the refined and cultivated Song court. During the ensuing Yuan dynasty, however, a split developed between scholars and the government. The Yuan (1279–1368 C.E.) was a foreign dynasty founded by the Mongols, a Central Asian people who had conquered China. The

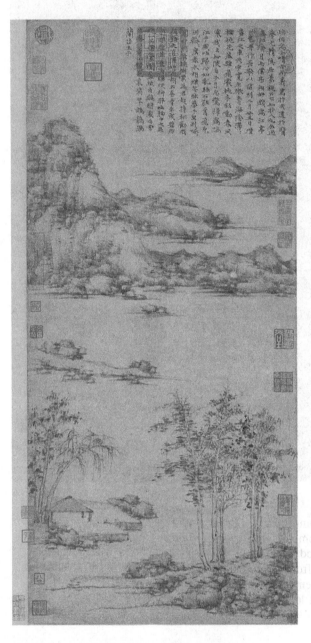

19.23 Ni Zan. *The Rongxi Studio*. Yuan dynasty, 1372. Hanging scroll, ink on paper, height 29 ⅜".
Photo © National Palace Museum, Taipei, Taïwan/Art Resource, NY

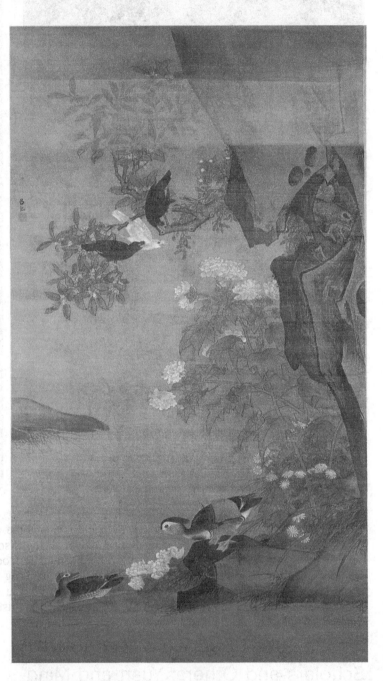

19.24 Lü Ji. *Mandarin Ducks and Hollyhocks*. Late 15th century. Hanging scroll, ink and colors on silk, 5' 8" × 3' 3".
The Metropolitan Museum of Art, New York. Ex coll. C. C. Wang Family, Gift of the Oscar L. Tang Family, 2005, 2005.494.2. Image © The Metropolitan Museum of Art

Mongol court continued to sponsor art, as had all China's past rulers, but scholars regarded everything connected with the court as illegitimate. They viewed themselves as the true inheritors of China's past.

Four scholar-painters of this time have come to be known as the Four Great Masters of the Yuan dynasty. One was Ni Zan, whose best-known work is the beautiful, lonely *Rongxi Studio* (**19.23**). Typical of scholar paintings, *The Rongxi Studio* is painted in monochrome ink on paper. Vivid color and silk were both considered too pretentious, too professional. The brushwork is spare and delicate. Compared with the carefully drawn temple in Li Cheng's *A Solitary Temple amid Clearing Peaks* (see 19.22), Ni Zan's little studio is almost childlike.

Like most scholar-painters, Ni Zan claimed that he painted merely to amuse himself, and that making a convincing likeness was the farthest thing from his mind. Also important is the inscription in Ni's own hand telling when, how, and for whom the picture was painted. Scholar-painters were not supposed to sell their work but to give it freely to one another as a token of friendship or in thanks for a favor. Their paintings almost always included an inscription and sometimes a poem as well. In their view, calligraphy and painting were closely related, for both consisted of brushstrokes that revealed character.

The Ming dynasty (1368–1644) returned Chinese rulers to the imperial throne. The scholar-painter ideal retained enormous prestige during this and the ensuing Qing dynasty (1644–1911), and Chinese writing about art focused on it almost exclusively. The writers, of course, were themselves scholars. In truth, scholar painting was only one of many types of art that were being made.

One lively sphere of artistic activity revolved around the large cities that had grown up during the late Song dynasty, especially in the south, and the wealthy middle-class patrons who lived in them. Another center of artistic patronage and production was the court itself. A beautiful example of Ming court taste in painting is *Mandarin Ducks and Hollyhocks*, a monumental hanging scroll by Lü Ji (**19.24**).

Born in southeastern China, Lü served with other court painters in the Hall of Benevolence and Wisdom and was eventually made a commander in the Imperial Guard. He specialized in bird-and-flower painting, a formerly intimate genre now conceived on a scale suitable for decorating the vast halls of the imperial palace. The brilliant colors, close observation, and meticulous detail of his lively composition are pleasures in themselves, but, as in much Chinese art, the objects depicted have symbolic value as well. Mandarin ducks were believed to mate for life, and so a pair of them, male and female, symbolizes marital fidelity. The nearby hollyhocks, *furong*, together with the branch of flowering cassia depicted above them, *gui*, allude to the phrase *furong qigui*, meaning "prosperous groom, honorable bride." Such a lavish painting would have made a suitable wedding gift in the rarefied circles of the imperial court.

Into the Modern Era

The Qing dynasty lasted until 1911, although not without experiencing major changes. A war with England over trade left the island of Hong Kong in British hands. Civil unrest challenging imperial authority and foreign involvement in Chinese affairs were met with brutal responses. Yet the Qing dynasty could not stem the changing tide, and China became a republic in 1912. Following World War II, China became the People's Republic of China, led by Chairman Mao Zedong. Social and economic reforms imposed Communist ideologies that promoted agrarian productivity and the redistribution of wealth.

Art created during the early days of the People's Republic aimed to teach Communist ideals. The poster on the next page (**19.25**) pictures Chairman Mao on the right, alongside Soviet leader Joseph Stalin, Russian revolutionary Vladimir Lenin, and German Socialist Friedrich Engels, who helped Karl Marx (on the far left) write *The Communist Manifesto* (1848). The imagery has little in common with traditional Chinese drawing. Instead, the artist embraced the naturalism of Western art and a clear, informational approach. The purpose of the poster and its

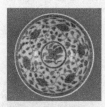

12.2 Bowl with lotus petals and floral scrolls

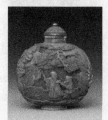

12.14 Snuff bottle with figures in a landscape

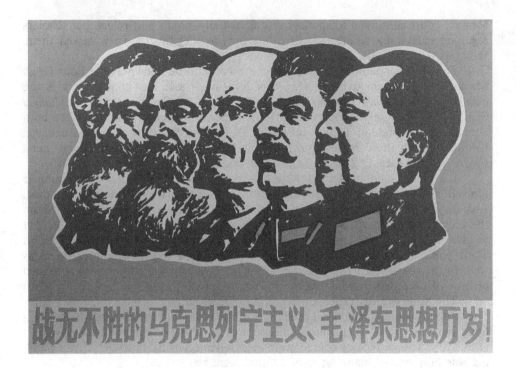

19.25 *Poster with Mao, Stalin, Lenin, Engels, and Marx.* ca. 1960. Screenprint.
colaimages/Alamy Stock Photo

inspirational slogan was to inform, not to entertain or delight with its beauty. It purpose as a propaganda tool promoting Socialist or Communist values led scholars to call this approach Socialist Realism.

Arts of Japan

Separated from the Asian landmass by the Sea of Japan, the islands of Japan form an arc curving northward from the tip of the Korean Peninsula. Neolithic cultures were established on the islands by 10,000 B.C.E. The ceramics they produced are not only among the oldest known pottery in the world, but also some of the most fanciful, shaped with a seemingly playful streak that resurfaces regularly in Japanese art.

Japanese culture comes into clearer focus during the first centuries of our common era. Large burial mounds from that time have yielded earthenware figures such as the horse illustrated here (**19.26**). Called *haniwa*, they embody a taste for simple forms and natural materials that is one of the themes of Japanese art. We can see these characteristics again in an early form of shrine architecture called *shinmei*.

The most famous example of *shinmei* is a shrine complex at Ise (**19.27**). Erected during the first century C.E., the shrine at Ise has been ritually rebuilt regularly since then, an unusual custom that allows this very early style to appear before our eyes in all its original freshness. The simple cylindrical shapes of the *haniwa* horse are echoed here in the wooden piles that raise the structures off the ground and the horizontal logs that hold the precisely trimmed thatched roofs in place. The buildings are left unpainted, just as *haniwa* were left unglazed.

Housed in the shrine, which can be entered only by members of the imperial family and certain priests, are a sword, a mirror, and a jewel—the three sacred symbols of Shinto. Shinto is often described as the native religion of Japan, but religion is perhaps too formal a word. Shinto involves a belief in numerous nature deities that are felt to be present in such picturesque sites as gnarled trees, imposing mountains, and waterfalls. A simple, unpainted wooden gate may be erected to mark a particularly sacred site. The chief deity of Shinto is female, the sun goddess. Purification through water plays an important role, as does the communion with

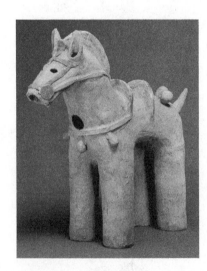

19.26 *Haniwa* figure of a horse. Japan. 3rd–6th century C.E. Earthenware with traces of pigment, height 23 ½".
Japanese School/Cleveland Museum of Art, Ohio/The Norweb Collection/ Bridgeman Images

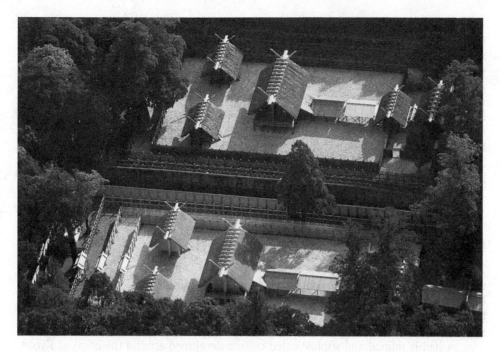

19.27 Overhead view of the shrine complex at Ise, showing the rebuilding of 2008–13 nearing completion and the previous rebuilding not yet dismantled.
The Asahi Shimbun/Getty Images

and appeasement of spirits, including spirits of the newly dead. The constant presence of nature in Japanese art, together with a respect for natural materials simply used, reflects the continuing influence of these ancient beliefs.

New Ideas and Influences: Asuka

Japan was profoundly transformed during the Asuka period (552–646 C.E.), when elements of Chinese culture reached the islands through the intermediary of Korea. One profound and lasting acquisition was the religion of Buddhism, accompanied by the art and architecture that China had developed to go with it. A perfected example of early Japanese Buddhist architecture is the temple compound Horyu-ji (**19.28**). Dating from the 7th century, Horyu-ji contains the oldest surviving wooden buildings in the world. The architecture reflects the elegant style of the Six Dynasties period in China.

RELATED WORKS

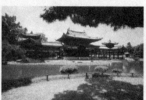

13.6 Byodo-in Temple

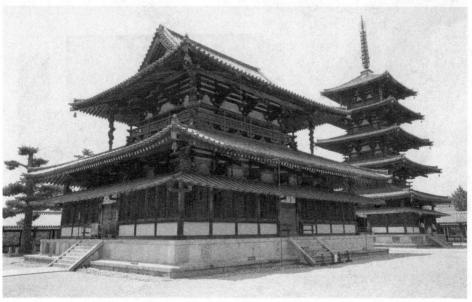

19.28 *Kondo* (main hall) and pagoda of Horyu-ji, Nara, Japan.
CulturalEyes—AusGS2/Alamy Stock Photo

Inside the gateway and to the left stands a pagoda, a slender tower with multiple roof lines. The equivalent of an Indian stupa (see 19.3), a pagoda serves as a shrine for the relics of a buddha or saintly person. Its ancestors are the tall, multistoried watchtowers of Han dynasty China. When Buddhism entered China, Chinese architects adapted the watchtower form to this new sacred purpose. To the right of the pagoda is the *kondo* ("golden hall"). Used for worship, the *kondo* houses devotional sculpture also based on Chinese models.

Buddhism did not eclipse Shinto, which continued to exist alongside it. Similarly, the earlier architectural ideas that produced the shrine at Ise were continued along with the newer Chinese-inspired forms. This ability to absorb and transform new ideas while keeping older traditions vital is one of the enduring strengths of Japanese culture.

Refinements of the Court: Heian

At the beginning of the Asuka period, Japan was ruled by powerful aristocratic clans, each of which controlled its own region. Inspired by the highly developed bureaucracy of China, the country moved toward unification under a centralized government. In 710 C.E., the imperial capital was established at Nara. The capital was soon moved to Kyoto, marking the beginning of the Heian period (794–1185 C.E.).

A highly refined and sophisticated culture developed around the court at Kyoto. Taste was paramount, and both men and women were expected to be accomplished in several arts. Perhaps the most important art was poetry. Through the miniature thirty-one-syllable form known as *tanka*, men and women communicated their feelings for each other, but always indirectly. The emphasis on literary accomplishment resulted in what many consider to be the greatest work of Japanese literature, *The Tale of Genji* by Murasaki Shikibu. A lady of the court, Murasaki wove aristocratic manners into a long narrative of love and loss that is often called the world's first novel.

Some of the earliest examples of secular painting in Japan survive in a copy of *The Tale of Genji* made during the 12th century (**19.29**). Written out and illustrated as a series of handscrolls (another imported Chinese idea), the monumental project brought together the specialized talents of several teams of artists. The illustration here depicts an episode from late in the tale. Yugiri, Genji's son, sits before a writing box, reading a letter he has just received. His wife, Kumoinokari, has crept up behind him and is about to snatch the letter from his hand, sure that it is from a woman he is in love with. On the opposite side of a partition, two anonymous ladies-in-waiting go about their duties, unseen by the protagonists although visible to us.

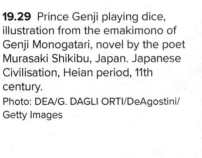

19.29 Prince Genji playing dice, illustration from the emakimono of Genji Monogatari, novel by the poet Murasaki Shikibu, Japan. Japanese Civilisation, Heian period, 11th century.
Photo: DEA/G. DAGLI ORTI/DeAgostini/ Getty Images

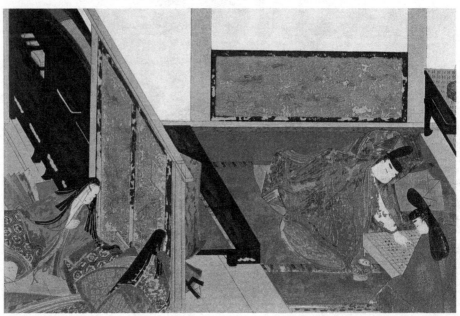

As in all the *Genji* illustrations, we are given a bird's-eye view of an interior with the roof conveniently removed so we can see inside. The painting's space tilts up. The artist uses thin outlines and flat areas of color without modeling. At first glance, all the characters seem to be wearing the same conventional masklike face—two dashes for eyes, a bent line for a nose, two heavier dashes for eyebrows, a small red mouth. Emotion is never betrayed by expressions or gestures in the *Genji* paintings. Just as Heian aristocrats maintained a facade of flawless manners and communicated their feelings through poems, so the artists of the *Genji* scrolls conveyed emotion by other means. Here, the protagonists are hemmed in by their narrow architectural setting and the presence of the ladies-in-waiting, suggesting the emotional and social pressures that bear down on them.

Buddhism remained central to Japanese life during the Heian period. Heian aristocrats at first favored esoteric Buddhism, an intellectually challenging faith that involved a hierarchy of deities as complicated as the hierarchy of the court itself. Later, as troubles grew, the simpler and more comforting message of Pure Land Buddhism became popular, as it had in China. In earlier chapters, we looked at one of the loveliest masterpieces of Heian Pure Land Buddhist art, the Byodo-in Temple (see 13.6).

Samurai Culture: Kamakura and Muromachi

The last decades of the Heian period were increasingly troubled by the rise of regional warriors, samurai. During the 12th century, civil war broke out as powerful regional clans, each with its army of samurai, battled for control of the country. With the triumph of the Minamoto clan in 1185, a military government was installed. The office of emperor was retained, but true power resided with the commander-in-chief, the shogun. A military capital was established at Kamakura, far from the distractions of the Heian court.

We can appreciate the life of a Kamakura period (1185–1392) samurai warrior through his armor (**19.30**). Made for a samurai who fought on horseback, the *yoroi* is a protective chest-piece and skirt. It is made of lacquered leather panels laced together with plates of leather-covered iron over vital areas. The small, rectangular and X-shaped markings are stitches in the leather. These were once made of white and colored silk, with colors and patterns determined by the warrior's clan and rank. An image of the Buddha is stenciled in the center of the leather chest-piece. The helmet has a large gilt copper crest and the samurai's face was covered by a mask, now lost. Armored sleeves and shin guards also once accompanied this suit. While undoubtedly protective, the *yoroi* could be quite heavy, and some examples weighed nearly half as much as their owners.

The painting of the Kamakura period depicted Buddhist themes, such as this painting of a subject called *raigo* (**19.31**). It represents a buddha and his attendants streaming down from Heaven in the light of their own glory. Literally "welcoming approach," *raigo* depicts the Amida Buddha arriving to escort a believer's soul to the Western Paradise. The gold on this *raigo* makes the heavenly procession shimmer as it descends toward Earth. The painting style, with thin, black outlines, flat areas of color, and conventional rather than individualized anatomy, is typical of this period. The tall, graceful Amida stands on a lotus blossom. The details of his robe are drawn in thin, gold lines. He is preceded by

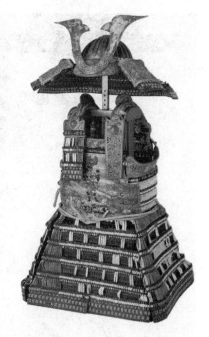

19.30 *Yoroi* (armor). 14th century. Iron, lacquer, leather, silk, 37 ½ × 22". Metropolitan Museum of Art, New York. Gift of Bashford Dean, 1914

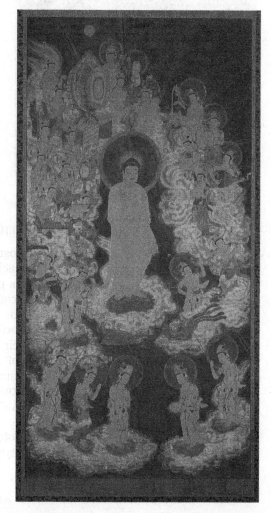

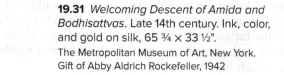

19.31 *Welcoming Descent of Amida and Bodhisattvas*. Late 14th century. Ink, color, and gold on silk, 65 ¾ × 33 ½". The Metropolitan Museum of Art, New York. Gift of Abby Aldrich Rockefeller, 1942

19.32 Bokushō Shūshō. *Splashed-Ink Landscape* (in the *haboku* technique). Early 16th century. Hanging scroll, ink on paper, 59 ¹³⁄₁₆ × 14 ³⁄₁₆". The Metropolitan Museum of Art, New York. Mary Griggs Burke Collection, Gift of the Mary and Jackson Burke Foundation, 2015

numerous bodhisattvas, and celestial musicians play all around him. *Raigo* were taken to the homes of the dying in the hopes that the vision they depicted might come true.

Pure Land Buddhism continued to win the hearts of ordinary people during the Kamakura period. Also popular was the worship of the Shinto deity Hachiman, who was claimed by the Minamoto clan as an ancestor. We looked at a statue of Hachiman in Chapter 11, Kaikei's *Hachiman in the Guise of a Monk* (see 11.17), carved in the new realistic style of the time.

Toward the end of the 14th century, the Ashikaga family gained control of the shogunate, and the military capital was moved to the Muromachi district of Kyoto. During the Muromachi period (1392–1568), a new type of Buddhism, Zen, became the leading cultural force in Japan. Zen reached Japan from China, where it was already highly developed. Following the example of the historical Buddha, it stressed personal enlightenment through meditation. Centuries of accumulated writings and scripture were cast aside in favor of direct, one-on-one teaching, master to student. The best-known Zen teaching tools are *koan*, irrational questions designed to "short-circuit" logical thought patterns. "What is the sound of one hand clapping?" is a well-known *koan*. Zen training was (and is) spartan and rigorous, qualities that appealed to the highly disciplined samurai.

Enlightenment in Zen is above all *sudden*. Zen priest-painters embodied this sudden appearance of meaning out of chaos in a painting technique called *haboku*, "splashed ink." Bokushō Shūshō's *Splashed-Ink Landscape* (**19.32**) is a masterpiece of this difficult technique—difficult because most attempts end in a mess. Bokushō drew together his "splashes" with a few expertly placed dark strokes, giving us all the clues we need to see a forested hillside by the water, and a rocky outcropping emerging above from the mist. A village nestles on the far side of the hill, and a bridge crosses the mostly unseen water. Bokushō was a painter, scholar, poet, and Zen monk. His quiet, subtle landscape painting embodies Zen's simplicity and solitary meditation.

Splendor and Silence: Momoyama

The shogun's control over regional lords and their samurai weakened during the Muromachi period, and devastating civil wars broke out. After the Ashikaga family fell from power in 1568, three strong leaders controlled the shogunate in succession. The decades of their rule are known as the Momoyama period (1573–1615).

For all its turbulence, the Momoyama period was a time of splendor for the arts. Fortified castles and great residences were built by powerful regional lords, and their interiors were decorated by the finest painters. We get a glimpse of the inside of a Momoyama period residence in this replica of a *shōin*, or study (**19.33**). The room features typical Japanese *tatami* grass mats covering the floor, and the paper-covered *fusuma* (sliding doors) that defined spaces within all kinds of structures. An alcove for sitting and contemplating a Zen Buddhist landscape is on the left. The *fusuma* on the far wall reflect the ostentatious tastes of the regional lords. Their gold background and gnarled tree embody the bold and highly colored decorative style that was much imitated in later Japanese art.

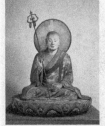

11.17 Kaikei, *Hachiman in the Guise of a Monk*

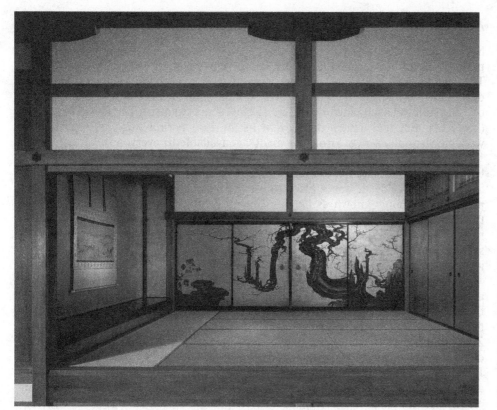

19.33 *Shōin* room. 1989 replica of Momoyama period room.
Image copyright © The Metropolitan Museum of Art, New York. Image source: Art Resource, NY

RELATED WORKS

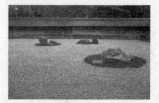

3.25 Stone and gravel garden, Ryoan-ji Temple

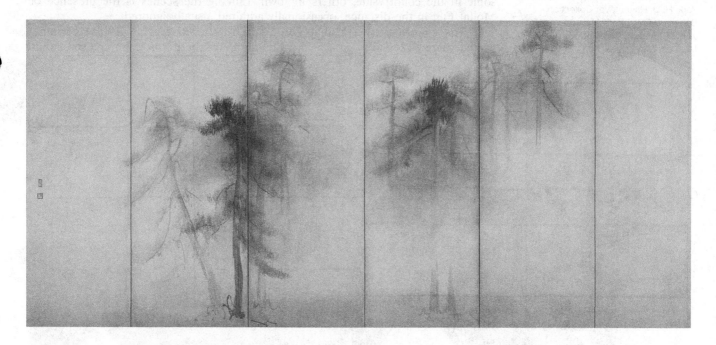

Showy displays on golden screens represent only one side of Momoyama taste. The other side is almost the exact opposite: a hushed and understated monochrome such as we see in Hasegawa Tōhaku's *Pine Wood* (**19.34**). *Pine Wood* consists of a pair of six-panel folding screens, of which we show one. Painted with great simplicity in ink on paper, the ghostly trees appear through veils of mist. The trees' setting is suggested but not shown. Instead, we see a fragment of a larger place. The paper itself, although technically blank, seems full of presences—trees we cannot see at the moment, or perhaps the edge of a lake. Tōhaku's genius was to fashion monumental, decorative works from a fundamentally intimate style.

19.34 Hasegawa Tōhaku. *Pine Wood*. Momoyama period, late 16th century. Ink on paper; one of a pair of six-panel screens, height 5' 1". Tokyo National Museum. HIP/Art Resource, NY

5.12 Sōtatsu,
*The Zen Priest
Choka*

19.35 Katsushika Hokusai. *The
Great Wave at Kanagawa*, from
Thirty-Six Views of Mount Fuji. ca.
1830–32. Polychrome woodblock
print; ink and color on paper,
10 ⅛ × 14 ¹⁵⁄₁₆".
The Metropolitan Museum of Art, New
York. H. O. Havemeyer Collection,
Bequest of Mrs. H. O. Havemeyer, 1929,
JP1847. Image © The Metropolitan
Museum of Art

Art for Everyone: Edo

Still another shift in the control of the shogunate signaled the beginning of the Edo period (1615–1868), named as before for the new capital city (present-day Tokyo). The many types of art that had been set in motion over the centuries continued during the Edo period. The tradition of ink painting and the continuing influence of Zen produced such playful wonders as Nonomura Sōtatsu's *The Zen Priest Choka* (see 5.12). But the great artistic event of the Edo period was the popularity of woodblock prints, a new form that made art available to everyone.

With theaters, tea houses, brothels, baths, wrestling matches, and other entertainments, the pleasure quarter and theater district of Edo became known as *ukiyo*, the "floating world." It was a place to escape life's difficulties. Edo era woodblock prints have become known as *ukiyo-e*, "images of the floating world," for they had their roots in this new urban playground, where townspeople and samurai went to relax. Beautiful women, famous actors, scenes set in tea houses and bath houses, scenes from folktales and ghost stories—these were some of the most popular subjects of *ukiyo-e*.

The production of woodblock prints was a team effort that brought together artists, block cutters, and printers. It was coordinated by a publisher, who marketed the results. In 1831, a publisher named Nishimuraya Yohachi announced the publication of a new series of prints, *Thirty-Six Views of Mount Fuji*, by "the old man Zen Hokusai Iitsu," one of the names used by Katsushika Hokusai. It would turn out to be one of the most popular series of prints ever produced. In the *Thirty-Six Views*, Hokusai left behind the traditional subject matter of *ukiyo-e* and turned his attention to a new subject, landscape. We meet pilgrims, laborers, merchants, farmers, fishermen, travelers, and sightseers, all going about their busy, fleeting lives, some in the countryside, others in town. Linking the scenes is the presence of Mount Fuji in the distance, occasionally admired, usually ignored.

The cowering fishermen of *The Great Wave at Kanagawa* (**19.35**) certainly cannot spare a second to gaze at the mountain. Yet there it is, calm and serene, its

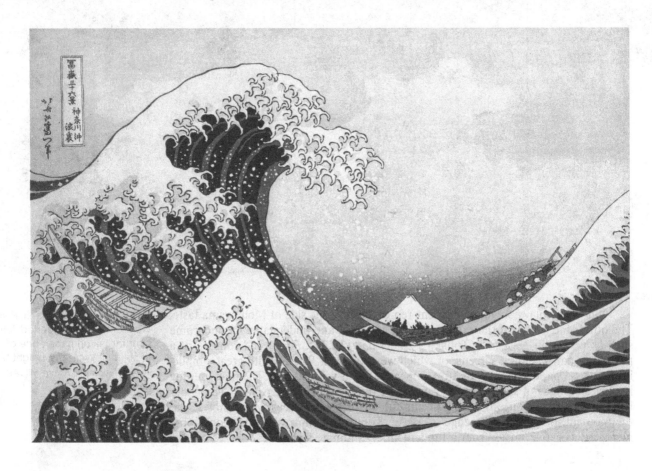

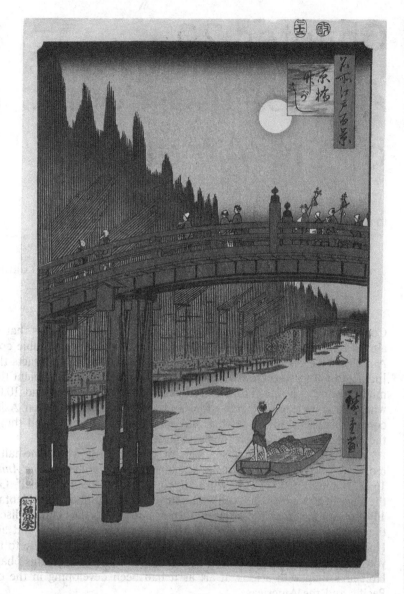

19.36 Ando Hiroshige. *Riverside Bamboo Market, Kyobashi*. View 76 from *One Hundred Famous Views of Edo*. 1857. Woodblock print, 14 ³⁄₁₆ × 9 ¼".
The Metropolitan Museum of Art, New York. The Howard Mansfield Collection, Purchase, Rogers Fund, 1936

RELATED WORKS

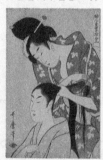

2.22 Utamaro, *Hairdressing*

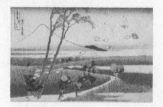

3.27 Hokusai, *Ejiri in Suruga Province*

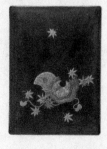

12.15 Lacquer writing box

sloping sides leading up to a majestic snowcapped peak. What a contrast it provides with the angry wave rearing with claws of foam, threatening to crush the slender boats below. A second wave in the foreground echoes the shape of Mount Fuji. But it will have this form for only a fraction of a second, whereas Fuji is eternal and unchanging. *The Great Wave at Kanagawa* has become an icon of Japanese art, famous around the world, thanks to Hokusai's brilliant design.

Like Hokusai, Ando Hiroshige produced series of views of a specific location. His *Riverside Bamboo Market, Kyobashi* (**19.36**) is one of a hundred views of Edo he published in 1857. It features people crossing a bridge in the moonlight while a boatman moves merchandise up the river. Bundled stalks of bamboo line the shore and float like rafts on the water. The artist has used a fragment to represent the whole busy market. The composition is so tightly cropped that we do not see either the beginning or the end of the bridge. It is as if the evening traffic on and under the bridge is captured for a moment before people and water move on. The moment is fleeting, yet by leafing through all one hundred views of the city we develop an appreciation of the daily lives of Edo's residents.

Chapter 20

Arts of the Pacific and of the Americas

In this chapter, you will learn to

LO1   explain the art of Pacific cultures, and

LO2   describe the art and architecture of the diverse cultures of the Americas.

Continuing eastward around the world, we come to two regions that together cover almost half the globe: the vast ocean of the Pacific and the double continent of the Americas. We began the previous chapter by stressing the contacts that had linked India and China to the evolving Mediterranean world since ancient times. Here, we might do the opposite. From the end of the last Ice Age around 10,000 years ago, when rising waters submerged the land bridge that once linked Asia and Alaska, contact between Europe, Africa, and Asia on the one hand and the Americas and the Pacific Islands on the other was largely cut off.

In Chapter 16, there is a sign of the moment when one-half of the world rediscovered the other. If you look again at Hans Holbein's *The Ambassadors* (see 16.18), painted in 1533, you will notice a globe on the lower shelf. Globes were all the rage in the early 16th century, spurred by Columbus's accidental discovery in 1492 of lands across the Atlantic Ocean and Vasco da Gama's discovery in 1498 that it was indeed possible to sail all the way around Africa and arrive in India. Holbein's globe is placed so that Europe is facing us. If you were to turn it around, you would see an emerging idea of the rest of the world. In this chapter, we fill in Holbein's map with a look at art as it had been developing in the cultures of the Pacific and the Americas.

Pacific Cultures

The lands of the Pacific include the continent of Australia and the thousands of islands grouped together as Oceania, "lands of the ocean." Australia was settled by the ancestors of the peoples today known as Aborigines, who arrived by sea from Southeast Asia as early as 50,000 years ago. The neighboring island of New Guinea was settled around the same time. The peopling of the rest of the Pacific Islands was the result of centuries of maritime courage, as seafaring settlers set out across uncharted waters in search of land they could not have known existed. Among the first islands to be settled, beginning around 1500 B.C.E., were those to the east of New Guinea. These are grouped with New Guinea as the cultural region of Melanesia. The last to be settled were the widely scattered islands of Polynesia, the easternmost cultural region of Oceania, which includes Hawaii (settled around 500 C.E.) and New Zealand (settled between 800 and 1200 C.E.).

The oldest examples of Pacific art are the earliest rock engravings of the Aborigines, some of which may date to 30,000 B.C.E. The meanings of these images are not known, but more recent Aboriginal art is intimately connected with the religious beliefs known as Dreamtime, or the Dreaming. Dreamtime includes

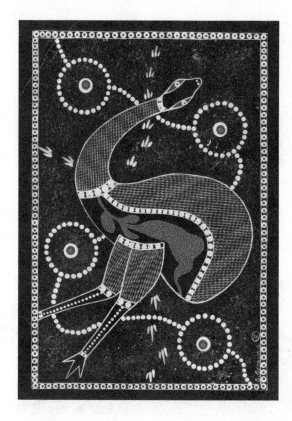

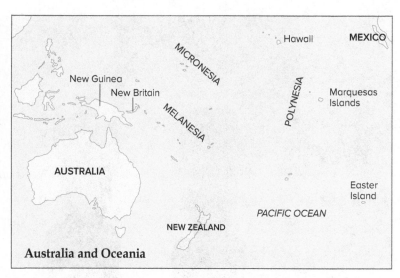

20.1 Stanley Geebung. Dot painting of an emu. ca. 1995. Ocher on card. Paul Pegler/E+/Getty Images

20.2 Asmat people. *Bis* pole. 1950s. Wood, paint, and fiber, height 216".
The Michael C. Rockefeller Memorial Collection, Bequest of Nelson A. Rockefeller, 1979. Inv. 1979.206.1611 © 2018. Image copyright The Metropolitan Museum of Art/Art Resource, NY

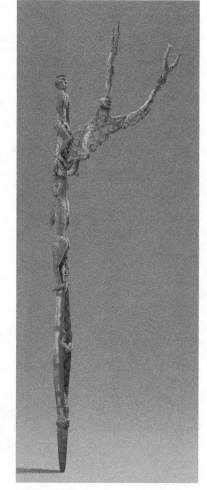

the distant past, when ancestral beings emerged from the Earth. Their actions shaped the landscape and gave rise to all forms of life within it, including humans. Dreamtime also exists in the present, and each individual is connected to it. With age a person draws closer to the realm of ancestors, and at death the spirit is reabsorbed into the Dreaming.

Art associated with the Dreaming pictures humans and animals, like the emu seen here (20.1). Aborigines consider the emu to be the king of all birds, thanks to its size. A Dreamtime story explains that the emu is flightless because a turkey was jealous of its status and tricked the emu into cutting off its wings. This and other legends appear in art related to the Dreaming. The emu is drawn in two dimensions against a flat background. It is defined by outlines and filled with repeating patterns of dots, circles, and lozenges in earth tones. The space the emu occupies is abstracted and gives the bird an otherworldly setting appropriate to its spiritual purpose.

The Asmat people of New Guinea, to the north of Australia, developed another way of representing their connection to the supernatural world. They erected huge monuments to honor deceased ancestors. With little contact with outsiders until the early 20th century, the Asmat people had hunted and fished in this Indonesian territory since settling the area almost 30,000 years ago. When explorers and traders encountered Asmat villages in the 19th and early 20th centuries, they found tall, carved wood *bis* poles (20.2) standing outside homes.

In Asmat belief all deaths are caused by human or supernatural enemies. The death must be avenged by living heirs to restore harmony in the world. The poles functioned in concert with ritual feasts held to honor the recent dead and confirm this obligation on the living. Once the feast was over and the death avenged, the pole was discarded and left to decay.

All the figures on an Asmat *bis* pole are family members. Each represents a specific person, not as a naturalistic portrait but as a conventionalized type. The figures are elongated and have thick necks and large eyes. The entire pole is cut from a single tree, with a root for the phallus that projects from near the top. The pole therefore connects death and fertility as two forces with a powerful influence on Asmat life.

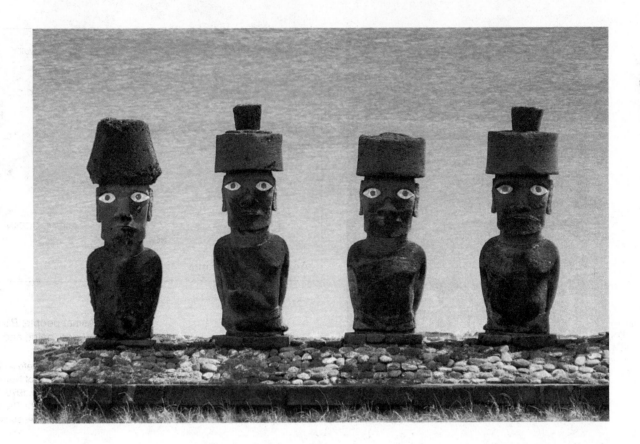

20.3 Stone figures on Ahu Nau Nau, Anakena, Easter Island (Rapanui), Chile.

Photo by Bernard Annebicque/Sygma via Getty Images

Among the most well-known works of the Pacific are the monumental stone figures of Easter Island (Rapanui), the most remote and isolated island of Polynesia (**20.3**). Almost one thousand of the monolithic statues have been found. Scholars believe they were carved as memorials to dead rulers or other important ancestors. Whatever purpose the statues served, the islanders must have believed it to be vital to their community, for they went to heroic efforts to erect them. The stones were quarried and partially carved in the island's volcanic mountains. The average height of the figures is about 36 feet, and each one weighs tens of tons, yet somehow they were dragged for miles across the island and set upright on elevated stone platforms that probably served as altars.

Easter Islanders seem to have begun erecting the figures around 900 C.E. Six centuries later, conflicts apparently broke out on the island, and a period of warfare ensued. Most of the figures were knocked down and destroyed. The statues photographed here were restored in 1978, their heads crowned again with red stone topknots and their faces set with white coral eyes. Stones that had slumbered for centuries suddenly awoke. Lined up once more along the shoreline, they stare hypnotically inland in an eternal vigil whose purpose we may never fully understand.

Polynesian peoples believed that certain materials were sacred to the gods. Among those materials were feathers. Rulers and other high-ranking members of society traced their descent from the gods, and they adorned themselves with feathered garments as a sign of their status. With their bold geometric designs and brilliant colors, the feather cloaks of Hawaii are the most spectacular products of this unique art form (**20.4**). Although both men and women of the Hawaiian elite wore many types of feathered garments, majestic cloaks such as this, reaching from the shoulders to the ground, belonged exclusively to the highest-ranking men. The creation of such a cloak was itself a ritual activity limited to high-ranking men. As the makers wove and knotted the cloak's plant-fiber foundation, they chanted the names of the ancestors of the man who would eventually wear it. The names were thus captured in the cloak, imbuing it with protective spiritual power. Feathers were tied onto the completed fiber netting in overlapping rows. Feathers were collected by commoners, who offered them as part of their yearly tribute to their rulers.

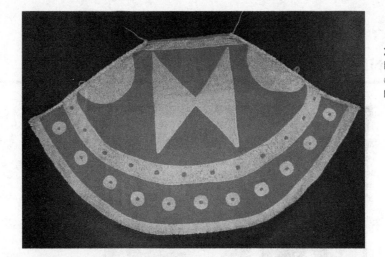

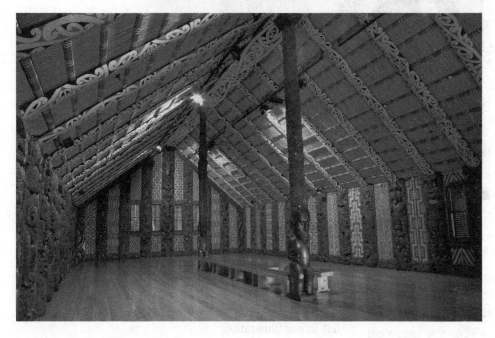

The feather cloaks of Hawaii embody ideas about the order of society, the respective roles of men and women, the continuing presence of ancestors, and the protective power of the gods. Similar concerns are given architectural form in the men's meeting houses of the Maori people of New Zealand, the southernmost of the Polynesian islands (**20.5**). The house is understood as the body of the sky father, the supreme deity of the Maori. The ridgepole is his spine, and the rafters are his ribs. His face is carved on the exterior, where other elements symbolize his embracing arms. Meetings thus take place within the god, which is to say under his protection, sanction, and authority.

The freestanding figures that support the ridgepole from inside portray ancestors. Their knees are bent in the aggressive posture of the war dance, reminding the living of their courage and great deeds. They are stylized according to Maori taste, with enlarged heads and squat proportions. More stylized portrayals of snarling, powerful ancestors are carved in the series of reliefs that line the walls. Each relief panel meets a rafter whose lower portion is carved with still more ancestors. Everywhere, iridescent shell eyes gleam and glimmer as they catch the light. Ancestors were believed to participate in the discussions held in the house, and these sculptures make their watchful presence felt. The reliefs along the walls alternate with panels of lattice woven in symbolic patterns that relate to stories about Maori deities and heroes. The panels were woven by women. Women, however, were not permitted to enter the meeting house, and so they wove the panels from the back, standing outside.

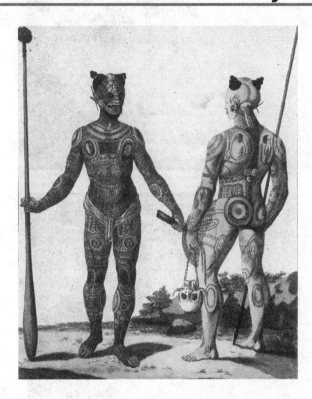

Do you have piercings? Tattoos? How do these body modifications relate to historical practices? Why do we as humans modify our bodies?

The patterns that swirl over the surfaces of the rafter and carved poles of the meeting house echo the tattoo patterns that ornament the bodies of Maori men and women. All Polynesian peoples practiced tattooing, but nowhere was the art cultivated with greater virtuosity than among the inhabitants of the Marquesas Islands in the South Pacific. The illustration here shows two Marquesan men in different stages of the lifelong tattooing process. The mature man at the left is completely tattooed from head to foot, whereas the younger man at the right is only partially ornamented. If life granted him enough time, prestige, and wealth, he gradually had the remaining blank areas of his skin decorated.

Like all other arts, the act of tattooing was considered sacred by the Marquesans. It was performed ritually by a specialist, a *tukuka*, who invoked the protective presence of specific deities. The designs were created using a bone tool that resembled a small comb with sharp, fine teeth. The specialist dipped the teeth in black pigment made of soot or ground charcoal, set them against his client's skin, then gave the tool a sharp rap with a stick to puncture the skin and insert the pigment. Because tattooing was expensive and painful, only a small area of the body was usually decorated during each session. Nearly all adult Marquesans, both male and female, wore tattoos, although only the wealthiest and most highly regarded chiefs and warriors reached the allover patterning of the man to the left in our illustration.

Tattooing and other forms of body art are not unique to the Pacific islands. Humans around the world have modified their bodies since prehistory. The famous Stone Age "Iceman" discovered frozen in the mountains of Europe has tattoos dating back 5,300 years. Women's mummies from ancient Egypt bear tattoos. In both cases, recent analysis suggests that the tattoos may have been intended to alleviate the physical pain of age or childbirth.

Scarification—the act of raising scars on the skin in decorative or symbolic patterns—was practiced by the African Yoruba peoples. The head of a king from Ife that we studied earlier (see 2.16) bears thin lines that are believed to be scars to denote social rank. Other forms of modification have included changing the ways our bodies develop. Chinese women had their feet bound to impede growth, and the ancient Maya used boards to elongate babies' heads. While today we may find these practices unsettling, both cultures believed the modifications to be beautiful.

Inhabitants of the island of Nuku Hiva. 1813. Hand-colored copperplate engraving after original drawings by Wilhelm Gottlieb Tilesius von Tilenau. akg-images.

The Americas

No one knows for sure when humans first occupied the double continent of the Americas, or where those people came from. The most widely accepted theory is that sometime before 13,000 years ago—and possibly as early as 25,000 years ago—migrating peoples crossed over a now-submerged land bridge linking Siberia with Alaska, then gradually pushed southward, seeking hospitable places in which to dwell. Firm evidence of human presence at the tip of South America has recently been dated to about 12,500 years ago, indicating that by then both continents were populated, if only sparsely.

By 3000 B.C.E., we can identify developed cultures in three important centers: the Northwest Coast of North America, the fertile plateaus and coastal lowlands of Mesoamerica, and the Pacific Coast of South America. During the ensuing centuries, peoples in these and other territories created rich and sophisticated artistic expressions. Their early art has sometimes been called "pre-Columbian," meaning that it was created before Columbus's voyages to the Americas. The term acknowledges that the arrival of Europeans changed everything, and that the civilizations of the Americas were interrupted as decisively as if they had been hit by a meteor. Yet it is best to approach them on their own terms and not to think of them as "before" something else. After all, they did not think of themselves as coming "before" anything but, rather, *after* their many predecessors, whose achievements they knew and admired.

Mesoamerica

"Mesoamerica" describes a region that extends from north of the Valley of Mexico (the location of present-day Mexico City) through the western portion of modern Honduras. Mesoamerica is a cultural and historical designation as well as a geographical one, for the civilizations that arose in this region shared many features,

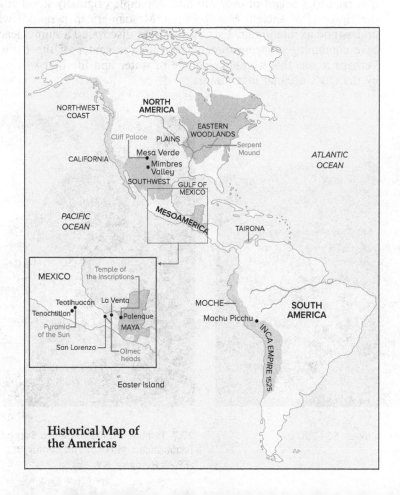

Historical Map of the Americas

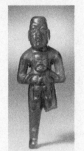

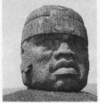

including the cultivation of corn, the building of pyramids, a 260-day ritual calendar, similar deities, an important ritual ball game, and a belief in the role of human blood in sustaining the gods and the universe. Mesoamerican peoples themselves were conscious of their common cultural background. Thus, the Aztecs, who were the most powerful culture in the region at the time of the Spanish conquests of the early 16th century, collected and admired jade sculptures by the Olmec, whose civilization had flourished more than two thousand years earlier.

Olmec civilization, which flourished between about 1500 and 300 B.C.E., is often called the "mother culture" of Mesoamerica, for it seems to have institution-alized the features that mark later civilizations of the region. The principal Olmec centers were concentrated in a small region on the Gulf Coast of Mexico, but the influence of Olmec culture extended over a much broader area. Chapter 11 illustrated one of the colossal stone heads carved by Olmec sculptors (see 11.10). Chapter 2 included a finely worked Olmec jade depicting a shaman (see 2.38). Olmec leaders may have derived their power by claiming ability as shamans. Rulers in later Mesoamerican societies were also expected to have privileged access to the sacred realm.

A few centuries after the decline of the Olmecs, the city of Teotihuacán, to the northeast of present-day Mexico City, began its rise to prominence. At its height, between 350 and 650 C.E., Teotihuacán was one of the largest cities in the world. Laid out in a grid pattern with streets at right angles, the city covered 9 square miles and had a population of around 200,000. Teotihuacán exerted great influence over the rest of Mesoamerica, although whether this was through trade or through conquest we do not know.

The heart of the city was its ceremonial center, a complex of pyramids and temples lining a 3-mile-long thoroughfare known as the Avenue of the Dead. To the Aztecs, who arrived in the region long after Teotihuacán had been abandoned, it seemed hardly possible that humans were capable of such wonders. They viewed the city as a sacred site where the gods had created the universe, and it was they who named its largest structure the Pyramid of the Sun (**20.6**). Made of stone using the stacking and piling technique of load-bearing architecture, the Pyramid of the Sun rises to a height of over 210 feet. A temple originally stood at its summit. Like the ziggurats of ancient Mesopotamia, Mesoamerican pyramids were symbolically understood as mountains. Excavations have discovered a tunnel leading to a natural cave containing a spring directly beneath the center of the Pyramid of the Sun. Perhaps it was this womblike source of water and life that was considered sacred by the city's original inhabitants.

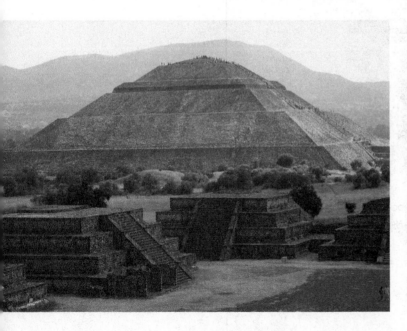

20.6 Pyramid of the Sun, Teotihuacán, Mexico. 50–200 C.E.
Getty Images/Moment/Nils Axel Braathen

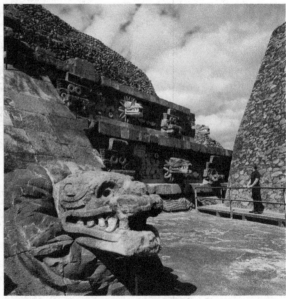

20.7 Temple of the Feathered Serpent, the Ciudadela, Teotihuacán, Mexico. 2nd century C.E.
SEF/Art Resource, NY

Farther north along the Avenue of the Dead is a large sunken plaza surrounded by temple platforms. The focal point of this complex, the Temple of the Feathered Serpent, gives us our first look at a deity shared by many of the Mesoamerican civilizations (**20.7**). The Olmec pantheon included a feathered serpent, although its exact meaning is unclear. To the Aztecs, the feathered serpent was Quetzalcoatl, the god of windstorms that bring rain. Here, representations of the deity—its aggressive head emerging from a collar of feathers—alternate with the more abstract figure of the god of rain, distinguished by his goggle eyes. Rain and the wind that brought it were essential to the agricultural societies of Mesoamerica.

One of the most fascinating of all Mesoamerican civilizations was that of the Maya, which arose in the southeastern portion of Mesoamerica, primarily in the Yucatán Peninsula and present-day Guatemala. Mayan culture began to form around 1000 B.C.E., probably under the influence of the Olmecs. The Maya themselves come into focus just after the final decline of Olmec civilization around 300 B.C.E. Maya civilization flourished most spectacularly between 250 and 900 C.E. It was still in existence when the Spanish arrived in the early 16th century, however, and speakers of Maya languages live in the region today.

Among their other accomplishments (including astronomy, biology, and the mathematical concept of zero), the Maya developed the most sophisticated version of the Mesoamerican calendar and the most advanced of the region's many writing systems. Scholars began to crack the code of Maya writing in the 1960s, and since then the steady deciphering of inscriptions has provided new insights into Maya civilization, in the process overturning much of what earlier scholars assumed.

The Maya were not a single state but a culture with many centers, each ruled by a hereditary lord and an elite class of nobles. Warfare between the centers was common, and its purpose was not conquest but capture: Prisoners of war were needed for the human sacrifices that were thought necessary to sustain the gods and maintain the universe. The official and ceremonial architecture of the Maya was meant to impress, and it does (**20.8**). This photograph shows the structures known as the Palace and the Temple of the Inscriptions at Palenque, in the Chiapas region of Mexico. The royal dynasty of Palenque was founded in 431 C.E. and rose to prominence under Lord Pacal, who died in 683 C.E. He was buried in a small chamber far below the Temple of the Inscriptions.

The palace probably served as an administrative and ceremonial center. Set on a raised terrace built using the load-bearing system, it is constructed on two levels around three courtyards. Like the Temple of the Inscriptions atop the pyramid, the buildings of the palace take the form of long, many-chambered galleries. The square pillars of their open porches support massive stone ceilings with corbeled vaulting.

20.8 Palace and Temple of the Inscriptions, Palenque, Mexico. Maya, 7th century C.E.
© Danny Lehman/Corbis

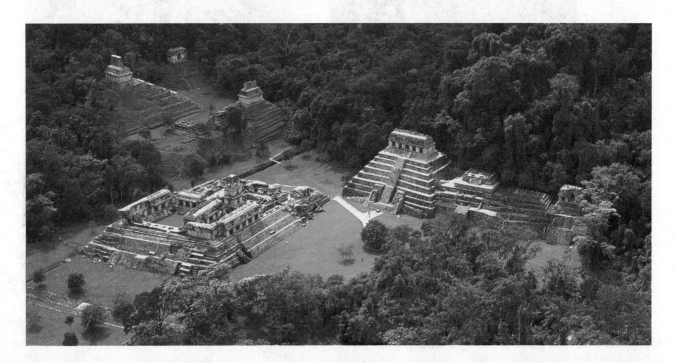

Maya palaces, temples, and burials were filled with art, from relief carvings to mural paintings. They also included painted vessels such as this cup from Guatemala (**20.9**). Made using the **coil technique**, cups like this served as gifts and grave goods. The painted scene represents a ruler seated on his throne, with offerings nearby. His elongated profile is the result of the cranial modifications made to Maya babies in the quest for beauty. The seated ruler wears an elaborate headdress, a pectoral necklace, bracelets, and anklets. While his body is seen frontally, his head is in profile. This is because just beyond our view are two other figures who have come to pay him homage. The seated ruler leans over to address them. Like the ruler, these figures are also drawn in graceful black outlines and painted in red, white, and brown pigments.

The first scholars to study the Maya believed that their art was primarily sacred and depicted cosmic events such as stories of the gods. Thanks to our understanding of Maya writing, we now realize that Maya art is almost entirely concerned with history. Like the vessel, it memorializes rulers and portrays important moments of their reigns. Preeminent among Maya arts are narrative stone relief carvings such as this lintel from a building in Yaxchilan, Mexico (**20.10**).

The scene shown on the lintel is the second in a sequence of three compositions that portray a royal bloodletting ceremony. Bloodletting was a central Maya practice, and almost every ritually important occasion was marked by it. Lady Xoc, the principal wife of Lord Shield Jaguar, is seated at the lower right. The previous panel showed her pulling a thorn-lined rope through her tongue in the presence of Shield Jaguar himself. Here, she experiences the hallucinatory vision that was the purpose of the ceremony. From the bowl of blood and ritual implements on the floor before her there rises the Vision Serpent. A warrior, possibly one of Shield Jaguar's

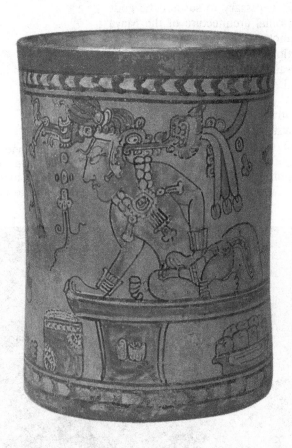

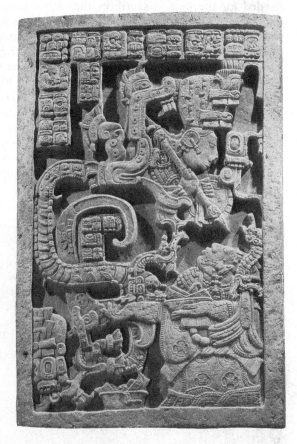

20.9 Vessel with throne scene. Maya, late 7th–8th century. Ceramic and pigment, height 8 ½".
The Metropolitan Museum of Art, New York. Gift of Charles and Valerie Diker, 1999

20.10 Lintel 25 (*The Vision of Lady Xoc*), Yaxchilan, Chiapas, Mexico. Maya, 725 C.E. Limestone, 5 13/16 × 34 × 4".
The British Museum, London. Photo © Justin Kerr K2888

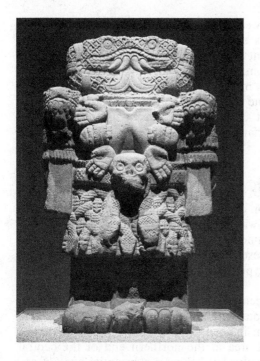

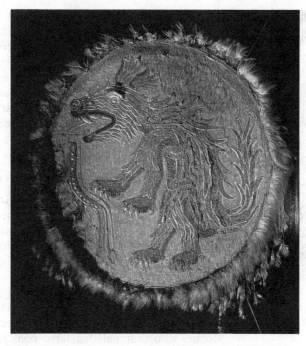

20.11 *Coatlicue*. Aztec, 1500 C.E. Basalt, height 101".
Francesco Palermo/Alamy Stock Photo

20.12 Ceremonial shield. Aztec, early 16th century. Feather mosaic and gold on wicker base, diameter 27 ½".
Museum für Völkerkunde, Vienna. Erich Lessing/Art Resource, NY

ancestors, issues from its gaping jaws. The ceremony, which probably marked the accession of Shield Jaguar as ruler, took place on the Maya equivalent of October 23, 681 C.E. We know the date and the names of the characters involved thanks to the Maya writing that appears above and to the left of the figures.

The last Mesoamerican empire to arise before the arrival of European conquerors was built by the Aztecs. According to their own legends, the Aztecs migrated into the Valley of Mexico during the 13th century C.E. from their previous home near the mythical Lake Aztlan (hence Aztec). They settled finally on an island in Lake Tezcoco, and there they began to construct their capital, Tenochtitlán. Tenochtitlán grew to be a magnificent city, built on a cluster of islands connected by canals and linked by long causeways to cities on the surrounding shores. Massive pyramids and temple platforms towered over the ritual precincts, and in the market squares goods from all over Mesoamerica changed hands. By 1500, Aztec power reached its height, and much of central Mexico paid them tribute.

Tenochtitlán is still somewhat visible in the plan and archaeological sites of modern Mexico City, despite the fact that Spanish conquerors razed its pyramids, burned its books, and melted its precious metal objects for gold and silver. The colossal sculpture of the Aztec goddess Coatlicue (**20.11**) was fortunate to have survived the destruction. Although other Aztec representations of Coatlicue picture her head as a human skull, this sculpture uses two serpents. She wears a necklace of human hearts and hands, and a skirt of snakes. Unlike the graceful lines of Maya art, Aztecs preferred more geometric and solid forms. We see this blockiness in Coatlicue's massive legs and thick body. Standing over 8 feet tall, this massive goddess is fearsome and powerful. When the sculpture was excavated in the late 18th century, Spanish colonial authorities feared that it would rekindle Aztec beliefs if left in public view. They re-buried the sculpture in a patio at the university, although it was excavated again and put on public display following Mexico's War of Independence.

Even while they destroyed many items in their quest to convert Aztecs to Christianity, the Spaniards were deeply impressed by the arts they found, and many objects were sent back to Europe. The ceremonial shield pictured here (**20.12**) made the trans-Atlantic journey. It is made of feathers in a technique greatly prized in

RELATED WORKS

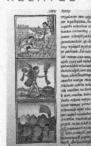

3.15 Sahagún, *Florentine Codex: Feather Workers*

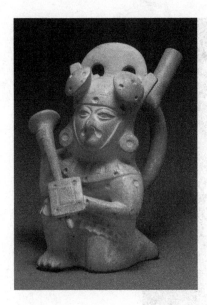

20.13 Stirrup vessel. Moche, 200–500 C.E. Earthenware with cream slip, height 9 ⅛".

The Metropolitan Museum of Art, New York. Gift of Nathan Cummings, 1963, 63.226.8. Image © The Metropolitan Museum of Art

Mesoamerica. A specialized group of weavers in Tenochtitlán produced feather headdresses, cloaks, and other garments exclusively for nobles and high officials. The heraldic coyote depicted in iridescent blue feather barbs edged in gold against red feathers is the Aztec god of war. From his mouth issues the term for war, written in the Aztec writing system. Rich in metaphors, Aztec speech also referred to warfare as "the song of the shields" and "flowers of the heart upon the plain." Feather shields such as this were part of the lavish dance costumes worn by warriors in ritual re-creations of the warfare of the gods.

South and Central America

Like Mesoamerica to the north, the region of the central Andes on the Pacific Coast of South America provided a setting in which numerous cultures developed. Pyramids, temple platforms, and other monuments have been found dating to the third millennium B.C.E., making them the oldest works of architecture in the Americas, contemporary with the pyramids of Egypt. Textiles of astonishing intricacy have also been found from this time.

Among the first South American peoples to leave a substantial record of art are the Nasca, whom we studied in Chapter 4. Their earth drawings (see 4.2) were so immense that they could not be seen in their entirety from ground level. The Moche, who dominated a large coastal area at the northern end of the central Andes during the first six centuries C.E., also left behind a substantial body of art. The Moche were exceptional potters and goldsmiths. Tens of thousands of Moche ceramics have been found, for one of their great innovations was the use of molds for mass production.

Kneeling warriors are a standard subject of Moche ceramic art (**20.13**). The large ear ornaments and elaborate headdress capped with a crescent-shaped element are typical of the costume on these figures. The warrior carries a shield and a war club; the heads of two more war clubs protrude from his headdress. His beaked nose probably links him to the barn owl, which was regarded as a warrior animal for its fierce and accurate nocturnal hunting abilities. Much of the finest Moche pottery takes the form of stirrup vessels, so called after their U-shaped spout (here attached to the warrior's back). The innovative spout pours well, can be carried easily, and minimizes evaporation. Yet such elaborate vessels cannot have been primarily practical. This vessel with its stylized figure composed of thick masses was likely reserved for ritual use.

One of the most spectacular archaeological sites in the world is the Inca city of Machu Picchu, in Peru (**20.14**). Beginning around 1430 and moving with amazing swiftness, the Inca created the largest empire of its time in the world. By 1500 their rule extended for some 3,400 miles along the Pacific Coast. Inca textiles are some of the finest in the long tradition of South American fiber work (see 12.10). Inca artists also excelled in sculptures and other objects of silver and gold. But the most original Inca genius expressed itself in stonework. Over 20,000 miles of stone-paved roads were built to speed communication and travel across the far-flung empire. The massive masonry walls of Inca buildings were constructed from large blocks of granite patiently shaped through abrasion. Masons shaped each stone until it fit into place in the load-bearing wall with no need for mortar.

Machu Picchu is set high in the Andes Mountains, overlooking a hairpin turn in the Urubamba River thousands of feet below. Builders leveled the site to create a small plateau and constructed terraces for houses and agriculture. Also visible at Machu Picchu is the wholly distinctive Inca sensitivity to the natural landscape. At the northern end of Machu Picchu, for example, a freestanding boulder was carved to resemble the silhouette of a peak that can be seen beyond it in the distance. Elsewhere a rounded building known as the Observatory accommodates a huge boulder in its walls and interior. Part of the boulder is subtly sculpted to create a staircase and chamber. The Inca believed stones and people to be equally alive and capable of changing into one another. This attitude seems to have resulted in their unique approach of relating architecture to its setting.

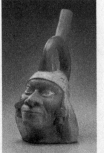

11.4 Stirrup-spout portrait vessel

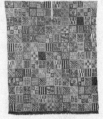

12.10 Inca tunic

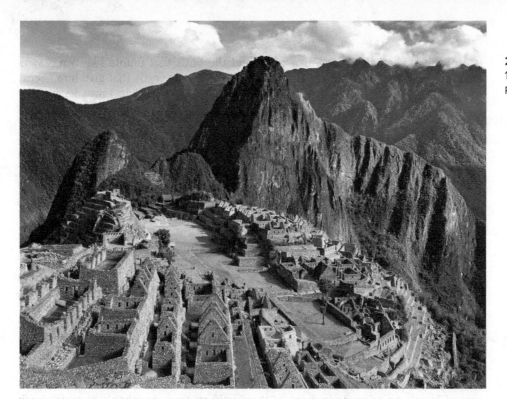

20.14 Machu Picchu, Peru. Inca, 15th–16th centuries.
Rob Kroenert/Getty Images

We end this section with an object made from the material that drove Spanish conquerors deep into the American continents: gold (**20.15**). Fashioned of a copper-and-gold alloy called *tumbaga*, this pendant figure was made by artists of the Tairona culture, which flourished in northern Colombia after about 1000 C.E. The Tairona belong to the cultural region of Central America, which extends from the southern part of present-day Honduras into northwestern Colombia, where a mountain range called the Cordillera Oriental forms a natural boundary. The knowledge of extracting and working gold was first developed to the south, in Peru. Over generations it spread northward, and the goldsmith's art became increasingly refined and technically advanced.

Cast using the **lost-wax** technique, the pendant here portrays a ruler. The figure is stylized, with squat proportions and a large head with oversized eyes. He

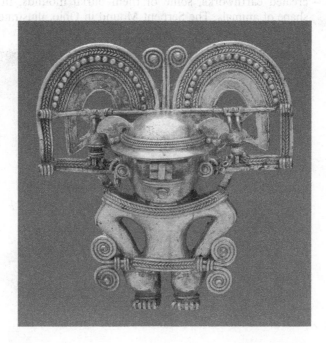

20.15 Tairona artist, active ca. 900–1550 CE; Figure Pendant; 900–1550; Culture: Colombia, Tairona style; 10th–16th Century; Cast gold; overall: 6.2 × 6.1 × 2.5 cm (2 7/16 × 2 3/8 × 1 in.)
The Cleveland Museum of Art, John L. Severance Fund 1998.3

is probably a shaman as well as a ruler, and the birds that unfold like wings symmetrically from either side of his head are the spirit alter egos that give him access to the other world. Tairona smiths added copper to the gold to lower its melting point and create a harder, more durable object. After casting, the pendant was bathed in acids that removed the outermost layer of copper particles, leaving the impression of solid gold. The taste for ornaments in precious metals spread from Central America northward into Mesoamerica. There the finest artists in precious metals were the Mixtec, who supplied the Aztecs with their legendary and now lost works. Earlier cultures such as the Olmecs and the Maya had preferred jade.

North America

It might be expected that those of us who live in North America would have a clear picture of the history of art on our own continent, since we are, after all, right here where it happened. Unfortunately, we do not. In general, the ancient arts of North America are much less available to us than are those of other parts of the world, for many reasons. These include a general lack of respect for Native American culture in the 19th and early 20th centuries, when the first histories of art were written in the United States. Early scholars preferred the art of Greece and Rome to the largely practical objects created by North America's native inhabitants. Materials also played a part in our inattention to Native American art, as the early inhabitants of North America made many of their artifacts from perishable materials such as wood and fiber. Also, patterns of life developed differently in the North, leaving few large urban centers to force our attention toward the people who built them.

Many arts of later North American peoples—Indians, as we have come to call them—are arts of daily life: portable objects such as baskets, clothing, and tools imbued with meaning that goes far beyond their practical functions. In Chapter 12, we used as an example of such arts a basket from the Pomo of California (see 12.9). Pomo thought links the basket to the story of the sun's journey across the sky, and a flaw woven deliberately into the basket provides a way for spirits to enter and leave. The basket is thus connected to the sacred realm and to ritual. And yet it is also a basket.

The first clearly identifiable culture group of North America populated an area known as the Eastern Woodlands—in parts of what are now Ohio, Indiana, Kentucky, Pennsylvania, and West Virginia—starting about 700 B.C.E. Several Eastern Woodlands cultures are known collectively as the "mound builders," because they created earthworks, some of them burial mounds, in geometric forms or in the shape of animals. The Serpent Mound in Ohio, illustrated in Chapter 11, is the most

20.16 Beaver effigy platform pipe. Hopewell, 100 B.C.E.–200 C.E. Pipestone, pearl, and bone, length 4 9/16".
The Thomas Gilcrease Museum, Tulsa, Oklahoma. © Dirk Bakker/ Bridgeman Images

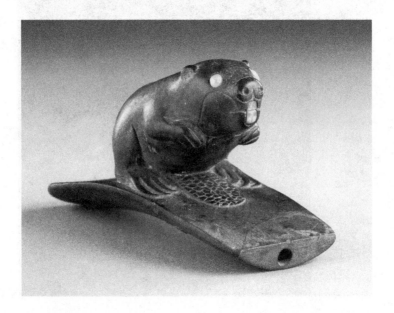

famous of the mounds still visible (see 11.24). Excavations of burial mounds have yielded beautifully crafted objects in sheet mica, copper, marine shell, silver, and obsidian—exotic materials obtained through an extensive trade network. Among the most compelling objects are hundreds of small stone pipes, their bowls carved as an effigy of an animal (**20.16**). The naturalistic beaver here assumes a fighting pose, its tail tucked beneath its body. The bared incisors were carved from actual beaver teeth. Two freshwater pearls serve for eyes. Their reflective luster signaled the spirit-life of the effigy.

Tobacco was considered a sacred substance by many North American peoples. First domesticated in the Andes around 3000 B.C.E., it made its way north via Mexico some two thousand years later. In North America, smoking tobacco became viewed as a form of prayer. The rising smoke faded into the other world, bidding its spirits to come and witness or sanction human events. Interestingly, although the knowledge of tobacco arrived from the South, the stone pipe itself is a North American invention.

Urban life was not entirely absent from North America. The people known to archaeologists as the Anasazi,[1] who lived in the southwestern part of the continent, created ambitious communal dwelling sites. One such dwelling at Mesa Verde, in Colorado, has become known as Cliff Palace (**20.17**). The Anasazi had been present in the region from the first several centuries B.C.E. Around the 12th century C.E., they began clustering their buildings in protected sites on the undersides of cliffs. A complex system of handholds and footholds made access difficult. (Modern tourists have been provided with an easier way in.) This arrangement allowed the Anasazi to ward off invaders and maintain a peaceful community life.

Cliff Palace, which dates to about 1200 C.E., has more than two hundred rooms constructed using the load-bearing system. The rooms are organized in apartment-house style, most of them living quarters but some at the back meant for storage. In addition, there are twenty-three *kivas*—large, round chambers, mostly underground and originally roofed, used for religious or other ceremonial purposes. The structures are of stone or adobe with timber, and so harmonious is the overall plan that many scholars believe a single architect must have been in charge. Cliff Palace was occupied for about a hundred years before being mysteriously abandoned in the early 14th century.

RELATED WORKS

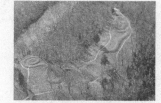

11.24 Serpent Mound

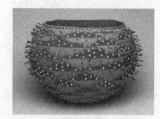

12.9 Pomo basket

20.17 Cliff Palace, Mesa Verde, Colorado. Anasazi, ca. 1200 C.E.
darekm101/RooM RF/Getty Images

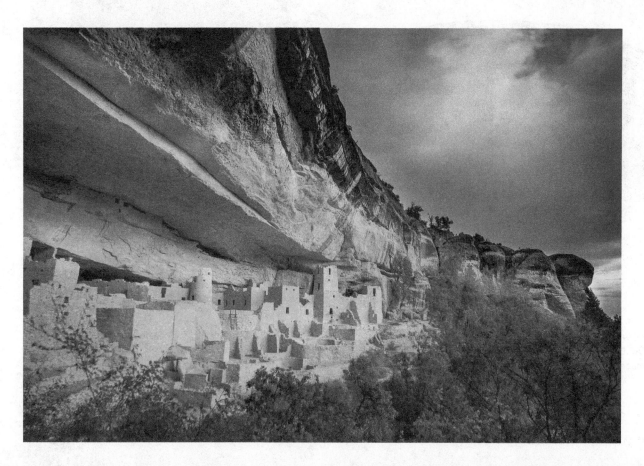

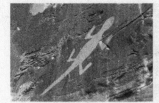

4.43 Fremont lizard petroglyph

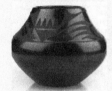

12.1 María and Julián Martínez, Jar

The Anasazi's neighbors in the Southwest were a people we know only as the Mogollon culture, which flourished in the Mimbres Valley of what is now New Mexico between the 3rd and 12th centuries C.E. Today the word *Mimbres* is associated with a type of ceramic vessel developed about 1000 C.E. Mimbres jars and bowls were made using the coil technique and decorated with black-on-white or brown-on-white geometric designs or with stylized figures of animals or humans. Often, these motifs appeared as paired figures (**20.18**). In this example, two sheep stand opposite each other, separated by stepped pyramids, swirls, and zig-zagging lines that may represent mountains, clouds, and lightning. Although Mimbres ceramics were probably used in households in some way, most examples that have come down to us have been recovered from burials. As grave goods the vessels often seem to have been ritually "killed," either by shattering or, as here, by being pierced with a hole. The act draws a parallel with the human body, which is a vessel for a soul. In death, the vessel is broken and the soul released.

Masks and masking played important roles in some Indian cultures. The Pueblo cultures of the Southwest acknowledge numerous supernatural beings called kachina (from the Hopi *katsina*). Danced by maskers, kachina enter into the community at important times to bring blessings. They may appear, for example, early in the year as auspicious presences so that rain will follow for the new crops. Later, after a successful growing season, they dance at harvest ceremonies. Over two hundred kachina have been identified, each with its own name, mask, character, dance movements, and powers.

Hopi and Zuni Indians make doll-size versions of kachina as educational playthings so that children may learn to identify and understand the numerous spirits (**20.19**). The dolls were believed to contain some of the power of the spirit they represented. The kachina themselves often presented the dolls to the young members of the community during their appearances. The doll illustrated here portrays

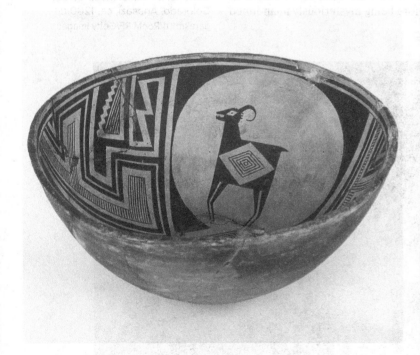

20.18 Bowl with mountain sheep. Mimbres, ca. 1000–1150 C.E. Painted pottery, diameter 10 ½".
Universal Images Group/Getty Images

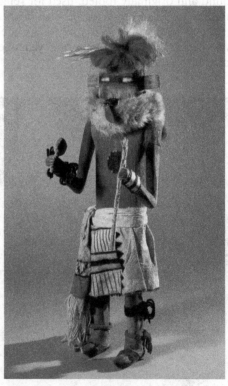

20.19 Kachina doll. Zuni, before 1903. Wood, pigments, hair, fur, hide, cotton, wool, and yucca, height 19".
Brooklyn Museum of Art, New York. Museum Expedition 1903, Museum Collection Fund, 03.325.4653

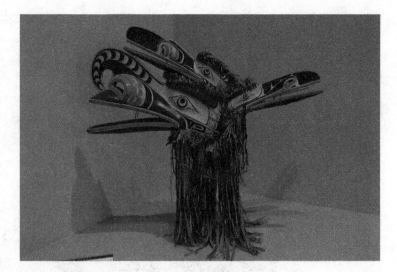

20.20 George Walkus. Four-headed hamat'sa mask. Late 19th century. Wood, paint, cedar bark, and string, height 17".
Album / Alamy Stock Photo

a kachina named Tamtam Kushokta. The spirit wears a white Hopi blanket around its waist and a coyote mask. A spectator who witnessed kachina maskers dancing in 1907 wrote, "In their right hands they carried a tortoise-shell rattle, which they shook with vigor when they danced, and in the left hand, a bundle of prayer sticks, tied up in corn husk, with a kind of handle attached by which it was held."[2] These handheld objects are faithfully represented on the doll.

Masks are also danced by many peoples of the Pacific Northwest, including the Kwakiutl, or Kwakwaka'wakw, who live along the southern coast of British Columbia. The flamboyant Kwakiutl mask illustrated here makes manifest the four mythical Cannibal Birds who live at the north end of the world and eat human flesh (**20.20**). The largest of them is the fearsome Crooked Beak. During the winter, the four monsters ritually invade the human community. They kidnap young men of noble families and turn them into cannibals. This kidnapping and transformation take place within the larger ceremony of potlatch, in which a host generously feeds guests from numerous villages over the course of many days. On the final day, the elders of the gathering ritually cure the young man of his cannibalism. The four Cannibal Bird masks dance as part of this ritual, after which they are banished for another year. Usually the birds are danced individually. This mask is exceptional in making all four of them present at once.

Cannibal Bird masks are carved to this day, both for use and to be sold to collectors. Their tremendous formal variety shows how much room for creativity and individual expression an artist actually has within forms that are too often thought of as unchanging and "traditional."

Whereas some Native American cultures were based on a settled way of life, the Plains culture that formed in the center of North America was nomadic, organized around the herds of buffalo that roamed the Great Plains. Initially Plains people moved on foot with the help of dogs, but by the 18th century the horses introduced by European explorers spread throughout Indian cultures, increasing mobility and becoming an essential part of buffalo hunts.

Buffalo hides provided not only clothing but also shelter in the form of coverings for tents, or tipis (also spelled "tepees"). Hides even provided a surface on which Plains men recorded their exploits as warriors (**20.21**). Drawn by Lakota warriors, the images here record a battle between the Lakota and the Crow, depicted with the vivid recall of participants.

The drawing style is similar to Howling Wolf's, as we saw in his ledger drawings in Chapter 6. It combines observed naturalism with outlines, flat areas of color, and limited exploration of space. This hide would have been worn around the shoulders as a robe. Other garments, such as shirts and leggings, were also painted.

20.21 Unknown (Lakota / Dakota (Sioux) atist, active 1860–1880); Robe; 1860s–1870s; Made in: United States, North AmericaHide and pigment; 96 × 72 in. (243.8 × 182.9 cm)
Thaw Collection, Fenimore Art Museum, Cooperstown, The Saint Louis Art Museum, Funds given by an anonymous donor, the John Allan Love Charitable Foundation, the Gateway Indian Art

RELATED WORKS

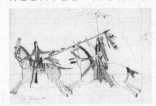

6.4 Howling Wolf, *Ute Indian*

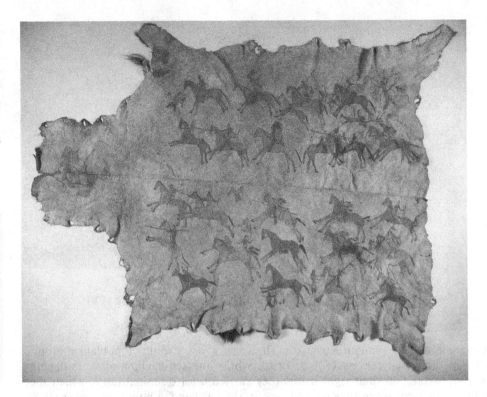

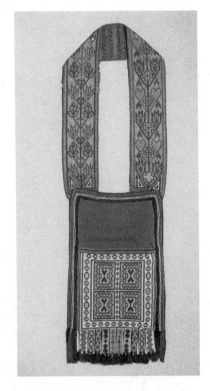

20.22 Ojibwe bandolier bag. 1870. Wool, cotton, and glass, 39 × 11 ¼". Artokoloro Quint Lox Limited/Alamy Stock Photo

Clearly visible are the feathered headdresses that were a distinctive feature of Plains costume. Headdresses were made from the tail feathers of eagles, which were identified with the thunderbird. Some offered protective spiritual power; others were merely finery. Only a proven warrior was permitted to wear one in battle, however.

Into the Modern Era

The arrival of Europeans did not just introduce horses into Native American culture. Other new materials acquired through trade or purchase changed the appearance of indigenous arts. Like the shopkeeper's ledgers Howling Wolf used for his drawings, aniline-dyed wool yarn arrived in the U.S. Southwest with the railroad and came to be incorporated into Navajo weavings such as the diamond-pattern blanket rug we saw in Chapter 4 (see 4.27). Native cultures that used porcupine quills for beadwork on textiles sometimes replaced these with colorful glass beads.

The Ojibwe bandolier bag (**20.22**) shown here uses glass beads to create its floral designs, and its very shape was derived from the ammunition satchels carried by U.S. soldiers. Worn across the body with the bag at the hip, bandolier bags were made of cotton, leather, wool, or even velvet. They were popular in the Eastern Woodlands, and early examples were purely ornamental, lacking any storage capability. This bag is decorated with stylized floral motifs on the strap and geometric patterns on the bag. The beads act like **tesserae** in a mosaic to define the forms and provide the color. They were not applied individually, however, and were instead strung together before being attached to the cloth.

Native American art in the 20th century did not just comprise traditional objects created with available materials. It also included works of painting and sculpture that participated in styles and trends practiced beyond native communities. Like artists around the world, some Native American artists received formal training in art schools, while others were self-taught. Some reflected their Native American heritage in the style of their art or the themes they addressed, but others took a different approach.

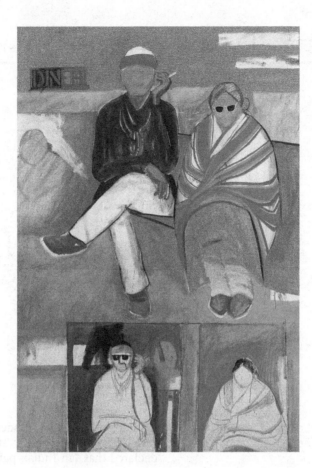

20.23 T. C. Cannon. *Mama and Papa Have the Going Home to Shiprock Blues.* 1966. Oil on canvas, 86 ⅞ × 62".
Image © Estate of Tee Cee Cannon. Reprinted with the permission of the Estate of Tee Cee Cannon, Joyce Cannon Yi, Executo

The artist T. C. Cannon combined aspects of Native American and non-indigenous cultures in paintings such as *Mama and Papa Have the Going Home to Shiprock Blues* (**20.23**). The painting features an elderly couple dressed in traditional Navajo clothes and jewelry. Yet they are not pictured in some nostalgic glimpse of a bygone era. They are instead part of the modern world, sitting on a bus station bench, wearing sunglasses, and smoking a cigarette. The style of the painting is also modern, and the figures and space are abstracted in a manner that was popular in the 1960s. A second pair of portraits of the couple appears below and looks to us like photographs tucked into the frame of a mirror, further abstracting time and space. Cannon's painting honors Native American culture by placing his figures in the here and now.

Notes to the Text

1. Although widely used by archaeologists since the 1930s, the name Anasazi is problematic, for it was originally a Navajo word meaning an ancient foreign or enemy people. Modern Pueblo peoples have objected to having their probable ancestors named in this way, but they have not yet agreed on an alternative from the numerous Pueblo languages now spoken. Some scholars have suggested referring to the culture as Ancestral Pueblo or Ancient Pueblo, but these, too, are problematic, since *pueblo* is a Spanish word and thus also imposes an identity from outside, in this case one framed by the region's conquerors and colonizers. Until a suitable alternative has been agreed on, Anasazi will probably remain the standard term, even if we are uneasy with it.

2. Quoted in Diana Fane, *Objects of Myth and Memory: American Indian Art at the Brooklyn Museum* (Brooklyn, NY: The Museum in association with the University of Washington Press, 1991), p. 107.

3. Quoted in Julie Tachick, "T. C. Cannon: Challenging the Parameters," *Points West* (Summer 2004), p. 23.

T. C. Cannon (1946–1978)

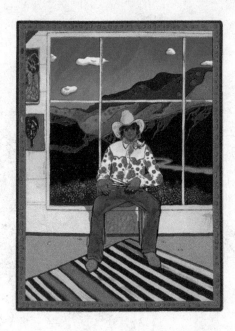

What is Native American art? What does it mean to be a Native American artist today? How did T. C. Cannon find his place in contemporary art?

Staring out from behind sunglasses that obscure our view of his eyes, T. C. Cannon sits in his New Mexico studio. His pose is confident, resting to one side of the chair, legs spread and feet firmly planted. Cigarette butts litter the floor and Cannon holds paintbrushes in his hand. He is an artist and he allows us to interrupt him for just a moment before he gets back to work.

T. C. Cannon was a member of the Caddo and Kiowa peoples, born in Oklahoma. He studied art at the Institute of American Indian Arts in Santa Fe, New Mexico, and at the San Francisco Art Institute. In 1967, Cannon enlisted in the U.S. Army and fought in Vietnam, earning two Bronze Stars for valor. Soon after his return, he exhibited his work at the Smithsonian Institution in a two-person show with his former teacher, the famous Native American artist Fritz Scholder. He was killed in a car accident just six years later.

Although his life was cut short, Cannon produced a substantial body of work that merged his Native American heritage and the trends of contemporary art. He was a member of a group of artists who felt constricted by the style of Native American art that collectors sought in the mid- to late 20th century. He and his peers wanted to pursue different, more modern approaches to art, not to be restricted to a particular style. Cannon is said to have declared that "an Indian painting is any painting that was done by an Indian."[3]

Yet Cannon and his group did not abandon tradition entirely. They became what has been called "bicultural," finding unique ways to freely combine Native culture and the American modernity around them. The painting *Mama and Papa Have the Going Home to Shiprock Blues*, for example, pictures a Navajo couple in a style inspired by the abstraction of European and American modernism.

The self-portrait seen here exhibits the style Cannon adopted near the end of this life. It is generally naturalistic, but the spaces and forms are flattened, textures are ornamental and decorative, and lines quiver ever so slightly. His colors are rich and vibrant and the image conveys a sense of bold confidence. Cannon depicts himself as a modern Native American man, his brown skin and dark hair testifying as much to his native heritage as his clothing and the view of the rugged Southwestern landscape. Yet the paintbrushes in his hand and the works of art tacked to the wall as sources of inspiration identify him as an artist like any other.

T. C. Cannon. *Self-Portrait in the Studio*. 1975. Color woodcut, 25 × 19 ½". Image © Estate of Tee Cee Cannon. Reprinted with the permission of the Estate of Tee Cee Cannon, Joyce Cannon Yi, Executor

Chapter 21

The Modern World: 1800–1945

In this chapter, you will learn to

LO1   identify Neoclassical and Romantic style and subjects,

LO2   describe the movement known as Realism,

LO3   discuss the forms and themes of Impressionism,

LO4   explain Post-Impressionist art,

LO5   classify the art of early avant-garde movements,

LO6   characterize art produced during and after World War I, and

LO7   summarize the key art movements dedicated to building more optimistic societies in the postwar period.

For 19th-century artists and writers, walking through the teeming city streets was the equivalent of today's scrolling through social media—one sensation followed quickly on another, offering fleeting glimpses of thousands of lives. They found it overwhelming—sometimes thrilling, sometimes disturbing—but they recognized it as new and they called it "modern." Modernity in Europe and North America reflected the emergence of a new kind of society in the wake of the French, American, and Industrial Revolutions discussed at the end of Chapter 17. Driven by technological progress and characterized by rapid change, the 19th century gave birth to our industrialized middle-class culture of mass production, mass advertising, and mass consumption, including the mass consumption of leisure activities such as shopping, going to entertainments, and visiting art museums.

Art museums themselves were a development of the 19th century, and they made art available to the public (including artists) in a way we now take for granted. The first national museum was the Louvre in Paris. Opened in 1793 during the fervor of the French Revolution, it placed the art that had been the private property of the kings of France on public view in what used to be the royal residence. Like everything else that used to belong to aristocrats, art was now for everybody, but what kind of art did everybody want? What kind of art was suited to a society dominated no longer by the Church or by the nobility, but by the middle class and its leaders of finance and industry? Debates about art and modernity began during the 19th century and continued into the 20th, resulting in the ever-increasing number of "isms" that appear in art history from this point on: Realism, Impressionism, pointillism, Fauvism, Cubism, Futurism, Surrealism—each one staking out a different viewpoint about what art can be, what subjects it can treat, and how it can look. During this time as well, photography revolutionized the making of images. From the Chauvet cave paintings of 30,000 B.C.E. until the first successful daguerreotype in 1837, images had been made by hand. Suddenly, there was another way, and it posed profound questions about the nature and purpose of art even as it opened up new possibilities.

The changes of modernity occurred everywhere in Europe and in nations affected by European colonialism, but the debates they provoked in the visual arts played out most dramatically in France, especially in Paris, and this brief survey largely focuses there.

Neoclassicism and Romanticism

As we saw in Chapter 17, France's foremost Neoclassical painter, Jacques-Louis David, was an ardent supporter of the Revolution and portrayed several of its heroes (see 17.20). David went on to become the official painter to Napoleon, a position that gave him great influence over the artistic life of France. When Napoleon fell from power in 1815, David went into exile, but Neoclassical style was carried forward into the new century by his students, the foremost of whom was Jean-Auguste-Dominique Ingres.

The flawless finish that Ingres learned from David can be seen in *Jupiter and Thetis* (**21.1**). The subject is drawn from Homer's *Iliad*, the Greek epic of the Trojan War. The nymph Thetis is shown pleading with Jupiter, ruler of the gods, to intervene in the war on behalf of her son, the warrior Achilles. To the left, hidden in the clouds, Jupiter's jealous wife, Juno, spies on the encounter. With its clear contours, clean colors, and precise draftsmanship, the painting clearly shows Ingres's debt to his teacher.

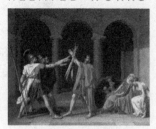
21.1 Jean-Auguste-Dominique Ingres. *Jupiter and Thetis*. 1811. Oil on canvas, 10' 8 ⅝" × 8' 6 ⁵⁄₁₆". Musée Granet, Aix-en-Provence, France. Erich Lessing/Art Resource, NY

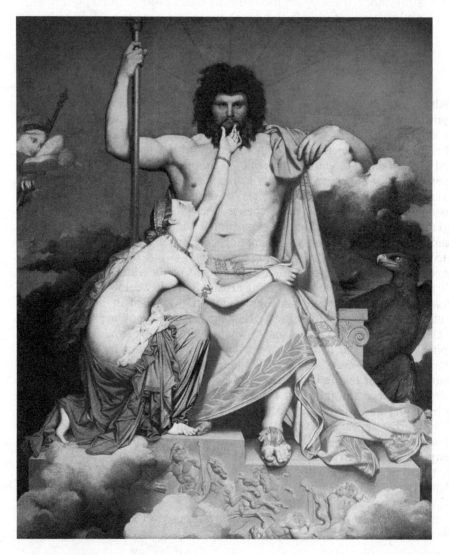

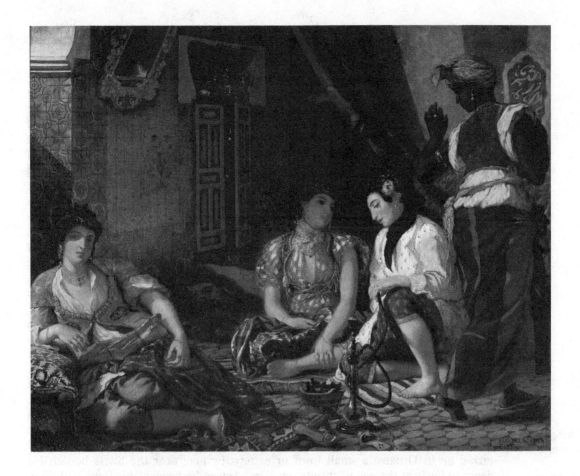

Although today Ingres's portraits and nudes are among his most admired works, Ingres himself staked his reputation on paintings such as *Jupiter and Thetis*. He had inherited the view that great art could be made only from great subject matter, and that the greatest subject matter of all was history—a category that included Classical mythology and biblical scenes. This viewpoint and the highly polished style that went with it became enshrined as academic art, the art that was encouraged by the official art schools and institutions of the 19th century.

The second dominant trend of the time, **Romanticism**, also had its roots in the preceding century. Romanticism was not a style so much as a set of attitudes and characteristic subjects. The 18th century is sometimes known as the Age of Reason, for its leading thinkers placed their faith in rationality, skeptical questioning, and scientific inquiry. Rebelling against those, Romanticism urged the claims of emotion, intuition, individual experience, and, above all, the imagination. Romantic artists gloried in such subjects as mysterious or awe-inspiring landscapes, picturesque ruins, extreme or tumultuous events and the struggle for liberty (see 3.7 and 5.17), and scenes of exotic cultures.

Geographically, the closest "exotic" cultures to Europe were the Islamic lands of North Africa. To European thinking, these were part of "the Orient," a realm imagined as sensuous and seductive, full of barbaric splendor and cruelty. Eugène Delacroix, the leading painter of the Romantic movement in France, spent several months in North Africa in 1832. Fascinated by all he saw, he filled sketchbook after sketchbook with drawings, watercolors, and observations. Later, he drew upon that material to create numerous paintings, including *The Women of Algiers* (**21.2**), which portrays three women and their servant in a harem, the women's apartment of an Islamic palace. Delacroix had apparently been allowed to visit an actual harem, a rare privilege for a man, not to mention a European. Compared with the cool perfection of Ingres's careful drawing and glazed colors, Delacroix's technique is freer and more painterly. Forms are built up with fully loaded brushstrokes, contours are blurred, and colors are broken.

21.2 Eugène Delacroix. *The Women of Algiers*. 1834. Oil on canvas, 5' 10 ⅞" × 7' 6 ⅛". Musée du Louvre, Paris. © RMN-Grand Palais/Art Resource, NY

RELATED WORKS

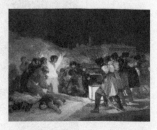

3.7 Delacroix, *Liberty Leading the People*

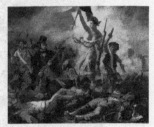

5.17 Goya, *Executions of the Third of May, 1808*

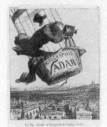

8.14 Daumier,
*Nadar Elevating
Photography to
the Heights of
Art*

Realism

The first art movement to be born in the 19th century was **Realism**, which arose as a reaction against both Neoclassicism and Romanticism. Realist artists sought to depict the everyday and the ordinary rather than the historic, the heroic, or the exotic. Their works unmasked for art viewers the true lives of the middle and lower classes. Taking advantage of lithography's rapid production, Honoré-Victorin Daumier brought the realities of modern life to a broad audience. While many of his images took a humorous approach to modern life (see 8.14), others tackled more serious topics.

Daumier's most poignant image of the difficult lives faced by France's poor is *Rue Transnonain* (**21.3**). The lithograph pictures a family lying dead in their apartment. The father, who died while trying to protect the child who lies beneath him, draws our attention. Daumier made him the focal point within the composition by his central location and the eerie moonlight that falls across his body. His lighting and pose are meant to remind us of paintings of Jesus taken down from the Cross.

Daumier associated the father with Jesus Christ to help us understand the tragic circumstances of his death. A rebellion raged in Paris in April 1834, when the government, led by a new king, imposed strict regulations. As the French military sought to quell the uprising, gunfire rained down on them. The soldiers entered a nearby apartment building and killed the occupants inside, regardless of their guilt or innocence. Parisians were outraged by the indiscriminate killing. Daumier's image of a humble family's innocent suffering was a scathing indictment of the king. Although government censors confiscated the lithographic stone and copies of the print, *Rue Transnonain* embodies Realism's truthfulness and unflinching social consciousness.

Another hero of the Realist cause was the painter Gustave Courbet. He had grown up in Ornans, a small town in eastern France, near the Swiss border. He came to Paris at the age of twenty, and, in a sense, he brought his town with him: The people he knew there, the lives they led, and the landscape of its region were

21.3 Honoré Daumier. *Rue Transnonain*. 1834. Lithograph, 11 ¼ × 17 ⅜".
Courtesy National Gallery of Art, Washington, D.C.

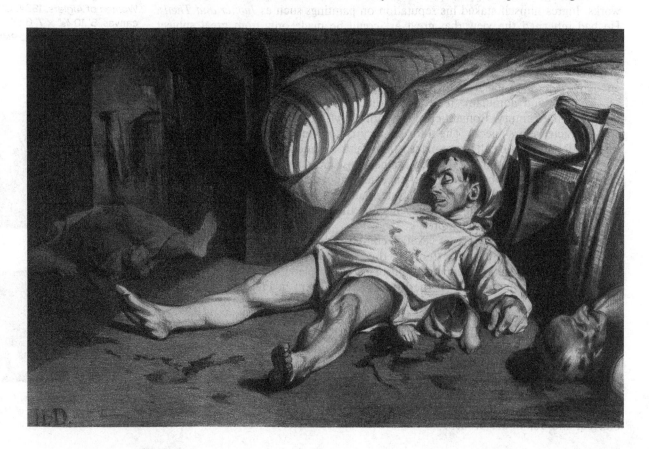

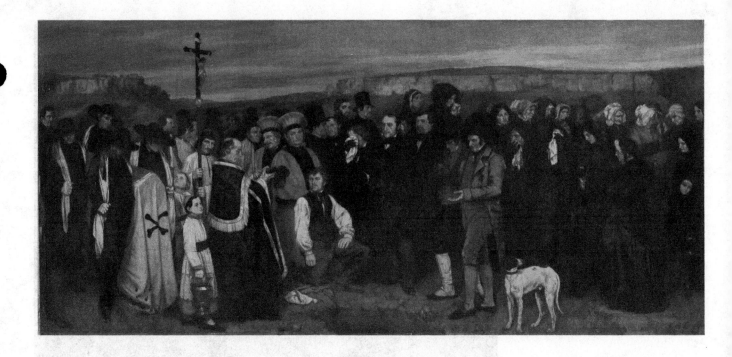

21.4 Gustave Courbet. *A Burial at Ornans*. 1849–50. Oil on canvas, 16' 10 ¾" × 21' 11".
Musée d'Orsay, Paris. Erich Lessing/Art Resource, NY

the subjects of his art. In 1849, after one of his paintings was awarded a gold medal at the Salon—the annual state-sponsored exhibition of new art—Courbet decided it was time for something truly ambitious. He returned to his hometown and worked through the winter on his first monumental painting, *A Burial at Ornans* (**21.4**). The subject is a burial—of whom we do not know. Courbet uses the event as a pretext for a group portrait of Ornans society. A priest, two red-robed beadles (lay officials in the Church), the mayor, a judge, male mourners, and a gravedigger have gathered around the open pit dug to receive the coffin, which is shown arriving at the left. Female mourners cluster to the right. A raised crucifix stands out clearly against the dull sky and distant chalk cliffs. Courbet persuaded the local authorities to pose for his painting: the mayor, judge, beadles, and priest are all portrayed as themselves. The painter's friends and family are present, and most of the other figures have been identified as well.

When the painting was shown at the Salon of 1850, a critic later recalled, it was as though a tornado had blown through the room. Admirers held that Realism had produced its first masterpiece. Detractors thought Courbet had pushed what they called "the cult of the ugly" about as far as it could go. The painting offended them on two counts. The first was its resolute refusal to beautify or sentimentalize the scene. It is a sad image, with drab colors and unidealized figures. The second was its scale: Monumental formats were traditionally reserved for history paintings full of important personages. This painting was full of nobodies, taken seriously as people.

Courbet's "we the people" artistic agenda was linked to radical political ideas. In 1871, his participation in a bloody Paris uprising earned him a prison sentence; two years later, still in trouble, he fled the country for Switzerland, where he died in 1877.

Manet and Impressionism

In 19th-century France, the mark of an artist's success was acceptance at the annual Salon. Artists submitted their work for consideration by an official jury, whose members varied from year to year but tended to be conservative, if not downright stodgy. In 1863, the Salon jury rejected almost three thousand of the submitted works, which caused such an uproar among the spurned artists and their supporters

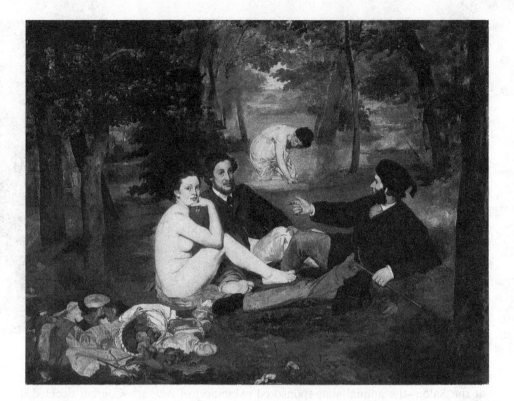

RELATED WORKS

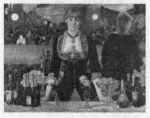

5.13 Manet, *A Bar at the Folies-Bergère*

that a second official exhibition was mounted: the "Salon des Refusés" ("showing of those who had been refused"). Among the works in the "refused" show—and very soon the most notorious among them—was Édouard Manet's painting *Le Déjeuner sur l'herbe* (**21.5**).

Luncheon on the Grass, as it is usually translated, shows a kind of outdoor picnic. Two men, dressed in the fashions of the day, relax and chat in a woodland setting. Their companion is a woman who has, for no apparent reason, taken off all her clothes. In the background another woman, wearing only a filmy garment, bathes in a stream.

Manet seems to have wanted to accomplish two goals with this work. The first was to join Courbet and other artists in painting modern life. But the other was to prove that modern life could produce eternal subjects worthy of the great masters of the museums. His solution was to "update" two famous Renaissance images, Titian's *Fête champêtre* and Raphael's *Judgment of Paris*. The public saw what Manet was doing: the Titian, after all, was in the Louvre Museum close by, and the Raphael was routinely copied by art students. They saw what he was doing, and they didn't like it. Surely Manet was making fun of them. In place of Titian's idealized and dignified nudes, he had painted what seemed to be a common woman of loose morals: Who else would sit there with no clothes on, meeting our gaze so frankly? The men in the painting, too, were completely undistinguished—not noble poets as in Titian, but ordinary students on holiday. One critic lamented that Manet was trying to achieve celebrity the easy way, by shocking his public. Others found the technique inept. Perhaps if Manet would learn something about perspective and drawing, they said, his taste might improve as well.

Manet's painting *is* odd, and art historians still debate just what he meant by it. In modeling his figures, he focused on the highest and lowest values, all but eliminating the middle, transitional tones. As a result, forms such as the nude woman's body appear flattened, as though illuminated by a sudden flash of light. The perspective is off: Contemporary viewers were quite right. The bather is as far away as the rowboat, but if you imagine her standing in it, you realize that she is a giantess. It was evidently more important to Manet to have her form the apex of his triangle of figures than to paint her in natural scale. This, too, flattens the painting, for the bather seems to move forward to join the rest of the figures, compressing the space between foreground and background. The spatial tension plays out in the landscape itself, too. On the left side of the painting, the ground recedes convincingly into the distance, but on the right side there is no recession—just flat, bright green that seems to sit on the surface of the canvas. Nor do we believe for a minute that these people are really sitting outdoors. Clearly, they are posing in a studio. The landscape is painted around them like a stage set or a photographer's backdrop. Finally, the borrowed composition *feels* borrowed, as though it were in quotation marks.

All these qualities—the public scandal, the flatness, the artificiality, the ambiguity, and the self-conscious relation to art history—have made the painting a touchstone of modern art. A painting in the modern era could no longer be a simple, transparent window on the world. It would also be increasingly conscious of itself *as* a painting.

During the years following Manet's sensation in the Salon des Refusés, young French artists increasingly sought alternatives to the Salon. One group in particular looked to Manet as their philosophical leader, although he never consented to exhibit with them. They thought of themselves as Realists, for, like Manet and Courbet, they believed that modern life itself was the most suitable subject for modern art. In 1874, they organized their first exhibition as the Anonymous Society of Artists, Painters, Sculptors, Printmakers, etc. A painting in the exhibition by Claude Monet called *Impression, Sunrise* (**21.6**), however, caught the attention of a critic named Jules-Antoine Castagnary, who used the title to explain what the artists had in common. They were not aiming for perfection, he wrote, but to capture an impression; they did not want to portray a landscape but the sensation of a landscape. All in all, he was quite taken with them: "I swear there's talent here, and a lot of it. These young people have a way of understanding nature that is neither dull nor banal. It's lively, nimble, light, ravishing. . . . It's admittedly sketchy, but how much of it rings true!"[1] He titled his review "The Impressionists." The name stuck in the public imagination, and the artists themselves largely accepted it.

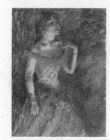

6.9 Degas, *The Singer in Green*

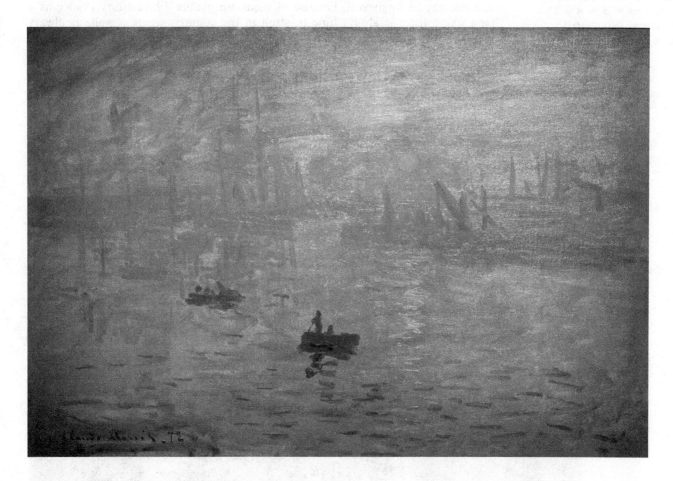

21.6 Claude Monet. *Impression, Sunrise*. 1872. Oil on canvas, 18 ⅞ × 24 ¾".
Musée Marmottan Monet, Paris. Peter Barritt/Alamy Stock Photo

With **Impressionism**, art moved outdoors—not the artificial outdoors of Manet, but the true outdoors. Painting until then had been a studio product, in part because of the cumbersome materials it involved. Thanks to the new availability of portable oil colors in tubes (as they are still manufactured today), many of the Impressionists took their canvases, brushes, and paints outside to be part of the shifting light they wanted to depict. While Monet painted *Impression, Sunrise* from a hotel-room window overlooking the harbor of Le Havre, France, he nevertheless captured the visual experience of a hazy sunrise over a foggy port. Little dabs and flicks of paint indicate the reflections of boats and masts, while small dashes of orange and red capture sunlight on the water's surface. The boats in the harbor and the factories and equipment on the shore are suggested by sketchy brushstrokes that evoke shapes but do not describe surfaces or textures. It is as if we see the entire scene through the rippled surface of the water, and the view will be gone in a moment.

The light in Pierre-Auguste Renoir's enchanting *Le Moulin de la Galette* (**21.7**) is a light we have not seen before in painting, the dappled, shifting light that filters through leaves stirred by a breeze. Traditional chiaroscuro required a steady and even source of light for modeling form. But light in nature wasn't always like that. It moved, it shifted, it danced. Like his friend Monet, Renoir sought to capture such optical sensations through fluid brushwork, a lightened palette, and colored shadows. We see these qualities in the spots of light on the seated man's jacket in the foreground and the patches of yellowy light and bluish shadow on the dance floor. Renoir would later modify his style to embrace more rigorously planned compositions and fully modeled forms, but here he is in his full Impressionist glory, capturing a moment's pleasure with flickering strokes of paint that record sensations of light, color, and movement.

Le Moulin de la Galette was an establishment on the outskirts of Paris where working people gathered on their days off to relax and enjoy themselves. Renoir paints a group of his friends there, dancing and talking, drinking and flirting. The leisure activities of the middle class were a favorite subject of the Impressionists, and we may be forgiven if, because of them, we picture 19th-century France as a land where there is always time to stroll in the country, where a waltz is always playing under the trees.

21.7 Pierre-Auguste Renoir. *Le Moulin de la Galette.* 1876. Oil on canvas, 4' 3 ½" × 5' 9". Musée d'Orsay, Paris. Scala/Art Resource, NY

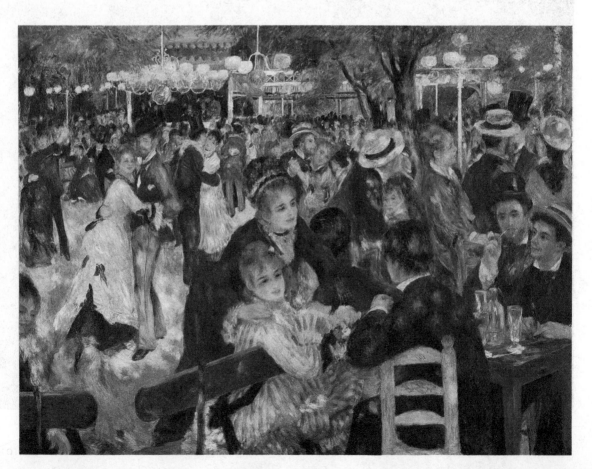

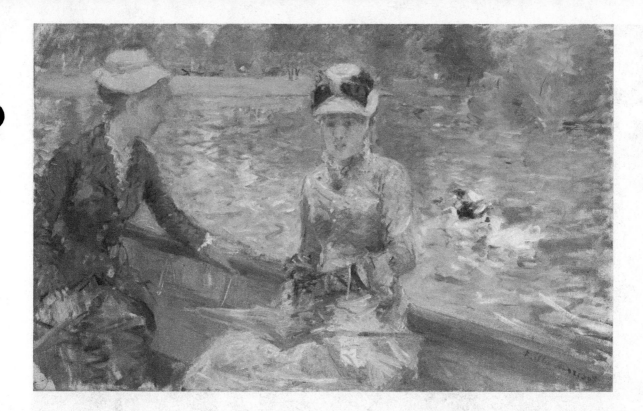

21.8 Berthe Morisot. *Summer's Day*. 1879. Oil on canvas, 18 × 29 ¼".
© National Gallery, London/Art Resource, NY

Another founding member of the Impressionist group was Berthe Morisot. Born into a well-to-do family, Morisot received private art lessons intended to prepare her for life as an accomplished amateur painter, wife to a husband whose career would presumably take precedence. But her great talent and passionate interest took her far beyond anything her parents may originally have had in mind. While still in her early twenties, she took up the new practice of "open air" painting and began exhibiting successfully in the official Salon. In 1874, she contributed nine paintings to the first Impressionist exhibit, and she remained a dedicated member of the group for the rest of her life. *Summer's Day* is a lovely example of her style (**21.8**). Two fashionably dressed young women are having an outing on a lake in a Parisian park. One gazes out at us, a sky-blue parasol folded on her lap. The other turns to look at the ducks swimming alongside. A hired boatman would have been responsible for rowing such fine young ladies, although we don't see him. The palette is light, and the brushwork is varied and free, as though painting were the easiest thing in the world. Looking at the water and the women's dresses, we see the rapid, sketchy brushwork characteristic of Impressionism. These areas seem to disintegrate into blotches of paint when we stand next to Morisot's work, only to be reconstituted as dresses or water when we step back from the painting. As a sympathetic critic of the day wrote, "No one represents Impressionism with a more refined talent or with more authority than Madame Morisot."[2]

Post-Impressionism

The next generation of artists admired many aspects of Impressionism, especially its brightened palette and direct painting technique. But they reacted in various ways to what they perceived as its shortcomings. Their styles are so highly personal that we commonly group them together under the neutral term **Post-Impressionists**, meaning simply the artists who came after Impressionism. They include Georges Seurat, Vincent van Gogh, Paul Gauguin, and Paul Cézanne.

Seurat wanted to place Impressionism's intuitive recording of optical sensations on a more scientific footing. His reading of color theories led him to develop the technique of pointillism, in which discrete dots and dashes of pure, complementary colors were supposed to blend in the viewer's eye (see 4.32). Seurat used

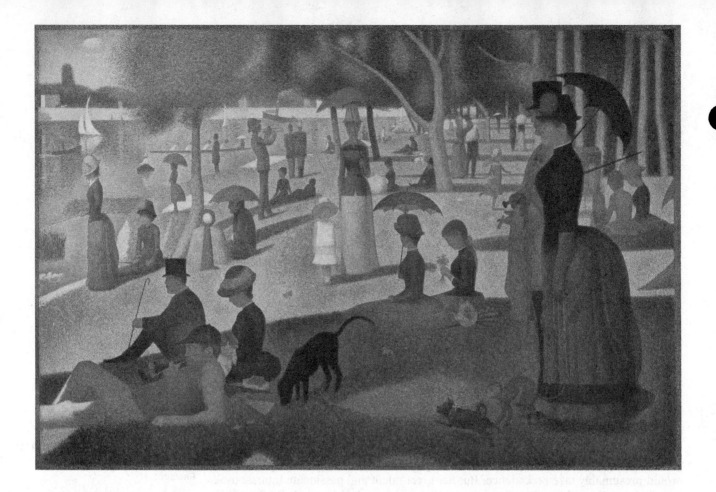

21.9 Georges Seurat. *A Sunday on La Grande Jatte*. 1884. Oil on canvas, 81 ¾ × 121 ¼".
The Art Institute of Chicago/Art Resource, NY

RELATED WORKS

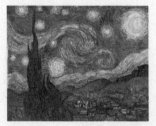

1.10 Van Gogh, *The Starry Night*

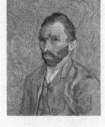

Chapter 1,
Artists
Van Gogh,
Self-Portrait

pointillism to its greatest effect in the monumental painting *A Sunday on La Grande Jatte* (**21.9**). Unlike the rapid and sketchy brushstrokes of Impressionist works, Seurat's tiny, precise spots of color merge to form his objects when seen at a distance. One effect of this technique is to make his paintings appear still. His landscape and figures do not change with the shifting light, but are instead stable and permanent. This stability is echoed in the linear forms throughout the canvas, from the upright posture of each of the figures, to the trees that surround them. Even the rounded shapes of the umbrellas, skirts, and boat sails are geometric and still. Despite picturing leisure time, Seurat's painting has nothing spontaneous or casual about it. We sense that the figures visit this location because it was expected of middle-class Parisians on their days off.

Of all the Post-Impressionists, Seurat was the most faithful to the idea of painting modern life. For other Post-Impressionists, the industrialized modern world was not something that needed to be confronted, but something that needed to be escaped. Vincent van Gogh arrived in Paris from Antwerp in 1886, but he stayed for only two years—just long enough to catch up with the latest developments in art. He settled instead in Arles, a small, rural town in the south of France, where he painted the landscape, people, and things closest to him. The high-key colors, agitated brushwork, and emotional intensity of such works as *The Starry Night* (see 1.10) and *Self-Portrait* (see p. 11) would be enormously influential on the next generation of artists.

Paul Gauguin worked in an Impressionist style early in his career, but he soon became dissatisfied. He felt the need for more substance, more solidity of form than could be found in optical perceptions of light. Beyond that, Gauguin was interested in expressing a spiritual meaning in his art. All these he sought on the sun-drenched islands of the South Pacific, where he journeyed to escape what he called "the disease of civilization." The brilliant high-key colors of his Tahitian paintings reveal his debt to Impressionism. To this lightened palette he added his own innovations: flattened forms and broad color areas, a strong outline, tertiary color harmonies, a taste for the exotic, an aura of mystery, and a quest for the "primitive."

Te Aa No Areois (*The Seed of the Areoi*) (**21.10**) was painted about a year into Gauguin's first long stay in Tahiti, and it shows all these characteristics. Whereas Monet's painting is woven together out of distinct brushstrokes, like a piece of fabric, Gauguin's seems pieced together with flat swatches, like a puzzle or a quilt. We can almost imagine assembling it by cutting the shapes from sheets of colored paper. The red ground is utterly flat. The white motifs on the blue cloth dance free of their ground, as do the yellow palm trees in the background. The effect reminds us of the flatness of the canvas even when other parts of the work are painted using linear and atmospheric perspective to create depth.

In the midst of all this whirling brilliance, a Tahitian woman sits in quiet dignity, holding a sprouting seed in the palm of her hand. Her pose—legs shown in profile, shoulders depicted frontally—is derived from Egyptian art. Gauguin believed that European art had been in thrall for too long to the legacy of Greece and Rome, and he looked to the art of Egypt, Islam, and Asia to renew it. The woman's gesture is mysterious, yet we sense that there is some profound meaning to it, if only we could understand what she is offering us. Although he painted a paradise, Gauguin in fact was bitterly disappointed in Tahiti. He felt that European missionaries and colonists had already ruined it. In the end, he painted what he dreamed of finding, because what he found was that there was no escape.

In contrast to Gauguin's search for what he considered "exotic" subjects, Paul Cézanne found everything he needed within walking distance of his home in the south of France. He admired the Impressionists' practice of working directly from nature, and he approved of their bright palette and their individual strokes of color. He was dissatisfied, though, with their casual compositions and their emphasis on what is transitory, such as the dappled sunlight on Renoir's spinning dancers. He felt that what had made painting great in the past was structure and order. Could the brushstrokes that the Impressionists used to register optical sensations be used to build something more solid and durable? Could an artist paint directly from nature and find in it the order and clarity of Classical art? These were the goals that Cézanne set for himself.

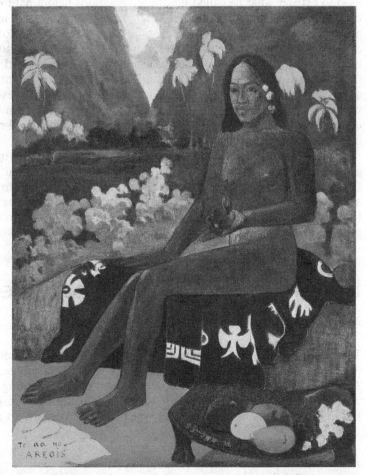

21.10 Paul Gauguin. *Te Aa No Areois* (*The Seed of the Areoi*). 1892. Oil on burlap, 36 ¼ × 28 ⅜". The Museum of Modern Art, New York. The William S. Paley Collection. SPC14.1990. Digital image © The Museum of Modern Art/Licensed by SCALA/Art Resource, NY

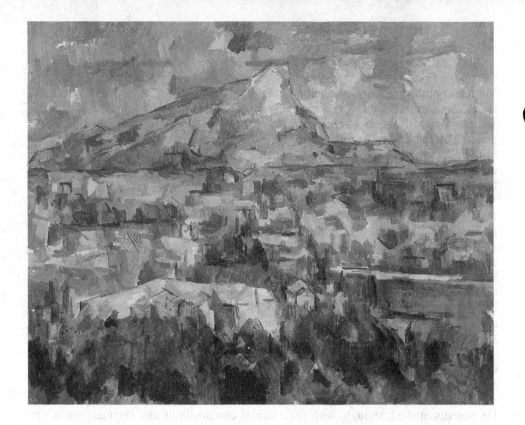

21.11 Paul Cézanne. *Mont Sainte-Victoire*. 1902–04. Oil on canvas, 27 ½ × 35 ¼".
The Philadelphia Museum of Art/The George W. Elkins Collection, 1936/Art Resource, NY

A favorite subject of Cézanne's last years was Mont Sainte-Victoire, a mountain near his home (**21.11**). Altogether he made seventy-five painted or drawn versions of the scene. The broad outlines of the composition are simple and noble: a rectangular band of landscape surmounted by the irregular pyramid of the mountain. This underlying geometry emerges clearly from hundreds of small, vivid patches of color. Each patch is composed of the terse, precise, parallel strokes that Cézanne used to register what he called his "little sensations before nature"—the impressions that colors shimmering in the hot southern sun made on his eyes. Near the foreground, the red tile roofs of farmhouses are like ready-made color patches. The roof of the isolated house near the center reproduces exactly the silhouette of the mountain. To the left, the upward diagonal of the ocher area around the group of three farmhouses is exactly parallel to the upward slope of the mountain. These echoes are a key to Cézanne's way of thinking: Major structural lines are echoed everywhere. The line of the horizon, for example, is broken into segments, none of them quite horizontal. Segments of almost-horizontal lines appear throughout the painting, even in the sky, which is also painted in patches of color.

With paintings such as *Mont Sainte-Victoire*, Cézanne's treatment of nature grew increasingly abstract. Repetitions and echoes of key contour lines help to unify the composition, but they have also begun to take on their own independent logic apart from the subject. Similarly, the terse strokes and color patches help to unify the painting's surface, but they tend to fracture the image into facets. The next generation of painters would study these devices and build on them.

Bridging the Atlantic: The Americas in the 19th Century

Thanks to links created during the colonial past, Europe remained an artistic touchstone during the 19th century in the western hemisphere. North and South American artists often went to Europe for part of their training, not only to study with European teachers, but also to see the collections of the great museums. In Europe, they could absorb more easily the history of Western art at first hand. There was no American substitute, for example, for wandering through the ruins of ancient Rome or visiting a Gothic cathedral. Some artists remained in Europe and spent their careers there. Similarly, some European artists emigrated to the United States or the newly independent nations of Latin America, where opportunity sometimes seemed greater. Neoclassicism, Romanticism, Realism, and Impressionism were broad trends in the Americas as they were in Europe, though without the intense battles they provoked in Paris.

Romanticism was a many-sided movement, and in the Americas it expressed itself most clearly through an attitude toward landscape, an almost mystical reverence for the natural beauty of the unspoiled land itself. The broad vista and threatening storm of Thomas Cole's *The Oxbow* (see 3.23) display one aspect of American Romanticism. Cole contrasts the sunlit cultivated fields that have benefited from human intervention with the wild and untamed lands still under darkened clouds. While picturing the awesome power of nature, Cole's painting also represents the virtue of American ingenuity as the nation marched west and turned wilderness into productive lands. In the 19th-century American context, this meant displacing the continent's native inhabitants in the name of progress and prosperity. Just before Cole made his painting, the U.S. government passed the Indian Removal Act, which permitted the forcible removal of Native Americans from their lands. Cole's painting has been interpreted to suggest that only with these "savages" removed from the wilderness will the skies clear for westward expansion.

While Cole's version of Romanticism celebrates the vast potential of the North American landscape, José María Velasco links the beauty of Mexico to the native peoples who occupied it. His *Valley of Mexico from the Santa Isabel Mountain Range* (**21.12**) offers a sweeping panorama of the site where the Aztec capital of Tenochtitlán stood before it fell to Spain in the 16th century. The effects of colonization remain visible, with the church dedicated to the miraculous image of the Virgin of Guadalupe barely visible in the center of the painting. Yet this shrine also celebrated Mexico's native population, since the painting of the Virgin Mary appeared to a local indigenous man. Other evidence of the past in Velasco's painting includes the volcanoes in the background, which were still known by their Aztec names. The woman and children walking in the foreground wear clothes that identify them as indigenous. They offer a charming picture of family life as they gather firewood accompanied by frolicking dogs. Velasco's image celebrates the beauty of

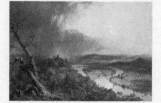

3.23 Cole, *The Oxbow*

21.12 José María Velasco. *The Valley of Mexico from the Santa Isabel Mountain Range.* 1875. Oil on canvas, 54 ⅛ × 89". Museo Nacional de Arte de Mexico. The Artchives/Alamy Stock Photo

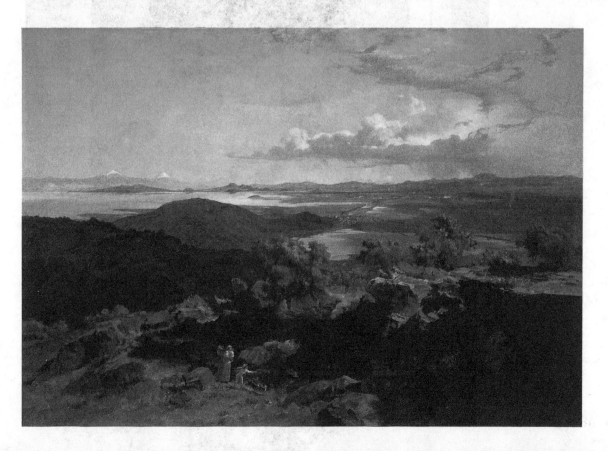

Mexico and its Aztec heritage. Yet, this romantic vision of Central Mexican indigenous peoples should not be taken at face value, just as Cole's picture *The Oxbow* hid political realities. The legacy of colonialism meant that the living heirs of the Aztecs suffered persistent discrimination and hardship.

The movement known as Realism also found its way to the Americas. Artists in the United States began exploring **genre** themes in the 1830s, picturing scenes of everyday American life. These representations of the lives of the lower and middle classes promoted American values and taught moral lessons about the virtues of hard work, independence, and democracy. Richard Woodville's *War News from Mexico* (**21.13**) offers a fictitious scene of Americans gathered to hear the latest news in the U.S. war with Mexico, which was fought from 1846 to 1848. They stand on the porch of a hotel that also serves as the town post office. One man reads the newspaper that has just arrived in the mail, while others listen. The painting promotes civic engagement but also pictures race relations in 19th-century America. The African-American man and child in the painting are not included among the group concerned with the war's progress. Off to the side, they represent the era's political debates over the expansion of slavery into new American territories.

Like Gustave Courbet, Woodville based his scene on observation. Each texture is carefully described, from the weathered paint and wood of the hotel to the crisp folds of the newspaper. The painting is filled with realistically portrayed figures of different ages and stations in life. The setting is humble and familiar. Woodville's Realism convinces us that the scene is true to real life, which helped persuade its viewers to its moralizing lessons.

21.13 Richard Woodville. *War News from Mexico*. 1848. Oil on canvas, 27 × 25".
Granger Historical Picture Archive/ Alamy Stock Photo

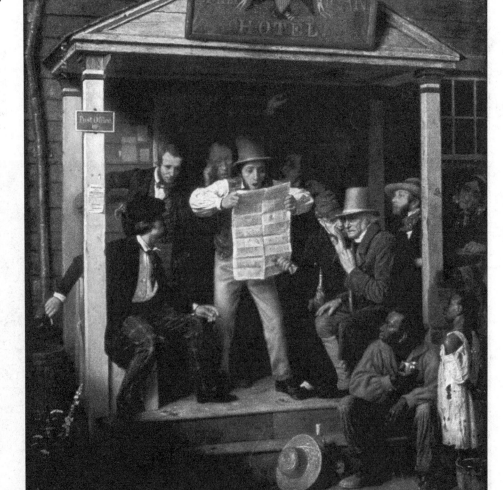

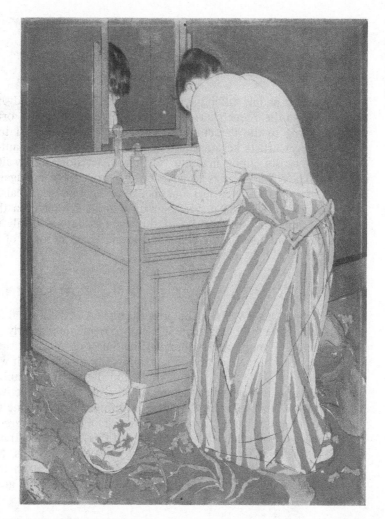

Realism found its finest U.S. practitioner in Thomas Eakins, whose *Biglin Brothers Racing* is illustrated in Chapter 4 (see 4.7). Eakins had studied in Paris and toured the museums of Europe, but he returned to Philadelphia to paint American lives. He had a distinguished career as a teacher. Among his students was Henry Ossawa Tanner, whose *Banjo Lesson* is illustrated in Chapter 5 (see 5.15). One of the first important African-American artists, Tanner moved in 1891 to Paris, where he turned increasingly to religious subjects and exhibited regularly in the Salon.

Another American artist who traveled to Paris and remained there was Mary Cassatt. Whereas her artistic training in America had been conservative and academic, her natural inclination drew her toward scenes from daily life, especially intimate domestic scenes of mothers and children—a world that men rarely depicted in art. Edgar Degas was impressed by the paintings Cassatt exhibited at the Salon during the 1870s, and he invited her to show with the Impressionists instead. "Finally I could work with absolute independence without concern for the eventual opinion of a jury," Cassatt later wrote. "I admired Manet, Courbet, and Degas. I detested conventional art. I began to live."[3]

Cassatt's *Woman Bathing* (**21.14**) is an intimate glimpse of private life. A woman stands with her back to us. Her face is hidden from our view and even her reflection in the mirror is obscured. Instead we see only the sink, pitcher, and carpet as we sneak a glimpse of this private moment. Cassatt's Realism lies in its honest depiction of this humble daily ritual. The bold, simplified forms and the broad areas of aquatint color reflect the influence of Japanese prints, which had been the subject of a major exhibition in Paris just a year prior. Many of these imported woodblock prints pictured beautiful women at their toilet, a theme Cassatt took up in this Realist print.

RELATED WORKS

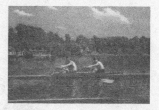

4.7 Eakins, *The Biglin Brothers Racing*

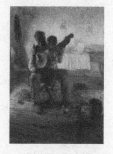

5.15 Tanner, *The Banjo Lesson*

Into the 20th Century:
The Avant-Garde

When you hear people talking about the newest, latest, most advanced art, you may hear them use the French term *avant-garde*. Avant-garde was originally a military term, referring to the detachment of soldiers that went first into battle. By the 1880s, younger artists began to refer to themselves as the avant-garde. They were the boldest artists, going first into uncharted territory and waiting for others to catch up. Their "battle" was to advance the progress of art against the resistance of conservative forces. Newness and change became artistic ideals. Each generation, even each group, believed it was their duty to go further than the one before. As the 20th century began, the idea of the avant-garde was firmly in place, and two of art's basic building blocks, color and form, were the focus of great innovation.

Freeing Color: Fauvism and Expressionism

Although it no longer wielded the power it once did, the annual Salon of Paris was still a conservative force in artistic life, and movements regularly arose against it. In 1903, a group of young artists founded the Salon d'Automne, the "autumn salon," as a progressive alternative. From the exhibits they organized, it was clear who their heroes were. In 1904, the artists of the Salon d'Automne organized a large exhibition of Cézanne, and in 1906, they mounted a major retrospective of Gauguin. But the most notorious exhibit of the Salon d'Automne was the one they organized for themselves in 1905. It was then that a critic dubbed them *fauves*, "wild beasts."

The artist who emerged as the leader of this "wild" new trend in painting was Henri Matisse. Not long after his art first alarmed the critics, Matisse completed *The Joy of Life* (**21.15**), a major work that he exhibited when the Fauves showed again in 1906. Pink sky, yellow earth, orange foliage, blue and green tree trunks—in

21.15 Henri Matisse. *The Joy of Life*. 1905–06. Oil on canvas, 5' 8 ½" × 7' 9 ¾".
The Barnes Foundation, Philadelphia, Pennsylvania/Bridgeman Images © 2019 Succession H. Matisse/Artists Rights Society (ARS), New York

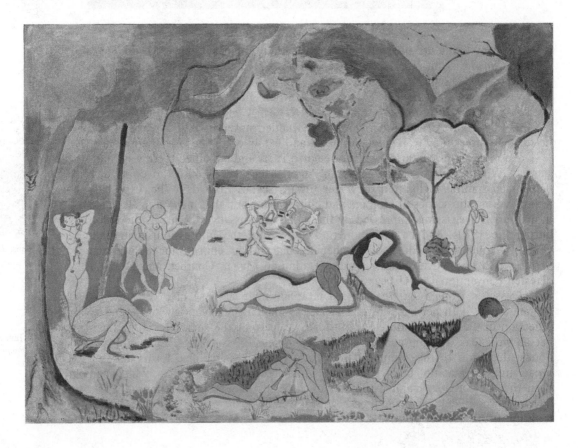

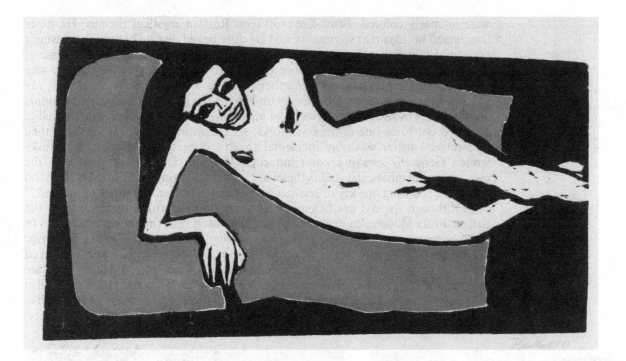

21.16 Erich Heckel. *Fränzi Reclining*. 1910. Woodcut, 8 15/16 × 16 ½".

Digital image © The Museum of Modern Art, New York/Licensed by SCALA/Art Resource, NY/© 2019 Artists Rights Society (ARS), New York/VG Bild-Kunst, Germany

the Fauvist vision, color was freed from its supporting role in describing objects to become a fully independent expressive element. With its broad areas of pure color floating free, *The Joy of Life* radiates a sense of harmony and well-being. Gauguin had painted Tahiti as a paradise. For Matisse, color itself became a paradise, a place to be.

Fauvism did not last long. By 1908, its painters had begun to go their separate ways. Yet, although brief, Fauvism was crucial for the development of modern art. Never again would artists feel they must confine themselves to replicating the "real" colors of the natural world.

Fauvism was part of a larger trend in Europe called expressionism, which arose as artists came to believe that the fundamental purpose of art was to express their intense feelings toward the world. **Expressionism**, broadly speaking, describes any style where the artist's subjective feelings take precedence over objective observation. Spelled with a capital E, it refers especially to an art movement that developed in Germany in the early 20th century, where the expressive ideal had its greatest influence. Like the Fauves, Expressionist artists looked to Gauguin and Van Gogh as their predecessors. They admired as well the stark works of the Norwegian artist Edvard Munch, who was then living in Berlin (see 4.36).

One important Expressionist group was Die Brücke (The Bridge), founded in Dresden in 1905, the same year as the Fauve exhibition in Paris. The bridge the artists had in mind was one they would build through their art to a better, more enlightened future. One of the founders was Erich Heckel, whose *Fränzi Reclining* we see here (**21.16**). The intense, arbitrary colors show Expressionism's link with Fauvism, and the wavering contours suggest the influence of Munch. The colored woodcut depicts a typical reclining nude like Titian's *Venus of Urbino* (see 16.13), but there is something upsetting about it. The drawing style is harsh and angular. The space is tilted and the figure is distorted. Unlike Titian's inviting, mature woman, Heckel's model is disturbingly young. Her masklike face displays no emotion as she lies displayed for our gaze. Like that of other Expressionists, Heckel's handling of form and subject is evocative and creates feelings of melancholy and angst.

Another Expressionist group was Der Blaue Reiter (The Blue Rider), organized in 1911 by the Russian painter Vasili Kandinsky. Kandinsky had been teaching law in Moscow when an exhibition of Impressionist paintings so moved him that he abandoned his career and moved to Germany to study art. His early paintings

RELATED WORKS

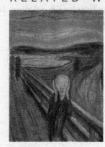

4.36 Munch, *The Scream*

were intensely colored, Fauve-like works on Russian mystical themes. He never abandoned his idea that spirituality and art were linked, but he became increasingly convinced that art's spiritual and communicative power lay in its own language of line, form, and color, and he was one of the first painters to take the decisive step of eliminating representation altogether, in such works as *Black Lines No. 189* (**21.17**). In his own telling, Kandinsky discovered the power of nonrepresentational art when he was struck by the beauty of a painting he didn't recognize in his studio. It turned out to be one of his own works, set the wrong way up. He realized then that subject matter was only incidental to art's impact. About color, Kandinsky wrote, "Generally speaking, color influences the soul. Color is the keyboard, the eyes are the hammers, the soul is the piano with many strings. The artist is the hand that plays, touching one key or another purposively, to cause vibrations in the soul."[4]

Although she did not belong to either group of German Expressionists, the painter Paula Modersohn-Becker has been associated with the movement thanks to her subjective use of color and form. Her *Kneeling Mother with a Child at her Breast* (**21.18**) portrays woman in her aspect of life-giver and nurturer. The woman's naked body is naturally proportioned, yet its color does not respond to nature. The face is instead a gray mask likely inspired by African or Oceanic art. Her body is also a mixture of pinks and grays that appear unnatural compared to the child's lifelike fleshiness. While the bodies are modeled and foreshortened as if having real, three-

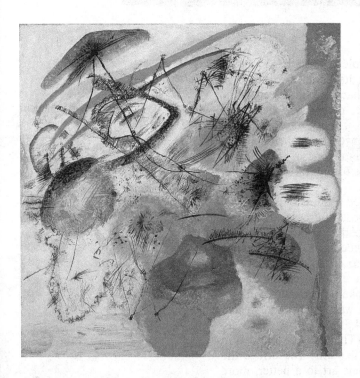

21.17 Vasili Kandinsky. *Black Lines No. 189*. 1913. Oil on canvas, 4' 3" × 4' 3 ⅝".

The Solomon R. Guggenheim Foundation/Art Resource, NY. Solomon R. Guggenheim Founding Collection, by gift. Photo David Heald. © Solomon R. Guggenheim Foundation, New York. © 2019 Artists Rights Society (ARS), New York

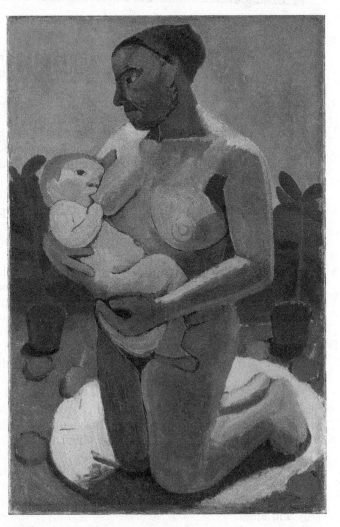

21.18 Paula Modersohn-Becker. *Kneeling Mother with a Child at her Breast*. 1907. Oil on canvas, 44 ½ × 29 ⅛".

bpk Bildagentur/Nationalgalerie, Staatliche Museen, Berlin/Photo: Jörg P. Anders/Art Resource, NY

dimensional volume, they occupy a flattened and unreal space. The effect of the painting is to make us see the child as real and alive but the mother as a kind of monument sculpted to support the child she holds.

Shattering Form: Cubism

While artists associated with Europe's many expressionist tendencies were exploring the possibilities of color, two artists in Paris were reducing the role of color to a minimum to concentrate on the problem of representing form in space. One of them was a young Spanish painter, Pablo Picasso. In 1907, at age twenty-six, Picasso had already painted what is widely regarded as a pivotal work in the development of 20th-century art, *Les Demoiselles d'Avignon* (**21.19**).

Les Demoiselles d'Avignon was not Picasso's title, but was given to the painting years later by a friend of his. It translates as "the young women of Avignon" and refers to the prostitutes of Avignon Street, a notorious district of Barcelona, Picasso's hometown. In early sketches for the painting, Picasso included a sailor entering at left to purchase a prostitute's services, but as the composition evolved, the sailor was eliminated. Instead, the prostitutes display themselves to us.

Picasso has chopped the figures up into planes—flat, angular segments that still hint at three-dimensionality but have no conventional modeling. Figure and ground lose their importance as separate entities; the "background"—that is, whatever is not the five figures—is treated in much the same way as the women's bodies. As a result, the entire picture appears flattened; we have no sense of looking "through" the painting into a world beyond, as with Delacroix or even Manet.

To many people who see *Les Demoiselles* for the first time, the faces cause discomfort. The three at left seem like reasonable enough, if abstract, depictions of

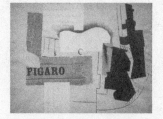

2.13 Picasso, *Bottle of Vieux Marc, Glass, Guitar and Newspaper*

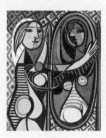

5.31 Picasso, *Girl Before a Mirror*

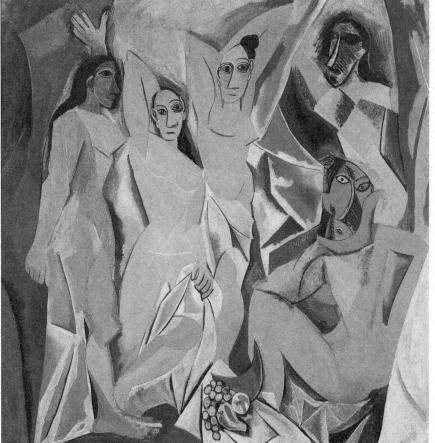

21.19 Pablo Picasso. *Les Demoiselles d'Avignon*. 1907. Oil on canvas, 8' × 7' 8".
The Museum of Modern Art, New York. Acquired through the Lillie P. Bliss Bequest. Digital image © The Museum of Modern Art/Licensed by SCALA/Art Resource, NY. © 2019 Estate of Pablo Picasso/Artists Rights Society (ARS), New York

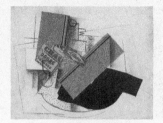
faces, except that the figure at far left, whose face is in profile, has an eye staring straight ahead, much as in an Egyptian painting. But the two faces at right are clearly masks—images borrowed from "primitive" art—and they create a disturbing effect when set atop the nude bodies of European females.

In *Les Demoiselles* Picasso was experimenting with several ideas that he would explore in his art for years to come. First, there is the inclusion of nontraditional elements. Picasso had recently seen sculptures from ancient Iberia (Spain before the Roman Empire), as well as art from Africa. In breaking with Western art conventions that reached back to ancient Greece and Rome, he looked for inspiration from other, equally ancient, traditions. Second, there is the merging of figure and ground, reflecting the assumption that all portions of the work participate in its expression. And third, there is the fragmenting of the figures and other elements into flat planes, especially evident in the breasts of the figure at upper right and the mask just below. This last factor proved especially significant for an artistic journey on which Picasso was soon to embark—the movement known as **Cubism**.

Picasso's partner in this venture was the artist Georges Braque. Braque was older than Picasso in years but younger as an artist. Picasso, after all, had been an artist since his early teens. He was one of the most naturally gifted artists in history, and his hand could produce any kind of style he asked it to. Braque was less precocious, but because of that, more disciplined and determined. He developed an intense personal identification with Cézanne, who also progressed from awkward beginnings to mastery. Picasso grew to share this interest, and for a time he renounced his natural gifts to pursue together with Braque this new line of investigation. Both artists emerged stronger for it.

Picasso and Braque began working together in 1909, and by 1910 their experiments were so closely intertwined that their styles became virtually identical. For a time, they even ceased signing their works. "We were prepared to efface our personalities in order to find originality," Braque later recalled.[5]

21.20 Georges Braque Man with a Guitar.
The Artchives/Alamy Stock Photo

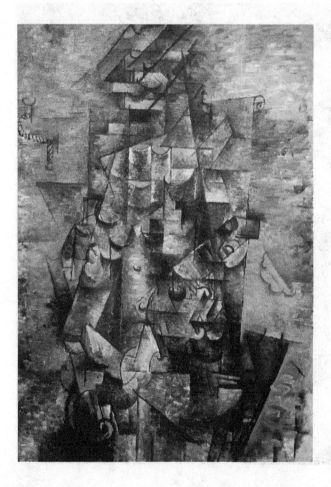

Braque's *Le Portugais* (*The Emigrant*) (**21.20**) demonstrates how Cézanne's methods led to something new. The figure of a seated man playing his guitar is broken into facets based on simple geometric shapes: triangle, circle, line. Because the forms are so basic, they easily echo throughout, unifying the composition. Color is reduced to gray warmed with ocher, allowing the shards of the foreground and background to interpenetrate at will. The principal lines of the composition suggest a classic Renaissance pyramid such as Leonardo used for *Mona Lisa* (see 2.1). Visual cues help viewers to orient themselves: the open hole and strings of the guitar, the player's mustache, the rope to the right that sets the scene on a dock. The addition of stenciled letters, an intrusion from the "real world," was Braque's innovation.

As Cubism progressed, the two artists experimented with incorporating other elements, such as newspaper, wallpaper, and fabric. The psychological tension of merging the "real" with the "not real" (the illusory world of paint on canvas) would have important applications for later 20th-century art. Picasso and Braque also realized that the geometric rhythms of an object could be assembled from multiple views. For example, if you look at a pitcher from the front, the side, the top, the bottom, you will see a number of versions, but your true understanding of a pitcher is the sum of all these. With Cubism, this sum of viewpoints could be painted. Cubism thus followed up on another discovery implicit in much of Cézanne's work: The eye is always moving, and motion is how we assimilate the world.

The great beauty of Cubism was that it offered the most original and powerful system for rethinking the representation of form and space since the Renaissance. Over the ensuing decade and more, many young artists in Europe passed through a Cubist phase to break free of the past.

Futurism

Cubism poured all of its energy into formal concerns. The subjects that Braque and Picasso treated while working out their discoveries were so traditional as to be neutral—a still life on a tabletop, a seated figure with a musical instrument, a landscape with some houses. Any of those subjects could have been painted in the 17th century. Other innovators, however, believed that art would move forward only through exploring new subjects.

A group of Italian artists calling themselves the **Futurists** decided that motion was the glory of the new 20th century, especially the motion of marvelous new machines. The view from an airplane, the feeling of racing through the countryside in an automobile—how could these new sensations not be reflected in art? Here, we see a work by the movement's foremost sculptor, Umberto Boccioni (**21.21**). *Unique Forms of Continuity in Space* represents a striding human figure as the Futurist imagined it to be in the light of contemporary science: a field of energy interacting with everything around it. "Sculpture," wrote Boccioni, "must give life to objects by making their extension in space palpable, systematic, and plastic, since no one can any longer believe that an object ends where another begins and that our body is surrounded by anything . . . that does not cut through it and section it in an arabesque of directional curves."[6]

Boccioni creates the illusion of the figure's interaction with its surroundings by distorting the body, much as our view of a car or train is distorted as it speeds by. Wind seems to pull at the figure. Light seems to reflect off it. Energy seems to emerge from it. We have no trouble imagining this body to be a machine in motion, struggling to move through space. For Boccioni and the Futurists, this machine was more beautiful than any work from the history of art.

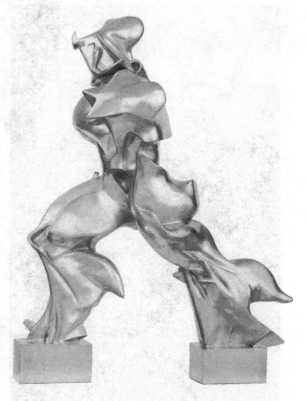

21.21 Umberto Boccioni. *Unique Forms of Continuity in Space.* 1913. Bronze, height 3' 7 ⅞".
The Museum of Modern Art, New York. Acquired through the Lillie P. Bliss Bequest, 231.1948. Digital image © The Museum of Modern Art/Licensed by SCALA/Art Resource, NY

World War I and After: Dada and Surrealism

In 1914, conflict broke out in the Balkan Peninsula. Soon, as the result of treaties and alliances, every major power in Europe was drawn into war. Soldiers with their heads full of gallant ideas about battle rushed headlong into the most horrible deaths imaginable. Trench warfare, poison gas, bombardment by air, machine guns, tanks, submarines—science and technology, in which the 19th century had put its faith, revealed their dark side. The ideal of progress was shown to be utterly hollow, and ten million people lost their lives in one of the bloodiest wars in history.

In 1916, a group of artists waiting out the war in Zurich, in neutral Switzerland, banded together as a protest art movement called Dada. What did Dada protest? Everything. Dada was anti. Anti art, anti middle-class society, anti politicians, anti good manners, anti business-as-usual, anti all that had brought about the war. In that sense, Dada was a big *no*. But Dada was also a big *yes*. Yes to creativity, to life, to silliness, to spontaneity. Dada was provocative and absurd. Above all, it refused to make sense or to be pinned down.

More an attitude than a coherent movement, Dada embraced as many kinds of art as there were artists. In Germany, Dada developed a biting political edge in the work of Hannah Höch and others (see 9.10). In France, its absurd and

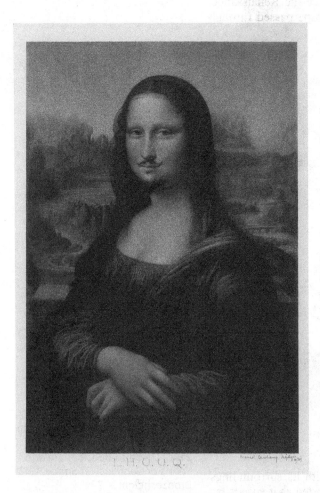

21.22 Marcel Duchamp, *L.H.O.O.Q.* 1919. Mixed media, 10 ¼ × 7".

Heritage Image Partnership Ltd/Alamy Stock Photo. © Association Marcel Duchamp/ADAGP, Paris/Artists Rights Society (ARS), New York 2019

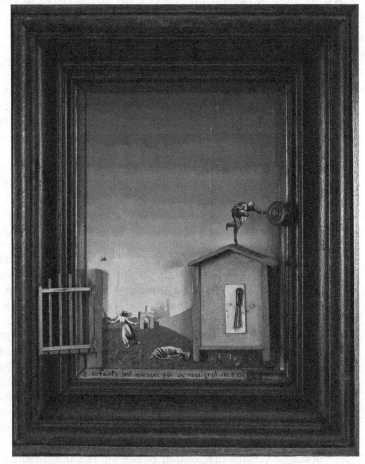

21.23 Max Ernst. *Two Children Are Threatened by a Nightingale.* 1924. Oil on wood and assemblage, 27 ½ × 22 ½".

Digital image © The Museum of Modern Art, New York/Licensed by SCALA/ Art Resource, NY © 2019 Artists Rights Society (ARS), New York/ADAGP, Paris

philosophical aspects came to the fore, especially in the work of Marcel Duchamp, whose "ready-mades" such as *Fountain* (see 2.2) probed the border between art and life in a way that later generations have returned to again and again.

Duchamp's *L.H.O.O.Q.* (**21.22**) also uses a found object as ready-made. In this case, it is an ordinary postcard of Leonardo da Vinci's *Mona Lisa* (see 2.1). As anyone who has bought a postcard or poster of a favorite work of art knows, even a cheap reproduction merits special treatment. We send them to loved ones, put them in albums, or tack them to the wall. Yet Duchamp did not treat the reproduction of Leonardo's venerable image as a treasured keepsake, let alone a priceless work of art. He drew on it instead, adding a mustache and goatee, much as street vandals do to bus-stop or subway advertisements. He also added letters that, when read in French, make a derogatory statement about Mona Lisa's anatomy. Like *Fountain*, these seemingly juvenile alterations called into question the nature of art (is this art?) and of artists (who is the maker?). It also comments on gender identity and our obsession with the great works from the history of art. By challenging beliefs, the work became an instant icon of the Dada movement.

A movement that grew out of Dada was **Surrealism**, which was formulated in Paris in the 1920s. Like Dada, Surrealism was not a style but a way of life. Fascinated by the theories of the psychoanalyst Sigmund Freud, who was then setting out his revolutionary ideas in Vienna, the Surrealists appreciated the power of dreams, the mystery of the unconscious, and the lure of the bizarre, the irrational, the incongruous, and the marvelous.

The Surrealist painter Max Ernst claimed to have been inspired by a dream when he made *Two Children Are Threatened by a Nightingale* (**21.23**). The work is an assemblage of printed images, paint, and wooden elements the artist constructed. A gate, house, and door knob project from the picture plane, pushing the image into our space. The work depicts a woman running with a knife, another woman lying on the ground, and a man on a rooftop carrying off a child. A tiny bird in the distance hardly seems to pose a threat to the figures at all, as the title suggests. Of course, searching for logic in Surrealist art is as difficult as searching for logic in a dream. Ernst stated that this scene played out in his sleep while he was suffering from a fever as a child. Like other Surrealists, he believed that dreams allow us to get beyond our rational minds and access a superior reality through our unconscious.

A distinctive contribution of Surrealism to art was the poetic object—not a sculpture as it had traditionally been understood, but a *thing*. Surrealist objects often juxtapose incongruous elements to provoke a shiver of strangeness or disorientation. One of the most famous and unsettling Surrealist objects is Meret Oppenheim's *Object (Luncheon in Fur)* (**21.24**). Perhaps Oppenheim witnessed two ladies taking tea together in their best fur coats, and melted them into a dreamlike object? Perhaps we really are supposed to imagine bringing the furry cup to our lips for lunch. Freud's theories famously claimed a large role for unconscious sexual desire, and Surrealist works often have erotic overtones.

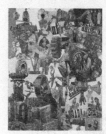
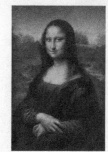
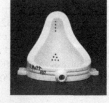
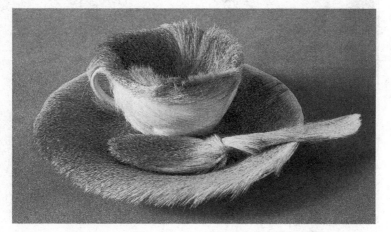

21.24 Meret Oppenheim. *Object (Luncheon in Fur)*. 1936. Fur-covered cup, saucer, and spoon, overall height 2 ⅞". The Museum of Modern Art, New York. Purchase, 130.1946.a-c. Digital image © The Museum of Modern Art/Licensed by SCALA/Art Resource, NY © 2019 Artists Rights Society (ARS), New York/ ProLitteris, Zürich

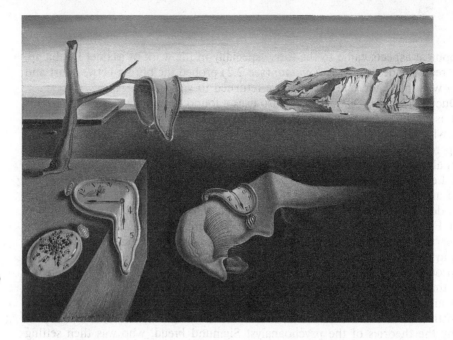

Possibly the most famous of all Surrealist works is Salvador Dalí's *The Persistence of Memory* (**21.25**), a small painting that many people call simply "the melted watches." Dalí's art, especially here, offers a fascinating paradox: His rendering of forms is precise and meticulous—we might say *super*-realistic—yet the forms could not possibly be real. *The Persistence of Memory* shows a bleak, arid, decayed landscape populated by an odd, fetal-type creature (some think representative of the artist) and several limp watches—time not only stopped but also melting away. Perhaps in this work Dalí's fantasy, his dream, is to triumph once and for all over time.

Joan Miró's *Carnival of the Harlequin* (**21.26**) offers a Surrealist view of one of the most famous of all Spanish paintings, *Las Meninas* by Velázquez (see 2.3). Miró's fantasy world is aswarm with odd little creatures—animals and fish and insects and perhaps a snake or two—as well as nameless abstract forms that participate in the artist's madcap party. Much of Miró's imagery suggests a cheerful sexuality, as though the whole space of the universe were occupied with lighthearted

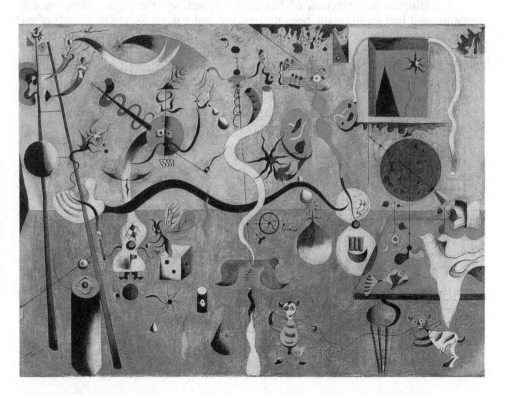

erotic play and reproduction. In contrast to the utter stillness of Dalí's *Persistence of Memory*, Miró's *Carnival* is all movement. There are even a few musical notes at the top to accompany the dance. As interpreted by Miró, Surrealism's dreams are lively ones.

Between the Wars: Building New Societies

Surrealism offered a personal solution to life during the years following the trauma of World War I. But in the view of many artists, society, and possibly even human nature itself, had to be transformed so that such a horror would not happen again. That art could play a central role in bringing about a better society was a 19th-century idea, yet it found renewed application after World War I in a collective approach. It was not through the personal insights of individual artists that the world would change, but through the cooperative endeavors of artists, designers, and architects. Together, they could create a new environment for living, one that was completely modern, purged of associations with the past, and comfortable with the new spirit of the machine age.

An even more radical opportunity presented itself in Mexico, where a successful revolution had toppled the old regime. The new government embraced lofty ideals of social and economic reform and a concern for ordinary workers, including native peoples who continued to suffer discrimination. In Chapter 7, we looked at a fresco commissioned from Diego Rivera by the revolutionary Mexican government (see 7.4). Before the Mexican Revolution, Rivera had been living in Paris and painting in an advanced Cubist style. On his return to Mexico, he developed a more accessible style for his murals, and he stayed with it for the rest of his career. His great desire was to communicate with everyone, to leave no one out.

The Mexican muralist José Clemente Orozco adopted a more expressive style, characterized by elongated and angular figures, dark colors, and high-keyed emotion. Orozco brought this style to the hallowed halls of Dartmouth College in New Hampshire, one of the oldest higher-education institutions in the United States. Over the course of two years, he painted a twenty-four-panel narrative titled *The Epic of American Civilization* (**21.27**) on the walls of the library. The mural cycle

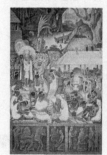

7.4 Rivera, *Mixtec Culture*

21.27 José Clemente Orozco. *The Epic of American Civilization*. 1932–34. Mural painting (detail). MacDuff Everton/Getty Images

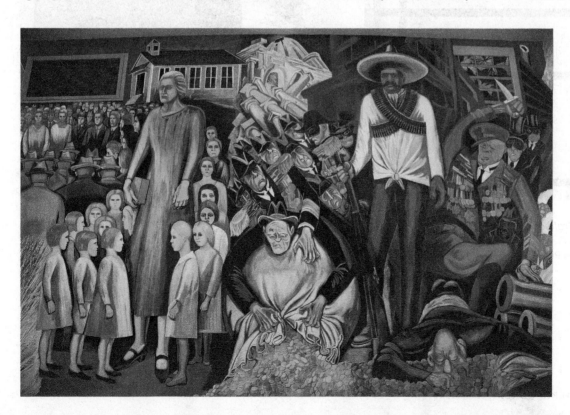

begins with the foundation of Aztec civilization and ends with the 1930s. While Rivera painted Mexico's native populations as peaceful and prosperous societies, Orozco's Aztecs are stern and fearsome, occasionally brutal and superstitious. The Spaniards who conquered them fare no better, and Orozco depicts Hernán Cortés destroying everything around him. Modern American society in the murals is filled with teachers brainwashing children, back-stabbing generals, dead war heroes, and skeletal academics witnessing the birth of another of their kind. Only the modern laborer escapes Orozco's criticism. Pictured reading during a break from building, the worker represents the socialist ideal that early 20th-century revolutionaries promoted.

Idealism also touched Europe, but the solution to the world's woes offered by De Stijl in the Netherlands differed radically from the Mexican muralists' public art. The artists of De Stijl reduced art to essential geometric shapes and primary colors, believing that these were a universally understood visual language. This pared-down art would promote harmony and order across national and ethnic boundaries. De Stijl broadcast its ideals in a magazine of the same name.

The most famous artist associated with De Stijl was Piet Mondrian. Beginning as a painter of flowers and landscapes, Mondrian distilled his art to what he considered to be the most universal signs of human order: vertical and horizontal lines, and the primary colors red, yellow, and blue (**21.28**). To him, these formal elements radiated a kind of intellectual beauty that was humanity's greatest

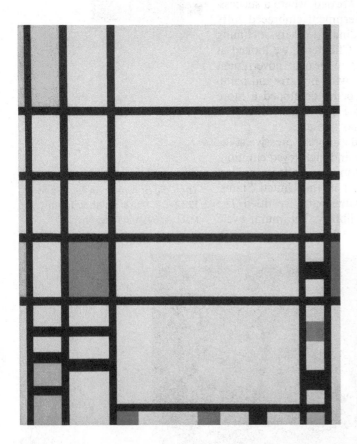

21.28 Piet Mondrian. *Trafalgar Square*. 1939–43. Oil on canvas, 4' 9 ¼" × 3' 11 ¼".
Asar Studios / Alamy Stock Photo

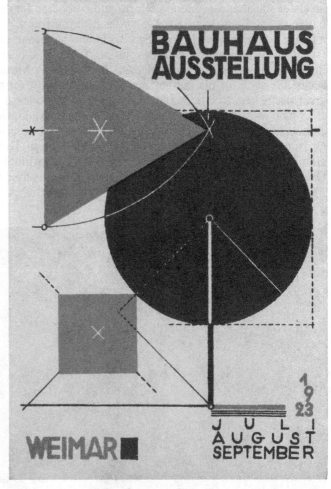

21.29 Herbert Bayer. *Bauhaus Ausstellung*. 1923. Lithograph, 5 ⅞ × 3 ¹⁵⁄₁₆".

achievement. Nature, with its irrationality and irregularity, encouraged humankind's primitive, animal instincts, resulting in such disasters as war. In Mondrian's vision of the world, people would be surrounded by rational beauty and thus become balanced themselves.

Mondrian thought of his canvases as places where we could turn to stabilize ourselves and restore our calm. He also believed that they would not be necessary—no art would be necessary—in a future in which people lived in houses that were also designed according to De Stijl principles. Central to these beliefs was that form should follow function without the need for decoration or ornamentation.

Functionalism was also a core principle of the German **Bauhaus**, a school of design founded in Germany in 1919 by the architect Walter Gropius. The Bauhaus was yet another incarnation of the ideal of collective artistic endeavor in the years following World War I. Students studied a variety of disciplines, and their education was designed to eliminate traditional divisions between painters, sculptors, architects, craft artists, graphic designers, and industrial designers. A poster for an exhibition of Bauhaus art and design by Herbert Bayer (**21.29**) shows the school's modern, rational aesthetic. Three geometric forms in primary colors rest on the picture plane. Arcing, dashed, and solid lines reveal the mathematics that underlie their shapes and positioning on the paper. The typography naming the exhibition and its dates and location lacks serifs and is as pared-down as the geometric shapes. The poster is easy to read and understand, with a modern, mass-produced appearance that seems to visualize the school's motto, "Art into Industry."

The word *Bauhaus* translates roughly as "building house," and its leaders sought to "build" new guiding principles of design compatible with 20th-century technology. Structures, rooms, furniture, and everyday household objects were stripped of superficial embellishment and pared down to clean lines. These principles are embodied in Marcel Breuer's armchair, designed in 1928 (**21.30**). Breuer, a teacher and former student at the Bauhaus, made his chair of canvas panels and steel tubing. These materials were not previously used in furniture, but Breuer chose them so that his chair would be economical to manufacture. Like other Bauhaus artists, he sought to create useful items that were nevertheless beautiful, making good design available to everyone. The armchair creates harmony between the individual life of its owner and 20th-century industry and technology. After the Nazis closed the Bauhaus in 1933, several of its most important members, including Breuer and Bayer, emigrated to the United States, and the school's influence continued to be felt in all design disciplines for decades.

The period following World War I also brought the flowering of art dedicated to building a better society in the United States. One of the most vibrant movements of the time arose in the New York neighborhood called Harlem. Harlem is the northeast section of Manhattan Island. It was and is home to many black Americans, of all economic classes. During the 1920s, Harlem served as a magnet for some of the greatest talents of that generation: artists, musicians, composers, actors, writers, poets, scientists, and educators. Louis Armstrong came to Harlem, and so did Duke Ellington. The writer Langston Hughes and the poet Countee Cullen were in residence. Creative energy was in the air, and for a time it seemed as though almost every Harlemite was doing something wonderful—a book, a play, a Broadway show, a sculpture series, a jazz opera, a public mural. This phenomenon came to be called the Harlem Renaissance.

Much of the spirit embodied in the Harlem Renaissance had to do with merging three experiences: the rich heritage of Africa, the ugly legacy of slavery in America (ended barely more than fifty years earlier), and the reality of modern urban life. There is no single style associated with artists of the Harlem Renaissance, but the work of the painter and illustrator Aaron Douglas is representative of the spirit and aspirations of the group. Douglas, who was born in Kansas, moved to Harlem in 1924. During the years of the Harlem Renaissance, he gradually developed a style that he called "geometric symbolism." This approach combines the flattened spaces of contemporary modern art with the narrative clarity of the Mexican muralists. Douglas worked prolifically throughout the 1920s, but is perhaps most noted for a series of murals he did a few years later, for the 135th Street

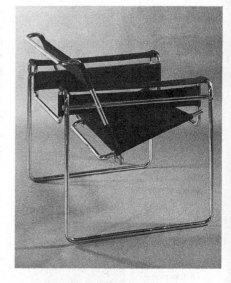

21.30 Marcel Breuer. Armchair. ca. 1928. Chrome-plated tubular steel with canvas slings.
The Museum of Modern Art, New York. Digital image © The Museum of Modern Art/Licensed by SCALA/Art Resource, NY

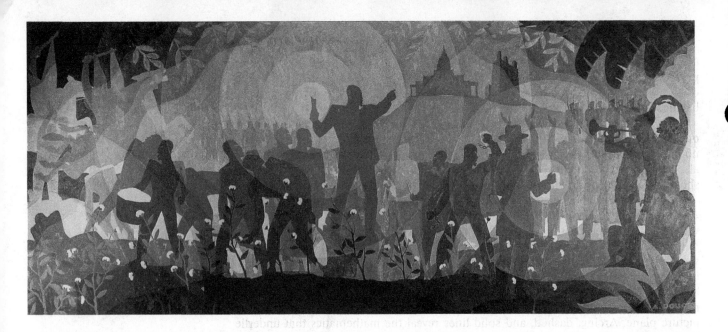

21.31 Aaron Douglas. *From Slavery Through Reconstruction*, from *Aspects of Negro Life*. 1934. Oil on canvas, 5' × 11' 7".

Schomburg Center for Research in Black Culture, The New York Public Library. © Art Resource, NY. Art © Heirs of Aaron Douglas/Licensed by VAGA, New York, NY

branch of the New York Public Library. The series is called *Aspects of Negro Life*. Our illustration shows the segment that Douglas called *From Slavery Through Reconstruction* (**21.31**).

To the right, figures rejoice at the reading of the Emancipation Proclamation, the 1863 executive order that freed slaves in rebelling states. Light radiates from the document in concentric circles. At the left, men pick cotton in the fields as members of the Ku Klux Klan loom menacingly in the background. Founded in the South at the end of the Civil War in 1865, the Klan terrorized newly free African Americans in an attempt to restore white supremacy. At the center, a man points toward the Capitol building, depicted high on a hill in the distance. In his left hand he holds another light-radiating document. It is a voting ballot. Voting rights had been granted to African Americans by constitutional amendment in 1870. However, they still were not secure when Douglas painted his mural, and they would not be for over thirty more years.

The Harlem Renaissance, as a movement, lasted only a decade: Its momentum was stopped by the stock market crash of 1929 and the ensuing Great Depression of the 1930s. Douglas's vision of a better society was actually painted during the early years of the Depression, as the dream of the Harlem Renaissance faded. It is nevertheless a vision of hope. Other artists continued to believe that art had a social mission during those difficult times. Dorothea Lange documented the dignity of ordinary people faced with extraordinary adversity in photographs such as *Migrant Mother* (see 9.6). The Depression was, in fact, worldwide. In Europe, severe hardship fueled nationalist resentment against the unjust settlement of World War I. Anger swept the fascist regimes of Hitler and Mussolini into power in Germany and Italy. In 1939, the world was plunged again into war.

RELATED WORKS

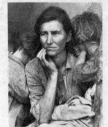

9.6 Lange, *Migrant Mother*

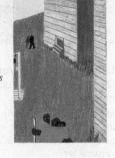

7.6 Lawrence, from *The Migration Series*

Notes to the Text

1. Jules-Antoine Castagnary, "Exposition du boulevard des Capucines: Les Impressionnistes," *Le Siècle*, April 29, 1874.
2. Gustave Geffroy, "L'Exposition des artistes indépendants," *La Justice*, April 19, 1881.
3. Quoted in Ian Dunlop, *Degas* (New York: Galley Press, 1979), p. 168.
4. Quoted in Hershel B. Chipp, *Theories of Modern Art: A Source Book by Artists and Critics* (Berkeley: University of California Press, 1968), pp. 154–55.
5. Quoted in William Rubin, *Picasso and Braque: Pioneering Cubism* (New York: Museum of Modern Art, 1989), p. 19.
6. From Hershel B. Chipp, *Theories of Modern Art: A Source Book by Artists and Critics* (Berkeley: University of California Press, 1968), p. 300.

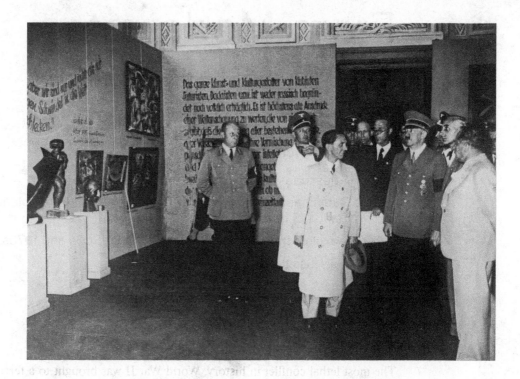

Why did Adolf Hitler object to modern art? What was the effect of Nazi condemnation of the art of the early 20th century?

Modern art flourished in Germany after World War I, and German museums and art collectors eagerly purchased works by Vincent van Gogh, Henri Matisse, Pablo Picasso, and the German Expressionists. All of this changed in 1933, when Adolf Hitler became Germany's chancellor. He immediately set about removing over 15,000 examples of avant-garde art from state-run museums. Art that had not been approved by the National Socialist Party could no longer be made or exhibited. The Bauhaus was immediately shuttered. In 1937, Hitler organized an exhibition of this art, which he called "degenerate." The photograph seen here shows Hitler touring the exhibition.

What did the Nazis find objectionable in modern art? Hitler claimed that abstraction was a sign of the artists' mental illness, immorality, and genetic inferiority. The artists and those who supported them were corrupt and sought to undermine German values. Hitler and the Nazis saw their work as part of an insidious plot against Germany, perpetrated by Jews.

The exhibition was organized to convince visitors of the danger of the art and its artists. Works were crowded onto the walls, and some were hung at odd angles. Text painted on the walls explained the danger and misguided nature of the works. The objects were organized into rooms dedicated to art by the insane, art by Jewish artists, objects that insulted religion, and works by Communists. When the exhibition was over, some of the art was sold at auction to fill Nazi coffers, while other works were burned.

At the same time, Hitler staged an exhibition that he called *Great German Art*. The works in this show depicted genre scenes of German life filled with idealized men and women, matching the Nazi propaganda promoting family, home, and Church. The objects selected for the exhibition displayed a naturalistic style based on Classical principles. This was the style of painting Hitler had practiced as a young man, when he had failed to be admitted to art school; his campaign against avant-garde art was at least in part his own revenge for that rejection.

Hitler Touring the Exhibition of Degenerate Art. 1937. Chronicle/Alamy Stock Photo

Chapter 22

From Modern to Postmodern

In this chapter, you will learn to

LO1   describe the art of the New York School,

LO2   summarize the goals and characteristics of assemblage
       and happenings,

LO3   explain the development of art in the 1960s and 1970s, and

LO4   discuss the art of the 1980s and 1990s.

The most lethal conflict in history, World War II was brought to a terrifying end on August 9, 1945, when the United States dropped an atomic bomb on the Japanese city of Nagasaki. Tens of millions of people had lost their lives over the course of the six-year conflict, most of them civilians. Many European cities lay in ruins.

In the aftermath of the war, the horrors of the Nazi death camps were brought to light. The United Nations was founded to promote peace. Yet already the United States and the Soviet Union, which had emerged from the war as the two dominant "superpowers," were entering into the prolonged, nuclear-armed standoff known as the Cold War.

As artistic life resumed in this new international climate, it gradually became clear to many observers that the most interesting new art was no longer originating in Paris. Rather, it was found in New York. The center of energy had shifted. Several developments had paved the way for this flowering of advanced art in America. One was the founding of the Museum of Modern Art in New York City in 1929. The first Western museum dedicated exclusively to modern art, the Museum of Modern Art began to assemble an important collection, and it mounted exhibitions of Cubism, nonrepresentational art, Dada, and Surrealism—all the important avant-garde trends. A number of progressive European artists spent the war years in exile in New York, including key members of the Surrealist movement. With them, there arrived an adventurous American collector and gallery owner named Peggy Guggenheim, who had been living in Paris and London. In New York, Guggenheim opened a gallery called Art of This Century, where she showed not only avant-garde European artists but also promising young Americans she discovered.

In short, New York now had many of the features of earlier European art capitals: direct contact with the latest directions in art, keen and engaged critics, forums for viewing and discussing new work, collectors ready to purchase, a national press prepared to trumpet artistic achievement, a confidence born of economic and political strength, and, most of all, the ability to attract talented and ambitious young artists.

Within a few decades, New York would become merely one important art center among many. But for a time, the story of Western art can be continued by looking at what happened there.

The New York School

Painters associated with the first major postwar art movement are commonly referred to as the New York School. Not a school in the sense of an institution or of instruction, the New York School was a convenient label under which to lump together a group of painters also known as the **Abstract Expressionists**. Primary among them were Jackson Pollock and Willem de Kooning. Abstract Expressionism had many sources, but the most direct influence was Surrealism, with its emphasis on the creative powers of the unconscious and its technique of automatism as a way to tap into them. The painters of the New York School developed highly individual and recognizable styles, but one element their paintings had in common was scale: Abstract Expressionist paintings are generally quite large, and this is important to their effect. Viewers are meant to be engulfed, to be swept into the world of the painting the way we may be swept into a film by sitting so close that the screen fills our entire field of vision.

The quintessential Abstract Expressionist was Jackson Pollock, who by the late 1940s had perfected his "drip technique." To create such works as *Number 1, 1949* (**22.1**), Pollock placed the unstretched canvas on the floor and painted on it indirectly, from above, by casting paint from a brush in controlled gestures or by dripping paint from a stir-stick. Layer after layer, color after color, the painting grew into an allover tangle of graceful arcs, dribbled lines, spatters, and pools of color. There is no focal point, no "composition." Instead, the paint rests on the surface of the canvas and we find ourselves in front of a field of energy like the spray of a crashing wave. A critic of the time coined the term **action painting** to describe the work of Pollock and others, for their paintings are not images in the traditional sense but traces of an act, the painter's dance of creation. Pollock said his method of working allowed him to be "in" the painting, to forget himself in the act of painting, and that is also the best way to look at his works, to lose ourselves in them.

Strictly speaking, Pollock's painting is not abstract but nonrepresentational. As always, the terminology of art evolved haphazardly and inconsistently as people

22.1 Jackson Pollock. *Number 1, 1949.* 1949. Enamel and metallic paint on canvas, 5' 3" × 8' 6".
The Museum of Contemporary Art, Los Angeles. The Rita and Taft Schreiber Collection. Given in loving memory of her husband, Taft Schreiber, by Rita Schreiber, 89.23. B Christopher/Alamy Stock Photo

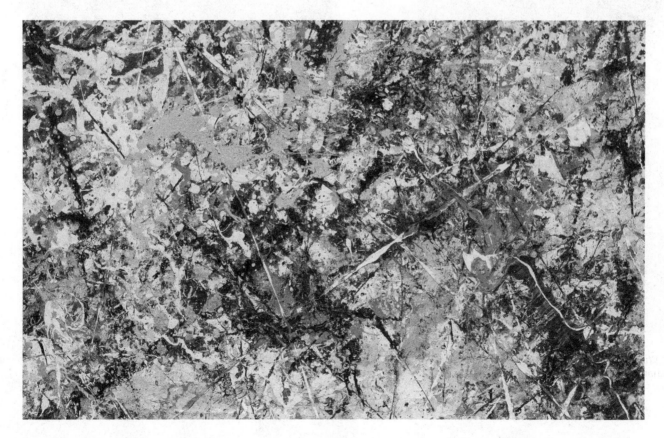

grasped for terms to speak about what was new. Critics and artists of the day used *abstract* and *nonrepresentational* interchangeably, and in casual speech and writing *abstract* is still the more common term. De Kooning's *Woman IV* is abstract in our strict sense (**22.2**). Like Pollock, de Kooning had developed a nonrepresentational, gestural style during the 1940s. During the next decade, however, he returned to the human figure, most notoriously in the *Women* series.

Even today the *Women* paintings retain their power to disturb. They are not beautiful, but grotesque. It is easy to understand why the acquisitions committee at the Museum of Modern Art called de Kooning's *Women* both vital and frightening when it considered purchasing one in the 1950s. We can see the paintings as reflecting de Kooning's conscious and unconscious feelings toward women. Yet they also record a struggle between two ways of thinking about art. Forceful gestures keep trying to establish a painting about the act of painting. Notice the slashing strokes of paint that remind us of the movement of the painter's hand. At the same time, the image keeps reasserting itself, demanding to be recognized with identifiable eyes here, arms and breasts there. The viewer is caught between seeing this as merely paint on canvas and reading that paint as a woman.

Whereas Pollock and de Kooning developed styles that exploit the visual impact of gestures—lively, often forceful movements of brush, hand, and arm—other Abstract Expressionists downplayed the drama of the gesture in favor of broad areas, or "fields," of color. This variety of Abstract Expressionism is sometimes known as **color field painting**. Few traces remain of the gestures that Mark Rothko used to apply paint to canvas in *Orange and Yellow* (**22.3**). Instead, we see two soft-edged, horizontal fields of color floating on the larger color rectangle of the canvas. Almost

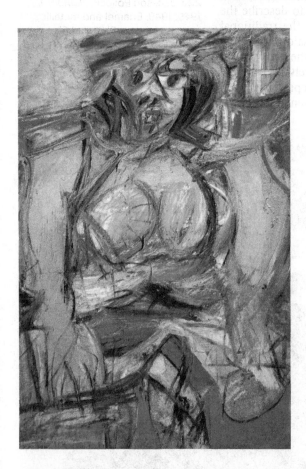

22.2 Willem de Kooning. *Woman IV*. 1952–53. Oil, enamel, and charcoal on canvas, 4' 10 ½" × 3' 9 ⅞".
Album / Prisma/Newscom

22.3 Mark Rothko. *Orange and Yellow*. 1956. Oil on canvas, 7' 7" × 5' 11".
Albright-Knox Art Gallery, Buffalo, New York, Gift of Seymour H. Knox Jr., 1956/Art Resource, NY © 1998 Kate Rothko Prizel & Christopher Rothko/Artists Rights Society (ARS), New York

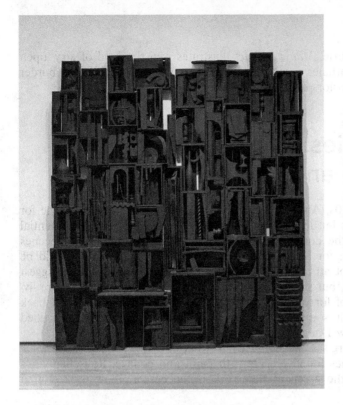

22.4 Louise Nevelson. *Sky Cathedral*. 1958. Painted wood, 11' 3 ½" × 10' ¼" × 18'.

The Museum of Modern Art, New York. Gift of Mr. and Mrs. Ben Mildwoff, 136.1958.1-57. Digital image, The Museum of Modern Art, New York/Scala, Florence. © 2019 Estate of Louise Nevelson/ Artists Rights Society (ARS), New York

22.5 Helen Frankenthaler. *Mauve District*. 1966. Polymer on unprimed canvas, 8' 7" × 7' 11".

The Museum of Modern Art, New York. Mrs. Donald B. Straus Fund, 2668.1967. Digital image © The Museum of Modern Art/Licensed by SCALA/Art Resource, NY. Artwork © 2019 Helen Frankenthaler Foundation, Inc./Artists Rights Society (ARS), New York

all Rothko's mature paintings consist of variations on this simple but fertile compositional idea: soft-edged horizontal fields of color on a vertical color ground; the rectangle of the canvas and its echoes. Where de Kooning emphasized the physicality of paint, Rothko did the opposite, thinning his colors so much that the pigment powder barely holds to the canvas.

Rothko's paintings have a luminous, meditative quality. A similarly contemplative mood infuses Louise Nevelson's wood assemblage *Sky Cathedral* (**22.4**). Nevelson was one of several New York-based sculptors whose work was associated with Abstract Expressionism. She began working with wood during World War II, at a time when colleagues such as David Smith were using iron and steel (see 11.11), but she later said that welding metal had reminded her too much of the war. Her son was in the war; everyone's son was in the war. She turned instead to cast-off bits of wood—odd scraps of lumber, fragments of furniture, broken pieces of architectural details. It was with these materials that she found her voice as an artist and created her most characteristic works, the monumental, monochromatic assemblages often referred to as "wall sculptures." *Sky Cathedral* is made of shallow wooden boxes filled with bits of scavenged wood, the whole painted black. At more than 11 feet in height, it shares the Abstract Expressionists' sense of scale. The monochrome paint unifies the diverse elements, emphasizing their formal qualities over their "previous lives," now muted.

The next generation of painters did not find much room to breathe in the heroic gestural style of action painting. Its famous practitioners were perhaps a little too famous to follow. The energy of color field painting, in contrast, was carried forward by a new generation of artists, who explored and extended its possibilities. First and foremost among these was Helen Frankenthaler, who pioneered a staining technique. To create such nonrepresentational paintings as *Mauve District*, Frankenthaler poured thinned paint onto unprimed canvas spread on the floor, and manipulated its flow in various ways (**22.5**). The colors soaked into the canvas like

RELATED WORKS

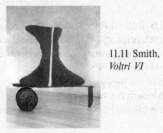

11.11 Smith, *Voltri VI*

dyes, binding with the fabric. *Mauve District* illustrates well the kind of airy, open composition that Frankenthaler excelled at. The white shape pushes at the border of the canvas, while the colors seem to expand outward.

Into the Sixties: Assemblage and Happenings

By the middle of the 1950s, Abstract Expressionism had been the "new" style for fifteen years. Many artists felt it was time to move on. One of the most influential voices of the time was the composer John Cage, whose writings and speeches suggested a different path for art to follow. Music and art, Cage said, should be "an affirmation of life—not an attempt to bring order out of chaos nor to suggest improvements in creation, but simply a way of waking up to the very life we're living."[1] Like the Dadaists of forty years earlier, young artists began mixing art back up with life as they found it, sometimes literally and often humorously. Critics called the trend Neo-Dada ("new Dada").

Robert Rauschenberg's *Canyon* (**22.6**) is what the artist called a *combine* because the work combines found objects with paint and collage. Rauschenberg's found objects came from the streets of New York, in this case a pillow and a stuffed

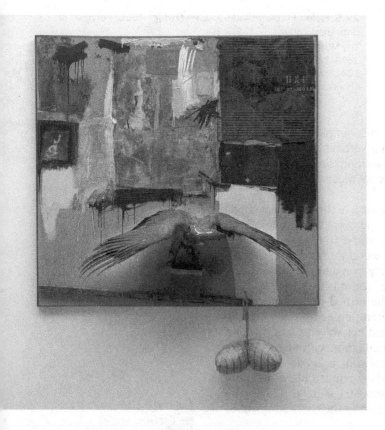

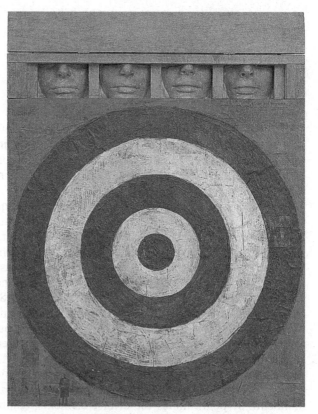

22.6 Robert Rauschenberg. *Canyon*. 1959. Oil, pencil, paper, metal, photograph, fabric, wood, canvas, buttons, mirror, taxidermied eagle, cardboard, pillow, paint tube and other materials, 81 ¾ × 70 × 24".

Gift of the family of Ileana Sonnabend. Digital image © The Museum of Modern Art, New York/Licensed by SCALA/Art Resource, NY. Art © Robert Rauschenberg Foundation/Licensed by VAGA, New York, NY

22.7 Jasper Johns. *Target with Four Faces*. 1955. Assemblage: encaustic on newspaper and collage on canvas with objects, 26" square, surmounted by four tinted plaster faces in wood box with hinged front; overall dimensions with box open 33 ⅝ × 26 × 3".

The Museum of Modern Art, New York. Gift of Mr. and Mrs. Robert C. Scull, 8.1958. Digital image © The Museum of Modern Art/Licensed by SCALA/Art Resource, NY. Art © Jasper Johns/Licensed by VAGA, New York, NY

eagle. To these the artist added newspaper clippings, a metal drum, a flattened tube of paint, bits of cardboard, a postcard of the Statue of Liberty, a photograph of his son, and a man's shirt. These are familiar items, even if they are found out of context in this work of art. Using them allowed Rauschenberg to challenge the nonrepresentational art of Abstract Expressionism. The artist gives viewers something to identify with and understand, although these are mostly in small bits and fragments. This hybrid work also challenges our definitions of art. Is it a two-dimensional painting? Is it a wall sculpture?

A more general term for Rauschenberg's combine paintings is **assemblage**. Another artist who made assemblages was Rauschenberg's friend Jasper Johns. Johns chose as his subjects some of the most familiar images one could imagine: the American flag, a map of the United States, numerals, letters of the alphabet, and targets (**22.7**). He said that if he chose these motifs, the work of composition had already been done for him, and he could concentrate on "other things." What other things? Paradoxes, for one. Painted in encaustic over newsprint, the target is textured, sensuous, and unique. Even in a photograph, we see the bumpy surface and the thick brushstrokes made by the artist's hand. Yet the idea of a target exists potentially in endless multiples. Above the target are portions of four faces. Johns took the casts from the same person, making a series of anonymous mechanical multiples from a unique individual. Like all Johns's favorite motifs, a target is not only familiar but also two-dimensional, abstract, and symbolic. Is the painting a representation of a target, or a target? What is the difference? It also teases us into thinking about aesthetics and emotional distance. For example, if we appreciate the painting as an abstract composition of concentric circles, does that spare us from thinking about it as a target and the blindfolded victims of a firing squad?

Cage had also suggested that visual art look to the lively art of theater for renewal. The composer's friend Allan Kaprow followed through on that suggestion by eliminating the art object and staging events he called **happenings**. Kaprow's *Courtyard* (**22.8**) happened in the courtyard of a seedy hotel. Kaprow and his assistants erected a five-story "mountain" of scaffolding covered with black paper. On a platform atop it they set an "altar" of mattresses. Over the mattresses was

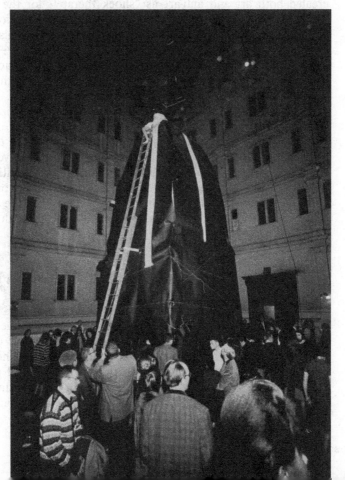

22.8 Allan Kaprow. *Courtyard.* 1962. Happening at the Mills Hotel, New York.

Metropolitan Museum of Art. Purchase, Frances Dittmer Gift, 2002 Photo: © Lawrence Shustak. Courtesy Allan Kaprow Estate and Hauser & Wirth

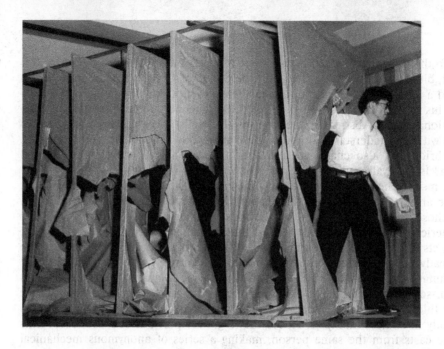

22.9 Saburo Murakami. *Laceration of Paper*. 1956.

Keystone Pictures USA/Alamy Stock Photo

RELATED WORKS

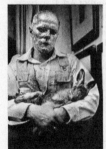

2.39 Beuys, *How to Explain Pictures to a Dead Hare*

suspended a large dome, also covered in black paper. After audience members helped to sweep the space clean, scraps of black paper were showered down from above. A woman in white danced around the base of the mountain and then climbed up to the mattresses. She was followed by photographers, who took pictures of her as she continued to dance. To the accompaniment of shrieks, sirens, and thunder effects, the dome was lowered over them.

Among the spectators at *Courtyard* was Hans Richter, one of the original members of Dada. None other than Marcel Duchamp, then living in New York, had drawn his attention to it. The Dadaists, too, had staged provocative events. "A Ritual!" Richter wrote. "It was a composition using space, color and movement, and the setting in which the Happening took place gave it a nightmarish, obsessive quality. . . ."[2] The Dadaists clearly recognized their successors. Just as Dada had created both art and anti-art as "shock therapy" for the complacent, conformist society that had produced World War I, this later generation was producing art and anti-art to jolt into awareness the complacent, conformist society of prosperous, postwar America.

Yet America was not the only location for interactive art events. In fact, Kaprow's happenings may have been inspired in part by the Japanese group known collectively as Gutai Art Association. Formed in 1954, Gutai performed public events as works of art. One of the most famous was Saburo Murakami's *Laceration of Paper* (**22.9**), in which the artist erected large sheets of paper in frames, then violently burst through them. Viewers not only witnessed the artist performing this act, but also heard the sound of the ripping paper. The event caused them to think about the nature of paper, about its material and its qualities. Like all performative art, it was the experience that Murakami created. No one could purchase it or display it on a wall. The fundamental characteristic of the work of art as a tangible object was undermined, as it has continued to be through to the present.

Art of the Sixties and Seventies

Does art exist in its own aesthetic realm apart from life? Is it important for us to have art as an alternative to our social experience, a refuge from everyday concerns that keeps us in touch with spiritual or abstract matters? Or is art deeply involved with life? Is it important for us to see the lives we live, the issues that concern us, our sense of what it is like to be in the world here and now given form through art? These questions have animated the history of art since the beginning of the modern era. As viewers, we have the luxury of appreciating all types of art, but artists have to choose one path or the other. During the sixties and seventies, the directions that had been set out in the previous decade were continued, questioned, and complicated by new trends.

Pop Art

Even the name is breezy: "pop," for popular. The artists of **Pop** found a gold mine of visual material in the mundane, mass-produced objects and images of America's popular culture: comic books, advertising, billboards, and packaging; the ever-expanding world of home appliances and other commodities; and photographic images from cinema, television, and newspapers. Like Neo-Dada, Pop drew art closer to life, but life as it had already been transformed into images by advertising and the media.

An example is Andy Warhol's *Gold Marilyn Monroe* (**22.10**). A glamorous but troubled film star, Monroe took her own life in August 1962. Warhol began a series of works devoted to her almost immediately. Significantly, the image is not a direct portrait of the actress herself but, rather, a silkscreen reproduction of one of her black-and-white publicity photographs. Warhol used the image in dozens of works, sometimes printing it several times across the canvas, like newspapers rolling off the press. He colored the image with silkscreen, garishly and clumsily. Monroe is at once debased by the crude, commercial treatment and glorified by the gold setting, like a sacred presence in a Byzantine icon (see 15.8). It is not quite her we see, but the mask of her fame. The son of eastern European immigrants, Warhol was brought up in the Eastern Orthodox faith, where the tradition of icons has been perpetuated. An astute observer, he noticed that images circulated with a similar force in American culture.

Warhol had started out as a highly successful commercial artist, and he brought this sensibility to his art. His many prints and paintings of Marilyn Monroe, Elizabeth Taylor, Jackie Kennedy, and, of course, the famous Coke bottles and

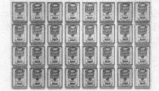

10.16 Warhol, *Campbell's Soup Cans*

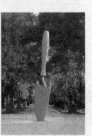

5.19 Oldenburg and Van Bruggen, *Plantoir*

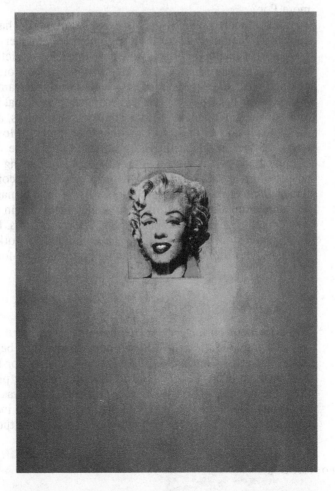

22.10 Andy Warhol. *Gold Marilyn Monroe*. 1962. Silkscreen ink on synthetic polymer paint on canvas, 6' 11 ¼" × 4' 9".

The Museum of Modern Art, New York. Gift of Philip Johnson, 316.1962. Digital image © The Museum of Modern Art/Licensed by SCALA/Art Resource, NY. © 2019 The Andy Warhol Foundation for the Visual Arts, Inc./Artists Rights Society (ARS), New York

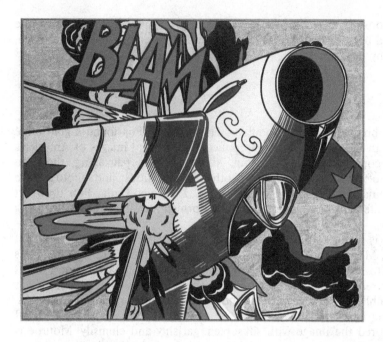

Campbell's soup cans have the appearance of slick advertising campaigns. Even their production was mechanized, as Warhol left much of the execution of his works to assistants. He liked to say that he was a "machine." He claimed to be devoid of emotion or feeling, just a machine that produced a product, called art, in a New York loft that he called the Factory. One of his much-quoted statements sums this up: "If you want to know all about Andy Warhol, just look at the surface: of my paintings and films and me, and there I am. There's nothing behind it."[3] After the celebration of the Abstract Expressionists as creative geniuses, Warhol claimed that he was as superficial and empty as mass-media advertising. What could be more Pop?

Roy Lichtenstein based his early paintings on hand-drawn advertising (then known as "commercial art") and comic-book imagery. He was intrigued by the conventions that these forms had developed for depicting the world—standardized ways of representing eyes, hair, glass, smoke, explosions, water, and even dripping brushstrokes. *Blam* (**22.11**) was adapted from a frame in the comic series *All-American Men of War*. Lichtenstein cropped the original image, rotated it 45 degrees, reduced the color scheme to the three primary colors, and simplified the depiction of the explosion to underscore its abstract quality. Most important, he enlarged it to over 5 feet in height, in the process enlarging the dot pattern of the printing. (Comic books then were printed on newsprint using a system that permitted a palette of up to sixty-four colors, all printed with four colors of dots; the background tint of *Blam* is made of painted dots.) By isolating images from their original context and dramatically shifting their scale, Lichtenstein draws our attention to the elements they are made of: black lines, flat colors, dots. He stopped drawing directly on comics within a few years, but he continued to work in his streamlined version of their style—cool, detached, seemingly mechanical—for the rest of his life.

Photorealism

Pop art's focus on imagery in the mass media inspired artists to look more closely at photographs. In a trend called **Photorealism**, they began to paint what they saw there. The artist Chuck Close asked friends to pose for his camera so that he could have faces to paint. He drew a grid over the resulting photograph, then a grid with the same number of squares over a much larger canvas (one work measures 9 feet in height). He copied each square of the photograph independently, one at a time, ignoring the larger image and focusing exclusively on the information in the square.

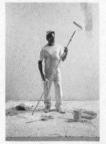
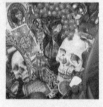

Similarly, Audrey Flack's *Wheel of Fortune (Vanitas)* (see 1.16) captures the visual experience of her assembled items in precise detail. We experience the mirrors, fruit, skull, and lipstick tube like a photographic record of their existence.

Minimalism and After

While Close and other painters turned their attention to photography and its effects, other artists continued to explore the possibilities of pure form. One group of sculptors wanted to rid art of representation and personal expression once and for all, and to allow viewers to see "the whole idea without any confusion." Critics tried to categorize their work in many ways—Primary Structures, Reductive art, Literalism—but the label that stuck, despite the artists' objections, was Minimalism.

Donald Judd's *Untitled (Stack)* embodies many of the characteristics associated with Minimalism (**22.12**). It is made of galvanized iron, a common industrial and construction material. The material is used literally; it does not try to depict or suggest anything else. The sculpture has the impersonal look of industrial fabrication; there is no trace of the artist's "hand" or "touch." In fact, *Untitled (Stack)* was manufactured by a metal workshop according to Judd's specifications. The composition consists of repeating units of simple geometric shapes, precisely positioned—in this case, boxes 9 inches in height displayed at 9-inch intervals. There is no focal point, no areas of greater or lesser interest. The sculpture is attached to the wall rather than exhibited on a pedestal, as traditional sculpture had been. Other Minimalist works were set on the floor.

Minimalist art did not reward the kind of looking skills that viewers had been taught were important, skills such as reading the subject (there was no content), analyzing the composition (this was quickly done), appreciating the use of formal elements (there weren't many), or sensing the artist's physical and emotional involvement (the work had been manufactured). It was almost as though appreciating Minimal art required different looking skills. Judd himself suggested what these might be. "A work of art needs only to be interesting," he wrote in 1965. "It isn't necessary for a work to have a lot of things to look at, to compare, to analyze one by one, to contemplate. The thing as a whole, its quality as a whole is what is interesting."[4]

Minimalism provoked strong reactions, not only among critics and the public, but also among artists. In a variety of interrelated trends, artists variously reacted against aspects of it or developed possibilities that it suggested. Collectively, these trends are known as **Postminimalism**, which unfolded from the mid-1960s through the mid-1970s. Neither styles nor movements in the traditional sense, the diverse trends of Postminimalism dramatically expanded—permanently, it seems—the ways in which art could be made, the materials it could be made from, and the kinds of objects and activities that could be offered and interpreted as art.

PROCESS ART A composition of repeating rectangular units links Eva Hesse's *Contingent* to Minimalism's exploration of form (**22.13**). Almost everything else about the work, however, stakes out a distance. Whereas Minimalism favored tough industrial materials associated with construction, *Contingent* consists of panels of flimsy cheesecloth, hung from the ceiling like banners. Each panel is encased in transparent fiberglass, and its center portion is painted with latex. In place of Minimalism's precise geometry and manufactured look, the rectangles of *Contingent* are casual and varied, and the piece is clearly handmade. And whereas Minimalist works were pointedly about nothing but their own clarity, *Contingent* feels more personal, intuitive, and intimate. Many viewers have sensed allusions to the human body in Hesse's works.

Hesse is one of a number of artists associated with **Process art**. In Process art, the meaning of a work embraced what it was made of and how it was made. Process artists were attracted to unconventional materials. They were willing to surrender complete control, to embrace chance and unpredictability, and to create

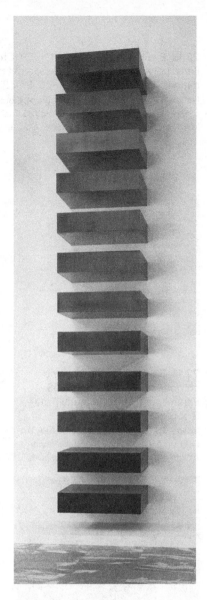

22.12 Donald Judd. *Untitled (Stack)*. 1967. Lacquer on galvanized iron, twelve units, each 9 × 40 × 31", installed vertically with 9" intervals.
The Museum of Modern Art, New York. Helen Acheson Bequest (by exchange) and gift of Joseph Helman. Digital image © The Museum of Modern Art/Licensed by SCALA/Art Resource, NY © Judd Foundation

RELATED WORKS

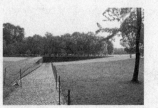

1.6 Lin, Vietnam Veterans Memorial

22.13 Eva Hesse. *Contingent*. 1969. Cheesecloth, latex, polyester resin, fiberglass; eight units, dimensions variable, 12' 4" × 20' 8" × 3' 7". National Gallery of Australia, Canberra. Courtesy the Estate of Eva Hesse, Galerie Hauser & Wirth, Zürich/Bridgeman Images © The Estate of Eva Hesse. Courtesy Hauser & Wirth

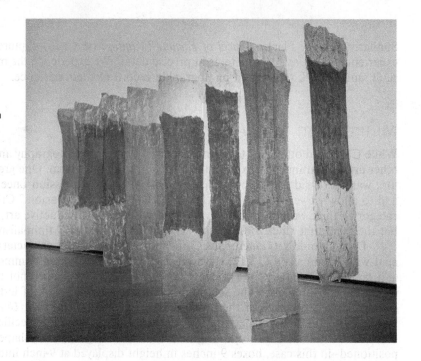

RELATED WORKS

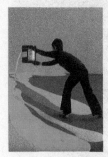

7.13 Benglis painting on the floor

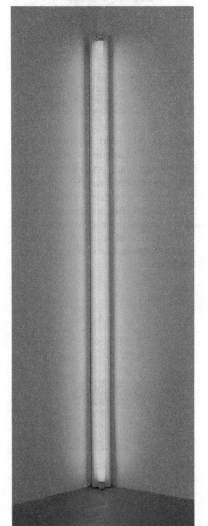

22.14 Dan Flavin. *pink out of a corner (to Jasper Johns)*. 1963. Fluorescent light and metal fixture, 8' × 6" × 5 ⅜".

Image © MoMA/Licensed by SCALA/Art Resource, NY © 2019 Stephen Flavin/ Artists Rights Society (ARS), New York

ephemeral or temporary works. The panels of *Contingent*, for example, "are the way they are and the way the material and fiberglass worked out," Hesse explained. "They are all different sizes and heights, but I said 'Well, if it happens, it happens'."[5] The latex has yellowed and grown brittle over the years, as Hesse knew it would; that her work would not have a long life was a trade-off she made for its impact in the moment.

INSTALLATION Minimalist sculptures were shown carefully positioned in the architectural spaces of a museum or gallery. In the words of one artist, a Minimalist sculpture was "one of the terms" in the space, all of which was interesting.[6] As the sculptors intended, viewers became conscious of their own bodily presence in the same space and attentive to their experience as they looked at the sculpture. Taking those ideas a step further, artists created installations—spaces conceived of as works of art for viewers to enter and experience. Dan Flavin's *pink out of a corner (to Jasper Johns)* (**22.14**) is precisely what the title suggests: pink coming out of a corner. The artist planned for the commercially made pink fluorescent light to be installed when he came up with the idea for the work. Installing the bulb in this way draws the viewer's attention to the shape of the room and the corners that are usually forgotten in gallery spaces. The installation also allows the walls to become part of the work. The pink light that reflects off the white walls that join in the corner creates a cylindrical halo around the bulb, magnifying its presence. The light also reflects off the viewers who approach the corner to get a better look. Each of these elements—bulb, corner, walls, visitors—becomes part of the installation. Dedicating the work to Jasper Johns, Flavin paid homage to another artist who made art with common and familiar items.

Installation art had numerous precedents. The Surrealists had sometimes exhibited their paintings in galleries decorated to look like a Surrealist painting come to life. Allan Kaprow, whose happening we looked at earlier (see 22.8), had also created places he called "environments"—rooms that viewers entered and explored. But it was in the climate of Postminimalism that the practice of creating spaces became widespread and that the name "installation" became standard.

BODY ART AND PERFORMANCE Many installations were temporary works: An existing space was transformed for the length of an exhibition, then returned to its original condition. Temporary installations were an attempt to move

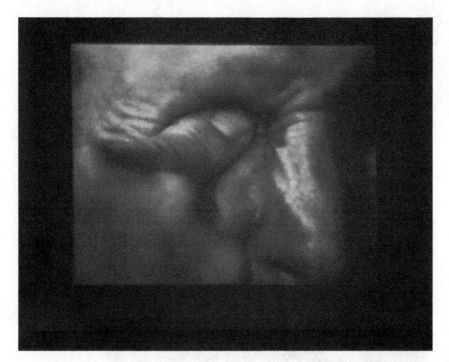

22.15 Bruce Nauman. *Poke in the Eye/Nose/Ear 3/8/94 Edit*. 1994. Video, 52 min.

Collection Walker Art Center, Minneapolis. T. B. Walker Acquisition Fund, 1994. © 2019 Bruce Nauman/ Artists Rights Society (ARS), New York

22.16 Marina Abramović and Ulay. *Imponderabilia*. 1977. Performance at the Galleria Comunale d'Arte Moderna, Bologna, Italy.

Photo Giovanna dal Magro. © 2015 Marina Abramović. Courtesy of Sean Kelly Gallery/2019 (ARS), New York

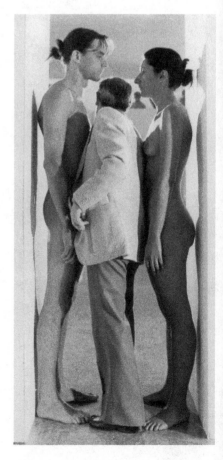

art away from the influence of the art market, which emphasized portable objects that could be bought and sold like luxury products. By making works that could not be sold, artists wanted to disrupt the association of art and money. A more radical move away from making objects was **Body art**, a practice in which artists made art using their own body as a material or medium. In Chapter 9, for example, we looked at a frame from a film that Bruce Nauman made to document his *Dance or Exercise on the Perimeter of a Square* (see 9.21). In *Poke in the Eye/Nose/ Ear 3/8/94 Edit* (**22.15**), the subject of the work is again Nauman's body. This time the artist filmed himself poking his own eye, nose, and ear. The framing is tight, the video is shot in slow motion, and the projection is huge. We watch in excruciating detail as his body reacts involuntarily to the violence. We feel sympathetic pain and discomfort with our bodies as we watch the artist's body. Should we choose to remain in the gallery, we can watch this action over and over again in the looped video.

Body art was a subcategory of a broader form called **Performance art**, in which the artist appears "live and in person." Performance had been a recurring presence in 20th-century art, beginning with events staged by Futurist and Dada artists in the first decades of the century and continuing through Kaprow's happenings (see 22.8). During the Postminimal years, such actions, events, and happenings became more formalized, and the name Performance art came into general use.

Much of the Performance art of the 1970s concerned the relationship between artist and spectator. An example is *Imponderabilia*, which the artist Marina Abramović performed with her then partner Ulay in a museum in Italy (**22.16**). The two stood facing each other in a narrow doorway, naked, eyes locked, immobile, and expressionless. Anyone wanting to enter the museum had to get by them, squeezing through sideways, brushing against their bodies. Which way would the spectators face? Where would they look? How would they hold their hands? It is easy to imagine their discomfort, but it is almost frightening to consider the extreme vulnerability of the artists, who were forbidden by the rules of the work to move or speak. Many of Abramović's works put her in a vulnerable position, and in some cases, the spectators grew menacing. We do not know what might have happened here, for after ninety minutes, the police were called to put an end to *Imponderabilia*.

Like Abramović, Ana Mendieta used her body in performances that she documented in photographs. She posed in different contexts, sometimes inside and

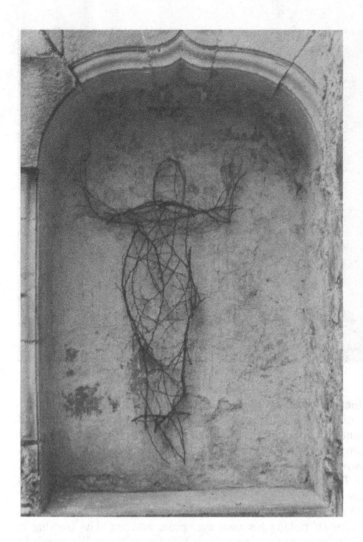

sometimes in nature. In *Untitled*, a work from her *Silueta Series* (**22.17**), the artist's arms are raised and her legs are together in a pose that suggested the soul moving through space. Mendieta let her body become integrated into the location, in this case a niche in the wall of a church. She arranged the sticks in the shape of her silhouette as a temporary trace of her presence. The photograph of the stick silhouette remains as the only evidence of her intervention on the location. In other works in this series, Mendieta covered her body with mud that camouflaged her against a tree, carved the shape of her body into the ground, and burned her silhouette into the earth using gunpowder. The artist called body-based performances "earth-body work" and "earth-body sculptures" to visualize what she described as a dialog between her body and the land.

LAND ART Mendieta's performative interventions on the natural landscape relate her to a movement known as Land art. Also known as **Earth art**, Land art was yet another way in which Postminimalist artists sought to separate art from issues of money and ownership, to escape from urban exhibition spaces such as galleries and museums, and to open up alternatives to the weighty traditions of painting and sculpture. In **Land art**, the artist intervenes in some way in a landscape. This can be as simple as aligning a sequence of found stones or as elaborate as creating a pathway that launches bravely out into a lake and then coils in on itself, as Robert Smithson did in *Spiral Jetty* (see 3.26). One of the most famous works of Land art is Walter De Maria's *Lightning Field* (**22.18**). Located in New Mexico in a remote region of high desert, it consists of four hundred highly polished steel poles arranged in a rectangular grid measuring 1 mile by just over 1 kilometer.

RELATED WORKS

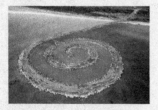

3.26 Smithson, *Spiral Jetty*

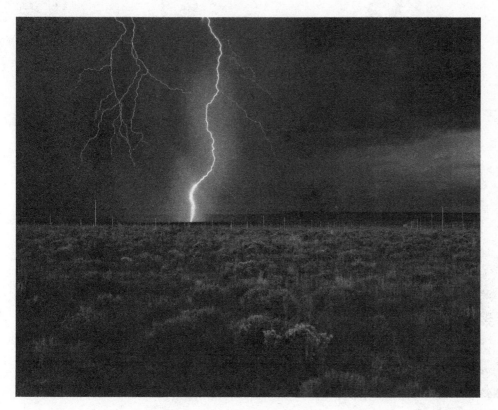

22.18 Walter De Maria. *The Lightning Field*. Quemado, New Mexico. 1977. Long-term installation, western New Mexico. Four hundred pointed steel rods, 1 mile × 1 kilometer.
© Estate of Walter De Maria. Photo: John Cliett. Courtesy Dia Art Foundation, New York

The poles are set so that their pointed tips describe a horizontal plane—that is, the artist explained, so that they would evenly support an imaginary sheet of glass. Their average height is over 20 feet. At dawn and dusk they are clearly visible in the raking light; at midday, with the sun directly overhead, they seem to vanish.

De Maria chose the location for its high incidence of lightning, and images such as the spectacular photograph illustrated here have captured the public's imagination. The poles do attract lightning when it occurs, yet their larger purpose is to provide a framework for visitors to have a heightened experience of light, space, landscape, and solitude. "The land is not the setting for the work but a part of the work," De Maria insisted.[7] He believed that isolation was essential to Land art, and he intended for *The Lightning Field* to be experienced alone or in the company of just a few people over a period of at least twenty-four hours. The foundation that owns the work is faithful to his wishes: Up to six visitors at a time are driven to the site, dropped off at a small cabin that has been made ready for them, and picked up the next day. If they have been wise, they will have separated to wander through the field, alone with their thoughts and alive to their sensations.

CONCEPTUAL ART **Conceptual art** is art in which ideas are paramount and the form that realizes those ideas is secondary—often lightweight, ephemeral, or unremarkable. Doris Salcedo's *Shibboleth* (see 1.11) is Conceptual art because the concepts it represents are just as significant as the crack in the floor. We are not meant to marvel at how well Salcedo crafted the crack. We are instead intended to think about what the crack represents and to focus on the concept behind the work. The same goes for Janine Antoni's *Gnaw* (see 2.28), in which the gnawed chocolate and lard raise ideas about love and self-image.

Arising in the mid-1960s as yet another echo of Dada, Conceptual art is especially indebted to Marcel Duchamp, whose self-proclaimed goal was to eliminate what he called the "retinal aspect" of art—its appeal solely to the eye—in favor of an engagement with ideas. His ready-mades, such as *Fountain* (see 2.2), can be considered Conceptual works, although they made their appearance before the term

RELATED WORKS

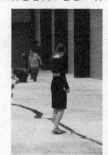

1.11 Salcedo, *Shibboleth*

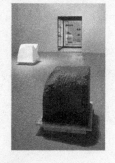

2.28 Antoni, *Gnaw*

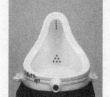

2.2 Duchamp, *Fountain*

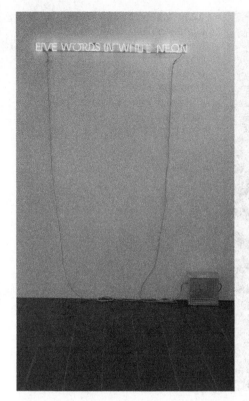

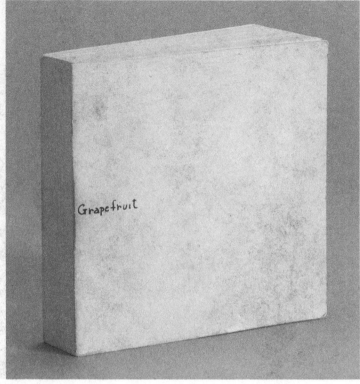

22.19 Joseph Kosuth. *Five Words in White Neon*, from *Tautology* series. 1965. Glass tubing, neon, and transformer, length of phrase 4' 11".
Private Collection/Bridgeman Images © 2019 Joseph Kosuth/Artists Rights Society (ARS), New York

22.20 Yoko Ono. *Grapefruit*. 1964. Artist's book, offset printed, 5 7/16 × 5 7/16".
Digital image © The Museum of Modern Art/Licensed by SCALA/Art Resource, NY

was invented. In itself, *Fountain* has no particular visual interest. But the shift brought about by calling a urinal *Fountain* and exhibiting it as art is food for thought.

Conceptualism is not a style but a way of thinking about art, and artists have put it to many different uses. Many Conceptual artists worked with language, for words, when written, take on a double life as image and idea. For example, Joseph Kosuth, one of the foremost practitioners and theorists of Conceptual art, made a work called *One and Three Chairs* by juxtaposing three elements: a chair, a black-and-white photograph of the same chair enlarged to life-size, and a photographic enlargement of a dictionary definition of the word *chair*. In true Conceptual fashion, the form is secondary, for the style of chair doesn't matter, any dictionary definition will do, and the three elements can be arranged in many ways. *One and Three Chairs* could thus take many forms. The work is not illustrated here, but it doesn't really need to be: You know all you need to know from the description.

In Kosuth's *Five Words in White Neon* (**22.19**), the form does matter, but it matters in a particular way. *Five Words in White Neon* is from Kosuth's *Tautology* series. A tautology is a restatement of the same idea in different terms. "The runners crossed the finish line one after the other in succession" is an example of a tautology, where "in succession" means the same thing as "one after the other." In logic, a tautology is a compound statement that is necessarily true, such as "it will rain tomorrow or it will not rain tomorrow." Kosuth's work is tautological in that it represents the phrase "five words in white neon" with five words in white neon.

Yoko Ono's *Grapefruit* (**22.20**) is a Conceptual artist's book. An artist's book is a work of art that is based on the idea of a book and what a book does. We accept that books are made of paper, are bound, and contain information. The artist's book plays on these "truths." Ono's book is filled with instructions, ranging from the practical to the illogical. One instruction asks the reader to walk through the city, stepping in every puddle. Another tells us to imagine one thousand suns in the sky, then make and eat one tuna sandwich. The book acts like a script, turning the reader into a performer within this work of art. It also challenges the traditional role of the artist as being in charge of all aspects of the work. Ono developed the instructions over an eleven-year period, gave them titles, and had them printed on paper in ordinary type in an edition of 500 copies. What happened afterward was beyond her control; readers could treat the book as a book and put it on a shelf, or follow the instructions and become Ono's performers.

New Media: Video

Portable video cameras were first made available to the general public in 1965, and the first two works of video art quickly followed within weeks of each other. One was by Andy Warhol, who had been asked by a magazine to experiment with one of the new devices. The other was by Nam June Paik, who recorded from a taxi his view of the papal motorcade during the Pope's historic visit to New York in 1965. Paik showed the video that very evening at a café that was popular with artists.

Video was ideally suited to an era that questioned whether artworks needed to be objects, in which performance had assumed an important role, and in which the power of television had begun to show its full force. Joan Jonas's *Glass Puzzle* illustrates the experimental nature of early video art (**22.21**). The video captures an unrehearsed performance by Jonas and another artist, Lois Lane. A mobile video camera operated by the filmmaker Babette Mangolte fed the live performance to a monitor. A second video camera was trained on the monitor, recording the video display. The second camera also captured the reflections of the room in the monitor's glass screen, creating a complex, puzzling space in which actions happening simultaneously appear to be layered over one another—one fed to the monitor by the mobile camera, the other visible in the reflection of the room in the glass. *Glass Puzzle* is an enigmatic work. The two women wear intimate clothing—short slips, a satin dressing gown, a white unitard. In some sequences, they appear together, one mimicking the other's gestures (as illustrated). In others, they appear to be waiting, marking time, or displaying themselves. One dances. The video records ambient sounds (traffic passing outdoors, dancing feet, rustling clothes, music playing), but the women do not speak.

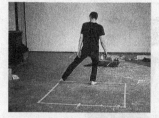

9.21 Nauman, *Dance or Exercise*

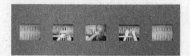

9.22 Korot, *Text and Commentary*

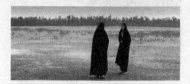

9.23 Neshat, *Women Without Men*

22.21 Joan Jonas. *Glass Puzzle*. 1973. Black-and-white video, 17:23 min. Performers: Joan Jonas and Lois Lane. Music: The Liquidators. Courtesy Electronic Arts Intermix (EAI), New York, and Yvon Lambert Paris © 2019 Joan Jonas/Artists Rights Society (ARS), New York

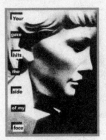

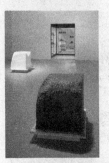

2.28 Antoni,
Gnaw

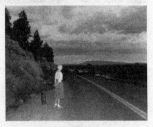

9.12 Sherman, *Untitled #48*

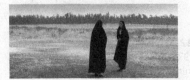

9.23 Neshat, *Women Without Men*

Feminism and Feminist Art

If you had been reading a book like this around 1968, the chapters of Part Five, "Arts in Time," would most likely not have introduced you to Sofonisba Anguissola (see 16.21), Artemisia Gentileschi (see 17.6), Élisabeth Vigée-Lebrun (see 17.19), Berthe Morisot (see 21.8), or Mary Cassatt (see 21.14). Art historians knew of works by these women; they just didn't make an effort to include them in their telling of the history of art. It was quite possible to come away from a course in art history or a visit to a museum believing that women had played little or no role in the art of the past. If you look forward in this book to the art of the eighties and nineties, you will find not only many more women but also greater diversity in general. This diversity accurately reflects the makeup of the contemporary art world, and it is due in large measure to the impact of feminism and related social and political movements of the 1970s.

Feminist organizations had originally been formed around such issues as equal rights and equal pay. Because images are powerful and pervasive in contemporary society, visual culture quickly became a feminist concern, both in art and in the media. Women art professionals organized to recover women's art of the past, to push for more equitable representation in museums and galleries, and to nurture contemporary women artists. During this first phase of feminism, a project that intrigued many artists was the creation of a specifically female art, rooted in the biological, psychological, social, and historical experience of women.

Judy Chicago's *Dinner Party* is perhaps the most important work from this time (**22.22**). A collaborative work, *The Dinner Party* was executed with the help of hundreds of women and several men. Arranged around a triangular table are thirty-nine place settings, each one created in honor of an influential woman, such as the Egyptian ruler Hatshepsut and the novelist Virginia Woolf. The names of an additional 999 important women are written on the tile floor. By using such craft techniques as ceramics, weaving, needlepoint, and **embroidery**, Chicago demanded artistic equality for media that had long been associated with "women's work." Confined to the domestic sphere, the vast majority of women throughout history had been limited to these expressive outlets—including the expressive outlet of set-

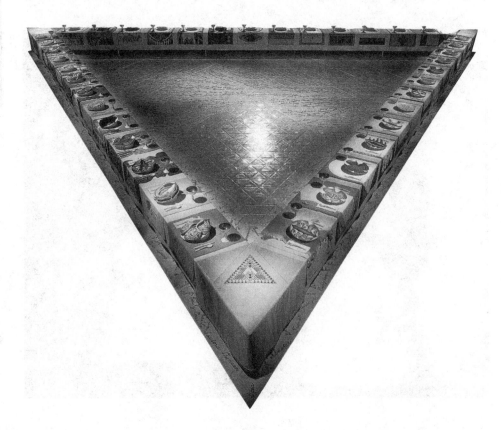

22.22 Judy Chicago. *The Dinner Party*. 1979. Mixed media, each side 48'.

Brooklyn Museum of Art, New York, Gift of The Elizabeth A. Sackler Foundation. Photo © Donald Woodman. © 2019 Judy Chicago/Artists Rights Society (ARS), New York

ting and decorating a table—and *The Dinner Party* honors them. The thirteen places on each side of the triangle intentionally evoke the seating arrangement of Leonardo's *Last Supper* (see 4.46), a central work in the history of Western art, and one that depicts an all-male gathering.

Chicago's choice to make her monumental work in clay and textiles was part of a reconsideration of crafts that began in the 1960s. Artists questioned the division between art and craft that had been in place for some two hundred years. Was there really such a clear difference between them, and, if so, what defined it? Materials? Techniques? Forms? Context? Makers? Crafts were traditionally ranked below painting and sculpture in the hierarchy of arts, in part because they were considered women's work. In the 1970s, women artists proudly chose to work in textiles or clay as a feminist act. As the artist Miriam Schapiro said of her work in fiber arts, "I wanted to validate the traditional activities of women, to connect myself to the unknown women artists who had made quilts, who had done the invisible 'women's work' of civilization. I wanted to acknowledge them, to honor them."[8] For Schapiro, Chicago, and others, craft's low status was a symptom of the widespread misogyny in the arts that they sought to overturn.

Art of the Eighties and Nineties: Postmodernism

Over the course of the 1970s, it became clear to many people that ideas about art that seemed to have been in place for much of the modern era were eroding and that something different was taking their place. This new climate of thought came to be called Postmodernism.

The term *Postmodern* was first used to describe architecture such as Renzo Piano and Richard Rogers's Georges Pompidou National Center of Art and Culture (**22.23**). Designed in 1971 and completed six years later, the Pompidou Center

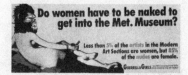
22.23 Renzo Piano and Richard Rogers. Georges Pompidou National Center of Art and Culture, Paris. 1977.
© Maria Breuer/imagebroker/Alamy

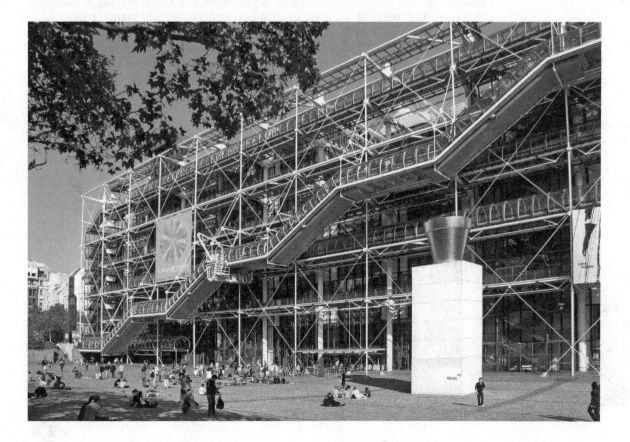

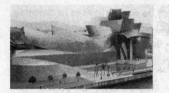

13.31 Gehry, Guggenheim
Museum Bilbao

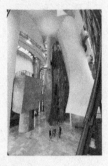

4.42 Gehry,
Guggenheim
Museum Bilbao
(interior)

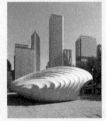

13.33 Hadid,
Burnham
Pavilion

22.24 Sherrie Levine. *Fountain
(after Marcel Duchamp: A. P.)*. 1991.
Bronze, 14 ½ × 14 ¼ × 25".
Walker Art Center, Minneapolis. T. B.
Walker Acquisition Fund, 1992. Courtesy
of the artist and David Zwirner Gallery,
New York

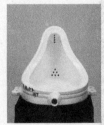

2.2 Duchamp,
Fountain

created a sensation. Encased in scaffolding, pipes, tubes, and funnels—all color-coded according to function—it looks like a building turned inside out. The architects themselves likened it to "a Jules Verne spaceship that can't fly."[9] The Pompidou Center was one of many buildings of the time that turned away from the International style that had dominated Western architecture after World War II (see 13.25). The International style had grown from the thinking of early 20th-century Modernist movements such as De Stijl and the Bauhaus (see Chapter 13). Its industrial materials, clean lines, and rectilinear forms sought not only to express the modern age, but also to create a luminous, rational environment in which humanity itself would progress. By the mid-1960s, however, many began to find International-style buildings oppressive and sterile. A new direction was called for, but instead of building on Modernist ideas and progressing *forward*, architects reached both *backward*—adapting ornaments and forms from traditions as distant as ancient Egypt—and *outward*—looking seriously at common, everyday architecture. Instead of the rational order of International style, they often emphasized other, equally human qualities such as playfulness, curiosity, and eccentricity.

The notion that there may be no such thing as "progress" in art is part of the web of related ideas that make up Postmodernism. Another is a more complex view of history. Feminism had shown clearly that within art history as it was usually told lay other histories that were untold. Art history was not the straightforward progression of one style to another that it had been made to seem. Rather, each historical moment was full of multiple directions, contradictions, and debates. Perhaps a fairer way to study history would be to study everything that happened, not just the "winners" whose style seemed to be part of "progress." This way of thinking led to the creation of the Gare d'Orsay museum in Paris, which displays 19th-century progressive art, such as Impressionist works, alongside conservative styles. It exhibits not just painting and sculpture, but also architecture, photography, popular arts and illustration, and decorative arts, to give a more inclusive view of the era. Applying these ideas to the present moment logically leads to pluralism, the idea that art can take many directions at the same time, all of them equally valid. Historians of the future should no longer select one as "correct" and sweep the rest under the carpet. Pluralism in turn recognizes that there is no longer any single leading artistic center. Rather, the world of art consists of many centers and has many levels.

Sherrie Levine's 1991 *Fountain (after Marcel Duchamp)* may be the ultimate Postmodern statement (**22.24**). *Fountain* was the most notorious of Duchamp's ready-mades, an ordinary porcelain urinal that he contributed to an art exhibition in 1917 (see 2.2). Levine presents a gleaming bronze version. She created a number of "after" works, restating images made originally by such artists as Constantin Brancusi, Man Ray, and the photographer Walker Evans. She has said that what interests her is the "almost-same"—Duchamp's *Fountain*, but with a slightly different urinal and cast in bronze; Brancusi's sculpture of a newborn, but cast in glass; a

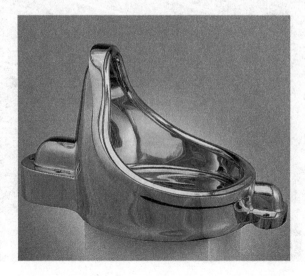

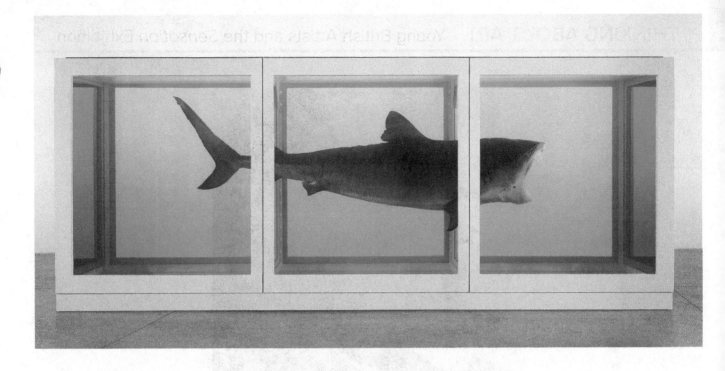

photograph of a photograph by Walker Evans. In exploring ideas about authorship and originality by repeating other artists' imagery, Levine was employing a post-modern practice known as **appropriation**. Loosely, appropriation refers to the artis-tic recycling of existing images. In this sense, it acknowledges that images circulate in such vast quantities through our society that they have become a kind of public resource that anyone can draw on. More strictly, appropriation is linked to Duchamp himself, who presented the creations of others (a urinal, or a postcard in *L.H.O.O.Q.*, see 21.22) as his own and in doing so gave them a new meaning. In music, many of the same ideas lie behind the practice of sampling—taking bits of music from prerecorded songs and giving them new meaning by placing them in a new context. Both appropriation and sampling form part of larger theories that question whether any artist is the sole creator of his or her work, or the final author-ity about what it means. All artists borrow ideas in one way or another, and the meaning of a work is unstable and varies from viewer to viewer. The creation of meaning, and thus of art, is a communal project.

Postmodern ideas about meaning, creativity, and the artist as authority are at play in Damien Hirst's *The Physical Impossibility of Death in the Mind of Someone Living* (**22.25**). The work, which was commissioned by a prominent London art collector, consists of a dead tiger shark that Hirst purchased and suspended in a tank of formaldehyde. In some ways, the work is a meditation on death, with the dead shark representing our own mortality. It is also an exploration of images in terms of what is real and what is a simulation. We are afraid of sharks mostly because of pictures, but this shark is real. Yet the shark here is treated as an art object by the commission and its display in the gallery. How is this a work of art? It looks like a specimen from a natural history museum. And how does this display relate to the title? The artist makes the meaning unclear to allow each viewer to bring a unique perspective to its interpretation.

22.25 Damien Hirst. *The Physical Impossibility of Death in the Mind of Someone Living.* 1991. Glass, painted steel, silicone, monofilament, shark, and formaldehyde solution, 85 ½" × 213 ⅖" × 70 ⁹⁄₁₀".

Words and Images, Issues and Identities

In works such as *Still Life on Table: "Gillette"* (see 6.13) and *Le Portugais (The Emigrant)* (see 21.20), Cubist artists at the beginning of the 20th century imported words into art. With the growth of advertising in the form of posters and newspa-pers, words had taken on a new visual presence in the environment, and Cubist

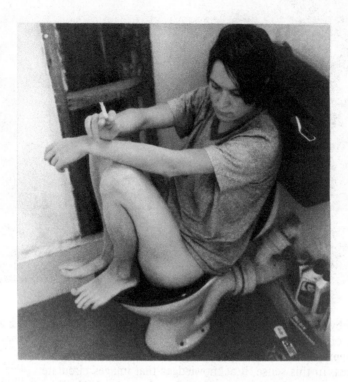

Who were the Young British Artists? What was the *Sensation* exhibition? Why did the exhibition upset so many people?

A dead cow and her calf suspended in formaldehyde. An image of the Madonna with elephant dung. A woman's unmade bed. A self-portrait made of frozen blood. Life-size, nude children with plastic bodies fused together.

In 1997, Charles Saatchi, the art collector who commissioned Damien Hirst's *Physical Impossibility of Death in the Mind of Someone Living*, staged an exhibition at the Royal Academy of Arts in London. Titled *Sensation*, the show featured work that Saatchi owned by Hirst, Sarah Lucas, and others, who had come to be known as the Young British Artists (YBAs). The YBAs did not practice a particular style or address a common theme. Instead, they were united by their use of found objects, their skill at marketing and self-promotion, and their refusal to limit themselves to a single medium. They were also known for their shocking images. Shown here is one of Lucas's photographic self-portraits, made the year after the exhibition.

The *Sensation* exhibition immediately attracted media attention, drawing visitors and protesters alike. The English public was particularly outraged by a portrait of Myra Hindley, who was convicted of killing five children in the 1960s. Her portrait by Marcus Harvey was made from the handprints of small children. When protests did not succeed in securing the painting's removal, it was attacked with ink and eggs. After cleaning, the painting was returned to the exhibition, but placed behind a shield.

Controversy followed the exhibition to the Brooklyn Museum of Art in New York. The focus of American outrage was Chris Ofili's image of the Madonna adorned with elephant dung and small pornographic photographs. The then mayor of New York City, Rudolph Giuliani, tried to evict the museum from its building and cut off its funding. He ultimately failed when advocates of free speech came to the museum's defense.

The *Sensation* exhibition did not just raise eyebrows for its controversial works. Some viewed the show as a publicity stunt designed to enrich Saatchi, who was not just a collector, but also the owner of a London gallery. The works in the show were part of the gallery's collection, which was for sale. In fact, Saatchi sold over a hundred of the works at auction following the London exhibition. This murky distinction between commercial and artistic endeavor troubled people in the art world, who viewed the show as just a slick marketing gimmick.

Sarah Lucas. *Human Toilet Revisited*. 1998. C-print. © Sarah Lucas, courtesy Tate, London, and Sadie Coles HQ, London. Photo © Tate, London, 2018

paintings were the first to acknowledge this. During the 1960s, Conceptual art often took the form of words, as in the work of Joseph Kosuth (see 22.19). By the 1980s, it had become clear to many that advertising was the prevalent visual reality of our time, and a number of artists adopted its techniques, most commonly to address political and social issues.

Jenny Holzer's *Protect Me From What I Want* (**22.26**) is one of a series of works in which the artist inserted words that closely resembled advertising slogans into public places. The photograph here shows the work installed at Caesar's Palace, a famous hotel and casino in Las Vegas. The photograph gives some idea of the dense advertising environment the sign was part of. Advertising, of course, is precisely about wanting, about creating desire. How many people noticed Holzer's prayerlike slogan shouting its warning amid the dazzling display of neon signs promoting hotels, casinos, restaurants, and other temptations? ("Win $5000 dollars!" reads a sign just visible in the lower right.) We have no way of knowing, of course, but those who did may have paused for a moment.

One of the most highly charged issues of the 1980s was the AIDS epidemic, which forced deep-lying prejudices to the surface of public life. The U.S. government was slow to act when the epidemic began to take its toll. President Ronald Reagan did not mention the disease in public until 1985, after more than five thousand victims had died. Activists believed that by not taking action, the government allowed the death toll to rise unnecessarily high. A group of activists in New York City known as the Silence=Death Project took up the cause to raise awareness and to mobilize people to political action. They designed the poster *Silence=Death* (**22.27**) in 1987. The work is simple, yet bold, with a pink triangle on a black background. The pink triangle was adapted from the badge the Nazis made gay male prisoners wear in concentration camps. The poster's designers chose the Nazi badge

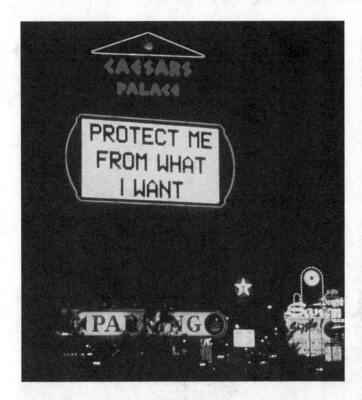

22.26 Jenny Holzer. *Protect Me From What I Want,* from *Survival*. 1983–85. Installation at Caesar's Palace, Las Vegas, Nevada, September 2–8, 1986, organized by Nevada Institute for Contemporary Art. Daktronics double-sided electronic sign.
© Jenny Holzer, Photo Thomas Holder. Courtesy Jenny Holzer/Art Resource, NY. © 2019 Jenny Holzer, member Artists Rights Society (ARS), New York

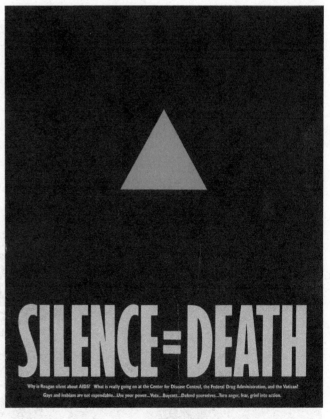

22.27 Silence=Death Project. *Silence=Death*. 1987. Poster. The New York Public Library/Art Resource, NY

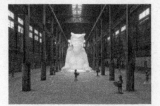

2.41 Walker, *A Subtlety*

10.2 Baker,
LGBT flag

22.28 Kara Walker. *African't*. 1996.
Cut paper on wall, 144 × 792".
Artwork © Kara Walker, courtesy of
Sikkema Jenkins & Co., New York.
Photo Jason Wyche

for its association with death, but inverted the triangle to empower the gay community. The poster's white sans serif uppercase type makes its powerful statement about the damaging effect of silence. Smaller text below questions Reagan's inaction and encourages the gay community to mobilize and exercise political power: "Turn anger, fear, grief into action." The poster's effect was immediate, and it quickly became a symbol of the fight against AIDS.

Artists associated with the feminist movement of the 1970s and the gay activism of the 1980s were instrumental in opening the art world to works that addressed human identities and issues, just as American culture in general became more aware of the many identities it embraced and, all too often, silenced. Perhaps the most complicated in America is race, most especially blackness and ideas about blackness both within and outside of the African-American community.

One artist working with historical and personal questions of blackness is Kara Walker. Her installation of paper silhouettes titled *African't* (**22.28**) uses biting wit to depict race relations before the U.S. Civil War. A host of characters drawn from Southern archetypes such as plantation owners and slaves are arrayed across the wall. Everyone engages in terrible and sometimes perverse acts. Seeing these acts takes time, because the paper silhouettes appear at first to be elegant and genteel. Silhouette portraits were common in 18th- and 19th-century America, made by tracing a profile onto a dark sheet of paper. They were especially popular in the Victorian era. Mothers kept silhouettes of their children, husbands kept them of their wives. Walker chose this medium for its lack of faces and other descriptive surface details. We can look at the subjects but not really see them. Walker considered this an appropriate metaphor for racism: We see it, but do not really see it. Her storytelling in *African't* offers a counter-narrative of the antebellum era, which has traditionally been romanticized in popular culture. She reminds us how horrific this period of enslavement, violence, and rape was for African Americans.

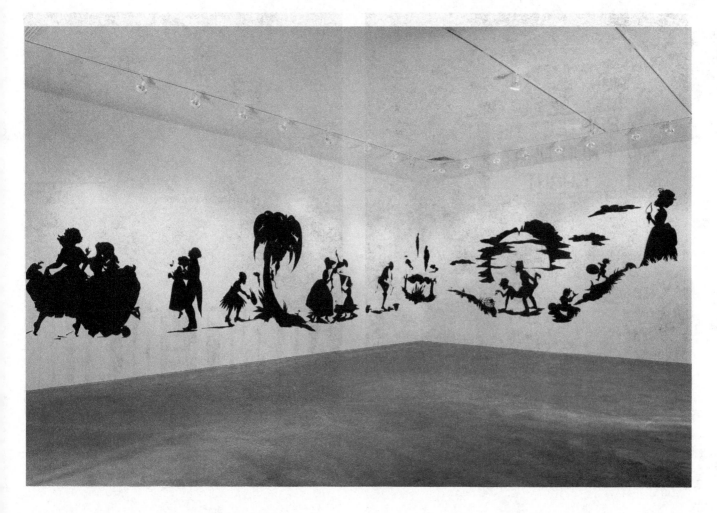

New Media: The Digital Realm

The rapid development of digital technology during the final two decades of the 20th century allowed images and sounds to be encoded and transmitted as patterns of numbers. Raw information—streams of numbers—came to flow rapidly around the world, decoded by machines into forms that have meaning for us, into text, into still and moving images, and into sound. During the 1990s, all those functions became concentrated in personal computers, which in turn were linked to the Internet and through it to the World Wide Web.

The Internet and the World Wide Web began to be colonized by artists almost as soon as they were up and running. Artists circulated e-mails, created Web sites, and wrote software programs as art. Coding gradually became recognized as a new medium, as necessary to making art for the Internet as learning how to use oil paint had been to making art during the Renaissance. Incorporeal and often ephemeral, Internet art exists for a time on the Internet, and although it can be commissioned or sponsored (and often is), it cannot truly be owned or sold.

One of the first pieces of Internet art to earn widespread recognition was a black-and-white, interactive, browser-based work by Olia Lialina called *My Boyfriend Came Back from the War* (**22.29**). Lialina created the work in 1996, the year that frames were added to HTML (HyperText Markup Language, the standard language used to create Web sites). Frames allowed designers to partition a Web page so that it could display more than one HTML document at a time. Lialina created *My Boyfriend Came Back from the War* to take advantage of the narrative possibilities that this new feature opened up. Through images and short sentences displayed in four independent frames, *My Boyfriend Came Back from the War* evokes the awkward conversation of a couple trying to reconnect after having been separated. Users cause the conversation to unfold by clicking on the frames. The low speed of the early Internet caused the frames to load slowly and haltingly, expressing a tentative, painful exchange full of silences.

One effect of the new technology was to expand the possibilities available to video artists. Newly developed digital video projectors allowed videos to be shown

22.29 Olia Lialina. *My Boyfriend Came Back from the War.* 1996. HyperText Markup Language (HTML), frames.
© Olia Lialina

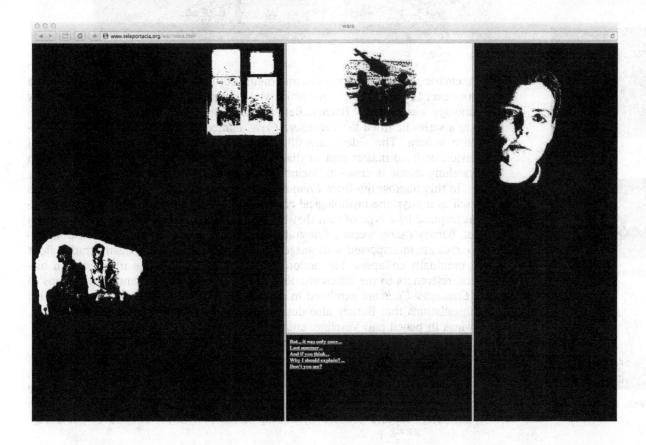

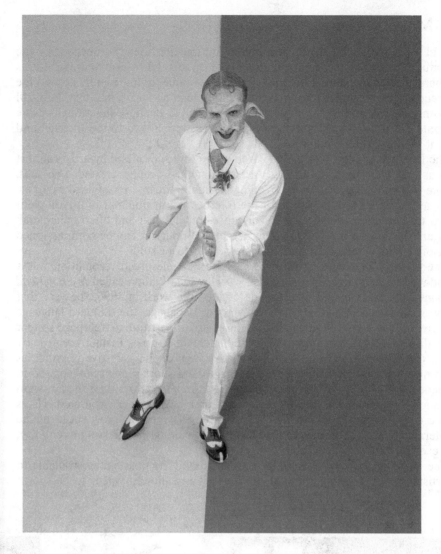

22.30 Matthew Barney. *Cremaster 4*. 1994. Film still.
Production still copyright Matthew Barney. Courtesy the artist and Gladstone Gallery, New York and Brussels. Photo: Michael James O'Brien

RELATED WORKS

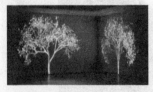

10.13 Curtis, *Graffiti Archaeology*

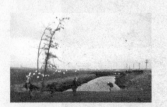

9.24 Bilal, *3rdi*

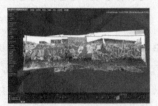

4.55 Steinkamp, *Dervish*

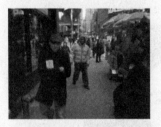

3.28 Wall, *A Sudden Gust of Wind*

at cinematic scale on gallery walls, and digital editing programs gave artists far more control over the final image. One artist who was quick to take advantage of the new technology was Matthew Barney. Between 1994 and 2002, Barney created five videos in a series he titled the *Cremaster Cycle*, named for a muscle in the male reproductive system. The videos are filled with odd characters engaged in unusual behavior, with no master plot or dialog. Barney plays many of the characters. An overarching theme is creation, including human reproduction.

In this photograph from *Cremaster 4* (**22.30**), the first video, Barney presents himself as a satyr, the mythological creature who is part man, part goat. The character is inspired by a type of ram that lives on England's Isle of Man, where the film is set. Barney's satyr wears a fine suit and is attended by fairies. Scenes of a motorcycle race are interspersed with images of the satyr dancing on a disintegrating floor that eventually collapses. The action continues to a final scene invested with biological references to the differentiation of the sexes. When this and other videos of the *Cremaster Cycle* are exhibited in galleries and museums, they are accompanied by installations that Barney also designs that include photographs from the films, drawings in pencil and Vaseline, and sculpture made of plastic and metal.

Digital technology has also opened up new possibilities in traditional media. Christiane Baumgartner's *Luftbild* ("Air Picture," **22.31**) uses woodcut, the oldest printmaking process, to make a technology-inspired image. Working on a large scale, Baumgartner begins with a video still taken by filming the monitor displaying the film. She manipulates the image using software to exaggerate the flickering effects of this image-capture process by adding horizontal lines. She traces the image

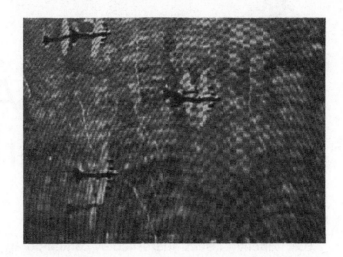

22.31 Christiane Baumgartner. *Luftbild*. 2009. Woodcut, 102 ⅜ × 137 ¹³⁄₁₆".
Christiane Baumgartner © VG Bild-Kunst Bonn/DACS, London, 2018. Courtesy Alan Cristea Gallery, London

onto the wood and cuts the relief print before printing it by hand. Using this technique, the artist slows the fast pace of video and draws attention to the passage of time. The image is true to its source, but it is also distorted by the artist's process. In *Luftbild*, Baumgartner uses a still from a documentary about World War II, choosing a moment depicting fighter planes flying through the sky.

Notes to the Text

1. John Cage, "Experimental Music" (1957), in *Silences* (Middletown, CT: Wesleyan University Press, 1961), p. 12.
2. Hans Richter, *Dada: Art and Anti-Art* (London: Thames & Hudson, 1965), p. 213.
3. Gretchen Berg, "Andy: My True Story," *Los Angeles Free Press*, March 17, 1967, p. 3; quoted in *Andy Warhol: A Retrospective*, ed. Kynaston McShine (New York: Museum of Modern Art, 1989), p. 460.
4. Donald Judd, "Specific Objects," *Arts Yearbook 8* (New York, 1965), pp. 74–82.
5. Eva Hesse, "A Conversation with Eva Hesse" (1970), interview with Cindy Nemser, reprinted in Mignon Nixon and Cindy Nemser, *Eva Hesse* (Cambridge, MA: MIT Press, 2002), pp. 21–22.
6. Robert Morris, "Notes on Sculpture" (1966), reprinted in Gregory Battcock, ed., *Minimal Art: A Critical Anthology* (Berkeley: University of California Press, 1995), p. 234.
7. Walter De Maria, "'The Lightning Field': Some Facts, Notes, Data, Information, Statistics and Statements," *Artforum*, vol. 18, no. 8 (April 1980), p. 52.
8. Miriam Schapiro, "Notes from a Conversation on Art, Feminism, and Work," in *Working It Out: 23 Women Writers, Artists, Scientists, and Scholars Talk About Their Lives and Work*, ed. Sara Ruddick and Pamela Daniels (New York: Pantheon, 1977), p. 296.
9. Quoted in Alan Riding, "Showcasing a Rise from Rebellion to Respectability," *New York Times*, March 5, 2000.

Chapter 23

Contemporary Art around the World

In this chapter, you will learn to

LO1   identify issues addressed by contemporary artists around
       the world.

Beginning in the 19th century and continuing through the 20th, transportation and communications technology made possible by science and industry opened up new possibilities for human interaction, compressing our experience of distance and quickening the pace of daily life. "All distances in time and space are shrinking," wrote the German philosopher Martin Heidegger in 1950, referring to the new phenomenon of air travel. "Man now reaches overnight, in planes, places which formerly took weeks and months of travel."[1] Astonished passengers had voiced similar sentiments about rail travel a century earlier. During the 1960s, when television took its place in homes alongside radio and the telephone, the phrase "global village" was proposed to characterize a worldwide community linked by electronic media. Two decades later, "globalization" came into common use to describe an intensified awareness that the world is being woven into a single place, a sensation reinforced on the most intimate level by the personal computer, the Internet, and the World Wide Web.

Over the course of the same centuries, countries around the world produced art that shared in global trends and respected local traditions. As the countries of Latin America gained their independence across the 19th century, for example, they maintained cultural ties with Europe while continuing to nurture regional art forms. Local modern movements flourished, just as they did in the United States, the Middle East, Africa, and Asia. In Japan, renewed contact with the West split Japanese art into two distinct strains for much of the 20th century: one that continued Japan's own traditions, and another that developed concepts pursued around the world.

As the 20th century drew to a close, the global art world—a term that embraces artists, curators, dealers, collectors, journalists, critics, and other professionals—became even more interconnected. Galleries, museums, and artists established presences on the Internet, and online magazines, newsletters, and blogs about art proliferated. Exhibition spaces opened in such newly energized centers as Tokyo, New Delhi, and Beijing, sometimes linked to galleries in Western art-market centers such as New York and London. The venerable and prestigious international biennial exhibitions of new art hosted by Venice (since 1895) and São Paulo (since 1951) were joined by similarly ambitious events in cities such as Sydney, Istanbul, Dakar, Singapore, Shanghai, Moscow, Seoul, and Berlin, creating an expanded network in which art from many points of origin circulates and becomes known. We close this brief survey of the arts in time by looking at contemporary art in our globalized world.

The Nigerian-British artist Yinka Shonibare, MBE, is known for installations featuring headless mannequins dressed in 18th- or 19th-century-style clothing made of colorful "African" cloth. *Cake Man* (**23.1**) bends under the weight of a tall stack of elaborately decorated cakes that he carries on his back. The gesture he makes with his left hand suggests that he has just tossed the last cake up there. Will the stack topple, or will he try for more? In place of a head he has a smooth black globe that tracks the rise and fall of a skittish stock market. Buy. Sell. Buy. Sell. "*Cake Man* is essentially about greed, the burden of carrying wealth and never having enough," Shonibare says. "Even though it weighs you down, you still want more."[2]

The textiles that Shonibare favors have an intriguing, global history. Although widely used in West Africa for clothing, they are not African in origin. They were first produced around 1900 by the Dutch, who developed them in imitation of the batik cloth made in Indonesia, which was at that time part of their colonial empire. The British soon began producing similar textiles, and both countries marketed them to West Africa, then part of the British and French colonial empires, where they became part of "traditional" dress. Still today, these "typical African" fabrics are made in England and the Netherlands. "Even things that were supposed to represent authentic Africa didn't turn out to fulfill the expectation of authenticity," says Shonibare.[3] The textiles invite us to meditate on the complex back-and-forth of these relationships, which destabilize simple ideas about cultural authenticity and national identity. More generally, they serve as the artist's visual marker. "I use the fabric to connect with my audience," he says. "When they see it, they know it's me talking to them, it's like a voice."[4]

RELATED WORKS

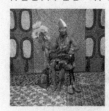

4.40 Fosso, *The Chief*

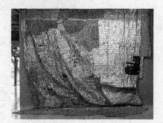

12.21 El Anatsui, *Sasa*

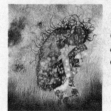

6.15 Mutu, *Hide and Seek, Kill or Speak*

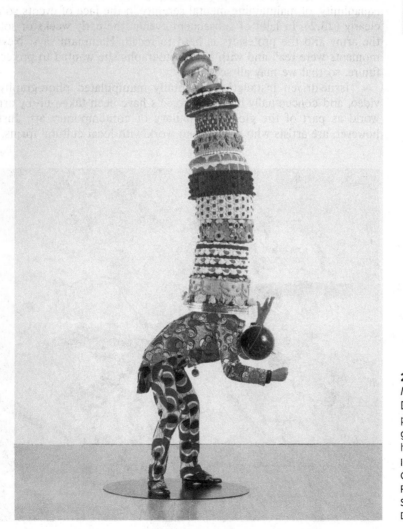

23.1 Yinka Shonibare, MBE. *Cake Man*. 2013. Fiberglass mannequin, Dutch wax-printed cotton textile, plaster, polystyrene, pocket watch, globe, leather, and steel baseplate, height 10' 4".
Image courtesy Stephen Friedman Gallery and Pearl Lam Galleries. Photo Stephen White. © Yinka Shonibare MBE. All Rights Reserved, DACS/ARS, NY 2019

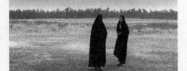

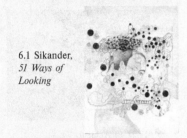

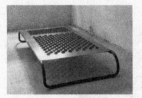

Yinka Shonibare is well positioned to explore cultural influence and cross-influence. Born in London to Nigerian parents, he moved to Nigeria with his family at the age of three, five years after the country had won its independence from Great Britain. Growing up, he spoke Yoruba at home and English at school; the academic year was spent in Africa, but summers were spent in England. "I think those who have actually had that colonial experience shouldn't necessarily be forced to choose one side, because their identity is formed from that mixture," he says. "I see it as making a new kind of global person."[5]

Taking up Shonibare's phrase, Nermine Hammam is also a new kind of global person. Born in Egypt, she was educated in the United Kingdom and the United States before returning to Cairo to live and work. In January 2011, during the early days of the Egyptian Revolution, Hammam went to Tahrir Square to photograph the arrival of the Egyptian army, which had been called in to guarantee order. Along with the protesters occupying the square, she watched with apprehension as the tanks and military vehicles arrived. But when the hatches opened and the vehicles emptied, what emerged were not the fierce, seasoned fighters she had expected but soldiers who were little more than boys—wide-eyed, slender, nervous, disoriented.

During the following weeks, as the protests continued under the protection of the army, Hammam photographed the soldiers in unguarded moments of daydreaming, vulnerability, flirtation, and kindness. "By the end of February, the exhaustion on their youthful faces was tangible," she writes. "I wanted to embrace them, to reassure them that everything would be ok. So I transported them to places in which they might find solace. . . . As an act of homage to these gentle youths, I stuck their images on postcards from all the pleasant destinations in the world."[6] Hammam titled her series of photographs *Upekkha*, after the Buddhist practice of equanimity, of maintaining mental serenity in the face of events so as to see things clearly (**23.2**). In light of subsequent events, the early weeks of solidarity between the army and the protesters is hard to recall, Hammam says. Nevertheless, those moments were real, and with her photographs she wanted to project them into the future, so that we may all see clearly.

Issue-driven installations, digitally manipulated photography, performance, video, and conceptually inspired projects have been taken up by artists around the world as part of the global vocabulary of contemporary art. Just as important, however, are artists who continue to work with local cultural forms, renewing them

23.2 Nermine Hammam. *Armed Innocence II*, from *Cairo Year One: Upekkha*. 2011. Digital print, 24 ⅜ × 33 ⅛".
Courtesy and © Nermine Hammam

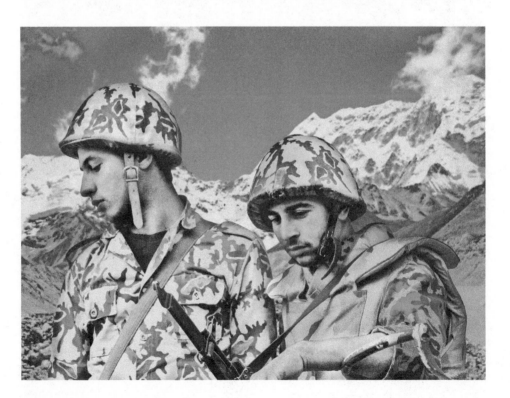

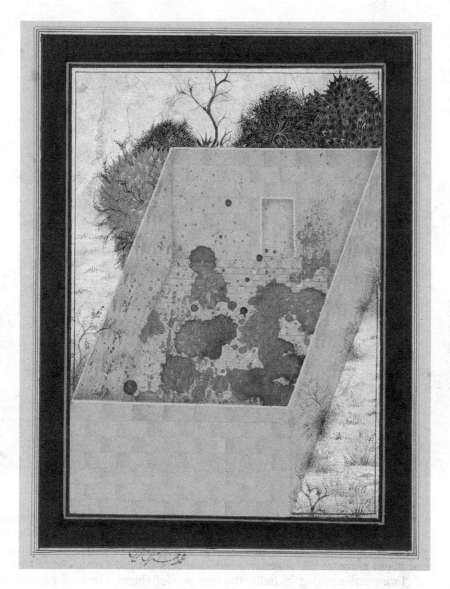

23.3 Imran Qureshi. *Blessings Upon the Land of My Love*, detail. 2011. Diptych: gouache and gold leaf on wasli paper, each painting 16 ⅝ × 13 ⅞".
Courtesy the artist and Corvi-Mora, London

to express contemporary concerns. In Pakistan, students at the National College of Arts in Lahore are required to study traditional Mughal miniature painting for one semester. Some of them become hooked, often to their own surprise.

Imran Qureshi entered the National College of Arts planning to study printmaking, but his professors convinced him that he was unusually gifted at miniature painting, and so he entered the school's rigorous two-year training program. For the first year and a half, students absorb the techniques and visual conventions of Mughal court painting by copying examples from the past. They learn how to make their own brushes and paper and process their own paints. Only during the final months of the program are they allowed to experiment with their own creative direction. In *Blessings Upon the Land of My Love*, Qureshi employs the conventions and techniques of Mughal painting. Notice the isometric perspective, brilliant color, and descriptive details of texture. Instead of picturing the heroic deeds of a king, however, Qureshi uses a Mughal-like style to portray what at first glance appears to be the aftermath of a violent incident (**23.3**). Something awful has occurred, an assassination or a massacre. A closer look, however, reveals that the pools of blood are composed of radiating petals, like flowers.

The painting transposes into another form an installation of the same name that Qureshi created for a biennial held in the emirate of Sharjah, where he covered a large courtyard with red splatters transformed into blossoms. The immediate inspiration for the works was the brutal murder of two young Pakistani boys, beaten

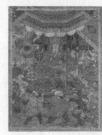

2.6 *Badi'uzzaman Fights Iraj to a Draw*

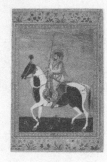

19.13 Payag, *Shah Jahan on Horseback*

541

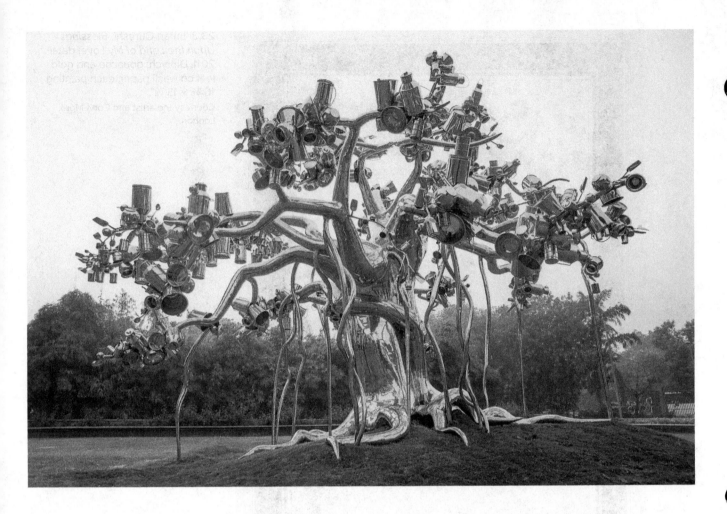

23.4 Subodh Gupta. *Dada*. 2010–14. Stainless steel and stainless-steel utensils, 22' 3 ¹¹⁄₁₆" × 30' 6 ⅛" × 30' 6 ⅛", dimensions variable. Installation view, *Subodh Gupta. Everything is Inside*, National Gallery of Modern Art, New Delhi, India, 2014.
Courtesy the artist and Hauser & Wirth. Photo Rahm Rahman. © Subodh Gupta

to death by an angry mob in broad daylight as a crowd that included members of the local police looked on. Captured on video, the sickening incident sparked a national outcry. The public's reaction seemed to Qureshi a sign of hope, that some good might come of the violence, that flowers might grow from the bloodshed.

From earliest times in India, the blessings of abundance have been celebrated and embodied in art. The facades of Hindu temples swarm with thousands of carved figures of gods and goddesses, radiating spiritual energy into the world (see 19.10). In works such as *Dada* (**23.4**), the Indian artist Subodh Gupta perpetuates his culture's generous aesthetic of abundance in purely secular terms. Named for the Hindu word for "grandfather" as well as the anarchic European art movement, *Dada* depicts a banyan tree, the national tree of India, bristling with stainless-steel pails, canisters, pots, pitchers, bowls, colanders, tiffin carriers, cups, spoons, ladles, and more. Stainless-steel vessels are ubiquitous in India, seen in the streets transporting food, and used at home for cooking and serving everyday meals. Replacing earlier vessels of pottery or copper, they are shining symbols of progress and rising living standards.

Gupta makes his flamboyant, entertaining art from the everyday objects of Indian culture. "There are times when there is nothing other than what is around us that makes us who we are," he writes. "For me, the great thinkers are the common people, with their everyday existence; their hurried lives and makeshift settlements. You must see this as the place I look to be inspired."[7]

Gupta insists that his sculpture is universal in its appeal, and we can certainly enjoy it purely for the spectacle it offers. Nevertheless, a little knowledge about contemporary India adds a layer of meaning, enriching our experience. In the same way, a little knowledge of Chinese history can enrich our experience of Feng Mengbo's *Long March: Restart* (**23.5**). The Long March was a famous event in 20th-century Chinese history, an episode from the prolonged civil war that pitted the Red Army

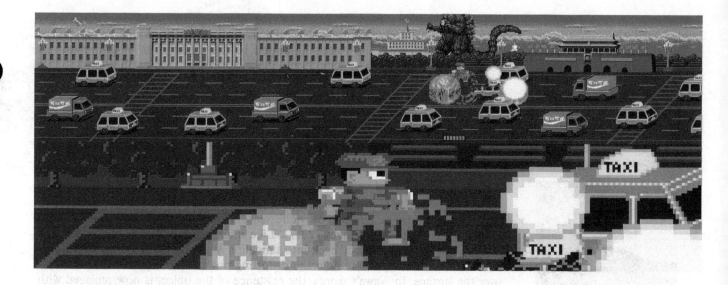

of the Chinese Communist Party against the Kuomintang, the army of the Chinese Nationalist Party, for control of the country. In 1934, encircled by the Kuomintang and certain that an attack was imminent, the Red Army decided on a tactical retreat. Breaking through the encirclement, they headed first west and then north, covering some 8,000 miles of often difficult terrain in 370 days. The march marked the rise to prominence of Mao Zedong (see 19.25), who established the People's Republic of China when the Red Army, now called the People's Liberation Army, finally triumphed in 1949.

Long March: Restart is an interactive video-game installation based on the Long March—but not too closely. The player character, a Red Army soldier, uses such unconventional weapons as Coca-Cola cans and faces such unhistorical enemies as space aliens, demons, and fireball monsters. Projected on an enormous screen approximately 20 feet in height and 80 feet long, *Long March: Restart* dwarfs the gamer and onlookers, who must dash to keep up with the soldier as he zips along from one challenge to another. Feng Mengbo created *Long March: Restart* using the 8-bit technology of the side-scrolling video games of the 1980s. East meets West and communism meets capitalism as icons, scenes, and characters drawn from popular video games of the time mingle with Chinese landmarks, slogans, and characters, as well as famous historical images such as Red Square in Moscow and the American moon landing. Long since superseded, the primitive 8-bit technology is now an object of nostalgia, giving *Long March: Restart* the look of an archaic, if much-loved, game from the past.

The past is a difficult subject in Cambodia, where almost a quarter of the population died of starvation, overwork, torture, or execution during the brutal four-year rule of the Khmer Rouge. The Cambodian sculptor Sopheap Pich was a young child when the Khmer Rouge came to power in 1975. Four years later, his family fled to a refugee camp on the Thai border, and in 1984, they came as refugees to the United States. Pich eventually studied art, earning a master's degree in 1999. In 2002, he moved back to Cambodia.

Pich had been a painter in America, but his work changed when he returned to Cambodia. He turned to two of the most common materials of Cambodian village life—rattan and bamboo—and he began weaving them into sculptural forms. "I sensed I was free from the art history that I knew," he recalls. "Working slowly, I gave up notions of what the final work should be like and what the forms meant."[8] Pich's first woven sculptures were based on the forms of inner organs, reflecting his time as a pre-med student, before he turned to art. He has made Buddhist images as well as memory sculptures of things he saw as a child during the Khmer Rouge years, but he resists pressure to address that time more directly in his work. "I don't believe I went through or saw the trauma the others did," he says simply. "I don't have an adult reading of it."[9]

23.5 Feng Mengbo. *Long March: Restart*. 2008. Video game (color, sound), custom computer software, wireless game controller, dimensions and duration variable. The Museum of Modern Art, New York. 1168.2008. Digital image © The Museum of Modern Art/Licensed by Scala/Art Resource, NY. © Feng Mengbo, courtesy Hanart TZ Gallery

RELATED WORKS

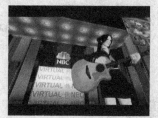

9.25 Cao Fei, *i.Mirror*

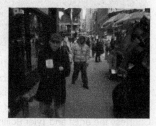

9.24 Bilal, *3rdi*

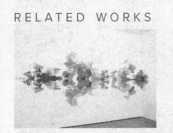

5.6 Kojin, *reflectwo*

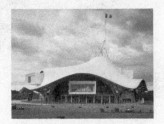

13.32 Ban, Centre Pompidou-Metz

More recently, Pich has been making nonrepresentational works that exist between painting and sculpture. An example is *Fertile Land* (**23.6**). Made of bamboo from the countryside and rattan harvested in the mountains, its grid crossings secured with tight twists of wire, *Fertile Land* is painted with earth pigments that Pich gathers on his travels around Cambodia and mixes with such materials as charcoal, warmed wax, and resin made by boiling sap. Burlap from used rice bags adds texture. Works such as *Fertile Land*, says Pich, "represent for me a kind of distillation of emotion, of remembrance, of reflections on what has influenced me, or the places I have been."[10]

Like many artists today, the Japanese artist Kohei Nawa works in series, each generated by a particular idea or strategy. For his series *PixCell (Beads)*, Nawa begins by searching Internet auction sites and purchasing an object. He thus knows the object only as a two-dimensional image made of pixels on the computer screen. When he receives the object, now quite real, he covers it with glass, crystal, and acrylic spheres of various sizes (**23.7**). Like mutant three-dimensional pixels, the spheres transpose the object back into unreality. We can still sense its broad contours, but detail disappears under the distorting power of the spheres that multiply over the surface. In Nawa's words, the existence of the object is now replaced with a "husk of light" that shows a new vision, the cells of an image, for which he invented the term PixCells.[11]

Nawa's *PixCell (Beads)* series includes toys, musical instruments, shoes, and numerous taxidermy animals. The animals carry a special charge, since they were once alive, and even as taxidermy they retain a lifelike presence and texture. In the context of traditional Japanese culture, *PixCell-Deer* is especially evocative. In Shinto belief, deer appear as messengers of the *kami*, nature spirits and natural phenomena that are worshiped as sacred beings. Deer are also associated with the Buddha, who gave his first sermon at Deer Park.

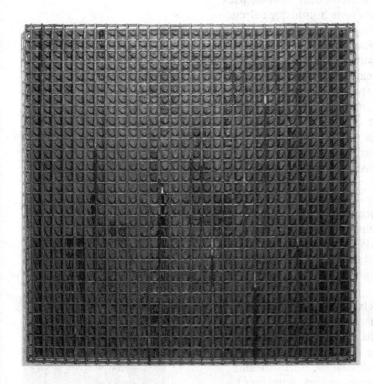

23.6 Sopheap Pich. *Fertile Land*. 2012. Bamboo, rattan, wire, burlap, plastics, beeswax, damar resin, earth pigment, charcoal, and oil paint, 7' 7" × 7' 7" × 3".
Courtesy the artist and Tyler Rollins Fine Art, New York

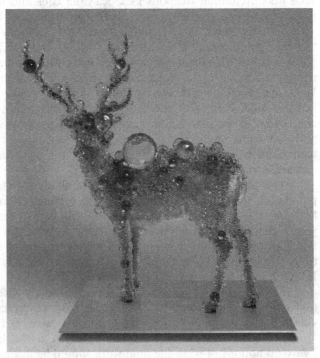

23.7 Kohei Nawa. *PixCell-Deer#24*. 2011. Stuffed deer and artificial crystal glass, height 6' 8 11/16".
The Metropolitan Museum of Art, New York. Purchase, Acquisitions Fund and Peggy and Richard M. Danziger Gift, 2011, 2011.493a–j.
Image copyright © The Metropolitan Museum of Art. Image source: Art Resource, NY

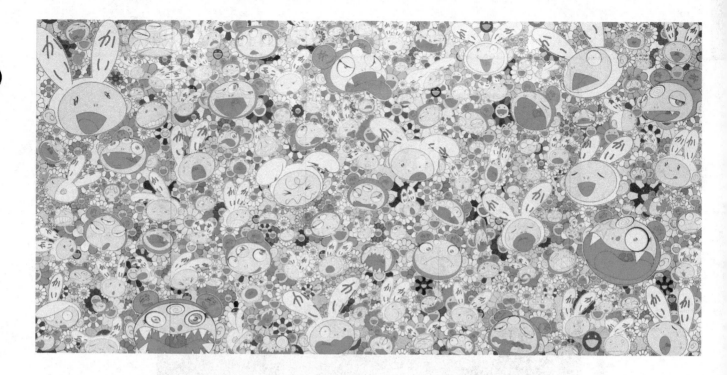

Takashi Murakami draws on contemporary Japanese culture in his art. Like Andy Warhol and Roy Lichtenstein, he loves pop culture, especially what the Japanese call the *otaku* lifestyle, a youthful fascination with toys, games, and cartoons (**23.8**). He is inspired by anime, a style of animation practiced in Japan (*anime* is short for *animation*) characterized by bright colors, vibrant effects, and expressive figures. He also draws on the style and pleasing themes of *ukiyo-e* woodblock prints, as well as the repetitive nature of mass production. In painting, fashion, film, and product design, Murakami's work is decorative, busy, and decadent, with brilliant colors, exaggerated forms, and a commercial feel. At the same time, he offers a critique of modern Japanese culture, which he considers hindered by *otaku*'s juvenile obsessions. The glossy world he creates is a sterile and dystopian society run amok. The smiling faces of toylike forms multiply and overwhelm, choking out anything that does not fit this mold.

Hustle'n'Punch by Kaikai and Kiki is an example of Murakami's "superflat" works. Superflat is a style of painting that was developed by Murakami and gained popularity in Japan and beyond at the beginning of the 2000s. As the name suggests, such works are entirely flat and do not create the illusion of three-dimensional space or forms. Every inch of this canvas is covered in smiling flowers in the bright colors of children's toys. Rabbit-like creatures that Murakami has named Kaikai and Kiki appear among the flowers and display different emotions: happiness, disgust, sadness, confusion, rage, and even a kind of drug-induced euphoria. For Murakami, the painting's lack of depth is a metaphor for the shallowness and emptiness of contemporary Japanese culture. Like a child's fairy tale, the painting attracts us with its cuteness, only revealing its terrifying characters and suffocating abundance upon close inspection.

As a child, the Mexican artist Damián Ortega used to get his older brother in trouble by pestering him to take apart household appliances. As the family toaster lay in dozens of pieces on the counter and his brother was being scolded, Ortega would be looking at the pieces, fascinated by the idea that the objects that lay before him were also a toaster. Ortega's taste for taking things apart accompanied him into adulthood. Most famously, he dismantled an entire car, a Volkswagen Beetle, and suspended the parts from the ceiling in relative position, as though the car had exploded outward in all directions at once.

Ortega takes apart not only objects but also ideas and systems, always to see how they are made. "I like to think that the importance of objects lies in what they

Sales and Value

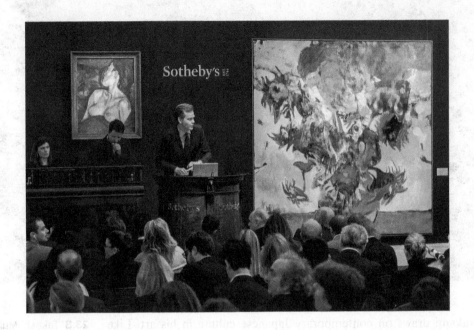

What gives a work of art its value? Should art be treated as an investment? Why does some art command such high prices?

The highest price ever paid at auction for a work of art so far is $450.3 million. A member of the Saudi royal family spent this immense sum in 2017 on a painting of Jesus Christ by the Italian Renaissance artist Leonardo da Vinci. Before this sale, the most anyone had paid for a work of art sold at auction was $179.4 million, for a painting by Pablo Picasso.

Why did these works command such enormous sums? Where does art get its value? There is nothing inherently valuable in a work of art. Most are made of cheap materials: paint, canvas, bronze, stone, paper. Most art can't be melted or broken down and sold for much money.

If high prices are not caused by the materials, what does make art valuable? Art collectors have traditionally been driven by a few basic desires. First, many of them love the art and want to look at it in their homes. Works of art are also status symbols: Owning them proves that you are both wealthy and cultured. Third, and this is a controversial point in the art world, people buy art because they think it will appreciate—which means to increase in value—to be resold.

The prices paid by art collectors are determined by the basic economic principle of supply and demand. When supply of a desired artist's work is low and demand is high, prices rise. But when the supply is high and demand is low, prices fall. Leonardo da Vinci is not around to make any more art. The supply of his art is very low, which means that on the rare occasions when one of his works comes up for sale, the price can go through the roof.

Another factor that contributes to rising art prices is competition between collectors. Since the late 20th century, the number of art collectors has risen dramatically, in part because of the growth of the economies of Russia, China, India, and the Gulf states. With many wealthy people competing to buy the same art, prices rise.

Why does a particular work become coveted? This is a complicated matter. As a rule of thumb, an individual artist's popularity among collectors rises and falls based on current tastes. Today, the art of the late 20th and early 21st century is very popular with bargain-hunting collectors who hope its value will rise. But who knows what will be popular tomorrow?

A contemporary art auction at Sotheby's, London, in 2016. Lucian Freud's *Pregnant Girl* (left) and Adrian Ghenie's *Sunflowers* sold for a hammer price of £14.2m and £2.65m respectively. Stephen Chung/Alamy Stock Photo

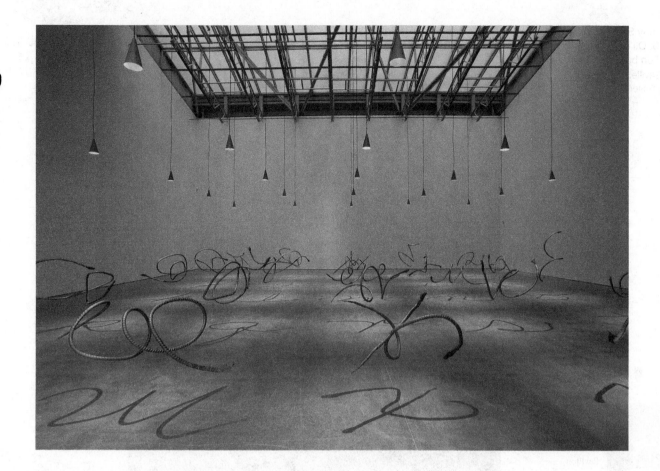

could generate as ideas," he has written. "I once read that, in Sanskrit, the concept of 'thing' is understood as an equivalent of 'event.' I found this incredibly interesting, because it implies playing down the importance of the object to emphasize the importance of its function, its production system, the technology employed in it, and its implications as a cultural and historical product."[12]

In *Harvest* the artist is thinking about language and its representation (**23.9**). Suspended from the ceiling, close to the floor, twenty-five lengths of steel turn and twist in the air—fragments, it seems, of some disaster that has left them broken and deformed. Each one is lit independently from above. Only if we shift our attention from the sculptures to the shadows they cast does sense begin to emerge: Each shadow takes the form of a letter of the alphabet. Ortega asked his mother, a school teacher, to write out the alphabet for him in the beautiful penmanship of her generation and profession. His sculptures reproduce it, but only in shadow. Critics have pointed out that the Latin word for the verb "to read," *legere*, also means to harvest or to gather. In reading, we harvest meaning from symbols, but only after we have the keys we need to decode them. How long might this new alphabet of writhing forms have resisted our attempts to make sense of it? Or might we even have decided that there was no meaning to be found?

Looking back to the art of the Renaissance, the painter Willem de Kooning once said that "flesh was the reason oil painting was invented."[13] Oil paint is uniquely suited to capturing the luminosity, the translucence, the sensual presence of human skin. An admirer of de Kooning, the British painter Jenny Saville cites his remark with approval. Flesh is her subject (**23.10**). Working in a loose, painterly style, Saville paints bodies—women's bodies. She paints them as landscapes of flesh shaped by time, pain, love, desire, illness, deformity, and violence. "I'm trying to find bodies that manifest in their flesh something of our contemporary age," she has said. "I'm drawn to bodies that emanate a sort of state of in-betweenness: a hermaphrodite, a transvestite, a carcass, a half-alive/half-dead head. If they are portraits, they are portraits of an idea or sensation."[14]

23.9 Damián Ortega. *Harvest*. 2013. Steel sculptures and lamps, dimensions variable.

© Damián Ortega. Courtesy Gladstone Gallery, New York and Brussels

RELATED WORKS

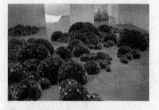

2.21 Donovan, *Untitled (Mylar)*

23.10 Jenny Saville. *Rosetta 2*. 2005–06. Oil on watercolor paper, mounted on board, 8' 3 ¼" × 6' 1 ¾".
© Jenny Saville. Courtesy of Gagosian Gallery

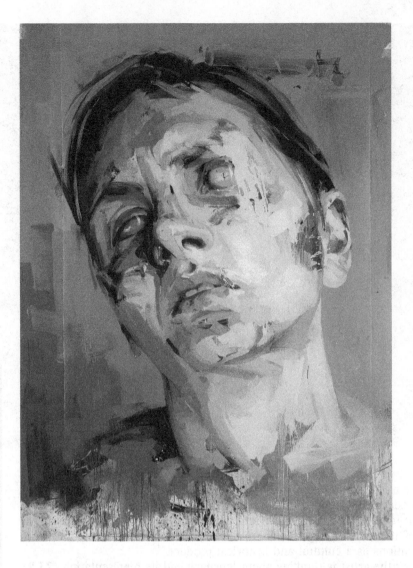

RELATED WORKS

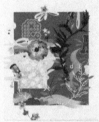

13.33 Hadid, Burnham Pavilion

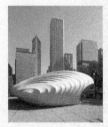

6.5 Ofili, *Prince Amongst Thieves with Flowers*

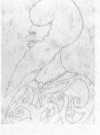

8.18 Rae, *Cute Motion!!*

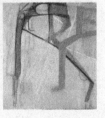

7.8 Sillman, *Nut*

Saville prefers working from photographs to working from a live model. She collects vast numbers of photographs, some of which she has taken herself, others of which she culls from medical textbooks, forensic science books, and the media. She has observed surgeons at work to understand what it is to cut into and enter a body. Her monumental paintings are often as disturbing as they are compelling. Their scale engulfs the viewer, and Saville intends this. She hopes that viewers will approach until the image dissolves in an intense, all-encompassing awareness of the sensuous physicality of the paint itself and the varied markings and densities on the surface.

The Brazilian sculptor Ernesto Neto has said that the space he would most like to create a work for, his ideal interior, would be a cave. Looking at *Leviathan Thot*, a sculpture he was invited to create for temporary installation in the Pantheon in Paris, we can see why he might feel that way. *Leviathan Thot* (**23.11**) transformed the Pantheon's cavernous Neoclassical interior into a sensuous, mysterious place filled with pendulous, organic forms. Weighted by sand and white plastic beads, elongated nylon sacks hung like soft, translucent stalactites from an openwork fabric membrane overhead, stretching it, tugging at it, opening it up in space, here like a web, there like a tent. "Leviathan" names a sea monster. Perhaps it has swallowed us up. The building has become a body, and we are inside.

Neto refers to the sacks in this work as columns, suggesting that we think of them in relation to the building's own columns, some of which are visible in the photograph shown here. The Pantheon's columns push upward against gravity, lifting the load of the vaulted ceilings and the central dome to open up an interior

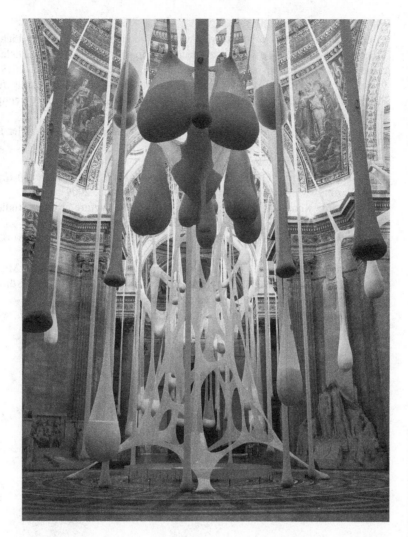

RELATED WORKS

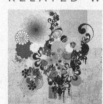

7.12 Milhazes, *Mariposa*

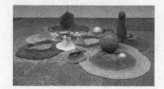

12.20 Nepomuceno, *Untitled*

space. Neto's sculpture works with gravity, is created by gravity, which pulls the elements earthward and gives the work form. "Every work I make is always about a relationship," he says. "One element interferes with the other element . . . and the result is a sociability from one to the other, so you should have an interaction that achieves a limit—a precise balance before equilibrium is lost."[15] Neto thinks of his work as a dance, another art of gravity, grace, balance, and interaction. "I always have a plan, but it's like the plan for a journey," he explains. "Once you're on the road, you change things. If nothing changes, if you end up with something that's just as you planned it, then you haven't created art."[16]

Notes to the Text

1. Martin Heidegger, "The Thing" (1950), trans. Albert Hofstadter, in *Poetry, Language, Thought* (New York: Harper & Row, 1971), p. 165.

2. Quoted in Stephanie Bailey, "Let Them Eat Cake: Interview with Yinka Shonibare," *ArtAsiaPacific*, January 3, 2014. Reproduced with permission.

3. Quoted in Richard Lacayo, "Decaptivating," *Time*, July 6, 2009. Reproduced with permission.

4. Quoted in Coline Milliard, "Yinka Shonibare MBE: Same But Different," *Catalogue*, Issue 1, September 2009. Reproduced with permission.

5. Quoted in Bailey, "Let Them Eat Cake." Reproduced with permission.

6. Nermine Hammam, "Upekkha: Artist Statement," www.nerminehammam.com. Reproduced with permission.

7. Quoted in *Subodh Gupta: The Imaginary Order of Things*, trans. by Laura A. E. Suffield

(Málaga: CAC Málaga, 2013), p. 121.

8. Quoted in Lisa Pollman, "Interview with Cambodian Artist Sopheap Pich: Sculpting with Bamboo," May 28, 2014. Available at theculturetrip.com/asia/cambodia/articles/interview-with-cambodian-artist-sopheap-pich-sculpting-with-bamboo, accessed April 27, 2018.

9. Quoted in Claire Knox, "Going Against the Grid: Moving Art Away from the Khmer Rouge," *The Phnom Penh Post*, November 30, 2012. Available at phnompenhpost.com/7days/going-against-grid-moving-art-away-khmer-rouge, accessed April 27, 2018.

10. Quoted in the press release for the exhibition *Sopheap Pich: Reliefs*, Tyler Rollins Fine Art, April 18–June 14, 2013.

11. Kohei Nawa, www.kohei-nawa.net. Reproduced with permission.

12. Quoted in Damián Ortega and Jessica Morgan, *Do It Yourself: Damián Ortega* (New York: Skira Rizzoli, with Institute of Contemporary Art, Boston, 2009), p. 168.

13. Willem de Kooning, "The Renaissance and Order," lecture given at Studio 35, 1949, published in *trans/formation*, vol. 1, no. 2 (1951), pp. 85–87.

14. Simon Schama, "Interview with Jenny Saville," in *Jenny Saville* (New York: Rizzoli, 2005), p. 124.

15. "Artworker of the Week #63: Ernesto Neto," an interview with Erin Mann, *Kultureflash*, no. 187, December 12, 2006, https://web.archive.org/web/20071015100715/http://kultureflash.net:80/archive/187/priview.html, accessed March 14, 2018.

16. Quoted in Dan Horch, "In the Studio: Ernesto Neto," *Art + Auction*, May 2008, p. 70. Reproduced with permission.

Pronunciation Guide

This guide offers pronunciations for names and foreign terms appearing in the text. It uses the sounds available in standard North American English to approximate the original languages. The phonetic system includes the following conventions:

ah—spa, hurrah
air—pair, there
an—plan, tan
aw—thaw, autumn
ay—play, say

dj—jump, bridge
j—mirage, barrage
eh—pet, get
er—her, fur
oh—toe, show

ow—cow, how
uh—bus, fuss
ye—pie, sky

Aachen AHK-en
Abakanowicz, Magdalena MAG-dah-LAY-nuh ah-bah-kah-NOH-vitch
Ahmed, Faig FAYG AHK-med
Akan AH-kahn
Akhenaten AH-keh-NAH-ten
Alberti, Leon Battista LAY-on bah-TEES-tuh ahl-BAIR-tee
Alhambra ahl-AHM-bruh
Anatsui, El el ah-nah-TSOO-ee
Andokides ahn-DOH-kee-dayz
Anguissola, Sofonisba soh-foh-NEEZ-bah ahn-gwee-SOH-lah
Antoni, Janine jah-NEEN an-TOH-nee
Aphrodite ah-froh-DYE-tee
Apoxyomenos ah-PAHK-see-oh-MEN-ohs
Ariwajoye ah-ree-wah-DJOH-yay
Arnolfini ahr-nohl-FEE-nee
Artemidoros ar-teh-mee-DOR-ohs
Asante ah-SAHN-tay
Athena Nike uh-THEE-nuh NYE-kee
Aurelius, Marcus aw-REE-lee-oos
auteur oh-TER
Avalokiteshvara ah-vah-loh-kih-TESH-vahr-uh
avant-garde AH-vawn GARD
Badi'uzzaman bah-DEE-OOZ-(ah)-MAHN
bas-relief BAH ruh-LYEF
Baule BOW-lay
Baumgartner, Christiane BOWM-gart-ner
Bellini, Giovanni djoh-VAHN-ee bell-EE-nee
Benin beh-NEEN
Bernini, Gianlorenzo djahn-loh-REN-zoh bayr-NEE-nee
Beuys, Joseph YOH-sef BOYZ
Bilal, Wafaa WAH-fah bee-LAHL
Bilbao bil-BAH-oh
Boccioni, Umberto oom-BAIR-toh boh-CHOH-nee
bodhisattva boh-dih-SUT-vuh
Borromini, Francesco frahn-CHESS-koh boh-roh-MEE-nee
Bosch, Hieronymus heer-AHN-ih-mus BAHSH
Botticelli, Sandro SAN-droh bot-ee-CHEL-ee
Bourgeois, Louise boor-JWAH
Brancusi, Constantin KAHN-stan-teen BRAHN-koosh; also, brahn-KOO-zee
Braque, Georges jorj BRAHK
Breuer, Marcel mahr-SELL BROY-er

Bronzino, Agnolo AHN-yoh-loh brahn-ZEE-noh
Bruegel, Pieter PEE-tur BROO-g'l; also, BROY-g'l
buon fresco boo-OHN FRES-koh
Byodo-in BYOH-doh-een
Callot, Jacques jahk kah-LOH
camera obscura KAM-er-uh ob-SKOOR-uh
Campin, Robert KAHM-pin
Caravaggio kah-rah-VAH-djoh
Carriera, Rosalba roh-SAHL-bah cah-RAY-rah
Cartier-Bresson, Henri awn-ree KAR-tee-ay bress-AWN
Cellini, Benvenuto behn-veh-NOO-toh cheh-LEE-nee
Cézanne, Paul POHL say-ZAHN
Chartres SHAR-tr'
Chauvet shoh-VAY
chiaroscuro kee-AH-roh-SKOOR-oh
Chihuly, Dale chi-HOO-lee
Cimabue chee-mah-BOO-ay
Coatlicue kwaht-LEE-kway
contrapposto trah-POH-stoh
Córdoba KOR-doh-buh
Courbet, Gustave goos-TAHV koor-BAY
Daguerre, Louis-Jacques-Mandé loo-ee JAHK mahn-DAY dah-GAIR
dai Libri, Giovanni djoh-VAHN-ee die LEE-bree
Dalí, Salvador sal-vah-DOHR DAH-lee
Dasavanta duh-shuh-VUHN-tuh
Daumier, Honoré OH-noh-ray DOH-mee-ay
David, Jacques-Louis jahk loo-EE dah-VEED
De Chirico, Giorgio DJOR-djoh deh-KEER-ee-koh
Deen Dayal, Lala LAH-lah deen DIE-ahl
Degas, Edgar ed-GAHR deh-GAH
de Kooning, Elaine duh KOON-ing
de Kooning, Willem VILL-um duh KOON-ing
Delacroix, Eugène uh-ZHEN duh-lah-KWAH
de La Tour, Georges jorj duh-lah-TUHR
De Maria, Walter dih-MAH-ree-uh
di Bartolomeo, Michelozzo mee-keh-LOH-tzo dee bahr-toh-loh-MAY-oh
diptych DIP-tik
dipylon DIH-pih-lon
Dogon doh-GAWN
Donatello dohn-ah-TELL-oh

Duccio doo-choh
Duchamp, Marcel mahr-sell doo-shawm
Dürer, Albrecht ahl-brekt door-er
Eakins, Thomas ay-kins
facade fuh-sahd
Fairey, Shepard fay-ree
Fanipdas fahn-neep-dahs
Fante fahn-tay
Fauve fohv
Feng Mengbo fung mung-boh
Flavin, Dan flay-vin
Fragonard, Jean-Honoré jawn aw-nor-ay fra-goh-nahr
Frankenthaler, Helen frank-en-thahl-er
fresco secco fres-koh sek-oh
Gauguin, Paul pohl goh-gan
Gehry, Frank gay-ree
Genji Monogatari gehn-jee mohn-oh-geh-tahr-ee
Gentileschi, Artemisia ahr-tuh-mee-zhuy djen-teel-ess-kee
Giorgione djor-djoh-nay
Giotto djoh-toh
Gijsbrechts, Cornelius Norbertus kohr-nay-lee-uhs nohr-bayr-tuhs
  hyes-brekts
Girodet de Roucy-Trioson, Anne-Louis djee-roh-day duh roo-see
  tree-oh-zohn
gouache gwahsh
Goya, Francisco de frahn-siss-koh day goy-ah
El Greco el gray-koh
Grien, Hans Baldung green
grisaille gree-zye
Grosse, Katharina kah-tah-ree-nah groh-suh
Grotjahn, Mark groht-djahn
Grünewald, Matthias mah-tee-ess groon-eh-vahlt
Guanyin gwahn-yeen
Guernica gwair-nih-kuh
Gupta, Subodh soo-bohd goop-tuh
Gutenberg, Johannes joh-hah-nehs goo-tehn-behrg
Hadid, Zaha zah-hah hah-deed
Hagia Sophia hye-uh soh-fee-uh
Hammam, Nermine nair-meen hah-mahm
Hamzanama hahm-zah-nah-mah
Hardouin-Mansart, Jules djool ahr-dwahn-mahn-sahr
Haruka Kojin hah-roo-kah koh-djin
Hasegawa Tōhaku ha-suh-gah-wuh toh-hah-koo
Hassam, Childe chyld hah-sahm
Hatoum, Mona hah-toom
Heian hay-ahn
Heiji Monogatari hay-djee mohn-oh-geh-tahr-ee
Hesse, Eva ay-vuh hess
Hiroshige, Ando ahn-doh heer-oh-shee-gay
Hokusai, Katsushika kat-s'-shee-kah hoh-k'-sye
Holbein, Hans hahns hohl-byne
Hon'ami Kōetsu hoh-nah-mee ko-eh-tsoo
Horyu-ji hor-yoo-djee
Huizong hway-dzung
hypostyle hye-poh-styel
Ife ee-fay
ijele ee-jay-lay
Iktinos ik-tin-ohs
Inca ing-keh
Ingres, Jean-Auguste-Dominique jawn oh-goost dohm-een-eek
  ang-gr'
intaglio in-tahl-yoh
Iraj ee-raj
Ise ee-say
iwan ee-wahn
Jacquette, Yvonne ee-vahn dja-ket
Jahangir ja-hahn-geer

Jain djayn
Jnanadakini ee-nuh-nuh-duh-kee-nee
Jocho djoh-choh
Kahlo, Frida free-da kah-loh
Kahn, Asif ah-seef kahn
Kaikei kye-kay
Kairouan kair-wahn
Kallikrates kah-lik-rah-teez
Kandariya Mahadeva kahn-dahr-yuh mah-hah-day-vuh
Kandinsky, Vasili vah-see-lee kan-din-skee
Kapoor, Anish ah-neesh kah-puhr
Käsebier, Gertrude gayr-trood kay-seh-beer
kente ken-tay
Khamerernebty kah-mair-air-neb-tee
Khusrau koos-row
Klimt, Gustav goos-tahv kleemt
Knossos naw-sos
Koblin, Aaron koh-blin
Kollwitz, Käthe kay-tuh kohl-vitz
Korot, Beryl bay-ril koh-roh
Kruger, Barbara kroo-ger
Kuma, Kengo keng-goh koo-mah
Lakshmana lahk-shmah-nah
Lange, Dorothea lang
Lascaux las-coh
Le Brun, Charles sharl le-bru(n)h
Le Corbusier luh kohr-boo-(zee)-ay
Lenzlinger, Jörg yohrg laynz-leen-gehr
Leonardo da Vinci lay-oh-nahr-doh dah veen-chee
Lialina, Olia oh-lee-ah lee-ah-lee-nah
Li Cheng lee cheng
Limbourg lam-boor
Lippi, Filippino fee-lee-pee-noh leep-pee
Louvre loov-r'
Lysippos lye-sip-os
Machu Picchu mah-choo peek-choo
Maderno, Carlo cahr-loh mah-dayr-noh
Mahavira mah-hah-vee-ruh
Manet, Édouard ayd-wahr mah-nay
Manohar mah-noh-hahr
Mapplethorpe, Robert may-p'l-thorp
Martínez, María & Julián mah-ree-uh & hoo-(lee)-ahn mahr-tee-nez
Masaccio mah-zah-choh
Matisse, Henri ahn-ree mah-tees
Maya mah-yah
Mehretu, Julie mair-eh-too
Mellan, Claude clohd may-lohn
Mendieta, Ana ah-nah mehn-dee-ai-tah
Menkaure men-kow-ray
Mesa Verde may-suh vair-day
Messager, Annette mess-ah-jay
mezzotint met-zoh-tint
Michelangelo mye-kel-an-jel-oh; *also,* mee-kel-ahn-jel-oh
mihrab mi-hrahb
Milhazes, Beatriz bay-ah-treez meel-yah-zess
Mimbres mim-bres
Miró, Joan hwahn meer-oh
Moche moh-chay
Modersohn-Becker, Paula moh-der-zun bek-er
Mondrian, Piet peet mohn-dree-ahn
Monet, Claude clohd moh-nay
Morimura, Yasumasa yah-soo-mah-sah moh-ree-moo-rah
Morisot, Berthe bayr-t' mohr-ee-zoh
Muafangejo, John moo-fahn-geh-joh
Mughal moo-gahl
Munch, Edvard ed-vahrd moonk
Murakami, Saburo sah-boo-roh moo-ruh-kah-mee

Murakami, Takashi tah-KAH-shee moo-ruh-KAH-mee
Muromachi MOOR-oh-MAH-chee
Mutu, Wangechi wang-GAY-shi moo-too
Muybridge, Eadweard ED-werd MY-bridj
Mycenae my-SEEN-ay, or my-SEEN-ee
Navajo NAH-vah-hoh
Nefertiti NEF-er-TEE-tee
Nepomuceno, Maria nap-oh-moo-SAY-noh
Neto, Ernesto NET-toh
Ni Zan nee DZAHN
nkisi nkondi en-KEE-see en-KOHN-dee
Nouvel, Jean jawne NOO-vail
Ofili, Chris oh-FEE-lee
Oldenburg, Claes klahs
Olmec OHL-mek
Olowe of Ise OH-loh-way of EE-say
Orozco, José Clemente hoh-SAY clay-MAYN-tay oh-ROH-scoh
Osorio, Pepón pay-POHN oh-ZOH-ree-oh
Paik, Nam June nahm djoon PYEK
Palenque pah-LENG-kay
Pantokrator pan-TAW-kruh-ter
Pérez de Aguilar, Antonio ahn-TOH-nee-oh PAY-rays duh AH-gee-lahr
Pettibon, Raymond PEH-tee-bahn
Piano, Renzo PYAH-noh
Piranesi, Giovanni Battista djoh-VAHN-eee bah-TEE-stah
  pee-rah-NAY-see
pointillism PWAN-tee-ism; also, POYN-till-izm
Pollock, Jackson PAHL-uck
Pompeii pahm-PAY
Pont du Gard pohn doo GAHR
Posada, José Guadalupe ho-SAY wah-dah-LOO-paye poh-SAH-dah
Puryear, Martin PUHR-yer
qibla KIB-luh
Qur'an koor-'AHN
Rae, Fiona fee-OH-nuh RAY
raigo rye-GOH
Rama RAH-mah
Raphael RAHF-yell; also, RAF-fye-ell
Rathnasambhava ruht-nuh-SUHM-buh-vuh
Rauschenberg, Robert ROW-shen-burg
Renoir, Pierre-Auguste pyair oh-GOOST rehn-WAHR
Rheims RANS
rhyton RYE-ton
Riemenschneider, Tilman TEEL-mahn REE-men-shnye-der
Rigaud, Hyacinthe YAH-sahnth REE-good
Rivera, Diego dee-AY-goh ree-VAIR-uh
Rococo roh-coh-COH
Rodchenko, Aleksandr roh-CHEHN-koh
Rodin, Auguste oh-GOOST roh-DAN
Rongxi rong-HSEE
Rousseau, Henri (le Douanier) ahn-REE roo-SOH (luh dwahn-YAY)
Ruscha, Ed roo-SHAY
Ryoan-ji RYOH-ahn-djee
Sahagún, Bernadino de behr-nah-DEE-noh day sah-ah-GOON
Sainte-Chapelle sant shah-PELL
Sainte-Foy sant FWAH
Salcedo, Doris DO-ris sal-SAY-doh
San Vitale san vee-TAHL-ay
Saville, Jenny SA-vil
Scher, Paula PAW-lah SHAYR
Seurat, Georges jorj sur-RAH
sfumato sfoo-MAH-toh
Shiva Nataraja SHEE-vuh NAH-tah-rah-juh
shōin SHOH-een
Shonibare, Yinka YING-kuh shoh-nee-BAHR-ay
Shravana SHRUH-vuh-nuh
Sikander, Shahzia SHAHZ-yuh sik-AN-dur

Sorolla y Bastida, Joaquín wah-KEEN soh-ROH-ya ee bah-STEE-dah
Sōtatsu, Nonomura noh-noh-MOOR-ah SOH-taht-s'
Steiner, Gerda GAYR-dah SHTYE-nayr
Stieglitz, Alfred STEEG-litz
stupa STOO-puh
Suh, Do Ho doh hoh suh
al-Suhrawardi, Ahmad AHK-mahd ah-soo-rah-WAHR-dee
Sze, Sarah zee
Taj Mahal tahj meh-HAHL
tathagata tah-tah-GAH-tah
Teotihuacán tay-OH-tee-hwah-CAHN
Titian TISH-an; also, TEE-shan
Todai-ji toh-DYE-djee
Toulouse-Lautrec, Henri de awn-REE duh too-LOOZ loh-TREK
trompe-l'oeil tromp-LOY
Tutankhamun toot-an-KAH-mun
Utamaro, Kitagawa kee-TAH-gah-wuh oo-TAH-mah-roh
Utzon, Jørn yern OOT-suhn
Valdés Leal, Juan de (hoo)-AHN day vahl-DAYS lay-AHL
Van Eyck, Jan YAHN van IKE
Van Gogh, Vincent van GOH; also, van GAWK
Van Herpen, Iris van HER-pehn
Van Ruisdael, Jacob YAH-cub van ROYS-dahl
Velasco, José María hoh-SAY mah-REE-ah vay-LAH-sko
Velázquez, Diego DYAY-goh vay-LASS-kess
Vermeer, Johannes yoh-HAH-ness vair-MAYR; also, vair-MEER
Verrocchio, Andrea del ahn-DRAY-ah del veh-ROH-kyo
Versailles vair-SYE
Vigée-Lebrun, Élisabeth ay-leez-eh-BETT vee-JAY leh-BRUN
Vishnu VISH-noo
Wang Jian wang JYAHN
Watteau, Antoine ahn-TWAHN wah-TOH; also, vah-TOH
Willendorf VILL-en-dohrf
Wojnarowicz, David voy-nyah-ROH-vitz
Xoc shawk
Xue, Lei lay shway
Yoruba YAW-roo-buh
Yucatán yoo-cuh-TAN
Zahadolzha zah-ha-DOHL-jah
Zhao Mengfu jow meng-FOO
Zhou Dynasty JOH
ziggurat ZIG-oor-aht

Suggested Readings

ON THE INTERNET

Many of the museums credited in the captions to the images in this book maintain Web sites. The most extensive museum sites offer a variety of resources such as online collections, thematic tours, timelines, informative texts and essays, glossaries, artists' biographies, video clips, and podcasts. Sites worth exploring in depth include those of the Metropolitan Museum of Art (metmuseum.org), the Museum of Modern Art (moma.org), the museums of the Smithsonian Institution (si.edu), the Art Institute of Chicago (artic.edu), the British Museum (britishmuseum.org), the Tate (tate.org.uk), and the J. Paul Getty Museum (getty.edu). Links to museums around the world can be found at artcyclopedia.com under "Art Museums Worldwide."

Most of the galleries credited in the captions maintain Web sites where recent works by contemporary artists can be viewed. Articles and press releases about the work may also be featured. Many individual artists maintain Web sites, as do a number of periodicals, including *Artforum*, *Art in America*, and *ARTnews*.

YouTube and other video-sharing sites feature numerous interviews with artists, tours of installations and works of architecture, and clips of video art. Particularly noteworthy is the United Nations Educational, Scientific, and Cultural Organization channel (UNESCO TV, youtube.com/user/unesco), which features videos of designated World Heritage properties such as the Alhambra and the Taj Mahal, and videos of Intangible Cultural Heritage items such as African masquerades.

Smarthistory.org offers videos and explanations of works of art and architecture from prehistory to the present. Objects are organized by art historical period and the entries feature links to additional images. For contemporary art, Art21.org has interviews with artists, organized by the themes that the artists explore in their work.

The Google Arts & Culture project (google.com/culturalinstitute/beta) brings together more than 32,000 works from over 150 participating institutions. Images labeled "gigapixel" can be enlarged to show details so fine that they escape the naked eye. Many of the institutions can also be explored room by room, showing how artworks are installed in their galleries.

GENERAL REFERENCE

Barnet, Sylvan. *A Short Guide to Writing about Art*, 11th ed. Upper Saddle River, NJ: Pearson, 2015.

Chilvers, Ian. *The Oxford Dictionary of Art and Artists*, 4th ed. Oxford: Oxford University Press, 2009.

Clarke, Michael. *The Concise Dictionary of Art Terms*, 2nd ed. Oxford: Oxford University Press, 2010.

Nelson, Robert S., and Richard Shiff, eds. *Critical Terms for Art History*, 2nd ed. Chicago: University of Chicago Press, 2003.

Turner, Jane, ed. *The Dictionary of Art*. 34 volumes. Oxford: Oxford University Press, 2003. Also available online by subscription at oxfordartonline.com.

PART 1
INTRODUCTION

Anderson, Richard L. *Calliope's Sisters: A Comparative Study of Philosophies of Art*, 2nd ed. Upper Saddle River, NJ: Pearson, 2004.

Arnheim, Rudolf. *Visual Thinking*, 1969. Berkeley: University of California Press, 2004.

Barrett, Terry. *Interpreting Art: Reflecting, Wondering, and Responding*. New York: McGraw-Hill, 2002.

Berger, John. *Ways of Seeing*. London: Penguin Books, 1990.

Carroll, Noël, ed. *Theories of Art Today*. Madison: University of Wisconsin Press, 2000.

Dutton, Denis. *The Art Instinct: Beauty, Pleasure, and Human Evolution*. New York: Bloomsbury Press, 2009.

Eldridge, Richard. *An Introduction to the Philosophy of Art*. Cambridge: Cambridge University Press, 2003.

Freeland, Cynthia. *Art Theory: A Very Short Introduction*. Oxford: Oxford University Press, 2007.

Shiner, Larry. *The Invention of Art: A Cultural History*. Chicago: University of Chicago Press, 2001.

Shipps, Steve. *(Re)Thinking "Art": A Guide for Beginners*. Oxford: Blackwell, 2008.

PART 2
THE VOCABULARY OF ART

Albers, Josef. *Interaction of Color*, 1963. New Haven: Yale University Press, 2006.

Arnheim, Rudolf. *The Power of the Center: A Study of Composition in the Visual Arts*. Berkeley: University of California Press, 2009.

Elam, Kimberly. *Geometry of Design: Studies in Proportion and Composition*, 2nd ed. New York: Princeton Architectural Press, 2011.

Gage, John. *Color and Meaning: Art, Science, and Symbolism*. Berkeley: University of California Press, 1999.

Puttfarken, Thomas. *The Discovery of Pictorial Composition*. New Haven: Yale University Press, 2000.

PART 3
TWO-DIMENSIONAL MEDIA

Baldwin, Gordon. *Looking at Photographs: A Guide to Technical Terms*, rev. ed. Los Angeles: J. Paul Getty Museum, 2009.

Barsam, Richard. *Looking at Movies: An Introduction to Film*, 4th ed. New York: Norton, 2012.

Doherty, Tiama, and Anne T. Woollett. *Looking at Paintings: A Guide to Technical Terms*, 2nd ed. Los Angeles: J. Paul Getty Museum, 2009.

Eskilson, Stephen J. *Graphic Design: A New History*, 2nd ed. New Haven: Yale University Press, 2012.

Fuga, Antonella. *Artists' Techniques and Materials*. Oxford: Oxford University Press, 2006.

Gascoigne, Bamber. *How to Identify Prints*, 2nd ed. London: Thames & Hudson, 2004.

Greene, Rachel. *Internet Art*. London: Thames & Hudson, 2004.

Hirsch, Robert. *Seizing the Light: A Social History of Photography*, 2nd ed. New York: McGraw-Hill, 2008.

Krug, Margaret. *An Artist's Handbook: Materials and Techniques*. London: Laurence King, 2012.

Lambert, Susan. *Prints: Art and Techniques*. London: V&A Publications, 2001.

Paul, Christiane. *Digital Art*, 2nd ed. London: Thames & Hudson, 2008.

Rush, Michael. *New Media in Art*, 2nd ed. London: Thames & Hudson, 2005.

PART 4

THREE-DIMENSIONAL MEDIA

Ballantyne, Andrew. *Architecture: A Very Short Introduction*. Oxford: Oxford University Press, 2002.

Beardsley, John. *Earthworks and Beyond: Contemporary Art in the Landscape*, 4th ed. New York: Abbeville Press, 2006.

Bishop, Claire. *Installation Art: A Critical History*. New York: Routledge, 2005.

Ching, Francis D. K. *A Visual Dictionary of Architecture*, rev. and expanded ed. Hoboken, NJ: Wiley, 2011.

Cooper, Emmanuel. *Ten Thousand Years of Pottery*, 4th ed. Philadelphia: University of Pennsylvania Press, 2010.

Fariello, M. Anna, and Paula Owen, eds. *Objects and Meaning: New Perspectives on Art and Craft*. Lanham, MD: Scarecrow Press, 2004.

Gissen, David, ed. *Big & Green: Toward Sustainable Architecture in the 21st Century*. New York: Princeton Architectural Press; Washington, D.C.: National Building Museum, 2002.

Harris, Jennifer, ed. *5000 Years of Textiles*. 1993. Washington, D.C.: Smithsonian Books, 2011.

Iwamoto, Lisa. *Digital Fabrications: Architectural and Material Techniques*. New York: Princeton Architectural Press, 2009.

Kaplan, Wendy. *The Arts & Crafts Movement in Europe & America: Design for the Modern World*. New York: Thames & Hudson in association with the Los Angeles County Museum of Art, 2004.

Keverne, Roger, ed. *Jade*. Leicester: Anness, 2010.

Magliaro, Joseph, and Shu Hung, eds. *By Hand: The Use of Craft in Contemporary Art*. New York: Princeton Architectural Press, 2007.

Mills, John W. *Encyclopedia of Sculpture Techniques*. London: B. T. Batsford, 2005.

Raizman, David. *History of Modern Design*, 2nd ed. Upper Saddle River, NJ: Pearson, 2010.

Salvadori, Mario. *Why Buildings Stand Up*. New York: Norton, 2002.

Schoeser, Mary. *World Textiles: A Concise History*. London: Thames & Hudson, 2003.

Stang, Alanna, and Christopher Hawthorne. *The Green House: New Directions in Sustainable Architecture*. New York: Princeton Architectural Press, 2005.

Tait, Hugh. *Five Thousand Years of Glass*, rev. ed. Philadelphia: University of Pennsylvania Press, 2004.

Trench, Lucy, ed. *Materials and Techniques in the Decorative Arts: An Illustrated Dictionary*. Chicago: University of Chicago Press, 2000.

Williams, Arthur. *The Sculpture Reference Illustrated: Contemporary Techniques, Terms, Tools, Materials, and Sculpture*. Gulfport, MS: Sculpture Books Publishing, 2005.

Yonemura, Ann. *Lacquer: An International History and Illustrated Survey*. New York: Abrams, 1984.

PART 5

ARTS IN TIME

Adams, Laurie Schneider. *Art across Time*, 4th ed. New York: McGraw-Hill, 2010.

Arnason, H. H., and Elizabeth Mansfield. *History of Modern Art*, 7th ed. Upper Saddle River, NJ: Pearson, 2012.

Arnold, Dieter. *The Encyclopedia of Ancient Egyptian Architecture*. Princeton: Princeton University Press, 2003.

Aruz, Joan, ed. *Art of the First Cities: The Third Millennium B.C. from the Mediterranean to the Indus*. New York: Metropolitan Museum of Art, 2003.

Bailey, Gauvin. *Baroque & Rococo*. London: Phaidon, 2012.

Beard, Mary, and John Henderson. *Classical Art: From Greece to Rome*. Oxford: Oxford University Press, 2001.

Berlo, Janet. *Native North American Art*. Oxford: Oxford University Press, 1998.

Blair, Sheila, and Jonathan Bloom. *The Art and Architecture of Islam, 1250–1800*. New Haven; London: Yale University Press, 1994.

Blier, Suzanne. *Royal Arts of Africa: The Majesty of Form*. New York: Abrams, 1998.

Bradley, Richard. *Image and Audience: Rethinking Prehistoric Art*. Oxford: Oxford University Press, 2009.

Britt, David, ed. *Modern Art: Impressionism to Post-Modernism*. London: Thames & Hudson, 2008.

Brown, David Blayney. *Romanticism*. London: Phaidon, 2001.

Clunas, Craig. *Art in China*, 2nd ed. Oxford: Oxford University Press, 2009.

Curatola, Giovanni, et al. *The Art and Architecture of Mesopotamia*. New York: Abbeville Press, 2007.

D'Alleva, Anne. *Art of the Pacific*. London: Weidenfeld & Nicolson, 1998.

Dehejia, Vidya. *Indian Art*. London: Phaidon, 1997.

Eisenman, Stephen. *Nineteenth-Century Art: A Critical History*, 4th ed. London: Thames & Hudson, 2011.

Ettinghausen, Richard, Oleg Graber, and Marilyn Jenkins-Madina. *Islamic Art and Architecture, 650–1250*. New Haven; London: Yale University Press, 2001.

Gale, Matthew. *Dada and Surrealism*. London: Phaidon, 1997.

Godfrey, Tony. *Conceptual Art*. London: Phaidon, 1998.

Harris, Ann Sutherland. *Seventeenth-Century Art & Architecture*, 2nd ed. Upper Saddle River, NJ: Pearson, 2008.

Hopkins, David. *After Modern Art, 1945–2000*. Oxford: Oxford University Press, 2000.

Irwin, David. *Neoclassicism*. London: Phaidon, 1997.

Lowden, John. *Early Christian & Byzantine Art*. London: Phaidon, 1997.

Miller, Mary Ellen. *The Art of Mesoamerica*, 5th ed. London: Thames & Hudson, 2012.

——, and Megan O'Neil. *Maya Art and Architecture*, 2nd ed. London: Thames & Hudson, 2014.

Mitter, Partha. *Indian Art*. Oxford: Oxford University Press, 2001.

Morphy, Howard. *Aboriginal Art*. London: Phaidon, 1998.

Nash, Susie. *Northern Renaissance Art*. Oxford: Oxford University Press, 2008.

Paoletti, John, and Gary M. Radke. *Art in Renaissance Italy*, 4th ed. Upper Saddle River, NJ: Pearson, 2011.

Pasztory, Esther. *Aztec Art*. Norman: University of Oklahoma Press, 1998.

Robins, Gay. *The Art of Ancient Egypt*, rev. ed. Cambridge, MA: Harvard University Press, 2008.

Sekules, Veronica. *Medieval Art*. Oxford: Oxford University Press, 2001.

Snyder, James, rev. L. Silver and H. Luttikhuizen. *Northern Renaissance Art*, 2nd ed. Upper Saddle River, NJ: Pearson, 2005.

Stanley-Baker, Joan. *Japanese Art*, rev. and expanded ed. London: Thames & Hudson, 2000.

Stokstad, Marilyn, and Michael W. Cothren. *Art History*, 6th ed. Upper Saddle River, NJ: Pearson, 2017.

Stone, Rebecca. *Art of the Andes: From Chavin to Inca*, 3rd ed. London: Thames & Hudson, 2012.

Sullivan, Michael. *The Arts of China*, 5th ed., rev. and expanded. Berkeley: University of California Press, 2009.

Taylor, Brandon. *Contemporary Art: Art Since 1970*. London: Laurence King, 2012.

Thapar, Bindia. *Introduction to Indian Architecture*. Singapore: Periplus Editions, 2004.

Thompson, Belinda. *Impressionism: Origins, Practice, Reception*. London: Thames & Hudson, 2000.

Visonà, Monica, et al. *A History of Art in Africa*, 2nd ed. Upper Saddle River, NJ: Pearson, 2008.

White, Randall. *Prehistoric Art: The Symbolic Journey of Humankind*. New York: Abrams, 2003.

Zanker, Paul. *Roman Art*. Los Angeles: J. Paul Getty Museum, 2010.

Glossary

Words in *italics* are also defined in the glossary. Numbers in **boldface** following the definitions refer to the numbers of figures in the text that illustrate the definitions.

abstract Descriptive of art in which the forms of the visual world are purposefully simplified, fragmented, or otherwise distorted. Compare *representational, naturalistic, stylized, nonrepresentational.* (**2.13**)

Abstract Expressionism An American art movement of the mid-20th century characterized by large ("heroic") scale and *nonrepresentational* imagery. An outgrowth of *Surrealism,* Abstract Expressionism emphasized the artist's spontaneous expression as it flowed from the subconscious, which in turn was believed to draw on primal energies. See also *action painting.* (**22.1**)

acrylic A synthetic plastic resin used as a *binder* for artists' paints. Also used in the plural to refer to the paints themselves: acrylics. (**7.12**)

action painting *Nonrepresentational* painting in which the physical act of applying paint to a support in bold, spontaneous gestures supplies the expressive content. First used to describe the work of certain *Abstract Expressionist* painters. (**22.1**)

adobe Sun-dried (as opposed to furnace-baked) brick made of clay mixed with straw. (**13.1**)

aesthetics The branch of philosophy concerned with the feelings aroused in us by sensory experiences such as seeing and hearing. Aesthetics examines, among other things, the nature of art and the nature of beauty.

afterimage An image that persists after the visual stimulus that first produced it has ceased. The mechanics of vision cause an afterimage to appear in the *complementary* hue of the original stimulus. (**4.31**)

aisle Generally, a passageway flanking a central area. In a *basilica* or cathedral, aisles flank the nave. (**15.5**)

alla prima Italian for "at first." In oil painting, the technique of painting directly in opaque colors, as opposed to constructing the image gradually by layering underpainting, opaque colors, and glazes over a detailed drawing. Also known as "direct painting" or "wet-on-wet." (**7.8**)

ambulatory In church architecture, a vaulted passageway for walking (ambulating) around the apse. An ambulatory allows visitors to walk around the altar and choir areas without disturbing devotions in progress. (**15.15**)

analogous harmony The juxtaposition of hues that contain the same color in differing proportions, such as red-violet, pink, and yellow-orange, all of which contain red. (**4.30**)

animal style A style in European and western Asian art in ancient and medieval times based in linear, *stylized* animal forms. Animal style is often found in metalwork. (**15.11**)

appropriation A Postmodern practice in which one artist reproduces an image created by another artist and claims it as his or her own. In Postmodern thought, appropriation is felt to challenge traditional ideas about authenticity and individuality, the location of meaning within a work of art, and copyright issues involving intellectual property. (**22.24**)

apse The semicircular, protruding niche at one or both ends of the *nave* of a Roman *basilica.* In basilica-based church architecture, an apse houses the altar and may be elongated to include a choir. (**15.5**)

aquatint An *intaglio* printmaking method in which areas of tone are created by dusting resin particles on a plate and then allowing acid to bite around the particles. Also, a *print* made by this method. (**8.12**)

arcade In architecture, a series of arches carried on columns or piers. (**13.9**)

arch In architecture, a curved structure, usually made of wedgeshaped stones, that serves to span an opening. An arch may be semicircular or rise to a point at the top. (**13.9**)

Archaic In the history of ancient Greece, the period between the 8th and the 6th centuries B.C.E., when what would later be leading characteristics of Greek art can be seen in their earliest form. (**14.22**)

architrave In *Classical* architecture, the lowest band of the *entablature.* (**13.5**)

assembling The technique of creating a sculpture by grouping or piecing together distinct elements, as opposed to *casting, modeling,* or *carving.* An assembled sculpture may be called an **assemblage.** (**11.11, 22.6**)

asymmetrical Not *symmetrical.* (**5.10, 5.11**)

atmospheric perspective *Perspective* is a system for portraying the visual impression of three-dimensional space and objects in it on a two-dimensional surface. **Atmospheric perspective** is based on the observation that distant objects appear less distinct, paler, and bluer than nearby objects because of the way moisture in the intervening atmosphere scatters light. (**4.49**)

auteur French for "author," the word describes a filmmaker, usually a director, who exercises extensive creative control over his or her films, imbuing them with a strong personal style. (**9.19**)

Baroque The period of European history from the 17th through the early 18th century, and the styles of art that flourished during it. Originating in Rome and associated at first with the Counter-Reformation of the Catholic Church, the dominant style of Baroque art was characterized by dramatic use of light, bold colors and value contrasts, emotionalism, a tendency to push into the viewer's space, and an overall theatricality. Pictorial composition often emphasized a diagonal axis, and sculpture, painting, and architecture were often combined to create ornate and impressive settings. (**17.1**)

barrel vault An arched masonry structure or roof that spans an interior space. A **barrel vault** is a half-round arch extended in depth. A **groin vault** is formed by the intersection of two barrel vaults of equal size at right angles. A **ribbed vault** is a groin vault in which the lines marking the intersection of the vaults are reinforced with a raised *rib.* (**13.10**)

bas-relief Anything that projects from a background. 1. Sculpture in which figures are attached to a background and project from it to some degree. In **low relief,** also called **bas-relief,** the figures project minimally, as on a coin. In **high relief**, figures project substantially from the background, often by half their full depth or more. In **sunken relief**, outlines are carved into the surface and the figure is modeled within them, from the surface down. 2. In printmaking, techniques in which portions of a block meant to be printed are raised. See *woodcut, linocut, wood engraving*. **(11.2)**

basilica   In Roman architecture, a standard type of rectangular building with a large, open interior. Generally used for administrative and judicial purposes, the basilica was adapted for early church architecture. Principal elements of a basilica are *nave, clerestory, aisle,* and *apse*. **(15.5)**

Bauhaus   A school of art and architecture in Germany from 1919 to 1933 whose influence was felt across the 20th century. Bauhaus instructors broke down the barriers between art, craft, and design, and they believed that artists could improve society by bringing the principles of good design to industrial mass production. **(21.29)**

bay   In architecture, a modular unit of space, generally cubic and generally defined by four supporting *piers* or columns. **(13.10)**

binder   A substance in paints that causes particles of *pigment* to adhere to one another and to a *support*.

Body art   A trend in *Postminimalism* in which the artist's body was used as a medium or material. Body art is a variety of *Performance art*. **(22.15)**

buttress, buttressing   In architecture, an exterior support that counteracts the outward thrust of an arch, dome, or wall. A **flying buttress** consists of a strut or arch segment running from a freestanding *pier* to an outer wall. **(13.12)**

cable-staying   In architecture, a structural system in which a horizontal element is supported from above by means of cables that rise diagonally to attach to a vertical mast or tower. **(13.26, 13.27)**

calligraphy   From the Greek for "beautiful writing," handwriting considered as an art, especially as practiced in China, Japan, and Islamic cultures. **(18.6)**

cantilever   In architecture, a horizontal structural element supported at one end only, with the other end projecting into space. **(13.29)**

capital   In architecture, the decorative sculpted block surmounting a column. In *Classical* architecture, the form of the capital is the most distinctive element of the various *orders*. **(13.3)**

Carolingian   The period in medieval European history dominated by the Frankish rulers of the Carolingian dynasty, roughly 750–850 c.e. In art, the term refers especially to the artistic flowering sponsored by Charlemagne (ruled 800–814). **(15.13)**

cartoon   A full-scale preparatory drawing for a *fresco* or *mural*.

carving   1. In sculpture, a subtractive technique in which a mass of material such as stone or wood is shaped by cutting and/or abrasion. 2. A work made by this method. Compare *modeling*. **(11.9)**

casting   The process of making a sculpture or some other object by pouring a liquid into a mold, letting it harden, and then releasing it. Common materials used for casting include bronze, plaster, clay, and synthetic resins. **(11.5)**

ceramic   Made of baked ("fired") clay. See also *terra cotta*. **(12.1)**

chiaroscuro   Italian for "light/dark." In two-dimensional, representational art, the technique of using *values* to record light and shadow, especially as they provide information about three-dimensional *form*. See *modeling*. **(4.20)**

chroma   The relative purity or brightness of a color. Also called *intensity* or *saturation*. **(4.26)**

chimera   A mythological creature composed of parts from different animals. **(19.17)**

Classical   Most narrowly, the "middle" period of ancient Greek civilization, beginning around 480 b.c.e. and lasting until around 323 b.c.e. More broadly, the civilizations of ancient Greece and ancient Rome, and the centuries during which they flourished. Most generally, and with a lowercase c, any art that emphasizes rational

order, balance, harmony, and restraint, especially if it looks to the art of ancient Greece and Rome for models. **(14.24)**

clerestory   The topmost part of a wall, extending above flanking elements such as *aisles*, and set with windows to admit light. In a *basilica* or church, the clerestory is the topmost zone of the *nave*. **(15.5)**

coffer   A recessed, geometrical panel in a ceiling, often used in multiples as a decorative element. **(13.15)**

coil technique   A process of making ceramics by coiling a thin strip of clay in circles. **(20.9)**

collage   From the French for "glue," the practice of pasting shapes cut from such real-world sources as magazines, newspapers, wallpaper, and fabric onto a surface. Also, a work of art made in this way. **(6.13)**

color field painting   A style of *nonrepresentational* painting featuring broad "fields" or areas of color. Arising in the 1950s after *Abstract Expressionism*, it shared that movement's fondness for large scale as well as its desire to transcend the visible world in favor of universal truths viewed as unconscious or spiritual. **(22.3)**

color wheel   A circular arrangement of hues used to illustrate a particular color theory or system. The most well-known color wheel uses the spectral *hues* of the rainbow plus the intermediary hue of red-violet. **(4.24)**

complementary colors   *Hues* that intensify each other when juxtaposed and dull each other when mixed (as pigment). On a *color wheel*, complementary hues are situated directly opposite each other. **(4.24)**

composition   The organization of lines, shapes, colors, and other art elements in a work of art. More often applied to two-dimensional art; the broader term is *design*.

Conceptual art   Art created according to the belief that the essence of art resides in a motivating idea, and that any physical realization or recording of this idea is secondary. Conceptual art arose during the 1960s as artists tried to move away from producing objects that could be bought and sold. Conceptual works are often realized physically in materials that have little or no inherent value, such as a series of photographs or texts that document an activity. They are often ephemeral. **(22.19, 22.20)**

Constructivism   A Russian art movement of the early 20th century. Based in the principles of geometric abstraction, Constructivism was founded around 1913 by Vladimir Tatlin and condemned in 1922 by the Soviet government. **(10.15)**

content   What a work of art is about, its meaning.

context   The personal, social, cultural, and historical setting in which a work of art was created, received, and interpreted.

contour   The perceived edges of a three-dimensional form such as the human body. **Contour lines** are lines used to indicate these perceived edges in two-dimensional art. **(4.5)**

contrapposto   A pose that suggests the potential for movement, and thus life, in a standing human figure. Developed by sculptors in ancient Greece, contrapposto places the figure's weight on one foot, setting off a series of adjustments to the hips and shoulders that produce a subtle S-curve. **(11.20)**

cool colors   Colors ranged along the blue curve of the *color wheel*, from green through violet. **(4.24)**

corbeling   In architecture, a construction technique in which each course of stone projects slightly beyond the one below. Corbeling can be used to create space-spanning forms that resemble the *arch*, the *vault*, and the *dome*, though they do not bear weight in the same way. **(13.20)**

Corinthian order   In *Classical* architecture, a system of standardized types. In ancient Greek architecture, three orders pertain: Doric, Ionic, and Corinthian. The orders are most easily distinguished by their columns. **Doric**: the shaft of the column may be smooth or fluted. It does not have a base. The capital is a rounded stone disk supporting a plain rectangular slab. **Ionic**: the shaft is fluted and rests on a stepped base. The capital is carved in graceful scrolling forms called *volutes*. **Corinthian**: the shaft is fluted and rests on a more detailed stepped base. The elaborate capital is carved with motifs based on stylized acanthus leaves. **(13.3)**

cornice In *Classical* architecture, the uppermost element of an *entablature*; a raking cornice frames the upper, slanting edges of a *pediment*. More generally, a horizontal, projecting element, usually molded and usually at the top of a wall. **(13.5)**

cross-hatching See *hatching*.

Cubism A movement developed during the early 20th century by Pablo Picasso and Georges Braque. In its most severe "analytical" phase, Cubism abstracted the forms of the visible world into fragments or facets drawn from multiple points of view, then constructed an image from them which had its own internal logic. A severely restricted palette (black, white, brown) and a painting technique of short, distinct "touches" allowed shards of figure and ground to interpenetrate in a shallow, shifting space. **(21.20)**

Dada An international art movement that emerged during World War I (1914–18). Believing that society itself had gone mad, Dada refused to make sense or to provide any sort of aesthetic refuge or comfort. Instead, it created "anti-art" that emphasized absurdity, irrationality, chance, whimsy, irony, and childishness. Deliberately shocking or provocative works, actions, and events were aimed at disrupting public complacency. **(21.22)**

daguerreotype The first practical photographic process. Invented by Louis Jacques Mandé Daguerre and made public in 1839, it produced a single permanent image directly on a prepared copper plate. **(9.3)**

design The organization of visual elements in a work of art. In two-dimensional art, often referred to as *composition*.

dome In architecture, a convex, evenly curved roof; technically, an *arch* rotated 360 degrees on its vertical axis. Like an arch, a dome may be hemispherical or pointed. **(13.13)**

Doric order In *Classical* architecture, a system of standardized types. In ancient Greek architecture, three orders pertain: Doric, Ionic, and Corinthian. The orders are most easily distinguished by their columns. **Doric**: the shaft of the column may be smooth or fluted. It does not have a base. The capital is a rounded stone disk supporting a plain rectangular slab. **Ionic**: the shaft is fluted and rests on a stepped base. The capital is carved in graceful scrolling forms called *volutes*. **Corinthian**: the shaft is fluted and rests on a more detailed stepped base. The elaborate capital is carved with motifs based on stylized acanthus leaves. **(13.3)**

drum In architecture, a cylindrical wall used as a base for a dome. **(13.18)**

drypoint An *intaglio* printmaking technique similar to *engraving* in which the design is scratched directly into a metal plate with a sharp, pointed tool that is held like a pen. As it cuts through the metal, the tool raises a rough edge called a burr, which, if left in place, produces a soft, velvety line when printed. Also, a print made by this method. **(8.9)**

Earth art Also known as *Land art*. Art, generally large in scale, made in a landscape from natural elements found there, such as rocks and dirt. Land art arose during the 1960s as a way to bypass conventional urban exhibition spaces and to make art that could not be sold as a commodity. A work of Land art may be referred to as an *earthwork*. **(3.26, 22.18)**

earthwork Also known as *Earth art*. Art, generally large in scale, made in a landscape from natural elements found there, such as rocks and dirt. Land art arose during the 1960s as a way to bypass conventional urban exhibition spaces and to make art that could not be sold as a commodity. A work of Land art may be referred to as an earthwork. **(3.26, 22.18)**

easel painting A portable painting executed on an easel or similar support. **(2.3)**

edition In printmaking, the total number of *prints* made from a given plate or block. According to contemporary practice, the size of an edition is written on each print, and the prints are individually numbered within it. The artist's signature indicates approval of the print and acts as a guarantee of the edition.

embroidery A technique of needlework in which designs or figures are stitched into a textile ground with colored thread or yarn.

encaustic Painting *medium* in which the *binder* is wax, which is heated to render the paints fluid. **(7.1)**

engraving An *intaglio* printmaking method in which lines are cut into a metal plate using a sharp tool called a burin, which creates a clean, V-shaped channel. Also, a print resulting from this technique. **(8.3)**

entablature In *Classical* architecture, the horizontal structure supported by capitals and supporting in turn the *pediment* or roof. An entablature consists of three horizontal bands: *architrave, frieze,* and *cornice*. **(13.5)**

entasis In *Classical* architecture, the slight swelling or bulge built into the center of a column to make the column seem straight visually. **(14.26)**

etching An *intaglio* printmaking method in which the design is bitten into the printing plate with acid. Also, the resultant print. To create an etching, a metal plate is covered with an acid-resistant *ground*. The design is drawn with a sharp, penlike tool that scratches the ground to reveal the metal beneath. The plate is then submerged in acid, which bites into the exposed metal. The longer the plate remains in contact with the acid, the deeper the bite, and the darker the line it will print. **(3.21, 8.11)**

Expressionism An art movement of the early 20th century, especially prevalent in Germany, which claimed the right to distort visual appearances to express psychological or emotional states, especially the artist's own personal feelings. More generally, and with a lowercase e, any art style that raises subjective feeling above objective observation, using distortion and exaggeration for emotional effect. **(21.16)**

Fauvism A short-lived but influential art movement in France in the early 20th century that emphasized bold, arbitrary, expressive color. **(21.15)**

figure See *figure-ground relationship*.

figure-ground relationship In two-dimensional images, the relationship between a *shape* we perceive as dominant (the figure) and the background shape we perceive it against (the ground). Figure shapes are also known as **positive shapes**, and the shapes of the ground are **negative shapes**. Psychologists have identified a list of principles we use to decide which shapes are figure and which ground. When none of those conditions is met, figure and ground may seem to shift back and forth as our brain organizes the information first one way and then another, an effect known as figure-ground ambiguity. **(4.12, 4.13, 4.14)**

flying buttress In architecture, an exterior support that counteracts the outward thrust of an arch, dome, or wall. A **flying buttress** consists of a strut or arch segment running from a freestanding *pier* to an outer wall. **(13.12)**

focal point An area of emphasis within a work of art.

foreshortening The visual phenomenon whereby an elongated object projecting toward or away from a viewer appears shorter than its actual length, as though compressed. In two-dimensional *representational* art, the portrayal of this effect. **(4.47)**

forging The technique of shaping metal, especially iron, usually by heating it until it softens and then beating or hammering it.

form 1. The physical appearance of a work of art—its materials, style, and *composition*. 2. Any identifiable shape or mass, as a "geometric form."

fresco A painting medium in which colors are applied to a plaster ground, usually a wall (*mural*) or a ceiling. In **buon fresco**, also called

true fresco, colors are applied before the plaster dries and thus bond with the surface. In *fresco secco* ("dry fresco"), colors are applied to dry plaster. **(7.3, 7.4)**

frieze Generally, any horizontal band of *relief* sculpture or painted decoration. In *Classical* architecture, the middle band of an *entablature*, between the *architrave* and the *cornice*, often decorated with relief sculpture. **(13.5)**

Futurism Art movement founded in Italy in 1909 and lasting only a few years. Futurism concentrated on the dynamic quality of modern technological life, emphasizing speed and movement. **(21.21)**

genre The daily lives of ordinary people considered as subject matter for art. Also, **genre painting**, painting that takes daily life for its subject. **(17.12)**

geodesic dome An architectural structure invented by R. Buckminster Fuller, based on triangles arranged into tetrahedrons (four-faceted solids). **(13.30)**

gesso A brilliant white undercoating made of inert *pigment* such as chalk or plaster and used as *ground* for paint, especially for *tempera*.

glaze In oil painting, a thin, translucent layer of color, generally applied over another color. (For example, blue glaze can be applied over yellow to create green.) In ceramics, a liquid that, upon firing, fuses into a vitreous (glasslike) coating, sealing the porous clay surface. Colored glazes are used to decorate ceramics. **(12.2)**

Gothic Style of art and architecture that flourished in Europe, especially northern Europe, from the mid-12th to the 16th century. Gothic architecture found its finest expression in cathedrals, which are characterized by soaring interiors and large stained glass windows, features made possible by the use of the pointed *arch* and the *flying buttress*. **(13.11)**

groin vault An arched masonry structure or roof that spans an interior space. A **barrel vault** is a half-round arch extended in depth. A **groin vault** is formed by the intersection of two barrel vaults of equal size at right angles. A **ribbed vault** is a groin vault in which the lines marking the intersection of the vaults are reinforced with a raised *rib*. **(13.10)**

ground 1. A preparatory coating of paint, usually white but sometimes colored, applied to the *support* for a painting or drawing. 2. An acid-resistant coating applied to a metal plate to ready it for use in *etching*. 3. The information that is perceived as secondary in a two-dimensional image; the background. See *figure-ground relationship*.

happening An event staged or directed by artists and offered as art. Coined in 1959 and widely used during the 1960s, the term has generally been replaced today by *Performance art*. Compared with contemporary Performance art, happenings were more open to spontaneity and often encouraged audience participation. **(22.8)**

hatching Closely spaced parallel lines that mix optically to suggest *values*. Hatching is a linear technique for modeling *forms* according to the principles of *chiaroscuro*. To achieve darker values, layers of hatching may be superimposed, with each new layer set at an angle to the one(s) beneath. This technique is called **cross-hatching**. **(4.21)**

Hellenistic Literally "Greek-like" or "based in Greek culture." Descriptive of the art produced in Greece and in regions under Greek rule or cultural influence from 323 B.C.E. until the rise of the Roman Empire in the final decades of the 1st century B.C.E. Hellenistic art followed three broad trends: a continuing classicism; a new style characterized by dramatic emotion and turbulence; and a closely observed *realism*. **(14.28, 14.29)**

hierarchical scale The representation of more important figures as larger than less important figures, as when a king is portrayed on a larger scale than his attendants. **(5.21)**

high relief Anything that projects from a background. 1. Sculpture in which figures are attached to a background and project from it to some degree. In **low relief**, also called **bas-relief**, the figures project minimally, as on a coin. In **high relief**, figures project substan-

tially from the background, often by half their full depth or more. In **sunken relief**, outlines are carved into the surface and the figure is modeled within them, from the surface down. 2. In printmaking, techniques in which portions of a block meant to be printed are raised. See *woodcut, linocut, wood engraving*. **(11.3)**

hue The "family name" of a color, independent of its particular *value* or *saturation*. **(4.24)**

hypostyle An interior space filled with rows of columns that serve to support the roof. **(13.2)**

icon In Byzantine and later Orthodox Christian art, a portrait of a sacred person or an image of a sacred event. **(15.10)**

iconography The identification, description, and interpretation of subject matter in art. **(2.29)**

illumination 1. The practice of adding hand-drawn illustrations and other embellishments to a manuscript. 2. An illustration or ornament thus added. **(15.12)**

impasto From the Italian for "paste," a thick application of paint.

Impressionism A movement in painting originating in the 1860s in France. Impressionism arose in opposition to the academic art of the day. In subject matter, Impressionism followed *Realism* in portraying daily life, especially the leisure activities of the middle class. Landscape was also a favorite subject, encouraged by the new practice of painting outdoors. In technique, Impressionists painters favored *alla prima* painting, which was put into the service of recording fleeting effects of nature and the rapidly changing urban scene. **(21.6)**

in the round In sculpture, a work fully finished on all sides and standing free of a background. Compare *relief*. **(11.1)**

installation An art form in which an entire room or similar space is treated as a work of art to be entered and experienced. More broadly, the placing of a work of art in a specific location, usually for a limited time. **(2.41)**

intaglio Printmaking techniques in which the lines or areas that will take the ink are incised into the printing plate, rather than raised above it (compare *relief*). *Aquatint, drypoint, etching, mezzotint*, and *photogravure* are intaglio techniques. **(8.7)**

intensity The relative purity or brightness of a color. Also called *chroma* or *saturation*. **(4.26)**

interlace Decoration composed of intricately intertwined strips or ribbons. Interlace was especially popular in medieval Celtic and Scandinavian art. **(15.11)**

intermediate colors Also known as *tertiary colors*. Colors made by mixing a primary color with a secondary color adjacent to it on the color wheel (for example, yellow and orange). **(4.24)**

International style A style that prevailed after World War II as the aesthetic of earlier Modernist movements such as de Stijl and the Bauhaus spread throughout the West and beyond. International style buildings are generally characterized by clean lines, rectangular geometric shapes, minimal ornamentation, and steel-and-glass construction. **(13.25)**

Ionic order In *Classical* architecture, a system of standardized types. In ancient Greek architecture, three orders pertain: Doric, Ionic, and Corinthian. The orders are most easily distinguished by their columns. **Doric**: the shaft of the column may be smooth or fluted. It does not have a base. The capital is a rounded stone disk supporting a plain rectangular slab. **Ionic**: the shaft is fluted and rests on a stepped base. The capital is carved in graceful scrolling forms called *volutes*. **Corinthian**: the shaft is fluted and rests on a more detailed stepped base. The elaborate capital is carved with motifs based on stylized acanthus leaves. **(13.3)**

isometric perspective *Perspective* is a system for portraying the visual impression of three-dimensional space and objects in it on a two-dimensional surface. **Isometric perspective** uses diagonal lines to convey recession, but parallel lines do not converge. It is principally used in Asian art, which is not based on a fixed viewpoint. **(4.51)**

keystone The wedge-shaped, central stone in an arch. Inserted last, the keystone locks the other stones in place. **(13.9)**

kinetic Having to do with motion. Kinetic art incorporates (rather than depicts) real or apparent movement. Broadly defined, kinetic art may include film, video, and *Performance art*. However, the term is most often applied to sculpture that is set in motion by motors or air currents. **(4.53)**

kore Greek for "maiden" or "girl," used as a generic name for the many sculptures of young women produced during the *Archaic* period of Greek civilization.

kouros Greek for "youth" or "boy," used as a generic name for the numerous sculptures of nude youths produced during the *Archaic* period of Greek civilization. **(14.22)**

Land art Also known as *Earth art*. Art, generally large in scale, made in a landscape from natural elements found there, such as rocks and dirt. Land art arose during the 1960s as a way to bypass conventional urban exhibition spaces and to make art that could not be sold as a commodity. A work of Land art may be referred to as an *earthwork*. **(3.26, 22.18)**

layout In graphic art, the disposition of text and images on a page, or the overall design of *typographic* elements on page, spread, or book.

linear perspective *Perspective* is a system for portraying the visual impression of three-dimensional space and objects in it on a two-dimensional surface. **Linear perspective** is based on the observation that parallel lines appear to converge as they recede from the viewer, finally meeting at a vanishing point on the horizon. Linear perspective relies on a fixed viewpoint. **(4.45)**

linocut A *relief* printmaking technique in which the printing surface is a thick layer of linoleum, often mounted on a wooden block for support. Areas that will not print are cut away, leaving raised areas to take the ink. **(8.6)**

lintel In architecture, a horizontal beam or stone that spans an opening. See *post-and-lintel*. **(13.2)**

lithography A *planographic* printmaking technique based on the fact that oil and water repel each other. The design to be printed is drawn in greasy crayon or ink on the printing surface—traditionally a block of fine-grained stone, but today more frequently a plate of zinc or aluminum. The printing surface is dampened, then inked. The oil-based ink adheres to the greasy areas and is repelled by the damp areas. **(8.14)**

logotype See *wordmark*. **(10.5)**

lost-wax casting A technique for *casting* sculptures or other objects in metal. A model of the object to be cast is created in wax, fitted with wax rods, then encased in a heat-resistant material such as plaster or clay, leaving the rods protruding. The ensemble is heated so that the wax melts and runs out (is "lost"), creating a mold. Molten metal is poured into the mold through the channels created by the melted wax rods, filling the void where the wax original used to be. When the metal has cooled, the mold is broken open to release the casting. **(11.6)**

low relief Anything that projects from a background. 1. Sculpture in which figures are attached to a background and project from it to some degree. In **low relief**, also called **bas-relief**, the figures project minimally, as on a coin. In **high relief**, figures project substantially from the background, often by half their full depth or more. In **sunken relief**, outlines are carved into the surface and the figure is modeled within them, from the surface down. 2. In printmaking, techniques in which portions of a block meant to be printed are raised. See *woodcut, linocut, wood engraving*. **(11.2)**

mandala In Hinduism and especially Buddhism, a diagram of a cosmic realm, from the Sanskrit for "circle." **(5.8)**

Mannerism From the Italian *maniera*, meaning "style" or "stylishness," a trend in 16th-century Italian art. Mannerist artists cultivated a variety of elegant, refined, virtuosic, and highly artificial styles, often featuring elongated figures, sinuous contours, bizarre effects of scale and lighting, shallow pictorial space, and intense colors. **(16.20)**

mass Three-dimensional *form*, often implying bulk, density, and weight. **(4.13)**

matrix In printmaking, a surface (such as a block of wood) on which a design is prepared before being transferred through pressure to a receiving surface (such as a sheet of paper).

medium 1. The material from which a work of art is made. 2. A standard category of art such as painting or sculpture. 3. A liquid compounded with *pigment* to make paint, also called a *vehicle* and often acting as a *binder*.

megalith A very large stone. **(1.4)**

metalpoint A drawing technique in which the drawing medium is a fine metal wire. When the metal employed is silver, the technique is known as **silverpoint**. **(6.6)**

mezzotint An *intaglio* printmaking technique in which the printing plate is first roughened with a special tool called a rocker, which creates a fine pattern of burrs. Inked and printed at this point, the plate would print a velvety black. *Values* are created by smoothing away the burrs in varying degrees (smoothing the plate altogether creates a nonprinting area, or white). Also, the resultant print. **(8.10)**

minaret A tower forming part of a mosque and serving as a place from which the faithful are called to prayer. **(18.1)**

Minimalism A broad tendency during the 1960s and 1970s toward simple, primary forms. Minimalist artists often favored industrial materials (sheet metal, bricks, plywood, fluorescent lights), and their sculptures (which they preferred to call objects) tended to be set on the floor or attached to the wall rather than placed on a pedestal. **(22.12)**

modeling 1. In sculpture, manipulating a plastic material such as clay or wax to create a *form*. 2. In figurative drawing, painting, and printmaking, simulating the effects of light and shadow to portray optically convincing *masses*. **(4.18)**

mold A casing containing a shaped void in which liquid metal, clay, or other material may be *cast*. **(11.6)**

monochromatic Having only one color. Descriptive of work in which one *hue*—perhaps with variations of *value* and *intensity*—predominates. **(4.29)**

monotype A *planographic* printmaking method resulting in a single impression. A typical technique is to paint the design in oil paint on a plate of glass or metal. While the paint is still wet, a piece of paper is laid over it, and pressure is applied to transfer the design from the plate to the paper. **(8.17)**

mosaic The technique of creating a design or image by arranging bits of colored ceramic, stone, glass, or other suitable materials and fixing them into a bed of cement or plaster. **(7.16, 7.17)**

mural Any large-*scale* wall decoration in painting, fresco, mosaic, or some other *medium*. **(3.8, 3.11)**

narrative Term used to describe art that appears to tell a story. **(3.9)**

narthex In early Christian architecture, the porch or vestibule serving as an entryway to a church. **(15.5)**

naturalistic Descriptive of an approach to portraying the visible world that emphasizes the objective observation and accurate imitation of appearances. Naturalistic art closely resembles the forms it portrays. Naturalism and *realism* are often used interchangeably, and both words have complicated histories. In this text, naturalism is construed as a broader approach, permitting a degree of idealization and embracing a stylistic range across cultures. *Realism* suggests a more focused, almost clinical attention to detail that refuses to prettify harsh or unflattering matters. **(2.12)**

nave In an ancient Roman *basilica*, the taller central space flanked by *aisles*. In a cruciform church, the long space flanked by *aisles* and leading from the entrance to the *transept*. **(13.10)**

negative shape See *figure–ground relationship*.

Neoclassicism Literally "new classicism," a Western movement in painting, sculpture, and architecture of the late 18th and early 19th centuries that looked to the civilizations of ancient Greece and Rome for inspiration. Neoclassical artists worked in a variety of individual styles, but in general, like any art labeled *Classical*, Neoclassical art emphasized order, clarity, and restraint. **(17.18)**

neutral Descriptive of colors that cannot be classified among the spectral hues and their intermediaries on the *color wheel*: black, white, gray, and the browns and brownish grays produced by mixing complementary colors. **(4.24)**

nonobjective Descriptive of art that does not represent or otherwise refer to the visible world outside itself. Synonymous with *nonrepresentational*. Compare *abstract, stylized*. **(2.20)**

nonrepresentational Descriptive of art that does not represent or otherwise refer to the visible world outside itself. Synonymous with *nonobjective*. Compare *abstract, stylized*. **(2.20)**

oculus A circular opening in a wall or at the top of a *dome*. **(13.14)**

open palette *Palette* refers here to the range of colors used by an artist or a group of artists, either generally or in a specific work. A **restricted palette** is limited to a few colors and their mixtures, tints, and shades. An **open palette** is one in which all colors are permitted. **(1.8)**

optical color mixture The tendency of the eyes to blend patches of individual colors placed near one another so as to perceive a different, combined color. Also, any art style that exploits this tendency, especially the *pointillism* of Georges Seurat. **(4.32)**

order In *Classical* architecture, a system of standardized types. In ancient Greek architecture, three orders pertain: Doric, Ionic, and Corinthian. The orders are most easily distinguished by their columns. **Doric**: the shaft of the column may be smooth or fluted. It does not have a base. The capital is a rounded stone disk supporting a plain rectangular slab. **Ionic**: the shaft is fluted and rests on a stepped base. The capital is carved in graceful scrolling forms called *volutes*. **Corinthian**: the shaft is fluted and rests on a more detailed stepped base. The elaborate capital is carved with motifs based on stylized acanthus leaves. **(13.3)**

palette 1. A surface used for mixing paints. 2. The range of colors used by an artist or a group of artists, either generally or in a specific work. An **open palette** is one in which all colors are permitted. A **restricted palette** is limited to a few colors and their mixtures, tints, and shades. **(4.25)**

pastel 1. A drawing medium consisting of sticks of color made of powdered *pigment* and a relatively weak *binder*. 2. A light-*value* color, especially a *tint*. **(6.9)**

pediment In *Classical* architecture, the triangular element supported by the columns of a portico. More generally, any similar element over a door or window. **(13.5)**

pendentive In architecture, a curving, triangular section that serves as a transition between a *dome* and the four walls of a rectangular building. **(13.16)**

Performance art An event or action carried out by an artist and offered as art. In widespread use since the 1970s, *Performance art* is an umbrella term that embraces earlier practices such as the *happenings* of the 1960s and the events staged by Dada artists in the 1920s. Performances may range from improvisatory to highly scripted, and from actions of daily life to elaborately staged spectacles. **(22.16)**

perspective A system for portraying the visual impression of three-dimensional space and objects in it on a two-dimensional surface. **Linear perspective** is based on the observation that parallel lines appear to converge as they recede from the viewer, finally meeting at a vanishing point on the horizon. Linear perspective relies on a fixed viewpoint. **Atmospheric perspective** is based on the observation that distant objects appear less distinct, paler, and bluer than nearby objects because of the way moisture in the intervening atmosphere scatters light. **Isometric perspective** uses diagonal lines to convey recession, but parallel lines do not converge. It is principally used in Asian art, which is not based in a fixed viewpoint. **(4.45)**

photogravure In *intaglio* printmaking, a method for printing a continuous-tone photographic image. To create a photogravure, a full-size positive transparency of the photographic image is placed over a piece of light-sensitized gelatin paper and exposed to ultraviolet light. Beginning at the surface and extending gradually downward, the gelatin hardens in proportion to the amount of light that reaches it through the transparency. Pale tones allow more light to pass through; dark tones allow less. After exposure, the gelatin tissue is attached face down to a copper plate. The plate is set in a bath of warm water, causing the paper backing to float free and the unhardened gelatin to dissolve. The hardened gelatin remains attached to the plate, where it reproduces the photographic image in relief, with lighter areas thicker and darker areas thinner. The gelatin surface is then dusted with resin, as for *aquatint*, and set in an acid bath, as for *etching*. The acid eats around the resin particles, through the gelatin, and into the plate, biting it to various depths according to the thickness of the gelatin. The plate is then removed from the acid and the gelatin layer cleaned away. When the plate is inked and printed, deeply bitten areas produce dark tones; lightly bitten areas produce pale tones. **(8.13)**

Photorealism A movement in painting and sculpture of the 1960s and 1970s that imitated the impersonal precision and wealth of minute detail associated with photography. Photorealist sculptors sometimes clothed their figures in real clothing, and painters sometimes took an actual photograph for their subject, faithfully depicting the effects of depth of field (sharp detail giving way to blurred areas), forced perspective, and other characteristics of the technology.

picture plane The literal surface of a painting imagined as a window, so that objects depicted in depth are spoken of as behind or receding from the picture plane, and objects in the extreme foreground are spoken of as up against the picture plane. A favorite trick of *trompe l'oeil* painters is to paint an object that seems to be projecting forward from the picture plane into the viewer's space.

pier A vertical support, often square or rectangular, used to bear the heaviest loads in an arched or vaulted structure. A pier may be styled to resemble a bundle of columns. **(13.12)**

pigment A coloring material made from various organic or chemical substances. When mixed with a *binder*, it creates a drawing or painting *medium*.

plane A flat surface. See *picture plane*.

planography Printmaking techniques in which the image areas are level with the surface of the printing plate. *Lithography* and *monotype* are planographic methods. **(8.1)**

plastic 1. Capable of being molded or shaped, as clay. 2. Any synthetic polymer substance, such as *acrylic*.

pointillism A quasi-scientific painting technique of the late 19th century, developed and promulgated by Georges Seurat and his followers, in which pure colors were applied in regular, small touches (points) that blended through *optical color mixture* when viewed at a certain distance. **(4.32)**

Pop art An art style of the 1960s, deriving its imagery from popular, mass-produced culture. Deliberately mundane, Pop art focused on the overfamiliar objects of daily life to give them new meanings as visual emblems. **(22.10)**

porcelain A *ceramic* ware, usually white, fired in the highest temperature ranges and often used for fine dinnerware, vases, and sculpture. **(12.2)**

portico A projecting porch with a roof supported by columns, often marking the entrance to a building. **(13.13)**

positive shape See *figure-ground relationship*.

post-and-lintel In architecture, a structural system based on two or more uprights (posts) supporting a horizontal crosspiece (*lintel* or beam). **(13.6)**

Post-Impressionism A term applied to the work of several artists—French or living in France—from about 1885 to 1905. Although all painted in highly personal styles, the Post-Impressionists were united in rejecting the relative absence of *form* characteristic of *Impressionism*. The group included Vincent van Gogh, Paul Cézanne, Paul Gauguin, and Georges Seurat. **(21.9)**

Postminimalism An umbrella term for the diverse trends that followed in the wake of *Minimalism*, including *Process art, Body art, Performance art, Installation, Land art*, and *Conceptual art*. Postminimalism was prevalent from the mid-1960s to the mid-1970s. **(22.14)**

primary color A *hue* that, in theory, cannot be created by a mixture of other hues. Varying combinations of the primary hues can be used to create all the other hues of the spectrum. In pigment, the primaries are red, yellow, and blue. **(4.24)**

primer A preliminary coating applied to a painting *support* to improve adhesion of paints or to create special effects. A traditional primer is *gesso*, consisting of a chalky substance mixed with glue and water. Also called a *ground*.

print An image created from a master wood block, stone, plate, or screen, usually on paper. Prints are referred to as multiples, because as a rule many identical or similar impressions are made from the same printing surface, the number of impressions being called an *edition*. See *relief, intaglio, lithography, screenprinting*. **(8.3)**

Process art A trend in *Postminimalism* in which the subject of a work of art was what it was made of (materials) and how it was made (processes). **(22.13)**

proportion Size relationships between parts of a whole, or between two or more items perceived as a unit; also, the size relationship between an object and its surroundings. Compare *scale*. **(5.20)**

radial balance A means of balancing a composition based on items emerging equally in all directions from a central point. **(5.8)**

Realism Broadly, any art in which the goal is to portray forms in the natural world in a highly faithful manner. Specifically, an art style of the mid-19th century, identified especially with Gustave Courbet, which fostered the idea that everyday people and events are fit subjects for important art. Compare *naturalistic*. **(21.3)**

refraction The bending of a ray of light, for example, when it passes through a prism. **(4.23)**

registration In printmaking, the precise alignment of impressions made by two or more printing blocks or plates on the same sheet of paper, as when printing an image in several colors. **(8.4)**

relief Anything that projects from a background. 1. Sculpture in which figures are attached to a background and project from it to some degree. In *low relief*, also called *bas-relief*, the figures project minimally, as on a coin. In *high relief*, figures project substantially from the background, often by half their full depth or more. In *sunken relief*, outlines are carved into the surface and the figure is modeled within them, from the surface down. 2. In printmaking, techniques in which portions of a block meant to be printed are raised. See *woodcut, linocut, wood engraving*. **(8.1)**

Renaissance The period in Europe from the 14th to the 16th century, characterized by a renewed interest in *Classical* art, architecture, literature, and philosophy. The Renaissance began in Italy and gradually spread to the rest of Europe. In art, it is most closely associated with Leonardo da Vinci, Michelangelo, and Raphael. **(16.9)**

representational Descriptive of a work of art that depicts *forms* in the natural world. **(2.12)**

restricted palette *Palette* refers here to the range of colors used by an artist or a group of artists, either generally or in a specific work. A **restricted palette** is limited to a few colors and their mixtures, tints, and shades. **(2.12)**

rib In architecture, a projecting band on a ceiling or a vault. **(13.11)**

Rococo A style of art popular in Europe in the first three quarters of the 18th century. Rococo architecture and furnishings emphasized ornate but small-*scale* decoration, curvilinear *forms*, and *pastel* colors. Rococo painting, also tending toward the use of pastels, has a playful, lighthearted, romantic quality and often pictures the aristocracy at leisure. **(17.15)**

Romanesque A style of architecture and art dominant in Europe from the 10th to the 12th century. Romanesque architecture, based on ancient Roman precedents, emphasizes the round *arch* and the *barrel vault*. **(13.10)**

Romanticism A movement in Western art of the late 18th and early 19th centuries, generally assumed to be in opposition to *Neoclassicism*. Romantic works are marked by intense colors, turbulent emotions, complex *composition*, soft outlines, and sometimes heroic or exotic subject matter. **(21.2)**

rotunda An open, cylindrical interior space, usually covered by a *dome*. **(13.15)**

saturation The relative purity or brightness of a color. Also called *chroma* or *intensity*. **(4.26)**

scale Size in relation to some "normal" or constant size. Compare *proportion*. **(5.18)**

screenprinting A printmaking method in which the image is transferred to paper by forcing ink through a fine mesh in which the areas not meant to print have been blocked; a stencil technique. **(8.16)**

secondary color A *hue* created by combining two *primary colors*, as yellow and blue mixed together yield green. In pigment, the secondary colors are orange, green, and violet. **(4.24)**

serigraphy A printmaking method in which the image is transferred to paper by forcing ink through a fine mesh in which the areas not meant to print have been blocked; a stencil technique. **(8.16)**

shade A color darker than a hue's normal value. Maroon is a shade of red. **(4.26)**

shape A two-dimensional area having identifiable boundaries, created by lines, color or *value* changes, or some combination of these. Broadly, *form*. **(4.12)**

silkscreen A printmaking method in which the image is transferred to paper by forcing ink through a fine mesh in which the areas not meant to print have been blocked; a stencil technique. **(8.16)**

simultaneous contrast The perceptual phenomenon whereby *complementary* colors appear most brilliant when set side by side. **(4.29)**

slip In ceramics, a liquid mixture used for casting consisting of powdered clay, water, and a deflocculant.

stained glass The technique of creating images or decorations from precisely cut pieces of colored glass held together with strips of lead. **(12.4)**

still life A painting or some other two-dimensional work in which the subject matter is an arrangement of objects—fruit, flowers, tableware, pottery, and so forth—brought together for their pleasing contrasts of shape, color, and texture. Also, the arrangement of objects itself. **(4.39, 17.13)**

stippling A pattern of closely spaced dots or small marks used to create a sense of three-dimensionality on a flat surface, especially in drawing and printmaking. See also *hatching*. **(4.22)**

stop out In printmaking, to protect selected areas of a plate from the bite of acid by coating them with a resistant varnish.

stupa A shrine, usually dome-shaped, associated with Buddhism. **(19.3)**

style A characteristic, or a number of characteristics, that we can identify as constant, recurring, or coherent. In art, the sum of such characteristics associated with a particular artist, group, or culture, or with an artist's work at a specific time.

stylized Descriptive of *representational* art in which methods for depicting *forms* have become standardized, and can thus be repeated without further observation of the real-world model. Compare *abstract*. **(2.18)**

subject matter In *representational* or *abstract* art, the objects or events depicted. **(2.25, 2.26)**

sunken relief Anything that projects from a background. 1. Sculpture in which figures are attached to a background and project from it to some degree. In **low relief**, also called **bas-relief**, the figures project minimally, as on a coin. In **high relief**, figures project substantially from the background, often by half their full depth or more. In **sunken relief**, outlines are carved into the surface and the figure is modeled within them, from the surface down. 2. In printmaking, techniques in which portions of a block meant to be printed are raised. See *woodcut, linocut, wood engraving*. **(14.16)**

support The surface on which a work of two-dimensional art is made; for example, canvas, paper, or wood.

Surrealism A movement of the early 20th century that emphasized imagery from dreams and fantasies. **(21.23)**

suspension In architecture, a structural system in which a horizontal element is supported from above by means of slender vertical cables attached to a thick main cable that describes a parabolic curve between two towers. **(13.26)**

symbol An image or sign that represents something else, because of convention, association, or resemblance. **(10.1)**

symmetrical Descriptive of a design in which the two halves of a composition on either side of an imaginary central vertical axis correspond to each other in size, shape, and placement. **(5.6)**

tapestry An elaborate textile meant to be hung from a wall and featuring images and motifs produced by various weaving techniques. **(7.18)**

tempera Paint in which the pigment is compounded with an aqueous, emulsified *vehicle* such as egg yolk. **(7.5)**

tensile strength In architecture, the ability of a material to withstand tension and thus to span horizontal distances without continuous support from beneath.

terra cotta Italian for "baked earth." A *ceramic* ware, usually reddish, fired in the low temperature ranges and somewhat porous and fragile; earthenware. **(11.4)**

tertiary colors Also known as *intermediate colors*. Colors made by mixing a primary color with a secondary color adjacent to it on the color wheel (for example, yellow and orange). **(4.24)**

tessera (pl. tesserae) In *mosaic*, a small, usually cubic piece of colored ceramic, stone, or glass used as the basic unit of composition.

tint A color lighter than a hue's normal value. Pink is a tint of red. **(4.26)**

transept The arm of a cruciform church perpendicular to the *nave*. The transept often marks the beginning of the *apse*. **(15.5, 15.15)**

triadic harmony A color scheme based in three *hues* equidistant from one another on the *color wheel*, such as yellow-orange, blue-green, and red-violet. **(2.19, 2.20)**

triptych A composition consisting of three panels side by side, generally hinged in such a way that the outer two panels can close like shutters over the central one. **(3.20)**

trompe l'oeil French for "fool the eye," *representational* art that mimics optical experience so faithfully that it may be mistaken momentarily for reality. **(2.15, 4.39)**

typeface In graphic design, a style of type. **(10.6)**

typography In graphic design, the arrangement and appearance of printed letter forms (type). **(10.7)**

value The relative lightness or darkness of a *hue*, or of a *neutral* varying from white to black. **(4.19)**

vanishing point In *linear perspective*, the point on the horizon where parallel lines appear to converge. **(4.45)**

vault An arched masonry structure or roof that spans an interior space. A **barrel vault** is a half-round arch extended in depth. A **groin vault** is formed by the intersection of two barrel vaults of equal size at right angles. A **ribbed vault** is a groin vault in which the lines marking the intersection of the vaults are reinforced with a raised *rib*. **(13.10)**

vehicle Another term for *medium*, in the sense of a liquid compounded with *pigment* to make paint.

visual weight The apparent "heaviness" or "lightness" of the forms arranged in a composition, as gauged by how insistently they draw the viewer's eye. **(5.9)**

volute In architecture, a spiral, scroll-like ornament such as the *capital* of a column in the *Ionic order*. **(13.3)**

warm colors Colors ranged along the orange curve of the *color wheel*, from red through yellow. **(4.24)**

wash Ink or *watercolor* paint thinned so as to flow freely onto a *support*. **(6.10)**

watercolor A painting *medium* in which the *binder* is gum Arabic. **(7.10)**

wood engraving Similar to *woodcut*, a *relief* printmaking process in which the image is cut on the end grain of a wood plank, resulting in a "white-line" impression. **(8.5)**

woodcut A *relief* printmaking method in which a block of wood is carved so as to leave the image areas raised from the background. Also, the resultant *print*. **(2.22, 8.2)**

wordmark In design, a logo that consists of text—generally the name of a company, an institution, or a product—given a distinctive graphic treatment. Also known as *logotype*. **(10.5)**

ziggurat In ancient Mesopotamian architecture, a monumental stepped structure symbolically understood as a mountain and serving as a platform for one or more temples. **(14.4)**

Index

Numbers in **bold** refer to illustrations.

A

Aachen 362–363; palace chapel 363, **363**
Aboriginal art 464–465, **465**
Abramović, Marina: *Imponderabilia* (with Ulay) 523, **523**
abstract art 34, 36, 38
Abstract Expressionism 512–515, 516, 520
academies 377, 413, **413**
Acropolis, Athens 345, **345**, 346
acrylic painting 171–172, **172**
action painting 513–514
Adam and Eve (Dürer) **389**, 389–390
Adams, Ansel 137; portrait (Weston) **137**; *The Tetons...* 136, **136**, 138
adobe 289, 290, 315
Adoration of the Shepherds (Giorgione) 41, **42**, 43, 44, 139, 385
Adoration of the Shepherds (Greco) 41, **42**, 43, 44, 139
advertising 16, **16**, 155, 204, 213, 230, 235, 238; *see also* posters
Aegean cultures 340–341
aesthetics 4, 6, 28, 30, 31
African art and architecture 421, 427, 428, 429; Asante 9, **9**, 47, **47**, 48; Baule 258, **259**; Benin **132**, 133, 429–430, **430**; Dogon 432, **432**; Ethiopian churches 428–429, **429**; Ghanaian 286; Ife 35, **35**; Igbo **433**, 433–434; Islamic architecture 289–290, 428; *kente* cloth 9, **9**, 286; Kenyan 157, **157**; Kush 428, **428**; Lesotho 315, **315**; masks and masquerades **51**, 51–52, 432–434, **433**; Namibian 186–187, **187**; *nkisi/ nkondi* figures 432, **432**; Nok 429, **429**; *see also* Egypt; Nigerian art
African-Americans 197; collage 156, **156**; etching 92–93, **93**; Harlem Renaissance 165, 509–510; installations 264–265, **265**, 534, **534**; lithography 197, **197**; painting 128–129, **129**, 164, **164**, 165, **165**, 497; sculpture **69**, 69–70, 116, **116**, 254, **254**, 255, **255**
African't (K. Walker) 534, **534**
afterimages 99, **99**
Agesander *et al.*: *Laocoön Group* 349, **349**, 350
Ahmed, Faig: rugs 284, **284**
aisles 358, **358**
Akan linguists 47, **47**; staff 47, **47**, 48
Akbar, Mughal emperor 26, 159, 444
Akhenaten 339; *Akhenaten and His Family* 339, **339**
Akkadians 331–332, 435–436
Albers, Josef 68
Alberti, Leon Battista: Sant'Andrea, Mantua 377, **377**
Alexander the Great 178, 179, 348, 354
Alexander the Great... (Bim Gujarati) 115, **115**
Algeria: Neolithic rock paintings 329, **329**
Alhambra, Granada, Spain 423–424, **424**
Alhazen (Abu Ali Hasan Ibn al-Haitham) 205
alla prima 167
Allegory... (Bronzino) **393**, 393–394
Alston, Charles 165
Altar to the Chases High School (Boltanski) 65, **65**
Amarna period 339
Ambassadors, The (Holbein) **391**, 391–392, 464
ambulatories 364, **364**

American Civil War 208, **208**, 209
American Revolution 49, 417
Amida Buddha 44–45, **45**, **459**, 459–460
amphora (Andokides) 343–344, **344**
Anasazi people 477; Cliff Palace 477, **477**
Anatsui, El: *Sasa* 286, **286**
...and Counting (Bilas) 227
And So Was His Grandfather (Goya) **192**, 193
Andokides: amphora 343–344, **344**
Angkor Wat, Cambodia **442**, 442–443
Anguissola, Sofonisba 394, 528; *Self-Portrait at the Easel* 394, **394**
animal hide drawings, Native American 145
Animal Locomotion (Muybridge) 217
animal style 362
animation 219–220; digital 117–118
anime 545
Anthemius of Tralles and Isidorus of Miletus: Hagia Sophia, Istanbul 299–399, **300**
Antoni, Janine: *Gnaw* 43–44, **44**, 525; *Lick and Lather* 250–251, **251**
Aphrodite of Melos 348, **348**
Apoxyomenos (*The Scraper*) (Lysippos) 259, **259**
applied arts 282
apprenticeships 25, 26
appropriation 24–25, 77, 531
apses 358, **358**, 364, **364**
aquamanile, lion 273, **273**
aquatints 187, **188**, 192, 193; Spanish **192**, 193
Aquila, Abruzzi, Italy (Cartier-Bresson) 84, **84**
Arapaho, the 146; art 64, **64**
arcades 294, 421
arch construction 294, 294–297, **295**, **296**
Arch of Constantine, Rome **356**, 356–357
architecture 4, 23, 106, 107, 152–153, 268, 288; American 106–107, **107**, 305–308, **305–307**, 310–312, **311**, **312**, 313, 316, **316**, 320, **320**, 323, 323–325, **325**; Australian 310, **310**, **322**, 322–323; Baroque **138**, 138–139, 396–397, **397**, 398, **398**; Bauhaus 509, 530; British 303, **303**; Buddhist 293, **293**, 437, **438**, 450, **450**, 452, 459; Byzantine 299–300, 300, 359, **359**, 422; Canadian 324, **324**; Carolingian 362–363, **363**; Chinese 292, **293**, 450, **450**, 452, 458; and Christianity 56, **56**; and community 318–321; and digital technology 312–314; Egyptian 290–291, **291**, 299, 337, **337**; fabric 314, **314**, 316, **316**, 318, **318**; French 134, **134**, 294, **294**, 295, **295**, 296, 296–297, **297**, 304, 304, 364, **364**, 366, 366–367, **367**, 404, **404**; German 320–321, **321**, 410, **410**, 509, 530; Gothic **296**, 296–297, **297**, 366, 366–367, **367**; Greek 291, 291–292, **292**, 293, 299, 342, **345**, 345–346, **346**; green 321–325; Hindu 441, **441**; Indian 300–301, **301**, 302, **302**, 423, 437, **438**, 441, **441**, 443, 444, 445; International style 307–308, 530; Islamic 56, **56**, 289–290, **290**, 299, 300–301, **301**, 421–424, **422–424**, 428–429, **429**; Italian **138**, 138–139, 375, **375**, 377, **377**, 383, **383**, 396–397, **397**, 398, **398**; Jain 302, **302**, 443; Japanese 292–293, **293**, 456, **457**, 457–458; Lesotho 315, **315**; Minoan 340, **341**; Mughal 300–301, **301**, 423, 444, 445; Neolithic 5–6, **6**, 7, 9, 328–329; Postmodern **529**, 529–530; Pueblo 315, **315**; Roman 133, 292, 294, **294**, 295, 297, **298**, 298–299, **299**, 353, **353**, 358, 373, 422; Romanesque 295, **295**, 296, 363–364, **364**, 366, 367; as social space 315; in Spain 106–107, **107**, 245, 313, **313**, 319, 319–320, 423–424, **424**; structural systems 288–312; Turkish 315, **315**
architraves **291**, 292
Ardabil carpets 276, **276**, 278
Aristotle 205
Ariwajoye I, Yoruba ruler 431, **431**
Ark Nova (Isozaki and Kapoor) 318, **318**
Armed Innocence II (Hammam) 540, **540**
Arnolfini Double Portrait (van Eyck) 45–46, **46**
art 21; collectors 30, 546; destruction 333, *see also*

iconoclasm; history 530; and meaning 41–49; preservation of 277, 329–330; and purpose 49–53; responding to 16–19
"art cinema" 221–222
Artemidoros, mummy case of 354, **354**
Artemis, Acrobats, Divas, and Dancers (Spero) 177, **177**
Artisans (Kunisada) 185, **185**
Arts and Crafts movement 283, 285, 286
Aryans 437
Asante people: *kente* cloth 9, **9**; staff 47, **47**, 48
Ascent of the Prophet Muhammad, The (Sultan Muhammad) 37, **37**, 98
Ashoka, King 437
Asmat people: *bis* pole 465, **465**
Aspects of Negro Life (Douglas) 509–510, **510**
assemblages **27**, 27–28, 68, 100–101, **101**, 121–122, **122**, 247, 252–254, **253**, **254**, 515, **515**, **516**, 516–517
Assumption (Titian) 48, 48–49
Assurnasirpal II 332; palace reliefs 332, **332**, 334, **334**
Assyrians 332; reliefs 332, **332**, 334, **334**
Ast, Balthasar van der: *Still Life with Fruit and Flowers* 408, 408–409
Asta su Abuelo (Goya) **192**, 193
Asuka period (Japan) 457; architecture **457**, 457–458
Athens 345; Acropolis 345, **345**; Dipylon Cemetery 343; Parthenon 292, **292**, 346, **346**, 347, 348; Plato's Academy 413; Temple of Athena Nike 292, **292**
Athos (Bhabha) 254, **254**
atmospheric perspective 113–114, 372
auctions, art 546, **546**
Aurelius, Marcus: equestrian statue **60**, 60–61
Australia 464; architecture 310, **310**, **322**, 322–323
Austria; figure from Willendorf 328, **328**; LISI House (Team Austria) 323, 323–324; painting 125, 125–126, 127
auteur (film director) 222
Autumn Colors... (Shen Zhou) 114, **114**, 154
Avalokiteshvara 247–248, **249**, 452
Azerbaijan rugs 284, **284**
Aztecs 41, 470–471, 473, 476, 495; sculpture 43, **473**; shield **473**, 473–474

B

Babylon 334; Ishtar Gate **334**, 334–335
Babylonians/Neo-Babylonians 332, 334–335
Baca, Judith: *Great Wall of Los Angeles* 64, 64–65
Badi'uzzaman Fights Iraq to a Draw (Dasavanta, Madhava Khurd, and Shravana) 26, **26**
Baghdad, Iraq 333, **333**, **424**, 426
Bahram Gur and the Princess... (Shaykhzada) 425, **425**
Baker, Gilbert: LGBT flag 232, **232**
balance (principle of design) 119, 122–127
Baldung Grien, Hans: *The Groom and the Witch* 111, **111**
balloon-frame construction 305, **305**
Bamiyan Buddhas, Afghanistan 58, **58**
Ban, Shigeru: Centre Pompidou-Metz, France 313–14, **314**
Bangladesh: architecture 320–321, **321**, 322
Banjo Lesson, The (Tanner) 128–129, **129**
Banksy: murals 53, **53**
Bar at the Folies-Bergère, A (Manet) 126–127, **127**
"barbarians" 361, 366
Barney, Matthew: *Cremaster Cycle* 536, **536**
Baroque era 395, 396, 410; architecture **138**, 138–139, 396–397, **397**, 398, **398**; painting 399, **399**, 400, **400**, **401**, 401–404, **402**, **403**, 405, 405–406; sculpture 397, 397–398
Bartholl, Aram: *Map* 228–229, **229**
bas-relief 245–246
basilicas, Roman 358, **358**
basketry, Pomo 275, **275**, 476
Basotho houses, Lesotho 315, **315**
Battle of the Granicus, The (Le Brun) 178, 178–179
Battleship Potemkin (Eisenstein) 221, **221**

Guernica (Picasso) **62**, 62–63; study for 143, **144**

Guerrilla Girls 79; "Do women have to be naked to get into the Met. Museum?" 79, **79**

Guggenheim Museum, Bilbao (Gehry) 106–107, **107**, 245, 313, **313**

Guggenheim, Peggy 512

Gupta, Subodh: *Dada* 542, **542**

Gutai Art Association 518, **518**

Gutenberg, Johannes 235; *Bible* **234**, 235

H

Hachiman in the Guise of a Monk (Kaikei) 257, **258**

Hadid, Zaha 317, **317**; Burnham Pavilion 316, **316**; Riverside Museum, Glasgow **317**

Haft Manzar (Hatifi) 425, **425**

Hagia Sophia, Istanbul 299–300, **300**, 359

Hairdressing (Utamaro) 39, **39**, 40

Haitian Revolution 418

Halley's comet 261

Halprin, Lawrence: Roosevelt Memorial 266

Hamilton, Gustavus: portrait (Carriera) 88, **88**, 89

Hammam, Nermine 540; *Armed Innocence II* 540, **540**

Hammurabi's Code 332

Hampton, James 27; *Throne of the Third Heaven of the Nations' Millennium General Assembly* **27**, 27–28

Hamzanama (Dasavanta, Madhava Khurd, and Shravana) 26, **26**, **444**

Han dynasty (China) 448, 449, 450; watchtowers 458

hand-/hanging scrolls: Chinese **66**, 66–67, **75**, 75–76, 114, **114**, 450, **450**, 452–453, **453**, **454**, 455; Japanese 126, **126**, **458**, 458–459, **460**

haniwa figure 456, **456**

Hanson, Duane 35; *Housepainter III* **34**, 35

happenings 68, **517**, 517–518, **518**, 523

Harappa: torso 436, **436**

Hardouin-Mansart, Jules: Palace of Versailles 404, **404**

Harlem Renaissance 165, 509–510

Harlot's Progress, A (Hogarth) 63, **63**, 181

Harvest (Ortega) 547, **547**

Harvest of Death, A (O'Sullivan) 208, **208**

Harvesters, The (Bruegel the Elder) 392, **392**

Harvey, Marcus: *Myra Hindley* 532

Hassam, Frederick Childe: *A North East Headland* 121, **121**

hatching 92, **93**, 148

Hatifi: *Haft Manzar* 425, **425**

Hatoum, Mona: *Dormiente* 103, **103**, 104; *Untitled (cut-out 4)* 157, **158**

Hatshepsut 528; statue **336**, 336–337; temple 337, **337**

Hawaii: feather cloaks 466–467, **467**

Heckel, Erich 499; *Fränzi Reclining* 499, **499**

Heian period (Japan) 458–459

Hellenistic era 348, 350; sculpture **348**, 348–349, **349**, 350, 373, 438, 439

Henderson, Frank: *Off to War* 64, **64**

Hendrix (Sperber) 100–101, **101**

Heringer, Anna 320; METI Handmade School 320–321, **321**, 322

Hernandez, Ester: *Sun Mad* 242, **242**

Herpen, Iris van 286–287; *Dress* 287, **287**

Hesse, Eva: *Contingent* 521–522, **522**

Hidden Relief (Sze) 82–83, **83**

Hide and Seek, Kill or Speak (Mutu) 157, **157**

hierarchical scale 133

High Performance Art (Pyke and Schmidt) 238, **238**

Hinduism/Hindu 58, 101, 143, 437, 440, 442; architecture 441, **441**; mandalas 124; sculpture 10, **10**, 246, **246**, 437, **440**, 440–441

Hiroshige, Ando: *Riverside Bamboo Market, Kyobashi* 181, 463, **463**

Hirschfeld Workshop (attr.): *krater* 342, 342–343

Hirst, Damien: *The Physical Impossibility of Death in the Mind of Someone Living* 531, **531**, 532

Hitchcock, John 202; *National Sanctuary* 202, **202**

Hitler, Adolf 62, 333, 510, 511, **511**

Höch, Hannah 213, 504; *Cut with the Kitchen Knife Dada...* 213–214, **214**

Hogarth, William 202; *A Harlot's Progress* 63, **63**, 181

Hokusai, Katsushika: *Ejiri in Suruga Province* 77, 78, **78**; *Great Wave at Kanagawa* **462**, 462–463

Holbein, Hans, the Younger 391; *The Ambassadors* **391**, 391–392, 464

Holy Virgin Mary, The (Ofili) 532

Holy Women at the Tomb (dai Libri) 163, 163–164

Holzer, Jenny: *Protect Me From What I Want* 533, **533**

Homer, Winslow: *Key West, Hauling Anchor* 170, **170**

homosexuality 232, **232**, **533**, 533–534

Honeywax (K. Smith) 260, **260**

Hopewell people 261; beaver effigy pipe 476, 477

Hopi Indians: blanket 479; kachina 478

Horse Galloping (Muybridge) 217, **217**, 219

Horyu-ji, Nara, Japan 457, 457–458

Houasse, Michel-Ange: *Drawing Academy* **413**

Housepainter III (Hanson) **34**, 35

How to Explain Pictures to a Dead Hare (Beuys) 51, **51**

Howling Wolf 146, 479, 480; *Howling Wolf and Feathered Bear* 146, **146**; *Ute Indian* 145, **145**

hues 96

Human Proportions... (Leonardo) 133, **133**, 377, 379

Human Toilet Revisited (Lucas) 532

humanism/humanists, Renaissance 372, 374, 377, 413

Hungarian photojournalism 210, 212

Hustle'n'Punch... (T. Murakami) 545, **545**

Hy-Fi (The Living) 324–325, **325**

I

ibn al-Fadl, Abdullah 426

iconoclasm 58

iconography 44–46

icons, Byzantine 361, **361**

Ideal Power (Fairey) 236, **236**

Ife, Nigeria 430; heads 35, **35**

Igbo people: *ijele* masks and masquerades 433, 433–434

Iktinos and Kallikrates: Parthenon 346, **346**

illuminated manuscripts **163**, 163–164, 362, **363**, 387, 387–388, 389

i.Mirror (Cao Fei) 228, **229**

impasto 171

Imponderabilia (Abramović and Ulay) 523, **523**

Impression, Sunrise (Monet) 489, **489**, 490

Impressionism 175, **489**, 489–491, **490**, **491**, 495

impressions 181

Incas 276; bridges 308–309; Machu Picchu 474, **475**; textiles 276, **276**, 474

India 27, 420, 426, 435, 436, 437, 445, 446, 546; architecture 300–301, **301**, 302, **302**, 423, 441, **441**, 443; Buddhism 437–439, 441; Jain architecture 302, **302**, 443; Jain art 443, **443**; map **435**; painting **108**, 109, **439**, 439–440, **443**, 443; photography 445, 445, 446, 447; sculpture 10, **10**, 246, 247–248, **248**, 437, **438**, 438–439, **439**, 440, 440–441, **442**, 542, **542**; *see also* Hinduism; Mughal dynasty

Indus River Valley 435, 436–437; torso 436, **436**; "yogi" seal 436–437, **437**

Industrial Revolution 230–231, 282, 304, 321, 419

Ingres, Jean-Auguste-Dominique 79, 484; *Jupiter and Thetis* 98, **484**, 484–485

ink drawings/paintings/washes 151–154, **152–154**; Chinese **75**, 75–76, 114, **114**; Japanese 126, **126**, 460, **460**, 461, **461**, 462

Inrush (Pearlman) 158, **158**

installations 52, 262–263; African-American 52–53, **53**, 264–265, **265**, 534, **534**; American 38, **38**, 43–44, **44**, 52, **52**, 82–83, **83**, 117, 117, 158, **158**, 177, **177**, 202, 202–203, **203**, 241, **241**, 263, **263**, 264, **265**, 522, **522**, 533, **533**; Brazilian **285**, 285–286, 548–549, **549**; British 117–118, **118**; Bulgarian 265, 267, **267**; Canadian 324–325, **325**; French 65, **65**; German 173–174, **174**, 228–229, **229**; Japanese 122–123, **123**; Swiss 263–264, **264**

intaglio prints **182**, 187, *see* aquatints, drypoint, engraving(s), etching(s), mezzotints, *and* photogravure

interlace patterns 362

International style architecture 307–308, 530

Internet, the 14, 215, 216, 226–229, 238, 535, 538

Ionic order 291, **291**, 353

Iran/Iranians 422; aquamaniles 273; architecture 422–423, **423**; coronation carpet 95, **95**; video installation 225, 225–226; woman's coat 427, **427**

Iraq/Iraqis: architecture 317, **317**; Internet art 226, 227, 228; sculpture 245, 245–246; ziggurat 331, **331**

iron construction 303, 303–304, **304**

Ise, Japan: shrine 456, **457**, 458

Isenheim Altarpiece (Grünewald) **390**, 390–391

Isfahan, Iran: Friday Mosque 422–423, **423**

Ishtar Gate, Babylon **334**, 334–335

Isidorus of Miletus *see* Anthemius of Tralles

Islam/Muslims 56, 58, 155, 278, 420–421; *see* Islamic culture

Islamic culture: architecture 56, **56**, 289–290, **290**, 299, 300–301, **301**, 421–424, **422–424**, 428–429, **429**; calligraphy 233, 424–426, **425**; carpets 95, **95**, 276, **276**, 278, 426; ceramics 426, 427, **427**; mosaics 422, 423, **423**; painting 114–115, **115**; scholars 426; textiles 425, 427, **427**

isometric perspective **114**, 114–115

Isozaki, Arata, and Kapoor, Anish: Ark Nova 318, **318**

Istanbul 299; Hagia Sophia 299–300, **300**, 359; *see also* Constantinople

Italy 510; architecture **138**, 138–139, 375, **375**, 377, **377**, 383, **383**, 396–397, 398, **398**; drawing 92, **93**, **148**, 148–149; mosaics **176**, 176–177; paintings and frescoes 13, 13–14, 21, **22**, 41, **42**, 43, **48**, 48–49, 57, **57**, 59, **88**, 88–89, **90**, 92, 98, 109, 110, 110–111, **161**, 161–162, **163**, 163–164, 370, 370–371, **371**, 375–378, **376**, **378**, 379, 381–383, **382**, **384**, **385**, 385–386, **386**, **393**, 393–395, **395**, 529; photography 121, **121**; prints 72–73, **73**, 181, **398**; sculpture 25, **25**, 211, 250, **250**, 374, 374–375, 381, **381**, 384, 397–398, **398**

ivory/ivories **123**, 123–124, 278, 279; Byzantine 361, **361**; Philippine **27**, 27, 47, 242, 279; Romanesque 365, **365**; Sapi 278, **278**, 279, **279**, 280

iwan 422, 423, **423**, 444

J

Jackson, Julia 208; photograph (Cameron) 208, **208**

Jacquette, Yvonne: *Three Mile Island, Night I* 149, **149**

jade 278, 280; Chinese **280**, 280–281, 447; Olmec 50, 50–51, 280, 470, 476

Jahangir... (Manohar) **9**, 9–10, 99

Jains: art 443, **443**; temples 302, **302**, 443

Jamestown, Virginia 396, 418

Japan 37, 318, 435, 436, 538; *anime* 545; architecture 292–293, **293**, 456, **457**, 457–458, 460; armor 459, **459**; Buddhism 457, 458, 459–460, **460**; Buddhist garden 76, **76**; calligraphy 233; ceramics 30, **30**, 269, 456, **456**; Conceptual art **526**, 526–527; contemporary art **544**, 544–545, **545**; *fusuma* 460, **461**; Gutai Art Association 518, **518**; hand- and hanging scrolls 126, **126**, **458**, 458–459, 460, **460**; ink paintings 126, **126**, **459**, 460, **460**, 461, **461**, 462; installation 122–123, **123**; *kami* 544; lacquerware **281**, 281–282; map **435**; photography 24, 24–25; samurai 459; sculpture 44–45, **45**, 257, **258**; Shinto 456–457, 458, 460, 544; shoguns 459, 460; *shōin* rooms 460–461, **461**; woodcuts/woodblock prints 39, **39**, 40, 77, 78, **78**, 185, **185**, **462**, 462–463, **463**, 497

Jeanne-Claude *see* Christo

Jesus Christ 355, 357, 358, 359, 360, **360**, 361, 362, 365, 401, 420, 428

Jnanadakini Mandala (Tibetan) 124, **124**, 127

nonrepresentational art 37–38
North East Headland, A (Hassam) 121, **121**
Nouvel, Ateliers Jean, and PTW Architects: One Central Park, Sydney **322**, 322–323
Nowo masks and masquerades 433, **433**
Nubia 428
nude, the 373, 374–375, 386
Number 1 (Pollock) **513**, 513–514
Numbers in Color (Johns) 160, **160**
Nut (Sillman) **167**, 167–168

O

007 goldeneye all characters cheat (Cortright) 175, **175**
Oath of the Horatii, The (David) 412, **412**, 414
Obey (Fairey) 237, **237**
Object (Oppenheim) 505, **505**
oculus 298, **299**
Off to War (Henderson) 64, **64**
Ofili, Chris: *The Holy Virgin Mary* 532; *Prince Amongst Thieves with Flowers* 147, 147–148
oil painting 43, 160, **166**, 166–168, **167**
oil pastels 150
Ojibwe bandolier bag 480, **480**
O'Keeffe, Georgia 169; portrait (Stieglitz) **169**; *White Shell with Red* 168, **168**, 169, 170
Oldenburg, Claes 131; *Plantoir* (with van Bruggen) 131, **131**
Olmecs 470, 471; colossal heads 251–252, **252**, 470; god 471; jade **50**, 50–51, 280, 470, 476
Olowe of Ise: *Olumeye* bowl **274**, 274–275
1 (from *51 Ways of Looking*) (Sikander) **142**, 143, 144
One and Three Chairs (Kosuth) 526
One Floor Up More Highly (Grosse) 174, **174**
Ono, Yoko: *Grapefruit* **526**, 526–527
Oppenheim, Meret: *Object (Luncheon in Fur)* 505, **505**
optical color mixing 93, 99–100
Orange and Yellow (Rothko) 514, **514**
Orozco, José Clemente 507; *The Epic of American Civilization* **507**, 507–508
Ortega, Damián 545, 547; *Harvest* 547, **547**
Osorio, Pepón: *You're Never Ready* **201**, 201–202
O'Sullivan, Timothy 208–209; *A Harvest of Death* 208, **208**
Ottomans 347; architecture 299–300, **300**, 315, **315**
outsider art 27–28
Oxbow, The (Cole) **74**, 74–75, 495, **495**

P

Pacific cultures 464–467, 468
Padua: Scrovegni Chapel frescoes (Giotto) 370–371, **371**
Paik, Nam June 527
Paine, Roxy 253; *Conjoined* 253, **253**
Painter's Cupboard (Pérez de Aguilar) 32, **32**, 33, 34, 99
painting 23, 174, 268, 282, 372, 373; African-American 128–129, **129**, 164, **164**, 165, **165**, 497; American **18**, 19, **36**, 40, **40**, **64**, 64–65, **74**, 74–75, **80**, 81, **85**, 85–86, 98, 113, 113–114, 121, **121**, 160, **160**, **167**, 167–168, **168**, **170**, 418, **418**, 495, 496, 496–497, **497**, **513**, 513–516, **514**, **515**, 520, **520**; Brazilian 172, **172**; British 532, **532**, 547–548, **548**; Buddhist 37, 57, **57**, 450, **450**; Chinese **66**, 66–67, **75**, 75–76, 450, **450**, 452–453, **453**, **454**, 455; digital 175, **175**; Dutch 10, **10**, **11**, 12, 39, 71, **71**, 98, 101, 102, **102**, 104, **104**, 105, **131**, **131**, 152, **152**, **191**, 191–192, 333, 405–406, **406**, 407, **407**, 408, 408–409, **409**, 492, **508**, 508–509; Egyptian 160, **160**, 337–338, **338**, 354, **354**; French **61**, 61–62, 73, **73**, 86–87, **87**, 98, 99–100, **100**, **126**, 126–127, **127**, 129, **129**, 402, 402–404, **403**, 411, 411–412, **412**, **413**, 414–415, **415**, 416, **416**, 417, **417**, **418**, 419, 484, 484–494, **485**, 487–**494**, 498, 498–499; German 101, 112, **112**, **390**, 390–392, **391**, **504**, 505, 511; Greek 144, 342, **342**, 343–344, **344**; Indian

and Mughal 9, **9**, 26, **26**, **108**, 109, **439**, 439–440, **443**, 443, **444**, 444–445; Islamic 114–115, **115**; Italian **13**, 13–14, 21, **22**, 41, **42**, 43, **48**, 48–49, 57, **57**, 59, **88**, 88–89, **90**, 92, 98, 109, **110**, 110–111, **161**, 161–162, **163**, 163–164, **370**, 370–371, **371**, 375–378, **376**, **378**, 379, 381–383, **382**, **384**, **385**, 385–386, **386**, **393**, 393–395, **395**, 529; Japanese 458, **458**, **459**, 459–460; Netherlandish 45–46, **46**, 71–72, **72**, **166**, 166–167, **387**, 387–389, **388**, 392, **392**; Pakistani 436, **541**, 541–542; Persian 37, **37**, 444; Roman 351–352, **352**; Russian 499–500, **500**; Spanish 17, 17–18, 19, **23**, 23–24, 26, 31, **31**, 77, 91, **91**, 130, **130**, 172, **192**, 193, 404–405, **405**, **506**, 506–507; Tibetan 57, **57**, 59; *see also* ink painting; landscape painting; paints; portraits
paints 159–160; acrylic 171–172; encaustic 160; fresco 160–162; gouache 170–171; oil 160, 166–168; tempera 163–164, 165, 166; watercolor 160, 170
Pakistani-Americans: art **142**, 143; sculpture 254, **254**
Palenque, Mexico 471, **471**
palettes 95; open 99; restricted 99
Palette of Narmer 335–336, **336**
Paleolithic era: cave art 4–5, **5**, 33, 53, 144, **326**, 327, 327–328; female statuettes 328, **328**
Palestinian art 103, **103**, 157, **158**
Pantheon, Rome 298, 298–299, **299**, 300, 377
paper 145, 155, 160; ledger paper drawings 145, **145**, 146, **146**; as medium 155–158
papier collé 156
papyrus 144; motif 274
parchment 144–145, **163**
Paris 61; Le Boulevard du Temple 206, **207**; Eiffel Tower 304, **304**, 321; Gare d'Orsay museum 530; Louvre 21, 49, **49**, 404, 483; Pompidou Center 313–14, **529**, 529–530; Saint-Denis 366; Sainte-Chapelle 56, **56**, 90; World's Fairs 62, 304
Parsons, Betty 68
Parthenon, Athens 292, **292**, 346, **346**; sculptures 347, **347**, 348, **348**
pastels 39, **39**, 40, 150, 151, **151**, 168, **168**, 170
patronage/patrons 374, 377, 380, 412, 420–421
pattern 81, 105
Paul, Saint 365
Paul III, Pope 383
Paxton, Joseph: Crystal Palace 303, **303**, 321
Payag: *Shah Jahan on Horseback* **444**, 444–445
Peale, Charles Willson: *Benjamin Franklin* 190, **190**–191
Pearlman, Mia 158; *Inrush* 158, **158**
pediments 292, 293
pencil drawings **147**, 147–148
pendentives 300
perception 16–17
Pérez de Aguilar, Antonio: *Painter's Cupboard* 32, **32**, 33, 34, 99
Performance art 51, **51**, 68, 523–524
Perikles 345
Perseus with the Head of Medusa (Cellini) 250, **250**
Persian painting 37, **37**, 444; *see also* Iran
Persistence of Memory, The (Dali) 506, **506**, 507
persistence of vision 218
perspective 373, 399; atmospheric (aerial) 113–114, 372; isometric **114**, 114–115; linear **109**, 109–111, 372
Peru: Nasca lines 82, **82**, 83
Pettibon, Raymond: *No Title (Not a single...)* 153–154, **154**
Phidias: Acropolis 345, 346, 348
Philip IV, of Spain 404, 405
Philippines, the: ivory 27, **27**, 47, 242, 279
photography 33, 92, 174, 204, 205, 206, 211, 483; African 105, **105**, 434, **434**; American 28, 29, 77–78, **78**, 121, **121**, 136, **136**, 137, **137**, 138, **169**, 173, **173**, 208, 208–210, **210**, 212–216, **214–216**, 241, 243, **243**; British 207–208, **208**, 217, **217**, 218; calotypes 207; Canadian 77–78, **78**; collodion process 207; color 215; daguerreotypes 206–207, **207**; documentary

209–210; Egyptian 540, **540**; French 84, **84**, 206–207, **207**; German 48, 48–49, 216, **216**; Indian 445, **445**, 446, 447; Japanese **24**, 24–25; Mexican 91, **92**; portraits 207–208, **208**; *see also* cameras *and below*
photogravure 187, **188**, 193–194, **194**
photojournalism 209–210, 212
Photorealism/Photorealists **18**, 19, 520–521
Physical Impossibility of Death in the Mind of Someone Living, The (Hirst) **531**, **531**, 532
Piano, Renzo and Rogers, Richard: Pompidou Center, Paris **529**, 529–530
Picasso, Pablo 32, 33, 62, 63, 143, 155, 501, 502, 503, 511, 546; *Bottle of Vieux Marc...* 32–33, **33**, 34, 38; *Les Demoiselles d'Avignon* **501**, 501–502; *Girl Before a Mirror* **139**, 139–140; *Guernica* **62**, 62–63, 143, **144**
Pich, Sopheap 543–544; *Fertile Land* 544, **544**
Pictorialism 212
picture plain 107
piers (architecture) **296**, 297, 300
Pietà (Michelangelo) 384
pigments 95, 97, 147, 159; mixing 97, **97**
pilgrimage churches 364, **364**
Pine Wood (Tōhaku) 461, **461**
pink out of a corner (to Jasper Johns) (Flavin) 522, **522**
Piranesi, Giovani Battista: *Il Carceri* 72–73, **73**; "The Sawhorse" 72, **73**, 181; *View of St. Peter's* 398
Piss Christ (Serrano) 211
PixCell (Beads) (Nawa) 544, **544**
pixels 100
pixilation 219
Plains people 479; feathered headdresses 480; painted hides 479–480, **480**
Plantoir (Oldenburg and van Bruggen) 131, **131**
Plato 373, 377, 413
Pliny [the Elder] 271
pluralism 530
pointillism 99–100, 105, 176, 491–492
Poke in the Eye/Nose/Ear... (Nauman) 523, **523**
Pollock, Jackson 173, 513; *Number 1* **513**, 513–14
Polynesia/Polynesians 464, 466–467; tattoos 468, **468**
polyptych **123**, 123–124
Pomo feathered baskets 275, **275**, 476
Pompeii 351; Villa of Mysteries 352, **352**
Pompidou Center, Paris 313–314, **529**, 529–530
Pompidou-Metz, Centre, France (Ban) 313–14, **314**
Pont du Gard, Nîmes, France 294, **294**
Pop art movement 222, 519–520
porcelain: Chinese 270, 408; German 410, 410
porticos 299
portraits: mezzotint 190, 190–191; paintings 36, 68, 88, **88**, 380, **384**, 385, **385**, **403**, 403–404, **418**, 419; photographic 137, **169**, 207–208, **208**; sculpture 333, **333**, 350–351, **351**; *see also* self-portraits
Portugais, Le (The Emigrant) (Braque) **502**, 503, 531
Posada, José Guadalupe: *Skeletons as Artisans* 186, **186**
post-and-lintel construction **290**, 290–293
poster paints 170
posters 155, 181, 213, 235; American 16, **16**, 79, **79**, 237, **237**, 242, **242**, 236, **236**, **533**, 533–534; French 120, 120–121, **235**, 235–236; German **508**, 509; Russian 240, **240**, 455–456, **456**; Swiss 128, **128**
Post-Impressionism 491–494, **492**–**494**
Postminimalism 521, 522, 523, 524
Postmodernism 529; in architecture **529**, 529–530; in art **530**, 530–531, **531**
potter's wheel 269–270
pottery *see* ceramics
"pre-Columbian" art 469
Pregnant Girl (L. Freud) 546
Presentation of the Portrait of Marie de' Medici (Rubens) **401**, 401–402
Primavera (Botticelli) 377–378, **378**, 380
primers 160
"primitive" art 30